MEET OUR AUTHORS

■ Donald J. Guerrieri

Donald J. Guerrieri is an accounting instructor at Norwin High School, North Huntingdon, Pennsylvania. He has taught accounting at both the secondary and college levels. He also has experience working for a firm of certified public accountants. Dr. Guerrieri has written numerous articles on the teaching of accounting for a variety of educational journals. He is also a program speaker at business education seminars and conferences.

■ F. Barry Haber

F. Barry Haber is Professor of Accounting at Fayetteville State University, Fayetteville, North Carolina. Dr. Haber has been teaching accounting principle courses for more than 35 years. He is a certified public accountant and has served on the American Institute of Certified Public Accountants (AICPA) Minority Doctoral Fellows Committee. In addition to teaching accounting principles, Dr. Haber has authored three other textbooks, as well as various articles and cases in accounting.

■ William B. Hoyt

William B. Hoyt is an accounting instructor at Wilton High School, Wilton, Connecticut. He has been involved in accounting curriculum development for many years. He was a member of the writing task force for the *National Standards for Business Education* and has published several articles in professional journals. In 1996, Mr. Hoyt was named Connecticut's *Outstanding Business Educator of the Year* and in 1997 was named *National Secondary Teacher of the Year* by the National Business Education Association.

■ Robert E. Turner

Robert E. Turner is the Vice President for Business Affairs at University of Louisiana at Monroe, Monroe, Louisiana. Mr. Turner has taught accounting and other business subjects at the high school and college levels. Mr. Turner has appeared on local, state, and national programs of a number of business education conferences. He is also a frequent speaker at educational seminars and workshops around the country.

Copyright © 2004 by Glencoe/McGraw-Hill, a division of The McGraw-Hill Companies. All rights reserved. Except as permitted under the United States Copyright Act, no part of this publication may be reproduced or distributed in any form or by any means, or stored in a database or retrieval system, without prior written permission of the publisher, Glencoe/McGraw-Hill.

Printed in the United States of America.

Send all inquiries to:
Glencoe/McGraw-Hill
21600 Oxnard Street, Suite 500
Woodland Hills, CA 91367-4906

ISBN 0-07-845670-3

3 4 5 6 7 8 9   071   08 07 06 05 04 03

GLENCOE Accounting

Real-World Applications & Connections

First-Year Course

Fifth Edition

Donald J. Guerrieri
Norwin High School
North Huntingdon,
Pennsylvania

F. Barry Haber
Fayetteville State University
Fayetteville,
North Carolina

William B. Hoyt
Wilton High School
Wilton,
Connecticut

Robert E. Turner
University of Louisiana at Monroe
Monroe,
Louisiana

Visit the *Glencoe Accounting* Web site at:
glencoeaccounting.glencoe.com

 **Glencoe**

New York, New York   Columbus, Ohio   Chicago, Illinois   Peoria, Illinois   Woodland Hills, California

EDUCATIONAL REVIEWERS

EDUCATIONAL CONSULTANTS

We wish to acknowledge the contributions of the following:

Jayne Abernathy, Xenia, OH
Jim Adams, New Albany, IN
G. Armstrong, Bath, NY
Ron Baldini, Pulaski, WI
Alan Balog, Ravenna, OH
B. A. Banks-Burke, Hudson, OH
Denise M. Barbaris, West Milford, NJ
E. Patricia Barnes, Evansville, IN
Lou Ellen Bass, Four Oaks, NC
Linda Becker, Cary, NC
Perry Beckerman, Brooklyn, NY
Kathleen Beetar, Houston, TX
Scott Behnke, Wales, WI
Len C. Bigler, Grand Rapids, MI
Jackie Billings, McAllen, TX
Lee Birnbaum, Farmingdale, NJ
Cheryl Birx, Canandaigua, NY
Linda J. Black, Mt. Airy, GA
Elbert F. Black, Hastings, MI
Cindi Blansfield, Auburn, WA
Josephine Bliss, Merced, CA
D. Bogataj, Flat Rock, MI
Kelly Brock, Columbus, GA
William A. Brogdon, German Town, TN
Rachelle Brown, Morocco, IN
Jessie Broxmeyer, Long Beach, NY
Margaret Broyles, Forest Park, OH
Gus Buchttolz, Wyoming, MI
Ronda K. Budd, Grove City, OH
Pete Bush, Leesburg, FL
Michelle Cardoza, Tulare, CA
Walter Carlson, Torrance, CA
Marisa Charles, Houston, TX
Bill Christianson, Spokane, WA
Jodi S. Clark, Warner Robins, GA
Anthony Paul Corbisiero, West New York, NJ
Ron Craig, Anaheim, CA
Lynn Crawford, Cudahy, WI
Claudia Cullari, Fair Lawn, NJ
Jo Damron, Abilene, TX
Jan Davis, Port Neches, TX
Toni DeFuria, Old Tappan, NJ
Denise Deltondo, Girard, OH
Carolyn Deshler, Moorpark, CA
Diane DeWitt, Freeport, IL
Wanda Drake, Jackson, TN
Buzz Drake, Barrington, IL
Ray Dunavant, Denison, TX
Tearle Dwiggins, Pendleton, IN
Susan España, Rocklin, CA
Morris P. Fair, Sr., Jackson, TN
Glenn Fong, Sacramento, CA
Julie Fox, Wisconsin Rapids, WI
Carolyn Francis, Baytown, TX
Cherilynn Frost, Livonia, MI
Patricia T. Gardella, Vineland, NJ
Robert D. Garrison, Belleview, FL
Kimberly Morris Gehres, Adrian, MI
JoAnn Gipson, Garland, TX
Nancy Glavic, New Concord, OH
Joyce Greemon, Gastonin, NC
Sheree Green, Teaneck, NJ
Andrea Gross, Vidor, TX
Guzzeta, Plant City, FL
Ronald L. Hainds, Jacksonville, IL
Kellie Hair, Kennesaw, GA

Sheryl J. Hane, Norco, CA
Janice Hanes, Forth Worth, TX
Marion Hanneld, Omaha, NE
Farolyn Hanscom, Riverside, CA
Wanda Harris, Eden, NC
Tammy Hatfield, Tullahoma, TN
Felicia S. Hatten, Detroit, MI
Debra R. Hauser, Shrub Oak, NY
Richard Heim, Latham, NY
Audrey M. Hendry, Huntington Beach, CA
John Hodgins, Marysville, WA
Helen Hogan, Lithonia, GA
Betty L. Holloway, Maplewood, NJ
Carol Huprich, Dover, OH
Antoinette Hutchings, Slate Hill, NY
David Ifkovic, Wilton, CT
Steve Ingmire, Indianapolis, IN
Waydene C. Jackson, Stone Mountain, GA
M. Jackson, Houston, TX
Irma D. James, Dayton, OH
Carol Jekel, Flushing, MI
Lori Jepson, Montclair, CA
Kay Jernigan, Vanceboro, NC
Glenn Johnson, Mukwonago, WI
Judy Jones, Amarillo, TX
Mary K. Jones, Neenah, WI
Ted Juske, Mundelein, IL
Beverly Kaeser, Appleton, WI
Linda Keats, Stevens Point, WI
Sue Kelley, Hubbard, OH
Mary Kay King, Dickson, TN
Carol Kinney, Eau Claire, WI
Ann Klingelsmith, Greenville, MI
Tammy Koch, Minocqua, WI
Patrick Kubeny, Rhinelander, WI
Cheryl M. Lagan, Ossining, NY
Amelia Lard, Memphis, TN
Marianna Larkin, Waxahachie, TX
Becky Larsen, Irvine, CA
Sharon Larson, Crystal Lake, IL
Inez Lauerman, Shingle Springs, CA
Annette Laughlin, Oswego, IL
Steve Leighton, Brooklyn, NY
James Leonard, Palos Hills, IL
Sue Lewis, Littlerock, CA
Stan Lewis, Champaign, IL
Donna Lewis, Morehead City, NC
Theresa Lueras, Daly City, CA
Sherry Lund, Port Angeles, WA
Linda Lupi, W. Bloomfield, MI
A. Mallette, New York, NY
John Matera, Kenosha, WI
Alice Matthews, Artesia, CA
Sarah McBride, Hickory, NC
Rebecca McKnight, Gainesville, FL
Pam Meyer, The Woodlands, TX
J. Miller, Madison, OH
Gloria Morris, Fort Worth, TX
Ralph A. Muro, Binghamton, NY
Dianne Murphy, Rancho Cucamonga, CA
Jill N. Murphy-Totten, Middletown, OH
John Murray, Fraser, MI
Karen Neuman, Parma, OH
William Nitch, Niles, OH
Bonnie N. Nute, Munford, TN
Betty O'Dell, Escondido, CA

Deborah Ottmers, San Antonio, TX
Donna Owens, Missouri City, TX
RaeNell Parker, Menomonie, WI
Ronda Patrick, Kirkland, WA
Diane Personett, Rushville, IN
Hank Petite, Bloomfield, NJ
Glenn Philpott, Belleville, IL
Kip Pichel, Auburn Hills, MI
Patti Pletcher, Bristol, IN
Mark G. Pretz, Harlingen, TX
Diane A. Prom, Oak Creek, WI
Lydia Quinones, Dunwoody GA
Mary C. Rabb, Winchester, TN
Margaret Ralph, Portland, IN
Glenda Razor, Santa Ana, CA
Tom Reach, Aliso Viejo, CA
C. Redmond, Lakewood, CA
Suzanne Reisert, Floral Park, NY
Edlyn Reneau, Corpus Christi, TX
Ruth Riley, Poland, OH
Melanie Rodges, Keller, TX
Rosalinda Rodriguez, McAllen, TX
Mary R. Roth, Warner Robins, GA
Frank Rudnesky, Pine Hill, NJ
Joyce Sadd, Hastings, NE
Lawrence Sakalas, Southgate, MI
Gary L. Schepf, Irving, TX
Donna M. Scheuerer, Farmingdale, NY
Jerry Schlecher, Hartland, MI
Sue Smith, Whittier, CA
Pete Smith, Mishawaka, IN
James Smith, Greensboro, NC
Linda Songer, Orange Park, FL
Linda Spellich, Belleville, MI
Carolyn R. Spencer, E. St. Louis, IL
Camille Sroka, Toms River, NJ
Will Stauske, Cedarburg, WI
Beverly Stergeos, Fort Worth, TX
Linda Stevens, Houston, TX
Anne Stewart, Clearwater, FL
Geoffrey Strauss, Endicott, NY
Amy C. Strickland, Columbus, GA
Debbie Stuebbe, Bakersfield, CA
Ken Swiergosz, Toledo, OH
Bonnie Toone, Evansville, IN
Robert Torres, Anaheim, CA
Jeff VanArsdel, W. Lafayette, IN
Jill Vicino, Darien, IL
Lina Volesky, West Bend, WI
Sandy Wainio, Durham, NC
David D. Weaver, Palmdale, CA
Irene Webb, Hackensack, NJ
Kathy Webb, Garland, TX
Gloria Wein, Aberdeen, NJ
Victoria Wenke, Burlington, WI
Donna Wheeler, Madison, IN
Patricia Williams, Tampa, FL
June Winkel, Plymouth, WI
Ann Wittmer, Waco, TX
Karen M. Wolf, West Carrollton, OH
William W. Wunrow, Green Bay, WI
Thomas F. YingLing, St. Marys, OH
Carol Young, Yorba Linda, CA
Cy Young, Garden Grove, CA
Cheri Zuccarelli, Phelan, CA

TABLE OF CONTENTS

TABLE OF CONTENTS

TABLE OF CONTENTS

Ben & Jerry's

TABLE OF CONTENTS

TABLE OF CONTENTS

Robert Half International Inc.

TABLE OF CONTENTS

TABLE OF CONTENTS

Sony Corporation of America

OUTER BANKS MARKETPLACE, INC.
An Accounting Simulation Using Special Journals
and Covering a Closely Held Merchandising Corporation

TABLE OF CONTENTS

TABLE OF CONTENTS

ELECTRONIC ARTS™

Bally Total Fitness

TABLE OF CONTENTS

DIGITAL EXPRESS
An Accounting Simulation Using Special Journals and
Covering a Closely Held Merchandising Corporation

TABLE OF CONTENTS

TABLE OF CONTENTS

TABLE OF CONTENTS

FOCUS ON FEATURES

ACCOUNTING CAREERS IN FOCUS

CONNECT TO ...

International ACCOUNTING

Exploring the Real World of Business

Dear Student...

The Fifth Edition focuses on **a business perspective** by using examples from the business world to illustrate accounting concepts. Information on featured companies, organizations, their products, and services is included for educational purposes only, and does not represent or imply endorsement of the *Glencoe Accounting* program. The following companies appear throughout the text:

Chapter 1
World Wildlife Fund
Home Office: Washington, D.C.
Web Address: www.worldwildlife.org

Chapter 2
Huey's Athletic Network
Home Office: Santa Monica, CA
Web Address: www.lahuey.com

Chapter 3
DreamWorks SKG
Home Office: Universal City, CA
Web Address: www.dreamworks.com

Chapter 4
American Airlines
Home Office: Fort Worth, TX
Web Address: www.aa.com

Chapter 5
Wendy's International
Home Office: Dublin, OH
Web Address: www.wendys.com

Chapter 6
Ben & Jerry's Homemade, Inc.
Home Office: South Burlington, VT
Web Address: www.benjerry.com

Chapter 7
King Ranch
Home Office: Kingsville, TX
Web Address: www.king-ranch.com

Chapter 8
Washington Metropolitan Area Transit Authority (WMATA)
Home Office: Washington, D.C.
Web Address: www.wmata.com

Chapter 9
New England Aquarium
Home Office: Boston, MA
Web Address: www.neaq.org

Chapter 10
ACTIONQuest
Home Office: Sarasota, FL
Web Address: www.actionquest.com

Chapter 11
The Timberland Company
Home Office: Stratham, NH
Web Address: www.timberland.com

Chapter 12
Robert Half International Inc.
Home Office: Menlo Park, CA
Web Address: www.rhii.com

Chapter 13
Rhino Records
Home Office: Westwood, CA
Web Address: www.rhino.com

Chapter 14
Rollerblade, Inc.
Home Office: Minneapolis, MN
Web Address: www.rollerblade.com

Chapter 15
Levi Strauss & Co.
Home Office: San Francisco, CA
Web Address: www.levistrauss.com

Chapter 16
Sony Corporation of America
Home Office: New York , NY
Web Address: www.sony.com

Chapter 17
PETCO Animal Supplies Inc.
Home Office: San Diego, CA
Web Address: www.petco.com

Chapter 18
Schwinn
Home Office: Boulder, CO
Web Address: www.schwinn.com

Chapter 19
Office Depot, Inc.
Home Office: Delray Beach, FL
Web Address: www.officedepot.com

Chapter 20
Bose Corporation
Home Office: Framingham, MA
Web Address: www.bose.com

Chapter 21
Microsoft Corporation
Home Office: Redmond, WA
Web Address: www.microsoft.com

Chapter 22
Outback Steakhouse
Home Office: La Jolla, CA
Web Address: www.outback.com

Chapter 23
Electronic Arts
Home Office: San Mateo, CA
Web Address: www.ea.com

Chapter 24
Bally Total Fitness
Home Office: Chicago, IL
Web Address: www.ballyfitness.com

Chapter 25
Gap
Home Office: New York, NY, San Francisco, CA
Web Address: www.gap.com

Chapter 26
Carnival Corporation
Home Office: Miami, FL
Web Address: www.carnival.com

Chapter 27
Intersal
Home Office: Boca Raton, FL
Web Address: www.ah.dcr.state.nc.us/qar
(N.C. Depart. of Cultural Resources)

Chapter 28
Plum Creek Timber Company
Home Office: Seattle, WA
Web Address: www.plumcreek.com

Chapter 29
Institute of Internal Auditors
Home Office: Altamonte Springs, FL
Web Address: www.theiia.org

INSIDE YOUR BOOK

Structure of This Book

Your book contains 6 units. Each unit is divided into chapters; each chapter is divided into sections. There are a total of 29 chapters. This structure, together with numerous special features, will help you learn and apply various accounting concepts and procedures to the real business world.

The **Unit Opener** includes a short introduction and a colorful topic photograph that sets the stage for what you will learn in the unit.

The **Chapter Opener** helps you organize your study of chapter concepts. Learning objectives let you preview what you will learn in the chapter. You also get a chance to explore a real world business. Special features like *Workplace Connections* provide an opportunity for you to apply your accounting knowledge.

The **Check Your Understanding** activities and problems provide immediate reinforcement and help you apply accounting concepts.

Source Documents accompany each Business Transaction Analysis Model to help you visualize the forms used by real businesses.

Business Transaction Analysis Models help you not only learn how to record transactions, but also help you think critically.

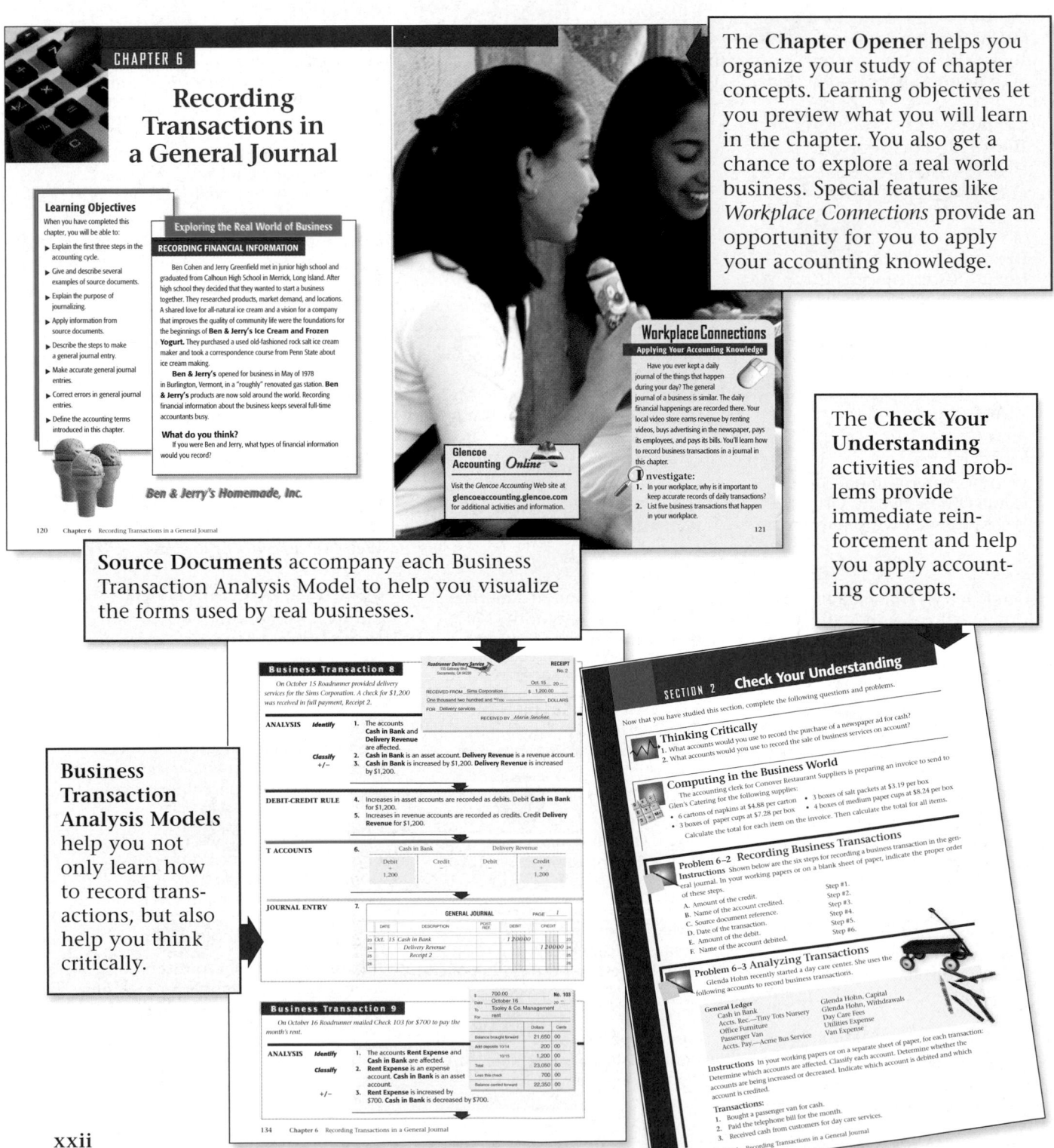

The **Chapter Summary** visually lists key concepts in the chapter for quick review and reference.

The **Chapter Review and Activities** help you review important accounting terms, concepts, and procedures. Various activities offer you an opportunity to apply your critical thinking and decision-making skills.

The **Chapter Problems** reinforce your accounting skills and enhance your accounting knowledge.

Computerized Accounting helps you make the transition from a manual system to a computerized system. You also learn how to apply the chapter content in the Peachtree system.

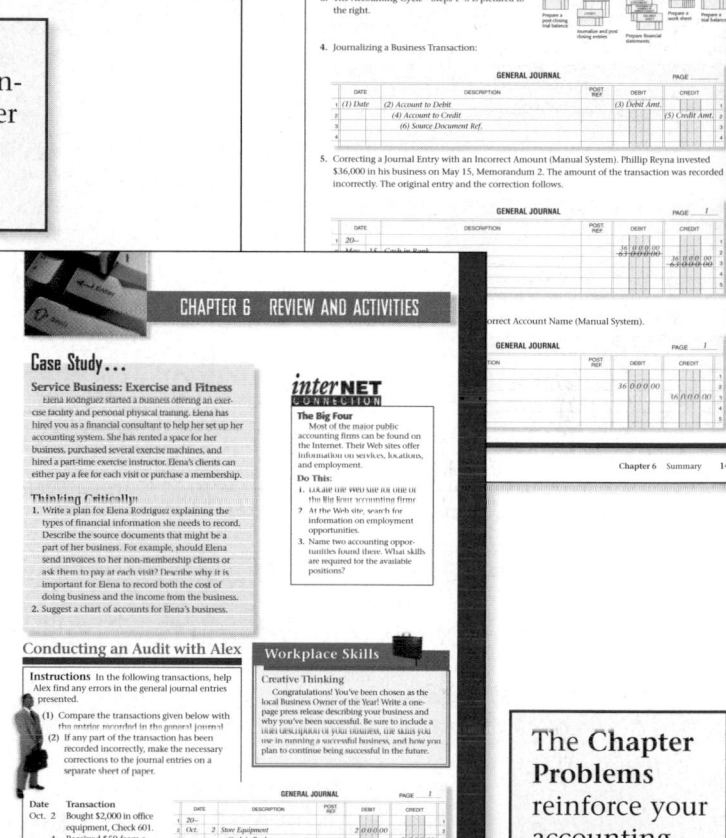

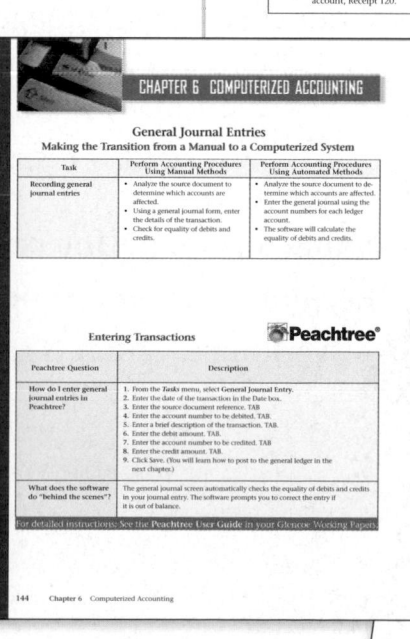

Introduction to Accounting

In this unit...

Accounting plays a vital role in the day-to-day activities of every business. In this first unit, you will learn about career planning, the variety of career opportunities available in accounting, and the importance of accounting in today's business environment. Accounting records and reports help businesses operate efficiently—and profitably—by keeping track of how much is earned and how much is spent.

Accounting is so much a part of the business world that much of its terminology has become a part of our everyday language. Throughout this book, you will learn why accounting has been called the "language of business."

Coming together is the beginning.
Keeping together is progress.
Working together is success.

—**Henry Ford**
American Automobile
Manufacturer

POWER READING STRATEGIES

To get the most out of your reading:

Predict what the section will be about.

Connect what you read with your own life.

Question as you read to make sure you understand the content.

Respond to what you've read.

In Your Journal . . .

Think of all your daily activities, either at school or work. How do you keep track of all your goals? Your future plans? Do you have a daily planner to keep track? This exercise will help you develop time management skills by setting priorities for completing work as scheduled.

In your journal, record the following:

1. During the next two weeks, make a list of at least three goals you would like to accomplish.

2. Next to the goals, write the steps you will take to achieve these goals.

3. Keep track of your daily progress by recording your ideas and experiences in a journal.

After the two weeks, review your journal to see if you have accomplished the goals.

CHAPTER 1

You and the World of Accounting

Learning Objectives

When you have completed this chapter, you will be able to:

▶ Describe how personal skills, values, and lifestyle goals affect career decisions.

▶ Find information about a variety of careers.

▶ Identify career opportunities in the accounting field.

▶ Set career goals.

▶ Describe the types of businesses and organizations that hire accountants.

▶ Compare for-profit businesses and non-profit organizations.

▶ Define the accounting terms introduced in this chapter.

Exploring the Real World of Business

THINKING ABOUT A CAREER

Do you know what tigers, black rhinos, and giant pandas have in common? All three have uncertain futures because their numbers are dwindling. Poachers and land development threaten their survival.

The **World Wildlife Fund,** a nonprofit organization, works to save endangered species. Not so long ago, the bald eagle—the national symbol of the United States—was on the endangered species list. Today, thanks to the **WWF** and other conservationists, the bald eagle is once again thriving and has been removed from the endangered list. The **WWF** raises and spends millions of dollars each year on its efforts to protect animals and their habitats.

The **World Wildlife Fund** employs accountants, writers, fund-raisers, and many other professionals who care about wildlife and their habitats.

What do you think?

1. What job skills or interests do you think you would need to work for an organization like the **World Wildlife Fund?**

2. What kinds of interests do you think would attract someone to such an organization?

World Wildlife Fund

Workplace Connections
Applying Your Accounting Knowledge

It's tough to figure out what you want to do with the rest of your life! Career counselors say that most people will have six to seven different careers throughout their lives. Some of us change careers entirely—from architect to teacher, or from freelance writer to photographer. Others stay within the same industry, but change specialties—from book designer to Web site designer, or from pediatrician to emergency care physician.

Investigate:

1. What type job do you have now or have you had in the past? Is it in a field you might continue to work in?
2. Imagine yourself in five years. What type of job do you have? Where are you living? What skills are you using?
3. Look at other people—your parents, other relatives, friends, coworkers, and people in the news. Do any of them have a career that you might enjoy? What skills would you need for this career?

Glencoe Accounting Online

Visit the *Glencoe Accounting* Web site at **glencoeaccounting.glencoe.com** for additional activities and information.

5

Exploring Careers

What You'll Learn

- How personal interests and skills, values, and lifestyle goals affect career decisions.
- Where to find information on possible careers.
- How to set career goals.

Why It's Important

A successful career begins with identifying your interests and skills and putting them to work for you. As consumers, we buy goods from merchandising businesses daily. Understanding the nature of these transactions is key to accounting for a merchandising business.

KEY TERMS

skills
values
lifestyle
personality
personal interest tests
networking

Film producer? Animation engineer? Web site designer? History teacher? Pediatrician? Financial analyst? Environmental conservation consultant? Who me?

Choosing a Career

Let's face it: Not many of us know what we want to do with the rest of our lives, especially when we're still in high school. You may be thinking, "I'll just take some liberal arts courses in college and something will come up" or "I'll just work for a while to make some money and then fall into a career." You know what? Something may come up, and you may just fall into a career; but if you ask people who really love what they do, odds are that they took some time to really get to know themselves and what turned them on.

Danielle and Steve have been friends since their freshman year. Like most students, they've been too wrapped up with classes, homework, and activities to give thought to what their lives will be like after high school. This all changed at the start of their final year. Steve sees his senior year as the end of a long haul, but Danielle sees it as the beginning of a whole new life.

Closing his locker door with his elbow, Steve turns to see Danielle smiling at him.

"Hey Dani! How's it going?"

"Great," says Danielle, holding up her class schedule. "They say the last year in high school is always the best."

"What are you taking?"

"Let's see. I've got chemistry, literature, algebra, speech, and accounting."

"Ouch, tough schedule! Did you say accounting? I would've never guessed you to be a number cruncher."

"I don't think I want to just 'crunch numbers.' I've always aced math, so I figured if I take accounting now, I'll know if I really like it enough to study it as a career. Besides, there are tons of ads in the paper for accounting jobs. If you're good at it, you can write your own ticket. Think about it: Companies need

*employees who know how to run their businesses. Plus it's not
just sitting at a desk crunching numbers. My aunt is a financial
advisor. She loves her job and travels all over the world."*

*"Slow down, Dani, it's only your senior year in high school. Don't you
think it's a bit too soon to be playing career woman?"*

"The sooner the better, Steve!"

"Maybe you're onto something here."

Unlike a job, which is simply work for pay, a career is built on a foundation of interest, knowledge, training, and experience. Have you given any thought to what you may want your career to be? If your answer is no, you're not alone.

Assess Your Career Vision

Before choosing a career, you'll want to do a little soul-searching. The more you know about yourself, the easier it will be to make career choices.

- What are your personal interests and skills?
- What are your values, and how will they affect your career?
- What lifestyle interests you?
- How will your personality affect a career choice?

Too many questions? You have all the answers; you just don't know it yet!

Your Interests, Skills, and Traits

You're more likely to enjoy a career that uses your individual interests, **skills**, and traits. Skills are activities that you do well. Take John King, for example. When John was a kid, he built an elaborate fort in his backyard. As a teenager John studied the architecture of major metropolitan cities. When he got out of high school, he was offered a job at a graphics company making calendars. The pay was good, but John lost interest and decided to go back to school to study his true passion, architecture. Today John is a partner in a successful architecture firm in Los Angeles, and he loves his job.

Are you good at math? Do you write well? Are you creative? Do you like to meet lots of new people, or like John, do you enjoy building things? Everyone has different skills and abilities—it's the combination that gives you a unique selling point. Here are some skills that employers have identified as being valuable. Although these skills are useful in a variety of situations, the chart on the next page provides examples of careers that require these skills and traits.

How many of these traits do you have? Make a list. It will come in handy when you begin to consider careers that interest you.

Values

One way to get to know yourself better is to examine your values. **Values** are the principles you live by and the beliefs that are important to you. It sounds good on paper, but values are really about actions, not words.

Key Points

Determining a Career Path

Assessing your interests, skills, and personality traits will help you determine a career path.

SKILLS & TRAITS	CAREER EXAMPLE
Creative thinking	Fine arts and humanities careers, such as actor, artist, or musician
Knowing how to learn	Training or teaching careers, such as business consultant or training coordinator
Responsibility	Health-related careers, such as surgeon, dental hygienist, or home health aide
Friendliness	Hospitality and recreation careers, including cruise director, hotel manager, or park ranger
Honesty	Child care workers, veterinarians, and other family and consumer science workers
Decision making	Financial planners, accountants, and other business and office careers
Analytical	Construction careers, including surveyors, general contractors, or electricians
Adaptability	Any of the public service careers, such as teaching, fire fighting, or serving in the armed forces
Self-control	Entrepreneur or manager
Self-esteem	Communications and media occupations, such as computer artist or book editor

For example, if you like to spend your free time volunteering at a local hospital or community center, one of your values might be helping others.

What you value and believe may change as you get older. Most people, though, have a basic set of values that they follow throughout their life. As you read this section, think about your personal beliefs. Remember, values are actions, not aspirations. Which values are important to you? Can you think of careers that would benefit from these values?

Responsibility. Being responsible means being dependable and taking positive actions, such as showing up on time to take a friend to an appointment or honoring a commitment. If you value responsibility, you might think about a career as a supervisor or manager.

Achievement. You value achievement if you want to be a success in whatever you do. I know, you're thinking, "Who doesn't want to be a success?" The truth is that wanting and achieving are two different things. For example, if you take the initiative to train outside of regular practices to make first string on the basketball team, you value achievement.

Relationships. If you especially value interaction with your friends and family, relationships are important to you.

After all, sharing the joy of your accomplishments is half the fun. Those who value these types of connections might avoid occupations that require a lot of travel and might base their career decisions on the ability to live close to family and friends.

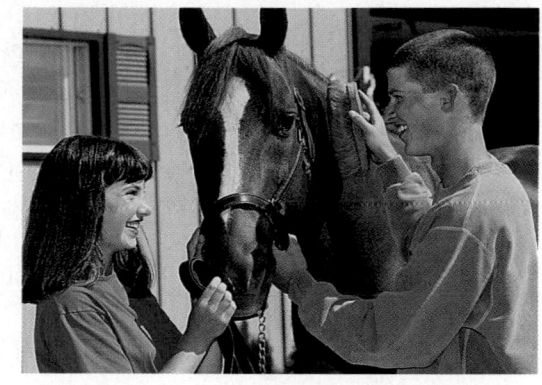

Compassion. Do you care deeply about people, animals, or special causes? For you, a compassionate career may outweigh all the money in the world. For example, if you love being around animals, you might enjoy a career in animal research or the marine sciences.

Courage. Courage is not just being brave in the face of physical danger. Courage is also the ability to overcome other fears. For example, it takes courage to make a speech to the whole school, even though you may be fearful or nervous. If you can put your beliefs on the line, you may be headed for a career in politics or law.

Recognition. If acknowledgement and appreciation of your work is important to you, then you value recognition. You might consider a career as a novelist or a television news reporter.

Many people share the same values, but how they apply them is unique to each person. To some, courage may be accepting the challenge of a job they know little about. To others, it may be turning down the big money to do something they really love. Think about your values. What can you learn from your values that will help you narrow your career choices?

Lifestyle Goals

Your **lifestyle** is the way you use your time, energy, and resources. For example, many people devote themselves to work, earn lots of money, and put off the benefits of free time until they're older. Others accept smaller paychecks and work fewer hours in order to spend more time with family and friends now. If you want to work as a business manager or accountant for a professional sports team, you'll have to live in a city that has such a team, even if the weather's bad! Or, if you want to perform in a touring theater company, you'll have to get ready for life on the road.

- What's really important to you?
- Do you want to go for the big bucks?
- Do you want to live in a big city with endless activities or a small town where everyone knows your name?
- Do you want to collaborate with a group of people, or do you prefer working solo?

Make a list of how you'd like to spend your time, energy, and resources. These are your lifestyle goals. Try to focus on careers that closely match them.

Personality Traits

Try to imagine what it would be like if all your friends had the same personality. What if they were all shy or all serious? Even worse, what if they all had the same sense of humor? It's a good thing we each have our own **personality** —a set of unique qualities that makes us different from all other people.

What is your personality? Are you confident, dependable, funny, friendly, sympathetic? Be honest. Do you like being with people, or would you rather

CONNECT TO . . .
GEOGRAPHY

Demographers study population density, distribution, and migration patterns. Using data from the census, records of vital statistics, and accounts of economic activity, demographers find out how different people react to certain events. For example, the rising cost of living has resulted in smaller families in America.

spend your time with things, such as reading books or working with computers? You're probably wondering what in the world this has to do with accounting. Well, your personality affects your preferences for working with data, people, or things.

As you collect information about yourself, you'll want to complete a personal career profile such as the one shown in **Figure 1–1**. Use this profile to help you evaluate whether the careers you're considering match your skills, interests, values, and personality.

Research the Possibilities

Once you have a clear vision of yourself and how you want to live, the next step is to begin researching careers to find the one that's right for you. Here are some great places to start:

- Guidance counselors do a lot more than just show you the quickest way to get from your homeroom to the cafeteria. They can help you identify the things you like to do. One way they accomplish this is through testing, called **personal interest tests**, which help you identify your preferences.
- **Networking** is a way to find out about particular careers by asking people to share information and advice.

Figure 1–1 Personal Career Profile Form

PERSONAL CAREER PROFILE FORM

Name Darla Johnson	Date December 12	Career Marketing Manager, Music Industry

Your Values I believe in equal opportunities for all people. I like to be creative.	**Career Values** All kinds of people work in the music industry. As a marketing manager, I would be able to use my creativity, as well as work with other creative people.
Your Interests I have a large collection of jazz and blues CDs and keep up with up-and-coming artists that are featured on independent labels. I love getting together with friends and having parties.	**Career Duties and Responsibilities** As a marketing manager, I would make contacts with music stores and distributors, labels and artists. I might send out press releases, arrange for artist appearances, and map out company marketing strategies to increase profits.
Your Personality I'm very outgoing and get bored with sitting in class or reading. I have a great imagination and love group discussions.	**Personality Type Needed** A marketing manager must work well with people. Sharp communications skills and attention to details are important.
Skills and Aptitudes My best subject is history, and I'm president of my school's debate team. I'm not big on writing letters or grammar, but love to communicate in person.	**Skills and Aptitudes Required** Good verbal communication skills are essential for a marketing professional. Although history may not be particularly important, good perceptions of what works and what doesn't work might be important.
Education/Training Acceptable I'd be interested in learning more about getting a business degree, but also believe that if I could get in on the ground level in the music industry and learn the ropes, I could be successful as well.	**Education/Training Required** I suppose a degree in marketing might open a lot of doors for me. A knowledge of how marketing and accounting fits into the big picture of a music corporation would definitely help.

- Print materials on every career imaginable can be found in your public library. Try books on careers or magazines that focus on your interests like *House & Garden, Metropolitan Home,* or *Business Week.*
- The Internet is a great source of educational and career information. Check out ideas for putting together the perfect résumé or browse through job opportunities at Paramount Studios!
- Professional organizations are groups of people who have common career interests. In the accounting field, the American Institute of Certified Public Accountants (AICPA) and the Institute of Management Accountants might lead to interesting careers.

Set Career Goals

Once you have a clear vision of your interests and the types of careers you want to pursue, it's time to put a plan into action.

Map Out a Plan

For starters you'll need to make a list of the careers you've researched and compare possibilities. The easiest way to do this is by making a chart. List the careers you're interested in along the top and list your personal information along one side. Where they meet, X marks the spot.

After selecting the career choices that look the most promising, decide which one you'll pursue. Reaching your ultimate career goal is not going to happen overnight. There are many intermediate goals to achieve along the way. **Figure 1–2** provides some ideas on setting career goals.

Education

Most careers require some education or training beyond high school. Unfortunately, deciding to further your education and coming up with the cash to pay for it are two different things. For ideas on help in paying tuition, you can turn to many of the same places you turned to for career information: books, the Internet, and your friend, the guidance counselor.

On-the-Job Training

Imagine going to school, taking only your favorite subject, and getting paid for it! That's how on-the-job training works. Suppose you're thinking about eventually opening your own accounting firm. While in school, you might work as an office assistant at a local accounting firm to learn how accounting services are provided. It's a great way to find out if accounting is the career for you, and you'll be paid for your efforts.

Internships

Another way to obtain career experience is to work as an intern. Many companies offer summer internships to students. Others offer longer internships. Some offer modest pay. Successful interns are often offered positions in the company once their internships are completed. The key is to become so valuable that they miss you when you're gone!

Key Points

Career Resources
- Guidance counselors
- Friends and family
- Print materials
- The Internet
- Professional organizations

Math Hints

Financial Aid

To find out if you qualify for financial aid, check with organizations such as:
- The College Board, or
- The U.S. Department of Education.

You can check their Web sites for more information.

Setting Career Goals

STEP 1 — Decide on a long-term goal.

A couple of years ago, Donald Yang began a part-time job working for an entrepreneur who started a business providing temporary employees to local companies. Donald decided that he wanted to be an entrepreneur someday, too.

STEP 2 — Decide on actions that will lead to the long-term goal.

Knowing that he lacked business experience, Donald realized that he had several things to learn before he could start a business. Donald's first action was to choose a college that offers business degrees. He researched financial aid packages and grants.

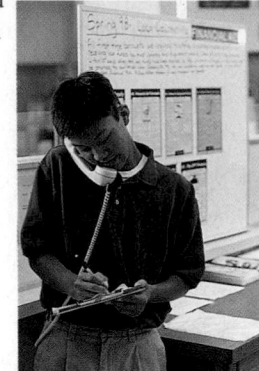

STEP 3 — Take action!

Donald got financial aid, enrolled in college, and worked for his business degree. As he neared graduation, Donald decided he wanted to learn the sports management business. After graduation he took a job with the New York Yankees. His job helped him learn about the costs of running a sports team. He also developed negotiation skills as he helped negotiate licensing fees for baseball souvenirs.

STEP 4 — Diversify your skills.

After gaining experience with the Yankees, Donald moved to a new job working for the Chicago Bulls basketball team. Here he learned more about operational costs and added negotiation of player salaries to his skills.

STEP 5 — Realize the long-term goal.

Through his work Donald has made a lot of contacts in the sports field. He's now ready to put his long-term goal into action by starting his own sports management business, where he will be a financial consultant to sports teams.

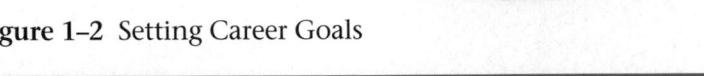

Figure 1–2 Setting Career Goals

A MATTER OF ETHICS

Padding a Résumé

Part of landing a great job is putting together a résumé that effectively represents your skills and background. Imagine that BMW has just opened a new regional headquarters in your area. You would like to work for BMW as a payroll clerk, but you're afraid you don't have the right qualifications. A friend suggests that you "change" your résumé to make yourself look better.

Ethical Decision Making:
- What are the ethical issues?
- What are the alternatives?
- Who are the affected parties?
- How do the alternatives affect the parties?
- What would you do?

Now that you have studied this section, complete the following questions and problems.

Thinking Critically

1. What consequences might result from choosing a career that conflicts with your values and lifestyle goals? Write one or two paragraphs describing these consequences.
2. Write three or four goals you can begin working toward now to help you choose a career. Include the steps you will need to take to reach each of your goals and the time within which you plan to accomplish each goal.

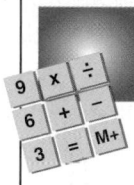

Computing in the Business World

Congratulations! The good news is that you've decided to attend a local community college after high school. The bad news is that tuition for an 18-week semester is $1,820. You estimate travel expenses of $20 per week and $300 for books and supplies. You plan to work 20 hours a week, earning $6.75 per hour. (I know it sounds weak, but hey, it's part-time!) Don't forget Uncle Sam. Social Security and income taxes will take about 15 percent of your earnings.

1. What is the total cost for a semester?
2. Assume that you've already saved $300 toward your first semester's costs. Approximately how long will it take to save enough to cover your tuition and books for one semester?

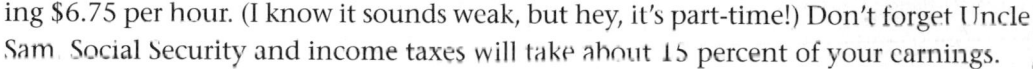

Problem 1–1 **Studying Yourself**

Instructions Think about the things you like to do and your particular skills. Make a list of at least five personal interests or skills, then use the career resource materials described in this section to identify one or more careers that match each interest or skill. Choose one career and write a one-page description of how your skills and interests fit this career.

Problem 1–2 **Gathering Career Resources**

Instructions Use the personal career profile form in **Figure 1–1** as a guide and compare three careers that you find interesting. Use the resources mentioned in this section to gather information: guidance counselors, networking, print materials, the Internet, and professional organizations. You may find other references in your school or local public library. After completing your comparison, write a brief summary; identify which of your choices you prefer and explain why.

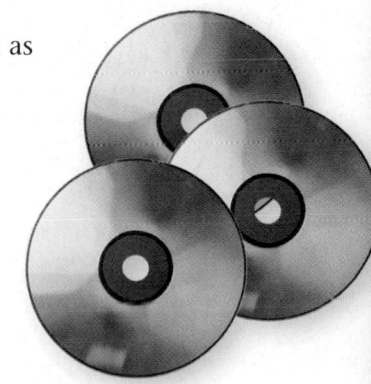

Accounting Careers: The Possibilities Are Endless!

What You'll Learn

- The variety of career opportunities available to accountants.
- The types of businesses and organizations that hire accountants.

Why It's Important

Explore all the careers available in accounting! You wouldn't want to miss a great opportunity just because you didn't know it existed.

KEY TERMS

accountant
for-profit business
not-for-profit organization
accounting clerk
certified public
   accountant
public accounting

Some people believe accounting is boring. There, we said it. It's a pretty safe bet that you didn't enroll in an accounting course because you thought it would lead to a career in the spotlight. How often do you see Brad Pitt starring in an action thriller about a jet-setting accountant? Exactly. However, who do you think develops and approves the budget for his films to go into production? Who do you think advises Mr. Pitt how to invest the hefty salary he makes? You got it—someone just like you, who is good with accounting concepts and knows how to handle money.

The point is: Accounting can be a lot of things you would never have imagined. So, if an accounting career matches up with some of your interests and goals, hang in there. We promise there's a lot more to it than crunching numbers!

The Changing Horizon

Sure, some careers in accounting can be a little dry, but there are many more that are dynamic and exciting. Think of any business— Warner Music, Nike, the Hard Rock Cafe. They all look to accountants to help run their businesses. Think of your favorite celebrities—maybe Jim Carrey or Cameron Díaz. Most have financial advisors. Movie producers hire accountants to track production costs. Publishers of magazines, like *PC World* and *Sports Illustrated,* depend on accountants to work with national advertisers to keep things running smoothly. In this chapter, you will identify career opportunities in the accounting field.

Accounting is not just adding and subtracting. An **accountant** handles a broad range of responsibilities, makes business decisions, and prepares and interprets financial reports. These are skills that successful businesses can't do without. If you're good, the sky's the limit. So, if you still picture accountants huddled over pages of numbers in back offices, the following scenarios should set you straight.

On the Road

"Okay, everybody. Show time in five minutes." The announcement comes as the members of the band adjust guitar straps and prepare to go out on stage. A crowd of 30,000 fans, dropping thirty-five bucks a head, waits for their entrance. Drew Taylor jokes with the band just offstage and then watches as they head out to the fans' applause.

Drew gets a rush being backstage amid all the excitement of a live show. As the financial assistant to the band's business manager, he often spends time at their performances. For Drew, working with numbers came as naturally as his love for music. He studied accounting throughout high school and college, and in his spare time he dabbled with the guitar and hung around recording studios with friends who were in the music business.

It wasn't long before they began to ask him for financial advice. His expertise landed him a position with one of the music industry's top business managers. Drew still dreams of recording his own music one day, but for now, he's quite content helping orchestrate the financial security of his music idols.

Accounting Professions in For-Profit Businesses. Entertainers perform to earn a profit. **For-profit businesses** operate to earn money for their owners. The majority of businesses in the United States are for-profit businesses.

Today, computers handle much of the basic accounting work, freeing accountants to do more planning for future operations. Computer technology means that accountants are no longer tied to a desk or an office. If you worked for artists like Moby, Radiohead, or Alicia Keys, you would probably spend part of your time traveling. Laptop computers and modems can connect you to your work as you travel to other cities and countries.

In order to explore accounting career opportunities, you need to compare the various forms of business organizations. Not all organizations are for-profit businesses.

For the Greater Good

"Listen up, folks! Here's the draft of the news release we're sending out tomorrow," shouts Darin Korman, waving a stack of papers in the air. "We need to get our position before the public while Congress is still considering the environmental legislation. Questions?"

"What else are we doing to alert voters to the potential value of this legislation?" a team member asks from the back of the room.

Darin, the team leader, opens a folder. "Here's our total plan. We begin filming a TV spot tomorrow. Next week, the art for our magazine ads will be finished, and they'll run in six different magazines. We'll also post a call-to-action on our Web site asking visitors for their support. We can all thank Maya for putting together a budget for the media campaign."

Accounting Professions in Not-For-Profit Organizations. Maya Cruz beams as her boss Darin describes a typical campaign put together for a group—like Sierra Club or Audubon Society—that works to protect and preserve the environment. Such groups operate as **not-for-profit organizations** , also known as *non-profit organizations*. When Maya was very young, her parents founded a similar group dedicated to cleaning up the waterways surrounding her hometown in New York. Maya helped her parents in the difficult task of soliciting donations within their community. As she grew older, Maya pursued the study of accounting with the sole purpose of continuing her involvement in environmental causes.

It is important to identify the various accounting functions involved with each form of business organization. Most not-for-profit organizations

have the goal of balancing their income with expenses rather than earning a profit for owners or investors. Some not-for-profit organizations, like United Way or Boy Scouts of America, get their income from donations. Other organizations get income through tax dollars. Government agencies, such as your school or a federal agency, fall under this category.

There are thousands of opportunities in the not-for-profit arena. Like Maya, it may be just the place for you to combine your interest in accounting with a cause that you hold close to your heart.

In the Know

"Shelly, the manufacturer is on the line in Hong Kong, and the designers are standing by in Vermont. We're ready to start the videoconference."

"All right, I'm set. Good morning, everyone. Let's get right to the point. As The Gap's financial consultant, it is my responsibility to inform you that costs on the new fall line are coming in slightly over budget. The purpose of this meeting is to find a way to cut costs without sacrificing quality. As manufacturer, Mr. Chu, you must have some ideas why our costs are higher than budgeted and what we can do to get back in line."

Shelly Hale loves her job. In high school Shelly could be counted on for two things—a keen fashion sense and the ease with which she breezed through math and logic. However, like most students, she was lukewarm to the idea of a career in accounting. That is, until an internship became available in the accounting department of The Gap. Shelly took the internship as an **accounting clerk**, an entry level job usually performing one or two accounting tasks. She eventually landed a position that allowed her to combine her talents and interests. Shelly continued to work at The Gap while attending school at night to become a **certified public accountant**, or CPA. CPAs pass a national test and meet specified experience and education standards to become "certified" to practice accounting.

Accounting Professions in Public Accounting Firms. With experience like Shelly's, you too might work as a financial consultant for a large company like The Limited or Levi Strauss. Or, you might choose to work for a **public accounting** firm and provide accounting services to their clients. Public accounting firms can be small or large—from a local business specializing in personal tax returns to an international firm such as Ernst & Young, which provides a variety of services to businesses all around the globe.

You might hear people refer to the "Big Four." These are the four major public accounting firms: PricewaterhouseCoopers, Deloitte & Touche, Ernst & Young, and KPMG. Accountants who work for these public accounting firms might work in tax planning or auditing. Auditing is the review of financial statements to confirm that they follow generally accepted accounting principles.

From entertainment to health care, conservation to entrepreneurship, the career possibilities in accounting are endless!

Key Points

Accountants in Demand

Every business must "account" for their financial activities.

It's something successful businesses can't do without!

Now that you have studied this section, complete the following questions and problems.

Thinking Critically

1. In business many decisions revolve around costs and potential earnings. For example, accountants might help create a picture, in numbers, of a proposed new product line; or they might be asked to suggest ways a company could cut its production costs. In addition to skill with numbers, what other skills do you think an accountant needs?
2. Make a list of five of your favorite products such as sports shoes, a favorite restaurant or food, or clothing. How do you think accountants who work for the companies that produce or sell these products might influence product decisions?

Communicating Accounting

Write a one-page article for a career newsletter. Describe the field of accounting and the types of businesses and organizations where accountants might work.

Problem 1–3 Checking Out Accounting Careers

Instructions Using the resources described in Section 1, research possible careers for people with accounting degrees. List at least five different careers and the formal training and work experience needed for each. Choose one career as your preference and write a paragraph describing why this career appeals to you.

Problem 1–4 Matching Interests and Careers

Instructions Using the three career examples described in this section, make a list of the personal interests and skills of the accountants described in each situation. Compare the list to your own interests and skills. Then think of three types of businesses (or actual companies) for which you might want to work. How would you learn about accounting career opportunities in those companies? Aside from pursuing needed training or education, what else would you do to prepare to work in that career? Share your ideas in class.

Problem 1–5 Researching Public Accounting Firms

Instructions Surf the World Wide Web or conduct research in your library to find information about the "Big Four" accounting firms. Create a table of information about each firm and the services the firm provides.

Problem 1–6 Interviewing Accountants

Instructions Interview members of the accounting field to investigate entry-level job requirements, career tracks for the profession, and projected trends for the future. Write a short report about your findings.

ACCOUNTING CAREERS IN FOCUS

JOYCE LUNDBOM
Senior Billing Manager
MCI

Q: What does your job entail?
A: I spend a lot of time answering revenue questions from other departments. I also answer my staff's questions and provide them with direction. I try to keep tabs on projects and keep them moving. I spend a lot of time problem-solving.

Q: What skills are most important to you?
A: Communication skills are critical. Analytical skills are also important. It's important to be able to see what has an impact on the profitability of a business. What appears to be small dollars could have a lot of significant numbers behind it. Knowing when to delve into something is a big part of the job.

Q: What do you like about your job?
A: I have a strong sense that my contribution to the company is relevant and that it is recognized. It is an exciting environment to work in. I like accounting because you take financial information and add meaning to it. You use your knowledge of the industry, the company, and the financial reports to understand trends. That's when you start contributing to the management of a company.

Tips from . . .

RHI Robert Half International Inc.

Money is not all a company can offer. Some companies offer benefits such as advancement opportunities, stock options, tuition reimbursement, training, telecommuting, flex-time and child-care. Employees who feel valued work harder.

CAREER FACTS

Nature of the Work: Oversee billing of wholesale customers, answer management questions, oversee projects, and guide staff.
Training or Education Needed: A bachelor's degree in accounting or business, the CPA exam, auditing experience, and continuing education.
Aptitudes, Abilities, and Skills: Communication skills, analytical skills, problem-solving skills, organizational skills, and good judgment.
Salary Range: $40,000 to $60,000 depending on company size and industry.
Career Path: Start as a staff accountant and gradually take on more challenges, and then move into management.

Thinking Critically: What attributes can make a company exciting to work for?

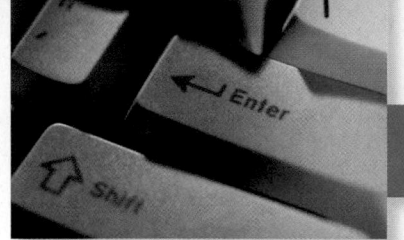

KEY CONCEPTS

1. A successful career begins with insight into your own personal skills, interests, goals, and lifestyle preferences.

2. Personal skills and traits play major roles in how successful you may be in certain careers. Get to know yourself. What you value and believe plays a vital role in deciding what you want to pursue as a career.

Responsibility   Compassion

Achievement   Courage

Relationships   Recognition

3. As you decide on a career, consider lifestyle goals and personality traits.

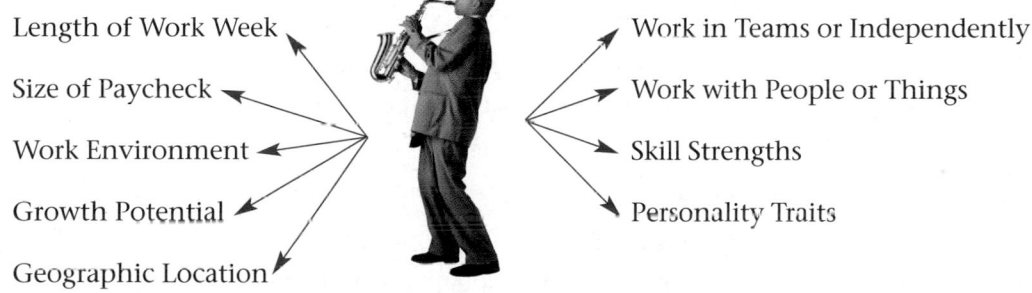

Length of Work Week   Work in Teams or Independently

Size of Paycheck   Work with People or Things

Work Environment   Skill Strengths

Growth Potential   Personality Traits

Geographic Location

4. Researching career possibilities can include sessions with a guidance counselor, networking with friends and family, magazines and books, the Internet, and seeking information from professional organizations. Do your homework. Research jobs, salaries, geographic locations, work environments, and growth potentials. You want to know what you are getting into, don't you?

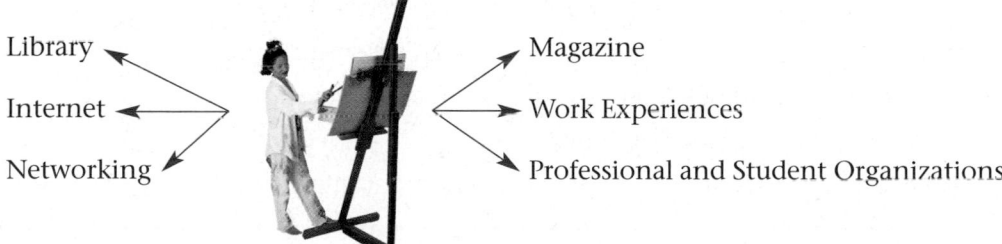

Library   Magazine

Internet   Work Experiences

Networking   Professional and Student Organizations

5. To set and accomplish career goals, map out a plan, consider the education required, find a part-time job to get some on-the-job training, and check into internships available in your field of interest.

6. Accountants work for almost any company you can think of. Find a company you're interested in, and you can bet there's an accountant in the picture planning next year's budget, chasing down an expense report from the owner, or advising managers on financial issues.

USING KEY TERMS

Suppose you are preparing to interview a person who works in the accounting field. On a separate sheet of paper, write a list of questions you'll be asking in the interview. Incorporate each of the following terms in your questions:

accountant
accounting clerk
career
certified public accountant
for-profit business

lifestyle
not-for-profit business
personal interest tests
values

Understanding Accounting Concepts and Procedures

Instructions

Answer the following questions on a separate sheet of paper:

1. Why should you consider your interests and skills when thinking about a career?

2. How does lifestyle affect career choices?

3. What are six common values that most people have?

4. Why should you consider your personality as you evaluate possible career choices?

5. List and describe at least three categories of career information resources.

6. Describe how networking is beneficial to career planning.

7. Describe how to create a personal career profile form.

8. Describe the five steps that are helpful when setting career goals.

9. List at least three types of organizations that offer accounting career opportunities.

10. What need would a not-for-profit organization have for an accounting professional?

11. Describe three ways that technology might be used by an accountant.

12. List three of the major public accounting firms.

13. List three possible functions that a Certified Public Accountant might provide for a business.

Case Study...

Career Advice

Sean Smith is a senior in high school. He's taking an accounting course this year because he wants to be an accountant. Sean likes working with numbers, but he also likes working with people. He plans to go to college but doesn't know which ones offer accounting programs and what costs are involved.

Thinking Critically:

Take the role of Sean's career counselor. Write a one-page report advising Sean. Include the following in your report:

- Information on how to find the resources he needs to choose a college.
- Details on how to set education and career goals.
- Define the steps Sean needs to take over the next several months.
- Prepare a list of resources Sean might use to learn more about accounting careers, colleges, and financial help.

inter NET CONNECTION

Finding Jobs on the Internet

Most large companies, and many smaller ones, can be found on the Internet. Along with product and service information, many companies post employment details and job openings.

Do This:

1. Find a company on the Internet that you might want to work for in the future. If you're not sure how to find a company on the Internet, ask your teacher for search engine sites like Yahoo, Excite, or Lycos.
2. What is the company's Web site address?
3. Does the company's site provide information about employment?
4. If employment information is provided, list the job opportunities you find.
5. Write a brief summary describing the company, its business purpose, and its products or services.

Workplace Skills

Acquiring and Evaluating Information

To make a decision, whether personal or business-related, you must be able to acquire and analyze data (information).

On the Job:

You've graduated and you're ready for that job that matches your skills and interests!

Thinking Critically:

1. Make a list of the businesses that advertise in one of your local or regional newspapers. You may want to use a Sunday issue since it's usually packed with ads.
2. Separate the businesses into for-profit and not-for-profit categories. For example, for-profit would include restaurants, retailers, entertainment providers (such as movie theaters or sports arenas), manufacturers, and so on. Not-for-profit may include schools, community organizations, and government agencies.
3. Write a summary of your findings, and describe the accounting career opportunities you think these businesses and organizations might offer.

Problem 1–7 Researching Careers in Your Library

Instructions Using a reference book (such as the *Occupational Outlook Handbook*), choose a career area that interests you. Research the skills, education, and experience you would need to work in that area. Your research can utilize any number of resources including books, magazines, and the Internet. Write a brief profile of your chosen career, including a description of jobs in the field, education or training requirements, potential earnings, and working conditions. Present your profile to the class.

Problem 1–8 Researching Careers in Your Local Newspaper

Instructions Review the employment ads in a local or regional newspaper. Collect information on at least 10 job titles plus the skills and education required for each. Include at least two job titles related to the accounting field. Present your information in table format. If you have access to a word processing program, use it to create and print your table for your teacher.

Problem 1–9 Assessing Your Skills and Interests

Instructions Complete an assessment of your personal skills and interests by answering the questions in your working papers. Use the survey included in the working papers, or you can ask your guidance counselor to administer a personal interest test. Using the results of the test, find at least three careers that match your skills and interests.

Problem 1–10 Working with Others

Instructions As an accountant for a large business, you might be put in charge of training new hires in the accounting department. Or, you might be asked to discuss project cost overruns with a department manager or to present operating results to senior managers. In these situations, you need skills other than just your accounting knowledge. For each situation, make a list of the skills needed, then decide whether you have those skills and, if not, how you plan to acquire them.

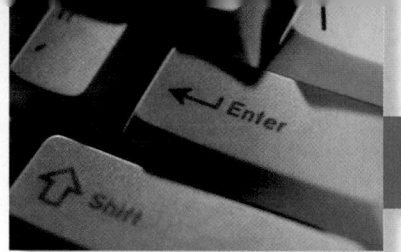

Problem 1–11 Summarizing Personal Traits

Instructions Sometimes you can learn about yourself by asking other people how they see you. Ask at least 10 people to name three words they think describe you. For example, someone might say you are dependable, fun, and quick-thinking. Do not just choose friends. Ask teachers, coworkers, relatives, and others who are willing to give you an honest opinion. Make a list of each person's descriptions; then summarize your findings by identifying the five characteristics or traits that were mentioned most often. Do these descriptions match your self-perception? Why or why not?

Problem 1–12 Gathering Career Information

Instructions Interview someone who currently works in a career area that interests you. Before the interview, prepare a list of the questions you want to ask. After the interview write two or three paragraphs describing your interview and the information you learned. Explain how this information will help you choose a career.

Problem 1–13 Exploring Careers in Accounting

Instructions Choose a local company that interests you, and find out who works as an accountant for the company. Call and ask whether you can observe the person at work for part of a day. Write a summary of your observations, and share the information with the class.

Problem 1–14 Exploring Global Careers

Instructions Many U.S. businesses operate in the global economy, which means they need accountants who understand international business. Find a local company that imports or exports products to or from one or more countries. Interview the accounting manager, and find out the skills, formal study, and personal traits they look for in an accountant who works in international accounting. Write a short report about your findings.

CHAPTER 2

The World of Business and Accounting

Learning Objectives

When you have completed this chapter, you will be able to:

▶ Describe the role of profit, risk-taking, and the entrepreneur in the U.S. economy.

▶ Describe the differences among service, merchandising, and manufacturing businesses.

▶ Compare the sole proprietorship, partnership, and corporate forms of business.

▶ List the advantages and disadvantages of each form of business organization.

▶ Describe the purpose of accounting.

▶ Explain the difference between financial and management accounting.

▶ Describe the three basic assumptions that underlie accounting principles.

▶ Define the accounting terms introduced in this chapter.

Exploring the Real World of Business

BECOMING AN ENTREPRENEUR

Sports superstars like Venus Williams, Alex Rodriguez, and Kobe Bryant are among the best-conditioned athletes in the world; but even super athletes occasionally pull a muscle or suffer a stress fracture. That's when Lynda Huey comes to the rescue.

Huey's Athletic Network (HAN) uses aquatic therapy to help injured athletes rebuild body strength. As a track star at San Jose State University, Lynda Huey taught herself that water is beneficial because the body's buoyancy in water reduces the strain on injured muscles and bones. After college, she worked as a college coach and in 1986 started **Huey's Athletic Network.** The company's first job was aquatic training for Olympic athletes.

Today, **HAN** provides personal training and consulting not only to sports stars, but also to entertainers and weekend warriors who want to stay fit. Entertainment clients include Ben Stiller and Barbra Streisand. Lynda Huey regularly appears on television programs and has written books and magazine articles on water exercise.

What do you think?

1. What knowledge and special skills do you think Lynda Huey needed to start and manage her business?
2. What makes an entrepreneur successful?

Huey's Athletic Network

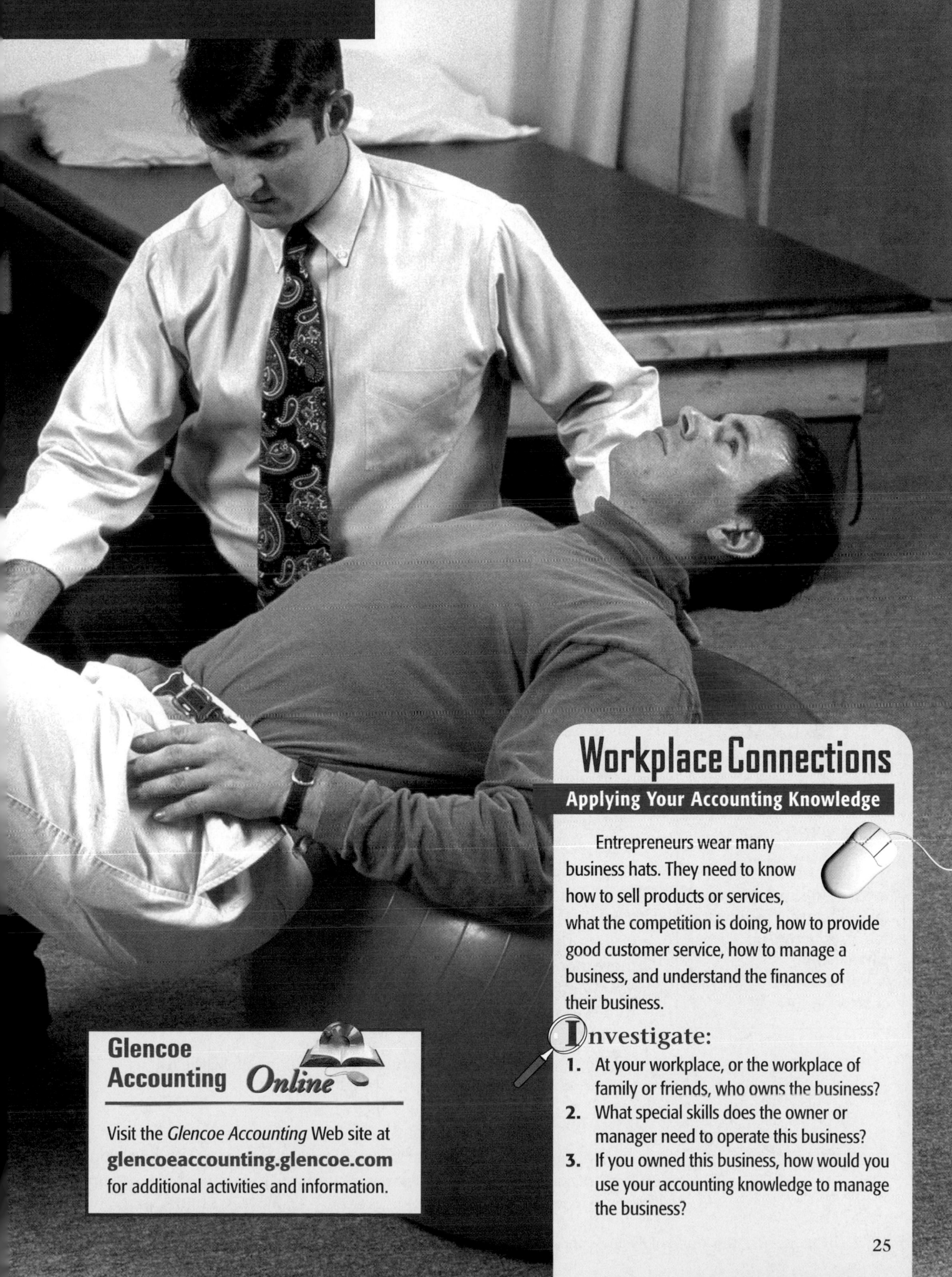

Workplace Connections

Applying Your Accounting Knowledge

Entrepreneurs wear many business hats. They need to know how to sell products or services, what the competition is doing, how to provide good customer service, how to manage a business, and understand the finances of their business.

Investigate:

1. At your workplace, or the workplace of family or friends, who owns the business?
2. What special skills does the owner or manager need to operate this business?
3. If you owned this business, how would you use your accounting knowledge to manage the business?

Glencoe Accounting *Online*

Visit the *Glencoe Accounting* Web site at **glencoeaccounting.glencoe.com** for additional activities and information.

25

Exploring the World of Business

In this chapter you will learn about different types of businesses and how they are organized. All businesses need information that is generated by accounting systems in the form of reports. You will learn about the different types of accounting and accounting reports.

In 1982 Howard Schultz joined Starbucks Coffee. When he purchased Starbucks, it consisted of six stores and fewer than 100 employees. Through his vision, energy, and imagination, he built the business to 4,000 stores with over 47,000 employees. By 2000 Starbucks was the top specialty coffee retailer in the nation, with coffee shops in 20 countries worldwide.

The Environment of Business

When you hear the word *business,* what do you think of? Nike, Microsoft, General Motors, IBM, Coca-Cola, or Tower Records? Large businesses like these are certainly players in the world of business today. Your neighborhood convenience store, clothing boutique, video rental store, and grocer are also important contributors in our free enterprise system. In a **free enterprise system** people are free to produce the goods and services they choose. Individuals are free to use their money as they wish: spend it, invest it, save it, or donate it. Business owners in this system must compete to attract the customers they need to continue operating.

One measure of success in a business operation is the amount of profit it earns. The amount of money earned over and above the amount spent to keep the business operating is called **profit** . Businesses that spend more money than they earn operate at a **loss** .

Whether small, medium, or large in size, a business must do two things to survive:

- It must operate at a profit.
- It must attract and keep an individual willing to take the risk to run it.

The Need for Profit

Continued operation and success of a business require profit. Your local pizza parlor must pay for raw materials (flour, sauce, cheese, toppings), equipment (mixers, ovens, freezers), employees, utilities, and rent.

The selling price of the pizza must be high enough to cover all costs. Once the owner pays these costs, the money left over is profit.

The Need for a Risk-Taker

Within a business many people play different roles in daily operations, planning, and management. Inventors create ideas for producing new products or services. Investors provide money to help businesses get started. Employees supply the labor needed to operate the business. Managers handle supervision and planning. The role of the entrepreneur is special. **Entrepreneurs** transform ideas for products or services into real-world businesses. They are motivated self-starters willing to take the necessary risks to create profitable and useful businesses.

Entrepreneurship: Who Me?

Have you ever considered owning a business? Owning a business can offer flexible schedules, self-direction, and financial gain. Yet business ownership is not free from risk. Examine **Figure 2–1** for some pros and cons of entrepreneurship.

Pros	Cons
• You are your own boss.	• You probably need to work long hours.
• You create opportunities for earning money.	• You lose the security of steady wages and medical benefits an employer provides.
• You create and control your work schedule.	• You market your own services or products.
• You choose the people you serve.	• You pay for your own operating expenses.
• You select the people who work with you.	• You must be motivated and energetic each day.
• You benefit from the rewards of your own hard work.	• You face the possibility of losing money.
• You choose your own work hours.	

Figure 2–1
Entrepreneurship:
Pros and Cons

Traits of Entrepreneurs

As you consider the path of entrepreneurship, take an inventory of your own skills and interests. Most entrepreneurs share certain behaviors and attitudes. Do you have good writing and speaking skills? Do you have a creative or mechanical mind? Are you a self-starter? Can you identify a community need and fill it? Do you have the capital to get started? Do you have accounting or marketing skills? Take a look at **Figure 2–2** to get an idea of the decisions that entrepreneurs face.

Owning your own business is not for everyone. An entrepreneur must possess the drive to overcome obstacles and be extremely resourceful. Strong organizational skills, marketing knowledge, and accounting skills are three areas of expertise that contribute to successful business ownership. If you are a visionary and have great energy and imagination, you may have the makings of an entrepreneur!

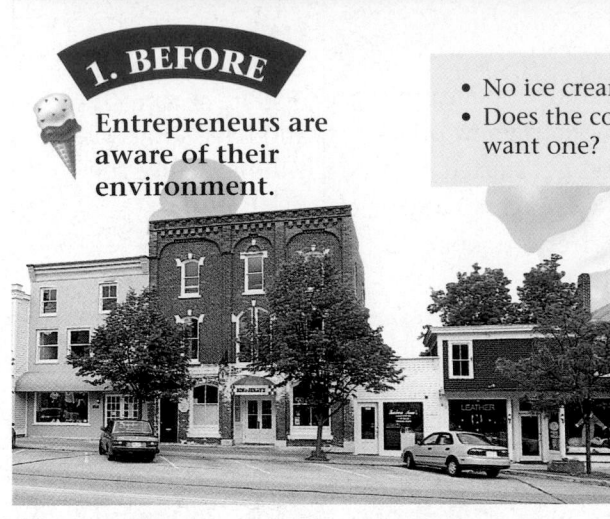

1. BEFORE

Entrepreneurs are aware of their environment.

- No ice cream shop.
- Does the community want one?

2. IN BETWEEN

Entrepreneurs evaluate alternatives.

- Customer preferences
- Architect plans
- Accountant's guidance

Figure 2–2

Types of Business Operations

In our free enterprise system there are three types of businesses that operate for profit: service, merchandising, and manufacturing.

Service, merchandising, and manufacturing businesses are alike in many ways. Each offers products or services, incurs expenses, and makes sales to customers. They differ from one another, however, in some basic ways. Each type of business needs money to begin and maintain operations. Money is needed to buy or to make products, and to cover operating costs like rent, utilities, and wages. Money supplied by investors, banks, or owners of a business is called **capital** .

Service Businesses

A **service business** provides a needed service for a fee. Service businesses include travel agencies, styling salons like Fantastic Sam's, movers, repair shops, real estate offices like Century 21, and medical centers.

Merchandising Businesses

A **merchandising business** buys finished products and resells them to individuals or other businesses. Department stores like JCPenney, new and used car dealers, supermarkets like Kroger, drugstores like Rite Aid, florists, and hobby shops are examples of merchandising businesses.

Manufacturing Businesses

A **manufacturing business** buys raw materials, such as wood or iron ore, and transforms them into finished products through the use of labor and capital. It then sells the finished products to individuals or other businesses. Manufacturing businesses range from a shipbuilder, like Atlantic Marine Shipyard of Mobile, Alabama, to the Pioneer Bakery in Venice, California.

Forms of Business Organization

To start a business, a potential owner must have a sufficient amount of money (capital) and must choose an appropriate form of business

---

ACCOUNTING *Flashbacks*

USING ELECTRONIC SPREADSHEETS

An electronic spreadsheet is software that can be used to create work sheets and trial balances and perform calculations. The first spreadsheet program, Visi-Calc, was released in 1978.

Key Points

Types of Businesses

There are three types of businesses:
- service
- merchandising
- manufacturing

Entrepreneurs seek the best solution.

 **3. AFTER**

Entrepreneurs turn ideas into actions.

• Ben & Jerry's is a worldwide producer of ice cream and frozen yogurt.

• Only used appliances are within budget guidelines.

organization. With a few exceptions, U.S. businesses are organized in one of three ways: sole proprietorship, partnership, or corporation, illustrated in **Figure 2–3**. Let's compare the various forms of business organization.

Type of Business	Form of Business		
	Sole Proprietorship	Partnership	Corporation
Service	X	X	X
Merchandising	X	X	X
Manufacturing	X	X	X

Figure 2–3 Forms of Business Organization

Key Points

Forms of Business Organization
There are three forms of business organization:
• sole proprietorship
• partnership
• corporation

Sole Proprietorship

Sole means "single" or "one." *Proprietor* means "owner." A **sole proprietorship**, therefore, is a business owned by one person. The term *proprietorship* is also used to describe this form of business organization. Being a sole proprietor does not mean working alone. Based on the size and scope of the operation, a sole proprietorship may have many managers and employees. The oldest and most common form of business organization, the sole proprietorship is the easiest form of business to start. Little or no legal paperwork (forms and documents) is required. The success or failure of the business depends heavily on the efforts and talent of the owner.

The advantages and disadvantages of organizing as a sole proprietorship are shown in **Figure 2–4**.

Did You Know?

Prices
Physical trainers and therapists charge from a low of about $30 an hour to more than $90 a session. Each session usually lasts from 30 to 60 minutes.

Advantages	Disadvantages
• Easy to set up	• Limited expertise
• All profits go to owner	• Hard to raise money
• Owner has total control	• Owner has all the risks
• Few regulations to follow	• Hard to attract talented employees

Figure 2–4 Advantages and Disadvantages of a Sole Proprietorship

Partnership

A **partnership** is a business owned by two or more persons, called partners, who agree to operate the business as co-owners. Business partners usually enter into a written, legal agreement. This agreement specifies the amount of money or property to be invested by each partner, the responsibilities of each partner, and how profits and losses are to be divided. Partnerships are often formed when the need for capital is greater than the amount of money one person can invest. Partnerships are not always small. For example, large accounting firms like Deloitte & Touche LLP are organized as partnerships and may have as many as 1,500 partners and over 20,000 employees. **Figure 2–5** provides advantages and disadvantages of the partnership.

Advantages	Disadvantages
• Easy to start • Skills and talents are pooled • More money available	• Conflicts between partners • Profits must be shared • Owners share all risks

Figure 2–5 Advantages and Disadvantages of a Partnership

Corporation

A **corporation** is a business organization that is recognized by law to have a life of its own. In contrast to a sole proprietorship and a partnership, a corporation must get permission from the state to operate. This legal permission, called a **charter**, gives a corporation certain rights and privileges. The charter spells out the rules under which the corporation is to operate.

Corporations often start out as sole proprietorships or partnerships. The owner(s) of a business may choose to "incorporate" to acquire additional money needed to expand. To raise this money, shares of stock are sold to hundreds or even thousands of people. These shares represent investments in and ownership of the corporation. *Shareholders,* who are also called stockholders, are the legal owners of a corporation. Starbucks is an example of a business organized as a corporation that has thousands of shareholders. **Figure 2–6** outlines a few advantages and disadvantages of organizing as a corporation.

Regardless of their form, sole proprietorship, partnership, or corporation, all businesses share common financial characteristics and methods for recording and reporting financial changes.

Setting Prices

When setting prices for products, most businesses:

• add all their costs of doing business,

• then calculate the prices to make an adequate profit.

Businesses might charge 20 or 25 percent over expenses.

Advantages	Disadvantages
• Easier to raise money • Easy to expand • Easy to transfer ownership • Losses limited to investment	• Costs more to start up • Complex to organize • More regulations • Higher taxes

Figure 2–6 Advantages and Disadvantages of a Corporation

Now that you have studied this section, complete the following questions and problem.

Thinking Critically

1. Would you say that the advantages of being an entrepreneur outweigh the disadvantages or vice versa? Why?
2. Explain how being influenced early in life by a role model might be critical to someone's success as an entrepreneur?

Communicating Accounting

Locate and read a current magazine article featuring a successful entrepreneur. Try periodicals like *Business Week, Forbes,* or *Working Woman.* Write a summary of the article, and explain why you think the person succeeded.

Problem 2–1 **Assess Your Entrepreneurship Potential**

Instructions The characteristics or traits needed to set up an owner operated business and to run it successfully are listed below. Rank yourself, indicating if this trait is most like you or least like you. Use the form provided in your working papers.

	Most Like Me			**Least Like Me**	
Persistent	5	4	3	2	1
Creative	5	4	3	2	1
Responsible	5	4	3	2	1
Inquisitive	5	4	3	2	1
Goal-oriented	5	4	3	2	1
Independent	5	4	3	2	1
Demanding	5	4	3	2	1
Self-confident	5	4	3	2	1
Risk-taking	5	4	3	2	1
Restless	5	4	3	2	1

List the categories in which you ranked 3 or lower. Identify experiences, activities, and ways in which you could improve your entrepreneurial potential.

Accounting: The Universal Language of Business

What You'll Learn

- How the accounting system works.
- Who uses financial accounting reports.
- Who uses management accounting reports.
- How accounting is used to help make business decisions.
- What assumptions provide the foundation for accounting systems.

Why It's Important

Understanding accounting systems is the key to understanding business.

KEY TERMS

accounting system
manual accounting
  system
computerized accounting
  system
GAAP
financial reports
financial accounting
management accounting
business entity
accounting period
going concern

Have you ever wondered how the band U2 determines which venues they will play, the cost of a tour, how profitable CD sales have been, or how much ticket prices should be? All these issues are probably tackled by the band's financial team: accountants, clerks, and financial advisors.

The Accounting System

Whether you are the accountant for a band or the financial manager for a chain of mountain bike stores, accounting methods are universal. The **accounting system** is designed to collect, document, and report on financial transactions affecting the business. In a **manual accounting system** the accounting information is processed by hand. In a **computerized accounting system** the financial information is recorded by entering it into a computer. Owners and investors who risk their money depend on accountants to report the results of operations and the financial condition of the businesses in which they invest. **Figure 2–7** outlines the inputs, processes, and outputs of an accounting system.

All accountants use the same set of rules, called **"generally accepted accounting principles"** or **GAAP** (pronounced "gap") to prepare their reports. Accounting principles provide a way to communicate financial information in a form understood by those interested in the operations and financial condition of a business. Because it is so fundamental to the communication of financial information, accounting is often called the "language of business." **Financial reports** are summarized information about the financial status of a business.

Key Points

GAAP

GAAP stands for "generally accepted accounting principles."

Inputs →	Processing →	Outputs
Source Documents	**Tasks**	**Financial and Management Accounting Reports**
• Checks	• Analyzing	• Financial condition
• Invoices	• Classifying	• Results of operations
• Sales Slips	• Recording	• Investments by and distributions to owners
• Receipts		

Figure 2–7 How the Accounting System Works

Using Accounting Reports for Making Business Decisions

The purpose of accounting is to provide financial information about a business or a not-for-profit organization. Individuals need financial information in order to make decisions.

The information found in accounting reports has a wide audience. In general, there are two groups that use accounting reports:

- individuals *outside* the business who have an interest in the business
- individuals *inside* the business

Financial Accounting

Financial accounting focuses on reporting information to external users. Financial accounting reports are prepared for individuals not directly involved in the day-to-day operations of the business. These reports are prepared using GAAP.

Who Uses Financial Accounting Reports?

- Suppose you wanted to invest in a business, such as Trek Mountain Bikes Inc. You would analyze financial accounting reports to estimate if an investment in the business would be profitable.
- Individuals or institutions, like banks that loan money to a business, use financial accounting reports to determine whether or not the business will be able to repay loans.
- Local, state, and federal governments review financial accounting reports. For example, the Internal Revenue Service may compare the tax return and financial reports of a business to determine whether the business is paying the proper amount of taxes.
- Workers, consumers, union leaders, and competitors are interested in the performance of businesses as presented in financial accounting reports.

Management Accounting

Management accounting, which focuses on reporting information to management, is often referred to as accounting for *internal* users of accounting information. Management accounting reports are prepared for managers involved in making the day-to-day operating decisions like purchasing, hiring, production, payments, sales, and collections.

Managers need accounting information so they can decide what to do, how to do it, when to do it, and whether or not the results match the plans for the future. **Figure 2–8** describes some of these decisions.

Accounting Assumptions

An assumption is something taken for granted as true. When you attend a movie, you assume the volume will be at a reasonable level, there will be a place to sit, and the film will be in focus. If these assumptions are wrong, the movie will be a disappointing experience.

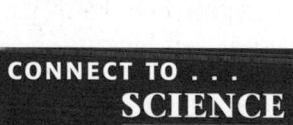

Owners and managers use financial reports to make decisions.

- Which flowers are the best sellers?
- Can we purchase a new delivery van?
- Should we hire more designers?
- Can we afford to attend floral conventions in Amsterdam?

Figure 2–8 Managerial Decisions

Each business sets up an accounting system according to its specific needs, but all businesses follow GAAP. These generally accepted accounting principles are based on three very important assumptions summarized by the following terms:

- business entity
- accounting period
- going concern

For accounting purposes, a business is a separate entity. A **business entity** exists independently of its owner's personal holdings. The accounting records and reports are maintained separately and contain financial information related only to the business. The business owner's personal financial activities or other investments are not included in the reports of the business. For example, the personal residence of a pet store owner, valued at $100,000, is not reported in the accounting records of the pet store. Buildings owned by the business, however, are included in the financial records and reports of the pet store.

For reporting purposes, the life of a business is divided into specific periods of time. A period of time covered by an accounting report is referred to as an **accounting period** . The accounting period can cover one month or three months (quarterly), but the most common period is one year. This assumption is necessary when accountants assign the cost of buildings and equipment over the estimated period of time they will be used. Comparison of reports from one period to the next also makes the accounting period concept necessary.

Unless there is evidence to the contrary, accountants assume that a business has the ability to survive and operate indefinitely. In other words, a business is expected to continue as a **going concern** . Although many businesses fail within the first five years, the accountant assumes the business will continue to operate unless it is clear that it cannot survive.

A MATTER OF ETHICS

Becoming an Entrepreneur

Imagine that you've been working for a local day-care center for several years. You attend a company meeting to discuss new ideas on improving day care. Several new services are discussed that would help your center stand out from its competition. You think that this is a great opportunity for you to become an entrepreneur—by opening your own day-care center offering the new services discussed in the meetings.

Ethical Decision Making:

- ☞ What are the ethical issues?
- ☞ What are the alternatives?
- ☞ Who are the affected parties?
- ☞ How do the alternatives affect the parties?
- ☞ What would you do?

Now that you have studied this section, complete the following questions and problems.

Thinking Critically

1. If a business owner failed to follow the assumption of "business entity," what complications might arise?
2. Consider creating an "accounting system" for your personal finances. How would you organize the system? What inputs would there be? How might you record your activities? How might you report on those activities?

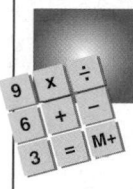

Computing in the Business World

Suppose you are opening a 1,000 square foot baseball card store in a shopping center. You have signed a lease that requires you to pay a monthly rent of $1.75 per square foot, plus 5% of your gross annual sales. What is the total amount of rent you will pay in one year if you have sales of $85,000?

Problem 2–2   Using Financial Information

Instructions Imagine that you are the manager for Valley Skateboard Shop. The accountant for the business delivered the news that sales are down by 15% compared to last month. She also reports that the rent on the building will be increasing next month by $100. You believe the shop needs a more experienced salesperson and that the building needs new paint and awnings. How might the information delivered by the accountant affect your decisions and course of action?

Problem 2–3   Identifying Accounting Assumptions

Suppose you work for a company called Greenwood Sky Divers as a sky-diving instructor. Since you have your pilot's license, you also give flying lessons on the side. You and the owner of Greenwood Sky Divers both belong to a local club, called the Greenwood Eagles, whose members get together for sky dives on weekends. Greenwood Sky Divers is a sole proprietorship that has been in business for six years. The owner of the company regularly reviews financial reports, and the company's accountant prepares end-of-the-year reports to compare results from one year to the next.

Instructions Decide what information in this paragraph is relevant to accounting for Greenwood Sky Divers. Identify the accounting assumptions for Greenwood, and give an example of each assumption from the information given here.

STERLING ELLSWORTH
Certified Public Accountant (CPA)

Q: Why did you choose accounting?
A: Because of its precision. I was a math major, but theoretical math, such as calculus, didn't interest me. I had taken an accounting class, and struggled with it, but enjoyed it at the same time. I took a second one and knew it was for me. It was challenging, but rewarding.

Q: What do you like about working for yourself?
A: I like the freedom to work when I want, take vacations when I want, to adjust my time around my workload. I work more intensely sometimes, but I have a lot of time off.

Q: How does your workload vary?
A: During tax season, I work 12 hours a day, or more, for about a 90-day period. It's very intense. Then it slows down. In late summer and early fall, I take a lot of four-day weekends. That's when I appreciate what I do.

Q: What skills are important to you?
A: Time management skills are the most critical. You have to be able to organize and work at maximum efficiency. You can't make mistakes that cost your client money, yet you have to work quickly. People skills are important too. Sometimes I have only 10 minutes to sell myself and convince clients they can trust me with their financial records.

Tips from . . .

RHI Robert Half International Inc.

Learn to manage your time by planning ahead. Get organized with a "to do" list. Gather your supplies and resources for each task, then set priorities and schedule similar tasks together.

CAREER FACTS

Nature of the Work: Consult with clients, prepare tax forms, attend IRS audits, give financial advice.

Training or Education Needed: A bachelor's degree in accounting or business, the CPA exam, and continuing education.

Aptitudes, Abilities, and Skills: Time-management skills, interpersonal skills, organizational skills, computer skills, and math.

Salary Range: Start at $40,000 to $200,000, depending on prior experience.

Career Path: Pass the CPA exam, work in an accounting field to gain work experience, build client base, then start your own business.

Thinking Critically: How would you convince clients that you can be trusted with their records?

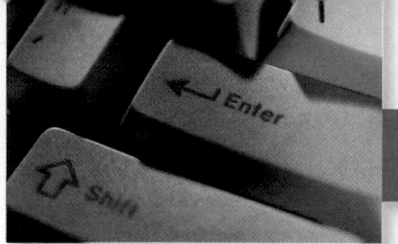

KEY CONCEPTS

1. The free enterprise system is based on individual freedoms.
2. Competition among businesses to attract customers is a key element of the free enterprise system.
3. Businesses need to operate profitably in order to continue.

| Money Earned from Sales | > | Money Spent to Operate Business | = | Profit |

4. Entrepreneurs are willing to take risks and make things happen in business.
5. While everyone is different, people who become successful entrepreneurs tend to have similar traits, such as a strong desire to succeed, the ability to solve problems, and creative ideas for business services or products.
6. The three types of businesses are service, merchandising, and manufacturing.
7. Sole proprietorships, partnerships, and corporations are three forms of business.
8. Sole proprietorships are owned by one person, partnerships by two or more partners, and corporations by many shareholders who own stock in the corporation.
9. Accountants use "generally accepted accounting principles" or GAAP to prepare financial accounting reports.
10. Financial accounting reports are often used by individuals outside the business to make decisions, such as whether to buy stock in a company or to loan money to the company.
11. Management accounting reports are used by individuals inside the business to make decisions, such as whether to cut costs or to hire more workers.
12. Three important accounting assumptions are business entity, going concern, and accounting period.

USING KEY TERMS

On a separate sheet of paper, write a brief definition for each of the following terms:

accounting period	GAAP
accounting system	going concern
business entity	management accounting
charter	manual accounting system
computerized accounting system	manufacturing business
	merchandising business
corporation	partnership
entrepreneur	service business
financial accounting	sole proprietorship
financial reports	
free enterprise system	

Understanding Accounting Concepts and Procedures

Instructions

On a separate sheet of paper, answer the following questions:

1. The United States economy is referred to as a free enterprise system. What are the major characteristics of this system?

2. What is one measure of the success of a business?

3. What is the major difference between a merchandising business and a manufacturing business?

4. List advantages and disadvantages of each form of business organization: sole proprietorship, partnership, corporation.

5. What does GAAP mean?

6. Describe the purpose of accounting.

7. What are the major differences between financial and management accounting?

8. What are the three basic assumptions of accounting, and what do they mean?

9. What are some characteristics of the entrepreneur?

10. Who are the users of management accounting information?

11. Who are the users of financial accounting reports?

Case Study...

Entrepreneurship

Thousands of entrepreneurs start new businesses each year. Locate two or three entrepreneurs in your local area to interview. If you need help finding entrepreneurs, check with your local chamber of commerce or other business organizations. Telephone each entrepreneur and ask for an interview. Schedule the interview, then prepare questions such as these:

- How did you get the idea for your business?
- How did you finance the business?
- What skills have helped you start and run the business? How did you acquire these skills?
- What personal qualities have helped you be successful?
- What has been your biggest challenge in starting a business?
- What advice would you offer to other would-be entrepreneurs?

Thinking Critically:

1. Conduct the interviews, then write a general profile of the qualities and skills of a successful entrepreneur. Use information from all your interviews.
2. After writing your profile, decide whether you're entrepreneurial material. Explain why or why not.

interNET
CONNECTION

The Small Business Administration

Some people dream of starting their own business because they want to be their own boss. Others desire financial independence or the opportunity to fully realize their creative freedom, skills, and knowledge. The Small Business Administration offers a wide variety of resources to the entrepreneur.

Do This:

1. Find the Small Business Administration Web site. What is the Web site address?
2. What features of the site do you think would be the most helpful to a person starting a business?
3. Based on information at the Web site, what goes into a business plan?

Workplace Skills

Individual Responsibility

High performance workers exhibit perseverance and excellence in their job duties. Working well and showing a high level of concentration on any task indicates you can assume individual responsibility for your work.

On the Job:

As an accounting clerk for Prints-in-a-Minute, a sole proprietorship, you prepare most of the financial statements for your employer, José Tirado. As you prepare for your year-end meeting with Mr. Tirado, you locate an error in the financial reports. How do you handle this situation?

Thinking Critically:

1. Mr. Tirado depends on you for accuracy. You write a memo to Mr. Tirado explaining what has occurred. Give Mr. Tirado a plan as to how you will correct the problem.
2. Mr. Tirado has read the memo and has called a conference with you. Pair up with another student and role-play the conference, one of you as the accounting clerk, the other as Mr. Tirado. Together discuss how you plan to fix the mistake.

Problem 2–4 Identifying Types of Businesses

Instructions In your working papers, indicate whether each of the following businesses is a service business, a merchandising business, or a manufacturing business.

1. International Business Machines (IBM)
2. The Gap
3. Glendale Medical Center
4. Avis Rent-a-Car
5. Ford Motor Company
6. The Chase Manhattan Bank
7. Ace Hardware Stores
8. Michigan City Animal Hospital
9. Office Depot
10. Wal-Mart Discount Department Store
11. Prudential Insurance Company of America
12. Bethlehem Steel Corporation

Problem 2–5 Understanding Accounting Assumptions

Instructions In your working papers, indicate the assumption from the list below that best matches each numbered statement.

Accounting Period   **Business Entity**   **Going Concern**

1. Accounting reports may cover a month, a quarter, or a year.
2. Accountants expect a business to last indefinitely.
3. The personal property of a business owner is not included in the accounting records of the business.
4. The business has been in operation for several years and is expected to continue.
5. An owner's personal activities or properties are not mixed with the business activities or properties.
6. The accountant's report shows how much profit the business earned for one month.

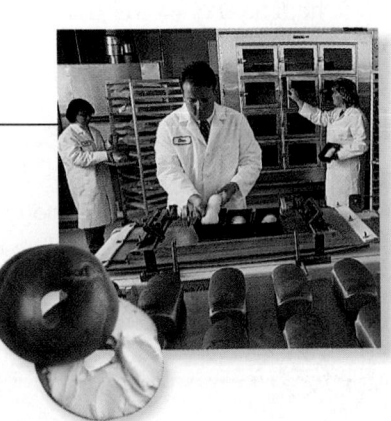

Problem 2–6 Understanding Business Operations

    Mary Torres owns and operates a bakery. During the past week she sold 500 loaves of bread at $2.25 per loaf. The raw materials for each loaf cost Ms. Torres $1.80.

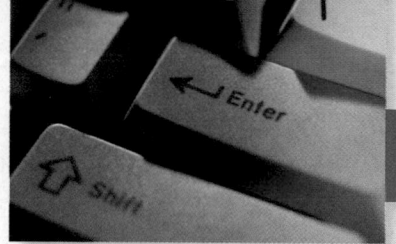

Instructions In your working papers, write the answers to the following questions:

1. What type of business does Ms. Torres operate?

2. What was the profit on bread sales for the week?

3. Aside from the costs for raw materials, what other costs will Ms. Torres use to calculate her profit for the week?

Problem 2–7 Categorizing Forms of Business Organizations

Instructions Match the letter next to each form of business with the appropriate items in the following list of advantages and disadvantages. You may use a letter more than once. Use the form provided in your working papers.

A. Sole Proprietorship B. Partnership C. Corporation

1. Easier to raise money
2. Limited expertise
3. Costs more to start up
4. Owner has total control
5. Must share the profits
6. Higher taxes
7. Fewer regulations to follow
8. Easy to transfer ownership
9. Conflict between owners
10. Easy to expand

Problem 2–8 Working as an Entrepreneur

Instructions Using the form in your working papers, identify each of the following as an advantage or disadvantage of being an entrepreneur. For each item you label a disadvantage, decide what actions you would take to overcome that disadvantage. Analyze and describe how your actions might affect the profit your business earns.

1. Risking the loss of your savings
2. Deciding what you and everyone else needs to do each day
3. Lacking steady wages and employee benefits
4. Choosing when and where to work
5. Keeping the financial benefits of your hard work
6. Choosing the people you want to work with
7. Paying all the expenses of a new business

UNIT 2

The Basic Accounting Cycle

In this unit...

All businesses keep financial records. In this unit, you will learn how business transactions affect the financial records of a business. Learning to analyze business transactions correctly is the first step toward learning accounting. The business used as an example in this unit is a sole proprietorship. The business, called **Roadrunner Delivery Service,** provides delivery services to its customers. After studying the chapters in this unit, you will have an understanding of the accounting cycle for a service business and will identify the accounting functions involved with a sole proprietorship.

We must use time creatively and forever realize that time is always hope to do great things.

—Martin Luther King, Jr.
American Civil
Rights Leader

To get the most out of your reading:

Predict what the section will be about.

Connect what you read with your own life.

Question as you read to make sure you understand the content.

Respond to what you've read.

In Your Journal . . .

The key to operating a successful business is keeping accurate accounting records. For one month, keep track of your personal accounting record by listing every transaction you make.

In your journal, record the following:

1. Write down the total amount of money you already have.

2. Add to the record the source of income (paycheck or allowance), the amount earned, and the date of transaction.

3. Then for every item you spend (movies, food, or shopping), record the amount spent, the item purchased, and the date of transaction.

After the month is over, review your list of transactions. How accurate is your accounting record?

43

CHAPTER 3

Business Transactions and the Accounting Equation

Learning Objectives

When you have completed this chapter, you will be able to:

▶ Appy basic accounting concepts.

▶ Apply basic accounting terminology.

▶ Describe the relationship between property and financial claims.

▶ Explain the meaning of *equity* as it is used in accounting.

▶ List and define each part of the accounting equation.

▶ Demonstrate the effects of transactions on the accounting equation.

▶ Check the balance of the accounting equation after a business transaction has been analyzed and recorded.

▶ Define the accounting terms introduced in this chapter.

Exploring the Real World of Business

INVESTING EQUITY

Born in Cincinnati, Ohio, Steven Spielberg shot his first movie in order to earn a Boy Scout merit badge. His homemade action film, called *Gunsmog,* featured a holdup, a sheriff, and a bad guy who plunged over a cliff. By the age of 46, Spielberg became a billionaire by producing movies like *ET, Back to the Future, Jurassic Park,* and several *Indiana Jones* movies.

DreamWorks SKG is a partnership he formed with Jeffrey Katzenberg and David Geffen. Each partner invested $33 million with plans to produce feature films and television series. **DreamWorks SKG** is located in Hollywood, California.

What do you think?

1. Making movies and television programs can cost millions of dollars. How do you think the money invested by the **DreamWorks'** partners helps the company operate?
2. What are the benefits of a partnership?

DreamWorks SKG

Glencoe Accounting *Online*

Visit the *Glencoe Accounting* Web site at **glencoeaccounting.glencoe.com** for additional activities and information.

Workplace Connections

Applying Your Accounting Knowledge

Every business has assets, liabilities, and owner's equity—the elements in the basic accounting equation that you'll study in this chapter. The business uses an accounting system to record its assets, liabilities, and owner's equity. Your local bakery's assets (what it owns) probably include kitchen equipment and ovens. Its liabilities (debts) may include unpaid bills to food suppliers, and the owner's equity of the business (what the business is worth) may be money that the owner invested to get the bakery up and running.

Investigate:

1. In your workplace, what assets does the business have?
2. What types of debts or liabilities would you imagine the business to have?

45

Property and Financial Claims

What You'll Learn

- The relationship between property and financial claims.
- The meaning of *equity* as it is used in accounting.
- The parts of the accounting equation.
- The definition of each part of the accounting equation.

Why It's Important

The accounting equation is the basis for keeping all accounting records in balance.

KEY TERMS

property
property rights
financial claims
credit
creditor
assets
investments
equity
owner's equity
liabilities
accounting equation

In Chapter 2, you learned that accounting is the language of business. In this chapter, you will learn how to apply basic accounting concepts and terminology. You will also learn how the accounting equation expresses the relationship between property and the rights, or claims, to the property.

United Parcel Service (UPS), a corporation that provides global delivery services, uses accounting reports to communicate to its managers, employees, and investors. The UPS financial reports identify the property used in the business, like airplanes, trucks, and computers. The reports also show how the company obtained the property, either from loans or from funds provided by investors.

Property: Ownership and Control

The right to own property is basic to a free enterprise system. **Property** is anything of value that is owned or controlled. When you own an item of property, you have a legal right or financial claim to that item. When you have control over an item, you have the right only to the use of the item. For example, suppose you paid $600 for a mountain bike. As a result of the payment, you own the bike. If you had rented the bike for the weekend instead of buying it, you would pay a much smaller amount of money, but you would have control of the bike for only a limited time. You would have the right to use the bike for the weekend, but you would not own it.

As you can see from this example, you can have certain rights, or claims, to the items that you either own or control. The following table illustrates the difference between ownership and control.

	Property Right	Financial Claim
Own	Yes	Yes
Control (like rent)	Yes	No

Businesses also own and control property. One of the purposes of accounting is to provide financial information about property and rights to that property. In accounting, property and financial claims are measured in dollar amounts. Dollar amounts measure both the cost of the property and the **property rights**, or **financial claims** to the property. In our mountain bike example, since you paid $600 cash to buy the bike, you have a property right *and* a financial claim of $600 to the bike. This relationship between property and financial claims is shown in the following equation.

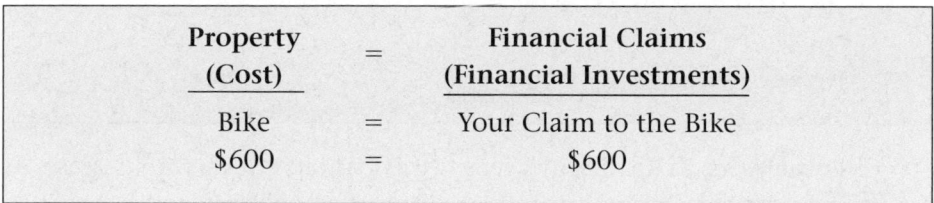

Property (Cost)	=	Financial Claims (Financial Investments)
Bike	=	Your Claim to the Bike
$600	=	$600

When you buy property with cash, you acquire all of the financial claims to that property at the time of purchase. What happens to the financial claim, however, when you don't pay for the property right away?

When you buy property and agree to pay for it later, you are buying on **credit**. The business or person selling you the property on credit is called a **creditor**. A creditor can be any person or business to which you owe money. When you buy property on credit, you do not have the only financial claim to the property. You share the financial claim to that property with your creditor. For example, suppose you want to buy a $100 lock for the mountain bike, but you have only $60. You pay the store $60 and sign an agreement to pay the remaining $40 over the next two months. Since you owe the store (the creditor) $40, you share the financial claim to the lock with the creditor. The creditor's financial claim to the lock is $40 and your claim is $60. The combined claims equal the cost of the property. Your purchase of the lock can be expressed in terms of the equation: PROPERTY = FINANCIAL CLAIMS.

Property	=	Financial Claims		
Bike Lock	=	Creditor's Financial Claim	+	Owner's Financial Claim
$100	=	$40	+	$60

As you can see, two (or more) people can have financial claims to the same property.

Financial Claims in Accounting

In accounting, property or items of value owned by a business are referred to as **assets**. Some examples of assets are cash, office equipment, manufacturing equipment, buildings, and land. The accounting term for the financial claims to these assets is **equity**. **Investments** are assets, generally long-term in nature, that are not intended to be converted to cash or to be used in the normal operations of the business in the next accounting period. If you have a financial claim to property, you are said to have equity in that property. Let's explore the meaning of the term equity by introducing Maria Sanchez and her new business, Roadrunner Delivery Service, organized as a sole proprietorship.

International ACCOUNTING

Overnight Guarantee

FedEx Corporation, the company that revolutionized the way people work, began when its founder Fred Smith was drawing a doodle of the distribution model—a hub and connecting spokes—used by major airlines to route flights. He proposed that if all mail were channeled through one major hub, it would reach its final destination more quickly. Smith's plan worked so well that FedEx was able to expand its overnight guarantee to include worldwide destinations.

ACCOUNTING Flashbacks

THE IRS WEB SITE
When the IRS put up its Web page in 1996, it received over a million hits during its first week. The site offers documents, guidelines, and help for taxpayers.

Using Algebra

You can calculate amounts in a financial equation using the rules of algebra.

The basic accounting equation is in the form of $a = b + c$.

- To find either b or c,
- re-write the equation as $b = a - c$, or $c = a - b$.

Suppose Roadrunner Delivery Service purchases a delivery truck for $10,000. Roadrunner makes a cash down payment of $3,000 to the seller. A local bank loans Roadrunner the remaining $7,000. Both Roadrunner and the bank now have financial claims to the truck.

Property	=	Creditor's Financial Claim	+	Owner's Financial Claim
Truck $10,000	=	$7,000	+	$3,000

Over the years, as Roadrunner repays the loan, its equity will increase. As less money is owed, the equity of the creditor (the bank) will decrease. When the loan is completely repaid, the creditor's financial claim will be canceled. In other words, the owner's equity will then equal the cost of the truck. Roadrunner will own the truck and will have full property rights to it.

As you can see from this example, equity is simply the claims—of both creditor(s) and owner(s)—to the assets of a business. In accounting, there are separate terms for owner's claims and creditor's claims. The owner's claims to the assets of the business are called **owner's equity**. Owner's equity is measured by the dollar amount of the owner's claims to the total assets of the business.

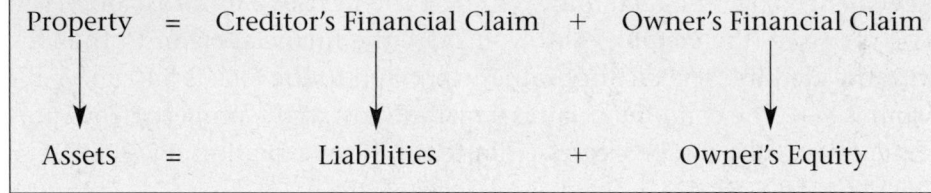

Property	=	Creditor's Financial Claim	+	Owner's Financial Claim
Assets	=	Liabilities	+	Owner's Equity

Key Points

Equity

Equity includes both the creditor's claims (liabilities) and the owner's claims (owner's equity).

The creditor's claims to the assets of the business are called **liabilities**. Liabilities are the debts of a business. They are measured by the amount of money owed by a business to its creditors. The relationship between assets and both types of equity (liabilities and owner's equity) is shown in the **accounting equation**:

$$\textbf{ASSETS} = \textbf{LIABILITIES} + \textbf{OWNER'S EQUITY}$$

A MATTER OF ETHICS

Company Property

Many companies provide office supplies for their employees' use while on the job. Imagine that you work for a large department store like JC Penney. Several of your co-workers take company supplies home for their personal use, such as pens, bags, hangers, and boxes. You need boxes to store some items at home, so you consider taking them from the supply room.

Ethical Decision Making:

- ☞ What are the ethical issues?
- ☞ What are the alternatives?
- ☞ Who are the affected parties?
- ☞ How do the alternatives affect the parties?
- ☞ What would you do?

Now that you have studied this section, complete the following questions and problems.

Thinking Critically

1. Explain the legal right of owning an item of property.
2. What is meant by having a financial claim to property?

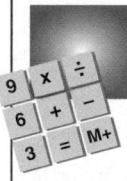

Computing in the Business World

Many types of work require you to convert fractions into decimals and vice versa. Convert the following fractions into decimals.

1. $\frac{1}{2}$
2. $\frac{1}{5}$
3. $\frac{1}{3}$
4. $\frac{4}{5}$
5. $\frac{7}{8}$
6. $\frac{7}{10}$

Convert the following decimals into fractions.

7. 0.889
8. 0.60
9. 0.375
10. 0.25
11. 0.667
12. 0.75

Problem 3–1   Balancing the Accounting Equation

Instructions Determine the missing dollar amount indicated by the question mark in each equation. Write each missing amount in your working papers.

	ASSETS	=	LIABILITIES	+	OWNER'S EQUITY
1.	$17,000	–	$ 7,000	+	?
2.	?	=	$ 6,000	+	$20,000
3.	$10,000	=	?	+	$ 7,000
4.	?	=	$ 9,000	+	$17,000
5.	$ 8,000	=	$ 2,000	+	?
6.	$20,000	=	$ 7,000	+	?
7.	?	=	$12,000	+	$ 4,000
8.	$30,000	=	?	+	$22,000
9.	$22,000	=	$ 1,000	+	?
10.	$25,000	=	$ 5,000	+	?
11.	?	=	$10,000	+	$25,000
12.	$ 7,500	=	?	+	$ 3,000

Transactions That Affect Owner's Investment, Cash, and Credit

The last time you purchased a new sweater, bought popcorn at the movies, or deposited money into your savings account, you were participating in business transactions. Business transactions involve the purchase, sale, or exchange of goods and services. Some businesses have hundreds, or even thousands, of business transactions every day. When a business transaction occurs, the financial position of the business changes.

Business Transactions

A **business transaction** is an economic event that causes a change—either an increase or a decrease—in assets, liabilities, or owner's equity. The change is reflected in the accounting system of the business. Let's look at an example.

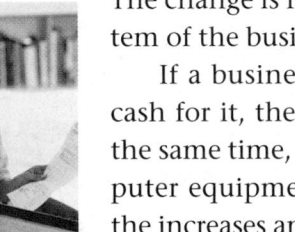

If a business buys a computer and pays cash for it, the amount of cash decreases. At the same time, the business increases its computer equipment. In an accounting system, the increases and decreases caused by business transactions are recorded in specific accounts. An **account** shows the balance for a specific item, such as cash or computer equipment. It also is a record of the increases or decreases for that specific item.

Accounts represent things in the real world, such as money invested in a business, office furniture, or money owed to a creditor. For example, an account for office furniture represents the dollar cost of all the office furniture owned by the business.

Every business sets up its accounts and its accounting system according to its needs. The number of accounts needed by a business will vary. Some businesses use only a few accounts, while others use hundreds. Regardless of the number of accounts a business has, all its accounts may be classified as either assets, liabilities, or owner's equity. Here are the accounts used by Roadrunner Delivery Service:

Assets	=	Liabilities	+	Owner's Equity
Cash in Bank		Accounts Payable		Maria Sanchez, Capital
Accounts Receivable				
Computer Equipment				
Office Equipment				
Delivery Equipment				

The second asset account listed is **Accounts Receivable**. **Accounts receivable** is the total amount of money owed to a business. It represents money to be received later because of the sale of goods or services on credit. The **Accounts Receivable** account is an asset because it represents a claim to the assets of other people or businesses. It represents a future value that eventually will bring cash into the business. When the business receives payment, the claim will be canceled.

The liability account listed is **Accounts Payable**. **Accounts payable** is the amount of money owed, or payable, to the creditors of a business. It is a future obligation requiring the payment of cash or services to other people or businesses.

Finally, note that the owner's equity account in a business is identified by the owner's name followed by a comma and the word "Capital." Capital, as you learned in Chapter 2, refers to the dollar value of assets contributed to the business.

Effects of Transactions on the Accounting Equation

When a business transaction occurs, an accounting clerk analyzes the transaction to see how it affects each part of the accounting equation. Analyzing business transactions is simple. Use the following steps.

Business Transaction		
ANALYSIS *Identify*	1. Identify the accounts affected.	
Classify	2. Classify the accounts affected.	
+/−	3. Determine the amount of increase or decrease for each account affected.	
Balance	4. Make sure the accounting equation remains in balance.	

The business transactions that follow are examples of transactions that occur in most businesses. To help you learn about various kinds of transactions, these examples are categorized as follows:

- investments by the owner,
- cash transactions,
- credit transactions,
- revenue and expense transactions, and
- withdrawals by the owner.

Key Points

Business Transactions
Every business transaction affects at least two accounts.

The first three categories are covered in this section. Transactions involving revenues, expenses, and withdrawals by the owner are covered in the next section.

Investments by the Owner

These transactions illustrate investments by the owner, Maria Sanchez, in her business, Road-runner Delivery Service. The first involves a cash investment, while the second concerns a transfer of property.

Business Transaction 1

Maria Sanchez took $25,000 from personal savings and deposited that amount to open a business checking account in the name of Roadrunner Delivery Service.

ANALYSIS	*Identify*	1. Cash transactions are recorded in the account **Cash in Bank.** Maria Sanchez is investing personal funds in the business. Her investment in the business is recorded in the account called **Maria Sanchez, Capital.**
	Classify	2. **Cash in Bank** is an asset account. **Maria Sanchez, Capital** is an owner's equity account.
	+/−	3. **Cash in Bank** is increased by $25,000. **Maria Sanchez, Capital** is increased by $25,000.
	Balance	4. The accounting equation remains in balance.

	Assets	=	**Liabilities**	+	**Owner's Equity**
	Cash in Bank				Maria Sanchez, Capital
Trans. 1	+$25,000	=	0	+	+$25,000

Business Transaction 2

*The owner, Maria Sanchez, took two telephones valued at $200 each (total $400) from her home and transferred them to the business as **Office Equipment**.*

ANALYSIS	*Identify*	1. The business received two telephones. Since a telephone is office equipment, the account **Office Equipment** is affected. Maria Sanchez invested a personal asset in the business, so the account **Maria Sanchez, Capital** is affected.
	Classify	2. **Office Equipment** is an asset account. **Maria Sanchez, Capital** is an owner's equity account.
	+/−	3. **Office Equipment** is increased by $400. **Maria Sanchez, Capital** is increased by $400.
	Balance	4. The accounting equation remains in balance.

	Assets		=	Liabilities	+	Owner's Equity
	Cash in Bank	Office Equipment				Maria Sanchez, Capital
Prev. Bal.	$25,000	0		0		$25,000
Trans. 2		+$400				+400
Balance	$25,000 +	$400	=	0	+	$25,400

Key Points

In Balance
After recording each transaction, the accounting equation must be in balance.

Cash Payment Transactions

Transaction 3 is an example of a transaction in which an asset is purchased for cash. Any asset that is purchased for cash will be recorded in the same manner, but the account name of the asset purchased may vary.

Business Transaction 3

Roadrunner issued a $3,000 check to purchase a computer system.

ANALYSIS	Identify	1. The **Computer Equipment** account is used to record transactions involving any type of computer equipment. The business paid cash for the computer system, so the account **Cash in Bank** is affected. (Payments made by check are treated as cash payments and are recorded in the **Cash in Bank** account.)
	Classify +/−	2. **Computer Equipment** and **Cash in Bank** are both asset accounts. 3. **Computer Equipment** is increased by $3,000. **Cash in Bank** is decreased by $3,000.
	Balance	4. The accounting equation remains in balance.

	Assets			=	Liabilities	+	Owner's Equity
	Cash in Bank	Computer Equipment	Office Equipment				Maria Sanchez, Capital
Prev. Bal.	$25,000	0	$400		0		$25,400
Trans. 3	−3,000	+$3,000					
Balance	$22,000 +	$3,000 +	$400	=	0	+	$25,400

Transaction 3 affects only the assets side of the equation. Roadrunner exchanged one asset (cash) for another asset (computer equipment).

Credit Transactions

Now that you have learned about cash transactions, let's look at how the use of credit affects the accounting equation. When a business buys an item on credit, it is buying **on account** . In the next four transactions, you will learn about a purchase on account, a sale on account, a payment made on account, and a payment received on account.

Business Transaction 4

Roadrunner bought a used truck on account from North Shore Auto for $12,000.

ANALYSIS

Identify
1. Roadrunner purchased a truck to be used as a delivery vehicle, so the account **Delivery Equipment** is affected. The business promised to pay for the truck at a later time. This promise to pay is a liability; therefore, the **Accounts Payable** account is affected.

Classify
2. **Delivery Equipment** is an asset account. **Accounts Payable** is a liability account.

+/−
3. **Delivery Equipment** is increased by $12,000. **Accounts Payable** is also increased by $12,000.

Balance
4. The accounting equation remains in balance.

		Assets			=	Liabilities	+	Owner's Equity
	Cash in Bank	Computer Equipment	Office Equipment	Delivery Equipment		Accounts Payable		Maria Sanchez, Capital
Prev. Bal.	$22,000	$3,000	$400	0		0		$25,400
Trans. 4				+$12,000		+$12,000		
Balance	$22,000 +	$3,000 +	$400 +	$12,000	=	$12,000	+	$25,400

Business Transaction 5

Roadrunner sold one telephone to Green Company for $200 on account.

ANALYSIS

Identify
1. Since Roadrunner has agreed to receive payment for the telephone at a later time, the **Accounts Receivable** account is affected. The business sold the telephone, so the account **Office Equipment** is also affected.

Classify
2. Both **Accounts Receivable** and **Office Equipment** are asset accounts.

+/−
3. **Accounts Receivable** is increased by $200. **Office Equipment** is decreased by $200.

Balance
4. The accounting equation remains in balance.

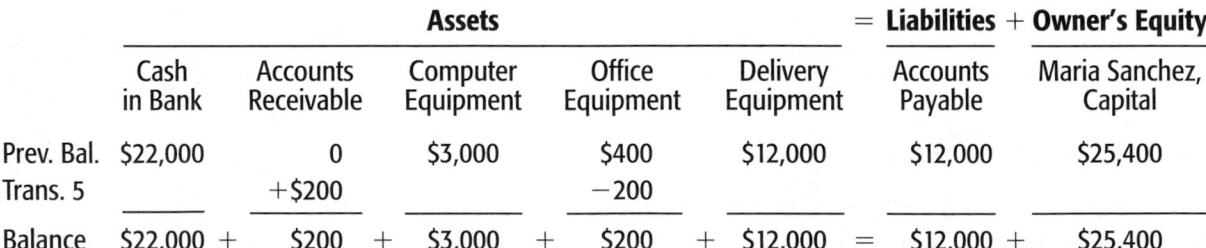

			Assets			=	Liabilities	+	Owner's Equity
	Cash in Bank	Accounts Receivable	Computer Equipment	Office Equipment	Delivery Equipment		Accounts Payable		Maria Sanchez, Capital
Prev. Bal.	$22,000	0	$3,000	$400	$12,000		$12,000		$25,400
Trans. 5		+$200		−200					
Balance	$22,000 +	$200 +	$3,000 +	$200 +	$12,000	=	$12,000	+	$25,400

Business Transaction 6

Roadrunner issued a check for $350 in partial payment of the amount owed to its creditor, North Shore Auto.

ANALYSIS	*Identify*	1. The payment decreased the total amount owed to the creditor, so **Accounts Payable** is affected. Payment was made by check, so the account **Cash in Bank** is affected.
	Classify +/−	2. **Accounts Payable** is a liability account. **Cash in Bank** is an asset account. 3. **Accounts Payable** is decreased by $350. **Cash in Bank** is also decreased by $350.
	Balance	4. The accounting equation remains in balance.

	Assets					= **Liabilities** +	**Owner's Equity**
	Cash in Bank	Accounts Receivable	Computer Equipment	Office Equipment	Delivery Equipment	Accounts Payable	Maria Sanchez, Capital
Prev. Bal.	$22,000	$200	$3,000	$200	$12,000	$12,000	$25,400
Trans. 6	−350					−350	
Balance	$21,650 +	$200 +	$3,000 +	$200 +	$12,000 =	$11,650 +	$25,400

Business Transaction 7

Roadrunner received and deposited a check for $200 from Green Co. The check received is full payment for the telephone sold on account in Transaction 5.

ANALYSIS	*Identify*	1. The check decreases the amount owed to Roadrunner, so **Accounts Receivable** is affected. A check is given in payment, so **Cash in Bank** is affected.
	Classify +/−	2. **Accounts Receivable** and **Cash in Bank** are asset accounts. 3. **Accounts Receivable** is decreased by $200. **Cash in Bank** is increased by $200.
	Balance	4. The accounting equation remains in balance.

	Assets					= **Liabilities** +	**Owner's Equity**
	Cash in Bank	Accounts Receivable	Computer Equipment	Office Equipment	Delivery Equipment	Accounts Payable	Maria Sanchez, Capital
Prev. Bal.	$21,650	$200	$3,000	$200	$12,000	$11,650	$25,400
Trans. 7	+200	−200					
Balance	$21,850 +	$0 +	$3,000 +	$200 +	$12,000 =	$11,650 +	$25,400

As you can see, each business transaction causes a change in assets, liabilities, or owner's equity. Analyzing each transaction to see how it affects the accounting equation keeps everything in balance.

Now that you have studied this section, complete the following questions and problems.

Thinking Critically

1. What is the difference between accounts receivable and accounts payable?
2. When a business transaction occurs, what is the role of the accountant or accounting clerk?

Communicating Accounting

In your business, Ace Tutoring Service, it is critical for your new accounting clerk to fully comprehend how a business transaction affects the accounts of your business. Using the four-step approach to transaction analysis, write a "tip sheet" to help your new employee remember the steps. Write a brief explanation and give an example of each step in the analysis. Create a business transaction to use in your explanation.

Problem 3–2 Determining the Effects of Transactions on the Accounting Equation

Instructions Use these accounts to analyze the business transactions of WordService.

Assets	=	Liabilities	+	Owner's Equity
Cash in Bank		Accounts Payable		Jan Swift, Capital
Accounts Receivable				
Computer Equipment				
Office Furniture				

On the form provided in your working papers, identify the accounts affected by each transaction and the amount of increase or decrease in each account. Make sure the accounting equation is in balance after each transaction. Your transaction analysis should be set up like Transactions 1 through 7 on pages 52–55.

1. Jan Swift, owner, deposited $30,000 in a checking account to start a business, WordService.
2. The owner transferred to the business a desk and chair valued at $700.
3. WordService issued a check for $4,000 for the purchase of a computer.
4. The business bought office furniture on account for $5,000 from Eastern Furniture Company.
5. The desk and chair previously transferred to the business by the owner were sold on account for $700.
6. WordService wrote a check for $2,000 in partial payment of the amount owed to Eastern Furniture Company.

Transactions That Affect Revenue, Expense, and Withdrawals by the Owner

United Parcel Service (UPS) has thousands of shareholders who expect a return on their investment in the business. The most common way for a business to provide a return is by selling goods or providing services. UPS earns revenue by providing a global delivery service. To  provide the delivery service, UPS incurs expenses like salaries, transportation, and insurance. In this section you will learn about revenue and expense transactions as well as owner's withdrawals.

Revenue and Expense Transactions

Income earned from the sale of goods or services is called revenue . Examples of revenue are fees earned for services performed and cash received from the sale of merchandise. Revenue increases owner's equity because it increases the assets of the business.

Both revenues and investments by the owner increase owner's equity, but these represent very different transactions. Revenue is income from the sale of goods and services. Investment by the owner is the dollar amount contributed to the business by the owner. To generate revenue by selling goods or services, most businesses must also incur expenses to buy goods, materials, and services. An expense is the price paid for goods or services used to operate a business. Examples of business expenses are rent, utilities, and advertising. Expenses decrease owner's equity because they decrease the assets of the business or increase liabilities.

What You'll Learn

- How revenue transactions affect the accounting equation.
- How expense transactions affect the accounting equation.
- How withdrawals by the owner affect the accounting equation.

Why It's Important

The experience you gain by analyzing revenue, expense, and withdrawal transactions will help you analyze transactions in real-world situations.

KEY TERMS

revenue
expense
withdrawal

Business Transaction 8

Roadrunner received a check for $1,200 from a customer, Sims Corporation, for delivery services.

ANALYSIS		
	Identify	1. Roadrunner received cash, so **Cash in Bank** is affected. The payment received is revenue. Revenue increases owner's equity, so **Maria Sanchez, Capital** is also affected.
	Classify	2. **Cash in Bank** is an asset account. **Maria Sanchez, Capital** is an owner's equity account.
	+/−	3. **Cash in Bank** is increased by $1,200. **Maria Sanchez, Capital** is also increased by $1,200.
	Balance	4. The accounting equation remains in balance.

	Assets					= Liabilities +	Owner's Equity
	Cash in Bank	Accounts Receivable	Computer Equipment	Office Equipment	Delivery Equipment	Accounts Payable	Maria Sanchez, Capital
Prev. Bal.	$21,850	$0	$3,000	$200	$12,000	$11,650	$25,400
Trans. 8	+1,200						+1,200
Balance	$23,050 +	$0 +	$3,000 +	$200 +	$12,000 =	$11,650 +	$26,600

Business Transaction 9

Roadrunner wrote a check for $700 to pay the rent for the month.

ANALYSIS	*Identify*	1. Roadrunner pays rent for use of building space. Rent is an expense. Expenses decrease owner's equity, so the account **Maria Sanchez, Capital** is affected. The business is paying cash for the use of the building, so **Cash in Bank** is affected.
	Classify	2. **Maria Sanchez, Capital** is an owner's equity account. **Cash in Bank** is an asset account.
	+/−	3. **Maria Sanchez, Capital** is decreased by $700. **Cash in Bank** is decreased by $700.
	Balance	4. The accounting equation remains in balance.

	Assets					= Liabilities +	Owner's Equity
	Cash in Bank	Accounts Receivable	Computer Equipment	Office Equipment	Delivery Equipment	Accounts Payable	Maria Sanchez, Capital
Prev. Bal.	$23,050	$0	$3,000	$200	$12,000	$11,650	$26,600
Trans. 9	−700						−700
Balance	$22,350 +	$0 +	$3,000 +	$200 +	$12,000 =	$11,650 +	$25,900

Withdrawals by the Owner

Generally, if a business earns revenue, the owner will take cash or other assets from the business for personal use. This transaction is called a **withdrawal**.

When the assets of a business are decreased because of a withdrawal by the owner, the owner's financial claim to the assets of the business is also decreased. A withdrawal, therefore, decreases both assets and owner's equity.

A withdrawal is not the same as an expense. Both expenses and owner's withdrawals decrease owner's equity, but these represent very different transactions. An expense is the price paid for goods and services used to operate a business. For example, a landscaping service might purchase fertilizer and lawncare supplies to conduct daily operations. Withdrawals by the owner are cash or other assets taken from the business for the owner's personal use. Transaction 10 illustrates the impact of a withdrawal on the accounting equation.

CONNECT TO . . .
HEALTH

Actuaries in the insurance industry determine how much it costs to care for different clients and generate rates accordingly. For example, health insurance actuaries keep track of how much more it costs to cover smokers than non-smokers and adjust their rates to compensate for the difference.

Business Transaction 10

Maria Sanchez withdrew $500 from the business for her personal use.

ANALYSIS	**Identify**	1. A withdrawal decreases the owner's claim to the assets of the business, so **Maria Sanchez, Capital** is affected. Cash is paid out, so the **Cash in Bank** account is affected.
	Classify	2. **Maria Sanchez, Capital** is an owner's equity account. **Cash in Bank** is an asset account.
	+/−	3. **Maria Sanchez, Capital** is decreased by $500. **Cash in Bank** is decreased by $500.
	Balance	4. The accounting equation remains in balance.

	Assets					**= Liabilities +**	**Owner's Equity**
	Cash in Bank	Accounts Receivable	Computer Equipment	Office Equipment	Delivery Equipment	Accounts Payable	Maria Sanchez, Capital
Prev. Bal.	$22,350	$0	$3,000	$200	$12,000	$11,650	$25,900
Trans. 10	−500						−500
Balance	$21,850	$0	+ $3,000	+ $200	+ $12,000	= $11,650	+ $25,400

The following summarizes the transactions of this chapter. Can you describe what is happening in each line?

	Cash in Bank	Accounts Receivable	Computer Equipment	Office Equipment	Delivery Equipment =	Accounts Payable +	Owner's Equity
Prev. Bal.	0	0	0	0	0	0	0
Trans. 1	+25,000						+25,000
Trans. 2				+400			+400
Trans. 3	−3,000		+3,000				
Trans. 4					+12,000	+12,000	
Trans. 5		+200		−200			
Trans. 6	−350					−350	
Trans. 7	+200	−200					
Trans. 8	+1,200						+1,200
Trans. 9	−700						−700
Trans. 10	−500						−500
Balance	$21,850	+ $0	+ $3,000	+ $200	+ $12,000 =	$11,650 +	$25,400

Now that you have studied this section, complete the following questions and problems.

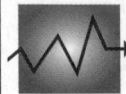 **Thinking Critically**

1. What effect does revenue have on a business?
2. What effect do withdrawals have on a business?

 **Analyzing Accounting**

Analyze the following transactions using the format shown below.

Analysis	Identify:	?
	Classify:	?
	+/− :	?
	Balance:	?

1. Paul Howard withdrew $500 from his business, Kite Supply, for his personal use.
2. Kite Supply issued a check for $250 to purchase an office desk and chair.

 **Problem 3–3 Determining the Effect of Transactions on the Accounting Equation**

Instructions Use the accounts of WordService, a secretarial service, to analyze these business transactions. The beginning balance for each account is shown following the account name.

Assets	=	Liabilities	+	Owner's Equity
Cash in Bank, $24,000		Accounts Payable		Jan Swift, Capital
Accounts Receivable, $700		$3,000		$30,700
Computer Equipment, $4,000				
Office Furniture, $5,000				

On the form provided in your working papers, identify the accounts affected by each transaction and the amount of the increase or decrease for each account. Make sure the accounting equation is in balance after each transaction.

1. Paid $50 for advertising in the local newspaper.
2. Received $1,000 as payment for preparing a report.
3. Wrote a $600 check for the month's rent.
4. Jan Swift withdrew $800 for her personal use.
5. Received $200 on account from the person who had purchased the old office furniture.

KEY CONCEPTS

1. For all property that is owned or controlled, there are corresponding financial claims equal to the cost of the property.
2. The accounting term for a financial claim to the assets of a business is *equity*.
3. Every business transaction changes one or more parts of the accounting equation.
4. When a business buys an item on account, the amount owed is called an account payable. When a business sells an item on account, the total amount to be received by the business is called an account receivable.
5. Revenues are earned by selling goods or services. Businesses must earn revenues to continue to operate and to provide a return on the owner's investment. Revenues increase the owner's equity in the business.
6. Expenses are the cost of items used in the operation of a business. Expenses decrease the owner's equity in the business.
7. Investments occur when an owner transfers cash or other assets to the business. Investments increase owner's equity.
8. Withdrawals occur when an owner takes cash or other assets from the business for personal use. Withdrawals decrease the owner's equity in the business.
9. The effects of typical business transactions on accounts are as follows:

Transaction	Effects On:		
	Assets	Liabilities	Owner's Equity
Investment of cash by owner	+		+
Investment of property	+		+
Cash payment, such as purchase of office equipment	+,−		
Purchase of an asset on account	+	+	
Sale of office equipment on account	,+		
Make a payment on account	−	−	
Record revenue from a cash sale	+		+
Record a cash payment for an expense	−		−
Record a cash withdrawal by the owner	−		−

USING KEY TERMS

Grouping, comparing, and contrasting terms often helps us understand definitions. Answer the following questions related to the terms in this chapter.

accounts payable	investments
accounts receivable	on account
credit	property
creditor	property rights
equity	revenue
expense	withdrawal
financial claims	

A. Which terms can be considered assets (or benefits) to the business? Why?

B. Which terms might be grouped under the heading "Owner's Equity"? Why?

C. Which terms relate to the liabilities of a business?

Understanding Accounting Concepts and Procedures

Instructions

Answer the following questions on a separate sheet of paper:

1. What is the relationship between property and financial claims?

2. List five examples of business assets. Explain why they are business assets rather than personal assets.

3. Name two types of equity in a business, and explain what each type represents. Give an example of each.

4. Why are accounts used in an accounting system?

5. Explain the difference between accounts receivable and accounts payable.

6. Why are at least two accounts affected by each business transaction?

7. What steps should be followed in analyzing a business transaction?

8. How does one determine if the accounting equation is in balance?

9. Why is it important for a business to earn revenue?

10. Explain the difference between revenue and expenses.

11. Explain the difference between revenue and owner's investment. How do transactions involving these items affect owner's equity?

12. Explain the difference between expense and owner's withdrawal. How do transactions involving these items affect owner's equity?

13. Why does withdrawal of cash by the owner for personal use decrease owner's equity?

Case Study...

Service Business: Health and Fitness

The Fitness Center, owned by Gail Chan, has been in business for two years. The business is successful with its expanded hours of operation and child care program. To meet the needs of its clients, the Fitness Center must buy additional exercise equipment.

You are a local business consultant and have worked with several other small businesses in the area. Ms. Chan has asked you about possible ways to obtain money for the new equipment. She has already borrowed money from family members and cannot use them as a source of more funds.

Thinking Critically:

1. As a consultant, your job is to evaluate possible sources of money for your client. Research alternatives with the Small Business Administration, the Chamber of Commerce, and local banks.
2. Make a list of alternatives. Include costs, interest rates, and advantages or disadvantages.
3. Make a recommendation to your client based on your list of alternatives.
4. Explain how the additional money will affect the accounting equation.

inter**NET** CONNECTION

Careers: Salary Expectations

Part of choosing a career means assessing your financial expectations. How much money do you hope to make? If you're considering a career in accounting, you'll want to check out the possibilities.

Do This:

1. Locate Web sites that offer salary guides. Some guides are profession-specific, while others are general salary surveys. What sites did you locate?
2. Do you see a job title that sounds interesting to you? What is the entry level for that position?
3. List three accounting occupations and the entry-level salaries for those positions.

Workplace Skills

Applying Technology

Whether you work in a small or large business, technology is critical to efficiency in the workplace. Employees must be able to apply the technology appropriate to their work tasks.

On the Job:

After graduating from college and working for a year as a junior accountant in a CPA's office, you decide to open an accounting business from your home. You'll need a computer, software, and office furniture to get started. Answer the questions below to help you analyze and select the appropriate technology for your needs.

Thinking Critically:

1. List the kinds of financial services you would like to provide to your customers.
2. Research three accounting software packages that would help you deliver the services you listed. List the name, price, system requirements, and features of each software package.
3. Select the software package that best meets your anticipated needs. Write a paragraph explaining why you selected this product.

Exploring Electronic Spreadsheets

Computer spreadsheets are important tools for organizing and analyzing data. A spreadsheet is made up of rows and columns. The columns are identified by letters and the rows are identified by numbers. As you create a spreadsheet, you will enter numbers, labels, and formulas into cells. Spreadsheet applications that are commonly used in the business world include Lotus 1-2-3 and Microsoft Excel. The following is an example of a basic electronic spreadsheet:

	A	B	C	D	E	F	G	H
1		Jan	Feb	March	April	May	June	July
2	Sales	2,500	5,000	1,650	10,000	3,100	8,200	12,500
3	Expenses	700	1,200	225	3,550	1,800	2,300	5,600
4	Net income	1,800	3,800	1,425	6,450	1,300	5,900	6,900
5								
6								

Before you create a computer spreadsheet, review the following spreadsheet terms.

	Spreadsheet Terms	Description
①	Row	Identified by numbers down the left side of the spreadsheet.
②	Column	Identified by letters along the top of the spreadsheet.
③	Cell address	Identified by a column letter and row number. For example, the cell address B4 indicates the cell where the number 1,800 is found.
④	Cell cursor	Indicated by a highlight of the cell.
⑤	Scroll arrows	Allows you to view other parts of the spreadsheet.
⑥	Labels	Text that identifies columns or rows of information; cannot be used for calculations.
⑦	Values	Numbers inserted in cells that can be used for calculations.
⑧	Formulas	Mathematical functions entered in a particular cell that tells the software to add, subtract, divide, or multiply values. For example, E2−E3 represents 10,000 − 3,550, or 6,450.

APPLICATION OPTIONS

Problem 3–4 Classifying Accounts

All accounts belong in one of the following classifications: Asset, Liability, Owner's Equity.

Instructions In your working papers indicate the classification for each of the following accounts.

1. John Jones, Capital
2. Cash in Bank
3. Accounts Receivable
4. Accounts Payable
5. Office Equipment

6. Delivery Equipment
7. Camping Equipment
8. Building
9. Land
10. Computer Equipment

Complete chapter problems one of two ways:

1 **Manual** Glencoe Working Papers

or

2 **Spreadsheet** Templates (Problem 3–9)

Problem 3–5 Completing the Accounting Equation

The following accounts are used in a business owned and operated by Mike Murray.

Instructions Look at the following list of accounts and determine the missing amount for each of the question marks.

Assets		=	Liabilities	+	Owner's Equity
Cash in Bank	$4,500		Accounts Payable		Mike Murray,
Accounts Receivable	1,350		?		Capital $9,250
Office Equipment	5,000				
	?				

Analyze: Is the accounting equation in balance?

Problem 3–6 Classifying Accounts Within the Accounting Equation

Listed below are the account names and balances for Wilderness Rentals.

Accounts Payable	$ 7,000	Cash in Bank	$ 5,000
Accounts Receivable	2,000	Office Equipment	3,000
Camping Equipment	12,000	Ronald Hicks, Capital	15,000

Continued ✒

Instructions Using these account names and balances:

(1) List and total the assets of the business.

(2) Determine the amount owed by the business.

(3) Give the amount of the owner's equity in the business.

Analyze: Is the accounting equation in balance?

Problem 3–7 Determining Increases and Decreases in Accounts

Hot Suds Car Wash uses the following accounts:

Assets	=	**Liabilities**	+	**Owner's Equity**
Cash in Bank		Accounts Payable		Regina Delgado,
Accounts Receivable				Capital
Office Equipment				
Office Furniture				
Car Wash Equipment				

Instructions Use a form similar to the one that follows. For each transaction:

(1) Identify the accounts affected.

(2) Classify the accounts.

(3) Determine the amount of the increase (+) or decrease (−) for each account affected.

The first transaction is completed as an example.

Trans.	Accounts Affected	Classification	Amount of Increase (+) or Decrease (−)
1.	Cash in Bank	Asset	+$25,000
	Regina Delgado, Capital	Owner's Equity	+$25,000

Date	Transactions
Jan. 1	**1.** Regina Delgado, the owner, invested $25,000 cash in the business.
4	**2.** Bought car wash equipment with cash for $12,000.
5	**3.** Purchased, on account, $2,500 of office equipment.
10	**4.** Wrote a check for the monthly rent, $800.
12	**5.** Received cash for services performed, $1,000.
15	**6.** The owner withdrew $600 cash from the business for personal use.
20	**7.** Purchased a desk for $1,000, paying $200 cash and agreeing to pay the balance of $800 in 30 days.
25	**8.** Provided services worth $600 on account.

Analyze: How many accounts are affected by Transaction 7?

Problem 3–8 Determining the Effects of Transactions on the Accounting Equation

After graduating from college, Abe Shultz decided to start a pet grooming service called Kits & Pups Grooming.

Instructions Use a form similar to the one that follows. For each of the following transactions:

(1) Identify the accounts affected, using the account names on the form.

(2) Determine the amount of the increase or decrease for each account.

(3) Write the amount of the increase (+) or decrease (−) in the space under each account affected.

(4) On the following line, write the new balance for each account.

(5) Transaction 1 is completed as an example.

	Assets				=	Liabilities	+	Owner's Equity
Trans.	Cash in Bank	Accts. Rec.	Office Equip.	Grooming Equip.	=	Accounts Payable	+	Abe Shultz, Capital
1	+$10,000							+$10,000

Date	Transactions
Jan. 2	1. Abe Shultz began the business by depositing $10,000 in a checking account at the Shoreline National Bank in the name of the business, Kits & Pups Grooming.
3	2. Bought grooming equipment for cash, $1,000.
8	3. Issued a check for $900 for the monthly rent.
9	4. Bought $6,000 worth of new office equipment on account for use in the business.
15	5. Received $700 cash for services performed for customers during the first week of business.
21	6. Issued a $2,000 check to the creditor as partial payment for the office equipment purchased on account.
29	7. Performed grooming services and agreed to be paid for them later, $500.

Analyze: What is the amount of total liabilities and owner's equity?

Problem 3–9 Determining the Effects of Business Transactions on the Accounting Equation

Juanita Ortega is the owner of a professional guide service called Outback Guide Service.

Instructions Use a form similar to the one below. For each of the following transactions:

(1) Identify the accounts affected.
(2) Write the amount of the increase (+) or decrease (−) in the space provided on the form in your working papers.
(3) Determine the new balance for each account.

	Assets					=	Liabilities	+	Owner's Equity
Trans.	Cash in Bank	Accts. Rec.	Hiking Equip.	Rafting Equip.	Office Equip.	=	Accounts Payable	+	Juanita Ortega, Capital

Date	Transactions
Jan. 3	1. Ms. Ortega, the owner, opened a checking account for the business by depositing $60,000 of her personal funds.
6	2. Paid by check the monthly rent of $3,000.
8	3. Bought hiking equipment for the business by writing a check for $3,000.
9	4. Purchased $24,000 of rafting equipment by writing a check.
11	5. Purchased office equipment on account for $4,000.
15	6. Received payment for guide services, $2,500.
18	7. Ms. Ortega contributed a desk valued at $450 to the business.
21	8. Withdrew $3,000 cash from the business for personal use.
26	9. Wrote a check to a creditor as partial payment on account, $1,500.
30	10. Took a group on a tour and agreed to accept payment later, $1,200.

Analyze: How much is owed to creditors after Transaction 10?

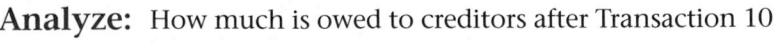

Problem 3–10 Describing Business Transactions

Showbiz Video is a business owned by Greg Failla. The transactions that follow are shown as they would appear in the accounting equation.

Instructions In your working papers, describe what has happened in each transaction. Transaction 1 is completed as an example.

Example:

1. The owner invested $30,000 in the business.

	Assets				=	Liabilities	+	Owner's Equity
Trans.	Cash in Bank	Accts. Rec.	Office Equip.	Video Equip.	=	Accounts Payable	+	Greg Failla, Capital
1	+$30,000							+$30,000
2	−$ 2,000		+$2,000					
3				+$8,000		+$8,000		
4	+$ 700							+$ 700
5		+$500						+$ 500
6			+$ 200					+$ 200
7	−$ 3,000					−$3,000		
8		+$200	−$ 200					
9	+$ 500	−$500						
10	−$ 1,000							−$ 1,000

Analyze: What is the balance in the account, **Greg Failla, Capital?**

 **Problem 3–11 Completing the Accounting Equation**

The account names and balances for Job Connect are listed below.

Instructions Determine the missing amount for each of the question marks. Use the form in your working papers and write in the missing amounts.

	Assets			=	Liabilities	+	Owner's Equity
Trans.	Cash in Bank	Accounts Receivable	Business Equipment	=	Accounts Payable	+	Richard Tang, Capital
1	?	$ 2,000	$ 1,000		$ 500		$ 7,500
2	$ 3,000	$ 9,000	?		$2,000		$16,000
3	$ 8,000	$ 1,000	$10,000		?		$15,000
4	$ 4,000	?	$ 4,000		$1,000		$17,000
5	$ 9,000	$ 7,000	$ 6,000		$5,000		?
6	$10,000	$14,000	?		$6,000		$32,000
7	$ 6,000	$ 4,000	$10,000		?		$15,000
8	?	$ 5,000	$ 9,000		$1,000		?

Hint: In line 8, total assets are $18,000.

Analyze: For line 8, if total liabilities and equity equals $20,000, what would the balance of **Cash in Bank** be?

CHAPTER 4

Transactions That Affect Assets, Liabilities, and Owner's Equity

Learning Objectives

When you have completed this chapter, you will be able to:

▶ Prepare a chart of accounts.

▶ Apply the rules of debit and credit to asset, liability, and owner's equity accounts.

▶ Use T accounts to analyze a business transaction into its debit and credit parts.

▶ Demonstrate the effects of transactions on the accounting equation using T accounts.

▶ Identify the normal balance of accounts.

▶ Calculate account balances after recording business transactions.

▶ Analyze transactions that increase or decrease assets, liabilities, and owner's capital and record them in T accounts.

▶ Define and use the accounting terms introduced in this chapter.

Exploring the Real World of Business

ANALYZING BUSINESS TRANSACTIONS

Cruising at 30,000 feet is just part of a normal day at **American Airlines. American** is one of the largest passenger airlines in the world and flies to over 170 destinations. The company employs nearly 125,000 people. The airline earns its revenue primarily from passenger tickets and cargo shipments.

When you're as big as **American Airlines,** the things you buy to operate the business can also be very large expenditures. Have you ever wondered how much a Boeing 757 costs? Between $90 and $105 million each! In addition to large purchases, the airline also buys food, fuel, and even coloring books for young travelers. Each transaction affects the airline's assets, liabilities, and total equity.

What do you think?

Name at least three business transactions that would affect the assets and liabilities of **American Airlines.**

AmericanAirlines®

Workplace Connections
Applying Your Accounting Knowledge

Business transactions occur around us everyday. A music store sells thousands of CDs in a day. You may stop by for a meal at a local sandwich shop. A cruise ship line may purchase new furniture for all its formal dining cabins. Successful businesses have hundreds, even thousands, of such transactions each day. Analyzing and recording these transactions are key duties of the accounting staff.

Investigate:

1. What types of business transactions occur in your workplace or the workplace of your family or friends?
2. Who records these transactions into the accounting records?

Accounts and the Double-Entry Accounting System

What You'll Learn

- How to use T accounts.
- Why you need a ledger.
- The rules of debit and credit.

Why It's Important

The rules of debit and credit are the basis for entering transactions into the records of a business.

KEY TERMS

ledger
chart of accounts
double-entry accounting
T account
debit
credit
normal balance

In Chapter 3 you learned about the accounting equation. In this chapter you will learn the double-entry accounting system that allows businesses to keep the accounting equation in balance. When The Coca-Cola Company records the dollar amount of a transaction in one account, it records an equal amount in another account. The same is true of the small computer repair shop or the McDonald's franchise in your community. In this chapter and following chapters, we will identify the various accounting functions involved in a sole proprietorship.

The Account

An account is a location within an accounting system in which the increases and decreases in a specific asset, liability, or owner's equity are recorded and stored. Accounts may have different physical forms, depending on the system. In a manual system, each account may be a separate page in a book or a separate card in a tray. In an electronic system, accounts are stored on disks or hard drives. Whether a system is manual or electronic, accounts are grouped together in a **ledger**. When people refer to "keeping the books," they are referring to maintaining accounts in the ledger. Grouping accounts in a ledger makes information easy to find. When financial statements are needed, the appropriate information is taken from the ledger and organized into reports.

The Chart of Accounts

To keep track of its accounts, a business develops a **chart of accounts**, or a list of all the accounts and their assigned account numbers. The number of accounts needed depends on the size of the business. A small business may require only 20 or 30 accounts. A large business may have several thousand accounts.

Numbering the Accounts

A system for numbering accounts makes it easy to locate individual accounts in the ledger. Account numbers have two or more digits. While a small company may use a three-digit system, a very large corporation may have 35 or more digits in its account numbers. The digits are used for sorting information based on the kinds of reports the business needs. A typical numbering system used to prepare a chart of accounts is as follows:

- Asset accounts begin with 1.
- Liability accounts begin with 2.
- Owner's equity accounts begin with 3.
- Revenue accounts begin with 4.
- Expense accounts begin with 5.

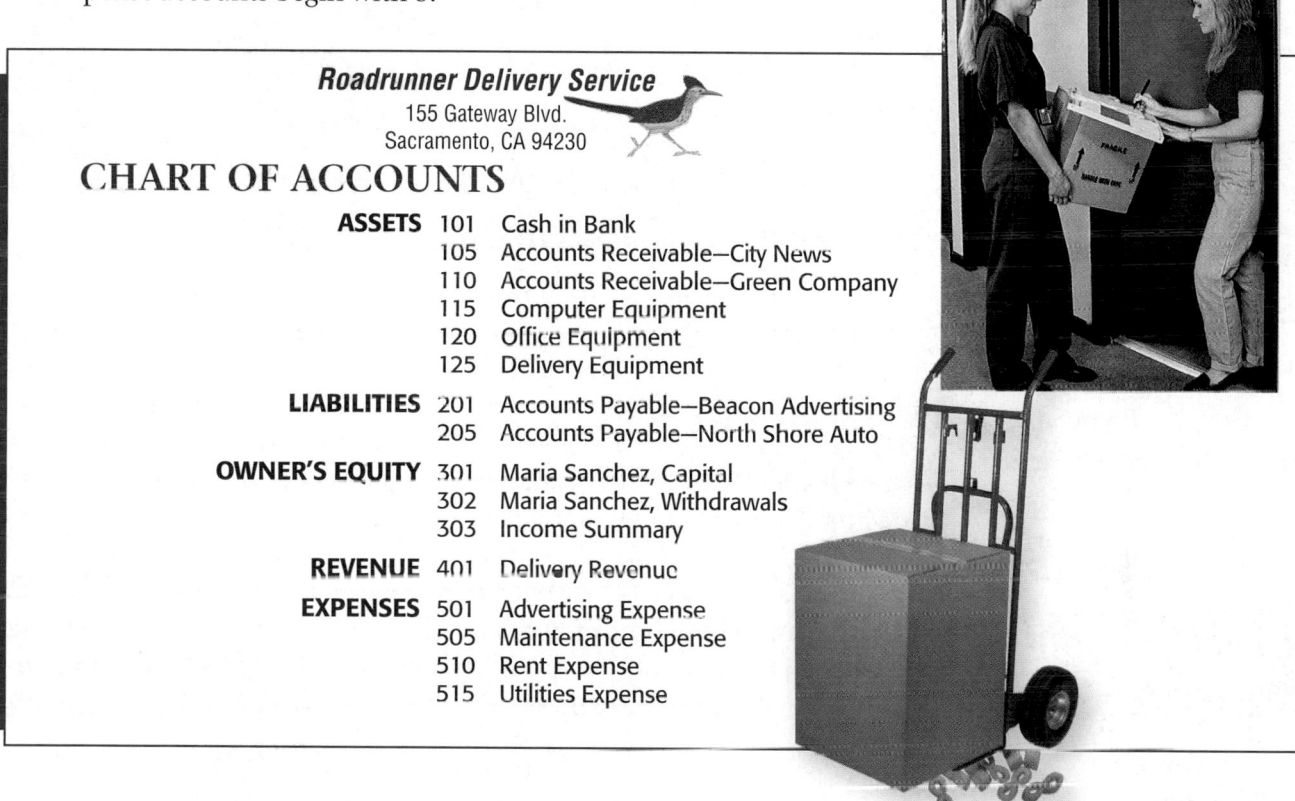

Roadrunner Delivery Service
155 Gateway Blvd.
Sacramento, CA 94230

CHART OF ACCOUNTS

ASSETS	101	Cash in Bank
	105	Accounts Receivable—City News
	110	Accounts Receivable—Green Company
	115	Computer Equipment
	120	Office Equipment
	125	Delivery Equipment
LIABILITIES	201	Accounts Payable—Beacon Advertising
	205	Accounts Payable—North Shore Auto
OWNER'S EQUITY	301	Maria Sanchez, Capital
	302	Maria Sanchez, Withdrawals
	303	Income Summary
REVENUE	401	Delivery Revenue
EXPENSES	501	Advertising Expense
	505	Maintenance Expense
	510	Rent Expense
	515	Utilities Expense

Double-Entry Accounting

The approach you used in Chapter 3 for analyzing and recording changes in account balances would work well if a business had only a few accounts. It becomes awkward, however, if a business has many accounts and many transactions to analyze. When accountants analyze and record a transaction, they use a system called **double-entry accounting** . Double-entry accounting is a system of recordkeeping in which each business transaction affects at least two accounts.

T Accounts

An efficient way to apply double-entry accounting is to use what accountants call a T account. The **T account** , so called because of its T shape, shows the dollar increase or decrease in an account that is caused

ACCOUNTING Flashbacks

ACCOUNTING TEXTBOOKS
Benjamin Workman published *The American Accountant,* the earliest-known American accounting textbook, in 1769. The State of New York passed its first CPA law 127 years later, in 1896.

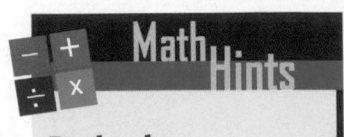
by a transaction. T accounts help the accountant analyze the parts of a business transaction.

As you can see from the illustration below, a T account has a place for an account name, a left side, and a right side. The top of the T is used for the account name. The left side of T accounts is *always* used for debit amounts. A **debit**, then, is an amount entered on the *left* side of the T account. The right side of T accounts is *always* used for credit amounts. A **credit** is an amount entered on the *right* side of the T account. The words *debit* and *credit* are simply the accountant's terms for *left* and *right*. Accountants sometimes use **DR** for debit and **CR** for credit.

Account Name	
Left Side	Right Side
Debit Side	Credit Side
Debit	Credit

The Rules of Debit and Credit

Debits and credits are used to record the increase or decrease in each account affected by a business transaction. Under double-entry accounting, for each debit entry made in one account, a credit of an equal amount must be made in another account. The rules of debit and credit vary according to whether an account is classified as an asset, a liability, or an owner's capital account. Regardless of the type of account, however, the left side of an account is always the debit side and the right side is always the credit side.

Each classification of account has a specific side that is its normal balance side. An account's **normal balance** is always on the side used to record increases to the account. The word *normal* used here means *usual*. Throughout this book, note that the normal balance side of each account will be shaded.

Rules for Asset Accounts

There are three rules of debit and credit for asset accounts:

1. An asset account is *increased* (+) on the *debit* side (left side).
2. An asset account is *decreased* (−) on the *credit* side (right side).
3. The *normal balance* for an asset account is the *increase side,* or the *debit side.* The normal balance side is shaded in the T account on the next page. Assets normally have debit balances.

We can illustrate these rules using an asset T account and the basic accounting equation. Look at the left side of the equation below.

ASSETS = LIABILITIES + OWNER'S EQUITY

Asset Accounts

Debit	Credit
+	−
(1) Increase Side	(2) Decrease Side
(3) Normal Balance	

For asset accounts the *increase* side is the debit (left) side of the T account. The *decrease* side is the credit (right) side of the T account. Notice the (+) and (−) signs. These signs are used to indicate the increase and decrease sides of the account. They do not mean the same thing as *debit* and *credit*.

Since the increase side of an asset account is always the debit side, asset accounts have a normal debit balance. For example, in the normal course of business, total increases to assets are larger than total decreases. You would expect an asset account, then, to have a normal debit balance.

Let's apply these rules to an actual asset account. Look at the entries in the T account for **Cash in Bank** below. The increases in the account are recorded on the left, or debit, side. The decreases in the account are recorded on the right, or credit, side. Total debits equal $350 ($200 + $150). Total credits equal $110 ($70 + $40). To find the balance, subtract total credits from total debits ($350 − $110). The debit balance is $240.

Cash in Bank

Debit	Credit
+	−
200	70
150	40
350	110
Bal. 240	

Rules for Liability and Owner's Capital Accounts

The rules of debit and credit for liability and owner's capital accounts are:

1. Liability and owner's capital accounts are *increased* on the *credit* side (right side).
2. Liability and owner's capital accounts are *decreased* on the *debit* side (left side).
3. The *normal balance* for liability and owner's capital accounts is the *increase side*, or the *credit side*. Liability and owner's capital accounts normally have credit balances.

To illustrate these rules, let's look again at the accounting equation and the T accounts. Remember, the normal balance side is shaded.

Assets		=	Liabilities		+	Owner's Equity	
Debit + Increase Side / Normal Balance	Credit − Decrease Side		Debit − (2) Decrease Side	Credit + (1) Increase Side / (3) Normal Balance		Debit − (2) Decrease Side	Credit + (1) Increase Side / (3) Normal Balance

For all three types of accounts, the debit side is always the left side of the T account, and the credit side is always the right side. Notice, however, that the increase (+) and decrease (−) sides of the liability and owner's capital accounts are the opposite of those for assets. This difference exists because accounts classified as liabilities and owner's capital are on the opposite side of the accounting equation from accounts classified as assets. As a result, debit and credit rules on one side of the accounting equation—and the T accounts within it—are mirror images of those on the other side.

Let's apply these rules to actual accounts. First, look at the entries in the T account below for the liability account **Accounts Payable.** The increases in the account are recorded on the right, or credit, side. The decreases in the account are recorded on the left, or debit, side. Total credits equal $375 ($200 + $175); total debits equal $175 ($100 + $75). To find the balance, subtract the total debits from the total credits ($375 − $175). The credit balance is $200.

Accounts Payable

Debit −	Credit +
100	200
75	175
175	375
	Bal. 200

Now look at the entries in the T account for the owner's equity account **Maria Sanchez, Capital.** Remember that the rules of debit and credit for the capital account are the same as for a liability account.

Increases to owner's capital are recorded on the right, or credit, side of the account. Decreases are recorded on the left, or debit, side. The capital account has a normal credit balance. If you subtract the total debits from the total credits ($4,000 − $550), you have a credit balance of $3,450.

Maria Sanchez, Capital

Debit −	Credit +
350	1,500
200	2,500
550	4,000
	Bal. 3,450

Now that you have studied this section, complete the following questions and problems.

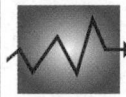

Thinking Critically

1. In a chart of accounts, why are the accounts numbered?
2. Explain why the normal balance of an asset account is on the debit side of the account.

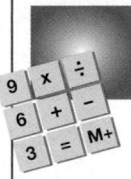

Computing in the Business World

During the month of December, Krusty's Pizza purchased computer equipment. According to your records, Krusty's Pizza took approximately $5,000 from the **Cash in Bank** account to purchase the computer equipment. Prior to that purchase, the owner's capital account had a credit balance of $10,000.

1. What is the balance in the owner's capital account after the purchase?
2. Is the owner's capital account balance a debit or a credit?

Problem 4–1   Applying the Rules of Debit and Credit

Speedy Appliance Repair, owned by R. Lewis, uses the following accounts:

General Ledger
    Cash in Bank
    Office Equipment
    Accounts Payable
    Accounts Receivable
    R. Lewis, Capital

Instructions In the form provided in your working papers:

(1) Classify each account as an asset, liability, or owner's capital account.

(2) Indicate whether the increase side is a debit or a credit.

(3) Indicate whether the decrease side is a debit or credit.

(4) Indicate whether the normal balance for the account is a debit or credit balance.

The **Cash in Bank** account is completed as an example.

Account Name	Account Classification	Increase Side	Decrease Side	Normal Balance
Cash in Bank	Asset	Debit	Credit	Debit

Applying the Rules of Debit and Credit

What You'll Learn

- How to analyze a transaction affecting assets, liabilities, and owner's equity.

Why It's Important

You need to analyze transactions properly so that you record them correctly.

Now that you are familiar with the rules of debit and credit for asset, liability, and owner's capital accounts, the next step is to apply those rules to the analysis of business transactions.

Business Transaction Analysis

Whether a business is buying a new computer system, paying its utility bills, or receiving money for sales, the accountant must analyze how the transaction should be recorded. When analyzing business transactions, you should use the following step-by-step method:

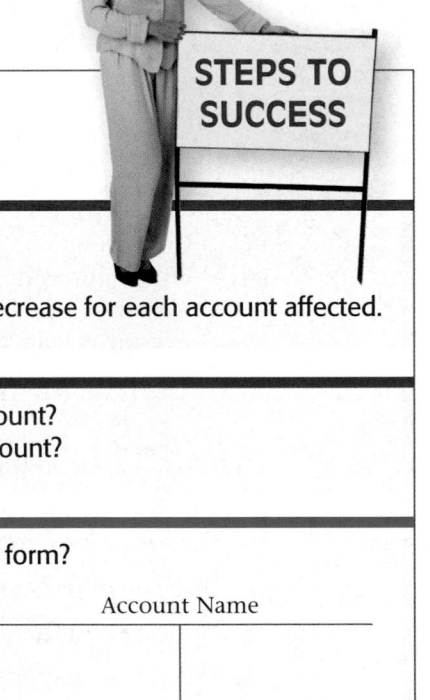

STEPS TO SUCCESS

Business Transaction

BUSINESS TRANSACTION ANALYSIS: Steps to Success

ANALYSIS	*Identify*	1. Identify the accounts affected.
	Classify	2. Classify the accounts affected.
	+/−	3. Determine the amount of increase or decrease for each account affected.

| **DEBIT-CREDIT RULE** | 4. Which account is debited? For what amount? |
| | 5. Which account is credited? For what amount? |

T ACCOUNTS   6. What is the complete entry in T-account form?

Account Name	Account Name

Key Points

Debits and Credits

For every transaction, total debits must equal total credits.

The business transactions that follow are for Roadrunner Delivery Service. Throughout the next several pages, you will learn how to analyze each Roadrunner transaction, apply the rules of debit and credit, and complete the entry in T-account form. The T accounts demonstrate the effects of transactions on the accounting equation. A debit in one account is offset by a credit in another account. Refer to the Roadrunner chart of accounts on page 73. These accounts will be used to analyze several business transactions.

Business Transaction 1

On October 1 Maria Sanchez took $25,000 from personal savings and deposited that amount to open a business checking account in the name of Roadrunner Delivery Service.

ANALYSIS	*Identify* *Classify* +/−	1. The accounts **Cash in Bank** and **Maria Sanchez, Capital** are affected. 2. **Cash in Bank** is an asset account. **Maria Sanchez, Capital** is an owner's capital account. 3. **Cash in Bank** is increased by $25,000. **Maria Sanchez, Capital** is increased by $25,000.
DEBIT-CREDIT RULE		4. Increases in asset accounts are recorded as debits. Debit **Cash in Bank** for $25,000. 5. Increases in the owner's capital account are recorded as credits. Credit **Maria Sanchez, Capital** for $25,000.

T ACCOUNTS	6.	Cash in Bank	Maria Sanchez, Capital
		Debit + 25,000	Credit + 25,000

Business Transaction 2

On October 2 Maria Sanchez took two telephones valued at $200 each from her home and transferred them to the business as office equipment.

ANALYSIS	*Identify* *Classify* +/−	1. The accounts **Office Equipment** and **Maria Sanchez, Capital** are affected. 2. **Office Equipment** is an asset account. **Maria Sanchez, Capital** is an owner's capital account. 3. **Office Equipment** is increased by $400. **Maria Sanchez, Capital** is increased by $400.
DEBIT-CREDIT RULE		4. Increases in asset accounts are recorded as debits. Debit **Office Equipment** for $400. 5. Increases in owner's capital accounts are recorded as credits. Credit **Maria Sanchez, Capital** for $400.

T ACCOUNTS	6.	Office Equipment	Maria Sanchez, Capital
		Debit + 400	Credit + 400

Business Transaction 3

On October 4 Roadrunner issued Check 101 for $3,000 to buy a computer system.

ANALYSIS	*Identify*	1. The accounts **Computer Equipment** and **Cash in Bank** are affected.
	Classify	2. **Computer Equipment** and **Cash in Bank** are asset accounts.
	+/−	3. **Computer Equipment** is increased by $3,000. **Cash in Bank** is decreased by $3,000.

| DEBIT-CREDIT RULE | 4. Increases in asset accounts are recorded as debits. Debit **Computer Equipment** for $3,000. |
| | 5. Decreases in asset accounts are recorded as credits. Credit **Cash in Bank** for $3,000. |

T ACCOUNTS   6.

Computer Equipment		Cash in Bank	
Debit + 3,000			Credit − 3,000

Business Transaction 4

On October 9 Roadrunner bought a used truck on account from North Shore Auto for $12,000.

ANALYSIS	*Identify*	1. The accounts **Delivery Equipment** and **Accounts Payable—North Shore Auto** are affected.
	Classify	2. **Delivery Equipment** is an asset account. **Accounts Payable—North Shore Auto** is a liability account.
	+/−	3. **Delivery Equipment** is increased by $12,000. **Accounts Payable—North Shore Auto** is increased by $12,000.

| DEBIT-CREDIT RULE | 4. Increases in asset accounts are recorded as debits. Debit **Delivery Equipment** for $12,000. |
| | 5. Increases in liability accounts are recorded as credits. Credit **Accounts Payable—North Shore Auto** for $12,000. |

T ACCOUNTS   6.

Delivery Equipment		Accounts Payable— North Shore Auto	
Debit + 12,000			Credit + 12,000

Business Transaction 5

On October 11 Roadrunner sold one phone on account to Green Company for $200.

ANALYSIS — *Identify*
1. The accounts **Accounts Receivable—Green Company** and **Office Equipment** are affected.

Classify
2. **Accounts Receivable—Green Company** is an asset account. **Office Equipment** is also an asset account.

+/−
3. **Accounts Receivable—Green Company** is increased by $200. **Office Equipment** is decreased by $200.

DEBIT-CREDIT RULE
4. Increases in asset accounts are recorded as debits. Debit **Accounts Receivable—Green Company** for $200.
5. Decreases in asset accounts are recorded as credits. Credit **Office Equipment** for $200.

T ACCOUNTS

6.

Accounts Receivable—Green Company		Office Equipment	
Debit + 200			Credit − 200

Business Transaction 6

On October 12 Roadrunner mailed Check 102 for $350 as the first installment payment on the truck purchased from North Shore Auto on October 9.

ANALYSIS — *Identify*
1. The accounts **Accounts Payable—North Shore Auto** and **Cash in Bank** are affected.

Classify
2. **Accounts Payable—North Shore Auto** is a liability account. **Cash in Bank** is an asset account.

+/−
3. **Accounts Payable—North Shore Auto** is decreased by $350. **Cash in Bank** is decreased by $350.

DEBIT-CREDIT RULE
4. Decreases in liability accounts are recorded as debits. Debit **Accounts Payable—North Shore Auto** for $350.
5. Decreases in asset accounts are recorded as credits. Credit **Cash in Bank** for $350.

T ACCOUNTS

6.

Accounts Payable—North Shore Auto		Cash in Bank	
Debit − 350			Credit − 350

On October 14, Roadrunner received and deposited a check for $200 from Green Company. The check is full payment for the telephone sold on account to Green Company on October 11.

ANALYSIS *Identify* 1. The accounts **Cash in Bank** and **Accounts Receivable—Green Company** are affected.

Classify 2. **Cash in Bank** is an asset account. **Accounts Receivable—Green Company** is an asset account.

+/− 3. **Cash in Bank** is increased by $200. **Accounts Receivable—Green Company** is decreased by $200.

DEBIT-CREDIT RULE 4. Increases in asset accounts are recorded as debits. Debit **Cash in Bank** for $200.

5. Decreases in asset accounts are recorded as credits. Credit **Accounts Receivable—Green Company** for $200.

T ACCOUNTS 6.

Cash in Bank		Accounts Receivable—Green Company	
Debit + 200			Credit − 200

A MATTER OF ETHICS

Software Piracy

Imagine that you're a bookkeeper for an attorney who likes to use state-of-the-art technology. The business just received the latest update on its Web site design software. You would like to use the software at home, so your assistant offers to make you a copy. Although you know that copyright laws protect software from unauthorized use, you figure that one little sale can't hurt a multimillion dollar software company; and besides, you're not doing the actual copying.

Ethical Decision Making:

☞ What are the ethical issues?

☞ What are the alternatives?

☞ Who are the affected parties?

☞ How do the alternatives affect the parties?

☞ What would you do?

Now that you have studied this section, complete the following questions and problem.

Thinking Critically

1. What is the debit-credit rule used in business transaction analysis?
2. In double-entry accounting, for each transaction there must be at least two entries. If you are increasing the **Cash in Bank** account, what other accounts might be affected?

Communicating Accounting

Philip Sanders, the owner of Bookworm Book Shops, believes his employees will be more responsible if they realize how their actions affect the records of the business. So Philip asks you to teach some basic accounting to the other managers in the company. You begin by explaining the double-entry accounting system. Explain how the purchase of delivery trucks used in the business affects different accounts.

1. Form a team. Divide the team into two groups.
2. Have one group explain the double-entry accounting system while the other group plays the role of the managers.

Problem 4–2 Identifying Increases and Decreases in Accounts

Alice Roberts uses the following accounts in her business:

General Ledger

Cash in Bank	Office Equipment
Accounts Receivable	Accounts Payable
Office Furniture	Alice Roberts, Capital

Instructions Analyze each of the following transactions. In your working papers, explain the debit and the credit. Use the format shown in the example.

Example:

On June 2 Alice Roberts invested $5,000 of her own money in a business called Roberts Employment Agency.

a. The asset account **Cash in Bank** is increased. Increases in asset accounts are recorded as debits.

b. The owner's capital account **Alice Roberts, Capital** is increased. Increases in the owner's capital account are recorded as credits.

Date	Transactions
June 3	1. Purchased a computer on account from Computer Inc. for $2,500.
9	2. Transferred a desk (Office Furniture) to the business. The desk is worth $750.
15	3. Made a partial payment on account of $1,000 to Computer Inc.

ANNA ALVAREZ
Business Consultant, MCI

Q: Why did you choose accounting?

A: Initially, I chose accounting because my older brother was taking it. He went on to another career, but I stuck with it. I like making sure things are in the right place where money is concerned. I enjoy it when everything balances.

Q: What kind of training did you have?

A: I worked for an accounting firm at 17 and went to school at night. I got a business administration degree with an emphasis in accounting. I learned the software side on the job by working with a variety of databases. I also learned through training classes offered by software companies. I go to one-week training classes about every four months. It's not required, but I'd fall behind if I didn't, everything changes so quickly.

Q: How did you get into consulting?

A: I was a project accountant at another firm when we updated our old accounting system. I worked closely with the consultants and they told me I would make a good consultant. When a co-worker went to MCI, he recommended me.

Q: Are computer classes necessary for accounting students?

A: Computer experience is necessary for anyone in accounting. Any computer science course helps. You should understand relational databases. You still have to know accounting—to understand that purchasing affects accounts payable, which affects inventory—so that when problems occur, you know the most likely place to look for causes.

Tips from . . .

RHI Robert Half International Inc.
When looking for a job, identify your ideal work environment. Do you want to work for a large or small company? Is pay or learning potential more important? Research companies at libraries, career centers, or through the Internet.

CAREER FACTS

Nature of the Work: Meet with and make presentations to business clients, install and debug financial systems, integrate new systems with the old, train new staff.

Training or Education Needed: A bachelor's or master's degree in accounting or business; experience in a variety of accounting areas.

Aptitudes, Abilities, and Skills: Computer skills, communication skills, analytical skills, business, and accounting.

Salary Range: Beginning consultant, $50,000 to $70,000; senior consultant, $85,000 to $100,000; managing consultant, $100,000 and up.

Career Path: Work in accounting in a variety of capacities, then move into a consulting firm.

Thinking Critically: What types of experience would you emphasize when applying for a job as a business consultant?

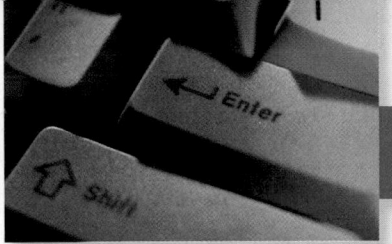

KEY CONCEPTS

1. Double-entry accounting is a system of record-keeping in which each business transaction affects at least two accounts.

Accounting Equation: ASSETS = LIABILITIES + OWNER'S EQUITY

2. The T account is a tool for analyzing the debit and credit parts of a business transaction.
3. The top of a T account is used for the account name. Debits are entered on the left side and credits on the right side of the T account.

T Accounts:

Account Name	
Debit	Credit

4. Every account has an increase and a decrease side (a debit and a credit side).
5. For asset accounts:
   - The increase side is the debit side (left).
   - The decrease side is the credit side (right).
   - The normal balance is a debit.

Asset Rule:

Asset Accounts	
Debit Increase Side + Normal Balance	Credit Decrease Side −

6. For liability and owner's capital accounts:
   - The increase side is the credit side (right).
   - The decrease side is the debit side (left).
   - The normal balance is a credit.

Liability and Owner's Equity Rule:

Liability and Owner's Capital Accounts	
Debit Decrease Side −	Credit Increase Side + Normal Balance

USING KEY TERMS

Your boss at Hillside Nurseries needs help understanding the concept of T accounts and the double-entry accounting system. Using the key terms listed below, draft a list of definitions and illustrations that would help in your explanation.

credit	ledger
chart of accounts	normal balance
debit	T account
double-entry accounting	

Understanding Accounting Concepts and Procedures

Instructions   Answer the following questions on a separate sheet of paper:

1. Why is a business transaction entered in at least two accounts?
2. Would double-entry accounting be used in an electronic accounting system? Explain.
3. Why do accountants use T accounts?
4. Name the three basic parts of a T account.
5. What is the left side of a T account called? The right side?
6. State briefly the rules of debit and credit for increasing and decreasing (a) asset accounts, (b) liability accounts, (c) the owner's capital account.
7. What is the normal balance side for asset accounts? Liability accounts? The owner's capital account?
8. Classify the following accounts.

   a. Office Equipment
   b. Delivery Truck
   c. Accounts Receivable
   d. Store Supplies
   e. Cash in Bank
   f. Lee Jones, Capital
   g. Office Supplies
   h. Accounts Payable

9. Explain briefly what is meant by each of the following phrases.

   a. A debit of $100 to **Cash in Bank.**
   b. A credit balance.
   c. A credit of $500 to **Accounts Payable.**
   d. A debit balance.

10. What are the six steps involved in analyzing a business transaction?

Case Study...

Service Business: Landscaping

While in school Martin Hamilton worked for a large landscaping company and gained work experience. Martin is planning to start a business called Landscapes and Beyond. Martin has made a list of everything he owns, with the estimated value for each.

Lawn mowers	$1,500
Shovels, and lawn-care tools	180
Truck	8,700
Stereo equipment	1,000
50 books on landscaping	400
Desk, chair, and file cabinet	700

Martin has also borrowed $5,000 from his family. He plans to repay the debt in one year.

Thinking Critically:

Write the accounting equation for Martin's new business, listing each item in the appropriate part of the equation.

*inter*NET CONNECTION

Currency Conversion

Traveling with family on a vacation to Brazil? Participating in an educational field trip to France? You'll want to know how much your U.S. dollar is worth in these locations. The Internet has the information you need.

Do This:

1. Locate a currency conversion site on the Internet. Use search terms: currency conversion or currency rates.
2. What is the name of the currency in Austria?
3. What is the current exchange rate for the Saudi Arabian riyal?
4. How much is the U.S. dollar worth in British pounds? In Japanese yen?

Conducting an Audit with Alex

In this and later chapters, you will be Conducting Audits with Alex. To audit means to examine and verify financial records and reports.

Instructions Review the T accounts below for errors. On a separate sheet of paper, make any corrections necessary.

1. Purchased a delivery truck for $27,000 on account from A-1 Trucks Inc.
2. Wrote a check for $1,500 to A-1 Trucks for payment on account.

Cash in Bank		Accounts Payable A-1 Trucks, Inc.	
	(2) 1,500	(1) 27,000	(2) 1,500

Delivery Equipment	
(1) 27,000	

Workplace Skills

Teaching Others

Keeping up with technology and learning new skills are important in today's workplace. Often, learning from co-workers and supervisors is the best way to increase your skills.

On the Job:

Assume that you work as the accountant for Westside Aquatics, a swim club in Florida. The club has 250 members. While some individuals pay cash on each visit, others are billed monthly for club use. A concession area featuring health foods and juices is a popular gathering place for members after swim lessons.

Thinking Critically:

List account names that would be used in a business like this. Describe to a classmate what kinds of transactions might affect each account. What is the normal balance side for each account?

Introduction to Computerized Accounting Systems
Making the Transition from a Manual to a Computerized System

Perform Accounting Procedures Using Manual Methods	Perform Accounting Procedures Using Automated Methods
• Transactions are recorded into journals by hand. • The details of each transaction are then posted in the general ledger. • Account balances are calculated and a trial balance is prepared. The accountant prepares a trial balance to verify that the accounting equation is still in balance. • Account names and balances are then transferred to the proper financial report (income statement, balance sheet, or statement of owner's equity) and the report is summarized (totaled).	• Transactions are keyed to the appropriate screen in the accounting system. • Posting to the general ledger accounts occurs automatically. • The trial balance is generated by the accounting system. • Financial reports are predefined to pull the appropriate accounts and their current balances from the general ledger computer files. The reports automatically summarize and can be printed when the user chooses.

A Quick Overview

Peachtree Question	Description
What types of transactions can be entered in Peachtree Complete® Accounting?	You name it! You can enter: • General journal entries • Sales and cash receipts • Purchases and cash payments • Inventory adjustments • Payroll entries
What else will Peachtree do for the accountant?	• Reconciles bank statements • Prepares financial reports automatically • Prints checks • Prints invoices • Closes the accounting period • Creates cash, collections, and payment management charts and graphs.

For detailed instructions: See the **Peachtree User Guide** in your Glencoe Working Papers.

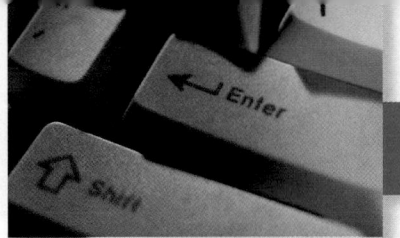

APPLICATION OPTIONS

Problem 4–3 Identifying Accounts Affected by Transactions

Ronald Hicks owns Wilderness Rentals and uses the following accounts in his business:

General Ledger
- 101 Cash in Bank
- 105 Accounts Receivable— Helen Katz
- 120 Office Equipment
- 125 Camping Equipment
- 201 Accounts Payable— Adventure Equipment Inc.
- 301 Ronald Hicks, Capital

Complete chapter problems one of two ways:

1 **Manual** Glencoe Working Papers

or

2 **Spreadsheet** Templates (Problem 4–6)

Instructions For each of the following transactions:

(1) Indicate the two accounts affected.

(2) Indicate whether each account is debited or credited.

Date	Transactions
May 11	1. Sold on account to Helen Katz an unneeded office typewriter.
19	2. Purchased camping equipment on credit from Adventure Equipment Inc. Payment is due within 30 days.
22	3. Ronald Hicks brought a filing cabinet from home and transferred it to the business (**Office Equipment**).
23	4. Purchased tents and sleeping bags for cash.

Analyze: Which transactions affect the **Cash in Bank** account?

Problem 4–4 Using T Accounts to Analyze Transactions

Regina Delgado owns a business called Hot Suds Car Wash. She uses the following accounts:

General Ledger
- 101 Cash in Bank
- 110 Accounts Receivable— Valley Auto
- 125 Office Equipment
- 130 Office Furniture
- 135 Car Wash Equipment
- 201 Accounts Payable— Allen Vacuum Systems
- 301 Regina Delgado, Capital

Continued

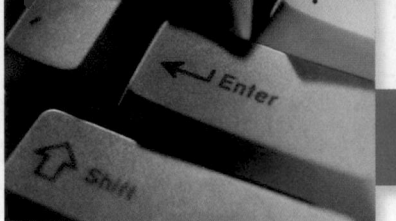

Instructions For each transaction:

(1) Determine which accounts are affected.

(2) Prepare T accounts for the accounts affected.

(3) Enter the debit and credit amounts in the T accounts.

Date	Transactions
May 5	**1.** Regina Delgado invested an additional $40,000 cash in her business.
12	**2.** Bought another car wash system on account for $27,000 from Allen Vacuum Systems.
17	**3.** Regina Delgado transferred some of her personal office furniture, valued at $3,750, to her business.
24	**4.** Hot Suds Car Wash purchased additional office equipment for $7,500. Payment was made by check.
29	**5.** Hot Suds Car Wash sold some surplus car washing equipment on account to Valley Auto for $1,200.

Analyze: What is the ending balance for the liability account **Accounts Payable—Allen Vacuum Systems**?

Problem 4–5 Analyzing Transactions into Debit and Credit Parts

Abe Shultz uses the following accounts for his business, Kits & Pups Grooming:

General Ledger

101 Cash in Bank	205 Accounts Payable—
115 Accounts Receivable—	Dogs & Cats Inc.
Martha Giles	301 Abe Shultz, Capital
125 Office Equipment	
130 Office Furniture	
140 Grooming Equipment	

Instructions For each transaction:

(1) In your working papers prepare a T account for each account listed.

(2) Using the appropriate T accounts, analyze and record each of the following business transactions. Identify each transaction by number.

(3) After recording all transactions, write the word "Balance" on the normal balance side of each T account. Then compute and record the balance for each account.

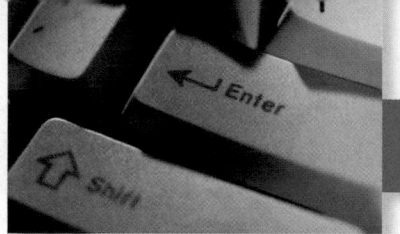

Date	Transactions
May 1	**1.** Abe Shultz invested an additional $45,000 cash in his business.
5	**2.** Bought grooming equipment on account from Dogs & Cats Inc. for $8,500.
10	**3.** Purchased an office lamp for $85, Check 150.
14	**4.** Abe Shultz transferred his personal typewriter, worth $200, to the business.
19	**5.** Made a $3,000 payment on the grooming equipment bought on account, Check 151.
22	**6.** Sold the typewriter on account to Martha Giles for $200.
29	**7.** Bought a photocopier for $1,500, Check 152.
31	**8.** Received a $100 payment for the typewriter sold on account.

Analyze: How much cash did the business spend in all the above transactions?

Problem 4–6 Analyzing Transactions into Debit and Credit Parts

Juanita Ortega runs Outback Guide Service. The accounts she uses to record and report business transactions are listed below.

General Ledger

101 Cash in Bank	205 Accounts Payable—
105 Accounts Receivable—	Peak Equipment Inc.
Mary Johnson	207 Accounts Payable—
130 Office Equipment	Premier Processors
140 Computer Equipment	301 Juanita Ortega, Capital
145 Hiking Equipment	
150 Rafting Equipment	

Instructions For each transaction:

(1) In your working papers, prepare a T account for each account.

(2) Analyze and record each of the following business transactions in the appropriate T accounts. Identify each transaction by number.

(3) After recording all transactions, compute and record the account balance on the normal balance side of each T account.

(4) Add the balances of those accounts with normal debit balances.

(5) Add the balances of those accounts with normal credit balances.

(6) Compare the two totals. Are they the same?

Continued 🍃

Date	Transactions
May 2	**1.** Juanita Ortega transferred an additional $53,250 from her personal savings account into the business checking account.
6	**2.** Bought hiking equipment for $550, Check 367.
7	**3.** Bought rafting equipment on account from Peak Equipment Inc. for $2,675.
11	**4.** Juanita Ortega transferred her own computer, valued at $850, to the business.
16	**5.** Bought a cash register for the office on account from Premier Processors for $1,250.
19	**6.** Sold the computer on credit for $850 to Mary Johnson.
22	**7.** Paid $500 on account to Peak Equipment Inc., Check 368.
24	**8.** Purchased shelves for the office for $650, Check 369.
28	**9.** Paid $1,250 on account to Premier Processors, Check 370.
31	**10.** Bought rafting oars for $175, Check 371.

Analyze: What is the ending balance in the **Computer Equipment** account?

CHALLENGE PROBLEM

Problem 4–7 Analyzing Transactions Recorded in T Accounts

Richard Tang owns and operates a job placement service, Job Connect. The T accounts on the next page summarize several business transactions for May.

Instructions Use a form similar to the one presented on the next page. For each of the 10 transactions:

(1) Identify the account debited, and record the account name in the appropriate column.

(2) Indicate whether the account debited is being increased or decreased.

(3) Identify the account credited, and write the account name in the appropriate column.

(4) Indicate whether the account credited is being increased or decreased.

(5) Write a short description of the transaction.

(1) Trans No.	(1) Account Debited	(2) Increase (I) or Decrease (D)	(3) Account Credited	(4) Increase (I) or Decrease (D)	(5) Description
1	Cash in Bank	I	Richard Tang, Capital	I	Richard Tang invested $15,000 in the business.

Cash in Bank

Debit +	Credit −
(1) 15,000	(4) 1,225
(9) 225	(6) 900
	(7) 995
	(8) 2,000

Accounts Receivable

Debit +	Credit −
(5) 225	(9) 225

Office Equipment

Debit +	Credit −
(2) 225	(5) 225
(3) 8,000	
(4) 1,225	

Office Furniture

Debit +	Credit
(6) 900	
(10) 145	

Computer Equipment

Debit +	Credit −
(7) 995	

Accounts Payable

Debit −	Credit +
(8) 2,000	(3) 8,000
	(10) 145

Richard Tang, Capital

Debit −	Credit +
	(1) 15,000
	(2) 225

Analyze: What is the ending balance for liabilities? For assets? For owner's equity?

CHAPTER 5

Transactions That Affect Revenue, Expenses, and Withdrawals

Learning Objectives

When you have completed this chapter, you will be able to:

▶ Explain the difference between permanent accounts and temporary capital accounts.

▶ List and apply the rules of debit and credit for revenue, expense, and withdrawals accounts.

▶ Use the six-step method to analyze transactions affecting revenue, expense, and withdrawals accounts.

▶ Test a series of transactions for equality of debits and credits.

▶ Define the new accounting terms introduced in this chapter.

Exploring the Real World of Business

ANALYZING REVENUE AND EXPENSES

Dave Thomas was the man behind **Wendy's International.** The original restaurant in Columbus, Ohio, opened in 1969 and is called **Wendy's Old Fashioned Hamburgers.** Now more than 6,000 restaurants offer salads, sandwiches, hamburgers, fries, and drinks.

When you buy a meal at **Wendy's,** you are helping the business earn revenue. That revenue is used to pay expenses and to build new restaurants. **Wendy's** grew to its size today by selling meals to people just like you. Dave Thomas' motto for the restaurants is "Quality, Service, Cleanliness, and Value." Have you ever wondered where **Wendy's** name came from? Dave named his restaurant after one of his daughters, Melinda Lou, whose nickname is Wendy.

What do you think?

Wendy's earns revenue by selling meals. Can you think of at least six examples of expenses that a **Wendy's** restaurant might have?

When you receive a paycheck, you probably think about the amount of money you have and the things you'd like to buy. Businesses also earn money and spend it on items used to operate the business. In this chapter, you'll learn to analyze transactions involving revenue and expenses of a business.

Investigate:

1. How does your workplace (or the workplace of family or friends) earn revenue?
2. What does the business buy with that revenue?
3. How do these revenue and expense transactions affect the profits of a business?

Glencoe Accounting *Online*

Visit the *Glencoe Accounting* Web site at **glencoeaccounting.glencoe.com** for additional activities and information.

Relationship of Revenue, Expenses, and Withdrawals to Owner's Equity

What You'll Learn

- The reason for having temporary and permanent accounts.
- The rules of debit and credit for the revenue, expense, and withdrawals accounts.

Why It's Important

The proper handling of transactions that affect temporary and permanent accounts is essential to maintaining accurate financial records.

KEY TERMS

temporary capital
accounts
permanent accounts

In Chapter 4 you learned how to record transactions in asset, liability, and owner's capital accounts. In this chapter you will learn how to record transactions in revenue, expense, and owner's withdrawals accounts. These accounts provide information about how well the business is doing. A pilot for American Airlines or Delta would never take off in a 747 equipped with only a speedometer and a gas gauge. These two instruments, although necessary, do not give a pilot all of the information needed to keep such a complex aircraft on course and operating smoothly. Operating a business is a bit like operating a 747. Information about revenues and expenses is needed by the owner to keep the business on course.

Revenue, Expenses, and Withdrawals Account Transactions

You learned earlier that the owner's capital account shows the amount of the owner's investment, or equity, in a business. Owner's equity is increased or decreased by transactions other than owner's investments. For example, the revenue, or income, earned by the business increases owner's equity. Both expenses and owner's withdrawals decrease owner's equity. (Remember that revenue is not the same as an owner's investment, and expense is not the same as an owner's withdrawal.)

Revenue, expenses, and withdrawals could be recorded as increases or decreases directly in the capital account. This method, however, makes classifying information about these transactions difficult. A more informative way to record transactions affecting revenue and expenses is to set up separate accounts for each type of revenue or expense. Such information helps the owner decide, for example, whether some expenses need to be reduced to save money.

Temporary Capital Accounts

As you learned in Chapter 2, accounting is an activity that is divided into periods of time or accounting periods. This means that once all of the activities are completed for a given accounting period, that period is closed. Then a new period starts, and transactions for the new period are entered into the accounting system. The process continues for as long as the business exists.

Revenue, expense, and withdrawals accounts are used to collect information for a single accounting period. These accounts are called **temporary capital accounts** . Temporary capital accounts start each new accounting period with zero balances. That is, the amounts in these accounts are not carried forward from one accounting period to the next. Temporary capital accounts are not temporary in the sense that they are used for a short time and then discarded. They continue to be used in the accounting system, but the amounts recorded in them accumulate for only one accounting period. At the end of that period, the balances in the temporary capital accounts are transferred to the owner's capital account. (The procedure for transferring these balances to owner's capital is explained in Chapter 10.)

Illustrating Temporary Capital Accounts. Let's use **Utilities Expense**, a temporary capital account, as an example. During an accounting period, business transactions related to utilities such as electricity and telephones are recorded in **Utilities Expense.** By using this separate account, the owner can see at a glance how much money is being spent on this expense. The individual transaction amounts accumulate in the account as the accounting period progresses. At the end of the period, the total spent is transferred to the owner's capital account and subtracted from the capital account balance. Remember, expenses decrease owner's capital. In **Figure 5–1**, the account, **Utilities Expense**, starts the next accounting period with a zero balance—ready for the transactions in the new period.

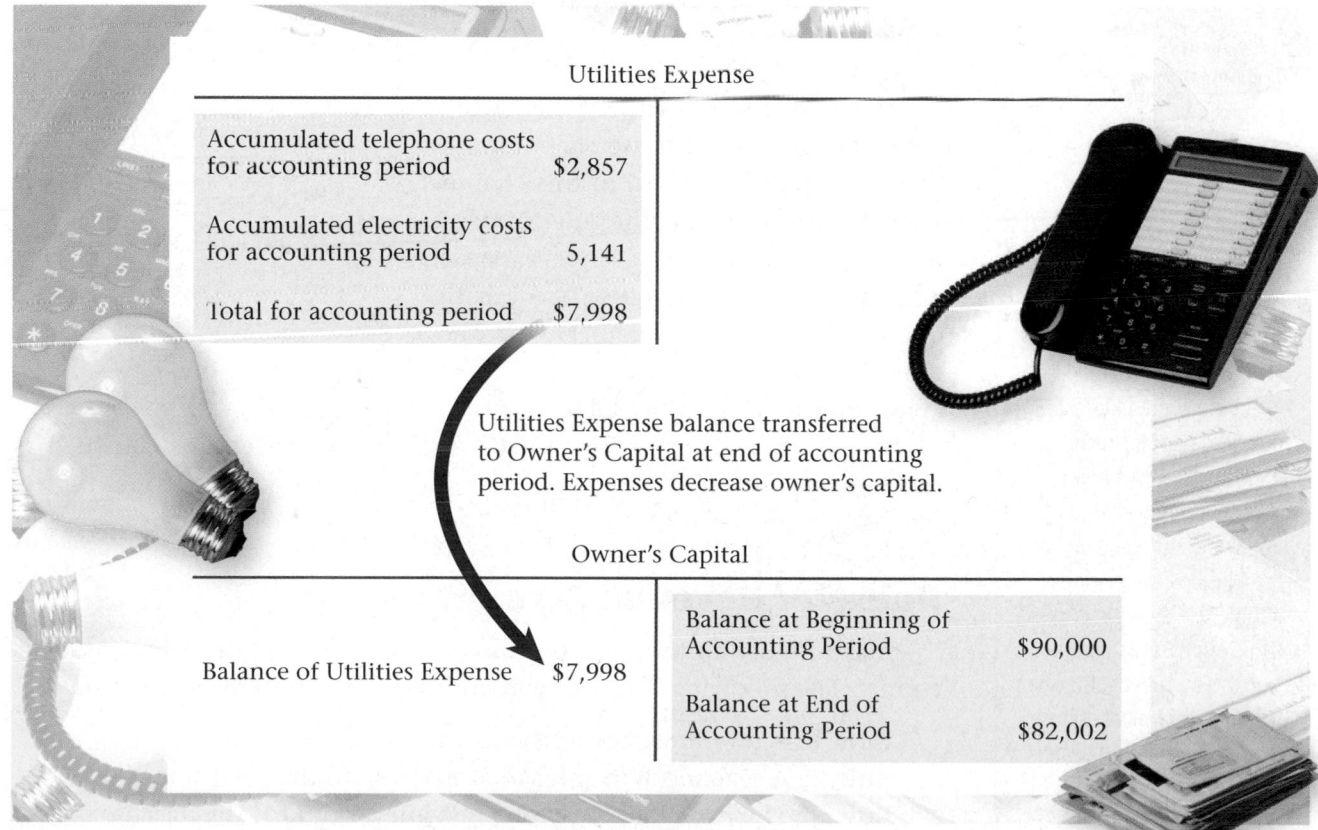

Figure 5–1 The Relationship of Temporary Capital Accounts to the Owner's Capital Account

Permanent Accounts

In contrast to the temporary accounts, the owner's capital account is a permanent account. Asset and liability accounts are also permanent accounts. **Permanent accounts** are continuous from one accounting period to the next. In permanent accounts, the dollar balances at the end of one accounting period become the dollar balances for the beginning of the next accounting period.

Illustrating Permanent Accounts. For example, if a business has supplies totaling $875 at the end of one accounting period, the business will start with $875 in supplies at the beginning of the next accounting period. That is, at the end of an accounting period, the ending balances in permanent accounts are carried forward to the next accounting period as the beginning balances.

End of Accounting Period		Beginning of Next Accounting Period	
Supplies		**Supplies**	
Debit	Credit	Debit	Credit
End Bal. 875		Beg. Bal. 875	

The permanent accounts show balances on hand or amounts owed at any time. They also show the day-to-day changes in assets, liabilities, and owner's capital.

The Rules of Debit and Credit for Temporary Capital Accounts

In Chapter 4 you learned the rules of debit and credit for the asset, liability, and owner's capital accounts. In this chapter we will continue with the rules of debit and credit, this time for revenue, expense, and withdrawals accounts. Before looking at these rules, let's review quickly the T account showing the rules of debit and credit for the owner's capital account.

Owner's Capital Account	
Debit	Credit
−	+
Decrease Side	Increase Side Normal Balance

As you will see, the rules of debit and credit for accounts classified as revenue, expense, and withdrawals accounts are related to the rules for the owner's equity account.

Rules for Revenue Accounts

Accounts set up to record business income are classified as revenue accounts. The following rules of debit and credit apply to revenue accounts:

Rule 1: A revenue account is *increased* (+) on the *credit* side.
Rule 2: A revenue account is *decreased* (−) on the *debit* side.
Rule 3: The *normal balance* for a revenue account is the *increase side,* or the *credit side*. Revenue accounts normally have credit balances.

Revenue earned from selling goods or services increases owner's capital. The relationship of revenue accounts to the owner's capital account is shown by the T accounts in **Figure 5–2.** Can you explain why the T account for revenue is used to represent the credit (right) side of the capital account?

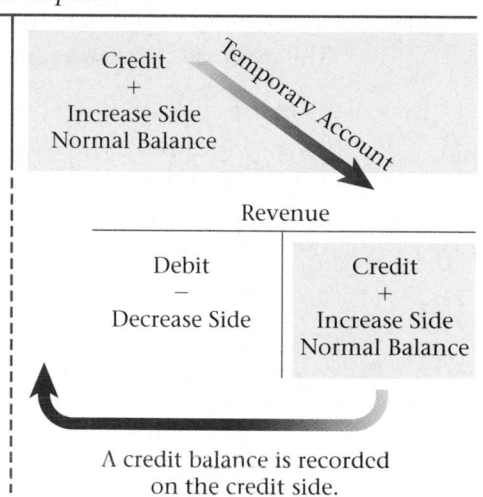

Permanent Account
Owner's Capital

Figure 5–2 Rules of Debit and Credit for Revenue Accounts

Increases in owner's capital are shown on the credit side of that account. Since revenue increases owner's capital, the revenue account is used to represent the credit side of the owner's capital account.

We can summarize the rules of debit and credit for revenue accounts with a T account illustration.

Revenue Accounts

Debit −	Credit +
(2) Decrease Side	(1) Increase Side
	(3) Normal Balance

Key Points

Normal Balances
The normal balance side of an account is the side used to increase the account.

Let's apply the rules of debit and credit to an actual revenue account. Look at the entries in the following T account for the revenue account called **Fees.** The increases to the revenue account are recorded on the right, or credit, side of the T account. The decreases are recorded on the left, or debit, side. To find the balance, subtract total debits ($200) from total credits ($500 + $1,000 + $2,000 = $3,500). You get a balance of $3,300 on the credit side, the normal balance side for a revenue account.

Fees

Debit −	Credit +
200	500
	1,000
	2,000
	Bal. 3,300

Rules for Expense Accounts

Accounts set up to record the costs of goods and services a business uses are expense accounts. The following rules of debit and credit apply to expense accounts:

Rule 1: An expense account is *increased* on the *debit* side.

Rule 2: An expense account is *decreased* on the *credit* side.

Rule 3: The *normal balance* for an expense account is the *increase side,* or the *debit side.* Expense accounts normally have debit balances.

Expenses are the costs of doing business. Expenses decrease owner's capital. Note that revenues have the exact opposite impact; revenues increase owner's capital. Look at the T accounts in **Figure 5–3.** Can you explain why the T account for expenses is used to represent the debit (left) side of the capital account?

Figure 5–3 Rules of Debit and Credit for Expense Accounts

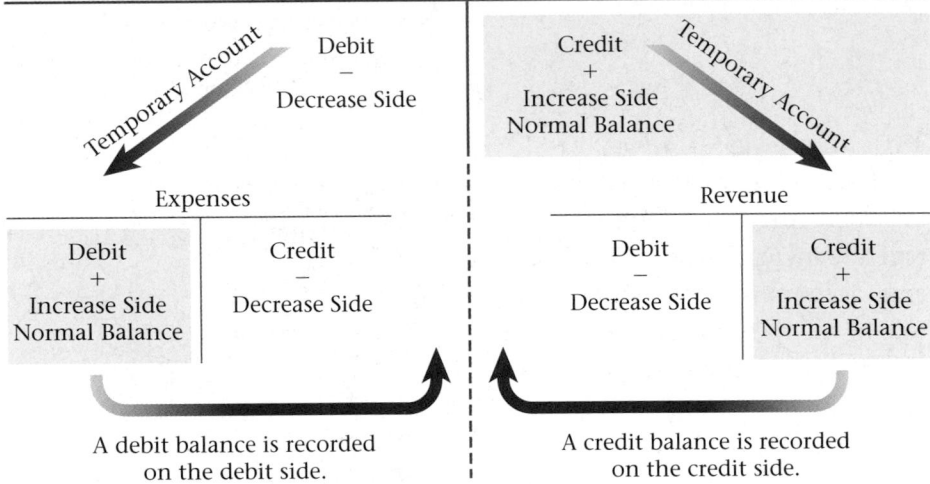

Permanent Account
Owner's Capital

Decreases in owner's capital are shown on the debit side of that account. Since expenses decrease owner's capital, expense accounts are used to represent the debit side of the owner's capital account.

Let's use a T account to summarize the rules of debit and credit for expense accounts.

Expense Accounts	
Debit +	Credit −
(1) Increase Side	(2) Decrease Side
(3) Normal Balance	

Now look at the entries recorded in the T account called **Advertising Expense.** The increases to the expense account are recorded on the left, or debit, side of the T account. The decreases to the account are recorded on the right, or credit, side of the T account. When total credits ($125) are subtracted from total debits ($600), there is a balance of $475 on the debit side, which is the normal balance side for expense accounts.

Advertising Expense

Debit +	Credit −
400	125
200	
Bal. 475	

Think different.

Rules for the Withdrawals Account

A withdrawal is an amount of money or an asset the owner takes out of the business. Since withdrawals do not occur as frequently as expenses, no separate classification is used for the withdrawals account. Rather, it is classified as a temporary owner's equity account. Withdrawals, like expenses, decrease capital, so the rules of debit and credit are the same as for expense accounts.

Rule 1: The withdrawals account is *increased* on the *debit* side.
Rule 2: The withdrawals account is *decreased* on the *credit* side.
Rule 3: The *normal balance* for the withdrawals account is the *increase side* or the *debit side*. The withdrawals account normally has a debit balance.

Withdrawals Account

Debit +	Credit −
(1) Increase Side	(2) Decrease Side
(3) Normal Balance	

Review the entries in the T account called **W. Smith, Withdrawals.** The increases are recorded on the left, or debit side, of the T account. The decreases are recorded on the right, or credit, side of the T account. When total credits ($200) are subtracted from total debits ($2,000), there is a balance of $1,800 on the debit side, which is the normal balance side for the withdrawals account.

W. Smith, Withdrawals

Debit +	Credit −
500	200
1,500	
Bal. 1,800	

Debits and Credits

Debits are used to:

1. Decrease (−) revenue.
2. Increase (+) expenses.
3. Increase (+) withdrawals.

Credits are used to:

1. Increase (+) revenue.
2. Decrease (−) expenses.
3. Decrease (−) withdrawals.

Summary of the Rules of Debit and Credit for Temporary Capital Accounts

Figure 5–4 summarizes the rules of debit and credit for the temporary capital accounts and the basic accounting relationships of these accounts to the owner's capital account.

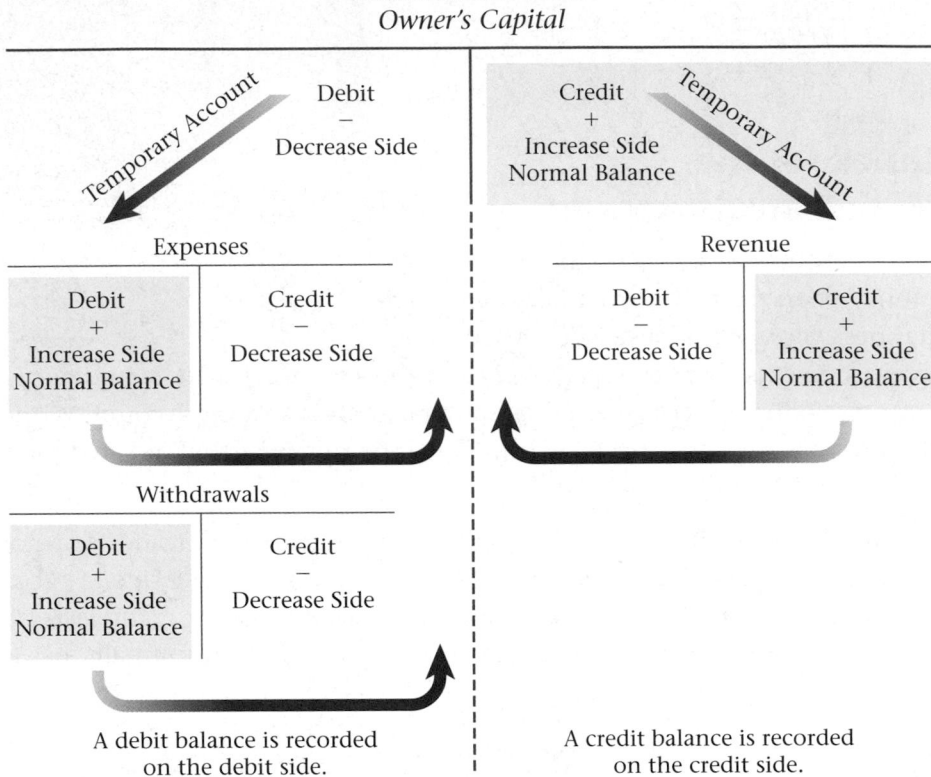

Figure 5–4 Rules of Debit and Credit for Temporary Capital Accounts

A MATTER OF ETHICS

Using a Toll-Free Number

Many businesses offer a toll-free telephone line for customers and business associates. Suppose you're an accountant for Procter & Gamble in Cincinnati, Ohio. Your friend Mike just moved to Houston and asks if your company has an 800 number he can use to call you. Your company does offer an 800 number, and you would like to hear from Mike. However, you also know that your company pays for each incoming call.

Ethical Decision Making:

☞ What are the ethical issues?

☞ What are the alternatives?

☞ Who are the affected parties?

☞ How do the alternatives affect the parties?

☞ What would you do?

Now that you have studied this section, complete the following questions and problems.

Thinking Critically

1. Changes to revenue accounts eventually affect another account. What other account is affected? Explain.
2. What type of transaction affects the debit side of the owner's capital account? Explain.

Communicating Accounting

As the financial director for the Southside Ballet Company, you determined it would be a good idea for Southside to open a ballet supply and dancewear shop. Write a memo to the ballet director and owner, Jonathan Booth, asking him to consider opening this shop. Explain how you view the impact of additional revenue on his capital account. Use the rules for revenue accounts in your explanation.

Problem 5–1   Applying the Rules of Debit and Credit

Caroline Palmer uses the following accounts in her San Francisco–Los Angeles commuter shuttle service.

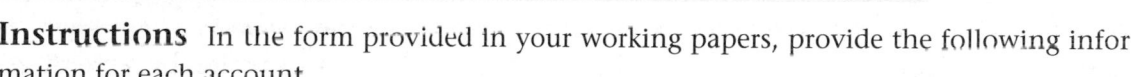

General Ledger

Cash in Bank	Caroline Palmer, Capital
Advertising Expense	Accounts Receivable
Caroline Palmer, Withdrawals	Food Expense
Airplanes	Flying Fees
Fuel and Oil Expense	Accounts Payable
Repairs Expense	

Instructions In the form provided in your working papers, provide the following information for each account.
(1) Classify the account as an asset, liability, owner's equity, revenue, or expense account.
(2) Indicate whether the increase side is a debit or a credit.
(3) Indicate whether the decrease side is a debit or a credit.
(4) Indicate whether the account has a normal debit balance or a normal credit balance. The first account is completed as an example.

Account Name	Account Classification	Increase Side	Decrease Side	Normal Balance
Cash in Bank	Asset	Debit	Credit	Debit

Applying the Rules of Debit and Credit to Revenue, Expense, and Owner's Equity Transactions

What You'll Learn

• How to analyze transactions that affect revenue, expense, and withdrawals accounts.

Why It's Important

You need to analyze revenue, expense, and owner's withdrawal transactions to record them correctly.

KEY TERMS

revenue recognition

In Section 1 you learned the rules of debit and credit for revenue, expense, and withdrawals accounts. Learning to apply these rules to typical business transactions is our next task. In the course of a week, a business might receive money, pay rent, or pay utility bills. Let's look at more transactions for Roadrunner Delivery Service.

Analyzing Transactions

In Chapter 4, Roadrunner's transactions dealt with asset and liability accounts and with the owner's equity account, **Maria Sanchez, Capital.** Using the rules of debit and credit, let's analyze several business transactions that affect revenue, expense, and owner's withdrawals accounts. Use the same six-step method you learned in Chapter 4. Refer to Roadrunner's chart of accounts on page 73 to analyze the following transactions.

Business Transaction 8

On October 15, Roadrunner provided delivery services for the Sims Corporation. A check for $1,200 was received in full payment.

ANALYSIS	*Identify* *Classify* +/−	1. The accounts **Cash in Bank** and **Delivery Revenue** are affected.
		2. **Cash in Bank** is an asset account. **Delivery Revenue** is a revenue account.
		3. **Cash in Bank** is increased by $1,200. **Delivery Revenue** is increased by $1,200.

DEBIT-CREDIT RULE	4. Increases in asset accounts are recorded as debits. Debit **Cash in Bank** for $1,200.
	5. Increases in revenue accounts are recorded as credits. Credit **Delivery Revenue** for $1,200.

T ACCOUNTS   6.

Cash in Bank		Delivery Revenue	
Debit +	Credit −	Debit −	Credit +
1,200			1,200

Business Transaction 9

On October 16, Roadrunner mailed Check 103 for $700 to pay the month's rent.

ANALYSIS *Identify*
1. The accounts **Rent Expense** and **Cash in Bank** are affected.

Classify
2. **Rent Expense** is an expense account. **Cash in Bank** is an asset account.

+/−
3. **Rent Expense** is increased by $700. **Cash in Bank** is decreased by $700.

DEBIT-CREDIT RULE
4. Increases in expense accounts are recorded as debits. Debit **Rent Expense** for $700.
5. Decreases in asset accounts are recorded as credits. Credit **Cash in Bank** for $700.

T ACCOUNTS 6.

Rent Expense		Cash in Bank	
Debit	Credit	Debit	Credit
+	−	+	−
700			700

Business Transaction 10

On October 18, Beacon Advertising prepared an advertisement for Roadrunner. Roadrunner will pay Beacon's $75 fee later.

ANALYSIS *Identify*
1. The accounts **Advertising Expense** and **Accounts Payable—Beacon Advertising** are affected.

Classify
2. **Advertising Expense** is an expense account. **Accounts Payable—Beacon Advertising** is a liability account.

+/−
3. **Advertising Expense** is increased by $75. **Accounts Payable—Beacon Advertising** is increased by $75.

DEBIT-CREDIT RULE
4. Increases in expense accounts are recorded as debits. Debit **Advertising Expense** for $75.
5. Increases in liability accounts are recorded as credits. Credit **Accounts Payable—Beacon Advertising** for $75.

T ACCOUNTS 6.

Advertising Expense		Accounts Payable— Beacon Advertising	
Debit	Credit	Debit	Credit
+	−	−	+
75			75

Business Transaction 11

On October 20, Roadrunner billed City News $1,450 for delivery services.

ANALYSIS	Identify	1.	The accounts **Accounts Receivable—City News** and **Delivery Revenue** are affected.
	Classify	2.	**Accounts Receivable—City News** is an asset account. **Delivery Revenue** is a revenue account.
	+/−	3.	**Accounts Receivable—City News** is increased by $1,450. **Delivery Revenue** is increased by $1,450.

| DEBIT-CREDIT RULE | | 4. | Increases in asset accounts are recorded as debits. Debit **Accounts Receivable—City News** for $1,450. |
| | | 5. | Increases in revenue accounts are recorded as credits. Credit **Delivery Revenue** for $1,450. |

T ACCOUNTS 6.

Accounts Receivable—City News		Delivery Revenue	
Debit + 1,450	Credit −	Debit −	Credit + 1,450

In Transaction 11 Roadrunner recorded revenue for services provided, even though the money had not been collected. Following the GAAP principle of **revenue recognition**, revenue should be recognized on the date earned, even if cash has not been received.

Business Transaction 12

On October 28, Roadrunner paid a $125 telephone bill with Check 104.

ANALYSIS	Identify	1.	The accounts **Utilities Expense** and **Cash in Bank** are affected.
	Classify	2.	**Utilities Expense** is an expense account. **Cash in Bank** is an asset account.
	+/−	3.	**Utilities Expense** is increased by $125. **Cash in Bank** is decreased by $125.

| DEBIT-CREDIT RULE | | 4. | Increases in expense accounts are recorded as debits. Debit **Utilities Expense** for $125. |
| | | 5. | Decreases in asset accounts are recorded as credits. Credit **Cash in Bank** for $125. |

T ACCOUNTS 6.

Utilities Expense		Cash in Bank	
Debit + 125	Credit −	Debit +	Credit − 125

Business Transaction 13

On October 29, Roadrunner wrote Check 105 for $600 to have the office repainted.

ANALYSIS	*Identify* *Classify* +/−	1. The accounts **Maintenance Expense** and **Cash in Bank** are affected. 2. **Maintenance Expense** is an expense account. **Cash in Bank** is an asset account. 3. **Maintenance Expense** is increased by $600. **Cash in Bank** is decreased by $600.
DEBIT-CREDIT RULE		4. Increases in expense accounts are recorded as debits. Debit **Maintenance Expense** for $600. 5. Decreases in asset accounts are recorded as credits. Credit **Cash in Bank** for $600.

T ACCOUNTS   6.

Maintenance Expense		Cash in Bank	
Debit + 600	Credit −	Debit +	Credit − 600

Business Transaction 14

On October 31, Maria Sanchez wrote Check 106 to withdraw $500 cash for personal use.

ANALYSIS	*Identify* *Classify* +/−	1. The accounts **Maria Sanchez, Withdrawals** and **Cash in Bank** are affected. 2. **Maria Sanchez, Withdrawals** is an owner's equity account. **Cash in Bank** is an asset account. 3. **Maria Sanchez, Withdrawals** is increased by $500. **Cash in Bank** is decreased by $500.
DEBIT-CREDIT RULE		4. Increases in the owner's withdrawals account are recorded as debits. Debit **Maria Sanchez, Withdrawals** for $500. 5. Decreases in assets are recorded as credits. Credit **Cash in Bank** for $500.

T ACCOUNTS   6.

Maria Sanchez, Withdrawals		Cash in Bank	
Debit + 500	Credit −	Debit +	Credit − 500

Testing for the Equality of Debits and Credits

In a double-entry accounting system, correct analysis and recording of business transactions should result in total debits being equal to total credits. Testing for the equality of debits and credits is one way of finding out whether you have made any errors in recording transaction amounts. To test for the equality of debits and credits, follow these steps:

Step 1. Make a list of the account titles used by the business.
Step 2. To the right of each account title, list the balance of the account. Use two columns, one for debit balances and the other for credit balances.
Step 3. Add the amounts in each column.

If you have recorded all the amounts correctly, the total of the debit column will equal the total of the credit column. The test for equality of debits and credits for the transactions in Chapters 4 and 5 shows that total debits are equal to total credits, so the ledger is in balance.

ACCOUNT NAME		DEBIT BALANCES	CREDIT BALANCES
101	Cash in Bank	$ 21,125	
105	Accounts Receivable—City News	1,450	
110	Accounts Receivable—Green Company		
115	Computer Equipment	3,000	
120	Office Equipment	200	
125	Delivery Equipment	12,000	
201	Accounts Payable—Beacon Advertising		$ 75
205	Accounts Payable—North Shore Auto		11,650
301	Maria Sanchez, Capital		25,400
302	Maria Sanchez, Withdrawals	500	
303	Income Summary		
401	Delivery Revenue		2,650
501	Advertising Expense	75	
505	Maintenance Expense	600	
510	Rent Expense	700	
515	Utilities Expense	125	
		$ 39,775	$ 39,775

Now that you have studied this section, complete the following questions and problem.

Thinking Critically

1. What is the normal balance of a withdrawals account?
2. What other temporary account carries a normal balance on the same side as the normal balance for a withdrawals account?
3. The two accounts referred to above temporarily represent a permanent account. What is the name of the permanent account?

Analyzing Accounting

Your accounting clerk has just handed you the bar chart shown at right reflecting the revenue and expense for the first quarter. What month was the most revenue? What month had the highest expense? Overall, did the business have a profit or loss?

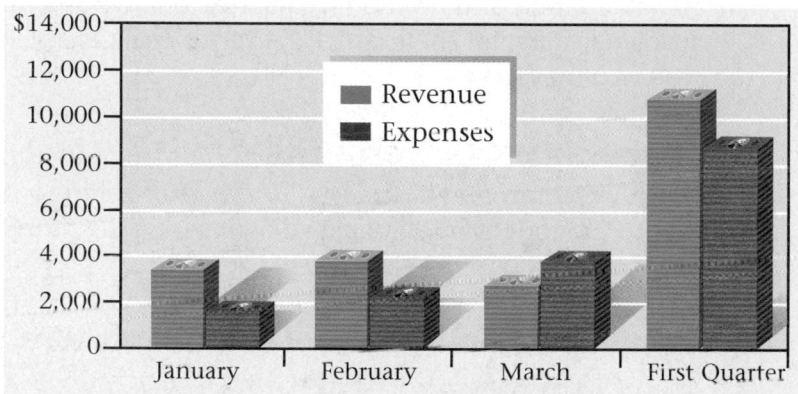

Problem 5-2 Identifying Accounts Affected by Transactions

John Albers uses the following accounts in his business.

General Ledger

Cash in Bank	John Albers, Capital	Advertising Expense
Accounts Receivable	John Albers, Withdrawals	Rent Expense
Office Equipment	Service Fees	Utilities Expense
Accounts Payable		

Instructions In your working papers:
(1) Identify the two accounts affected by each of the following transactions.
(2) Indicate whether each account is debited or credited.

Date	Transactions
July 1	1. Issued Check 543 to pay the electric bill for the month.
3	2. Billed a customer for services provided on account.
10	3. John Albers took cash from the business for his personal use.
17	4. Issued Check 544 to pay for an advertisement.

BILL ALBRETS
Chief Accountant, Lockheed Martin Technical Operations

Q: How did you get into accounting?

A: I was a bookkeeper and liked it, but bookkeeping has a limited career growth and pay. There were two paths to business management: the MBA (Masters of Business Administration) and the CPA. The MBA takes two years, and since I had a family and no money, that was out. Getting my CPA involved sitting for the exam. It's a very difficult exam. It took me two tries to pass it.

Q: Is getting a CPA worthwhile?

A: I highly recommend it. The first two years of getting your experience are tough. I didn't enjoy working for a CPA firm, but it has only helped me in my career.

Q: What do you recommend to students who want to go into management?

A: Accounting is a very good path into management. As an internal auditor, you see all the operations of your employer. That's how I got my job here. I came in to do an audit, they liked what they saw, and they gave me a tremendous job offer.

Q: What skills are most important?

A: Excellent communication skills. You don't move ahead with just technical skills. You need to show your ideas to management in a way they'll understand and remember. I teach public speaking classes in community college because I believe so strongly in it.

> **Tips from . . .**
>
> **RHI** Robert Half International Inc.
>
> Be enthusiastic and be ready to perform first-rate work no matter what you're asked to do. Enthusiasm can help you get a job done faster. You'll have time to take on exciting new challenges.

CAREER FACTS

Nature of the Work: Working with management on planning, guiding and directing staff, and doing accounting functions when necessary.

Training or Education Needed: A bachelor's degree in accounting, and the CPA exam.

Aptitudes, Abilities, and Skills: Accounting, time-management skills, problem-solving skills, communication skills and interpersonal skills.

Salary Range: $70,000 to $150,000 depending on company size and industry.

Career Path: Start as an internal auditor for a variety of firms to learn business, gain experience in lower management (such as project manager), and then move to chief accountant or controller.

Thinking Critically: In what ways would you use public speaking in your career?

KEY CONCEPTS

1. The accounts used by a business can be separated into permanent accounts and temporary capital accounts.
2. Asset and liability accounts and the owner's capital account are permanent accounts.
3. Revenue, expense, and withdrawals accounts are temporary capital accounts.
4. Temporary capital accounts start each new accounting period with zero balances.
5. Revenue accounts temporarily represent the credit side of owner's capital.
6. Expense and withdrawals accounts temporarily represent the debit side of owner's capital.
7. Revenue accounts are increased by credits and have normal credit balances.
8. Expense and withdrawals accounts are increased by debits and have normal debit balances.
9. The rules of debit and credit for the permanent accounts—assets, liabilities, and the owner's capital account—are summarized below using T accounts and the basic accounting equation.

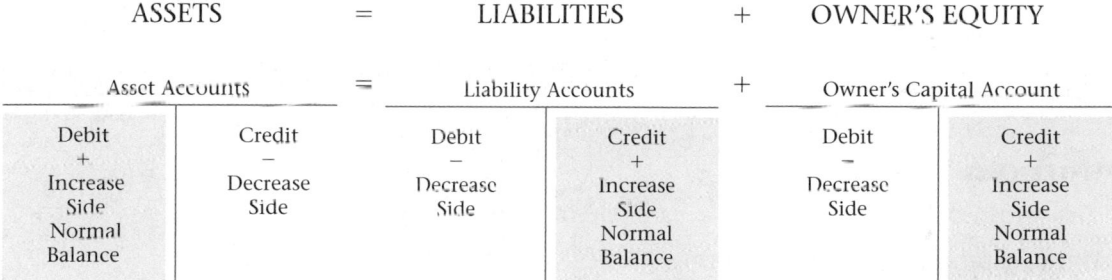

10. The rules of debit and credit for the temporary capital accounts—revenue, expenses, and the owner's withdrawals account—may also be summarized using T accounts.

Temporary Capital Accounts

Withdrawals		Expenses		Revenue	
Debit + Increase Side Normal Balance	Credit – Decrease Side	Debit + Increase Side Normal Balance	Credit – Decrease Side	Debit – Decrease Side	Credit + Increase Side Normal Balance

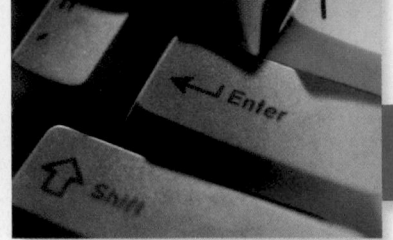

USING KEY TERMS

You have been asked to make a presentation to your company's owners. For the owners to understand the difference in the accounts you manage, you must be able to explain the following key terms:

| permanent accounts | temporary capital accounts |
| revenue recognition | |

Create three examples that could be used as overhead transparencies. Each example (master) should show a term, a brief definition, and an illustration or example.

Understanding Accounting Concepts and Procedures

Instructions

Answer the following questions on a separate sheet of paper:

1. Why are temporary capital accounts used?

2. What is the difference between a temporary capital account and a permanent account? Give three examples of each type of account.

3. State briefly the rules of debit and credit for increasing and decreasing (a) revenue accounts, (b) expense accounts, (c) withdrawals accounts.

4. List the normal balance side of (a) revenue accounts, (b) expense accounts, (c) withdrawals accounts, (d) asset accounts, (e) liability accounts, (f) the owner's capital account.

5. Why does a revenue account temporarily represent the credit side of the owner's capital account?

6. What effect does a revenue transaction have on owner's capital?

7. Explain why the expense accounts temporarily represent the debit side of the owner's capital account.

8. What effect does an expense transaction have on owner's capital?

9. How is a withdrawal different from an expense? How are they the same?

10. How is an investment different from revenue? How are they the same?

11. How would you test for the equality of debits and credits?

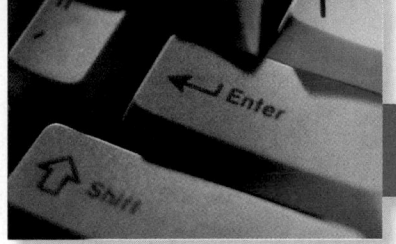

Case Study...

Service Business: Web Site Design

Colleen Chapelli owns Web Design Source, a service that creates Web sites for local businesses. While Colleen is an expert with computers and software programming, her business finance expertise is limited. She has hired you as her accountant to organize her business information and suggest business accounts. Here are some of the items Colleen uses in the business:

- Computer
- Printer
- Software
- Desk and chair
- Bookcases
- Computer supplies

Colleen has been advertising in the local newspaper to find new clients. She manages the business from her home and has a separate telephone line for the business.

Thinking Critically:

1. Prepare a chart of accounts for Web Design Source.
2. Explain to Colleen why it is important to collect and organize the financial information resulting from business transactions.

Conducting an Audit with Alex

Instructions Review the T accounts below to verify that the following transactions are reflected properly. On a separate sheet of paper, make any necessary corrections.

1. Received $425 from Marty Prichard for printing services.
2. Provided printing services to Marty Prichard on account, $325.
3. Paid for repairs to the copier, $127.

Cash in Bank		Printing Revenue	
(1) 425	(3)127	(3) 127	(2) 325
(2) 325			(1) 425

inter**NET** CONNECTION

Certified Public Accounting

The American Institute of Certified Public Accountants (AICPA) Web site offers an area for students that presents information on becoming a CPA.

Do This:

1. Locate the Web site for the AICPA. What is the Web site address?
2. Describe the features that exist on the AICPA site.
3. What other organizations might an accounting professional want to join?
4. List three scholarships available for accounting majors.

Workplace Skills

Acquiring and Analyzing Data

To make a decision, whether business or personal, you must be able to acquire and analyze data (information).

On the Job:

You are about to enter your senior year at Highland College, a small liberal arts college of 2,000 students in North Carolina. Eighty percent of the students live in dorms on campus or in apartments within one mile of the college. The student activities center closes at 9:00 P.M. during the school week, and students complain about the lack of a food and beverage service available for late night study sessions. You decide to analyze the market potential of starting a limited food and beverage delivery service.

Thinking Critically:

1. Develop a market survey of 5–10 questions related to the opening of an off-campus food and beverage delivery service.
2. Decide what type of food and beverage you can provide in a delivery service. How much investment would you need to begin? What do you anticipate your customer base to be?

The Chart of Accounts
Making the Transition from a Manual to a Computerized System

Task	Perform Accounting Procedures Using Manual Methods	Perform Accounting Procedures Using Automated Methods
Setting up the accounts in the general ledger	• Accounts are set up in the general ledger using general ledger account forms. • Accounts can be set up with or without beginning balances.	• Accounts are set up using defined account numbers and account types. • Accounts can be set up with or without beginning balances. • Peachtree offers hundreds of sample companies from which you can copy the chart of accounts instead of creating each account individually.

Chart of Accounts

Assets	Owner's Equity
Cash in Bank	Maria Sanchez, Capital
Accounts Receivable	Maria Sanchez, Withdrawals
Computer Equipment	
Office Equipment	**Revenue**
Delivery Equipment	Delivery Revenue
Liabilities	**Expenses**
Accounts Payable	Advertising Expense
	Maintenance Expense
	Rent Expense

Setting Up General Ledger Accounts

Peachtree Question	Description
How do I create general ledger accounts in Peachtree?	1. From the *Maintain* menu, select **Chart of Accounts**. 2. Enter the account number in the Account ID box. 3. Enter the account name in the Description box. 4. From the Account Type drop-down list, select the account type from options like accounts payable, accounts receivable, equity, expenses, income, and others.
What does the software do "behind the scenes"?	• General ledger accounts are opened for each account and stored in the chart of accounts. • These accounts will be accessible from a drop-down list for any transaction you wish to enter in the future. • Assigning each account an account type defines for the software where each account will be reported when you begin to print financial statements.

For detailed instructions: See the **Peachtree User Guide** in your Glencoe Working Papers.

APPLICATION OPTIONS

Problem 5–3 Identifying Increases and Decreases in Accounts

Ronald Hicks uses the following accounts in his business, Wilderness Rentals.

General Ledger

101 Cash in Bank	301 Ronald Hicks, Capital
105 Accounts Receivable— Helen Katz	305 Ronald Hicks, Withdrawals
	401 Equipment Rental Revenue
120 Office Equipment	505 Maintenance Expense
125 Camping Equipment	525 Utilities Expense

Instructions Analyze each of the following transactions using the format shown in the example below. Record your answers in your working papers.

a. Explain the debit.

b. Explain the credit.

Example:

On Jan. 2, Ronald Hicks paid the bill for office cleaning, $100.

a. The expense account **505 Maintenance Expense** is increased. Increases in expenses are recorded as debits.

b. The asset account **101 Cash in Bank** is decreased. Decreases in assets are recorded as credits.

Date	Transactions
Jan. 3	1. Ronald Hicks withdrew $500 from his business for his own use, Check 225.
8	2. The business received $1,200 cash in rental fees from various customers.
12	3. The business paid a telephone bill of $85, Check 226.

Analyze: By what amount did the **Cash in Bank** balance change?

Problem 5–4 Using T Accounts to Analyze Transactions

Regina Delgado, the owner of Hot Suds Car Wash, uses the following accounts:

Continued

Complete chapter problems one of three ways:

1 **Manual** Glencoe Working Papers

or

2 **Peachtree Complete Accounting** Software

or

3 **Spreadsheet** Templates (Problem 5–8)

Peachtree®

SMART GUIDE

Step–by–Step Instructions: Problem 5–3

1. Select the problem set for Wilderness Rentals (Prob. 5–3).
2. Rename the company and set the system date.
3. Print a Chart of Accounts using the **General Ledger** option in the **Reports** menu.
4. Review the Chart of Accounts.
5. End the session.

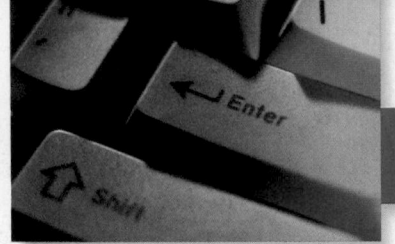

Peachtree®

SMART GUIDE

Step–by–Step Instructions: Problem 5–4

1. Select the problem set for Hot Suds Car Wash (Prob. 5–4).
2. Rename the company and set the system date.
3. Print a Chart of Accounts using the **General Ledger** option in the **Reports** menu.
4. Review the Chart of Accounts.
5. End the session.

TIP: You will learn how to enter transactions into the accounts in the next chapter.

General Ledger

101	Cash in Bank	401	Wash Revenue
125	Office Equipment	510	Maintenance Expense
205	Accounts Payable— O'Brian's Office Supply	520	Rent Expense
301	Regina Delgado, Capital		
305	Regina Delgado, Withdrawals		

Instructions In your working papers:

(1) Determine which accounts are affected for each transaction.

(2) Prepare T accounts for the accounts affected.

(3) Enter the amount of the debit and the amount of the credit in the T accounts.

Date	Transactions
Jan. 7	1. Received a check for $1,675 for car wash services.
12	2. Paid the monthly rent of $450 by writing Check 212.
15	3. Regina Delgado withdrew $250 for her personal use, Check 213.
29	4. Had the computer repaired at O'Brian's Office Supply for $245 and was given until next month to pay.

Analyze: Which transactions affect expense accounts?

Peachtree®

SMART GUIDE

Step–by–Step Instructions: Problem 5–5

1. Select the problem set for Kits & Pups Grooming (Prob. 5–5).
2. Rename the company and set the system date.
3. Add new general ledger accounts using the **Chart of Accounts** option in the **Maintain** menu.
4. Enter beginning balances using the **Chart of Accounts** option in the **Maintain** menu.
5. Print a Chart of Accounts using the **General Ledger** option in the **Reports** menu.
6. Proof your work.
7. End the session.

TIP: When a report list appears, double-click a report title to go directly to that report.

Problem 5–5 Analyzing Transactions into Debit and Credit Parts

Abe Shultz, owner of Kits & Pups Grooming, uses the following accounts to record transactions for the month.

General Ledger

101	Cash in Bank	401	Boarding Revenue
105	Accounts Receivable— Juan Alvarez	405	Grooming Revenue
140	Grooming Equipment	501	Advertising Expense
205	Accounts Payable— Dogs & Cats Inc.	505	Equipment Repair Expense
301	Abe Shultz, Capital	510	Maintenance Expense
305	Abe Shultz, Withdrawals	520	Rent Expense
		530	Utilities Expense

Instructions For each transaction:

(1) Prepare a T account for each account listed.

(2) Enter a balance of $15,000 in the **Cash in Bank** account; also enter a balance of $15,000 in the **Abe Shultz, Capital** account.

(3) Analyze and record each of the following business transactions, using the appropriate T accounts. Identify each transaction by number.

(4) After all the business transactions have been recorded, write the word "Balance" on the normal balance side of each account.

(5) Compute and record the balance for each account.

Date	Transactions
Jan. 1	1. Purchased grooming equipment for $12,700, Check 283.
10	2. Wrote Check 284 for advertising, $125.
12	3. Received $1,850 cash for dog boarding services.
15	4. Paid $150 for equipment repair, Check 285.
17	5. Purchased a dog cage on account from Dogs & Cats Inc. for $75.
20	6. Abe Shultz withdrew $150 for personal use, Check 286.
22	7. Billed Juan Alvarez for $775 covering grooming services for all of the dogs boarded at the kennels he owns. Payment will be received later.
23	8. Paid the first two weeks' rent by writing Check 287 for $325.
25	9. Paid the electric bill at a cost of $115, Check 288.

Analyze: If you were asked to prepare a check on January 30 for another expense, what check number would you use?

Problem 5-6 Analyzing Transactions into Debit and Credit Parts

Juanita Ortega operates Outback Guide Service. She uses the following accounts to record and summarize her business transactions.

General Ledger

101 Cash in Bank	301 Juanita Ortega, Capital
105 Accounts Receivable— Mary Johnson	302 Juanita Ortega, Withdrawals
150 Rafting Equipment	401 Guide Service Revenue
205 Accounts Payable— Peak Equipment Inc.	505 Maintenance Expense
	515 Rent Expense
	520 Utilities Expense

Instructions For each transaction:

(1) Prepare a T account for each account the business uses.

(2) Analyze and record each of the following transactions using the appropriate T accounts. Identify each transaction by number.

Peachtree®

SMART GUIDE

Step–by–Step Instructions: Problem 5–6

1. Select the problem set for Outback Guide Service (Prob. 5–6).
2. Rename the company and set the system date.
3. Add new general ledger accounts using the **Chart of Accounts** option in the **Maintain** menu.
4. Print a Chart of Accounts using the **General Ledger** option in the **Reports** menu.
5. Proof your work using the Chart of Accounts report.
6. End the session.

TIP: You can use General Ledger Navigation Aid to access the Maintain Chart of Accounts window.

Continued

(3) After recording all transactions, compute and record the account balance on the normal balance side of each T account.

(4) Test for the equality of debits and credits.

Date	Transactions
Jan. 2	**1.** Juanita Ortega invested $12,000 cash in her business.
7	**2.** Purchased two new whitewater rafts on account for $3,750 from Peak Equipment Inc.
10	**3.** Billed, but did not collect, $750 for guide services provided to Mary Johnson.
12	**4.** Repaired a raft at a cost of $123, Check 411.
14	**5.** Wrote Check 412 to pay the electric bill of $95.
17	**6.** Received $225 for guide service fees.
21	**7.** Paid the $225 rent for the month, Check 413.
24	**8.** Paid $1,750 toward the rafts bought on account, Check 414.
27	**9.** Juanita Ortega withdrew $250 cash for personal use, Check 415.
29	**10.** Received guide service fees of $250.

Analyze: How much revenue was earned?

Peachtree®

SMART GUIDE

Step–by–Step Instructions: Problem 5–7

1. Select the problem set for Showbiz Video (Prob. 5–7).
2. Rename the company and set the system date.
3. Add a new record for each of the general ledger accounts.
4. Print a Chart of Accounts.
5. Proof your work.
6. End the session.

TIP: Peachtree requires that you group accounts by type: asset, liability, equity, income, and expense.

Problem 5–7 Analyzing Transactions

Greg Failla owns Showbiz Video. He uses the following accounts to record business transactions.

General Ledger

101	Cash in Bank	
105	Accounts Receivable—Gabriel Cohen	
110	Accounts Receivable—James Coletti	
140	Computer Equipment	
145	Video Tapes	

205	Accounts Payable—Computer Horizons
207	Accounts Payable—New Media Suppliers
301	Greg Failla, Capital
305	Greg Failla, Withdrawals
401	Video Rental Revenue
405	VCR Rental Revenue
505	Equipment Repair Expense
520	Rent Expense
530	Utilities Expense

Instructions For each transaction:

(1) Prepare a T account for each account listed above.

(2) Analyze and record each of the following transactions using the appropriate T accounts. Identify each transaction by number.

(3) After recording all transactions, compute a balance for each account.

(4) Test for the equality of debits and credits.

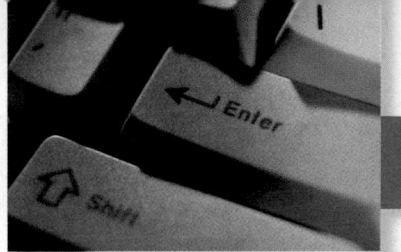
Date	Transactions
Jan. 1	**1.** Greg Failla invested $17,500 cash in Showbiz Video.
3	**2.** Purchased computer equipment on account from Computer Horizons for $2,400.
8	**3.** Purchased on account videos from New Media Suppliers for $375.
10	**4.** Paid monthly rent of $750, Check 1183.
13	**5.** Wrote Check 1184 to pay for new videos, $265.
14	**6.** Sent a bill for $67 to Gabriel Cohen for a VCR rental.
16	**7.** Deposited the receipts from video rentals, $233.
19	**8.** Paid the gas and electric bill of $125, Check 1185.
21	**9.** Sent Check 1186 for $375 to New Media Suppliers as payment on account.
22	**10.** Greg Failla withdrew $150 for his personal use, Check 1187.
25	**11.** Paid $45 for VCR repair, Check 1188.
30	**12.** Deposited VCR rental receipts of $264 in the bank.

Analyze: What liabilities does Showbiz have after these transactions?

CHALLENGE PROBLEM

Problem 5–8 Completing the Accounting Equation

SPREADSHEET SMART GUIDE

With the addition of temporary capital accounts, the basic accounting equation can be expanded as follows:

Assets = Liabilities + Owner's Equity − Withdrawals + Revenue − Expenses

Instructions Using the expanded equation, determine the missing amounts for the accounting equations shown below. Use the form in your working papers. The first equation is completed as an example.

Step–by–Step Instructions: Problem 5–8

1. Select the spreadsheet template for Problem 5–8.
2. Enter your name and the date in the spaces provided on the template.
3. Complete the spreadsheet using the instructions in your working papers.
4. Print the spreadsheet and proof your work.
5. Save your work and exit the spreadsheet program.

	Assets	=	Liabilities	+	Owner's Equity	−	Withdrawals	+	Revenue	−	Expenses
1.	$64,400		$8,200		$56,300		$ 500		$10,000		$ 9,600
2.	$22,150		525		18,800		1,200		12,100		?
3.	17,500		75		21,650		?		4,115		3,250
4.	49,450		?		47,840		1,500		20,300		17,610
5.	21,900		1,150		20,005		950		?		16,570
6.	72,640		2,790		?		10,750		67,908		39,749
7.	?		1,988		41,194		6,196		52,210		42,597
8.	?		3,840		61,774		?		40,163		21,637

(Expenses plus withdrawals equal $27,749.)

| 9. | 64,070 | | ? | | 49,102 | | 4,875 | | 53,166 | | ? |

(Total owner's equity after adding revenue and subtracting expenses and withdrawals is $50,643.)

Analyze: Increases in temporary capital accounts result in an increase or a decrease in owner's equity?

Recording Transactions in a General Journal

Learning Objectives

When you have completed this chapter, you will be able to:

▶ Explain the first three steps in the accounting cycle.

▶ Give and describe several examples of source documents.

▶ Explain the purpose of journalizing.

▶ Apply information from source documents.

▶ Describe the steps to make a general journal entry.

▶ Make accurate general journal entries.

▶ Correct errors in general journal entries.

▶ Define the accounting terms introduced in this chapter.

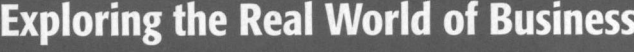

Exploring the Real World of Business

RECORDING FINANCIAL INFORMATION

Ben Cohen and Jerry Greenfield met in junior high school and graduated from Calhoun High School in Merrick, Long Island. After high school they decided that they wanted to start a business together. They researched products, market demand, and locations. A shared love for all-natural ice cream and a vision for a company that improves the quality of community life were the foundations for the beginnings of **Ben & Jerry's Ice Cream and Frozen Yogurt.** They purchased a used old-fashioned rock salt ice cream maker and took a correspondence course from Penn State about ice cream making.

Ben & Jerry's opened for business in May of 1978 in Burlington, Vermont, in a "roughly" renovated gas station. **Ben & Jerry's** products are now sold around the world. Recording financial information about the business keeps several full-time accountants busy.

What do you think?

If you were Ben and Jerry, what types of financial information would you record?

Ben & Jerry's Homemade, Inc.

Workplace Connections

Applying Your Accounting Knowledge

Have you ever kept a daily journal of the things that happen during your day? The general journal of a business is similar. The daily financial happenings are recorded there. Your local video store earns revenue by renting videos, buys advertising in the newspaper, pays its employees, and pays its bills. You'll learn how to record business transactions in a journal in this chapter.

Investigate:

1. In your workplace, why is it important to keep accurate records of daily transactions?
2. List five business transactions that happen in your workplace.

Glencoe Accounting Online

Visit the *Glencoe Accounting* Web site at **glencoeaccounting.glencoe.com** for additional activities and information.

121

The Accounting Cycle

In earlier chapters, you learned to use the accounting equation and T accounts to analyze business transactions. You also studied the rules of debit and credit for asset, liability, owner's equity, revenue, and expense accounts. In this chapter, you will learn how to record business transactions in a journal.

The Steps of the Accounting Cycle

The accounting period of a business is separated into activities that help the business keep its accounting records in an orderly fashion. These activities are called the **accounting cycle**. Take a look at **Figure 6–1**, which describes accounting activities and their sequence.

In this chapter, you will read about and use Steps 1, 2, and 3 of the accounting cycle. The remaining chapters in this unit will each cover at least one more step in the accounting cycle. After studying Chapters 3 through 10, you will have covered the accounting cycle for a service business organized as a sole proprietorship.

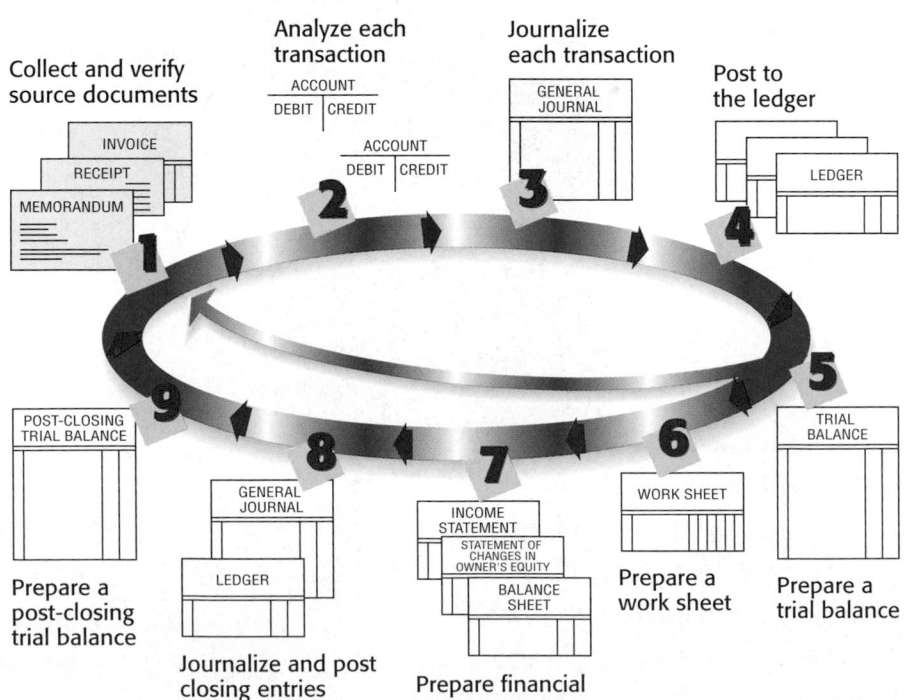

Figure 6–1 Steps in the Accounting Cycle with Steps 1, 2, 3 Highlighted

The First Step in the Accounting Cycle: Collecting and Verifying Source Documents

Most business transactions take place during the daily operations of a business. In the course of one day, a business may pay its rent, place an ad in a local newspaper, contract to have a Web site created, pay its employees, sell products, and purchase new equipment. When a business transaction occurs, a paper is prepared as evidence of that transaction. This paper is a **source document** . The business owner, accountant, or accounting clerk (depending on the size of the business) uses source documents generated by business transactions to keep the records of the business. The accounting cycle starts by collecting and verifying the accuracy of source documents. One important activity is to check the arithmetic on each source document.

There are several types of source documents that can be prepared by hand, by computer, or by a machine. The type of source document prepared depends on the nature of the transaction. **Figure 6–2** describes and illustrates commonly used source documents.

Spreadsheet Hints

Cell Addresses

Spreadsheets are divided into:

- Columns labeled A, B, C, and so on.
- Rows labeled 1, 2, 3, and so on.

The point where a column and a row meet is called a cell. Each cell has its own "address," identified by a letter and a number, such as A1.

Invoice

Lists specific information about a business transaction involving the buying or selling of an item. The invoice contains the date of the transaction, along with the quantity, description, and cost of each item.

Receipt

A record of cash received by a business. It indicates the date the payment was received, the name of the person or business from whom the payment was received, and the amount of the payment.

Memorandum

A brief written message that describes a transaction that takes place within a business. Often used if no other source document exists for the business transaction.

Check Stub

The check stub lists the same information that appears on a check: the date written, the person or business to whom the check was written, and the amount of the check. The check stub also shows the balance in the checking account before and after each check is written.

Figure 6–2 Source Documents

Key Points

Source Documents

Source documents are evidence of business transactions. They are the basis for the information recorded in the accounting system.

CONNECT TO . . . ENVIRONMENT

Because businesses sometimes find it cheaper to pollute and pay fines than to take measures that protect the environment, the government is often forced to offer economic incentives. When accountants compare these benefits to the costs of environmental safeguarding, they must also factor in civic responsibility and public relations.

The Second Step in the Accounting Cycle: Analyzing Business Transactions

After collecting and verifying source documents, the second step in the accounting cycle can begin—analyzing information on the source documents to determine the debit and credit parts of each transaction.

You have already learned how to analyze business transactions using the rules of debit and credit. When you learned to analyze transactions, you were given a description of each transaction, such as: Roadrunner Delivery Service bought a computer system from Info-Systems Inc. for $3,000 and issued Check 101 in payment. On the job, you won't get a description of the transaction. Instead, you must examine a source document to determine what occurred during a business transaction.

The Third Step in the Accounting Cycle: Recording Business Transactions in a Journal

You are now ready to apply information from source documents. The third step in the accounting cycle is to record the debit and credit parts of each business transaction in a journal. A **journal** is a record of all of the transactions of a business. Journals are kept in chronological order, that is, in the order that the transactions occur. The process of recording business transactions in a journal is called **journalizing** . Keeping a journal can be compared to keeping a diary in which all important events are written. A journal contains the most important information relating to a business transaction. It is the only place where complete details of a transaction, including both the debit and credit parts, are recorded. For this reason, the journal is often called a *record* or *"book" of original entry.*

The Accounting Period

As discussed in Chapter 2, accounting records are summarized for a certain period of time, called an accounting period. An accounting period may be for any designated length of time, such as a month, a quarter, or a year. Most businesses use a year as their accounting period. If the accounting period for a business begins on January 1 and ends on December 31, it is called a **calendar year** accounting period. A **fiscal year** is an accounting period of twelve months. Many businesses start their accounting periods in months other than January. For example, department stores often have fiscal years that begin on February 1 and end January 31 of the following year. School districts usually have fiscal years that begin on July 1 and end on June 30.

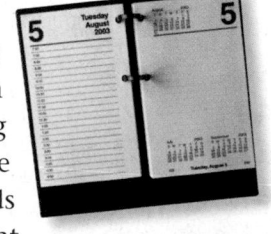

Now that you have studied this section, complete the following questions and problems.

Thinking Critically

1. Businesses separate their accounting records into accounting periods. Why is this procedure important for keeping meaningful accounting records?
2. How are source documents used?

Communicating Accounting

Write a paragraph describing the content of invoices, check stubs, memorandums, and receipts. Explain how to verify and analyze these source documents before an entry in the journal is made.

Problem 6–1 Analyzing a Source Document

Instructions Analyze the invoice shown below and answer the following questions.

JAYMAX OFFICE SUPPLY			**INVOICE NO. 479**	
554 Town Square				
Fort Myers, FL 33902		DATE:	Apr. 9, 20--	
		ORDER NO.:		
Dario's Accounting Services		SHIPPED BY:	Truck	
TO 5821 Gulf Blvd.		TERMS:	Payable in 30 days	
Naples, FL 33940				

QTY.	ITEM	UNIT PRICE	TOTAL
1	Fax Machine	$ 299.00	$ 299.00

1. What is the name of the company providing the service?
2. What is the name of the business receiving the service?
3. What is the date of the invoice?
4. What is the invoice number?
5. What item was sold?
6. What is the price for this item?
7. What are the payment terms?

Recording Transactions in the General Journal

In Section 1, you learned about the first three steps in the accounting cycle. Let's apply these steps to business transactions for Roadrunner Delivery Service.

Recording a General Journal Entry

Many kinds of accounting journals are used in business. One of the most common is the general journal. As its name suggests, the **general journal** is an all purpose journal in which all the transactions of a business may be recorded. **Figure 6–3** shows the general journal you will be using throughout the accounting cycle for Roadrunner Delivery Service. The general journal has two amount columns. The first amount column, the amount column on the left, is used to record debit amounts. (Remember that debit means left.) The second amount column, the amount column on the right, is used to record credit amounts. (Remember that credit means right.) Look at **Figure 6–3** to find where each component of a general journal entry appears.

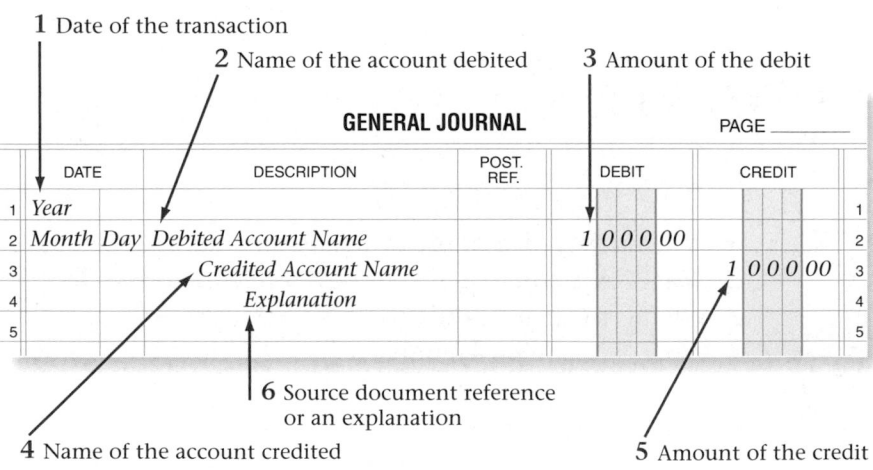

Figure 6–3 General Journal for Roadrunner Delivery Service

In Chapters 4 and 5, you learned a step-by-step method for analyzing business transactions. In this chapter, you will learn to complete the journal entry for a business transaction in the same manner. Review the following steps before you continue.

Business Transaction

BUSINESS TRANSACTION ANALYSIS: Steps to Success

ANALYSIS	*Identify*	1. Identify the accounts affected.
	Classify	2. Classify the accounts affected.
	+/−	3. Determine the amount of increase or decrease for each account affected.

| DEBIT-CREDIT RULE | 4. Which account is debited? For what amount? |
| | 5. Which account is credited? For what amount? |

| T ACCOUNTS | 6. What is the complete entry in T-account form? |

| JOURNAL ENTRY | 7. What is the complete entry in general journal form? |

Use these steps to determine the debit and credit parts of each journal entry. Remember, it is always helpful to use T accounts to analyze transactions. After analyzing many transactions, you will find that you need these tools less and less to determine the debit and credit parts of a journal entry.

Now, let's examine business transactions and their analysis for Roadrunner Delivery Service.

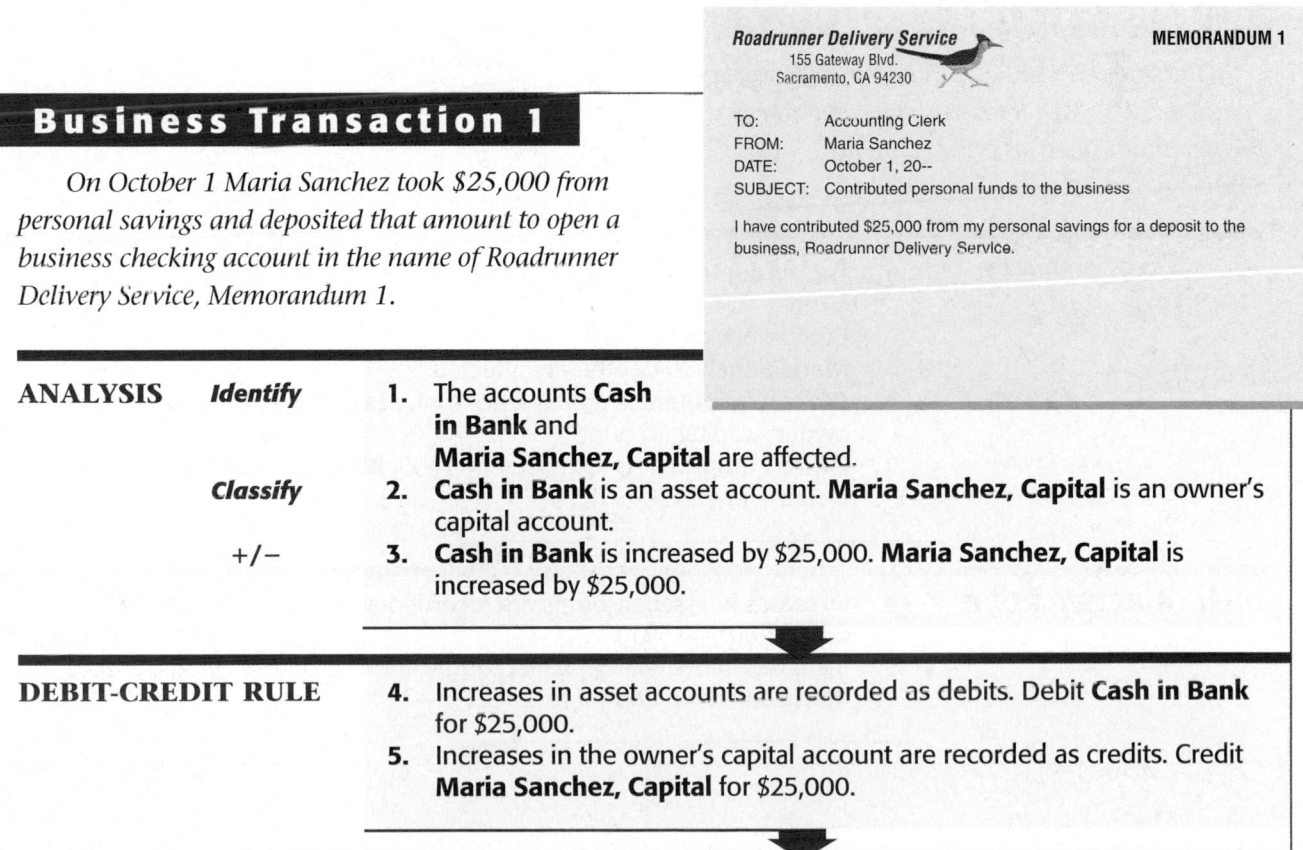

Roadrunner Delivery Service
155 Gateway Blvd.
Sacramento, CA 94230

MEMORANDUM 1

TO: Accounting Clerk
FROM: Maria Sanchez
DATE: October 1, 20--
SUBJECT: Contributed personal funds to the business

I have contributed $25,000 from my personal savings for a deposit to the business, Roadrunner Delivery Service.

Business Transaction 1

On October 1 Maria Sanchez took $25,000 from personal savings and deposited that amount to open a business checking account in the name of Roadrunner Delivery Service, Memorandum 1.

ANALYSIS	*Identify*	1. The accounts **Cash in Bank** and **Maria Sanchez, Capital** are affected.
	Classify	2. **Cash in Bank** is an asset account. **Maria Sanchez, Capital** is an owner's capital account.
	+/−	3. **Cash in Bank** is increased by $25,000. **Maria Sanchez, Capital** is increased by $25,000.

| DEBIT-CREDIT RULE | 4. Increases in asset accounts are recorded as debits. Debit **Cash in Bank** for $25,000. |
| | 5. Increases in the owner's capital account are recorded as credits. Credit **Maria Sanchez, Capital** for $25,000. |

T ACCOUNTS

6.

Cash in Bank		Maria Sanchez, Capital	
Debit + 25,000	Credit −	Debit −	Credit + 25,000

JOURNAL ENTRY

7.

GENERAL JOURNAL   PAGE ___1___

	DATE		DESCRIPTION	POST. REF.	DEBIT	CREDIT	
1	20--						1
2	Oct.	1	Cash in Bank		25 000 00		2
3			Maria Sanchez, Capital			25 000 00	3
4			Memorandum 1				4
5							5

Look again at the general journal entry shown above. Notice that in the upper right-hand corner there is a line for the page number. Journal pages are numbered in consecutive order; that is, 1, 2, 3, and so on. When you fill one page with journal entries, go on to the next page. Be sure to properly number each new page.

Roadrunner Delivery Service   MEMORANDUM 2
155 Gateway Blvd.
Sacramento, CA 94230

TO: Accounting Clerk
FROM: Maria Sanchez
DATE: October 2, 20--
SUBJECT: Contributed personal phones

I have contributed two telephones from my home to the business. The phones are valued at $200 each. Total contribution = $400.

Business Transaction 2

On October 2 Maria Sanchez took two telephones valued at $200 each from her home and transferred them to the business as office equipment, *Memorandum 2*.

ANALYSIS	*Identify*	1.	The accounts **Office Equipment** and **Maria Sanchez, Capital** are affected.
	Classify	2.	**Office Equipment** is an asset account. **Maria Sanchez, Capital** is an owner's capital account.
	+/−	3.	**Office Equipment** is increased by $400. **Maria Sanchez, Capital** is increased by $400.

DEBIT-CREDIT RULE		4.	Increases in asset accounts are recorded as debits. Debit **Office Equipment** for $400.
		5.	Increases in owner's capital accounts are recorded as credits. Credit **Maria Sanchez, Capital** for $400.

T ACCOUNTS

6.

Office Equipment		Maria Sanchez, Capital	
Debit + 400	Credit –	Debit –	Credit + 400

JOURNAL ENTRY

7.

		GENERAL JOURNAL			PAGE ___1___		
	DATE	DESCRIPTION	POST. REF.	DEBIT		CREDIT	
5	Oct. 2	Office Equipment		400 00			5
6		Maria Sanchez, Capital				400 00	6
7		Memorandum 2					7
8							8

Business Transaction 3

On October 4 Roadrunner issued Check 101 for $3,000 to buy a computer system.

$ 3,000.00		No. 101
Date October 4		20 --
To Info-Systems Inc.		
For computer		
	Dollars	Cents
Balance brought forward	25,000	00
Add deposits		
Total	25,000	00
Less this check	3,000	00
Balance carried forward	22,000	00

ANALYSIS *Identify*

1. The accounts **Computer Equipment** and **Cash in Bank** are affected.

Classify

2. **Computer Equipment** and **Cash in Bank** are asset accounts.

+/–

3. **Computer Equipment** is increased by $3,000. **Cash in Bank** is decreased by $3,000.

DEBIT-CREDIT RULE

4. Increases in asset accounts are recorded as debits. Debit **Computer Equipment** for $3,000.
5. Decreases in asset accounts are recorded as credits. Credit **Cash in Bank** for $3,000.

T ACCOUNTS

6.

Computer Equipment		Cash in Bank	
Debit + 3,000	Credit –	Debit +	Credit – 3,000

JOURNAL ENTRY   **7.**

			GENERAL JOURNAL			PAGE ___1___	
	DATE		DESCRIPTION	POST. REF.	DEBIT	CREDIT	
8	Oct.	4	Computer Equipment		3 000 00		8
9			Cash in Bank			3 000 00	9
10			Check 101				10
11							11

As you analyze a number of transactions, the rules of debit and credit will become clearer to you. Remember when you first learned to play a sport such as basketball? In the beginning you had to concentrate as you learned to dribble, shoot, and pass the ball. As you practiced, your skills improved. Learning to analyze business transactions is the same as learning anything else: The more you do it, the easier it gets.

Let's look at the remaining transactions for Roadrunner for the month of October.

North Shore Auto   **INVOICE NO. 200**
440 Lake Drive
Sacramento, CA 94230

DATE: Oct. 9, 20--
ORDER NO.: 99674
SHIPPED BY: n/a
TERMS: Installment

TO   Roadrunner Delivery Service
155 Gateway Blvd.
Sacramento, CA 94230

QTY.	ITEM	UNIT PRICE	TOTAL
1	Dodge Truck Used	$ 12,000.00	$ 12,000.00

Business Transaction 4

On October 9 Roadrunner bought a used truck on account from North Shore Auto for $12,000, Invoice 200.

ANALYSIS   *Identify*   1. The accounts **Delivery Equipment** and **Accounts Payable—North Shore Auto** are affected.

         Classify   2. **Delivery Equipment** is an asset account. **Accounts Payable—North Shore Auto** is a liability account.

         +/−   3. **Delivery Equipment** is increased by $12,000. **Accounts Payable—North Shore Auto** is increased by $12,000.

DEBIT-CREDIT RULE   4. Increases in asset accounts are recorded as debits. Debit **Delivery Equipment** for $12,000.

         5. Increases in liability accounts are recorded as credits. Credit **Accounts Payable—North Shore Auto** for $12,000.

T ACCOUNTS   6.

Delivery Equipment		Accounts Payable— North Shore Auto	
Debit + 12,000	Credit −	Debit −	Credit + 12,000

JOURNAL ENTRY   **7.**

	DATE		DESCRIPTION	POST. REF.	DEBIT	CREDIT	
			GENERAL JOURNAL			PAGE ___1___	
11	Oct.	9	Delivery Equipment		12 000 00		11
12			Accts. Pay.—North Shore Auto			12 000 00	12
13			Invoice 200				13
14							14

To separate the amounts to be paid to individual creditors, Roadrunner uses a different account name for each creditor. The account name consists of **Accounts Payable** followed by the name of the creditor. You may have to abbreviate the name to fit it on one line of the journal. An acceptable abbreviation in the preceding journal entry is **Accts. Pay.—North Shore Auto.**

Business Transaction 5

On October 11 Roadrunner sold one telephone on account to Green Company for $200, Memorandum 3.

Roadrunner Delivery Service   MEMORANDUM 3
155 Gateway Blvd.
Sacramento, CA 94230

TO: Accounting Clerk
FROM: Maria Sanchez
DATE: October 11, 20--
SUBJECT: Sold telephone

Sold one telephone on account to Green Company for $200.

ANALYSIS	*Identify*	1. The accounts **Accounts Receivable—Green Company** and **Office Equipment** are affected.
	Classify	2. **Accounts Receivable—Green Company** is an asset account. **Office Equipment** is also an asset account.
	+/−	3. **Accounts Receivable—Green Company** is increased by $200. **Office Equipment** is decreased by $200.

DEBIT-CREDIT RULE		4. Increases in asset accounts are recorded as debits. Debit **Accounts Receivable—Green Company** for $200.
		5. Decreases in asset accounts are recorded as credits. Credit **Office Equipment** for $200.

T ACCOUNTS   **6.**

Accounts Receivable—Green Company		Office Equipment	
Debit + 200	Credit −	Debit +	Credit − 200

JOURNAL ENTRY   **7.**

			GENERAL JOURNAL			PAGE 1
	DATE		DESCRIPTION	POST. REF.	DEBIT	CREDIT
14	Oct.	11	Accts. Rec.—Green Company		20000		14
15			Office Equipment			20000	15
16			Memorandum 3				16
17							17

To separate the amounts to be received from individual customers, Roadrunner uses a different account name for each customer. The account name consists of **Accounts Receivable** followed by the customer's name. You may have to abbreviate the name to fit it on one line of the journal. An acceptable abbreviation in the preceding journal entry is **Accts. Rec.—Green Co.**

$ 350.00		No. 102
Date October 12		20 --
To North Shore Auto		
For installment on truck		
	Dollars	Cents
Balance brought forward	22,000	00
Add deposits		
Total	22,000	00
Less this check	350	00
Balance carried forward	21,650	00

Business Transaction 6

On October 12 Roadrunner mailed Check 102 for $350 as the first installment payment on the truck purchased from North Shore Auto on October 9.

ANALYSIS	*Identify*	1.	The accounts **Accounts Payable—North Shore Auto** and **Cash in Bank** are affected.
	Classify	2.	**Accounts Payable—North Shore Auto** is a liability account. **Cash in Bank** is an asset account.
	+/–	3.	**Accounts Payable—North Shore Auto** is decreased by $350. **Cash in Bank** is decreased by $350.

DEBIT-CREDIT RULE		4.	Decreases in liability accounts are recorded as debits. Debit **Accounts Payable—North Shore Auto** for $350.
		5.	Decreases in asset accounts are recorded as credits. Credit **Cash in Bank** for $350.

T ACCOUNTS   **6.**

Accounts Payable— North Shore Auto		Cash in Bank	
Debit –	Credit +	Debit +	Credit –
350			350

JOURNAL ENTRY   **7.**

	DATE		DESCRIPTION	POST. REF.	DEBIT	CREDIT	
			GENERAL JOURNAL			PAGE ___1___	
17	Oct.	12	Accts. Pay.—North Shore Auto		3 5 0 00		17
18			Cash in Bank			3 5 0 00	18
19			Check 102				19
20							20

Roadrunner Delivery Service
155 Gateway Blvd.
Sacramento, CA 94230

RECEIPT
No. 1

Oct. 14   20 --

RECEIVED FROM   Green Company $ 200.00

Two hundred and ⁿᵒ/₁₀₀ ——————————— DOLLARS

FOR   Telephone

RECEIVED BY   *Maria Sanchez*

Business Transaction 7

On October 14 Roadrunner received and deposited a check for $200 from Green Company. The check is full payment for the telephone sold on account to Green on October 11, Receipt 1.

ANALYSIS	*Identify*	1.	The accounts **Cash in Bank** and **Accounts Receivable–Green Company** are affected.
	Classify	2.	**Cash in Bank** is an asset account. **Accounts Receivable–Green Company** is an asset account.
	+/−	3.	Cash in Bank is increased by $200. **Accounts Receivable–Green Company** is decreased by $200.

DEBIT-CREDIT RULE	4.	Increases in asset accounts are recorded as debits. Debit **Cash in Bank** for $200.
	5.	Decreases in asset accounts are recorded as credits. Credit **Accounts Receivable–Green Company** for $200.

T ACCOUNTS   **6.**

Cash in Bank		Accounts Receivable— Green Company	
Debit + 200	Credit −	Debit +	Credit − 200

JOURNAL ENTRY   **7.**

	DATE		DESCRIPTION	POST. REF.	DEBIT	CREDIT	
			GENERAL JOURNAL			PAGE ___1___	
20	Oct.	14	Cash in Bank		2 0 0 00		20
21			Accts. Rec.—Green Company			2 0 0 00	21
22			Receipt 1				22
23							23

Business Transaction 8

On October 15 Roadrunner provided delivery services for the Sims Corporation. A check for $1,200 was received in full payment, Receipt 2.

Roadrunner Delivery Service
155 Gateway Blvd.
Sacramento, CA 94230

RECEIPT
No. 2

Oct. 15   20 --

RECEIVED FROM Sims Corporation $ 1,200.00

One thousand two hundred and no/100 —————————— DOLLARS

FOR Delivery services

RECEIVED BY *Maria Sanchez*

ANALYSIS	*Identify*	1.	The accounts **Cash in Bank** and **Delivery Revenue** are affected.
	Classify	2.	**Cash in Bank** is an asset account. **Delivery Revenue** is a revenue account.
	+/−	3.	**Cash in Bank** is increased by $1,200. **Delivery Revenue** is increased by $1,200.

DEBIT-CREDIT RULE	4.	Increases in asset accounts are recorded as debits. Debit **Cash in Bank** for $1,200.
	5.	Increases in revenue accounts are recorded as credits. Credit **Delivery Revenue** for $1,200.

T ACCOUNTS   6.

Cash in Bank			Delivery Revenue	
Debit + 1,200	Credit −		Debit −	Credit + 1,200

JOURNAL ENTRY   7.

GENERAL JOURNAL   PAGE ___1___

	DATE		DESCRIPTION	POST. REF.	DEBIT	CREDIT	
23	Oct.	15	Cash in Bank		1 200 00		23
24			Delivery Revenue			1 200 00	24
25			Receipt 2				25
26							26

Business Transaction 9

On October 16 Roadrunner mailed Check 103 for $700 to pay the month's rent.

$ 700.00   No. 103
Date October 16   20 --
To Tooley & Co. Management
For rent

	Dollars	Cents
Balance brought forward	21,650	00
Add deposits 10/14	200	00
10/15	1,200	00
Total	23,050	00
Less this check	700	00
Balance carried forward	22,350	00

ANALYSIS	*Identify*	1.	The accounts **Rent Expense** and **Cash in Bank** are affected.
	Classify	2.	**Rent Expense** is an expense account. **Cash in Bank** is an asset account.
	+/−	3.	**Rent Expense** is increased by $700. **Cash in Bank** is decreased by $700.

| DEBIT-CREDIT RULE | **4.** Increases in expense accounts are recorded as debits. Debit **Rent Expense** for $700. |
| | **5.** Decreases in asset accounts are recorded as credits. Credit **Cash in Bank** for $700. |

T ACCOUNTS   **6.**

Rent Expense		Cash in Bank	
Debit +	Credit −	Debit +	Credit −
700			700

JOURNAL ENTRY   **7.**

		GENERAL JOURNAL		PAGE ___1___	

	DATE	DESCRIPTION	POST. REF.	DEBIT	CREDIT	
26	Oct. 16	Rent Expense		700 00		26
27		Cash in Bank			700 00	27
28		Check 103				28
29						29

Business Transaction 10

On October 18 Beacon Advertising prepared an advertisement for Roadrunner. Roadrunner will pay Beacon's $75 fee later, Invoice 129.

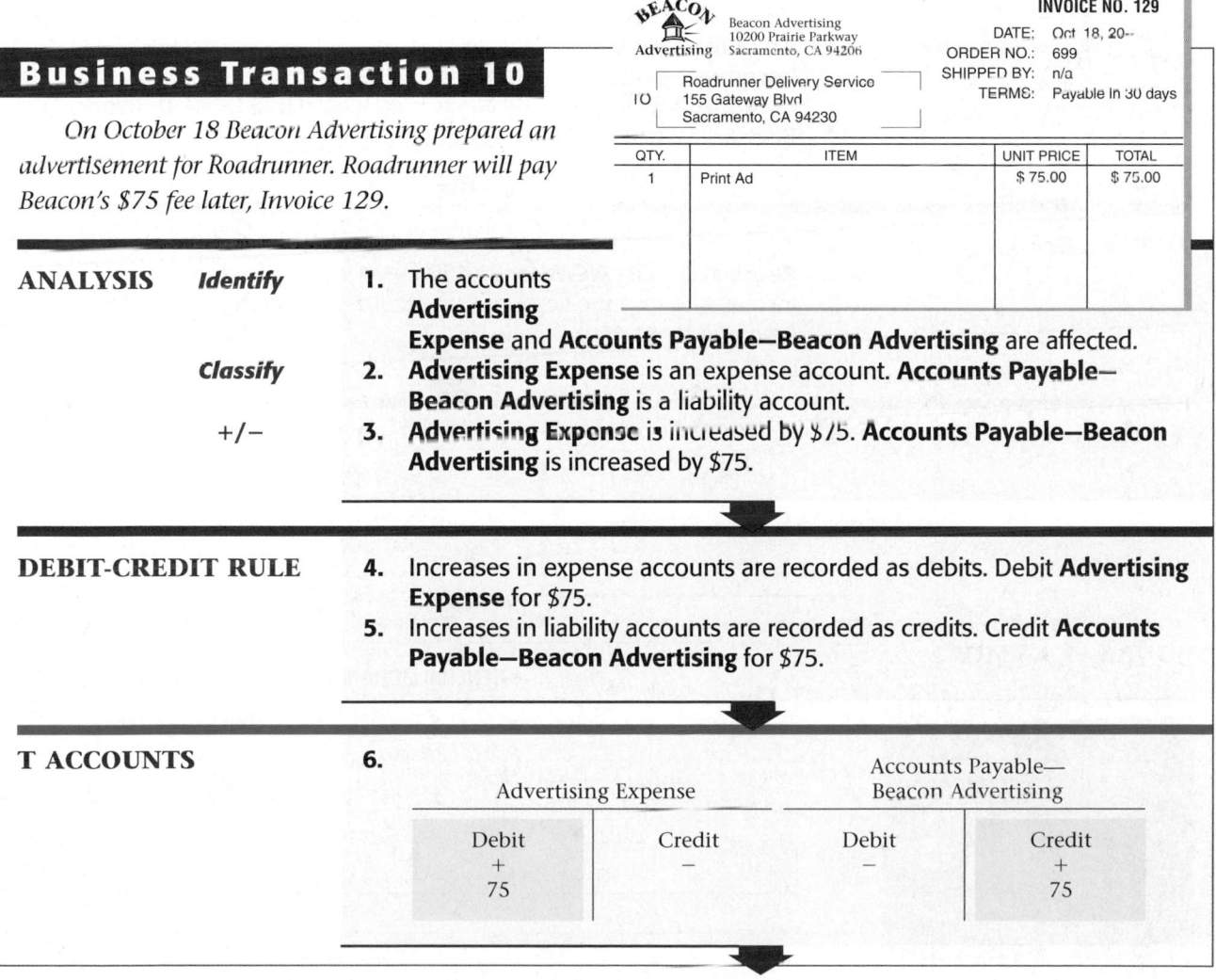

		INVOICE NO. 129
Beacon Advertising	Beacon Advertising 10200 Prairie Parkway Sacramento, CA 94206	DATE: Oct 18, 20-- ORDER NO.: 699
TO	Roadrunner Delivery Service 155 Gateway Blvd Sacramento, CA 94230	SHIPPED BY: n/a TERMS: Payable in 30 days

QTY.	ITEM	UNIT PRICE	TOTAL
1	Print Ad	$ 75.00	$ 75.00

ANALYSIS	*Identify*	**1.** The accounts **Advertising Expense** and **Accounts Payable—Beacon Advertising** are affected.
	Classify	**2.** **Advertising Expense** is an expense account. **Accounts Payable—Beacon Advertising** is a liability account.
	+/−	**3.** **Advertising Expense** is increased by $75. **Accounts Payable—Beacon Advertising** is increased by $75.

| DEBIT-CREDIT RULE | **4.** Increases in expense accounts are recorded as debits. Debit **Advertising Expense** for $75. |
| | **5.** Increases in liability accounts are recorded as credits. Credit **Accounts Payable—Beacon Advertising** for $75. |

T ACCOUNTS   **6.**

Advertising Expense		Accounts Payable— Beacon Advertising	
Debit +	Credit −	Debit −	Credit +
75			75

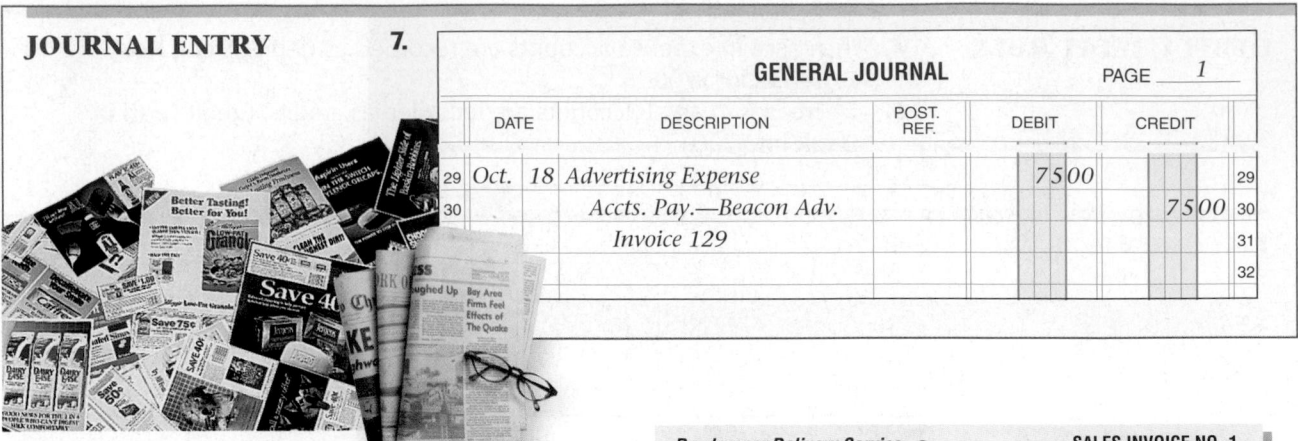

JOURNAL ENTRY   7.

GENERAL JOURNAL   PAGE _1_

	DATE		DESCRIPTION	POST. REF.	DEBIT	CREDIT	
29	Oct.	18	Advertising Expense		75 00		29
30			Accts. Pay.—Beacon Adv.			75 00	30
31			Invoice 129				31
32							32

Roadrunner Delivery Service
155 Gateway Blvd.
Sacramento, CA 94230

SALES INVOICE NO. 1
DATE: Oct. 20, 20--
ORDER NO.: 300
SHIPPED BY: n/a
TERMS: Payable in 30 days

TO   City News
10900 Main St.
Sacramento, CA 94230

QTY.	ITEM	UNIT PRICE	TOTAL
1	Delivery Services	$ 1,450.00	$ 1,450.00

Business Transaction 11

On October 20 Roadrunner provided delivery services for a customer, City News. Roadrunner billed City News $1,450, Sales Invoice 1.

ANALYSIS   *Identify*
1. The accounts **Accounts Receivable—City News** and **Delivery Revenue** are affected.

Classify
2. **Accounts Receivable—City News** is an asset account. **Delivery Revenue** is a revenue account.

+/−
3. **Accounts Receivable—City News** is increased by $1,450. **Delivery Revenue** is increased by $1,450.

DEBIT-CREDIT RULE
4. Increases in asset accounts are recorded as debits. Debit **Accounts Receivable—City News** for $1,450.
5. Increases in revenue accounts are recorded as credits. Credit **Delivery Revenue** for $1,450.

T ACCOUNTS   6.

Accounts Receivable—City News		Delivery Revenue	
Debit +	Credit −	Debit −	Credit +
1,450			1,450

JOURNAL ENTRY   7.

GENERAL JOURNAL   PAGE _1_

	DATE		DESCRIPTION	POST. REF.	DEBIT	CREDIT	
32	Oct.	20	Accts. Rec.—City News		1 450 00		32
33			Delivery Revenue			1 450 00	33
34			Sales Invoice 1				34
35							35

Business Transaction 12

On October 28 Roadrunner paid a $125 telephone bill with Check 104.

		No. 104
$ 125.00		
Date October 28		20 --
To Pacific Bell Telephone		
For telephone bill		

	Dollars	Cents
Balance brought forward	22,350	00
Add deposits		
Total	22,350	00
Less this check	125	00
Balance carried forward	22,225	00

ANALYSIS

Identify
1. The accounts **Utilities Expense** and **Cash in Bank** are affected.

Classify
2. **Utilities Expense** is an expense account. **Cash in Bank** is an asset account.

+/−
3. **Utilities Expense** is increased by $125. **Cash in Bank** is decreased by $125.

DEBIT-CREDIT RULE
4. Increases in expense accounts are recorded as debits. Debit **Utilities Expense** for $125.
5. Decreases in asset accounts are recorded as credits. Credit **Cash in Bank** for $125.

T ACCOUNTS

6.

Utilities Expense		Cash in Bank	
Debit + 125	Credit −	Debit +	Credit − 125

JOURNAL ENTRY

7.

GENERAL JOURNAL PAGE 1

	DATE	DESCRIPTION	POST. REF.	DEBIT	CREDIT	
35	Oct. 28	Utilities Expense		125 00		35
36		Cash in Bank			125 00	36
37		Check 104				37
38						38

Business Transaction 13

		No. 105
$ 600.00		
Date October 29		20 --
To Rainbow Painting		
For office painted		

On October 29 Roadrunner wrote Check 105 for $600 to have the office repainted.

	Dollars	Cents
Balance brought forward	22,225	00
Add deposits		
Total	22,225	00
Less this check	600	00
Balance carried forward	21,625	00

ANALYSIS

Identify
1. The accounts, **Maintenance Expense** and **Cash in Bank,** are affected.

Classify
2. **Maintenance Expense** is an expense account. **Cash in Bank** is an asset account.

+/−
3. **Maintenance Expense** is increased by $600. **Cash in Bank** is decreased by $600.

| DEBIT-CREDIT RULE | **4.** Increases in expense accounts are recorded as debits. Debit **Maintenance Expense** for $600. |
| | **5.** Decreases in asset accounts are recorded as credits. Credit **Cash in Bank** for $600. |

T ACCOUNTS

6.

Maintenance Expense		Cash in Bank	
Debit + 600	Credit −	Debit +	Credit − 600

JOURNAL ENTRY

7.

GENERAL JOURNAL

PAGE __1__

	DATE		DESCRIPTION	POST. REF.	DEBIT	CREDIT	
38	Oct.	29	Maintenance Expense		600 00		38
39			Cash in Bank			600 00	39
40			Check 105				40
41							41

Business Transaction 14

On October 31 Maria Sanchez wrote Check 106 to withdraw $500 cash for personal use.

$ ____500.00____		No. 106
Date ___October 31___		20 --
To ___Maria Sanchez___		
For ___withdrawal___		
	Dollars	Cents
Balance brought forward	21,625	00
Add deposits		
Total	21,625	00
Less this check	500	00
Balance carried forward	21,125	00

ANALYSIS	*Identify*	**1.** The accounts **Maria Sanchez, Withdrawals** and **Cash in Bank** are affected.
	Classify	**2.** **Maria Sanchez, Withdrawals** is an owner's withdrawals account. **Cash in Bank** is an asset account.
	+/−	**3.** **Maria Sanchez, Withdrawals** is increased by $500. **Cash in Bank** is decreased by $500.

| DEBIT-CREDIT RULE | **4.** Increases in the owner's withdrawals account are recorded as debits. Debit **Maria Sanchez, Withdrawals** for $500. |
| | **5.** Decreases in asset accounts are recorded as credits. Credit **Cash in Bank** for $500. |

T ACCOUNTS

6.

Maria Sanchez, Withdrawals		Cash in Bank	
Debit + 500	Credit −	Debit +	Credit − 500

JOURNAL ENTRY **7.**

	GENERAL JOURNAL			PAGE _1_	
DATE	DESCRIPTION	POST. REF.	DEBIT	CREDIT	
41 Oct. 31	Maria Sanchez, Withdrawals		500 00		41
42	Cash in Bank			500 00	42
43	Check 106				43
44					44

Correcting Errors in General Journal Entries

Occasionally, errors occur when journalizing transactions. When an error is discovered, it must be corrected.

In a manual system, *an error should never be erased.* An erasure looks suspicious. It might be seen as an attempt to cover up a mistake or, worse, to change the accounting records illegally. To correct errors, use a pen and a ruler to draw a horizontal line through the entire incorrect item and write the correct information above the crossed-out error. A correction for an erroneous amount is shown in the general journal as follows:

	GENERAL JOURNAL			PAGE _1_	
DATE	DESCRIPTION	POST. REF.	DEBIT	CREDIT	
1 20--					1
2 Oct. 1	Cash in Bank		25 000 00 / ~~52 000 00~~		2
3	Maria Sanchez, Capital			25 000 00 / ~~52 000 00~~	3
4	Memorandum 1				4
5					5

To correct an error for an erroneous account name, cross out the incorrect information and write the correct names above.

Key Points

General Journal Entries
- Every transaction requires a debit and a credit entry.
- Debits are recorded before credits.
- Source document references are entered on a separate line.

A MATTER OF ETHICS

Gossip in the Workplace

Let's say that you are an accounting clerk for a large insurance company like Farmers Insurance. Your boss introduces you to the newest hire, and you recognize her as a former classmate from high school named Sally. You remember that Sally had been suspended from school for a series of locker thefts. During lunch, you consider telling other co-workers about Sally's history. You also wonder if your boss knows.

Ethical Decision Making:
- What are the ethical issues?
- What are the alternatives?
- Who are the affected parties?
- How do the alternatives affect the parties?
- What would you do?

Now that you have studied this section, complete the following questions and problems.

Thinking Critically

1. What accounts would you use to record the purchase of a newspaper ad for cash?
2. What accounts would you use to record the sale of business services on account?

Computing in the Business World

The accounting clerk for Conover Restaurant Suppliers is preparing an invoice to send to Glen's Catering for the following supplies:

- 6 cartons of napkins at $4.88 per carton
- 3 boxes of salt packets at $3.19 per box
- 3 boxes of paper cups at $7.28 per box
- 4 boxes of medium paper cups at $8.24 per box

Calculate the total for each item on the invoice. Then calculate the total for all items.

Problem 6–2 Recording Business Transactions

Instructions Shown below are the six steps for recording a business transaction in the general journal. In your working papers or on a blank sheet of paper, indicate the proper order of these steps.

A. Amount of the credit.   Step #1.
B. Name of the account credited. Step #2.
C. Source document reference.   Step #3.
D. Date of the transaction.   Step #4.
E. Amount of the debit.   Step #5.
F. Name of the account debited.   Step #6.

Problem 6–3 Analyzing Transactions

Glenda Hohn recently started a day care center. She uses the following accounts to record business transactions.

General Ledger

Cash in Bank	Glenda Hohn, Capital
Accts. Rec.—Tiny Tots Nursery	Glenda Hohn, Withdrawals
Office Furniture	Day Care Fees
Passenger Van	Utilities Expense
Accts. Pay.—Acme Bus Service	Van Expense

Instructions In your working papers or on a separate sheet of paper, for each transaction: Determine which accounts are affected. Classify each account. Determine whether the accounts are being increased or decreased. Indicate which account is debited and which account is credited.

Transactions:

1. Bought a passenger van for cash.
2. Paid the telephone bill for the month.
3. Received cash from customers for day care services.

CHAPTER 6 SUMMARY

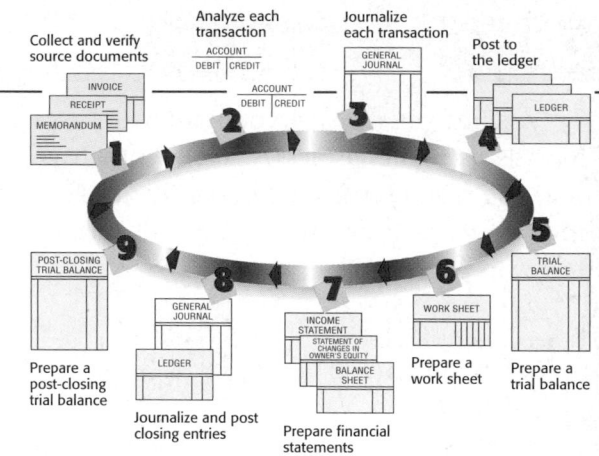

Analyze each transaction

Journalize each transaction

Collect and verify source documents

Post to the ledger

Prepare a post-closing trial balance

Journalize and post closing entries

Prepare financial statements

Prepare a work sheet

Prepare a trial balance

KEY CONCEPTS

1. Accounting records are maintained in separate time periods called accounting periods.
2. The activities involved in maintaining the accounting records make up the accounting cycle.
3. The Accounting Cycle—Steps 1–3 is pictured to the right.

4. Journalizing a Business Transaction:

GENERAL JOURNAL   PAGE _____

	DATE	DESCRIPTION	POST. REF.	DEBIT	CREDIT	
1	(1) Date	(2) Account to Debit		(3) Debit Amt.		1
2		(4) Account to Credit			(5) Credit Amt.	2
3		(6) Source Document Ref.				3
4						4

5. Correcting a Journal Entry with an Incorrect Amount (Manual System). Phillip Reyna invested $36,000 in his business on May 15, Memorandum 2. The amount of the transaction was recorded incorrectly. The original entry and the correction follows.

GENERAL JOURNAL   PAGE ___1___

	DATE		DESCRIPTION	POST. REF.	DEBIT	CREDIT	
1	20--						1
2	May	15	Cash in Bank		36 000 00 ~~63 000 00~~		2
3			Phillip Reyna, Capital			36 000 00 ~~63 000 00~~	3
4			Memorandum 2				4
5							5

6. Correcting a Journal Entry with an Incorrect Account Name (Manual System).

GENERAL JOURNAL   PAGE ___1___

	DATE		DESCRIPTION	POST. REF.	DEBIT	CREDIT	
1	20--						1
2	May	15	Cash in Bank ~~Office Supplies~~		36 000 00		2
3			Phillip Reyna, Capital			36 000 00	3
4			Memorandum 2				4
5							5

USING KEY TERMS

Assume you are an accountant who keeps financial records for small businesses. Write a one-page newsletter that you might send to potential clients describing the importance of accounting records. Use each of the terms below in your report.

accounting cycle	journal
calendar year	journalizing
check stub	memorandum
fiscal year	receipt
general journal	source document
invoice	

Understanding Accounting Concepts and Procedures

Instructions

On a separate sheet of paper, answer the following questions:

1. What is meant by the term "fiscal year"?
2. List the nine steps of the accounting cycle.
3. What is the purpose of a source document?
4. List four source documents and explain when each is used.
5. Why is a journal sometimes called the book of original entry?
6. Why is it important for businesses to keep accurate financial records?
7. How are the two amount columns of the general journal used to record dollar amounts?
8. What six types of information are included in each general journal entry?
9. List the seven steps used to analyze a business transaction.
10. What procedure is used for correcting an error in a journal entry in a manual system?

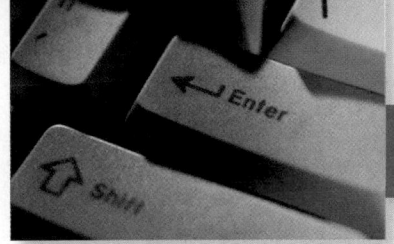

Case Study...

Service Business: Exercise and Fitness

Elena Rodriguez started a business offering an exercise facility and personal physical training. Elena has hired you as a financial consultant to help her set up her accounting system. She has rented a space for her business, purchased several exercise machines, and hired a part-time exercise instructor. Elena's clients can either pay a fee for each visit or purchase a membership.

Thinking Critically:

1. Write a plan for Elena Rodriguez explaining the types of financial information she needs to record. Describe the source documents that might be a part of her business. For example, should Elena send invoices to her non-membership clients or ask them to pay at each visit? Describe why it is important for Elena to record both the cost of doing business and the income from the business.

2. Suggest a chart of accounts for Elena's business.

interNET CONNECTION

The Big Four

Most of the major public accounting firms can be found on the Internet. Their Web sites offer information on services, locations, and employment.

Do This:

1. Locate the Web site for one of the Big Four accounting firms.

2. At the Web site, search for information on employment opportunities.

3. Name two accounting opportunities found there. What skills are required for the available positions?

Conducting an Audit with Alex

Instructions In the following transactions, help Alex find any errors in the general journal entries presented.

(1) Compare the transactions given below with the entries recorded in the general journal.

(2) If any part of the transaction has been recorded incorrectly, make the necessary corrections to the journal entries on a separate sheet of paper.

Workplace Skills

Creative Thinking

Congratulations! You've been chosen as the local Business Owner of the Year! Write a one page press release describing your business and why you've been successful. Be sure to include a brief description of your business, the skills you use in running a successful business, and how you plan to continue being successful in the future.

Date	Transaction
Oct. 2	Bought $2,000 in office equipment, Check 601.
4	Received $50 from a charge customer, Jack Lane, to apply to his account, Receipt 120.

GENERAL JOURNAL PAGE ___1___

	DATE		DESCRIPTION	POST. REF.	DEBIT	CREDIT	
1	20--						1
2	Oct.	2	Store Equipment		2 0 0 0 00		2
3			Cash in Bank			2 0 0 0 00	3
4			Check 601				4
5		4	Cash in Bank		5 0 0 00		5
6			Accts. Rec.—Jack Lane			5 0 0 00	6
7			Receipt 102				7
8							8

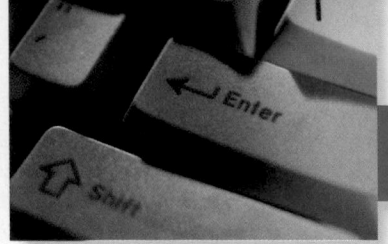

General Journal Entries

Making the Transition from a Manual to a Computerized System

Task	Perform Accounting Procedures Using Manual Methods	Perform Accounting Procedures Using Automated Methods
Recording general journal entries	• Analyze the source document to determine which accounts are affected. • Using a general journal form, enter the details of the transaction. • Check for equality of debits and credits.	• Analyze the source document to determine which accounts are affected. • Enter the general journal using the account numbers for each ledger account. • The software will calculate the equality of debits and credits.

Entering Transactions

Peachtree Question	Description
How do I enter general journal entries in Peachtree?	1. From the *Tasks* menu, select **General Journal Entry.** 2. Enter the date of the transaction in the Date box. 3. Enter the source document reference. TAB 4. Enter the account number to be debited. TAB. 5. Enter a brief description of the transaction. TAB. 6. Enter the debit amount. TAB. 7. Enter the account number to be credited. TAB 8. Enter the credit amount. TAB. 9. Click *Save*. (You will learn how to post to the general ledger in the next chapter.)
What does the software do "behind the scenes"?	The general journal screen automatically checks the equality of debits and credits in your journal entry. The software prompts you to correct the entry if it is out of balance.

For detailed instructions: See the **Peachtree User Guide** in your Glencoe Working Papers.

APPLICATION OPTIONS

Problem 6–4 Recording General Journal Transactions

Ronald Hicks owns and operates Wilderness Rentals. The following accounts are needed to journalize the month's transactions.

General Ledger

101	Cash in Bank	301	Ronald Hicks, Capital
105	Accts. Rec.—Helen Katz	305	Ronald Hicks, Withdrawals
110	Accts. Rec.—Polk and Co.	310	Income Summary
120	Office Equipment	401	Equipment Rental Revenue
125	Camping Equipment	501	Advertising Expense
201	Accts. Pay.—Adventure	505	Maintenance Expense
	Equipment Inc.	515	Rent Expense
203	Accts. Pay.—Digital Tech	520	Salaries Expense
	Computers	525	Utilities Expense
205	Accts. Pay.—Greg Mollaro		

Instructions Record the following transactions on page 1 of the general journal in your working papers. For each transaction:

(1) Enter the date. Use the current year.
(2) Enter the name of the account debited.
(3) Enter the amount of the debit.
(4) Enter the name of the account credited.
(5) Enter the amount of the credit.
(6) Enter a source document reference.

Date	Transactions
Jan. 1	Wrote Check 310 for the part-time secretary's salary, $270.
3	Bought $2,000 of camping equipment on account from Adventure Equipment Inc., Invoice 320.
5	Received $500 from a client for equipment rental, Receipt 150.
7	Wrote Check 311 to pay the electricity bill of $110.
11	Billed a client, Polk and Co., $1,700 for rental equipment, Sales Invoice 262.
12	Ronald Hicks withdrew $800 for personal use, Check 312.
14	Bought a $300 scanner for the office computer from Digital Tech Computers, on account, Invoice 270.
16	Wrote Check 313 for $1,000 as an installment payment toward the amount owed to Adventure Equipment Inc.
25	Received $1,700 from Polk and Co. in payment on their account, Receipt 151.
30	Paid Digital Tech Computers $300 for the amount owed, Check 314.

Analyze: How much cash was deducted from the **Cash in Bank** account in January?

Complete chapter problems one of three ways:

1 **Manual** Glencoe Working Papers

or

2 **Peachtree Complete Accounting** Software

or

3 **QuickBooks®** Templates (Problems 6–4, 6–5)

Peachtree®

SMART GUIDE

Step–by–Step Instructions: Problem 6–4

1. Select the problem set for Wilderness Rentals (Prob. 6–4).
2. Rename the company and set the system date.
3. Enter all of the general journal transactions using the **General Journal Entry** option in the *Tasks* menu.
4. Print a General Journal report.
5. Proof your work and make any needed corrections.
6. Answer the Analyze question.
7. End the session.

Peachtree®

SMART GUIDE

**Step–by–Step Instructions:
Problem 6–5**

1. Select the problem set for Hot Suds Car Wash (Prob. 6–5).
2. Rename the company and set the system date.
3. Enter all of the general journal transactions using the **General Journal Entry** option in the *Tasks* menu.
4. Print a General Journal report.
5. Proof your work and make any needed corrections.
6. Answer the Analyze question.
7. End the session.

TIP: You can use General Ledger Navigation Aid as an alternative way to access the General Journal Entry window.

Problem 6–5 Recording General Journal Transactions

Regina Delgado owns a business called Hot Suds Car Wash. She uses the following chart of accounts.

General Ledger

101	Cash in Bank	401	Wash Revenue
105	Accts. Rec.—Linda Brown	405	Wax Revenue
110	Accts. Rec.—Valley Auto	410	Interior Detailing Revenue
125	Office Equipment	501	Advertising Expense
130	Office Furniture	505	Equipment Rental Expense
135	Car Wash Equipment	510	Maintenance Expense
201	Accts. Pay.—Allen Vacuum Systems	520	Rent Expense
205	Accts. Pay.—O'Brian's Office Supply	525	Salaries Expense
		530	Utilities Expense
301	Regina Delgado, Capital		
305	Regina Delgado, Withdrawals		
310	Income Summary		

Instructions Record the following transactions on page 1 of the general journal in your working papers.

Date	Transactions
Jan. 1	Regina Delgado invested $12,000 in the business, Memorandum 41.
5	Purchased $5,000 in desks, chairs, and cabinets from O'Brian's Office Supply on account, Invoice 1632.
8	Deposited $1,600 for income received from car washes for the week, Receipt 101.
10	Paid the *Village Bulletin* $75 for running an ad, Check 301.
13	Regina Delgado withdrew $900 for personal use, Check 302.
17	Billed Valley Auto $400 for interior detailing, Sales Invoice 102.
18	Paid O'Brian's Office Supply $2,500 as an installment payment on account, Check 303.
20	Regina Delgado transferred to the business an electronic calculator valued at $350, Memorandum 42.
22	Wrote Check 304 for $600 to Shadyside Realty for the office rent.
24	Purchased $1,500 in car wash equipment from Allen Vacuum Systems on account, Invoice 312.
26	Received a $400 check from Valley Auto in full payment of its account, Receipt 102.
30	Issued Check 305 for $2,500 to O'Brian's Office Supply for the balance due on account.

Analyze: What is the amount of total assets for Hot Suds Car Wash at January 31?

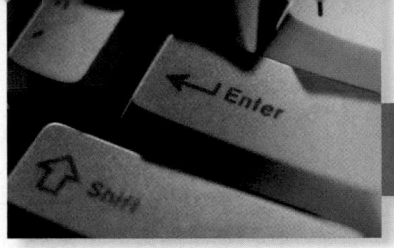

Problem 6–6 Recording General Journal Transactions

Abe Shultz owns and operates a pet grooming business called Kits & Pups Grooming. The following accounts are used to journalize transactions.

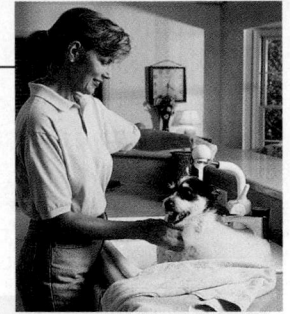

General Ledger

101 Cash in Bank	207 Accts. Pay.—Pet Gourmet
105 Accts. Rec.—Juan Alvarez	301 Abe Shultz, Capital
110 Accts. Rec.—N. Carlsbad	305 Abe Shultz, Withdrawals
115 Accts. Rec.—Martha Giles	310 Income Summary
125 Office Equipment	401 Boarding Revenue
130 Office Furniture	405 Grooming Revenue
135 Computer Equipment	501 Advertising Expense
140 Grooming Equipment	505 Equipment Repair Expense
145 Kennel Equipment	510 Maintenance Expense
201 Accts. Pay.—Able Store Equipment	520 Rent Expense
	525 Salaries Expense
205 Accts. Pay.—Dogs & Cats Inc.	530 Utilities Expense

Instructions Record the following transactions on page 7 of the general journal in your working papers.

Date	Transactions
Jan. 1	Received $125 for boarding a client's dog for one week, Receipt 300.
3	Abe Shultz contributed to the business a computer valued at $2,500, Memorandum 33.
5	Billed a client, Juan Alvarez, $80 for grooming his pets, Sales Invoice 212.
9	Wrote Check 411 to Allegheny Power Co. for $150 in payment for the month's electricity bill.
11	Abe Shultz withdrew $700 for personal use, Check 412.
14	Purchased kennel equipment for $2,600 from Dogs & Cats Inc., on account, Invoice DC92.
16	Paid the part-time receptionist's salary of $400 by issuing Check 413.
18	Abe Shultz took from the business for his personal use a ten-key adding machine valued at $65, Memorandum 34.
23	Juan Alvarez sent a check for $80 in full payment of his account, Receipt 301.
28	Purchased on credit $250 in grooming equipment from the Pet Gourmet, Invoice PG333.
31	Issued Check 414 for $1,300 as an installment payment for the amount owed to Dogs & Cats Inc.

Analyze: What is the total of the Accounts Receivable accounts at January 31?

Peachtree®

SMART GUIDE

**Step–by–Step Instructions:
Problem 6–7**

1. Select the problem set for Outback Guide Service (Prob. 6–7).
2. Rename the company and set the system date.
3. Enter all of the general journal transactions.
4. Print a General Journal report.
5. Proof your work and make any needed corrections.
6. Answer the Analyze question.
7. End the session.

TIP: Press **SHIFT+?** in an *Account No.* field to display an account list.

Problem 6–7 Recording General Journal Transactions

Juanita Ortega is the owner of Outback Guide Service. The following accounts are used to record the transactions of her business.

General Ledger

101 Cash in Bank	205 Accts. Pay.—Peak Equipment Inc.
105 Accts. Rec.—M. Johnson	207 Accts. Pay.—Premier Processors
110 Accts. Rec.—Feldman, Jones, & Ritter	301 Juanita Ortega, Capital
	302 Juanita Ortega, Withdrawals
115 Accts. Rec.—Podaski Systems Inc.	310 Income Summary
	401 Guide Service Revenue
130 Office Equipment	501 Advertising Expense
135 Office Furniture	505 Maintenance Expense
140 Computer Equipment	515 Rent Expense
145 Hiking Equipment	520 Salaries Expense
150 Rafting Equipment	525 Utilities Expense
201 Accts. Pay.—A–1 Adventure Warehouse	

Instructions Record the following transactions on page 1 of the general journal in your working papers.

Date	Transactions
Jan. 1	Juanita Ortega contributed the following assets to her business: cash, $1,500; hiking equipment, $2,000; rafting equipment, $2,500; and office furniture, $500; Memorandum 21.
2	Issued Check 515 to *Town News* for a $75 ad.
4	Purchased $3,000 in rafting equipment on account from A-1 Adventure Warehouse, Invoice AW45.
6	A group from Feldman, Jones, & Ritter went on a hiking trip. The group was billed $4,800 for guide services, Sales Invoice 300.
10	Paid $300 to Dunn's Painting and Interior Co. for painting the office, Check 516.
13	Made a $1,000 payment to A-1 Adventure Warehouse toward the amount owed, Check 517.
15	Received a check for $4,800 from Feldman, Jones, & Ritter in payment of their account, Receipt 252.
18	Juanita Ortega paid herself $600 by issuing Check 518.
22	Billed a client, Mary Johnson, $1,200 for completing guide services on a hiking expedition, Sales Invoice 301.
25	Paid the monthly telephone bill for $175 by issuing Check 519.
30	Purchased a $3,600 computer system from Premier Processors. Made a down payment for $1,800 and agreed to pay the balance within 30 days, Check 520 and Invoice 749.

Analyze: Did any of Outback's customers pay cash for services in January?

CHALLENGE PROBLEM ✕

Problem 6–8
Recording
General Journal Transactions

SOURCE DOCUMENT PROBLEM

Greg Failla operates Showbiz Video. The following accounts are used to record business transactions.

General Ledger

101 Cash in Bank	207 Accts. Pay.—New Media Suppliers
105 Accts. Rec.—G. Cohen	209 Accts. Pay.—Palace Films
110 Accts. Rec.—J. Coletti	301 Greg Failla, Capital
113 Accts. Rec.—S. Flannery	305 Greg Failla, Withdrawals
115 Accts. Rec.—Spring Branch School District	310 Income Summary
	401 Video Rental Revenue
130 Office Equipment	405 VCR Rental Revenue
135 Office Furniture	501 Advertising Expense
140 Computer Equipment	505 Equipment Repair Expense
145 Video Tapes	510 Maintenance Expense
150 Video Equipment	520 Rent Expense
201 Accts. Pay.—Broad Street Office Supply	525 Salaries Expense
	530 Utilities Expense
205 Accts. Pay.—Computer Horizons	

Instructions Record the following transactions on page 5 of the general journal in your working papers.

Date	Transactions
Jan. 1	Deposited $3,400 in receipts. Of that amount, $1,900 was VCR rentals and $1,500 was video tape rentals, Receipt 435.
3	Wrote Check 1250 for $325 of equipment repairs.
5	Purchased $400 in video tapes from Palace Films on account, Invoice PF32.
7	Bought from New Media Suppliers $2,600 in video equipment. Made a down payment of $600 and agreed to pay the balance in two installments, Check 1251 and Invoice NM101.
10	Rented videos to Spring Branch School District. The school district agreed to pay $1,800 at a later date, Sales Invoice 1650.
12	Issued Check 1252 for $750 to Computer Horizons for the amount owed to them.
15	Deposited $5,600 in receipts. VCR rentals amounted to $4,400 and video tape rentals were $1,200, Receipt 436.
18	Paid Clear Vue Window Cleaners $100 for monthly window cleaning, Check 1253.
25	Made a $1,000 installment payment toward the amount owed to New Media Suppliers by issuing Check 1254.

Analyze: What were the total expenses incurred in January?

Peachtree®

SMART GUIDE

Step–by–Step Instructions: Problem 6–8

1. Select the problem set for Showbiz Video (Prob. 6–8).
2. Rename the company and set the system date.
3. Enter all of the general journal transactions.
4. Print a General Journal report.
5. Proof your work and make any needed corrections.
6. Answer the Analyze question.
7. End the session.

SOURCE DOCUMENT PROBLEM

Problem 6–8

Use the source documents in your working papers to record the transactions for this problem.

CHAPTER 7

Posting Journal Entries to General Ledger Accounts

Learning Objectives

When you have completed this chapter, you will be able to:

▶ Describe the steps in the posting process.

▶ Post general journal entries.

▶ Prepare a trial balance.

▶ Locate and correct trial balance errors.

▶ Record correcting entries in the general journal.

▶ Define the accounting terms introduced in this chapter.

Exploring the Real World of Business

ACCOUNTS AND THE GENERAL LEDGER

Can you imagine living on a ranch and riding a horse to work? One world-famous ranch on which you might work is the **King Ranch** in Texas. The ranch covers 825,000 acres, which is larger than the entire state of Rhode Island! It employs around 350 people full-time and another 350 as part-timers.

King Ranch is noted as the producer of the first registered American Quarter Horse and as the original breeder of Santa Gertrudis cattle. It is one of the oldest working ranches in the U.S. and also makes money from cotton crops, gas, and oil wells.

Accounting for an operation like **King Ranch** means keeping track of the number of calves born each year or the pounds of cotton produced. Computers handle much of the routine work of recording ranch information, leaving the ranch managers free to make decisions about how many horses to sell or how much feed to buy.

What do you think?

What are some general ledger accounts that might be used by **King Ranch?** List at least two accounts in each category (assets, liabilities, revenue, and expenses).

King Ranch

Workplace Connections
Applying Your Accounting Knowledge

In the last chapter, you learned how to record financial transactions in a journal. These journal entries show individual daily activities, but do not show the total of all transactions. You'll learn in this chapter that posting the journal entries is a means of organizing all the transactions affecting the accounts of a business. For example, all the transactions that might affect an account called "Revenue" are summarized and totaled. All the transactions that might affect an account called "Utilities Expense" are summarized and totaled.

Investigate:

What types of accounts would you imagine are used for accounting in your workplace?

151

The General Ledger

In Chapter 6 you learned how to analyze business transactions and enter those transactions in a general journal.

In this chapter you will learn how to post journal entries to the general ledger and how to prepare a trial balance (Steps 4 and 5 in the accounting cycle illustrated in **Figure 7–1**). The Jeep dealership in your area records all business transactions in the journal and posts those transactions to the general ledger. An up-to-date ledger allows the accountant for the Jeep dealership to provide management with information such as:

- sales of vehicles
- service income
- salary and commission expense

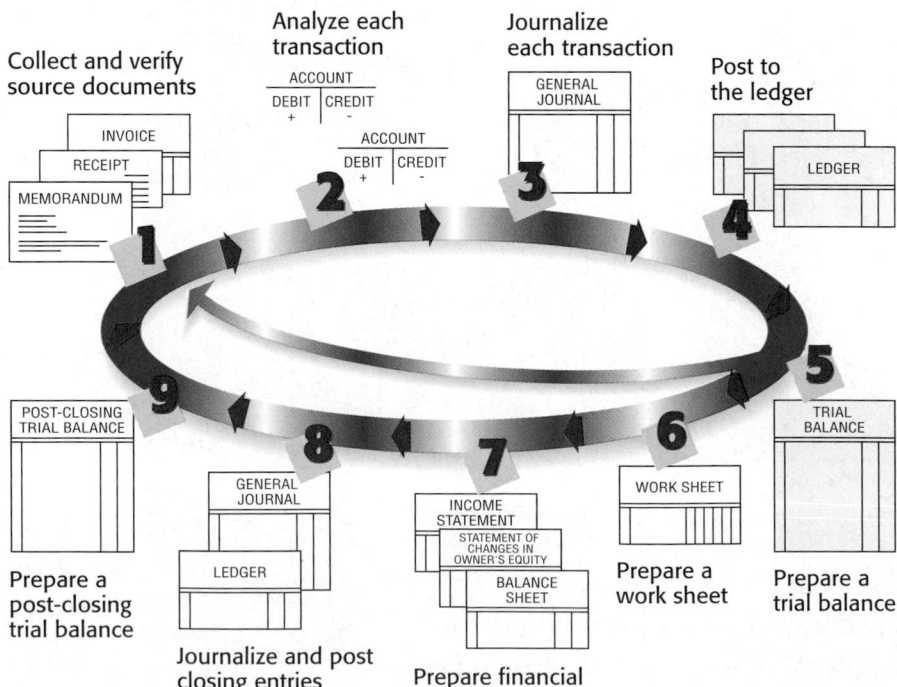

Figure 7–1 The Accounting Cycle with Steps 4 and 5 Highlighted

Setting Up the General Ledger

In a manual accounting system, the accounts used by a business are kept on separate pages or cards. These pages or cards are kept together in a book or file called a ledger. In a computerized accounting system, the electronic files containing the accounts are still referred to as the ledger, or the ledger accounts. In either system, the ledger is often called a **general ledger**.

Posting journal entries to the ledger accounts creates a record of the impact of business transactions on each account used by a business. After journal entries have been posted, a business owner or manager can look at a specific account and easily find its current balance. If, for example, Maria Sanchez wants to know how much money Roadrunner Delivery Service has in its bank account, she can simply look at the balance of the **Cash in Bank** account.

The Four-Column Ledger Account Form

In a manual accounting system, the accounting stationery used to record financial information about specific accounts is a **ledger account form**. There are several common ledger account forms. These forms—as well as other accounting stationery—are usually described by the number of amount columns they have. In other words, the number of columns refers only to those columns in which dollar amounts are recorded. For example, Roadrunner uses a four-column ledger account form.

The four-column account form has spaces to enter the account name, the account number, the date, a description of the entry, and the posting reference. It also has four columns in which to record dollar amounts. Look at the four-column account form shown in **Figure 7–2**.

ACCOUNT				ACCOUNT NO.		
DATE	DESCRIPTION	POST. REF.	DEBIT	CREDIT	BALANCE DEBIT	CREDIT

Figure 7–2 Four-Column Ledger Account Form

Notice the four amount columns: the debit column, the credit column, the debit balance column, and the credit balance column. The first two amount columns are used to enter debit and credit amounts posted from journal entries. The last two amount columns are used to enter the new account balance after a journal entry is posted. The balance columns show the current balance in the account. The type of account (expense, revenue, asset, etc.) determines which balance column to use. For example, accounts with a normal debit balance—such as asset or expense accounts—use the debit balance column. Accounts with a normal credit balance—such as liability or revenue accounts—use the credit balance column.

Opening Accounts in the Ledger

Before journal entries can be posted, a general ledger account is opened for each account that appears on the chart of accounts. The number of steps required to open an account depends on whether or not the account has a zero balance.

Opening an Account with a Zero Balance

There are two steps required to open an account with a zero balance:

(1) Write the account name at the top of the ledger account form.
(2) Write the account number on the ledger account form.

These two steps are performed each time a new ledger account page is needed. The accounts that are opened for the first three asset accounts on Roadrunner's chart of accounts (page 73) are shown in **Figure 7–3.**

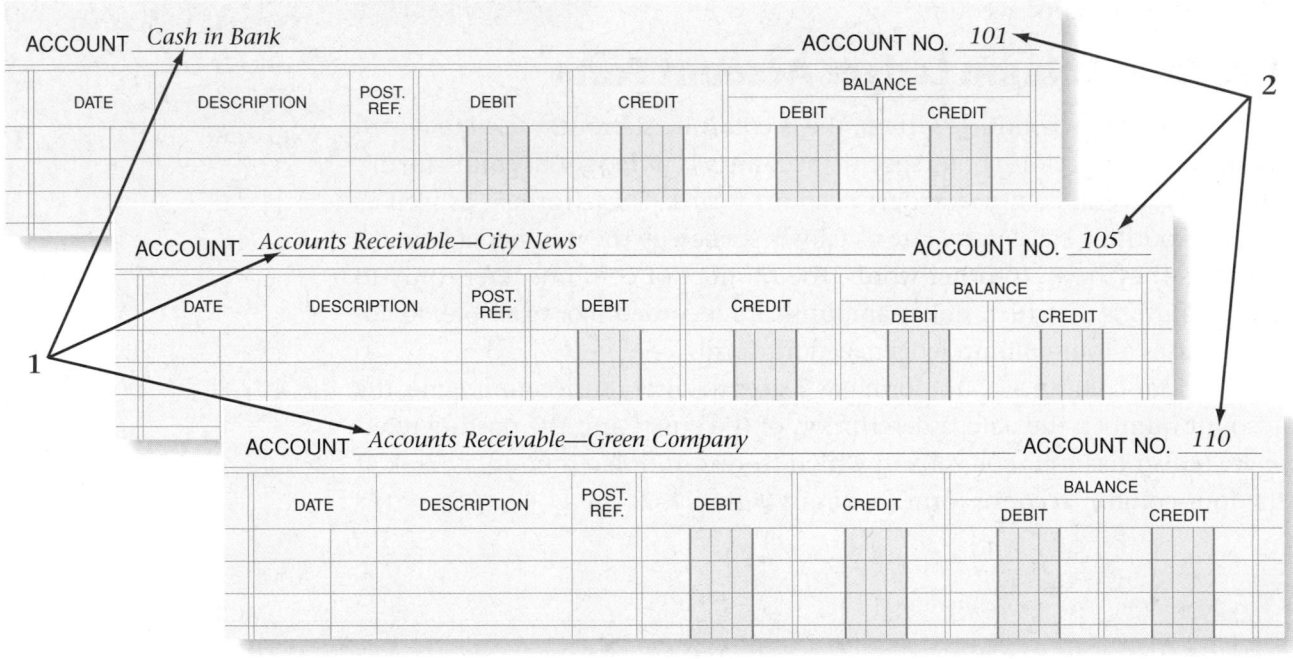

Figure 7–3 Opening General Ledger Accounts with Zero Balances

In a computerized accounting system, the procedure is similar. An account is opened by entering the account name and number on the chart of accounts. Computerized accounting systems vary, but all of them require that information such as the account numbers and names be entered into the computer files.

Opening an Account with a Balance

To open an account with a balance, six steps are required:

(1) Write the account name at the top of the ledger account form.

(2) Write the account number on the ledger account form.

(3) Enter the complete date (year, month, and day) in the date column.

(4) Write the word "Balance" in the Description column.

(5) Place a check mark (✓) in the Posting Reference column to show the amount entered on this line is not being posted from a journal.

(6) Enter the balance in the appropriate balance column of the ledger account form. Usually asset, expense, and owner's withdrawals accounts have debit balances. Liability, owner's capital, and revenue accounts have credit balances.

Figure 7–4 shows an example of an entry made to open an account with a balance.

	DATE	DESCRIPTION	POST. REF.	DEBIT	CREDIT	BALANCE DEBIT	BALANCE CREDIT
ACCOUNT *Cash in Bank* **1**						ACCOUNT NO. *101* **2**	
3 20-- Oct. 1		*Balance* **4**	**5** ✓			**6** 25 0 0 0 00	

Figure 7–4 Opening General Ledger Accounts with a Balance

The Usefulness of Journals and Ledgers to Managers

Managers continually make use of the information contained in the accounting records. To obtain information about a specific business transaction, a manager might refer to the journal entry. To learn the current balance of important accounts like **Cash in Bank**, **Accounts Receivable**, and **Accounts Payable**, managers will look to the ledger accounts. The organization of accounting data in ledgers makes it possible for managers to obtain summarized information before the financial statements are prepared.

A MATTER OF ETHICS

Meeting a Deadline

Imagine that you are an accounting clerk for Ace Hardware. The store manager has asked you to prepare the trial balance for the month. The totals on the trial balance are not equal and you cannot find the error. You also realize that the trial balance is due at the end of the day. You are frustrated and consider changing one of the account balances just to get the trial balance to balance.

Ethical Decision Making:

☞ What are the ethical issues?

☞ What are the alternatives?

☞ Who are the affected parties?

☞ How do the alternatives affect the parties?

☞ What would you do?

Now that you have studied this section, complete the following questions and problem.

Thinking Critically

1. List the steps involved in opening an account with a zero balance.
2. List the steps involved in opening an account with a balance.

Communicating Accounting

Often the way we say things has a big impact on how our listeners respond to us. Angry words can bring an equally angry response, and no real communication will have taken place. Communication occurs when one person is able to express an idea in words and tone that are heard and understood in the way the speaker intended. See if you can identify why communication did not take place in the following examples. How would you have said things differently?

1. Supervisor: (Angrily) "You are late again, Wiley. If you're not here on time every day from now on, you're out of a job."
   Employee: "Aw, man. Get off my back. I'm trying as hard as I can."
2. First Employee: "I'm tired of always making the decisions and teaching you how to do your job. You should know how to open ledger accounts by yourself by now."
   Second Employee: "Well, you don't have to work with me anymore then. I'll find someone else to help me."

Problem 7–1 Opening Ledger Accounts

Instructions Use the step-by-step processes presented in this chapter to open the following ledger accounts. Use the accounting stationery provided in your working papers. January 1 of the current year is the date.

Account Name	Account Number	Balance
Cash in Bank	101	$10,000
Accounts Receivable— Mark Cohen	104	2,000
Accounts Payable— Jenco Industries	203	1,000
Tom Torrie, Capital	301	35,000
Admissions Revenue	401	- 0 -

The Posting Process

In the last section you learned how to open accounts in the general ledger. In this section you will learn how to post general journal entries to the ledger. **Posting** is the process of transferring information from the general journal to individual general ledger accounts, the fourth step in the accounting cycle. To provide current information to management, the accountant for the Jeep dealership in your area probably posts journal entries to the general ledger every day.

What You'll Learn

- The purpose and importance of posting.
- How often a business posts transactions.
- The six steps in the posting process.
- How to compute an account balance.
- How to show an account with a zero balance.

Why It's Important

Posting brings the records of the business up-to-date. If a business did not post its transactions, the balances in ledger accounts would not be current.

KEY TERMS

posting

The Fourth Step in the Accounting Cycle: Posting

The general journal is a sort of business diary containing all the transactions of a business. It is not easy to see the increases and decreases taking place in the account by looking at journal entries. To provide a clear picture of how each account is affected by a business transaction, the information in a journal entry is posted to the general ledger accounts. The purpose of posting, therefore, is to show the impact of business transactions on the individual accounts.

The size of the business, the number of transactions, and whether the accounting system is manual or computerized all affect how often posting occurs. Ideally, businesses post daily to keep their accounts up-to-date. Regardless of how often posting is performed, the process remains the same.

As in journalizing a transaction, posting to a ledger account is completed from left to right. Let's look at a journal entry for Roadrunner that is ready to be posted to the ledger.

Posting to the Roadrunner General Ledger

Roadrunner's first transaction affects two accounts: **Cash in Bank** and **Maria Sanchez, Capital.** The information in the journal entry is transferred item by item from the journal to each of the accounts affected. As you read about each step in the posting process, refer to **Figure 7–5.**

Locate the account to be debited in the ledger; in this example, **Cash in Bank** is to be debited.

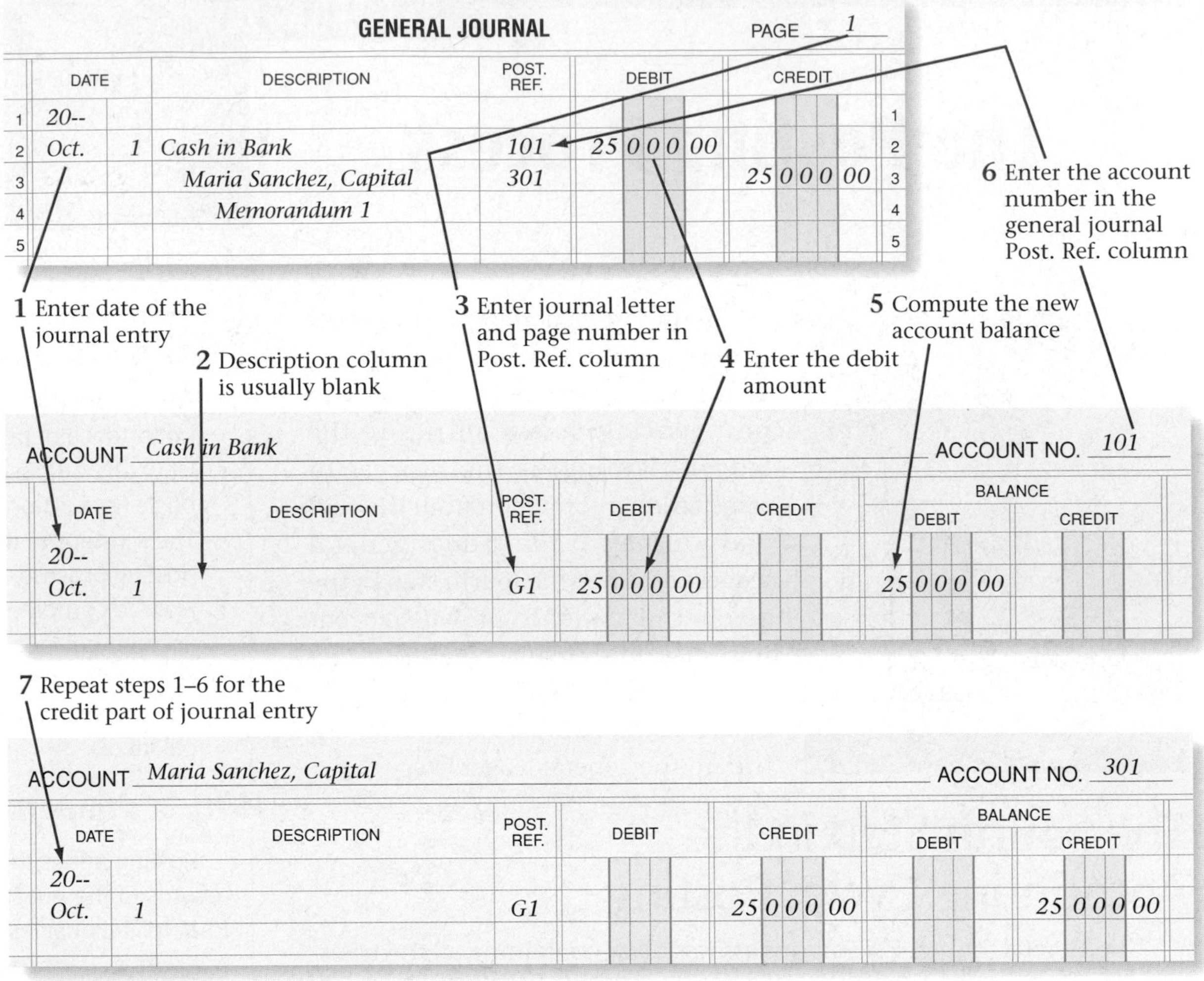

GENERAL JOURNAL   PAGE ___1___

	DATE		DESCRIPTION	POST. REF.	DEBIT	CREDIT	
1	20--						1
2	Oct.	1	Cash in Bank	101	25 000 00		2
3			Maria Sanchez, Capital	301		25 000 00	3
4			Memorandum 1				4
5							5

1 Enter date of the journal entry

2 Description column is usually blank

3 Enter journal letter and page number in Post. Ref. column

4 Enter the debit amount

5 Compute the new account balance

6 Enter the account number in the general journal Post. Ref. column

ACCOUNT _Cash in Bank_   ACCOUNT NO. _101_

DATE		DESCRIPTION	POST. REF.	DEBIT	CREDIT	BALANCE DEBIT	BALANCE CREDIT
20--							
Oct.	1		G1	25 000 00		25 000 00	

7 Repeat steps 1–6 for the credit part of journal entry

ACCOUNT _Maria Sanchez, Capital_   ACCOUNT NO. _301_

DATE		DESCRIPTION	POST. REF.	DEBIT	CREDIT	BALANCE DEBIT	BALANCE CREDIT
20--							
Oct.	1		G1		25 000 00		25 000 00

Figure 7–5 Posting from the General Journal to Ledger Accounts

1. Enter the date of the journal entry in the Date column of the account debited. Use the date of the journal entry, not the date on which the posting is done. Write the year and month in the left side of the Date column. It is not necessary to write the year and month for other postings to the same account on the same page unless the month or year changes. The day, however, is always entered.

2. The Description column on the ledger account is usually left blank. Some businesses use this space to write in the source document number.

3. In the ledger account Posting Reference (Post. Ref.) column, identify where the journal entry is recorded. Enter a letter for the journal and the journal page number. In this example, the letter "G" represents the general journal and the "1" indicates page one of the general journal.

4. Enter the debit amount in the Debit column of the ledger account.

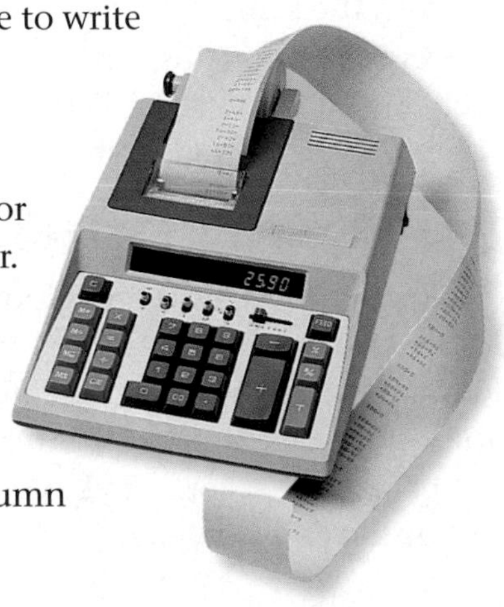

5. Compute and record the new account balance in the appropriate balance column. Every amount posted will either increase or decrease the balance of that account.

6. Return to the journal and, in the Posting Reference column, enter the ledger account number of the account to which you just posted the debit part of the journal entry. Be sure it is entered on the same line as the debit entry. In this example, enter 101 in the Posting Reference column on the line for **Cash in Bank.**

    This step in the posting process is very important. The notation in the Posting Reference column of the journal indicates that the journal entry has been posted. The posting reference also shows the account to which the entry was posted. If the posting process is interrupted, perhaps by a telephone call, the posting reference signals the point at which posting stopped. *Never* write an account number in the posting reference column until *after* you have posted.

7. Repeat steps 1–6 for the credit part of the journal entry.
   - Locate the account to be credited. In this example, **Maria Sanchez, Capital,** is to be credited.
   - Enter the date.
   - Enter the posting reference on the ledger account form. In this example, G1 represents the first page of the general journal.
   - Enter the credit amount.
   - Compute the new account balance.
   - Enter the account number in the Posting Reference column of the general journal. In the example, enter 301 to show that the credit was posted to **Maria Sanchez, Capital.**

The journal entries made in Chapter 6 for Roadrunner's transactions are shown in **Figure 7–6.**

The Importance of Posting

    Posting organizes business transaction details into the proper accounts. As discussed earlier, transactions that are itemized in the general journal are helpful, but do not summarize similar transactions into the same location. Posting summarizes all business transactions so managers can see the cumulative effects on accounts like **Utilities** Expense or **Salaries** Expense.

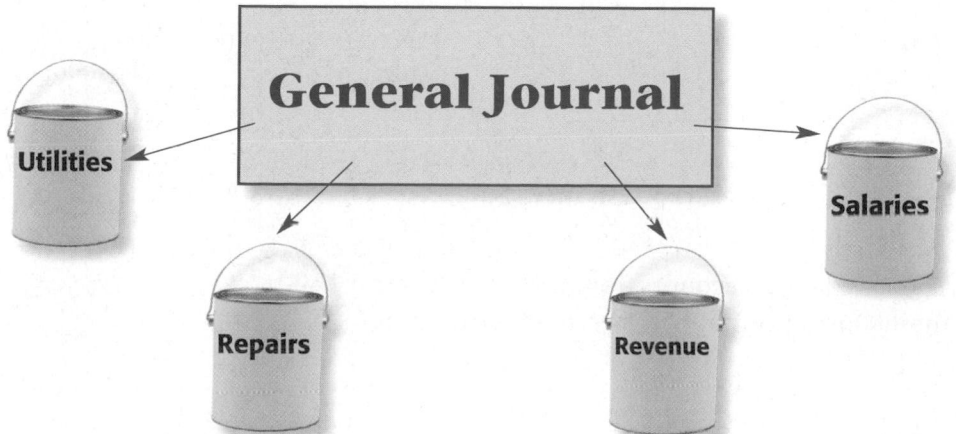

	DATE		DESCRIPTION	POST. REF.	DEBIT	CREDIT	
1	20--						1
2	Oct.	1	Cash in Bank	101	25 000 00		2
3			Maria Sanchez, Capital	301		25 000 00	3
4			Memorandum 1				4
5		2	Office Equipment	120	400 00		5
6			Maria Sanchez, Capital	301		400 00	6
7			Memorandum 2				7
8		4	Computer Equipment	115	3 000 00		8
9			Cash in Bank	101		3 000 00	9
10			Check 101				10
11		9	Delivery Equipment	125	12 000 00		11
12			Accounts Payable—North Shore Auto	205		12 000 00	12
13			Invoice 200				13
14		11	Accounts Receivable—Green Co.	110	200 00		14
15			Office Equipment	120		200 00	15
16			Memorandum 3				16
17		12	Accounts Payable—North Shore Auto	205	350 00		17
18			Cash in Bank	101		350 00	18
19			Check 102				19
20		14	Cash in Bank	101	200 00		20
21			Accounts Receivable—Green Co.	110		200 00	21
22			Receipt 1				22
23		15	Cash in Bank	101	1 200 00		23
24			Delivery Revenue	401		1 200 00	24
25			Receipt 2				25
26		16	Rent Expense	510	700 00		26
27			Cash in Bank	101		700 00	27
28			Check 103				28
29		18	Advertising Expense	501	75 00		29
30			Accounts Payable—Beacon Advertising	201		75 00	30
31			Invoice 129				31
32		20	Accounts Receivable—City News	105	1 450 00		32
33			Delivery Revenue	401		1 450 00	33
34			Sales Invoice 1				34
35		28	Utilities Expense	515	125 00		35
36			Cash in Bank	101		125 00	36
37			Check 104				37
38		29	Maintenance Expense	505	600 00		38
39			Cash in Bank	101		600 00	39
40			Check 105				40
41		31	Maria Sanchez, Withdrawals	302	500 00		41
42			Cash in Bank	101		500 00	42
43			Check 106				43
44							44

Figure 7–6 General Journal Entries for October Business Transactions

The postings made to the general ledger accounts from these entries are shown in **Figure 7–7**. Study these illustrations to check your understanding of the posting process.

ACCOUNT Cash in Bank   ACCOUNT NO. 101

DATE		DESCRIPTION	POST. REF.	DEBIT	CREDIT	BALANCE	
						DEBIT	CREDIT
20--							
Oct.	1		G1	25 000 00		25 000 00	
	4		G1		3 000 00	22 000 00	
	12		G1		3 50 00	21 650 00	
	14		G1	2 00 00		21 850 00	
	15		G1	1 200 00		23 050 00	
	16		G1		7 00 00	22 350 00	
	28		G1		1 25 00	22 225 00	
	29		G1		6 00 00	21 625 00	
	31		G1		5 00 00	21 125 00	

ACCOUNT Accounts Receivable—City News   ACCOUNT NO. 105

DATE		DESCRIPTION	POST. REF.	DEBIT	CREDIT	BALANCE	
						DEBIT	CREDIT
20--							
Oct.	20		G1	1 450 00		1 450 00	

ACCOUNT Accounts Receivable—Green Company   ACCOUNT NO. 110

DATE		DESCRIPTION	POST. REF.	DEBIT	CREDIT	BALANCE	
						DEBIT	CREDIT
20--							
Oct.	11		G1	2 00 00		2 00 00	
	14		G1		2 00 00	—	

ACCOUNT Computer Equipment   ACCOUNT NO. 115

DATE		DESCRIPTION	POST. REF.	DEBIT	CREDIT	BALANCE	
						DEBIT	CREDIT
20--							
Oct.	4		G1	3 000 00		3 000 00	

ACCOUNT Office Equipment   ACCOUNT NO. 120

DATE		DESCRIPTION	POST. REF.	DEBIT	CREDIT	BALANCE	
						DEBIT	CREDIT
20--							
Oct.	2		G1	4 00 00		4 00 00	
	11		G1		2 00 00	2 00 00	

ACCOUNT Delivery Equipment   ACCOUNT NO. 125

DATE		DESCRIPTION	POST. REF.	DEBIT	CREDIT	BALANCE	
						DEBIT	CREDIT
20--							
Oct.	9		G1	12 000 00		12 000 00	

ACCOUNT Accounts Payable—Beacon Advertising   ACCOUNT NO. 201

DATE		DESCRIPTION	POST. REF.	DEBIT	CREDIT	BALANCE	
						DEBIT	CREDIT
20--							
Oct.	18		G1		7 5 00		7 5 00

Figure 7–7 Postings to General Ledger Accounts for the Month of October

ACCOUNT Accounts Payable—North Shore Auto   **ACCOUNT NO.** 205

DATE		DESCRIPTION	POST. REF.	DEBIT	CREDIT	BALANCE DEBIT	BALANCE CREDIT
20--							
Oct.	9		G1		12 000 00		12 000 00
	12		G1	3 50 00			11 650 00

ACCOUNT Maria Sanchez, Capital   **ACCOUNT NO.** 301

DATE		DESCRIPTION	POST. REF.	DEBIT	CREDIT	BALANCE DEBIT	BALANCE CREDIT
20--							
Oct.	1		G1		25 000 00		25 000 00
	2		G1		4 00 00		25 400 00

ACCOUNT Maria Sanchez, Withdrawals   **ACCOUNT NO.** 302

DATE		DESCRIPTION	POST. REF.	DEBIT	CREDIT	BALANCE DEBIT	BALANCE CREDIT
20--							
Oct.	31		G1	5 00 00		5 00 00	

ACCOUNT Income Summary   **ACCOUNT NO.** 303

DATE	DESCRIPTION	POST. REF.	DEBIT	CREDIT	BALANCE DEBIT	BALANCE CREDIT

ACCOUNT Delivery Revenue   **ACCOUNT NO.** 401

DATE		DESCRIPTION	POST. REF.	DEBIT	CREDIT	BALANCE DEBIT	BALANCE CREDIT
20--							
Oct.	15		G1		1 200 00		1 200 00
	20		G1		1 450 00		2 650 00

ACCOUNT Advertising Expense   **ACCOUNT NO.** 501

DATE		DESCRIPTION	POST. REF.	DEBIT	CREDIT	BALANCE DEBIT	BALANCE CREDIT
20--							
Oct.	18		G1	75 00		75 00	

ACCOUNT Maintenance Expense   **ACCOUNT NO.** 505

DATE		DESCRIPTION	POST. REF.	DEBIT	CREDIT	BALANCE DEBIT	BALANCE CREDIT
20--							
Oct.	29		G1	6 00 00		6 00 00	

ACCOUNT Rent Expense   **ACCOUNT NO.** 510

DATE		DESCRIPTION	POST. REF.	DEBIT	CREDIT	BALANCE DEBIT	BALANCE CREDIT
20--							
Oct.	16		G1	7 00 00		7 00 00	

ACCOUNT Utilities Expense   **ACCOUNT NO.** 515

DATE		DESCRIPTION	POST. REF.	DEBIT	CREDIT	BALANCE DEBIT	BALANCE CREDIT
20--							
Oct.	28		G1	1 25 00		1 25 00	

Figure 7–7
Postings to
General Ledger
Accounts for the
Month of October
(Continued)

Computing a New Account Balance

On a four-column ledger account form, each time you post to an account, you also compute a new account balance. An easy rule of thumb for determining a new balance is that debits are added to debits, credits are added to credits, but debits and credits are subtracted. In other words, after you post to an account, you compute the new account balance as follows:

When the existing account balance is a debit, and

- the amount posted is a debit, ADD the amounts
- the amount posted is a credit, SUBTRACT the amounts.

When the existing account balance is a credit, and

- the amount posted is a debit, SUBTRACT the amounts
- the amount posted is a credit, ADD the amounts.

A ledger account usually has space for several postings. Often, blank lines remain after the journal entries for the month are posted. To save space, the journal entries for more than one month are entered on the same ledger page. Both the new month and day are entered in the Date column, as shown below in **Figure 7–8.**

Key Points

Calculating Balances
- Debit amounts are added together.
- Credit amounts are added together.
- Debit and credit amounts are subtracted.

ACCOUNT _Cash in Bank_   ACCOUNT NO. _101_

DATE		DESCRIPTION	POST. REF.	DEBIT	CREDIT	BALANCE DEBIT	BALANCE CREDIT
20--							
Oct.	1		G1	25 000 00		25 000 00	
	31		G2		5 00 00	24 500 00	
Nov.	1		G2		1 25 00	24 375 00	

Figure 7–8 A Ledger Account with Several Postings

Showing a Zero Balance in a Ledger Account

Sometimes a ledger account will have a zero balance. To show a zero balance, a line should be drawn across the center of the column—where the normal balance would appear. For example, on October 11, Roadrunner sold a phone for $200 on account to Green Company. On October 14, Green Company paid for the phone in full with a $200 check. When the October 14 journal entry is posted, **Accounts Receivable—Green Company** has a zero balance. Look at the ledger account in **Figure 7–9.** The line across the debit balance column means that the account has a zero balance. The line is drawn in the debit column because the normal balance for this account is a debit.

ACCOUNT _Accounts Receivable—Green Company_   ACCOUNT NO. _110_

DATE		DESCRIPTION	POST. REF.	DEBIT	CREDIT	BALANCE DEBIT	BALANCE CREDIT
20--							
Oct.	11		G1	2 00 00		2 00 00	
	14		G1		2 00 00	—	

Figure 7–9 Showing a Ledger Account with a Zero Balance

Now that you have studied this section, complete the following questions and problem.

Thinking Critically

1. Explain the purpose for posting.
2. Explain the process of posting from a journal to the ledger.

Analyzing Accounting

As an employee of Always Fresh Bakery, you have been asked to analyze the impact that different sales levels have on the ultimate profit or loss of the business. After posting is completed, you prepare the following line graph to illustrate the sales figures for Always Fresh Bakery. Review the line graph and write a one-paragraph analysis of the impact of sales on the bakery's profit.

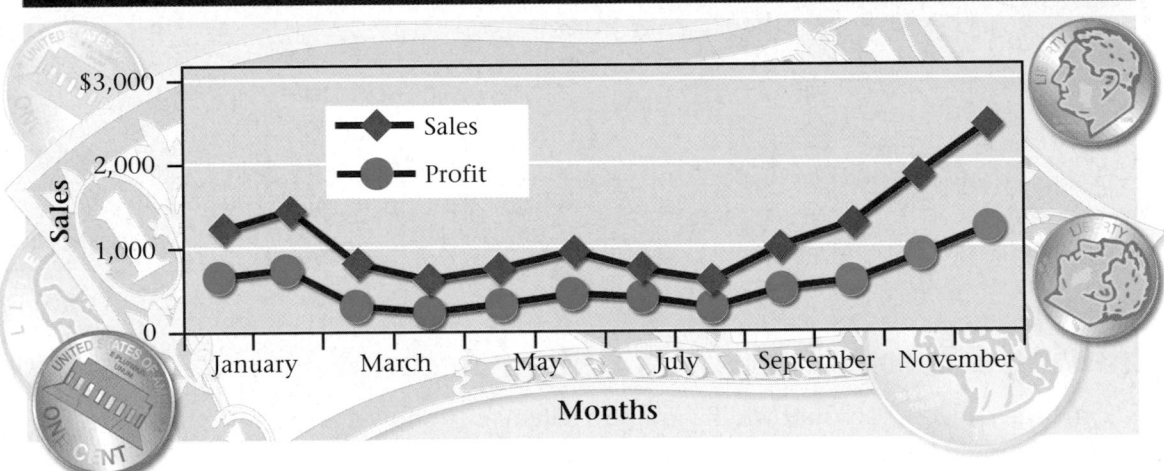

ANNUAL SALES AND REVENUE

Problem 7–2 **Posting from the General Journal to the Ledger**

Instructions David Serlo made the following cash investment in his business. Use the six-step process to post the entry to the ledger accounts in your working papers.

GENERAL JOURNAL   PAGE ___1___

	DATE		DESCRIPTION	POST. REF.	DEBIT	CREDIT	
1	20--						1
2	May	1	Cash in Bank		10 0 0 0 00		2
3			David Serlo, Capital			10 0 0 0 00	3
4			Memorandum 101				4
5							5

LORA HURRELBRINK
**Accounts Payable Manager,
National Veterinary Associates**

Q: How did you get into accounting?

A: I started in a retail clothing warehouse tagging merchandise. Soon my responsibilities included checking receipts sent in by all the stores. That got boring, and I needed something more challenging and people-interactive. So, I became an accounts payable clerk. After a while, I wanted more responsibilities. So, I became an accounts payable bookkeeper and gained experience for five years. Then I applied for a supervisory position. I loved it! I have been a manager ever since.

Q: Why do you like managing?

A: I like being the boss, and I like teaching.

Q: What kind of degree do you need?

A: If someone wants to be an accounts payable manager, they don't necessarily need an accounting degree, although some companies like to see it. I've never been asked why I don't have one. If you want to move up to staff accountant, or controller, though, you need an accounting degree and a CPA. Business training is important. The best thing is to get experience while you're in school. Work anywhere you deal with money and math.

Tips from . . .

RHI Robert Half International Inc.

In business, success is usually a team effort. Help out whenever your help is necessary, even if it is "not your job." Show initiative, and give credit to the group when someone compliments a job well done.

CAREER FACTS

Nature of the Work: Oversee accounts payable staff, make decisions, and report to management.

Training or Education Needed: A bachelor's degree in accounting, or five to ten years experience.

Aptitudes, Abilities, and Skills: Analytical skills, problem-solving skills, computer skills, interpersonal skills, and communication skills.

Salary Range: $27,000 to $60,000 depending on company size and industry.

Career Path: First start as a clerk, then you can move to a lead clerk, and eventually move into management.

Thinking Critically: What qualities do you think employers look for when hiring?

Preparing a Trial Balance

What You'll Learn

- The purpose of a trial balance.
- How to prepare a trial balance.
- How to identify and locate trial balance errors.

Why It's Important

To present accurate financial statements, the accounts must be in balance. The purpose of a trial balance is to prove that the general ledger is in balance.

KEY TERMS

proving the ledger
trial balance
transposition error
slide error
correcting entry

ACCOUNTING TIPS

Trial Balance

When preparing a trial balance, be sure to list all the general ledger accounts, in the order in which they appear in the ledger and on the chart of accounts. List even those accounts with a zero balance. Every account is listed to avoid omitting an account (and its balance) from the trial balance.

In the last section you learned how to post to the ledger. In this section you will learn how to prepare a trial balance. A trial balance is how accountants prove that the accounting system is in balance. Preparing a trial balance is the fifth step in the accounting cycle. Every time the accountant for the Jeep dealership in your area posts to the ledger, he or she prepares a trial balance. The trial balance provides assurance that the journal entries are posted properly.

The Fifth Step in the Accounting Cycle: The Trial Balance

After the journal entries are posted to the accounts in the general ledger, the total of all the debit balances should equal the total of all the credit balances. Adding all the debit balances, then adding all the credit balances, and finally comparing the two totals to see whether they are equal is called **proving the ledger**.

A formal way to prove that debits equal credits is to prepare a **trial balance**. A trial balance is a list of all the account names and their current balances. All of the debit balances are added. All of the credit balances are added. The totals are compared. If the totals are the same, the trial balance is in balance. If the totals are not equal, an error was made in journalizing, posting, or preparing the trial balance. You must find the error and correct it before continuing with the next step in the accounting cycle.

The trial balance for Roadrunner Delivery Service for the month of October is shown in **Figure 7–10.** The trial balance was prepared on two-column accounting stationery. The account numbers are listed in the far left column. The account names are listed in the next column. All of the debit balances are entered in the first amount column, and all of the credit balances are entered in the second amount column. Trial balances do not have to be prepared on accounting stationery. They can be handwritten on plain paper, typed, or prepared on a computer.

Roadrunner Delivery Service
Trial Balance
October 31, 20--

		Debit	Credit
101	Cash in Bank	21 1 2 5 00	
105	Accounts Receivable—City News	1 4 5 0 00	
110	Accounts Receivable—Green Company		
115	Computer Equipment	3 0 0 0 00	
120	Office Equipment	2 0 0 00	
125	Delivery Equipment	12 0 0 0 00	
201	Accounts Payable—Beacon Advertising		7 5 00
205	Accounts Payable—North Shore Auto		11 6 5 0 00
301	Maria Sanchez, Capital		25 4 0 0 00
302	Maria Sanchez, Withdrawals	5 0 0 00	
303	Income Summary		
401	Delivery Revenue		2 6 5 0 00
501	Advertising Expense	7 5 00	
505	Maintenance Expense	6 0 0 00	
510	Rent Expense	7 0 0 00	
515	Utilities Expense	1 2 5 00	
	Totals	39 7 7 5 00	39 7 7 5 00

Figure 7–10 Trial Balance

Finding Errors

Most trial balance errors can be located easily and quickly. When total debits do not equal total credits, follow these steps:

1. Add the debit and credit columns again. You may have added one or both of the columns incorrectly.
2. Find the difference between the debit and credit columns. This is the amount that you are out of balance. If this amount is 10, 100, 1,000, and so on, you probably made an addition error. Suppose, for example, you have total debits of $35,245 and total credits of $35,345. The difference between the debits and credits is $100, which indicates an addition error is likely. Add the columns again to find the error.
3. Check if the amount you are out of balance is evenly divisible by 9. For example, suppose the difference between the debits and credits is $27. That amount is evenly divisible by 9 (27 ÷ 9 = 3). If the difference between the columns is evenly divisible by 9, you may have a transposition error or a slide error. A **transposition error** occurs when two digits within an amount are accidentally reversed, or transposed. For example, the amount $325 may have been written as $352.

   A **slide error** occurs when a decimal point is moved by mistake. For example, if you write $1,800 as either $180 or $18,000, you made a slide error.

   To find a transposition error or a slide error, check the trial balance amounts against the general ledger account balances to make sure you copied the balances correctly.
4. Make sure that you have included all of the general ledger accounts in the trial balance. Look in the general ledger for an account balance equal

to the amount you are out of balance. For example, if the difference between total debits and credits is $725, look in the general ledger for an account with a balance of $725.

5. If all the general ledger accounts and their balances are included in the trial balance, one of the account balances could be recorded in the wrong column. That is, a debit is entered in the credit column or a credit is entered in the debit column. To find out if this happened, divide the out-of-balance amount by 2 and check if the result matches the balance of an account. For example, suppose that the difference between the two columns is $300; $300 divided by 2 is $150. Look in the debit and credit columns for an account balance of $150. Then check to see if the $150 is entered in the wrong column.

6. If you still have not found the error, recompute the balance in each ledger account. You may have an addition or subtraction error on a ledger account form.

7. Finally, check the general ledger accounts to verify that the correct amounts are posted from the journal entries. Also, check to make sure that debit amounts are posted to the debit column and credit amounts are posted to the credit column.

Correcting Entries

Anyone who works in accounting understands the saying, "To err is human..." When mistakes are made in accounting, one rule applies: *Never erase an error*.

The method for correcting an error depends on when and where the error is found. There are three types of errors:

- Error in a journal entry that is not posted.
- Error in posting to the ledger when the journal entry is correct.
- Error in a journal entry that is posted.

In Chapter 6 you learned that when an error in a journal entry is discovered before posting, you draw a single line through the incorrect item in the journal and write the correction directly above. If the journal entry is correct but is posted incorrectly to the ledger, you draw a single line through the incorrect item in the ledger and write the correction directly above.

When an error in a journal entry is discovered *after* posting, make a **correcting entry** to fix the error.

On November 15, the accountant for Roadrunner found an error in a journal entry made on November 2. A $100 check to pay the electricity bill was journalized and posted to the **Maintenance Expense** account by mistake. The original journal entry is shown in the following T accounts.

Maintenance Expense		Cash in Bank	
Debit + 100	Credit −	Debit +	Credit − 100

"Never erase an error"

The following T accounts show how the transaction *should* have been recorded.

Utilities Expense			Cash in Bank	
Debit + 100	**Credit** –		**Debit** +	**Credit** – 100

As you can see, the $100 credit to **Cash in Bank** is correct. The error is in the debit part of the November 2 transaction. **Maintenance Expense** is incorrectly debited for $100. To correct the error, **Maintenance Expense** is credited for $100 and **Utilities Expense** is debited for $100.

The accountant wrote Memorandum 70 to notify the accounting clerk of the mistake. The correcting entry, recorded in the general journal, is shown in **Figure 7–11**.

GENERAL JOURNAL   PAGE ___3___

	DATE		DESCRIPTION	POST. REF.	DEBIT	CREDIT	
1	20--						1
2	Nov.	15	*Utilities Expense*		100 00		2
3			*Maintenance Expense*			100 00	3
4			*Memorandum 70*				4
5							5

Figure 7–11 Correcting Entry

Posting a correcting entry is similar to any other posting. In the Description column of the ledger accounts, however, the words "Correcting Entry" are written. **Figure 7–12** shows how the correcting entry is posted to the **Maintenance Expense** and **Utilities Expense** accounts.

ACCOUNT _Maintenance Expense_   ACCOUNT NO. _505_

DATE		DESCRIPTION	POST. REF.	DEBIT	CREDIT	BALANCE DEBIT	BALANCE CREDIT
20--							
Oct.	29		G1			600 00	
Nov.	2		G2	100 00		700 00	
	15	Correcting Entry	G3		100 00	600 00	

ACCOUNT _Utilities Expense_   ACCOUNT NO. _515_

DATE		DESCRIPTION	POST. REF.	DEBIT	CREDIT	BALANCE DEBIT	BALANCE CREDIT
20--							
Oct.	28		G1	125 00		125 00	
Nov.	15	Correcting Entry	G3	100 00		225 00	

Figure 7–12 Posting of Correcting Entry

Now that you have studied this section, complete the following questions and problems.

Thinking Critically

1. List some common errors made when posting. Give a brief description of each.
2. What is the best way to correct an error?

Computing in the Business World

1. Compare the numbers in Column 1 to those in Column 2. Find any transposition, slide, or omission errors. Identify the type of error for each line.

Column 1	Column 2
$18.00	$180.00
$15,000	$1,500
$222.52	$222.25
$187,235,499.05	$187,235,499.50
$47,988	$47,988
$578,334.99	$5,778,334.99

2. Using a calculator or adding machine, total Column 1. Correct any errors in Column 2, and then total Column 2. Do the totals of Columns 1 and 2 match?

Problem 7–3 Analyzing a Source Document

Instructions Analyze the transaction described in Memorandum 47, then record and post the required correcting entry in your working papers.

FUNTIME
AMUSEMENT ARCADE

MEMORANDUM 47

TO: Accounting Clerk
FROM: Dan Vonderhaar
DATE: May 20, 20--
SUBJECT: Correction of error

On May 10, we purchased an office copier for $1,500. I noticed in the general journal that the entry was recorded and posted to the Computer Equipment account. Please record the necessary entry to correct this error.

Problem 7–4 Recording and Posting a Correcting Entry

Instructions On July 7, Video Connection's accounting supervisor discovered a July 3 transaction was recorded incorrectly. The transaction, involving the purchase of advertising in the local newspaper with a $300 check, was incorrectly journalized and posted to the **Rent Expense** account. In your working papers, record and post the correcting entry using Memorandum 13 as the source document.

VIDEO
Connection

MEMORANDUM 13

TO: Accounting Clerk
FROM: Accounting Manager
DATE: July 7, 20--
SUBJECT: Correction of error

On July 3, we paid $300 for advertising in the *Daily News Record* that was incorrectly journalized and posted to the Rent Expense account. Please record the necessary entry to correct this error.

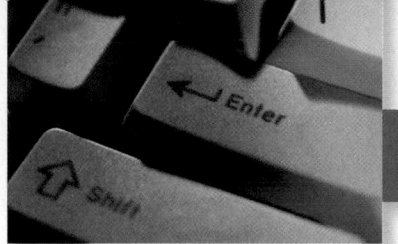

KEY CONCEPTS

1. Posting is the fourth step in the accounting cycle. It is the process of transferring information from a journal entry to specific accounts in the ledger.

2. The accounts used by a business are kept in the ledger. In a manual accounting system, each ledger account appears on its own page or card.

3. Ledger accounts are opened before posting can begin. An account is opened by writing the account name and its number at the top of the ledger account form.

4. A four-column ledger account form has four amount columns: one for a debit entry, one for a credit entry, one for a debit balance, and one for a credit balance.

5. Posting from the general journal to ledger accounts is illustrated below.

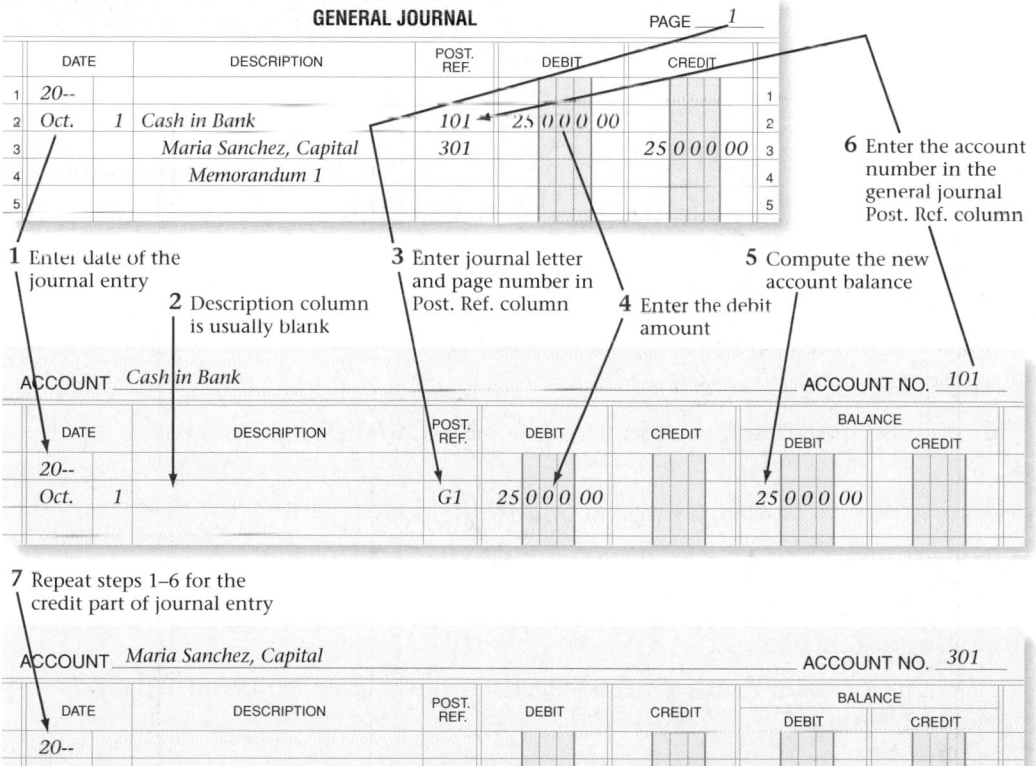

6. After posting is complete, the equality of the ledger is proved. A trial balance is prepared to prove that total debits equal total credits. Preparing a trial balance is the fifth step in the accounting cycle.

7. The most common errors made in accounting records are addition and subtraction errors, transpositions, slides, omissions, and incorrect debiting or crediting.

8. Errors discovered after posting require a correcting entry in both the general journal and the ledger.

USING KEY TERMS

As a junior accounting clerk for Action Sports Outfitters, you are being evaluated for a raise. Your boss wants to see how well you understand basic accounting terminology. He asks you to write a sentence for each term below, showing how you would use each term in connection with Action Sports Outfitters.

correcting entry	proving the ledger
general ledger	slide error
ledger account form	transposition error
posting	trial balance

Understanding Accounting Concepts and Procedures

Instructions

On a separate sheet of paper, answer the following questions:

1. What step in the accounting cycle is the posting process?

2. What is the purpose of posting?

3. How is the information posted in the ledger accounts helpful to the business owner or manager?

4. What two steps are required to open a ledger account with a zero balance?

5. What six steps are required to open a ledger account that has a balance?

6. What determines the frequency of posting?

7. List the steps in the posting process.

8. Although the Description column in a general ledger account is often left blank, what do some businesses record there?

9. What two things are indicated by the journal posting reference?

10. How is a zero balance shown in a ledger account?

11. What steps should be followed to locate trial balance errors?

12. How does an accounting clerk correct a journal entry that has not been posted?

13. How does an accounting clerk correct an error in a journal entry that was posted?

Case Study...

Service Business: Accounting Services

Joel Rivlin studied accounting in college, then worked as an accountant for a local real estate company. After becoming a CPA, Joel decided to start his own company, Joel Rivlin, CPA.

Robert's Excavating Services came to Joel with a problem. The company's trial balance shows total debits of $76,240 and total credits of $75,090. The owner knows that clients paid for services worth at least $2,500 during the month, but the **Service Revenue** account balance is only $800. The owner also wrote a check for $550 for advertising, but the **Advertising Expense** account shows a zero balance.

Thinking Critically:

1. Describe what Joel should do to find the problems.
2. Suggest probable causes for the trial balance being out of balance.

*inter*NET CONNECTION

Peachtree Accounting Software

Assume that you are working part time and your employer is planning to change from a manual accounting system to a computerized system. She is not familiar with Peachtree software. She asks you to provide her with information about Peachtree software and how Peachtree can help her manage her business.

Do This:

1. Locate the Peachtree software Web site.
2. What Peachtree software is available for small businesses?
3. What is the cost?
4. Identify three advantages that Peachtree describes about its products.

Conducting an Audit with Alex

Instructions The owner of Frank Palmer's Flying School has given you the final general ledger balances and has provided the trial balance in your working papers. He has told you the Accounts Payable balance is wrong. Prepare a corrected trial balance on a separate sheet of paper.

Cash in Bank	$ 4,700
Accounts Receivable	1,600
Airplanes	90,000
Accounts Payable	2,680
Frank Palmer, Capital	68,650
Frank Palmer, Withdrawals	3,000
Flying Fees	40,000
Advertising Expense	150
Fuel and Oil Expense	5,600
Repairs Expense	6,200

Workplace Skills

Interpreting and Communicating Information

Every worker must learn how to interpret information and communicate effectively with co-workers, customers, and superiors.

On the Job:

As an accounting clerk for New Wave Inc., a surfboard manufacturer, one of your duties is to audit the accounting records and make the necessary corrections. Former employees did not always maintain the records accurately. The owner, Ron Lee, has asked you to provide written explanations for each error discovered in your audit.

Thinking Critically:

1. During an audit you discover a transposition error. An invoice for $510.00 payable to Marketing Pros was recorded and posted as $150.00. How do you correct this error?
2. Using word processing software, write a memo to Mr. Lee explaining how you corrected the error.

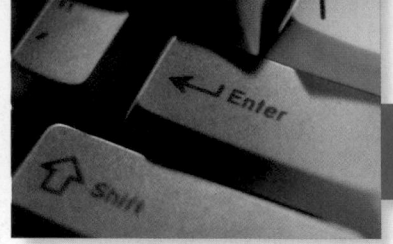

Posting to the General Ledger

Making the Transition from a Manual to a Computerized System

Task	Perform Accounting Procedures Using Manual Methods	Perform Accounting Procedures Using Automated Methods
Posting to the General Ledger	1. Transfer the details of each journal entry to individual ledger accounts. 2. Calculate the new account balance for each ledger account.	1. After each journal entry is entered, amounts are posted automatically into the general ledger. 2. New account balances are calculated for you.

Posting to the General Ledger

Peachtree Question	Description
How do I post general journal transactions?	• After entering a journal entry, click Save.
What does the software do "behind the scenes?"	• The software automatically posts the debit and credit amounts to the accounts you have indicated in the journal entry. New account balances are calculated for each account affected. • The software will not allow an out-of-balance journal entry to be posted. Therefore, the software always keeps the accounting records in balance (debits always equal credits).
What if I find an error in my journal entry after it has been posted?	Changes to journal entries can be made before or after the entry has been posted. 1. From the General Journal Entry window, drop down the *Edit* menu. Select **Edit Record.** 2. Select the entry you want to change. 3. Make the correction. 4. Click *OK*, then click the *Save* button.
What does the software do "behind the scenes"?	• When journal entries are edited, only the correct entry appears in the ledger account. Account balances are updated after each posting.

For detailed instructions: See the **Peachtree User Guide** in your Glencoe Working Papers.

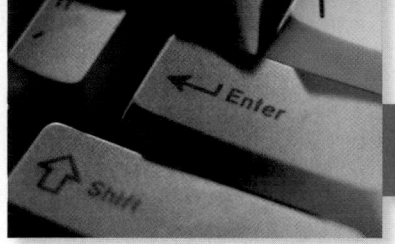

APPLICATION OPTIONS

Problem 7–5 Posting General Journal Transactions

The accounts used by Wilderness Rentals have been opened and are included in the working papers accompanying this textbook. The general journal transactions for March of the current year are also included.

Instructions Post the transactions recorded on page 1 of the general journal to the accounts in the general ledger.

Analyze: After posting, what is the balance in the **Cash in Bank** account?

Problem 7–6 Preparing a Trial Balance

The ledger accounts for Hot Suds Car Wash are shown in your working papers.

Instructions Prepare a trial balance for the month of March of the current year.

Analyze: What is the amount of total debits?

Problem 7–7 Journalizing and Posting Business Transactions

A partial chart of accounts for Kits & Pups Grooming is provided below.

General Ledger

101	Cash in Bank	301	Abe Shultz, Capital
105	Accts. Rec.—J. Alvarez	305	Abe Shultz, Withdrawals
120	Grooming Supplies	401	Boarding Revenue
130	Office Furniture	405	Grooming Revenue
140	Grooming Equipment	525	Salaries Expense
205	Accts. Pay.—Dogs & Cats Inc.		

Instructions

(1) In your working papers, open an account in the general ledger for each account above.
(2) Record the March transactions on page 1 of the general journal.
(3) Post each journal entry to the appropriate ledger account.
(4) Prove the ledger by preparing a trial balance.

Date		Transactions
Mar.	1	Abe Shultz invested $5,000 in the business, Memorandum 51.
	3	Abe Shultz transferred a desk and chairs valued at $1,200 to the business, Memorandum 52.
		Continued ☛

Complete chapter problems one of three ways:

1 **Manual** Glencoe Working Papers

or

2 **Peachtree Complete Accounting** Software

or

3 **QuickBooks** Templates (Problems 7–5, 7–6, 7–7)

Peachtree®
SMART GUIDE

Step–by–Step Instructions: Problem 7–5

1. Select the problem set for Wilderness Rentals (Prob. 7–5).
2. Rename the company and set the system date.
3. Print a General Ledger report.
4. Answer the Analyze question.
5. End the session.

Peachtree®
SMART GUIDE

Step–by–Step Instructions: Problem 7–6

1. Select the problem set for Hot Suds Car Wash (Prob. 7–6).
2. Rename the company and set the system date.
3. Print a General Ledger Trial Balance report.
4. Answer the Analyze question.
5. End the session.

Peachtree®

SMART GUIDE

Step–by–Step Instructions:
Problem 7–7

1. Select the problem set for Kits & Pups Grooming (Prob. 7–7).
2. Rename the company and set the system date.
3. Enter all of the general journal transactions.
4. Print a General Journal report.
5. Proof your work.
6. Print a General Ledger report and a General Ledger Trial Balance report.
7. Answer the Analyze question.
8. End the session.

TIP: As a shortcut, you can enter just the day of the month for a transaction date.

Peachtree®

SMART GUIDE

Step–by–Step Instructions:
Problem 7–8

1. Select the problem set for Outback Guide Service (Prob. 7–8).
2. Rename the company and set the system date.
3. Enter all of the general journal transactions.
4. Print a General Journal report.
5. Proof your work.
6. Print a General Ledger report and a General Ledger Trial Balance report.
7. Answer the Analyze question.
8. End the session.

TIP: Always double-check the account numbers and amounts in a general journal entry before you post it.

Date	Problem 7–7 (cont.) Transactions
Mar. 5	Issued Check 551 for $300 for grooming supplies.
7	Bought grooming equipment on account for $1,800 from Dogs & Cats Inc., Invoice DC201.
9	Groomed Juan Alvarez's show dogs on account, $400, Sales Invoice 350.
12	Paid Dogs & Cats Inc. $900 on account, Check 552.
15	Issued Check 553 for $500 to pay the office secretary's salary.
18	Abe Shultz withdrew $1,000 cash from the business, Check 554.
20	Deposited $1,400 received from clients for boarding their pets, Receipts 477-480.
24	Wrote Check 555 for $900 to Dogs & Cats Inc. to apply on account.
26	Received a check for $400 from Juan Alvarez on account, Receipt 481.

Analyze: What are the total debits on the trial balance on March 31?

SOURCE DOCUMENT PROBLEM

Problem 7–8 Journalizing and Posting Business Transactions

The chart of accounts for Outback Guide Service is listed below.

General Ledger

101 Cash in Bank	301 Juanita Ortega, Capital
115 Accts. Rec.—Podaski Systems Inc.	302 Juanita Ortega, Withdrawals
140 Computer Equipment	401 Guide Service Revenue
145 Hiking Equipment	501 Advertising Expense
150 Rafting Equipment	
205 Accts. Pay.—Peak Equipment Inc.	
207 Accts. Pay.—Premier Processors	

Instructions

(1) In your working papers, open an account in the general ledger for each account in the chart of accounts.
(2) Record the following transactions on page 1 of the general journal.
(3) Post each journal entry to the appropriate accounts in the ledger.
(4) Prove the ledger by preparing a trial balance.

Date	Transactions
Mar. 1	Invested $20,000 in cash and transferred rafting equipment valued at $5,000 to the business, Memorandum 35.
3	Purchased $600 in hiking equipment on account from Peak Equipment Inc., Invoice 101.
	Continued

Date	Problem 7–8 (cont.) Transactions
Mar. 5	Bought a $2,800 computer from Premier Processors and agreed to pay for it within 60 days, Invoice 616.
7	Deposited $700 cash received from clients, Receipts 310–315.
9	Paid $400 to the *Daily Courier* for an ad, Check 652.
12	Sent a bill for $900 to Podaski Systems Inc. for conducting a group rafting trip for them, Sales Invoice 352.
15	Juanita Ortega wrote a check for $800 for personal use, Check 653.
18	Paid Premier Processors $1,400 to apply on account, Check 654.
22	Received $900 from Podaski Systems Inc. in full payment for the amount owed, Receipt 316.
27	Bought a $500 television ad with LIVE TV, Check 655.
28	Paid Peak Equipment Inc. $600 by writing Check 656.

SOURCE DOCUMENT PROBLEM

Problem 7–8

Use the source documents in your working papers to record the transactions for this problem.

Analyze: What is the balance of **Cash in Bank** at March 28?

Problem 7–9 Recording and Posting Correcting Entries

An auditor reviewed the accounting records of Showbiz Video. The auditor wrote a memo, outlined below, regarding the number of errors discovered in the March records. The general journal for March and a portion of the general ledger are included in your working papers.

Instructions

(1) Record correcting entries on general journal page 22.

(2) Use Memorandum 50 as the source document for all correcting entries and March 31 as the date. Some errors will not require correcting entries, but will require a general ledger correction. Make the appropriate general ledger corrections.

(3) Post all correcting entries to the general ledger accounts.

Peachtree®

SMART GUIDE

Step–by–Step Instructions: Problem 7–9

1. Select the problem set for Showbiz Video (Prob. 7–9).
2. Rename the company and set the system date.
3. Correct the general journal entries based on the auditor's report.
4. Print a General Journal report and a General Ledger report.
5. Proof your work.
6. Answer the Analyze question.
7. End the session.

TIP: Use the **General Journal Entry** task option to edit the general journal entries.

Date	Transactions
Mar. 3	The $125 purchase was for office supplies.
7	A $200 payment to a creditor, Broad Street Office Supply, was not posted to the account.
13	Greg Failla withdrew $1,200 from the business for personal use.
17	Cash totaling $2,000 was received for video rentals.
19	A $75 receipt from Shannon Flannery was posted as $57.
27	Greg Failla invested an additional $3,000 in the business.
29	The revenue of $1,000 was for video rentals.

Analyze: Once correcting entries have been posted, what are the balances of the owner's equity accounts?

Setting Up Accounting Records for a Sole Proprietorship

Canyon.com Web Sites

Company Background: Whether you're interested in a Web site for your new hair salon or a corporate intranet site, Canyon.com provides design, hosting, and maintenance services for the small mom-and-pop business and the multi-national corporation alike. Jack Hines, owner of Canyon.com Web Sites is known for his unique and dynamic presentations on the Web. His creativity and knowledge of Web culture makes him a success in electronic content delivery.

Organization: Canyon.com is organized as a sole proprietorship. The business is fully owned and operated by Jack Hines.

Your Job Responsibilities: As the accounting clerk for the business, use the accounting stationery in your workbook to complete the following:

(1) Open a general ledger account for each account in the chart of accounts.
(2) Analyze each business transaction.
(3) Enter each business transaction in the general journal, page 1.
(4) Post each journal entry to the appropriate accounts in the general ledger.
(5) Prove the general ledger by preparing a trial balance.

What **You'll Learn**

- How to analyze business transactions.
- How to record business transactions in the general journal.
- How to post business transactions in the general ledger accounts.
- How to prepare a trial balance.

Why **It's Important**

Learning to apply the first five steps of the accounting cycle will prepare you to perform these accounting tasks for any service business organized as a sole proprietorship.

APPLICATION OPTIONS

Complete activities one of three ways:

1 **Manual** Glencoe Working Papers

or

2 **Peachtree Complete Accounting** Software

or

3 **QuickBooks** Templates

CHART OF ACCOUNTS
Canyon.com Web Sites

ASSETS

101	Cash in Bank
105	Accts. Rec.–Andrew Hospital
110	Accts. Rec.–Indiana Trucking
115	Accts Rec.–Sunshine Products
130	Office Supplies
135	Office Equipment
140	Office Furniture
145	Web Server

LIABILITIES

205	Accts. Pay.–Computer Specialists Inc.
210	Accts. Pay.–Office Systems
215	Accts. Pay.–Service Plus Software Inc.

OWNER'S EQUITY

301	Jack Hines, Capital
305	Jack Hines, Withdrawals

REVENUE

401	Web Service Fees

EXPENSES

505	Membership Expense
506	Telecommunications Expense
507	Rent Expense
508	Utilities Expense

Canyon.com Web Sites

Business Transactions: Jack Hines, owner of Canyon.com Web Sites, began business operations on May 1 of this year. During the month of May, the business completed the transactions that follow.

Peachtree®

SMART GUIDE

Step–by–Step Instructions:
1. Select the problem set for Canyon.Com Web Sites (MP-1).
2. Rename the company and set the system date.
3. Record all of the business transactions using the **General Journal Entry** option.
4. Print a General Journal report.
5. Proof your work.
6. Print a General Ledger report.
7. Print a Trial Balance.
8. Answer the Analyze questions and complete the Audit Test.
9. End the session.

Date	Transactions
May 1	Jack Hines invested $50,000 in the business, Memorandum 1.
2	The owner, Jack Hines, invested a desktop computer and printer (Office Equipment) $3,500, Memorandum 2.
2	Issued Check 101 for $125 for the purchase of office supplies.
3	Bought office furniture for $2,700 on account from Office Systems, Invoice 457.
7	Bought a Web server from Computer Specialists Inc. on account for $35,000, Invoice WS4658421.
9	Received $1,000 from James Market for Web site services, Receipt 101.
11	Completed Web site design services for Andrew Hospital to be paid later, Invoice 101, $3,000.
12	Bought software for the Web server (Web Server) on account from Service Plus Software Inc., Invoice 876, $10,000.
14	Wrote Check 102 for $118 to pay the electric bill.
15	Jack Hines withdrew $2,500 for personal expenses, Check 103.
17	Completed Web site design on account for Sunshine Products, Invoice 102, $5,000.
18	Bought a filing cabinet (Office Furniture) for $275, Check 104.
19	Received a check for $4,000 as payment for Web site maintenance for one year to a client, Receipt 102.
20	Provided design services on account to Indiana Trucking, Invoice 103 for $2,000.
21	Prepared Receipt 103, $2,500, received on account, Sunshine Products.
22	Paid $4,900 for telecommunication services for the period May 1–May 31, Check 105.
22	Wrote check 106 for $3,333 to Service Plus Software Inc. as payment on account.
25	Sent Check 107 for $2,000 to Office Systems as payment on account.
26	Received $1,000 for two months of Web services, Receipt 104.
27	Paid the dues for membership in the All Inclusive Group for $7,000, Check 108.
30	Wrote Check 109 for the monthly rent $750.
30	Withdrew $2,500 for personal expenses, Check 110.
30	Sent Check 111 for $25,000 to Computer Specialists Inc., as payment on account.

Analyze: How many checks were written by the business during May? What was the total of all checks written?

CHAPTER 8

The Six-Column Work Sheet

Learning Objectives

When you have completed this chapter, you will be able to:

▶ Explain the purpose of the work sheet.

▶ Describe the parts of a six-column work sheet.

▶ Prepare a six-column work sheet.

▶ Calculate net income and net loss.

▶ Define the accounting terms introduced in this chapter.

Exploring the Real World of Business

SUMMARIZING RESULTS

Public transportation began as early as 1630. Today, most cities have public buses, and larger cities also have subway or rail lines.

The Washington D.C. metro system is the fourth largest transit system in the United States. The subway trains travel 103 miles of track each day and stop at 83 different stations in Washington and nearby communities in Maryland and Virginia.

The Metro system is operated by the **Washington Metropolitan Area Transit Authority (WMATA),** a not-for-profit organization. Revenues and expenses are monitored carefully by the **WMATA** managers since revenues must pay the full operating costs of the system. If they do not, fares must be increased. Work sheets that summarize the total revenue from fares and the expenses of operating the system help managers keep track of whether the system's income is in balance with its expenses.

What do you think?

If you worked for the **Washington Metro,** what information would you look for in monthly work sheets to alert you to revenue or expense problems?

Washington Metropolitan Area Transit Authority (WMATA)

Workplace Connections

Applying Your Accounting Knowledge

When you prepare to write a research paper, you probably use note cards or a database program to collect and organize information. You may also write a rough draft of your paper, further organizing the information. In accounting, a work sheet serves to organize financial information. You'll learn how to create a work sheet in this chapter.

Investigate:

1. How might your ability to organize information be valuable to your employer?
2. Why is it important for financial and other information to be organized in a certain way?

Glencoe Accounting Online

Visit the *Glencoe Accounting* Web site at **glencoeaccounting.glencoe.com** for additional activities and information.

Preparing the Work Sheet

As you learned in Chapter 6, the length of an accounting period can vary. The maximum period covered by the accounting cycle is one year. The first five steps of the accounting cycle are performed frequently during the cycle. The last four steps—preparing a work sheet, preparing financial statements, journalizing and posting closing entries, and preparing a post-closing trial balance—are performed at the end of the accounting period. Look at **Figure 8–1**. In this chapter you will learn how to prepare a work sheet, the sixth step of the accounting cycle. With this step, businesses like your local Midas Muffler shop or a Nike Outlet collect information from their ledger accounts and record this information on a single form.

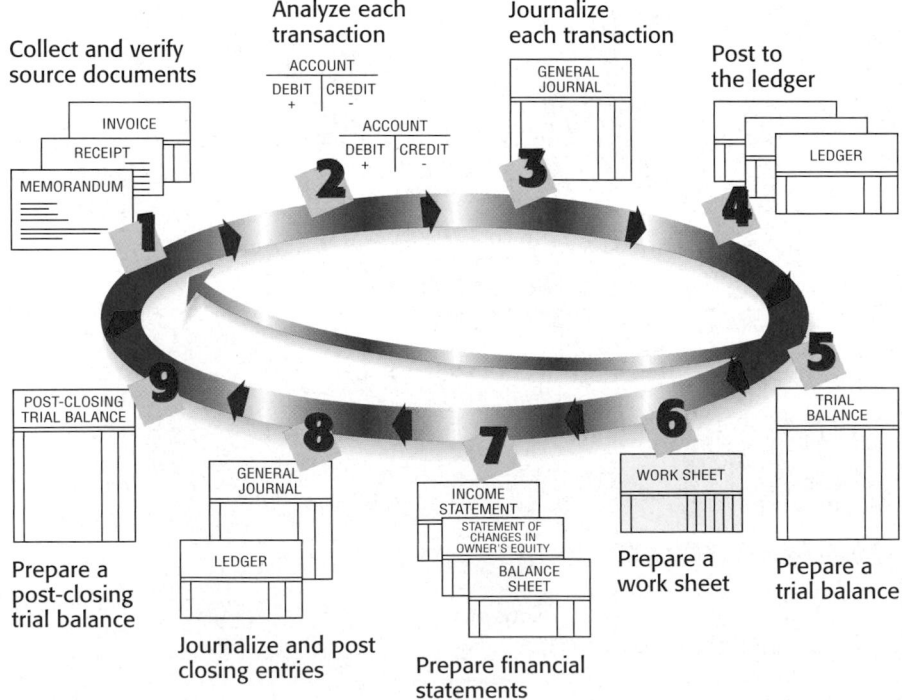

Figure 8–1 Steps in the Accounting Cycle with Step 6 Highlighted

The Sixth Step of the Accounting Cycle: The Work Sheet

A **work sheet** is just what its name implies—a working paper used to collect information from the ledger accounts in one place. Like the T account, the work sheet is a tool that the accountant uses. With the work sheet, an accountant gathers all the information needed to prepare the financial statements and to complete the other end-of-period activities.

A work sheet may be prepared in pencil on standard multi-column accounting paper. The paper comes in several sizes and is usually printed without column headings. Blank spaces for column headings allow the accountant to enter the headings needed by a particular business. The work sheet can also be prepared using computer spreadsheet software.

The Roadrunner Delivery Service work sheet, shown in **Figure 8–2**, has five sections:

(1) the Heading
(2) the Account Name section
(3) the Trial Balance section
(4) the Income Statement section
(5) the Balance Sheet section.

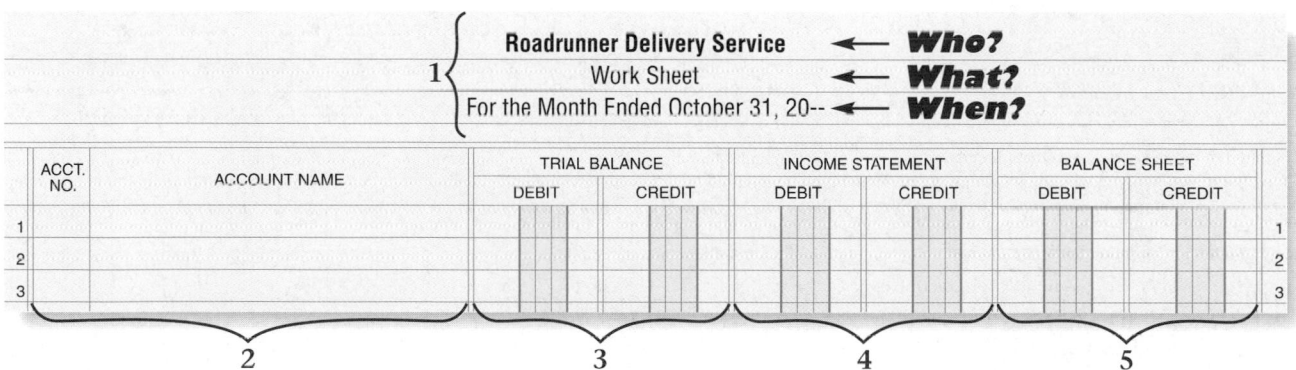

Figure 8–2 Six-Column Work Sheet

The Account Name section includes a column for the account number and a column for the account name. The Trial Balance, Income Statement, and Balance Sheet sections have debit and credit amount columns. The six amount columns give this work sheet its name: the six-column work sheet.

The Work Sheet Heading

The work sheet heading contains three kinds of information:

(1) The name of the business **(Who?)**
(2) The name of the accounting form **(What?)**
(3) The period covered by the work sheet **(When?)**

Notice how these elements are positioned on the work sheet in **Figure 8–2**. Follow this format when preparing the heading of any work sheet.

Rules

A *single rule* means that the column of figures is to be added or subtracted. *Double rules* mean that the last figure is a total and that no more entries are to be made below.

The Account Name and Trial Balance Sections

Information for the Account Name and Trial Balance sections comes from the general ledger accounts. In Chapter 7, you prepared a trial balance by listing the account names and their final balances. A trial balance can be prepared at any time during the fiscal period to prove the general ledger. When a trial balance is prepared at the end of an accounting period, though, it is prepared as a part of the work sheet.

Account Name Section. Look at the work sheet in **Figure 8–3**. The account numbers and names are from Roadrunner's general ledger and are listed on the work sheet in the same order that they appear in the general ledger. The order is:

- Assets
- Liabilities
- Owner's equity
- Revenues
- Expenses

Roadrunner Delivery Service
Work Sheet
For the Month Ended October 31, 20--

	ACCT. NO.	ACCOUNT NAME	TRIAL BALANCE DEBIT	TRIAL BALANCE CREDIT	INCOME STATEMENT DEBIT	INCOME STATEMENT CREDIT	BALANCE SHEET DEBIT	BALANCE SHEET CREDIT	
1	101	Cash in Bank	21125 00						1
2	105	Accts. Rec.—City News	1450 00						2
3	110	Accts. Rec.—Green Company	—						3
4	115	Computer Equipment	3000 00						4
5	120	Office Equipment	200 00						5
6	125	Delivery Equipment	12000 00						6
7	201	Accts. Pay.—Beacon Advertising		75 00					7
8	205	Accts. Pay.—North Shore Auto		11650 00					8
9	301	Maria Sanchez, Capital		25400 00					9
10	302	Maria Sanchez, Withdrawals	500 00						10
11	303	Income Summary	—	—					11
12	401	Delivery Revenue		2650 00					12
13	501	Advertising Expense	75 00						13
14	505	Maintenance Expense	600 00						14
15	510	Rent Expense	700 00						15
16	515	Utilities Expense	125 00						16
17									17

Figure 8–3 Work Sheet with Account Names and Trial Balance Amounts

Key Points

The Work Sheet
On the work sheet, enter the number, name, and end-of-period balance of *every* account in the general ledger.

All the general ledger accounts are listed on the work sheet, even those that have a zero balance. Listing all the accounts avoids accidentally omitting an account and ensures that the work sheet contains all the accounts needed to prepare the financial reports.

Trial Balance Section. The end-of-period balance in the general ledger for each account is entered in the appropriate amount column of the Trial Balance section. Accounts with debit balances are entered in the Trial

Balance debit column. Accounts with credit balances are entered in the Trial Balance credit column. If an account has a zero balance at the end of the period, a line is drawn in the normal balance column. Notice in **Figure 8–3** that a line was drawn in the Trial Balance debit column for Accounts Receivable—Green Company. Lines were also recorded in the Trial Balance debit and credit columns for Income Summary since this account does not have a normal balance side. You'll learn more about the Income Summary account in Chapter 10.

Ruling and Totaling the Trial Balance Section

Ruling means "drawing a line." In accounting, a single rule drawn under a column of amounts means that the entries above the rule are to be added or subtracted. After all account names and balances are entered on the work sheet, a single line is drawn under the last entry and across both amount columns of the Trial Balance section as shown in **Figure 8–4**. The debit and credit columns are now ready for totaling. If the ledger balances, the total debits will equal the total credits. Look again at **Figure 8–4**. The totals match, with each column totaling $39,775. Since total debits equal total credits, a double rule is drawn across both amount columns just beneath the totals. This double rule means that the amounts just above are totals and that no other entries will be made in the Trial Balance columns.

If the total debits do not equal the total credits, there is an error. Find and correct the error before completing the work sheet. Procedures for locating errors are discussed in Chapter 7.

Roadrunner Delivery Service

Work Sheet

For the Month Ended October 31, 20--

	ACCT. NO.	ACCOUNT NAME	TRIAL BALANCE		INCOME STATEMENT		BALANCE SHEET		
			DEBIT	CREDIT	DEBIT	CREDIT	DEBIT	CREDIT	
1	101	Cash in Bank	21 125 00						1
2	105	Accts. Rec.—City News	1 450 00						2
3	110	Accts. Rec.—Green Company	—						3
4	115	Computer Equipment	3 000 00						4
5	120	Office Equipment	200 00						5
6	125	Delivery Equipment	12 000 00						6
7	201	Accts. Pay.—Beacon Advertising		75 00					7
8	205	Accts. Pay.—North Shore Auto		11 650 00					8
9	301	Maria Sanchez, Capital		25 400 00					9
10	302	Maria Sanchez, Withdrawals	500 00						10
11	303	Income Summary	—	—					11
12	401	Delivery Revenue		2 650 00					12
13	501	Advertising Expense	75 00						13
14	505	Maintenance Expense	600 00						14
15	510	Rent Expense	700 00						15
16	515	Utilities Expense	125 00						16
17			39 775 00	39 775 00					17
18									18

Figure 8–4 Work Sheet with Trial Balance Section Completed

Now that you have studied this section, complete the following questions and problems.

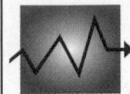

Thinking Critically

1. What is the purpose of the work sheet?
2. What is the purpose of ruling in accounting?

Communicating Accounting

Your accounting firm, AccountFast, volunteered to provide mentors to area schools for accounting and math programs. As a mentor, you are assigned to work with three accounting students. Your topic for this week is "Ruling and Totaling the Trial Balance." Create a handout to explain and illustrate this topic. Use any company, accounts, and account balances you wish. Remember, it is helpful to provide step-by-step instructions.

Problem 8–1 Entering Account Balances on the Work Sheet

The following accounts appear on the work sheet for Lee's Bike Shop.

Store Equipment	Scott Lee, Capital	Scott Lee, Withdrawals
Rent Expense	Advertising Expense	Maintenance Expense
Service Fees Revenue	Accts. Rec.—John Langer	Office Supplies
Accts. Pay.—Rubino Supply		

Instructions Use a form similar to the one below in your working papers. Classify each account and use an "x" to indicate whether the account balance is entered in the debit or the credit column of the Trial Balance section. The first account is completed as an example.

Account Name	Classification	Trial Balance	
		Debit	Credit
Store Equipment	Asset	X	

Problem 8–2 Analyzing a Source Document

Instructions Based on the invoice presented here, answer the following questions in your working papers.

1. Which company shipped the supplies?
2. Which company ordered the supplies?
3. On what date were the supplies received?
4. What does one box of file folders cost?
5. How many ring binders were ordered?
6. What is the invoice number?

Hailey Office Supply		**INVOICE NO. 220**
2763 East Meadow Ave.		
Richardson, TX 75080	DATE:	June 3, 20--
	ORDER NO.:	PO304
Garmot Electrical Co.	SHIPPED BY:	Truck
TO 15638 Lone Star Highway	TERMS:	Net 30
Plano, TX 75074		

QTY.	ITEM	UNIT PRICE	TOTAL
2	Ring Binders, 37546	$ 2.94	$ 5.88
1	Bond Paper, 27361	5.83	5.83
2	Rotary Cards, 62744	1.75	3.50
4	Fine-Tip Markers, 28733	.84	3.36
4	File Folders, Box 36206	6.23	24.92
			$43.49
	Sales Tax		2.17
REC'D 6/15/20--	Total		$45.66

Extending Amounts Across the Work Sheet

In the previous section you learned how to prepare and prove the Trial Balance section of the work sheet. In this section, you will learn how to extend account balances across the work sheet to the Balance Sheet section and the Income Statement section.

The Balance Sheet Section

The Balance Sheet section of the work sheet contains the "balance sheet accounts"—asset, liability, and owner's equity accounts. After the Trial Balance section is proved, the next step is to *extend,* or transfer, the appropriate amounts to the Balance Sheet section. To do this, copy the Trial Balance section amounts for the asset, liability, and owner's equity accounts to the appropriate Balance Sheet amount columns. Start with the first account and extend each account balance. Extend debit amounts to the Balance Sheet debit column. Extend credit amounts to the Balance Sheet credit column. The work sheet in **Figure 8–5** shows the balances extended to the Balance Sheet section.

The Income Statement Section

The next step in completing the work sheet is to extend the appropriate account balances to the Income Statement section. The Income Statement section of the work sheet contains the revenue and expense accounts. After the asset, liability, and owner's equity account balances are extended to the Balance Sheet section, the revenue and expense account balances are transferred to the Income Statement section. Because revenue accounts have a normal credit balance, revenue account balances are extended to the credit column of the Income Statement section. Since expense accounts have a normal debit balance, expense account balances are transferred to the debit column of the Income Statement section. Notice the amounts in the debit and credit columns of the Income Statement section in **Figure 8–6.**

What You'll Learn

- How to extend amounts to the Balance Sheet and Income Statement sections.
- The importance of the matching principle.
- How to calculate and show the net income or net loss on the work sheet.

Why It's Important

Preparing the work sheet helps you understand the relationship of all ledger accounts and where they are reported.

KEY TERMS

matching principle
net income
net loss

Roadrunner Delivery Service

Work Sheet

For the Month Ended October 31, 20--

	ACCT. NO.	ACCOUNT NAME	TRIAL BALANCE DEBIT	TRIAL BALANCE CREDIT	INCOME STATEMENT DEBIT	INCOME STATEMENT CREDIT	BALANCE SHEET DEBIT	BALANCE SHEET CREDIT	
1	101	Cash in Bank	21125 00				21125 00		1
2	105	Accts. Rec.—City News	1450 00				1450 00		2
3	110	Accts. Rec.—Green Company	—				—		3
4	115	Computer Equipment	3000 00				3000 00		4
5	120	Office Equipment	200 00				200 00		5
6	125	Delivery Equipment	12000 00				12000 00		6
7	201	Accts. Pay.—Beacon Advertising		75 00				75 00	7
8	205	Accts. Pay.—North Shore Auto		11650 00				11650 00	8
9	301	Maria Sanchez, Capital		25400 00				25400 00	9
10	302	Maria Sanchez, Withdrawals	500 00				500 00		10
11	303	Income Summary							11
12	401	Delivery Revenue		2650 00					12
13	501	Advertising Expense	75 00						13
14	505	Maintenance Expense	600 00						14
15	510	Rent Expense	700 00						15
16	515	Utilities Expense	125 00						16
17			39775 00	39775 00					17
18									18

Figure 8–5 Work Sheet with Trial Balance Amounts Extended to Balance Sheet Section

Roadrunner Delivery Service

Work Sheet

For the Month Ended October 31, 20--

	ACCT. NO.	ACCOUNT NAME	TRIAL BALANCE DEBIT	TRIAL BALANCE CREDIT	INCOME STATEMENT DEBIT	INCOME STATEMENT CREDIT	BALANCE SHEET DEBIT	BALANCE SHEET CREDIT	
1	101	Cash in Bank	21125 00				21125 00		1
2	105	Accts. Rec.—City News	1450 00				1450 00		2
3	110	Accts. Rec.—Green Company	—				—		3
4	115	Computer Equipment	3000 00				3000 00		4
5	120	Office Equipment	200 00				200 00		5
6	125	Delivery Equipment	12000 00				12000 00		6
7	201	Accts. Pay.—Beacon Advertising		75 00				75 00	7
8	205	Accts. Pay.—North Shore Auto		11650 00				11650 00	8
9	301	Maria Sanchez, Capital		25400 00				25400 00	9
10	302	Maria Sanchez, Withdrawals	500 00				500 00		10
11	303	Income Summary	—	—					11
12	401	Delivery Revenue		2650 00		2650 00			12
13	501	Advertising Expense	75 00		75 00				13
14	505	Maintenance Expense	600 00		600 00				14
15	510	Rent Expense	700 00		700 00				15
16	515	Utilities Expense	125 00		125 00				16
17			39775 00	39775 00					17
18									18

Figure 8–6 Work Sheet with Trial Balance Amounts Extended to Income Statement Section

Totaling the Income Statement and Balance Sheet Sections

After all the amounts in the Trial Balance section are extended to the Balance Sheet and Income Statement sections, each section is totaled. A single rule is drawn across the four debit and credit columns to indicate that the columns are ready to be added. Look now at **Figure 8–7.** After the four columns are totaled, notice that the debit and credit columns in each section are not equal. Unlike the Trial Balance section debit and credit totals, the column totals in these two sections will not be equal until the net income or net loss for the period is added.

Roadrunner Delivery Service
Work Sheet
For the Month Ended October 31, 20--

	ACCT. NO.	ACCOUNT NAME	TRIAL BALANCE DEBIT	TRIAL BALANCE CREDIT	INCOME STATEMENT DEBIT	INCOME STATEMENT CREDIT	BALANCE SHEET DEBIT	BALANCE SHEET CREDIT	
1	101	Cash in Bank	21125 00				21125 00		1
2	105	Accts. Rec.—City News	1450 00				1450 00		2
3	110	Accts. Rec.—Green Company	—				—		3
4	115	Computer Equipment	3000 00				3000 00		4
5	120	Office Equipment	200 00				200 00		5
6	125	Delivery Equipment	12000 00				12000 00		6
7	201	Accts. Pay.—Beacon Advertising		75 00				75 00	7
8	205	Accts. Pay.—North Shore Auto		11650 00				11650 00	8
9	301	Maria Sanchez, Capital		25400 00				25400 00	9
10	302	Maria Sanchez, Withdrawals	500 00				500 00		10
11	303	Income Summary	—	—	—				11
12	401	Delivery Revenue		2650 00		2650 00			12
13	501	Advertising Expense	75 00		75 00				13
14	505	Maintenance Expense	600 00		600 00				14
15	510	Rent Expense	700 00		700 00				15
16	515	Utilities Expense	125 00		125 00				16
17			39775 00	39775 00	1500 00	2650 00	38275 00	37125 00	17
18									18

Figure 8–7 Work Sheet with Income Statement and Balance Sheet Sections Totaled

Showing Net Income on the Work Sheet

The Income Statement section of the work sheet includes both the revenue and the expenses for the period. In accounting, expenses incurred in an accounting period are matched with the revenue earned during the same period. This comparison is referred to as the **matching principle** . Matching expenses of a period with revenue of the same period provides a reliable measure of profit, because it shows the cost (expense) of producing the revenue. This information helps the business owner or manager analyze results and then make decisions.

After the Income Statement section columns are totaled, total expenses (the debit column total) are subtracted from total revenue (the credit column total) to find the net income. **Net income** is the amount of revenue that remains after expenses for the period are subtracted. Net income is entered as a debit at the bottom of the Income Statement section of the work sheet. Look at **Figure 8–8.** Roadrunner's net income is $1,150.

1. Skip a line after the last account and write the words "Net Income" in the Account Name column. **A**
2. On the same line, enter the net income amount in the Income statement debit column. **B**
3. On the same line, enter the net income amount in the Balance sheet credit column. **C**

Roadrunner Delivery Service

Work Sheet

For the Month Ended October 31, 20--

	ACCT. NO.	ACCOUNT NAME	TRIAL BALANCE		INCOME STATEMENT		BALANCE SHEET		
			DEBIT	CREDIT	DEBIT	CREDIT	DEBIT	CREDIT	
1	101	Cash in Bank	21 125 00				21 125 00		1
2	105	Accts. Rec.—City News	1 450 00				1 450 00		2
3	110	Accts. Rec.—Green Company	—				—		3
4	115	Computer Equipment	3 000 00				3 000 00		4
5	120	Office Equipment	200 00				200 00		5
6	125	Delivery Equipment	12 000 00				12 000 00		6
7	201	Accts. Pay.—Beacon Advertising		75 00				75 00	7
8	205	Accts. Pay.—North Shore Auto		11 650 00				11 650 00	8
9	301	Maria Sanchez, Capital		25 400 00				25 400 00	9
10	302	Maria Sanchez, Withdrawals	500 00				500 00		10
11	303	Income Summary	—	—	—	—			11
12	401	Delivery Revenue		2 650 00		2 650 00			12
13	501	Advertising Expense	75 00		75 00				13
14	505	Maintenance Expense	600 00		600 00				14
15	510	Rent Expense	700 00		700 00				15
16	515	Utilities Expense	125 00		125 00				16
17			39 775 00	39 775 00	1 500 00	2 650 00	38 275 00	37 125 00	17
18		Net Income			1 150 00			1 150 00	18
19									19

A   B   C

Figure 8–8 Partial Work Sheet with Net Income

The amount of net income is also reflected in the Balance Sheet section of the work sheet. Remember, revenue and expense accounts are temporary capital accounts. As you can see in **Figure 8–9,** revenues increase capital, while expenses decrease capital. Net income, therefore, increases capital since revenues exceed expenses. During the accounting period, revenue and expense amounts are recorded in the temporary capital accounts (like **Delivery Revenue** and **Utilities Expense**). At the end of the period, net income is transferred to the owner's capital account. Since the capital account is increased by credits, the amount of the net income is entered in the credit column of the Balance Sheet section of the work sheet.

The Effects of Income or Loss on Capital

Revenues   >   Expenses   =   Net income   Capital increases

Revenues   <   Expenses   =   Net loss   Capital decreases

Figure 8–9 The Effects of Income or Loss on Capital

To check the accuracy of the net income amount in the Balance Sheet section, subtract the total of the credit column from the total of the debit column. If the result equals the net income computed in the Income Statement section, enter the net income in the credit column of the Balance Sheet section. If the result does not equal net income, there is an error. Before continuing, you must find and correct the error. To find the error, check that the amounts from the Trial Balance section are extended correctly and that the totals of all columns are added correctly.

Completing the Work Sheet

The completed work sheet for Roadrunner is shown in **Figure 8–10.** To complete the Income Statement and Balance Sheet sections, follow these steps:

1. On the line under the net income amount, draw a single rule across the four columns. **D**
2. In the Income Statement section debit column, add the net income amount to the previous total and enter the new total. Bring down the total of the Income Statement section credit column. Total debits should equal total credits. **E**

	ACCT. NO.	ACCOUNT NAME	TRIAL BALANCE DEBIT	TRIAL BALANCE CREDIT	INCOME STATEMENT DEBIT	INCOME STATEMENT CREDIT	BALANCE SHEET DEBIT	BALANCE SHEET CREDIT	
1	101	Cash in Bank	21125 00				21125 00		1
2	105	Accts. Receivable—City News	1450 00				1450 00		2
3	110	Accts. Receivable—Green Company	—				—		3
4	115	Computer Equipment	3000 00				3000 00		4
5	120	Office Equipment	200 00				200 00		5
6	125	Delivery Equipment	12000 00				12000 00		6
7	201	Accts. Payable—Beacon Advertising		75 00				75 00	7
8	205	Accounts Pay.—North Shore Auto		11650 00				11650 00	8
9	301	Maria Sanchez, Capital		25400 00				25400 00	9
10	302	Maria Sanchez, Withdrawals	500 00				500 00		10
11	303	Income Summary	—	—					11
12	401	Delivery Revenue		2650 00		2650 00			12
13	501	Advertising Expense	75 00		75 00				13
14	505	Maintenance Expense	600 00		600 00				14
15	510	Rent Expense	700 00		700 00				15
16	515	Utilities Expense	125 00		125 00				16
17			39775 00	39775 00	1500 00	2650 00	38275 00	37125 00	17
18		Net Income			1150 00			1150 00	18
19					2650 00	2650 00	38275 00	38275 00	19
20									20

A   B D   E   F   G C

Figure 8–10 Completed Work Sheet

3. In the Balance Sheet section credit column, add net income to the previous total and enter the new total. Bring down the total of the Balance Sheet section debit column. The total debit amount should equal the total credit amount. **F**

4. In the Balance Sheet and Income Statement sections, draw a double rule under the four column totals. The double rule indicates that the debit and credit columns are equal and that no more amounts are to be entered in these columns. **G**

Showing a Net Loss on the Work Sheet

When total expenses are greater than total revenue, a **net loss** occurs. A net loss decreases owner's equity. This decrease is shown as a debit to the capital account. On the work sheet when a net loss occurs, the Income Statement section debit column total (total expenses) is greater than the Income Statement section credit column total (total revenue). The steps

to complete the work sheet are the same as described for Net Income except that the words "Net Loss" are written in the Account Name column and the net loss amount is entered in the credit column of the Income Statement section and the debit column of the Balance Sheet section. The partial work sheet in **Figure 8–11** shows a net loss. Expenses exceed revenue by $746.

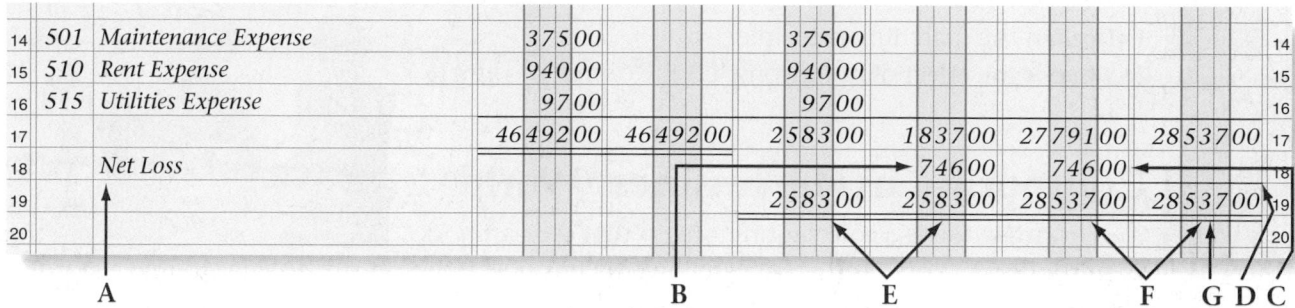

14	501	Maintenance Expense	375 00			375 00					14
15	510	Rent Expense	940 00			940 00					15
16	515	Utilities Expense	97 00			97 00					16
17			46492 00	46492 00		2583 00	1837 00	27791 00	28537 00		17
18		Net Loss					746 00		746 00		18
19						2583 00	2583 00	28537 00	28537 00		19
20											20

A   B   E   F G D C

Figure 8–11 Partial Work Sheet Showing a Net Loss

A Review of the Steps in Preparing a Six-Column Work Sheet

Follow these steps when preparing a six-column work sheet:

1. Write the heading on the work sheet.
2. In the Account Name and Trial Balance sections, enter the account numbers, names, and balances for all accounts in the general ledger.
3. Prove the equality of total debits and total credits in the Trial Balance section.
4. Extend the amounts of the Trial Balance section to the appropriate columns in the Balance Sheet and Income Statement sections.
5. Total the columns in the Income Statement and Balance Sheet sections.
6. Determine the amount of the net income or the net loss for the period.
7. Enter the amount of the net income or the net loss in the appropriate columns in the Income Statement and Balance Sheet sections.
8. Total and rule the Income Statement and Balance Sheet sections.

A MATTER OF ETHICS

Padding Expense Accounts

Imagine that you're an auditor for an accounting firm like PricewaterhouseCoopers. You and a co-worker, Mark, have been sent to Chicago to perform an audit. You have an allowance of $200 a day to cover lodging, meals, and transportation. At the end of the trip, you are to turn in an expense account report detailing how you spent the allowance. Mark adds a few dollars to each of his expenses so he can have some extra cash. You figure that the firm won't miss a few dollars, so you consider doing the same.

Ethical Decision Making:

☞ What are the ethical issues?

☞ What are the alternatives?

☞ Who are the affected parties?

☞ How do the alternatives affect the parties?

☞ What would you do?

Now that you have studied this section, complete the following questions and problem.

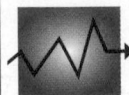

Thinking Critically

1. Explain the matching principle.
2. What is the effect of net income on the capital account?

Computing in the Business World

For Art's Sake is a sole proprietorship that sells artwork. Even though the operating costs are low, the business relies on steady sales to make a profit. The first two quarterly financial statements for this year have been grim. Using the revenue and expense information for the third quarter, calculate the net profit or loss. (Balances of the Accounts Receivable accounts represent third-quarter revenue.) Compare the third quarter figure with the figures from the first and second quarters. What do you predict the future of For Art's Sake will be?

Third Quarter

Rent Expense	$2,000
Utilities Expense	800
Advertising Expense	3,000
Maintenance Expense	1,200
Accounts Receivable—Sammy Wong	500
Accounts Receivable—The Artist Collection	5,525
Accounts Receivable—Vera Samuels	3,200

Second Quarter   Net Loss = $2,000

First Quarter   Net Loss = $1,200

Problem 8-3 Extending Amounts Across the Work Sheet

The following account balances appear in the Account Name section of the work sheet for Lee's Bike Shop.

Store Equipment	Advertising Expense
Rent Expense	Accounts Receivable—John Langer
Service Fees Revenue	Scott Lee, Withdrawals
Accounts Payable—Rubino Supply	Maintenance Expense
Scott Lee, Capital	Office Supplies

Instructions Use a form similar to the one below in your working papers or on a separate sheet of paper. For the above accounts, enter an "X" in the column where the account balance is transferred. The first account has been completed as an example.

Account Name	Income Statement		Balance Sheet	
	Debit	Credit	Debit	Credit
Store Equipment			X	

KEY CONCEPTS

1. Preparing a work sheet is the sixth step in the accounting cycle.
2. A work sheet gathers all the information needed to complete the end-of-period work.
3. The work sheet heading contains three kinds of information:

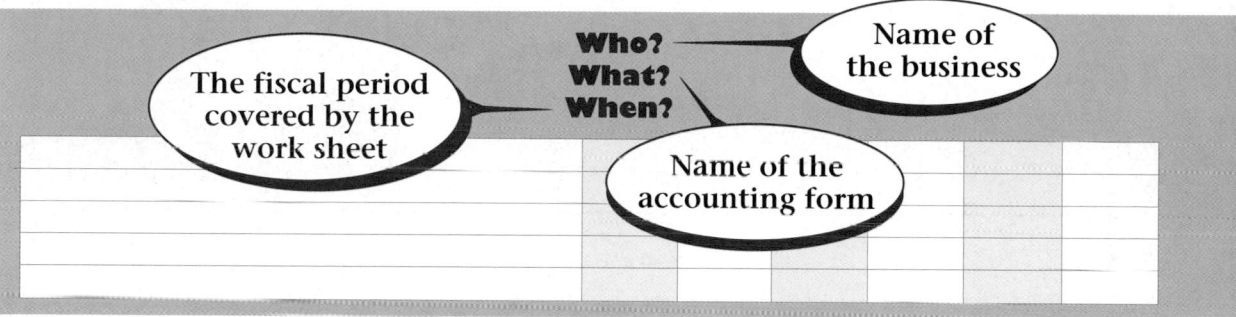

The fiscal period covered by the work sheet

Who? What? When?

Name of the business

Name of the accounting form

4. The Account Name section of the work sheet lists all general ledger account names, along with the account numbers.
5. Complete the Trial Balance section of the work sheet first. Total debits and total credits in the Trial Balance section must be equal.
6. Extend amounts from the Trial Balance section to the Balance Sheet section and then to the Income Statement section.
7. Use the work sheet to calculate the net income or net loss for the period. A net income results when revenue is greater than expenses. A net loss results when expenses are greater than revenue.
8. Show a net income as a debit on the Income Statement section and as a credit on the Balance Sheet section.

Account Name	Income Statement		Balance Sheet	
	Debit	Credit	Debit	Credit
Net Income	X			X

9. Show a net loss as a credit on the Income Statement section and as a debit on the Balance Sheet section.

Account Name	Income Statement		Balance Sheet	
	Debit	Credit	Debit	Credit
Net Loss		X	X	

10. A double rule means that the amount immediately above is a total and that no additional amounts will be entered in the amount column.

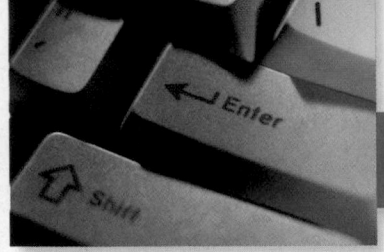

USING KEY TERMS

You just finished the work sheet for the third quarter and it looks like your company will make considerable profits. In the second quarter the company had experienced a net loss. On a separate sheet of paper, write a memo to your boss, Tonya Newman, asking her to review your trial balance and work sheet. Use the terms listed below in your memo.

matching principle	ruling
net income	work sheet
net loss	

Understanding Accounting Concepts and Procedures

Instructions

On a separate sheet of paper, answer the following questions:

1. Preparing the work sheet is which step of the accounting cycle?
2. Explain why a work sheet is prepared.
3. List the items that should be included in the work sheet heading.
4. Name and briefly describe the five parts of a six-column work sheet.
5. In what order are the account names listed on the work sheet?
6. Why are all accounts, including those with zero balances, listed on the work sheet?
7. What does the Trial Balance section of the work sheet prove when it has been totaled and ruled?
8. Which types of accounts are extended to the Balance Sheet section of the work sheet?
9. Which types of accounts are extended to the Income Statement section of the work sheet?
10. Why is the matching principle important?
11. Explain how to record net income on the work sheet.
12. Explain how to record a net loss on the work sheet.
13. What effect does net income have on owner's equity?
14. What effect does a net loss have on owner's equity?
15. What does a double rule on the work sheet indicate?

Case Study...

Service Business: Advertising Agency

You work for Creative Advertising as an assistant to the company's accountant. You're preparing a work sheet for the month of July. The trial balance totals are $127,750 and you've extended the account balances to the amount columns in the Balance Sheet and Income Statement sections. After adding the Balance Sheet and Income Statement columns and calculating net income, you find that the totals do not balance.

Thinking Critically:
1. What steps would you take to find the problem?
2. Provide a likely reason why the net income amounts do not match.

*inter*NET CONNECTION

The Big Four
The largest public accounting firms are often referred to as the "Big Four." These firms practice internationally and provide accounting and business services to clients of all sizes.

Do This:
1. Consult the AICPA Web site, or other accounting-related Web sites to find the names of the "Big Four" firms.
2. List the Web site for each firm.
3. Do any of these firms have offices near you? If so, where are these offices located?

Conducting an Audit with Alex

Instructions The trial balance below is out of balance. Find and correct the errors, re-total the debit and credit columns, and prove the correctness of the account balances.

ACCT NO.	ACCOUNT NAME	DEBIT	CREDIT
101	Cash in Bank	7 3 4 1 00	
105	Accts. Rec.—Jon Vasi	2 1 9 00	
110	Accts. Rec.—Sheila Henry	3 4 6 00	
115	Accts. Rec.—Frank Gawle	8 0 00	
120	Supplies		3 1 9 00
125	Office Furniture	3 6 8 3 00	
130	Store Equipment	2 0 4 7 00	
135	Computer Equipment	6 4 2 0 00	
205	Accts. Pay.—Westport Supply		2 3 1 00
210	Accts. Pay.—Bradley Co.		1 8 2 9 00
215	Accts. Pay.—Jackson Brothers	2 1 6 3 00	
301	James Haily, Capital		14 1 9 8 00
302	James Haily, Withdrawals		1 8 0 0 00
303	Income Summary		
405	Delivery Revenue	1 8 1 4 00	
410	Repair Revenue		7 2 0 3 00
501	Advertising Expense		6 0 0 00
505	Maintenance Expense	1 3 8 4 00	
510	Miscellaneous Expense	7 6 00	
515	Rent Expense	2 3 0 0 00	
520	Repair Expense	3 0 5 00	
525	Utilities Expense		5 1 8 00
		28 1 7 8 00	26 6 9 8 00

Workplace Skills

Understanding Social and Organizational Systems
- Can you read and interpret a company's organizational chart?
- Can you identify who reports to whom?
If you can answer "yes" to these questions, then you can probably work and operate effectively within an organizational system.

On the Job:
Your employer, The Teen Scene, was just bought out by a large, national clothing chain—Natural Fibers. The buyout has created a massive reorganization.

Thinking Critically:
1. The change from a small clothing store to a national chain store has affected employee morale. What do you think would help build loyalty to Natural Fibers?
2. How would an organizational chart that depicts who reports to whom help with the transition?

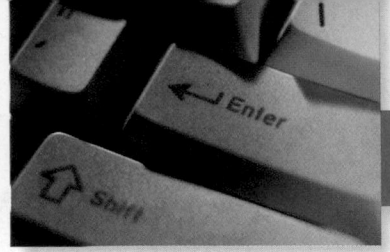

CHAPTER 8 COMPUTERIZED ACCOUNTING

The Trial Balance

Making the Transition from a Manual to a Computerized System

Task	Perform Accounting Procedures Using Manual Methods	Perform Accounting Procedures Using Automated Methods
Preparing the trial balance	1. After all journal entries have been posted and all general ledger balances have been updated, list account names and balances on two column accounting stationery. 2. List debit balances in one column and credit balances in the other. 3. Add all debit balances. 4. Add all credit balances. 5. Compare the totals. If totals are not in balance, locate and correct any journalizing or posting errors. 6. The trial balance is correct when total debits equal total credits.	1. Although the Trial Balance is not necessary to check the equality of debits and credits since out-of-balance entries cannot be posted, it is one of the most commonly used accounting statements. It provides a clear list format for reviewing accounts.

Preparing a Trial Balance

Peachtree Question	Description
How do I generate a trial balance in Peachtree?	1. Select **General Ledger** from the ***Reports*** menu. 2. Select General Ledger Trial Balance from the Reports list. 3. Click *Print*.
What does the software do "behind the scenes?"	• The software automatically pulls up all account names and their current balances and lists them on a preformatted report. • The software will not allow an out-of-balance journal entry to be posted. Therefore, the accounting records stay in balance.

For detailed instructions: See the Peachtree User Guide in your Glencoe Working Papers.

198   **Chapter 8**   Computerized Accounting

APPLICATION OPTIONS

Problem 8–4 Preparing a Six-Column Work Sheet

The ending balances in the general ledger accounts of Wilderness Rentals for the period ended May 31 follow.

		Debit Balances	Credit Balances
101	Cash in Bank	$5,814	
105	Accts. Rec.—Helen Katz	717	
110	Accts. Rec.—Polk and Co.	590	
115	Office Supplies	847	
120	Office Equipment	4,360	
125	Camping Equipment	6,130	
201	Accts. Pay.—Adventure Equipment Inc.		$ 1,680
203	Accts. Pay.—Digital Tech Computers		3,554
205	Accts. Pay.—Greg Mollaro		635
301	Ronald Hicks, Capital		12,760
305	Ronald Hicks, Withdrawals	1,200	
310	Income Summary	—	—
401	Equipment Rental Revenue		9,716
501	Advertising Expense	1,940	
505	Maintenance Expense	1,083	
515	Rent Expense	3,500	
525	Utilities Expense	2,164	

Instructions Prepare a work sheet for the period ended May 31.

1. Write the heading on the work sheet.
2. List all of the accounts in the Account Name and Trial Balance sections. For each account, include the account number, name, and balance.
3. Total and rule the Trial Balance section. Do total debits equal total credits? If not, find and correct the problem before continuing.
4. Extend the appropriate amounts to the Balance Sheet section.
5. Extend the appropriate amounts to the Income Statement section.
6. Total the amount columns in the Income Statement and Balance Sheet sections.
7. Enter the amount of net income or net loss in the appropriate columns in the Income Statement and Balance Sheet sections.
8. Total and rule the Income Statement and Balance Sheet sections.

Analyze: What is the net income or net loss for the period?

Complete chapter problems one of four ways:

1 **Manual** Glencoe Working Papers

or

2 **Peachtree Complete Accounting** Software

or

3 **QuickBooks** Templates (Problems 8–5, 8–6)

or

4 **Spreadsheet** Templates (Problems 8–4, 8–8)

SPREADSHEET SMART GUIDE

Step–by–Step Instructions: Problem 8–4

1. Select the spreadsheet template for Problem 8–4.
2. Enter your name and the date in the spaces provided on the template.
3. Complete the spreadsheet using the instructions in your working papers.
4. Print the spreadsheet and proof your work.
5. Save your work and exit the spreadsheet program.

Peachtree®

SMART GUIDE

Step–by–Step Instructions:
Problem 8–5

1. Select the problem set for Hot Suds Car Wash (Prob. 8–5).
2. Rename the company and set the system date.
3. Print a General Ledger Trial Balance.
4. End the session.

TIP: As a shortcut, you can choose to print the trial balance from the **General Ledger** Navigation Aid.

Problem 8–5 Preparing a Six-Column Work Sheet

The general ledger for Hot Suds Car Wash shows the following account balances on May 31, the end of the period.

101	Cash in Bank	$9,400
105	Accts. Rec.—Linda Brown	429
110	Accts. Rec.—Valley Auto	372
115	Detailing Supplies	694
120	Detergent Supplies	418
125	Office Equipment	15,195
130	Office Furniture	2,029
135	Car Wash Equipment	7,486
201	Accts. Pay.—Allen Vacuum Systems	4,346
205	Accts. Pay.—O'Brian's Office Supply	2,730
301	Regina Delgado, Capital	26,530
305	Regina Delgado, Withdrawals	2,500
310	Income Summary	
401	Wash Revenue	7,957
405	Wax Revenue	5,329
410	Interior Detailing Revenue	2,970
501	Advertising Expense	1,940
505	Equipment Rental Expense	3,836
510	Maintenance Expense	1,424
520	Rent Expense	3,500
530	Utilities Expense	639

Instructions Prepare a work sheet for Hot Suds Car Wash in your working papers.

Analyze: Why are there three revenue accounts?

Peachtree®

SMART GUIDE

Step–by–Step Instructions:
Problem 8–6

1. Select the problem set for Kits & Pups Grooming (Prob. 8–6).
2. Rename the company and set the system date.
3. Print a General Ledger Trial Balance.
4. End the session.

Problem 8–6 Preparing a Six-Column Work Sheet

The account balances in the general ledger of Kits & Pups Grooming at the end of May are:

101	Cash in Bank	$11,194
105	Accts. Rec.—Juan Alvarez	357
110	Accts. Rec.—Nathan Carlsbad	547
115	Accts. Rec.—Martha Giles	1,450
120	Grooming Supplies	842
125	Office Equipment	4,147
130	Office Furniture	935
135	Computer Equipment	2,200
140	Grooming Equipment	1,948
145	Kennel Equipment	7,305
201	Accts. Pay.—Able Store Equipment	7,945
205	Accts. Pay.—Dogs & Cats Inc.	1,205
207	Accts. Pay.—Pet Gourmet	2,846
301	Abe Shultz, Capital	23,048

305	Abe Shultz, Withdrawals	2,500
310	Income Summary	—
401	Boarding Revenue	11,596
405	Grooming Revenue	4,496
501	Advertising Expense	3,675
505	Equipment Repair Expense	932
510	Maintenance Expense	2,658
520	Rent Expense	7,500
530	Utilities Expense	2,946

Instructions Prepare a work sheet for the month ended May 31 for Kits & Pups Grooming in your working papers.

Analyze: The balances of revenue and expense accounts are extended to which work sheet section?

Problem 8–7 Preparing a Six-Column Work Sheet

The general ledger account balances on May 31 for Outback Guide Service are:

101	Cash in Bank	$ 2,834
105	Accts. Rec.—Mary Johnson	384
125	Office Supplies	307
130	Office Equipment	5,902
135	Office Furniture	2,804
140	Computer Equipment	3,295
145	Hiking Equipment	922
150	Rafting Equipment	8,351
205	Accts. Pay.—Peak Equipment Inc.	1,204
301	Juanita Ortega, Capital	20,419
302	Juanita Ortega, Withdrawals	1,800
310	Income Summary	—
401	Guide Service Revenue	9,179
501	Advertising Expense	795
505	Maintenance Expense	125
515	Rent Expense	2,000
525	Utilities Expense	1,283

Instructions Prepare a work sheet for Outback Guide Service for the period ended May 31 in your working papers.

Analyze: What is the total of all of Outback's assets?

Peachtree®

SMART GUIDE

Step–by–Step Instructions: Problem 8–7

1. Select the problem set for Outback Guide Service (Prob. 8–7).
2. Rename the company and set the system date.
3. Print a General Ledger Trial Balance.
4. End the session.

SPREADSHEET SMART GUIDE

Step–by–Step Instructions: Problem 8–8

1. Select the spreadsheet template for Problem 8–8.
2. Enter your name and the date in the spaces provided on the template.
3. Complete the spreadsheet using the instructions in your working papers.
4. Print the spreadsheet and proof your work.
5. Save your work and exit the spreadsheet program.

Problem 8–8 Completing the Work Sheet

The work sheet for Job Connect appears in your working papers. The amounts that have been entered are correct. Several amounts, however, are missing from various columns.

Instructions Calculate all missing amounts and complete the work sheet.

Analyze: What is the net income or net loss for Job Connect?

CHAPTER 9

Financial Statements for a Sole Proprietorship

Learning Objectives

When you have completed this chapter, you will be able to:

- ▶ Explain the purpose of the income statement.

- ▶ Prepare an income statement.

- ▶ Explain the purpose of a statement of changes in owner's equity.

- ▶ Prepare a statement of changes in owner's equity.

- ▶ Explain the purpose of the balance sheet.

- ▶ Explain and compute the return on sales percentage.

- ▶ Calculate liquidity ratios and explain their function.

- ▶ Prepare a balance sheet.

- ▶ Define the accounting terms introduced in this chapter.

Exploring the Real World of Business

PREPARING FINANCIAL REPORTS

Imagine yourself just inches from the jaws of a shark—of course, from behind a thick glass wall.

The **New England Aquarium** in Boston allows you to do just that. Public aquariums date from the mid-1800s when it was discovered that marine life could live in glass containers. Modern aquariums do much more than just exhibit various forms of marine life, though. The **New England Aquarium** also supports projects that protect endangered whales and conserve coral reefs in the Indian Ocean. Staff members rescue hundreds of stranded seals, dolphins, whales, and turtles from local beaches each year.

As a public organization, the **New England Aquarium** funds its operations in several different ways. Sources of funds include memberships sold to the general public, admission fees, sales of **Aquarium**-sponsored books and films, and grants from corporate sponsors like Fleet Bank or Pepsi. The **Aquarium's** financial statements show the amounts of revenue from each source as well as how that revenue was spent during the year.

What do you think?

Why is it important for the **New England Aquarium** to prepare financial statements even though their purpose is not to earn a profit?

New England Aquarium

Workplace Connections
Applying Your Accounting Knowledge

A sole proprietorship can be a small business with a few employees or a large business with thousands of employees. In a small business, one person may handle the accounting duties. A larger business might have several employees working in an accounting department. Whether large or small, the preparation of financial statements is an important task.

Investigate:

1. Do you work for a sole proprietorship, a corporation, or a partnership?
2. In your work location, approximately how many people are employed?
3. If you were an accountant, do you think you would prefer to work for a large organization or a small one? Why?

The Income Statement

To operate a business profitably, a business owner needs to have current financial information. Businesses ranging from Mobil Corporation to a rural dairy farm must organize financial information to evaluate profits or losses. **Financial statements** are prepared to summarize the changes resulting from business transactions that occur during an accounting period. As you can see from **Figure 9–1**, the preparation of financial statements is the seventh step in the accounting cycle.

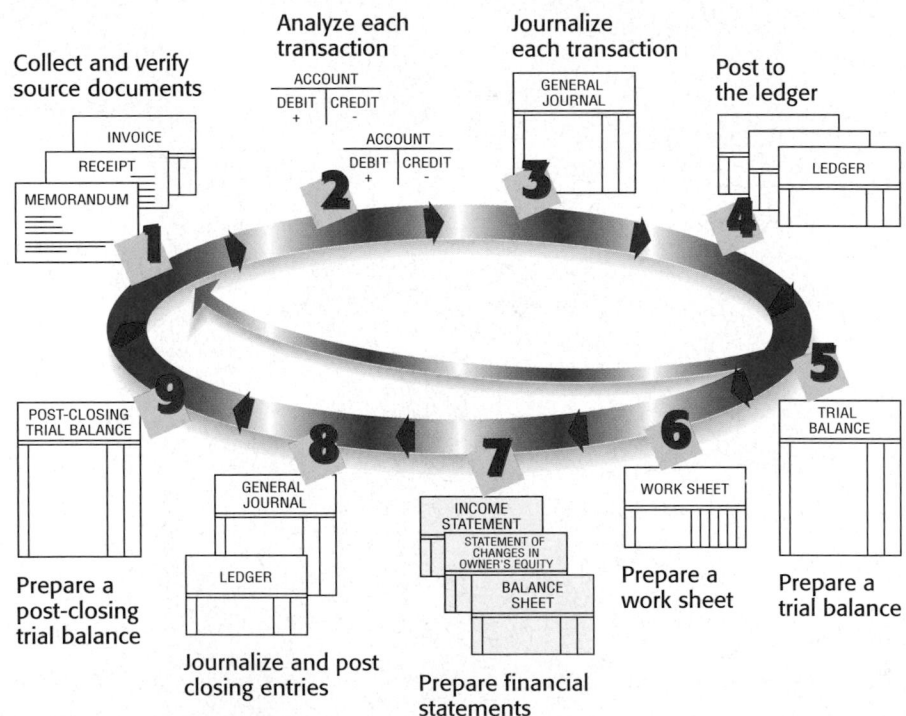

Figure 9–1 The Accounting Cycle with the Seventh Step Highlighted

Financial Statements

The primary financial statements prepared for a sole proprietorship are the income statement and the balance sheet. A third statement, the statement of changes in owner's equity, is also often prepared. The financial statements may be handwritten or typed but most often are prepared on a computer. When using a computerized accounting system, the information for preparing the financial statements is stored in the computer. When a business owner needs financial statements, he or she can use the computer to generate them without first preparing a work sheet. Let's learn how to prepare financial statements for a service business such as Roadrunner.

The Income Statement

The **income statement** reports the net income or net loss for the period. As you recall from Chapter 8, net income or net loss is the difference between total revenue and total expenses. The main purpose of the income statement is to provide a report of the revenue earned and the expenses incurred over a specific period of time. For this reason, it is sometimes called a "profit-and-loss statement" or an "earnings statement."

The income statement contains the following sections:

- the heading
- the revenue for the period
- the expenses for the period
- the net income or net loss for the period

The Heading

Like the work sheet heading, the heading of an income statement has three parts:

1. The name of the business **(Who?)**
2. The name of the report **(What?)**
3. The period covered **(When?)**

The heading for the Roadrunner Delivery Service income statement is shown in **Figure 9–2.** Each line of the heading is centered on the width of the statement.

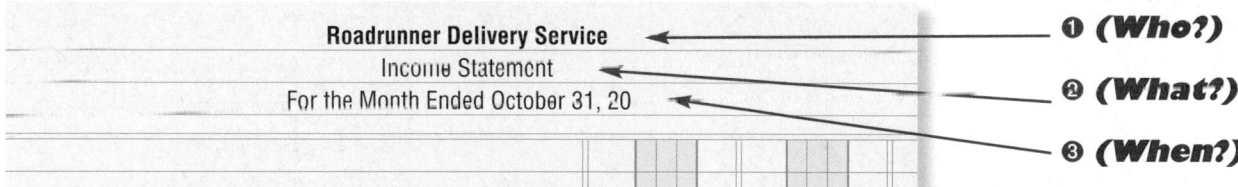

Roadrunner Delivery Service ◄——— ❶ **(Who?)**
Income Statement ◄——— ❷ **(What?)**
For the Month Ended October 31, 20-- ◄——— ❸ **(When?)**

Figure 9–2 The Heading for an Income Statement

When preparing an income statement heading, be sure to follow the wording and capitalization shown in **Figure 9–2.** The wording of the date line is especially important. The reporting period will vary from business to business and must be clearly identified.

When preparing financial statements, a business owner uses the same fiscal periods year after year. This consistency allows the owner to compare and analyze the data on financial statements from one period to the next. This comparison is difficult if one statement covers a period of one month while another statement covers a period of six months.

Reporting Period	Wording of Date Line
One month	For the Month Ended October 31, 20--
One quarter	For the Quarter Ended March 30, 20--
One year	For the Year Ended June 30, 20--

The Revenue Section

After the heading is complete, enter the revenue earned for the period. Look at **Figure 9–3.** The Income Statement section of the work sheet is the information source used in preparing the income statement.

Figure 9–3 Preparing an Income Statement

Roadrunner Delivery Service
Work Sheet
For the Month Ended October 31, 20--

	ACCT. NO.	ACCOUNT NAME	TRIAL BALANCE DEBIT	TRIAL BALANCE CREDIT	INCOME STATEMENT DEBIT	INCOME STATEMENT CREDIT	BALANCE SHEET DEBIT	BALANCE SHEET CREDIT	
1	101	Cash in Bank	21 125 00				21 125 00		1
2	105	Accts. Rec.—City News	1 450 00				1 450 00		2
3	110	Accts. Rec.—Green Company	—				—		3
4	115	Computer Equipment	3 000 00				3 000 00		4
5	120	Office Equipment	200 00				200 00		5
6	125	Delivery Equipment	12 000 00				12 000 00		6
7	201	Accts. Pay.—Beacon Advertising		75 00				75 00	7
8	205	Accts. Pay.—North Shore Auto		11 650 00				11 650 00	8
9	301	Maria Sanchez, Capital		25 400 00				25 400 00	9
10	302	Maria Sanchez, Withdrawals	500 00				500 00		10
11	303	Income Summary	—						11
12	401	Delivery Revenue		2 650 00		2 650 00			12
13	501	Advertising Expense	75 00		75 00				13
14	505	Maintenance Expense	600 00		600 00				14
15	510	Rent Expense	700 00		700 00				15
16	515	Utilities Expense	125 00		125 00				16
17			39 775 00	39 775 00	1 500 00	2 650 00	38 275 00	37 125 00	17
18		Net Income			1 150 00			1 150 00	18
19					2 650 00	2 650 00	38 275 00	38 275 00	19
20									20

Roadrunner Delivery Service
Income Statement
For the Month Ended October 31, 20--

Revenue: **A**			
Delivery Revenue **B**		2 650 00 **C**	
Expenses: **D**			
Advertising Expense	75 00		
Maintenance Expense **E**	600 00	**E**	
Rent Expense	700 00		
Utilities Expense **F**	125 00		
Total Expenses **G**		**H** 1 500 00	**I**
Net Income **K**		**J** 1 150 00	**L**

The income statement for Roadrunner is prepared on standard accounting stationery, which has a column for account names and two amount columns. The two amount columns are used to separate individual account balances from totals. The first amount column is used to enter the balances of the individual revenue and expense accounts. The second amount column is used to enter totals: total revenue, total expenses, and net income (or net loss).

Refer to **Figure 9–3** as you read the procedures for preparing an income statement:

1. Write "Revenue:" on the first line at the left side of the form. **A**
2. Enter the revenue account names beginning on the second line, indented about a half inch from the left edge of the form. **B**
3. Enter the balance of the revenue account(s). Since Roadrunner has only one revenue account, **Delivery Revenue**, total revenue is the same as the balance of the one revenue account. The balance is thus written in the second, or totals, column. **C**

Roadrunner uses one revenue account, which represents its only source of revenue. Many businesses have more than one source of revenue and thus have a separate revenue account for each source. For example, a swim club might have revenue accounts such as **Membership Fees**, **Pool Rental**, and **Instruction Revenue**.

If a business has more than one revenue account, the individual account balances are entered in the first amount column. Total revenue is then written on a separate line in the second amount column. **Figure 9–4** illustrates the revenue section of the income statement for a business with more than one revenue account. Notice that the words "Total Revenue" are indented about one inch from the left edge of the form.

Revenue:		
Rental Revenue	11 2 3 0 00	
Repair Revenue	4 8 5 0 00	
Total Revenue		16 0 8 0 00

Figure 9–4 Income Statement with More Than One Revenue Account

The Expenses Section

After total revenue is entered, the expenses incurred during the period are reported. The expense account names and the balances in the Income Statement section of the work sheet are used to prepare the expenses section of the income statement. Refer to **Figure 9–3** as you read the following instructions:

1. On the line following the revenue section, write "Expenses:" at the left side of the form. **D**
2. On the following lines, write the names of the expense accounts, indented half an inch, in the order that they appear on the work sheet. Since there are several expense accounts, enter the individual balances in the first amount column. **E**

3. Draw a single rule under the last expense account balance. **F**
4. Write the words "Total Expenses" on the line following the last expense account name, indented about one inch. **G**
5. Add the balances for all the expense accounts. Write the total expenses amount in the second amount column, one line below the last expense account balance. **H**

The Net Income Section

The next step is to enter net income. Net income, remember, occurs when total revenue is greater than total expenses. Refer to **Figure 9–3** as you read the following instructions for the preparation of the net income section.

1. Draw a single rule under the total expenses amount. **I**
2. Subtract the total expenses from the total revenue to find net income. Enter the net income in the second amount column under the total expenses amount. **J**
3. On the same line, write the words "Net Income" at the left side of the form. **K**
4. If the amount of net income matches the amount shown on the work sheet, draw a double rule under the net income amount. **L**

The income statement is complete.

If the amount of net income shown on the work sheet does not equal the amount shown on the income statement, there is an error. Since the work sheet is balanced and ruled, the error probably occurred while the income statement was being prepared. An account balance may be omitted or entered incorrectly, or there may be an error in addition or subtraction. Find and correct the error.

Showing a Net Loss

If total expenses are greater than total revenue, there is a net loss. To determine the amount of net loss, subtract total revenue from total expenses. Enter the net loss in the second amount column under total expenses amount. Write the words "Net Loss" on the same line at the left side of the form. **Figure 9–5** illustrates how to report a net loss.

Revenue:				
Delivery Revenue			3 1 7 0 00	
Expenses:				
Advertising Expense	2 7 5 00			
Maintenance Expense	7 5 0 00			
Miscellaneous Expense	2 7 0 00			
Rent Expense	1 9 0 0 00			
Utilities Expense	3 2 5 00			
Total Expenses			3 5 2 0 00	
Net Loss			3 5 0 00	

Figure 9–5 Income Statement Showing a Net Loss

Now that you have studied this section, complete the following questions and problems.

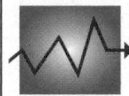

Thinking Critically

1. What three financial statements are prepared for a sole proprietorship?
2. Why is it important to divide the income statement into sections?

Communicating Accounting

Anna is the accounting clerk for the New Country Deli. For several months, Anna has tried to convince the owner to purchase a computer. Anna believes that a computer would save time, especially when financial statements are being prepared. She has explained that the information for preparing financial statements can be stored in the computer files. Then, when the financial statements are needed, it is not necessary to prepare a work sheet. The owner believes that a computer will cost too much money. What would you say to convince the owner that a computer should be purchased for use in the business?

Problem 9–1   Analyzing a Source Document

Instructions   Based on the receipt shown below, answer the following questions in your working papers.

1. What is the name of the business that received the money?
2. How much money was received?
3. Who paid the money?
4. Why was the money paid?
5. When was the payment made?
6. Who received the money and made out the receipt?
7. Where is the business that received the money located?

Stratford Learning Center
243 Eastern Road
Roxbury, NY 14752

RECEIPT
No. 1834

Aug. 21   20 --

RECEIVED FROM___Sandra Miller___ $ 832.00

Eight hundred thirty-two and no/100 ——————————— DOLLARS

FOR___On account___

RECEIVED BY___Rose Hughes___

The Statement of Changes in Owner's Equity

One of the most important concerns of a business owner is whether the owner's equity in the business has increased or decreased during the period. An increase in owner's equity means the owner's claims to the assets of the business have grown. A decrease means the owner's claims to the assets of the business have been reduced.

The Statement of Changes in Owner's Equity

The **statement of changes in owner's equity** summarizes changes in the owner's capital account as a result of business transactions during the period. This statement is prepared at the end of the period and, as you will see in the next section, is a supporting document of the balance sheet.

The heading of the statement of changes in financial position is set up in the same manner as the heading for the income statement.

1. The first line consists of the name of the business *(Who?)*
2. The second line indicates the name of the statement *(What?)*
3. The third line indicates the period covered *(When?)*

Because the statement of changes in financial position and the income statement cover the same period, the third line of the heading of both statements will include the same wording and date.

The information to prepare this statement is found in three places:

- the work sheet
- the income statement
- the owner's capital account in the general ledger

Completing the Statement of Changes in Owner's Equity

Look at **Figure 9–6** to see the statement of changes in owner's equity for Roadrunner Delivery Service for the month ended October 31.

In order to complete the statement of changes in owner's equity, follow these steps:

1. On the first line, write the words "Beginning Capital" followed by a comma and then by the first day of the period. For Roadrunner, that date is October 1, 20--. A

Roadrunner Delivery Service			
Statement of Changes in Owner's Equity			
For the Month Ended October 31, 20--			
Beginning Capital, October 1, 20-- A			B
C Add: Investments by Owner	D 25 400 00		
Net Income	E 1 150 00		
Total Increase in Capital		26 550 00	F
Subtotal		26 550 00	G
Less: Withdrawals by Owner		500 00	H
Ending Capital, October 31, 20-- I		26 050 00	J

Figure 9–6 Statement of Changes in Owner's Equity

2. In the second amount column, enter the balance of the capital account at the beginning of the period. The source of this information is the capital account. Since Roadrunner was formed after the beginning of the period, there is no beginning capital balance. Place a line in the second amount column. **B**

3. Next, enter the *increases* to the capital account: investments by the owner and net income. Investments made by the owner during the period are recorded in the capital account. Maria Sanchez, the owner of Roadrunner, invested a total of $25,400 during October. This includes $25,000 cash and two phones valued at $400. Write "Add: Investments by Owner." **C** Enter the total investment in the first amount column. **D**

Roadrunner Delivery Service
155 Gateway Blvd.
Sacramento, CA 94230

On the next line, write the words "Net Income." Indent so that "Net Income" aligns on the left with "Investments by Owner" above. In the first amount column, enter the net income amount from the income statement. Draw a single rule under the net income amount. **E**

4. Write the words "Total Increase in Capital" on the next line at the left side of the form. Add the investments by owner and net income amounts and enter the total in the second amount column. Draw a single rule under the amount. **F**

5. Write "Subtotal" on the next line, at the left side of the form. Add the amounts for beginning capital and total increase in capital. Enter the result in the second amount column. **G**

6. The next section of the statement lists the *decreases* to the capital account: withdrawals and net loss. Since Roadrunner did not have a net loss for the period, write the words "Less: Withdrawals by Owner" at the left side of the form. Find the withdrawals amount on the work sheet. Enter the withdrawals amount in the second amount column. Draw a single rule under the withdrawals amount. **H**

7. On the next line, at the left side of the form, write the words "Ending Capital" followed by a comma and the last day of the period. **I**

8. Subtract the withdrawals amount from the subtotal to determine the ending balance of the capital account. Finally, draw a double rule below the ending capital amount. **J**

Statement of Changes in Owner's Equity for an Ongoing Business

To prepare the statement of changes in owner's equity, you need to know the beginning balance of the owner's capital account. For an ongoing business, the balance entered on the work sheet for the capital account *may not* be the balance at the beginning of the period. If the owner made additional investments during the period, the investments would be recorded in the general journal, posted to the general ledger, and included in the amount shown on the work sheet.

For example, suppose the owner of Garo's Tree Service, James Garo, invested an additional $1,000 during the period. Look at **Figure 9–7**. The ledger account reflects the additional capital investment. The amount entered on the work sheet for **James Garo, Capital** includes the balance at the beginning of the period ($23,800) and the investment made during the period ($1,000).

Figure 9–7 Statement of Changes in Owner's Equity for an Ongoing Business

ACCOUNT	James Garo, Capital							ACCOUNT NO.	301

DATE		DESCRIPTION	POST. REF.	DEBIT	CREDIT	BALANCE DEBIT	BALANCE CREDIT
20--							
Apr.	1	Balance	✓				23 800 00
	15		G1		1 000 00		24 800 00

Garo's Tree Service
Work Sheet
For the Month Ended April 30, 20--

	ACCT. NO.	ACCOUNT NAME	TRIAL BALANCE DEBIT	TRIAL BALANCE CREDIT	INCOME STATEMENT DEBIT	INCOME STATEMENT CREDIT	BALANCE SHEET DEBIT	BALANCE SHEET CREDIT	
12	301	James Garo, Capital		24 800 00				24 800 00	12
13	302	James Garo, Withdrawals	700 00				700 00		13
20	525	Utilities Expense	620 00		620 00				20
21			21 924 00	21 924 00	6 033 00	9 309 00	29 877 00	26 601 00	21
22		Net Income			3 276 00			3 276 00	22
23					9 309 00	9 309 00	29 877 00	29 877 00	23
24									24

Garo's Tree Service
Statement of Changes in Owner's Equity
For the Month Ended April 30, 20--

Beginning Capital, April 1, 20--			23 800 00
Add: Investments by Owner	1 000 00		
Net Income	3 276 00		
Total Increase in Capital		4 276 00	
Subtotal		28 076 00	
Less: Withdrawals by Owner		700 00	
Ending Capital, April 30, 20--		27 376 00	

There are two ways to determine the owner's capital account balance at the beginning of the period. One way is to look at the ledger. The other way is to subtract the additional investments from the account balance shown on the work sheet. For **James Garo, Capital,** the $1,000 additional investment is subtracted from the $24,800 account balance shown on the work sheet to arrive at the beginning account balance of $23,800.

Figure 9–7 shows the statement of changes in owner's equity for an ongoing business.

Statement of Changes in Owner's Equity Showing a Net Loss

Figure 9–8 shows a statement of changes in owner's equity for an ongoing business with a net loss. Notice that since there is only one item that increases capital, investments by owner, the amount of the individual item is entered in the second amount column. Since there are two items that decrease capital, withdrawals by owner and net loss, the amounts of the individual items are entered in the first amount column. The total decrease in capital is entered in the second amount column.

Island Burgers												
Statement of Changes in Owner's Equity												
For the Month Ended April 30, 20--												
Beginning Capital, April 1, 20--										13	8 4 8	00
Add: Investments by Owner										1	5 0 0	00
Subtotal										15	3 4 8	00
Less: Withdrawals by Owner						9 0 0	00					
Net Loss						8 3 5	00					
Total Decrease in Capital										1	7 3 5	00
Ending Capital, April 30, 20--										13	6 1 3	00

Figure 9–8 Statement of Changes in Owner's Equity Showing a Net Loss

A MATTER OF ETHICS

Financial Report or Repair?

Your favorite uncle, who owns a restaurant, has asked you to help with his bookkeeping. He desperately needs a bank loan and wants you to prepare the financial statements. After going over his accounting records, you don't believe a bank will give him a loan; but you notice that by leaving out an expense or two, your uncle's business could look more promising. After all, he does have some good ideas for improving the business.

Ethical Decision Making:

☞ What are the ethical issues?

☞ What are the alternatives?

☞ Who are the affected parties?

☞ How do the alternatives affect the parties?

☞ What would you do?

Now that you have studied this section, complete the following questions and problems.

Thinking Critically

1. Where do you find the data needed to prepare a statement of changes in owner's equity?
2. How can the statement of changes in owner's equity help to determine the short- and long-term success of a business?

Analyzing Accounting

Tracy Murphy is a fashion designer who works from her home. She contributed her own funds and equipment to the business. She also continues to add new clients and increase her revenue. Tracy's investments in her business and the revenue she has earned over the past ten months are shown below. Create a line graph, by date, comparing Tracy's investments to her revenue. What can you determine from this chart?

Investments		
1/01/20--	Cash	$20,000
1/01/20--	Sewing machines	6,000
1/01/20--	Mannequins	3,500
1/01/20--	Material	25,000
1/01/20--	Computer equipment	5,600
1/01/20--	Business cards	500
2/15/20--	Cash	12,000
3/10/20--	Material	7,500
Total Investments		$80,100

Revenue	
2/01/20--	$5,000
3/01/20--	6,000
4/01/20--	12,000
5/01/20--	15,000
6/01/20--	17,500
7/01/20--	19,000
8/01/20--	20,000
9/01/20--	26,000
10/01/20--	20,000

Problem 9–2 Determining Ending Capital Balances

The financial transactions affecting the capital accounts of several different businesses are summarized below.

Instructions Use the form in your working papers. Determine the ending capital balance for each business.

	Beginning Capital	Investments	Revenue	Expenses	Withdrawals
1.	$60,000	$ 500	$ 5,100	$2,400	$ 700
2.	24,075	0	13,880	7,240	800
3.	28,800	1,000	6,450	6,780	0
4.	0	10,500	5,320	4,990	200
5.	6,415	0	4,520	3,175	700
6.	20,870	1,300	13,980	9,440	1,700

ACCOUNTING CAREERS IN FOCUS

ALFRED A. PEGUERO
Partner
PricewaterhouseCoopers LLP

Q: How did you become interested in accounting?

A: I was an economics major in college, but in my senior year I took two accounting classes that I really enjoyed. I realized that this is where the opportunities are. Accounting as a general profession is very broad. The basic principles are the same but you can focus on areas and industries that really interest you—anything from technology to farming. As an accountant, you have the opportunity to choose your industry.

Q: Which skills are most important?

A: Analytical and reasoning skills are critical. Mathematical ability can be helpful. Communication skills are essential.

Q: What do you enjoy most about your job?

A: I enjoy being able to offer solutions to my clients. Helping real people solve their problems and achieve peace of mind over their financial matters is very rewarding.

Q: What advice do you have for accountants just beginning their careers?

A: Find a good mentor—this is really important. Always follow through with what you say you're going to do and don't be afraid to ask questions.

Tips from . . .

RHI Robert Half International Inc.

Many companies look for leadership potential in new employees. Look beyond your immediate area of responsibility. Help your colleagues, learn what motivates and inspires people, and take on new challenges.

CAREER FACTS

Nature of the Work: Specialize in personal financial and business consulting. Advise clients on complex accounting issues.

Training or Education Needed: Bachelor's degree in business administration, accounting, or economics (minor in communications and technology particularly useful); and the CPA exam.

Aptitudes, Abilities, and Skills: Communication skills, analytical skills, reasoning skills, and math.

Salary Range: $150,000 to $400,000 as a new partner, and up to $2,000,000 with more experience, based on the firm's performance.

Career Path: Gather hands-on experience with either a major accounting firm or a reputable local firm. Once you have a taste for the areas that most interest you, consider getting a master's degree. It usually takes about 10 to 15 years to make partner at most firms.

Thinking Critically: What kind of advice would you ask of a mentor?

The Balance Sheet

The third financial report that is prepared at the end of a period is the balance sheet. The balance sheet provides a record of assets, and claims against those assets, for a business.

Your local bakery might prepare this statement to include amounts for items such as kitchen equipment, cash, and accounts receivable, as well as amounts for bills outstanding and owner's equity.

The Balance Sheet

The **balance sheet** is a report of the balances in all asset, liability, and owner's equity accounts at the end of the period. These accounts, you'll remember, are called permanent accounts. The main purpose of the balance sheet is to provide a record of the assets of the business and a summary of the claims (of both creditors and owners) against those *assets on a specific date.* In other words, the balance sheet states the financial position of a business at a specific point in time. It pinpoints what a business owns, owes, and is worth. For this reason, the balance sheet is sometimes called a *financial position statement.*

The balance sheet is prepared from the information in the Balance Sheet section of the work sheet and from the statement of changes in owner's equity. The balance sheet may be handwritten, typed, or, as in most cases, prepared by computer. Let's look at the sections of the balance sheet:

- the heading
- the assets section
- the liabilities and owner's equity sections

The Heading

Like the heading of the income statement, the heading of the balance sheet answers the questions *who? what? when?* The balance sheet heading includes:

1. The name of the business *(Who?)*
2. The name of the financial statement *(What?)*
3. The date of the balance sheet *(When?)*

As you recall, the income statement reports the amount of net income (or net loss) for the period. Unlike the income statement, which covers the entire period, the balance sheet covers only one day in the period, the last day. The amounts shown on the balance sheet are the general ledger balances in the accounts on the last day of the period. Look at **Figure 9–9.** Notice the difference between the date lines on the income statement and on the balance sheet.

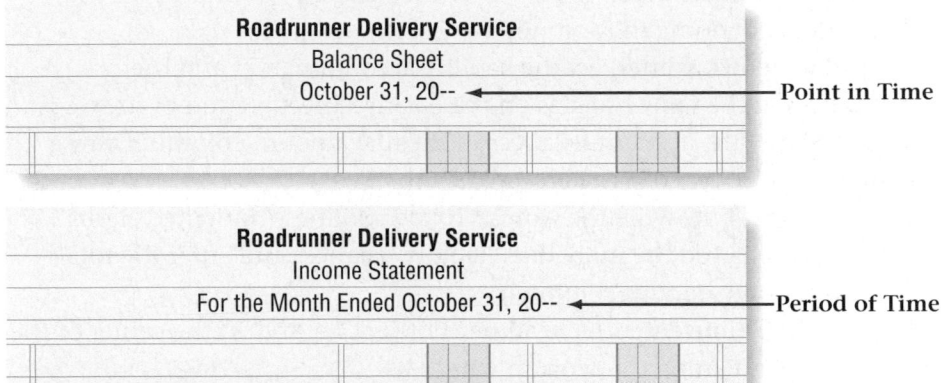

Figure 9–9 Headings of Financial Statements

The Assets Section

Refer to Roadrunner's balance sheet in **Figure 9–10** as you read how to prepare the balance sheet. Roadrunner's work sheet and statement of changes in owner's equity are also included to show the information sources used to prepare the balance sheet. Note that Roadrunner's balance sheet is prepared in report form. In **report form** , the balance sheet accounts are shown one under the other.

The asset section of the balance sheet is prepared as follows:

1. Write the word "Assets" on the first line in the center of the column containing the account names. **A**
2. On the following lines, enter the asset account names and their balances. List them in the same order as they appear in the Balance Sheet section of the work sheet. Enter the account balances in the first amount column. Draw a single rule under the last account balance. **B**
3. On the next line, write the words "Total Assets," indented about half an inch. Add the individual asset balances and enter the total in the second amount column. **C**

Do *not* draw a double rule under the total at this time. The double rule is entered when the liabilities and owner's equity sections are complete and equal to total assets.

The Liabilities and Owner's Equity Sections

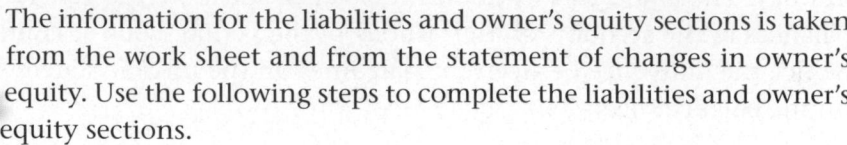

The information for the liabilities and owner's equity sections is taken from the work sheet and from the statement of changes in owner's equity. Use the following steps to complete the liabilities and owner's equity sections.

1. On the line after "Total Assets" enter the heading "Liabilities" in the column containing the account names. **D**
2. On the following lines, list the liability account names and their balances in the same order as on the Balance Sheet section of the work sheet. Enter the account balances in the first amount column. Draw a single rule under the last account balance. **E**
3. On the next line, write the words "Total Liabilities," indented about half an inch. Add the individual liability balances and enter the total in the second amount column. **F**
4. On the next line enter the heading "Owner's Equity" in the center of the column containing the account names. **G**
5. On the next line, write the name of the capital account. In the second amount column, enter the ending balance of the capital account as shown on the statement of changes in owner's equity. **H**

Proving the Equality of the Balance Sheet

You learned in earlier chapters that the basic accounting equation must always be in balance. The balance sheet represents the basic accounting equation; thus, the assets section total must equal the total of the liabilities and owner's equity sections.

Assets = Liabilities + Owner's Equity

To prove the equality of the balance sheet, follow these steps:

1. Draw a single rule under the balance of the capital account. On the next line, write the words "Total Liabilities and Owner's Equity," indented about half an inch. **I**
2. Add the total liabilities amount and the ending capital balance. Enter the total in the second amount column. **J** This total must equal the total assets amount. If the totals are not equal, there is an error. Most errors occur when transferring amounts from the work sheet or from the statement of changes in owner's equity. Verify that each account balance has been transferred properly. Find and correct the error and then complete the balance sheet.
3. When total assets equal total liabilities and owner's equity, draw a double rule under the total assets amount *and* under the total liabilities and owner's equity amount. **K** The balance sheet is now complete.

Review the amounts and their placement in **Figure 9–10** again. As you can see, completion of the work sheet is the basis of all financial statement preparation.

Roadrunner Delivery Service
Work Sheet
For the Month Ended October 31, 20--

ACCT. NO.	ACCOUNT NAME	TRIAL BALANCE DEBIT	TRIAL BALANCE CREDIT	INCOME STATEMENT DEBIT	INCOME STATEMENT CREDIT	BALANCE SHEET DEBIT	BALANCE SHEET CREDIT	
101	Cash in Bank	21 125 00				21 125 00		1
105	Accts. Rec.—City News	1 450 00				1 450 00		2
110	Accts. Rec.—Green Company	—				—		3
115	Computer Equipment	3 000 00				3 000 00		4
120	Office Equipment	200 00				200 00		5
125	Delivery Equipment	12 000 00				12 000 00		6
201	Accts. Pay.—Beacon Advertising		75 00				75 00	7
205	Accts. Pay.—North Shore Auto		11 650 00				11 650 00	8
301	Maria Sanchez, Capital		25 400 00				25 400 00	9
302	Maria Sanchez, Withdrawals	500 00				500 00		10
303	Income Summary	—	—	—	—			11
401	Delivery Revenue		2 650 00		2 650 00			12
501	Advertising Expense	75 00		75 00				13
505	Maintenance Expense	600 00		600 00				14
510	Ren…							15
515	Util…							16
							37 125 00	17
	Net…						1 150 00	18
							38 275 00	19
								20

Roadrunner Delivery Service
Statement of Changes in Owner's Equity
For the Month Ended October 31, 20--

Beginning Capital, October 1, 20--			
Add: Investments by Owner	25 400 00		
Net Income	1 150 00		
Total Increase in Capital		26 550 00	
Subtotal		26 550 00	
Less: Withdrawals by Owner		500 00	
Ending Capital, October 31, 20--		26 050 00	

Roadrunner Delivery Service
Balance Sheet
October 31, 20--

A Assets			
Cash in Bank	21 125 00		
Accounts Receivable—City News	1 450 00		
Accounts Receivable—Green Company	—		
Computer Equipment	3 000 00		
Office Equipment	200 00		
Delivery Equipment	12 000 00		
C Total Assets		37 775 00	**K**
D Liabilities			
Accounts Payable—Beacon Advertising		75 00	
Accounts Payable—North Shore Auto	11 650 00		
F Total Liabilities		11 725 00	
G Owner's Equity			
H Maria Sanchez, Capital		26 050 00	
I Total Liabilities and Owner's Equity	**J**	37 775 00	**K**

B E H

Figure 9–10 Preparing a Balance Sheet

Ratio Analysis

Ratio analysis involves the comparison of two amounts on a financial statement and the evaluation of the relationship between these amounts. A manager uses ratio analysis to determine the financial strength, activity, or debt-paying ability of a business.

Profitability ratios are used to evaluate the earnings performance of the business during the accounting period. The earning power of a business is an important measure of its ability to grow and continue to earn revenue. One commonly used profitability ratio is return on sales.

Return on Sales

Sales is a revenue account representing the sale of merchandise. Business owners use the **return on sales** ratio to examine the portion of each sales dollar that represents profit. To calculate this ratio, divide net income by sales. For example, the return on sales for Roadrunner Delivery Service is calculated as follows:

$$\frac{\$1{,}150 \text{ net income}}{\$2{,}650 \text{ sales}} = .434 \text{ or } 43.4\%$$

This percentage indicates that each dollar of sales produced 43.4 cents of profit for Roadrunner. It can be compared to other accounting periods to determine whether it is increasing or decreasing.

For example, if net income next year is $2,750 and net sales are $5,000, the return on sales would be computed as follows:

$$\frac{\$2{,}750 \text{ net income}}{\$5{,}000 \text{ sales}} = .550 \text{ or } 55.0\%$$

As you can see, profit per sales dollar would increase by 11.6 cents.

Liquidity Ratios

Liquidity refers to the ease with which an asset can be converted to cash. A **liquidity ratio** is a measure of the ability of a business to pay its current debts as they become due and to provide for unexpected needs of cash. Two common ratios used to determine liquidity follow.

Current Ratio. The **current ratio** is the relationship between current assets and current liabilities. The current ratio is calculated by dividing the dollar amount of current assets by the dollar amount of current liabilities. **Current assets** are those used up or converted to cash during the normal operating cycle of the business. These might include **Accounts Receivable**, **Cash in Bank**, and **Supplies. Current liabilities** are debts of the business that must be paid within the next accounting period. **Accounts Payable** is an example of current liabilities. The current ratio for Roadrunner based on the balance sheet in **Figure 9–10** is:

$$\frac{\text{Current Assets}}{\text{Current Liabilities}} = \text{Current Ratio} \qquad \frac{\$22{,}575}{\$11{,}725} = 1.92 \text{ or } 1.9{:}1$$

The current liabilities of a business must be paid within a year. These liabilities are paid from current assets.

A ratio of 2:1 or higher is considered favorable by creditors. It indicates that a business is able to pay its debts, that a business has current assets which are two times its current liabilities. A low ratio may indicate that a company could have trouble paying its debts.

Quick Ratio. A **quick ratio** is a measure of the relationship between short-term assets and current liabilities. Short-term liquid assets—those that can be quickly converted to cash—are cash and net receivables. The quick ratio is computed by dividing the total cash and receivables by total current liabilities.

The quick ratio for Roadrunner based on the Balance Sheet in **Figure 9–10** is:

$$\frac{\text{Cash and Receivables}}{\text{Current Liabilities}} = \text{Quick Ratio} \qquad \frac{\$22,575}{\$11,725} = 1.92{:}1$$

In some instances, the current ratio and the quick ratio can be the same, as in the case in this example.

A quick ratio of 1:1 is considered adequate. This indicates that a business can pay its current debts with cash in incoming receivables. If a business has a quick ratio of 1:1 or higher, the business has $1 in liquid assets for each $1 of its current liabilities.

Quick ratios may also be compared from one year to the next. For example, if cash and receivables for the previous year were $48,653 and current liabilities were $53,245, then that year's quick ratio would be computed as:

$$\frac{\$48,653}{\$53,245} = 0.91{:}1$$

As you can see, Roadrunner would have improved its liquidity position in the current year. $1.92 in liquid assets per $1 in current liabilities (current year) is stronger than $.91 in liquid assets per $1 in current liabilities (previous year).

ANALYZING FINANCIAL REPORTS

Return on Sales

In this chapter, you've learned about three basic financial reports that present different types of information about a business. One of these is the income statement. Owners and managers use the income statement to analyze the profit earned by the business and are especially interested in the return on sales.

To review, **return on sales** is calculated by dividing the net income by revenue, or sales. Take a look at the following example:

$$\frac{\text{Net Income}}{\text{Revenue}} = \frac{\$3,600}{\$42,500} = 8.5 \text{ percent}$$

The resulting percentage shows the proportion of each revenue dollar that is profit to the business.

▶ **Interpret the Report:**
Use the income statement for Roadrunner Delivery Service on page 206 to complete these activities. Record your answers on a separate sheet of paper.
1. Calculate the return on sales for Roadrunner Delivery Service for the month of October.
2. Assume that total sales for Roadrunner are roughly equal from month to month. If return on sales decreases each month, what conclusions might you draw about the business? What suggestions would you offer to improve the return on sales?

Now that you have studied this section, complete the following questions and problems.

Thinking Critically

1. On the balance sheet, if the total of liabilities and owner's equity does not equal the total assets, where did the error most likely occur?
2. What is the difference between the heading sections of the income statement and the balance sheet?

Communicating Accounting

Interactive Communication is a company that specializes in voice and data communications. They have just experienced a fantastic year in sales and service. Team up with a classmate and, using the balance sheet provided below, give a brief presentation about the purpose and use of the balance sheet.

Interactive Communication			
Balance Sheet			
December 31, 20--			
Assets			
Cash in Bank	944 0 0 0 00		
Accounts Receivable—Chamber of Commerce	200 0 0 0 00		
Office Equipment	850 0 0 0 00		
Computer Equipment	1,000 0 0 0 00		
Total Assets		2,994 0 0 0 00	
Liabilities			
Accounts Payable—Tip Top Advertising	275 5 0 0 00		
Interest Payable	1 3 0 0 00		
Salaries Payable	2 1 0 0 00		
Total Liabilities		278 9 0 0 00	
Owner's Equity			
Chuck Thompson, Capital		2,715 1 0 0 00	
Total Liabilities and Owner's Equity		2,994 0 0 0 00	

Problem 9–3 Calculating Return on Sales

The Gawle Company is a family-owned and operated appliance rental and repair business. The income statement for the month ended August 31 includes the following:

Rental Revenue	$3,256	Rent Expense	$2,100
Repair Revenue	2,140	Utilities Expense	483
Advertising Expense	575	Net Income	1,108
Maintenance Expense	1,130		

Instructions Calculate the return on sales for the month for the Gawle Company.

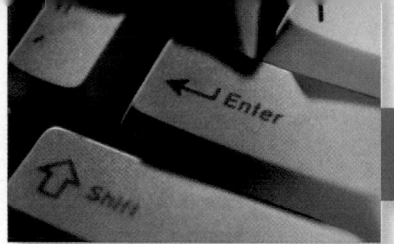

KEY CONCEPTS

1. Preparing financial reports is the seventh step in the accounting cycle. The primary reports are the income statement and the balance sheet. Also, the statement of changes in owner's equity is often prepared.

2. The income statement reports the net income or net loss for the period.

3. The statement of changes in owner's equity summarizes the impact the period's business transactions had on the capital account.

4. The balance sheet reports the balances of asset, liability, and owner's equity accounts at the end of the period.

5. Financial reports may be handwritten, typewritten, or prepared using a computer.

6. The following chart lists the source of information and a description for each financial report.

Financial Report	Description	Source of Information
Income Statement	This statement reports revenue earned and the expenses incurred for a specific period of time. It also reports the net income or net loss for the period.	Work Sheet
Statement of Changes in Owner's Equity	This statement is a supporting document for the balance sheet. It reports the increases and decreases in the owner's capital account for the period.	Work Sheet General Ledger (Capital Account) Income Statement
Balance Sheet	This statement reports the financial position of the business on a specific date.	Work Sheet Statement of Changes in Owner's Equity

7. Ratio analysis is used to determine the financial strength, activity, or debt-paying ability of a business.

8. Liquidity ratios measure the ability of a business to pay its current debts as they become due.

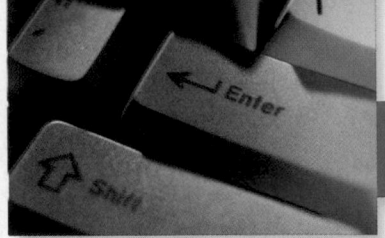

USING KEY TERMS

Imagine that you are the owner of a video arcade. Develop an information sheet for your manager and explain the importance of financial statement preparation. Use each of the following key terms in your report.

balance sheet
current assets
current liabilities
current ratio
financial statements
income statement
liquidity ratio

profitability ratio
quick ratio
ratio analysis
report form
return on sales
statement of changes in
   owner's equity

Understanding Accounting Concepts and Procedures

Instructions

On a separate sheet of paper, answer the following questions:

1. Why are financial statements prepared?

2. What is the purpose of the income statement?

3. Why does a business need to be consistent in the fiscal period it uses for its financial reports?

4. What is the source of information used to prepare the income statement?

5. What is the purpose of the statement of changes in owner's equity?

6. What sources of information are used to prepare the statement of changes in owner's equity?

7. What is the purpose of the balance sheet?

8. What sources of information are needed to prepare the balance sheet?

9. How does the date in the heading of a balance sheet differ from the date in the heading of an income statement and a statement of changes in owner's equity?

10. Which financial statement represents the basic accounting equation?

11. What is the purpose of computing ratios from amounts on financial statements?

12. Why might a creditor be interested in the liquidity ratios of a business?

13. How are the current ratio and the quick ratio similar? different?

14. Who might be interested in the profitability ratios of a business?

Case Study...

Service Business: Video Arcade

Taki Yamamoto owns a video arcade business called Arcadia.

Taki hired your accounting firm to record Arcadia's financial information. Taki hands you a folder containing these documents:

- Canceled checks with June dates: $800 for rent, $120 for electricity, $70 for telephone service, $180 for insurance, $250 for newspaper advertising, and $200 for a cleaning service.
- Invoice dated June 16 for a used video game that was sold on account for $2,000.
- Cash register tapes for June showing total cash sales of $5,890.

Thinking Critically:

1. Using the preceding information, make a list of accounts needed to record the transactions indicated by the financial documents Taki gave you.
2. Prepare an income statement for Arcadia for the month of June.

interNET CONNECTION

Preparing Financial Statements

Many national companies began as proprietorships or partnerships. Whether a company is a sole proprietorship or a corporation, financial statements provide information for making financial and operating decisions. Hoover's Online contains information about more than 18,000 public and private companies.

Do This:

1. Find the Hoover's Online Web site.
2. Within the site, locate financial information about The Gap and The Limited, Inc.
3. What was the amount of each company's sales last year?
4. What was the net income for each company?

Conducting an Audit with Alex

Instructions Using the amounts that are given below, calculate the missing amounts. Write the missing amounts on a separate sheet of paper.

SweepIt Carpet Cleaning Company
Statement of Changes in Owner's Equity
For the Month Ended July 31, 20--

Beginning Capital, July 1, 20--		?
Add: Investments by Owner	1 5 0 0 00	
Subtotal:		?
Less: Withdrawals by Owner	1 6 0 0 00	
Net Loss	?	
Total Decrease in Capital		2 7 5 1 00
Ending Capital, July 31, 20--		19 7 2 9 00

Workplace Skills

Using Computers

Businesses of all sizes are becoming automated. Computers are integral to most business operations. The ability to use computers and software is essential to complete most business tasks.

On the Job:

As the accounting clerk for Jewels, Gems, and Treasures, a costume jewelry and gift shop, you are to prepare the quarterly income statement using a spreadsheet program. In the past you have prepared this statement using accounting stationery and a pencil.

Thinking Critically:

Prepare a list of reasons why using a spreadsheet program is an improvement over manually preparing financial reports.

Preparing Financial Statements

Making the Transition from a Manual to a Computerized System

Task	Perform Accounting Procedures Using Manual Methods	Perform Accounting Procedures Using Automated Methods
Preparing an income statement	1. Transfer all revenue and expense accounts and their balances from the work sheet. 2. Subtract expenses from revenue to determine net income or net loss.	1. Select **Income Statement** from the *Reports* menu. 2. Click Print.
Preparing a statement of changes in owner's equity	1. Transfer the beginning balance of the capital account from the work sheet. 2. Add additional investments and net income or loss. 3. Subtract withdrawals. 4. Calculate the ending balance for the capital account.	1. Since the software automatically computes the ending balance of the capital account for you, it is not necessary to prepare this statement.
Preparing a balance sheet	1. Transfer permanent accounts and their balances from the work sheet. 2. Transfer the ending capital account balance from the statement of changes in owner's equity. 3. Total all asset account balances. 4. Total all liabilities and owner's equity account balances. 5. Verify that assets equal liabilities and owner's equity.	1. Select **Balance Sheet** from the *Reports* menu. 2. Click Print.

Preparing Financial Statements

Peachtree Question	Description
How do I prepare financial statements in Peachtree?	1. Select **Financial Statements** from the *Reports* menu. 2. Choose the statement you wish to print from the Reports list. 3. Click *Print* when the statement appears on the screen.
What does the software do "behind the scenes"?	• The software automatically reads through the general ledger accounts, pulling account balances and names into the appropriate pre-formatted statements.

For detailed instructions: See the Peachtree User Guide in your Glencoe Working Papers.

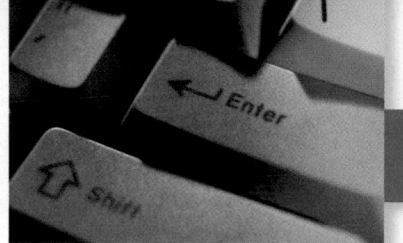

APPLICATION OPTIONS

Problem 9–4 Preparing an Income Statement

The work sheet for Wilderness Rentals for the month ended September 30, 20-- is in your working papers.

Instructions Using the work sheet, prepare an income statement for Wilderness Rentals.

Analyze: What is the return on sales for the period?

Problem 9–5 Preparing a Statement of Changes in Owner's Equity

Instructions Using the work sheet for Wilderness Rentals in your working papers and the income statement prepared in Problem 9–4, prepare a statement of changes in owner's equity and a balance sheet. Ronald Hicks made an additional investment in the business of $500 during the period.

Analyze: What is the current ratio for Wilderness Rentals for this statement period?

Problem 9–6 Preparing Financial Statements

The trial balance for the Hot Suds Car Wash is listed below and in your working papers.

Instructions

1. Complete the work sheet in your working papers.
2. Prepare an income statement for the quarter ended September 30, 20--.
3. Prepare a statement of changes in owner's equity. Regina Delgado made no additional investments during the period.
4. Prepare a balance sheet in report form.

Analyze: What is the return on sales for the period?

Complete chapter problems one of four ways:

1 **Manual** Glencoe Working Papers

or

2 **Peachtree Complete Accounting** Software

or

3 **QuickBooks** Templates (Problem 9–6)

or

4 **Spreadsheet** Templates (Problem 9–8)

Peachtree®

SMART GUIDE

Step–by–Step Instructions: Problem 9–4, 9–5

1. Select the problem set for Wilderness Rentals (Prob. 9–4, 5).
2. Rename the company and set the system date.
3. Print a General Ledger Trial Balance.
4. Print an Income Statement.
5. Print a Statement of Changes in Owner's Equity.
6. Print a Balance Sheet.
7. Answer the Analyze question.
8. End the session.

Hot Suds Car Wash
Trial Balance
For the Quarter Ended September 30, 20--

		Debit	Credit
101	Cash in Bank	8 4 5 7 00	
105	Accts. Rec.—Linda Brown	5 8 4 00	
110	Accts. Rec.—Valley Auto	6 1 9 00	
115	Detailing Supplies	8 1 0 00	
120	Detergent Supplies	4 6 0 00	
125	Office Equipment	15 2 4 0 00	
130	Office Furniture	2 1 6 0 00	
135	Car Wash Equipment	7 5 2 2 00	
201	Accts. Pay.—Allen Vacuum Systems		3 5 2 8 00
205	Accts. Pay.—O'Brian's Office Supply		1 2 1 5 00
301	Regina Delgado, Capital		23 8 4 5 00
305	Regina Delgado, Withdrawals	1 5 0 0 00	
310	Income Summary		
401	Wash Revenue		9 6 2 3 00
405	Wax Revenue		8 0 1 9 00
410	Interior Detailing Revenue		2 6 2 8 00
501	Advertising Expense	1 9 6 3 00	
505	Equipment Rental Expense	4 1 3 7 00	
510	Maintenance Expense	1 1 8 6 00	
520	Rent Expense	3 5 0 0 00	
530	Utilities Expense	7 2 0 00	
		48 8 5 8 00	48 8 5 8 00

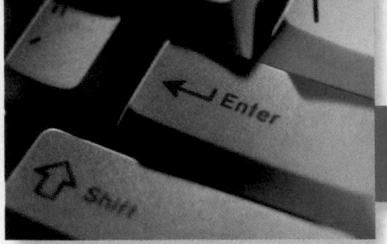

Peachtree®

SMART GUIDE

Step–by–Step Instructions:
Problem 9–6

1. Select the problem set for Hot Suds Car Wash (Prob. 9–6).
2. Rename the company and set the system date.
3. Print a General Ledger Trial Balance.
4. Print an Income Statement.
5. Print a Statement of Changes in Owner's Equity.
6. Print a Balance Sheet.
7. Answer the Analyze question.
8. End the session.

Peachtree®

SMART GUIDE

Step–by–Step Instructions:
Problem 9–7

1. Select the problem set for Kits & Pups Grooming (Prob. 9–7).
2. Rename the company and set the system date.
3. Print a General Ledger Trial Balance.
4. Print an Income Statement.
5. Print a Statement of Changes in Owner's Equity.
6. Print a Balance Sheet.
7. Answer the Analyze question.
8. End the session.

Problem 9–7 Preparing Financial Statements

The general ledger accounts and balances for Kits & Pups Grooming follow.

General Ledger

101	Cash in Bank	$ 4,296
105	Accts. Rec.—Juan Alvarez	1,528
110	Accts. Rec.—Nathan Carlsbad	904
115	Accts. Rec.—Martha Giles	1,219
120	Grooming Supplies	1,368
125	Office Equipment	8,467
130	Office Furniture	3,396
135	Computer Equipment	2,730
140	Grooming Equipment	1,974
145	Kennel Equipment	7,412
201	Accts. Pay.—Able Store Equipment	3,876
205	Accts. Pay.—Dogs & Cats Inc.	2,746
207	Accts. Pay.—Pet Gourmet	1,281
301	Abe Shultz, Capital	30,928
305	Abe Shultz, Withdrawals	1,900
310	Income Summary	—
401	Boarding Revenue	11,989
405	Grooming Revenue	4,420
501	Advertising Expense	3,934
505	Equipment Repair Expense	943
510	Maintenance Expense	2,483
520	Rent Expense	8,850
530	Utilities Expense	3,836

Instructions

1. Prepare a work sheet for the month ended September 30, 20--.
2. Prepare an income statement for the period.
3. Prepare a statement of changes in owner's equity. Abe Shultz made an additional investment of $2,500 during the period.
4. Prepare a balance sheet in report form.

Analyze: What is the quick ratio for Kits & Pups Grooming?

Problem 9–8 Preparing a Statement of Changes in Owner's Equity

Instructions Use the balance sheet and income statement shown to prepare a statement of changes in owner's equity. (The owner made an additional investment of $4,000 and withdrew $1,500 during the period.)

Outback Guide Service
Income Statement
For the Month Ended September 30, 20--

Revenue:								
Guide Service Revenue					8	9 1 3	00	
Expenses:								
Advertising Expense		3 7 5	00					
Maintenance Expense		1 3 8	00					
Rent Expense	1	2 5 0	00					
Salaries Expense	1	5 0 0	00					
Utilities Expense	1	1 6 1	00					
Total Expenses					4	4 2 4	00	
Net Income					4	4 8 9	00	

SPREADSHEET SMART GUIDE

Step–by–Step Instructions: Problem 9–8

1. Select the spreadsheet template for Problem 9–8.
2. Enter your name and the date in the spaces provided on the template.
3. Complete the spreadsheet using the instructions in your working papers.
4. Print the spreadsheet and proof your work.
5. Save your work and exit the spreadsheet program.

Outback Guide Service
Balance Sheet
September 30, 20--

Assets							
Cash in Bank	3	1 1 7	00				
Accounts Receivable—Mary Johnson		4 2 3	00				
Accounts Receivable—Feldman, Jones, & Ritter		4 4 3	00				
Accounts Receivable—Podaski Systems Inc.	1	0 0 8	00				
Hiking Supplies		1 5 3	00				
Office Supplies		3 3 8	00				
Office Equipment	6	4 9 2	00				
Office Furniture	3	0 8 4	00				
Computer Equipment	3	6 2 4	00				
Hiking Equipment	1	0 1 5	00				
Rafting Equipment	9	1 8 6	00				
Total Assets				28	8 8 3	00	
Liabilities							
Accounts Payable—A-1 Adventure Warehouse	6	5 4 5	00				
Accounts Payable—Peak Equipment Inc.	1	3 2 5	00				
Accounts Payable—Premier Processors		6 4 2	00				
Total Liabilities				8	5 1 2	00	
Owner's Equity							
Juanita Ortega, Capital				20	3 7 1	00	
Total Liabilities and Owner's Equity				28	8 8 3	00	

Analyze: What was the largest expense for this business during the period?

CHAPTER 10

Completing the Accounting Cycle for a Sole Proprietorship

Learning Objectives

When you have completed this chapter, you will be able to:

▶ Explain why it is necessary to update accounts through closing entries.

▶ Explain the purpose of the Income Summary account.

▶ Explain the relationship between the Income Summary account and the capital account.

▶ Analyze and journalize closing entries.

▶ Post the closing entries to the general ledger.

▶ Prepare a post-closing trial balance.

▶ Define the accounting terms introduced in this chapter.

Exploring the Real World of Business

LOOKING AT FISCAL YEAR-END ACTIVITIES

Grind the winch? Trim the sail? Inflate your BCD? If any of these terms sound intriguing, you might be interested in sailing or scuba diving. **ActionQuest** is a company that offers certification in both. The company specializes in programs for teens, and you can even earn high school or college credits as you live aboard a sailing yacht and study marine sciences, oceanography, and tropical marine biology.

Located in Sarasota, Florida, **ActionQuest** trains teens from all over the United States, the Far East, South America, and Europe. Each voyage, which takes place in the waters of the Caribbean Islands, Mediterranean and Fiji, lasts from two and a half to three weeks. Instruction is provided by professional diving instructors and U.S. Coast Guard licensed skippers.

ActionQuest's revenue comes from fees teens pay for diving and sailing instruction. At the end of each fiscal period, the company closes its accounts and analyzes the revenue and costs of its diving and sailing programs. Part of the analysis might be looking at expenses or deciding whether fees are at an appropriate level to cover operating costs.

What do you think?

If you worked for **ActionQuest,** why would you want to be able to compare operating expenses from one fiscal period to another?

Workplace Connections

Applying Your Accounting Knowledge

Preparing financial statements can be a hectic time for an accounting staff. Professional accountants learn to manage stressful times using good organizational skills. Once the financial statements have been prepared, other tasks must be completed to close one accounting cycle and begin another. You will learn about these tasks in this chapter.

Investigate:

1. In your workplace, are there especially hectic times of the day or year?
2. How do you and your co-workers handle these busy times?

Glencoe Accounting Online

Visit the *Glencoe Accounting* Web site at **glencoeaccounting.glencoe.com** for additional activities and information.

Preparing Closing Entries

In Chapter 9 you learned how to prepare the following financial statements:

- The income statement reports revenue, expenses, and net income or net loss for the period.
- The statement of changes in owner's equity summarizes the impact of the business transactions on the owner's capital account.
- The balance sheet reports the financial position of the business at the end of the period.

In a company like Mattel Toys, accountants prepare financial statements and then journalize and post closing entries. A post-closing trial balance is prepared to verify that the accounting records are still in balance.

Completing the Accounting Cycle

During the accounting period, the accountant records transactions involving revenue, expenses, and withdrawals in temporary capital accounts. At the end of the period, the accountant transfers the balances in the temporary capital accounts to the owner's capital account to bring it up to date and to prepare the accounting records for the next period.

Closing entries are journal entries made to close, or reduce to zero, the balances in the temporary capital accounts and to transfer the net income or net loss for the period to the capital account.

After the closing entries are journalized and posted, a trial balance is prepared to prove the equality of the general ledger after the closing process. The trial balance prepared after closing is called a post-closing trial balance. As you can see in **Figure 10–1**, the closing process and the post-closing trial balance complete the accounting cycle.

Starting the Eighth Step in the Accounting Cycle: Journalizing the Closing Entries

Preparing financial records for the start of a new period is a little like keeping stats for a basketball team. In keeping basketball stats, individual and team scores are recorded for every game, but each new game starts with a score of zero. Similarly, in keeping the stats or accounting for a

Figure 10–1 The Accounting Cycle with Steps 8 and 9 Highlighted

Collect and verify source documents

INVOICE
RECEIPT
MEMORANDUM

1

Analyze each transaction

ACCOUNT
DEBIT | CREDIT
+ | -

ACCOUNT
DEBIT | CREDIT
+ | -

2

Journalize each transaction

GENERAL JOURNAL

3

Post to the ledger

LEDGER

4

TRIAL BALANCE

5

WORK SHEET

6

Prepare a work sheet

Prepare a trial balance

INCOME STATEMENT
STATEMENT OF CHANGES IN OWNER'S EQUITY
BALANCE SHEET

7

Prepare financial statements

GENERAL JOURNAL
LEDGER

8

Journalize and post closing entries

POST-CLOSING TRIAL BALANCE

9

Prepare a post-closing trial balance

business, entries are recorded in the accounts during the year (game), but the temporary accounts (**Rent Expense, Maintenance Expense, Revenue,** etc.) start each new year (game) with zero balances.

The income statement, you'll remember, reports the net income or net loss for *one accounting period.* The statement is prepared from information recorded and accumulated in the revenue and expense accounts. At the end of the period, entries are recorded to close, or reduce to zero, the revenue and expense accounts because their balances also apply to only one accounting period. These closing entries also transfer the net income or net loss for the period to the capital account.

The need to complete the closing process can be seen in **Figure 10–2.**

- Prior to the closing process, you know that net income or net loss is calculated on the work sheet. **A**
- The net income or net loss amount then appears on the income statement. **B**
- On the statement of changes in owner's equity, the ending balance of the capital account includes net income or net loss. **C**
- The ending balance of the capital account then appears on the balance sheet. **D**
- At this point, however, the balance of the capital account in the general ledger does not equal the amount on the balance sheet because the closing entries need to be journalized and posted. **E**

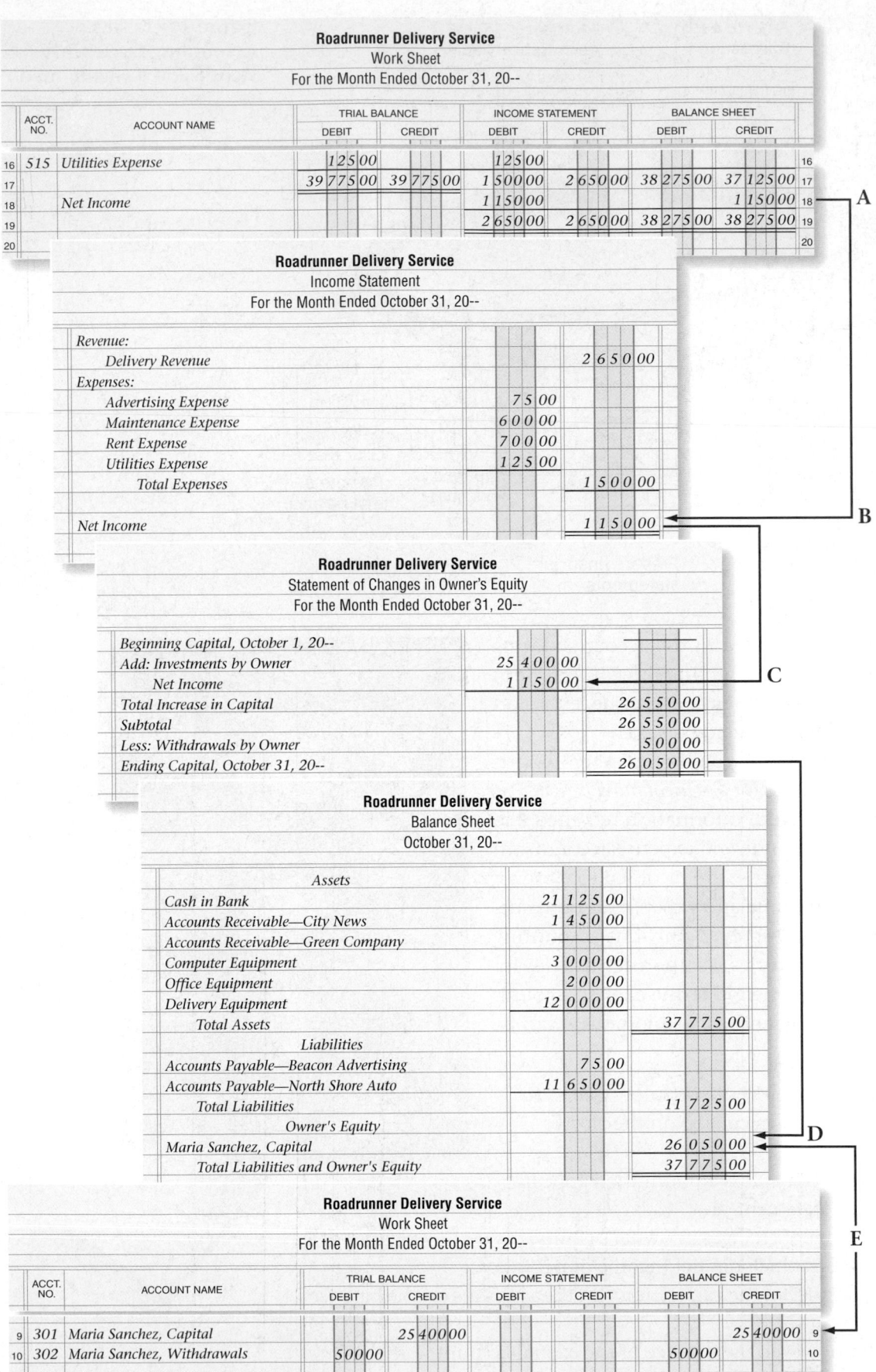

Figure 10–2 The Closing Process

For example, the balance for **Maria Sanchez, Capital** on the work sheet is $25,400 but the balance on the balance sheet is $26,050. These two amounts differ because the withdrawals and the net income are not yet recorded in the capital account in the general ledger. The closing process is used to update accounts through closing entries. The balance of the general ledger capital account is brought up-to-date.

The Income Summary Account

Before the closing entries are journalized and posted, there is no single account in the general ledger that shows all of the revenue and expenses for the period. This information is scattered among the individual revenue and expense accounts. There is, however, one general ledger account that, up to this point, has not been used. That is the **Income Summary** account.

The **Income Summary account** is used to accumulate and summarize the revenue and expenses for the period. This account serves as a simple income statement in the ledger. Expenses, which have debit balances, are transferred as debits to **Income Summary.** Revenues, which have credit balances, are transferred as credits to **Income Summary.** The balance of the account equals the net income or net loss for the fiscal period.

Look on page 73 at the chart of accounts for Roadrunner Delivery Service. Notice that **Income Summary** is located in the owner's equity section of the general ledger. It is located there because of its relationship to the owner's capital account. Remember, the revenue and expenses transferred to **Income Summary** actually represent increases and decreases to owner's equity. The balance of **Income Summary** (the net income or net loss for the period) is transferred to the capital account at the end of the closing process.

Like the withdrawals account, **Income Summary** is a temporary capital account. **Income Summary** is quite different, however, from the other temporary capital accounts.

- **Income Summary** is used only at the end of the fiscal year to summarize the balances from the revenue and expense accounts.
- **Income Summary** does not have a normal balance, which means that it does not have an increase or a decrease side. As shown in the T account below, the debit and credit sides of the account are simply used to summarize the period's revenue and expenses.

	Income Summary	
Debit		Credit
Expenses		Revenue

If Revenue > Expenses ⟶ Balance is net income

If Revenue < Expenses ⟶ Balance is net loss

Adding Columns

To avoid errors in adding a column of figures, as for a post-closing trial balance, be sure to vertically align:

- the tens,
- the hundreds, and
- the thousands.

- The balance of the **Income Summary** account before and after the closing process is zero.
- The **Income Summary** account does not appear on any financial statement.

Preparing Closing Entries

Four journal entries are prepared to close the temporary capital accounts for Roadrunner.

1. The balance of the revenue account is transferred to the credit side of the **Income Summary** account.
2. The expense account balances are transferred to the debit side of the **Income Summary** account.
3. The balance of the **Income Summary** account is transferred to the capital account (net income to the credit side; net loss to the debit side).
4. The balance of the withdrawals account is transferred to the debit side of the capital account.

Closing the Balance of the Revenue Account to Income Summary

The first step in the closing procedure is to transfer the balance of the revenue account to **Income Summary**. The balance for the revenue account is found in the Income Statement section of the work sheet. (Refer to the work sheet in **Figure 9–3** on page 206 when reading about closing entries.)

Closing Entry

First Closing Entry—Close Revenue to Income Summary

ANALYSIS	*Identify*	1. Roadrunner has only one revenue account, **Delivery Revenue.** The accounts affected are **Delivery Revenue** and **Income Summary.**
	Classify	2. **Delivery Revenue** is a revenue account. **Income Summary** is a temporary capital account.
	+/−	3. The **Delivery Revenue** account balance is decreased by $2,650 to zero. That amount, $2,650 is transferred to the **Income Summary** account.

| **DEBIT-CREDIT RULE** | 4. Decreases in revenue accounts are recorded as debits. Debit **Delivery Revenue** for $2,650. |
| | 5. To transfer the revenue to the **Income Summary** account, credit **Income Summary** for $2,650. |

T ACCOUNTS 6.

Delivery Revenue			Income Summary	
Debit	Credit		Debit	Credit
−	+			
Closing 2,650	Balance 2,650			Closing 2,650

JOURNAL ENTRY

	DATE		DESCRIPTION	POST. REF.	DEBIT	CREDIT	
	20--		*Closing Entries*				1
	Oct.	31	Delivery Revenue		2 650 00		2
			Income Summary			2 650 00	3
							4

GENERAL JOURNAL   PAGE ___3___

To record closing entries in the general journal, follow these steps:

1. Enter "Closing Entries" in the center of the description column.
2. Enter the date (the last day of the fiscal period).
3. Enter the name(s) of the account(s) to be debited and the amount(s) to be debited.
4. Enter the name of the account, **Income Summary**, to be credited and the amount to be credited.

Closing the Balances of the Expense Accounts to Income Summary

The second closing entry transfers the balances of the expense accounts to **Income Summary**. The balances of the expense accounts are found in the Income Statement section of the work sheet.

Closing Entry

Second Closing Entry—Close Expenses to Income Summary

ANALYSIS

Identify
1. The accounts affected by the second closing entry are **Advertising Expense, Maintenance Expense, Rent Expense, Utilities Expense**, and **Income Summary**.

Classify
2. **Advertising Expense, Maintenance Expense, Rent Expense**, and **Utilities Expense** are expense accounts. **Income Summary** is a temporary capital account.

+/−
3. The balances of the four expense accounts are decreased to zero; the total decrease is $1,500. The total amount, $1,500, is transferred to the **Income Summary** account.

DEBIT-CREDIT RULE
4. To transfer the expenses to the **Income Summary** account, debit **Income Summary** for $1,500.
5. Decreases in expense accounts are recorded as credits. Credit **Advertising Expense**, $75; **Maintenance Expense**, $600; **Rent Expense**, $700; **Utilities Expense**, $125.

T ACCOUNTS

6.

Income Summary	
Debit	Credit
Closing 1,500	

Advertising Expense	
Debit +	Credit −
Balance 75	Closing 75

Maintenance Expense	
Debit +	Credit −
Balance 600	Closing 600

Rent Expense	
Debit +	Credit −
Balance 700	Closing 700

Utilities Expense	
Debit +	Credit −
Balance 125	Closing 125

JOURNAL ENTRY

7.

GENERAL JOURNAL PAGE 3

	DATE		DESCRIPTION	POST. REF.	DEBIT	CREDIT	
5	*Oct.*	*31*	*Income Summary*		*1 500 00*		5
6			*Advertising Expense*			*75 00*	6
7			*Maintenance Expense*			*600 00*	7
8			*Rent Expense*			*700 00*	8
9			*Utilities Expense*			*125 00*	9
10							10

It is not necessary to use a separate closing entry for each expense account. As you can see, the above entry has one debit and four credits. A journal entry with two or more debits or two or more credits is called a **compound entry**. A compound entry saves both space and posting time. For example, each of Roadrunner's expense accounts could be closed to **Income Summary** separately. That, however, requires four entries and postings to the **Income Summary** account instead of one entry and posting.

Key Points

Closing Entries

To Close Revenue Accounts:
- Debit revenue account(s)
- Credit **Income Summary** account

To Close Expense Accounts:
- Debit **Income Summary** account
- Credit expense account(s)

Closing the Balance of the Income Summary Account to Capital

The third closing entry transfers the balance of the **Income Summary** account to the capital account. As shown in the T account, after closing Roadrunner's revenue and expense accounts, **Income Summary** has a credit balance of $1,150.

Income Summary			
2 Closing entry for expenses	1,500	1 Closing entry for revenue	2,650
		Balance	1,150

A credit balance indicates net income for the period. It is the same amount that appears on the work sheet.

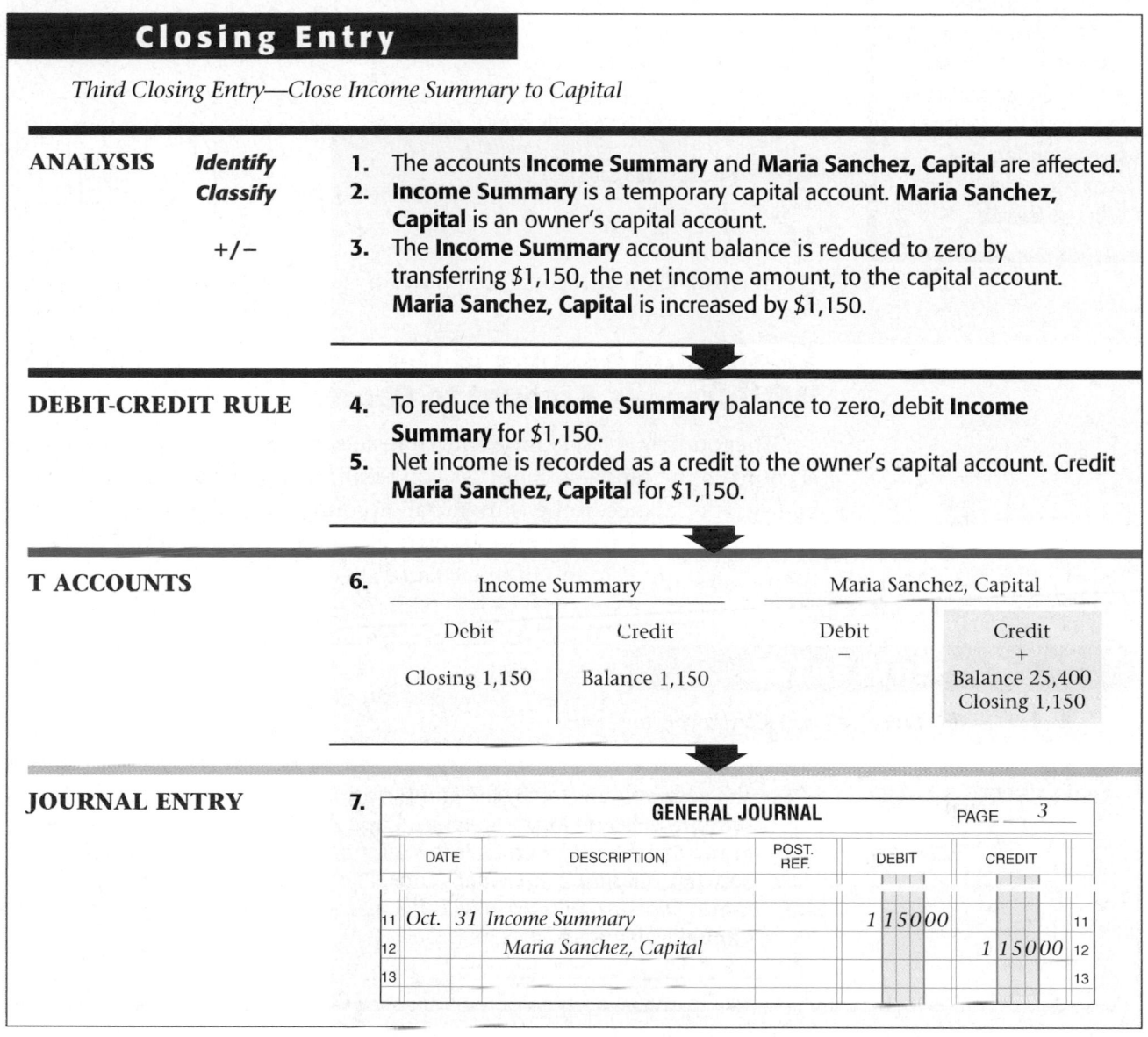

After the third closing entry is posted, the **Income Summary** account appears as follows:

Income Summary			
2 Closing entry for expenses	1,500	1 Closing entry for revenue	2,650
3 Closing balance to owner's capital account	1,150		

If a business reports a net loss for the period, **Income Summary** has a debit balance. In that situation, the third closing entry is a debit to the capital account and a credit to **Income Summary** for the amount of the net loss. **Figure 10–3** shows this entry as it appears in the general journal.

	DATE		DESCRIPTION	POST. REF.	DEBIT	CREDIT	
1	20--		*Closing Entries*				1
2	Oct.	31	Maria Sanchez, Capital		7 0 0 00		2
3			*Income Summary*			7 0 0 00	3
4							4

GENERAL JOURNAL · PAGE 3

Figure 10–3 Closing Income Summary for the Amount of Net Loss

Closing the Balance of the Withdrawals Account to Capital

The fourth and last closing entry transfers the balance of the withdrawals account to the capital account. As you recall, withdrawals decrease owner's equity. The balance of the withdrawals account is transferred to the capital account to reflect the decrease in owner's equity. The balance of the withdrawals account is found in the Balance Sheet section of the work sheet.

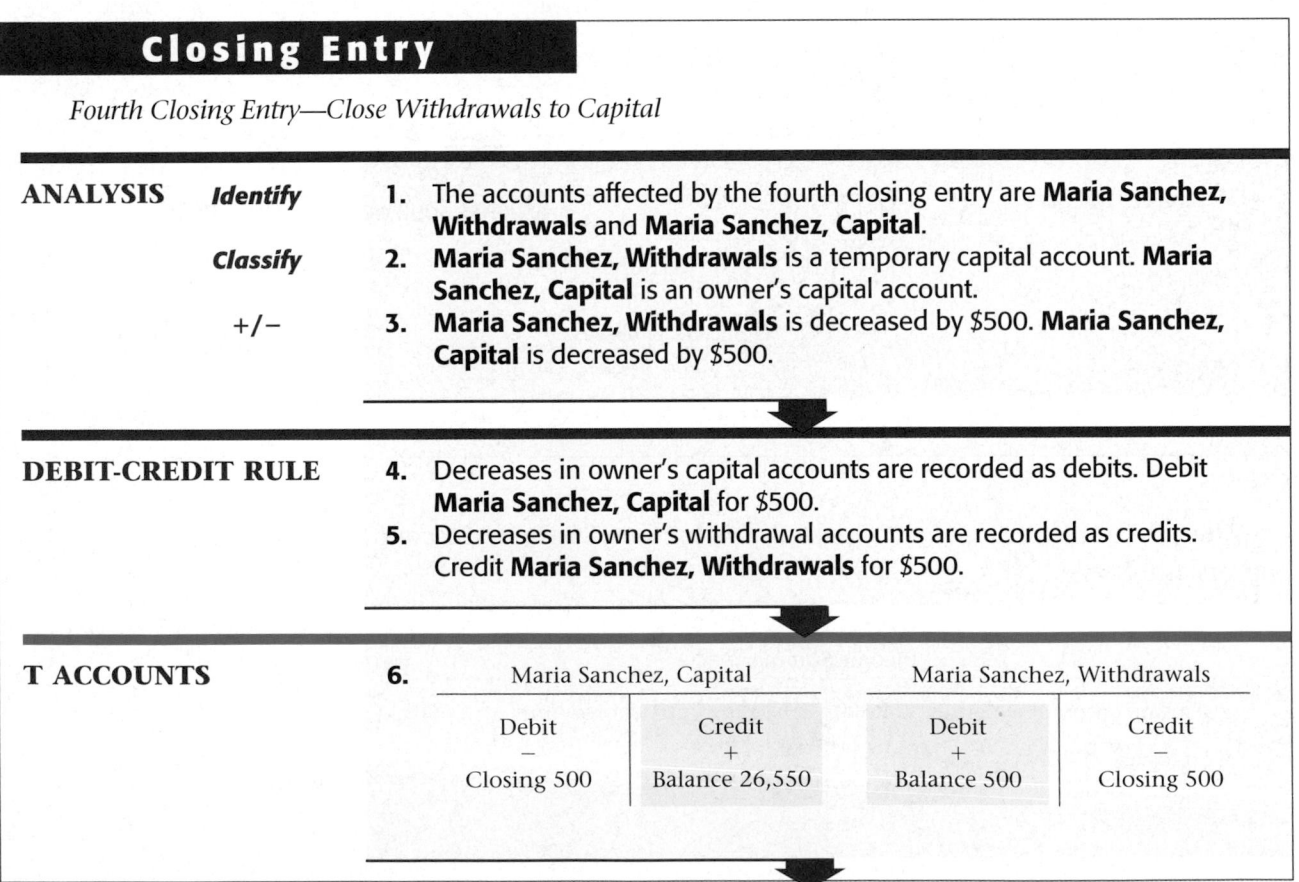

Closing Entry

Fourth Closing Entry—Close Withdrawals to Capital

ANALYSIS *Identify* 1. The accounts affected by the fourth closing entry are **Maria Sanchez, Withdrawals** and **Maria Sanchez, Capital**.

Classify 2. **Maria Sanchez, Withdrawals** is a temporary capital account. **Maria Sanchez, Capital** is an owner's capital account.

+/− 3. **Maria Sanchez, Withdrawals** is decreased by $500. **Maria Sanchez, Capital** is decreased by $500.

DEBIT-CREDIT RULE 4. Decreases in owner's capital accounts are recorded as debits. Debit **Maria Sanchez, Capital** for $500.

5. Decreases in owner's withdrawal accounts are recorded as credits. Credit **Maria Sanchez, Withdrawals** for $500.

T ACCOUNTS 6.

Maria Sanchez, Capital		Maria Sanchez, Withdrawals	
Debit −	Credit +	Debit +	Credit −
Closing 500	Balance 26,550	Balance 500	Closing 500

JOURNAL ENTRY   **7.**

	GENERAL JOURNAL			PAGE 3	
DATE	DESCRIPTION	POST. REF.	DEBIT	CREDIT	
14	Oct. 31	Maria Sanchez, Capital		500 00		14
15		Maria Sanchez, Withdrawals			500 00	15
16						16

The journal entries made to close the temporary capital accounts for Roadrunner are shown in **Figure 10–4.**

			GENERAL JOURNAL		PAGE 3				
	DATE		DESCRIPTION	POST. REF.	DEBIT		CREDIT		
1	20--		Closing Entries						1
2	Oct.	31	Delivery Revenue		2 650 00				2
3			Income Summary				2 650 00		3
4									4
5		31	Income Summary		1 500 00				5
6			Advertising Expense				75 00		6
7			Maintenance Expense				600 00		7
8			Rent Expense				700 00		8
9			Utilities Expense				125 00		9
10									10
11		31	Income Summary		1 150 00				11
12			Maria Sanchez, Capital				1 150 00		12
13									13
14		31	Maria Sanchez, Capital		500 00				14
15			Maria Sanchez, Withdrawals				500 00		15
16									16

Figure 10–4 Journalizing the Closing Entries

A MATTER OF ETHICS

Computer Viruses

Computer viruses are small computer programs that "reproduce" themselves into other programs, slowing entire systems or, worse, destroying data. Imagine that you're a part-time accounting clerk for a big corporation like Adidas. Your friend gives you a computer game with a harmless virus to play with. To add some fun to your work, you decide to load the game onto the company's network system.

Ethical Decision Making:

☞ What are the ethical issues?

☞ What are the alternatives?

☞ Who are the affected parties?

☞ How do the alternatives affect the parties?

☞ What would you do?

Now that you have studied this section, complete the following questions and problems.

Thinking Critically

1. Why are closing entries for revenue and expense accounts recorded?
2. What is the purpose of the **Income Summary** account?

Communicating Accounting

It is 8:00 A.M. and your boss, Gregory Levi, posted a note on your phone asking you to come see him. He does not understand why his owner's equity account shows a decrease. You determine that the reason for the decrease in owner's equity is the amount of withdrawals made this quarter. Before you see your boss, you make a few notes. Write out some discussion points to help you explain the situation. Then pick a colleague to listen to your explanation, which should include proof that you understand the closing of the balance of a withdrawals account to a capital account.

Please see me... Gregory

Problem 10–1 **Preparing Closing Entries**

Instructions Prepare closing entries for the following in your working papers.
1. A closing entry must be made for the account **Ticket Revenue**, which has a balance of $6,000.
2. A business has three expense accounts: **Gas and Oil Expense** (balance, $700), **Miscellaneous Expense** (balance, $600), and **Utilities Expense** (balance, $1,800). The end of the fiscal year is June 30.

Problem 10–2 **Analyzing a Source Document**

Instructions Using the source document:
1. Journalize the transaction in a general journal in your working papers.
2. Post the entry to the appropriate T accounts.
3. Assume it is the end of the accounting period. Record the closing entry for this account in the general journal.
4. Post the closing entry to the appropriate T accounts.

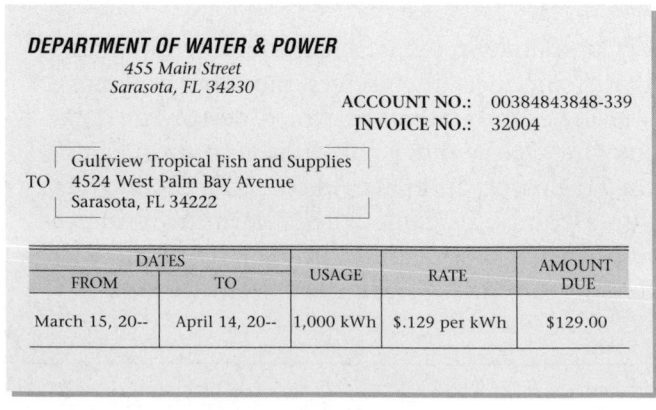

DEPARTMENT OF WATER & POWER
455 Main Street
Sarasota, FL 34230

ACCOUNT NO.: 00384843848-339
INVOICE NO.: 32004

TO Gulfview Tropical Fish and Supplies
4524 West Palm Bay Avenue
Sarasota, FL 34222

DATES		USAGE	RATE	AMOUNT DUE
FROM	TO			
March 15, 20--	April 14, 20--	1,000 kWh	$.129 per kWh	$129.00

Posting Closing Entries and Preparing a Post-Closing Trial Balance

Completing the Eighth Step in the Accounting Cycle: Posting Closing Entries to the General Ledger

In the last section you learned how to prepare four closing entries. The next step in the closing process is to post the closing entries to the general ledger accounts. The posting procedure is the same as for any other general journal entry, with one exception. The word "Closing" is written in the Description column of the general ledger account. The posting of the closing entries for Roadrunner is shown in **Figure 10–5.**

What You'll Learn

- How to record closing entries in the general ledger.
- The purpose of a post-closing trial balance.
- How to prepare a post-closing trial balance.

Why It's Important

A post-closing trial balance verifies that the closing entries are properly recorded in the general ledger and that you are ready to start the next accounting period.

KEY TERMS

post-closing trial balance

GENERAL JOURNAL   PAGE _____3_____

	DATE		DESCRIPTION	POST. REF.	DEBIT	CREDIT	
1	20--		*Closing Entries*				1
2	Oct.	31	Delivery Revenue	401	2 6 5 0 00		2
3			Income Summary	303		2 6 5 0 00	3
4							4
5		31	Income Summary	303	1 5 0 0 00		5
6			Advertising Expense	501		7 5 00	6
7			Maintenance Expense	505		6 0 0 00	7
8			Rent Expense	510		7 0 0 00	8
9			Utilities Expense	515		1 2 5 00	0
10							10
11		31	Income Summary	303	1 1 5 0 00		11
12			Maria Sanchez, Capital	301		1 1 5 0 00	12
13							13
14		31	Maria Sanchez, Capital	301	5 0 0 00		14
15			Maria Sanchez, Withdrawals	302		5 0 0 00	15
16							16

ACCOUNT _Maria Sanchez, Capital_   ACCOUNT NO. _301_

DATE		DESCRIPTION	POST. REF.	DEBIT	CREDIT	BALANCE DEBIT	BALANCE CREDIT
20--							
Oct.	1		G1		25 0 0 0 00		25 0 0 0 00
	2		G1		4 0 0 00		25 4 0 0 00
	31	Closing	G3		1 1 5 0 00		26 5 5 0 00
	31	Closing	G3	5 0 0 00			26 0 5 0 00

Figure 10–5 Closing Entries Posted to the General Ledger

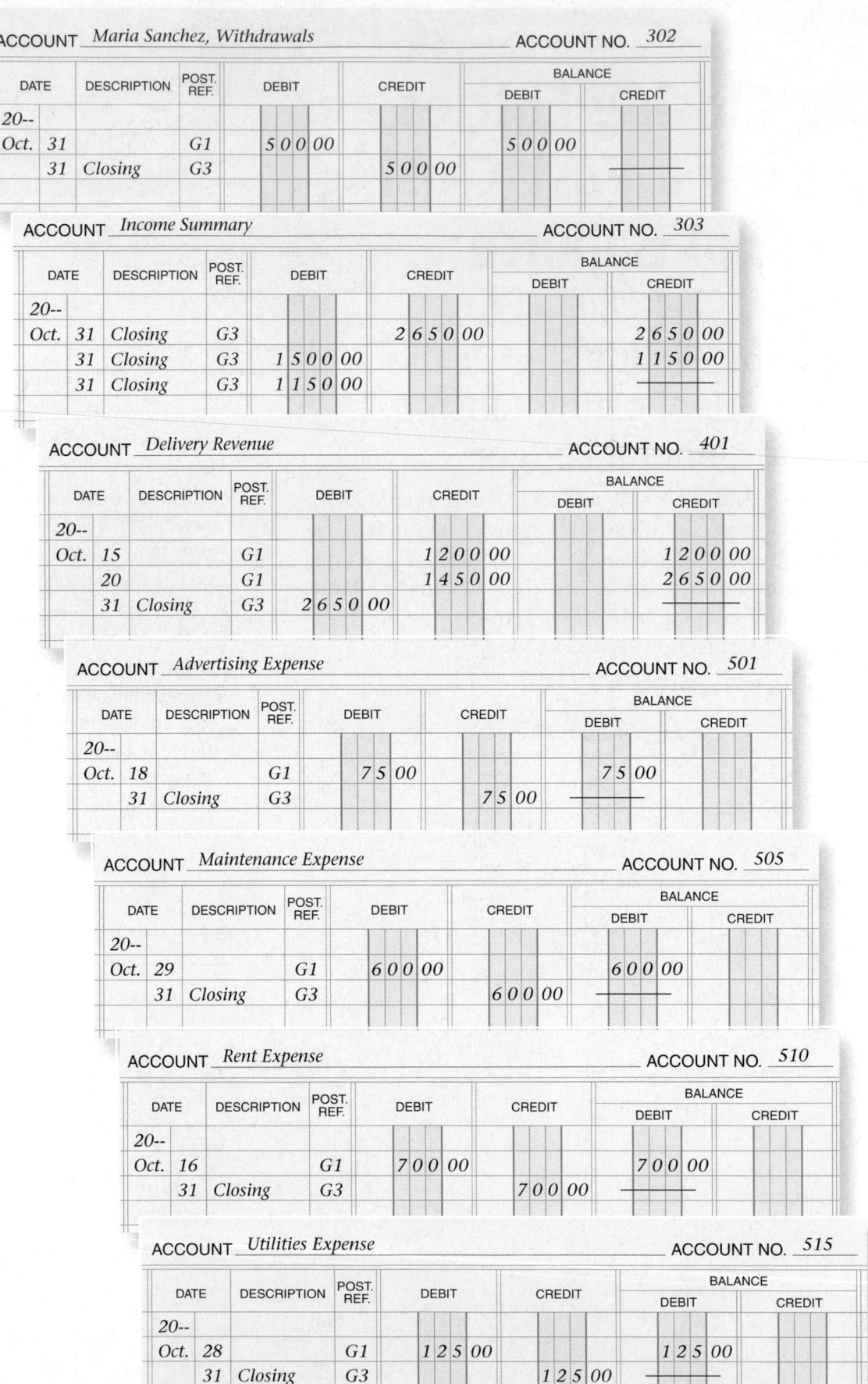

ACCOUNT Maria Sanchez, Withdrawals   **ACCOUNT NO.** 302

DATE	DESCRIPTION	POST. REF.	DEBIT	CREDIT	BALANCE DEBIT	BALANCE CREDIT
20--						
Oct. 31		G1	500 00		500 00	
31	Closing	G3		500 00		

ACCOUNT Income Summary   **ACCOUNT NO.** 303

DATE	DESCRIPTION	POST. REF.	DEBIT	CREDIT	BALANCE DEBIT	BALANCE CREDIT
20--						
Oct. 31	Closing	G3		2650 00		2650 00
31	Closing	G3	1500 00			1150 00
31	Closing	G3	1150 00			

ACCOUNT Delivery Revenue   **ACCOUNT NO.** 401

DATE	DESCRIPTION	POST. REF.	DEBIT	CREDIT	BALANCE DEBIT	BALANCE CREDIT
20--						
Oct. 15		G1		1200 00		1200 00
20		G1		1450 00		2650 00
31	Closing	G3	2650 00			

ACCOUNT Advertising Expense   **ACCOUNT NO.** 501

DATE	DESCRIPTION	POST. REF.	DEBIT	CREDIT	BALANCE DEBIT	BALANCE CREDIT
20--						
Oct. 18		G1	75 00		75 00	
31	Closing	G3		75 00		

ACCOUNT Maintenance Expense   **ACCOUNT NO.** 505

DATE	DESCRIPTION	POST. REF.	DEBIT	CREDIT	BALANCE DEBIT	BALANCE CREDIT
20--						
Oct. 29		G1	600 00		600 00	
31	Closing	G3		600 00		

ACCOUNT Rent Expense   **ACCOUNT NO.** 510

DATE	DESCRIPTION	POST. REF.	DEBIT	CREDIT	BALANCE DEBIT	BALANCE CREDIT
20--						
Oct. 16		G1	700 00		700 00	
31	Closing	G3		700 00		

ACCOUNT Utilities Expense   **ACCOUNT NO.** 515

DATE	DESCRIPTION	POST. REF.	DEBIT	CREDIT	BALANCE DEBIT	BALANCE CREDIT
20--						
Oct. 28		G1	125 00		125 00	
31	Closing	G3		125 00		

Figure 10–5 Closing Entries Posted to the General Ledger (continued)

Permanent Accounts

After closing, the only accounts with balances are permanent accounts.

The Ninth Step in the Accounting Cycle: Preparing a Post-Closing Trial Balance

The last step in the accounting cycle is to prepare a post-closing trial balance. The **post-closing trial balance** is prepared to make sure total debits equal total credits after the closing entries are posted. The post-closing trial balance for Roadrunner is shown in **Figure 10–6.**

Notice that only accounts with balances are listed on the post-closing trial balance. After the closing process, only permanent accounts have balances. Temporary accounts have zero balances, so there is no need to list those accounts on the post-closing trial balance.

ACCOUNTING Flashbacks

ACCOUNTING TEXTBOOKS

Friar Luca Pacioli published the first complete accounting textbook, *Summa de Arithmetica, Geometria: Proportioni et Proportionalita* in 1494. The double-entry system he described is still used today.

Roadrunner Delivery Service				
Post-Closing Trial Balance				
October 31, 20--				
Cash in Bank	21 1 2 5 00			
Accounts Receivable—City News	1 4 5 0 00			
Computer Equipment	3 0 0 0 00			
Office Equipment	2 0 0 00			
Delivery Equipment	12 0 0 0 00			
Accounts Payable—Beacon Advertising			7 5 00	
Accounts Payable—North Shore Auto			11 6 5 0 00	
Maria Sanchez, Capital			26 0 5 0 00	
Total	37 7 7 5 00		37 7 7 5 00	

Figure 10–6 Post-Closing Trial Balance

ANALYZING FINANCIAL REPORTS

Calculating Return on Owner's Equity

The statement of changes in owner's equity reports the amount of the owner's interest in the business. If the business is successful and growing, owner's equity should increase each fiscal period. One measure of business success is the **return on owner's equity.** Look at the following example.

$$\frac{\text{Net Income}}{\text{Beginning Owner's Equity} - \text{Withdrawals}} = \frac{\$3,600}{\$34,500 - \$2,500} = 11.25\%$$

The resulting percentage shows the amount earned during the period on each dollar invested by the owner.

▶ **Analyze the Report:**

Use the income statement on page 206 and the statement of changes in owner's equity for Roadrunner Delivery Service on page 211 to answer these questions.

1. Calculate the return on owner's equity for the month of October.
2. If you were the owner of Roadrunner Delivery Service, how would you evaluate the return on equity? For example, if current rates on savings paid by banks is 5 percent, how does your return on equity compare?

Now that you have studied this section, complete the following questions and problems.

Thinking Critically

1. After the closing process, what types of accounts have balances other than zero, and what types of accounts have zero balances?
2. What is the purpose of the eighth and ninth steps in the accounting cycle?

Communicating Accounting

The Electric Light Company has a large accounting department, and every accounting clerk has specific duties. Your co-worker, Denise Doster, is ill today, and she usually completes the post-closing trial balance. You are too busy with your own work to complete this task, and Denise cannot be reached by phone, so you have to show another accounting clerk how to prepare the post-closing trial balance. Explain where the balances are pulled from and how to set up the post-closing trial balance. Using your computer or lined paper, draft an example for the accounting clerk to follow.

Problem 10–3 Determining Accounts Affected by Closing Entries

The following list contains some of the accounts used by the Living Well Health Spa.

General Ledger

Accts. Pay.—The Fitness Shop Membership Fees
Accts. Rec.—Linda Brown Miscellaneous Expense
Advertising Expense Office Furniture
Cash in Bank Rent Expense
Exercise Class Revenue Repair Tools
Exercise Equipment Ted Chapman, Capital
Income Summary Ted Chapman, Withdrawals
Laundry Equipment Utilities Expense
Maintenance Expense

Instructions Using the form in your working papers:

1. In the first column, indicate the financial statement where each account appears: balance sheet or income statement.
2. In the next column, indicate whether or not the account is affected by a closing entry.
3. In the last column, indicate whether or not the account appears on the post-closing trial balance.

The first account is shown as an example.

Account Name	Financial Statement	Is the account affected by a closing entry?	Does the account appear on the post-closing trial balance?
Accts. Pay.—The Fitness Shop	Balance Sheet	No	Yes

KEY CONCEPTS

1. The eighth step in the accounting cycle is to journalize and post the closing entries.
2. The ninth step in the accounting cycle is to prepare a post-closing trial balance.
3. Closing is the process of transferring the balances in the temporary capital accounts to the owner's capital account. The work sheet shows the balances of the temporary capital accounts.
4. Only temporary capital accounts are closed. The asset, liability, and owner's capital accounts are never closed.
5. The first closing entry transfers the balance of the revenue account(s) to **Income Summary.**
6. The second closing entry transfers the balances of the expense accounts to **Income Summary.**
7. The third closing entry transfers the balance of the **Income Summary** account (the net income or net loss for the period) to the owner's capital account.
8. The fourth closing entry transfers the balance of the withdrawals account to the owner's capital account.

1	*20--*						1
2	*Dec.*	*31*	*Revenue Account*	*X X X XX*			2
3			*Income Summary*		*X X X XX*		3
4		*31*	*Income Summary*	*X X X XX*			4
5			*Expense Account*		*X X X XX*		5
6			*Expense Account*		*X X X XX*		6
7			*Expense Account*		*X X X XX*		7
8		*31*	*Income Summary*	*X X X XX*			8
9			*Owner's Capital Account*		*X X X XX*		9
12		*31*	*Owner's Capital Account*	*X X X XX*			12
13			*Withdrawals Account*		*X X X XX*		13

9. After the closing entries are journalized, they are posted to the general ledger. A post-closing trial balance is prepared to verify the equality of total debits and total credits in the general ledger after the closing entries are posted.

Roadrunner Delivery Service		
Post-Closing Trial Balance		
December 31, 20--		
Cash in Bank	21 1 2 5 00	
Accts. Rec.—City News	1 4 5 0 00	
Computer Equipment	3 0 0 0 00	
Office Equipment	2 0 0 00	
Delivery Equipment	12 0 0 0 00	
Accts. Pay.—Beacon Advertising		7 5 00
Accts. Pay.—North Shore Auto		11 6 5 0 00
Maria Sanchez, Capital		26 0 5 0 00
Totals	37 7 7 5 00	37 7 7 5 00

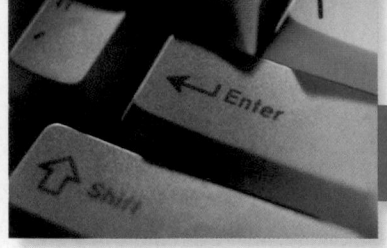

USING KEY TERMS

On a separate sheet of paper, write a brief definition for each term below.

closing entries
compound entry

Income Summary account
post-closing trial balance

Understanding Accounting Concepts and Procedures

Instructions

On a separate sheet of paper, answer the following questions:

1. Why are the temporary capital accounts closed at the end of the fiscal year?

2. Which accounts are considered temporary capital accounts?

3. What is the purpose of the **Income Summary** account?

4. Explain the relationship between the **Income Summary** account and the capital account.

5. How is the **Income Summary** account different from the other temporary capital accounts?

6. Why doesn't the **Income Summary** account have a normal balance?

7. List the steps for closing the temporary capital accounts.

8. What is the source of information for the closing entries?

9. Why is a compound entry useful when closing the expense accounts?

10. How does the closing procedure for net loss differ from the closing procedure for net income?

11. Why is the balance of the withdrawals account closed to the capital account?

12. How are the posting procedures for closing entries and for other general journal entries different?

13. Why is the post-closing trial balance prepared?

14. Why do only the balances of permanent accounts appear on the post-closing trial balance?

Case Study...

Service Business: Computer Consulting

You are the accountant for Computer Works, a computer consulting business. After preparing financial statements and completing the closing entries below, you notice that the owner's capital account balance in the general ledger of $34,400 differs from the ending capital balance of $43,400 on the statement of changes in owner's equity. The capital account balance was $38,900 at the beginning of the month.

Date	Description	Debit	Credit
Aug. 31	Consulting Fee Revenue	9,240	
	Income Summary		9,240
Aug. 31	Income Summary	870	
	Advertising Expense		300
	Internet Access Expense		20
	Rent Expense		550
Aug. 31	Rex Moran, Capital	8,100	
	Income Summary		8,100

Thinking Critically:

1. Identify the mistakes in the closing entries.
2. What is the correct capital account balance?

Conducting an Audit with Alex

The work sheet and financial statements for Bennett Company for November are complete. The balances of revenue, expense and equity accounts are:

Service Revenue	$ 6,200
Advertising Expense	900
Miscellaneous Expense	300
Rent Expense	1,400
Utilities Expense	600
Dale Bennett, Capital	30,000
Dale Bennett, Withdrawals	2,000

Instructions Answer the following questions about the closing entries that will be prepared:

1. What is the amount of the debit to the **Income Summary** to close out the expense accounts?
2. What is the amount of the credit to the **Income Summary** to close out the revenue account?

inter NET CONNECTION

Accounting Publications

When using the Internet, the accountant has many resources at his or her fingertips. Whether you're interested in the latest tax laws, accounting software, or professional conduct tips, you'll find publications that cover these topics and others.

Do This:

1. Locate and list five accounting publications on the Internet.
2. Describe the information each publication contains.
3. Imagine you have landed your first accounting job in a CPA office. Which publication do you think would be most helpful?

Workplace Skills

Working in a Team

Completion of projects at work often requires a variety of talents and skills. You may be asked to work as part of a team to complete a budget for your department or create a presentation on your group's latest achievement.

On the Job:

Imagine that you work in the accounting department for the multimedia division of MTV. The CD-ROM project manager wants to produce a new CD-ROM that will contain clips from the latest music videos to sell in stores. You and your co-workers in accounting have questions:

- What are the engineering costs for the CD-ROM?
- When will the CD-ROM be on the shelves at music stores?
- What will be the price of the product?

Thinking Critically:

1. Form a team of five students. Outline other questions you may have for the project manager.
2. Compile your questions and opinions about the product (from a financial perspective) into a one-page report.
3. Present your report to the class.

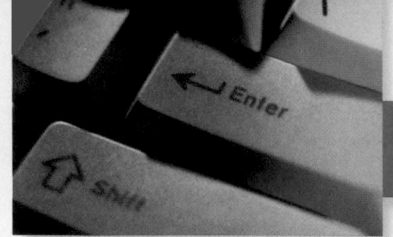

Closing the Accounting Period
Making the Transition from a Manual to a Computerized System

Task	Perform Accounting Procedures Using Manual Methods	Perform Accounting Procedures Using Automated Methods
Closing Entries	• Using a general journal form, prepare closing entries for revenue, expense, income summary, and withdrawals accounts. Post the closing entries in the general ledger accounts.	• It is not necessary to journalize closing entries. Closing entries are performed by the computerized system.

Closing the Accounting Period

Peachtree Question	Description
What is the difference between changing the accounting period and closing the fiscal year in Peachtree?	• At the end of an accounting period (usually at month-end), you should change to the next accounting period. For example, at March 30, 20— you would select the next accounting period, April 1, 20— through April 30, 20—. • The fiscal year should be closed only when you are sure that all entries have been recorded and all reports have been printed for the year.
How do I change the accounting period?	When you finish entering all transactions for the month and are ready to move to the next month, you must change the accounting period. 1. Select **System** from the *Tasks* menu. 2. Select Change Accounting Period. 3. Select the next accounting period from the pull-down menu. 4. Peachtree asks if you would like to print monthly reports before continuing. Do so if necessary. Click *OK*.
What does the software do "behind the scenes"?	• The software will change the accounting period and it will appear in the status bar at the bottom of the screen. • Now you may enter transactions for the new month.
How do I close the fiscal year?	1. Post and print all journal entries before closing the fiscal year. Closing the fiscal year cannot be reversed. 2. From the *Tasks* menu, select **System**. 3. Select Year-End Wizard. 4. You will be prompted to complete Year-End closing procedures.
What does the software do "behind the scenes"?	• Closing the fiscal year will zero all income and expense accounts and post them to the Retained Earnings account, essentially preparing and posting all closing entries.

For detailed instructions: See the Peachtree User Guide in your Glencoe Working Papers.

APPLICATION OPTIONS

Problem 10–4 Preparing Closing Entries

A portion of the work sheet for Wilderness Rentals for the period ended December 31 appears below.

Instructions Using the information from the work sheet, prepare the journal entries to close the temporary capital accounts.

1. Record the closing entry for the revenue account.
2. Record the closing entry for the expense accounts.
3. Record the closing entry for the **Income Summary** account.
4. Record the closing entry for the withdrawals account.

Complete chapter problems one of four ways:

1 **Manual** Glencoe Working Papers

or

2 **Peachtree Complete Accounting** Software

or

3 **QuickBooks** Templates (Problems 10–8, 10–9)

or

4 **Spreadsheet** Templates (Problem 10–9)

Peachtree®

SMART GUIDE

Step–by–Step Instructions: Problem 10–4

1. Select the problem set for Wilderness Rentals (Prob. 10–4).
2. Rename the company and set the system date.
3. Select **System** from the **Tasks** menu and then choose **Year-End Wizard.**
4. Answer the Analyze question.
5. End the session.

TIP: Print the General Ledger or General Ledger Trial Balance report to find an account balance.

Wilderness Rentals
Work Sheet
For the Period Ended December 31, 20--

	ACCT. NO.	ACCOUNT NAME	INCOME STATEMENT DEBIT	INCOME STATEMENT CREDIT	BALANCE SHEET DEBIT	BALANCE SHEET CREDIT	
1	101	Cash in Bank			7 000 00		1
2	105	Accts. Rec.—Helen Katz			2 000 00		2
3	110	Accts. Rec.—Polk and Co.			1 000 00		3
4	115	Office Supplies			900 00		4
5	120	Office Equipment			12 000 00		5
6	125	Camping Equipment			6 000 00		6
7	201	Accts. Pay.—Adventure Equip. Inc.				900 00	7
8	203	Accts. Pay.—Digital Tech Computers				400 00	8
9	205	Accts. Pay.—Greg Mollaro				500 00	9
10	301	Ronald Hicks, Capital				19 775 00	10
11	305	Ronald Hicks, Withdrawals			2 350 00		11
12	310	Income Summary					12
13	401	Equipment Rental Revenue		14 965 00			13
14	501	Advertising Expense	1 500 00				14
15	505	Maintenance Expense	1 560 00				15
16	515	Rent Expense	1 000 00				16
17	525	Utilities Expense	1 230 00				17
18			5 290 00	14 965 00	31 250 00	21 575 00	18
19		Net Income	9 675 00			9 675 00	19
20			14 965 00	14 965 00	31 250 00	31 250 00	20
21							21

Analyze: What is the capital account balance after posting the closing entries?

Problem 10–5 Preparing a Post-Closing Trial Balance

Instructions Use the accounts shown on the next two pages to prepare a Dec. 31 post-closing trial balance for Hot Suds Car Wash.

Continued

Peachtree®

SMART GUIDE

**Step–by–Step Instructions:
Problem 10–5**

1. Select the problem set for Hot Suds Car Wash (Prob. 10–5).
2. Rename the company and set the system date.
3. Print a General Ledger Trial Balance.
4. Answer the Analyze question.
5. End the session.

TIP: Print the General Ledger Trial Balance after you complete the closing process to generate a post-closing trial balance.

Cash in Bank

Debit +	Credit −
Balance 8,000	

Accounts Receivable— Valley Auto

Debit +	Credit −
Balance 5,050	

Office Furniture

Debit +	Credit −
Balance 9,000	

Accounts Payable— Allen Vacuum Systems

Debit −	Credit +
	Balance 41,000

Regina Delgado, Capital

Debit −	Credit +
Closing 1,500	35,925
	Closing 16,000

Income Summary

Debit	Credit
Closing 19,000	Closing 35,000
Closing 16,000	

Wax Revenue

Debit −	Credit +
Closing 8,000	Balance 8,000

Advertising Expense

Debit +	Credit −
Balance 2,500	Closing 2,500

Accounts Receivable— Linda Brown

Debit +	Credit −
Balance 875	

Office Equipment

Debit +	Credit −
Balance 6,000	

Car Wash Equipment

Debit +	Credit −
Balance 65,000	

Accounts Payable— O'Brian's Office Supply

Debit −	Credit +
	Balance 2,500

Regina Delgado, Withdrawals

Debit +	Credit −
Balance 1,500	Closing 1,500

Wash Revenue

Debit −	Credit +
Closing 15,000	Balance 15,000

Interior Detailing Revenue

Debit −	Credit +
Closing 12,000	Balance 12,000

Equipment Rental Expense

Debit +	Credit −
Balance 3,000	Closing 3,000

Continued

Maintenance Expense	
Debit + Balance 5,000	Credit − Closing 5,000

Rent Expense	
Debit + Balance 5,000	Credit − Closing 5,000

Utilities Expense	
Debit + Balance 3,500	Credit − Closing 3,500

Analyze: What is the balance of the temporary accounts after the closing entries are posted?

Peachtree®

SMART GUIDE

Step–by–Step Instructions: Problem 10–6

1. Select the problem set for Kits & Pups Grooming (Prob. 10–6).
2. Rename the company and set the system date.
3. Close the current fiscal year.
4. Answer the Analyze question.
5. End the session.

Problem 10–6 Journalizing Closing Entries

The following account names and balances appear on the work sheet for Kits & Pups Grooming for the month ended December 31.

Kits & Pups Grooming
Work Sheet
For the Month Ended December 31, 20--

ACCT NO.	ACCOUNT NAME	INCOME STATEMENT DEBIT	INCOME STATEMENT CREDIT	BALANCE SHEET DEBIT	BALANCE SHEET CREDIT	
1	Cash in Bank			9 300 00		1
2	Accts. Rec.—Juan Alvarez			3 000 00		2
3	Accts. Rec.—Nathan Carlsbad			10 000 00		3
4	Accts. Rec.—Martha Giles			5 000 00		4
5	Office Equipment			8 000 00		5
6	Office Furniture			10 000 00		6
7	Computer Equipment			9 000 00		7
8	Grooming Equipment			15 000 00		8
9	Kennel Equipment			21 000 00		9
10	Accts. Pay.—Able Store Equip.				5 000 00	10
11	Accts. Pay.—Dogs & Cats Inc.				1 500 00	11
12	Accts. Pay.—Pet Gourmet				15 000 00	12
13	Abe Shultz, Capital				52 700 00	13
14	Abe Shultz, Withdrawals			7 000 00		14
15	Income Summary					15
16	Boarding Revenue		20 000 00			16
17	Grooming Revenue		8 000 00			17
18	Advertising Expense	700 00				18
19	Equipment Repair Expense	1 200 00				19
20	Maintenance Expense	500 00				20
21	Rent Expense	1 700 00				21
22	Utilities Expense	800 00				22

Instructions Using the above information, record the closing entries for Kits & Pups Grooming. Use general journal page 11.

Analyze: What was the change in the capital account for the period?

Peachtree®

SMART GUIDE

**Step–by–Step Instructions:
Problem 10–7**

1. Select the problem set for Outback Guide Service (Prob. 10–7).
2. Rename the company and set the system date.
3. Close the fiscal year.
4. Print a General Ledger Trial Balance.
5. Answer the Analyze question.
6. End the session.

Problem 10–7 Posting Closing Entries and Preparing a Post-Closing Trial Balance

The closing entries for Outback Guide Service for the period ended December 31 appear below.

	DATE		DESCRIPTION	POST. REF.	DEBIT	CREDIT	
1	20--		*Closing Entries*				1
2	*Dec.*	31	Guide Service Revenue		16 3 0 0 00		2
3			Income Summary			16 3 0 0 00	3
4		31	Income Summary		10 0 0 0 00		4
5			Advertising Expense			3 0 0 0 00	5
6			Maintenance Expense			1 1 0 0 00	6
7			Rent Expense			4 0 0 0 00	7
8			Utilities Expense			1 9 0 0 00	8
9		31	Income Summary		6 3 0 0 00		9
10			Juanita Ortega, Capital			6 3 0 0 00	10
11		31	Juanita Ortega, Capital		4 0 0 0 00		11
12			Juanita Ortega, Withdrawals			4 0 0 0 00	12

GENERAL JOURNAL — PAGE 1

Instructions In your working papers:

1. Post the closing entries to the appropriate general ledger accounts.
2. Using the general ledger in your working papers, prepare a post-closing trial balance.

Analyze: What is the balance of the capital account after closing?

Peachtree®

SMART GUIDE

**Step–by–Step Instructions:
Problem 10–8**

1. Select the problem set for Showbiz Video (Prob. 10–8).
2. Rename the company and set the system date.
3. Print a General Ledger Trial Balance.
4. Print an Income Statement, a Statement of Changes in Owner's Equity, and a Balance Sheet.
5. Close the fiscal year.
6. Print a General Ledger Trial Balance.
7. Answer the Analyze question.
8. End the session.

TIP: You can use the General Ledger navigation aid to access the financial statements.

Problem 10–8 Completing End-of-Period Activities

The general ledger for Showbiz Video shows the following at December 31:

General Ledger

101	Cash in Bank	12,000	207	Accts. Pay.—	
105	Accts. Rec.—G. Cohen	3,000		New Media Suppliers	3,000
110	Accts. Rec.—J. Coletti	900	209	Accts. Pay.—Palace Films	14,000
113	Accts. Rec.—S. Flannery	1,800	301	Greg Failla, Capital	33,775
115	Accts. Rec.—Spring		305	Greg Failla, Withdrawals	4,000
	Branch School District	1,500	310	Income Summary	—
130	Office Equipment	5,000	401	Video Rental Revenue	9,600
135	Office Furniture	8,000	405	VCR Rental Revenue	3,500
140	Computer Equipment	10,000	501	Advertising Expense	1,600
145	Video Tapes	20,000	505	Equipment Repair	
150	Video Equipment	9,000		Expense	1,200
201	Accts. Pay.—Broad Street		510	Maintenance Expense	400
	Office Supply	400	520	Rent Expense	1,000
205	Accts. Pay.—		530	Utilities Expense	375
	Computer Horizons	15,500			

Instructions Using the preceding account names and balances:

1. Prepare the six-column work sheet. The period covered is one month.
2. Prepare the financial statements. Greg Failla invested $10,000 during the month.
3. Record the closing entries on page 12 of the general journal.
4. Post the closing entries.
5. Prepare a post-closing trial balance.

Analyze: What is the total amount of all the accounts receivable accounts on December 31?

 **Problem 10–9   Completing End-of-Period Activities**   **CHALLENGE PROBLEM**

At the end of December, the general ledger for Job Connect showed the following account balances:

General Ledger

101	Cash in Bank	6,000	207	Accts. Pay.—Wildwood Furniture Sales	2,000
105	Accts. Rec.—CompuRite Systems	1,000	301	Richard Tang, Capital	23,600
110	Accts. Rec.—Marquez Manufact.	500	302	Richard Tang, Withdrawals	3,000
113	Accts. Rec.—Roaring Rivers Water Park	600	303	Income Summary	—
115	Accts. Rec.—M. Spencer	200	401	Placement Fees Revenue	6,900
130	Office Equipment	7,000	405	Technology Classes Revenue	2,400
135	Office Furniture	5,000	501	Advertising Expense	3,000
140	Computer Equipment	8,500	505	Maintenance Expense	800
201	Accts. Pay.—Micro Solutions Inc.	2,800	510	Miscellaneous Expense	800
205	Accts. Pay.—Vega Internet Services	1,600	520	Rent Expense	2,000
			530	Utilities Expense	900

Instructions Using the preceding account names and balances:

1. Prepare the six-column work sheet. The period covered is one month.
2. Prepare the financial statements.
3. Record the closing entries on page 28 of the general journal.
4. Post the closing entries.
5. Prepare a post-closing trial balance.

Analyze: What was the greatest expenditure for the period?

CHAPTER 11

Cash Control and Banking Activities

Learning Objectives

When you have completed this chapter, you will be able to:

► Describe the internal controls used to protect cash.

► Describe the forms needed to open and use a checking account.

► Accurately record information on check stubs.

► Prepare a check correctly.

► Prepare bank deposits.

► Reconcile a bank statement.

► Journalize and post entries relating to bank service charges.

► Define the terms introduced in this chapter.

Exploring the Real World of Business

CONTROLLING CASH

If you're shopping for waterproof boots or a new waistpack, you could be looking at **Timberland**® products.

The Timberland Company designs and sells footwear, clothing, and accessories. **Timberland**® products are sold in more than 90 countries through specialty and department stores, in addition to its own retail locations. The company's flagship store is on Madison Avenue in New York. When you shop at a **Timberland**® store, you might pay for your purchase in cash or use a credit card.

What do you think?

If you worked at a **Timberland**® store, what are at least three cash controls you would use to help protect money received by the company?

Workplace Connections

Applying Your Accounting Knowledge

You cash your paycheck, stuff the cash in your wallet, and before you know it, it's gone! It's easy to lose track of how you spend your money. Businesses also have to watch their money carefully. One way of safeguarding cash is to keep it in the bank and write checks to make payments. You'll learn about a business checking account in this chapter.

Investigate:

1. Do you handle cash, checks, or credit cards in your job?
2. What procedures are in place to help protect cash?

Glencoe Accounting Online

Visit the *Glencoe Accounting* Web site at **glencoeaccounting.glencoe.com** for additional activities and information.

Banking Procedures

What You'll Learn

- What controls a business uses to protect cash and why these controls are needed.
- To complete forms used to open a checking account.
- To record information on check stubs.
- To prepare a check correctly.

Why It's Important

Cash is a valuable asset. It must be protected and processed properly.

KEY TERMS

internal controls
external controls
checking account
check
depositor
signature card
deposit slip
endorsement
restrictive endorsement
payee
drawer
drawee
voiding a check

In any business, cash (currency, coins, and checks) is used in daily transactions. A business receives cash in return for the goods or services it sells. It pays out cash to purchase goods and services and to pay its expenses. An important part of accounting for a business, therefore, involves tracking the cash received and paid out. For example, McDonald's has established procedures for processing the cash received from the sale of food and drinks. McDonald's also has a system of monitoring and controlling cash paid out for wages, utilities, supplies, and the numerous other expenses involved in operating a restaurant.

Cash needs protection to prevent loss or waste. One of the most commonly used controls is a checking account. The use of a checking account not only helps protect cash but also provides a separate record of cash transactions.

Protecting Cash

It is important to protect cash from loss, waste, theft, forgery, and embezzlement. Cash is protected through internal controls and external controls. **Internal controls** refer to those steps the business itself takes to protect cash and other assets. Internal controls for cash include:

1. Limiting the number of persons handling cash.
2. Separating accounting tasks involving cash. For example, one person handles cash receipts and payments, and a different person keeps the accounting records showing the amounts received or paid.
3. Bonding (insuring) employees who handle cash or cash records.
4. Using a cash register and a safe.
5. Depositing cash receipts in the bank daily.
6. Using checks to make all cash payments.

External controls are the measures and procedures provided outside the business to protect cash and other assets. For example, banks maintain controls to protect the funds their customers deposit. These controls include verifying the accuracy of signatures on checks and maintaining records of monetary transactions.

Opening a Checking Account

A **checking account** allows a person or business to deposit cash in a bank and to write checks against the account balance. A **check** is a written order from a depositor telling the bank to pay a stated amount of cash to the person or business named on the check. A **depositor** is a person or business that has cash on deposit in a bank.

Signature Card

To open a checking account, a business owner fills out a **signature card** and deposits cash in the bank. A signature card contains the signature(s) of the person(s) authorized to write checks on the account. The signature card is kept on file so that it can be matched against signed checks presented for payment. The use of a signature card protects both the account holder and the bank against checks with forged signatures. **Figure 11–1** shows the signature card used to open the checking account for Roadrunner Delivery Service.

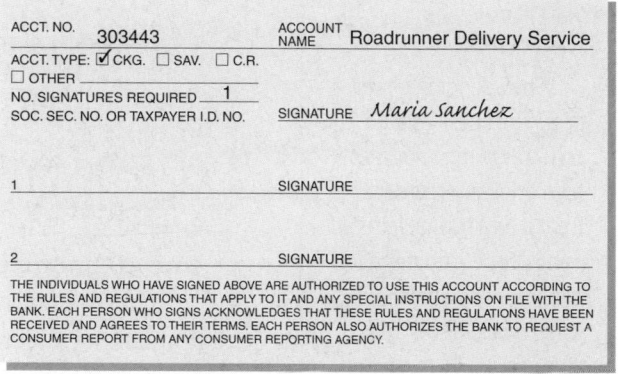

Figure 11–1 Checking Account Signature Card

Checkbook

When a depositor opens a checking account, checks are printed for the depositor's use. Printed checks are packaged together in *checkbooks* shown in **Figure 11–2**, which looks like a spiral-bound notebook. Each page has several detachable checks attached to check stubs, both numbered in sequence. Using checks with preprinted numbers helps a business keep track of every check that is written, an important internal control.

ABA Number

In addition to the check number, each check is printed with the account number and an American Bankers Association (ABA) number. The ABA number is the fractional number printed in the upper right corner of a check, just below the check number. The ABA number is a code that identifies the bank. For example, look at the ABA number on the check in **Figure 11–3**. The number above the line and to the left of the hyphen represents the city or state where the bank is located. The number to the right of the hyphen indicates the specific bank. The number below the line is the code for the Federal Reserve district where the bank is located.

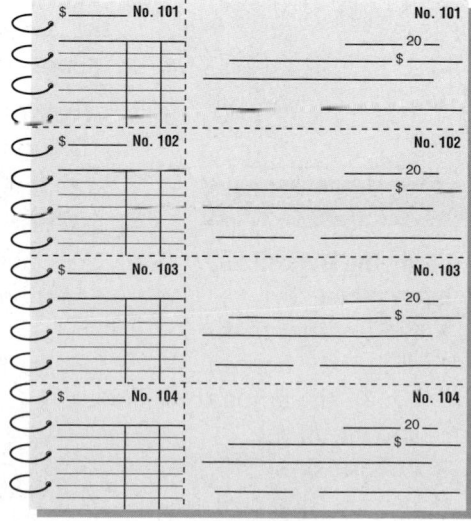

Figure 11–2 Checkbook

Figure 11–3 Printed Check

Roadrunner Delivery Service
155 Gateway Blvd.
Sacramento, CA 94230

No. 101

71-627
3222

DATE _____ 20 ____

PAY TO THE
ORDER OF _____ $ _____

_____ DOLLARS

❖ *American National Bank*
SACRAMENTO, CALIFORNIA

MEMO _____ _____

⑈322271627⑈ 303443⑈ 101

The ABA number was developed to speed the sorting of checks by hand. An updated version of the ABA number is also printed on the bottom of each check for electronic sorting. The ABA number, the depositor's account number, and sometimes the check number are printed at the bottom of the check in a special ink and typeface. These specially printed numbers are called MICR (magnetic ink character recognition) numbers. Can you identify the MICR numbers on the check in **Figure 11–3?**

Making Deposits to a Checking Account

Businesses make regular deposits to protect the currency, coins, and checks received. Most businesses make daily deposits. These deposits are accompanied by a **deposit slip**, a bank form listing the cash and checks to be deposited. The deposit slip, also called a deposit ticket, gives both the depositor and the bank a detailed record of the deposit. Most banks provide deposit slips with the depositor's name, address, and account number printed on the form. A deposit slip for Roadrunner Delivery Service is shown in **Figure 11–4.**

Let's learn how to prepare commercial bank deposits. To complete a deposit slip, follow these steps:

1. Write the date on the Date line.
2. On the Cash line, indicate the total amount of currency and coins to be deposited.
3. List checks separately by their ABA numbers. Write on the deposit slip only the two numbers that appear above the line in the ABA number. If there are many checks, list the checks by amount on a calculator tape and attach the tape to the deposit slip. On the first Checks line, write "See tape listing," followed by the total amount of the checks.
4. Add the cash and checks amounts, and write the total amount to be deposited on the Total line.

When the deposit slip is completed, the checks are arranged in the order listed on the deposit slip. The deposit slip and the cash and checks are handed to a bank teller. The teller verifies the deposit and gives the depositor a receipt. The deposit receipt may be a copy of the deposit slip stamped and initialed by the teller or it may be a machine-printed form.

Key Points

Verify the Deposit Slip Information

- Be sure that the cash to be deposited equals the amount shown on the deposit slip.
- Be sure each check to be deposited is listed on the deposit slip by ABA number.

Figure 11–4
Deposit Slip

Endorsing Checks

A check is a form of property. When a business receives a check in payment for a product or service, it acquires the right to that check. To deposit the check in a checking account, the depositor endorses the check to transfer ownership to the bank. An **endorsement** is an authorized signature written or stamped on the back of a check representing a promise to pay.

Burton Company wrote a check to Roadrunner to pay for delivery services. After Roadrunner endorses the check on the back, the check is deposited in Roadrunner's account at American National Bank. The endorsement by Roadrunner authorizes American National Bank to add the amount of the check to Roadrunner's account. Suppose American National Bank cannot collect the amount of the check from Burton Company—that is, Burton's account does not have sufficient funds to cover the check. Roadrunner must go back to Burton Company to collect payment.

There are several types of endorsements, but most businesses use restrictive endorsements. A **restrictive endorsement** limits, or restricts, how a check may be handled. To protect checks from being cashed by anyone else, Roadrunner stamps a restrictive endorsement, "For Deposit Only," on the back of each check as soon as it is received. By doing so, Roadrunner ensures that the check will be deposited in its checking account. See Figure 11–5 for a typical restrictive endorsement.

Figure 11–5 Restrictive Endorsement

Recording Deposits in the Checkbook

The check stubs in the checkbook are a record of the **Cash in Bank** account. That is, the completed stubs reflect all checking account transactions: payments, deposits, and bank service charges.

To see how to record a deposit in the checkbook, refer to **Figure 11–6** and follow these procedures:

1. Enter the date of the deposit on the Add Deposits line of the check stub for the next unused check.
2. Enter the total amount of the deposit on the same line in the Dollars and Cents (amount) columns.
3. Add the deposit amounts to the amount on the Balance Brought Forward line. Enter the result on the Total line. This total is the new checkbook balance.

Figure 11–6 Recording a Deposit in the Checkbook

Writing Checks

Writing a check involves a simple procedure. You need to follow a few important rules, however, to ensure correct recordkeeping and proper handling of the money represented by the check.

- Write checks in ink, or prepare typewritten or computer-generated checks. It is difficult to alter checks written in ink, prepared on a typewriter, or generated on a computer. Checks written in pencil are not acceptable because they can be easily altered.
- Complete the check stub *before* writing the check. This reduces the chance of forgetting to complete the stub. Because the stub serves as a permanent record of the check, it is important that the stub be complete and accurate.

Completing the Check Stub

A check stub is divided into two parts. The upper part summarizes the details of the cash payment transaction. The lower part is a record of how the transaction affects the checking account. It contains the balance before the transaction, any current deposits, the transaction amount, and the balance after the transaction. To see how to complete the check stub, refer to **Figure 11–7** and follow these steps:

1. In the upper part of the stub, enter the amount of the check, the date, the name of the payee (on the To line), and the purpose of the check (on the For line). A **payee** is the person or business to whom a check is written.
2. If it is not already done, enter the balance on the Total line on the lower part of the stub.
3. Enter the amount of the check on the Less This Check line. This amount is the same as the amount shown on the first line in the upper part of the stub.
4. Subtract the check amount from the total. Enter the new balance on the Balance Carried Forward line.
5. Enter the new balance on the first line of the bottom part of the *next* check stub, the Balance Brought Forward line.

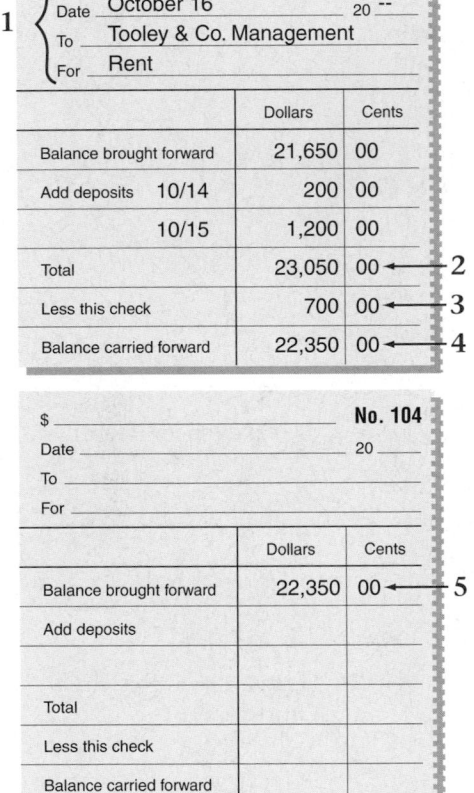

Figure 11–7 Filling Out the Check Stub

Filling Out the Check

When the check stub is complete, the next step is to write the check. Remember to write the check in ink so that it cannot easily be changed. To see how to write a check, refer to **Figure 11–8** and follow these steps:

1. Write the date on which the check is being issued.
2. Write the payee's name on the Pay To The Order Of line. Start the payee's name as far left as possible.
3. Enter the amount of the check in numbers. Write clearly, and begin the first number as close to the printed dollar sign as possible.
4. On the next line, write the dollar amount of the check *in words*. Start at the left edge of the line. Write any cents as a fraction. For example, write 22 cents as 22/100. Draw a line from the cents fraction to the word "Dollars."

> ### Key Points
>
> **The Check Stub**
> Always complete the check stub *before* you write a check.

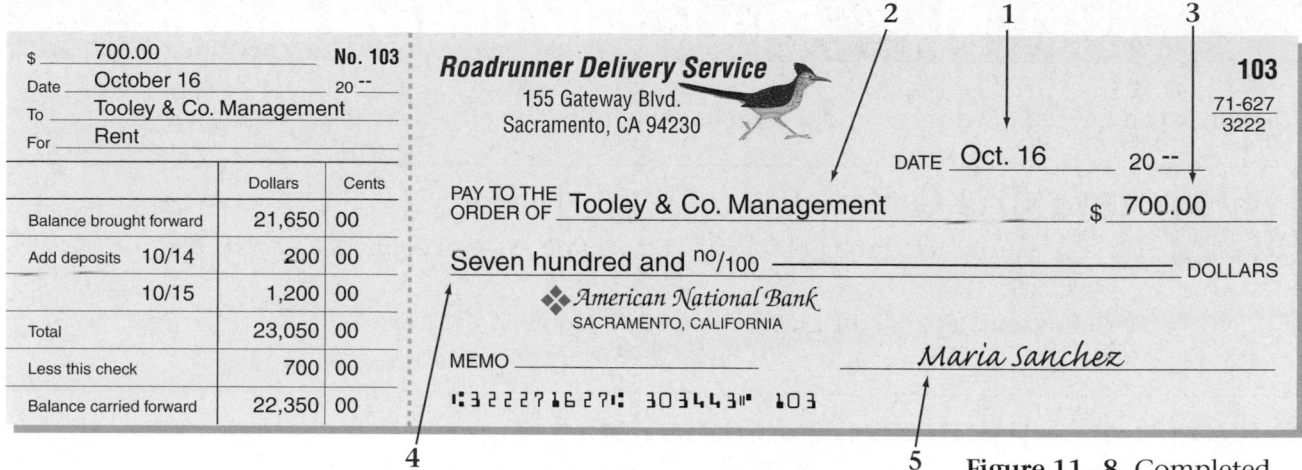

$ 700.00		No. 103
Date October 16		20 --
To Tooley & Co. Management		
For Rent		

	Dollars	Cents
Balance brought forward	21,650	00
Add deposits 10/14	200	00
10/15	1,200	00
Total	23,050	00
Less this check	700	00
Balance carried forward	22,350	00

Roadrunner Delivery Service
155 Gateway Blvd.
Sacramento, CA 94230

103

71-627
3222

DATE Oct. 16 20 --

PAY TO THE ORDER OF Tooley & Co. Management $ 700.00

Seven hundred and no/100 ———————————— DOLLARS

American National Bank
SACRAMENTO, CALIFORNIA

MEMO ———————— *Maria Sanchez*

⑆322271627⑆ 303443⑈ 103

Figure 11–8 Completed Check and Stub

5. Sign the check. Only an authorized person—one who has signed the signature card for the account—may sign the check. The person who signs a check is the **drawer** . The bank on which the check is written is the **drawee** .

The checkbook is now ready for the next transaction.

Some businesses prepare checks using a check-writing machine, which perforates the amount of the check in words on the Dollars line. These perforations protect a check from alteration, since the holes in the check are almost impossible to alter.

Voiding a Check

If an error is made while writing a check, that check is not used. Corrected checks look suspicious to banks. Instead, the incorrect check is marked "Void" and a new check is prepared. Writing the word "Void" in large letters across the front of a check (in ink) is known as **voiding a check** . When a check is voided, the stub is also voided.

Since a business needs to account for each check used, a voided check is never destroyed. Instead it is filed with the business records. A voided check may be placed in a special file, or it may simply be folded and stapled to the check stub.

A MATTER OF ETHICS

Pocketing Differences

Imagine that you are a cashier at a grocery store like Ralphs. In a four-hour shift, you handle thousands of dollars. At the end of your shift, you total receipts and cash to see if they match. One day, cash comes up short, and you report the discrepancy to the manager. A few weeks later, cash is over by two dollars. You know a couple of cashiers who pocket extra cash. You wonder who would miss two dollars.

Ethical Decision Making:

☛ What are the ethical issues?

☛ What are the alternatives?

☛ Who are the affected parties?

☛ How do the alternatives affect the parties?

☛ What would you do?

Now that you have studied this section, complete the following questions and problems.

Thinking Critically

1. Cash is protected through internal controls and external controls. Describe controls over cash.
2. Define and describe the purpose of an ABA number.

Communicating Accounting

Assume you work for a sporting goods store that is open six days a week from 9:00 A.M. to 9:00 P.M. Due to a major promotion, the store is making record sales and the manager has been too busy to make daily cash deposits. Discuss with your classmates and teacher why it is important to take time each day to deposit cash receipts.

Problem 11–1 Preparing a Deposit Slip and Writing Checks

On August 14, Loretta Harper, owner of Peabody Cards and Gifts, deposited the following items in the checking account of the business.

Cash: $784.29

Checks: Charles Ling, drawn on American Bank of Commerce, ABA No. 32-7091; $39.44

Keith Lopez, drawn on People's Bank, ABA No. 84-268; $22.95

Marjorie Luke, drawn on Horizon Federal Savings and Loan, ABA No. 84-6249; $52.95

Mable Parker, drawn on Security National Bank, ABA No. 84-2242; $67.45

On August 15, Peabody Cards and Gifts received a bill from Northeast Telephone for $214.80 for July telephone services.

On August 17, Peabody received a bill from the Bayside News for $275.00.

Instructions Using the forms provided in your working papers:

1. Complete a deposit slip.
2. Record the deposit on the check stub for Check 41.
3. Check 41 is issued to pay the telephone bill on August 16. Record the information for Check 41 on the check stub and complete the check stub.
4. Prepare Check 41 to pay the telephone bill. Use August 16 as the date and sign your name as drawer.
5. Prepare Check 42 to pay the bill for advertising. Use August 17 as the date and sign your name as drawer.

Reconciling the Bank Account

Have you ever forgotten to record a cash withdrawal from your bank account and then been surprised to find that you have less money than you thought? If so, you understand the importance of reconciling (bringing into agreement) your checkbook with your bank statement. Business owners and their accountants also need to keep their records up-to-date when it comes to cash. An important part of accounting for cash for both large multinational companies, like General Motors, and small local companies, like the video game arcade at the mall, is the comparison and reconciliation of the bank statement with company records.

Proving Cash

The balance in the **Cash in Bank** account in the general ledger is regularly compared with the balance in the checkbook. If all cash receipts are deposited, all cash payments are made by check, and all transactions are journalized and posted, the **Cash in Bank** account balance should agree with the checkbook balance. Comparing these two cash balances regularly is part of the internal control of cash. Some businesses prove cash daily or weekly, while others prove cash on a monthly basis.

If the **Cash in Bank** balance does not agree with the checkbook balance, and the trial balance is proved, the error is probably in the checkbook. A checkbook error is usually the result of **(1)** faulty addition or subtraction, **(2)** failure to record a deposit or a check, or **(3)** a mistake in copying the balance forward amount to the Balance Brought Forward line of the next check stub.

If an error is made in the checkbook, the proper place to enter the correction is on the next unused check stub. For example, suppose Check 22 for $84.60 was recorded on the check stub as $48.60. The error is found when cash is proved. By this time, several other checks have been written, so the next unused check stub is 31. In this case, the amount of the error ($84.60 − $48.60 = $36.00) is subtracted from the balance brought forward on Check Stub 31 (see **Figure 11–9**). A note is made on Check Stub 22 to indicate that the error is corrected on Check Stub 31.

What You'll Learn

- Why a business reconciles a bank statement.
- How to journalize and post entries relating to bank service charges.
- The accounting procedure for stopping payment on a check.
- How to record an NSF check.
- How electronic funds transfer systems enable banks to transfer funds quickly and accurately.

Why It's Important

Reconciling the bank account ensures that a business owner is aware of all transactions that affect cash.

KEY TERMS

bank statement
canceled checks
reconciling the bank
 statement
outstanding checks
outstanding deposits
bank service charge
stop payment order
NSF check
electronic funds transfer
 system (EFTS)

	No. 31
$ _____	
Date _____	20 --
To _____	
For _____	

	Dollars	Cents
Balance brought forward	4,750	00
Add deposits		
Less: Error corr. Ck. 22	36	00
Total	4,714	00
Less this check		
Balance carried forward		

Figure 11–9 Entering an Error Correction on the Check Stub

Key Points

Bank Service Charges

Before reconciling the bank statement, record in the checkbook those bank service charges and other deductions listed on the bank statement, but not previously entered in the checkbook.

The Bank Statement

A **bank statement** is an itemized record of all the transactions in a depositor's account over a given period, usually a month. Typical bank statements include the following information:

(1) the checking account balance at the beginning of the period
(2) a list of all deposits made by the business during the period
(3) a list of all checks paid by the bank
(4) a list of any other deductions from the depositor's account
(5) the checking account balance at the end of the period

Find each of these items on the bank statement for Roadrunner Delivery Service in **Figure 11–10**.

When a bank sends a statement to a depositor, it may return the checks paid by the bank and deducted from the depositor's account. These returned checks are called **canceled checks**. Canceled checks are stamped or marked with the word "Paid" and the date of payment. They can be used to verify the information on the bank statement. These checks should be kept in a file or storage box in case they are needed later as proof of payment.

❖ *American National Bank*
SACRAMENTO, CALIFORNIA

Roadrunner Delivery Service
155 Gateway Boulevard
Sacramento, CA 94230

Account Number: 303443

FDIC

Statement Date: 10/31/20--

Balance Last Statement	Deposits & Other Credits		Checks & Other Debits		Balance This Statement
	No.	Amount	No.	Amount	
1 00.00	3	26,400.00	5	4,183.00	5 22,217.00

Description	Checks & Other Debits	Deposits & Other Credits	Date	Balance
Balance Forward				00.00
Deposit		25,000.00	10/01	25,000.00
Check 101	3,000.00		10/04	22,000.00
Deposit		200.00	10/14	22,200.00
Check 102	350.00		10/15	21,850.00
Deposit		1,200.00	10/16	23,050.00
Check 103	700.00		10/20	22,350.00
Check 104	125.00		10/31	22,225.00
Service Charge	4 8.00		10/31	22,217.00

PLEASE EXAMINE YOUR STATEMENT AT ONCE. IF NO ERROR IS REPORTED IN 10 DAYS THE ACCOUNT WILL BE CONSIDERED CORRECT AND VOUCHERS GENUINE. ALL ITEMS ARE CREDITED SUBJECT TO FINAL PAYMENT.

The Bank for All Your Business Needs

Figure 11–10 Bank Statement

Upon receipt, the bank statement is compared to the checkbook. The process of determining any differences between the bank statement and the checkbook is called **reconciling the bank statement**. The ending balance on the bank statement seldom agrees with the balance in the checkbook. There are three common reasons why the bank statement balance and the checkbook balance disagree:

- outstanding checks
- outstanding deposits
- bank charges

Outstanding Checks and Deposits

In banking terms, the word "outstanding" simply means "not yet received." **Outstanding checks**, therefore, are checks that have been written but have not yet been presented to the bank for payment. It is not unusual for checks written in one statement period to reach the bank in a later period. **Outstanding deposits** are deposits that have been made and recorded in the checkbook but do not appear on the bank statement. Deposits made the same day the bank statement is prepared may not appear on the statement.

Bank Service Charges

The bank statement balance also reflects any service charges made by the bank during the statement period. A **bank service charge** is a fee the bank charges for maintaining bank records and processing bank statement items for the depositor. This charge varies from bank to bank, but is frequently based on either the number of checks and deposits handled during the statement period or the balance in the depositor's account. The bank subtracts the service charge from the depositor's account. The depositor usually does not know about the service charge, or other bank charges handled in the same manner, until the statement is received.

Before the bank statement is reconciled, the checkbook balance is adjusted by the amount of the bank service charge. As shown in **Figure 11–11**, the words "Less: Service Charge" are written on the next unused check stub on the line above the Total line. The amount of the service charge is entered in the amount column, preceded by a minus sign. The balance is recalculated and entered on the Total line.

Reconciling a Bank Statement

Promptly reconciling the bank statement is a good way to ensure orderly cash records and guard against cash losses. The bank expects to be notified immediately of any errors on the statement. Failure to do so may release the bank from responsibility for the errors.

On the back of the bank statement is a form for reconciling the bank statement. This form documents the differences between the bank balance and the checkbook balance. Refer to **Figure 11–12** and follow these steps to reconcile a bank statement:

	No. 107	
$ _____		
Date _____	20 __	
To _____		
For _____		
	Dollars	Cents
Balance brought forward	21,125	00
Add deposits		
Less: Svc. Charge	−8	00
Total	21,117	00
Less this check		
Balance carried forward		

Figure 11–11 Entering a Bank Service Charge on the Check Stub

BANK RECONCILIATION FORM

PLEASE EXAMINE YOUR STATEMENT AT ONCE.
ANY DISCREPANCY SHOULD BE REPORTED TO
THE BANK IMMEDIATELY.

1. Record any transactions appearing on this statement but not listed in your checkbook.

2. List any checks still outstanding in the space provided to the right.

3. Enter the balance shown on this statement here.

4. Enter deposits recorded in your checkbook but not shown on this statement.

5. Total lines 3 and 4 and enter here.

6. Enter total checks outstanding here.

7. Subtract line 6 from line 5. This adjusted bank balance should agree with your checkbook balance.

2	22,217 00
3	— —
	22,217 00
4	1,100 00
5	21,117 00

CHECKS OUTSTANDING

Number	Amount
105	600 00
106	500 00
TOTAL	**1,100 00**

Figure 11–12 Bank Reconciliation Using a Bank Statement Form

1. Arrange the canceled checks in numerical order. Compare the canceled checks with those listed on the statement and with the stubs. When you match a check and a stub, place a check mark beside the check amount on the bank statement and on the check stub. After all the checks and stubs are matched, list on the reconciliation form, by number and amount, all the stubs without check marks. These stubs indicate the outstanding checks.

2. Enter the ending balance shown on the bank statement.

3. Compare deposits listed on the bank statement to deposits listed in the checkbook. Enter the total of any outstanding deposits on the reconciliation form. Add this total to the bank statement balance and enter the result on the form.

4. Subtract the total of the outstanding checks from the amount calculated in Step 3. The result is the adjusted bank balance.

5. Compare the adjusted bank balance to the checkbook balance. When the balances match, the bank statement is reconciled.

Figure 11–13 illustrates the same bank reconciliation using a two-column account form.

If the adjusted bank balance does not match the checkbook balance, find and correct the error. Notify the bank immediately if it is a bank error. It is more likely, however, that the error is in the checkbook. Check the addition

Did You Know?

Ticket Sales

Ticketmaster is the world's largest computerized ticketing service. The company sells more than 86 million tickets a year and earns annual revenue of $600 million to $675 million on ticket sales.

Roadrunner Delivery Service
Bank Reconciliation Statement
October 31, 20--

Balance on bank statement			22 2 1 7 00
Additions:			
Deposits in transit		— —	
			22 2 1 7 00
Deductions for outstanding checks:			
Check 105	6 0 0 00		
Check 106	5 0 0 00		
Total outstanding checks		1 1 0 0 00	
Adjusted bank balance		21 1 1 7 00	

Figure 11–13 Bank Account Reconciliation Using a Two Column Account Form

and subtraction on the check stubs and on the bank reconciliation form. Also look for any outstanding checks or deposits that are not included in your calculations.

Recording Bank Service Charges

Like any other business, banks charge fees for their services. A bank service charge is an expense that is recorded in the accounting records.

The bank deducted the service charge from Roadrunner's account, so it is not necessary to write a check for this expense. The bank statement is the source document for recording the bank service charge.

Business Transaction

On November 1 Roadrunner received the bank statement. A bank service charge of $8 appeared on the statement.

ANALYSIS	*Identify*	1.	Bank service charges are often recorded in the **Miscellaneous Expense** account. Therefore, **Miscellaneous Expense** and **Cash in Bank** are affected.
	Classify	2.	**Miscellaneous Expense** is an expense account. **Cash in Bank** is an asset account.
	+/−	3.	**Miscellaneous Expense** is increased by $8. **Cash in Bank** is decreased by $8.

DEBIT-CREDIT RULE	4.	Increases in expense accounts are recorded as debits. Debit **Miscellaneous Expense** for $8.
	5.	Decreases in asset accounts are recorded as credits. Credit **Cash in Bank** for $8.

T ACCOUNTS 6.

Miscellaneous Expense		Cash in Bank	
Debit + 8	Credit −	Debit +	Credit − 8

JOURNAL ENTRY 7.

GENERAL JOURNAL   PAGE __42__

	DATE		DESCRIPTION	POST. REF.	DEBIT	CREDIT	
1	20--						1
2	Nov.	1	Miscellaneous Expense		8 00		2
3			Cash in Bank			8 00	3
4							4

Check Stub for Stopped Check

$ 500.00		No. 633
Date January 12		20 --
To Smith Engineering		
For Electrical Work		
	Dollars	Cents
Balance brought forward	12,723	00
Add deposits		
	STOPPED PAYMENT	
Total		
Less this check	500	00
Balance carried forward	12,223	00

Next Unused Check Stub

$		No. 652
Date		20
To		
For		
	Dollars	Cents
Balance brought forward	10,452	00
Add deposits Stopped		
Payment on Ck 633	500	00
Total	10,952	00
Less this check		
Balance carried forward		

Figure 11–14 Recording a Stopped Check on the Check Stub

Calculator Hints

Subtracting the Same Number

If you're subtracting one number several times, such as $20 three times in a row:

- enter the number once,
- then press the = key for each additional time you want to subtract the number.

Special Banking Procedures

Checks are usually written or received and deposited without any problems. However, two problems that may happen are:

- A business does not want the bank to pay a check that was issued.
- A business receives and deposits a check from a customer whose account does not have enough money to cover the check.

Stopping Payment on a Check

Occasionally, a drawer (Roadrunner) will order the drawee (bank) not to honor, or pay, a check. A **stop payment order** is a demand by the drawer that the bank not honor a certain check. A stop payment order is often used when a check is lost. The drawer must issue a stop payment order *before* the check is presented to the bank for payment. Usually, a stop payment order is made in writing.

To record a stop payment order, the accountant writes the words "Stopped Payment" on the check stub for the stopped check. The accountant then adds the amount of the stopped check on the next unused check stub, illustrated in **Figure 11–14.** If appropriate, the accountant then issues a replacement check.

Most banks charge a fee for a stop payment order. The fee appears on the bank statement and is subtracted from the checkbook balance. A journal entry, similar to that made for the bank service charge, is prepared. Most businesses record the fee in **Miscellaneous Expense.** The source document for this entry is the bank statement.

Recording NSF Checks

An **NSF check** is a check returned to the depositor by the bank because there are not sufficient funds in the drawer's checking account to cover the check. For example, suppose Roadrunner deposits a check from a customer. If the customer does not have enough money in the bank to cover the check, Roadrunner's bank deducts the amount of the check from Roadrunner's account and returns the check to Roadrunner. Roadrunner notifies the customer that the bank returned the check. The customer then deposits enough money in the bank to cover the check or finds another means of payment.

When the bank returns an NSF check, the amount of the check is subtracted from the checkbook balance, and a journal entry is made to record the returned check.

On November 15 a check for $450, written by Burton Company for payment on account and deposited by Roadrunner, was returned by the bank due to insufficient funds in Burton's account.

ANALYSIS	**Identify** **Classify**	1. **Accounts Receivable—Burton Company** and **Cash in Bank** are affected.
		2. **Accounts Receivable—Burton Company** and **Cash in Bank** are both asset accounts.
	+/−	3. **Accounts Receivable—Burton Company** is increased by the amount of the check returned by the bank, $450. **Cash in Bank** is decreased by $450.

DEBIT-CREDIT RULE		4. Increases in asset accounts are recorded as debits. Debit **Accounts Receivable—Burton Company** for $450.
		5. Decreases in asset accounts are recorded as credits. Credit **Cash in Bank** for $450.

T ACCOUNTS

6.

Accounts Receivable—Burton Company		Cash in Bank	
Debit + 450	Credit −	Debit +	Credit − 450

JOURNAL ENTRY

7.

		GENERAL JOURNAL		PAGE 43	
	DATE	DESCRIPTION	POST. REF.	DEBIT	CREDIT
1	20--				
2	Nov. 15	Accts. Rec.—Burton Company		450 00	
3		Cash in Bank			450 00
4					

Electronic Funds Transfer System

Look at **Figure 11–15**. It illustrates the route a check follows from the time it is written until the time it is returned with the bank statement.

Since millions of checks are written each day, the transfer of checks and funds is routine. This transfer of funds among banks is a huge job, however. To handle such a large volume of transfers, banks use the **electronic funds transfer system (EFTS)**. The EFTS allows banks to transfer funds among accounts quickly and accurately without the exchange of checks.

An example of EFTS is the direct deposit of payroll. Many employees do not receive paychecks. Their pay is electronically transferred from the employer's account to the employees' accounts using the EFTS.

In the United States, the EFTS is not fully implemented because the general public does not yet want a completely check-less system.

Roadrunner Delivery Service

1 Roadrunner writes Check 103 to Tooley & Co. Management for $700 for rent.

Tooley & Co. Management

2 Tooley & Company Management deposits the check in its account at First National Bank.

FIRST NATIONAL BANK

3 First National Bank increases the balance in Tooley's checking account by $700.

Tooley's account increased $700

American National Bank

4 First National Bank sends the $700 check to American National Bank, Roadrunner's bank, for collection.

Roadrunner's account decreased $700

5 American National Bank sends $700 to First National Bank and deducts this amount from Roadrunner's account.

6 American National Bank returns the paid check to Roadrunner with the monthly bank statement.

American National Bank
SACRAMENTO, CALIFORNIA

Roadrunner Delivery Service
155 Gateway Boulevard
Sacramento, CA 94230

Account Number: 303443

FDIC — Statement Date: 10/31/20--

Balance Last Statement	Deposits & Other Credits		Checks & Other Debits		Balance This Statement
	No.	Amount	No.	Amount	
00.00	3	26,400.00	5	4,183.00	22,217.00

Description	Checks & Other Debits	Deposits & Other Credits	Date	Balance
Balance Forward				00.00
Deposit		25,000.00	10/01	25,000.00
Check 101	3,000.00		10/04	22,000.00
Deposit		200.00	10/14	22,200.00
Check 102	350.00		10/15	21,850.00
Deposit		1,200.00	10/16	23,050.00
Check 103	700.00		10/20	22,350.00
Check 104	125.00		10/31	22,225.00
Service Charge	8.00		10/31	22,217.00

PLEASE EXAMINE YOUR STATEMENT AT ONCE. IF NO ERROR IS REPORTED IN 10 DAYS THE ACCOUNT WILL BE CONSIDERED CORRECT AND VOUCHERS GENUINE. ALL ITEMS ARE CREDITED SUBJECT TO FINAL PAYMENT.

The Bank for All Your Business Needs

Figure 11–15 Routing of Checks

ANALYZING FINANCIAL REPORTS

Evaluating Working Capital

When analyzing the balance sheet, one thing owners and managers want to know is whether the business has enough assets to pay its debts. One measure of a company's ability to pay debts is its working capital.

Working Capital = Current Assets − Current Liabilities

Current assets are cash and assets that will be converted to cash within the next accounting period. *Current liabilities* are debts that must be paid within the next accounting period.

▶ **Analyze the Report:**

Use the balance sheet for Roadrunner Delivery Service on page 219 to answer these questions.

1. What is the total amount of current assets?
2. What is the total amount of current liabilities?
3. Calculate the working capital for Roadrunner Delivery Service.

Now that you have studied this section, complete the following questions and problems.

Thinking Critically

1. List the standard information that appears on a bank statement.
2. If you have problems reconciling a bank statement, what steps may uncover the errors?

Computing in the Business World

The balance in the checkbook of Valleyview Tennis Center on April 30 is $2,944.20. The balance shown on the April bank statement is $3,085.95. A deposit of $345.00 was made on April 29, and another deposit of $290.00 was made on April 30. Neither of these deposits appears on the bank statement. The service charge for the month was $5.25. Valleyview has four outstanding checks:

| Check 344 | $202.00 | Check 350 | $ 25.00 |
| Check 346 | 55.00 | Check 351 | 500.00 |

Instructions
1. Record the bank service charge in the checkbook.
2. Reconcile the bank statement.

Problem 11–2
Analyzing a Source Document

Instructions Review the Global Travel Agency bank statement and answer the following questions in your working papers.

1. What is the amount of the returned check?
2. What is the bank charging Global Travel Agency for the returned check?
3. What account will be debited for the $12 bank service charge?

Security National Bank
155 Flower Street, Cambridge, MA 02138

STATEMENT

Global Travel Agency
200 Brattle Street
Cambridge, MA 02138

Account Number: 2649-84
Statement Date: 2/28/20--

FDIC

Balance Last Statement	Deposits & Other Credits No.	Amount	Checks & Other Debits No.	Amount	Balance This Statement
2,714.00	3	2,395.00	7	4,036.00	1,073.00

Checks & Other Debits	Deposits & Other Credits	Date	Balance
	1,250.00	2/05	3,964.00
700.00		2/10	3,264.00
900.00		2/10	2,364.00
	845.00	2/15	3,209.00
600.00		2/15	2,609.00
(R) 100.00		2/20	2,509.00
(S) 25.00		2/20	2,484.00
725.00		2/25	1,759.00
600.00		2/25	1,159.00
(S) 12.00		2/26	1,147.00
214.00		2/26	933.00
	300.00	2/27	1,233.00
160.00		2/27	1,073.00

PLEASE EXAMINE YOUR STATEMENT AT ONCE. IF NO ERROR IS REPORTED IN 10 DAYS THE ACCOUNT WILL BE CONSIDERED CORRECT AND VOUCHERS GENUINE. ALL ITEMS ARE CREDITED SUBJECT TO FINAL PAYMENT.

C=CERTIFIED CHECK   T=DEBIT OR CREDIT   S=SERVICE CHARGE   L=LIST   CR=OVERDRAFT   R=RETURNED CHECK

ACCOUNTING CAREERS IN FOCUS

KEVIN HART
Controller
Pittsburgh Penguins

Q: What are some of the special concerns of a controller for a hockey team?

A: You have to handle personnel with more care than you would in another organization. You have young fellows making a lot of money and their superstar status creates some problems. You have to have superb people skills.

Q: What kinds of reporting do you do?

A: We have the regular reporting requirements everyone has: state, local, federal, and the reports to our lending institution. We also make reports to the National Hockey League. We let them know what's happened after each game and after each payroll.

Q: Do you enjoy your work?

A: It's a lot of fun. I enjoy talking to the league or to players or to their agents. I can walk into the locker room when I want and talk to players and coaches about questions I have for them or questions they have for me.

Q: How did you get this job?

A: I joined a large public accounting firm out of college. I worked on the acquisition of the Penguin franchise from its previous owners. It took about four months. During that time I got familiar with the organization and they got familiar with me. They offered me the position.

Tips from . . .

RHI Robert Half International Inc.

Communication is very important in a team-oriented work environment. Learn to communicate your ideas to others through written memos or verbal updates. Always keep your supervisor updated on the status of your projects.

CAREER FACTS

Nature of the Work: Supervise accounting and finance, motivate and oversee staff, oversee accounts receivable, accounts payable and payroll, and meet reporting deadlines.

Training or Education Needed: A bachelor's degree in accounting.

Aptitudes, Abilities, and Skills: Accounting, time-management skills, problem-solving skills, communication skills, and interpersonal skills.

Salary Range: $50,000 to $100,000 depending on the team's city.

Career Path: Work for an accounting firm and become familiar with a variety of organizations, and then move to the right job when it becomes available.

Thinking Critically: In what ways could a sports team player's "superstar status" create problems for a controller?

KEY CONCEPTS

1. The use of a checking account by a business provides an important control of cash. The checking account protects cash and also serves as a record of all cash transactions.
2. Deposit slips are prepared when cash and checks are deposited in a bank account. Copies of deposit slips are the proof of deposits.
3. Checks are endorsed before they are deposited. Most businesses stamp a restrictive endorsement on checks as soon as the checks are received. A restrictive endorsement limits how checks are handled and helps protect the checks from misuse.
4. Correctly written checks and accurate check stubs help prevent cash loss through carelessness or fraud.
5. As a part of their control of cash, businesses regularly prove cash by comparing the **Cash in Bank** balance to the checkbook balance. The reasons for any differences between the two balances are determined, and appropriate corrections are made.
6. A bank statement is sent to each depositor, usually once a month. A bank statement is reconciled promptly upon receipt. Any errors found on the bank statement are reported to the bank immediately.
7. Before reconciling the bank statement, record bank service charges and NSF checks in the checkbook.
8. Follow these steps when reconciling a bank statement:
   a. Arrange the canceled checks in numerical order.
   b. On the bank reconciliation form, enter the ending balance shown on the bank statement.
   c. Identify outstanding deposits and add them to the bank statement balance.
   d. Identify outstanding checks and subtract them from the bank statement balance.
   e. Compare the adjusted bank statement balance with the checkbook balance. When the amounts are equal, the bank statement is reconciled.
9. After the bank statement is reconciled, journalize and post the bank service charges, stop payment order charges, and NSF checks.

	GENERAL JOURNAL			PAGE __1__	
DATE	DESCRIPTION	POST. REF.	DEBIT	CREDIT	
1	20--				1
2	Date	Miscellaneous Expense		x x x x		2
3		Cash in Bank			x x x x	3
4		10/31/20—Bank Statement				4
5						5

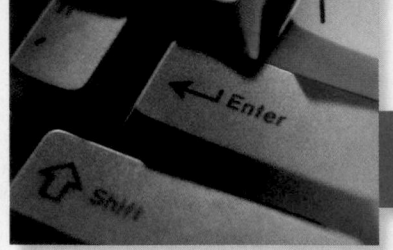

USING KEY TERMS

The manager of Valley View Bowling Center is concerned about cash control and banking procedures for his business. On a separate sheet of paper, write a paragraph explaining how the list of terms relates to each of the four group headings.

External Controls
check
checking account
depositor
signature card

Internal Controls
deposit slip
drawee
drawer
endorsement
payee
restrictive endorsement

Personal Banking Controls
bank statement
canceled checks
reconciling the bank
   statement
voiding a check

Financial Record Controls
bank service charge
electronic funds transfer
   system (EFTS)
NSF check
outstanding checks
outstanding deposits
stop payment order

Understanding Accounting Concepts and Procedures

Instructions

On a separate sheet of paper, answer the following questions:

1. Why is it important for businesses to protect cash?
2. What internal controls can businesses use to protect cash?
3. What external controls help businesses protect cash?
4. Describe the forms that are needed to open and use a checking account.
5. What is the purpose of a check endorsement?
6. Why should you always complete the check stub *before* writing the check?
7. What information does a bank statement contain?
8. List the steps to reconcile a bank statement.
9. Explain how bank service charges are recorded in the checkbook and in the accounting records of a business.
10. Explain how NSF checks and related charges are recorded in the checkbook and in the accounting records of a business.

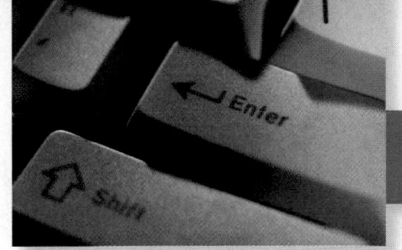

Case Study...

Service Business: Entertainment

Dexter Shuman owns a bowling alley called Ten Pin Alley. Each night, Dexter counts the cash in the two cash registers and makes a night deposit at the local bank. For the month of May, Dexter made deposits totaling $6,400.

During May, Dexter wrote checks totaling $2,900. The last three checks he wrote were Check 1408 for $180; Check 1409 for $560; and Check 1410 for $212. The beginning cash balance for the month was $13,840, which is the amount shown as the beginning balance on the May bank statement. The May bank statement also includes a $12 service charge and an $18 charge for printing new checks.

Thinking Critically:

1. What is the ending bank statement balance if all checks written have cleared?
2. If Checks 1408, 1409, and 1410 are outstanding, what is the ending bank statement balance?
3. After reconciling the bank statement, what is the ending balance in the cash account?

Conducting an Audit with Alex

The accountant for Jack's Produce received the March bank statement. While proving cash and reviewing the bank statement, the accountant discovered the following:

1. A stop payment bank charge for $20, dated March 12, found on the March bank statement, was not recorded in the accounting records.
2. A monthly bank service charge for $15, dated March 31, was not recorded in the accounting records, but appeared on the March bank statement.

Instructions Record these bank charges in the general journal on a separate sheet of paper.

*inter*NET CONNECTION

Cash Control and Banking Activities

The Federal Reserve System is the central bank of the United States. Locate the Web site for the Board of Governors of the Federal Reserve System and complete the following activities.

Do This:

1. From the Board of Governors' site, access the related Web site for the National Information Center of Banking. Name the three largest banks and the headquarters of each bank.
2. From the Board of Governors' site, access the site for Federal Reserve Banks. The United States is divided into 12 federal reserve districts. In which district is your city located?

Workplace Skills

Serving Customers

Working with others and satisfying expectations are essential skills in any work environment. Listening, communicating, and solving problems shows your employer you have strong interpersonal skills.

On the Job:

You are a personal banker for Citizens First National Bank. Your job duties include opening personal bank accounts, taking loan applications, and serving bank customers. Today, Ms. Kelly Myer wants to open a bank account. How will you assist her?

Thinking Critically:

1. Before you can assist Ms. Myer, you put together a packet of information and forms needed to open her account. List the items that are in her packet.
2. Review with Ms. Myer how to write a check and complete a deposit ticket. Use examples from your textbook to explain how to complete each document. Pair up with a student and role-play this situation.

Reconciling the Bank Statement
Making the Transition from a Manual to a Computerized System

Task	Perform Accounting Procedures Using Manual Methods	Perform Accounting Procedures Using Automated Methods
Reconciling the bank statement	1. Using the form on the back of the bank statement or accounting stationery, follow the steps on page 268 to reconcile the bank statement.	1. Before attempting to reconcile the bank statement, make sure all transactions of the month have been posted. 2. A computerized system will list all cash transactions and allow you to check off the appropriate cleared items. 3. You may enter adjustments such as bank fees. These will be posted to the general ledger.

Reconciling the Bank Statement

Peachtree Question	Description
How do I reconcile the cash account in Peachtree?	1. Select **Account Reconciliation** from the *Tasks* menu. 2. Select the cash account to be reconciled. 3. Enter the bank statement date. 4. Enter the ending bank statement balance. 5. Click the *Clear* box for all items that appear on the bank statement. 6. When the unreconciled difference is $0.00, the account has been reconciled. 7. Click *OK* to save the reconciliation.
How do I enter an adjustment to the cash account?	1. When reconciling the bank statement, you may find bank charges that have not yet been entered into the accounting records. 2. After you have cleared all items listed on the bank statement, click the *Adjust* button at the top of the screen. 3. Enter the account number that the adjustment should be posted to and enter the amount. 4. Click *OK*.
What does the software do "behind the scenes"?	1. Peachtree automatically pulls up a list of cash transactions to help you verify bank statement activity. 2. Any adjustments that must be entered at the time of the reconciliation are posted to the general ledger accounts, updating the balances of each account.

For detailed instructions: See the **Peachtree User Guide** in your Glencoe Working Papers.

APPLICATION OPTIONS

Problem 11–3 Handling Deposits

On October 4, the owner of Wilderness Rentals deposited the following in the checking account at First National Bank. The beginning balance in the account is $3,306.54 before these transactions.

Cash: Currency, $374.00; Coins, $7.42

Checks: Bob Warner, drawn on Consumers Bank, ABA No. 63-706; $64.98
Joan Walkman, drawn on Mountain Bank, ABA No. 63-699; $349.81
Ernesto Garcia, drawn on Progressive Savings and Loan, ABA No. 63-710; $29.44

Instructions   In your working papers:

1. Place a restrictive endorsement on each check. Use "Wilderness Rentals."
2. Fill out a deposit slip. Use the ABA number to identify each check.
3. Record the deposit in the checkbook on Check Stub 651.

Analyze: What is the checkbook balance after recording the deposit on the check stub?

Problem 11–4 Maintaining the Checkbook

As the accounting clerk for Hot Suds Car Wash, you write checks and make deposits. The current checkbook balance is $3,486.29.

Instructions   For each transaction:

1. Record the necessary information on the check stub. Determine the new balance and carry the balance forward.
2. Prepare the necessary checks and sign your name as drawer.

Date	Transactions
Oct. 3	Issued Check 504 for $868.45 to Custom Construction for construction supplies.
3	Deposited $601.35 in the checking account.
6	Issued Check 505 for $299.60 to CP Lumber for paint.
7	Issued Check 506 to Laverne Brothers for $1,000.00 for completing a painting job.
10	Deposited $342.80 in the checking account.
10	Issued Check 507 to Union Utilities for the September electricity bill of $175.50.

Analyze: What is the balance brought forward amount on Check Stub 508?

Complete chapter problems one of four ways:

1 **Manual** Glencoe Working Papers

or

2 **Peachtree Complete Accounting** Software

or

3 **QuickBooks** Templates (Problems 11–5, 11–7)

or

4 **Spreadsheet** Templates (Problem 11–6)

Peachtree®

SMART GUIDE

Step–by–Step Instructions: Problem 11–4

1. Select the problem set for Hot Suds Car Wash (Prob. 11–4).
2. Rename the company and set the system date.
3. Use the **Payments** option in the **Tasks** menu to record the checks issued.
4. Record the deposits using the **General Journal Entry** option.
5. Print an Account Register report using the **Account Reconciliation** option from the **Reports** menu.
6. Answer the Analyze question.
7. End the session.

Peachtree®

SMART GUIDE

**Step–by–Step Instructions:
Problem 11–5**

1. Select the problem set for Kits & Pups Grooming (Prob. 11–5).
2. Rename the company and set the system date.
3. Reconcile the bank statement using the **Account Reconciliation** option in the *Tasks* menu.
4. Print the following Account Reconciliation reports: Account Register, Account Reconciliation, Deposits in Transit, and Outstanding Checks.
5. Answer the Analyze question.
6. End the session.

TIP: Peachtree automatically updates the general ledger when you record an adjustment such as a bank service charge.

**SPREADSHEET
SMART GUIDE**

**Step–by–Step Instructions:
Problem 11–6**

1. Select the spreadsheet template for Problem 11–6.
2. Enter your name and the date in the spaces provided on the template.
3. Complete the spreadsheet using the instructions in your working papers.
4. Print the spreadsheet and proof your work.
5. Save your work and exit the spreadsheet program.

Problem 11–5 Reconciling the Bank Statement

On October 31, George Flaum, the accountant for Kits & Pups Grooming, received the bank statement dated October 30. After comparing the company's checkbook with the bank statement, George found the following:

1. The checkbook balance on October 31 is $960.
2. The ending bank statement balance is $1,380.
3. The bank statement shows a service charge of $10.
4. A deposit of $405 was made on October 30, but does not appear on the bank statement.
5. Check 768 for $529 and Check 772 for $306 are outstanding.

Instructions In your working papers:

1. Record the bank service charge in the checkbook.
2. Reconcile the bank statement.
3. Journalize the bank service charge in the general journal, page 4.
4. Post the bank service charge journal entry to the appropriate general ledger accounts.

Analyze: How many checks are outstanding? What is the total amount outstanding?

 ## Problem 11–6 Reconciling the Bank Statement

On October 31, Juanita Ortega, owner of Outback Guide Service, received a bank statement dated October 30. Juanita found the following:

1. The checkbook has a balance of $2,551.34.
2. The bank statement shows a balance of $2,272.36.
3. The statement shows a bank service charge of $20.00.
4. A check from Podaski Systems for $62.44, deposited on October 18, was returned by the bank. There is no fee for handling the NSF check.
5. A deposit of $672.48 made on October 30 does not appear on the bank statement.
6. These checks are outstanding:
   Check 872 for $126.84   Check 883 for $192.80
   Check 881 for   87.66   Check 887 for   68.64

Instructions Using the preceding information:

1. Record the service charge and the NSF check in the checkbook.
2. Reconcile the bank statement.
3. Record the service charge and NSF check on page 7 of the general journal.
4. Post the journal entries to the appropriate general ledger accounts.

Analyze: Review the **Miscellaneous Expense** account found in your working papers. What is the balance of the **Miscellaneous Expense** account after posting the October 31 entry?

Problem 11–7 Reconciling the Bank Statement

On October 31, Showbiz Video received the bank statement dated October 30. After comparing the company's checkbook with the bank statement, the accountant found the following:

1. The checkbook balance on October 31 is $13,462.96.
2. The ending bank statement balance is $13,883.80.
3. The bank statement shows a service charge of $17.50.
4. Deposits of $675.00 on October 28 and $925.00 on October 29 do not appear on the bank statement.
5. The following checks are outstanding:

| Check 1766 | $125.00 | Check 1770 | $1,462.19 |
| Check 1768 | 69.42 | Check 1771 | 381.73 |

Instructions In your working papers:

1. Record the bank service charge in the checkbook in your working papers.
2. Reconcile the bank statement.
3. Record the entry for the bank service charge on general journal page 13.
4. Post the bank service charge journal entry to the appropriate ledger accounts.

Analyze: What is the balance of the **Cash in Bank** account after posting the October 31 entry? Does it agree with the adjusted checkbook balance?

CHALLENGE PROBLEM

Problem 11–8 Reconciling the Bank Statement Using the Account Form

SOURCE DOCUMENT PROBLEM

On Oct. 20, Job Connect received its bank statement dated Oct. 18.
1. The checkbook balance on Oct. 20 is $880.84.
2. The ending bank statement balance is $344.58.
3. A $14.00 service charge appears on the bank statement.
4. The following checks are outstanding:

| Check 864 | $ 88.41 | Check 871 | $129.88 |
| Check 869 | 69.34 | Check 873 | 14.25 |

5. A $68.42 check from Tom McCrary deposited on Oct. 13 was returned by the bank for insufficient funds. The bank charged Job Connect's account $7.00 for the NSF check. No journal entry was made for the NSF check.
6. A deposit of $938.72 made on Oct. 19 does not appear on the bank statement.
7. A check for $200.00 to Fontenot Inc. was lost in the mail and has not been deposited. A stop payment order, which cost $10.00, was issued on Oct. 15. No new check was issued.

Instructions Reconcile the bank statement using the account form in your working papers.

Analyze: What accounts will be debited for the NSF check and the bank handling charge on the check?

Peachtree®

SMART GUIDE

Step–by–Step Instructions:
Problem 11–7

1. Select the problem set for Showbiz Video (Prob. 11–7).
2. Rename the company and set the system date.
3. Reconcile the bank statement using the **Account Reconciliation** option in the **Tasks** menu.
4. Print the Account Reconciliation reports.
5. Answer the Analyze question.
6. End the session.

TIP: Make sure that you mark any adjustments as "cleared."

Peachtree®

SMART GUIDE

Step–by–Step Instructions:
Problem 11–8

1. Select the problem set for Job Connect (Prob. 11–8).
2. Rename the company and set the system date.
3. Reconcile the bank statement.
4. Print the Account Reconciliation reports.
5. Answer the Analyze question.
6. End the session.

SOURCE DOCUMENT PROBLEM

Problem 11–8

Use the source documents in your working papers to record the transactions for this problem.

Completing the Accounting Cycle for a Sole Proprietorship

FAST TRACK
TUTORING
SERVICES

Fast Track Tutoring Service

Company Background: Fast Track Tutoring Service is owned and managed by Jennifer Rachael. The business is organized as a sole proprietorship and provides tutoring services for students from pre-kindergarten through high school. The business earns revenue from tuition charged from one-on-one instruction and special classes.

What You'll Learn

- How to analyze, journalize, and post.
- How to prepare a trial balance, a work sheet, and financial statements.
- How to journalize and post closing entries.
- How to prepare a post-closing trial balance.
- How to prepare a bank reconciliation.

Why It's Important

This mini practice set will help to pull together all the concepts and procedures that you've learned.

Your Job Responsibilities: As the accounting clerk for this business, use the accounting stationery in your working papers to complete the following activities.

(1) Open a general ledger account for each account in the chart of accounts.

(2) Analyze each business transaction.

(3) Enter each business transaction in the general journal. Begin on journal page 1.

(4) Post each journal entry to the appropriate accounts in the general ledger.

(5) Reconcile the bank statement that was received on December 31. The statement is dated December 30. The checkbook has a current balance of $9,631. The bank statement shows a balance of $9,844. The bank service charge is $15. These checks are outstanding: Check 108 $183 and Check 109 $45. There are no outstanding deposits.

(6) Make any necessary adjustments to the checkbook balance.

(7) Journalize and post the entry for the bank service charge.

(8) Prepare a trial balance and complete the work sheet.

(9) Prepare an income statement, a statement of changes in owner's equity, and a balance sheet.

(10) Journalize and post the closing entries.

(11) Prepare a post-closing trial balance.

Business Transactions: Fast Track Tutoring Service began business operations on December 1 of this year.

APPLICATION OPTIONS

CHART OF ACCOUNTS
Fast Track Tutoring Service

ASSETS

101 Cash in Bank
110 Accts. Rec.—Carla DiSario
120 Accts. Rec.—George McGarty
140 Office Supplies
150 Office Equipment
155 Instructional Equipment

LIABILITIES

210 Accts. Pay.—Educational Software
215 Accts. Pay.—T & N School Equip.

OWNER'S EQUITY

301 Jennifer Rachael, Capital

305 Jennifer Rachael, Withdrawals
310 Income Summary

REVENUE

401 Group Lessons Fees
405 Private Lessons Fees

EXPENSES

505 Maintenance Expense
510 Miscellaneous Expense
515 Rent Expense
525 Utilities Expense

Complete activities
one of three ways:

1 **Manual** Glencoe
Working Papers

or

2 **Peachtree**
Complete
Accounting
Software

or

3 **QuickBooks**
Templates

Date	Transactions
Dec. 1	Jennifer Rachael invested $25,000 in Fast Track Tutoring Service, Memorandum 1.
2	Bought a cash register (**Office Equipment**) for $525, Check 101.
2	Purchased $73 in office supplies, Check 102.
5	Purchased educational instructional computers for $13,924, Check 103.
5	Received $950 for private instruction, Receipt 1.
6	Bought $8,494 of instructional material, Invoice 395, from Educational Software on account.
8	Carla DiSario billed for two group classes, $36, Invoice 101.
9	Wrote Check 104 for $850 for the December rent.
10	Billed George McGarty $275 for special group classes, Invoice 102.
10	Received Invoice 5495 for a $2,375 microcomputer system, for office use, bought on account from T & N School Equipment.
11	Prepared Receipt 2 for $695 for 20 private lessons given between December 1 and December 10.
13	Received $36 from Carla DiSario on account, Receipt 3.
14	Sent Check 105 for $200 to Educational Software on account.
15	Wrote Check 106 for $750 to repaint two classrooms.
18	Jennifer Rachael withdrew $500 for personal use, Check 107.
20	Sent Check 108 for the electric bill of $183.
24	Issued Check 109 for $45 for stamps (**Miscellaneous Expense**).

Peachtree®

SMART GUIDE

Step–by–Step Instructions:

1. Select the problem set for Fast Track Tutoring Service (MP–2).
2. Rename the company and set the system date.
3. Record all of the transactions.
4. Reconcile the bank statement.
5. Print the Account Reconciliation reports.
6. Print a General Journal report and proof your work.
7. Print a General Ledger report and a Trial Balance.
8. Print the financial statements.
9. Close the fiscal year.
10. Print a Post-Closing Trial Balance.
11. Answer the Analyze questions and complete the Audit Test.
12. End the session.

Analyze: To which creditors did Fast Track Tutoring Service owe the most money on December 31?

UNIT 3

Accounting for a Payroll System

In this unit. . .

You have now learned how to record business transactions for a service business. Service businesses and merchandising businesses, like the ones you'll learn about in Unit 4, employ people and must keep records on the money paid to their employees and on the taxes paid to local, state, and federal governments. In this unit, you will learn how to perform payroll procedures. You will learn how to keep records on employee earnings and how to record the payment of wages in the accounting records of the business.

> Success is having a flair for the thing that you are doing; knowing that is not enough, you have got to have hard work and a sense of purpose.
>
> **—Margaret Thatcher**
> **Former Prime Minister of England**

In Your Journal . . .

The next time you get paid, take a good look at your pay stub. If you're not employed, ask your parents if you can take a look at their paycheck. Record your responses to the following questions in a journal entry.

1. What do you think of when you hear the word taxes?

2. Now take a close look at the pay stub. What percentage of your income was withheld from your paycheck?

3. What are the different types of taxes?

4. Where do you think your tax dollars go?

285

Payroll Accounting

Learning Objectives

When you have completed this chapter, you will be able to:

▶ Explain the importance of accurate payroll records.

▶ Compute gross pay using different methods.

▶ Explain and compute employee-paid withholdings.

▶ Compute net pay.

▶ Prepare payroll registers.

▶ Explain and determine methods of dissemination of payroll funds.

▶ Prepare an employee's earnings record.

▶ Define the accounting terms introduced in this chapter.

Exploring the Real World of Business

MOVING INTO THE WORKFORCE

It's graduation day! You've studied hard, and now you're ready for the next big step—looking for your first job. Where do you start looking? How will you know whether you'll like the company? How do you prepare for a job interview? What will you earn? **Robert Half International** can help!

Robert Half is an international staffing service that specializes in matching employers and workers for jobs in accounting, finance, and information systems. The company offers job placement for both full-time and temporary jobs. Job seekers can find a database of job listings for openings around the world. If you choose temporary work, you might find assignments lasting from a few weeks to several months. Such assignments give you an opportunity to work at a variety of jobs.

What do you think?

Why do you think it is beneficial for some companies to hire temporary employees rather than full-time staff? Give at least two specific examples.

 Robert Half International Inc.

286   Chapter 12   Payroll Accounting

Workplace Connections

Applying Your Accounting Knowledge

When you get your paycheck, do you look at it carefully to see how much you've earned and what amounts have been deducted from the total? Employers are required to make certain deductions from your pay. You'll learn about those deductions in this chapter.

Investigate:

1. Look at your last pay stub. Was money deducted from your earnings?
2. What do you think those deductions were taken for?

Calculating Gross Earnings

In a private enterprise economy, people are free to work for any business they choose—as long as they meet the requirements for employment. Employers such as Ford Motor Company, Pier 1, and Borders Books & Music rely on their employees to operate the business and pay their employees for the services they perform. In paying their employees, businesses follow certain guidelines. For example, both federal and state laws require businesses to keep accurate payroll records and to report on employees' earnings.

Most companies set up a payroll system to ensure that their employees are paid on time and that payroll checks are accurate. In this chapter, you will learn about the payroll system.

The Importance of Payroll Records

A **payroll** is a list of the employees and the payments due to each employee for a specific pay period. A **pay period** is the amount of time over which an employee is paid. Most businesses use weekly, biweekly (every two weeks), semimonthly (twice a month), or monthly pay periods.

The payroll expense is a major expense for most companies. To compute salary expenses, most businesses set up a payroll system for recording and reporting employee earnings information. A well-designed payroll system achieves two goals:

(1) The collection and processing of all the information needed to prepare and issue payroll checks.
(2) The generation of payroll records needed for accounting purposes and for reporting to government agencies, management, and others.

Businesses with many employees often hire a **payroll clerk** who is responsible for preparing the payroll. The payroll clerk:

- Makes sure employees are paid on time.
- Makes sure each employee is paid the correct amount.
- Completes payroll records.
- Submits payroll reports.
- Pays payroll taxes.

All payroll systems have certain tasks in common, as shown in **Figure 12–1.**

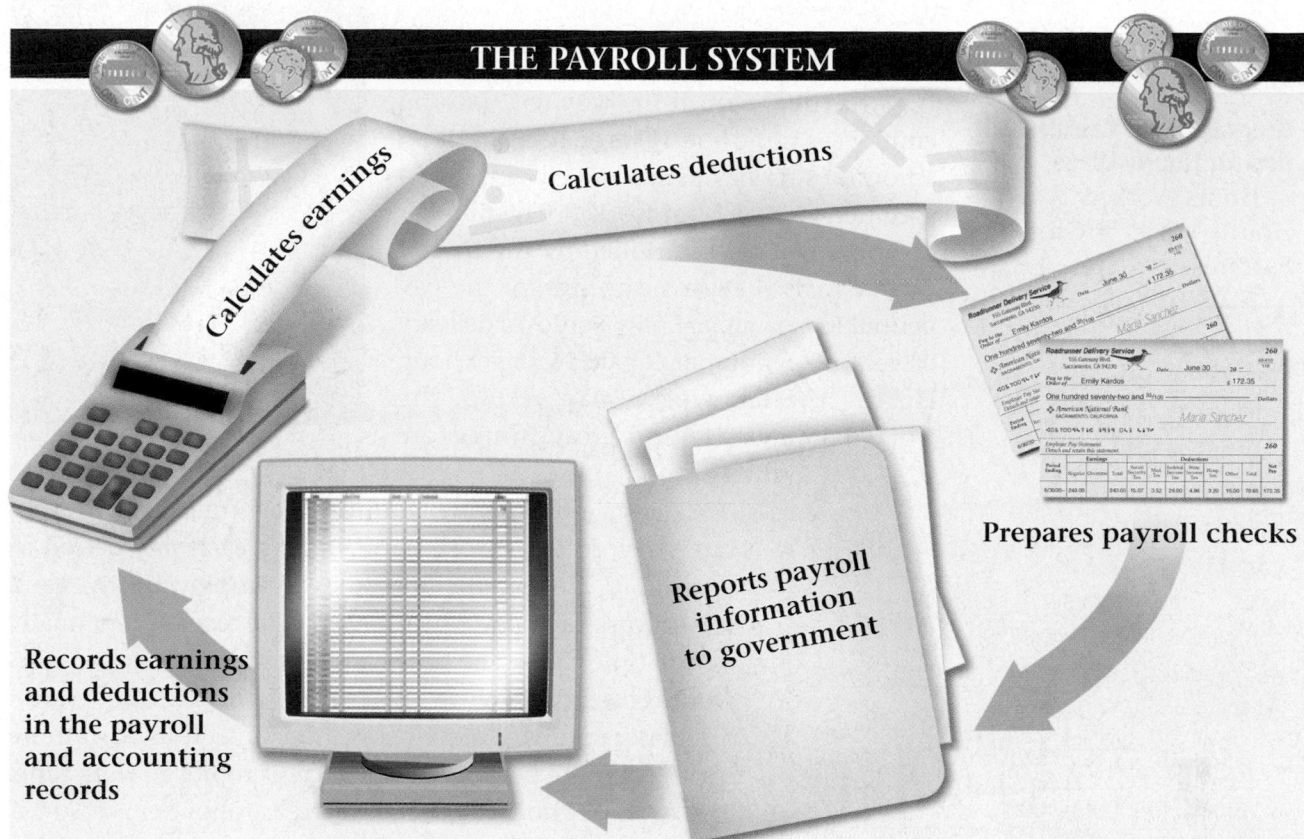

Calculates earnings

Calculates deductions

Prepares payroll checks

Reports payroll information to government

Records earnings and deductions in the payroll and accounting records

Figure 12–1 The Payroll System

Computing Gross Pay

Most employees are paid for the specific amount of time they work during a pay period. The total amount of money an employee earns in a pay period is the employee's **gross earnings**, or *gross pay*. The gross earnings expense is sometimes called salary expense. The method used to compute gross pay depends on the basis on which an employee is paid. An employee's pay can be based on:

- salary
- hourly wage
- commission
- salary plus commission or bonus
- overtime pay

Let's look at each method of paying employees.

Salary

One common method of paying employees, especially those who are managers or supervisors, is by salary. A **salary** is a fixed amount of money paid to an employee for each pay period. In other words, an employee who is paid a salary earns the same amount regardless of the number of hours worked during the pay period. For example, Paula Ferguson, an administrative assistant, is paid a salary of $2,000 a month. Her gross earnings are $2,000 for each monthly pay period. Paula may work 160 hours in one month and 170 hours in the next, but her gross earnings for each of the two months are the same—$2,000.

> **Did You Know?**
>
> **Teen Income**
> Teens get a large portion of the money they spend from parents, who provide 55 percent of teen income. Other sources of income are part-time jobs, allowances, and even full-time jobs.

Hourly Wage

Another common way of paying employees is the hourly wage. A **wage** is an amount of money paid to an employee at a specified rate per hour worked. The number of hours worked multiplied by the hourly wage equals the gross earnings for the pay period. For example, Emily Kardos, a delivery driver for Roadrunner, is paid $6.75 per hour. During the last weekly pay period, she worked 36 hours. Emily's gross earnings are $243.00 (36 hours × $6.75).

Many employees are required to use time cards to accurately record their work hours during each pay period. A **time card** is a record of the times an employee arrives and leaves work each day. The times may be recorded manually or by a time clock. The time card also shows the total hours worked each day. **Figure 12–2** shows a manual time card.

Many companies divide an hour into four 15-minute quarters for the purpose of measuring employee work time. These quarter hours are determined as follows:

Quarter Hour	Example	
On the hour	2:00	P.M.
15 minutes after the hour	2:15	P.M.
30 minutes after the hour	2:30	P.M.
45 minutes after the hour	2:45	P.M.

Employees seldom arrive and leave exactly on the quarter hour. As a result, some companies round arrival and departure times to the nearest quarter hour. Employees, therefore, are paid for working to the nearest quarter hour. Look at **Figure 12–2**. The times appearing on the time card for Emily Kardos for Monday will be rounded to the nearest quarter hour as follows:

Actual Time Recorded	Nearest Quarter Hour
7:58 A.M.	8:00 A.M.
12:25 P.M.	12:30 P.M.
1:32 P.M.	1:30 P.M.
4:18 P.M.	4:15 P.M.

Emily will be paid for working on Monday from 8:00 A.M. to 12:30 P.M. (4 ½ hours) and from 1:30 P.M. to 4:15 P.M. (2 ¾ hours) for a total of 7¼ hours.

Some businesses use computer technology to track employee arrival and departure times. One method uses **electronic badge readers** . With this method the employee is issued an identification badge with a magnetic strip that contains employee information. When the employee inserts the identification badge into a badge reader, the magnetic strip is scanned and the following information is transferred directly to the computer: the employee's name,

NO. __11__

NAME   Emily Kardos

SOC. SEC. NO.   201-46-8319

WEEK ENDING   6/30/20--

DAY	IN	OUT	IN	OUT	IN	OUT	TOTAL
M	7:58	12:25	1:32	4:18			7¼
T	8:00	12:00	12:45	4:00			7¼
W	7:56	12:01	1:10	4:15			7
Th	8:01	11:55	1:02	4:16			7¼
F	7:45	12:02	1:05	3:58			7¼
S							
S							
					TOTAL HOURS		36

	HOURS	RATE	AMOUNT
REGULAR	36	$6.75	$243.00
OVERTIME	0		
		TOTAL EARNINGS	$243.00

SIGNATURE *Emily Kardos*   DATE 6/30/20--

Figure 12–2 An Employee Time Card

the department or area where the employee works, and the arrival or departure times.

This electronic equipment makes it fast and easy to prepare a daily print-out on employee work hours.

Regardless of how employee work hours are recorded (manually, time clock, or electronic reader), business owners and supervisors check the accuracy of the hours reported and analyze the labor costs for every pay period.

Commission

A **commission** is an amount paid to an employee based on a percentage of the employee's sales. Sales employees are often paid a commission to encourage them to increase their sales. For example, Joyce Torrez is paid a 5% commission on all her sales. Last week Joyce's total sales were $8,254. Joyce's gross earnings for the week are $412.70 ($8,254 × .05).

Salary Plus Commission or Bonus

Some salespeople earn a base salary plus a commission or a bonus on the amount of their sales. For example, Juan Espito, who works at a car stereo shop, is paid a salary of $200 per week plus a commission of 3% of his sales. Juan's sales were $4,810 last week. His gross earnings are $344.30 [$200 + ($4,810 × .03)].

Overtime Pay

State and federal laws regulate the number of hours some employees may work in a week. Generally, employers are required to pay overtime when employees covered by these laws work more than 40 hours per week. The **overtime rate**, set by the Fair Labor Standards Act of 1938, is 1½ (1.5) times the employee's regular hourly pay rate. For example, Jesse Dubow, a photo-lab clerk at Fast Photo, worked 43 hours last week. Jesse's hourly rate of pay is $6.60. His hourly overtime rate is $9.90 ($6.60 × 1.5). His gross earnings for the week are $293.70 determined as follows:

	Hours		Rate		
Regular	40	×	$6.60	=	$264.00
Overtime	3	×	$9.90	=	29.70
Total					$293.70

Some employees who are paid a salary are also entitled to overtime pay. If a salaried employee is paid overtime, the salary is converted to an hourly rate using a standard number of hours for the period covered by the salary. Then the hourly overtime rate is calculated. For example, Jim Halley's salary is $600 per week. His hourly rate is $15 assuming a standard 40-hour work week. His hourly overtime rate is $22.50 ($15 × 1.5). Jim's gross earnings for a 44-hour week are $690, determined as follows:

	Hours		Rate		
Regular				=	$600.00
Overtime	4	×	$22.50	=	90.00
Total					$690.00

Key Points

Overtime Pay
Some employees who work more than 40 hours per week are paid overtime. The usual overtime rate is 1½ times the employee's hourly rate of pay.

Now that you have studied this section, complete the following questions and problems.

Thinking Critically

1. List the two goals a payroll system should achieve.
2. How does an electronic badge reader record the correct arrival and departure times?

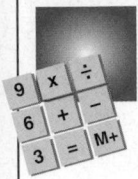

Computing in the Business World

You have been interviewing with several financial consulting firms for entry-level management positions, and you received two job offers. One company, Bryson Consulting, offers you a starting salary of $30,000 with a 2% bonus (on salary) if you can bring 10 new clients into the firm. The other company, The Charleston Group, offers a salary of $25,000 plus a 3% commission on all new client billings. Which job offers the highest earnings potential? Explain.

Problem 12–1 Calculating Gross Earnings

Cleary's Music Center has nine employees. The employees are paid weekly with overtime after 40 hours per week. The overtime rate is 1½ times the regular rate of pay. Payroll information for the week ending June 12 follows:

Employee	Pay Rate	Hours
David Clune	$6.95	33½
Richard Lang	$7.80	38
Jane Longas	$7.25	43
Betty Quinn	$8.30	44¼
John Sullivan	$8.30	39½
Kelly Talbert	$7.50	40
Gene Trimbell	$9.75	42½
Heidi Varney	$8.75	34¼
Kevin Wallace	$9.25	46

Instructions Prepare a form similar to the one that follows. Calculate regular earnings, overtime earnings, and gross earnings for each employee.

Employee	Total Hours	Pay Rate	Regular Earnings	Overtime Earnings	Gross Earnings
Clune, David	33½	$6.95	$232.83	– 0 –	$232.83

Payroll Deductions

Whether you work at Target, McDonald's, or CompUSA, your earnings and deductions are prepared in the same manner. In this section, you will learn how to compute employee-paid withholdings.

Computing Employee-Paid Withholdings

The first time you received a payroll check, you were probably surprised to see that the amount of the check was less than your gross earnings. Various amounts are taken out of gross earnings. An amount that is subtracted from gross earnings is called a **deduction** . Deductions include those required by law and those an employee wishes to have withheld from earnings.

Deductions Required by Law

An employer is required by law to withhold payroll taxes. These taxes include the federal income tax and the social security tax. In addition, most cities and states require employers to withhold city and state income tax.

Federal Income Tax. Most people pay the federal government a tax based on their annual income. To ensure that employees have the funds to pay their income taxes, employers are required to withhold a certain amount of money from each payroll check. The employer sends the money withheld to the federal government. The employer, thus, acts as a collection agent for the federal government.

The amount of income tax withheld is based on an estimate of the amount of income tax the employee will actually owe. The exact amount of income tax is determined when the employee prepares an income tax return. If too much money is withheld, the Internal Revenue Service (IRS) will refund the overpayment. If too little money is withheld, the employee pays the amount due when the income tax return is filed. To avoid penalties, an employee should have at least 90% of the actual tax liability deducted from his or her pay.

Form W-4. The amount withheld for federal income taxes depends on three factors:

(1) the employee's marital status
(2) the number of allowances claimed by the employee
(3) the employee's gross earnings

What **You'll Learn**

- Why deductions are calculated and reported.
- How to calculate deductions required by the federal government.
- How to determine voluntary deductions.

Why **It's Important**

To prepare the payroll accurately and to comply with the law, both mandatory and voluntary deductions must be calculated correctly.

KEY TERMS

deduction
allowance
401(k) plan

The first two items of information are found on Form W-4, the Employee's Withholding Allowance Certificate. Form W-4 is filled out by each employee when starting a job. A revised Form W-4 is filed if the employee's marital status or number of allowances changes. Employers keep a current Form W-4 on file for each employee.

Figure 12–3 shows the completed Form W-4 for Emily Kardos. As you can see, Form W-4 includes the employee's name, address, social security number, and marital status. In addition, the employee lists the number of allowances claimed (see line 4). An **allowance** reduces the amount of income tax to be withheld. The greater the number of allowances claimed by a taxpayer, the lower the amount of income tax withheld from earnings. Usually, a taxpayer is allowed one personal allowance and one allowance for each person the taxpayer supports, such as a child or an elderly parent.

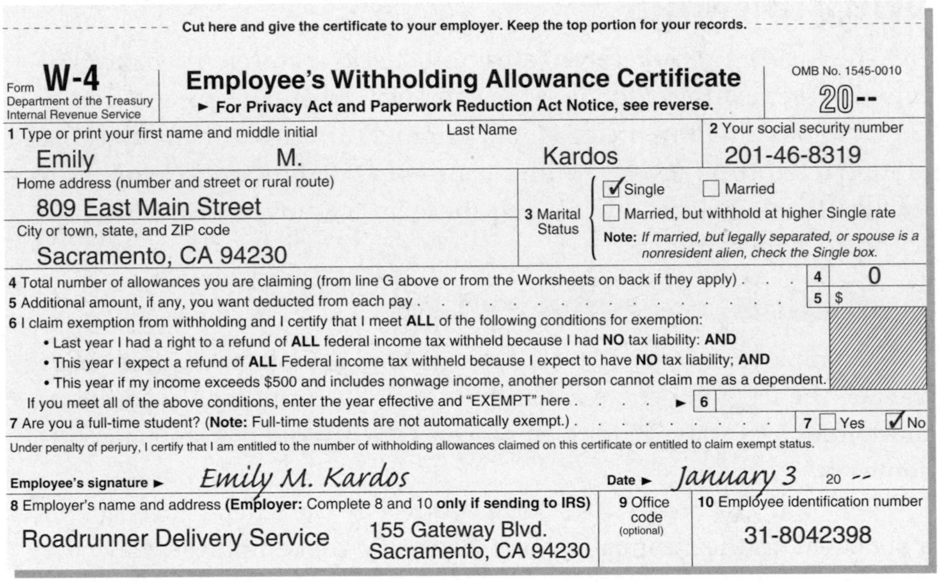
Cut here and give the certificate to your employer. Keep the top portion for your records.

Form **W-4** Department of the Treasury Internal Revenue Service

Employee's Withholding Allowance Certificate

► **For Privacy Act and Paperwork Reduction Act Notice, see reverse.**

OMB No. 1545-0010 **20--**

1 Type or print your first name and middle initial: Emily M. — Last Name: Kardos — 2 Your social security number: 201-46-8319

Home address (number and street or rural route): 809 East Main Street

City or town, state, and ZIP code: Sacramento, CA 94230

3 Marital Status: ☑ Single ☐ Married ☐ Married, but withhold at higher Single rate

Note: *If married, but legally separated, or spouse is a nonresident alien, check the Single box.*

4 Total number of allowances you are claiming (from line G above or from the Worksheets on back if they apply) . . . 4 | 0

5 Additional amount, if any, you want deducted from each pay . . . 5 | $

6 I claim exemption from withholding and I certify that I meet **ALL** of the following conditions for exemption:

- Last year I had a right to a refund of **ALL** federal income tax withheld because I had **NO** tax liability: **AND**
- This year I expect a refund of **ALL** Federal income tax withheld because I expect to have **NO** tax liability; **AND**
- This year if my income exceeds $500 and includes nonwage income, another person cannot claim me as a dependent.

If you meet all of the above conditions, enter the year effective and "EXEMPT" here . . . ► 6

7 Are you a full-time student? (**Note:** Full-time students are not automatically exempt.) . . . 7 ☐ Yes ☑ No

Under penalty of perjury, I certify that I am entitled to the number of withholding allowances claimed on this certificate or entitled to claim exempt status.

Employee's signature ► *Emily M. Kardos* **Date** ► *January 3* 20 --

8 Employer's name and address (**Employer:** Complete 8 and 10 **only if sending to IRS**): Roadrunner Delivery Service, 155 Gateway Blvd. Sacramento, CA 94230 — 9 Office code (optional) — 10 Employee identification number: 31-8042398

Figure 12–3 Employee's Withholding Allowance Certificate—Form W-4

In certain circumstances as defined in the tax laws, some employees do not pay federal income tax. An employee who does not pay federal income tax can be "exempt" from withholding if he or she:

- Did not have a federal income tax liability in the previous year.
- Expects no tax liability this year.
- Has income of $700 or less including nonwage income such as interest on a savings account.
- Cannot be claimed as a dependent on someone else's tax return.

If an employee writes "EXEMPT" on Form W-4, the employer will not withhold federal income taxes.

Tax Tables. An employee's gross earnings also affect the amount withheld for federal income taxes. Once gross earnings are calculated, most employers use tables supplied by the IRS to determine the amount of federal tax to withhold. **Figure 12–4** shows tables for single and married persons who are paid weekly. Other tax tables are available.

Let's use the tables to determine the tax withheld for Emily Kardos. Emily is single and claims no allowances. For the week ending June 30, she earned

SINGLE Persons—WEEKLY Payroll Period

If the wages are –		And the number of withholding allowances claimed is –										
At least	But less than	0	1	2	3	4	5	6	7	8	9	10
		The amount of income tax to be withheld is –										
$0	$55	0	0	0	0	0	0	0	0	0	0	0
55	60	1	0	0	0	0	0	0	0	0	0	0
60	65	2	0	0	0	0	0	0	0	0	0	0
65	70	2	0	0	0	0	0	0	0	0	0	0
70	75	3	0	0	0	0	0	0	0	0	0	0
75	80	4	0	0	0	0	0	0	0	0	0	0
80	85	5	0	0	0	0	0	0	0	0	0	0
85	90	5	0	0	0	0	0	0	0	0	0	0
90	95	6	0	0	0	0	0	0	0	0	0	0
95	100	7	0	0	0	0	0	0	0	0	0	0
100	105	8	0	0	0	0	0	0	0	0	0	0
105	110	8	1	0	0	0	0	0	0	0	0	0
110	115	9	2	0	0	0	0	0	0	0	0	0
115	120	10	2	0	0	0	0	0	0	0	0	0
120	125	11	3	0	0	0	0	0	0	0	0	0
125	130	11	4	0	0	0	0	0	0	0	0	0
130	135	12	5	0	0	0	0	0	0	0	0	0
135	140	13	5	0	0	0	0	0	0	0	0	0
140	145	14	6	0	0	0	0	0	0	0	0	0
145	150	14	7	0	0	0	0	0	0	0	0	0
150	155	15	8	0	0	0	0	0	0	0	0	0
155	160	16	8	1	0	0	0	0	0	0	0	0
160	165	17	9	1	0	0	0	0	0	0	0	0
165	170	17	10	2	0	0	0	0	0	0	0	0
170	175	18	11	3	0	0	0	0	0	0	0	0
175	180	19	11	4	0	0	0	0	0	0	0	0
180	185	20	12	4	0	0	0	0	0	0	0	0
185	190	20	13	5	0	0	0	0	0	0	0	0
190	195	21	14	6	0	0	0	0	0	0	0	0
195	200	22	14	7	0	0	0	0	0	0	0	0
200	210	23	15	8	0	0	0	0	0	0	0	0
210	220	25	17	9	2	0	0	0	0	0	0	0
220	230	26	18	11	3	0	0	0	0	0	0	0
230	240	28	20	12	5	0	0	0	0	0	0	0
240	250	29	21	14	6	0	0	0	0	0	0	0
250	260	31	23	15	8	0	0	0	0	0	0	0
260	270	32	24	17	9	2	0	0	0	0	0	0
270	280	34	26	18	11	3	0	0	0	0	0	0
280	290	35	27	20	12	5	0	0	0	0	0	0
290	300	37	29	21	14	6	0	0	0	0	0	0
300	310	38	30	23	15	8	0	0	0	0	0	0
310	320	40	32	24	17	9	1	0	0	0	0	0
320	330	41	33	26	18	11	3	0	0	0	0	0
330	340	43	35	27	20	12	4	0	0	0	0	0
340	350	44	36	29	21	14	6	0	0	0	0	0

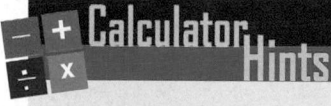

Calculating Gross Earnings

To calculate gross earnings:

- multiply the pay rate by the hours worked,
- place that amount in memory by pressing M I,
- then multiply the regular rate by 1.5 and the number of overtime hours,
- press MR,
- then + to find the total.

MARRIED Persons—WEEKLY Payroll Period

If the wages are –		And the number of withholding allowances claimed is –										
At least	But less than	0	1	2	3	4	5	6	7	8	9	10
		The amount of income tax to be withheld is –										
$0	$125	0	0	0	0	0	0	0	0	0	0	0
125	130	1	0	0	0	0	0	0	0	0	0	0
130	135	1	0	0	0	0	0	0	0	0	0	0
135	140	2	0	0	0	0	0	0	0	0	0	0
140	145	3	0	0	0	0	0	0	0	0	0	0
145	150	4	0	0	0	0	0	0	0	0	0	0
150	155	4	0	0	0	0	0	0	0	0	0	0
155	160	5	0	0	0	0	0	0	0	0	0	0
160	165	6	0	0	0	0	0	0	0	0	0	0
165	170	7	0	0	0	0	0	0	0	0	0	0
170	175	7	0	0	0	0	0	0	0	0	0	0
175	180	8	0	0	0	0	0	0	0	0	0	0
180	185	9	1	0	0	0	0	0	0	0	0	0
185	190	10	2	0	0	0	0	0	0	0	0	0
190	195	10	3	0	0	0	0	0	0	0	0	0
195	200	11	3	0	0	0	0	0	0	0	0	0
200	210	12	5	0	0	0	0	0	0	0	0	0
210	220	14	6	0	0	0	0	0	0	0	0	0
220	230	15	8	0	0	0	0	0	0	0	0	0
230	240	17	9	1	0	0	0	0	0	0	0	0
240	250	18	11	3	0	0	0	0	0	0	0	0
250	260	20	12	4	0	0	0	0	0	0	0	0
260	270	21	14	6	0	0	0	0	0	0	0	0
270	280	23	15	7	0	0	0	0	0	0	0	0
280	290	24	17	9	1	0	0	0	0	0	0	0
290	300	26	18	10	3	0	0	0	0	0	0	0
300	310	27	20	12	4	0	0	0	0	0	0	0
310	320	29	21	13	6	0	0	0	0	0	0	0
320	330	30	23	15	7	0	0	0	0	0	0	0
330	340	32	24	16	9	1	0	0	0	0	0	0

Figure 12–4 Internal Revenue Service Tax Tables

$243. This amount falls between $240 and $250 on the tax table for single persons. Reading across this line to the column for zero withholding allowances, you find that $29 is withheld from Emily's gross earnings for federal income taxes.

Social Security Tax. In addition to federal income tax, employers also collect social security taxes for the federal government. The present social security system was established by the Federal Insurance Contributions Act (FICA) in 1935. Social security taxes are therefore often referred to as FICA taxes. The FICA taxes finance programs that provide income to certain individuals:

1. The old-age and disability insurance programs provide income to retired and disabled persons and their dependent children.
2. The survivors' benefits program provides income to the spouse and dependent children of a deceased worker.
3. The Medicare program provides health insurance benefits for the elderly.

The FICA taxes are exact taxes in that, unlike the federal income tax, they do not involve estimation and are not affected by allowances or marital status. The FICA tax rates are set by Congress, and can be changed at any time. Most employees are subject to FICA taxes, even those who are exempt from federal income taxes.

There are two FICA taxes: social security and Medicare. Each tax is separately recorded on payroll documents. The tax rates are as follows:

Social security tax	6.20%
Medicare tax	1.45%
Total FICA taxes	7.65%

The social security tax is deducted from each employee's earnings until the maximum taxable earnings amount for the year is reached. This amount increases each year. For 2002, the maximum taxable earnings amount is $84,900. Therefore the maximum amount of social security tax that can be withheld from an employee in one year is $5,263.80 ($84,900 × .062). There is no maximum taxable earnings amount for the Medicare tax. For example, Lisa Gustavson earns $87,000 per year as a manager at a CPA firm. The $6,525.30 in FICA taxes withheld from her earnings is calculated as follows:

	Earnings Subject to Tax	Tax Rate		Tax
Social security tax	$84,900	× .062	=	$5,263.80
Medicare tax	87,000	× .0145	=	1,261.50
Total withheld				$6,525.30

State and Local Income Taxes. Most states and cities tax the earnings of the people who live or work within their boundaries. In some states and cities, the tax rates are set as a percentage of gross earnings, like social security taxes. In others, the amounts to be deducted are indicated on tables similar to the ones used for federal income tax.

Voluntary Deductions

Most employers agree to deduct other amounts from their employees' payroll check to accommodate the wishes of the employees. Once an employee requests that deductions be made, they are withheld from each payroll check until the employee notifies the employer to stop. Common voluntary deductions include:

- union dues
- health insurance payments
- life insurance payments
- pension and other retirement contributions
- credit union deposits and payments
- U.S. savings bonds
- charitable contributions.

A popular payroll deduction is a contribution to a **401(k) plan**. An employee contributes a portion of gross earnings to an account in the 401(k) plan. The employee does not pay income tax on the contributed earnings. In other words, taxable income is reduced by the amount of the contribution. The 401(k) contribution and earnings on the contribution are not taxed until the money is withdrawn from the plan, usually after age 59½. In some 401(k) plans, employers make matching and profit-sharing contributions to their employees' accounts.

Angelo Cappelli, a graphic artist, earns $644 each week and contributes $75 to his 401(k) account. Angelo will pay income tax on $569 ($644 − $75). He will not pay income tax on his $75 contribution until it is withdrawn from his 401(k) account.

CONNECT TO . . .
CIVICS

The Internal Revenue Service is the number-one employer of accountants in the world. Sixty-three district offices across the United States hire Revenue Agents, Revenue Officers, Special Agents, Tax Auditors, and Computer Specialists. Together, they use their accounting backgrounds in reviewing tax returns and investigating tax fraud.

ANALYZING FINANCIAL REPORTS

Analyzing Employee Productivity

The cost of wages and benefits is often one of a company's largest expenses. Before hiring additional employees, managers and owners carefully calculate whether another person will contribute to the overall profitability of the company.

One measure of profitability is the average sales dollars generated by each employee. This measure is calculated by dividing the total revenue by the number of all employees.

$$\frac{\text{Total Revenue}}{\text{Number of Employees}} = \text{Sales per Employee}$$

For example, in a company with total revenue of $1,480,000 and 20 employees, sales per employee are $74,000. Calculating this measure of profitability from period to period or from one part of a company to another allows an owner to see changes in employee productivity. If sales per employee increase or decrease greatly, the owner would want to learn why.

▶ **Analyze the Report:**

Use the income statement for Roadrunner Delivery Service on page 206 to answer these questions.

1. Assume that Roadrunner Delivery Service has two employees, including the owner. What is the monthly revenue per employee?
2. Suppose Maria Sanchez hires two more delivery people. The revenue for the next month increases to $5,400.00. How has the productivity per employee changed?

HELP WANTED

Now that you have studied this section, complete the following questions and problems.

Thinking Critically

1. Which taxes are required to be withheld from employees' pay?
2. What three factors determine the amount of federal income tax withheld each pay period?

Computing in the Business World

As the president of Creative Craft Memory Books, you have decided to add five new sales consultants to your sales force. You offer these sales consultants a gross salary of $23,000 each, but the consultants will not take home $23,000. Calculate the FICA taxes to be withheld from each consultant's gross pay. What remains of their gross pay after you deduct FICA taxes?

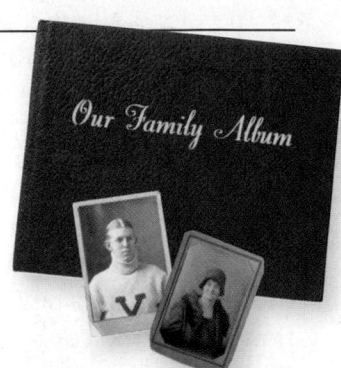

Problem 12–2 Determining Taxes on Gross Earnings

Information related to the just-completed pay period of MegaCom Computer Upgrades is provided in the chart below. Determine the amounts to be withheld from each employee's gross earnings for FICA and income taxes. It is a weekly pay period, so use the tables on page 295 to determine the amount of federal income tax to be withheld. The state income tax is 2% of gross earnings. The social security tax rate is 6.2%, and the Medicare tax rate is 1.45%. Use the format shown in your working papers.

Employee	Marital Status	Allowances	Gross Earnings
Cleary, Kevin	S	0	$155.60
Halley, James	S	1	184.10
Hong, Kim	S	0	204.65
Jackson, Marvin	M	1	216.40
Sell, Richard	M	2	196.81
Total			$957.56

Problem 12–3 Analyzing a Source Document

Examine the following partially completed payroll check stub. The employee, Melanie Galvin, is single and claims one allowance.

What amount should be deducted for:

1. Medicare tax?

2. Social Security tax?

3. Federal Income tax?

Employee Pay Statement											260
Detach and retain this statement.											
	Earnings			Deductions							Net Pay
Period Ending	Regular	Overtime	Total	Social Security Tax	Med. Tax	Federal Income Tax	State Income Tax	Hosp. Ins.	Other	Total	
1/15/20--	315.00		315.00								

Payroll Records

In the previous sections you learned how to calculate gross earnings and deductions. Now you will learn how to compute net pay, prepare the payroll records for each period, and prepare payroll checks. Whether a business has many employees, like the Boeing Corporation, or a small staff, like a veterinarian's office, it is essential that the payroll be prepared on time and accurately.

What You'll Learn

- The purpose of a payroll register.
- How to prepare a payroll register.
- How to prepare a payroll check.
- The purpose of an employee's earnings record.
- How to prepare an employee's earnings record.

Why It's Important

To comply with federal and state laws, payroll records must be kept accurately.

KEY TERMS

payroll register
net pay
direct deposit
employee's earnings record
accumulated earnings

Preparing the Payroll Register

Federal and state laws require businesses to keep accurate payroll records. To help meet these requirements, businesses use a payroll register. The **payroll register** is a form that summarizes information about employees' earnings for each pay period. Let's learn how to prepare payroll registers.

Figure 12–5 shows the payroll register for Roadrunner. As you can see, the payroll register lists each employee's I.D. number, name, marital status, and the number of allowances claimed. Refer to **Figure 12–5** as you read the descriptions of the payroll register.

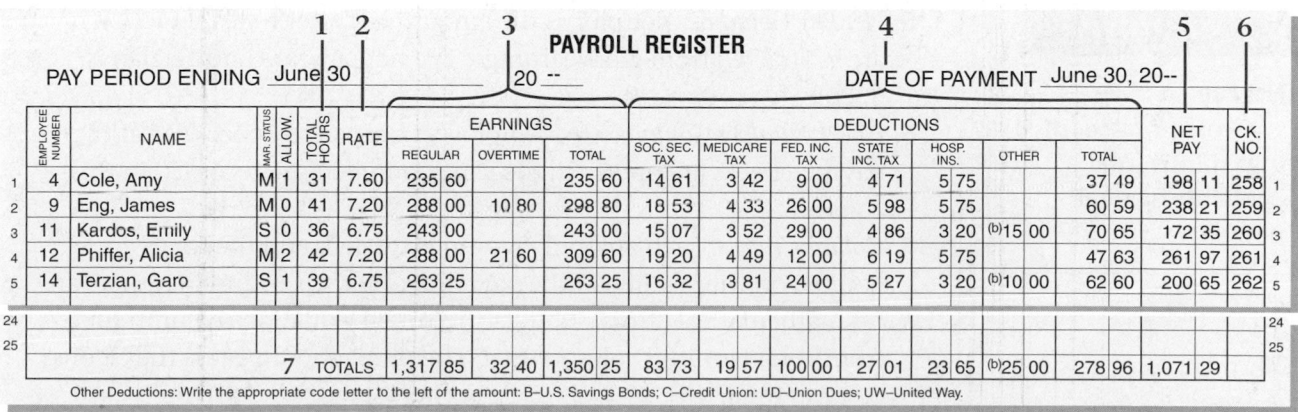

PAYROLL REGISTER

PAY PERIOD ENDING June 30 ___ 20 -- ___ DATE OF PAYMENT June 30, 20--

	EMPLOYEE NUMBER	NAME	MAR. STATUS	ALLOW.	TOTAL HOURS	RATE	EARNINGS REGULAR	EARNINGS OVERTIME	EARNINGS TOTAL	SOC. SEC. TAX	MEDICARE TAX	FED. INC. TAX	STATE INC. TAX	HOSP. INS.	OTHER	TOTAL	NET PAY	CK. NO.	
1	4	Cole, Amy	M	1	31	7.60	235 60		235 60	14 61	3 42	9 00	4 71	5 75		37 49	198 11	258	1
2	9	Eng, James	M	0	41	7.20	288 00	10 80	298 80	18 53	4 33	26 00	5 98	5 75		60 59	238 21	259	2
3	11	Kardos, Emily	S	0	36	6.75	243 00		243 00	15 07	3 52	29 00	4 86	3 20	(b)15 00	70 65	172 35	260	3
4	12	Phiffer, Alicia	M	2	42	7.20	288 00	21 60	309 60	19 20	4 49	12 00	6 19	5 75		47 63	261 97	261	4
5	14	Terzian, Garo	S	1	39	6.75	263 25		263 25	16 32	3 81	24 00	5 27	3 20	(b)10 00	62 60	200 65	262	5
24																			24
25																			25
				7	TOTALS		1,317 85	32 40	1,350 25	83 73	19 57	100 00	27 01	23 65	(b)25 00	278 96	1,071 29		

Other Deductions: Write the appropriate code letter to the left of the amount: B–U.S. Savings Bonds; C–Credit Union: UD–Union Dues; UW–United Way.

Figure 12–5 Completed Payroll Register

1. *Total Hours Column.* Regular and overtime hours from the employee's time card are added together, and the total is entered in this column.
2. *Rate Column.* This column shows the employee's current rate of pay, found on the employee's earnings record.
3. *Earnings Section.* The earnings section is divided into three columns: regular, overtime, and total earnings. To complete these columns, the payroll clerk multiplies the hours worked by the employee's regular hourly rate or, when applicable, overtime hourly rate.

Employee 4, Amy Cole, worked 31 hours. Her regular hourly rate is $7.60. Amy earned $235.60 (31 × $7.60) for the week. Since there are no overtime hours, regular and total earnings are the same.

Alicia Phiffer, Employee 12, worked 2 overtime hours in addition to 40 regular hours. Her regular hourly rate is $7.20. Her overtime hourly rate is $10.80 ($7.20 × 1.5). Her regular earnings are $288.00 (40 × $7.20) and her overtime earnings are $21.60 (2 × $10.80). Her total earnings are $309.60 ($288.00 + $21.60).

4. *Deductions Section.* The illustrated payroll register has seven deduction columns. The number of deduction columns, however, varies among businesses depending on the specific needs of each business. In the illustration, columns are provided for the deductions required by law—FICA taxes (social security and Medicare), federal income tax, and state income tax. Columns are also provided for voluntary deductions. Certain voluntary deductions taken by many employees on a regular basis will usually have their own columns, such as the column shown in the illustration for hospital insurance. Deductions taken less frequently are often placed in a column titled "Other." In the illustration these deductions include credit union, union dues, savings bonds, and charitable contributions. Finally, a column is provided for the total deductions of each employee.

Look at the deductions for Garo Terzian, Employee 14. Garo's deductions include the taxes required by law. He also has two voluntary deductions, $3.20 for hospital insurance and $10.00, shown in the Other column, for U.S. Savings Bonds. The total deductions for Garo are $62.60 as shown in the "Total" column.

5. *Net Pay Column.* **Net pay** is the amount left after total deductions are subtracted from gross earnings. The net pay for Garo Terzian is $200.65.
6. *Check Number Column.* Most employees are paid by check. After the payroll checks are prepared, the check numbers are recorded in this column.
7. *Column Totals.* Each amount column is totaled, and the totals are entered on the last line of the payroll register. To ensure that there are no mathematical errors, subtract the Total Deductions column total from Total Earnings column total. The result should equal the Net Pay column total.

Key Points

Net Pay

Gross (total) earnings minus total deductions equal net pay.

Preparing Payroll Checks

Once the accuracy of the payroll register is verified, a payroll check is prepared for each employee. Most businesses pay their employees by check as a means of cash control. When a company has only a few employees, payroll checks are written from the company's regular checking account. Companies with many employees have a separate checking account for payroll.

When a separate payroll checking account is used, funds are transferred to this account each pay period. A check for the total net pay amount is written from the company's regular checking account and deposited in the payroll checking account. Then, individual payroll checks are issued to employees from the payroll account.

The payroll register is the source of information for preparing the payroll checks. Along with a payroll check, each employee is given a written or printed explanation showing how the employee's net pay is calculated. This explanation is provided on a stub attached to the payroll check. **Figure 12–6** shows a typical payroll check and stub. Notice that for Emily Kardos, the amounts on the stub are the same as the amounts in the payroll register. After each payroll check is written, the check number is recorded in the payroll register.

Employees are not always paid by check. The accountant reviews the records to determine methods of dissemination of payroll funds, for example, direct deposit, and mail. With **direct deposit**, the net pay is deposited in the employee's personal bank account by the employer. No payroll check is prepared. The employee does, however, receive a printed record of the payroll calculation. Direct deposits are made through electronic funds transfer. With this system, the employer informs the employee's bank of the amount to be deposited.

International ACCOUNTING

Voltage Power

Accountants who travel frequently and carry laptop computers should be aware of the voltage used in the countries of their destination. Power in the United States is 110V, but in most other countries it is 220V.

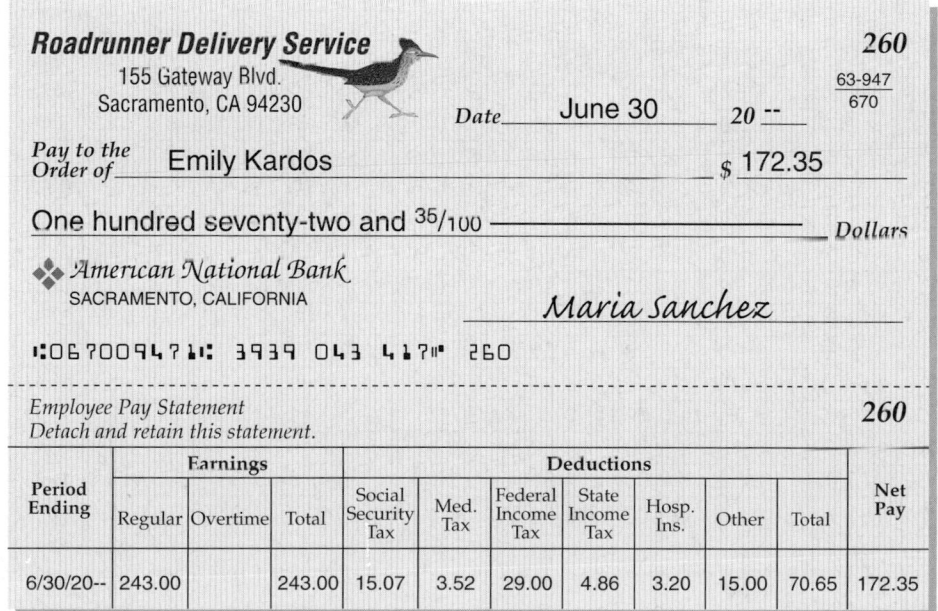

Period Ending	Earnings			Deductions							Net Pay
	Regular	Overtime	Total	Social Security Tax	Med. Tax	Federal Income Tax	State Income Tax	Hosp. Ins.	Other	Total	
6/30/20--	243.00		243.00	15.07	3.52	29.00	4.86	3.20		15.00	70.65	172.35

Figure 12–6 Completed Payroll Check and Stub

The Employee's Earnings Record

ACCOUNTING TIPS

Work Experience

Research shows that employers would rather hire people who can do things rather than people who know about things. If you can get experience doing anything in the accounting field, you'd have a better chance of getting a job than an applicant who has taken the same classes as you have but doesn't have your work experience.

In addition to the payroll register, an employer must also keep an **employee's earnings record** for each employee. This record contains all of the payroll information related to an employee. **Figure 12–7** shows an example of an employee's earnings record. The earnings record has the same amount columns that appear on the payroll register. An additional column for the employee's accumulated earnings is also provided. **Accumulated earnings** are the employee's year-to-date gross earnings, or the employee's gross earnings from the beginning of the year through the end of each pay period. The accumulated earnings for Emily Kardos as of June 30 are computed by adding her gross earnings for the pay period just completed to her accumulated earnings for the previous pay period as follows:

Gross Earnings for Pay Period Just Completed	+	Accumulated Earnings for Previous Pay Period	=	Accumulated Earnings for Pay Period Just Completed
$243.00	+	$4,178.60	=	$4,421.60

Businesses keep employee's earnings records on a quarterly basis. This makes it easier to complete government reports that are required each

This amount was carried forward from the previous quarter's record.

EMPLOYEE'S EARNINGS RECORD FOR QUARTER ENDING June 30, 20--

Kardos (Last Name) Emily (First) M (Initial)
809 East Main Street (Address)
Sacramento, CA 94230

EMPLOYEE NO. 11 MARITAL STATUS S ALLOWANCES 0
POSITION Delivery Driver
RATE OF PAY 6.75 SOC. SEC. NO. 201-46-8319

PAY PERIOD		EARNINGS			DEDUCTIONS							NET PAY	ACCUMULATED EARNINGS
NO.	ENDED	REGULAR	OVERTIME	TOTAL	SOC. SEC. TAX	MEDICARE TAX	FED. INC. TAX	STATE INC. TAX	HOSP. INS.	OTHER	TOTAL		1,490 39
1	4/07/--	199 13		199 13	12 35	2 89	22 00	3 98	3 20	(B) 15 00	59 42	139 71	1,689 52
2	4/14/--	205 88		205 88	12 76	2 99	23 00	4 12	3 20		46 07	159 81	1,895 40
3	4/21/--	270 00	30 38	300 38	18 62	4 36	38 00	6 01	3 20		70 19	230 19	2,195 78
4	4/28/--	222 75		222 75	13 81	3 23	26 00	4 46	3 20		50 70	172 05	2,418 53
5	5/05/--	229 50		229 50	14 23	3 33	26 00	4 59	3 20	(B) 15 00	66 35	163 15	2,648 03
6	5/12/--	162 00		162 00	10 04	2 35	17 00	3 24	3 20		35 83	126 17	2,810 03
7	5/19/--	256 50		256 50	15 90	3 72	31 00	5 13	3 20		58 95	197 55	3,066 53
8	5/26/--	270 00	20 25	290 25	18 00	4 21	37 00	5 81	3 20		68 22	222 03	3,356 78
9	6/02/--	204 19		204 19	12 66	2 96	23 00	4 08	3 20	(B) 15 00	60 90	143 29	3,560 97
10	6/09/--	212 63		212 63	13 18	3 08	25 00	4 25	3 20		48 71	163 92	3,773 60
11	6/16/--	189 00		189 00	11 72	2 74	20 00	3 78	3 20		41 44	147 56	3,962 60
12	6/23/--	216 00		216 00	13 39	3 13	25 00	4 32	3 20		49 04	166 96	4,178 60
13	6/30/--	243 00		243 00	15 07	3 52	29 00	4 86	3 20	(B) 15 00	70 65	172 35	4,421 60
	QUARTERLY TOTALS	2,880 58	50 63	2,931 21	181 73	42 51	342 00	58 63	41 60	60 00	726 47	2,204 74	

Other Deductions: B—U.S. Savings Bonds; C—Credit Union; UD—Union Dues; UW—United Way.

Figure 12–7 Employee's Earnings Record

This amount will be carried forward to the next quarter's record.

quarter. At the end of a quarter, the amount columns on each employee's earnings record are totaled. The final amount in the Accumulated Earnings column is carried forward to the top of the employee's earnings record for the next quarter, (refer to **Figure 12–7**).

As you can see from this chapter, preparing payroll is time consuming and detail oriented. A mistake that is not promptly detected and corrected can mean hours of rework. To reduce simple mathematical errors and to improve productivity, many businesses use computers and special software to prepare payroll. In a computerized system, the computer:

- performs all the payroll calculations
- prepares and prints the payroll register
- prints the payroll checks and stubs
- maintains the employee's earnings records

Managerial Implications for Payroll Accounting

Payroll procedures and records must comply with state, federal, and local laws. Withholding amounts must be accurately computed and care should be taken that necessary reports are prepared on time.

Wages and salaries form a large part of the expenses of a business. Thus, an adequate set of payroll records is essential as an aid to management in controlling expenses. These records help pinpoint the labor cost for each area of the business by showing management exactly what amounts have been spent. These records also indicate how much of the amount spent was for overtime. Although overtime is fully justified in many cases, it may also be a sign of inefficiency. Large or frequent expenditures for overtime should therefore be investigated by management. To prevent errors or fraud, management should make sure that the payroll records are audited carefully and that payroll procedures are evaluated periodically.

A MATTER OF ETHICS

Payroll Information

Payroll clerks have access to some very personal information about employees, such as rate of pay and marital status. Imagine that you're the payroll clerk for a clothing store like The Gap. Your friend Janet, who also works at the store, is interested in one of the sales clerks. She wants you to find out how much money he makes and also if he's married.

Ethical Decision Making:

- ☛ What are the ethical issues?
- ☛ What are the alternatives?
- ☛ Who are the affected parties?
- ☛ How do the alternatives affect the parties?
- ☛ What would you do?

Now that you have studied this section, complete the following questions and problems.

Thinking Critically

1. Describe the direct deposit process.
2. What is the difference between a payroll register and an employee's earnings record?

Analyzing Accounting

While reviewing payroll records from the past three years for Sports Junction, an athletic supply store, you notice that the increasing payroll cost could be holding down overall company profits. Review the graph comparing the cost of payroll with the revenue realized. Make a recommendation to the management of Sports Junction about the salary levels. Do you recommend downsizing to increase profit?

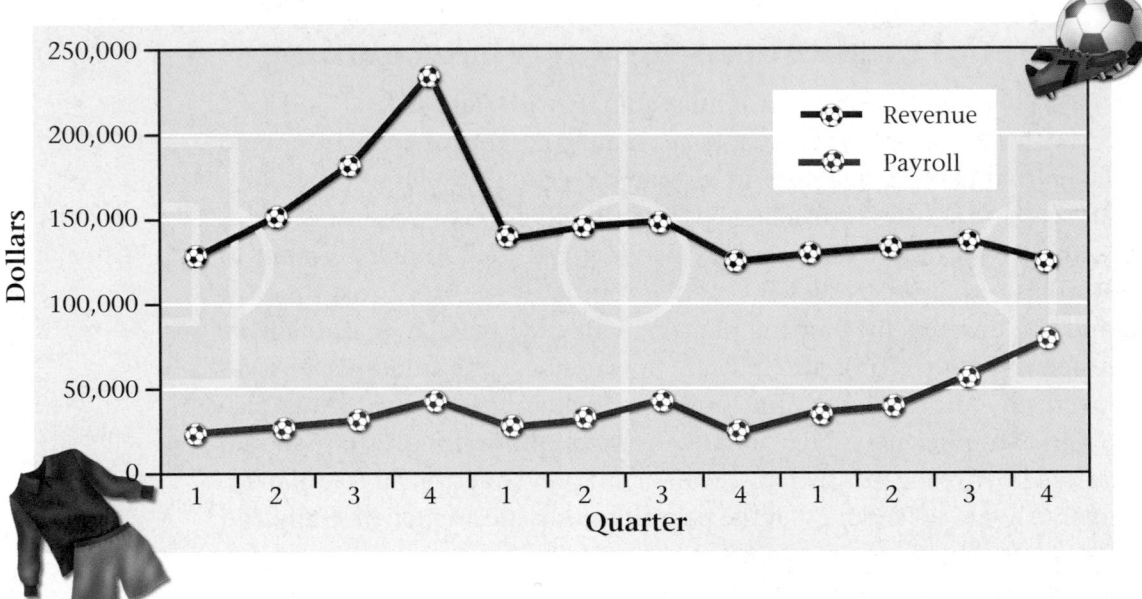

Problem 12–4 Preparing a Payroll Check

Use the information on the payroll register for Heather's Dance School and the form in the working papers to prepare a payroll check for Janice Burns for the week ending March 23, 20—.

PAYROLL REGISTER

PAY PERIOD ENDING March 23 _____ 20 -- _____   DATE OF PAYMENT March 23, 20--

	EMPLOYEE NUMBER	NAME	MAR. STATUS	ALLOW.	TOTAL HOURS	RATE	EARNINGS			DEDUCTIONS							NET PAY	CK. NO.	
							REGULAR	OVERTIME	TOTAL	SOC. SEC. TAX	MEDICARE TAX	FED. INC. TAX	STATE INC. TAX	HOSP. INS.	OTHER	TOTAL			
1	18	Burns, Janice	S	1	42	7.80	312 00	23 40	335 40	20 79	4 86	35 00	6 71	4 10	——	71 46	263 94	79	1
2																			2

KEY CONCEPTS

1. Federal and state laws require employers to keep accurate records of all payroll information. Most employers have a payroll system to ensure that employees are paid on time and that their payroll checks and payroll records are accurate.

2. Gross earnings may be calculated by various methods including:
   - salary,
   - hourly wage,
   - commission,
   - overtime pay, or
   - a combination of these methods.

3. Some employees who work more than 40 hours in a week are paid overtime. Usually the overtime rate is 1½ times the regular rate of pay.

Regular Hourly Rate			**Overtime Hourly Rate**
$8.20	×	1.5 =	$12.30

4. Some deductions from gross earnings are required by law. Other deductions are voluntary.

Deductions Required By Law	**Voluntary Deductions**
federal income tax	union dues
social security tax	insurance payments
medicare tax	401(k) plans
city and state tax	charitable contributions
	other retirement-related contributions

5. Form W-4 is used to determine federal income tax withholding.

6. Payroll Deductions
   - Federal income tax withholding is determined by tables.
   - Social security tax rate is 6.2% (.062) of gross earnings.
   - Medicare tax rate is 1.45% (.0145) of gross earnings.
   - State income tax is determined by each state.
   - Voluntary deductions are agreed to by employer and employees.

7. A payroll register, prepared for each pay period, summarizes the payroll information for all employees.

8. The employee's earnings record contains all of the payroll information, including earnings and deductions, for an employee for each period.

9. Gross pay is the amount that an employee earns before deductions.

10. Net pay is the amount of money actually received by an employee.
    Gross Pay − Total Payroll Deductions = Net Pay

11. Many businesses use computers to process payroll. In a computerized payroll system, the computer is used to perform all the calculations and to prepare and print the payroll register, the employee payroll checks and stubs, and the employee's earnings records.

USING KEY TERMS

You are the payroll clerk for Wild West Amusement Park. The new sales manager for the Western region, Will Klein, called and asked you to explain the items on his payroll check, dated January 31, 20--. He also asked you to explain any relevant company payroll procedures. Use the following key terms in your written explanation of his payroll check and the payroll process. Use your imagination!

401(k) plan	net pay
accumulated earnings	overtime rate
allowance	pay period
commission	payroll
deduction	payroll clerk
direct deposit	payroll register
electronic badge readers	salary
employee's earnings record	time card
gross earnings	wage

Understanding Accounting Concepts and Procedures

Instructions

On a separate sheet of paper, answer the following questions:

1. What are the two goals of a payroll system?

2. What five tasks does an effective payroll system perform?

3. What is the difference between a salary and a wage?

4. Why do some businesses pay their employees on a commission basis?

5. List the three federal taxes that businesses are required to withhold from employees' wages.

6. List three factors that determine the amount of federal income tax withheld from employee earnings each pay period.

7. Why do all employees complete Form W-4?

8. Describe the three programs that are financed by the Federal Insurance Contributions Act (FICA).

9. Explain the statement, "The social security tax is an exact tax."

10. What are some common voluntary deductions that are withheld from employee payroll checks?

Case Study...

Payroll: Financial Planning

You are employed by Tallman Financial Advisors, owned by Marcy Tallman. Parker's Framing hired Tallman to design its payroll system. Parker's Framing will offer group health insurance to its employees and a retirement plan that will require contributions from both the employer and employees. Marcy has assigned the Parker's Framing payroll project to you.

Thinking Critically:

Write a one-page report describing the payroll system you would design for Parker's Framing. Include information on:
- payroll forms
- how hours worked will be collected
- payroll deductions

interNET CONNECTION

Payroll and Tax Records

The federal government makes available a great deal of information related to wages and earnings.

Do This:

Use key words from the following questions to search the Internet for payroll-related statistics.

1. What is the current minimum hourly wage?
2. What are the annual earnings for a full-time employee who earns the minimum wage?
3. What is the average hourly wage in the United States?
4. What are the average annual earnings in the United States?
5. How many people are employed in the United States?

Conducting an Audit with Alex

Philip Wagner is paid an hourly rate of $8.20. Last week Philip worked 41 hours. He is paid overtime for all work over 40 hours. The social security tax is 6.2%, the Medicare tax is 1.45%, and the state income tax is 2.5% of gross earnings. Philip is single and claims one allowance.

Instructions Examine the following check. Check all calculations, and create a replacement check using a separate sheet of paper.

Horizons Garden Supply
5295 Southwest Parkway
Cape Coral, Florida 33990

58

63-947
670

Date____August 19____20 --

Pay to the
Order of____Philip Wagner_____$ 291.14____

Two hundred ninety-one and 14/100 ———————————— Dollars

State Street Bank
CAPE CORAL, FLORIDA

Angela Armstrong

⑆06700947⑈: 3939 043 417⑈ 58

Employee Pay Statement
Detach and retain this statement.

58

| Period Ending | Earnings | | | Deductions | | | | | | | Net Pay |
	Regular	Overtime	Total	Social Security Tax	Med. Tax	Federal Income Tax	State Income Tax	Hosp. Ins.	Other	Total	
8/19/20--	328.00	36.90	364.09	22.57	5.28	36.00	9.10	6.25	—	72.95	291.14

Workplace Skills

Integrity

Employees who demonstrate integrity are persons who can make ethical decisions. Employers expect you to have integrity on the job. Your ability to make decisions that uphold your company's codes, operating standards, and practices will indicate that you have integrity.

On the Job:

As a payroll clerk for the Fun 'n Games Amusement Park, you have access to confidential payroll information about all park employees. Your friend and co-worker, Mark Arnold, asked you to divulge payroll information about his associate, Melissa Porter. Melissa and Mark have the same job title. Melissa just received a pay raise. Mark did not.

Thinking Critically:

How do you respond to Mark's request? Write a few sentences explaining your response.

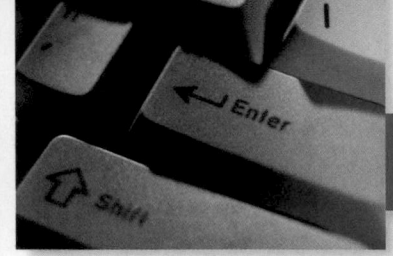

Preparing the Payroll
Making the Transition from a Manual to a Computerized System

Task	Perform Accounting Procedures Using Manual Methods	Perform Accounting Procedures Using Automated Methods
Enter and maintain employee information; process payroll.	1. Calculate employee gross earnings based on time cards or salary information. 2. Calculate required and voluntary deductions for each employee. 3. Complete the payroll register. 4. Prepare payroll checks. 5. Update employee earnings records. 6. Prepare journal entries. 7. Post journal entries to the general ledger.	1. Set up information related to employee earnings and deductions in employees' records. 2. Based on rate, deduction, and withholding information for each employee, the software automatically calculates gross earnings and deductions. 3. The payroll checks, journal entries, and ledger postings are generated automatically.

Preparing the Payroll

Peachtree Question	Description
How do I set up payroll information for employees in Peachtree?	1. Standard or default information for each employee can be entered and maintained by using the *Maintain* menu. 2. Click on **Employees/Sales Reps**. 3. Enter employee names, addresses, deductions, tax rates, rates of pay, and filing status.
How do I process a payroll?	1. Select **Payroll Entry** from the *Tasks* menu. 2. Select the employee(s) to be paid. 3. Verify the pay amounts that are automatically entered for you. (These amounts are pulled from employee records stored in the system.) 4. Click *Save*. 5. To print payroll checks, click on *Open* then *OK* to select checks to print. 6. Click *Print*.
What does the software do "behind the scenes?"	• Gross pay, taxes, and other deductions are calculated automatically. • Journal entries are prepared and posted automatically. • Earnings and deductions are posted to employee earnings records.

For detailed instructions: See the **Peachtree User Guide** in your Glencoe Working Papers.

APPLICATION OPTIONS

Problem 12–5
Calculating Gross Pay

Wilderness Rentals pays employees either an hourly wage or a salary plus commission based on rental revenue. Hourly wage employees can earn overtime. The overtime rate is 1½ times the regular hourly rate of pay for hours worked over 40 in a week.

Instructions For each of the following employees, determine the total gross pay for the pay period.

John Gilmartin
- Earns an hourly wage of $6.80.
- Worked 43 hours this week.

Arlene Stone
- Receives a salary of $250 per week plus a 3% commission on rental revenue.
- Had rental revenue of $760 this week.

Tom Driscoll
- Earns an hourly wage of $7.35.
- Worked 39 hours this week.

Ann Ryan
- Receives a salary of $185 per week plus 3% commission.
- Had rental revenue of $1,235 this week.

Analyze: Which employee had the smallest gross pay for the week?

 ## Problem 12–6
Preparing a Payroll Register

Hot Suds Car Wash has four employees. They are paid on a weekly basis with overtime paid for all hours worked over 40 in a week. The overtime rate is 1½ times the regular rate of pay. The payroll information follows.

Employee	Employee Number	Rate per Hour	Marital Status	Allowances	Union Member
James Dumser	108	$6.40	Single	0	No
Gail Job	112	$7.22	Married	1	Yes
James Liptak	102	$6.70	Married	2	Yes
Bruce Stern	109	$7.80	Single	1	Yes

During the week ending October 9, Dumser worked 39 hours, Job worked 41 hours, and Liptak and Stern each worked 36 hours.

Continued ✒

Complete chapter problems one of three ways:

1 **Manual** Glencoe Working Papers

or

2 **Peachtree Complete Accounting** Software

or

3 **Spreadsheet Templates** (Problem 12–6)

Peachtree®

SMART GUIDE

Step–by–Step Instructions: Problem 12–5

1. Select the problem set for Wilderness Rentals (Prob. 12-5).
2. Rename the company and set the system date.
3. Enter John Gilmartin's regular and overtime pay rates using the **Employees/Sales Reps** option.
4. Calculate the employees' gross pay using the **Payroll Entry** option.
5. Print a Payroll Register report.
6. Proof your work and make any needed corrections.
7. Answer the Analyze question.
8. End the session.

SPREADSHEET SMART GUIDE

Step–by–Step Instructions: Problem 12–6

1. Select the spreadsheet template for Problem 12–6.
2. Enter your name and the date in the spaces provided on the template.
3. Complete the spreadsheet using the instructions in your working papers.
4. Print the spreadsheet and proof your work.
5. Save your work and exit the spreadsheet program.

Instructions On the forms provided in your working papers:

1. Prepare a payroll register for the week ending October 9. The date of payment is also October 9. List employees in alphabetical order by *last* name. Use the tables on page 295 to determine the federal income tax withholding. The rate for the state income tax is 2%. Compute social security tax at 6.2% and Medicare tax at 1.45%. Union members pay weekly dues of $4.50. Both Gail Job and Bruce Stern had $6.75 deducted for health and hospital insurance.
2. Total the amount columns. Subtract total deductions from total earnings. Does the result equal the sum of the Net Pay column? If not, find and correct any error(s) on the payroll register.

Analyze: Which employee had the greatest amount withheld for federal income tax for the week?

Problem 12–7 Preparing Payroll Checks and Employee's Earnings Records

The payroll register for Kits & Pups Grooming is presented below and also appears in your working papers.

PAYROLL REGISTER

PAY PERIOD ENDING October 17   20 --   DATE OF PAYMENT October 17, 20--

	EMPLOYEE NUMBER	NAME	MAR. STATUS	ALLOW.	TOTAL HOURS	RATE	EARNINGS REGULAR	EARNINGS OVERTIME	EARNINGS TOTAL	SOC. SEC. TAX	MEDICARE TAX	FED. INC. TAX	STATE INC. TAX	HOSP. INS.	OTHER	TOTAL	NET PAY	CK. NO.	
1	162	Hurd, Mildred	S	0	38	7.60	288 80		288 80	17 91	4 19	35 00	7 22		(B) 5 00	69 32	219 48		1
2	157	Montego, José	S	1	39	7.90	308 10		308 10	19 10	4 47	30 00	7 70	5 10		66 37	241 73		2
3	151	Pilly, Amanda	M	2	36	8.10	291 60		291 60	18 08	4 23	10 00	7 29	7 60	(B) 5 00	52 20	239 40		3
4	163	Steams, Margaret	S	0	41	7.60	304 00	11 40	315 40	19 55	4 57	40 00	7 89			72 01	243 39		4
24																			24
25																			25
		TOTALS					1,192 50	11 40	1,203 90	74 64	17 46	115 00	30 10	12 70	(B)10 00	259 90	944 00		

Other Deductions: Write the appropriate code letter to the left of the amount: B–U.S. Savings Bonds; C–Credit Union; UD–Union Dues; UW–United Way.

Peachtree® SMART GUIDE

Step–by–Step Instructions: Problem 12–7

1. Select the problem set for Kits & Pups Grooming (Prob. 12–7).
2. Rename the company and set the system date.
3. Print payroll checks using the **Payroll Entry** option.
4. Print a Payroll Register report and a Current Earnings report.
5. End the session.

Instructions On the forms in your working papers:

1. Prepare a payroll check and stub for each employee. Where would you record the check numbers in the payroll register?
2. Record the payroll information in the employee's earnings records for José Montego and Amanda Pilly.

Analyze: What was the net pay for José Montego for this week?

Problem 12–8 Preparing the Payroll

Outback Guide Service has six employees and pays each week. Hourly employees are paid overtime for all hours worked over 40 in a week. The overtime rate is 1½ times the regular rate of pay. Outback pays its employees by hourly rate, salary, or salary plus a 5% commission on total sales.

Method of Computing Earnings

Employee	Hourly Wage	Salary	Salary Plus Commission
Cummings, Carol		$270.00	
Dame, Ted	$6.95		
Lengyel, Tom			$160.00 plus 5%
Robinson, Jean			$140.00 plus 5%
Usdavin, James	$6.65		
Wong, Kim			$140.00 plus 5%

Employee deductions include federal income taxes (use the tables on page 295), FICA taxes at 6.2% for social security and 1.45% for Medicare, state income taxes of 1.5%, and hospital insurance premiums of $5.43 for single employees and $9.37 for married employees. Also, Kim Wong and Tom Lengyel have $10.00 withheld each week to purchase U.S. savings bonds.

During the pay period ending October 17, the sales were: Tom Lengyel $1,204.76, Jean Robinson $1,925.80, and Kim Wong $2,135.65.

The hourly employees filled in the following time cards.

Peachtree®

SMART GUIDE

Step–by–Step Instructions: Problem 12–8

1. Select the problem set for Outback Guide Service (Prob. 12–8).
2. Rename the company and set the system date.
3. Record the payroll and print a check for each employee using the **Payroll Entry** option.
4. Print a Payroll Register report and a Current Earnings report.
5. Proof your work and make any needed corrections.
6. Answer the Analyze question.
7. End the session.

TIP: Use the Windows calculator accessory if you need to make a calculation (e.g., commission)

NO. __73__

NAME __Ted Dame__

SOC. SEC. NO. __093-48-7423__

WEEK ENDING __10/17/20--__

DAY	IN	OUT	IN	OUT	IN	OUT
M	8:58	12:03	12:55	5:09		
T	8:55	11:55	1:00	4:00		
W	9:30	12:10	1:04	3:30		
Th	8:57	12:03	12:59	6:00		
F	0:58	12.00	1:00	6:05		
S	9:00	12:00				
S						

TOTAL HOURS _____

	HOURS	RATE
REGULAR		
OVERTIME		

TOTAL EARNINGS _____

SIGNATURE _____ DATE _____

NO. __92__

NAME __James Usdavin__

SOC. SEC. NO. __087-46-3875__

WEEK ENDING __10/17/20--__

DAY	IN	OUT	IN	OUT	IN	OUT	TOTAL
M	8:55	12:06	1:01	5:35			
T	7:58	11:01	12:03	6:38			
W	9:03	1:10	2:00	6:00			
Th	7:59	11:55	1:10	4:51			
F	9:01	12:06	1:05	3:47			
S	9:00	12:03					
S							

TOTAL HOURS _____

	HOURS	RATE	AMOUNT
REGULAR			
OVERTIME			

TOTAL EARNINGS _____

SIGNATURE _____ DATE _____

Continued ✎

Instructions On the forms in your working papers:
1. Complete the time cards to the nearest quarter hour.
2. Prepare a payroll register for the week ending October 17. The date of payment is also October 17. Each employee's number, marital status, and number of allowances claimed are listed on her or his employee's earnings record.
3. Prepare a payroll check and stub for each employee.
4. Record the payroll information for each employee on her or his employee's earnings record.

Analyze: What is the total amount deducted from employees' gross pay for FICA taxes (social security and Medicare)?

Peachtree®

SMART GUIDE

Step–by–Step Instructions: Problem 12–9

1. Select the problem set for Showbiz Video (Prob. 12-9).
2. Rename the company and set the system date.
3. Record the payroll for each employee.
4. Print a Payroll Register report.
5. Proof your work and make any needed corrections.
6. Answer the Analyze question.
7. End the session.

Problem 12–9 Preparing the Payroll Register

Showbiz Video has six employees who are paid weekly. The hourly employees are paid overtime for hours worked over 40 in a week, at a rate 1½ times their regular rate of pay. Employee information follows:

Employee	Employee Number	Marital Status	Allowances
Mary Arcompora	105	Married	2
Barbara Fox	137	Married	1
John French	135	Single	1
Chris German	141	Married	4
David Ifkovic	139	Single	0
Susan Tilbert	129	Married	1

Mary Arcompora, the store manager, is paid a salary of $300.00 per week plus 1% of all rental sales. Barbara Fox and John French, salespeople, are paid a salary of $200.00 per week plus a 6% commission on all rentals from the "Oldies but Goodies" section. Chris German and David Ifkovic, office workers, are paid an hourly wage of $7.25. Susan Tilbert, a stock person, is paid $6.40 per hour.

The payroll deductions include federal income tax, social security tax of 6.2%, Medicare tax of 1.45%, and state income tax of 1.8%. Chris German and Susan Tilbert have $12.50 deducted each week for hospital insurance.

NO. __141__

NAME __Chris German__

SOC. SEC. NO. __449-42-6721__

WEEK ENDING __October 24, 20--__

DAY	IN	OUT	IN	OUT	IN	OUT	TOTAL
M	8:05	12:03	1:00	5:05			
T	8:00	12:05	1:10	5:00			
W	9:05	12:05	1:15	6:05			
Th	8:30	11:55	1:15	6:00			
F	8:00	12:00	1:00	6:15			
S							
S							
					TOTAL HOURS		

	HOURS	RATE	AMOUNT
REGULAR			
OVERTIME			
		TOTAL EARNINGS	

During the week ending October 24, "Oldies but Goodies" rentals were $484.90 for Barbara Fox and $641.70 for John French. Total rental revenue for the week was $3,917.30.

Instructions

Prepare a payroll register in your working papers for the week ending October 24. Use the federal income tax tables provided in the chapter.

Analyze: What is the total net pay of all employees for the pay period?

NO. 139

NAME   David Ifkovic

SOC. SEC. NO.   461-24-4422

WEEK ENDING   October 24, 20--

DAY	IN	OUT	IN	OUT	IN	OUT
M	8:00	12:05	1:00	5:00		
T	8:10	12:00	1:00	5:05		
W	8:05	12:30	1:30	5:00		
Th	8:00	12:00	1:00	5:10		
F	8:05	12:05	1:05	3:30		
S						
S						

TOTAL HOURS

	HOURS	RATE
REGULAR		
OVERTIME		
TOTAL EARNINGS		

SIGNATURE_____ DATE_____

NO. 129

NAME   Susan Tilbert

SOC. SEC. NO.   401-32-0977

WEEK ENDING   October 24, 20--

DAY	IN	OUT	IN	OUT	IN	OUT	TOTAL
M	8:05	12:00	1:00	5:00			
T	8:10	12:00	1:15	5:00			
W	8:30	12:00	1:00	6:00			
Th	9:00	12:00	12:45	5:00			
F	9:00	11:50					
S							
S							

TOTAL HOURS

	HOURS	RATE	AMOUNT
REGULAR			
OVERTIME			
TOTAL EARNINGS			

SIGNATURE_____ DATE_____

Problem 12–10 Calculating Gross Earnings

SOURCE DOCUMENT PROBLEM

Job Connect has 7 employees, all of whom are paid weekly. For hourly wage employees, overtime is paid at 1½ times the regular rate of pay for hours worked over 40 in a week.

Barbara Miller, the office manager, is paid a salary of $375.00 per week plus a bonus of 3% of all revenue *over* $6,000 per week. Lynn Austin, an office assistant, is paid a salary of $250.00 per week plus 5% of all telephone sales made in the office. Charlene Womack, the office secretary, is paid a salary of $230.00 per week. Susan Dilloway and Doris Franco, placement workers, are paid an hourly wage of $8.95. Pam Darrah is also a placement worker but is paid a commission of $35.00 for every job placement that she completes. David Facini, a part-time maintenance worker, is paid $6.75 per hour.

For the week ending October 24, the office recorded the following payroll information.

- Total office sales for the week were $8,420.00.
- Susan Dilloway worked a total of 38½ hours.
- Doris Franco worked a total of 41¼ hours.
- Phone sales for the week were $1,375.00.
- Pam Darrah made seven job placements.
- David Facini worked a total of 23 hours.

Instructions Using the form provided in your working papers, calculate the gross earnings for the workers at Job Connect for the week ending October 24.

Analyze: Who had the largest gross earnings?

Peachtree®

SMART GUIDE

Step–by–Step Instructions: Problem 12–10

1. Select the problem set for Job Connect (Prob. 12–10).
2. Rename the company and set the system date.
3. Calculate the employees' gross pay using the **Payroll Entry** option.
4. Print a Payroll Register report.
5. Proof your work.
6. Answer the Analyze question.
7. End the session.

SOURCE DOCUMENT PROBLEM

Problem 12–10

Use the source documents in your working papers to record the transactions for this problem.

CHAPTER 13

Payroll Liabilities and Tax Records

Learning Objectives

When you have completed this chapter, you will be able to:

▶ Record payroll transactions in the general journal.

▶ Describe the employer's payroll taxes.

▶ Compute and complete payroll tax expense forms.

▶ Record the payment of tax liabilities in the general journal.

▶ Complete payroll tax reports.

▶ Define the accounting terms introduced in this chapter.

Exploring the Real World of Business

EVALUATING PAYROLL COSTS

Back in the early '70s, Richard Foos sold used records from the trunk of his car. Eventually, Richard sold so many records that he opened up a store. He hired a store manager, and together they turned the business into one of the hippest record stores in Los Angeles. Thus, **Rhino Records** was born. Soon after, the owner created his own record label.

Rhino Records' issues of *Billboard Top Hits* include '50s and '60s rhythm and blues and pop-rock, '70s and '80s disco, hip-hop, show tunes, and television theme songs. The company does more than just earn money. Its mission is to "put out great stuff, have some fun, make some money, learn from each other, and make a difference where we can." The company donates money to charitable causes and encourages employees to volunteer for community programs by allowing them time off during work hours to do so.

What do you think?

How do you think **Rhino Records'** commitment to social responsibility affects its payroll costs?

Workplace Connections

Applying Your Accounting Knowledge

Almost everyone must pay taxes. You learned about the taxes you pay on your earnings in the last chapter. Your employer also pays taxes on what you and other employees earn. That money must then be paid to the appropriate government agency within a certain amount of time. You'll learn about the employer's payroll taxes in this chapter.

Investigate:

1. Do you receive your paycheck in person, in the mail, or by direct deposit?
2. What do you imagine would happen if the accounting department failed to pay the taxes collected to the appropriate government agencies?

Glencoe Accounting *Online*

Visit the *Glencoe Accounting* Web site at **glencoeaccounting.glencoe.com** for additional activities and information.

315

Journalizing and Posting the Payroll

What You'll Learn

- How to compute the business payroll deductions.
- How to record the payroll entry in the general journal.

Why It's Important

Payroll deductions are liabilities of the business. It is essential that payroll deductions are journalized and posted in a timely manner.

KEY TERMS

Salaries Expense

Employees, ranging from design engineers at Ford Motor Company to the waitresses at a neighborhood coffee shop, expect their payroll checks to arrive on time and to be accurate. You have learned that various amounts are withheld from employees' earnings for taxes and other voluntary deductions. Once the payroll register is complete, the payroll entry is journalized and the amounts are posted to the general ledger.

Journalizing and Posting the Payroll

After the payroll is prepared, a check is written to transfer the *total net pay* amount from the regular checking account of a business to the payroll checking account. The check is deposited in the payroll account, and all payroll checks for the period are written on the payroll account. The next step is to record the payroll in the accounting records.

Analyzing the Payroll Transaction

Let's analyze the effect of payroll on the employer's accounting system. Each pay period, the business pays out a certain amount of money to its employees in the form of wages and salaries. Employee earnings are a normal operating expense of a business. The expense account often used to record employees' earnings is called **Salaries Expense** . To increase the amount in **Salaries Expense**, the account is debited for the gross earnings for the pay period.

Various deductions, such as income and FICA taxes, are withheld from gross earnings each pay period. The employer retains the amounts withheld until it is time to pay the appropriate government agencies and businesses. The amounts withheld but not yet paid are liabilities of the business. Remember, a liability is an amount *owed* by a business.

Each type of payroll liability is recorded in a separate account.

Type of Deduction	Ledger Account
Federal income tax	**Employees' Federal Income Tax Payable**
Medicare tax	**Medicare Tax Payable**
Hospital insurance premiums	**Hospital Insurance Premiums Payable**

Depending on the business, it is possible that several different types of deductions are recorded in the Other Deductions column of the payroll register. If so, the total for each type of deduction is credited to the appropriate liability account. Refer to the Roadrunner Delivery Service payroll register shown in **Figure 12–5** on page 299. To accommodate the deductions that may appear in the Other Deductions column, Roadrunner's ledger includes:

- **U.S. Savings Bonds Payable**,
- **Credit Union Payable**,
- **Union Dues Payable**, and
- **United Way Payable**.

The credit part of the payroll journal entry is made up of several items. The largest item is for net pay. Net pay is the amount actually paid out in cash by the employer to the employees. **Cash in Bank** is credited for total net pay.

The difference between gross earnings and net pay equals the employer's payroll liabilities. Each payroll liability account is separately credited for the total amount shown on the payroll register.

Business Transaction

Roadrunner's payroll register in Figure 12–5 on page 299 is the source document for the payroll journal entry.

ANALYSIS

Identify   1. The accounts **Salaries Expense, Employees' Federal Income Tax Payable, Employees' State Income Tax Payable, Social Security Tax Payable, Medicare Tax Payable, Hospital Insurance Premiums Payable, U.S. Savings Bonds Payable**, and **Cash in Bank** are affected.

Classify   2. **Salaries Expense** is an expense account. **Employees' Federal Income Tax Payable, Employees' State Income Tax Payable, Social Security Tax Payable, Medicare Tax Payable, Hospital Insurance Premiums Payable**, and **U.S. Savings Bonds Payable** are liability accounts. **Cash in Bank** is an asset account.

+/−   3. **Salaries Expense** is increased by $1,350.25; **Employees' Federal Income Tax Payable** is increased by $100.00; **Employees' State Income Tax Payable** is increased by $27.01; **Social Security Tax Payable** is increased by $83.73; **Medicare Tax Payable** is increased by $19.57; **Hospital Insurance Premiums Payable** is increased by $23.65; **U.S. Savings Bonds Payable** is increased by $25.00; **Cash in Bank** is decreased by $1,071.29

DEBIT-CREDIT RULE

4. Increases in expense accounts are recorded as debits. Debit **Salaries Expense** for $1,350.25.

5. Decreases in asset accounts are recorded as credits. Credit **Cash in Bank** for $1,071.29. Increases in liability accounts are recorded as credits. Credit **Employees' Federal Income Tax Payable** for $100; **Employees' State Income Tax Payable** for $27.01; **Social Security Tax Payable** for $83.73; **Medicare Tax Payable** for $19.57; **Hospital Insurance Premiums Payable** for $23.65; **U.S. Savings Bonds Payable** for $25.00.

T ACCOUNTS

6.

Salaries Expense	
Debit + 1,350.25	Credit –

Employees' Federal Income Tax Payable	
Debit –	Credit + 100.00

Employees' State Income Tax Payable	
Debit –	Credit + 27.01

Social Security Tax Payable	
Debit –	Credit + 83.73

Medicare Tax Payable	
Debit –	Credit + 19.57

Hospital Insurance Premiums Payable	
Debit –	Credit + 23.65

U.S. Savings Bonds Payable	
Debit –	Credit + 25.00

Cash in Bank	
Debit +	Credit – 1,071.29

JOURNAL ENTRY

7.

	GENERAL JOURNAL			PAGE 29	
	DATE	DESCRIPTION	POST. REF.	DEBIT	CREDIT
1	20--				
2	June 30	Salaries Expense		1 3 5 0 25	
3		Emplys' Fed. Inc. Tax Pay.			1 0 0 00
4		Emplys' State Inc. Tax Pay.			27 01
5		Social Sec. Tax Pay.			83 73
6		Medicare Tax Pay.			19 57
7		Hosp. Ins. Premiums Pay.			23 65
8		U.S. Savings Bonds Pay.			25 00
9		Cash in Bank			1 0 7 1 29
10		Pay. Reg. 6/30—Ck 186			
11					

The payroll expense is $1,350.25. The employees receive $1,071.29 in cash (net pay). Later the business will pay the federal government $203.30 ($100.00 federal income tax, $83.73 social security tax, and $19.57 Medicare tax). The business will also pay the state $27.01 for state income tax. A check for $23.65 will be written to the insurance company for hospital insurance premiums. Finally, a check for $25 will be sent to the federal government to purchase savings bonds.

In the next section, you will learn about the payroll tax liabilities of the employer and how those liabilities are calculated and recorded.

Posting the Payroll Entry to the General Ledger

Figure 13–1 shows the general journal entry and the individual ledger accounts after posting.

Key Points

The Payroll Entry

Gross pay
 Amount debited to
 Salaries Expense

Net pay
 Amount credited to
 Cash in Bank

Payroll deductions
 Amounts credited
 to various liability
 accounts

GENERAL JOURNAL PAGE ___29___

	DATE		DESCRIPTION	POST. REF.	DEBIT	CREDIT	
1	20--						1
2	June	30	Salaries Expense	514	1 3 5 0 25		2
3			Employees' Fed. Inc. Tax Pay.	210		1 0 0 00	3
4			Employees' State Inc. Tax Pay.	215		2 7 01	4
5			Social Security Tax Pay.	220		8 3 73	5
6			Medicare Tax Pay.	225		1 9 57	6
7			Hosp. Ins. Premiums Pay.	230		2 3 65	7
8			U.S. Savings Bonds Pay.	235		2 5 00	8
9			Cash in Bank	101		1 0 7 1 29	9
10			Payroll Reg. 6/30—Ck. 186				10
11							11

ACCOUNT _Salaries Expense_ ACCOUNT NO. _514_

DATE		DESCRIPTION	POST. REF.	DEBIT	CREDIT	BALANCE DEBIT	BALANCE CREDIT
20--							
June	23	Balance	✓			3 4 6 8 3 10	
	30		G29	1 3 5 0 25		3 6 0 3 3 35	

ACCOUNT _Employees' Federal Income Tax Payable_ ACCOUNT NO. _210_

DATE		DESCRIPTION	POST. REF.	DEBIT	CREDIT	BALANCE DEBIT	BALANCE CREDIT
20--							
June	23	Balance	✓				2 9 3 18
	30		G29		1 0 0 00		3 9 3 18

ACCOUNT _Employees' State Income Tax Payable_ ACCOUNT NO. _215_

DATE		DESCRIPTION	POST. REF.	DEBIT	CREDIT	BALANCE DEBIT	BALANCE CREDIT
20--							
June	23	Balance	✓				3 2 1 12
	30		G29		2 7 01		3 4 8 13

ACCOUNT _Social Security Tax Payable_ ACCOUNT NO. _220_

DATE		DESCRIPTION	POST. REF.	DEBIT	CREDIT	BALANCE DEBIT	BALANCE CREDIT
20--							
June	23	Balance	✓				2 5 0 35
	30		G29		8 3 73		3 3 4 08

Figure 13–1 Posting the Payroll Entry to the General Ledger

Continued

ACCOUNT Medicare Tax Payable   **ACCOUNT NO.** 225

DATE		DESCRIPTION	POST. REF.	DEBIT	CREDIT	BALANCE DEBIT	BALANCE CREDIT
20--							
June	23	Balance	✓				5 8 63
	30		G29		1 9 57		7 8 20

ACCOUNT Hospital Insurance Premiums Payable   **ACCOUNT NO.** 230

DATE		DESCRIPTION	POST. REF.	DEBIT	CREDIT	BALANCE DEBIT	BALANCE CREDIT
20--							
June	23	Balance	✓				4 73
	30		G29		2 3 65		2 8 38

ACCOUNT U.S. Savings Bonds Payable   **ACCOUNT NO.** 235

DATE		DESCRIPTION	POST. REF.	DEBIT	CREDIT	BALANCE DEBIT	BALANCE CREDIT
20--							
June	23	Balance	✓				7 5 00
	30		G29		2 5 00		1 0 0 00

ACCOUNT Cash in Bank   **ACCOUNT NO.** 101

DATE		DESCRIPTION	POST. REF.	DEBIT	CREDIT	BALANCE DEBIT	BALANCE CREDIT
20--							
June	23	Balance	✓			1 9 6 1 0 30	
	30		G29		1 0 7 1 29	1 8 5 3 9 01	

Figure 13–1 Posting the Payroll Entry to the General Ledger (continued)

A MATTER OF ETHICS

Money Shuffling

Suppose you're an accounting clerk at the Cybercafé and Bookstore, a sole proprietorship. The business owner has asked you to use the money from the employees' 401(k) withholdings to pay off a pressing debt. The owner believes she will have the money to replace the employees' 401(k) funds within a couple of months. The owner doesn't think that the employees will lose very much by not having their money invested during that time. The owner justifies the transfer of funds saying, "It's all out of the same pocket anyway."

Ethical Decision Making:
☛ What are the ethical issues?
☛ What are the alternatives?
☛ Who are the affected parties?
☛ How do the alternatives affect the parties?
☛ What would you do?

Now that you have studied this section, complete the following questions and problems.

Thinking Critically

1. Why are income and FICA taxes that are withheld from employees' gross earnings considered liabilities to the employer?
2. What is the source of information for recording the payroll transaction in the general journal? What accounts are debited and what accounts are credited?

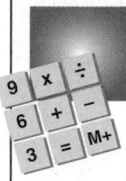

Computing in the Business World

You are the payroll clerk for Queen City Motors. As you review the payroll records, you notice that two employees are nearing the $84,900 limit for social security tax. As commission-only sales employees, Marcie Laliberte and Kevin Hogan have earned $74,500 and $78,500 respectively.

1. How much more must Marcie and Kevin earn in commission to reach the social security tax limit?
2. If Marcie and Kevin are paid 7% commission on each sale, how much more in sales must each make to reach the social security tax limit?

Problem 13–1   Determining Payroll Amounts

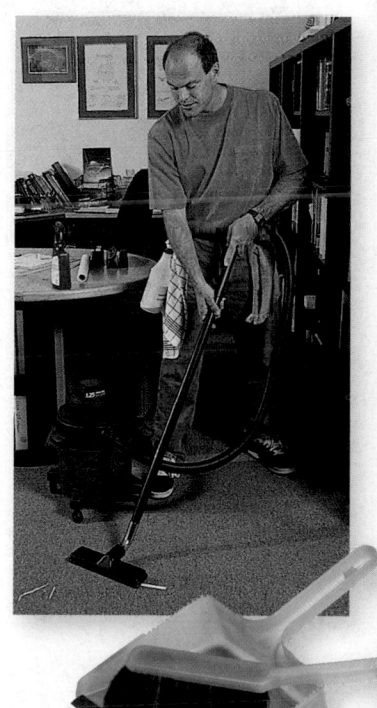

The SweepIt Cleaning Service reported the following amounts for the week ending November 4. The total amount earned by all employees is $2,193.40. The amount withheld for federal income tax is $263.00. Social security tax is $136.00, and Medicare tax is $31.80. Three employees each have $11.25 deducted for hospital insurance. The amount withheld for state income tax is $38.70.

Instructions Answer the following questions concerning the November 4 payroll for the SweepIt Cleaning Service.

1. What amount is recorded in the **Salaries Expense** account?
2. What amount is recorded in the **Medicare Tax Payable** account?
3. What is the total amount of liabilities for the weekly payroll?
4. What amount is entered in the **Hospital Insurance Premiums Payable** account?
5. What amount is recorded as a credit for the **Cash in Bank** account?

Employer's Payroll Taxes

What You'll Learn

- How to calculate the employer's FICA taxes.
- How to calculate federal and state unemployment taxes.
- How to journalize and post employer's payroll taxes.

Why It's Important

In addition to the amounts withheld from employees' payroll checks, the employer owes taxes based on the weekly payroll. These taxes are liabilities of the business.

KEY TERMS

Federal Unemployment Tax Act (FUTA)
State Unemployment Tax Act (SUTA)
unemployment taxes
Payroll Tax Expense

Key Points

FICA Taxes

Both employees and employers pay FICA taxes using the same tax rates.

In Section 1, you learned how to journalize and post the payroll entry. This entry, in part, records taxes employees are required to pay on their earnings. Your local florist, employing designers, delivery workers, and sales clerks, must also pay taxes on their worker's earnings. These amounts need to be calculated, journalized, and posted.

Computing Payroll Tax Expenses

In addition to withholding taxes from employees' wages, the employer *pays* taxes on these wages. The employer's taxes, considered operating expenses of the business, consist of the employer's FICA taxes, the federal unemployment tax, and the state unemployment tax.

The Employer's FICA Taxes

Under the Federal Insurance Contributions Act, both the employee and the employer pay FICA taxes. As you recall, the employer withholds a percentage of gross earnings for social security and Medicare taxes. In addition, the employer pays FICA taxes using the same percentage of gross earnings. Recall that the current rates are 6.2% for social security tax and 1.45% for Medicare tax.

The employer and the employee pay social security tax on gross earnings up to the maximum taxable limit per employee ($84,900 in 2002). The employer and the employee pay Medicare tax on all gross earnings; there is no maximum taxable limit. The payroll clerk checks the accumulated earnings on each employee's earnings record to determine if that employee has reached the maximum taxable amount. When an employee reaches the limit, the social security tax is no longer computed.

In determining social security tax and Medicare tax for both employee and employer, it makes no difference if the employees are full-time, part-time, temporary, or permanent. A full-time adult employee and a student employed part-time only for the summer are subject to the same taxes.

At Roadrunner Delivery Service for the week ending June 30, the employees' total social security taxes are $83.73 and total Medicare taxes are $19.57. The employer's taxes on the total gross earnings are $83.72

(6.2% of $1,350.25) and $19.58 (1.45% of $1,350.25) respectively. Notice that the social security tax for the employees ($83.73) and the employer ($83.72) do not match. The same situation exists for the Medicare tax. This is because the employer's tax is calculated on the total gross earnings ($1,350.25). The employees' taxes are calculated on each employee's gross earnings and the individual tax amounts are totaled. This may result in small differences between the employees' and employer's taxes.

Federal and State Unemployment Taxes

The **Federal Unemployment Tax Act (FUTA)** and the **State Unemployment Tax Act (SUTA)** require employers to pay unemployment taxes. Unemployment taxes are based on a percentage of the employees' gross earnings. **Unemployment taxes** are collected to provide funds for workers who are temporarily unemployed.

The employer pays both federal and state unemployment taxes. The maximum federal unemployment tax is 6.2% on the first $7,000 of an employee's annual wages. State unemployment tax rates and maximum taxable amounts vary among states. Employers may deduct up to 5.4% of the state unemployment taxes from federal unemployment taxes. Most employers, therefore, pay a federal tax of .8% (6.2%–5.4%) of taxable gross earnings.

In a few states, employees are also required to pay unemployment taxes. The percentage amounts vary among these states.

For Roadrunner, since none of the employees has reached the maximum taxable amount, the federal unemployment tax for the week ended June 30 is $10.80 ($1,350.25 × .8%). The state unemployment tax is $72.91 ($1,350.25 × 5.4%).

Journalizing the Employer Payroll Taxes

The employer's payroll taxes are business expenses recorded in the **Payroll Tax Expense** account. Until paid, the employer's payroll taxes are liabilities of the business.

Use the **Social Security Tax Payable** and the **Medicare Tax Payable** accounts to record both the employees' and the employer's FICA taxes. Record the employer's unemployment taxes in the **Federal Unemployment Tax Payable** and **State Unemployment Tax Payable** accounts.

In the next business transaction we will analyze the accounts affected when an employer pays its payroll taxes. This entry takes place in each payroll period.

Business Transaction

Roadrunner's payroll register in **Figure 12–5** on page 299 is the source document for the payroll tax journal entry.

ANALYSIS	*Identify*	1. The accounts **Payroll Tax Expense**, **Social Security Tax Payable**, **Medicare Tax Payable**, **State Unemployment Tax Payable**, and **Federal Unemployment Tax Payable** are affected.
	Classify	2. **Payroll Tax Expense** is an expense account. **Social Security Tax Payable**, **Medicare Tax Payable**, **State Unemployment Tax Payable**, and **Federal Unemployment Tax Payable** are liability accounts.
	+/−	3. **Payroll Tax Expense** is increased by $187.01; **Social Security Tax Payable** is increased by $83.72; **Medicare Tax Payable** is increased by $19.58; **State Unemployment Tax Payable** is increased by $72.91; **Federal Unemployment Tax Payable** is increased by $10.80.

DEBIT-CREDIT RULE

4. Increases in expense accounts are recorded as debits. Debit **Payroll Tax Expense** for $187.01.
5. Increases in liability accounts are recorded as credits. Credit **Social Security Tax Payable** for $83.72; **Medicare Tax Payable** for $19.58; **State Unemployment Tax Payable** for $72.91; **Federal Unemployment Tax Payable** for $10.80.

T ACCOUNTS

6.

Payroll Tax Expense			Social Security Tax Payable	
Debit + 187.01	Credit −		Debit −	Credit + 83.72

Medicare Tax Payable			State Unemployment Tax Payable	
Debit −	Credit + 19.58		Debit −	Credit + 72.91

Federal Unemployment Tax Payable	
Debit −	Credit + 10.80

JOURNAL ENTRY

7.

| | | GENERAL JOURNAL | | | PAGE 30 |

	DATE	DESCRIPTION	POST. REF.	DEBIT	CREDIT	
1	20--					1
2	June 30	Payroll Tax Expense		187 01		2
3		Social Security Tax Pay.			83 72	3
4		Medicare Tax Pay.			19 58	4
5		State Unemplymnt. Tax Pay.			72 91	5
6		Fed. Unemplymnt. Tax Pay.			10 80	6
7		Payroll Reg. 6/30				7

Posting Payroll Taxes to the General Ledger

Figure 13–2 shows the individual ledger accounts after posting the payroll taxes entry.

Notice that the **Social Security Tax Payable** and the **Medicare Tax Payable** accounts have two entries for the June 30 payroll. The first entry is the amount of taxes withheld from the *employees'* earnings. The second entry is the amount of taxes paid by the *employer*.

ACCOUNT _Payroll Tax Expense_   ACCOUNT NO. _520_

DATE		DESCRIPTION	POST. REF.	DEBIT	CREDIT	BALANCE DEBIT	BALANCE CREDIT
20--							
June	23	Balance	✓			4 7 8 4 10	
	30		G30	1 8 7 01		4 9 7 1 11	

ACCOUNT _Social Security Tax Payable_   ACCOUNT NO. _220_

DATE		DESCRIPTION	POST. REF.	DEBIT	CREDIT	BALANCE DEBIT	BALANCE CREDIT
20--							
June	23	Balance	✓				2 5 0 35
	30		G29		8 3 73		3 3 4 08
	30		G30		8 3 72		4 1 7 80

ACCOUNT _Medicare Tax Payable_   ACCOUNT NO. _225_

DATE		DESCRIPTION	POST. REF.	DEBIT	CREDIT	BALANCE DEBIT	BALANCE CREDIT
20--							
June	23	Balance	✓				5 8 63
	30		G29		1 9 57		7 8 20
	30		G30		1 9 58		9 7 78

ACCOUNT _State Unemployment Tax Payable_   ACCOUNT NO. _240_

DATE		DESCRIPTION	POST. REF.	DEBIT	CREDIT	BALANCE DEBIT	BALANCE CREDIT
20--							
June	23	Balance	✓				7 9 3 41
	30		G30		7 2 91		8 6 6 32

ACCOUNT _Federal Unemployment Tax Payable_   ACCOUNT NO. _245_

DATE		DESCRIPTION	POST. REF.	DEBIT	CREDIT	BALANCE DEBIT	BALANCE CREDIT
20--							
June	23	Balance	✓				1 1 8 80
	30		G30		1 0 80		1 2 9 60

Figure 13–2 General Ledger Accounts after Posting the Payroll Taxes Entry

Now that you have studied this section, complete the following questions and problems.

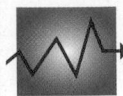

Thinking Critically

1. What does the Federal Insurance Contributions Act require of employers and employees?
2. Explain why the employer's payroll taxes are a liability of the business.

Communicating Accounting

As the payroll clerk for Fashion Square Gift Shop, you are to explain the deductions from employees' payroll checks.

1. Prepare an outline of the items you'll need to discuss.
2. Team up with a classmate and present your list of deductions. Explain each deduction.

Problem 13–2 Calculating Employer's Payroll Taxes

For the week ending June 30, EZ Copy Center's payroll has total gross earnings of $4,836.60. Calculate the employer's payroll taxes. Use the following percentages:

Social security tax	6.2%
Medicare tax	1.45%
Federal unemployment tax	.8%
State unemployment tax	5.4%

Problem 13–3 Identifying Entries for Payroll Liabilities

The following list includes several payroll-related items used in preparing the weekly payroll for Outdoor Adventures. These items are included in either the entry to record the payroll or the entry to record the employer's payroll taxes.

Employees' federal income tax	Employees' state income tax
Employer's social security tax	Union dues
U.S. savings bonds	Employees' social security tax
Employer's Medicare tax	State unemployment tax
Federal unemployment tax	Employees' Medicare tax

Instructions Use the form provided in your working papers. Place a check mark in the column that describes the entry in which the item is recorded: the entry to record the payroll, or the entry to record the employer's payroll taxes.

Tax Liability Payments and Tax Reports

After the payroll entries are journaled and posted, the amounts owed to government agencies and other institutions (credit unions, charitable organizations, etc.) must be paid in a timely manner. Depending on the balance, the payroll liabilities are paid biweekly, monthly, or quarterly. Payroll reports and payroll tax returns are also prepared and filed. In this section you will learn how to complete payroll tax forms.

Paying the Payroll Tax Liabilities

At regular intervals, the payroll taxes and the amounts withheld from employees are paid by the employer. These items include (1) FICA and employees' federal income taxes, (2) employees' state income taxes, (3) federal and state unemployment taxes, and (4) amounts voluntarily withheld from employees' earnings.

FICA and Federal Income Taxes

One payment is made for:

- social security and Medicare taxes (both the employees' and the employer's shares), and
- employees' federal income taxes withheld.

The payment is made at an authorized financial institution or a Federal Reserve Bank. For most small businesses, like Roadrunner, this payment is made monthly. The payment is due by the 15th day of the month following the payroll month. For example, for the month ending June 30, the payment is due by July 15. Larger businesses make the payment every two weeks, or even within days of the payroll date.

For many small businesses, the **Federal Tax Deposit Coupon** (Form 8109) is prepared and sent with the check. The form identifies the type of tax and the tax period. **Figure 13-3** shows Form 8109 for Roadrunner. Notice the ovals on the right side of the form. One oval, 941, is filled in to indicate FICA and federal income taxes. Another oval, 2nd Quarter, is filled in to indicate the period ending June 30.

What You'll Learn

- How to pay payroll tax liabilities.
- Which tax reports are prepared and filed.

Why It's Important

Business owners must pay their payroll liabilities and file payroll tax reports promptly and accurately.

KEY TERMS

Federal Tax Deposit Coupon
Electronic Federal Tax Payment System (EFTPS)
Form W-2
Form 940
Form 941
Form W-3

International ACCOUNTING

Netiquette
Make considerations for foreign users who browse your Web site. Using simple text with few colloquialisms will help accommodate foreign users.

Figure 13–3 Federal Tax Deposit Coupon (Form 8109) for FICA and Federal Income Taxes

Larger businesses deposit income tax payments by electronic funds transfer through the **Electronic Federal Tax Payment System (EFTPS)**. Eventually even small businesses will make payments using EFTPS.

Business Transaction

After recording the June 30 payroll and the employer's payroll taxes, Roadrunner pays its payroll tax liabilities of $908.76, which include employees' federal income taxes of $393.18 (refer to ledger account in **Figure 13–1**), *social security taxes of $417.80, and Medicare taxes of $97.78 on July 15 (refer to ledger accounts in* **Figure 13–2**).

ANALYSIS

Identify
1. The accounts **Employees' Federal Income Tax Payable**, **Social Security Tax Payable**, **Medicare Tax Payable**, and **Cash in Bank** are affected.

Classify
2. **Employees' Federal Income Tax Payable**, **Social Security Tax Payable**, and **Medicare Tax Payable** are liability accounts. **Cash in Bank** is an asset account.

+/−
3. **Employees' Federal Income Tax Payable** is decreased by $393.18; **Social Security Tax Payable** is decreased by $417.80; **Medicare Tax Payable** is decreased by $97.78; **Cash in Bank** is decreased by $908.76.

DEBIT-CREDIT RULE
4. Decreases in liability accounts are recorded as debits. Debit **Employees' Federal Income Tax Payable** for $393.18; **Social Security Tax Payable** for $417.80; **Medicare Tax Payable** for $97.78.
5. Decreases in asset accounts are recorded as credits. Credit **Cash in Bank** for $908.76.

T ACCOUNTS
6.

Employees' Federal Income Tax Payable	
Debit −	Credit +
393.18	

Social Security Tax Payable	
Debit −	Credit +
417.80	

Medicare Tax Payable	
Debit −	Credit +
97.78	

Cash in Bank	
Debit +	Credit −
	908.76

JOURNAL ENTRY 7.

	GENERAL JOURNAL			PAGE 31	
DATE	DESCRIPTION	POST. REF.	DEBIT	CREDIT	
1	20--					1
2	July 15 Emplys' Fed. Inc. Tax Pay.		393 18		2
3	Social Security Tax Pay.		417 80		3
4	Medicare Tax Pay.		97 78		4
5	Cash in Bank			908 76	5
6	Check 208				6
7					7

State Income Taxes

At regular intervals, businesses pay the amounts withheld for state income taxes. Each state determines how and when the payments are made and what reports are filed.

Business Transaction

Roadrunner pays $348.13 to the state. This is the amount of state income tax withheld from employees earnings, as indicated in the **Employees' State Income Tax Payable** account shown in **Figure 13–1**.

ANALYSIS

Identify
1. The accounts **Employees' State Income Tax Payable** and **Cash in Bank** are affected.

Classify
2. **Employees' State Income Tax Payable** is a liability account. **Cash in Bank** is an asset account.

+/–
3. **Employees' State Income Tax Payable** is decreased by $348.13. **Cash in Bank** is decreased by $348.13.

DEBIT-CREDIT RULE
4. Decreases in liability accounts are recorded as debits. Debit **Employees' State Income Tax Payable** for $348.13.
5. Decreases in asset accounts are recorded as credits. Credit **Cash in Bank** for $348.13.

T ACCOUNTS 6.

Employees' State Income Tax Payable			Cash in Bank	
Debit –	Credit +		Debit +	Credit –
348.13				348.13

JOURNAL ENTRY 7.

	GENERAL JOURNAL			PAGE 32	
DATE	DESCRIPTION	POST. REF.	DEBIT	CREDIT	
1	20--				1
2	July 15 Emplys' State Inc. Tax Pay.		348 13		2
3	Cash in Bank			348 13	3
4	Check 209				4
5					5

Federal Unemployment Taxes

Most businesses pay the federal unemployment or FUTA tax quarterly. If a business has accumulated federal unemployment taxes of less than $100 for the year, only one annual payment is necessary.

Business Transaction

*Roadrunner pays $129.60 for FUTA taxes. This is the balance of the **Federal Unemployment Tax Payable** account shown in **Figure 13–2**.*

ANALYSIS

Identify
1. The accounts **Federal Unemployment Tax Payable** and **Cash in Bank** are affected.

Classify
2. **Federal Unemployment Tax Payable** is a liability account. **Cash in Bank** is an asset account.

+/−
3. **Federal Unemployment Tax Payable** is decreased by $129.60. **Cash in Bank** is decreased by $129.60.

DEBIT-CREDIT RULE
4. Decreases in liability accounts are recorded as debits. Debit **Federal Unemployment Tax Payable** for $129.60.
5. Decreases in asset accounts are recorded as credits. Credit **Cash in Bank** for $129.60.

T ACCOUNTS

6.

Federal Unemployment Tax Payable		Cash in Bank	
Debit	Credit	Debit	Credit
−	+	+	−
129.60			129.60

JOURNAL ENTRY

7.

	GENERAL JOURNAL			PAGE 33	

	DATE	DESCRIPTION	POST. REF.	DEBIT	CREDIT	
1	20--					1
2	July 15	Fed. Unemployment Tax Pay.		129 60		2
3		Cash in Bank			129 60	3
4		Check 210				4
5						5

When a business pays the FUTA tax, a Federal Tax Deposit Coupon (Form 8109) is prepared and sent with the check. When FUTA taxes are paid, the "940" oval is filled in instead of the "941" oval. **Figure 13–4** shows the Form 8109 that Roadrunner sends with the federal unemployment tax payment.

Figure 13-4 Federal Tax Deposit Coupon (Form 8109) for Federal Unemployment Taxes

State Unemployment Taxes

State unemployment taxes are usually paid on a quarterly basis.

Business Transaction

*Roadrunner pays $866.32 to the state, as shown in **Figure 13-2**.*

ANALYSIS	*Identify*	1. The accounts **State Unemployment Tax Payable** and **Cash in Bank** are affected.
	Classify	2. **State Unemployment Tax Payable** is a liability account. **Cash in Bank** is an asset account.
	+/−	3. **State Unemployment Tax Payable** is decreased by $866.32. **Cash in Bank** is decreased by $866.32.

DEBIT-CREDIT RULE	4. Decreases in liability accounts are recorded as debits. Debit **State Unemployment Tax Payable** for $866.32.
	5. Decreases in asset accounts are recorded as credits. Credit **Cash in Bank** for $866.32.

T ACCOUNTS 6.

State Unemployment Tax Payable		Cash in Bank	
Debit −	Credit +	Debit +	Credit −
866.32			866.32

JOURNAL ENTRY 7.

GENERAL JOURNAL PAGE __34__

	DATE	DESCRIPTION	POST. REF.	DEBIT	CREDIT	
1	20--					1
2	July 15	State Unemployment Tax Pay.		866 32		2
3		Cash in Bank			866 32	3
4		Check 211				4
5						5

Other Payroll Liabilities

In addition to the payroll taxes, employers pay the appropriate organizations for all voluntary deductions. For Roadrunner, these deductions are for insurance premiums and U.S. savings bonds. Other types of voluntary deductions include union dues, charitable contributions, and so on.

Business Transaction

On July 15, Roadrunner pays $28.38 for hospital insurance premiums. This is the balance of the **Hospital Insurance Premiums Payable** account shown in **Figure 13–1**, page 320.

ANALYSIS	*Identify*	**1.**	The accounts **Hospital Insurance Premiums Payable** and **Cash in Bank** are affected.
	Classify	**2.**	**Hospital Insurance Premiums Payable** is a liability account. **Cash in Bank** is an asset account.
	+/–	**3.**	**Hospital Insurance Premiums Payable** is decreased by $28.38. **Cash in Bank** is decreased by $28.38.

DEBIT-CREDIT RULE	**4.**	Decreases in liability accounts are recorded as debits. Debit **Hospital Insurance Premiums Payable** for $28.38.
	5.	Decreases in asset accounts are recorded as credits. Credit **Cash in Bank** for $28.38.

T ACCOUNTS   **6.**

Hospital Insurance Premiums Payable		Cash in Bank	
Debit	Credit	Debit	Credit
–	+	+	–
28.38			28.38

JOURNAL ENTRY   **7.**

		GENERAL JOURNAL			PAGE 35
	DATE	DESCRIPTION	POST. REF.	DEBIT	CREDIT
1	20--				
2	July 15	Hospital Ins. Premiums Pay.		28 38	
3		Cash in Bank			28 38
4		Check 212			
5					

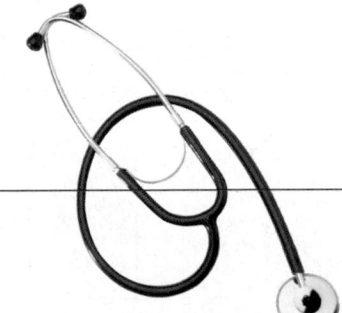

Posting the Payment of Payroll Liabilities

After the payments for the employer's payroll liabilities are journalized, the entries are posted to the appropriate general ledger accounts. **Figure 13–5** shows Roadrunner's general ledger accounts after posting.

ACCOUNT Employee's Federal Income Tax Payable   **ACCOUNT NO.** 210

DATE		DESCRIPTION	POST. REF.	DEBIT	CREDIT	BALANCE DEBIT	BALANCE CREDIT
20--							
June	23	Balance	✓				2 9 3 18
	30		G29		1 0 0 00		3 9 3 18
July	15		G31	3 9 3 18			

ACCOUNT Employee's State Income Tax Payable   **ACCOUNT NO.** 215

DATE		DESCRIPTION	POST. REF.	DEBIT	CREDIT	BALANCE DEBIT	BALANCE CREDIT
20--							
June	23	Balance	✓				3 2 1 12
	30		G29		2 7 01		3 4 8 13
July	15		G32	3 4 8 13			

ACCOUNT Social Security Tax Payable   **ACCOUNT NO.** 220

DATE		DESCRIPTION	POST. REF.	DEBIT	CREDIT	BALANCE DEBIT	BALANCE CREDIT
20--							
June	23	Balance	✓				2 5 0 35
	30		G29		8 3 73		3 3 4 08
	30		G30		8 3 72		4 1 7 80
July	15		G31	4 1 7 80			

ACCOUNT Medicare Tax Payable   **ACCOUNT NO.** 225

DATE		DESCRIPTION	POST. REF.	DEBIT	CREDIT	BALANCE DEBIT	BALANCE CREDIT
20--							
June	23	Balance	✓				5 8 63
	30		G29		1 9 57		7 8 20
	30		G30		1 9 58		9 7 78
July	15		G31	9 7 78			

ACCOUNT Hospital Insurance Premium Payable   **ACCOUNT NO.** 230

DATE		DESCRIPTION	POST. REF.	DEBIT	CREDIT	BALANCE DEBIT	BALANCE CREDIT
20--							
June	23	Balance	✓				4 73
	30		G29		2 3 65		2 8 38
July	15		G35	2 8 38			

ACCOUNT State Unemployment Tax Payable   **ACCOUNT NO.** 240

DATE		DESCRIPTION	POST. REF.	DEBIT	CREDIT	BALANCE DEBIT	BALANCE CREDIT
20--							
June	23	Balance	✓				7 9 3 41
	30		G30		7 2 91		8 6 6 32
July	15		G34	8 6 6 32			

ACCOUNT Federal Unemployment Tax Payable   **ACCOUNT NO.** 245

DATE		DESCRIPTION	POST. REF.	DEBIT	CREDIT	BALANCE DEBIT	BALANCE CREDIT
20--							
June	23	Balance	✓				1 1 8 80
	30		G30		1 0 80		1 2 9 60
July	15		G33	1 2 9 60			

Preparing Payroll Tax Reports

Employers must complete a variety of payroll-related tax forms.

Form	Name of Form	Filed
W-2	Wage and Tax Statement	Annually
940	Employer's Annual Federal Unemployment (FUTA) Tax Return	Annually
941	Employer's Quarterly Federal Tax Return	Quarterly
W-3	Transmittal of Wage and Tax Statements	Annually

Wage and Tax Statement

The Wage and Tax statement, **Form W-2**, summarizes an employee's earnings and withholdings for the calendar year. Form W-2 reports:

(1) gross earnings

(2) federal income tax withheld

(3) FICA taxes withheld

(4) state and local income taxes withheld

Each employee receives a Form W-2 by January 31 of the following year. The information reported on Form W-2 assists employees in preparing their individual income tax returns. **Figure 13–6** shows Emily Kardos' Form W-2.

Employers prepare many copies of Form W-2. The employer sends Copy A to the IRS and gives Copies B and C to the employee. The employer keeps Copy D. Additional copies are sent to city or state government if necessary.

Figure 13–6 Form W-2 Wage and Tax Statement

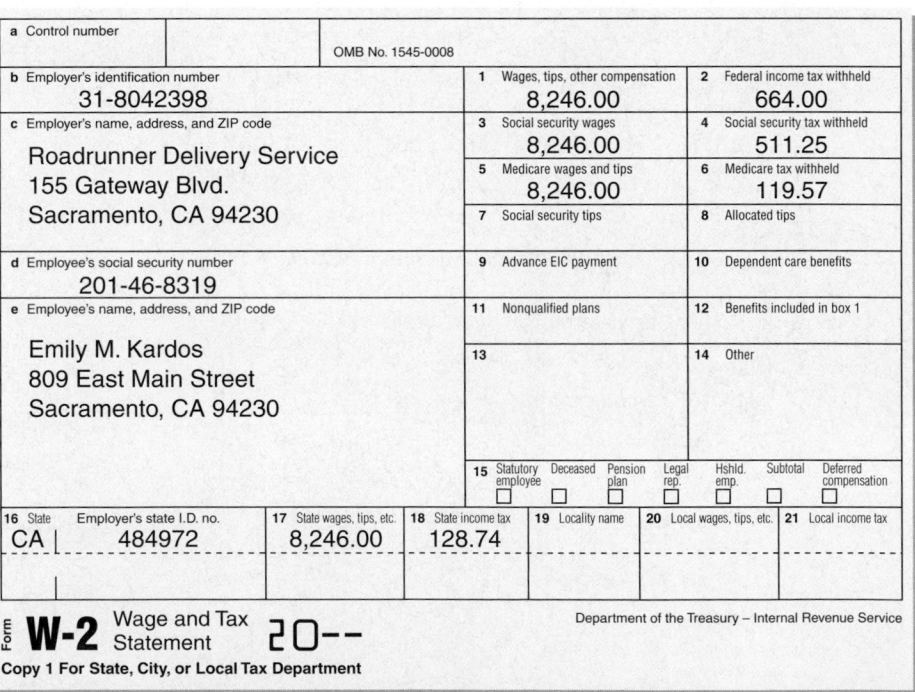

Forms 940 and 941

Use **Form 940** to report the employer's unemployment (state and federal) taxes. **Form 941** illustrated in **Figure 13–7**, is the employer's quarterly federal tax return on which accumulated amounts of FICA and federal income tax withheld from employees' earnings, as well as FICA tax owed by the employer, are reported.

Form **941**	**Employer's Quarterly Federal Tax Return**		OMB No. 1545-0029

Form **941**

Department of the Treasury
Internal Revenue Service

Employer's Quarterly Federal Tax Return

▶ **See separate instructions for information on completing this return.**

Please type or print.

OMB No. 1545-0029

Enter state code for state in which deposits were made ONLY if different from state in address to the right ▶ ⬚ (see page 3 of instructions).

Name (as distinguished from trade name)

Roadrunner Delivery Service

Trade name, if any

Address (number and street)

155 Gateway Blvd.

Date quarter ended

June 30, 20--

Employer identification number

31-8042398

City, state, and ZIP code

Sacramento, CA 94230

T	
FF	
FD	
FP	
I	
T	

If address is different from prior return, check here ▶ ⬚

IRS Use

1 1 1 1 1 1 1 1 1 1 2 3 3 3 3 3 3 3 4 4 4 5 5 5

6 7 8 8 8 8 8 8 8 8 9 9 9 9 10 10 10 10 10 10 10 10 10

If you do not have to file returns in the future, check here ▶ ⬚ and enter date final wages paid ▶

If you are a seasonal employer, see **Seasonal employers** on page 1 of the instructions and check here ▶ ⬚

1	Number of employees in the pay period that includes March 12th . ▶	**1**		
2	Total wages and tips, plus other compensation	**2**	9,252	96
3	Total income tax withheld from wages, tips, and sick pay	**3**	747	64
4	Adjustment of withheld income tax for preceding quarters of calendar year	**4**	0	00
5	Adjusted total of income tax withheld (line 3 as adjusted by line 4—see instructions) . . .	**5**	773	55
6	Taxable social security wages . . . . . **6a** 9,252 96 × 12.4% (.124) =	**6b**	1,147	37
	Taxable social security tips . . . . . **6c** × 12.4% (.124) =	**6d**	0	00
7	Taxable Medicare wages and tips . . . **7a** 9,252 96 × 2.9% (.029) =	**7b**	268	33
8	Total social security and Medicare taxes (add lines 6b, 6d, and 7b). Check here if wages are not subject to social security and/or Medicare tax . . . . ▶ ⬚	**8**	1,415	70
9	Adjustment of social security and Medicare taxes (see instructions for required explanation) Sick Pay $ _____ ± Fractions of Cents $ _____ ± Other $ _____ =	**9**	0	00
10	Adjusted total of social security and Medicare taxes (line 8 as adjusted by line 9—see instructions) . . .	**10**	1,415	70
11	**Total taxes** (add lines 5 and 10)	**11**	2,163	34
12	Advance earned income credit (EIC) payments made to employees	**12**	0	00
13	Net taxes (subtract line 12 from line 11). **This should equal line 17, column (d) below (or line D of Schedule B (Form 941))**	**13**	2,163	34
14	Total deposits for quarter, including overpayment applied from a prior quarter	**14**	2,163	34
15	**Balance due** (subtract line 14 from line 13). See instructions	**15**	0	00
16	**Overpayment,** if line 14 is more than line 13, enter excess here ▶ $ _____ and check if to be: ⬚ Applied to next return **OR** ⬚ Refunded.			

- **All filers:** If line 13 is less than $500, you need not complete line 17 or Schedule B (Form 941).
- **Semiweekly schedule depositors:** Complete Schedule B (Form 941) and check here . . . . ▶ ⬚
- **Monthly schedule depositors:** Complete line 17, columns (a) through (d), and check here . . . . ▶ ⬚

17	**Monthly Summary of Federal Tax Liability.** Do not complete if you were a semiweekly schedule depositor.		
(a) First month liability	**(b)** Second month liability	**(c)** Third month liability	**(d)** Total liability for quarter
627.29	627.29	908.76	2,163.34

Sign Here

Under penalties of perjury, I declare that I have examined this return, including accompanying schedules and statements, and to the best of my knowledge and belief, it is true, correct, and complete.

Signature ▶ *Maria Sanchez*   Print Your Name and Title ▶ Maria Sanchez, Owner   Date ▶ **6/30/20--**

Figure 13–7—Form 941

Transmittal of Wage and Tax Statements

The employer files **Form W-3**, Transmittal of Wage and Tax Statements, with the federal government. Form W-3 summarizes the information contained on the employees' Forms W-2. Form W-3 is due by February 28. Along with Form W-3, the employer includes Copy A of each employee's Form W-2. The federal government uses the Form W-2 information to check individual income tax returns. **Figure 13–8** shows Roadrunner's Form W-3.

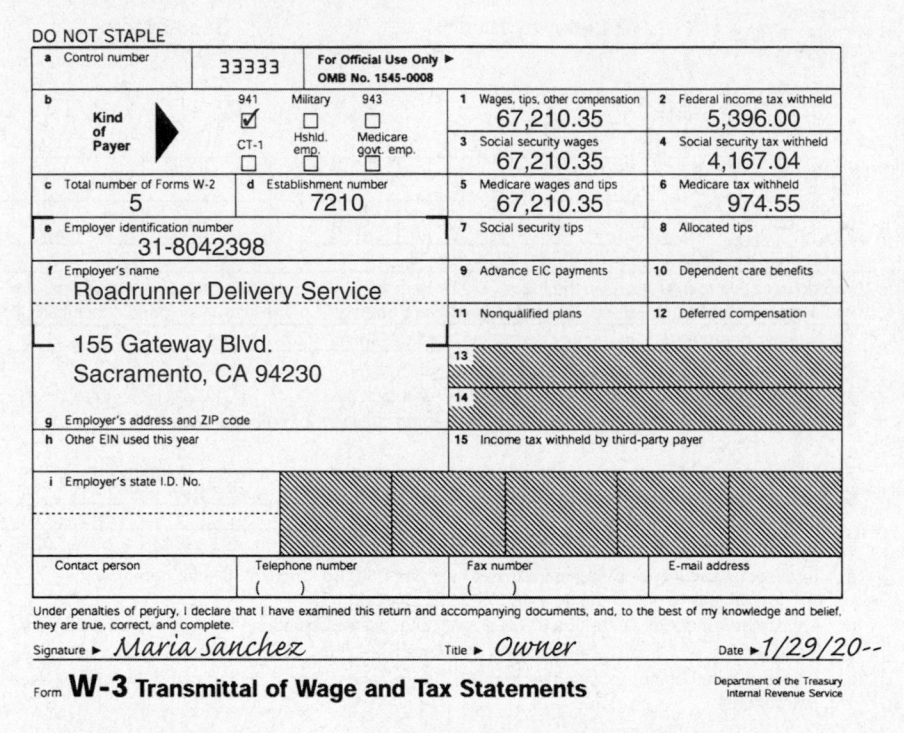

Figure 13–8 Transmittal of Wage and Tax Statements

ANALYZING FINANCIAL REPORTS

Employee Costs

Business owners and managers monitor employee costs by tracking the number of employees, total salary costs, and the cost of providing employee benefits. Employee benefits might include paid vacations, employer contributions to employee retirement plans, and health insurance. Many employers calculate the cost of benefits as a percentage of total salaries. For example, if a company's total costs for salaries are $58,600 and the cost of benefits paid by the company is $12,900, benefits as a percentage of salaries are 22%. Owners and managers use this percentage when calculating the total cost of hiring a new employee.

▶ **Analyze the Report:**

Use the payroll register on page 299 and payroll tax information in this chapter to answer these questions.

1. If the company's employee benefits cost 24% of employee earnings, what would be the benefits cost for this salary period?
2. If a new employee is to be hired for a 40-hour work week at wages of $7 an hour, what would be the total cost for the new employee? The company estimates its employee benefits cost at 22%.

Now that you have studied this section, complete the following questions and problems.

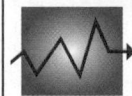

Thinking Critically

1. What accounts are affected when a business pays the federal unemployment tax?
2. What information is included on a Form W-2?

Analyzing Accounting

Small businesses (those with revenues less than $200,000 per year) pay their federal taxes by the 15th day of the month following the payroll month. Large businesses pay their taxes every two weeks. Review the graph, and answer the following questions.

Annual Revenue in Dollars

$125,000
$158,000 $215,000 ■ Morgan Manufacturing
■ Ziggy's Ice Cream
Lights and More
■ Beverly Drive Spa
Stanford Tools
$420,000
Plains Educational Supply
$95,000 $220,000

1. Which businesses pay their taxes every two weeks?
2. What percent of businesses represented in the circle graph are large businesses?

Problem 13–4 **Payment of Payroll Liabilities**

The following account balances appear in the general ledger for Soap Box Laundry on April 30.

General Ledger
Social Security Tax Payable	$318.55
State Income Tax Payable	205.60
Medicare Tax Payable	113.28
Employees' Federal Income Tax Payable	286.00

Instructions Record the payment of the four liability accounts on page 34 of the general journal. (Hint: Two checks are written.)

Problem 13–5 **Analyzing a Source Document**

PAYROLL REGISTER

PAY PERIOD ENDING May 19   20 --   DATE OF PAYMENT May 19, 20--

EMPLOYEE NUMBER	NAME	MAR. STATUS	ALLOW.	TOTAL HOURS	RATE	EARNINGS			DEDUCTIONS							NET PAY	CK. NO.
						REGULAR	OVERTIME	TOTAL	SOC. SEC. TAX	MEDICARE TAX	FED. INC. TAX	STATE INC. TAX	HOSP. INS.	OTHER	TOTAL		
25					TOTALS	1,218 93	109 14	1,328 07	82 34	19 26	184 00	26 56	20 00	—	332 16	995 91	25

Other Deductions: Write the appropriate code letter to the left of the amount: B–U.S. Savings Bonds; C–Credit Union; UD–Union Dues; UW–United Way.

Instructions Based on the payroll register above, record the appropriate journal entry in your working papers. Use page 14 in the general journal.

GRACE KIM
Tax Specialist
KPMG LLP

Q: How did you get into accounting?

A: I was an economics major as an undergraduate, and I wanted to do something practical in which I could be licensed. I like numbers because they're so concrete. You have to be creative when you work with words, but numbers are given to you as a fact. I see a lot of different issues and deal with a lot of different companies.

Q: What's the most difficult part of your job?

A: I have a hard time asking for help when I run into a wall. When I was in school, I didn't take any group study classes. I worked on my own, but anyone going into public accounting has to develop interpersonal skills and be willing to ask for help.

Q: Is tax season difficult?

A: Tax season gets the juices flowing. I find it exciting, and it's never so long that a person can't handle it. You can always see the light at the end of the tunnel.

Q: How should students present themselves at an on-campus interview?

A: Be mature and confident and talk about yourself articulately. Also, having an idea of what you want to be doing in the next five years will be helpful.

Q: What is the future like for tax specialists?

A: It's definitely good. The field is moving toward tax consultants who can advise companies about changing tax laws.

Tips from . . .

RHI Robert Half International Inc.

Numbers are important to accountants, but 96 percent of financial executives say communication skills are essential.

Learn what it takes to clearly put your ideas into writing, and practice speaking to large groups of people.

CAREER FACTS

Nature of the Work: Prepare tax returns and research tax questions.

Training or Education Needed: A bachelor's or master's degree in accounting or tax, and the CPA exam.

Aptitudes, Abilities, and Skills: Accounting, time-management skills, problem-solving skills, analytical skills, computer skills, communication skills, interpersonal skills, and willingness to learn.

Salary Range: $60,000 to $100,000 with a master's degree.

Career Path: Do an on-campus interview to find a job with a public accounting firm.

Thinking Critically: Why is it important to be willing to ask for help?

KEY CONCEPTS

1. Employees' earnings are an operating expense of the business. The total gross earnings is debited to the **Salaries Expense** account.
2. Amounts withheld from employees' earnings are liabilities of the business. The employer makes regular payments of the amounts withheld to the appropriate government agencies, businesses, and organizations.
3. Employers pay taxes on their employees' gross earnings. These taxes are operating expenses of the business. The amounts are debited to the **Payroll Tax Expense** account. Employer's payroll taxes include FICA taxes (Social security & Medicare) and Unemployment taxes (Federal & State).
4. Both employees and employers are liable for payroll taxes. Payroll tax rates can change and vary by state. To calculate the tax, multiply gross earnings by the tax rate.
5. To journalize various payroll items, the related journal entries include the following:

Payroll Item	Required in Journal Entry
Total gross earnings ⟶	Debit to **Salaries Expense**
Total net pay ⟶	Credit to **Cash in Bank**
Federal income tax withholding ⟶	Credit to **Employees' Federal Income Tax Payable**
Social security tax withholding ⟶	Credit to **Social Security Tax Payable**
Medicare tax withholding ⟶	Credit to **Medicare Tax Payable**
State income tax withholding ⟶	Credit to **State Income Tax Payable**

6. The payroll register is the source of information for preparing the entry to record the payment of the payroll.
7. When payroll liabilities accounts are paid, the related liability accounts are debited and **Cash in Bank** is credited.

	DATE	DESCRIPTION	POST. REF.	DEBIT	CREDIT	
1	20					1
2	*Date*	Medicare Tax Payable		x x x x x		2
3		State Income Tax Payable		x x x x x		3
4		Cash in Bank			x x x x x	4
5						5

GENERAL JOURNAL   PAGE _12_

8. Employers file quarterly and annual tax reports on employee earnings and on taxes paid by the employee and the employer.
9. Employers report earnings and tax information to employees once a year on Form W-2.

USING KEY TERMS

You are the owner of Accurate Financial Services. You have just been hired by Brad Justice, the owner of a new company called Snack Shack, to help establish a payroll system. As a new business owner, Brad understands the importance of complying with government requirements, but he is concerned that he may not be aware of all of the requirements related to payroll. Using the following key terms, prepare a presentation for Brad describing the government requirements for payroll.

Electronic Federal Tax
   Payment System (EFTPS)
Federal Tax Deposit Coupon
   (Form 8109)
Federal Unemployment Tax
   Act (FUTA)
Form 940
Form 941
Form W-2

Form W-3
Payroll Tax Expense
Salaries Expense
State Unemployment Tax Act
   (SUTA)
unemployment taxes

Understanding Accounting
Concepts and Procedures

Instructions

On a separate sheet of paper, answer the following questions:

1. Explain why gross earnings, not net pay, is debited to the **Salaries Expense** account.

2. Explain why the amounts withheld from employees' payroll checks are liabilities of the employer.

3. What account is credited for net pay?

4. How is the employer's share of FICA tax calculated?

5. How is the employee's share of FICA tax calculated?

6. State and federal unemployment taxes are percentages of what amount?

7. The debit to **Payroll Tax Expense** is the total of what amounts?

8. What payroll taxes are deposited monthly in a Federal Reserve Bank or other authorized financial institution?

9. When does an employee receive a Form W-2?

10. Explain how different copies of Form W-2 are distributed.

11. What information is reported on Form W-2?

12. What is the difference between a Form 940 and Form 941?

13. What information is contained on Form W-3?

Case Study...

Payroll: Warehousing Center

Morrison Distribution Center offers warehousing services to local businesses. Morrison has 40 full-time employees and operates two shifts. The company is considering adding a third shift, which would require 12 additional employees.

The accountant estimates that a third shift could bring in additional revenue of $390,000. Prepare an estimate of the third shift payroll costs. Assume: (1) The average warehouse employee earns $21,000 per year. (2) The state unemployment tax is 5.4%, and the federal unemployment tax is 0.8%. (Both applied to the first $7,000 of earnings.) (3) The employer's cost of health insurance averages 22% of an employee's earnings.

Thinking Critically:

1. What is the salary expense related to adding the new employees?
2. How much in additional payroll taxes will Morrison pay?
3. What is the total cost to add the third shift?

inter**NET** CONNECTION

The Internal Revenue Service

The Internal Revenue Service (IRS), the largest agency in the Department of the Treasury, employs 100,000 people. The IRS processes approximately 226 million tax returns in a year while assisting more than 100 million taxpayers by telephone and at more than 400 walk-in offices throughout the country.

Do This:

1. Locate the IRS Web site online. What is the Web site address?
2. Name 6 services or kinds of information that the Web site offers.
3. Who is the Commissioner of the IRS?
4. What is e-file?

Conducting an Audit with Alex

The journal entry for the March 12 payroll was recorded in the general journal of Milan's Painting. Later some water spilled on the journal making two amounts illegible.

Instructions

Based on the remaining amounts shown below, determine what the illegible amounts should be.

	DATE	DESCRIPTION	POST. REF.	DEBIT	CREDIT	
1	20--					1
2	Mar. 12	Salaries Expense		3 840 00		2
3		Empl. Fed. Inc. Tax Pay.			274 00	3
4		Social Security Tax Pay.			?	4
5		Medicare Tax Pay.			55 68	5
6		State Income Tax Payable			63 00	6
7		Hosp. Ins. Premiums Pay.			?	7
8		Cash in Bank			3 144 24	8
9						9

GENERAL JOURNAL   PAGE   14

Workplace Skills

Self-Management

Are you a "self-starter"? If the answer is yes, then you have strong self-management skills. People who possess these skills can assess their own abilities and skills, set attainable goals, and motivate themselves to accomplish those goals. Employers are always eager to hire and promote employees with self-management skills.

On the Job:

As an accounting clerk in the payroll department of Trendy Threads, you are responsible for processing all payroll and tax reports. It is December, and your tax reports are due soon. What steps do you need to take now to make sure you process your reports on time?

Thinking Critically:

Describe the reports you'll need to file and what payroll ledgers and registers you'll need to complete each one.

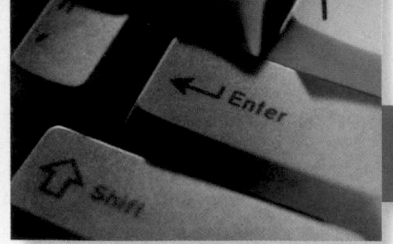

Recording and Paying Payroll Tax Liabilities

Making the Transition from a Manual to a Computerized System

Task	Perform Accounting Procedures Using Manual Methods	Perform Accounting Procedures Using Automated Methods
Record and post payroll entries; pay payroll tax liabilities	1. Prepare the journal entry based on the payroll register totals for the employee and employer's tax liabilities. 2. Post the payroll entries to the general ledger. 3. Prepare tax liability checks to pay federal, state, and local taxing authorities. 4. Prepare journal entries to record the payment of the liabilities.	1. When the payroll checks are generated, the payroll tax journal entries are automatically prepared and posted.

Recording and Paying Payroll Taxes

Peachtree Question	Description
How do I journalize the employer's tax liabilities?	• When payroll checks were issued, the software automatically journalized the tax liabilities.
How do I pay the payroll tax liabilities?	• Select **Payments** from the *Tasks* menu. • Select the taxing authority ID to be paid. • Enter the amount and cash account number. • Enter description and general ledger account (tax liability account). • Click *Print*.
What does the software do "behind the scenes?"	• When payroll checks are issued, the software automatically journalizes and posts both the tax liabilities of the employee and the employer. • When a check is prepared to pay a tax liability, the software automatically journalizes and posts the payment. • Employee earnings records are updated for you.

For detailed instructions: See the **Peachtree User Guide** in your Glencoe Working Papers.

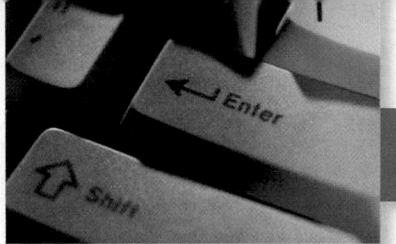

APPLICATION OPTIONS

Problem 13–6 Calculating Employer's Payroll Taxes

Instructions For each of the following total gross earnings amounts recorded in the past five pay weeks for Hot Suds Car Wash, determine the employer's FICA taxes (social security 6.2%, Medicare 1.45%), the federal unemployment tax (.8%), and the state unemployment tax (5.4%). Use the form provided in the working papers. None of the employees has reached the taxable earnings limit.

Total gross earnings:

1. $914.80
2. $1,113.73
3. $2,201.38
4. $791.02
5. $1,245.75

Analyze: Explain the relationship between federal and state unemployment tax rates.

Problem 13–7 Recording the Payment of the Payroll

The totals of the payroll register for Kits & Pups Grooming are shown in your working papers. On December 31, the owner, Abe Shultz, wrote Check 1400 to pay the payroll.

Instructions In your working papers:

1. Record the payroll entry in the general journal.
2. Post the entry to the general ledger accounts.

Analyze: Which payroll liability account has the largest credit entry?

Problem 13–8 Journalizing Payroll Transactions

The Outback Guide Service payroll register for the week ending Dec. 31 appears on the next page.

Complete chapter problems one of four ways:

1 **Manual** Glencoe Working Papers

or

2 **Peachtree Complete Accounting** Software

or

3 **QuickBooks** Templates (Problems 13–8, 13–9)

or

4 **Spreadsheet** Templates (Problem 13–6)

SPREADSHEET SMART GUIDE

Step–by–Step Instructions: Problem 13–6

1. Select the spreadsheet template for Problem 13–6.
2. Enter your name and the date in the spaces provided on the template.
3. Complete the spreadsheet using the instructions in your working papers.
4. Print the spreadsheet and proof your work.
5. Save your work and exit the spreadsheet program.

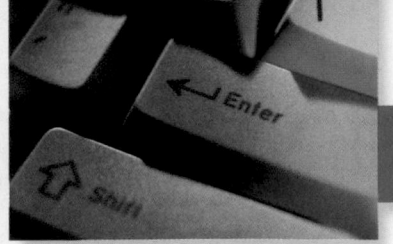

Peachtree®

SMART GUIDE

Step–by–Step Instructions: Problem 13–7

1. Select the problem set for Kits & Pups Grooming (Prob. 13–7).
2. Rename the company and set the system date.
3. Record the payroll entry using the **General Journal Entry** option.
4. Print a General Journal report and a General Ledger report.
5. Proof your work.
6. Answer the Analyze question.
7. End the session.

TIP: As a shortcut, you can type just the day in most date fields.

Peachtree®

SMART GUIDE

Step–by–Step Instructions: Problem 13–8

1. Select the problem set for Outback Guide Service (Prob. 13–8).
2. Rename the company and set the system date.
3. Record the payment of the payroll and the employer's payroll taxes.
4. Print a General Journal report.
5. Proof your work.
6. Answer the Analyze question.
7. End the session.

TIP: You can press ALT+S to post a General Journal entry.

SOURCE DOCUMENT PROBLEM

Problem 13–9

Use the source documents in your working papers to record the transactions for this problem.

PAYROLL REGISTER

PAY PERIOD ENDING Dec. 31 _____ 20 -- _____   DATE OF PAYMENT Dec. 31, 20--

EMPLOYEE NUMBER	NAME	MAR. STATUS	ALLOW	TOTAL HOURS	RATE	EARNINGS			DEDUCTIONS							NET PAY	CK. NO.
						REGULAR	OVERTIME	TOTAL	SOC. SEC. TAX	MEDICARE TAX	FED. INC. TAX	STATE INC. TAX	HOSP. INS.	OTHER	TOTAL		
31	Coleman, Clarence	M	1	41	7.60	304 00	11 40	315 40	19 55	4 57	21 00	6 31			51 43	263 97	1
28	Lorman, Victoria	S	1	30	8.00	240 00		240 00	14 88	3 48	21 00	4 80		(UD)5 40	49 56	190 44	2
33	Peterson, Peg	S	1	38	7.25	275 50		275 50	17 08	3 99	26 00	5 51			52 58	222 92	3
35	Torrez, Joyce	M	2	36	7.25	261 00		261 00	16 18	3 78	6 00	5 22		(UD)5 40	36 58	224 42	4
24																	24
25																	25
	TOTALS					1,080 50	11 40	1,091 90	67 69	15 82	74 00	21 84	—	10 80	190 15	901 75	

Other Deductions: Write the appropriate code letter to the left of the amount: B–U.S. Savings Bonds; C–Credit Union; UD–Union Dues; UW–United Way.

Instructions In your working papers:

1. Record the entry for the payment of the payroll on page 15 of the general journal. (Check 1201, dated Dec. 31).
2. Use the information in the payroll register to compute the employer's payroll taxes. These include FICA taxes (6.2% for social security, 1.45% for Medicare) and federal (.8%) and state (5.4%) unemployment taxes. None of the employees has reached the taxable earnings limit.
3. Record the entry for the employer's payroll taxes on page 15 of the general journal.

Analyze: In the entry recording the payment of payroll, which account, **Social Security Tax Payable** or **Employees' Federal Income Tax Payable**, had the largest credit?

SOURCE DOCUMENT PROBLEM

Problem 13–9 Recording and Posting Payroll Transactions

Showbiz Video completed the following payroll transactions during the first two weeks of December. Showbiz Video pays its employees on a biweekly (every two weeks) basis.

Instructions In your working papers:

1. Record the December 13 transactions on page 38 in the general journal.
2. Post both payroll entries to the appropriate general ledger accounts.
3. Journalize and post the December 16 transactions.

Date	Transactions
Dec. 13	Wrote Check 2206 to pay the payroll of $3,840.58 (gross earnings) for the pay period ending December 13. The following amounts were withheld: FICA taxes, $238.12 for social security and $55.69 for Medicare; employees' federal income taxes, $639.00; employees' state income taxes, $96.02; insurance premium, $21.00; U.S. savings bonds, $20.00.
13	Recorded the employer's payroll taxes (FICA tax rates, 6.2% for social security and 1.45% for Medicare; federal unemployment tax rate, 0.8%; state unemployment tax rate, 5.4%). No employee has reached the maximum taxable amount.
	Continued

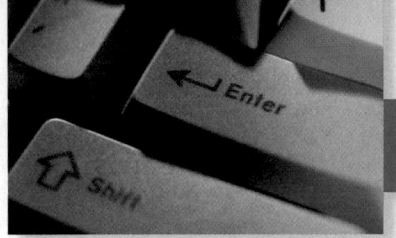
Date	Transactions (cont.)
16	Paid the amounts owed to the federal government for employees' federal income taxes and FICA taxes, Check 2215.
16	Purchased U.S. savings bonds for employees for $100.00, Check 2216.
16	Paid $148.00 to American Insurance Company for employees' insurance, Check 2217.

Analyze: Which payroll accounts have a balance after entries are posted?

Problem 13–10 Recording and Posting Payroll Transactions

Job Connect pays its employees twice a month. Employee earnings and tax amounts for the pay period ending December 31 are:

Gross Earnings	$12,543.40
Social Security Tax	777.69
Medicare Tax	181.88
Employees' Federal Income Tax	662.00
Employees' State Income Tax	250.87

Instructions In your working papers:

1. Prepare Check 1602 (payable to "Job Connect Payroll Account") to transfer the net pay amount to the payroll checking account.
2. On page 19 of the general journal, record the payment of the payroll.
3. Post the payroll transaction to the general ledger.
4. Compute payroll tax expense forms and journalize the entry to record employer's payroll taxes. (Social security rate = 6.2%; Medicare rate = 1.45%; state unemployment rate = 5.4%; federal unemployment rate = .8%.) No employee has reached the taxable earnings limit.
5. Post the entry to the general journal.
6. Prepare checks dated December 31 to pay the following payroll liabilities:
   (a) Federal unemployment taxes, payable to First City Bank (Check 1603).
   (b) State unemployment taxes, payable to the State of North Carolina (Check 1604).
   (c) Employees' federal income taxes and FICA taxes, payable to First City Bank (Check 1605).
7. Journalize and post the entries for the payment of the payroll liabilities.
8. Complete payroll tax expense forms. Prepare a Form 8109 for each of the two federal tax deposits paid in Instruction 6, parts (a) and (c). The oval for FICA and federal income tax is 941. The oval for the federal unemployment tax is 940.

Analyze: What is the balance in the **Salaries Expense** account on December 31 after the payroll entries have been posted?

Peachtree®

SMART GUIDE

Step–by–Step Instructions:
Problem 13–9

1. Select the problem set for Showbiz Video (Prob. 13-9).
2. Rename the company and set the system date.
3. Record the December transactions.
4. Print a General Journal report and a General Ledger report.
5. Proof your work.
6. Answer the Analyze question.
7. End the session.

Peachtree®

SMART GUIDE

Step–by–Step Instructions:
Problem 13–10

1. Select the problem set for Job Connect (Prob. 13-10).
2. Rename the company and set the system date.
3. Record all of the entries using the **General Journal Entry** option.
4. Print a General Journal report and a General Ledger report.
5. Proof your work.
6. Manually prepare Form 8109 for the federal tax deposits.
7. Answer the Analyze question.
8. End the session.

Payroll Accounting

GREEN THUMB *Plant Service*

What You'll Learn

- How to calculate employees' gross earnings and deductions.
- How to calculate employees' net pay.
- How to prepare a payroll register.
- How to write payroll checks and stubs for employees.
- How to record payroll information on employees' earnings records.
- How to journalize and post the payroll transaction.
- How to calculate, journalize, and post the employer's payroll taxes.
- How to journalize and post the payment of FICA taxes, employees' federal income taxes, and insurance premiums.
- How to prepare Form 8190.

Why It's Important

To review and apply what you've learned about the procedures involved in a payroll system as you prepare the payroll and maintain the payroll records for a sole proprietorship.

Green Thumb Plant Service

Company Background: Green Thumb Plant Service is a plant maintenance company located in Kingsbury, Michigan. It is a service business that is organized as a sole proprietorship. It is owned and operated by Joanna Ecke. The company places and maintains plants, flowers, and small trees in offices and corporate buildings.

The business has been in operation for almost five years. During that time, its revenue has increased each year, additional employees have been hired, and the business is now showing a good profit.

Payroll Information: The business presently employs eight people. A Form W-4 is on file for each employee. The list that follows summarizes the data on those documents.

Michael Alter	Single	claims 1 exemption
Christine Cuddy	Single	claims 0 exemptions
Jesse Dubow	Single	claims 0 exemptions
Joclyn Filley	Single	claims 1 exemption
Greg Millette	Married	claims 2 exemptions
Heather Repicky	Married	claims 3 exemptions
Daniel Ripp	Married	claims 2 exemptions
Yourself	Single	claims 1 exemption

The business pays its employees on a weekly basis. Overtime is paid at the rate of $1\frac{1}{2}$ times the regular rate of pay for all hours worked over 40. The weekly pay period runs from Monday through Saturday, with employees being paid on Saturday for the week's work. Because most office buildings are closed on Sunday, the business is also closed.

The employees are paid by one of three methods: hourly rate, salary, or salary plus 10% commission on any new accounts they acquire for the company. The following table lists the employees, the method by which their wages are computed, and other pertinent information. Next, you'll find the time cards for the employees who are paid on an hourly basis.

Green Thumb Plant Service

Employee	Empl. No.	Position	Employee Status	Rate of Pay
Heather Repicky	010	Manager	Full-time	$725.00/weekly salary
Greg Millette	011	Salesperson	Full-time	$450.00/week plus 10% Commission
Jesse Dubow	012	Bookkeeper	Part-time	$250.00/week
Joclyn Filley	013	Supply clerk	Full-time	$7.40/hour
Daniel Ripp	016	Service	Full-time	$8.30/hour
Christine Cuddy	018	Service	Full-time	$8.30/hour
Michael Alter	019	Supply clerk	Part-time	$7.10/hour
Yourself	022	Accounting clerk	Part-time	$175.00/week

Peachtree®

SMART GUIDE

Step–by–Step Instructions:

1. Select the problem set for Green Thumb Plant Service (MP–3).
2. Rename the company and set the system date.
3. Enter your name for employee record 022.
4. Record the weekly payroll and print checks for all employees using the **Payroll Entry** option.
5. Print a Payroll Register for the current week and proof your work.
6. Print a Payroll Journal report.
7. Calculate and record the employer's payroll tax expense using the **General Journal Entry** option.
8. Record the deposit for the taxes owed to the federal government and enter the monthly insurance premium using the **General Journal Entry** option.
9. Manually complete Form 8109.
10. Print a General Journal report and proof your work.
11. Print a General Ledger report.
12. Print Quarterly Earnings reports for Michael Alter and Greg Millette.
13. Answer the Analyze questions.
14. End the session.

The time cards for the employees who are paid on an hourly rate are listed below.

NO. 019
NAME Michael Alter
SOC. SEC. NO. 049-71-8436
WEEK ENDING 7/25/20--

DAY	IN	OUT	IN	OUT	IN	OUT	TOTAL
M			2:00	5:00			
T			2:00	6:00			
W			3:00	5:00			
Th			2:00	6:00			
F			2:00	6:00			
S			9:00	2:00			
S							

NO. 018
NAME Christine Cuddy
SOC. SEC. NO. 223-56-0992
WEEK ENDING 7/25/20--

DAY	IN	OUT	IN	OUT	IN	OUT	TOTAL
M	9:00	12:00	12:30	5:00			
T	9:00	11:30	12:00	5:00			
W	9:00	1:00					
Th	9:00	12:00	12:30	4:00			
F	8:30	1:00	1:30	3:00			
S	9:00	1:30					
S							

NO. 013
NAME Joclyn Filley
SOC. SEC. NO. 042-97-3814
WEEK ENDING 7/25/20--

DAY	IN	OUT	IN	OUT	IN	OUT	TOTAL
SIGN. M	9:00	12:00	1:00	3:00			
T	9:00	12:00	1:00	5:00			
W	8:00	12:00	1:00	5:00			
Th	9:00	12:00	1:00	3:30			
F	9:00	12:00	1:00	4:00			
S	9:00	12:00					
S							

	TOTAL HOURS			
	HOURS	RATE	AMOUNT	
REGULAR				
OVERTIME				
	TOTAL EARNINGS			

SIGNATURE_____ DATE_____

NO. 016
NAME Daniel Ripp
SOC. SEC. NO. 011-79-2118
WEEK ENDING 7/25/20--

DAY	IN	OUT	IN	OUT	IN	OUT	TOTAL
SIGN. M	9:00	12:00	12:30	5:00			
T	9:00	12:30	1:00	6:00			
W	9:00	12:00	1:00	4:30			
Th	8:30	12:30	1:00	5:00			
F	9:00	11:30	12:00	5:00			
S	9:00	1:00					
S							

	TOTAL HOURS			
	HOURS	RATE	AMOUNT	
REGULAR				
OVERTIME				
	TOTAL EARNINGS			

SIGNATURE_____ DATE_____

Federal tax tables are used to determine income taxes to be withheld. The table is included in the working papers. The current rate for other taxes are as follows:

State income tax:	2%
FICA: Employee and employer contributions	
Social Security Tax:	6.2%
Medicare Tax:	1.45%
State unemployment tax:	5.4%
Federal unemployment tax:	0.8%

APPLICATION OPTIONS

Complete activities one of two ways:

1 **Manual** Glencoe Working Papers

or

2 **Peachtree Complete Accounting** Software

YOUR JOB RESPONSIBILITIES
Green Thumb Plant Service

The business entered the third quarter of its fiscal year at the beginning of July. It is presently the last week of July. Jesse Dubow, the bookkeeper, is leaving on vacation. In his absence, you are to prepare this week's payroll.

(1) Complete the timecards for the four hourly employees. Enter the total hours worked at the bottom of each card.

(2) Greg Millette recorded additional clients that brought in $925.00 in new business. Calculate his commission and add it to his salary to determine his gross earnings.

(3) Enter the payroll information for all employees in the payroll register. Each employee was recently assigned an employee number because the business is soon converting to an automated payroll preparation system. Since this payroll is being prepared manually, list the employees in the payroll register in alphabetical order by last name.

(4) Use the following information to complete the payroll register.

(a) Use the federal tax chart to determine income tax amounts to be withheld.

(b) Michael Alter, Christine Cuddy, Joclyn Filley, and Greg Millette each have $5.00 deducted for the purchase of U.S. savings bonds.

(c) Jesse Dubow, Heather Repicky, and Daniel Ripp each have $4.00 deducted for donations to the United Way.

(d) All employees pay an insurance premium each week. Married employees pay $9.00 and single employees pay $6.00.

(e) None of Green Thumb's employees has reached the maximum taxable amount for the social security tax.

(5) Calculate the net pay for each employee.

(6) Total all amount columns in the payroll register. Prove the accuracy of the totals.

(7) Write Check 972 on the business's regular checking account for the amount of the total net pay. Make the check payable to the Green Thumb Plant Service—Payroll Account. In Jesse's absence, Joanna Ecke will sign the check for you. Complete the deposit slip for the payroll account.

(8) Record the payroll transaction in the general journal, page 21. Use the information contained in the payroll register and Check 972 as the source documents. Post the transaction to the general ledger accounts.

(9) Write the paychecks for the employees. Use the information in the payroll register to complete the check stubs. After a check has been written for an employee, enter the check number in the payroll register.

(10) Enter this week's payroll information on the employee's earnings records for Michael Alter and Greg Millette only. Be sure to add the current

gross earnings amount to the accumulated total.

(11) Calculate and record the employer's taxes for this pay period in the general journal. The source of information is the payroll register. Post the journal entry to the general ledger.

(12) Make a deposit for the taxes owed to the federal government. The total includes the amounts withheld for employees' federal income tax, social security tax, and medicare tax. Complete Form 8109 by entering the amount owed. Write Check 973, payable to the First Federal Bank for the taxes.

(13) Enter the transaction in the general journal and post the entry to the general ledger.

(14) Pay the monthly insurance premium by writing Check 974 to the American Insurance Company for $228.00. Record the payment in the general journal and post the entry to the general ledger.

Analyze:
1. What is the total net pay for this pay period?
2. For what amount is the deposit to the federal government for taxes owed?

UNIT 4

The Accounting Cycle for a Merchandising Corporation

In this unit...

You will learn how to keep the accounting records for a business that sells merchandise. The business we will use in our examples is organized as a corporation. You will study the complete accounting cycle for the merchandise business called **On Your Mark Athletic Wear.** We'll examine cash sales, sales on account, cash receipts, cash payments, and purchases. In addition, you'll learn how to record adjusting entries, prepare financial statements for a corporation, and prepare closing entries. The chart of accounts for **On Your Mark Athletic Wear** is shown on page 355.

Where profit is, loss is hidden nearby.

Japanese Proverb

POWER READING STRATEGIES

To get the most out of your reading:

Predict what the section will be about.

Connect what you read with your own life.

Question as you read to make sure you understand the content.

Respond to what you've read.

In Your Journal...

The next time you visit your local CD store, examine the inventory—the various types of products that are available to purchase. The managers of merchandising businesses are responsible for the quality and popularity of their stores.

In your journal, record the following:

1. Make a list of all the product groups for sale (CDs, tapes, magazines, t-shirts, etc).

2. What items are the least expensive for sale? Most expensive?

3. Make a list of items that the store does not currently carry that you feel would be a beneficial addition.

CHAPTER 14

Accounting for Sales and Cash Receipts

Learning Objectives

When you have completed this chapter, you will be able to:

▶ Explain the difference between a service business and a merchandising business.

▶ Analyze transactions relating to the sale of merchandise.

▶ Explain the difference between a retailer and a wholesaler.

▶ Record a variety of sales and cash receipt transactions in a general journal.

▶ Define the accounting terms introduced in this chapter.

Exploring the Real World of Business

ANALYZING SALES

Twenty years ago, the now-popular sport of in-line skating didn't exist. Today, in-line skating attracts nearly 29 million participants and is one of the fastest growing sports in the U.S.

Rollerblade, a leading producer of in-line skates based in Minnesota, was created when two brothers found a used pair of in-line skates while rummaging through a sporting goods store. In the basement of their parents' home, they modified the skates for their off-season hockey training. Other hockey players and skiers in training soon adapted the in-line skates into their training routines. Professional marketing efforts helped the sport gain public attention, and soon in-line skaters were a common sight along city streets, beaches, and college campuses.

Although the company does not release its accounting records because it is privately owned, it has become a multi-million dollar business, maintaining a 33 percent market share.

What do you think?

1. What products and accessories do you think a company like **Rollerblade** sells?

2. When **Rollerblade** sells its products to sporting goods stores and skate shops, what general ledger accounts do you imagine would be affected?

Workplace Connections

Applying Your Accounting Knowledge

Making sales is key to the financial success of a business. Sales dollars come from selling products or services to customers. In Chapters 3 through 11, you learned about accounting for a business that sells services to its customers. In this Unit, you'll learn about selling merchandise to customers and how to record these sales into the accounting records.

Investigate:

1. Does your work or the work of friends or family involve selling merchandise to customers?
2. What products are sold?
3. What information from these sales do you think should be recorded into the accounting records?

Glencoe Accounting *Online*

Visit the *Glencoe Accounting* Web site at **glencoeaccounting.glencoe.com** for additional activities and information.

353

Accounting for a Merchandising Business

As you remember, a service business is one that provides a service to the public for a fee. In contrast, a merchandising business buys goods (such as computers, clothing, or furniture) and then sells those goods to customers for a profit. You're probably familiar with merchandising businesses like Tower Records or Wal-Mart. Most merchandising businesses operate either as retailers or as wholesalers. Some merchandising businesses are both retailers and wholesalers. A **retailer** is a business that sells to the final user, that is, to you—the consumer. A **wholesaler** is a business that sells to retailers. In this chapter, we will analyze transactions relating to the sale of merchandise for On Your Mark Athletic Wear, a retailer. Refer to the chart of accounts for On Your Mark Athletic Wear.

The Operating Cycle of a Merchandising Business

A merchandising business produces revenue through a series of transactions called the operating cycle, as illustrated in **Figure 14–1** below.

The collection of cash from sales enables the business to purchase more items to sell, pay expenses, and make a profit. As long as the company is in business, this is a continuous, repeating sequence.

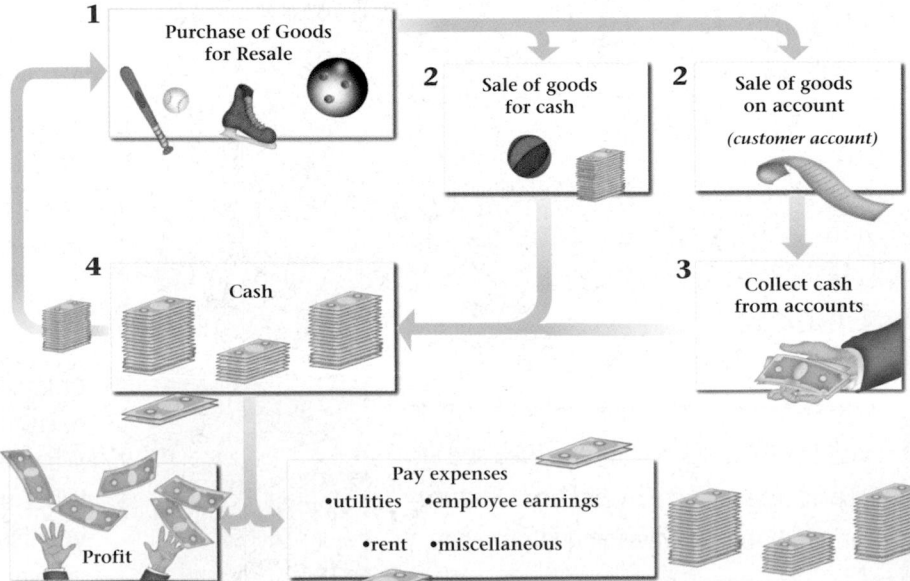

Figure 14–1 The Operating Cycle for a Merchandising Business

ON YOUR MARK
ATHLETIC WEAR
595 Leslie Street, Dallas, TX 75207

CHART OF ACCOUNTS

ASSETS

101 Cash in Bank	130 Supplies
105 Change Fund	135 Prepaid Insurance
110 Petty Cash Fund	140 Delivery Equipment
115 Accounts Receivable	142 Accumulated Depreciation—Delivery Equipment
117 Allowance for Uncollectible Accounts	145 Office Equipment
118 Notes Receivable	147 Accumulated Depreciation—Office Equipment
120 Interest Receivable	150 Store Equipment
125 Merchandise Inventory	152 Accumulated Depreciation—Store Equipment

LIABILITIES

201 Accounts Payable	212 Social Security Tax Payable
202 Notes Payable	213 Medicare Tax Payable
203 Discount on Notes Payable	214 Federal Unemployment Tax Payable
204 Federal Corporate Income Tax Payable	215 State Unemployment Tax Payable
205 Employees' Federal Income Tax Payable	220 Sales Tax Payable
211 Employees' State Income Tax Payable	

STOCKHOLDERS' EQUITY

301 Capital Stock	310 Income Summary
305 Retained Earnings	

REVENUE

401 Sales	410 Sales Returns and Allowances
405 Sales Discounts	415 Interest Income

COST OF MERCHANDISE

501 Purchases	510 Purchases Discounts
505 Transportation In	515 Purchases Returns and Allowances

EXPENSES

601 Advertising Expense	645 Loss/Gain on Disposal of Plant Assets
605 Bankcard Fees Expense	650 Maintenance Expense
610 Cash Short and Over	655 Miscellaneous Expense
612 Delivery Expense	657 Payroll Tax Expense
615 Depreciation Expense—Delivery Equipment	660 Rent Expense
620 Depreciation Expense—Office Equipment	665 Salaries Expense
625 Depreciation Expense—Store Equipment	670 Supplies Expense
630 Federal Corporate Income Tax Expense	675 Uncollectible Accounts Expense
635 Insurance Expense	680 Utilities Expense
640 Interest Expense	

▶ Accounts Receivable Subsidiary Ledger

BRE	Break Point Sports Club
DIM	Dimaio, Joe
GAL	Galvin, Robert
KLE	Klein, Casey
MON	Montero, Anita
RAH	Rahim, Shashi
RAM	Ramos, Gabriel
SOU	South Branch High School Athletics
SUL	Sullivan, Megan
TAM	Tammy's Fitness Club
WON	Wong, Kim
YOU	Young, Lara

▶ Accounts Payable Subsidiary Ledger

CHA	Champion Store Supply
COM	Computer Solutions
DAR	Dara's Delivery Service
FAS	FastLane Athletics
GEA	Geary Office Supply
PRO	Pro Runner Warehouse
SLF	Sports Link Footwear
SNS	Sports Nutrition Supply

CONNECT TO . . .
EDUCATION

A study performed by the Federation of Schools of Accountancy determined that writing and speaking are the subjects in which accounting students require the most extra work. The Federation also found that most accounting students would benefit from extra courses on multinational accounting, ethics, and other liberal-arts courses.

Merchandise Inventory Account

A merchandising business buys goods from a wholesaler or a manufacturing business and then sells these goods to its customers. Goods bought for resale are called **merchandise** . The items of merchandise the business has in stock are referred to as **inventory** . The inventory is represented in the general ledger by the asset account **Merchandise Inventory.** Increases to **Merchandise Inventory** are recorded as debits, and decreases are recorded as credits. The normal balance of the **Merchandise Inventory** account is a debit. At the beginning of each period, the dollar amount of merchandise in stock is indicated by the debit balance in the **Merchandise Inventory** account.

Merchandise Inventory	
Debit + Increase Side Normal Balance	Credit − Decrease Side

During the business operating cycle, the merchandise in stock is sold, and new inventory items are purchased to replace the ones sold. Separate accounts are used to record the sale of merchandise and the purchase of new merchandise.

Sales Account

When a retail merchandising business sells goods to a customer, the amount of the merchandise sold is recorded in the **Sales** account. **Sales** is a revenue account. Increases to the **Sales** account are recorded as credits, and decreases are recorded as debits. The normal balance of the **Sales** account is a credit. Both sales for cash and on account are recorded as credits to the **Sales** account.

Sales	
Debit − Decrease Side	Credit + Increase Side Normal Balance

Sales on account will affect the **Accounts Receivable** account, while cash sales will affect the **Cash in Bank** account.

A MATTER OF ETHICS

Confidentiality

Imagine that you work as an accounting clerk for a fast-food franchise like Taco Bell. You have access to all the accounting records for the business.

A friend of yours has promised to hire you as an accountant when he opens his own Mexican food restaurant. He has asked you to share information about Taco Bell's sales and expenses.

Ethical Decision Making:

☛ What are the ethical issues?

☛ What are the alternatives?

☛ Who are the affected parties?

☛ How do the alternatives affect the parties?

☛ What would you do?

Now that you have studied this section, complete the following questions and problems.

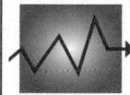

Thinking Critically

1. Explain the two types of merchandising businesses.
2. What type of account is **Merchandise Inventory?**

Communicating Accounting

You and your best friend, Inga Swenson, graduated from a prestigious art school. You have a degree in art history and business management; Inga has a degree in fine art. Inga is an award-winning weaver and creates wall hangings that are extremely popular in your community. Together you decide to form a business partnership. You want to open a retail store. Inga wants to sell directly to the customers at fairs and art shows. Draft a report to Inga that explains why selling art through a retail store is more profitable than seasonal shows and fairs.

Problem 14–1 Recording Merchandising Transactions

Instructions Record the following transactions in T-account form in your working papers for Sharp Shot Camera Shop. A partial chart of accounts follows:

General Ledger
Cash in Bank
Accounts Receivable
Merchandise Inventory
Accounts Payable
Sales

Date	Transactions
Apr. 4	Sold 10 Canon cameras on account for $3,000, Sales Slip 224.
10	Sold 2 dozen photo albums for $150, cash, Sales Slip 225.
20	Sold 4 rolls of 35mm film for $24 cash, Sales Slip 226.
25	Sold a Canon camera to a customer for $380 cash, Sales Slip 227.

SECTION 2

Analyzing Sales Transactions

What You'll Learn

- How to record the sale of merchandise on account.
- How to use the accounts receivable subsidiary ledger.
- How to post to the accounts receivable subsidiary ledger.
- The use of the **Sales Tax Payable** account, and its rules of debit and credit.
- The use of the **Sales Returns and Allow-ances** account, and its rules of debit and credit.

Why It's Important

It is essential to record sales transactions correctly as they reflect the revenue of the business.

KEY TERMS

sale on account
charge customer
credit cards
sales slip
sales tax
credit terms
accounts receivable
   subsidiary ledger
subsidiary ledger
controlling account
sales return
sales allowance
credit memorandum
contra account

In a merchandising business, the most frequent transaction is the sale of merchandise. Some businesses sell on a cash only basis. Others sell only on credit. Most businesses handle both cash and credit sales. Think about how many sales transactions a single Sears store records on a December day. Some customers pay with cash, some use a Sears credit card, and others use a bankcard such as VISA, MasterCard, or Discover. Each transaction is recorded so that at the end of the day, the store can report sales by each category (cash, credit card, and bankcard) and total sales. In this section, you will learn how to analyze transactions relating to sale of merchandise on account.

The sale of merchandise that will be paid for at a later date is called a **sale on account**, a charge sale, or a credit sale. The sale on account is made to a **charge customer**. Charge customers use **credit cards** issued by the business to make their purchases. A credit card, imprinted with the customer's name and account number, facilitates the sale on account.

The Sales Slip

A **sales slip** is a form that lists the details of a sale:

- The date of the sale.
- The name of the customer.
- The description, quantity, and price of the item(s) sold.

The description may include the physical details (such as "white athletic socks"), a stock number, or both. A sales slip is usually prepared in multiple copies. The customer receives the original as a receipt and as proof of purchase. The number of copies kept by the business varies with its needs. A copy is always used for accounting purposes as the source document for recording the journal entry.

Pre-numbered sales slips help businesses keep track of all sales made on account. On Your Mark uses pre-numbered sales slips printed with its name and address. On Your Mark's sales slip is shown in **Figure 14–2**.

Notice that the total amount on the sales slip includes cost of the items sold and sales tax.

Sales Tax

Most states and some cities tax the retail sale of goods and services. This tax is called a **sales tax** . Items subject to sales tax and sales tax rates vary from state to state. The sales tax rate is usually stated as a percentage of the sale, such as 5%. Sales tax rates are determined by each state's taxing authority.

The sales tax is paid by the customer and collected by the business. The business acts as the collection agent for the state or city government. (In the future, we will refer only to the state government.) At the time of the sale, the business adds the sales tax to the total selling price of the goods. Periodically, the business sends the collected sales tax to the state. Until the state is paid, however, the sales tax collected from customers represents a liability of the business. The business keeps a record of the sales tax owed to the state in a liability account called **Sales Tax Payable**. For **Sales Tax Payable**, the increase and balance side is a credit and the decrease side is a debit.

Sales Tax Payable	
Debit	Credit
−	+
Decrease Side	Increase Side
	Normal Balance

ON YOUR MARK			
ATHLETIC WEAR			
595 Leslie Street, Dallas, TX 75207			
DATE: December 1, 20--			NO. 50
SOLD TO	Casey Klein 3345 Spring Creek Parkway Plano, Texas 75074		
CLERK B.E.	CASH	CHARGE ✓	TERMS n/30
QTY.	DESCRIPTION	UNIT PRICE	AMOUNT
1	Pair Running Shoes	$ 100.00	$ 100 00
6	Pair Athletic Socks	10.00	60 00
1	Vinyl Jacket/Pants	40.00	40 00
		SUBTOTAL	$ 200 00
		SALES TAX	12 00
Thank You!		TOTAL	$ 212 00

Figure 14–2 On Your Mark Athletic Wear Sales Slip

Calculating Sales Tax

To calculate the sales tax, multiply the total selling price of the merchandise by the sales tax rate. Refer to **Figure 14–2**. Casey Klein bought $200 worth of merchandise. The sales tax rate is 6%. The sales clerk multiplied $200 by 6% (.06) to compute the $12 sales tax. The total transaction amount is $212.

Not all sales of retail merchandise are taxed. In most states, sales made to tax-exempt organizations, such as schools, are not taxed. For example, South Branch High School purchased $1,500 worth of merchandise on account. Since schools are tax exempt, no sales tax is added to the amount of the sale.

Credit Terms

On the sales slip in **Figure 14–2**, space is provided to indicate the credit terms of the sale. **Credit terms** state the time allowed for payment. The credit terms for the sale to Casey Klein are n/30. The "n" stands for the *net*, or total, amount of the sale. The "30" stands for the number of days the customer has to pay for the merchandise. Casey Klein owes On Your Mark $212 (the net amount) by December 31 (30 days after December 1).

The Accounts Receivable Ledger

Businesses with few charge customers usually include an Accounts Receivable account for each customer in the general ledger. A large business, however, with many charge customers, sets up a separate ledger that contains an account for each charge customer. This ledger is the **accounts receivable subsidiary ledger** . A **subsidiary ledger** is a ledger, or book, that contains detailed data summarized to a controlling account in the

Did You Know?

Teen Spending
Teens are major consumers in the U.S. economy, spending over $103 billion each year. Transactions per teen average $67 per week on clothing, health and beauty aids, and entertainment.

general ledger. For example, the accounts receivable subsidiary ledger contains details of all the individuals and businesses that owe money to a company. Summary information about accounts receivable appears in the **Accounts Receivable** account in the general ledger. **Accounts Receivable** is a **controlling account** because its balance equals the total of all the account balances in the subsidiary ledger. The balance of **Accounts Receivable** thus serves as a control on the accuracy of the balances in the accounts receivable subsidiary ledger after all posting is complete.

General Ledger

Accounts Receivable—controlling account $10,000

Accounts Receivable Subsidiary Ledger

Individual Accounts Within Ledger:

Brown, Joshua	$2,000
Clark, Gillian	3,000
Greene, Jason	1,000
Perez, Sarita	4,000
Total	$10,000

> Controlling account balance equals total of accounts in subsidiary ledger.

The Accounts Receivable Subsidiary Ledger Form

Figure 14–3 shows the accounts receivable subsidiary ledger form used by On Your Mark.

The subsidiary ledger account form has lines at the top for the name and address of the customer. In a manual accounting system, subsidiary ledger accounts are arranged in alphabetical order. They are not usually numbered. In a computerized system, however, each charge customer is assigned a specific account number.

Notice that the subsidiary ledger account form has only three amount columns. The Debit and Credit columns are used to record increases and decreases to the customer's account. There is only one Balance column. Since **Accounts Receivable** is an asset account, the normal balance is a debit, so one balance amount is sufficient.

NAME						
ADDRESS						
DATE	DESCRIPTION	POST. REF.	DEBIT	CREDIT	BALANCE	

Figure 14–3 Subsidiary Ledger Account Form

Recording Sales on Account

Recall that Roadrunner Delivery Service is a service business organized as a sole proprietorship. When Roadrunner provides delivery services and bills the customer, the **Accounts Receivable** and **Delivery Revenue** accounts are affected. Let's compare that transaction to a sale on account for a merchandising business, On Your Mark Athletic Wear.

Business Transaction

On December 1 On Your Mark sold merchandise on account to Casey Klein for $200 plus sales tax of $12, Sales Slip 50.

ON YOUR MARK
ATHLETIC WEAR
595 Leslie Street, Dallas, TX 75207

DATE: December 1, 20--   NO. 50

SOLD TO	Casey Klein 3345 Spring Creek Parkway Plano, Texas 75074

CLERK B.E.	CASH	CHARGE ✓	TERMS n/30

QTY.	DESCRIPTION	UNIT PRICE	AMOUNT
1	Pair Running Shoes	$ 100.00	$ 100 00
6	Pair Athletic Socks	10.00	60 00
1	Vinyl Jacket/Pants	40.00	40 00
		SUBTOTAL	$ 200 00
		SALES TAX	12 00
Thank You!		TOTAL	$ 212 00

ANALYSIS   *Identify*

1. The accounts affected are **Accounts Receivable** (controlling), **Accounts Receivable–Casey Klein** (subsidiary), **Sales,** and **Sales Tax Payable.**

Classify

2. **Accounts Receivable** (controlling) and **Accounts Receivable–Casey Klein** (subsidiary) are asset accounts. **Sales** is a revenue account. **Sales Tax Payable** is a liability account.

+/–

3. **Accounts Receivable** (controlling) and **Accounts Receivable–Casey Klein** (subsidiary) are increased by the total amount, $212 (dollar amount of merchandise sold plus sales tax). **Sales** is increased by the dollar amount of merchandise sold, $200. **Sales Tax Payable** is increased by the amount of sales tax charged, $12.

DEBIT-CREDIT RULE

4. Increases to asset accounts are recorded as debits. Debit **Accounts Receivable** (controlling) for $212. Also debit **Accounts Receivable– Casey Klein** (subsidiary) for $212.
5. Increases to revenue and liability accounts are recorded as credits. Credit **Sales** for $200 and **Sales Tax Payable** for $12.

T ACCOUNTS

6.

Accounts Receivable			Sales	
Debit + 212	Credit –		Debit –	Credit + 200

Accounts Receivable Subsidiary Ledger Casey Klein			Sales Tax Payable	
Debit + 212	Credit –		Debit –	Credit + 12

JOURNAL ENTRY

7.

GENERAL JOURNAL   PAGE _20_

	DATE		DESCRIPTION	POST. REF.	DEBIT	CREDIT	
1	20--						1
2	Dec.	1	Accts. Rec./Casey Klein		212 00		2
3			Sales			200 00	3
4			Sales Tax Payable			12 00	4
5			Sales Slip 50				5
6							6

Notice that the debit in the general journal entry is to "Accounts Receivable/Casey Klein." The slash indicates that two accounts are debited: **Accounts Receivable** (controlling) and **Accounts Receivable—Casey Klein** (subsidiary).

As mentioned earlier, when merchandise is sold to tax-exempt organizations, such as school districts, sales tax is not charged. An example of such a transaction follows.

This transaction is analyzed and recorded in the same manner as the December 1 entry for Casey Klein *except* there is no sales tax. On Your Mark's accountant debits **Accounts Receivable/South Branch High School Athletics** for $1,500 and credits the **Sales** account for $1,500.

Business Transaction

On December 3 On Your Mark sold merchandise on account to South Branch High School Athletics for $1,500, Sales Slip 51.

JOURNAL ENTRY

ON YOUR MARK
ATHLETIC WEAR
595 Leslie Street, Dallas, TX 75207

DATE: December 3, 20--   NO. 51

SOLD TO	South Branch High School 1750 Rutgers Dr. Dallas, TX 75207		
CLERK B.E.	CASH	CHARGE ✓	TERMS 2/10, n/30

QTY.	DESCRIPTION	UNIT PRICE	AMOUNT	
15	Baseball Uniforms	$ 40.00	$ 600	00
15	Baseball Caps	20.00	300	00
15	Baseball Mitts	35.00	525	00
2	Baseballs	15.00	30	00
3	Baseball Bats	15.00	45	00
		SUBTOTAL	$ 1,500	00
		SALES TAX	0	00
Thank You!		TOTAL	$ 1,500	00

GENERAL JOURNAL   PAGE __20__

	DATE	DESCRIPTION	POST. REF.	DEBIT	CREDIT	
6	3	Accts. Rec./So. Branch H.S.		1 500 00		6
7		Sales			1 500 00	7
8		Sales Slip 51				8
9						9

Sales Returns and Allowances

All merchandising businesses expect that some customers will be dissatisfied with their purchases. The reasons for dissatisfaction vary. An item may be damaged or defective. The color or size may be incorrect. Whatever the reason, merchants usually allow dissatisfied customers to return merchandise. Any merchandise returned for credit or a cash refund is called a **sales return** .

Sometimes a customer discovers that merchandise is damaged or defective but still usable. When this happens, the merchant may reduce the sales price for the damaged merchandise. A price reduction granted for damaged goods kept by the customer is called a **sales allowance** .

The Credit Memorandum. If the sales return or allowance occurs on a charge sale, the business usually prepares a credit memorandum. A **credit memorandum** lists the details of a sales return or allowance. The charge customer's account is credited (decreased) for the amount of the return or allowance.

Figure 14–4 shows a credit memorandum, or credit memo, used by On Your Mark. The credit memo was prepared when Gabriel Ramos returned merchandise that he bought on account on November 29. Note that the credit memo includes a description of the returned item, the reasons for the return, and the amount to be credited to Gabriel Ramos' account.

On Your Mark's credit memo also includes spaces for the date and sales slip number of the original sale. Notice too that the total on the credit memo includes the sales tax charged on the original sale.

The same form is used if Gabriel Ramos is instead given a sales allowance. Of course, the amount credited to his account would be less. The credit granted for an allowance is the difference between the original sales price and the reduced price.

On Your Mark's credit memos are pre-numbered and prepared in duplicate. The original is given to the customer. The copy is kept by the business and is the source document used for the journal entry to record the transaction.

The Sales Returns and Allowances Account. Sales returns and allowances decrease the total revenue earned by a business. This decrease, however, is not recorded in the **Sales** account. Instead, a separate account called **Sales Returns and Allowances** is used. **Sales Returns and Allowances** summarizes the total returns and allowances for damaged, defective, or otherwise unsatisfactory merchandise. If the **Sales Returns and Allowances** account balance is large in proportion to the **Sales** account balance, there may be merchandising problems. The **Sales Returns and Allowances** account is carefully analyzed to detect any trouble.

The **Sales Returns and Allowances** account is a contra account. As a **contra account**, its balance decreases the balance of its related account. **Sales Returns and Allowances** is more specifically classified as a *contra revenue* account because it is related to a revenue account, **Sales**. Since the normal balance side of **Sales** is a credit, the normal balance side of **Sales Returns and Allowances** is a debit. This relationship is shown below:

CREDIT MEMORANDUM   NO. 124

ON YOUR MARK
ATHLETIC WEAR
595 Leslie Street, Dallas, TX 75207

ORIGINAL SALES DATE	ORIGINAL SALES SLIP	APPROVAL	☒ MDSE RET
Nov. 29, 20--	No. 35	J.R.	

DATE: December 4, 20--

NAME: Gabriel Ramos

ADDRESS: 278 Summit Avenue
Dallas, TX 75206

Gabriel Ramos
CUSTOMER SIGNATURE

QTY	DESCRIPTION	AMOUNT
1	Athletic Suit	$ 150 00

REASON FOR RETURN		
wrong color	SUB TOTAL	$ 150 00
THE TOTAL SHOWN AT THE RIGHT WILL BE CREDITED TO YOUR ACCOUNT.	SALES TAX	9 00
	TOTAL	$ 159 00

Figure 14–4 Credit Memorandum

	Sales	
Debit		Credit
–		+
Decrease Side		Increase Side
		Normal Balance

Sales Returns and Allowances	
Debit	Credit
+	–
Increase Side	Decrease Side
Normal Balance	

Cash Refunds

Sometimes a merchant will give a customer a cash refund instead of a credit. On Your Mark's store policy is to give a cash refund only if the original sale was a cash sale. For cash refunds, the **Cash in Bank** account is credited instead of **Accounts Receivable**.

Key Points

Contra Accounts
A contra account balance decreases the balance of its related account. The normal balance side of any contra account is always the opposite of the normal balance side of its related account.

Business Transaction

On December 4 On Your Mark issued Credit Memorandum 124 to Gabriel Ramos for the return of merchandise purchased on account, $150 plus $9 sales tax.

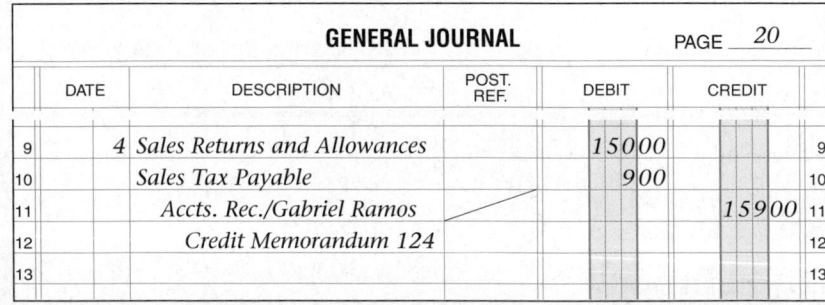

ON YOUR MARK
ATHLETIC WEAR
595 Leslie Street, Dallas, TX 75207

CREDIT MEMORANDUM			NO. 124
ORIGINAL SALES DATE	ORIGINAL SALES SLIP	APPROVAL	☒ MDSE RET
Nov. 29, 20--	No. 35	J.R.	

DATE: December 4, 20--

NAME: Gabriel Ramos

ADDRESS: 278 Summit Avenue
Dallas, TX 75206

QTY	DESCRIPTION	AMOUNT
1	Athletic Suit	$ 150 00

REASON FOR RETURN wrong color

SUB TOTAL		$ 150 00
THE TOTAL SHOWN AT THE RIGHT WILL BE CREDITED TO YOUR ACCOUNT.	SALES TAX	9 00
	TOTAL	$ 159 00

Gabriel Ramos
CUSTOMER SIGNATURE

ANALYSIS

Identify
1. The accounts affected are **Accounts Receivable** (controlling), **Accounts Receivable—Gabriel Ramos** (subsidiary), **Sales Returns and Allowances,** and **Sales Tax Payable.**

Classify
2. **Accounts Receivable** (controlling) and **Accounts Receivable—Gabriel Ramos** (subsidiary) are asset accounts. **Sales Returns and Allowances** is a contra revenue account. **Sales Tax Payable** is a liability account.

+/−
3. **Sales Returns and Allowances** is increased by $150. **Sales Tax Payable** is decreased by $9. **Accounts Receivable** (controlling) and **Accounts Receivable—Gabriel Ramos** (subsidiary) are decreased by $159.

DEBIT-CREDIT RULE

4. Increases to a contra revenue account are recorded as debits. Debit **Sales Returns and Allowances** for $150. Decreases to liability accounts are recorded as debits. Debit **Sales Tax Payable** for $9.
5. Decreases to asset accounts are recorded as credits. Credit **Accounts Receivable** (controlling) for $159. Also credit **Accounts Receivable—Gabriel Ramos** (subsidiary) for $159.

T ACCOUNTS

6.

Accounts Receivable		Sales Returns and Allowances	
Debit +	Credit − 159	Debit + 150	Credit −

Accounts Receivable Subsidiary Ledger Gabriel Ramos		Sales Tax Payable	
Debit +	Credit − 159	Debit − 9	Credit +

JOURNAL ENTRY

7.

GENERAL JOURNAL   PAGE _20_

	DATE	DESCRIPTION	POST. REF.	DEBIT	CREDIT	
9	4	Sales Returns and Allowances		150 00		9
10		Sales Tax Payable		9 00		10
11		Accts. Rec./Gabriel Ramos	/		159 00	11
12		Credit Memorandum 124				12
13						13

Posting to the Accounts Receivable Subsidiary Ledger

Refer to **Figure 14–5**. Look at the general journal entry. The credit is to **Accts Rec./Gabriel Ramos.** The slash indicates that both **Accounts Receivable** (controlling) and **Accounts Receivable—Gabriel Ramos** (subsidiary) are credited. Notice that a diagonal line is entered in the Post. Ref. column. This diagonal line indicates that the amount, $159, is posted in *two* places: *first* to the **Account Receivable** controlling account in the general ledger and *then* to the **Gabriel Ramos** account in the accounts receivable subsidiary ledger.

After the amount is posted to the Accounts Receivable controlling account, the account number (115) is entered to the *left* of the diagonal line in the Posting Reference column. After the amount is posted to the subsidiary ledger account, Gabriel Ramos, a check mark (✓) is entered to the *right* of the diagonal line.

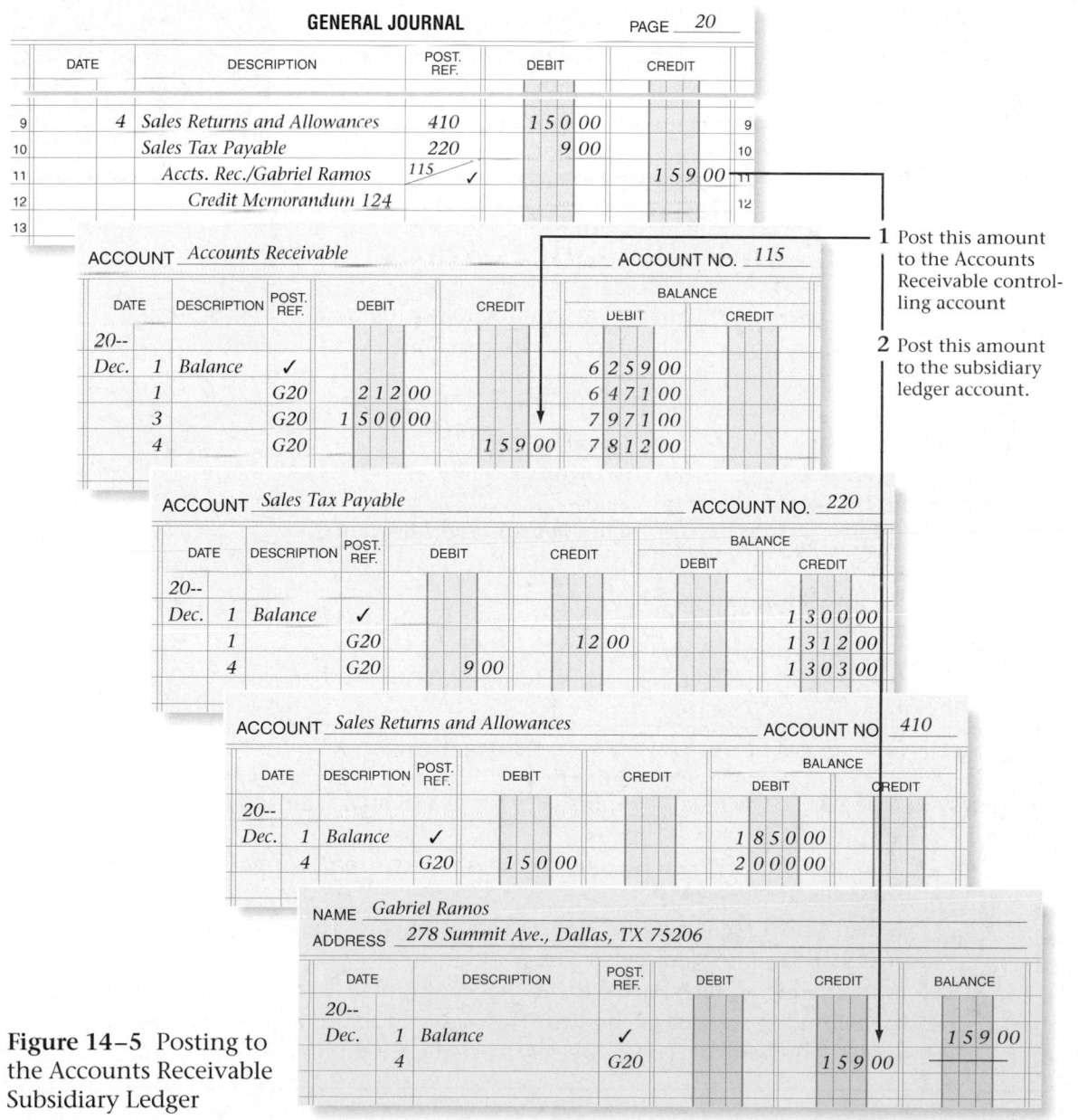

Figure 14–5 Posting to the Accounts Receivable Subsidiary Ledger

Now that you have studied this section, complete the following questions and problems.

Thinking Critically

1. Businesses collect sales tax from customers. In what account is the sales tax recorded?
2. Explain this term: n/30.
3. The normal balance for an Accounts Receivable subsidiary account is a debit. Under what circumstances would a customer's account have a credit balance?

Analyzing Accounting

From Rags to Riches is a local consignment clothing store. You are the office manager for the store. The owner, Patty Potter, has extended quite a bit of "in store credit" to her customers. As you analyze the books, you can see that sales on account are significant and many accounts may be uncollectible. To help Patty understand her problem, design a diagram to show the operating cycle for sales on account. Pair up with a classmate and explain your diagram.

Problem 14–2 Recording Sales on Account and Sales Returns and Allowances Transactions

Instructions In your working papers, record the following transactions of Alpine Ski Shop on page 2 of the general journal. Use the following accounts:

General Ledger

Cash in Bank	Sales Tax Payable
Accounts Receivable	Accounts Payable
Merchandise Inventory	Sales
	Sales Returns and Allowances

Accounts Receivable Subsidiary Ledger
Palmer, James
Rodriguez, Anna

Date	Transactions
Sept. 1	Sold $300 in merchandise plus sales tax of $18 on account to James Palmer, Sales Slip 101.
4	Sold $600 in merchandise plus $36 sales tax to Anna Rodriguez on account, Sales Slip 102.
7	Issued Credit Memorandum 15 to James Palmer for the return of $300 in merchandise plus sales tax of $18.
19	Anna Rodriguez telephoned the manager of Alpine Ski Shop and said that the zipper on her ski jacket is broken. The manager agreed to give her a $40 credit on her purchase, plus a $2.40 sales tax credit, Credit Memorandum 16.

Analyzing Cash Receipt Transactions

Whether it's the Los Angeles Metropolitan Transit Authority collecting fares from its bus passengers or Baskin-Robbins ringing up sales for ice cream, each business must account for cash receipts. In this section, you'll explore cash sales, charge sales, bankcard sales, and cash discounts.

Kinds of Cash Receipts

A transaction in which money comes in to a business is referred to as a **cash receipt**. The three most common sources of cash for a merchandising business are payments from charge customers, cash sales, and bankcard sales. Cash is also received, though much less frequently, from such transactions as the sale of an asset other than merchandise inventory. Let's learn how to handle these four kinds of cash receipts.

Cash Sales

In a **cash sale** transaction, the business receives full payment for the merchandise sold *at the time of the sale*. The proof of sale and the source document generated by a cash sale transaction differ from those for a sale on account.

Most retailers use a cash register to record cash sales. Instead of using preprinted sales slips, cash sales are recorded on two rolls of paper tape inside the cash register. When a cash sale occurs, the details of the sale are printed on the two tapes at the same time. The portion of one tape that contains a record of the sale is torn off and handed to the customer as a receipt. The other tape remains in the register.

Totaling Cash Sales

At the end of the day, the cash register is totaled and cleared. The total cash sales and the total sales taxes collected on those sales are listed on the cash register tape. The tape also shows the total charge sales for the day. A proof is usually prepared to show that the amount of cash in the cash register equals the amount of cash sales and sales tax recorded on the cash register tape. The proof and the tape are sent to the accounting clerk, who uses the tape, **Figure 14–6**, as the source document for the journal entry to record the day's cash sales.

What You'll Learn

- How to record cash receipt transactions.
- The use of the **Sales Discounts** account, and its rules of debit and credit.

Why It's Important

It is essential to understand the various ways that businesses receive cash and how to record the receipt of cash.

KEY TERMS

cash receipt
cash sale
bankcard
cash discount
sales discount

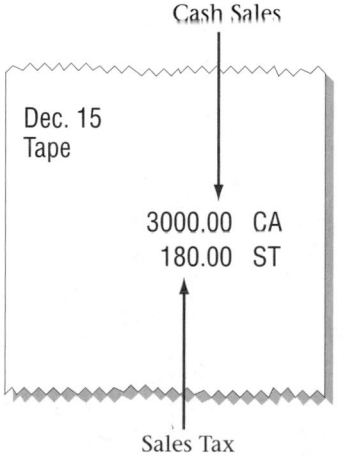

Cash Sales

Dec. 15
Tape

3000.00 CA
180.00 ST

Sales Tax

Figure 14–6 Cash Register Tape

Cash from Charge Customers

Businesses record cash received on account from charge customers by preparing receipts. A receipt, shown in **Figure 14–7**, is a form that serves as a record of cash received. Receipts are pre-numbered and may be prepared in multiple copies. The receipt is a source document for the journal entry. As you can see, the receipt lists the date the cash was received, the customer's name, the amount received, and an explanation of the transaction.

Figure 14–7 Receipt for Cash Received from a Charge Customer

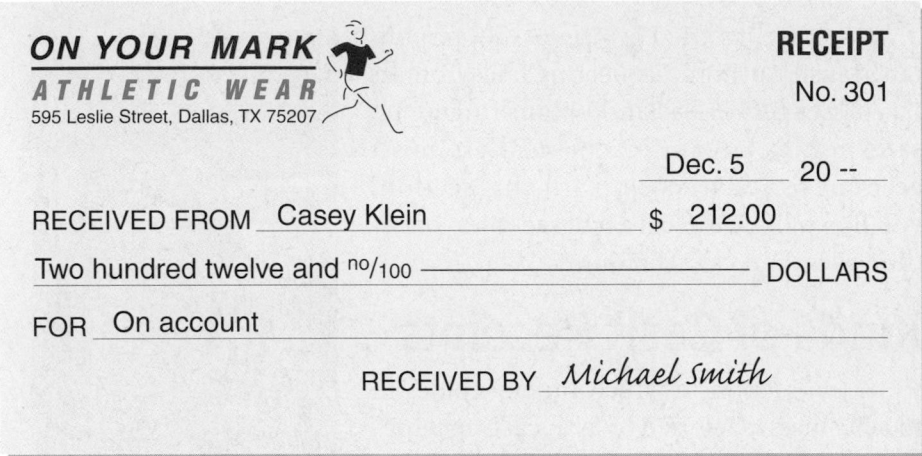

ON YOUR MARK
ATHLETIC WEAR
595 Leslie Street, Dallas, TX 75207

RECEIPT
No. 301

Dec. 5   20 --

RECEIVED FROM   Casey Klein $ 212.00

Two hundred twelve and ⁿᵒ/₁₀₀ ——————————— DOLLARS

FOR   On account

RECEIVED BY   *Michael Smith*

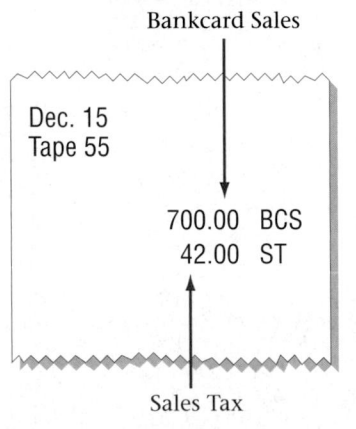

Bankcard Sales

Dec. 15
Tape 55

700.00 BCS
42.00 ST

Sales Tax

Figure 14–8 Bankcard Sales Tape

Bankcard Sales

Many businesses accept bankcards. Unlike a credit card, which is issued by a business and is used for purchases only at that business, a **bankcard** is issued by a bank and honored by many businesses. The most widely used bankcards in North America are VISA, MasterCard, and Discover.

Bankcard sales are processed differently from a store's credit card sales. Since the bankcard holder has an account with the bank that issued the card, and not with the businesses where the card is used, a store receives cash from the bank soon after it deposits its bankcard sales slips. The store does not have to wait until the bank collects from the card holder. Therefore, bankcard sales are recorded as though they are cash sales.

Processing Bankcard Sales. When a bankcard sale occurs, the sales clerk completes a multi-copy bankcard sales slip. The sales slip is inserted into the cash register, which records the details of the sale on both the sales slip and the cash register tape. When the cash register is totaled at the end of the day, the total bankcard sales and the sales taxes for those sales are listed on the cash register tape. Since the cash register tape includes the bankcard sales, those sales are included on the daily cash proof. Bankcard sales are journalized from the same tape as the cash sales for the day. **Figure 14–8** shows a cash register tape indicating the day's bankcard sales and related sales tax.

A business deposits all bankcard sales slips in its checking account, using a special deposit slip. Deposits of bankcard sales slips are treated the same as cash deposits. There is often a three or four-day delay before the amount of the deposit is credited to the business's checking account. This is due to the time it takes the bank to collect the funds from the various banks that issued the customers' bankcards.

Other Cash Receipts

Most of the cash receipts of a merchandising business result from the sale of merchandise. Cash may also be received from infrequently occurring transactions, such as the sale of assets other than merchandise or a loan from a bank.

When such transactions do occur, a receipt is prepared to indicate the source of the cash received. This receipt is similar to that prepared for cash received from a charge customer. All the information needed for the journal entry is listed on the explanation line.

Cash Discounts

To encourage charge customers to pay promptly, some merchandising businesses offer a cash discount. A **cash discount**, or **sales discount**, is the amount a customer can deduct from the amount owed for purchased merchandise if payment is made within a certain time. A cash discount is an advantage to both the buyer and seller. Therefore, the buyer gets merchandise at a reduced cost, and the seller receives cash quickly.

Businesses do not automatically offer cash discounts to all customers. Some businesses may offer cash discounts only to business customers. On Your Mark offers a cash discount to charge customers who buy merchandise in large quantities. Its credit terms are *2/10, n/30*. These terms mean that the customer can deduct 2% of the cost of the merchandise if payment is made within 10 days of the sale date. Otherwise, the full (net) amount is due within 30 days. A cash discount, then, decreases the amount the business actually receives from the sale. Let's look at an example.

Cash Discount Transactions

On December 3 On Your Mark sold $1,500 worth of merchandise on account to South Branch High School Athletics. This transaction was recorded as a credit to **Sales** and a debit to **Accounts Receivable** for $1,500. If South Branch pays within 10 days (by December 13), On Your Mark will receive $1,470, or the original price less the cash discount of $30. These amounts are determined as follows:

1.

Merchandise Sold	×	Discount Rate	=	Discount
$1,500	×	.02	=	$30

2.

Sales Slip Amount	−	Discount Amount	=	Amount Paid Within Discount Period
$1,500	−	$30	=	$1,470

Which accounts are involved in this cash receipt transaction? **Cash in Bank** is debited for $1,470, the amount of cash actually received. **Accounts Receivable** is credited for the full $1,500 because the customer paid for the merchandise and doesn't owe any more on the purchase. The difference between $1,500 and $1,470, $30, is the discount amount.

A separate account is used to record cash discounts taken by customers. The $30 discount is entered in a contra revenue account called **Sales Discounts**, which reduces the revenue earned from sales. The normal balance of the **Sales** account is a credit. The normal balance of the **Sales Discounts** account is a debit.

Sales		Sales Discounts	
Debit − Decrease Side	Credit + Increase Side Normal Balance	Debit + Increase Side Normal Balance	Credit − Decrease Side

A cash discount is recorded only when the customer pays for the merchandise within the time stated. The discount is on the price of the merchandise *before* taxes.

Recording Cash Received from Charge Customers

Let's look at a business transaction involving receipt of cash from a charge customer.

Business Transaction

On December 5 On Your Mark received $212 from Casey Klein to apply to her account, Receipt 301.

ON YOUR MARK	RECEIPT
ATHLETIC WEAR 595 Leslie Street, Dallas, TX 75207	No. 301

Dec. 5   20 --

RECEIVED FROM   Casey Klein $ 212.00

Two hundred twelve and no/100 ———————— DOLLARS

FOR   On account

RECEIVED BY   *Michael Smith*

ANALYSIS   *Identify*

1. The accounts affected are **Cash in Bank, Accounts Receivable** (controlling), **Accounts Receivable—Casey Klein** (subsidiary).

     Classify

2. **Cash in Bank, Accounts Receivable** (controlling), and **Accounts Receivable—Casey Klein** (subsidiary) are asset accounts.

     +/−

3. **Cash in Bank** is increased by $212. **Accounts Receivable** (controlling) and **Accounts Receivable—Casey Klein** (subsidiary) are decreased by $212.

DEBIT-CREDIT RULE

4. Increases to asset accounts are recorded as debits. Debit **Cash in Bank** for $212.

5. Decreases to asset accounts are recorded as credits. Credit **Accounts Receivable** (controlling) for $212. Also credit **Accounts Receivable—Casey Klein** (subsidiary) for $212.

T ACCOUNTS

6.

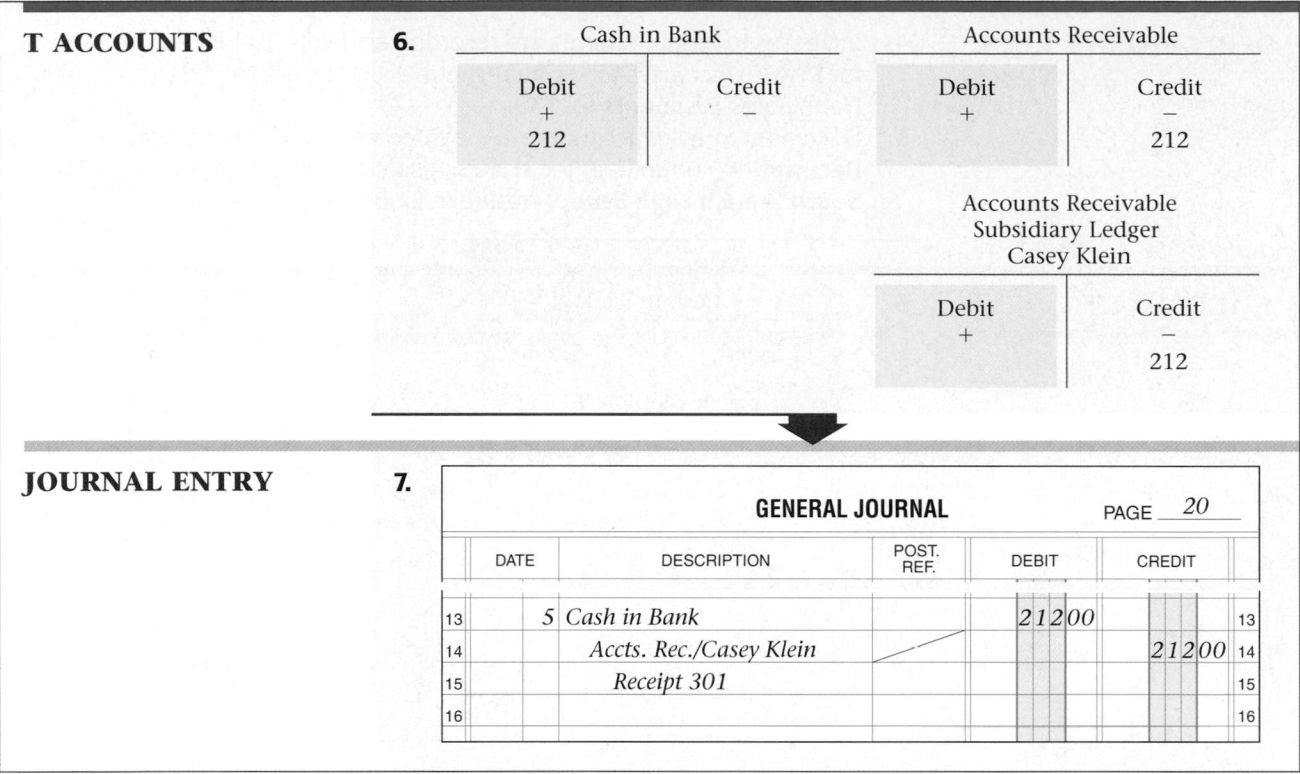

Cash in Bank

Debit +	Credit −
212	

Accounts Receivable

Debit +	Credit −
	212

Accounts Receivable
Subsidiary Ledger
Casey Klein

Debit +	Credit −
	212

JOURNAL ENTRY

7.

GENERAL JOURNAL PAGE __20__

	DATE	DESCRIPTION	POST. REF.	DEBIT	CREDIT	
13	5	Cash in Bank		2 1 2 00		13
14		Accts. Rec./Casey Klein			2 1 2 00	14
15		Receipt 301				15
16						16

Recording Cash Received on Account with a Cash Discount

When a customer pays for a purchase on account within the discount period, the amount paid equals the amount of the invoice less the cash discount. Let's record a cash discount transaction.

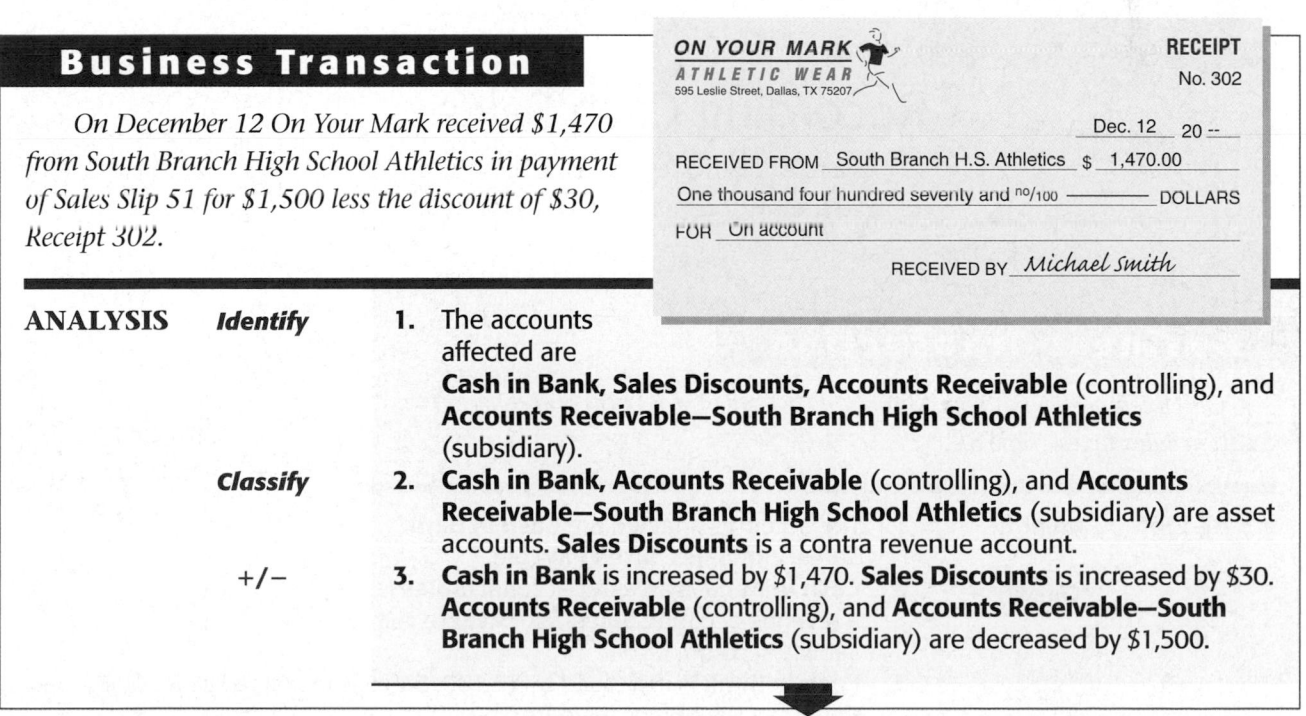

Business Transaction

On December 12 On Your Mark received $1,470 from South Branch High School Athletics in payment of Sales Slip 51 for $1,500 less the discount of $30, Receipt 302.

ON YOUR MARK
ATHLETIC WEAR
595 Leslie Street, Dallas, TX 75207

RECEIPT
No. 302

Dec. 12 20 --

RECEIVED FROM South Branch H.S. Athletics $ 1,470.00

One thousand four hundred seventy and no/100 ———— DOLLARS

FOR On account

RECEIVED BY Michael Smith

ANALYSIS

Identify 1. The accounts affected are **Cash in Bank, Sales Discounts, Accounts Receivable** (controlling), and **Accounts Receivable—South Branch High School Athletics** (subsidiary).

Classify 2. **Cash in Bank, Accounts Receivable** (controlling), and **Accounts Receivable—South Branch High School Athletics** (subsidiary) are asset accounts. **Sales Discounts** is a contra revenue account.

+/− 3. **Cash in Bank** is increased by $1,470. **Sales Discounts** is increased by $30. **Accounts Receivable** (controlling), and **Accounts Receivable—South Branch High School Athletics** (subsidiary) are decreased by $1,500.

| DEBIT-CREDIT RULE | 4. | Increases to asset accounts are recorded as debits. Debit **Cash in Bank** for $1,470. Increases to contra revenue accounts are recorded as debits. Debit **Sales Discounts** for $30. |
| | 5. | Decreases to asset accounts are recorded as credits. Credit **Accounts Receivable** (controlling) for $1,500. Also credit **Accounts Receivable—South Branch High School Athletics** (subsidiary) for $1,500. |

T ACCOUNTS

6.

Cash in Bank	
Debit +	Credit −
1,470	

Accounts Receivable	
Debit +	Credit −
	1,500

Sales Discounts	
Debit +	Credit −
30	

Accounts Receivable Subsidiary Ledger South Branch High School Athletics	
Debit +	Credit −
	1,500

JOURNAL ENTRY

7.

		GENERAL JOURNAL			PAGE 20	
	DATE	DESCRIPTION	POST. REF.	DEBIT	CREDIT	
16	12	Cash in Bank		1 470 00		16
17		Sales Discounts		30 00		17
18		Accts. Rec./South Br. H.S.			1 500 00	18
19		Receipt 302				19
20						20

Recording Cash Sales

As a rule, businesses journalize cash sales and make cash deposits daily. Let's analyze transactions relating to sale of merchandise for cash on December 15.

Business Transaction

On December 15 On Your Mark had cash sales of $3,000 and collected $180 in sales taxes, Tape 55.

```
Dec. 15
Tape 55

                3000.00  CA
                 180.00  ST
```

ANALYSIS	Identify	1.	The accounts affected are **Cash in Bank, Sales,** and **Sales Taxes Payable.**
	Classify	2.	**Cash in Bank** is an asset account. **Sales** is a revenue account. **Sales Tax Payable** is a liability account.
	+/−	3.	**Cash in Bank** is increased by $3,180. **Sales** is increased by $3,000. **Sales Tax Payable** is increased by $180.

| DEBIT-CREDIT RULE | **4.** | Increases in asset accounts are recorded as debits. Debit **Cash in Bank** for $3,180. |
| | **5.** | Increases in revenue and liability accounts are recorded as credits. Credit **Sales** for $3,000, and **Sales Tax Payable** for $180. |

T ACCOUNTS   **6.**

Cash in Bank			Sales	
Debit + 3,180	Credit −		Debit −	Credit + 3,000

Sales Tax Payable	
Debit −	Credit + 180

JOURNAL ENTRY   **7.**

GENERAL JOURNAL   PAGE ___20___

	DATE		DESCRIPTION	POST. REF.	DEBIT	CREDIT	
20	20	15	Cash in Bank		3 180 00		20
21			Sales			3 000 00	21
22			Sales Tax Payable			180 00	22
23			Tape 55				23
24							24

Recording Bankcard Sales

Now let's record sales paid by bankcard. Notice how this is similar to recording cash sales.

Business Transaction

On Your Mark had bankcard sales of $700 and collected $42 in related sales taxes on December 15, Tape 55.

Dec. 15
Tape 55

700.00 BCS
42.00 ST

ANALYSIS	*Identify*	**1.**	The accounts affected are **Cash in Bank, Sales,** and **Sales Tax Payable.**
	Classify	**2.**	**Cash in Bank** is an asset account. **Sales** is a revenue account. **Sales Tax Payable** is a liability account.
	+/−	**3.**	**Cash in Bank** is increased by $742. **Sales** is increased by $700. **Sales Tax Payable** is increased by $42.

| DEBIT-CREDIT RULE | **4.** | Increases in asset accounts are recorded as debits. Debit **Cash in Bank** for $742. |
| | **5.** | Increases in revenue and liability accounts are recorded as credits. Credit **Sales** for $700 and **Sales Tax Payable** for $42. |

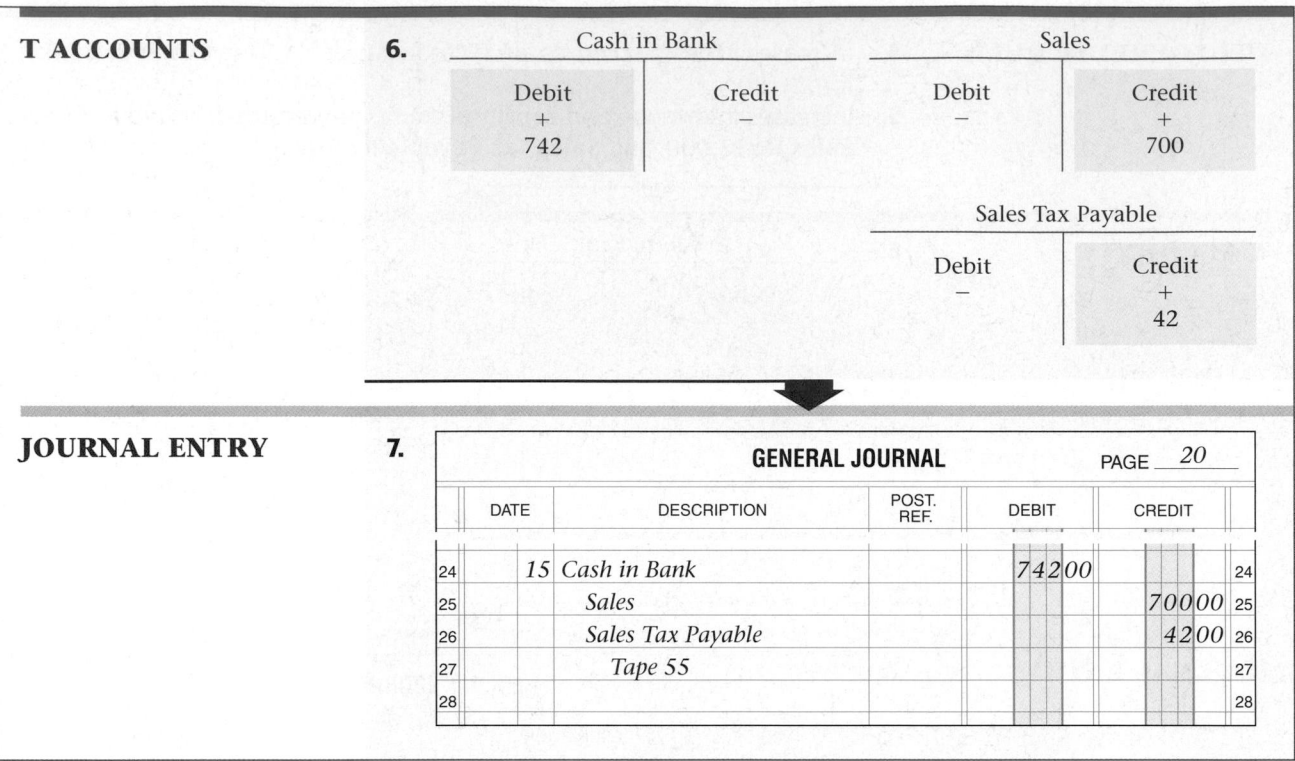

T ACCOUNTS

6.

Cash in Bank			Sales	
Debit + 742	Credit −		Debit −	Credit + 700

	Sales Tax Payable	
	Debit −	Credit + 42

JOURNAL ENTRY

7.

GENERAL JOURNAL   PAGE __20__

	DATE	DESCRIPTION	POST. REF.	DEBIT	CREDIT	
24	15	Cash in Bank		742 00		24
25		Sales			700 00	25
26		Sales Tax Payable			42 00	26
27		Tape 55				27
28						28

Recording Other Cash Receipts

Occasionally a business receives cash from a transaction that does not involve the sale of merchandise. The **Sales** account is not used because the item is not a *merchandise* item.

ON YOUR MARK
ATHLETIC WEAR
595 Leslie Street, Dallas, TX 75207

RECEIPT
No. 303

Dec. 16   20 --

RECEIVED FROM   Mandy Harris $ 30.00

Thirty and ⁿᵒ/100 ———————————— DOLLARS

FOR   calculator

RECEIVED BY   *Michael Smith*

Business Transaction

On December 16 On Your Mark received $30 from Mandy Harris, an office employee. She purchased a calculator that the business was no longer using, Receipt 303.

JOURNAL ENTRY

GENERAL JOURNAL   PAGE __20__

	DATE	DESCRIPTION	POST. REF.	DEBIT	CREDIT	
28	16	Cash in Bank		30 00		28
29		Office Equipment			30 00	29
30		Receipt 303				30
31						31

Figure 14–9 presents all the transactions discussed and illustrated in this chapter.

Figure 14–9 Sales and Cash Receipt Transactions

GENERAL JOURNAL   PAGE ___20___

	DATE		DESCRIPTION	POST. REF.	DEBIT	CREDIT	
1	20--						1
2	Dec.	1	Accts. Rec./Casey Klein		2 1 2 00		2
3			Sales			2 0 0 00	3
4			Sales Tax Payable			1 2 00	4
5			Sales Slip 50				5
6		3	Accts. Rec./South Branch H.S.		1 5 0 0 00		6
7			Sales			1 5 0 0 00	7
8			Sales Slip 51				8
9		4	Sales Returns and Allowances		1 5 0 00		9
10			Sales Tax Payable		9 00		10
11			Accts. Rec./Gabriel Ramos			1 5 9 00	11
12			Credit Memorandum 124				12
13		5	Cash in Bank		2 1 2 00		13
14			Accts. Rec./Casey Klein			2 1 2 00	14
15			Receipt 301				15
16		12	Cash in Bank		1 4 7 0 00		16
17			Sales Discounts		3 0 00		17
18			Accts. Rec./South Branch H.S.			1 5 0 0 00	18
19			Receipt 302				19
20		15	Cash in Bank		3 1 8 0 00		20
21			Sales			3 0 0 0 00	21
22			Sales Tax Payable			1 8 0 00	22
23			Tape 55				23
24		15	Cash in Bank		7 4 2 00		24
25			Sales			7 0 0 00	25
26			Sales Tax Payable			4 2 00	20
27			Tape 55				27
28		16	Cash in Bank		3 0 00		28
29			Office Equipment			3 0 00	29
30			Receipt 303				30
31							31

Annual Report

Now that you have studied this section, complete the following questions and problems.

Thinking Critically

1. Explain the process behind a bankcard transaction.
2. Explain the benefits of a cash discount.
3. The balance of the controlling account should equal the sum of the related subsidiary ledger accounts. What error might cause the sum of the subsidiary ledger accounts to be less than the controlling account balance? How would you find the error?

Analyzing Accounting

The following graph illustrates the sales of flowers throughout the year for Randy's Florist.

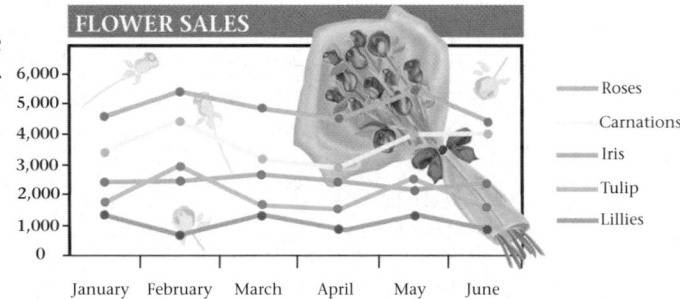

1. The sale of tulips was highest in which month?
2. Which type of flower sells at a steady rate, regardless of the month?
3. How would this graph be helpful in planning purchases for the year? Explain.

Problem 14–3 Analyzing a Source Document

As the accounting clerk for Super Cycle Shop, you record the business transactions. The store's manager hands you the source document shown here.

Instructions Analyze the source document and record the necessary entries on page 17 of the general journal.

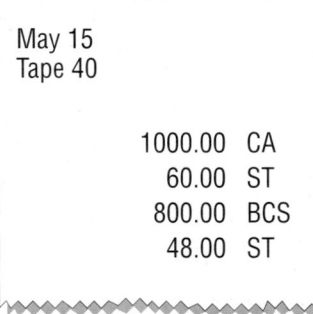

May 15
Tape 40

1000.00	CA
60.00	ST
800.00	BCS
48.00	ST

Problem 14–4 Recording Cash Receipts

Commerce Technology, a computer equipment retailer, had the following selected transactions in March.

Instructions Record each transaction on page 4 of the general journal in your working papers.

Date	Transactions
Mar. 1	Sold one modem for $130 plus $10.40 sales tax, Sales Slip 49.
5	Sold one computer monitor to Kelly Wilson on account for $300 plus $24 sales tax, Sales Slip 55.
17	Bankcard sales totaled $750 plus $60 sales tax, Tape 65.

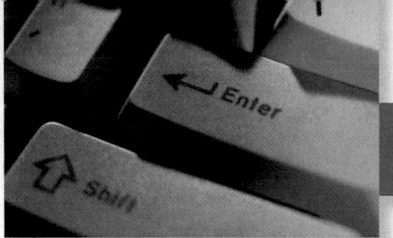

KEY CONCEPTS

1. Retail firms buy merchandise to resell to consumers. Two of the accounts used by merchandising businesses are **Merchandise Inventory** and **Sales.**

2. The **Merchandise Inventory** account is an asset account used to record the value of the merchandise in stock.

Merchandise Inventory	
Debit + Increase Side Normal Balance	Credit − Decrease Side

3. The **Sales** account is a revenue account used to record business income.

4. A sales slip, prepared in multiple copies, lists the details of a sale on account. It is the source document for the journal entry.

Sales	
Debit − Decrease Side	Credit + Increase Side Normal Balance

5. Most states and some cities tax the retail sale of goods. Businesses collect sales tax and record it as a liability in the **Sales Tax Payable** account. Later the business sends a check to the state for the sales tax collected.

Sales Tax Payable	
Debit − Decrease Side	Credit + Increase Side Normal Balance

6. The **Sales Returns and Allowances** account is used to record the credit granted to charge customers for returned or damaged merchandise.

Sales Returns and Allowances	
Debit + Increase Side Normal Balance	Credit − Decrease Side

7. The cash received by a business is recorded on receipts and cash register tapes. These receipts and tapes are the source documents for the journal entries.

8. Bankcard sales are recorded as cash sales.

9. Some merchandising businesses grant cash discounts to customers who pay for their credit purchases within a certain time period. The time period and amount of the discount are indicated in the credit terms of the purchases.

10. The **Sales Discounts** account is used to record the amount of any cash discount taken by charge customers.

Sales Discounts	
Debit + Increase Side Normal Balance	Credit − Decrease Side

11. **Accounts Receivable** is a controlling account. Its balance must equal the sum of the customer account balances in the accounts receivable subsidiary ledger.

USING KEY TERMS

You have just hired Geoffrey Hillman to be the accounting clerk for the Hats Off Corporation, a merchandiser of hats, caps, and scarves. Geoffrey worked as a payroll clerk, but not in sales or cash receipts jobs. To help him, you've offered to write on note cards the definitions of the following terms. Provide an example of each term when possible.

accounts receivable subsidiary ledger	inventory
bankcard	merchandise
cash discount	retailer
cash receipt	sale on account
cash sale	**Sales**
charge customer	sales allowance
contra account	sales discount
controlling account	sales return
credit cards	sales slip
credit memorandum	sales tax
credit terms	subsidiary ledger
	wholesaler

Understanding Accounting Concepts and Procedures

Instructions:

On a separate sheet of paper, answer the following questions:

1. Contrast the characteristics of a service and a merchandising business.
2. What is the difference between a wholesaler and a retailer?
3. Classify the following accounts: Merchandise Inventory, Sales, Sales Returns and Allowances, Sales Discounts, and Sales Tax Payable.
4. How does a merchandising business act as a collection agency for the state government?
5. What four accounts are affected by a sale of merchandise on account?
6. Why is a diagonal line drawn in the posting reference column when journalizing a sale of merchandise on account?
7. What are the source documents for recording cash sales, bankcard sales, and cash received from a charge customer?
8. Why are bankcard sales considered a form of cash sales?
9. Why would a business offer a cash discount to its customers?
10. Which accounts are affected when a business receives a payment from a charge customer who has taken a cash discount?

Case Study...

Merchandising Business: Videotapes

Felix Andersen is a film buff. His business, Video Source, specializes in foreign titles and classic film collections. Video Source uses a manual accounting system. Sales are recorded from cash register tapes at the end of the day. Felix is thinking of updating to an electronic cash register that records sales information directly into a computerized accounting system.

Thinking Critically:

1. What are the benefits of converting to an electronic system?
2. Explain how an analysis of sales would help when making decisions about what types of videos to stock.

*inter*NET CONNECTION

Becoming Part of an Organization

Becoming part of an organization helps us feel vibrant and involved. The same holds true in the world of work. Accounting organizations provide a place for professionals to exchange ideas, discuss issues, and gather information about current trends.

Do This:

1. Find out which accounting organizations have Web sites. Make a list of three accounting organizations you find on the Internet.
2. For each organization, where would you write or call for membership information?
3. How would membership in this organization help accounting students?

Conducting an Audit with Alex

You are an accounting intern for Computer Solutions Incorporated. Your supervisor, Lisa Lane, would like you to review the accounts receivable subsidiary ledger. You decide to prepare a schedule of accounts receivable.

Instructions

Use the information below to prepare the schedule on a separate sheet of paper. Does the controlling account balance equal the sum of the subsidiary accounts?

Accounts Receivable Subsidiary Ledger

Amanda Shively	$ 47.90
Kate Right	98.50
St. Andrews Community Center	359.60
West Heights School District	885.45
Randy Sabin	145.50

Accounts Receivable

Controlling Account Balance	$1,536.95

Workplace Skills

Allocating Time, Money, Materials, Space, and Staff

When you operate a business, you are constantly evaluating the effective use of your company's resources. These resources include time, money, materials, space, and staff.

On the Job:

You are the owner of the Retro Café, a late-night spot for young professionals and college students. The café is open from 11:00 A.M. until midnight. You review the month's financial reports and find that the café is showing a net loss for the third month in a row.

Thinking Critically:

1. To help you gather information from your employees, design a staff evaluation form regarding menu, staffing, and hours of operation.
2. In reviewing sales figures, you discover that most of your sales happen after 3:00 P.M. What are the possible staffing implications?

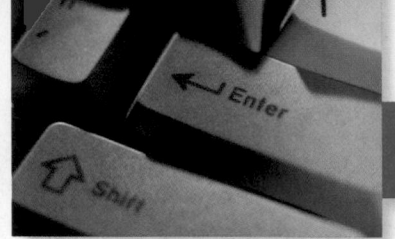

Sales and Cash Receipts

Making the Transition from a Manual to a Computerized System

Task	Perform Accounting Procedures Using Manual Methods	Perform Accounting Procedures Using Automated Methods
Recording Sales Transactions	1. General journal entries are prepared based on a sales slip or an invoice. 2. Journal entries are prepared and posted to the appropriate general ledger accounts. 3. New account balances must be calculated.	1. Invoices can be created with the software and posted to the general ledger accounts at the same time. 2. New account balances are calculated for you.
Recording Cash Receipts Transactions	1. Journal entries are prepared based on deposit slips, receipts, or cash register tapes. 2. Journal entries are prepared and posted to the appropriate general ledger accounts. 3. New account balances must be calculated.	1. Deposits are recorded and posted to the general ledger using the cash receipts task item. 2. General ledger accounts are updated automatically.

Entering Sales and Cash Receipts

Peachtree Question	Description
How do I record a cash sale or a miscellaneous receipt?	1. From the *Tasks* menu, select **Receipts.** 2. Enter a reference number (generally the customer's check number). 3. In the Cash Account list, enter the bank account in which the receipt is deposited. 4. Select the *Apply to Revenues* tab. Then, enter the line items on the receipt. (For a miscellaneous receipt, select the appropriate general ledger account. The Sales account is the default account.) 5. Click *Save.*
How do I record a sale on account?	1. From the *Tasks* menu, select **Sales/Invoicing.** 2. Enter customer ID and invoice number. 3. Click on the *Apply to Sales* tab. 4. Enter details of the invoice and amount. 5. Click *Save.*
How do I record a cash receipt from a customer on account?	1. From the *Tasks* menu, select **Receipts.** 2. Enter a reference number (generally the customer's check number). 3. In the Cash Account list, enter the bank account in which the receipt is to be deposited. 4. Select the *Apply to Invoices* tab. Then, select the invoices being paid. 5. Click *Save.*

For detailed instructions: See the **Peachtree User Guide** in your Glencoe Working Papers.

APPLICATION OPTIONS

Problem 14–5 Recording Sales and Cash Receipts

Sunset Surfwear, a California-based merchandising store, had the following sales and cash receipt transactions for January. The partial chart of accounts for Sunset Surfwear follows.

General Ledger

101	Cash in Bank	401	Sales
115	Accounts Receivable	405	Sales Discounts
215	Sales Tax Payable	410	Sales Returns and Allowances

Accounts Receivable Subsidiary Ledger

ADA	Adams, Martha	MOU	Moulder, Nate
HAM	Hamilton, Alex	WES	Westwood High School Athletics
JUN1	Jun, Helen		

Instructions Record the following transactions on page 20 of the general journal.

Date	Transactions
Jan. 1	Sold $300 in merchandise plus a sales tax of $18 on account to Martha Adams, Sales Slip 777.
5	Sold $1,500 in merchandise on account to Westwood High School Athletics, Sales Slip 778.
7	Received $400 from Alex Hamilton on account, Receipt 345.
10	Issued Credit Memorandum 102 to Martha Adams for $318 covering $300 in returned merchandise plus $18 sales tax.
15	Recorded cash sales of $800 plus $48 in sales tax, Tape 39.
15	Recorded bankcard sales of $900 plus $54 in sales tax, Tape 39.
20	Received $1,500 from Westwood High School Athletics in payment of Sales Slip 778, Receipt 346.
25	Sold $1,200 in merchandise plus sales tax of $72 on account to Helen Jun, Sales Slip 779.
28	Granted a $106 sales allowance to Helen Jun, which includes $100 for damaged merchandise she kept and sales tax of $6, Credit Memorandum 103.
30	Received $500 from a charge customer, Nate Moulder, in payment of his $500 account, Receipt 347.

Analyze: What is the sum of all the debits to the **Sales Returns and Allowances** account during January?

Complete chapter problems one of three ways:

1 **Manual** Glencoe Working Papers

or

2 **Peachtree Complete Accounting** Software

or

3 **QuickBooks** Templates (Problems 14–5, 14–7)

Peachtree®

SMART GUIDE

Step–by–Step Instructions: Problem 14–5

1. Start Peachtree and open Sunset Surfwear (Prob. 14-5).
2. Rename the problem set by using your initials.
3. Enter all sales on account transactions using the **Sales/Invoicing** option in the *Tasks* menu.
4. Process all credit memorandums using the **Sales/Invoicing** and **Receipts** options.
5. Record all cash receipts transactions using the Receipts option.
6. Print a Sales Journal report and a Cash Receipts Journal report.
7. Proof your work and make any needed corrections.
8. Print a GL report to answer the Analyze question.
9. End the session.

Peachtree®

SMART GUIDE

Step–by–Step Instructions: Problem 14–6

1. Start Peachtree and open InBeat CD Shop (Prob. 14–6).
2. Rename the problem set by using your initials.
3. Choose **General Ledger** from the **Reports** menu.
4. Print a General Ledger report.
5. Select the Accounts Receivable report area.
6. From the list on the right, select and print the Customer Ledgers report.
7. Compare each GL entry in your working papers to the GL report and Customer Ledgers report.
8. Use the GL report to answer the Analyze question.
9. End the session.

Problem 14–6 Posting Sales and Cash Receipts

The January transactions for InBeat CD Shop are recorded on page 15 of the general journal.

Instructions Post the transactions to the general ledger and subsidiary ledger in your working papers.

GENERAL JOURNAL PAGE __15__

	DATE		DESCRIPTION	POST. REF.	DEBIT	CREDIT	
1	20--						1
2	Jan.	1	Cash in Bank		3 8 8 00		2
3			Sales Discounts		1 2 00		3
4			Accts. Rec./Alicia Alvarez			4 0 0 00	4
5			Receipt 92				5
6		4	Accts. Rec./Dena Greenburg		7 3 5 00		6
7			Sales			7 0 0 00	7
8			Sales Tax Payable			3 5 00	8
9			Sales Slip 60				9
10		6	Cash in Bank		2 1 0 0 00		10
11			Sales			2 0 0 0 00	11
12			Sales Tax Payable			1 0 0 00	12
13			Tape 32				13
14		6	Cash in Bank		3 1 5 0 00		14
15			Sales			3 0 0 0 00	15
16			Sales Tax Payable			1 5 0 00	16
17			Tape 32				17
18		8	Sales Returns and Allowances		7 0 0 00		18
19			Sales Tax Payable		3 5 00		19
20			Accts. Rec./ Dena Greenburg			7 3 5 00	20
21			Credit Memorandum 15				21
22		10	Cash in Bank		1 3 5 8 00		22
23			Sales Discounts		4 2 00		23
24			Accts. Rec./Joe Montoya			1 4 0 0 00	24
25			Receipt 93				25
26		15	Accts. Rec./Alicia Alvarez		4 2 0 00		26
27			Sales			4 0 0 00	27
28			Sales Tax Payable			2 0 00	28
29			Sales Slip 61				29
30		27	Cash in Bank		1 3 6 5 00		30
31			Accts. Rec./Chelsea Wright			1 3 6 5 00	31
32			Receipt 94				32
33							33

Analyze: What is the ending balance in the **Sales Discounts** account for January?

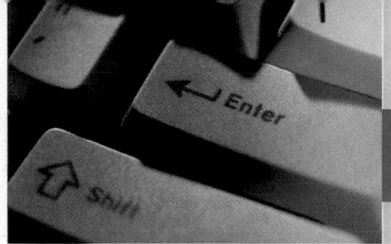

Problem 14–7 Recording Sales and Cash Receipts

Shutterbug Cameras had the following transactions during January. The partial chart of accounts for Shutterbug is shown below.

General Ledger

101 Cash in Bank	401 Sales
115 Accounts Receivable	405 Sales Discounts
130 Supplies	410 Sales Returns and Allowances
215 Sales Tax Payable	

Accounts Receivable Subsidiary Ledger

DIA Diaz, Arturo		**NAK** Nakata, Yoko	
FAS FastForward Productions		**SUL** Sullivan, Heather	

Instructions Record the transactions on page 5 of the general journal in your working papers.

Date	Transactions
Jan. 1	Sold merchandise on account to Yoko Nakata for $250 plus a 4% sales tax of $10, Sales Slip 90.
3	Received $50 in cash from the sale of supplies to Betty's Boutique, Receipt 201.
7	Sold $300 in merchandise plus a sales tax of $12 to Arturo Diaz on account, Sales Slip 91.
12	Sold on account $1,500 in merchandise plus a sales tax of $60 to FastForward Productions, credit terms 2/10, n/30, Sales Slip 92.
13	Issued Credit Memorandum 20 for $312 to Arturo Diaz, which includes $300 in merchandise returned by him plus sales tax of $12.
14	Received a check for $260 from Yoko Nakata in full payment of his account, Receipt 202.
15	Cash sales amounted to $2,500 plus $100 in sales tax, Tape 75.
15	Bankcard sales were $3,000 plus $120 in sales tax, Tape 75.
21	Received a check for $1,530 from FastForward Productions in payment of their $1,560 account balance less a cash discount of $30, Receipt 203.
28	Granted Heather Sullivan a $104 allowance for damaged merchandise of $100 plus a 4% sales tax of $4, Credit Memorandum 21.

Analyze: What is the net amount of sales tax for the month based on these transactions?

Peachtree®

SMART GUIDE

Step–by–Step Instructions:
Problem 14–7

1. Start Peachtree and open Shutterbug Cameras (Prob. 14–7).
2. Rename the problem set by using your initials.
3. Enter all sales on account transactions using the **Sales/Invoicing** option.
4. Process all credit memorandums using the **Sales/Invoicing** and **Receipts** options.
5. Record all cash receipts using the **Receipts** option.
6. Print a Sales Journal and a Cash Receipts Journal report.
7. Proof your work. Make any needed corrections.
8. Print a GL report to answer the Analyze question.
9. End the session.

Peachtree®

SMART GUIDE

Step–by–Step Instructions:
Problem 14–8

1. Start Peachtree and open River's Edge (Prob. 14–8).
2. Rename the problem set by using your initials.
3. Enter all sales on account transactions using the **Sales/Invoicing** option.
4. Process all credit memorandums using the **Sales/Invoicing** and **Receipts** options.
5. Record all cash receipts using the **Receipts** option.
6. Print a Sales Journal and Cash Receipts journal report.
7. Proof your work. Make any needed corrections.
8. Print a GL report to answer the Analyze question.
9. End the session.

Problem 14–8 Recording Sales and Cash Receipt Transactions

River's Edge Canoe & Kayak is a merchandising business in Wyoming. The partial chart of accounts follows:

General Ledger

101	Cash in Bank	401	Sales
115	Accounts Receivable	405	Sales Discounts
135	Supplies	410	Sales Returns and Allowances
215	Sales Tax Payable		

Accounts Receivable Subsidiary Ledger

ADV	Adventure River Tours	WILD	Wildwood Resorts
DRA	Drake, Paul	WU	Wu, Kim

Instructions Record January transactions on page 10 of the general journal.

Date	Transactions
Jan. 1	Sold $2,000 in merchandise on account to Wildwood Resorts, a tax-exempt agency, credit terms 3/15, n/30, Sales Slip 103.
5	Granted Wildwood Resorts a $150 credit allowance for defective merchandise, Credit Memorandum 33.
8	Received $485 from Adventure River Tours for $500 in merchandise sold to them on Dec. 27 less a 3% cash discount of $15, Receipt 96.
10	Sold $500 in merchandise plus a 5% sales tax of $25 to Paul Drake on account, credit terms 3/15, n/30, Sales Slip 104.
12	Received a check for $1,794.50 from Wildwood Resorts on account ($1,850 less a 3% cash discount of $55.50), Receipt 97.
15	Cash sales were $3,500 plus sales tax of $175, Tape 22.
15	Bankcard sales amounted to $4,000 plus sales tax of $200, Tape 22.
20	Sold to Adventure River Tours $75 in supplies. Cash received recorded on Receipt 98.
22	Granted Kim Wu $63 credit for $60 in damaged merchandise sold to her last month and 5% sales tax of $3 on the merchandise, Credit Memorandum 34.
25	Paul Drake sent a check for $510 in payment of his account. The account balance was $525 ($500 in merchandise and $25 sales tax). He took a 3% cash discount of $15 on the merchandise, Receipt 99.

Analyze: If customers had not taken any cash discounts, how much more cash would have been collected in the month of January?

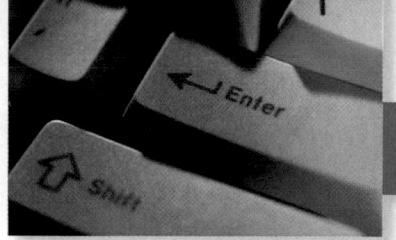

CHALLENGE PROBLEM

Problem 14–9 Recording and Posting Sales and Cash Receipts

SOURCE DOCUMENT PROBLEM

Peachtree®

SMART GUIDE

Step–by–Step Instructions: Problem 14–9

1. Start Peachtree and open Buzz Newsstand (Prob. 14–9).
2. Rename the problem set by using your initials.
3. Enter all sales on account transactions.
4. Process all credit memorandums.
5. Record all cash receipts.
6. Print the following reports: Sales Journal, Cash Receipts Journal, Customer Ledgers, and General Ledger.
7. Proof your work. Make any needed corrections.
8. Use the GL report to answer the Analyze question.
9. End the session.

Buzz Newsstand had the following transactions for the month of January.

General Ledger

101 Cash in Bank	401 Sales
115 Accounts Receivable	405 Sales Discounts
135 Supplies	410 Sales Returns and Allowances
215 Sales Tax Payable	

Accounts Receivable Subsidiary Ledger

ADK Adkins, Lee	NAD Nadal, Saba
JAV Java Shops Inc.	ROL Rolling Hills Pharmacies

Instructions

1. Record the transactions on page 9 of the general journal.

2. Post each transaction to the appropriate general ledger and accounts receivable subsidiary ledger accounts. A partial general ledger and accounts receivable subsidiary ledger are included in the working papers. The current account balances are recorded in the accounts.

Date	Transactions
Jan. 1	Lee Adkins returned $200 in damaged merchandise purchased on account last month, issued Credit Memorandum 10 for $212 ($200 in merchandise plus 6% sales tax of $12).
3	Received a check from Rolling Hills Pharmacies for $2,256.62 in payment of their account of $2,300 less a 2% cash discount of $43.38, Receipt 75.
7	Gave credit to Saba Nadal for the return of $300 in merchandise sold to him on account, plus sales tax of $18. Issued Credit Memorandum 11 for $318.
10	Java Shops Inc. sent a check for $1471.70 in payment of their account of $1,500 less a 2% cash discount of $28.30, Receipt 76.
15	Cash sales were $2,500 plus $150 in sales tax, Tape 25.
15	Bankcard sales were $2,000 plus $120 in sales tax, Tape 25.
20	Janson Lee, a neighboring store, needed supplies urgently. Sold them $40 in supplies and received cash from the sale, Receipt 77.
25	Received a check for $636 from Lee Adkins on account, Receipt 78.
31	Sold $3,000 in merchandise plus sales tax of $180 on account to Rolling Hills Pharmacies, Sales Slip 114.

SOURCE DOCUMENT PROBLEM

Problem 14–9

Use the source documents in your working papers to record the transactions in this problem.

Analyze: What is the balance of the **Sales** account at January 31?

CHAPTER 15

Accounting for Purchases and Cash Payments

Learning Objectives

When you have completed this chapter, you will be able to:

▶ Explain the procedures for processing a purchase on account.

▶ Describe the accounts used in the purchasing process.

▶ Analyze transactions relating to the purchase of merchandise.

▶ Record a variety of purchases and cash payment transactions.

▶ Post to the accounts payable subsidiary ledger.

▶ Define the accounting terms introduced in this chapter.

Exploring the Real World of Business

ANALYZING PURCHASES

Levi's® jeans are one of the oldest and most successful products ever made. **Levi Strauss** is the largest manufacturer of branded clothing in the world, with recent sales of over $4 billion. That's a lot of jeans!

Born in Bavaria, Levi Strauss emigrated to New York in 1847. Several years later, he moved to San Francisco and started a small dry-goods store. In 1873, Strauss and a tailor, Jacob Davis, received a patent for riveted men's pants. Originally called waist overalls, the pants were made of denim purchased from the Amoskeag Mill in New Hampshire and were fastened with copper rivets. Around 1890, the company started numbering their styles and the 501® style came into existence. These original pants were made only for men. It was not until 1981 that 501® jeans for women were introduced.

Today, **Levi Strauss** operates not only as a wholesaler, but also as a retailer of its products from its own retail stores.

What do you think?

Levi Strauss buys denim for making its jeans from a fabric manufacturer. What are at least three other items the company might purchase for use in making its jeans?

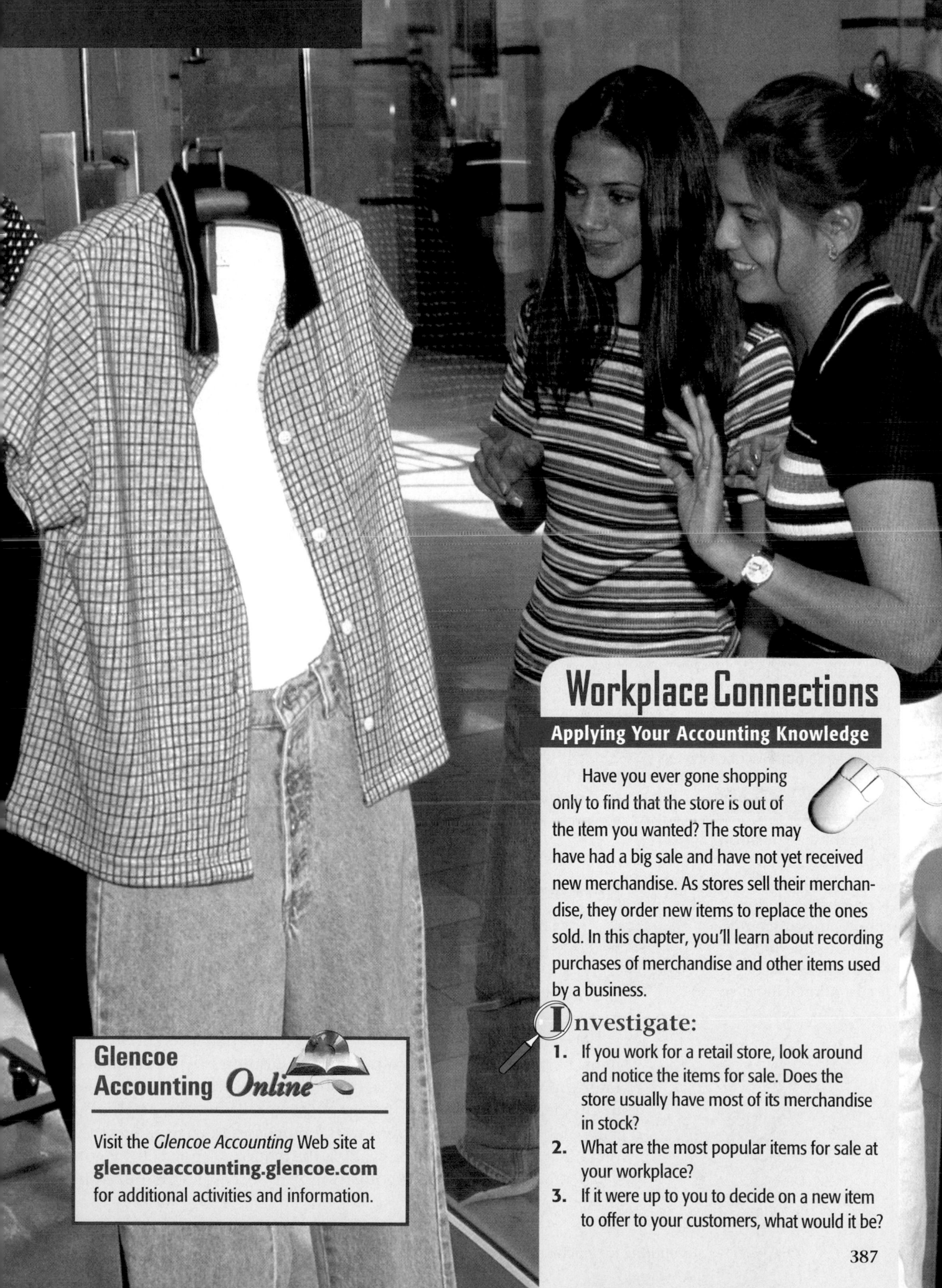

Workplace Connections

Applying Your Accounting Knowledge

Have you ever gone shopping only to find that the store is out of the item you wanted? The store may have had a big sale and have not yet received new merchandise. As stores sell their merchandise, they order new items to replace the ones sold. In this chapter, you'll learn about recording purchases of merchandise and other items used by a business.

Investigate:

1. If you work for a retail store, look around and notice the items for sale. Does the store usually have most of its merchandise in stock?
2. What are the most popular items for sale at your workplace?
3. If it were up to you to decide on a new item to offer to your customers, what would it be?

Purchasing Items Needed by a Business

What You'll Learn

- About the paperwork involved in the purchasing process.
- The purpose of the **Purchases Discounts** account.
- The purpose of the **Purchases** account and its rules of debit and credit.

Why It's Important

It is essential that businesses establish controls and procedures for handling the purchase of assets in a systematic manner because the purchasing process results in a large outflow of cash.

KEY TERMS

purchase requisition
purchase order
packing slip
processing stamp
purchases discount
discount period
Purchases account
cost of merchandise

In Chapter 14 you learned that the primary source of income for a merchandising business is from the sale of its merchandise. However, to sell merchandise, a business must first buy the items. The items you find for sale at Wal-Mart— housewares, clothing, sporting goods, jewelry—are all purchased from wholesalers and suppliers. In this chapter you will learn how to analyze transactions relating to the purchase of merchandise.

The Purchasing Process

All businesses, from the corner grocery store to a giant international corporation, are involved in the purchasing process. Retail businesses need shopping bags for customers, sales slips, and cash register tapes. They also need to purchase supplies, equipment, and merchandise.

The purchase of supplies, equipment, and merchandise is divided into four stages:

- requesting needed items
- ordering from a supplier
- verifying items received
- processing the supplier's invoice

Let's take a look at each of these stages.

Requesting Needed Items

In a small business, the owner does all the buying. In a large business, a separate purchasing department buys items for the entire company. When the company needs to buy equipment or supplies, or when the inventory of merchandise on hand is low, a purchase requisition is prepared.

A **purchase requisition** is a written request that a certain item or items be purchased. Usually a purchase requisition is a pre-numbered, multicopy form. The purchase requisition is approved by the manager of the department requesting the purchase. Then, the original of the purchase requisition is sent to the purchasing department or the purchasing agent. The person making the request keeps a copy. **Figure 15–1** shows the purchase requisition form used by On Your Mark Athletic Wear.

ON YOUR MARK ATHLETIC WEAR
PURCHASE REQUISITION

NO. 9421

FOR DEPARTMENT Shoes DATE Nov. 12, 20--

NOTIFY Vic Ventura ON DELIVERY DATE WANTED Dec. 15, 20--

QUANTITY	DESCRIPTION	STOCK NO.
20 Pair	Soft Cushion, White	94682
10 Pair	Soft Cushion, Black	94788
10 Pair	Low Cut, White	94281
10 Pair	Low Cut, Black	94666

ORDER FROM Pro Runner Warehouse APPROVED BY *Jennifer Mack*
SHOE DEPARTMENT MANAGER

Figure 15–1
Purchase Requisition

Ordering from a Supplier

A **purchase order** is a written *offer* to a supplier to buy certain items. Much of the information on the purchase order comes directly from the purchase requisition. Other information may be obtained from the supplier's catalog.

Look at the purchase order prepared by On Your Mark in **Figure 15–2**. The purchase order contains:

1. quantity
2. description
3. unit price
4. total cost
5. supplier's name and address
6. date needed
7. shipping method (optional)

The purchase order is a pre-numbered multi-copy form. The original of the purchase order is sent to the supplier. One copy of the purchase order is sent to the department requesting the items. Another copy is kept in the purchasing department.

Key Points

Forms Used in Purchasing

The purchase requisition stays inside the company (from the department making the request to the purchasing department). The purchase order is sent outside (from the purchasing department to the supplier).

ON YOUR MARK
ATHLETIC WEAR
595 Leslie Street, Dallas, TX 75207

PURCHASE ORDER
No. 9784

To Pro Runner Warehouse 5
22009 Ben White Blvd.
Austin, TX 78705

Date: November 15, 20-- 6
Date Needed: December 15, 20--

Quantity 1	Item 2	Unit Price 3	Total 4
20 pair	Soft Cushion: White, #94682	$ 50.00	$ 1,000.00
10 pair	Soft Cushion: Black #94788	50.00	500.00
10 pair	Low Cut: White, #94281	40.00	400.00
10 pair	Low Cut: Black, #94666	40.00	400.00
	Total		$ 2,300.00

Figure 15–2
Purchase Order

CONNECT TO . . . ART

At television and motion picture awards ceremonies, accounting firms are called on to tally and verify vote results. The accounting firms' involvement with such programs adds authenticity to the vote counting and lends exposure to the accounting industry.

Verifying Items Received

Note that a purchase order is only an *offer* to buy items. Until the items are actually received, the buyer does not know whether or not the supplier has accepted the offer. A supplier may not be able to fill the purchase order because an item is out of stock or has been discontinued. The mailing of a purchase order, therefore, does not require a journal entry. A supplier accepts a purchase order by shipping the items requested and billing the buyer for these items.

When an order is shipped to a buyer, a packing slip is included with the order. A **packing slip** is a form that lists the items included in the shipment. When a shipment is received, it is immediately unpacked and checked against the quantities and items listed on the packing slip. If the contents of the shipment do not agree with those listed on the packing slip, a note about the differences is made on the packing slip. The packing slip is then sent to the accounting department to be checked against both the purchase order and the supplier's bill. A buyer does not have to pay for items that were not received or for damaged or unordered items that were returned to the supplier.

Processing the Supplier's Invoice

When items are shipped to a buyer, the supplier prepares a bill called an invoice. An invoice lists the credit terms; the quantity, description, unit price, and total cost of the items shipped; the buyer's purchase order number; and the method of shipment.

The invoice is sent directly to the buyer's accounting department, where it is date stamped to indicate when the invoice was received. The accounting clerk checks each detail (item, quantity, and price) on the invoice against the packing slip and the purchase order. This procedure verifies that the buyer is billed for the quantities and items actually ordered and received and that the prices are correct.

Once verified, the invoice is the source document for a journal entry. Before the invoice is recorded, a **processing stamp** is placed on the invoice to enter the following information: the date the invoice is to be paid, the discount amount, if any, the amount to be paid, and the check number.

The first three lines on the processing stamp are completed at the time the invoice is received. The check number is entered later, when the check is issued.

Look at the invoice in **Figure 15–3.** Notice the date stamp, which indicates when the invoice was received. The processing stamp information is complete except for the check number, which means that the invoice has been verified but not yet paid.

Purchases Discounts

Suppliers frequently offer charge customers a cash discount for early payment. For the buyer, this discount is called a **purchases discount**. A purchases discount and cash discount are calculated in the same way.

■ Key Points

Purchase Order

A purchase order is only an *offer* to buy and does not require a journal entry.

■ Key Points

Recording an Invoice

After a supplier's invoice is verified, a journal entry is made to record the amount owed.

Figure 15–3 Invoice

QTY.	ITEM	UNIT PRICE	TOTAL

PRO RUNNER WAREHOUSE
22009 Ben White Blvd.
Austin, TX 78705

REC'D DEC. 14, 20--

INVOICE NO. 7894

TO   On Your Mark Athletic Wear
     595 Leslie Street
     Dallas, TX 75207

DATE: Dec. 14, 20--
ORDER NO.: 9784
SHIPPED BY: Federal Trucking
TERMS: 2/10, n/30

QTY.	ITEM	UNIT PRICE	TOTAL
20 pair	Soft Cushion: White, #94682	$ 50.00	$ 1,000.00
10 pair	Soft Cushion: Black, #94788	50.00	500.00
10 pair	Low Cut: White, #94281	40.00	400.00
10 pair	Low Cut: Black, #94666	40.00	400.00
		Total	$ 2,300.00

Due Date: _____12/24_____
Discount: _____$ 46.00_____
Net Amount: _$ 2,254.00_
Check No.: _____

For example, On Your Mark purchased $2,300 of merchandise on account from Pro Runner Warehouse. **Figure 15–3** shows the invoice dated December 14. The credit terms are 2/10, n/30. If On Your Mark pays for the merchandise on or before December 24, it may deduct 2% of the value of the merchandise. The 10 days, called the **discount period**, is the time within which an invoice must be paid if the discount is taken. If On Your Mark does not pay for the merchandise within the discount period, it pays the net, or total, amount within 30 days of the invoice date.

On Your Mark can save $46 if the invoice is paid within the 10-day discount period ending December 24. The end of the discount period can be determined by adding 10 days to the date of the invoice (December 14 + 10 days = December 24). The amount to be paid within the discount period is calculated as follows:

1.
Merchandise Purchased	×	Discount Rate	=	Discount
$2,300	×	.02	=	$46

2.
Invoice Amount	−	Discount Amount	=	Amount Paid Within Discount Period
$2,300	−	$46	=	$2,254

The Purchases Account

When a business buys merchandise to sell to customers, the cost of the merchandise is recorded in the **Purchases account**. The **Purchases** account is a temporary account, classified as a **cost of merchandise** account. Cost of merchandise accounts contain the actual cost to the business of the merchandise sold to customers.

Merchandise that is purchased for resale is a cost of doing business. Therefore, the **Purchases** account follows the rules of debit and credit for expense accounts. The **Purchases** account is increased by debits and decreased by credits. The normal balance of the **Purchases** account is a debit.

Purchases

Debit + Increase Side Normal Balance	Credit − Decrease Side

Now that you have studied this section, complete the following questions and problems.

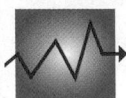

Thinking Critically

1. Explain the steps in the purchasing process from the request for merchandise to the payment of the invoice.
2. When a business purchases merchandise for resale, what accounts are affected?

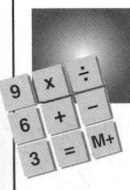

Computing in the Business World

As a new accountant for the South City School District, one of your primary duties involves preparing purchase requisitions. For each item ordered, you compute the extensions (quantity ordered multiplied by the cost per unit). On a separate sheet of paper, calculate the extensions for each of the following items ordered.

Quantity	Item Description	Unit Price
1	Box of copy paper	$34.00/box
5	Reams of art paper	$12/ream
2	Globes	$55/ea.
100	No. 2 pencils	$.12/ea.
4 doz.	Transparency markers	$6.50/doz.

Problem 15–1 Analyzing a Purchase Order

Instructions Analyze the purchase order shown below and answer the following questions in your working papers.

1. What company ordered the merchandise?
2. What company was asked to supply the merchandise?
3. What is the purchase order number?
4. When was the purchase order prepared?
5. When is the merchandise needed?
6. How many gallons of paint were ordered?
7. How many different colors of paint were ordered?
8. What colors were ordered?
9. How much does each gallon of paint cost?
10. What is the total cost of the order?

CASE CONSTRUCTION COMPANY
601 Mt. Lebanon Road, Shaker Heights, OH 44120

PURCHASE ORDER
No. 7894

To: Westmoreland Paint and Supply Co.
1714 Peak Road
Cleveland, OH 44109

Date: November 15, 20--
Date Needed: December 1, 20--

Quantity	Item	Unit Price	Total
4 gal.	Exterior paint, white, #682	$ 20.00	$ 80.00
4 gal.	Exterior paint, gray, #788	20.00	80.00
6 gal.	Exterior paint, brown, #281	20.00	120.00
6 gal.	Exterior paint, beige, #66	20.00	120.00
5 gal.	Exterior paint, peach, #711	20.00	100.00
	Total		$ 500.00

Analyzing and Recording Purchases on Account

In the previous section, you learned about the purchasing process. In this section you will learn how to record transactions involving the purchases of merchandise and other assets on account. You will also learn how to record purchases returns and purchases allowances.

A small retailer may rely on a bookkeeper or part-time accountant to record purchase transactions. A large company, like Kohl's Department Store, can have thousands of suppliers and therefore needs an entire accounts payable department to verify invoices and handle any discrepancies before recording purchases in the accounting records.

Analyzing Purchases of Assets on Account

Regardless of its type, size, or purpose, a retail business needs to buy supplies, equipment, and other assets. Most importantly, it needs to buy merchandise to resell to customers. These items may be bought on a cash basis or on account. Purchases on account are recorded in the accounts payable subsidiary ledger.

The Accounts Payable Subsidiary Ledger

In Chapter 14 you learned that when a business sells to many customers on credit, it is efficient to set up an accounts receivable subsidiary ledger. Likewise, when a business purchases from many suppliers on account, it is efficient to set up an **accounts payable subsidiary ledger** that contains an account for each supplier or creditor. The individual accounts in the accounts payable subsidiary ledger are summarized in the general ledger controlling account, **Accounts Payable.** The balance of the **Accounts Payable** controlling account and the total of all the account balances in the accounts payable subsidiary ledger must agree after posting.

What You'll Learn

- How the accounts payable subsidiary ledger is used.
- How to record the purchase of merchandise on account.
- How to record the purchase of other assets on account.
- How to record purchases returns and allowances transactions.
- How to post to creditor accounts in the accounts payable subsidiary ledger.

Why It's Important

Purchasing is a critical, ongoing process in a merchandising business; therefore, it is essential that you learn how to record the different kinds of purchases transactions.

KEY TERMS

accounts payable
    subsidiary ledger
tickler file
due dates
purchases returns
purchases allowances
debit memorandum

General Ledger	
Accounts Payable—controlling account	$4,500

Accounts Payable Subsidiary Ledger	
Individual Accounts Within Ledger:	
Sandals Etc.	$ 900
Shoe Warehouse	2,100
Shoe Wholesale Inc.	1,000
Store Supply Shop	500
Total	$4,500

Controlling account balance equals total of accounts in subsidiary ledger.

The Accounts Payable Subsidiary Ledger Form

The ledger account form used for the accounts payable subsidiary ledger, shown in **Figure 15–4**, is the same form that is used for the accounts receivable subsidiary ledger.

Figure 15–4 Subsidiary Ledger Account Form

NAME						
ADDRESS						
DATE	DESCRIPTION	POST. REF.	DEBIT	CREDIT	BALANCE

As you can see, the ledger account form has lines at the top for the creditor's name and address. In a manual accounting system, the accounts payable subsidiary ledger is arranged in alphabetical order. There are no account numbers. In a computerized accounting system, each creditor is assigned an account number.

The ledger account form has three amount columns. The Debit column records decreases to the account. Therefore, payments to creditors on account are recorded in the Debit column. The Credit column records increases to the account. Therefore, purchases on account are recorded in the Credit column. The Balance column shows the amount that is owed to the creditor. The normal balance of an Accounts Payable subsidiary account is a credit.

Recording the Purchase of Merchandise on Account

On Your Mark's first purchase transaction in December involves a purchase of merchandise on account.

Business Transaction

On December 14 On Your Mark purchased $2,300 in merchandise on account from Pro Runner Warehouse, Invoice 7894.

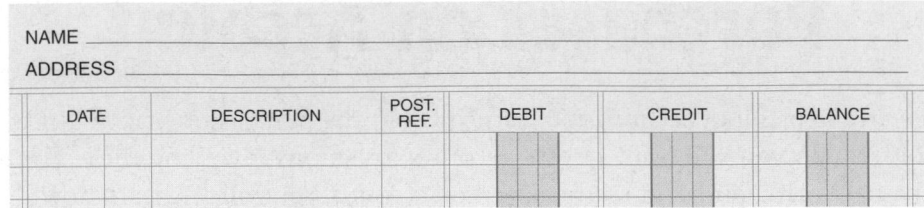

		INVOICE NO. 7894
PRO RUNNER WAREHOUSE 22009 Ben White Blvd. Austin, TX 78705	REC'D DEC. 14, 20--	DATE: Dec. 14, 20-- ORDER NO.: 9784 SHIPPED BY: Federal Trucking TERMS: 2/10, n/30
TO On Your Mark Athletic Wear 595 Leslie Street Dallas, TX 75207		

QTY.	ITEM	UNIT PRICE	TOTAL
20 pair	Soft Cushion: White, #94682	$ 50.00	$ 1,000.00
10 pair	Soft Cushion: Black, #94788	50.00	500.00
10 pair	Low Cut: White, #94281	40.00	400.00
10 pair	Low Cut: Black, #94666	40.00	400.00
	Total		$ 2,300.00

Due Date: 12/24
Discount: $ 46.00
Net Amount: $ 2,254.00
Check No.: _____

ANALYSIS

Identify 1. The accounts affected are **Purchases, Accounts Payable** (controlling), and **Accounts Payable—Pro Runner Warehouse** (subsidiary).

Classify 2. **Purchases** is a cost of merchandise account. **Accounts Payable** (controlling) and **Accounts Payable—Pro Runner Warehouse** (subsidiary) are liability accounts.

+/− 3. **Purchases** is increased by $2,300. This is the cost of the merchandise purchased. **Accounts Payable** (controlling) and **Accounts Payable—Pro Runner Warehouse** (subsidiary) are increased by $2,300.

| DEBIT-CREDIT RULE | **4.** Increases to cost of merchandise accounts are recorded as debits. Debit **Purchases** for $2,300. |
| | **5.** Increases to liability accounts are recorded as credits. Credit **Accounts Payable** (controlling) for $2,300. Also credit **Accounts Payable—Pro Runner Warehouse** (subsidiary) for $2,300. |

T ACCOUNTS 6.

Purchases		Accounts Payable	
Debit + 2,300	Credit −	Debit −	Credit + 2,300

Accounts Payable
Subsidiary Ledger
Pro Runner Warehouse

Debit −	Credit + 2,300

JOURNAL ENTRY 7.

GENERAL JOURNAL PAGE 21

	DATE	DESCRIPTION	POST. REF.	DEBIT	CREDIT	
1	20--					1
2	Dec. 14	Purchases		2 30000		2
3		Accts. Pay./Pro Runner Whs.			2 30000	3
4		Invoice 7894				4
5						5

When this entry is recorded in the journal, a diagonal line is entered in the Posting Reference column to indicate that the credit amount is posted in *two* places.

- *First* post to the **Accounts Payable** controlling account in the general ledger.
- *Then* post to the **Pro Runner Warehouse** account in the accounts payable subsidiary ledger.

After the invoice from Pro Runner Warehouse is journalized, it is placed in a tickler file. A **tickler file** has a folder for each day of the month. Invoices are placed in the folders according to their **due dates**, that is, the dates that they are to be paid. For example, an invoice due on December 24 is placed in the folder marked "24."

Recording Other Purchases on Account

On Your Mark purchases assets other than merchandise, such as supplies, computer equipment, and store equipment. The following example illustrates the purchase of store equipment on account.

> **Key Points**
>
> **Recording and Posting a Purchase on Account**
> The purchase of merchandise on account is recorded in the journal as a debit to **Purchases** and a credit to **Accounts Payable.** The credit is posted to **Accounts Payable** (controlling) and to the accounts payable subsidiary ledger.

On December 15 On Your Mark received Invoice 3417, dated December 13, from Champion Store Supply for store equipment bought on account for $1,200, terms n/30.

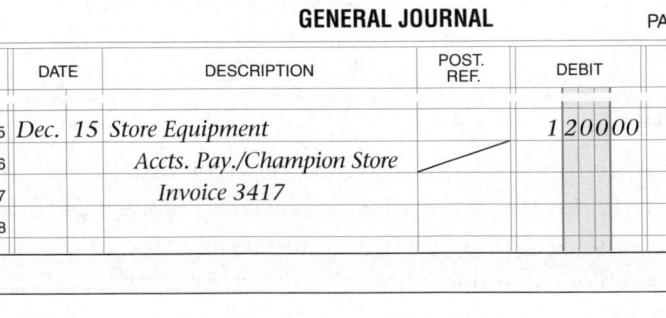

CHAMPION STORE SUPPLY
47249 Randall Parkway
Dallas, TX 75207

REC'D DEC. 15, 20--

INVOICE NO. 3417

DATE:	Dec. 13, 20--	
ORDER NO.:	9795	
SHIPPED BY:	Federal Trucking	
TERMS:	n/30	

TO On Your Mark Athletic Wear
595 Leslie Street
Dallas, TX 75207

QTY.	ITEM	UNIT PRICE	TOTAL
3	Corner Shelf Units	$ 300.00	$ 900.00
1	Shirt Rack	300.00	300.00
	Total		$ 1,200.00

Due Date: _1/12_
Discount: _$0.00_
Net Amount: _$1,200.00_
Check No.: _____

ANALYSIS	*Identify*	**1.** The accounts affected are **Store Equipment, Accounts Payable** (controlling), and **Accounts Payable–Champion Store Supply** (subsidiary).
	Classify	**2.** **Store Equipment** is an asset account. **Accounts Payable** (controlling) and **Accounts Payable–Champion Store Supply** (subsidiary) are liability accounts.
	+/–	**3.** **Store Equipment** is increased by $1,200. **Accounts Payable** (controlling) and **Accounts Payable–Champion Store Supply** (subsidiary) are increased by $1,200.

DEBIT-CREDIT RULE

4. Increases to asset accounts are recorded as debits. Debit **Store Equipment** for $1,200.

5. Increases to liability accounts are recorded as credits. Credit **Accounts Payable** (controlling) for $1,200. Also credit **Accounts Payable–Champion Store Supply** (subsidiary) for $1,200.

T ACCOUNTS

6.

Store Equipment		Accounts Payable	
Debit + 1,200	Credit –	Debit –	Credit + 1,200

Accounts Payable
Subsidiary Ledger
Champion Store Supply

Debit –	Credit + 1,200

JOURNAL ENTRY

7.

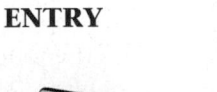

	GENERAL JOURNAL			PAGE _21_
DATE	DESCRIPTION	POST. REF.	DEBIT	CREDIT
Dec. 15	Store Equipment		1 200 00	
	Accts. Pay./Champion Store			1 200 00
	Invoice 3417			

Purchases Returns and Allowances

Occasionally, a business buys merchandise that, upon inspection, is unacceptable. A **purchases return** occurs when a business returns merchandise to the supplier for full credit. A **purchases allowance** occurs when a business keeps less than satisfactory merchandise and pays a reduced price.

A **debit memorandum**, or debit memo, is used to notify suppliers (creditors) of a return or to request an allowance. The "debit" in debit memorandum indicates that the creditor's account will be debited, or decreased.

Figure 15–5 shows a debit memorandum prepared by On Your Mark. As you can see, the debit memorandum is prenumbered and has spaces for the creditor's name and address, and the invoice number. The original is sent to the creditor. The copy is the source document for the journal entry.

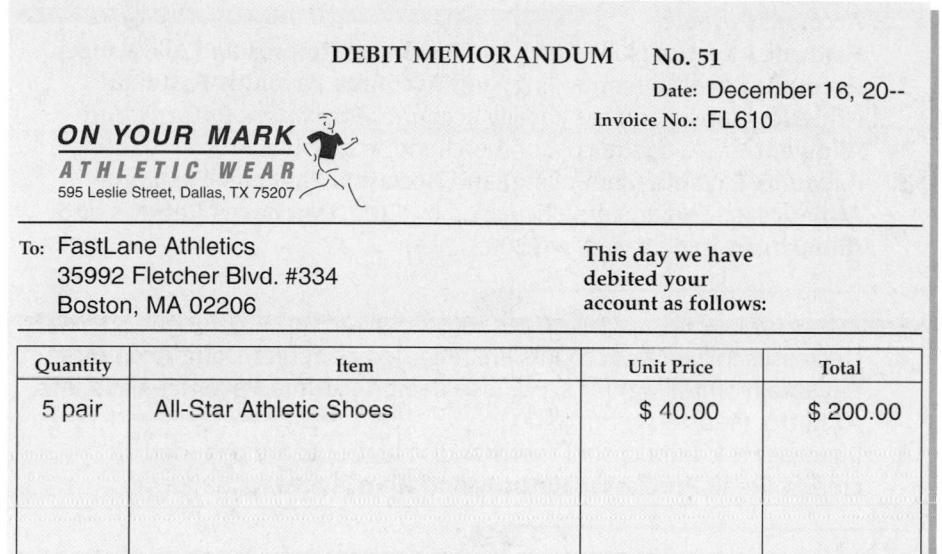

DEBIT MEMORANDUM   No. 51

Date: December 16, 20--
Invoice No.: FL610

ON YOUR MARK
ATHLETIC WEAR
595 Leslie Street, Dallas, TX 75207

To: FastLane Athletics
35992 Fletcher Blvd. #334
Boston, MA 02206

This day we have debited your account as follows:

Quantity	Item	Unit Price	Total
5 pair	All-Star Athletic Shoes	$ 40.00	$ 200.00

Figure 15–5 Debit Memorandum

A debit memorandum always results in a debit (decrease) to the **Accounts Payable** controlling account in the general ledger and to the creditor's account in the subsidiary ledger. The account credited depends upon whether the debit memorandum is for merchandise or for some other asset.

The **Purchases Returns and Allowances** account is used to record the return of merchandise to a supplier or to record an allowance. **Purchases Returns and Allowances** is classified as a *contra cost of merchandise* account. As a contra account, its balance reduces the balance of the related account, **Purchases**. The normal balance of **Purchases** is a debit, so the normal balance of **Purchases Returns and Allowances** is a credit. This relationship is shown in the T accounts below.

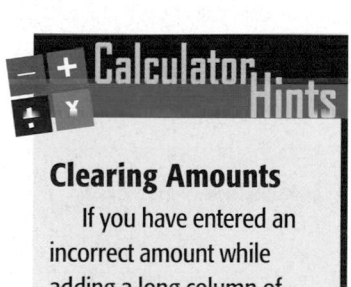

Calculator Hints

Clearing Amounts
If you have entered an incorrect amount while adding a long column of numbers:
- press the CE button *once* to clear that amount;
- previously entered numbers will not be deleted,
- and you can continue entering amounts to find the total.

Purchases		Purchases Returns and Allowances	
Debit + Increase Side Normal Balance	Credit – Decrease Side	Debit – Decrease Side	Credit + Increase Side Normal Balance

Recording a Purchases Returns and Allowances Transaction

Now let's record a purchases return. On Your Mark prepared and sent the debit memorandum shown in **Figure 15–5**.

On December 16 On Your Mark issued Debit Memorandum 51 for the return of $200 in merchandise purchased on account from FastLane Athletics.

DEBIT MEMORANDUM		No. 51	
		Date: December 16, 20--	
ON YOUR MARK		Invoice No.: FL610	
ATHLETIC WEAR			
595 Leslie Street, Dallas, TX 75207			

To: FastLane Athletics
35992 Fletcher Blvd. #334
Boston, MA 02206

This day we have debited your account as follows:

Quantity	Item	Unit Price	Total
5 pair	All-Star Athletic Shoes	$ 40.00	$ 200.00

ANALYSIS *Identify*

1. The accounts affected are **Accounts Payable** (controlling), **Accounts Payable—FastLane Athletics** (subsidiary), and **Purchases Returns and Allowances**.

Classify

2. **Accounts Payable** (controlling) and **Accounts Payable—FastLane Athletics** (subsidiary) are liability accounts. **Purchases Returns and Allowances** is a contra cost of merchandise account.

+/−

3. **Accounts Payable** (controlling) and **Accounts Payable—FastLane Athletics** (subsidiary) are decreased by $200. **Purchases Returns and Allowances** is increased by $200.

DEBIT-CREDIT RULE

4. Decreases to liability accounts are recorded as debits. Debit **Accounts Payable** (controlling) for $200. Also debit **Accounts Payable—FastLane Athletics** (subsidiary) for $200.

5. Increases to contra cost of merchandise accounts are recorded as credits. Credit **Purchases Returns and Allowances** for $200.

T ACCOUNTS

6.

Accounts Payable			Purchases Returns and Allowances	
Debit − 200	Credit +		Debit −	Credit + 200

Accounts Payable
Subsidiary Ledger
FastLane Athletics

Debit − 200	Credit +

JOURNAL ENTRY

7.

	GENERAL JOURNAL		PAGE 21	
DATE	DESCRIPTION	POST. REF.	DEBIT	CREDIT
Dec. 16	Accts. Pay./FastLane Athletics		200 00	
	Purchases Returns and Allow.			200 00
	Debit Memorandum 51			

Posting to the Accounts Payable Subsidiary Ledger

In **Figure 15–6** notice how the transaction is posted. The $200 debit amount is posted to two accounts—the **Accounts Payable** controlling account and the accounts payable subsidiary ledger account, **FastLane Athletics**. After the amount is posted to **Accounts Payable**, the account number *201* is entered to the *left* of the diagonal in the Posting Reference column. After the amount is posted to **FastLane Athletics**, a check mark (✓) is entered to the *right* of the diagonal line.

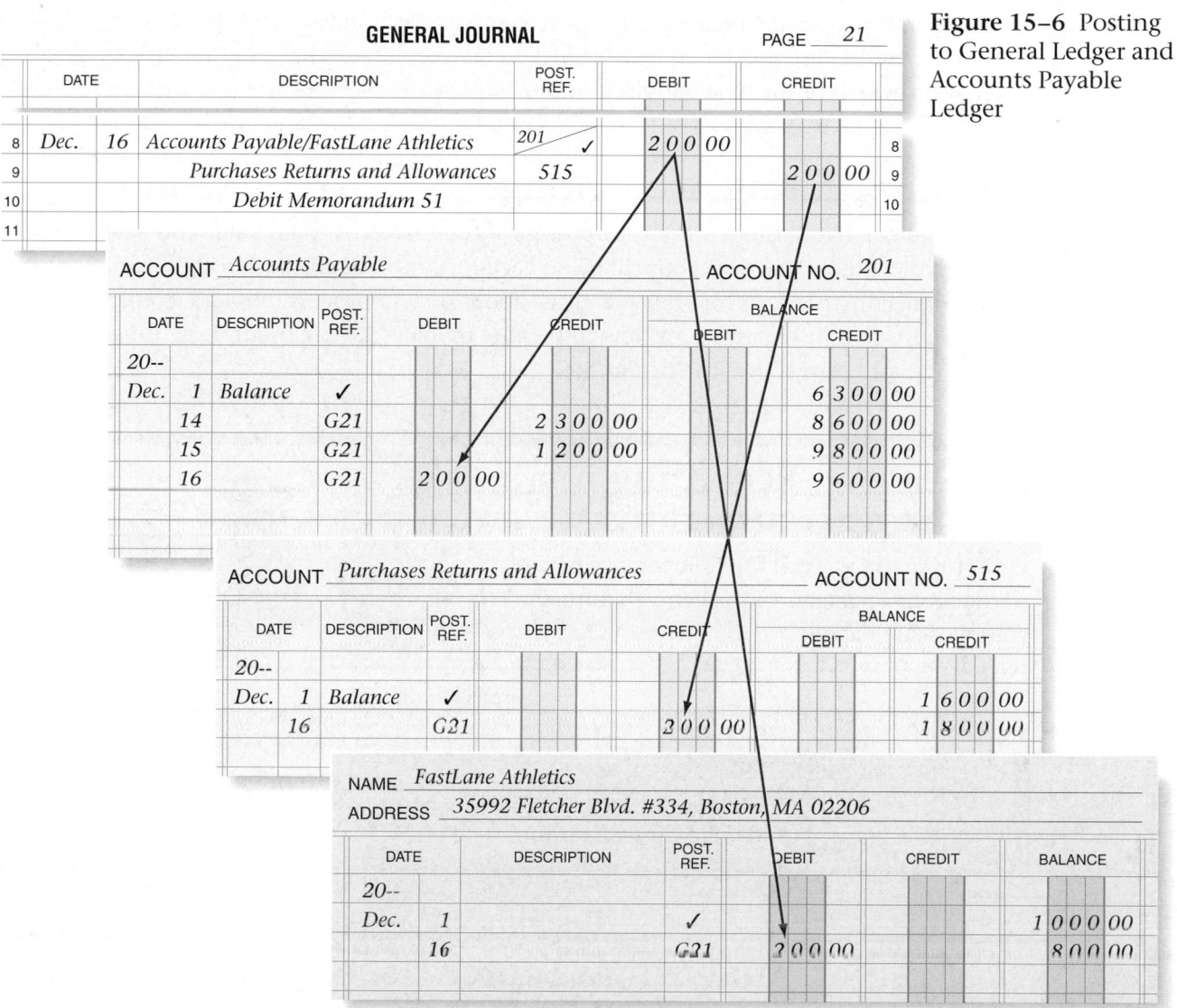

Figure 15–6 Posting to General Ledger and Accounts Payable Ledger

Identifying Corporate Goals

The information in an annual report is directed to a number of different audiences: potential buyers of company stock; existing shareholders; financial analysts and advisors; government regulators, such as the Securities and Exchange Commission (SEC); employees; and creditors.

▶ **Analyze the Report:**

Use the pages labeled "To Our Shareholders" at the back of your textbook. Answer these questions using the section titled "Forging Ahead."

1. List three goals for Office Depot.
2. How does Office Depot plan to communicate the differences between the company and its competitors?

Now that you have studied this section, complete the following questions and problems.

Thinking Critically

1. When and why would a business use an accounts payable subsidiary ledger?
2. When merchandise purchased by a business is unacceptable, what can the business do to recover the cost of the merchandise?

Communicating Accounting

Your job at The Writer's Desk is to process all the invoices to be paid. You keep a tickler file of invoices due. This year you will be on vacation from March 13 through April 2, so you leave detailed instructions for your substitute about how to process invoices. Prepare a memo with step-by-step instructions on how to prepare invoices for payment, how to record journal entries, and how to use the tickler file.

Problem 15–2 Recording Purchases Transactions

Instructions Record the following purchases transactions on page 7 of the general journal in your working papers.

Date	Transactions
Sept. 2	Purchased $900 in merchandise on account from Sunrise Novelty Supply, Invoice SN110.
7	Issued Debit Memorandum 18 to Sunrise Novelty Supply for a $50 allowance granted on damaged merchandise.

Problem 15–3 Analyzing a Source Document

As an accounting intern for Kaleidoscope Comics, you are expected to perform a variety of accounting tasks. Kaleidoscope's accountant gives you the debit memorandum shown at right.

Instructions

1. Analyze the source document. Determine which accounts are to be debited or credited.
2. Record the entry on page 15 of the general journal in your working papers.

DEBIT MEMORANDUM   No. 559

Date: November 12, 20--
Invoice No.: 2260

Kaleidoscope Comics
2110 Brady Lane, Austin, TX 78748

To: Randall's Cafe and Bookstore

This day we have debited your account as follows:

Quantity	Item	Unit Price	Total
1 dz	Best of Dilbert	$ 7.50	$ 7.50
1 dz	Banzai Anime	8.50	8.50
			$ 16.00

MICHELE MOLYNEUX
Credit Analyst
3Com Corporation

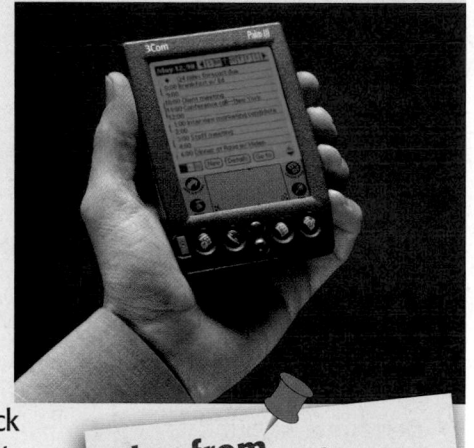

Q: How do you evaluate a company's credit?
A: I get reports from agencies such as Dun & Bradstreet and the SEC. I analyze financial statements. I look at the type of business, the number of years in business, and how the company is run.

For international businesses, I may get an opinion on the country from the state department, or read about it in a periodical such as the *Economist* or *The Wall Street Journal.* I also check with people who specialize in research. Then I make a judgment.

Q: What do you like about your work?
A: I like the variety, the challenges, and the diversity. I work with people all over the world.

Q: What kind of attitude do you need?
A: Curiosity. You need to want to know the big picture. Because most companies do a lot of work overseas, you need an international perspective or you'll lose ground very quickly in this profession.

Q: Do you suggest learning another language?
A: I highly recommend proficiency in an Asian language. A Latin-American language and one of the European languages would also be helpful.

Q: Is a degree necessary?
A: I'm just finishing my bachelor's degree. Without it, I have been handicapped in terms of promotions and getting other jobs. Get your education early. You just can't compete without it.

> **Tips from . . .**
>
> **RHI** Robert Half International Inc.
>
> When focusing on an accounting career, consider learning a second language. Among executives surveyed, 63 percent said Spanish is the most important language to know as business becomes more global.

CAREER FACTS

Nature of the Work: Analyze credit worthiness of corporate customers, evaluate credit risk and set credit line, and decide whether to extend credit.

Training or Education Needed: A bachelor's degree in accounting or finance, and a good working knowledge of one or two other languages.

Aptitudes, Abilities, and Skills: Time management skills, accounting, good judgement, investigative skills, analytical skills, communication skills, and interpersonal skills.

Salary Range: $30,000 to $65,000

Career Path: Get experience in different areas of accounting, purchasing, or customer service, then move into credit analysis.

Thinking Critically: In determining credit worthiness, why would it be important to get information about the country in which the company is located?

Analyzing and Recording Cash Payments

What You'll Learn

- The different kinds of cash payments made by a business.
- The rules of debit and credit for the **Purchases Discounts** account.
- How shipping charges are recorded and whether the buyer or the seller pays for them.

Why It's Important

About half of all business transactions result in the outflow of cash; therefore, it is essential that you understand how businesses record various cash payment transactions.

KEY TERMS

premium
FOB destination
FOB shipping point
bankcard fee

International ACCOUNTING

International Cuisine

When inviting international clients to a meal, consider the customary diets of different religions and cultures.

If cash is the lifeblood of a business, the accounting department is its heart. All cash entering or leaving a business is "pumped" through the accounting department at some time. If it is not, cash losses may occur.

Controls over Cash

Earlier chapters explained ways to guard against losses of cash receipts. For example, businesses should deposit all cash receipts in a bank account. Cash payments must also be properly managed so that losses don't occur. The following are procedures to manage cash payments:

- Authorize all cash payments. Each payment is supported by an approved source document, such as an invoice.
- Write checks for all payments. Only authorized persons can sign checks.
- Use prenumbered checks.
- Retain and account for spoiled checks. Mark these checks "Void," and file them in sequence.

Analyzing Cash Payment Transactions

Businesses buy merchandise and other assets on account or by paying cash. At On Your Mark, all cash payments are made by check. When a cash payment is made, the details are recorded on the check stub. The check stub is the source document for the journal entry. Then, a check is prepared and signed by an authorized person. Let's look at two cash payment transactions that occur frequently.

Recording Cash Purchase of Insurance

Businesses buy insurance to protect against losses from hazards such as theft, fire, and flood. Insurance policies cover varying time periods, such as six months or one year. The cost of insurance protection is called the **premium** . A premium is paid in advance at the beginning of the covered period. Insurance paid in advance is an asset because until the insurance protection expires, it represents a benefit to the company. The insurance premium is recorded in the asset account, **Prepaid Insurance**.

Business Transaction

On December 17 On Your Mark paid $1,500 to Keystone Insurance Company for the premium on a six-month insurance policy, Check 1001.

ON YOUR MARK
ATHLETIC WEAR
595 Leslie Street, Dallas, TX 75207

1001
22-523
4210

DATE _Dec. 17_ 20 --

PAY TO THE ORDER OF _Keystone Insurance Company_ $ _1,500.00_

One thousand five hundred and ⁿᵒ/100 ———————— DOLLARS

Security National Bank
DALLAS, TEXAS

MEMO _____ _Michael Brown_

⑄421022523⑊ 727546⑊ 1001

ANALYSIS	*Identify*	1. The accounts affected are **Prepaid Insurance** and **Cash in Bank.**
	Classify +/−	2. Both **Prepaid Insurance** and **Cash in Bank** are asset accounts. 3. **Prepaid Insurance** is increased by $1,500. **Cash in Bank** is decreased by $1,500.

DEBIT-CREDIT RULE		4. Increases to asset accounts are recorded as debits. Debit **Prepaid Insurance** for $1,500. 5. Decreases to asset accounts are recorded as credits. Credit **Cash in Bank** for $1,500.

T ACCOUNTS   6.

Prepaid Insurance		Cash in Bank	
Debit + 1,500	Credit −	Debit +	Credit − 1,500

JOURNAL ENTRY   7.

	GENERAL JOURNAL			PAGE _21_		
	DATE	DESCRIPTION	POST. REF.	DEBIT	CREDIT	
11	Dec. 17	Prepaid Insurance		1 50000		11
12		Cash in Bank			1 50000	12
13		Check 1001				13
14						14

Recording Cash Purchases of Merchandise

Usually businesses purchase merchandise on account. Sometimes a business buys merchandise for cash. Let's look at an example of a cash purchase of merchandise.

ON YOUR MARK
ATHLETIC WEAR
595 Leslie Street, Dallas, TX 75207

1002
22-523
4210

DATE _Dec. 19_ 20 --

PAY TO THE ORDER OF _FastLane Athletics_ $ _1,300.00_

One thousand three hundred and ⁿᵒ/100 ———————— DOLLARS

Security National Bank
DALLAS, TEXAS

MEMO _____ _Michael Brown_

⑄421022523⑊ 727596⑊ 1002

Business Transaction

On December 19 On Your Mark purchased merchandise from FastLane Athletics for $1,300, Check 1002.

ANALYSIS	*Identify*	1. The accounts affected are **Purchases** and **Cash in Bank.**
	Classify +/−	2. **Purchases** is a cost of merchandise account. **Cash in Bank** is an asset account. 3. **Purchases** is increased by $1,300. **Cash in Bank** is decreased by $1,300.

| DEBIT-CREDIT RULE | **4.** Increases to cost of merchandise accounts are recorded as debits. Debit **Purchases** for $1,300.
5. Decreases to asset accounts are recorded as credits. Credit **Cash in Bank** for $1,300. |

T ACCOUNTS   **6.**

Purchases		Cash in Bank	
Debit + 1,300	Credit −	Debit +	Credit − 1,300

JOURNAL ENTRY   **7.**

		GENERAL JOURNAL			PAGE 21	
	DATE	DESCRIPTION	POST. REF.	DEBIT	CREDIT	
14	Dec. 19	Purchases		1 300 00		14
15		Cash in Bank			1 300 00	15
16		Check 1002				16
17						17

Key Points

Recording Purchases

Regardless of when payment is made, now (cash) or later (on account), the **Purchases** account is debited when merchandise for resale is purchased.

Recording Cash Payments for Items Purchased on Account

An invoice received by a business is verified for items, quantities, and prices, recorded in the journal, and filed by due date in a tickler file.

Each day, the invoices due for payment are removed from the tickler file. Checks are prepared, signed by an authorized person, and mailed to creditors.

The amount of the check in payment of an invoice depends on the credit terms and the payment date. For example, On Your Mark purchased $2,300 of merchandise on account from Pro Runner Warehouse. The invoice, dated December 14, listed credit terms of 2/10, n/30. If On Your Mark pays for the merchandise on or before December 24, it can take a discount of $46.

When the invoice is paid on December 24, On Your Mark debits **Accounts Payable** (controlling) and **Accounts Payable—Pro Runner Warehouse** for the full amount of the invoice, $2,300. On Your Mark is paying for all of the merchandise and doesn't owe any more money on this purchase. **Cash in Bank** is credited for $2,254, the actual amount of the check. The difference between $2,300 and $2,254 is the cash discount, which is debited to the **Purchases Discounts** account.

The **Purchases Discounts** account tracks the cash discounts a business takes. **Purchases Discounts** is a contra cost of merchandise account. Its balance reduces the balance of the **Purchases** account. Its normal balance is therefore a credit.

Key Points

Purchases discounts

Taking all purchases discounts is a good business practice. Over a period of time, these discounts can add up to sizable cost savings.

Purchases	
Debit + Increase Side Normal Balance	Credit − Decrease Side

Purchases Discounts	
Debit − Decrease Side	Credit + Increase Side Normal Balance

Business Transaction

On December 24 On Your Mark paid $2,254 to Pro Runner Warehouse for merchandise purchased on account, $2,300 less a discount of $46, Check 1003.

ON YOUR MARK · **ATHLETIC WEAR**
595 Leslie Street, Dallas, TX 75207

No. 1003
22-523
4210

DATE Dec. 24 20 --

PAY TO THE ORDER OF Pro Runner Warehouse · $ 2,254.00

Two thousand two hundred fifty-four and ⁿᵒ/100 ———— DOLLARS

Security National Bank
DALLAS, TEXAS

MEMO ———— *Michael Brown*

⑆421022523⑆ 727596⑈ 1003

ANALYSIS	*Identify*	1.	The accounts affected are **Accounts Payable** (controlling), **Accounts Payable—Pro Runner Warehouse** (subsidiary), **Cash in Bank,** and **Purchases Discounts.**
	Classify	2.	**Accounts Payable** (controlling) and **Accounts Payable—Pro Runner Warehouse** (subsidiary) are liability accounts. **Cash in Bank** is an asset account. **Purchases Discounts** is a contra cost of merchandise account.
	+/−	3.	**Accounts Payable** (controlling) and **Accounts Payable—Pro Runner Warehouse** (subsidiary) are decreased by $2,300. **Cash in Bank** is decreased by $2,254. **Purchases Discounts** is increased by $46.

DEBIT-CREDIT RULE	4.	Decreases to liability accounts are recorded as debits. Debit **Accounts Payable** (controlling) for $2,300. Also debit **Accounts Payable—Pro Runner Warehouse** (subsidiary) for $2,300.
	5.	Decreases to asset accounts are recorded as credits. Credit **Cash in Bank** for $2,254. Increases to contra cost of merchandise accounts are recorded as credits. Credit **Purchases Discounts** for $46.

T ACCOUNTS   6.

Accounts Payable				Cash in Bank	
Debit − 2,300	Credit +			Debit +	Credit − 2,254

Accounts Payable Subsidiary Ledger Pro Runner Warehouse				Purchases Discounts	
Debit − 2,300	Credit +			Debit −	Credit + 46

JOURNAL ENTRY   7.

	GENERAL JOURNAL				PAGE 21
	DATE	DESCRIPTION	POST. REF.	DEBIT	CREDIT
17	Dec. 24	Accts. Pay./Pro Runner Ware.		2 300 00	
18		Cash in Bank			2 254 00
19		Purchases Discounts			46 00
20		Check 1003			
21					

Other Cash Payments

When a company buys merchandise from a supplier, there is often a charge for shipping the goods. The shipping terms determine who will pay the shipping charges, either the buyer or the supplier.

Shipping terms are stated as either FOB destination or FOB shipping point. "FOB" stands for "free on board." **FOB destination** means that the

supplier pays the shipping cost to the buyer's destination or location. **FOB shipping point** means that the *buyer* pays the shipping charge from the supplier's shipping point.

Terms	Shipping Cost Paid By
FOB destination	Supplier
FOB shipping point	Buyer

A shipping charge is an additional cost of the merchandise. The account set up to handle shipping charges is **Transportation In**, which is a cost of merchandise account. **Transportation In** follows the rules of debit and credit for expense accounts. **Transportation In** is increased by debits and decreased by credits. The normal balance of **Transportation In** is a debit.

Here is an example of the payment of shipping charges.

Transportation In	
Debit + Increase Side Normal Balance	Credit − Decrease Side

Business Transaction

On December 24 On Your Mark issued Check 1004 for $275 to Dara's Delivery Service for shipping charges on merchandise purchased from Sports Link Footwear.

ON YOUR MARK
ATHLETIC WEAR
595 Leslie Street, Dallas, TX 75207

1004
22-523
4210

DATE Dec. 24 20 --
PAY TO THE ORDER OF Dara's Delivery Service $275.00
Two hundred seventy-five and no/100 ———— DOLLARS
Security National Bank
DALLAS, TEXAS
MEMO ———— Michael Brown
⑉⑊⑈⑉①⑈②②⑊②③⑉ ⑦②⑦⑊⑈⑥⑊⑊ ①⑈⑈①

JOURNAL ENTRY

GENERAL JOURNAL PAGE 21

	DATE	DESCRIPTION	POST. REF.	DEBIT	CREDIT	
21	Dec. 24	Transportation In		275 00		21
22		Cash in Bank			275 00	22
23		Check 1004				23
24						24

Recording Bankcard Fees

The following transaction is made to record the bankcard fee deducted from the business checking account. Banks charge a fee for handling bankcard sales slips. This **bankcard fee** is usually a percentage of the total of the amounts recorded on the bankcard sales slips processed.

Business Transaction

On December 31 On Your Mark records the bankcard fee of $75, December bank statement.

JOURNAL ENTRY

GENERAL JOURNAL PAGE 21

	DATE	DESCRIPTION	POST. REF.	DEBIT	CREDIT	
24	Dec. 31	Bankcard Fees Expense		75 00		24
25		Cash in Bank			75 00	25
26		December Bank Statement				26
27						27

The journal entries for all the transactions discussed and illustrated in this chapter are shown in **Figure 15–7.**

GENERAL JOURNAL

PAGE ___21___

	DATE		DESCRIPTION	POST. REF.	DEBIT	CREDIT	
1	20--						1
2	Dec.	14	Purchases		2 3 0 0 00		2
3			Accounts Payable/Pro Runner Warehouse	/		2 3 0 0 00	3
4			Invoice 7894				4
5		15	Store Equipment		1 2 0 0 00		5
6			Accounts Payable/Champion Store Supply	/		1 2 0 0 00	6
7			Invoice 3417				7
8		16	Accounts Payable/FastLane Athletics	/	2 0 0 00		8
9			Purchases Returns & Allowances			2 0 0 00	9
10			Debit Memorandum 51				10
11		17	Prepaid Insurance		1 5 0 0 00		11
12			Cash in Bank			1 5 0 0 00	12
13			Check 1001				13
14		19	Purchases		1 3 0 0 00		14
15			Cash in Bank			1 3 0 0 00	15
16			Check 1002				16
17		24	Accounts Payable/Pro Runner Warehouse	/	2 3 0 0 00		17
18			Cash in Bank			2 2 5 4 00	18
19			Purchases Discounts			4 6 00	19
20			Check 1003				20
21		24	Transportation In		2 7 5 00		21
22			Cash in Bank			2 7 5 00	22
23			Check 1004				23
24		31	Bankcard Fees Expense		7 5 00		24
25			Cash in Bank			7 5 00	25
26			December Bank Statement				26
27							27

Figure 15–7 Journal Entries for December Business Transactions

A MATTER OF ETHICS

Showing Favoritism

Manufacturers, like any other business, must make purchases to carry out their business. Imagine that you work in the purchasing department of a large toy manufacturer like Mattel. You are responsible for placing orders for the toy parts that make up some of their cars and trucks. One supplier, whose prices are only slightly higher than others, has indicated that they would send free tickets to a sports event if you order most of the supplies from them.

Ethical Decision Making:

☛ What are the ethical issues?

☛ What are the alternatives?

☛ Who are the affected parties?

☛ How do the alternatives affect the parties?

☛ What would you do?

Now that you have studied this section, complete the following questions and problems.

Thinking Critically

1. What steps are involved in the payment of an invoice?
2. How do businesses record premium payments for insurance coverage?

Analyzing Accounting

Clara's Designs is a crafts store with a large inventory of seasonal crafts items. As the inventory clerk, you are to create a chart or graph to compare the cost of the items purchased and the related shipping charges. Using the data given below, design a chart or graph that depicts both sets of data. What conclusions can you draw from your chart or graph?

	Cost of Item	Shipping Charges
Holiday decorator ribbon	$2,000	$200
Door wreaths and hangers	3,200	320
Potpourri	1,200	120
Styrofoam trees	4,350	435

Problem 15–4 Recording Cash Payment Transactions

Meadow Link Golf Club had the following cash payment transactions.

Instructions Record the following transactions on page 6 of the general journal in your working papers.

Date	Transactions
May 1	Purchased $10,500 in golf equipment (merchandise) from TopMax Golf Manufacturers, Check 1150.
5	Issued Check 1151 for $325 to Franco's Trucking for delivery charges on merchandise bought from TopMax Golf Manufacturers.
7	Paid Lone Star Insurance Company $2,500 for the annual premium on an insurance policy, Check 1152.

KEY CONCEPTS

1. There are four documents used in the purchasing process:
   - The purchase requisition is a request to order goods.
   - The purchase order is an offer to buy goods.
   - The packing slip is a list of the goods shipped.
   - The invoice lists the quantity, description, unit price, and total cost of the items shipped to the buyer.

2. When an invoice is received by the accounting department, it is checked against the purchase order and the packing slip for items, quantities, and prices.

3. After the invoices are recorded in the journal, they are filed according to their due dates in a tickler file. A tickler file contains a folder for each day of the month.

4. The **Purchases** account is used to record the cost of merchandise purchased during the period. **Purchases** is a cost of merchandise account. The rules of debit and credit for **Purchases** are the same as those for expense accounts.

5. Suppliers may offer cash discounts to their credit customers to encourage prompt payment. Buyers who take a cash discount record it in the **Purchases Discounts** account. **Purchases Discounts** is a contra cost of merchandise account.

6. When the buyer receives credit for returned or damaged merchandise, the amount is recorded in the **Purchases Returns and Allowances** account. **Purchases Returns and Allowances** is a contra cost of merchandise account.

7. The shipping charges for merchandise purchased from suppliers are considered an additional cost of merchandise. Shipping charges are debited to the **Transportation In** account, which is a cost of merchandise account.

8. The accounts payable subsidiary ledger contains an account for each creditor. The total of the account balances in the accounts payable subsidiary ledger must match the balance of the **Accounts Payable** controlling account in the general ledger.

9. The premium paid for insurance coverage is debited to **Prepaid Insurance. Prepaid Insurance** is an asset account.

10. Good internal controls include proper management of cash payments. All cash payments should be authorized, all cash payments should be made by check, and all checks should be signed by an authorized person.

Purchases

Debit	Credit
+	−
Increase Side	Decrease Side
Normal Balance	

Purchases Discounts

Debit	Credit
−	+
Decrease Side	Increase Side
	Normal Balance

Purchases Returns and Allowances

Debit	Credit
−	+
Decrease Side	Increase Side
	Normal Balance

Transportation In

Debit	Credit
+	−
Increase Side	Decrease Side
Normal Balance	

Prepaid Insurance

Debit	Credit
+	−
Increase Side	Decrease Side
Normal Balance	

USING KEY TERMS

Work with a partner to pair these terms. Discuss the relationship between the terms. Is one the result of another? Are they opposite? Once you agree, write out your explanation for each pair.

accounts payable subsidiary ledger	premium
bankcard fee	processing stamp
cost of merchandise	purchase order
debit memorandum	purchase requisition
discount period	**Purchases** account
due dates	purchases allowances
FOB destination	purchases discount
FOB shipping point	purchases returns
packing slip	tickler file

Understanding Accounting Concepts and Procedures

Instructions

On a separate sheet of paper, answer the following questions:

1. Why is an invoice checked against both the purchase order and the packing slip?
2. What information is included on a processing stamp?
3. Why do suppliers give cash discounts to credit customers?
4. What is a tickler file? How are invoices filed in a tickler file?
5. What is a purchases return? What is a purchases allowance?
6. List four procedures that a business should use to control its cash payments.
7. Why are shipping charges an additional cost of merchandise purchased for resale?
8. What is the source document for recording the bank card fees?
9. On what amount is the bank card fee based?
10. To which account are bank card fees debited?

Case Study...

Merchandising Business: Sportswear Store

The Sports Loft is a retail store that sells sports clothing, accessories, and equipment. Janet wants you to design a more automated system for ordering merchandise that will free her for other management duties.

Thinking Critically:

1. Identify issues involved in creating a new purchasing process. For example, how is low stock to be identified? If you think an electronic system is needed, specify the information it should collect and how new orders would be triggered.
2. Write a one-page report suggesting a purchasing system for The Sports Loft. Include a description of any forms needed. Draw a diagram if necessary.

*inter*NET CONNECTION

Fraud Detection

The Association of Certified Fraud Examiners considers occupational fraud and abuse to be a serious problem in the U.S. Most accountants believe that fraud cannot be eliminated, but that it can be reduced.

Do This:

Locate sites on the Internet related to occupational fraud and abuse and answer the following questions.

1. What organizations are most vulnerable to occupational fraud and abuse? Why?
2. Are regular audits designed to detect fraud and abuse?
3. How is most fraud discovered?

Conducting an Audit with Alex

The following entries were made in the general journal for Nova Shoe Shop.

Instructions

Review each transaction and record any errors on a separate sheet of paper.

On June 1 Nova issued Check 557 for $105 to Don's Deliveries for shipping charges on merchandise purchased from E-Z Shoe Supply.

	GENERAL JOURNAL				PAGE 3	
	DATE	DESCRIPTION	POST. REF.	DEBIT	CREDIT	
1	20--					1
2	June 6	Purchases		105 00		2
3		Cash in Bank			105 00	3
4		Check 557				4
5						5

On June 6 Nova purchased $200 in supplies from Bayside Office Supply, Check 558.

	GENERAL JOURNAL				PAGE 3	
	DATE	DESCRIPTION	POST. REF.	DEBIT	CREDIT	
1	20--					1
2	June 9	Purchases		200 00		2
3		Cash in Bank			200 00	3
4		Check 585				4
5						5

Workplace Skills

Monitoring and Correcting Performance of Systems

Identifying trends, predicting changes, finding problems, and applying solutions are skills of a "systems thinker."

On the Job:

After working for Action Athletics for one year, you recognize your customers' growing interest in cycling. Your community is hosting a large mountain bike competition. You see an opportunity for Action Athletics to increase sales of cycling gear. You recommend to management that they adjust and upgrade their cycling merchandise line to appeal to this growing market.

Thinking Critically:

1. Pair up with a student and role play your "sales pitch" to persuade your employer to add to their current merchandise line.
2. Using a spreadsheet program, make a list of 10 biking accessories to add to the inventory. For each item, provide reasonable estimates for price and one month's sales. Assume that approximately 200 cyclists will visit the store in one month.

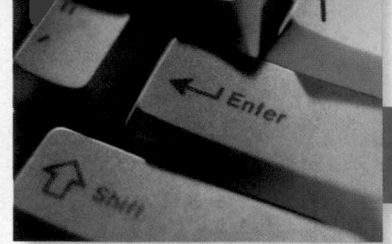

Recording Purchases and Cash Payments
Making the Transition from a Manual to a Computerized System

Task	Perform Accounting Procedures Using Manual Methods	Perform Accounting Procedures Using Automated Methods
Recording purchases transactions	1. General journal entries are prepared and then posted based on an invoice for merchandise purchased on account or for cash.	1. The purchase can be recorded when the merchandise is received, when the invoice is received, or when the cash purchase is made. Journal entries are automatically generated from the invoice information and posted to the general ledger.
Recording cash payment transactions	1. Checks are prepared in payment of an invoice or memorandum. 2. Journal entries are prepared to record the check. 3. Journal entries are posted to the general ledger. 4. New account balances are calculated.	1. Journal entries are automatically generated as the check for payment is prepared. 2. Journal entries are posted and account balances updated.

Recording Purchases and Cash Payments

Peachtree Question	Description
How do I record the purchase of merchandise on account?	1. Select **Purchases/Receive Inventory** from the *Tasks* menu. 2. Enter Vendor ID, Invoice No., and Date. 3. Select the *Apply to Purchases* tab. 4. Enter quantity, description, GL account, and unit price for each item. 5. Click *Save*.
How do I record cash (check) purchases for merchandise or miscellaneous expenses?	1. Select **Payments** from the *Tasks* menu. 2. Enter the Vendor ID, Check No., Date, and Cash GL account number. 3. Click the *Apply to Expenses* tab. 4. Enter quantity, description, GL account, and unit price for each item. 5. Click *Save*.
How do I record payments on account?	1. Select **Payments** from the *Tasks* menu. 2. Enter the Vendor ID, Check No., Date, and Cash GL account number. 3. Click the *Apply to Invoices* tab. 4. Select the invoice to be paid. 5. Verify or enter the amount being paid. Click *Save*.
What does the software do "behind the scenes"?	• For purchases and cash payments, the software automatically updates the vendor's or creditor's account and the general ledger accounts.

For detailed instructions: See the Peachtree User Guide in your Glencoe Working Papers.

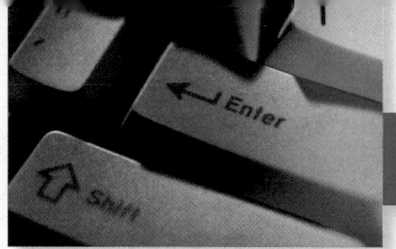

APPLICATION OPTIONS

Problem 15–5
Determining Due Dates and Discount Amounts

Sunset Surfwear frequently purchases merchandise on account. When invoices are received, a processing stamp is placed on the invoice indicating the due date, the amount of any discount, and the amount to be paid. The following invoices were received during March.

	Invoice Number	Invoice Date	Credit Terms	Invoice Amount
1.	24574	March 5	2/10, n/30	$3,000.00
2.	530992	March 7	3/10, n/30	5,550.00
3.	211145	March 12	2/15, n/60	729.95
4.	45679	March 16	n/45	345.67
5.	34120	March 23	2/10, n/30	1,526.50
6.	00985	March 27	n/30	700.00

Instructions Prepare a form similar to the one shown below. The first invoice has been completed as an example. For each invoice:

1. Determine the due date. Assume that Sunset Surfwear always pays invoices within the discount period.
2. Compute the discount amount, if any.
3. Compute the amount to be paid.

Invoice Number	Invoice Date	Credit Terms	Invoice Amount	Due Date	Discount Amount	Amount To Be Paid
24574	Mar. 5	2/10, n/30	$3,000.00	Mar. 15	$60.00	$2,940.00

Analyze: If all discounts are taken, how much money will Sunset Surfwear save?

Complete chapter problems one of four ways:

1 **Manual** Glencoe Working Papers

or

2 **Peachtree Complete Accounting** Software

or

3 **QuickBooks** Templates (Problems 15–7, 15–9)

or

4 **Spreadsheet** Templates (Problem 15–5)

SPREADSHEET SMART GUIDE

Step–by–Step Instructions: Problem 15–5

1. Select the spreadsheet template for Problem 15–5.
2. Enter your name and the date in the spaces provided on the template.
3. Complete the spreadsheet using the instructions in your working papers.
4. Print the spreadsheet and proof your work.
5. Save your work and exit the spreadsheet program.

Peachtree®

SMART GUIDE

Step–by–Step Instructions:
Problem 15–6

1. Select the problem set for InBeat CD Shop (Prob. 15–6).
2. Rename the company and set the system date.
3. Enter all of the purchases on account transactions using the **Purchases/ Receive Inventory** option in the **Tasks** menu.
4. Process all debit memorandums using the **Purchases/Receive Inventory** and the **Payments** options.
5. Record all cash payments using the **Payments** option.
6. Print a Purchases Journal report and a Cash Disbursements Journal report.
7. Proof your work and make any needed corrections.
8. Print a General Ledger report to answer the Analyze question.
9. End the session.

TIP: To save time entering transactions, group them by type and then enter the transactions in batches.

Problem 15–6 Analyzing Purchases and Cash Payments

InBeat CD Shop had the following transactions in March.

Instructions Use the T accounts in your working papers. For each transaction:
1. Determine which accounts are affected.
2. Enter the debit and credit amounts in the T accounts.

Date	Transactions
Mar. 2	Purchased merchandise on account from NightVision and Company, $2,000, Invoice NV-20, terms 2/10, n/30.
6	Issued Check 250 for $85 to Penn Trucking Company for delivering merchandise from NightVision and Company.
7	Purchased $300 in supplies on account from Temple Store Supply, Invoice 6011, terms n/30.
12	Issued Check 251 for $1,960 to NightVision and Company in payment of Invoice NV-20 for $2,000 less a cash discount of $40.
15	Paid Keystone Insurance Company $2,500 for the annual premium on business insurance, Check 252.
16	Purchased $3,000 in merchandise on account from NightVision and Company, Invoice NV-45, terms 2/10, n/30.
18	Issued Debit Memorandum 25 for $100 to NightVision and Company for the return of merchandise.
20	Purchased $900 in merchandise from Dandelion Records, Check 253.
22	Issued Check 254 to Temple Store Supplies for $300 for Invoice 6011.

Analyze: What is the Purchases account balance at the end of March?

Problem 15–7 Recording Purchases Transactions

Shutterbug Cameras, a retail merchandising store, had the following purchases transactions in March.

Instructions In your working papers, record the transactions on page 31 of the general journal.

Date	Transactions
Mar. 3	Purchased $4,500 in merchandise on account from Photo Emporium, Invoice 1221, terms 2/10, n/30.
5	Bought $750 in supplies on account from State Street Office Supply, Invoice 873, terms n/30.

Continued

Date	Prob. 15–7 (cont.) Transactions
Mar. 9	Returned $225 in merchandise to Photo Emporium, issued Debit Memorandum 72.
10	Purchased $3,600 in merchandise on account from Video Optics Inc., Invoice VO94, terms 3/15, n/45.
15	State Street Office Supply granted a $60 credit for damaged supplies purchased on August 5, Debit Memorandum 73.
20	Bought $4,800 in store equipment from Digital Precision Equipment on account, Invoice 1288, terms n/30.
25	Issued Debit Memorandum 74 to Video Optics Inc. for the return of $120 in merchandise.
28	Purchased $1,800 in merchandise on account from U-Tech Products, Invoice UT66, terms n/30.
29	Bought $270 in supplies on account from ProStudio Supply, Invoice 4574, terms n/30.
30	Returned $150 in merchandise to U-Tech Products, Debit Memorandum 75.
31	Issued Debit Memorandum 76 to ProStudio Supply for the return of $35 in supplies bought on March 29.

Analyze: What are the total credits made to the **Purchases Returns and Allowances** account for the month?

Problem 15–8 Recording Cash Payment Transactions

Cycle Tech Bicycles had the following cash payment transactions in March.

Instructions In your working papers, record the transactions on page 19 of the general journal.

Date	Transactions
Mar. 1	Purchased $1,800 in merchandise from Summit Bicycles, Check 2111.
3	Issued Check 2112 for $2,450 to Spaulding Inc. in payment of the $2,500 account balance less a 2% cash discount of $50.
7	Issued Check 2113 for $3,100 to Desert Palms Insurance Company for the annual business insurance premium.
12	Paid $175 to Viking Express for delivery of merchandise purchased from Schwinn Inc., FOB shipping point, Check 2114.
17	Issued Check 2115 to Suspension Specialists for $3,880 in payment of Invoice 1492 for $4,000 less a 3% cash discount of $120.

Continued ✎

Peachtree®

SMART GUIDE

Step–by–Step Instructions: Problem 15–7

1. Select the problem set for Shutterbug Cameras (Prob. 15–7).
2. Rename the company and set the system date.
3. Enter all of the purchases on account transactions using the **Purchases/ Receive Inventory** option in the *Tasks* menu.
4. Process all debit memorandums using the **Purchases/Receive Inventory** and the **Payments** options.
5. Print a Purchases Journal report and a Cash Disbursements Journal report.
6. Proof your work. Make any needed corrections.
7. Print a GL report to answer the Analyze question.
8. End the session.

TIP: Using the **Vendors** option, Peachtree lets you set the terms offered by each vendor.

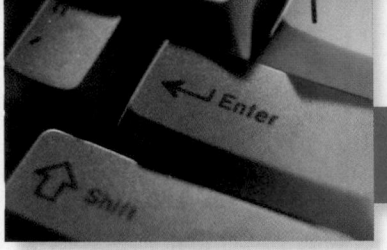

Peachtree®

SMART GUIDE

Step–by–Step Instructions:
Problem 15–8

1. Select the problem set for Cycle Tech (Prob. 15–8).
2. Rename the company and set the system date.
3. Record all cash payments using the **Payments** option.
4. Print a Cash Disbursements Journal report.
5. Proof your work. Make any needed corrections.
6. Answer the Analyze question.
7. End the session.

TIP: Remember that you may need to change the G/L Account in the Payments window to enter a cash payment for the purchase of an asset (e.g., supplies, office equipment).

Peachtree®

SMART GUIDE

Step–by–Step Instructions:
Problem 15–9

1. Select the problem set for River's Edge (Prob. 15–9).
2. Rename the company and set the system date.
3. Enter all of the purchases on account.
4. Process all debit memorandums.
5. Record all cash payments.
6. Print the following reports: Purchases Journal, Cash Disbursements Journal, and General Ledger.
7. Proof your work.
8. Answer the Analyze question.
9. End the session.

TIP: Peachtree automatically calculates a purchases discount if the terms are included in a vendor's account.

Date	Prob. 15–8 (cont.) Transactions
Mar. 20	Received the March bank statement and recorded bankcard fees of $275.
24	Paid All-Star News $130 to run an advertisement promoting the store, Check 2116.
28	Bought $100 in supplies and $700 in store equipment from Superior Store Equipment Inc., Check 2117 for $800.
31	Issued Check 2118 for $2,185.50 in payment of monthly wages of $3,000 less deductions for the following taxes: Employees' Federal Income Tax Payable, $480; Employees' State Income Tax Payable, $105; Social Security Tax Payable, $186; and Medicare Tax Payable, $43.50.

Analyze: What is the total decrease to the checking account for the month?

Problem 15–9 Recording Purchases and Cash Payment Transactions

River's Edge Canoe & Kayak had the following purchases and cash payment transactions for the month of March.

Instructions In your working papers, record the following transactions on page 16 of the general journal.

Date	Transactions
Mar. 1	Purchased $8,200 in merchandise on account from Trailhead Canoes, Invoice TC202, terms 2/10, n/30.
5	Issued Check 887 for $98 to Santini Trucking Company for delivery of merchandise purchased from Trailhead Canoes.
7	Bought $230 in supplies on account from StoreMart Supply, Invoice SM101, terms n/30.
9	Issued Check 888 to World-Wide Insurance Company for $2,500 in payment of business insurance premium.
11	Issued Check 889 to Trailhead Canoes for $8,036 in payment of Invoice TC202 for $8,200 less a 2% cash discount of $164.
15	Purchased $6,200 in merchandise on account from Mohican Falls Kayak Wholesalers, Invoice 45332, terms 3/15, n/45.
18	Issued Debit Memorandum 67 for $25 to StoreMart Supply for damaged supplies purchased on March 7.
21	Paid StoreMart Supply the balance due on their account, $205 ($230 less $25 credit), Check 890.
25	Returned $200 in merchandise to Mohican Falls Kayak Wholesalers, Debit Memorandum 68.
28	Rollins Plumbing Service completed $120 in repair work (**Maintenance Expense**) on account, Invoice RP432.

Analyze: What are the total debits to the **Purchases** account for the month?

CHALLENGE PROBLEM

Problem 15–10 Recording and Posting Purchases and Cash Payment Transactions

SOURCE DOCUMENT PROBLEM

Buzz Newsstand's purchases and cash payment transactions for the month of March are described below.

Instructions In your working papers:
1. Record the transactions in the general journal, page 7.
2. Post the transactions to the ledger accounts.

Peachtree®

SMART GUIDE

Step–by–Step Instructions: Problem 15–10

1. Select the problem set for Buzz Newsstand (Prob. 15–10).
2. Rename the company and set the system date.
3. Enter all of the purchases on account.
4. Process all debit memorandums.
5. Record all cash payments.
6. Print the following reports: Purchases Journal, Cash Disbursements Journal, Vendor Ledgers, and General Ledger.
7. Proof your work.
8. Answer the Analyze question.
9. End the session.

SOURCE DOCUMENT PROBLEM

Problem 15–10

Use the source documents in your working papers to record the transactions for this problem.

Date	Transactions
Mar. 1	Purchased $5,600 in merchandise on account from ADC Publishing, Invoice 785, terms 3/15, n/45.
3	Issued Check 1400 for $735 to Pine Forest Publications in payment of Invoice PFP98 for $750 less a 2% cash discount of $15.
5	Issued Check 1401 for $275 to Rizzo's Trucking Company for transportation charges.
7	Issued Check 1402 for $588 to Delta Press in payment of Invoice DP166 for $600 less a 2% cash discount of $12.
9	American Trend Publishers granted a $100 allowance for damaged merchandise, Debit Memorandum 33.
11	Issued Check 1403 for $3,200 to Keystone Insurance Company for the annual premium for business insurance.
15	Issued Check 1404 for $5,432 to ADC Publishing in payment of Invoice 785 for $5,600 less a 3% cash discount of $168.
18	Bought $2,800 in merchandise on account from Delta Press, Invoice DP204, terms 2/10, n/30.
22	Issued Debit Memorandum 34 to Delta Press for the return of $300 in merchandise.
28	Paid American Trend Publishers the balance due on their account, $800, no discount, Check 1405.
30	Bought $120 in merchandise for cash from ADC Publishing, Check 1406.

Analyze: How much did Buzz Newsstand save in March by taking cash discounts available?

CHAPTER 16

Special Journals: Sales and Cash Receipts

Learning Objectives

When you have completed this chapter, you will be able to:

▶ Identify the special journals and explain how they are used in a merchandising business.

▶ Record transactions in sales and cash receipts journals.

▶ Post from the sales and cash receipts journals to customer accounts in the accounts receivable subsidiary ledger.

▶ Foot, prove, total, and rule the sales and cash receipts journals.

▶ Post column totals from the sales and cash receipts journals to general ledger accounts.

▶ Prepare a schedule for the accounts receivable subsidiary ledger.

▶ Define the accounting terms introduced in this chapter.

Sony Corporation

Exploring the Real World of Business

ANALYZING SALES GROWTH

Imagine yourself with your headphones on, jamming to the latest release of REM. Perhaps you're using a Sony Walkman cassette player, a product that started a revolution in personal music listening.

Sony Corporation was the first to see the potential for a portable, battery-operated cassette player. **Sony** has a lot of other firsts, a few of which are the home videotape recorder, the world's smallest color TV, the water-resistant Sports Walkman, and the digital video disc. The company has dozens of electronic products that have become market leaders.

If you've listened to music, been to the movies, watched music videos, or watched television recently, chances are you've come into contact with something made by **Sony.** The **Sony** brands include Columbia Pictures, Epic Records, and PlayStation game consoles. **Sony Corporation of America** has annual sales of more than $18 billion. The company has grown to this size because sales of its early products helped to pay for the research needed to develop even better electronics products that consumers want to buy.

What do you think?

If you were making a presentation to a group of potential investors, what would you say about **Sony's** sales?

Workplace Connections

Applying Your Accounting Knowledge

In this chapter, you will learn more about the cycle of buying and selling merchandise. Dollars from sales are used to buy merchandise, which is in turn sold to customers. Some sales dollars come from customers who pay cash, while others come from sales on credit. Both types are recorded in the accounting records.

Investigate:

1. In your job, do you handle cash and personal checks?
2. Do you handle credit card sales?
3. If a business did not accept credit cards, how do you think it would affect overall sales?

Glencoe Accounting Online

Visit the *Glencoe Accounting* Web site at **glencoeaccounting.glencoe.com** for additional activities and information.

The Sales Journal

What You'll Learn

- To identify the special journals and how they are used.
- How to record sales of merchandise on account in a sales journal.
- How to post from the sales journal to the accounts receivable subsidiary ledger accounts.
- How to foot, prove, total, and rule the sales journal.
- How to post column totals from the sales journal to the general ledger.

Why It's Important

The use of the sales journal provides a systematic method of keeping track of sales on account.

KEY TERMS

special journals
sales journal
footing

You have learned how to record a variety of business transactions in a general journal. A merchandising business can record all of its transactions in a general journal. However, each transaction requires at least three journal lines—one line for the debit, one line for the credit, and one line for the explanation. Each debit and credit is posted separately to the general ledger. For merchandising businesses with many sales transactions, such as Crate & Barrel, this would be very time consuming. To improve efficiency many merchandising businesses use special journals. In this chapter and the next chapter, you will learn how to record transactions in special journals.

Special Journals

Special journals have amount columns used to record debits and credits to specific general ledger accounts. Most transactions are recorded on one line. Special journals thus simplify the journalizing and posting process. The four most commonly used special journals and the type of transaction recorded in each journal are:

Journal	Transaction
Sales journal	sale of merchandise on account
Cash receipts journal	receipt of cash
Purchases journal	purchase of any asset on account
Cash payments journal	payment of cash, including payment by check

Businesses that use special journals still need the general journal to record transactions that cannot be entered in the special journals. Let's now look at the sales journal.

The Sales Journal

The **sales journal** is a special journal used to record sales of merchandise on account. **Figure 16–1** shows the sales journal used by On Your Mark Athletic Wear.

Like the general journal, the sales journal has a space for the page number and columns for the date and the posting reference. There is a separate column in which to record the sales slip number and a column in which to record the name of the charge customer. There are also three special amount columns. **Figure 16–1** illustrates what is to be recorded in each column.

Figure 16–1 Sales Journal

SALES JOURNAL PAGE _____

	DATE	SALES SLIP NO.	CUSTOMER'S ACCOUNT DEBITED	POST. REF.	SALES CREDIT	SALES TAX PAYABLE CREDIT	ACCOUNTS RECEIVABLE DEBIT	
1								1
2								2
3								3

Record the amount of the merchandise sold on account ——————

Record the amount of sales tax on the sale ——————

Record the total amount to be received from the customer on account ——————

Recording Sales of Merchandise on Account

Are you ready to record a sale on account in the sales journal? It's simple. Let's look at the same transactions you analyzed in Chapter 14 for On Your Mark Athletic Wear. This time we'll record transactions using the sales journal.

ON YOUR MARK
ATHLETIC WEAR
595 Leslie Street, Dallas, TX 75207

DATE: December 1, 20-- NO. 50

SOLD TO	Casey Klein 3345 Spring Creek Parkway Plano, Texas 73004		
CLERK B.E.	CASH	CHARGE ✓	TERMS n/30

QTY.	DESCRIPTION	UNIT PRICE	AMOUNT
1	Pair Running Shoes	$ 100.00	$ 100 00
6	Pair Athletic Socks	10.00	60 00
1	Vinyl Jacket/Pants	40.00	40 00
		SUBTOTAL	$ 200 00
		SALES TAX	12 00
	Thank You!	TOTAL	$ 212 00

Business Transaction

On December 1 On Your Mark sold merchandise on account to Casey Klein for $200 plus $12 sales tax, Sales Slip 50.

JOURNAL ENTRY

SALES JOURNAL PAGE 12

	DATE	SALES SLIP NO.	CUSTOMER'S ACCOUNT DEBITED	POST. REF.	SALES CREDIT	SALES TAX PAYABLE CREDIT	ACCOUNTS RECEIVABLE DEBIT	
1	20--							1
2	Dec. 1	50	Casey Klein		200 00	12 00	212 00	2
3	**1**	**2**	**3**		**4**	**5**	**6**	3

To record the transaction in the sales journal, journalize from left to right by following these steps.

1. Enter the date of the sales slip in the Date column.
2. Enter the sales slip number in the Sales Slip No. column.
3. Enter the name of the customer in the Customer's Account Debited column.
4. Enter the total of the merchandise sold in the Sales Credit column. (This is the amount shown in the subtotal box of the sales slip.)
5. Enter the amount of the sales tax in the Sales Tax Payable Credit column.

6. Enter the total amount to be received from the customer in the Accounts Receivable Debit column. (This is the amount shown in the total box of the sales slip.)

You learned in Chapter 14 that sales tax is not imposed on sales of merchandise to tax-exempt organizations. The next transaction involves a tax-exempt sale.

ON YOUR MARK
ATHLETIC WEAR
595 Leslie Street, Dallas, TX 75207

DATE: December 3, 20--   NO. 51

SOLD TO	South Branch High School 1750 Rutgers Dr. Dallas, TX 75207		
CLERK B.E.	CASH	CHARGE ✓	TERMS 2/10, n/30

QTY.	DESCRIPTION	UNIT PRICE	AMOUNT
15	Baseball Uniforms	$ 40.00	$ 600 00
15	Baseball Caps	20.00	300 00
15	Baseball Mitts	35.00	525 00
2	Baseballs	15.00	30 00
3	Baseball Bats	15.00	45 00
		SUBTOTAL	$ 1,500 00
		SALES TAX	0 00
	Thank You!	TOTAL	$ 1,500 00

Business Transaction

On December 3 On Your Mark sold merchandise on account to South Branch High School Athletics for $1,500, Sales Slip 51.

JOURNAL ENTRY

SALES JOURNAL   PAGE ___12___

	DATE	SALES SLIP NO.	CUSTOMER'S ACCOUNT DEBITED	POST. REF.	SALES CREDIT	SALES TAX PAYABLE CREDIT	ACCOUNTS RECEIVABLE DEBIT	
3	3	51	South Branch H.S. Ath.		1 500 00		1 500 00	3
4	**1**	**2**	**3**		**4**		**5**	4

This transaction is analyzed in the same manner as the previous transaction—except there is no sales tax. There are only five steps involved in journalizing this transaction. The first four steps are the same. The fifth step is to skip the Sales Tax Payable Credit column. Enter the total amount to be received from the customer in the Accounts Receivable Debit column.

For sales that do not include a sales tax, amounts entered in the Sales Credit column and in the Accounts Receivable Debit column are the same.

Posting a Sales Journal Entry to the Accounts Receivable Subsidiary Ledger

In Chapter 14 you learned about posting to the accounts receivable subsidiary ledger. To keep the balances of the customer accounts current, sales journal transactions are posted daily to the accounts receivable subsidiary ledger. Whether you use the general journal or the sales journal when posting to the accounts receivable subsidiary ledger, the process is similar. Refer to **Figure 16–2** and follow these steps.

1. Enter the date of the transaction in the Date column of the subsidiary ledger account. Use the same date as the journal entry.
2. In the Posting Reference column of the subsidiary ledger account, enter the journal letter and the journal page number. "S" is the letter used for the sales journal.
3. In the Debit column of the subsidiary ledger account, enter the total amount to be received from the customer.
4. Compute the new balance and enter it in the Balance column. To find the new balance, add the amount in the Debit column to the previous balance amount.

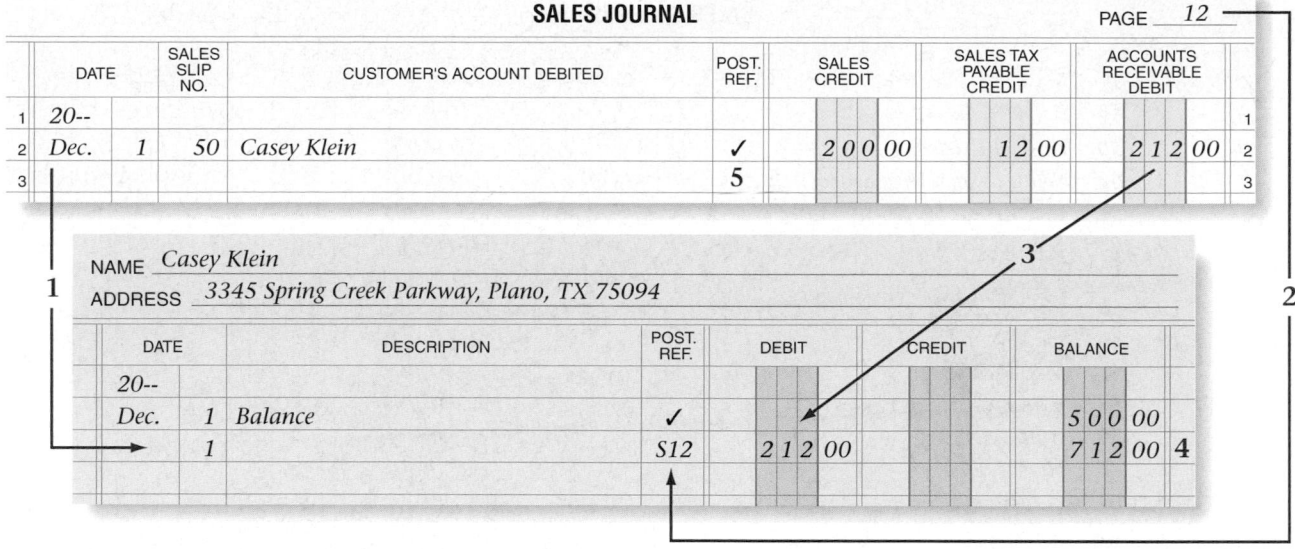

SALES JOURNAL   PAGE 12

	DATE	SALES SLIP NO.	CUSTOMER'S ACCOUNT DEBITED	POST. REF.	SALES CREDIT	SALES TAX PAYABLE CREDIT	ACCOUNTS RECEIVABLE DEBIT	
1	20--							1
2	Dec.	1	50	Casey Klein	✓	2 0 0 00	1 2 00	2 1 2 00	2
3					5				3

NAME _Casey Klein_

ADDRESS _3345 Spring Creek Parkway, Plano, TX 75094_

DATE		DESCRIPTION	POST. REF.	DEBIT	CREDIT	BALANCE	
20--							
Dec.	1	Balance	✓			5 0 0 00	
	1		S12	2 1 2 00		7 1 2 00	4

Figure 16–2 Posting a Sales Journal Entry to the Accounts Receivable Subsidiary Ledger

5. Return to the sales journal and enter a check mark (✓) in the Posting Reference column. The check mark indicates that the transaction has been posted to the accounts receivable subsidiary ledger. In manual accounting systems, customer accounts are not numbered, so a check mark is used in the Posting Reference column.

Completing the Sales Journal

All special journals have amount columns used to record debits and credits to specific general ledger accounts. These amount columns simplify posting. Instead of posting each transaction separately to the general ledger, only the amount column totals are posted. For the sales journal, the column totals posted are the Sales Credit, the Sales Tax Payable Credit, and the Accounts Receivable Debit. Therefore, only three postings are made to the general ledger from the sales journal.

Footing, Totaling, Proving, and Ruling the Sales Journal

Before amounts are posted to the general ledger, the accountant calculates and verifies the column totals. Refer to **Figure 16–3** as you follow each step.

1. Draw a single rule across the three amount columns, just below the last transaction.
2. Foot the amount columns. A **footing** is a column total written in small penciled figures. A footing must be verified. It is written in pencil so that it can be erased if a mistake is discovered.
3. On a separate sheet of paper, test for the equality of debits and credits. The total of the debit column should equal the total of the two credit columns.

Debit Column		**Credit Columns**	
Accounts Receivable	$11,305	Sales Tax Payable	$ 555
		Sales	10,750
Total	$11,305	Total	$11,305

> ### Key Points
>
> **Posting from a Special Journal**
>
> When posting from a special journal, post information from left to right across the ledger form. By following this procedure, you will remember to enter all the information from the journal entry.

SALES JOURNAL

	DATE	SALES SLIP NO.	CUSTOMER'S ACCOUNT DEBITED	POST. REF.	SALES CREDIT	SALES TAX PAYABLE CREDIT	ACCOUNTS RECEIVABLE DEBIT	
1	20--							1
2	Dec. 1	50	Casey Klein	✓	200 00	12 00	212 00	2
3	3	51	South Branch High School Athletics	✓	1 500 00		1 500 00	3
4	5	52	Break Point Sports Club	✓	3 500 00	210 00	3 710 00	4
5	9	53	Gabriel Ramos	✓	300 00	18 00	318 00	5
6	10	54	Kim Wong	✓	100 00	6 00	106 00	6
7	12	55	Robert Galvin	✓	250 00	15 00	265 00	7
8	18	56	Joe Dimaio	✓	400 00	24 00	424 00	8
9	20	57	Megan Sullivan	✓	500 00	30 00	530 00	9
10	24	58	Tammy's Fitness Club	✓	1 000 00	60 00	1 060 00	10
11	26	59	Anita Montero	✓	350 00	21 00	371 00	11
12	28	60	Shashi Rahim	✓	200 00	12 00	212 00	12
13	30	61	Lara Young	✓	2 450 00	147 00	2 597 00	13
14	31		Totals		10 750 00	555 00	11 305 00	14
15								15

Figure 16–3 Totaled and Ruled Sales Journal

4. In the Date column, on the line below the single rule, enter the date the journal is being totaled.
5. On the same line, in the Customer's Account Debited column, enter the word "Totals."
6. Enter the column totals, in ink, just below the footings.
7. Double-rule the three amount columns. A double rule, as you know, indicates that the totals have been verified.

After the sales journal is footed, proved, totaled, and ruled, the column totals are posted to the general ledger.

Posting the Total of the Sales Credit Column

Refer to **Figure 16–4** as you read the procedure for posting the total of the Sales Credit column to the **Sales** account in the general ledger.

1. In the Date column of the **Sales** account in the general ledger, enter the date from the "Totals" line of the sales journal.
2. Enter the sales journal letter and page number in the Posting Reference column. Remember, "S" is the letter for the sales journal.
3. In the Credit column, enter the total from the Sales Credit column of the sales journal.
4. Compute the new balance and enter it in the Credit Balance column. To determine the new balance, add the amount entered in the Credit column to the previous balance.
5. Return to the sales journal and enter the **Sales** account number, in parentheses, below the double rule in the Sales Credit column. The number written in parentheses indicates that the column total has been posted to the general ledger account.

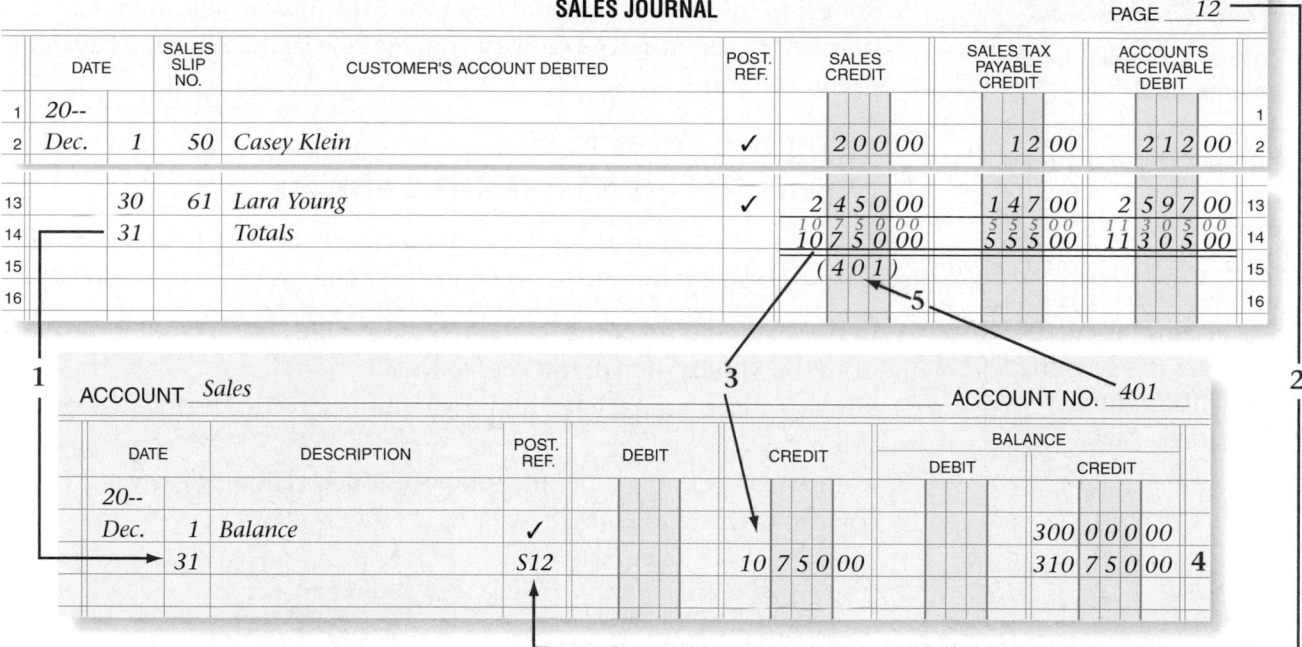

Figure 16–4 Posting the Sales Credit Total to the General Ledger Account

Posting the Total of the Sales Tax Payable Credit Column

The next amount to be posted is the Sales Tax Payable Credit column total. Refer to **Figure 16–5** as you read the following procedure.

1. In the Date column of the **Sales Tax Payable** account, enter the date from the "Totals" line of the sales journal.
2. Enter the sales journal letter and page number in the Posting Reference column.
3. In the Credit column, enter the total from the Sales Tax Payable Credit column of the sales journal.

Figure 16–5 Posting the Sales Tax Payable Credit Total to the General Ledger

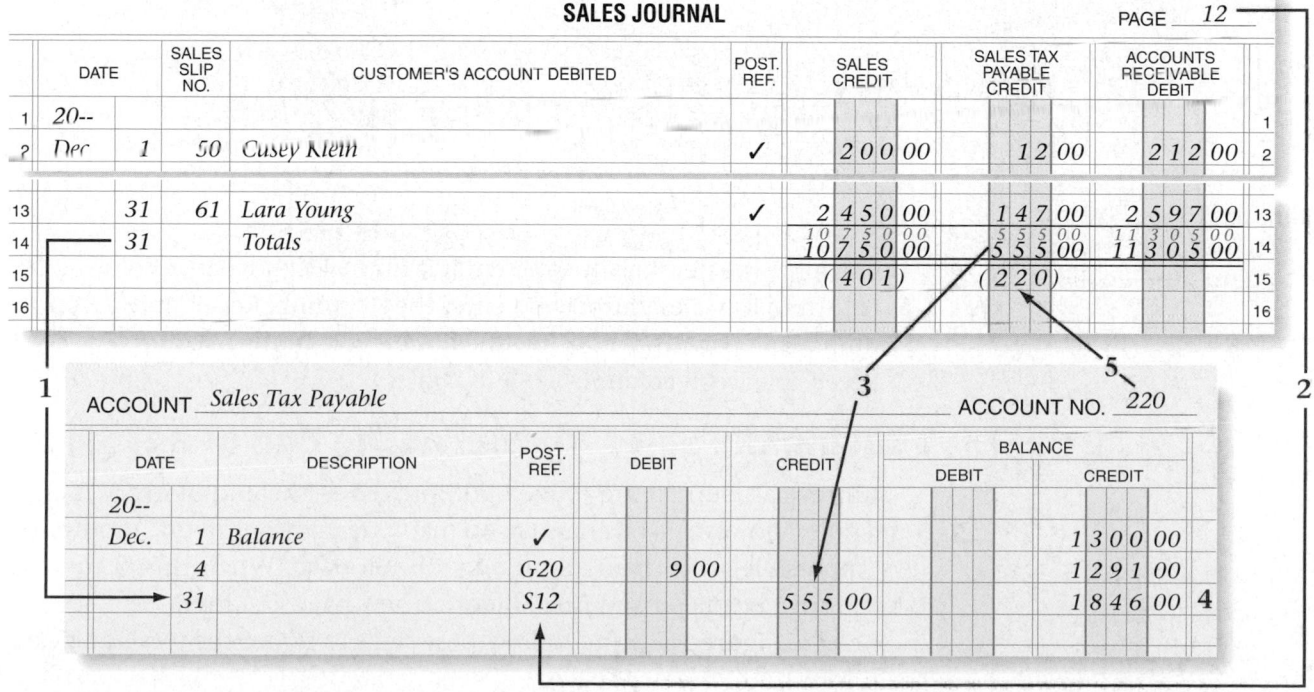

Posting a Special Journal Column Total

Entering an account number in parentheses under a column total means that the column total has been posted to the general ledger. The account number indicates the account where the column total was posted.

4. Compute the new balance and enter it in the Credit Balance column.
5. Return to the sales journal and enter the Sales Tax Payable account number, in parentheses, below the double rule in the Sales Tax Payable Credit column.

Posting the Total of the Accounts Receivable Debit Column

The last column of the sales journal to be posted is the Accounts Receivable Debit column. Refer to **Figure 16–6** as you read these steps.

1. In the Date column of the **Accounts Receivable** account, enter the date from the "Totals" line of the sales journal.
2. Enter the sales journal letter and page number in the Posting Reference column.
3. In the Debit column, enter the total from the Accounts Receivable Debit column of the sales journal.

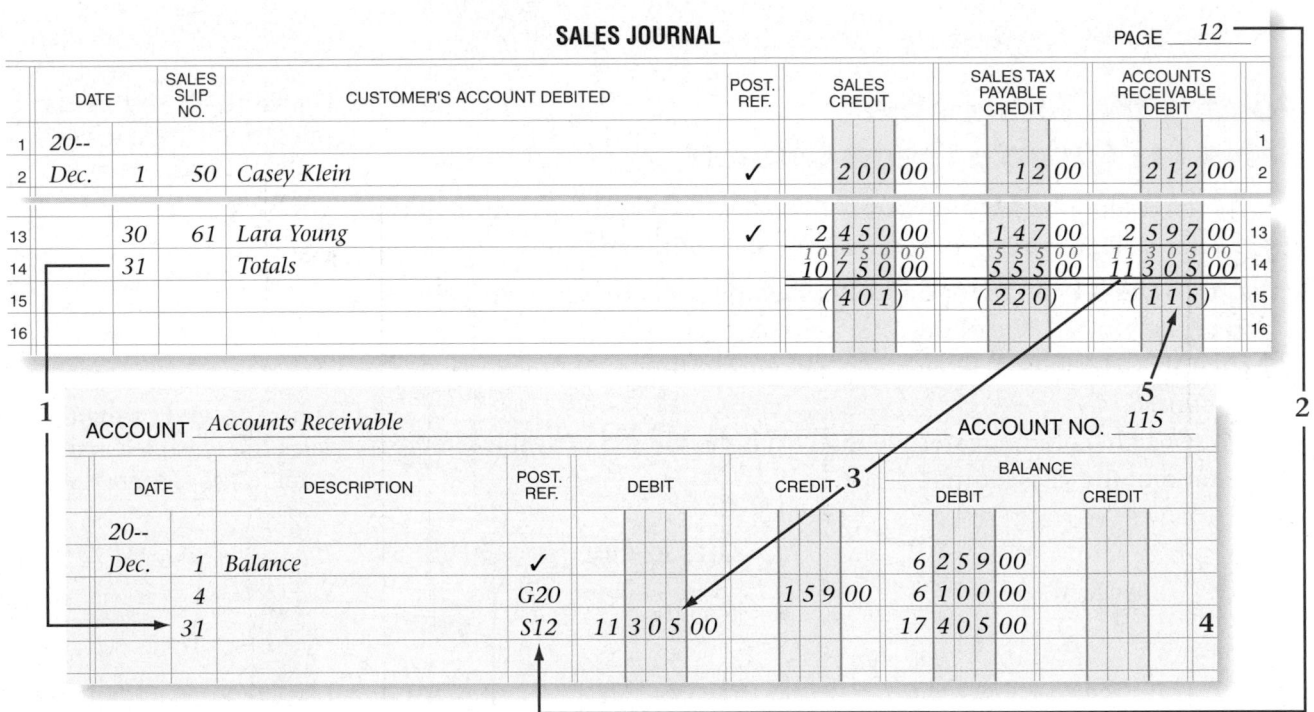

Figure 16–6 Posting Accounts Receivable Debit Total to the General Ledger

4. Compute the new balance and enter it in the Debit Balance column.
5. Return to the sales journal and enter the **Accounts Receivable** account number, in parentheses, below the double rule in the Accounts Receivable Debit column.

Proving the Sales Journal at the End of a Page

All special journals are totaled and proved at the end of every month. Sometimes, however, a business has so many transactions in one month that it is impossible to fit them all on one journal page. When this occurs, the journal page is totaled and ruled before a new page is started.

Refer to **Figure 16–7** and follow these steps to record the totals and carry them forward to the next page.

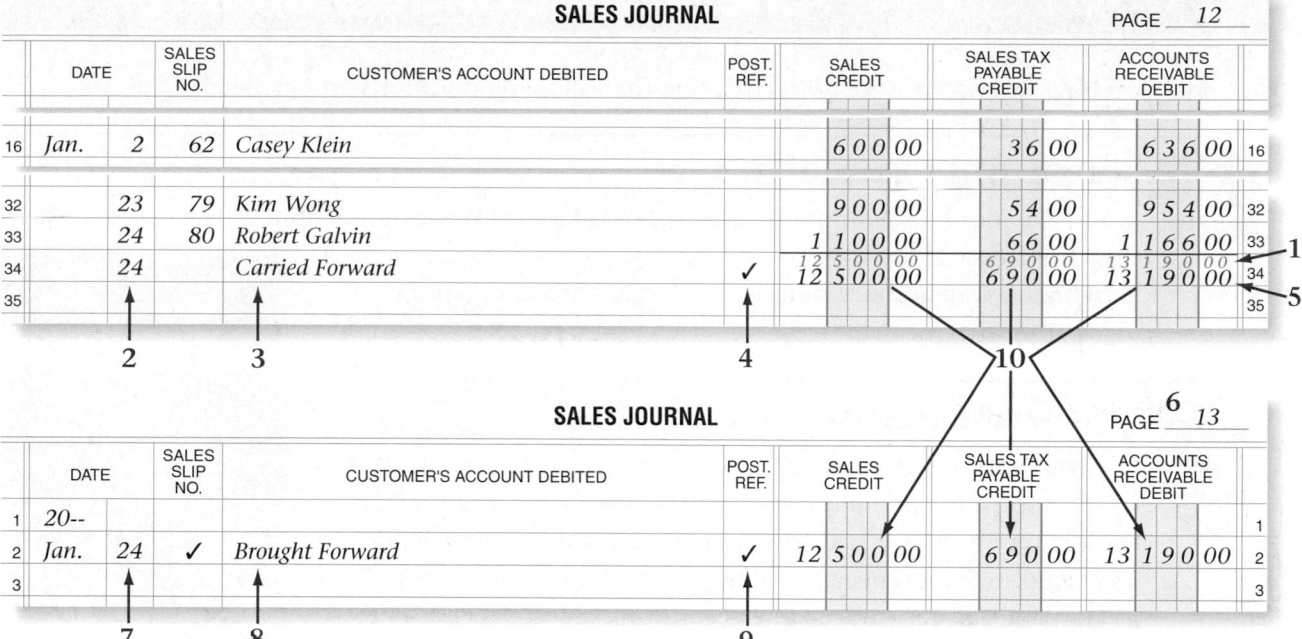

SALES JOURNAL PAGE 12

	DATE	SALES SLIP NO.	CUSTOMER'S ACCOUNT DEBITED	POST. REF.	SALES CREDIT	SALES TAX PAYABLE CREDIT	ACCOUNTS RECEIVABLE DEBIT	
16	Jan. 2	62	Casey Klein		6 0 0 00	3 6 00	6 3 6 00	16
32	23	79	Kim Wong		9 0 0 00	5 4 00	9 5 4 00	32
33	24	80	Robert Galvin		1 1 0 0 00	6 6 00	1 1 6 6 00	33
34	24		Carried Forward	✓	12 5 0 0 00	6 9 0 00	13 1 9 0 00	34
35								35

2   3   4   10

SALES JOURNAL PAGE 6 13

	DATE	SALES SLIP NO.	CUSTOMER'S ACCOUNT DEBITED	POST. REF.	SALES CREDIT	SALES TAX PAYABLE CREDIT	ACCOUNTS RECEIVABLE DEBIT	
1	20--							1
2	Jan. 24	✓	Brought Forward	✓	12 5 0 0 00	6 9 0 00	13 1 9 0 00	2
3								3

7   8   9

Figure 16–7 Starting a New Journal Page

1. Draw a single rule across the three amount columns below the last transaction. Foot the columns and prove the equality of debits and credits.
2. On the line following the last transaction, enter the date of the last transaction in the Date column.
3. In the Customer's Account Debited column, write "Carried Forward."
4. Place a check mark (✓) in the Posting Reference column. This check mark indicates that these totals are not to be posted.
5. Enter the column totals in ink. *Do not* double-rule the columns.
6. On the next journal page, enter the new page number.
7. On line 1 and 2 enter the complete date (year, month, and day) in the Date column. Use the same date as on the last line of the previous page.
8. Write "Brought Forward" in the Customer's Account Debited column.
9. Place a check mark (✓) in the Posting Reference column.
10. Enter the column totals from the previous page on line 2.

The journal page is now ready for the recording of the next transaction.

International ACCOUNTING

Laptop Safety
Business travelers who carry a laptop should test the phone lines to make sure that power surges don't ruin their computers.

A MATTER OF ETHICS

Working for a Competitor

Accounting clerks use sales journals to record sales on account, which means they have direct access to the company's customer lists. Imagine that you are an accounting clerk at a furniture store like Haverty's. A co-worker named Bob also works as an accounting clerk, but only part-time. Recently, Bob has confided in you that during the mornings, he works at World Classic Furniture, a competitor of Haverty's.

Ethical Decision Making:
☞ What are the ethical issues?
☞ What are the alternatives?
☞ Who are the affected parties?
☞ How do the alternatives affect the parties?
☞ What would you do?

Now that you have studied this section, complete the following questions and problems.

Thinking Critically

1. List the four most commonly used special journals. What transactions are recorded in each of these special journals?
2. What does an account number written in parentheses under a column total mean?

Communicating Accounting

You work for Equestrian Steps—Horse Boarding and Lessons, which sponsored an equestrian competition last weekend. During the competition you had to purchase grain on account from the local feed store. You need to tell the accountant about the purchase so that she can record it in the accounting records. On a separate sheet of paper, write a brief memo explaining the transaction. The grain cost $85. The feed store charged a 6% sales tax.

Problem 16–1 Posting Column Totals from the Sales Journal

Instructions Here are the column totals of the sales journal for the month of April. In your working papers, post these totals to the appropriate general ledger accounts.

SALES JOURNAL PAGE ___4___

	DATE	SALES SLIP NO.	CUSTOMER'S ACCOUNT DEBITED	POST. REF.	SALES CREDIT	SALES TAX PAYABLE CREDIT	ACCOUNTS RECEIVABLE DEBIT	
1	20--							1
2	Apr. 1	47	Amy Anderson	✓	800 00	48 00	848 00	2
32	30		Totals		12 000 00	720 00	12 720 00	32
33								33

Problem 16–2 Analyzing a Source Document

Metro Sports Distributors had the following transaction on June 15.

Instructions

1. Analyze the sales slip shown. In your working papers, record the required entry on page 3 of the sales journal.
2. Post to the customer's account in the accounts receivable subsidiary ledger.

SPORTS DISTRIBUTORS
Kingston Mall, Williamsburg, Virginia 23185

DATE: June 15, 20--   NO. 113

SOLD TO	M&M Consultants 2816 Mt. Odin Drive Williamsburg, VA 23185		
CLERK RDP	CASH	CHARGE ✓	TERMS 3/15, n/45

QTY.	DESCRIPTION	UNIT PRICE	AMOUNT
10	Golf Bags	$ 50.00	$ 500 00
2 doz.	Ladies Golf Shirts	100.00/doz	200 00
20	Golf Caps	6.00	120 00
		SUBTOTAL	$ 820 00
		SALES TAX	41 00
	Thank You!	TOTAL	$ 861 00

The Cash Receipts Journal

In Chapter 14 you learned about cash receipts. The three most common sources of cash for a merchandising business are payments from charge customers, cash sales, and bank card sales. Cash is also received, though less frequently, from the sale of other business assets.

Think about cable television, electric, and telephone companies in your area. Can you imagine how many checks these companies receive every day? You can be sure they have streamlined the cash receipts process so that checks are recorded as efficiently as possible and deposited in the bank promptly. In this section, you will learn a more efficient way to record cash receipts by using a special journal called the six-column cash receipts journal.

The Cash Receipts Journal

The **cash receipts journal** is a special journal used to record all cash receipt transactions. Every transaction recorded in the cash receipts journal requires a debit to the **Cash in Bank** account, so there is always a Cash in Bank Debit column. The number of credit columns varies, depending on the needs of the business.

The cash receipts journal used by On Your Mark Athletic Wear is shown in **Figure 16–8**. In addition to the date, source document, account name and posting reference columns, it contains six amount columns.

To keep the customer account balances current, the entries in the Accounts Receivable Credit column are posted daily to the accounts receivable subsidiary ledger. The entries in the General Credit column are posted daily to the individual general ledger accounts. At the end of the month, the totals of all the special amount columns are posted to the general ledger accounts named in the column headings.

What **You'll Learn**

- How to record transactions in the cash receipts journal.
- How to post from the cash receipts journal to accounts receivable subsidiary ledger accounts.
- How to post amounts in the General Credit column of the cash receipts journal to general ledger accounts.
- How to post column totals from the cash receipts journal to the general ledger.
- How to prepare a schedule of accounts receivable.

Why **It's Important**

Use of the cash receipts journal will save time and reduce errors.

KEY TERMS

cash receipts journal
schedule of accounts
　receivable

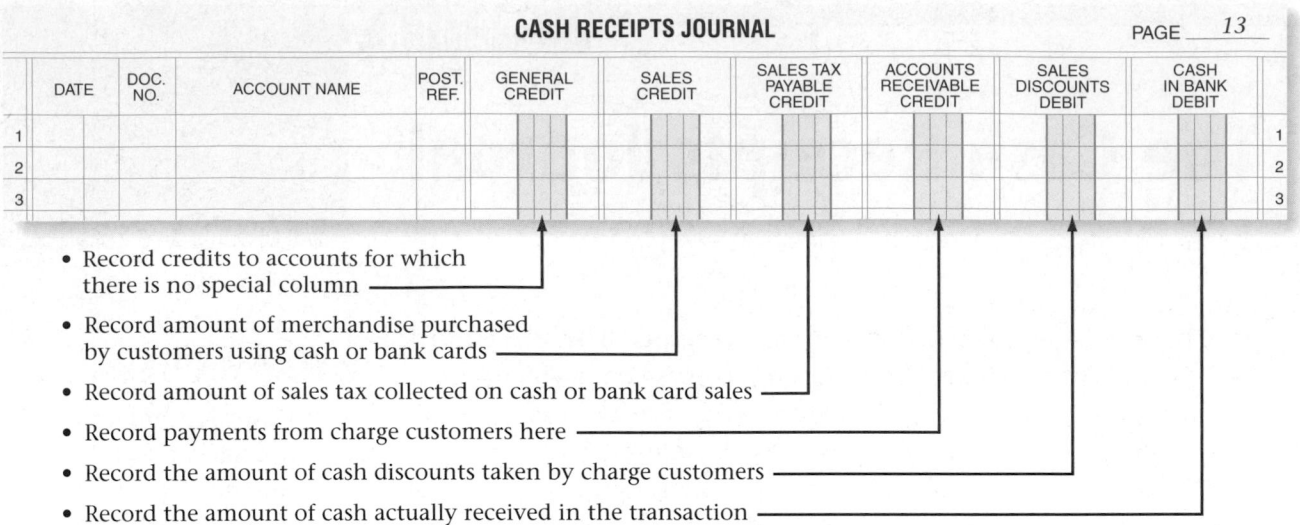

Figure 16–8 Cash Receipts Journal

Recording Cash from Charge Customers

Let's record a transaction for cash received from a charge customer. The source document for this transaction is the receipt.

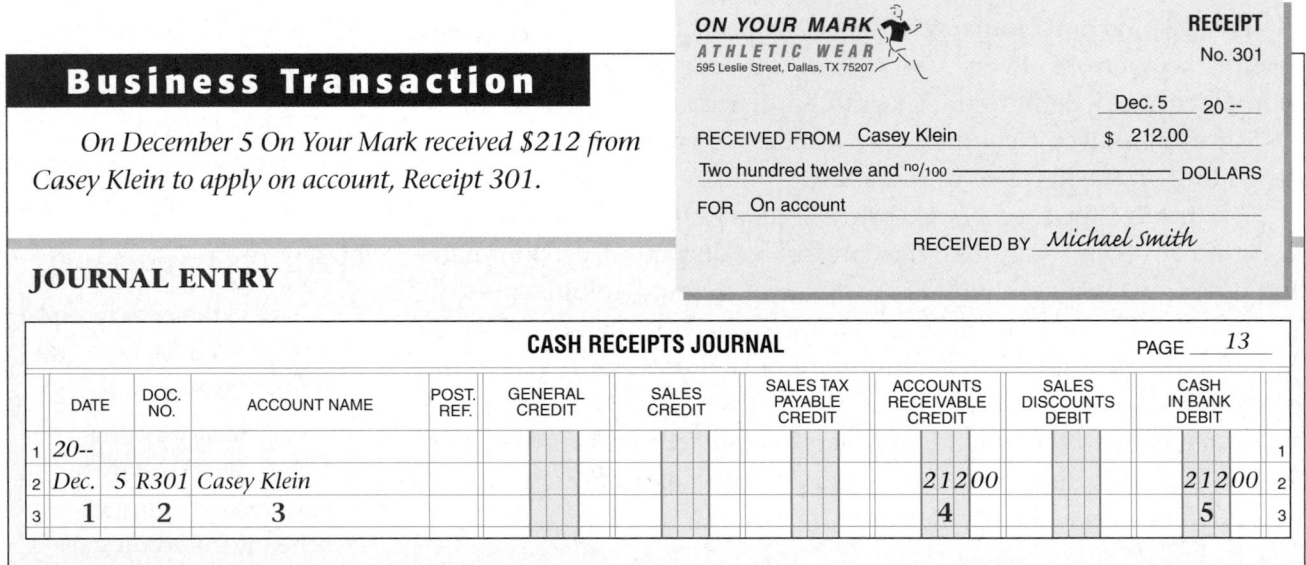

Follow these steps when journalizing cash receipts from charge customers:

1. Enter the date of the transaction in the Date column.
2. Enter the receipt number in the Document Number column. Write the letter "R" (for receipt) before the receipt number.
3. Enter the name of the customer in the Account Name column.
4. Enter the decrease in the amount owed by the customer in the Accounts Receivable Credit column.
5. Enter the amount of cash received in the Cash in Bank Debit column.

When this entry is posted to the customer's account in the accounts receivable subsidiary ledger, a check mark (✓) is entered in the Posting Reference column of the cash receipts journal.

Recording Cash Received on Account, Less a Cash Discount

Now let's record a cash receipt transaction with a cash discount.

Business Transaction

On December 12 On Your Mark received $1,470 from South Branch High School Athletics in payment of Sales Slip 51 for $1,500 less the discount of $30, Receipt 302.

ON YOUR MARK
ATHLETIC WEAR
595 Leslie Street, Dallas, TX 75207

RECEIPT
No. 302

Dec. 12   20 --

RECEIVED FROM   South Branch H.S. Athletics $ 1,470.00

One thousand four hundred seventy and no/100 ———— DOLLARS

FOR   On account

RECEIVED BY   *Michael Smith*

JOURNAL ENTRY

CASH RECEIPTS JOURNAL PAGE ___13___

	DATE	DOC. NO.	ACCOUNT NAME	POST. REF.	GENERAL CREDIT	SALES CREDIT	SALES TAX PAYABLE CREDIT	ACCOUNTS RECEIVABLE CREDIT	SALES DISCOUNTS DEBIT	CASH IN BANK DEBIT	
3	12	R302	South Branch H.S. Ath.					1 500 00	30 00	1 470 00	3
4	**1**	**2**	**3**					**4**	**5**	**6**	4

Follow these steps to journalize this transaction:

1. Enter the date of the receipt in the Date column.
2. Enter the receipt number in the Document Number column. Remember to write the letter "R" before the receipt number.
3. Enter the name of the customer in the Account Name column.
4. In the Accounts Receivable Credit column, enter the amount of the original sales transaction (the amount that was debited in the sales journal) less any related sales returns or allowances.
5. Enter the cash discount amount in the Sales Discounts Debit column.
6. Enter the amount of cash received in the Cash in Bank Debit column.

Recording Cash Sales

Many businesses journalize cash sales and make cash deposits daily. In this chapter, however, we assume that On Your Mark records cash sales every two weeks.

Business Transaction

On December 15 On Your Mark records the cash sales for the first two weeks of December, $3,000, and $180 in related sales taxes, Tape 55.

Dec. 15
Tape 55

3000.00   CA
180.00   ST

JOURNAL ENTRY

CASH RECEIPTS JOURNAL PAGE ___13___

	DATE	DOC. NO.	ACCOUNT NAME	POST. REF.	GENERAL CREDIT	SALES CREDIT	SALES TAX PAYABLE CREDIT	ACCOUNTS RECEIVABLE CREDIT	SALES DISCOUNTS DEBIT	CASH IN BANK DEBIT	
4	15	T55	Cash Sales	—		3 000 00	180 00			3 180 00	4
5	**1**	**2**	**3**	**4**		**5**	**6**			**7**	5

**Journalizing
Cash Receipts**

When journalizing a cash receipt transaction involving a sales discount, be sure to credit **Accounts Receivable** for the amount of the original sales transaction less any related sales returns or allowances.

Follow these steps when entering cash sales in the cash receipts journal. The source document for this transaction is the cash register tape.

1. Enter the date written on the cash register tape in the Date column.
2. Enter the number of the tape in the Document Number column. Write the letter "T" (for tape) before the tape number.
3. Enter the words "Cash Sales" in the Account Name column.
4. Enter a dash in the Posting Reference column. The amounts recorded in the cash sales entry are posted to the general ledger as part of the column totals at the end of the month. The dash indicates that the entry is not posted individually to the general ledger accounts.
5. Enter the amount of merchandise sold in the Sales Credit column.
6. Enter the amount of the sales taxes collected in the Sales Tax Payable Credit column.
7. Enter the total cash received in the Cash in Bank Debit column.

Recording Bankcard Sales

A business can record and deposit bankcard sales slips at any interval. For illustration purposes, we assume that On Your Mark processes bankcard sales every two weeks. Let's record a bankcard sales transaction. Notice how this is similar to recording a cash sale.

Business Transaction

On December 15 On Your Mark recorded bankcard sales of $700 for the first two weeks of December and related sales taxes of $42, Tape 55.

Dec. 15
Tape 55

700.00 BCS
42.00 ST

JOURNAL ENTRY

	DATE	DOC. NO.	ACCOUNT NAME	POST. REF.	GENERAL CREDIT	SALES CREDIT	SALES TAX PAYABLE CREDIT	ACCOUNTS RECEIVABLE CREDIT	SALES DISCOUNTS DEBIT	CASH IN BANK DEBIT	
5	15	T55	Bankcard Sales	—		700 00	42 00			742 00	5
6	1	2	3	4		5	6			7	6

CASH RECEIPTS JOURNAL PAGE ___13___

Follow these steps when entering bankcard sales in the cash receipts journal. The source document for this entry is the cash register tape.

1. Enter the date of the cash register tape in the Date column.
2. Enter the number of the tape in the Document Number column. Remember to write the letter "T" before the tape number.
3. Enter the words "Bankcard Sales" in the Account Name column.
4. Enter a dash in the Posting Reference column. The amounts recorded in the bankcard sales entry are posted to the general ledger as part of the column totals at the end of the month.
5. Enter the amount of merchandise sold in the Sales Credit column.

6. Enter the amount of sales taxes collected in the Sales Tax Payable Credit column.
7. Enter the total cash received in the Cash in Bank Debit column.

Recording Other Cash Receipts

Occasionally, a retail business will receive cash from a transaction that does not involve the sale of merchandise. Since the business is receiving cash, the transaction is entered in the cash receipts journal.

Business Transaction

On December 16 On Your Mark received $30 from Mandy Harris, an office employee. She purchased a calculator that the business was no longer using, Receipt 303.

ON YOUR MARK ATHLETIC WEAR 595 Leslie Street, Dallas, TX 75207	RECEIPT No. 303
	Dec. 16 20 --
RECEIVED FROM Mandy Harris	$ 30.00
Thirty and no/100	DOLLARS
FOR calculator	
RECEIVED BY Michael Smith	

JOURNAL ENTRY

	DATE	DOC. NO.	ACCOUNT NAME	POST. REF.	GENERAL CREDIT	SALES CREDIT	SALES TAX PAYABLE CREDIT	ACCOUNTS RECEIVABLE CREDIT	SALES DISCOUNTS DEBIT	CASH IN BANK DEBIT	
CASH RECEIPTS JOURNAL										PAGE 13	
6	16	R303	Office Equipment		30 00					30 00	6
7	1	2	3		4					5	7

Follow these steps to enter this transaction into the cash receipts journal:

1. Enter the date of the receipt in the Date column.
2. Enter the letter "R" and the receipt number in the Document Number column.
3. Enter "Office Equipment" in the Account Name column.
4. Enter the amount of the credit in the General Credit column. Use the General Credit column whenever the credit part of the entry is to an account that does not have a special amount column.
5. Enter the amount of cash received in the Cash in Bank Debit column.

Posting to the Accounts Receivable Subsidiary Ledger

Daily postings are made from the Accounts Receivable Credit column to the accounts receivable subsidiary ledger. This ensures that customer accounts are always current. To post a cash receipt transaction to an account in the accounts receivable subsidiary ledger, refer to **Figure 16–9** and follow these steps.

1. Enter the date of the transaction in the Date column of the subsidiary ledger account.
2. In the Posting Reference column of the subsidiary ledger, enter the journal letters and the page number. Use the letters "CR" for the cash receipts journal.

3. In the Credit column of the subsidiary ledger account, enter the amount shown in the Accounts Receivable Credit column of the cash receipts journal.
4. Compute the new balance and enter it in the Balance column. If the account has a zero balance, draw a line through the Balance column.
5. Return to the cash receipts journal and enter a check mark (✓) in the Posting Reference column.

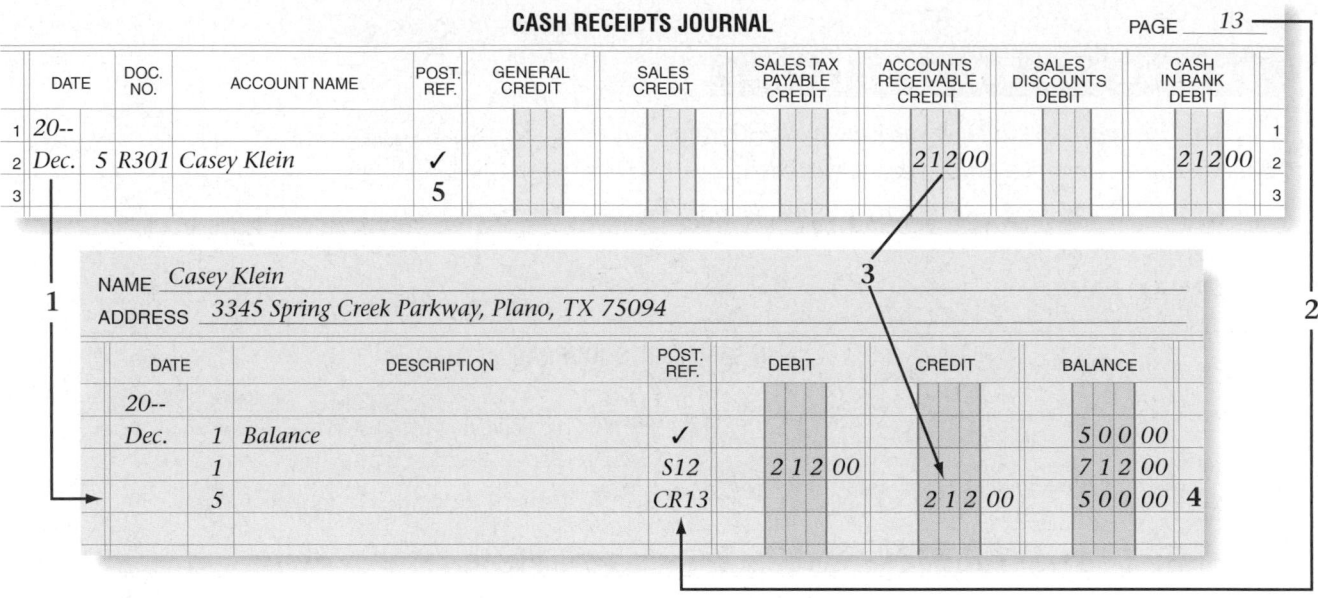

Figure 16–9 Posting from the Cash Receipts Journal to the Accounts Receivable Subsidiary Ledger

Posting the General Credit Column

Daily postings are made from the General Credit column of the cash receipts journal to the appropriate accounts in the general ledger. Refer to **Figure 16–10** as you read the steps for posting amounts from this column.

1. Enter the date of the transaction in the Date column of the general ledger account.
2. Enter the journal letters and page number in the Posting Reference column of the ledger account. Be sure to use the letters "CR" for cash receipts journal.
3. In the Credit column of the ledger account, enter the amount from the General Credit column of the cash receipts journal.
4. Compute and enter the new account balance in the proper Balance column. For the **Office Equipment** account shown in **Figure 16–10**, the Debit Balance column is used. If the account has a zero balance, draw a line through the appropriate Balance column.
5. Return to the cash receipts journal and enter the general ledger account number in the Posting Reference column.

The cash receipts journal entry for the December 16 transaction is now posted. All transactions recorded in the General Credit column are posted in the same manner.

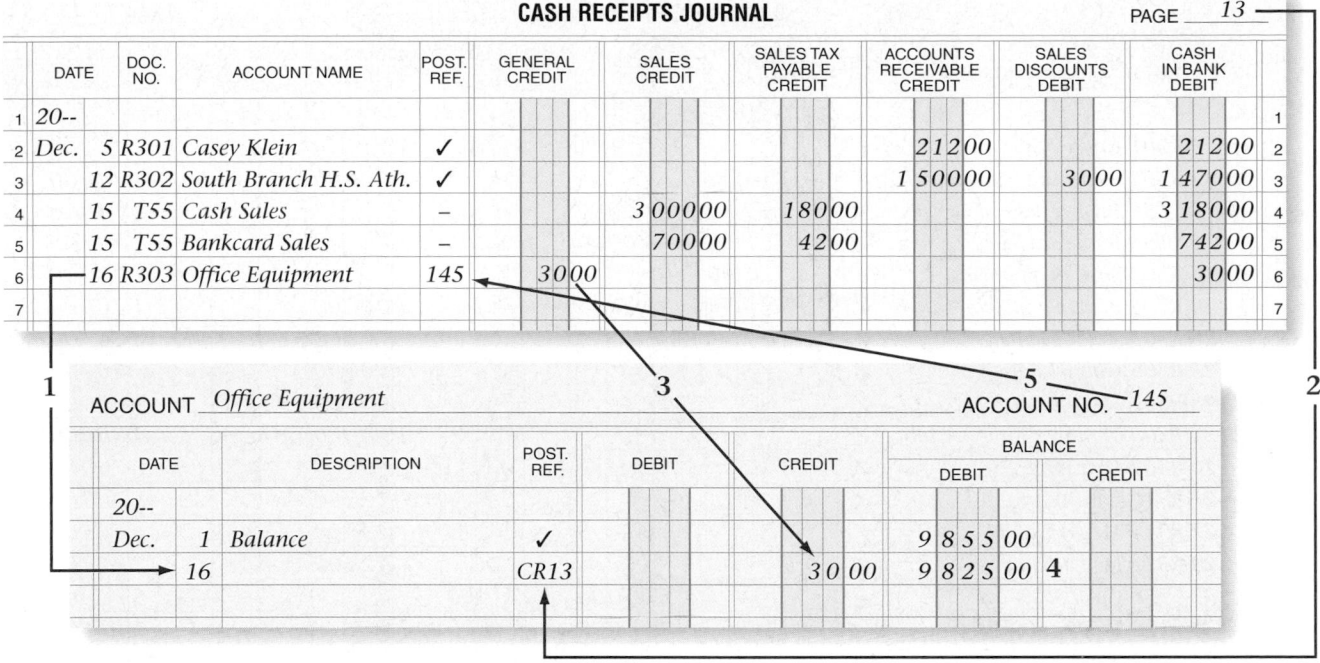

CASH RECEIPTS JOURNAL

	DATE	DOC. NO.	ACCOUNT NAME	POST. REF.	GENERAL CREDIT	SALES CREDIT	SALES TAX PAYABLE CREDIT	ACCOUNTS RECEIVABLE CREDIT	SALES DISCOUNTS DEBIT	CASH IN BANK DEBIT	
1	20--										1
2	Dec. 5	R301	Casey Klein	✓				2 1 2 00		2 1 2 00	2
3	12	R302	South Branch H.S. Ath.	✓				1 5 0 0 00	3 0 00	1 4 7 0 00	3
4	15	T55	Cash Sales	–		3 0 0 0 00	1 8 0 00			3 1 8 0 00	4
5	15	T55	Bankcard Sales	–		7 0 0 00	4 2 00			7 4 2 00	5
6	16	R303	Office Equipment	145	3 0 00					3 0 00	6
7											7

ACCOUNT __Office Equipment__   ACCOUNT NO. __145__

DATE	DESCRIPTION	POST. REF.	DEBIT	CREDIT	BALANCE DEBIT	BALANCE CREDIT
20--						
Dec. 1	Balance	✓			9 8 5 5 00	
16		CR13		3 0 00	9 8 2 5 00	

Figure 16–10 Posting from the General Credit Column of the Cash Receipts Journal

Footing, Totaling, Proving, and Ruling the Cash Receipts Journal

To complete the cash receipts journal, refer to **Figure 16–11** and follow these steps:

1. Draw a single rule across the six amount columns, just below the last transaction.
2. Foot the columns.
3. Test for the equality of debits and credits.

Debit Columns			**Credit Columns**		
Sales Discounts	$	30	General	$	30
Cash in Bank		17,283	Sales		9,700
			Sales Tax Payable		582
			Accounts Receivable		7,001
Total	$	17,313	Total	$	17,313

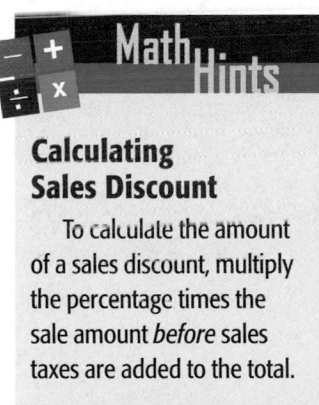

Math Hints

Calculating Sales Discount

To calculate the amount of a sales discount, multiply the percentage times the sale amount *before* sales taxes are added to the total.

4. In the Date column, on the line below the single rule, enter the date the journal is being totaled.
5. On the same line in the Account Name column, enter the word "Totals."
6. Enter the column totals, in ink, just below the footings.
7. Double-rule the amount columns.

Take a look at the completed Cash Receipts Journal. As you can see, a business saves time by using this special journal to record its cash receipts in one location instead of using many general journal pages.

After the cash receipts journal is footed, proved, totaled, and ruled, the column totals are posted to the general ledger.

DATE	DOC. NO.	ACCOUNT NAME	POST. REF.	GENERAL CREDIT	SALES CREDIT	SALES TAX PAYABLE CREDIT	ACCOUNTS RECEIVABLE CREDIT	SALES DISCOUNTS DEBIT	CASH IN BANK DEBIT	
20--										1
Dec. 5	R301	Casey Klein	✓				212 00		212 00	2
12	R302	South Branch H.S. Ath.	✓				1 500 00	30 00	1 470 00	3
15	T55	Cash Sales	–		3 000 00	180 00			3 180 00	4
15	T55	Bankcard Sales	–		700 00	42 00			742 00	5
16	R303	Office Equipment	145	30 00					30 00	6
18	R304	Break Point Sports Club	✓				100 00		100 00	7
20	R305	Anita Montero	✓				100 00		100 00	8
22	R306	Gabriel Ramos	✓				500 00		500 00	9
23	R307	South Branch H.S. Ath.	✓				100 00		100 00	10
24	R308	Tammy's Fitness Club	✓				1 300 00		1 300 00	11
26	R309	Kim Wong	✓				300 00		300 00	12
27	R310	Lara Young	✓				200 00		200 00	13
27	R311	Robert Galvin	✓				465 00		465 00	14
28	R312	Joe Dimaio	✓				424 00		424 00	15
31	T56	Cash Sales	–		5 000 00	300 00			5 300 00	16
31	T56	Bankcard Sales	–		1 000 00	60 00			1 060 00	17
31		Totals		30 00	9 700 00	582 00	7 001 00	30 00	17 283 00	18
				(✓)						19

Figure 16–11 Totaled and Ruled Cash Receipts Journal

Posting Column Totals to the General Ledger

There are six amount columns in the cash receipts journal used by On Your Mark. Only five of the column totals, however, are posted to the general ledger. The total of the General Credit column is *not* posted. The entries in this column have already been posted, individually, to the general ledger accounts. (See **Figure 16–10**.)

As shown in **Figure 16–12**, the total in each of the other five amount columns is posted to the general ledger account named in the column heading. The column heading indicates whether the amount is to be posted to the Debit or Credit column of the ledger account.

Refer to **Figure 16–12** and follow these steps:

1. Place a check mark in parenthesis under the General column total to indicate that this total is not posted.
2. Post the **Sales** total to the **Sales** account Credit column.
3. Post the **Sales Tax Payable** total to the **Sales Tax Payable** account Credit column.
4. Post the **Accounts Receivable** total to the **Accounts Receivable** controlling account Credit column.
5. Post the **Sales Discount** total to the **Sales Discounts** account Debit column.
6. Post the **Cash in Bank** total to the **Cash in Bank** account Debit column.
7. Compute new balances for each general ledger account.
8. Write the number of each account below the double rule in the cash receipts journal.

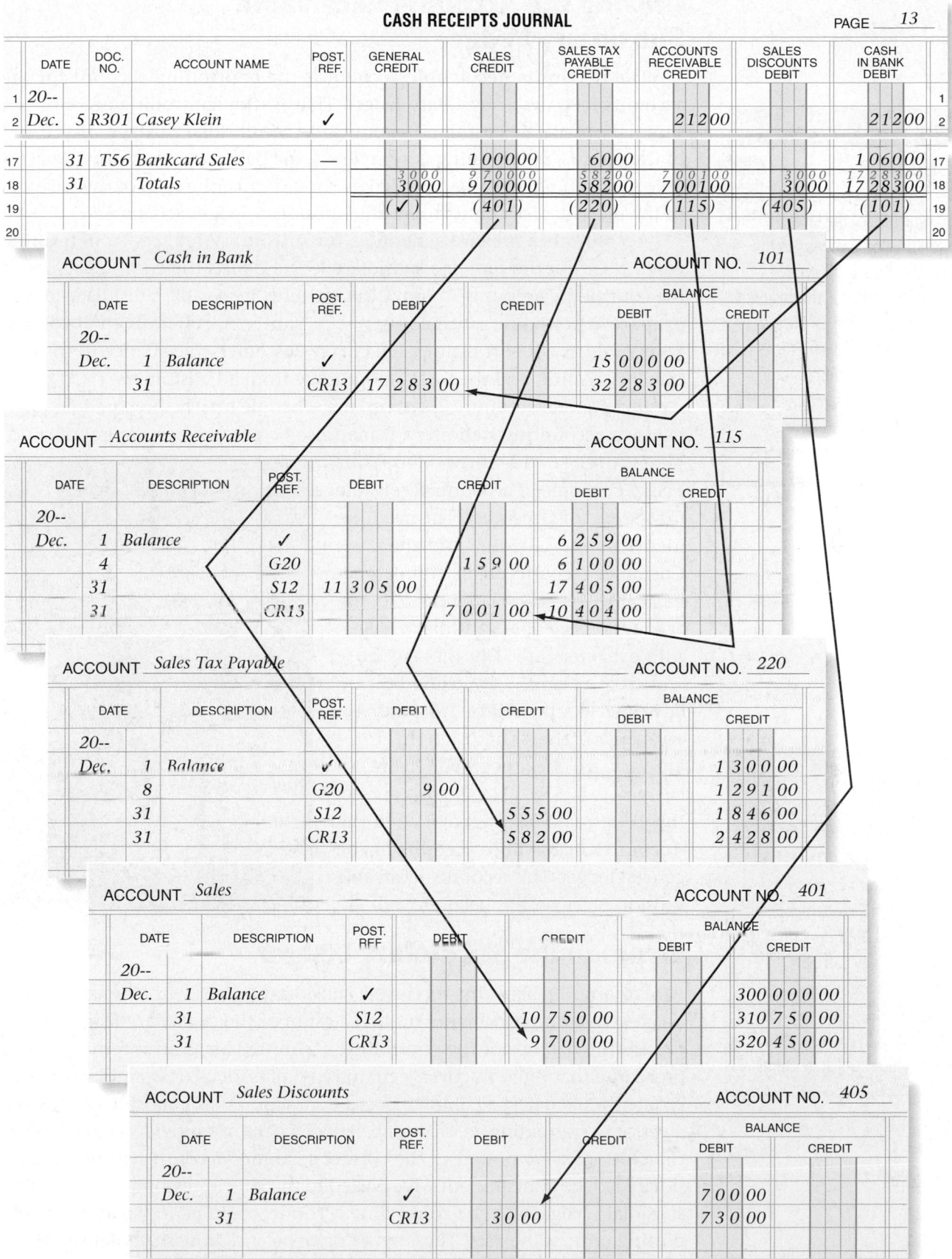

Figure 16–12 Posting Column Totals from the Cash Receipts Journal

Proving the Accounts Receivable Subsidiary Ledger

The **Accounts Receivable** account is the controlling account for the accounts receivable subsidiary ledger. That is, the controlling account is a summary of all the customer accounts in the subsidiary ledger. At the end of the month, after posting is completed, the balance of **Accounts Receivable** (controlling) in the general ledger should equal the total of the balances of the individual accounts receivable subsidiary ledger accounts.

Accountants prepare schedules for subsidiary ledgers to determine whether or not the sum of a subsidiary ledger equals the ending balance of the controlling account. To prove the accounts receivable subsidiary ledger, prepare a schedule of accounts receivable. A **schedule of accounts receivable** is a report listing each charge customer, the balance in the customer's account, and the total amount due from all customers.

In a manual accounting system, the schedule may be prepared on plain paper or accounting stationery. It may also be prepared on a computer.

Figure 16–13 shows On Your Mark's schedule of accounts receivable for the end of December. The heading identifies the schedule and the date. Customer accounts are listed in alphabetical order, as they appear in the accounts receivable subsidiary ledger. All customers are listed, even those with zero balances, to ensure that no customer is omitted by mistake. According to the schedule, the total amount to be received from all customers is $10,404. As you can see, this total matches the balance of the **Accounts Receivable** account in the general ledger. The accounts receivable subsidiary ledger has been proved.

Errors in the Subsidiary Ledger

Proving the accounts receivable subsidiary ledger with the controlling account determines whether or not the sum of the subsidiary ledger equals the ending balance of the controlling account. This is an internal control procedure that often uncovers certain types of errors. For example, this procedure should detect a failure to post a transaction to the subsidiary ledger or an error in computing an account balance. It does **not** provide assurance that transactions were posted to the correct customer account within the subsidiary ledger. If an amount were posted to the wrong customer account, the subsidiary ledger and the controlling account would be in balance, but the posting error still exists. These types of errors are difficult to detect. These errors are often detected by a customer who finds the error on a monthly billing.

ACCOUNT _Accounts Receivable_   ACCOUNT NO. _115_

DATE		DESCRIPTION	POST. REF.	DEBIT	CREDIT	BALANCE DEBIT	BALANCE CREDIT
20--							
Dec.	1	Balance	✓			6 2 5 9 00	
	4		G20		1 5 9 00	6 1 0 0 00	
	31		S12	11 3 0 5 00		17 4 0 5 00	
	31		CR13		7 0 0 1 00	10 4 0 4 00	

On Your Mark Athletic Wear
Schedule of Accounts Receivable
December 31, 20--

Break Point Sports Club	3 7 1 0 00	
Joe Dimaio		
Robert Galvin		
Casey Klein	5 0 0 00	
Anita Montero	3 7 1 00	
Shashi Rahim	2 1 2 00	
Gabriel Ramos	3 1 8 00	
South Branch High School Athletics	1 0 0 0 00	
Megan Sullivan	5 3 0 00	
Tammy's Fitness Club	1 0 6 0 00	
Kim Wong	1 0 6 00	
Lara Young	2 5 9 7 00	
		10 4 0 4 00

The balance of the **Accounts Receivable** account should equal the total of the schedule of accounts receivable.

Figure 16–13 Schedule of Accounts Receivable

ANALYZING FINANCIAL REPORTS

Operating Results

As you learned earlier, public corporations publish the financial results of their business operations each year in an annual report. The annual report contains much more than just financial data about the business. The company usually includes a description of the business activities of the past fiscal period, new products in development, and the business actions taken by the company's management to help make the business successful in the future.

The description of business activities includes management's analysis and interpretation of the financial data. For example, if revenue has decreased, the description might provide reasons for the decrease and projections for the next fiscal period.

▶ **Analyze the Report:**

Refer to the "Results of Operations" section on pages A-43–A-44 for Office Depot to answer these questions.

1. Did sales increase or decrease over the prior year?
2. What reasons are given for the change in sales from the prior fiscal period?
3. Why do you think an analysis of sales would be important to people reading an annual report?

Now that you have studied this section, complete the following questions and problems.

Thinking Critically

1. Explain the rules of debit and credit for recording bank card sales.
2. What is included in a schedule of accounts receivable? Explain how to prove the accounts receivable subsidiary ledger.

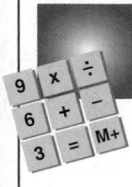

Computing in the Business World

You are hired to audit the books for a computer software retailer, Software Biz. As you review the books, you realize that the sales tax was not calculated on a sales slip. You also want to estimate cash receipts from a sale. On a separate sheet of paper, make the following calculations:

1. Accounts Receivable—Business World; Sales Slip 47: software for $550; sales tax at 6%. What is the total due?
2. Accounts Receivable—Cindy Caskey; Sales Slip 48:

Software	$46.53
Sales tax	2.79
Total	$49.32

Terms: 1/10, n/30.
How much will be received if paid within the discount period?

Problem 16-3 Completing the Cash Receipts Journal

The cash receipts journal for the month of January is provided in your working papers and illustrated below.

Instructions In your working papers, foot, prove, total, and rule the cash receipts journal.

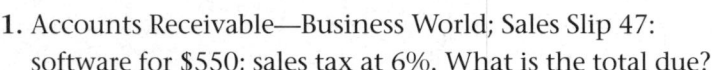

CASH RECEIPTS JOURNAL PAGE __10__

	DATE	DOC. NO.	ACCOUNT NAME	POST. REF.	GENERAL CREDIT	SALES CREDIT	SALES TAX PAYABLE CREDIT	ACCOUNTS RECEIVABLE CREDIT	SALES DISCOUNTS DEBIT	CASH IN BANK DEBIT	
1	20--										1
2	Jan. 3	R502	Jennifer Smith	✓				80 00		80 00	2
3	5	R503	Wilton High School	✓				3 100 00	62 00	3 038 00	3
4	8	R504	Store Equipment	155	75 00					75 00	4
5	15	T42	Cash Sales	—		5 000 00	300 00			5 300 00	5
6	15	T42	Bankcard Sales	—		1 200 00	72 00			1 272 00	6
7	20	R505	Norwin High School	✓				2 400 00	48 00	2 352 00	7
8	30	R506	Supplies	115	30 00					30 00	8
9											9

KEY CONCEPTS

1. Special journals are used by businesses that have many transactions. The most commonly used special journals are: the sales journal, the cash receipts journal, the purchases journal, and the cash payments journal.

2. A sales journal is used to record all sales of merchandise on account. The entry to record the sale of merchandise on account in the sales journal is illustrated below.

SALES JOURNAL   PAGE ___1___

	DATE	SALES SLIP NO.	CUSTOMER'S ACCOUNT DEBITED	POST. REF.	SALES CREDIT	SALES TAX PAYABLE CREDIT	ACCOUNTS RECEIVABLE DEBIT	
1	Date	Sales	Customer's Account Name		x x x xx	x x xx	x x x xx	1
2		Slip						2
3		No.						3

3. Daily postings are made from the Accounts Receivable Debit column to customer accounts in the accounts receivable subsidiary ledger. At the end of the month, the totals of the amount columns in the sales journal are posted to the accounts named in the column headings.

4. The cash receipts journal is used to record all cash received by a business.

5. The following illustrates the use of the cash receipts journal:
   (a) the receipt of cash from a charge customer
   (b) the receipt of cash from a charge customer less a cash discount
   (c) the receipt of cash from cash sales
   (d) the receipt of cash from bankcard sales
   (e) the receipt of cash from the sale of other assets

CASH RECEIPTS JOURNAL   PAGE ___1___

		DATE	DOC. NO.	ACCOUNT NAME	POST. REF.	GENERAL CREDIT	SALES CREDIT	SALES TAX PAYABLE CREDIT	ACCOUNTS RECEIVABLE CREDIT	SALES DISCOUNTS DEBIT	CASH IN BANK DEBIT	
(a)	1	Date of Receipt	Receipt No.	Customer's Name					x x x xx		x x x xx	1
(b)	2	Date of Receipt	Receipt No.	Customer's Name					x x x xx	x x xx	x x x xx	2
(c)	3	Date of Deposit	Tape No.	Cash Sale			x x x xx	x x xx			x x x xx	3
(d)	4	Date of Deposit	Tape No.	Bankcard Sales			x x x xx	x x xx			x x x xx	4
(e)	5	Date of Receipt	Receipt No.	Account Affected		x x x xx					x x x xx	5

6. The schedule of accounts receivable lists all charge customers and the amount each customer owes.

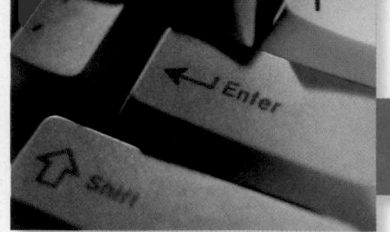

USING KEY TERMS

Imagine that you are the accounting manager for EarthWear Clothing. Recently you noticed that several sales associates are not keeping good records of sales transactions. Write an informational memorandum to the sales staff about the need for accurate, complete sales records. Use the terms listed below, and describe a systematic method to track sales.

cash receipts journal	schedule of accounts receivable
footing	special journals
sales journal	

Understanding Accounting Concepts and Procedures

Instructions

Answer the following questions on a separate sheet of paper.

1. When are special journals used in an accounting system?

2. Name and describe four commonly used special journals.

3. What three accounts are affected by a sale on account?

4. When are sales transactions posted to the accounts receivable subsidiary ledger? Why?

5. What are the source documents for transactions recorded in the cash receipts journal?

6. Why does a cash receipts journal always have a Cash in Bank Debit column.

7. What are the two kinds of postings made from the cash receipts journal?

8. When are amounts in the Accounts Receivable Credit column of the cash receipts journal posted to the accounts receivable subsidiary ledger?

9. Why is a check mark in parentheses placed below the double rule in the General Credit column of the cash receipts journal?

10. What is the purpose of preparing a schedule of accounts receivable?

Case Study...

Merchandising Business: Movie Theater

You work in the accounting department for Springdale Movie Theaters and have been asked to analyze ticket and concession food sales. The owners are considering enlarging the concession area to offer a greater variety of foods. No theater seats would be lost. The cost of enlarging the concession area to one and one-half times its current size is estimated at $200,000. Review the following sales figures for the past three years.

Year	Ticket Sales	Concession Sales
Year 1	$4,800,000	$1,800,000
Year 2	5,100,000	1,600,000
Year 3	5,400,000	1,480,000

Thinking Critically:

1. What percentage of sales are ticket sales and concession sales for each year?
2. What percentage increase in concession revenue would be needed to pay for the renovation costs in the first year?

*inter*NET CONNECTION

Bankcards

As you learned in Chapter 14, VISA and MasterCard are the two most widely used bankcards. Locate the Internet site for each company and answer the following questions.

Do This:

1. Which card, VISA or Master-Card, has greater acceptance or use by shoppers?
2. How many merchants accept VISA and MasterCard? What volume of sales is charged to each card?
3. List at least three additional services offered by the two major bankcard companies.
4. What is the cost to a merchant for accepting these bankcards?

Conducting an Audit with Alex

Alex is the chief auditor for the Mega Byte Corporation. You are working as an accounting intern under Alex's supervision. In April a number of errors are discovered in the sales journal. Alex asked you to identify and correct the errors. All sales were made on account and are taxable at a rate of 6%.

Instructions

1. What possible error has been made in the Sales Slip No. column?
2. What errors have been made in the three amount columns?

SALES JOURNAL PAGE ___1___

	DATE	SALES SLIP NO.	CUSTOMER'S ACCOUNT DEBITED	POST. REF.	SALES CREDIT	SALES TAX PAYABLE CREDIT	ACCOUNTS RECEIVABLE DEBIT	
1	20--							1
2	Apr. 25	3110	Suzette Simons		330 00		330 00	2
3	25	3101	John Joyce		450 00	27 00	477 00	3
4	26	3102	Fred Woodburn		170 00		190 00	4
5								5

Workplace Skills

Designing and Improving Systems

The ultimate in "systems thinking" is predicting trends, making adjustments, and improving the current system to benefit the organization.

On the Job:

At Ice Cream Express, you keep the financial records and maintain inventory. You noticed that some ice cream flavors are only popular during certain seasons of the year. For example, peppermint-flavored ice cream is very popular during the winter season, but sales decrease dramatically in the summer. You decide to get feedback from regular customers.

Thinking Critically:

1. Design a survey that will help determine the likes and dislikes of your customers. Include questions that will gather information about the gender, age, and income levels of respondents.
2. What incentives might prompt customers to participate?

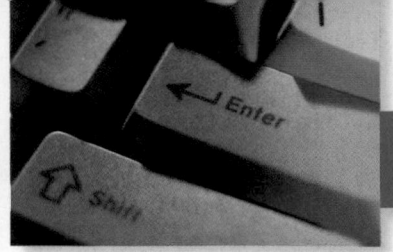

Mastering Sales and Cash Receipts

Making the Transition from a Manual to a Computerized System

Task	Perform Accounting Procedures Using Manual Methods	Perform Accounting Procedures Using Automated Methods
Setting up customer records	1. Ledger sheets or cards are prepared with customer account details such as customer name, address, and contact information. 2. Account activities are posted to the customer's subsidiary ledger account.	1. Assign each customer an ID code. 2. Record details of customer accounts into customer records. 3. The software will access this information automatically each time the ID code is used. 4. The customer's sales and payment history is maintained automatically.
Issuing and Recording a Credit Memorandum	1. A credit memorandum is prepared. 2. A journal entry is prepared to record the credit memorandum. 3. The journal entry is posted to the customer's account and to the general ledger.	1. A credit memorandum is prepared. 2. Record the credit memorandum as a negative amount using the Sales/Invoice option. 3. The software applies the credit memorandum to the appropriate outstanding invoice and posts the amount to the customer's account and to the general ledger.

Mastering Sales and Cash Receipts

Peachtree Question	Description
How do I set up a new customer account?	1. Select **Customers/Prospects** from the *Maintain* menu. 2. Assign a Customer ID to the customer account. 3. Enter customer name and contact information. 4. Click on the *Sales Defaults* tab. 5. Verify or enter the appropriate sales default GL account number. 6. Click *Save*.
How do I issue and record a credit memorandum?	1. Select **Sales/Invoicing** from the *Tasks* menu. 2. Enter a reference number, usually the Credit Memorandum number. 3. Enter the return or allowance as a negative amount for the appropriate invoice listed. 4. Click *Save*.
What does the software do "behind the scenes"?	• Using Customer ID codes, the software can update customer sales and payment history records when you enter invoices or cash receipts. • Credit memorandums are applied directly to the appropriate outstanding invoice and posted to the general ledger and subsidiary ledger automatically.

For detailed instructions: See the **Peachtree User Guide** in your Glencoe Working Papers.

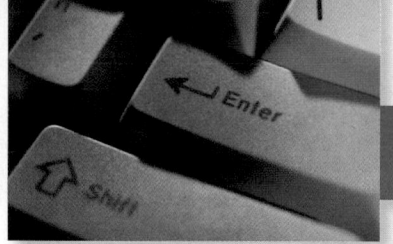

APPLICATION OPTIONS

Problem 16–4 Recording and Posting Sales Transactions

Shutterbug Cameras uses special journals for recording its transactions. The accounts receivable subsidiary ledger and certain general ledger accounts are included in your working papers.

Instructions In your working papers:

1. Record each transaction on page 12 of the sales journal or on page 13 of the cash receipts journal.
2. Post to the customer accounts in the accounts receivable subsidiary ledger on a daily basis.
3. Foot, prove, total, and rule the sales journal.
4. Post the column totals from the sales journal and the cash receipts journal to the general ledger accounts named in the column headings.
5. Prepare a schedule of accounts receivable.

Date		Transactions
May	1	Sold merchandise on account to Yoko Nakata, $500 plus 4% sales tax of $20, Sales Slip 220.
	3	Sold to Click Studios $1,500 in camera equipment plus sales tax of $60, Sales Slip 221.
	7	Sold telescopic lens to Jimmy Thompson for $200 plus sales tax of $8, Sales Slip 222.
	9	Sold merchandise on account to Heather Sullivan for $100 plus sales tax of $4, Sales Slip 223.
	12	Sold camera tripod to Arturo Diaz for $400 plus sales tax of $16, Sales Slip 224.
	15	Sold $3,000 in merchandise on account to FastForward Productions plus sales tax of $120, Sales Slip 225.
	18	Sold merchandise on account to Yoko Nakata, $200 plus sales tax of $8, Sales Slip 226.

Analyze: Based on the transactions above, how much cash was collected for the month?

Problem 16–5 Recording and Posting Cash Receipts

River's Edge Canoe & Kayak uses special journals and an accounts receivable subsidiary ledger for recording business transactions. The accounts receivable subsidiary ledger accounts and certain general ledger accounts are included in your working papers. The current account balances are recorded in the accounts.

Continued 🍂

Complete chapter problems one of three ways:

1 **Manual** Glencoe Working Papers

or

2 **Peachtree Complete Accounting** Software

or

3 **QuickBooks** Templates (Problems 16–5, 16–6)

Peachtree®

SMART GUIDE

Step–by–Step Instructions: Problem 16–4

1. Select the problem set for Shutterbug Cameras (Prob. 16–4).
2. Rename the company and set the system date.
3. Enter all sales on account transactions using the **Sales/Invoicing** option.
4. Record all cash sales using the **Receipts** option.
5. Print a Sales Journal report and a Cash Receipts Journal report.
6. Proof your work. Make any needed corrections.
7. Print a General Ledger report and Customer Ledgers report.
8. Answer the Analyze question.
9. End the session.

TIP: When you print a report, such as the General Ledger, you can use the filter options to customize the information that appears on the report.

Peachtree®

SMART GUIDE

Step–by–Step Instructions: Problem 16–5

1. Select the problem set for River's Edge Canoe & Kayak (Prob. 16–5).
2. Rename the company and set the system date.
3. Record all cash receipts using the **Receipts** option.
4. Print the following reports: Cash Receipts Journal, General Ledger, and Customer Ledgers.
5. Proof your work. Make any needed corrections.
6. Answer the Analyze question.
7. End the session.

TIP: You can apply a partial payment from a customer.

Instructions In your working papers:

1. Record the transactions on page 7 in the cash receipts journal.
2. Post the amounts from the Accounts Receivable Credit column to the customers' accounts in the accounts receivable subsidiary ledger. Post the individual amounts in the General Credit column to the general ledger accounts.
3. Foot, prove, total, and rule the cash receipts journal.
4. Post the column totals to the general ledger accounts named in the column headings.
5. Prepare a schedule of accounts receivable.

Date	Transactions
May 2	Received $400 from Paul Drake to apply on his account, Receipt 505.
5	Received $2,940 from Adventure River Tours in payment of their $3,000 account less a 2% cash discount of $60, Receipt 506.
7	Sold old shelving (**Store Equipment**) for $50, Receipt 507.
10	Wildwood Resorts sent us a check for $2,425 in payment of their account, $2,500 less a 3% cash discount of $75, Receipt 508.
15	Cash sales totaled $2,000 plus $100 in sales tax, Tape 20.
15	Bankcard sales were $3,000 plus $150 in sales tax, Tape 20.
18	Celeste Everett sent us a check for $150 to apply on her account, Receipt 509.
20	Isabel Rodriquez sent us $100 to apply on her account, Receipt 510.
30	Cash sales were $4,500 plus $225 sales tax, Tape 21. Bankcard sales totaled $3,800 plus sales tax of $190, Tape 21.

Analyze: What source document would be used to record bankcard sales and cash sales?

SOURCE DOCUMENT PROBLEM

Problem 16–6

Use the source documents in your working papers to record the transactions for this problem.

Problem 16–6 Recording and Posting Sales and Cash Receipts

SOURCE DOCUMENT PROBLEM

Buzz Newsstand had the following sales and cash receipt transactions for May. In your working papers, the accounts receivable subsidiary ledger and general ledger accounts have been opened with current balances.

Instructions

1. Record the sales and cash receipts for May on page 11 of the sales journal and page 11 of the cash receipts journal.
2. Post to the customer accounts in the accounts receivable subsidiary ledger on a daily basis.
3. Post from the General Credit column of the cash receipts journal on a daily basis.

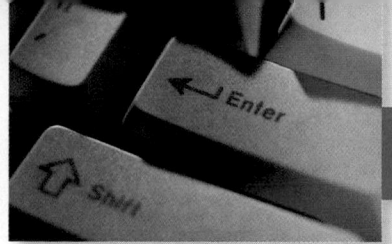

4. Foot, prove, total, and rule both journals.
5. Post the column totals of the sales journal to the general ledger accounts named in the column headings.
6. Post the column totals from the cash receipts journal to the general ledger accounts named in the column headings.
7. Prepare a schedule of accounts receivable.

Date	Transactions
May 1	Sold $300 in merchandise plus 6% sales tax of $18 on account to Ilya Bodonski, Sales Slip 170.
3	Received $490.00 from Katz Properties in payment of their $500 account balance less a 2% discount of $10.00, Receipt 145.
5	As a favor, sold $60 in supplies to Straka Stores, received cash, Receipt 146.
7	Rothwell Management Inc. sent us a check for $294.00 in payment of their $300 account balance less a $6.00 cash discount, Receipt 147.
9	Sold $100 in merchandise plus $6 sales tax on account to Saba Nadal, Sales Slip 171.
10	Sold $600 in merchandise plus $36 sales tax on account to Java Shops Inc., terms 2/10, n/30, Sales Slip 172.
12	Sold $50 in merchandise plus $3 sales tax on account to Lee Adkins, Sales Slip 173.
15	Received a check for $196.00 from Rolling Hills Pharmacies in payment of their $200 account less a 2% cash discount of $4.00, Receipt 148.
15	Cash sales were $2,400 plus $144 sales tax, Tape 33.
15	Bankcard sales totaled $2,000 plus sales tax of $120, Tape 33.
18	Sold $1,000 in merchandise plus sales tax of $60 on account to Katz Properties, terms 2/10, n/30, Sales Slip 174.
20	Received $100 from Ilya Bodonski to apply on her account, Receipt 149.
22	Sold $800 in merchandise plus $48 sales tax on account to Rothwell Management Inc., terms 2/10, n/30, Sales Slip 175.
23	Lee Adkins sent us a check for $53 in payment of his account, Receipt 150.
24	Received a $106 check from Saba Nadal to apply on account, Receipt 151.
26	Java Shops Inc. sent us a check for $200 to apply on account, Receipt 152.
27	Sold $200 in merchandise plus sales tax of $12 on account to Lee Adkins, Sales Slip 176.
28	Received $75 from the sale of excess store equipment, Receipt 153.
30	Cash sales totaled $2,600 plus $156 sales tax, Tape 34.
30	Bankcard sales were $2,200 plus sales tax of $132, Tape 34.

Analyze: If all Buzz Newsstand's customers pay their accounts within the cash discount period, what total amount will be forfeited by Buzz?

Peachtree®

SMART GUIDE

Step–by–Step Instructions: Problem 16–6

1. Select the problem set for Buzz Newsstand (Prob. 16–6).
2. Rename the company and set the system date.
3. Enter all sales on account transactions.
4. Record all cash receipts.
5. Print a Sales Journal report and a Cash Receipts Journal report.
6. Proof your work.
7. Print a General Ledger report and Customer Ledgers report.
8. Answer the Analyze question.
9. End the session.

CHAPTER 17

Special Journals: Purchases and Cash Payments

Learning Objectives

When you have completed this chapter, you will be able to:

▶ Explain the purpose of the purchases and cash payments journals.

▶ Record transactions in the purchases and cash payments journals.

▶ Record payroll transactions in the cash payments journal.

▶ Post from the purchases and cash payments journals to the general and accounts payable subsidiary ledgers.

▶ Total, prove, and rule the purchases and cash payments journals.

▶ Prepare a schedule of accounts payable.

▶ Prove cash.

▶ Define the accounting terms introduced in this chapter.

Exploring the Real World of Business

LOOKING AT THE ROLE OF PURCHASES

The U.S. population loves pets, spending $23 billion a year on pet-care products and services.

PETCO is one of the country's largest providers of these products and services. In addition to large selections of pet foods, toys, grooming supplies, books, and pet care accessories, the company also sells fish, birds, snakes, cats, dogs, and other companion animals.

Operating in 42 states, plus the District of Columbia, **PETCO** has 575 pet food, supply and services stores. An expanded product line offers more products to customers and provides more supplies used in their grooming service operations. Using its accounting records to analyze which products and services pet owners buy helps the company anticipate future demand. Offering the right products and services is the key to continued growth.

What do you think?

Name at least three different products that **PETCO** might purchase for resale to its customers. Name three products the company might buy for use in operating the business.

PETCO.

Workplace Connections

Applying Your Accounting Knowledge

Do you, or anyone you know, make regular payments to anyone—perhaps for car insurance or for a purchase you made on an installment plan? Businesses make a lot of similar payments. Retail businesses buy the merchandise they sell to customers. They also buy many items used to operate the business, such as china and silverware for a restaurant. Businesses buy most items on credit and must keep track of when payments are due. You'll learn how that's done through the accounting records as you study this chapter.

Investigate:

1. What items might your employer buy on credit?
2. Do you have any ideas on how you might keep track of purchases and when payments are due on those items?

449

The Purchases Journal

In the last chapter, you learned that businesses use special journals to record transactions that are similar and occur frequently. If the accounting system is like a transit system, then special journals help accountants avoid accounting traffic jams. Special journals channel incoming data into appropriate "lanes" and provide a shortcut for much of the data headed for the general ledger.

In the last chapter, you learned that the sales and cash receipts journals record the sale of merchandise and other assets. In this chapter you'll learn about purchases and cash payments journals and how these journals are used to record the purchase of merchandise and other assets. You will also learn about the accounts payable subsidiary ledger.

Kmart purchases merchandise for resale from hundreds of suppliers. Businesses like Kmart use purchases and cash payments journals to simplify the purchase and payment processes.

The Purchases Journal

The **purchases journal** is a special journal used to record all purchases on account. **Figure 17–1** shows the purchases journal used by On Your Mark Athletic Wear.

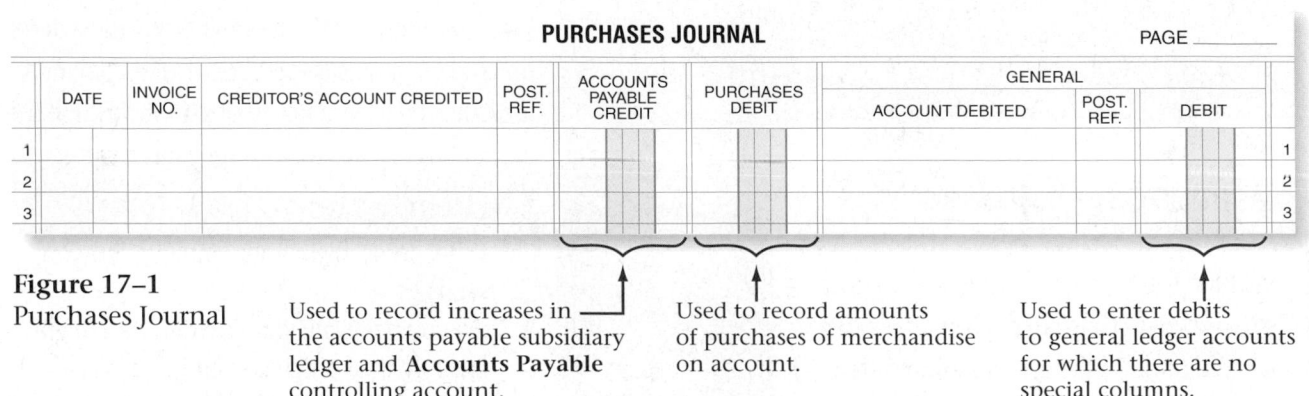

Figure 17–1
Purchases Journal

Used to record increases in the accounts payable subsidiary ledger and **Accounts Payable** controlling account.

Used to record amounts of purchases of merchandise on account.

Used to enter debits to general ledger accounts for which there are no special columns.

The purchases journal includes: space for the page number, a column for the date, a column for the invoice number, a column for the name of the creditor, and a column for the posting reference. There are also three amount columns. Refer to **Figure 17–1** for a description of what amounts should be recorded in each column.

Recording the Purchase of Merchandise on Account

After an invoice is verified by the accounting clerk, the purchase is recorded in the purchases journal.

PRO RUNNER WAREHOUSE				INVOICE NO. 7894	
22009 Ben White Blvd. Austin, TX 78705			REC'D DEC. 14, 20--	DATE:	Dec. 14, 20--
				ORDER NO.:	9784
TO	On Your Mark Athletic Wear 595 Leslie Street Dallas, TX 75207			SHIPPED BY:	Federal Trucking
				TERMS:	2/10, n/30

QTY.	ITEM	UNIT PRICE	TOTAL
20 pair	Soft Cushion: White, #94682	$ 50.00	$ 1,000.00
10 pair	Soft Cushion: Black, #94788	50.00	500.00
10 pair	Low Cut: White, #94281	40.00	400.00
10 pair	Low Cut: Black, #94666	40.00	400.00
	Total		$ 2,300.00

Due Date: _12/24_
Discount: _$ 46.00_
Net Amount: _$ 2,254.00_
Check No.: _____

Business Transaction

On December 14 On Your Mark received Invoice 7894 from Pro Runner Warehouse for merchandise purchased on account, $2,300, terms 2/10, n/30.

JOURNAL ENTRY

PURCHASES JOURNAL   PAGE   12

	DATE	INVOICE NO.	CREDITOR'S ACCOUNT CREDITED	POST. REF.	ACCOUNTS PAYABLE CREDIT	PURCHASES DEBIT	GENERAL			
							ACCOUNT DEBITED	POST. REF.	DEBIT	
6	14	7894	Pro Runner Warehouse		2 300 00	2 300 00				6
7	**1**	**2**	**3**		**4**	**5**				7

Refer to the purchases journal and follow these steps:

1. Enter the date in the Date column. Use the date the invoice was *received,* not the date the invoice was prepared.
2. Enter the invoice number in the Invoice Number column.
3. Enter the creditor's name in the Creditor's Account Credited column.
4. Enter the *total* of the invoice in the Accounts Payable Credit column.
5. For purchases of merchandise on account, enter the total amount of the invoice in the Purchases Debit column.

After the invoice from Pro Runner Warehouse is journalized, it is placed in a tickler file by due date. In this case, it is filed in the December 24 folder. On Your Mark plans to take the discount, and December 24 is ten days after the invoice date.

Journalizing Other Purchases on Account

On Your Mark also purchases supplies and other assets on account. These purchases do not occur often enough to set up special columns in the purchases journal. When these purchases do occur, they are recorded in the General Debit column of the purchases journal.

Key Points

Recording a Purchase on Account

A purchase of merchandise on account is recorded as a debit to **Purchases** and a credit to **Accounts Payable.**

On December 15 On Your Mark received Invoice 3417, dated December 13, from Champion Store Supply for store equipment bought on account, $1,200, terms n/30.

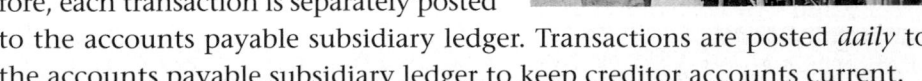

			INVOICE NO. 3417
★CHAMPION *STORE SUPPLY*			
47249 Randall Parkway			DATE: Dec. 13, 20--
Dallas, TX 75207	REC'D DEC. 15, 20--		ORDER NO.: 9795
On Your Mark Athletic Wear			SHIPPED BY: Federal Trucking
TO 595 Leslie Street			TERMS: n/30
Dallas, TX 75207			

QTY.	ITEM	UNIT PRICE	TOTAL
3	Corner Shelf Units	$ 300.00	$ 900.00
1	Shirt Rack	300.00	300.00
	Total		$ 1,200.00

Due Date: __1/12__
Discount: __$0.00__
Net Amount: __$1,200.00__
Check No.: __

JOURNAL ENTRY

PURCHASES JOURNAL   PAGE ___12___

	DATE	INVOICE NO.	CREDITOR'S ACCOUNT CREDITED	POST. REF.	ACCOUNTS PAYABLE CREDIT	PURCHASES DEBIT	GENERAL			
							ACCOUNT DEBITED	POST. REF.	DEBIT	
7	15	3417	Champion Store Supply		1 200 00		Store Equipment		1 200 00	7
8	1	2	3		4		5		6	8

Refer to the purchases journal above and follow these steps:

1. Enter the date the invoice was *received* in the Date column.
2. Enter the invoice number in the Invoice Number column.
3. Enter the creditor's name in the Creditor's Account Credited column.
4. Enter the *total* of the invoice in the Accounts Payable Credit column.
5. Store equipment is not merchandise purchased for resale, so this transaction is not recorded in the Purchases Debit column. Instead, it is recorded in the General columns. Write the name of the general ledger account being debited in the General Account Debited column.
6. Enter the total amount of the invoice in the General Debit column.

After journalizing the invoice, the accounting clerk places it in the tickler file. Because Champion Store Supply does not offer its credit customers a cash discount, the due date is January 12, 30 days after the date of the invoice. The invoice is filed in folder "12" to indicate the bill is to be paid on January 12.

Posting to the Accounts Payable Subsidiary Ledger

Each transaction in the purchases journal is a purchase on account. Therefore, each transaction is separately posted to the accounts payable subsidiary ledger. Transactions are posted *daily* to the accounts payable subsidiary ledger to keep creditor accounts current.

Refer to **Figure 17–2** as you read about posting to the accounts payable subsidiary ledger.

1. In the Date column of the subsidiary ledger account, enter the date of the transaction.

Math Hints

Proving Cash

Proving cash is easy when you remember a simple formula:

- Beginning balance
  + Cash in
  − Cash out
  Ending balance
- The ending balance is then compared with the ending checkbook balance.

2. In the Posting Reference column of the subsidiary ledger account, record the journal letter and the page number. "P" is the letter used for the purchases journal.

3. In the Credit column of the subsidiary ledger account, enter the amount owed to the creditor.

4. Compute the new account balance by adding the amount in the Credit column to the previous balance amount. Since there was no previous balance in Pro Runner's account, enter $2,300 in the Balance column.

5. Return to the purchases journal and place a check mark (✓) in the *first* Posting Reference column (the column following the Creditor's Account Credited column).

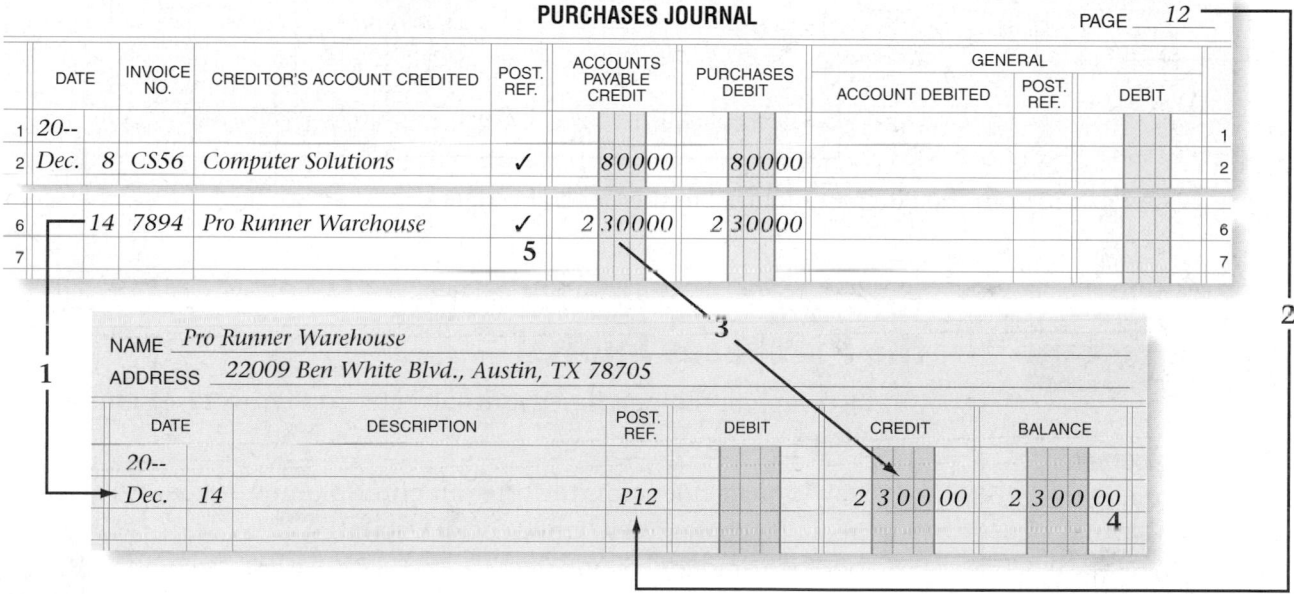

Figure 17–2 Posting from the Purchases Journal to the Accounts Payable Subsidiary Ledger

Posting from the General Debit Column

Daily postings are made from the General Debit column of the purchases journal to the appropriate accounts in the general ledger.

Refer to **Figure 17–3** as you read the following steps:

1. Enter the date of the transaction in the Date column of the general ledger account.

2. In the Posting Reference column of the general ledger account, record the journal letter and page number. Be sure to use the letter "P" for purchases journal.

3. In the Debit column of the general ledger account, enter the amount recorded in the General Debit column of the purchases journal.

4. Compute and record the new balance in the Debit Balance column.

5. Return to the purchases journal and place the general ledger account number in the General Posting Reference column (the column following the General Account Debited column).

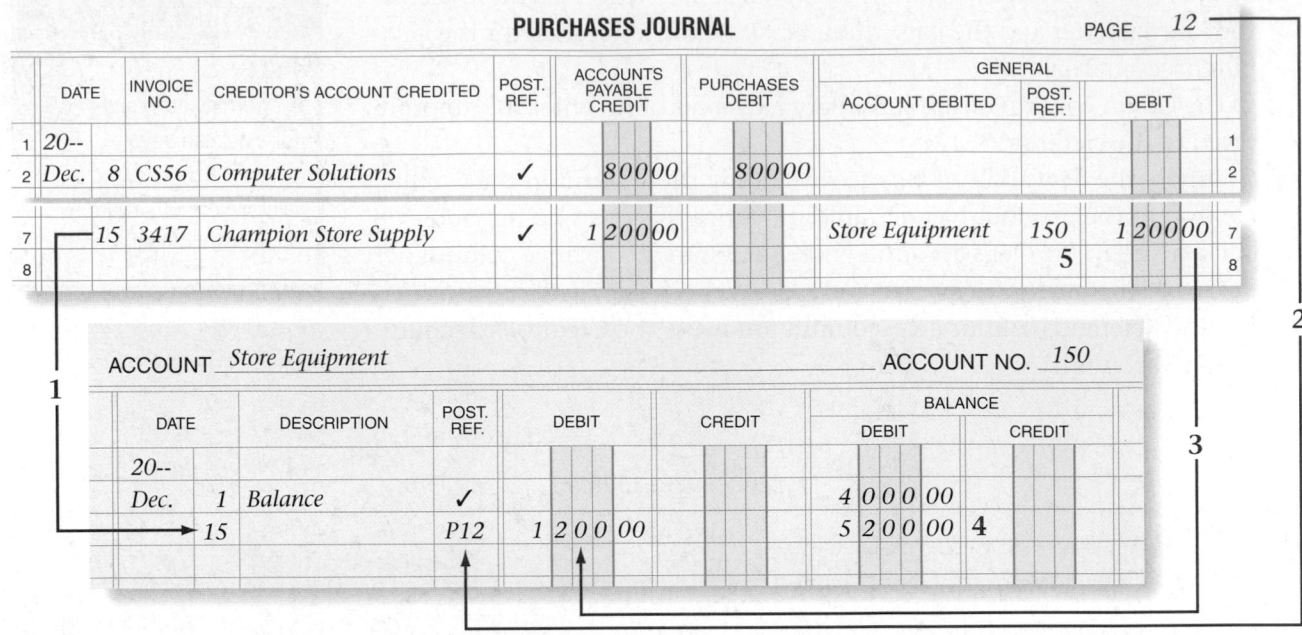

PURCHASES JOURNAL PAGE __12__

	DATE	INVOICE NO.	CREDITOR'S ACCOUNT CREDITED	POST. REF.	ACCOUNTS PAYABLE CREDIT	PURCHASES DEBIT	GENERAL			
							ACCOUNT DEBITED	POST. REF.	DEBIT	
1	20--									1
2	Dec. 8	CS56	Computer Solutions	✓	80000	80000				2
7	15	3417	Champion Store Supply	✓	1 20000		Store Equipment	150	1 20000	7
8								5		8

1

2

ACCOUNT _Store Equipment_ ACCOUNT NO. _150_

DATE	DESCRIPTION	POST. REF.	DEBIT	CREDIT	BALANCE	
					DEBIT	CREDIT
20--						
Dec. 1	Balance	✓			4 000 00	
15		P12	1 200 00		5 200 00 4	

3

Figure 17–3 Posting from the Purchases Journal to the General Ledger

Totaling, Proving, and Ruling the Purchases Journal

To complete the purchases journal, refer to **Figure 17–4** and follow these steps:

1. Draw a single rule across the three amount columns: Accounts Payable Credit, Purchases Debit, and General Debit.
2. Foot each amount column.
3. Test for the equality of debits and credits.

Debit Columns		**Credit Column**	
Purchases	$15,400	Accounts Payable	$16,850
General	1,450		
	$16,850		$16,850

4. In the Date column, on the line below the single rule, enter the date the journal is being totaled.
5. On the same line, write the word "Totals" in the Creditor's Account Credited column.
6. Enter the three column totals, in ink, just below the footings.
7. Draw a double rule across the three amount columns.

The completed purchases journal is a quick reference tool for the accountant to review current transactions that affect the **Purchases** account and the **Accounts Payable** account. Miscellaneous purchases are also reflected here. If a general journal had been used, these transactions would have been mingled with other transactions (cash receipts, payments, and more) of the period.

PAGE __12__

	DATE	INVOICE NO.	CREDITOR'S ACCOUNT CREDITED	POST. REF.	ACCOUNTS PAYABLE CREDIT	PURCHASES DEBIT	GENERAL ACCOUNT DEBITED	POST. REF.	DEBIT	
1	20--									1
2	Dec. 8	CS56	Computer Solutions	✓	8 0 0 00	8 0 0 00				2
3	10	4692	Sports Link Footwear	✓	4 0 0 0 00	4 0 0 0 00				3
4	12	SN63	Sports Nutrition Supply	✓	6 0 0 00	6 0 0 00				4
5	14	2560	FastLane Athletics	✓	3 0 0 0 00	3 0 0 0 00				5
6	14	7894	Pro Runner Warehouse	✓	2 3 0 0 00	2 3 0 0 00				6
7	15	3417	Champion Store Supply	✓	1 2 0 0 00		Store Equipment	150	1 2 0 0 00	7
8	15	9881	Geary Office Supply	✓	2 5 0 00		Supplies	130	2 5 0 00	8
9	18	8560	FastLane Athletics	✓	2 0 0 0 00	2 0 0 0 00				9
10	20	6593	Computer Solutions	✓	1 2 0 0 00	1 2 0 0 00				10
11	27	5200	Sports Link Footwear	✓	1 5 0 0 00	1 5 0 0 00				11
12	31		Totals		16 8 5 0 00	15 4 0 0 00			1 4 5 0 00	12
13										13

Figure 17–4 The Completed Purchases Journal

What else can the accountant verify from the completed purchases journal? A quick review of the Post. Ref. column tells the accountant that amounts have been posted to the accounts payable subsidiary ledger.

Posting the Special Column Totals of the Purchases Journal

After the purchases journal is totaled and ruled, post the totals of the Accounts Payable Credit column and the Purchases Debit column to the general ledger accounts. Calculate the new balance for each account, and enter the new balance in the appropriate Balance column. **Figure 17–5** shows the posting of these column totals.

After posting each column total, write the general ledger account number, in parentheses, in the column below the double rule as shown in **Figure 17–5**. The total of the General Debit column is not posted because the individual amounts were posted during the month. Place a check mark (✓) in parentheses below the double rule in the General Debit column to indicate that the total is not posted.

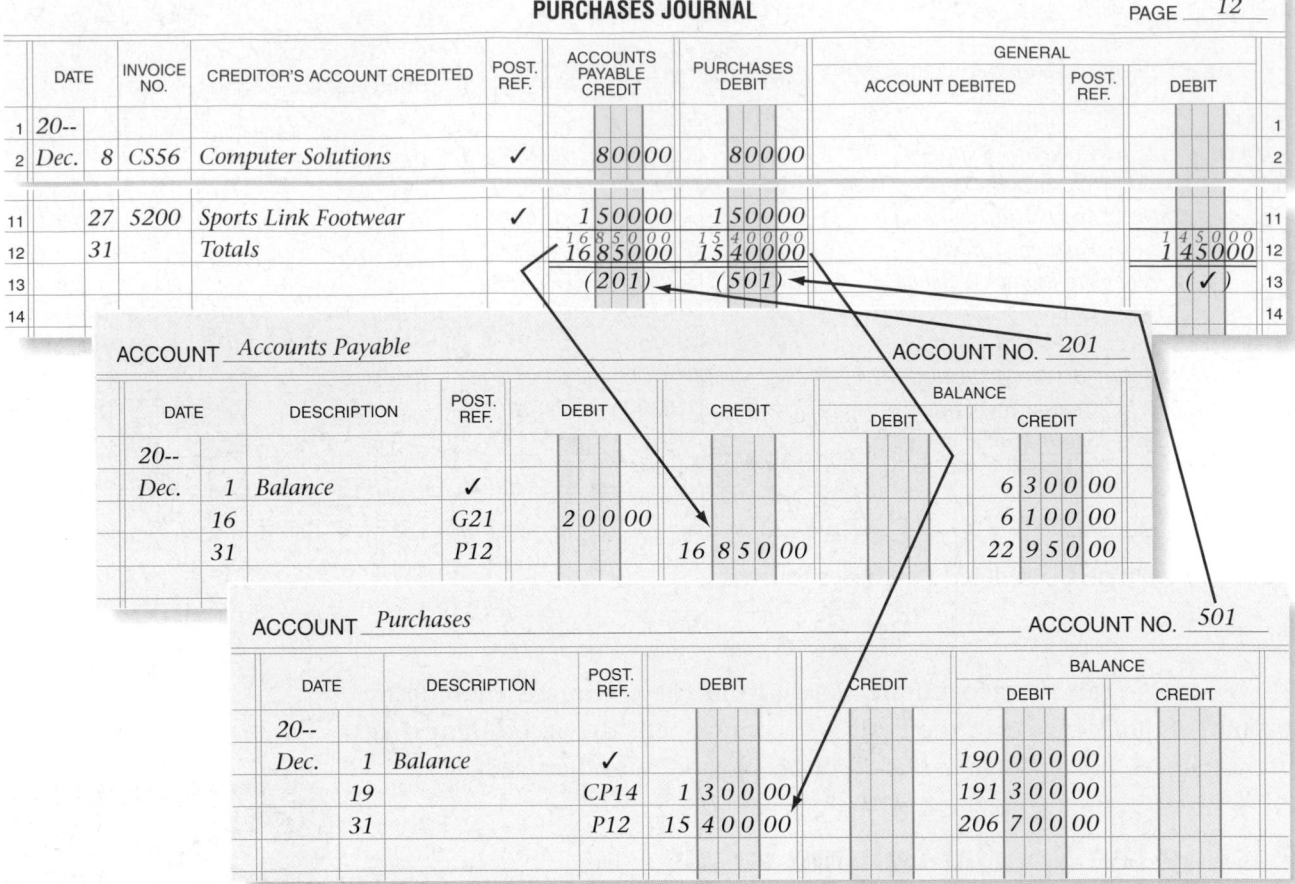

Figure 17–5 Posting Column Totals from the Purchases Journal to the General Ledger

---

A MATTER OF ETHICS

Insufficient Funds

Imagine that you own a sporting goods store, and you manage your own accounting records. Your delivery van has been in the shop for repairs. The mechanic calls to give you the cost of his work. The bill is much more than you expected, but you authorize the work.

You need the van back as soon as possible to make deliveries to your customers, but you don't have enough money in your checking account to cover the mechanic's bill. If you write a check for the expense, you believe that you will have enough money in the account by the time the mechanic cashes the check.

Ethical Decision Making:

☛ What are the ethical issues?

☛ What are the alternatives?

☛ Who are the affected parties?

☛ How do the alternatives affect the parties?

☛ What would you do?

Now that you have studied this section, complete the following questions and problems.

Thinking Critically

1. Describe the two types of purchases on account that are recorded in the purchases journal.
2. In the purchases journal, the General Debit column *total* is not posted. Explain why.

Communicating Accounting

Thomas Sampson is a purchasing agent for Complete Offices, a small office supply company. He recently returned from a 10-day business trip to California and gave you an envelope full of receipts. He did not provide any explanations about the purchases represented by the receipts. Write a memo to Thomas asking him to identify which receipts represent purchases for cash and which receipts represent purchases on account. Explain the information you need to analyze the transactions. Refer specifically to payment terms.

Problem 17–1 Recording Transactions in the Purchases Journal

The Design Den, a retail merchandising business, uses special journals. On page 3 of the purchases journal in the working papers, record the following purchases:

Date	Transactions
Feb. 1	Purchased $1,400 in merchandise on account from Woodstock Furnishings, terms 3/15, n/30, Invoice WF39.
2	Bought $900 in store equipment on account from Holmes Equipment Company, terms n/30, Invoice 98.
4	Purchased $700 in merchandise from Fuller Fabrics, terms 3/10, n/30, Invoice 72.
7	Purchased computer speakers on account for $50 from Digital Solutions, terms 2/10, n/30, Invoice AB220.
10	Purchased fabric from Valley Upholstery for $1,500, terms 2/10, n/30, Invoice 947.

The Cash Payments Journal

What You'll Learn

- The purpose of the cash payments journal.
- How to record trans-actions in the cash payments journal.
- How to post from the cash payments journal.
- How to prepare a sched-ule of accounts payable.
- How to prove cash.

Why It's Important

Cash is a major asset of a business; therefore, it is essential that a business keep accurate records of both the inflow and the outflow of cash.

KEY TERMS

cash payments journal
schedule of accounts
    payable
proving cash

You have learned about three special journals: the sales journal, the cash receipts journal, and the purchases journal. Now you will study the cash payments journal. For many businesses, like grocers who must pay for the purchases of a wide variety of merchandise and florists who constantly pay to keep fresh flowers in stock, frequent payments make the use of the cash payments journal necessary.

The Cash Payments Journal

The **cash payments journal** is used to record all transactions in which cash is paid out or decreased. These transactions include: payments to creditors for items bought on account, cash purchases of merchandise and other assets, payments for various expenses, payments for wages and salaries, and cash decreases for bank service charges and bank card fees. The source documents for the journal entries are check stubs and the bank statement.

Figure 17–6 shows the cash payments journal used by On Your Mark. Notice that there are five amount columns.

The seven transactions that follow are typical of those recorded in the cash payments journal. Note that each transaction in the cash payments journal results in a credit to the **Cash in Bank** account.

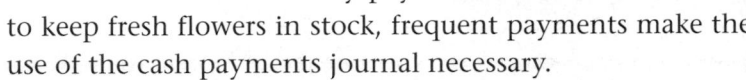

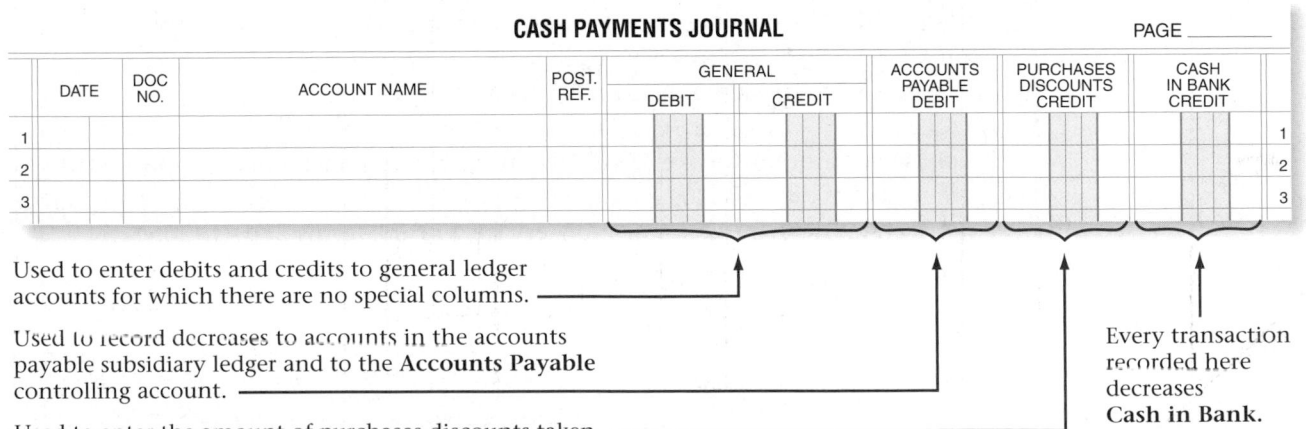

CASH PAYMENTS JOURNAL   PAGE _____

DATE	DOC. NO.	ACCOUNT NAME	POST. REF.	GENERAL		ACCOUNTS PAYABLE DEBIT	PURCHASES DISCOUNTS CREDIT	CASH IN BANK CREDIT	
				DEBIT	CREDIT				
1									1
2									2
3									3

Used to enter debits and credits to general ledger accounts for which there are no special columns. ⟶

Used to record decreases to accounts in the accounts payable subsidiary ledger and to the **Accounts Payable** controlling account. ⟶

Used to enter the amount of purchases discounts taken. ⟶

Every transaction recorded here decreases **Cash in Bank.**

Figure 17–6 Cash Payments Journal

Recording the Cash Purchase of an Asset

Cash purchases of various assets are recorded in the cash payments journal. One asset commonly purchased for cash is insurance. Let's record a transaction involving a cash purchase of insurance.

Business Transaction

On December 17 On Your Mark paid $1,500 to Keystone Insurance Company for the premium on a six-month insurance policy, Check 1001.

Check 1001

ON YOUR MARK
ATHLETIC WEAR
595 Leslie Street, Dallas, TX 75207

No. 1001
22-523
4210

DATE Dec. 17 20 --

PAY TO THE ORDER OF Keystone Insurance Company $ 1,500.00

One thousand five hundred and no/100 ———————— DOLLARS

Security National Bank
DALLAS, TEXAS

MEMO _____ Michael Brown

⑆421022523⑆ 727596⑈ 1001

JOURNAL ENTRY

CASH PAYMENTS JOURNAL PAGE 14

	DATE	DOC NO.	ACCOUNT NAME	POST. REF.	GENERAL DEBIT	GENERAL CREDIT	ACCOUNTS PAYABLE DEBIT	PURCHASES DISCOUNTS CREDIT	CASH IN BANK CREDIT	
1	20--									1
2	Dec. 17	1001	Prepaid Insurance		1 500 00				1 500 00	2
3	**1**	**2**	**3**		**4**				**5**	3

Refer to the cash payments journal above and follow these steps:

1. Enter the date of the transaction in the Date column.
2. Enter the check number in the Document Number column.
3. Enter the name of the account debited in the Account Name column.
4. Because there is no special column for **Prepaid Insurance**, enter the amount of the debit in the General Debit column.
5. Enter the amount of the credit in the Cash in Bank Credit column.

After payment, the invoice for the insurance is filed.

Recording a Cash Purchase of Merchandise

Retail businesses are constantly purchasing merchandise for resale. While most purchases are on account, many are for cash. Let's record a cash purchase of merchandise for resale.

Business Transaction

On December 19 On Your Mark purchased merchandise from FastLane Athletics for $1,300, Check 1002.

Check 1002

ON YOUR MARK
ATHLETIC WEAR
595 Leslie Street, Dallas, TX 75207

No. 1002
22-523
4210

DATE Dec. 19 20 --

PAY TO THE ORDER OF FastLane Athletics $ 1,300.00

One thousand three hundred and no/100 ———————— DOLLARS

Security National Bank
DALLAS, TEXAS

MEMO _____ Michael Brown

⑆421022523⑆ 727596⑈ 1002

JOURNAL ENTRY

CASH PAYMENTS JOURNAL PAGE 14

	DATE	DOC NO.	ACCOUNT NAME	POST. REF.	GENERAL DEBIT	GENERAL CREDIT	ACCOUNTS PAYABLE DEBIT	PURCHASES DISCOUNTS CREDIT	CASH IN BANK CREDIT	
3	19	1002	Purchases		1 300 00				1 300 00	3
4	**1**	**2**	**3**		**4**				**5**	4

Refer to the cash payments journal and follow these steps:

1. Enter the date of the transaction in the Date column.
2. Enter the check number in the Document Number column.
3. Enter the name of the account debited in the Account Name column.
4. Because there is no special column for **Purchases**, enter the amount of the debit in the General Debit column.
5. Enter the amount of the check in the Cash in Bank Credit column.

After recording the transaction, the receipt for the cash purchase is filed.

Recording a Payment on Account

Now let's learn how to make a payment on account and take a purchase discount.

Business Transaction

On December 24 On Your Mark paid $2,254 to Pro Runner Warehouse for merchandise purchased on account, $2,300 less a discount of $46, Check 1003.

ON YOUR MARK
ATHLETIC WEAR
595 Leslie Street, Dallas, TX 75207

1003
22-523
4210

DATE Dec. 24 20 --

PAY TO THE ORDER OF Pro Runner Warehouse $ 2,254.00

Two thousand two hundred fifty-four and no/100 —————— DOLLARS

Security National Bank
DALLAS, TEXAS

MEMO _____ Michael Brown

⑆421022523⑆ 727596⑈ 1003

JOURNAL ENTRY

CASH PAYMENTS JOURNAL PAGE 14

	DATE	DOC NO.	ACCOUNT NAME	POST. REF.	GENERAL DEBIT	GENERAL CREDIT	ACCOUNTS PAYABLE DEBIT	PURCHASES DISCOUNTS CREDIT	CASH IN BANK CREDIT	
4	24	1003	Pro Runner Warehouse				2 300 00	46 00	2 254 00	4
5	1	2	3				4	5	6	5

Refer to the purchases journal above and follow these steps:

1. Enter the date of the transaction in the Date column.
2. Enter the check number in the Document Number column.
3. Enter the creditor's name in the Account Name column.
4. Enter the amount of the original purchase in the Accounts Payable Debit column.
5. Enter the amount of the purchase discount in the Purchases Discounts Credit column.
6. Enter the amount of the check in the Cash in Bank Credit column.

Remember that a processing stamp is placed on each invoice when it is verified. After the cash payment is journalized, the accounting clerk records the check number on the "Check No." line of the processing stamp. The paid invoice is then filed.

For some purchases a discount is not offered. For others a discount is offered, but the business cannot pay within the discount period. In these cases the check is written for the amount of the purchase.

Recording Other Cash Payments

Let's record a check written to pay for shipping charges when merchandise is sent FOB shipping point.

Business Transaction

On December 24 On Your Mark issued Check 1004 for $275 to Dara's Delivery Service for shipping charges on merchandise purchased from Sports Link Footwear.

ON YOUR MARK	1004
ATHLETIC WEAR	22-523
595 Leslie Street, Dallas, TX 75207	4210

DATE Dec. 24 20 --

PAY TO THE ORDER OF Dara's Delivery Service $ 275.00

Two hundred seventy-five and no/100 ———————— DOLLARS

Security National Bank
DALLAS, TEXAS

MEMO _____ Michael Brown

⑆421022523⑆ 727596⑆ 1004

JOURNAL ENTRY

CASH PAYMENTS JOURNAL   PAGE ___14___

	DATE	DOC NO.	ACCOUNT NAME	POST. REF.	GENERAL DEBIT	GENERAL CREDIT	ACCOUNTS PAYABLE DEBIT	PURCHASES DISCOUNTS CREDIT	CASH IN BANK CREDIT	
5	24	1004	Transportation In		275 00				275 00	5
6	**1**	**2**	**3**		**4**				**5**	6

Refer to the cash payments journal above and follow these steps:

1. Enter the date of the transaction in the Date column.
2. Enter the check number in the Document Number column.
3. Enter the name of the account debited in the Account Name column.
4. Because there is no special column for **Transportation In**, enter the amount of the expense in the General Debit column.
5. Enter the amount of the check in the Cash in Bank Credit column.

Recording Payment of Payroll

In an earlier chapter, you learned how to record the payroll entry in the general journal. When a business uses special journals, the entry for payment of the payroll is recorded in the cash payments journal. The information to record payroll transactions in journals is taken from the payroll register.

To record the payroll transaction, refer to the cash payments journal and follow these steps:

1. On the first line of the entry, enter the date of the transaction in the Date column.
2. Enter the check number in the Document Number column.
3. Enter the name of the account debited in the Account Name column.
4. Enter the amount of the payroll (gross pay) in the General Debit column.
5. Enter the net pay in the Cash in Bank Credit column.
6. On the next four lines, enter the names of the accounts credited in the Account Name column. Enter the amount of each liability in the General Credit column.

On December 31 On Your Mark wrote Check 1012 for $2,974 to pay the payroll of $4,000 (gross earnings) for the pay period ended December 31. The following amounts were withheld: Employees' Federal Income Tax, $640; Employees' State Income Tax, $80; Social Security Tax, $248; and Medicare Tax, $58.

JOURNAL ENTRY

	DATE	DOC NO.	ACCOUNT NAME	POST. REF.	GENERAL DEBIT	GENERAL CREDIT	ACCOUNTS PAYABLE DEBIT	PURCHASES DISCOUNTS CREDIT	CASH IN BANK CREDIT	
CASH PAYMENTS JOURNAL									PAGE 14	
13	31	1012	Salaries Expense **3**		4 000 00				**5** 2 974 00	13
14	**1**	**2**	Employees' Fed. Inc. Tax Pay.		**4**	640 00				14
15			Employees' State Inc. Tax Pay.			80 00				15
16			Social Security Tax Pay.		**6**	248 00				16
17			Medicare Tax Pay.			58 00				17
18										18

Recording Bank Service Charges

Bank service charges are automatically deducted from the checking account. No check is written. Since the charges result in decreases to **Cash in Bank**, the transactions are recorded in the cash payments journal.

On December 31 On Your Mark recorded a bank service charge for $20 indicated on the bank statement.

JOURNAL ENTRY

	DATE	DOC NO.	ACCOUNT NAME	POST. REF.	GENERAL DEBIT	GENERAL CREDIT	ACCOUNTS PAYABLE DEBIT	PURCHASES DISCOUNTS CREDIT	CASH IN BANK CREDIT	
CASH PAYMENTS JOURNAL									PAGE 14	
18	31		Miscellaneous Expense		20 00				20 00	18
19										19

Recording Bankcard Fees

Most banks charge a fee for handling bankcard sales. This fee is automatically deducted from the business's checking account. On Your Mark's bank deducted a bankcard fee of $75. The fee appeared on the bank statement as a deduction from the checking account balance. This decrease in cash is recorded in the cash payments journal.

On December 31 On Your Mark recorded the bankcard fee of $75 that appeared on the bank statement.

JOURNAL ENTRY

	DATE	DOC. NO.	ACCOUNT NAME	POST. REF.	GENERAL DEBIT	GENERAL CREDIT	ACCOUNTS PAYABLE DEBIT	PURCHASES DISCOUNTS CREDIT	CASH IN BANK CREDIT	
19	31		Bankcard Fees Expense		75 00				75 00	19
20										20

CASH PAYMENTS JOURNAL — PAGE 14

The bank charges are also entered in the checkbook records. **Figure 17–7** illustrates one way to adjust the balance on the check stub. The deposit heading is crossed out, and the words "Bankcard Fees" are written in its place. A deduction of $75 is entered on the stub. On the next line, the words "Less Bank Service Charge" are written and an entry is made for the $20 deduction. Both amounts are subtracted from the balance brought forward.

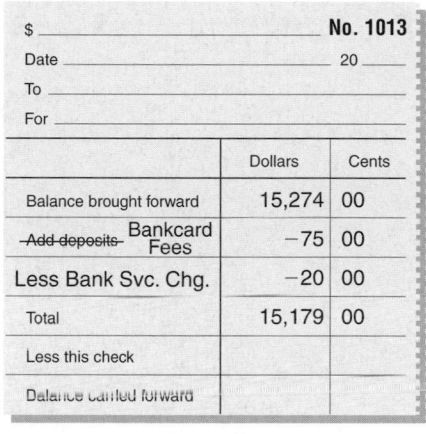

$ _____		No. 1013
Date _____ 20 __		
To _____		
For _____		
	Dollars	Cents
Balance brought forward	15,274	00
~~Add deposits~~ Bankcard Fees	−75	00
Less Bank Svc. Chg.	−20	00
Total	15,179	00
Less this check		
Balance carried forward		

Figure 17–7 Recording Bankcard Fees and Service Charges in the Checkbook

Posting to the Accounts Payable Subsidiary Ledger

To keep creditors' accounts current, daily postings are made from the Accounts Payable Debit column to the accounts payable subsidiary ledger. Refer to **Figure 17–8** and follow these steps:

1. Enter the date of the transaction in the Date column of the subsidiary ledger account.
2. In the subsidiary ledger account's Posting Reference column, enter the journal letters and the page number. The letters "CP" represent the cash payments journal.
3. In the Debit column of the subsidiary ledger account, enter the amount recorded in the Accounts Payable Debit column of the journal.
4. Compute the new account balance and enter it in the Balance column. If the account has a zero balance, draw a line through the Balance column.

5. Return to the cash payments journal and enter a check mark (✓) in the Posting Reference column.

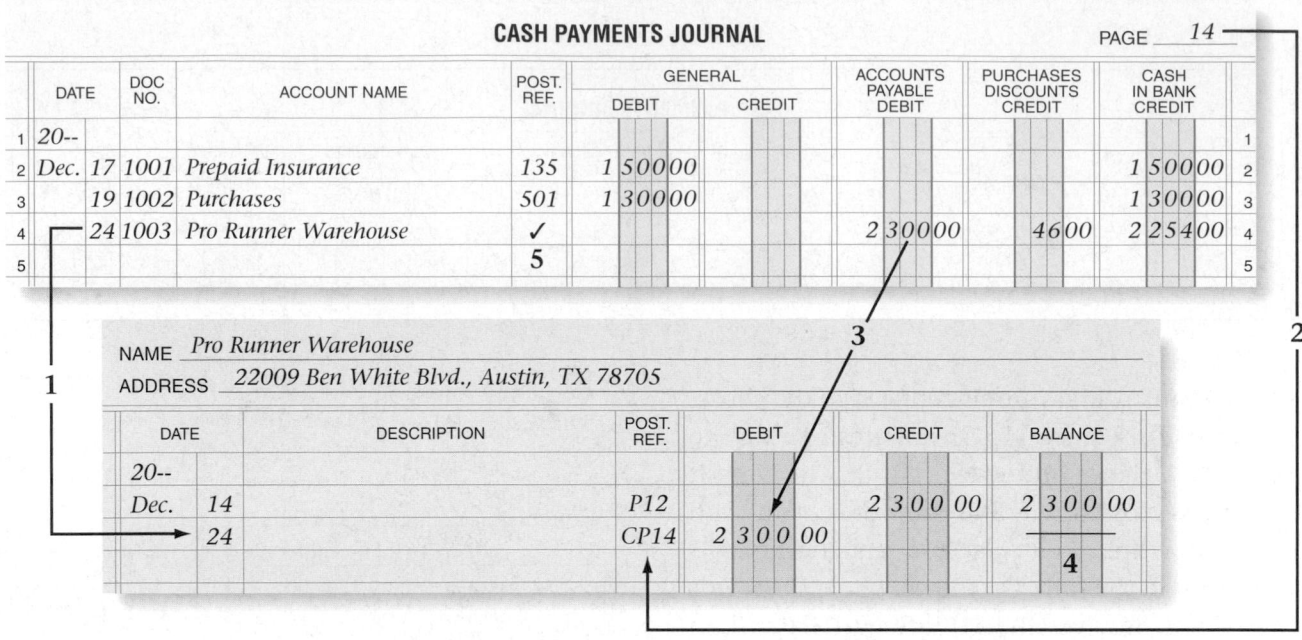

Figure 17–8 Posting from the Cash Payments Journal to the Accounts Payable Subsidiary Ledger

Figure 17–9 shows On Your Mark's accounts payable subsidiary ledger after all postings are completed. Notice that the accounts contain entries from the purchases, cash payments, and general journals.

NAME *Champion Store Supply*

ADDRESS *99455 Williams Lane #334, Dallas, TX 75214*

DATE		DESCRIPTION	POST. REF.	DEBIT	CREDIT	BALANCE
20--						
Dec.	1	Balance	✓			1 0 0 0 00
	15		P12		1 2 0 0 00	2 2 0 0 00
	26		CP14	1 2 0 0 00		1 0 0 0 00

NAME *Computer Solutions*

ADDRESS *6990 Baker Circle, Dallas, TX 75219*

DATE		DESCRIPTION	POST. REF.	DEBIT	CREDIT	BALANCE
20--						
Dec.	1	Balance	✓			5 0 0 00
	8		P12		8 0 0 00	1 3 0 0 00
	20		P12		1 2 0 0 00	2 5 0 0 00
	31		CP14	1 2 0 0 00		1 3 0 0 00

Figure 17–9 The Completed Accounts Payable Subsidiary Ledger

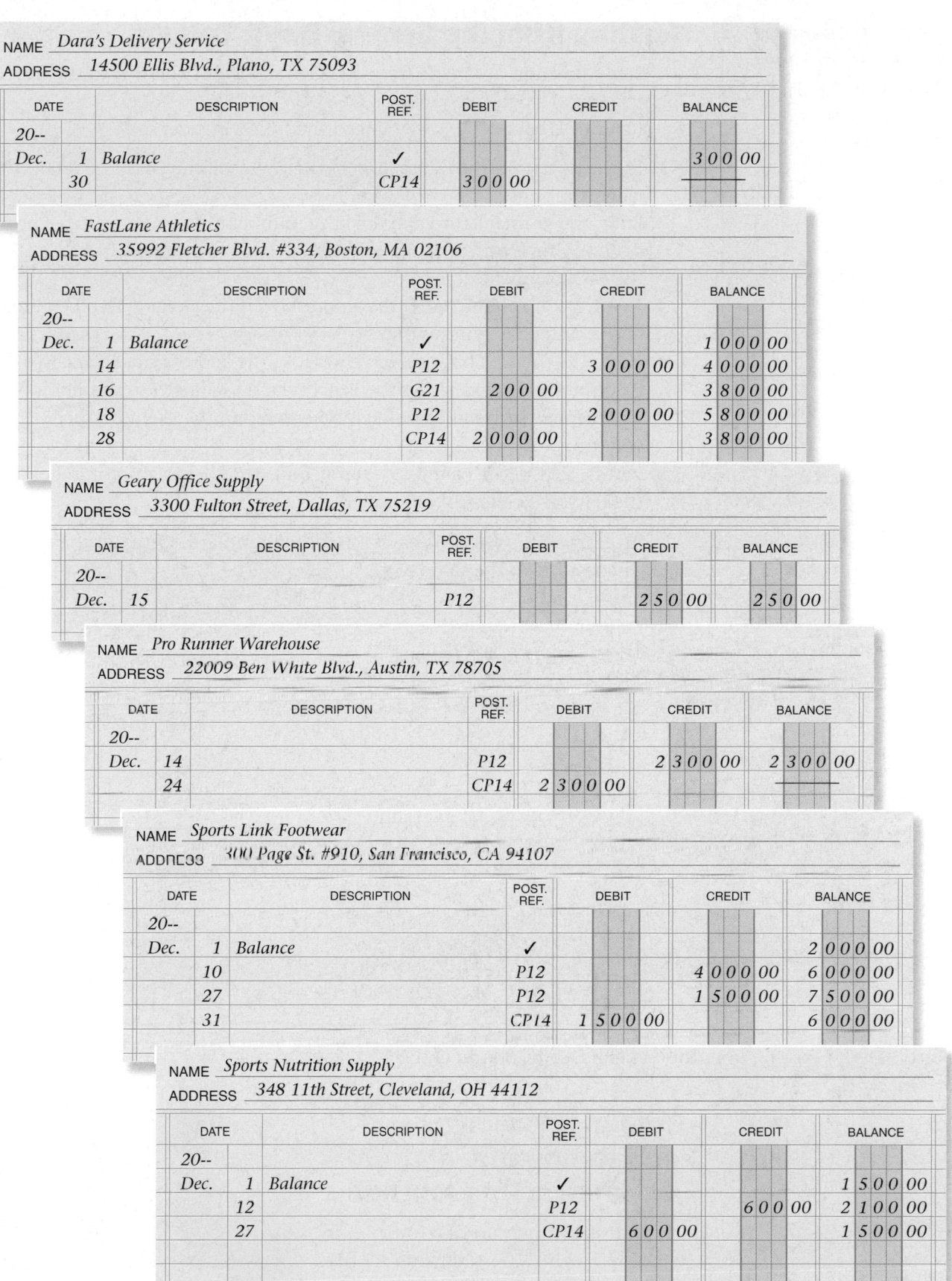

NAME Dara's Delivery Service

ADDRESS 14500 Ellis Blvd., Plano, TX 75093

DATE		DESCRIPTION	POST. REF.	DEBIT	CREDIT	BALANCE
20--						
Dec.	1	Balance	✓			3 0 0 00
	30		CP14	3 0 0 00		

NAME FastLane Athletics

ADDRESS 35992 Fletcher Blvd. #334, Boston, MA 02106

DATE		DESCRIPTION	POST. REF.	DEBIT	CREDIT	BALANCE
20--						
Dec.	1	Balance	✓			1 0 0 0 00
	14		P12		3 0 0 0 00	4 0 0 0 00
	16		G21	2 0 0 00		3 8 0 0 00
	18		P12		2 0 0 0 00	5 8 0 0 00
	28		CP14	2 0 0 0 00		3 8 0 0 00

NAME Geary Office Supply

ADDRESS 3300 Fulton Street, Dallas, TX 75219

DATE		DESCRIPTION	POST. REF.	DEBIT	CREDIT	BALANCE
20--						
Dec.	15		P12		2 5 0 00	2 5 0 00

NAME Pro Runner Warehouse

ADDRESS 22009 Ben White Blvd., Austin, TX 78705

DATE		DESCRIPTION	POST. REF.	DEBIT	CREDIT	BALANCE
20--						
Dec.	14		P12		2 3 0 0 00	2 3 0 0 00
	24		CP14	2 3 0 0 00		

NAME Sports Link Footwear

ADDRESS 300 Page St. #910, San Francisco, CA 94107

DATE		DESCRIPTION	POST. REF.	DEBIT	CREDIT	BALANCE
20--						
Dec.	1	Balance	✓			2 0 0 0 00
	10		P12		4 0 0 0 00	6 0 0 0 00
	27		P12		1 5 0 0 00	7 5 0 0 00
	31		CP14	1 5 0 0 00		6 0 0 0 00

NAME Sports Nutrition Supply

ADDRESS 348 11th Street, Cleveland, OH 44112

DATE		DESCRIPTION	POST. REF.	DEBIT	CREDIT	BALANCE
20--						
Dec.	1	Balance	✓			1 5 0 0 00
	12		P12		6 0 0 00	2 1 0 0 00
	27		CP14	6 0 0 00		1 5 0 0 00

Figure 17–9 The Completed Accounts Payable Subsidiary Ledger (continued)

Posting from the General Debit Column

Footing and Totaling a Special Journal

First, columns are footed with the total entered in pencil. Verified totals are then written in ink.

Daily postings are made from the General Debit column to the appropriate general ledger accounts.

Refer to **Figure 17–10** as you read the following steps.

1. Enter the date of the transaction in the Date column of the general ledger account.
2. Enter the journal letters and the page number in the Posting Reference column of the general ledger account. Be sure to use the letters "CP" for the cash payments journal.
3. In the Debit column, enter the amount from the General Debit column of the cash payments journal.
4. Compute the new balance and enter it in the appropriate Balance column. (In this example there is no previous balance, so the amount recorded in the Debit column is also entered in the Debit Balance column.)
5. Return to the cash payments journal and enter the account number in the Posting Reference column.

All transactions in the General Debit column are posted to the general ledger accounts in the same way.

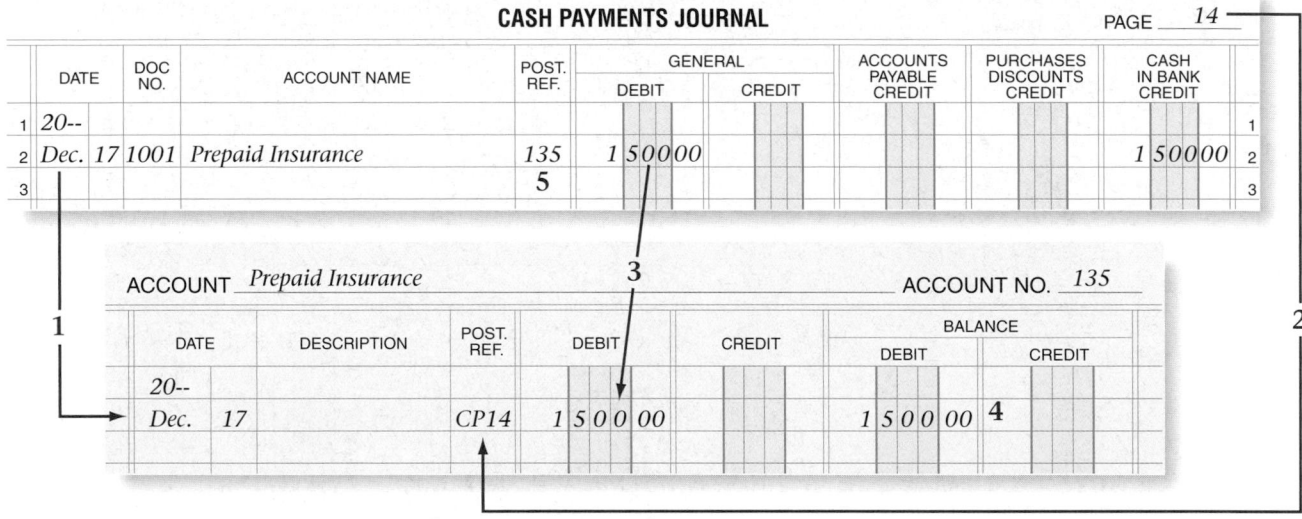

Figure 17–10 Posting from the General Debit Column of the Cash Payments Journal

Totaling, Proving, and Ruling the Cash Payments Journal

The cash payments journal is totaled in the same manner as the other special journals. Before the journal is ruled, prove the equality of debits and credits.

	Debit Columns		Credit Columns	
	General	$ 9,170	General	$ 1,026
	Accounts Payable	9,100	Purchases Discounts	140
			Cash in Bank	17,104
		$18,270		$18,270

Since debits equal credits, the cash payments journal can be double-ruled, as shown in **Figure 17–11**.

CASH PAYMENTS JOURNAL   PAGE ___14___

	DATE	DOC. NO.	ACCOUNT NAME	POST. REF.	GENERAL DEBIT	GENERAL CREDIT	ACCOUNTS PAYABLE DEBIT	PURCHASES DISCOUNTS CREDIT	CASH IN BANK CREDIT	
1	20--									1
2	Dec. 17	1001	Prepaid Insurance	135	1 500 00				1 500 00	2
3	19	1002	Purchases	501	1 300 00				1 300 00	3
4	24	1003	Pro Runner Warehouse	✓			2 300 00	46 00	2 254 00	4
5	24	1004	Transportation In	505	275 00				275 00	5
6	26	1005	Champion Store Supply	✓			1 200 00		1 200 00	6
7	27	1006	Sports Nutrition Supply	✓			600 00		600 00	7
8	28	1007	FastLane Athletics	✓			2 000 00	40 00	1 960 00	8
9	30	1008	Dara's Delivery Service	✓			300 00		300 00	9
10	31	1009	Rent Expense	660	2 000 00				2 000 00	10
11	31	1010	Computer Solutions	✓			1 200 00	24 00	1 176 00	11
12	31	1011	Sports Link Footwear	✓			1 500 00	30 00	1 470 00	12
13	31	1012	Salaries Expense	665	4 000 00				2 974 00	13
14			Employee's Federal Inc. Tax Pay.	205		640 00				14
15			Employee's State Inc. Tax Pay.	211		80 00				15
16			Social Security Tax Payable	212		248 00				16
17			Medicare Tax Payable	213		58 00				17
18	31	—	Miscellaneous Expense	655	20 00				20 00	18
19	31	—	Bankcard Fees Expense	605	75 00				75 00	19
20	31		Totals		9 170 00	1 026 00	9 100 00	140 00	17 104 00	20
21										21

Figure 17–11 The Completed Cash Payments Journal

Posting Column Totals to the General Ledger

At the end of the month, the total of each special amount column is posted to the general ledger account named in the column heading. For the cash payments journal, column totals are posted to **Accounts Payable, Purchases Discounts,** and **Cash in Bank. Figure 17–12** shows the posting of the three special column totals to the general ledger accounts. Note that the account numbers for the three general ledger accounts are written in parentheses below the double rule in the appropriate columns of the cash payments journal.

The totals of the General Debit and Credit columns are not posted. Each entry in those columns was posted individually to the general ledger accounts. A check mark (✓) is entered below the double rule in the General Debit and Credit columns.

Key Points

General Columns in Special Journals

To show that General column totals are not posted, place a check mark in parentheses (✓) below the double rule.

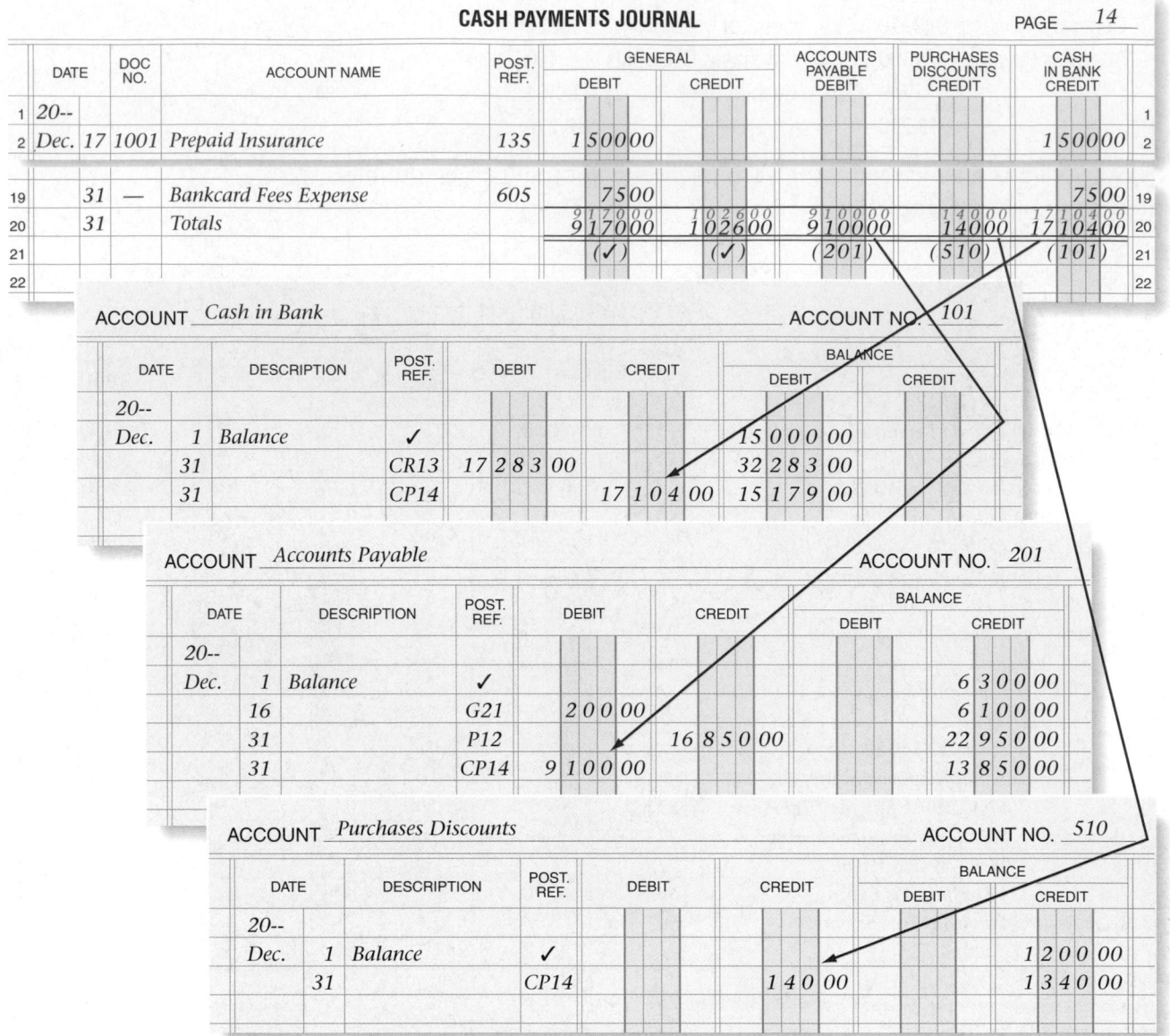

Figure 17–12 Posting Column Totals from the Cash Payments Journal

Proving the Accounts Payable Subsidiary Ledger

After the column totals are posted, prepare a **schedule of accounts payable** . This schedule lists all creditors in the accounts payable ledger, the balance in each account, and the total amount owed to all creditors. The accounts payable subsidiary ledger is proved when the total of the schedule of accounts payable agrees with the balance of the **Accounts Payable** (controlling) account in the general ledger.

Figure 17–13 shows On Your Mark's schedule of accounts payable for December. The accounts are listed in alphabetical order. All creditors are listed, even those with zero balances. Notice that the total listed on the schedule ($13,850) agrees with the balance of the **Accounts Payable** account.

ACCOUNT _Accounts Payable_   ACCOUNT NO. _201_

DATE		DESCRIPTION	POST. REF.	DEBIT	CREDIT	BALANCE DEBIT	BALANCE CREDIT
20--							
Dec.	1	Balance	✓				6 3 0 0 00
	16		G21	2 0 0 00			6 1 0 0 00
	31		P12		16 8 5 0 00		22 9 5 0 00
	31		CP14	9 1 0 0 00			13 8 5 0 00

On Your Mark Athletic Wear
Schedule of Accounts Payable
December 31, 20--

Champion Store Supply	1 0 0 0 00	
Computer Solutions	1 3 0 0 00	
Dara's Delivery Service	—	
FastLane Athletics	3 8 0 0 00	
Geary Office Supply	2 5 0 00	
Pro Runner Warehouse	—	
Sports Link Footwear	6 0 0 0 00	
Sports Nutrition Supply	1 5 0 0 00	
Total Accounts Payable		13 8 5 0 00

The balance of the Accounts Payable account should equal the total of the schedule of accounts payable.

Figure 17–13 Schedule of Accounts Payable

Proving Cash

Proving cash is the process of verifying that cash recorded in the accounting records agrees with the amount entered in the checkbook. Ideally businesses prove cash each day. When a business uses special journals, however, the **Cash in Bank** account in the general ledger is updated at the end of the month. For many businesses, then, proving cash is done at the end of the month.

Preparing a Cash Proof

The cash proof may be prepared on plain paper, on accounting stationery, on a special cash proof form, or on a computer. The cash proof for On Your Mark, shown in **Figure 17–14**, is prepared on two-column accounting stationery. To prove cash, follow these steps:

1. On the first line, record the beginning balance of **Cash in Bank** according to the general ledger account.
2. On the next line, enter the total cash received during the month. This is the total of the Cash in Bank Debit column from the cash receipts journal.
3. Add the first and second lines.
4. From the subtotal, subtract the cash payments for the month. This is the total of the Cash in Bank Credit column from the cash payments journal.
5. Compare this figure to the balance shown on the last check stub in the checkbook. If the ending balance of **Cash in Bank** and the balance on

the check stub match, cash is proved. The ending balance of **Cash in Bank** is $15,179. The balance shown on the last check stub is also $15,179; therefore, cash is proved.

If the balances are not equal, the error should be located and corrected. Errors can occur if a bank service charge or a bankcard fee was recorded in the checkbook, but not recorded in the general ledger. Next, you should verify that all disbursements and deposits were recorded in the accounting records. If cash is being proved at month-end, the accountant can then continue with month-end entries.

On Your Mark Athletic Wear		
Cash Proof		
December 31, 20--		
Beginning Cash in Bank Balance		15 000 00
Plus: Cash Receipts for the Month		17 283 00
Subtotal		32 283 00
Less: Cash Payments for the Month		17 104 00
Ending Cash in Bank Balance		15 179 00
Check Stub Balance		15 179 00

Figure 17–14 Cash Proof

ANALYZING FINANCIAL REPORTS

Cost of Goods Sold

For most corporations, increasing profits is a primary goal. To increase profits, either sales must increase or costs must decrease. Managers analyze both sales and costs carefully, and share information about both in the corporation's annual report. For example, in the Office Depot annual report at the back of your textbook, you'll see a section labeled "Management's Discussion and Analysis of Financial Condition and Results of Operations" on pages A-43–A-44. This section contains information about sales and the cost of goods sold.

Management's discussion refers to the company's gross profit, which is sometimes called gross margin. Here's how gross profit is calculated:

> Sales
> − Cost of goods sold
> Gross Profit

In the Office Depot Financial reports, occupancy costs such as rent and common area maintenance are included in cost of goods sold based on the industry's general practices.

▶ **Analyze the Report:**
 1. For Office Depot, what other items do you think would be included in cost of goods sold?
 2. By what percentage did "cost of goods sold and occupancy costs" change from 2000 to 2001? Was this an increase or a decrease?

Now that you have studied this section, complete the following questions and problems.

Thinking Critically

1. How is the accounts payable subsidiary ledger proved?
2. How does an accountant prove cash? How often is cash proved?

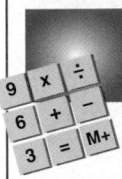

Computing in the Business World

At Car Wash Palace, hourly-wage earners are paid weekly. These employees earned $8,000 in total gross earnings this week.

1. Calculate each withholding amount.
2. What is the total net pay for this week?

Tax	Rate
Social Security	6.2%
Medicare	1.45%
Federal Unemployment	0.8%
State Unemployment	5.4%
State Income	4%

Problem 17–2 Preparing a Cash Proof

The Apple Tree Boutique uses special journals. On September 30 the total of the Cash in Bank Debit column of the cash receipts journal is $18,750.12. The total of the Cash in Bank Credit column of the cash payments journal is $16,890.43. The checkbook balance on September 30 is $5,610.59.

Instructions Prepare a cash proof for September in your working papers. The balance of **Cash in Bank** on September 1 is $3,750.90.

Problem 17–3 Analyzing a Source Document

The Country Peddler, which is a retail merchandising store, had the following transaction on November 2.

Instructions Analyze Check Stub 104 shown here. In your working papers, record the necessary entry on page 11 of the cash payments journal.

$ 873.00		No. 104
Date November 2		20 --
To Colonial Products Inc.		
For Inv. 323 $900 less 3% disc. $27.00		

	Dollars	Cents
Balance brought forward	3,468	29
Add deposits		
Total	3,468	29
Less this check	873	00
Balance carried forward	2,595	29

SETH PRATT, CPA
Software Developer
Peachtree Software, Inc.

Q: What is your background?

A: After I got my Bachelor of Science in accounting, I worked for three and a half years as a junior accountant and an accountant. Then I passed the CPA exam and went to work for a local CPA firm. I had my own business for a while, but I got excited about computers in the late 1970s. So I went to work for a computer store, then worked as a programmer. After a year and a half, I started a software company and developed accounting software for Windows. Peachtree noticed me and bought my company.

Q: Now what do you do?

A: I lead a team that produces new releases of the product. We improve the product by finding out what our customers complain about and what the competition is doing. We try to see opportunities that no one has thought of.

Q: What skills are most important?

A: Simple math is really important, especially the ability to do word problems. The ability to write concisely is also important. Have the desire to learn new things.

Q: What advice do you have for students interested in developing accounting software?

A: Study accounting in school rather than programming. Programming technology changes rapidly, but accounting procedures don't. Then learn as much about accounting as you can in a small company where you get the opportunity to look at the big picture.

Tips from . . .

RHI Robert Half International Inc.

When hiring, many companies find applicants who do not have basic math, reading, writing or leadership skills. You can improve your chances of being hired by working on weaknesses in these areas before you go to a job interview.

CAREER FACTS

<u>Nature of the Work:</u> Talk to clients, evaluate products on the market, and design products to fit niches.

<u>Training or Education Needed:</u> A bachelor's degree in accounting, the CPA exam, and broad computer experience.

<u>Aptitudes, Abilities, and Skills:</u> Accounting, problem-solving skills, computer skills, communication skills, listening skills, and analytical skills.

<u>Salary Range:</u> $50,000 to $100,000

<u>Career Path:</u> Start by getting accounting experience in a small firm. Then gain some experience in computer sales, programming, and eventually move into development.

Thinking Critically: Why is it important for software designers to be able to see the big accounting picture?

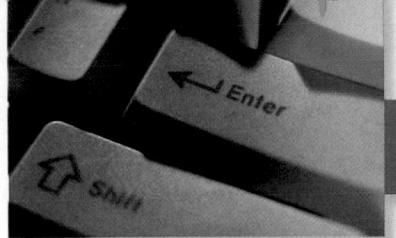

KEY CONCEPTS

1. The purchases journal is used to record all purchases on account. The source document for a purchases journal entry is an invoice.

PURCHASES JOURNAL   PAGE ___12___

	DATE	INVOICE NO.	CREDITOR'S ACCOUNT CREDITED	POST. REF.	ACCOUNTS PAYABLE CREDIT	PURCHASES DEBIT	GENERAL		
							ACCOUNT DEBITED	POST. REF.	DEBIT
1	Date	Invoice No.	Creditor's Name		xx xx	xx xx			
2									
3									

2. The accounts payable subsidiary ledger contains an account for each creditor. The total of the account balances in the accounts payable subsidiary ledger must match the balance of the **Accounts Payable** controlling account in the general ledger.

3. Transactions are posted from the purchases journal to the accounts payable subsidiary ledger daily. Transactions entered in the General Debit column of the purchases journal are posted daily to the general ledger accounts.

4. At the end of the month, the totals of the special amount columns of special journals are posted to the general ledger.

5. Good internal controls require that all cash payments are authorized, all payments are made by check, and all checks are signed by an authorized person.

6. The cash payments journal, illustrated below, is used to record all transactions in which cash is paid out. The source documents for the journal entry are check stubs and the bank statement.

CASH PAYMENTS JOURNAL   PAGE ___14___

	DATE	DOC NO.	ACCOUNT NAME	POST. REF.	GENERAL		ACCOUNTS PAYABLE DEBIT	PURCHASES DISCOUNTS CREDIT	CASH IN BANK CREDIT
					DEBIT	CREDIT			
1	Date	Ck #	Purchases		xx xx				xx xx
2	Date	Ck #	Creditor's Account Name				xx xx		xx xx
3	Date	Ck #	Creditor's Account Name				xx xx	xx xx	xx xx
4	Date	---	Account Name to be Debited		xx xx				xx xx
5									

7. Transactions are posted from the cash payments journal to the accounts payable subsidiary ledger daily. Transactions entered in the General Debit column of the cash payments journal are posted daily to the general ledger accounts.

8. A schedule of accounts payable is a list of all creditors, the amount owed to each, and the total amount owed to all creditors. The total of the schedule of accounts payable must agree with the balance of the **Accounts Payable** controlling account in the general ledger.

9. At the end of the month, cash is proved by verifying that the cash recorded in the accounting records agrees with the amount shown in the checkbook.

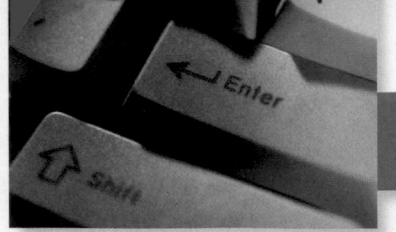

USING KEY TERMS

Imagine that you are an applicant for an accounting clerk position with PETCO. You are asked to write definitions for the terms listed below. You really want to get the job, so make sure you connect your knowledge of these accounting terms to the financial activities you believe take place at PETCO.

cash payments journal	purchases journal
proving cash	schedule of accounts payable

Understanding Accounting Concepts and Procedures

Instructions

On a separate sheet of paper, answer the following questions:

1. What kinds of transactions are recorded in the purchases journal?

2. Which account is credited when merchandise is purchased on account?

3. How often are amounts in the Accounts Payable Credit column of the purchases journal posted? Explain.

4. What is the normal balance of an account in the accounts payable subsidiary ledger? Explain.

5. Explain why the total of the General Debit column in the purchases journal is not posted.

6. What kinds of transactions are recorded in the cash payments journal?

7. What information is available in the accounts payable subsidiary ledger that cannot be found in the **Accounts Payable** controlling account?

8. Should the balance of the **Accounts Payable** account in the general ledger always equal the total of the accounts payable subsidiary ledger? Explain.

9. Why is a schedule of accounts payable prepared?

10. List the steps to prove cash at the end of the month.

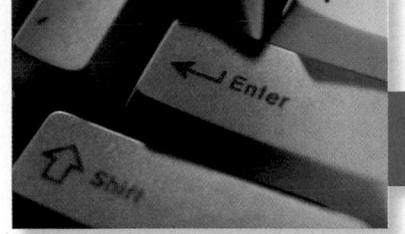

Case Study...

Merchandising Business:
Books & More

Books & More is a retail store that sells hardcover and paperback books, plus a large selection of music tapes and CDs. Books & More keeps a large stock of merchandise on hand and places frequent orders for new merchandise. For fast-selling items, such as a popular new CD, the store may place an order each week.

You work in the accounting department for Books & More. Recently, you noticed two invoices for three dozen CDs ordered from the same music wholesaler. The CDs ordered and the amounts are identical on both invoices.

Thinking Critically:

1. How would you determine whether the invoices are for two different orders or are duplicate invoices for one order?
2. What steps would you take to ensure that payments are not made for duplicate invoices?

Conducting an Audit with Alex

Alpha Enterprises had the following business transactions in May:
- Alpha issued a check to Metro Ace Realty for rent, $800.
- Alpha issued a check to Cray Hardware for $1,940 in payment for a $2,000 invoice due, less cash discount of $60.
- Alpha paid $300 to Ron's Paint Shop for painting supplies.

The accounting clerk for Alpha Enterprises made the following postings:
$800 was posted as a credit to **Rent Expense;**
$1,940 was posted as a debit to **Accounts Payable;**
$300 was posted as a credit to **Paint Supplies.**

Instructions Determine whether the transactions were posted correctly. If not, what error(s) were made?

*inter*NET CONNECTION

Electronic Commerce
Electronic commerce on the Internet is becoming increasingly popular. You should be aware of the basics of e-commerce and its benefits.

Do This:
Explore e-commerce on the Internet and then answer the following questions:
1. Define electronic commerce.
2. A smart card is one method for making electronic payments. Locate an Internet site that discusses smart cards. What is a smart card?
3. List two advantages electronic commerce provides for consumers.

Workplace Skills

Selecting Equipment and Tools
For your business to be competitive, you must be able to look at your company's needs, assess the best technology to help solve problems, and find the best equipment to produce results.

On the Job:
Web Works is an online computer assistance service for people who use computers. The company specializes in applications accessible through the Internet. In a recent staff meeting, Shelly Lazarus, your manager, asked you to assess online banking and invoice payment.

Thinking Critically:
1. Investigate online banking on the Internet. Find out what type of computer equipment is required, and how much the service will cost. Prepare a table showing comparative data.
2. Next, review different options for paying invoices online. Look at software product reviews and prepare a table showing the comparative data for this type of service.
3. Write a memorandum with your recommendations to Ms. Lazarus for the types of equipment Web Works will need to facilitate both online banking and online invoice payment.

Mastering Purchases and Cash Payments

Making the Transition from a Manual to a Computerized System

Task	Perform Accounting Procedures Using Manual Methods	Perform Accounting Procedures Using Automated Methods
Setting up vendor records	1. Ledger sheet or card is prepared with vendor details such as name, address, and contact information. 2. Account activities are posted to the vendor subsidiary ledger accounts.	1. Assign each vendor an ID code. 2. Record details of vendor accounts into vendor records. 3. The software will access this information automatically each time the ID code is used.
Recording a debit memorandum	1. A debit memorandum is prepared when merchandise is damaged or an allowance is due. 2. A journal entry is prepared to record the debit memorandum. 3. The journal entry is posted to the subsidiary account and to the general ledger.	1. Record the debit memorandum as a negative amount using the Purchases/Receive Inventory option. 2. The debit memorandum will appear on the outstanding invoices list. 3. The debit memorandum data is posted automatically to the vendor's account record and the general ledger.

Mastering Purchases and Cash Payments

Peachtree Question	Description
How do I set up a new vendor record?	1. Select **Vendors** from the *Maintain* menu. 2. Assign a Vendor ID to the new vendor. 3. Enter vendor name and contact information. 4. Click on the *Purchase Defaults* tab. 5. Verify or enter the appropriate purchase default GL account number. 6. Click *Save*.
How do I record a debit memorandum?	1. Select **Purchases/Receive Inventory** from the *Tasks* menu. 2. Select the appropriate Vendor ID from the pull-down list. 3. Enter the Debit Memorandum number in the Invoice field. 4. Select or verify the GL A/P account number. 5. Enter the line items of the return or allowance as a negative amount. 6. Click *Save*.
What does the software do "behind the scenes"?	• Using Vendor ID codes, the software can update vendor purchases and payments when purchase or cash payments are recorded. • Debit memorandums are applied directly to the appropriate vendor account and posted to the general ledger and subsidiary ledger automatically.

For detailed instructions: See the **Peachtree User Guide** in your Glencoe Working Papers.

APPLICATION OPTIONS

Problem 17–4
Recording Payment of the Payroll

Denardo's Country Store pays its employees on a biweekly basis. This week the payroll is $2,000. You issued Check 949 for $1,487 in payment of the payroll less the following amounts: Employees' Federal Income Tax, $320; Employees' State Income Tax, $40; Social Security Tax, $124; and Medicare Tax, $29.

Instructions In your working papers, record the July 15 payroll on page 4 of the cash payments journal.

Analyze: Calculate the total deductions from employees wages for federal, state, social security, and Medicare taxes. What percentage of gross payroll is this amount?

Complete chapter problems one of three ways:

1 **Manual** Glencoe Working Papers

or

2 **Peachtree Complete Accounting** Software

or

3 **QuickBooks** Templates (Problems 17–5, 17–8)

Problem 17–5 Recording Transactions in the Purchases Journal

Sunset Surfwear had the following purchases transactions for July.

Instructions Use the purchases journal in your working papers.
1. Record the following transactions on page 4 of the purchases journal.
2. Foot, prove, total, and rule the purchases journal.

Date	Transactions
July 1	Purchased merchandise on account from Waverunner Designs for $1,200, Invoice WD121.
3	Received Invoice CA552 from Capital Accessories for the purchase of $1,600 in merchandise on account.
5	Purchased $2,000 in store equipment on account from Neilson Store Equipment, Invoice NS444.
9	Purchased $870 in merchandise on account from Kelley Apparel Inc., Invoice KA772.
12	Purchased $250 in supplies from Moore Paper & Office Supply Co., Invoice MPS266.
15	Purchased $1,800 in merchandise on account from AcaTan Products, Invoice ATP99.

Continued

Peachtree®

SMART GUIDE

Step–by–Step Instructions: Problem 17–4

1. Select the problem set for Denardo's Country Store (Prob. 17–4).
2. Rename the company and set the system date.
3. Record the payment of the payroll using the **Payments** option.
4. Print a Cash Disbursements Journal report.
5. Proof your work.
6. Print a General Ledger report and a Vendor Ledgers report.
7. Answer the Analyze question.
8. End the session.

TIP: Remember to update the *G/L Account* field for each line of a multi-part cash payment transaction.

Peachtree®

SMART GUIDE

Step–by–Step Instructions:
Problem 17–5

1. Select the problem set for Sunset Surfwear (Prob. 17–5).
2. Rename the company and set the system date.
3. Record all of the purchases on account using the **Purchases/Receive Inventory** option.
4. Print a Purchases Journal report.
5. Proof your work.
6. Answer the Analyze question.
7. End the session.

TIP: Remember to change the *G/L Account* field as needed for general purchases.

Peachtree®

SMART GUIDE

Step–by–Step Instructions:
Problem 17–6

1. Select the problem set for Shutterbug Cameras (Prob. 17–6).
2. Rename the company and set the system date.
3. Record all of the purchases on account using the **Purchases/Receive Inventory** option.
4. Print a Purchases Journal report.
5. Proof your work.
6. Print a General Ledger report and a Vendor Ledgers report.
7. Answer the Analyze question.
8. End the session.

TIP: Remember to change the *G/L Account* field for purchases other than merchandise.

Date	Problem 17–5 (cont.) Transactions
July 18	Purchased $500 in office equipment on account from Moore Paper & Office Supply Co., Invoice MPS275.
22	Received Invoice WD156 from Waverunner Designs for the purchase of $900 in merchandise on account.
25	Purchased $475 in merchandise on account from Capital Accessories, Invoice CA560.
28	Purchased from Kelley Apparel Inc. $390 in merchandise on account, Invoice KA800.
30	Received Invoice NS460 from Neilson Store Equipment for the purchase of $1,200 in store equipment on account.

Analyze: What are the total purchases on account for the month?

Problem 17–6 Recording and Posting Purchases

Shutterbug Cameras, a retail merchandising business, had the following purchases on account for the month of July. In the working papers, the beginning balances in the accounts are opened for you.

Instructions In your working papers:
1. Record July's transactions on page 18 of the purchases journal.
2. Post to the accounts payable subsidiary ledger accounts daily.
3. Post amounts entered in the General Debit column daily.
4. Foot, prove, total, and rule the purchases journal at the end of the month.
5. Post the column totals at the end of the month to the account named in the column heading.
6. Prepare a schedule of accounts payable.

Date	Transactions
July 1	Purchased $1,200 in merchandise on account from U-Tech Products, Invoice UT220.
3	Purchased $140 in supplies on account from State Street Office Supply, Invoice 983, n/30.
6	Received Invoice 1338 from Photo Emporium for the purchase of $150 in merchandise on account, 2/10, n/30.
9	Invoice 445 for $90 was sent by Allen's Repair for plumbing repairs completed at the store (**Maintenance Expense**).
12	Purchased $800 in merchandise on account from Video Optics Inc., Invoice VO167, 3/15, n/45.
15	Received Invoice 1322 from Digital Precision Equipment for the purchase of $2,500 in store equipment on account, n/30.

Continued 🖎

Date	Problem 17–6 (cont.) Transactions
July 18	Purchased $1,300 in merchandise on account from U-Tech Products, Invoice UT257.
20	Purchased $400 in supplies on account from ProStudio Supply, Invoice 4677.
23	Photo Emporium sent Invoice 1359 for the purchase of $600 of merchandise on account.
26	Received Invoice 478 for $120 from Allen's Repair for additional plumbing work completed at the store.
28	Purchased $200 in merchandise on account from Video Optics Inc., Invoice VO183.

Analyze: If the transaction of July 23 (Photo Emporium) was posted to the accounts payable subsidiary ledger as $60, what problems would occur?

Problem 17–7 Recording and Posting Cash Payments

River's Edge Canoe & Kayak is a retail merchandising business located in Jackson Hole, Wyoming. The beginning balances of the accounts needed to complete this problem are opened in your working papers.

Instructions In your working papers:
1. Record the transactions on page 19 of the cash payments journal.
2. Post the individual amounts in the Accounts Payable Credit column on a daily basis to the creditors' accounts.
3. Post the individual amounts in the General Debit and Credit columns on the date the transaction occurred.
4. Foot, prove, total, and rule the cash payments journal.
5. Post the column totals at the end of the month.
6. Prepare a schedule of accounts payable.
7. Prove cash at the end of the month. The beginning **Cash in Bank** balance was $8,000; cash receipts were $7,000; and the ending check stub balance is $8,402.

Date	Transactions
July 1	Issued Check 1405 for $1,372 to North American Waterways Suppliers in payment on account of $1,400 invoice less a 2% discount.
3	Received insurance premium statement from Rocky Mountain Insurance Company. Issued Check 1406 for $1,800.

Continued 🌱

Peachtree®

SMART GUIDE

Step–by–Step Instructions: Problem 17–7

1. Select the problem set for River's Edge Canoe & Kayak (Prob. 17–7).
2. Rename the company and set the system date.
3. Record all of the cash payments using the **Payments** option.
4. Print a Cash Disbursements Journal report.
5. Proof your work.
6. Print a General Ledger report and a Vendor Ledgers report.
7. Answer the Analyze question.
8. End the session.

TIP: Sometimes you may have to manually enter a cash discount when you record a cash payment.

Date	Problem 17–7 (cont.) Transactions
July 5	Issued Check 1407 to Pacific Wholesalers for $500 to apply on account.
8	Received an invoice for $300 from Jackson News for advertising. Issued Check 1408.
12	Issued Check 1409 for $686 to Trailhead Canoes in payment on account of $700 invoice less a 2% discount.
15	Issued Check 1410 for $200 to Rollins Plumbing Service in full payment of the amount owed on account.
18	Issued Check 1411 for $75 to Ben Jacobs for completing odd jobs in the store (Miscellaneous Expense).
20	Purchased $90 in supplies from StoreMart Supply by issuing Check 1412.
22	Paid StoreMart Supply $400 to apply on account, Check 1413.
24	Issued Check 1414, $700 to Office Max, store equipment.
25	Paid Mohican Falls Kayak Wholesalers $200 to apply on account, Check 1415.
26	Issued Check 1416 to Office Max, $150 to apply on account.
28	Paid transportation charges of $125 to Stein's Trucking, Check 1417.

Analyze: At month end, how much does River's Edge owe to its creditors?

Peachtree®

SMART GUIDE

Step–by–Step Instructions: Problem 17–8

1. Select the problem set for Buzz Newsstand (Prob. 17-8).
2. Rename the company and set the system date.
3. Enter the purchases on account.
4. Record all of the cash payments.
5. Print the following reports: Purchases Journal, Cash Disbursements Journal, and Vendor Ledgers.
6. Proof your work.
7. Print a General Ledger report.
8. Answer the Analyze question.
9. End the session.

SOURCE DOCUMENT PROBLEM

Problem 17–8

Use the source documents in your working papers to record the transactions for this problem.

CHALLENGE PROBLEM

Problem 17–8 Recording and Posting Purchases and Cash Payments

SOURCE DOCUMENT PROBLEM

Buzz Newsstand had the following purchases and cash payment transactions for July. The balance in the accounts payable subsidiary ledger and general ledger accounts are opened in the working papers.

Instructions In your working papers:

1. Record the purchases and cash payment transactions on page 12 of the purchases journal and page 12 of the cash payments journal.
2. Post to the creditors' accounts in the accounts payable subsidiary ledger daily.
3. Post from the General Debit and Credit columns of the journals on the date the transaction occurred.
4. Foot, prove, total, and rule both journals.
5. Post the column totals of the purchases journal to the general ledger accounts named in the column headings.
6. Post the column totals of the cash payments journal to the general ledger accounts named in the column headings.
7. Prepare a schedule of accounts payable.

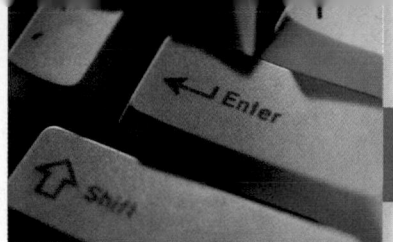

8. Prepare a cash proof at the end of the month. The beginning **Cash in Bank** balance was $9,000. Cash receipts were $10,500. The check stub balance on July 31 is $10,178.

Date	Transactions
July 1	Issued Check 2455 for $1,552 to ADC Publishing in payment on account of $1,600 invoice less a 3% discount.
2	Purchased $400 in merchandise on account from Pine Forest Publications, Invoice PFP144, terms 2/10, n/30.
2	Paid Candlelight Software $1,358 in payment of $1,400 account less a 3% discount, Check 2456.
4	Issued Check 2457 to Nomad Computer Sales for $350 to apply on account.
5	Purchased $2,000 in store equipment on account from CorpTech Office Supply, Invoice CT67.
7	Issued Check 2458 for $125 to Wolfe Trucking for transportation charges.
9	Purchased $900 in merchandise on account from American Trend Publishers, Invoice ATP98.
12	Purchased $300 in supplies on account from CorpTech Office Supply, Invoice CT72.
14	Issued Check 2459 to Delta Press for $750 to apply on account.
15	Received insurance premium statement from SeaTac Insurance Co. for $1,600. Issued Check 2460.
16	Check 2461 was issued for $882 to American Trend Publishers in payment of $900 account less a 2% discount.
18	Purchased $500 in merchandise on account from Candlelight Software, Invoice CS101, terms n/30.
20	Purchased $200 in merchandise on account from Nomad Computer Sales, Invoice NC56, terms 2/10, n/30.
22	Paid Pine Forest Publications $100 to apply on account, Check 2462.
23	Issued Check 2463 for $2,000 to CorpTech Office Supply to apply on account.
25	Purchased $600 in merchandise on account from ADC Publishing, Invoice ADC70.
28	Issued Check 2464 for $450 to Nomad Computer Sales to apply on account.
30	Recorded the bank service charge of $25. Recorded the bankcard fees, $130. July bank statement.

Analyze: Of the purchases made during July, what dollar amount increased merchandise inventory?

CHAPTER 18

Adjustments and the Ten-Column Work Sheet

Learning Objectives

When you have completed this chapter, you will be able to:

▶ Describe the parts of a ten-column work sheet.

▶ Generate trial balances and end-of-period adjustments.

▶ Determine which general ledger accounts are adjusted.

▶ Calculate the adjustments.

▶ Prepare a ten-column work sheet.

▶ Journalize the adjustments.

▶ Define the accounting terms introduced in this chapter.

Exploring the Real World of Business

ANALYZING ADJUSTMENTS

The Black Phantom rides again! Is it a superspy? Batman's sidekick? A new James Bond car? Actually, it's a bicycle. The original Black Phantom was made in 1949 and was recently re-introduced as a collector's item by the **Schwinn Bicycle Company.** Since 1895, German engineer Ignaz Schwinn has been making bicycles in his factory in Chicago.

Today, if you visit any local health club, you might find Schwinn stationary bicycles, treadmills, weight stacks, and steppers. Many health clubs use **Schwinn's** Johnny G SPINNER stationary bikes, which give users the same exercise as if they were cycling through hilly terrain. The SPINNER bike was developed by **Schwinn** with Johnny Goldberg, a world-class cyclist who used the bike to train for the Race Across America.

Schwinn counts these and its other products as part of its inventory. Each year, items in inventory are counted and adjustments are made to show changes in beginning and ending inventories. Analysis of inventory shortages or excesses often help companies make production decisions and develop marketing strategies.

What do you think?

What other adjustments do you think **Schwinn** would need to make at the end of their fiscal period?

Workplace Connections

Applying Your Accounting Knowledge

A merchandising business uses the work sheet for collecting and organizing financial information. In really big businesses, several people might work on different parts of the work sheet. For example, one person might be responsible for accounts payable information and others for accounts receivable and payroll. The staff works as a team to prepare the work sheet.

Investigate:

1. In your workplace, are you asked to participate in group or team assignments?
2. How do team members work with each other?
3. What skills are needed to work well in a team?

483

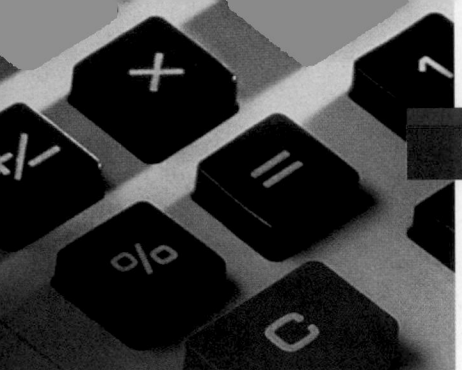

Identifying Accounts To Be Adjusted and Adjusting Merchandise Inventory

The work sheet in Chapter 8 had six amount columns. The work sheet in this chapter, however, has ten amount columns. The additional columns are for the Adjustments and Adjusted Trial Balance sections. Companies like Taco Bell make adjustments at the end of each accounting period. In this chapter you will learn how to generate trial balances and end-of-period adjustments.

Completing End-of-Period Work

The general ledger summarizes the effects of business transactions on individual accounts for an accounting period. However, managers, stockholders, and creditors need more than a list of account totals to evaluate performance. They need to know net income and the value of owners' equity. Sound business decisions cannot be made without this vital information.

The purpose of all end-of-period reports is to provide essential information about the financial position of a business organization. In Chapters 8 and 9, you learned about the work sheet prepared for a service business organized as a sole proprietorship. In this chapter you will prepare a work sheet for a merchandising business organized as a corporation. This work sheet is the basis for preparing end-of-period financial statements and journal entries.

The Ten-Column Work Sheet

The ten-column work sheet is prepared in the same way as the six-column work sheet. The ten-column work sheet, however, has five amount sections instead of three. The five sections are:

- Trial Balance
- Adjustments
- Adjusted Trial Balance
- Income Statement
- Balance Sheet

Completing the Trial Balance Section

A trial balance is prepared to prove the equality of debits and credits in the general ledger. **Figure 18–1** shows the end-of-period trial balance for On Your Mark Athletic Wear.

To prepare the trial balance, the number and name of each account in the general ledger are entered on the work sheet in the Account Number

	ACCT. NO.	ACCOUNT NAME	TRIAL BALANCE DEBIT	TRIAL BALANCE CREDIT
1	101	Cash in Bank	15 179 00	
2	115	Accounts Receivable	10 404 00	
3	125	Merchandise Inventory	84 921 00	
4	130	Supplies	5 549 00	
5	135	Prepaid Insurance	1 500 00	
6	140	Delivery Equipment	19 831 00	
7	145	Office Equipment	9 825 00	
8	150	Store Equipment	5 200 00	
9	201	Accounts Payable		13 850 00
10	204	Fed. Corp. Inc. Tax Payable		
11	205	Employees' Fed. Inc. Tax Pay.		640 00
12	211	Employees' State Inc. Tax Pay.		80 00
13	212	Social Security Tax Payable		248 00
14	213	Medicare Tax Payable		58 00
15	214	Fed. Unemployment Tax Payable		18 36
16	215	State Unemployment Tax Payable		114 73
17	220	Sales Tax Payable		2 428 00
18	301	Capital Stock		75 000 00
19	305	Retained Earnings		19 771 19
20	310	Income Summary		
21	401	Sales		320 450 00
22	405	Sales Discounts	730 00	
23	410	Sales Returns & Allowances	2 000 00	
24	501	Purchases	206 700 00	
25	505	Transportation In	4 036 18	
26	510	Purchases Discounts		1 340 00
27	515	Purchases Returns & Allowances		1 800 00
28	601	Advertising Expense	2 450 00	
29	605	Bankcard Fees Expense	4 199 27	
30	630	Fed. Corp. Income Tax Expense	9 840 00	
31	635	Insurance Expense		
32	650	Maintenance Expense	3 519 25	
33	655	Miscellaneous Expense	348 28	
34	657	Payroll Tax Expense	3 826 83	
35	660	Rent Expense	14 000 00	
36	665	Salaries Expense	29 374 60	
37	670	Supplies Expense		
38	680	Utilities Expense	2 364 87	
39			435 798 28	435 798 28
40				

Figure 18–1 The Trial Balance Section of the Work Sheet

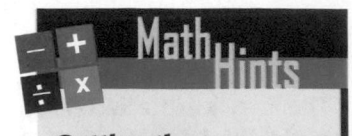

and Account Name columns. The accounts are listed in the order that they appear in the general ledger (Asset, Liability, Owner's Equity, Revenue, Cost of Merchandise, Expense). The balance of each account is entered in the appropriate column, either the Debit or the Credit column, of the Trial Balance section. Notice that every general ledger account is listed, even those with zero balances. After all balances are entered, the Trial Balance Debit and Credit columns are ruled, totaled, and proved. Then, a double rule is drawn across both columns.

Calculating Adjustments

Not all changes in account balances are the result of daily business transactions. Some changes result from the internal operations of the business or from the passage of time. For example, supplies such as paper, pens, shopping bags, and sales slips are bought for use by the business. They are recorded in an asset account called **Supplies.** These supplies are used gradually during the accounting period. Another example is insurance premiums, which cover a certain period of time. The premiums are recorded in an asset account called **Prepaid Insurance.** During the period, some of the insurance is used up, or expires. At the end of the period, the balances in accounts such as **Supplies** and **Prepaid Insurance** are brought up-to-date.

To illustrate, suppose that supplies costing $500 were purchased during an accounting period and recorded in the **Supplies** account. At the end of the period, the **Supplies** account balance is $500; however, only $200 of supplies are still on hand. The account balance for **Supplies** is adjusted downward to show that the business used $300 of supplies.

Up to this point, the general ledger account balances have been changed by journal entries made to record transactions that are supported by source documents. There are no source documents, however, for the changes in account balances caused by the internal operations of a business or the passage of time. Such changes are recorded through adjustments made at the end of the period to the account balance. An **adjustment** is an amount that is added to or subtracted from an account balance to bring that balance up-to-date. Every adjustment affects at least one permanent account and one temporary account.

At the end of the period, adjustments are made to transfer the costs of the assets consumed from the asset accounts (permanent accounts) to the appropriate expense accounts (temporary accounts). Accountants say that these assets are "expensed" because the costs of consumed assets are expenses of doing business. Thus, when an adjustment is recorded, the expenses for a given period are matched with the revenue for that period.

The Adjustments section of the work sheet is used to record the adjustments made at the end of the period to bring various account balances up-to-date.

Determining the Adjustments Needed

How do you generate end-of-period adjustments? Review each account balance in the Trial Balance columns of the work sheet. If the balance shown for an account is not up-to-date *as of the last day of the fiscal period,* then that account balance must be adjusted.

Refer to **Figure 18–1.** The first account listed is **Cash in Bank.** All cash received or paid out during the period was journalized and posted to the **Cash in Bank** account. The balance in this account is up-to-date. The next account, **Accounts Receivable** (controlling), is also up-to-date since all amounts owed or paid by charge customers were journalized and posted.

The third account is **Merchandise Inventory,** used to report the cost of merchandise on hand. The balance reported in the Trial Balance section ($84,921) is the merchandise on hand at the *beginning* of the period.

The amount of merchandise on hand is constantly changing during the period. The changes are not recorded in the **Merchandise Inventory** account. During the period the cost of merchandise purchased is recorded in the **Purchases** account. As inventory is reduced by the sale of merchandise, the amount of each sale is recorded in the **Sales** account. No entries are posted to **Merchandise Inventory.** At the end of the period, the balance in the **Merchandise Inventory** account does not reflect the amount of merchandise on hand. So, the **Merchandise Inventory** account balance must be adjusted.

The other account balances on the work sheet are reviewed in the same manner. Additional adjustments are made as described later in this chapter.

Adjusting the Merchandise Inventory Account

Merchandise Inventory is an asset account used by merchandising businesses. **Beginning inventory** is the merchandise a business has on hand and available for sale at the *beginning* of a period. **Ending inventory** is the merchandise a business has on hand at the *end* of a period. The ending inventory for one period becomes the beginning inventory for the next period.

The account balance of **Merchandise Inventory** does not change during the period. It is changed *only* when a physical inventory is taken. A **physical inventory** is an actual count of all the merchandise on hand and available for sale. A physical inventory can be taken at any time. One is always taken at the end of a period.

Key Points

Adjustments
Adjustments help match expenses with related revenue.

For example, if inventory is counted in a toy store at the end of a period, the cost of inventory can be calculated. This is done by multiplying the quantity of each item by its unit cost.

At the end of each period, after the physical inventory is taken and the cost of ending inventory is calculated, the beginning inventory amount recorded in **Merchandise Inventory** is replaced by the ending inventory amount. This is accomplished by an adjustment to **Merchandise Inventory.**

Calculating the Adjustment for Merchandise Inventory

When calculating the adjustment for **Merchandise Inventory,** you need to know:

- The **Merchandise Inventory** account balance
- The physical inventory amount

For On Your Mark:

Merchandise Inventory account balance	$84,921
Physical inventory	81,385

The effect of all the purchases and sales during the period is a decrease to **Merchandise Inventory** of $3,536 ($84,921 − $81,385). This reduction in inventory needs to be recorded as an adjustment in the accounting records. The two accounts affected by the inventory adjustment are **Merchandise Inventory** and **Income Summary**.

Adjustment

*To adjust the **Merchandise Inventory** account to reflect the physical inventory amount ($81,385), the following transaction is recorded.*

ANALYSIS	*Identify*	1. The accounts **Merchandise Inventory** and **Income Summary** are affected.
	Classify	2. **Merchandise Inventory** is an asset account (permanent). **Income Summary** is a stockholder's equity account.
	+/−	3. **Merchandise Inventory** is decreased by $3,536. This amount is transferred to **Income Summary**.

DEBIT-CREDIT RULE		4. To transfer the decrease in **Merchandise Inventory**, debit **Income Summary** for $3,536.
		5. Decreases to asset accounts are recorded as credits. Credit **Merchandise Inventory** for $3,536.

T ACCOUNTS 6.

Income Summary			Merchandise Inventory	
Debit	Credit		Debit +	Credit −
3,536				3,536

Key Points

Adjustment to Merchandise Inventory
When beginning inventory is greater than ending inventory, credit **Merchandise Inventory**. When beginning inventory is less than ending inventory, debit **Merchandise Inventory**.

If ending inventory is greater than beginning inventory, **Merchandise Inventory** is debited and **Income Summary** is credited. For example, suppose that the beginning inventory was $84,921 and the ending inventory is $88,226. Inventory increased by $3,305 ($88,226 − $84,921). The **Merchandise Inventory** account is debited for $3,305, and **Income Summary** is credited for $3,305.

Merchandise Inventory			Income Summary	
Debit +	Credit −		Debit	Credit
3,305				3,305

Entering the Adjustment for Merchandise Inventory on the Work Sheet

Adjustments are entered in the Adjustments columns of the work sheet. The debit and credit parts of each adjustment are given a unique label. The label consists of a small letter in parentheses and is placed just above and to the left of the adjustment amounts. The adjustments are labeled as follows:

First adjustment   (a)
Second adjustment   (b)
Third adjustment   (c)

The number of adjustments vary depending on the business. Once the adjustments are entered, the work sheet provides the information needed to make the adjusting journal entries.

Use the T accounts in step 6 of the preceding example as a guide to entering the inventory adjustment on the work sheet. Refer to **Figure 18–2**. To record the adjustment for **Merchandise Inventory:**

1. In the Adjustments Debit column, enter the debit amount of the adjustment on the Income Summary line. Label this amount (a).
2. In the Adjustments Credit column, enter the credit amount of the adjustment on the Merchandise Inventory line. Label this amount (a) also.

Key Points

Adjustments on the Work Sheet
Label the debit and credit amounts of each adjustment.

	ACCT. NO	ACCOUNT NAME	TRIAL BALANCE		ADJUSTMENTS	
			DEBIT	CREDIT	DEBIT	CREDIT
1	101	Cash in Bank	15 179 00			
2	115	Accounts Receivable	10 404 00			
3	125	Merchandise Inventory	84 921 00			(a) 3 536 00
20	310	Income Summary			(a) 3 536 00	
21						

Figure 18–2 Recording the Adjustment for Merchandise Inventory on the Work Sheet

A MATTER OF ETHICS

Out-of-Date Goods

Imagine that you work as an accounting clerk for a local bakery. At your company, day-old baked goods are not to be sold. Employees are allowed to eat them or take them home. You think this policy is wasteful. One day, a mother with three children asks if she can buy some day-old donuts because she can't afford fresh ones. You consider giving her several pastries that are about to be thrown away.

Ethical Decision Making:

- What are the ethical issues?
- What are the alternatives?
- Who are the affected parties?
- How do the alternatives affect the parties?
- What would you do?

Now that you have studied this section, complete the following questions and problems.

Thinking Critically

1. What would you do if the Debit and Credit columns of the Trial Balance section of the work sheet are not equal?
2. After the physical inventory is taken, what happens to the **Merchandise Inventory** account?

Analyzing Accounting

Jim Warren, accounting manager, asked you to analyze inventory for the past three years. Your company, Photo Shots, is looking to expand its merchandise, but Jim wants to analyze inventory data for the last three years before he recommends expansion. Using the data given, create a bar graph to depict the total amount of merchandise sold by year. Write a paragraph summarizing your analysis of inventory trends.

	Merchandise Inventory		
Year	Beginning	Ending	Purchases
2001	900	1,000	5,000
2002	1,000	2,000	8,000
2003	2,000	1,500	7,500

Problem 18–1 Analyzing the Adjustment for Merchandise Inventory

The Ely Corporation, a custom furniture manufacturer, has a general ledger account balance of $73,395 for **Merchandise Inventory** as of July 1. On the following June 30, the end of the fiscal period, Ely took a physical inventory and determined there was $74,928 in merchandise on hand. In your working papers, answer the following questions regarding the adjustment for **Merchandise Inventory:**

1. Is the value of the ending inventory greater than or less than the value of the beginning inventory?
2. What is the amount of the inventory adjustment?
3. Which account is debited?
4. Which account is credited?

Adjusting Supplies, Prepaid Insurance, and Federal Corporate Income Tax

In Section 1 you learned that the **Merchandise Inventory** account is updated at the end of the period. Other accounts in the general ledger are also adjusted. For example, high-risk businesses, like building construction and demolition, spend a lot of money on insurance. Therefore, it is important that the financial statements reflect the proper insurance expenses each period. Supplies and federal corporate income taxes also represent significant expenses that must be reported accurately.

Adjusting the Supplies Account

A merchandising business buys various supplies to be used by employees in the everyday operations of the business. Pencils, pens, computer paper, shopping bags, sales slips, price tags, and cash register tapes are purchased, and the cost is debited to the **Supplies** account.

Supplies are used every day. As they are consumed, they become expenses of the business. It is inefficient to keep daily records of each item as it is used, so the **Supplies** account is updated at the end of the period.

In the Trial Balance section of the work sheet in **Figure 18–1**, the balance of the **Supplies** account is $5,549. This amount is the cost of the supplies on hand on January 1 *plus* the cost of the additional supplies purchased during the period.

At the end of December, On Your Mark took a physical inventory and found that there were $1,839 of supplies on hand. This means that $3,710 of supplies were used during the period ($5,549 − $1,839 = $3,710). The amount of supplies on hand decreased by $3,710. Therefore, **Supplies** (a permanent asset account) is credited for $3,710. **Supplies Expense** (a temporary account) is debited (increased) to record the cost of supplies used during the period.

What You'll Learn

- Why the **Supplies**, **Prepaid Insurance**, and **Federal Corporate Income Tax Expense** accounts are adjusted.
- How to calculate the adjustments for supplies, insurance, and federal corporate income tax.
- How to enter the adjustments on the work sheet.

Why It's Important

Account balances related to supplies, insurance, and federal corporate income tax require adjustment in order to prepare accurate financial reports.

Adjustment

Record the adjustment for supplies.

ANALYSIS	*Identify*	1.	The accounts affected are **Supplies** and **Supplies Expense**.
	Classify	2.	**Supplies** is an asset account (permanent). **Supplies Expense** is an expense account (temporary).
	+/−	3.	**Supplies** is decreased by $3,710. **Supplies Expense** is increased by $3,710.

DEBIT-CREDIT RULE	4. Increases to expense accounts are recorded as debits. Debit **Supplies Expense** for $3,710.
	5. Decreases to asset accounts are recorded as credits. Credit **Supplies** for $3,710.

T ACCOUNTS	6.	Supplies Expense		Supplies	
		Debit +	Credit −	Debit +	Credit −
		3,710			3,710

The adjustment for supplies is shown in **Figure 18–3.** To enter the adjustment on the work sheet, follow these steps:

1. In the Adjustments Debit column, enter the debit amount of the adjustment on the Supplies Expense line. Since this is the second adjustment, label it (b).
2. In the Adjustments Credit column, enter the credit amount of the adjustment on the Supplies line. Label it (b) also.

Adjusting the Prepaid Insurance Account

On December 17 On Your Mark purchased an insurance policy. The insurance coverage is for six months, mid-December through mid-May. The premium of $1,500 ($250 per month) was debited to the **Prepaid Insurance** account.

At the end of December, the balance of **Prepaid Insurance** is $1,500, as shown in the Trial Balance section of the work sheet in **Figure 18–1.** However, the coverage for half of a month, costing $125, has expired. Since the value of the unexpired portion of the coverage has decreased to $1,375 ($1,500 − $125), **Prepaid Insurance** is adjusted with a credit for $125 to bring its balance up-to-date. The adjustment records the expired portion of the coverage as a business expense.

Adjustment

Record the adjustment for the expiration of one-half month's insurance coverage.

ANALYSIS	*Identify*	1. The accounts affected are **Insurance Expense** and **Prepaid Insurance.**
	Classify	2. **Insurance Expense** is an expense account (temporary). **Prepaid Insurance** is an asset account (permanent).
	+/−	3. **Insurance Expense** is increased by $125. **Prepaid Insurance** is decreased by $125.

DEBIT-CREDIT RULE	4. Increases to expense accounts are recorded as debits. Debit **Insurance Expense** for $125.
	5. Decreases to asset accounts are recorded as credits. Credit **Prepaid Insurance** for $125.

T ACCOUNTS

6.

Insurance Expense		Prepaid Insurance	
Debit +	Credit −	Debit +	Credit −
125			125

	ACCT. NO.	ACCOUNT NAME	TRIAL BALANCE		ADJUSTMENTS	
			DEBIT	CREDIT	DEBIT	CREDIT
1	101	Cash in Bank	15 179 00			
2	115	Accounts Receivable	10 404 00			
3	125	Merchandise Inventory	84 921 00			(a) 3 536 00
4	130	Supplies	5 549 00			(b) 3 710 00
5	135	Prepaid Insurance	1 500 00			(c) 125 00
6	140	Delivery Equipment	19 831 00			
7	145	Office Equipment	9 825 00			
8	150	Store Equipment	5 200 00			
9	201	Accounts Payable		13 850 00		
10	204	Fed. Corp. Inc. Tax Payable				(d) 155 00
11	205	Employees' Fed. Inc. Tax Pay.		640 00		
12	211	Employees' State Inc. Tax Pay.		80 00		
13	212	Social Security Tax Payable		248 00		
14	213	Medicare Tax Payable		58 00		
15	214	Fed. Unemployment Tax Payable		18 36		
16	215	State Unemployment Tax Payable		114 73		
17	220	Sales Tax Payable		2 428 00		
18	301	Capital Stock		75 000 00		
19	305	Retained Earnings		19 771 19		
20	310	Income Summary			(a) 3 536 00	
21	401	Sales		320 450 00		
22	405	Sales Discounts	730 00			
23	410	Sales Returns and Allowances	2 000 00			
24	501	Purchases	206 700 00			
25	505	Transportation In	4 036 18			
26	510	Purchases Discounts		1 340 00		
27	515	Purchases Returns and Allowances		1 800 00		
28	601	Advertising Expense	2 450 00			
29	605	Bankcard Fees Expense	4 199 27			
30	630	Fed. Corp. Income Tax Expense	9 840 00		(d) 155 00	
31	635	Insurance Expense			(c) 125 00	
32	650	Maintenance Expense	3 519 25			
00	655	Miscellaneous Expense	348 28			
34	657	Payroll Tax Expense	3 826 83			
35	660	Rent Expense	14 000 00			
36	665	Salaries Expense	29 374 60			
37	670	Supplies Expense			(b) 3 710 00	
38	680	Utilities Expense	2 364 87			
39			435 798 28	435 798 28	7 526 00	7 526 00
40						

Figure 18–3 Recording the Adjustments on the Work Sheet

The adjustment for **Prepaid Insurance** is shown in **Figure 18–3**. To enter the adjustment on the work sheet, follow these steps:

1. In the Adjustments Debit column, enter the debit amount of the adjustment on the Insurance Expense line. Since this is the third adjustment, label it (c).

2. In the Adjustments Credit column, enter the credit amount of the adjustment on the Prepaid Insurance line. Label it (c) also.

Adjusting the Federal Corporate Income Tax Expense Account

On Your Mark is organized as a corporation. A corporation is considered to be a legal entity separate from its owners. On Your Mark owns assets, pays its own debts, and enters into legal contracts.

A corporation pays federal corporate income taxes on its net income. Many states and cities also tax corporate income. For now, we will discuss only federal corporate income taxes. A corporation estimates its federal corporate income taxes for the coming year and pays that amount to the federal government in quarterly installments. At the end of the year, the exact net income and the tax on that income are determined. If the corporation owes additional taxes, they are paid when the corporate income tax return is filed.

At the beginning of the year, On Your Mark's accountant estimated that federal corporate income taxes would be $9,840. The business made quarterly payments of $2,460 in March, June, September, and December. These payments were journalized as debits to **Federal Corporate Income Tax Expense** and credits to **Cash in Bank.**

At the end of the year, On Your Mark's accountant determines that the federal corporate income tax for the year is $9,995. Since On Your Mark has already paid $9,840, the business owes an additional $155 ($9,995 − $9,840).

To bring the accounting records up-to-date, **Federal Corporate Income Tax Expense** and **Federal Corporate Income Tax Payable** must both be increased by $155. The T accounts below illustrate this adjustment.

Federal Corporate Income Tax Expense		Federal Corporate Income Tax Payable	
Debit + 155	Credit −	Debit −	Credit + 155

The adjustment for **Federal Corporate Income Tax Expense** is shown in **Figure 18–3.** Since this is the fourth adjustment, it is labeled (d).

Totaling and Ruling the Adjustments Section

After all adjustments are entered, the Adjustments section of the work sheet is totaled and ruled. Each adjustment has an equal debit and credit, so the totals of the Adjustments Debit and Credit columns should be the same. When the Adjustments section is proved, a double rule is drawn under the totals and across both columns, as shown in **Figure 18–3.**

Now that you have studied this section, complete the following questions and problems.

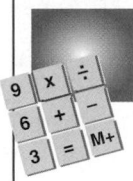

Thinking Critically

1. Explain how to record the cost of supplies purchased for use in a business.
2. Explain how to make an adjustment for prepaid insurance.

Computing in the Business World

You own a personal-training franchise called Your Body. You want to provide health insurance for your ten employees. As you review the alternative plans, you have to make a decision based not only on affordability, but also on total benefits. Determine the total annual premium of each plan and decide which plan best fits your needs.

Type of plan	Plan #1	Plan #2	Plan #3
Monthly cost per employee	$600	$500	$800
Co-pay for each employee	$10	$20	None

Problem 18–2   Analyzing Adjustments

Information related to accounts requiring adjustment on the work sheet for the year ended December 31 for Star City Resorts Corporation follows. Indicate in your working papers the amount of each adjustment, which account is debited, and which account is credited.

1. The Trial Balance section shows a balance of $3,347.45 for **Supplies**. The amount of supplies actually on hand is $892.75.
2. Star City paid an annual insurance premium of $4,440 on November 1.
3. Star City made quarterly federal corporate income tax payments of $945 each. Its actual tax, calculated at the end of the year, is $3,885.

Completing the Work Sheet and Journalizing and Posting the Adjusting Entries

What You'll Learn

- How to complete the Adjusted Trial Balance section.
- How to extend amounts to the Income Statement and Balance Sheet sections.
- How to report the net income or net loss for the period.
- How to journalize the adjusting entries in the general journal.
- How to post the adjusting entries to the general ledger.

Why It's Important

The work sheet is the source of information for journalizing the adjusting entries and preparing the financial statements.

Once the adjustments are entered in the Adjustments section of the work sheet, it is important to prove that the accounts are still in balance. This is done by completing an adjusted trial balance. Once the Adjusted Trial Balance section is proved, the work sheet can be completed.

Completing the Adjusted Trial Balance Section

After all the adjustments are entered on the work sheet, the Adjusted Trial Balance section can be completed. This section of the work sheet shows the updated balances of all the general ledger accounts. To complete this section, the balance of each account in the Trial Balance section is combined with the adjustment, if any, in the Adjustments section. The new balance is then entered in the appropriate Adjusted Trial Balance column.

Refer to **Figure 18–4** and look at how new balances are computed. If there is no adjustment, the account balance shown in the Trial Balance section is simply extended to the same column (Debit or Credit) in the Adjusted Trial Balance section. There are no adjustments for the first two accounts, **Cash in Bank** and **Accounts Receivable**, so those balances are extended to the Adjusted Trial Balance Debit column.

If the account balance in the Trial Balance section has an adjustment, a new balance is calculated. The amount of the adjustment (from the Adjustments section) is added to or subtracted from the amount in the Trial Balance section. Add debits to debits; add credits to credits; subtract debits and credits.

The first account in the Trial Balance section to have an adjustment is **Merchandise Inventory. Merchandise Inventory** has an unadjusted debit balance of $84,921. Adjustment (a) is a credit of $3,536. To calculate the new balance, the credit adjustment is subtracted from the debit balance. The adjusted balance of $81,385 ($84,921 − $3,536) is extended to the Adjusted Trial Balance Debit column.

The adjusted balances for **Supplies, Prepaid Insurance,** and **Federal Corporate Income Tax Expense** are calculated in the same way.

If an account has a zero balance in the Trial Balance section, the amount listed in the Adjustments section is extended to the Adjusted Trial Balance section. **Federal Corporate Income Tax Payable,** for example, has a zero

	ACCT. NO.	ACCOUNT NAME	TRIAL BALANCE DEBIT	TRIAL BALANCE CREDIT	ADJUSTMENTS DEBIT	ADJUSTMENTS CREDIT	ADJUSTED TRIAL BALANCE DEBIT	ADJUSTED TRIAL BALANCE CREDIT	
1	101	Cash in Bank	15 179 00				15 179 00		
2	115	Accounts Receivable	10 404 00				10 404 00		
3	125	Merchandise Inventory	84 921 00			(a) 3 536 00	81 385 00		
4	130	Supplies	5 549 00			(b) 3 710 00	1 839 00		
5	135	Prepaid Insurance	1 500 00			(c) 125 00	1 375 00		
6	140	Delivery Equipment	19 831 00				19 831 00		
7	145	Office Equipment	9 825 00				9 825 00		
8	150	Store Equipment	5 200 00				5 200 00		
9	201	Accounts Payable		13 850 00				13 850 00	
10	204	Fed. Corp. Inc. Tax Payable				(d) 155 00		155 00	
11	205	Employees' Fed. Inc. Tax Pay.		640 00				640 00	
12	211	Employees' State Inc. Tax Pay.		80 00				80 00	
13	212	Social Security Tax Payable		248 00				248 00	
14	213	Medicare Tax Payable		58 00				58 00	
15	214	Fed. Unemployment Tax Payable		18 36				18 36	
16	215	State Unemployment Tax Payable		114 73				114 73	
17	220	Sales Tax Payable		2 428 00				2 428 00	
18	301	Capital Stock		75 000 00				75 000 00	
19	305	Retained Earnings		19 771 19				19 771 19	
20	310	Income Summary			(a) 3 536 00		3 536 00		
21	401	Sales		320 450 00				320 450 00	
22	405	Sales Discounts	730 00				730 00		
23	410	Sales Returns and Allowances	2 000 00				2 000 00		
24	501	Purchases	206 700 00				206 700 00		
25	505	Transportation In	4 036 18				4 036 18		
26	510	Purchases Discounts		1 340 00				1 340 00	
27	515	Purchases Returns and Allowances		1 800 00				1 800 00	
28	601	Advertising Expense	2 450 00				2 450 00		
29	605	Bankcard Fees Expense	4 199 27				4 199 27		
30	630	Fed. Corp. Income Tax Expense	9 840 00		(d) 155 00		9 995 00		
31	635	Insurance Expense			(c) 125 00		125 00		
32	650	Maintenance Expense	3 519 25				3 519 25		
33	655	Miscellaneous Expense	348 28				348 28		
34	657	Payroll Tax Expense	3 826 83				3 826 83		
35	660	Rent Expense	14 000 00				14 000 00		
36	665	Salaries Expense	29 374 60				29 374 60		
37	670	Supplies Expense			(b) 3 710 00		3 710 00		
38	680	Utilities Expense	2 364 87				2 364 87		
39			435 798 28	435 798 28	7 526 00	7 526 00	435 953 28	435 953 28	
40									

Figure 18–4 Extending Balances to the Adjusted Trial Balance Section of the Work Sheet

balance in the Trial Balance section. Adjustment (d) is a credit of $155. This amount is extended to the Adjusted Trial Balance Credit column.

After all account balances are extended to the Adjusted Trial Balance section, both columns are totaled. If total debits equal total credits, this section is proved. A double rule is drawn under the totals and across both columns. If total debits do not equal total credits, there is an error. To find the error, re-add each column. Also, make sure amounts in the Trial Balance and Adjustments sections are extended properly to the Adjusted Trial Balance section.

Extending Amounts to the Balance Sheet and Income Statement Sections

Beginning with line 1, each account balance in the Adjusted Trial Balance section is extended to the appropriate column of either the Balance Sheet section or the Income Statement section. **Figure 18–5** shows these extensions.

Figure 18–5 On Your Mark Athletic Wear Completed Work Sheet

	ACCT. NO.	ACCOUNT NAME	TRIAL BALANCE DEBIT	TRIAL BALANCE CREDIT	ADJUSTMENTS DEBIT	ADJUSTMENTS CREDIT
1	101	Cash in Bank	15 179 00			
2	115	Accounts Receivable	10 404 00			
3	125	Merchandise Inventory	84 921 00			(a) 3 536 00
4	130	Supplies	5 549 00			(b) 3 710 00
5	135	Prepaid Insurance	1 500 00			(c) 125 00
6	140	Delivery Equipment	19 831 00			
7	145	Office Equipment	9 825 00			
8	150	Store Equipment	5 200 00			
9	201	Accounts Payable		13 850 00		
10	204	Fed. Corp. Inc. Tax Payable				(d) 155 00
11	205	Employees' Fed. Inc. Tax Pay.		640 00		
12	211	Employees' State Inc. Tax Pay.		80 00		
13	212	Social Security Tax Payable		248 00		
14	213	Medicare Tax Payable		58 00		
15	214	Fed. Unemployment Tax Payable		18 36		
16	215	State Unemployment Tax Payable		114 73		
17	220	Sales Tax Payable		2 428 00		
18	301	Capital Stock		75 000 00		
19	305	Retained Earnings		19 771 19		
20	310	Income Summary			(a) 3 536 00	
21	401	Sales		320 450 00		
22	405	Sales Discounts	730 00			
23	410	Sales Returns and Allowances	2 000 00			
24	501	Purchases	206 700 00			
25	505	Transportation In	4 036 18			
26	510	Purchases Discounts		1 340 00		
27	515	Purchases Returns and Allowances		1 800 00		
28	601	Advertising Expense	2 450 00			
29	605	Bankcard Fees Expense	4 199 27			
30	630	Fed. Corp. Income Tax Expense	9 840 00		(d) 155 00	
31	635	Insurance Expense			(c) 125 00	
32	650	Maintenance Expense	3 519 25			
33	655	Miscellaneous Expense	348 28			
34	657	Payroll Tax Expense	3 826 83			
35	660	Rent Expense	14 000 00			
36	665	Salaries Expense	29 374 60			
37	670	Supplies Expense			(b) 3 710 00	
38	680	Utilities Expense	2 364 87			
39			435 798 28	435 798 28	7 526 00	7 526 00
40		Net Income				
41						

The Income Statement section contains the balances of all the temporary accounts. This section includes **Income Summary** and all revenue, cost of merchandise, and expense accounts.

The Balance Sheet section contains the balances of all the permanent accounts. Here you will find all asset, liability, and capital accounts (**Capital Stock** and **Retained Earnings**).

Athletic Wear
Sheet
December 31, 20--

ADJUSTED TRIAL BALANCE		INCOME STATEMENT		BALANCE SHEET		
DEBIT	CREDIT	DEBIT	CREDIT	DEBIT	CREDIT	
15 179 00				15 179 00		1
10 404 00				10 404 00		2
81 385 00				81 385 00		3
1 839 00				1 839 00		4
1 375 00				1 375 00		5
19 831 00				19 831 00		6
9 825 00				9 825 00		7
5 200 00				5 200 00		8
	13 850 00				13 850 00	9
	155 00				155 00	10
	640 00				640 00	11
	80 00				80 00	12
	248 00				248 00	13
	58 00				58 00	14
	18 36				18 36	15
	114 73				114 73	16
	2 428 00				2 428 00	17
	75 000 00				75 000 00	18
	19 771 19				19 771 19	19
3 536 00		3 536 00				20
	320 450 00		320 450 00			21
730 00		730 00				22
2 000 00		2 000 00				23
206 700 00		206 700 00				24
4 036 18		4 036 18				25
	1 340 00		1 340 00			26
	1 800 00		1 800 00			27
2 450 00		2 450 00				28
4 199 27		4 199 27				29
9 995 00		9 995 00				30
125 00		125 00				31
3 519 25		3 519 25				32
348 28		348 28				33
3 826 83		3 826 83				34
14 000 00		14 000 00				35
29 374 60		29 374 60				36
3 710 00		3 710 00				37
2 364 87		2 364 87				38
435 953 28	435 953 28	290 915 28	323 590 00	145 038 00	112 363 28	39
		32 674 72			32 674 72	40
		323 590 00	323 590 00	145 038 00	145 038 00	41
						42
						43

Figure 18–5 On Your Mark Athletic Wear Completed Work Sheet (continued)

CONNECT TO . . .
MUSIC

When you buy a CD, your money doesn't just go to the performer. Music company accountants also have to consider writers, publishers, and administrative fees when checking royalty payments. Keeping track of who gets paid can get even more complicated when a song incorporates samples of other songs.

Completing the Work Sheet

After all amounts are extended to the Balance Sheet and Income Statement sections, a single rule is drawn across the columns in these sections. All four columns are then totaled as shown in **Figure 18–5.** As you learned in Chapter 8, the totals of the debit and credit columns within the Balance Sheet and Income Statement sections are not equal at this point. The difference between the two column totals in each section is the amount of net income (or net loss) for the period.

After the net income (or net loss) is recorded, the columns in the Balance Sheet and Income Statement sections are ruled and totaled as shown in **Figure 18–5.** Notice that the words "Net Income" are written in the Account Name column on the same line as the net income amount.

If the totals of the two Income Statement columns are equal, and the totals of the two Balance Sheet columns are equal, a double rule is drawn across all four columns. The double rule indicates that these sections of the work sheet are proved.

Journalizing Adjustments

The journal entries that update the general ledger accounts at the end of a period are called adjusting entries. The source of information for journalizing the adjusting entries is the Adjustments section of the work sheet. The accounts debited and credited in the Adjustments section are entered in the general journal.

Before recording the first adjusting entry, the words "Adjusting Entries" are written in the Description column of the general journal. This heading eliminates the need to write an explanation after each adjusting entry.

Refer to **Figure 18–6.** The following entries are recorded in the Adjustments columns of the work sheet:

(a) adjusting merchandise inventory
(b) adjusting supplies
(c) adjusting insurance
(d) adjusting income tax

The first adjustment, labeled **(a)** on the work sheet, is recorded in the general journal as a debit to **Income Summary** for $3,536 and a credit to **Merchandise Inventory** for $3,536. The label **(a)** is not recorded in the general journal.

Remaining adjustments are entered in the general journal in the same manner, with the debit part of the entry recorded first. The date for each adjusting entry is the last day of the period.

GENERAL JOURNAL

	DATE		DESCRIPTION	POST. REF.	DEBIT	CREDIT	
1	20--		*Adjusting Entries*				1
2	Dec.	31	Income Summary		3 5 3 6 00		2
3			Merchandise Inventory			3 5 3 6 00	3
4		31	Supplies Expense		3 7 1 0 00		4
5			Supplies			3 7 1 0 00	5
6		31	Insurance Expense		1 2 5 00		6
7			Prepaid Insurance			1 2 5 00	7
8		31	Fed. Corporate Income Tax Exp.		1 5 5 00		8
9			Fed. Corp. Income Tax Pay.			1 5 5 00	9
10							10

Figure 18–6 Recording Adjusting Entries in the General Journal

Posting Adjusting Entries to the General Ledger

After the adjusting entries are recorded in the general journal, they are posted to the general ledger accounts. Once the adjusting entries are posted, the general ledger accounts are up-to-date. The balances in the general ledger accounts all agree with the amounts entered on the Income Statement and Balance Sheet sections of the work sheet.

Once these entries are posted, the following has been accomplished:

- The **Supplies Expense** account has been "charged" with the value of the supplies used in the period.
- The **Supplies** account now reflects only the amount of items still remaining in inventory.
- The **Merchandise Inventory** account now reflects the correct inventory value.
- The **Income Summary** account has been "charged" with the cost of goods sold for the period.
- The **Insurance Expense** account now reflects the appropriate insurance expense for the period.
- The **Prepaid Insurance** account has been reduced by the amount of insurance expired.
- The **Federal Corporate Income Tax Expense** account now reflects the tax expense for the period.
- The **Federal Corporate Income Tax Payable** account has been increased to reflect the appropriate payable amount.

Figure 18–7 shows the general journal and the general ledger accounts after the posting of the adjusting entries is completed. Notice that the words "Adjusting Entry" are written in the Description column of the general ledger accounts.

GENERAL JOURNAL

	DATE		DESCRIPTION	POST. REF.	DEBIT	CREDIT	
1	20--		*Adjusting Entries*				1
2	Dec.	31	Income Summary	310	3 5 3 6 00		2
3			Merchandise Inventory	125		3 5 3 6 00	3
4			Supplies Expense	670	3 7 1 0 00		4
5			Supplies	130		3 7 1 0 00	5
6			Insurance Expense	635	1 2 5 00		6
7			Prepaid Insurance	135		1 2 5 00	7
8			Fed. Corporate Income Tax Exp.	630	1 5 5 00		8
9			Fed. Corp. Income Tax Pay.	204		1 5 5 00	9
10							10
11							11

ACCOUNT _Merchandise Inventory_   ACCOUNT NO. _125_

DATE		DESCRIPTION	POST. REF.	DEBIT	CREDIT	BALANCE DEBIT	BALANCE CREDIT
20--							
Jan.	1	Balance	—			84 9 2 1 00	
Dec.	31	Adjusting Entry	G22		3 5 3 6 00	81 3 8 5 00	

ACCOUNT _Supplies_   ACCOUNT NO. _130_

DATE		DESCRIPTION	POST. REF.	DEBIT	CREDIT	BALANCE DEBIT	BALANCE CREDIT
20--							
Dec.	1	Balance	✓			5 2 9 9 00	
	15		P12	2 5 0 00		5 5 4 9 00	
	31	Adjusting Entry	G22		3 7 1 0 00	1 8 3 9 00	

ACCOUNT _Prepaid Insurance_   ACCOUNT NO. _135_

DATE		DESCRIPTION	POST. REF.	DEBIT	CREDIT	BALANCE DEBIT	BALANCE CREDIT
20--							
Dec.	17	Balance	CP14	1 5 0 0 00		1 5 0 0 00	
	31	Adjusting Entry	G22		1 2 5 00	1 3 7 5 00	

ACCOUNT _Federal Corporate Income Tax Payable_   ACCOUNT NO. _204_

DATE		DESCRIPTION	POST. REF.	DEBIT	CREDIT	BALANCE DEBIT	BALANCE CREDIT
20--							
Dec.	31	Adjusting Entry	G22		1 5 5 00		1 5 5 00

Figure 18–7 Adjusting Entries Posted to the General Ledger

ACCOUNT Income Summary — ACCOUNT NO. 310

DATE		DESCRIPTION	POST. REF.	DEBIT	CREDIT	BALANCE DEBIT	BALANCE CREDIT
20--							
Dec.	31	Adjusting Entry	G22	3 5 3 6 00		3 5 3 6 00	

ACCOUNT Federal Corporate Income Tax Expense — ACCOUNT NO. 630

DATE		DESCRIPTION	POST. REF.	DEBIT	CREDIT	BALANCE DEBIT	BALANCE CREDIT
20--							
Dec.	1	Balance	—			9 8 4 0 00	
	31	Adjusting Entry	G22	1 5 5 00		9 9 9 5 00	

ACCOUNT Insurance Expense — ACCOUNT NO. 635

DATE		DESCRIPTION	POST. REF.	DEBIT	CREDIT	BALANCE DEBIT	BALANCE CREDIT
20--							
Dec.	31	Adjusting Entry	G22	1 2 5 00		1 2 5 00	

ACCOUNT Supplies Expense — ACCOUNT NO. 670

DATE		DESCRIPTION	POST. REF.	DEBIT	CREDIT	BALANCE DEBIT	BALANCE CREDIT
20--							
Dec.	31	Adjusting Entry	G22	3 7 1 0 00		3 7 1 0 00	

Figure 18–7 Adjusting Entries Posted to the General Ledger (continued)

ANALYZING FINANCIAL REPORTS

The Income Statement: Return on Sales

One use of the income statement is to analyze the return on sales. You first analyzed return on sales for a sole proprietorship in Chapter 9. Analyzing return on sales for a corporation is similar. Look at the following example:

$$\text{Return on Sales} = \frac{\text{Net Income}}{\text{Net Sales}} = \frac{\$59,000}{\$5,655,000} = 0.0104 = 1.04\%$$

▶ **Analyze the Report:**

Use the information found on the Office Depot income statement and "To Our Shareholders" letter to answer these questions. Note that Office Depot chooses to use the term "Consolidated Statements of Earnings" instead of "income statement." For our purposes, they are the same. Net income is called "net earnings" and net sales is called "sales."

1. Calculate the return on sales for each of the three years given.
2. What possible factors affected the return on sales over the last two years?

Now that you have studied this section, complete the following questions and problems.

Thinking Critically

1. Which types of general ledger accounts appear in the Balance Sheet section of the work sheet?
2. What accounts are affected by the adjustment for prepaid insurance?

Communicating Accounting

You are making a presentation to the board of directors of your organization, Kids-n-Teens. As you review the financial statements for this quarter, you notice that the bookkeeper extended the account balances from the Adjusted Trial Balance section to the Balance Sheet section but not to the Income Statement section. What a mistake! You can fix it this time, but you need to explain to the bookkeeper how to extend to both sections of the work sheet. Select a classmate and practice your explanation.

Problem 18–3 Analyzing the Work Sheet

Refer to **Figure 18–5** and answer the following questions in your working papers:

1. What amount is extended to the Income Statement section for **Federal Corporate Income Tax Expense**?
2. To which section of the work sheet is the balance of **Prepaid Insurance** extended?
3. What is the total amount of supplies consumed during the period?
4. What is the total amount still owed to the federal government for corporate income tax?

Problem 18–4 Analyzing a Source Document

Based on the debit memorandum, answer the following questions.

1. Which company is returning the merchandise?
2. How many items are being returned?
3. What amount is entered in the journal entry?
4. Which account is debited?
5. Which account is credited?

	DEBIT MEMORANDUM	No. 284	
		Date: May 4, 20--	
		Invoice No.: 378456	

ROTARY SUPPLY CORPORATION
634 West Washington Avenue, Lincoln, SC 30856

To: K & L Electrical
845 Morgan Street
Plantsville, SC 30455

This day we have
debited your
account as follows:

Quantity	Item	Unit Price	Total
4	Locking Fixture #27304-78	$ 36.95	$ 147.80
2	Mirror/Reflectors #8935-231	11.24	22.48
	Subtotal		$ 170.28
	Tax		6.81
	Total		$ 177.09

KEY CONCEPTS

1. The work sheet is prepared, either manually or on a spreadsheet, to organize all the data needed to update the accounts, to prepare the financial statements, and to record end-of-period adjusting journal entries.

2. The ten-column work sheet contains columns for the following:
   - trial balance
   - adjustments
   - adjusted trial balance
   - income statement
   - balance sheet

3. The Trial Balance section of the work sheet includes all accounts listed in the chart of accounts, even those with zero balances. The ending balances for all accounts are listed, and the equality of debits and credits is proved.

4. Some general ledger accounts must be updated at the end of a period by entering adjustments. Adjustments are often made to the following accounts:
   - inventory
   - supplies
   - insurance
   - tax liabilities

5. Every adjustment affects one permanent and one temporary general ledger account.

6. The beginning inventory is the amount of merchandise a business has on hand at the beginning of a period. The ending inventory is the amount of merchandise on hand at the end of a period. The balance of the **Merchandise Inventory** account changes after the physical inventory count, when it is adjusted to reflect the actual amount of merchandise on hand.

7. A corporation pays income taxes on its net income for the year.

8. All account balances are extended to the Adjusted Trial Balance section of the work sheet. Adjustments are reflected in the balances entered in the Adjusted Trial Balance section.

9. The Balance Sheet section of the work sheet contains the balances of all the permanent accounts, including assets, liabilities, and owners' equity.

10. The Income Statement section of the work sheet contains the balances of all the temporary accounts, including **Income Summary** and revenue, cost of merchandise, and expense accounts.

11. The completed work sheet lists all general ledger accounts and their updated balances and shows the net income (or net loss) for the period.

USING KEY TERMS

As the accounting manager for several Homemade Fresh Ice Cream stores in your region, it is your responsibility to oversee the preparation of end-of-period financial statements. Before you complete your end-of-period reports, you need your staff to verify their work sheets and trial balances. Write a memorandum to the staff to remind them to verify their data, make adjustments where needed, give beginning and ending inventory figures, and complete a physical inventory. In the body of your memorandum, provide a brief definition of each term.

adjustment	ending inventory
beginning inventory	physical inventory

Understanding Accounting Concepts and Procedures

Instructions

On a separate sheet of paper, answer the following questions:

1. Why is a work sheet completed before the financial statements are prepared?
2. What are the five sections of the ten-column work sheet?
3. Why are general ledger accounts with zero balances entered in the Trial Balance section of the work sheet?
4. Why are some general ledger accounts updated at the end of the period?
5. Name four accounts of a merchandising business that are typically adjusted at the end of the period.
6. What is meant by "expensing" an asset?
7. Why does the balance of the **Merchandise Inventory** account not change during the period?
8. What is the purpose of completing the Adjusted Trial Balance section of the work sheet?
9. Which accounts are included on the Balance Sheet section of the work sheet?
10. Which accounts are included on the Income Statement section of the work sheet?

Case Study...

Merchandising Business: Training Videos

You're an accountant for Millennium Training Systems, a company that creates and sells training videos. The company CEO asks you to prepare financial statements for the month without the appropriate adjusting entries.

Thinking Critically:

1. Look at the information for adjustments:

	Beginning	Ending
Supplies	$5,000	$1,200
Prepaid Insurance	6,400	800

Net income, before adjustments, is $22,400. What is net income after the adjustments are made?

2. Explain why the financial statements do not present an accurate picture of the company without considering the adjusting entries.

inter NET CONNECTION

Purchase versus Lease

Whether you are ready to buy your first car or your business needs to replace a delivery vehicle, you can use the Internet to research the costs and convenience factors of purchasing or leasing a vehicle.

Do This:

1. Select an automobile that you wish to purchase or lease.
2. Find the lowest interest rate for new cars in your area.
3. Locate an online calculator that will calculate the cost:
   - if you take a loan on the car
   - if you lease the vehicle

   What is the cost of each option over a four-year term?
4. Will you lease or purchase the vehicle? Explain your decision.

Conducting an Audit with Alex

Florence Loch works part-time as a clerk at Tiger Corporation. She was asked to take a physical count of the lamp area and complete an inventory sheet. Her completed sheet is presented below. Check Florence's work.

Instructions Locate any errors on the inventory sheet. On a separate sheet of paper, make a list of the corrections.

INVENTORY SHEET

STOCK NO.	ITEM	UNIT	QUANTITY	UNIT COST	TOTAL VALUE
27485	Lamp Shade	Each	23	$ 27 56	$ 633 88
27847	Lamp Socket	Each	162	3 85	579 96
23186	Electrical Wire	Feet	895	73	653 35
21965	Lamp Shade	Each	11	32 05	325 55
22625	Lamp Shade	Each	13	29 11	378 43
52335	Lamp Base	Each	9	27 30	245 00
55894	Lamp Base	Each	17	24 91	423 47
			TOTAL FOR THIS SHEET		$ 3,239 64

Workplace Skills

Leadership

Effective leaders are those who provide positive examples for others to follow. Leaders listen, encourage, motivate, persuade, and take initiative.

On the Job:

You have just been promoted to director of accounting for a national toy store chain. In reviewing the end-of-period financial reports, you notice that the net income was not as great as past reporting periods. In your weekly management meeting, you mention to the director of marketing that perhaps a new line of toys should be considered to boost the net income for the next financial reporting period.

Thinking Critically:

Prior to the management meeting, you meet with Leonard Rainwater, Director of Marketing. Leonard has been with the company for 25 years, and his decisions are rarely questioned. How would you approach Leonard to discuss a new line of toys being added to the inventory?

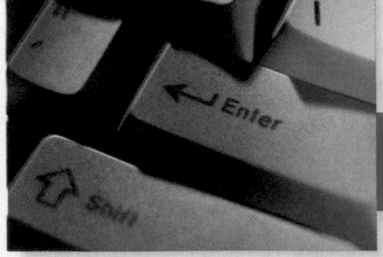

Adjusting Entries
Making the Transition from a Manual to a Computerized System

Task	Perform Accounting Procedures Using Manual Methods	Perform Accounting Procedures Using Automated Methods
Recording adjusting entries	1. From the general ledger, prepare a trial balance in the first two columns of a work sheet. 2. Record adjustments on the work sheet. 3. Calculate adjusted account balances in the Adjusted Trial Balance columns. 4. Extend account balances to Income Statement or Balance Sheet columns of work sheet. 5. Calculate net income (loss) for the accounting period. 6. Record adjusting entries in the general journal. 7. Post adjusting entries to general ledger accounts.	1. Print a Trial Balance. 2. Record the adjusting entries in the general journal. 3. General ledger accounts are automatically updated.

Recording Adjusting Entries

Peachtree Question	Description
How do I generate a trial balance for use in preparing adjustments?	1. Choose **General Ledger** from the *Reports* menu. 2. From the Report list, select Working Trial Balance. 3. Click the *Print* button.
How do I journalize the adjusting entries?	1. List necessary adjustments on the Working Trial Balance form. 2. From the *Tasks* menu, select **General Journal Entry**. 3. Enter the adjusting entries. 4. Click *Save*.
What does the software do "behind the scenes?"	1. Peachtree automatically updates the general ledger accounts when the adjusting entries are posted. 2. A trial balance can be generated at any time.

For detailed instructions: See the **Peachtree User Guide** in your Glencoe Working Papers.

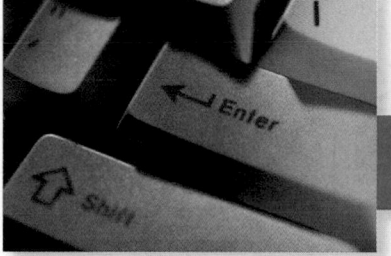

APPLICATION OPTIONS

Problem 18–5 Completing a Ten-Column Work Sheet

The August 31 trial balance for InBeat CD Shop is entered on the work sheet in your working papers. Listed below is the data needed to make the adjustments.

Instructions In your working papers, complete the ten-column work sheet for InBeat CD Shop for the month ended August 31.

Data for Adjustments

Merchandise Inventory, August 31	$ 77,872
Supplies consumed during the period	2,171
Insurance premium expired during the period	489
Additional federal corporate income taxes owed	118

Analyze: After the adjustments are made on the work sheet, which expense account has the highest balance?

Complete chapter problems one of four ways:

1 **Manual** Glencoe Working Papers

or

2 **Peachtree Complete Accounting** Software

or

3 **QuickBooks** Templates (Problems 18–7, 18–8)

or

4 **Spreadsheet** Templates (Problem 18–5)

Problem 18–6 Completing a Ten-Column Work Sheet

The August 31 trial balance for Shutterbug Cameras is listed on the next page. Also listed is the data needed for the adjustments.

SPREADSHEET SMART GUIDE

Step–by–Step Instructions: Problem 18–5

1. Select the spreadsheet template for Problem 18–5.
2. Enter your name and the date in the spaces provided on the template.
3. Complete the spreadsheet using the instructions in your working papers.
4. Print the spreadsheet and proof your work.
5. Save your work and exit the spreadsheet program.

Instructions In your working papers, complete the ten-column work sheet for Shutterbug Cameras for the month ended August 31.

Continued

Peachtree®

SMART GUIDE

Step–by–Step Instructions:
Problem 18–6

1. Select the problem set for Shutterbug Cameras (Prob. 18–6).
2. Rename the company and set the system date.
3. Print a Working Trial Balance and use it to help you prepare the adjustments.
4. Record the adjustments using the **General Journal Entry** option.
5. Print a General Journal report and proof your work.
6. Print a General Ledger Trial Balance report.
7. Answer the Analyze question.
8. End the session.

TIP: Use the Inventory Adjustment account, not the Income Summary account, to record the adjustment for Merchandise Inventory.

		Trial Balance	
		Debit	Credit
101	Cash in Bank	$13,873	
115	Accounts Receivable	5,382	
125	Merchandise Inventory	82,981	
130	Supplies	2,397	
135	Prepaid Insurance	1,350	
140	Store Equipment	30,769	
201	Accounts Payable		$ 8,481
207	Federal Corporate Income Tax Payable		—
210	Employees' Federal Income Tax Payable		194
211	Employees' State Income Tax Payable		48
212	Social Security Tax Payable		119
213	Medicare Tax Payable		25
215	Sales Tax Payable		381
216	Federal Unemployment Tax Payable		19
217	State Unemployment Tax Payable		92
301	Capital Stock		80,000
305	Retained Earnings		28,568
310	Income Summary	—	—
401	Sales		95,487
405	Sales Discounts	37	
410	Sales Returns and Allowances	945	
501	Purchases	39,491	
505	Transportation In	2,039	
510	Purchases Discounts		656
515	Purchases Returns and Allowances		219
601	Advertising Expense	128	
605	Bankcard Fees Expense	219	
620	Federal Corporate Income Tax Expense	1,580	
630	Insurance Expense	—	
640	Maintenance Expense	2,513	
645	Miscellaneous Expense	652	
647	Payroll Tax Expense	1,953	
650	Rent Expense	9,000	
655	Salaries Expense	18,631	
660	Supplies Expense	—	
670	Utilities Expense	349	

Data for Adjustments

Merchandise Inventory, August 31	$78,672
Supplies on hand, August 31	389
Insurance premium expired during the period	490
Additional federal income taxes owed	252

Analyze: On the Balance Sheet section, which account has the higher balance, **Accounts Payable** or **Accounts Receivable**?

Problem 18–7 Completing a Ten-Column Work Sheet

The balances of the general ledger accounts of Cycle Tech Bicycles, as of August 31, are listed below. Also listed is the data needed for the adjustments.

Instructions In your working papers:

Prepare a ten-column work sheet for Cycle Tech Bicycles for the month ended August 31.

101	Cash in Bank	$ 22,323
115	Accounts Receivable	1,737
125	Merchandise Inventory	23,654
130	Supplies	3,971
135	Prepaid Insurance	1,800
140	Store Equipment	25,395
145	Office Equipment	15,239
201	Accounts Payable	11,051
210	Federal Corporate Income Tax Payable	—
211	Employees' Federal Income Tax Payable	519
212	Employees' State Income Tax Payable	142
213	Social Security Tax Payable	408
214	Medicare Tax Payable	137
215	Sales Tax Payable	1,871
216	Federal Unemployment Tax Payable	51
217	State Unemployment Tax Payable	263
301	Capital Stock	40,000
305	Retained Earnings	14,908
310	Income Summary	—
401	Sales	128,231
405	Sales Discounts	214
410	Sales Returns and Allowances	1,289
501	Purchases	67,118
505	Transportation In	1,172
510	Purchases Discounts	810
515	Purchases Returns and Allowances	322
601	Advertising Expense	2,938
605	Bankcard Fees Expense	185
625	Federal Corporate Income Tax Expense	3,650
630	Insurance Expense	—
645	Maintenance Expense	2,450
650	Miscellaneous Expense	3,929
655	Payroll Tax Expense	834
657	Rent Expense	10,750
660	Salaries Expense	4,670
665	Supplies Expense	—
675	Utilities Expense	5,395

Peachtree®

SMART GUIDE

Step–by–Step Instructions: Problem 18–7

1. Select the problem set for Cycle Tech Bicycles (Prob. 18–7).
2. Rename the company and set the system date.
3. Print a Working Trial Balance and use it to help you prepare the adjustments.
4. Record the adjustments using the **General Journal Entry** option.
5. Print a General Journal report and proof your work.
6. Print a General Ledger Trial Balance report.
7. Answer the Analyze question.
8. End the session.

Continued

Data for Adjustments

Ending merchandise inventory	$ 24,188
Ending supplies inventory	1,049
Insurance premium expired	675
Federal income tax expense for the month	3,827

Analyze: Which section of the work sheet had the higher balance for **Merchandise Inventory**, the Trial Balance section or the Balance Sheet section?

Peachtree®

SMART GUIDE

Step–by–Step Instructions: Problem 18–8

1. Select the problem set for River's Edge Canoe & Kayak (Prob. 18–8).
2. Rename the company and set the system date.
3. Print a Working Trial Balance and use it to help you prepare the adjustments.
4. Record the adjustments using the **General Journal Entry** option.
5. Print a General Journal report and proof your work.
6. Print a General Ledger report.
7. Print a General Ledger Trial Balance report.
8. Answer the Analyze question.
9. End the session.

TIP: Enter the adjustments as one multi-part entry to save time.

Problem 18–8 Completing a Ten-Column Work Sheet

The balances of the general ledger accounts of River's Edge Canoe & Kayak, as of August 31, are listed below.

Instructions   In your working papers:

(1) Prepare a ten-column work sheet for River's Edge Canoe & Kayak for the month ended August 31. The account names are entered on the work sheet. The data for the adjustments follows:

   (a) The cost of the ending merchandise inventory is $45,669.
   (b) The cost of the supplies on hand on August 31 is $619.
   (c) The one-year insurance premium of $1,680 was paid on April 1.
   (d) The total federal income taxes owed for the year are $2,635.

(2) Enter the journal entries for the adjustments on page 31 of the general journal.

(3) Post the journal entries to the general ledger accounts.

101	Cash in Bank	$ 15,387
115	Accounts Receivable	2,852
130	Merchandise Inventory	49,205
135	Supplies	3,027
140	Prepaid Insurance	1,680
145	Delivery Equipment	19,437
150	Store Equipment	29,504
201	Accounts Payable	13,339
204	Federal Corporate Income Tax Payable	—
210	Employees' Federal Income Tax Payable	632
211	Employees' State Income Tax Payable	117
212	Social Security Tax Payable	472
213	Medicare Tax Payable	108
215	Sales Tax Payable	2,931
216	Federal Unemployment Tax Payable	77
217	State Unemployment Tax Payable	315
219	U.S. Savings Bonds Payable	150
301	Capital Stock	50,000
305	Retained Earnings	25,425
310	Income Summary	—

401	Sales	144,945
405	Sales Discounts	203
410	Sales Returns and Allowances	1,381
501	Purchases	79,310
505	Transportation In	1,192
510	Purchases Discounts	1,292
515	Purchases Returns and Allowances	576
601	Advertising Expense	3,151
605	Bankcard Fees Expense	288
625	Federal Corporate Income Tax Expense	2,480
635	Insurance Expense	—
650	Maintenance Expense	1,381
655	Miscellaneous Expense	3,772
658	Payroll Tax Expense	1,219
660	Rent Expense	10,350
665	Salaries Expense	11,965
670	Supplies Expense	—
680	Utilities Expense	2,595

Analyze: How much in discounts did River's Edge earn by paying the amounts owed to creditors within the discount period?

CHALLENGE PROBLEM

Problem 18–9 Locating Errors on the Work Sheet

The Trial Balance and adjustment sections for Buzz Newsstand have been prepared in your working papers. It is apparent from the totals on the work sheet that errors have been made in preparing these portions of the work sheet.

The accounting records show:

1. The merchandise on hand at the end of the month is valued at $12,950.
2. The supplies on hand on August 31 are valued at $529.
3. The insurance premium was paid on August 1. The premium was $980 and covers the period from August 1 to November 30.
4. The total federal income tax owed for the period is $249.

Instructions   In your working papers:

(1) Find and correct the error(s) in the Trial Balance section.
(2) On the line provided on the work sheet, write in the corrected totals for the Trial Balance section.
(3) Find and correct the error(s) in the Adjustments section.
(4) Write in the corrected totals for the Adjustments columns.

Analyze: Explain your calculations for the Merchandise Inventory adjustment.

CHAPTER 19

Financial Statements for a Corporation

Learning Objectives

When you have completed this chapter, you will be able to:

► Explain how to record ownership of a corporation.

► Explain the relationship between the work sheet and the financial statements for a merchandising corporation.

► Explain how the financial statements for a corporation differ from those for a sole proprietorship.

► Prepare an income statement, balance sheet, and statement of retained earnings for a merchandising corporation.

► Analyze the financial data contained on the statements.

► Define the accounting terms introduced in this chapter.

Office DEPOT.

Exploring the Real World of Business

ANALYZING CORPORATE FINANCIAL STATEMENTS

Whether you need a backpack and a three-ring binder for school, or an assortment of office supplies, desks, chairs, and computers for your new business, **Office Depot** can serve you in 21 countries at over 1,000 company-owned and licensed stores and from its worldwide delivery channel through catalog sales, contract account sales, or one of its 20 unique Web sites. Founded in 1986, the company began with one modest store in Fort Lauderdale, Florida. In two short years, **Office Depot** went public and by the end of 1990, customers could shop at 173 stores in 27 states.

International joint ventures and licensing agreements placed **Office Depot** in countries like France, Japan, Mexico, Israel, Poland, and Hungary. In addition, an impressive Internet presence boosted sales by approximately $1.6 billion in 2001.

As **Office Depot** grows and strengthens, the owners of the corporation must be properly informed of the financial value and condition of the entity through the issuance of audited financial statements. Other parties like creditors, government agencies, employees, and internal managers must also be given relevant and reliable financial data upon which decisions can be based.

What do you think?

As a potential investor in **Office Depot** stock, what types of information would you be interested in?

Workplace Connections

Applying Your Accounting Knowledge

Once the work sheet is completed, the accounting staff is ready to prepare financial statements. If you've listened to the evening news on television, you might remember an announcer reporting earnings increases or decreases for a large national corporation. This information is found in the financial statements or annual reports of the company.

Investigate:

1. Is your employer a public corporation?
2. Are the financial statements available for you to look at?
3. Can they be found on the Internet or in your local library?

The Ownership of a Corporation

What You'll Learn

- Which equity accounts are used in corporation accounting.
- How equity earned through business profits is reported.
- Which end-of-period financial statements are prepared for a corporation.

Why It's Important

To properly prepare end-of-period financial reports for a corporation, you need to understand how equity for a corporation is handled and the differences in equity between corporations and sole proprietorships.

KEY TERMS

Capital Stock
stockholders' equity
retained earnings
comparability
reliability
relevance
full disclosure
materiality

In Chapter 18 you learned that some accounts in the general ledger are not up-to-date at the end of a period. You learned how to determine which accounts to adjust, how to calculate the amount of each adjustment, and how to enter each adjustment on a ten-column work sheet.

The work sheet is a working paper, organizing all the accounting data needed to prepare the financial statements and the end-of-period journal entries. In this chapter you will use the information on the work sheet to prepare the financial statements for a merchandising corporation. Businesses like John Deere & Co. focus a lot of time and attention on the preparation of financial statements.

Accounting for a Corporation

A sole proprietorship is owned by one person. A corporation may be owned by one person or by thousands of people. The ownership of a corporation is represented by shares of stock. After completing this chapter and following chapters, you will be able to identify the various accounting functions involved with a corporation.

Recording the Ownership of a Corporation

As you recall, investments made by the owner of a sole proprietorship are recorded in the owner's capital account. An owner's investment of $25,000 in a sole proprietorship is recorded as shown in the T accounts. **Cash in Bank** is debited for $25,000, and **Maria Sanchez, Capital** is credited for $25,000.

Cash in Bank		Maria Sanchez, Capital	
Debit + 25,000	Credit −	Debit −	Credit + 25,000

If a business is organized as a corporation, the owner's capital account used in a sole proprietorship is replaced by an account named **Capital Stock. Capital Stock** represents the investments in the corporation by its stockholders (owners).

Capital Stock is classified as a stockholders' equity account. **Stockholders' equity** is the value of the stockholders' claims to the corporation. Like the owner's capital account in a sole proprietorship, increases to the **Capital Stock** account are recorded as credits and decreases are recorded as debits.

Business Transaction

On January 1 stockholders invested $25,000 in exchange for shares of stock of the corporation, Receipt 997.

ANALYSIS	*Identify*	1.	The accounts affected are **Cash in Bank** and **Capital Stock.**
	Classify	2.	**Cash in Bank** is an asset account. **Capital Stock** is a stockholders' equity account.
	+/−	3.	**Cash in Bank** is increased by $25,000. **Capital Stock** is increased by $25,000.

DEBIT-CREDIT RULE		4.	Increases to asset accounts are recorded as debits. Debit **Cash in Bank** for $25,000.
		5.	Increases to stockholders' equity accounts are recorded as credits. Credit **Capital Stock** for $25,000.

T ACCOUNTS   6.

	Cash in Bank		Capital Stock	
Debit + 25,000	Credit −	Debit −	Credit + 25,000

JOURNAL ENTRY   7.

		GENERAL JOURNAL				PAGE 1	
	DATE	DESCRIPTION	POST. REF.	DEBIT	CREDIT		
1	20--						1
2	Jan. 1	Cash in Bank		25 000 00			2
3		Capital Stock			25 000 00		3
4		Receipt 997					4

Reporting Stockholders' Equity in a Corporation

The form of business organization does not affect the amount of equity in the business. That is, one person may have an ownership interest in a sole proprietorship worth $80,000, or ten people may have shares of stock in a corporation worth a total of $80,000. The difference is in the way these two amounts are reported on the balance sheet.

A sole proprietorship reports the balance of the owner's capital account in the owner's equity section of the balance sheet. For a corporation the owner's equity section of the balance sheet is called stockholders' equity. The law requires that stockholders' equity be reported in two parts: (1) equity contributed by stockholders and (2) equity earned through business profits.

Equity Contributed by Stockholders

The first part of stockholders' equity is the amount of money invested by stockholders. This amount is comparable to the investments made by the owner in a sole proprietorship. In a corporation stockholders contribute to equity by buying shares of stock issued by the corporation. Stockholders' investments are recorded in the **Capital Stock** account.

Equity Earned Through Business Profits

The second part of stockholders' equity is the amount of accumulated net income earned and retained by the corporation. This amount is comparable to the amount of net income less any withdrawals by the owner in a sole proprietorship. In a corporation this amount, called **Retained Earnings**, represents the increase in stockholders' equity from the portion of net income not distributed to the stockholders.

Earnings retained by a corporation are recorded in the **Retained Earnings** account. **Retained Earnings** is classified as a stockholders' equity account. Like the **Capital Stock** account, it is increased by credits and decreased by debits. **Retained Earnings** has a normal credit balance.

Retained Earnings	
Debit	Credit
−	+
Decrease Side	Increase Side
	Normal Balance

In a sole proprietorship, net income increases owner's capital. This increase in owner's capital represents an increase in the assets of the business. In a corporation net income increases retained earnings, which represents the growth, or increase, in the assets of the corporation.

Balance Sheet Presentation

A comparison of the capital section of the balance sheet for a sole proprietorship and for a corporation follows:

Sole Proprietorship	**Corporation**
Owner's Equity:	Stockholders' Equity:
Owner's Capital	Capital Stock
	Retained Earnings

Characteristics of Financial Information

At the end of a period, a business prepares various financial statements. These statements summarize the changes that have taken place during the period and report the financial condition of the business at the end of the period. Financial statements are used by many groups:

- Managers analyze the financial statements to help evaluate past performance and to make informed decisions and predictions that will affect future operations.
- Stockholders are interested in the performance, potential future growth, and success of the business.
- Creditors want to know the ability of the business to pay its debts in a timely manner and the amount of credit that should be extended to the business.
- Government agencies, employees, consumers, and the general public are also interested in the financial position of the business.

Key Points

The Accounting Equation

The basic accounting equation applies to the accounting system in any business regardless of the form of business organization:

Assets = Liabilities + Stockholders' (Owner's) Equity

Increases in owner's capital or in retained earnings also represent increases in assets.

Comparability

For accounting information to be useful, it must be understandable and comparable. Thus, for the financial reports to be useful, the data must be presented in a way that lets users recognize similarities, differences, and trends from one period to another. **Comparability** allows accounting information to be compared from one fiscal period to another. The same types of statements, therefore, are prepared at the end of each period. The length of time covered by the financial statements is the same from one period to another (for example, one month or one year). By comparing financial statements in different periods of equal length, financial patterns and relationships can be identified and analyzed and the information from the analysis can be used in making decisions regarding business operations. Comparability also allows the comparison of financial information between businesses.

Reliability

Users of accounting data assume that the data are reliable. **Reliability** relates to the confidence users have that the financial information is reasonably free from bias and error.

Relevance

Not all information about a business is relevant to financial decision making. In accounting, **relevance** means that the information "makes a difference" to a user in reaching a business decision.

Full Disclosure

To "disclose" means "to uncover or to make known." **Full disclosure** means that financial reports include enough information so that the report is complete.

Materiality

If something is "material," it is important. In accounting, materiality means that information deemed relative should be included in financial reports.

Computerized Accounting Systems

Today most businesses rely on automated equipment or computers to maintain the general and subsidiary ledgers and to prepare the end-of-period financial statements. Computers offer the advantages of speed and accuracy. Even small businesses can afford computers and accounting software designed for their needs. On the other hand, some businesses prefer to have an outside company maintain their accounting records and prepare their financial statements.

Financial Statements for a Merchandising Corporation

On Your Mark Athletic Wear, a merchandising corporation, prepares three financial statements: the income statement, the statement of retained earnings, and the balance sheet. The first two statements report the changes that have taken place over the period. The third statement, the balance sheet, shows the financial position of the business on a specific date—the last day of the period. The data needed to complete all three statements come from the work sheet.

A MATTER OF ETHICS

Reporting a Mistake

Imagine that you're an accounting clerk for a major league sports franchise like the Green Bay Packers. Your job responsibilities do not include any end-of-period activities, but you discover that a co-worker has made a significant error when she prepared the work sheet. You know the error will affect the financial statements. You wonder if you should report the error or assume that someone else will catch the mistake.

Ethical Decision Making:
- What are the ethical issues?
- What are the alternatives?
- Who are the affected parties?
- How do the alternatives affect the parties?
- What would you do?

Now that you have studied this section, complete the following questions and problems.

Thinking Critically

1. What two parts of stockholders' equity are required by law to be reported on the balance sheet?
2. What is the purpose of preparing the same types of financial statements at the end of each period?

Communicating Accounting

As the CEO of First Rate Products, you are expected to present accurate financial statements at your next stockholders' meeting. It is imperative that your recently-hired accounting clerk, Vanessa Fuller, understand the importance of the end-of-period financial statements. Write a clear, concise memorandum to her outlining the end-of-period financial statements you are required to present at the meeting. Make sure Vanessa understands the importance of each financial statement and the relationships of those statements to the overall performance of First Rate Products.

Problem 19–1 Analyzing Stockholders' Equity Accounts

1. An investment of $60,000 by Kevin Cleary in his sole proprietorship is recorded as a credit to which account?
2. The sale of 100 shares of stock, for $8,500, by the Sims Corporation is recorded as a credit to which account?
3. Stockholders' equity consists of which two accounts?

Problem 19–2 Analyzing a Source Document

A sales slip for Cindy's Curtains is presented at right. The accountant noticed errors in the calculations.

Instructions Check all calculations and recalculate the sales tax using a rate of 4 percent.

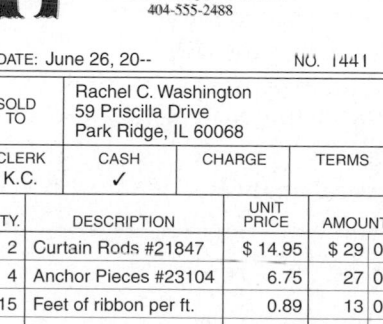

Cindy's Curtains
432 Meadowbrook Street
Wilcoxson, Georgia 30345-8417
404-555-2488

DATE: June 26, 20--   NO. 1441

SOLD TO	Rachel C. Washington 59 Priscilla Drive Park Ridge, IL 60068		
CLERK K.C.	CASH ✓	CHARGE	TERMS

QTY.	DESCRIPTION	UNIT PRICE	AMOUNT
2	Curtain Rods #21847	$ 14.95	$ 29 09
4	Anchor Pieces #23104	6.75	27 00
15	Feet of ribbon per ft.	0.89	13 00
		SUBTOTAL	$ 69 09
		SALES TAX	2 76
	Thank You!	TOTAL	$ 71 85

The Income Statement

- What is included in each of the five sections of the income statement.
- How to prepare an income statement using four amount columns.
- How to calculate the cost of merchandise sold.
- How to calculate the gross profit on sales.
- How to analyze the information on the income statement.

Why It's Important

The income statement reports the net income or loss for the period and indicates whether or not the business is operating efficiently.

KEY TERMS

net sales
net purchases
gross profit on sales
operating expenses
selling expenses
administrative expenses
operating income
vertical analysis

In Section 1 you learned that there are three financial statements prepared by corporations at the end of each period. In this section you will learn how to prepare and analyze the income statement. Every year John Deere & Co. expects the March income statement to show a large profit as farmers get ready for the new growing season.

The Income Statement

As you know, the income statement reports the net income or loss earned by a business. In Chapter 9 you prepared an income statement for Roadrunner Delivery Service, a service business organized as a sole proprietorship. You subtracted total expenses from revenue to determine the net income or loss for the period.

Merchandising businesses have an additional cost—the cost of the merchandise that is purchased and then resold to customers. The income statement for a merchandising business is thus expanded to include the cost of merchandise sold.

An income statement for a merchandising business has five sections:

- Revenue
- Cost of Merchandise Sold
- Gross Profit on Sales
- Operating Expenses
- Net Income (or Loss)

A comparison of the income statements for a service business and for a merchandising business follows:

Service Business	**Merchandising Business**
Roadrunner Delivery Service	*On Your Mark Athletic Wear*
Revenue	Revenue
− Expenses	− Cost of Merchandise Sold
Net Income (Loss)	Gross Profit on Sales
	− Operating Expenses
	Net Income (Loss)

As you can see from **Figure 19–1,** On Your Mark's income statement has four amount columns. The far right column is used to enter totals. The other columns are used to enter balances that are added or subtracted. Note that the format of a computer-generated income statement may vary from the format of an income statement prepared manually on accounting stationery. Regardless of how an income statement is prepared, the formats are very similar.

On Your Mark Athletic Wear				
Income Statement				
For the Year Ended December 31, 20--				
Revenue:				
Sales			320 450 00	
Less: Sales Discounts		730 00		
Sales Returns and Allowances		2 000 00	2 730 00	
Net Sales				317 720 00

Figure 19–1 The Heading and Revenue Section of the Income Statement

All of the information needed to prepare the income statement comes from the work sheet, particularly the Income Statement section. As with all other financial statements, the income statement begins with a three-line heading. The income statement for On Your Mark is prepared for the year ended December 31.

The Revenue Section

The first section on the income statement is the revenue section. This section reports the net sales for the period. The balances of the **Sales** revenue account and the **Sales Discounts** and **Sales Returns and Allowances** contra revenue accounts are reported in this section. Remember, contra revenue accounts decrease the revenue account. Therefore, **net sales** is the amount of sales for the period less any sales discounts, returns, and allowances. Refer to **Figure 19–1** as you learn how to complete the revenue section.

1. On the first line, enter the classification "Revenue:" at the left edge of the stationery.
2. On the second line, enter the name of the revenue account "**Sales**," indented about half an inch. Enter the balance of the account in the *third* amount column.
3. On the next lines, enter the deductions from **Sales.** Write the word "Less:" followed by the names and balances of the two contra revenue accounts. (You may have to abbreviate the account names.) Enter the balances of the accounts in the *second* amount column.
4. Add the balances of the two contra revenue accounts. Write the total below the **Sales** balance on the fourth line, in the *third* amount column.
5. On the next line, enter the words "Net Sales," indented about an inch. Subtract the total of the two contra accounts from the balance of the **Sales** account. Enter the amount in the *fourth* amount column. On Your Mark's net sales for the year are $317,720.

The Cost of Merchandise Sold Section

The next section reports the cost of merchandise sold. As the words indicate, the "cost of merchandise sold" is the actual cost to the business of the merchandise that was sold to customers during the period.

The cost of merchandise sold is calculated as follows:

Beginning Merchandise Inventory
+ Net Purchases During the Period
Cost of Merchandise Available for Sale
— Ending Merchandise Inventory
Cost of Merchandise Sold

There are two steps involved in calculating the cost of merchandise sold. The first step is to determine the cost of all the merchandise available for sale. The second step is to calculate the cost of merchandise sold.

Net Purchases

To calculate the cost of merchandise available for sale, add net purchases to the beginning inventory amount. **Net purchases** is all the costs related to merchandise purchased during the period. To calculate net purchases, add the transportation charges for the period (**Transportation In**) to the **Purchases** balance and then subtract the balances of **Purchases Discounts** and **Purchases Returns and Allowances**.

Purchases
+ Transportation In
Cost of Delivered Merchandise
— Purchases Discounts
— Purchases Returns and Allowances
Net Purchases

Cost of Merchandise Sold

To calculate the cost of merchandise sold, subtract the ending merchandise inventory amount from the cost of merchandise available for sale. Refer to **Figure 19–2** as you learn how to complete the cost of merchandise sold section.

1. On the line below net sales, enter the words "Cost of Merchandise Sold:" at the left edge.
2. Next, enter "Merchandise Inventory, January 1, 20—" indented about half an inch. Enter the amount of the beginning inventory in the *third* amount column. (The beginning inventory is found on the work sheet, in the Trial Balance section, on the Merchandise Inventory line.)
3. Next, enter "Purchases", indented about half an inch, and place the **Purchases** account balance in the *first* amount column.
4. On the next line, enter "Plus: Transportation In" indented about half an inch. Enter the balance of the **Transportation In** account in the *first* amount column, below the **Purchases** amount. Draw a line across the *first* amount column under the **Transportation In** amount.
5. On the next line, enter "Cost of Delivered Merchandise" indented about half an inch. Add the balances of the **Purchases** and **Transportation In** accounts. Enter the result in the *second* amount column.
6. On the next line, enter "Less: Purchases Discounts," indented about half an inch, and place the **Purchases Discounts** account balance in the *first* amount column.

On Your Mark Athletic Wear

Income Statement

For the Year Ended December 31, 20--

Revenue:					
Sales				320 450 00	
Less: Sales Discounts		7 30 00			
Sales Returns and Allowances		2 000 00	2 730 00		
Net Sales					317 720 00
Cost of Merchandise Sold:					
Merchandise Inventory, January 1, 20--				84 921 00	
Purchases	206 700 00				
Plus: Transportation In	4 036 18				
Cost of Delivered Merchandise		210 736 18			
Less: Purchases Discounts	1 340 00				
Purchases Returns and Allowances	1 800 00	3 140 00			
Net Purchases			207 596 18		
Cost of Merchandise Available			292 517 18		
Merchandise Inventory, December 31, 20--			81 385 00		
Cost of Merchandise Sold				211 132 18	
Gross Profit on Sales				106 587 82	

Figure 19–2 Income Statement Through Gross Profit on Sales

7. On the next line, enter "Purchases Returns and Allowances" indented about half an inch, and place the **Purchases Returns and Allowances** account balance in the *first* amount column.

8. To find the total deduction from **Purchases**, add the balances of the **Purchases Discounts** and **Purchases Returns and Allowances** accounts. Enter the total, on the Purchases Returns and Allowances line, in the *second* amount column. Draw a line across the *first* and *second* amount columns under this total.

9. On the next line, enter "Net Purchases" indented about half an inch. Subtract the total of the **Purchases Discounts** and **Purchases Returns and Allowances** accounts from the cost of delivered merchandise. The difference is the net purchases for the period. Enter the amount in the *third* amount column. Draw a line across the *third* amount column under this amount.

10. On the next line, enter "Cost of Merchandise Available" indented about half an inch. Add the net purchases amount to the beginning inventory amount. The total is the cost of merchandise available for sale. Enter the total in the *third* amount column.

11. On the next line, write "Merchandise Inventory, December 31, 20—" indented about half an inch. Enter the amount of the ending inventory in the *third* amount column. (The ending inventory is found on the work sheet, in the Balance Sheet section, on the Merchandise Inventory line.) Draw a line across the *third* amount column under this amount.

12. On the next line, enter "Cost of Merchandise Sold" indented about one inch. Subtract the ending inventory amount from the cost of merchandise available for sale. The difference is the cost of merchandise sold during the period. Enter the amount in the *fourth* amount column. Draw a line across the *fourth* amount column under this amount.

The Gross Profit on Sales Section

Once the cost of merchandise sold is calculated, the gross profit on sales can be determined. The **gross profit on sales** is the profit made during the period before operating expenses are deducted. Gross profit on sales is found by subtracting the cost of merchandise sold from net sales. "Gross Profit on Sales" is entered at the left edge, and the amount is placed in the *fourth* amount column. In **Figure 19–2** you can see that On Your Mark's gross profit on sales is $106,587.82.

The Operating Expenses Section

The next section of the income statement shows the operating expenses for the period. **Operating expenses** are the costs of the goods and services used in the process of earning revenue for the business. Some businesses choose to further classify operating expenses into **selling expenses** (incurred to sell or market the merchandise sold) and **administrative expenses** (costs related to the management of the business). Look at **Figure 19–3.** "Operating Expenses" is entered at the left edge on the line following the gross profit on sales. On the following lines, the names and balances of all expense accounts except **Federal Corporate Income Tax Expense** are listed in the same order as on the work sheet. While federal corporate income tax is a normal expense for a corporation, it is not considered to be an operating expense. Rather than a cost related to earning revenue, income tax represents a cost *resulting* from the revenue earned.

Notice that the balances of the expense accounts are entered in the *third* amount column. The balances are totaled. The total, $63,918.10, is entered in the *fourth* amount column.

The Net Income Section

The final section of the income statement reports the net income (or net loss) for the period, both before and after federal corporate income taxes. It is customary to present the federal corporate income tax amount separately on the income statement. This is done so that the income statement shows the amount of operating income. **Operating income** is the amount of income earned before federal corporate income taxes are deducted.

Look at **Figure 19–3** again. To calculate operating income, subtract the total operating expenses from the gross profit on sales. On Your Mark's operating income for the period is $42,669.72.

To calculate net income:

1. Enter "Less: Federal Corporate Income Tax Expense" on the next line, indented about half an inch.
2. Enter the amount of income taxes, $9,995, in the *fourth* amount column. Federal corporate income taxes appear in the Income Statement section of the work sheet. Draw a line across the *fourth* column under this amount.
3. Enter "Net Income" (or "Net Loss") on the next line at the left edge.
4. Subtract the amount of federal corporate income taxes from the operating income. The result is net income or net loss.
5. Enter the difference, $32,674.72, in the *fourth* amount column. Net income on the income statement must agree with the net income

On Your Mark Athletic Wear

Income Statement

For the Year Ended December 31, 20--

Revenue:				
Sales			320 450 00	
Less: Sales Discounts		730 00		
Sales Returns and Allowances		2 000 00	2 730 00	
Net Sales				317 720 00
Cost of Merchandise Sold:				
Merchandise Inventory, January 1, 20--			84 921 00	
Purchases	206 700 00			
Plus: Transportation In	4 036 18			
Cost of Delivered Merchandise		210 736 18		
Less: Purchases Discounts	1 340 00			
Purchases Returns and Allowances	1 800 00	3 140 00		
Net Purchases			207 596 18	
Cost of Merchandise Available			292 517 18	
Merchandise Inventory, December 31, 20--			81 385 00	
Cost of Merchandise Sold				211 132 18
Gross Profit on Sales				106 587 82
Operating Expenses:				
Advertising Expense			2 450 00	
Bank Card Fees Expense			4 199 27	
Insurance Expense			125 00	
Maintenance Expense			3 519 25	
Miscellaneous Expense			348 28	
Payroll Tax Expense			3 826 83	
Rent Expense			14 000 00	
Salaries Expense			29 374 60	
Supplies Expense			3 710 00	
Utilities Expense			2 364 87	
Total Operating Expenses				63 918 10
Operating Income				42 669 72
Less: Federal Corporate Income Tax Expense				9 995 00
Net Income				32 674 72

Figure 19–3 On Your Mark's Completed Income Statement

shown on the work sheet. If it does, draw a double rule under the amount to show that the income statement is proved and complete. If it does not, check the addition and subtraction on the income statement. Also check that all the accounts and balances in the Income Statement section of the work sheet appear correctly on the income statement.

Analyzing Amounts on the Income Statement

The income statement is analyzed to evaluate the financial performance of the business. The information reported on the income statement and other financial statements is expressed in dollars. Although dollar amounts are useful, the analysis of financial statements can be expanded and made more meaningful by expressing the dollar amounts as percentages. These percentages more clearly indicate the relationships among the items on the financial statements. They also enable users of the financial statements to compare the relationships within an accounting period and changes in these relationships between accounting periods.

One type of analysis is called **vertical analysis**. With vertical analysis, each dollar amount reported on a financial statement is also reported as a percentage of another amount, called a base amount, appearing on that same statement. For example, on the income statement, each amount is reported as a percentage of net sales. Current-period percentages can be compared with percentages from past periods or with percentages from other companies within the same industry.

Figure 19–4 illustrates a comparative income statement. As you can see, the net sales amount for each year is assigned a percentage of 100. Every other amount on the income statement is stated as a percentage of the net sales amount. Notice that net income was 14.68 percent of net sales in the previous year and only 10.28 percent of net sales for the current year. Analysis of this and other percentages will help management make informed decisions regarding the operation of the business.

Figure 19–4 Comparative Income Statement Showing Vertical Analysis

On Your Mark Athletic Wear
Comparative Income Statement
For the Current and Previous Years Ended December 31

	Current Year		Previous Year	
	Dollars	Percent	Dollars	Percent
Revenue:				
Sales	$ 320,450.00	100.86 %	$ 296,350.00	100.79 %
Less: Sales Discounts	730.00	0.23	625.00	0.21
Sales Ret. and Allow.	2,000.00	0.63	1,700.00	0.58
Net Sales	$ 317,720.00	100.00 %	$ 294,025.00	100.00 %
Cost of Merchandise Sold:				
Merch. Inventory, Jan. 1	$ 84,921.00	26.73 %	$ 82,100.00	27.92 %
Net Purchases	207,596.18	65.34	186,836.56	63.54
Merch. Available for Sale	292,517.18	92.07 %	$ 268,936.56	91.47 %
Merch. Inventory, Dec. 31	81,385.00	25.62	84,921.00	28.88
Cost of Merchandise Sold	$ 211,132.18	66.45 %	$ 184,015.56	62.59 %
Gross Profit on Sales	$ 106,587.82	33.55 %	$ 110,009.44	37.41 %
Operating Expenses:				
Advertising Expense	$ 2,450.00	0.77 %	$ 1,779.00	0.61 %
Bankcard Fees Expense	4,199.27	1.32	3,569.37	1.21
Insurance Expense	125.00	0.04	0.00	0.00
Maintenance Expense	3,519.25	1.11	3,308.10	1.13
Miscellaneous Expense	348.28	0.11	742.00	0.25
Payroll Tax Expense	3,826.83	1.20	3,444.15	1.17
Rent Expense	14,000.00	4.41	13,200.00	4.49
Salaries Expense	29,374.60	9.25	26,437.14	8.99
Supplies Expense	3,710.00	1.17	2,968.00	1.01
Utilities Expense	2,364.87	0.74	2,305.75	0.78
Total Operating Expenses	$ 63,918.10	20.12 %	$ 57,753.51	19.64 %
Operating Income	$ 42,669.72	13.43 %	$ 52,255.93	17.77 %
Fed. Corp. Inc. Tax Exp.	9,995.00	3.15	9,085.00	3.09
Net Income	$ 32,674.72	10.28 %	$ 43,170.93	14.68 %

Now that you have studied this section, complete the following questions and problems.

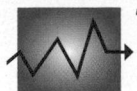

Thinking Critically

1. An income statement for a merchandising business has five sections. Name and briefly describe each section.
2. How do transportation charges affect the cost of merchandise?

Analyzing Accounting

Look at the comparative income statement at the right and answer the following questions about the vertical analysis of this financial statement.

1. What is the trend in sales?
2. How is that trend affecting the net income?
3. What expenses have decreased in the past year?
4. Are there any significant changes in inventory?
5. What is the largest expense?
6. Would you invest your money in this business? Why or why not?

Comparative Income Statement
For the Current and Previous Years Ended December 31

| | Current Year | | Previous Year | |
	Dollars	Percent	Dollars	Percent
Revenue:				
Sales	$ 1,500,000	100.13 %	$ 850,000	100.26 %
Less: Sales Ret. and Allow.	2,000	0.13	2,200	0.26
Net Sales	$ 1,498,000	100.00 %	$ 847,800	100.00 %
Cost of Merchandise Sold:				
Merch. Inventory, Jan. 1	$ 250,000	16.69 %	$ 100,000	11.80 %
Net Purchases	800,000	53.40	650,000	76.67
Merch. Available for Sale	$ 1,050,000	70.09 %	$ 750,000	88.46 %
Merch. Inventory, Dec. 31	60,000	4.01	250,000	29.49
Cost of Merchandise Sold	$ 990,000	66.09 %	$ 500,000	58.98 %
Gross Profit on Sales	$ 508,000	33.91 %	$ 347,800	41.02 %
Operating Expenses:				
Advertising Expense	$ 50,000	3.34 %	$ 25,000	2.95 %
Bankcard Fees Expense	10,000	0.67	8,000	0.94
Insurance Expense	5,300	0.35	5,300	0.63
Maintenance Expense	9,000	0.60	7,500	0.88
Payroll Tax Expense	6,200	0.41	3,200	0.38
Rent Expense	20,000	1.34	20,000	2.36
Salaries Expense	58,000	3.87	48,000	5.66
Supplies Expense	3,000	0.20	2,200	0.26
Utilities Expense	2,400	0.16	1,850	0.22
Total Operating Expenses	$ 163,900	10.94 %	$ 121,050	14.28 %
Operating Income	$ 344,100	22.97 %	$ 226,750	26.75 %
Fed. Corp. Inc. Tax Exp.	44,940	3.00	25,434	3.00
Net Income	$ 299,160	19.97 %	$ 201,316	23.75 %

Problem 19–3 Calculating Amounts on the Income Statement

Instructions

For each group of figures that follows, determine the missing amount.

1. Beginning merchandise inventory $81,367
   Net purchases   15,139
   Cost of merchandise available for sale   ?
2. Net sales $52,935
   Cost of merchandise sold   36,232
   Gross profit on sales   ?
3. Purchases $26,472
   Transportation in   1,311
   Cost of delivered merchandise   ?
4. Cost of merchandise available for sale $49,769
   Ending merchandise inventory   32,621
   Cost of merchandise sold   ?

RAJ KHANNA
Recruiting Manager
Robert Half

Q: How did you become a recruiter?

A: Like most people, I sort of fell into recruiting. I was a CPA for eight years, working in both public and private accounting, when my sister introduced me to a friend who owned a small recruiting firm. I had been there just a few months when the firm was acquired by Robert Half. That's when things really started to happen for me. I had the opportunity to travel and attend key training workshops, which really gave my career momentum.

Q: What are some factors that have been key to your success?

A: Intense daily activity is critical, and, in providing customer service, thinking outside the box is also important. These factors have enabled me to establish long-standing relationships with my clients and candidates.

Q: What advice do you have for people considering a degree in accounting?

A: It is still one of the most solid business foundations out there. Even in light of recent developments, accounting and finance is a discipline that transcends any industry and is relevant at any level throughout one's career.

Tips from . . .

Robert Half International Inc.

The way you present yourself is important throughout your career, not just during a job interview. Be confident and friendly. Always be prompt, and work hard. Put in the hours necessary to do first-rate work.

CAREER FACTS

Nature of the Work: Identify qualified candidates for available employment opportunities with client companies.

Training or Education Needed: For recruiting firm specializing in accounting and finance, a bachelor's degree in accounting or related experience.

Aptitudes, Abilities, and Skills: Interpersonal skills; communication skills; aptitude for sales. To work with a specialized recruiter in accounting and finance, familiarity with industry jobs.

Salary Range: $50,000 to $150,000, depending on personal performance, company size and performance.

Career Path: Work in a public accounting firm or corporate accounting department to gain experience and knowledge; transfer to a recruiting position with a specialized recruiting firm in accounting and finance.

Thinking Critically: What might a job applicant look for in deciding whether or not a company's culture is right?

The Statement of Retained Earnings and the Balance Sheet

In the previous section, you learned how to prepare and analyze the income statement, which reports the net income or loss for the period. In this section you will learn how to prepare and analyze the statement of retained earnings and the balance sheet. The stockholders of John Deere & Co. study the balance sheet to understand the financial position of the company.

The Statement of Retained Earnings

In a corporation there are two stockholders' equity accounts: **Capital Stock** and **Retained Earnings**. The **Capital Stock** account represents the stockholders' investment in the corporation. The balance of this account changes only when additional shares of stock are issued by the corporation. The **Retained Earnings** account summarizes the accumulated profits of a corporation less any amounts paid to stockholders as returns on their investments.

In Chapter 9 you learned how to prepare a statement of changes in owner's equity for a sole proprietorship to show the changes that occur in the owner's capital account during the period. A similar statement, the statement of retained earnings, is prepared for a corporation. A **statement of retained earnings** reports the changes that take place in the **Retained Earnings** account during the period. These changes result from business operations and the distribution of earnings to stockholders through dividends.

The changes to **Retained Earnings** are summarized as follows:

Retained Earnings	
Debit	Credit
−	+
Decreased by:	Increased by:
net loss	net income
dividends	

What You'll Learn

- How to prepare a statement of retained earnings for a merchandising corporation.
- How to prepare a balance sheet for a merchandising corporation.
- How to analyze the balance sheet.

Why It's Important

The statement of retained earnings reports how the Retained Earnings stockholders' equity account changes from the beginning to the end of the period. The balance sheet reports the financial position of the business on the last day of the period.

KEY TERMS

statement of retained earnings
horizontal analysis
base year
working capital

The statement of retained earnings is prepared from information found on the work sheet. The statement of retained earnings is a supporting document for the balance sheet. The final balance of the **Retained Earnings** account, as calculated on the statement of retained earnings, is used when preparing the balance sheet.

Figure 19–5 shows the statement of retained earnings for On Your Mark. The first line shows the balance of the **Retained Earnings** account at the beginning of the period. This balance comes from the Balance Sheet section of the work sheet. The second line is the net income for the period. This is from the Income Statement columns of the work sheet. Add net income to the beginning balance of the **Retained Earnings** account. Since On Your Mark did not distribute any of its net income to stockholders during the period, there are no deductions from **Retained Earnings**. The new balance of the **Retained Earnings** account is $52,445.91.

On Your Mark Athletic Wear					
Statement of Retained Earnings					
For the Year Ended December 31, 20--					
Retained Earnings, January 1, 20--				19 7 7 1 19
Net Income				32 6 7 4 72
Retained Earnings, December 31, 20--				52 4 4 5 91

Figure 19–5 Statement of Retained Earnings

The Balance Sheet

The balance sheet reports the balances of all asset, liability, and stockholders' equity accounts for a specific date. The balance sheet is prepared from the information in the Balance Sheet section of the work sheet and from the statement of retained earnings.

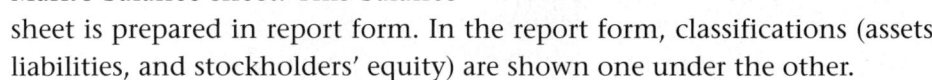

Figure 19–6 shows On Your Mark's balance sheet. This balance sheet is prepared in report form. In the report form, classifications (assets, liabilities, and stockholders' equity) are shown one under the other.

The assets are listed first. The classification "Assets" is centered on the first line. The account names are listed at the left edge in the same order as they appear on the work sheet. The individual balances are entered in the first amount column. "Total Assets" is entered on the line below the last account name, indented about half an inch. The total assets amount is entered in the second amount column. The double rule, however, is not entered until the Liabilities and Stockholders' Equity sections are complete, and the total of these two sections equals the total of the Assets section.

On Your Mark Athletic Wear
Balance Sheet
December 31, 20--

Assets			
Cash in Bank	15 1 7 9 00		
Accounts Receivable	10 4 0 4 00		
Merchandise Inventory	81 3 8 5 00		
Supplies	1 8 3 9 00		
Prepaid Insurance	1 3 7 5 00		
Delivery Equipment	19 8 3 1 00		
Office Equipment	9 8 2 5 00		
Store Equipment	5 2 0 0 00		
Total Assets		145 0 3 8 00	
Liabilities			
Accounts Payable	13 8 5 0 00		
Federal Corporate Income Tax Payable	1 5 5 00		
Employees' Federal Income Tax Payable	6 4 0 00		
Employees' State Income Tax Payable	8 0 00		
Social Security Tax Payable	2 4 8 00		
Medicare Tax Payable	5 8 00		
Federal Unemployment Tax Payable	1 8 36		
State Unemployment Tax Payable	1 1 4 73		
Sales Tax Payable	2 4 2 8 00		
Total Liabilities		17 5 9 2 09	
Stockholders' Equity			
Capital Stock	75 0 0 0 00		
Retained Earnings	52 4 4 5 91		
Total Stockholders' Equity		127 4 4 5 91	
Total Liabilities and Stockholders' Equity		145 0 3 8 00	

Figure 19–6 On Your Mark's Balance Sheet

The Liabilities section begins on the second line below the total assets. "Liabilities" is centered on this line. Again, the account names are listed at the left edge in the same order as they appear on the work sheet. The individual balances are entered in the first amount column. "Total Liabilities" is entered on the line below the last account name, indented about half an inch. The total liabilities amount is entered in the second amount column.

Next, the Stockholders' Equity section begins on the second line below total liabilities. "Stockholders' Equity" is centered on this line. Stockholders' equity consists of two accounts: **Capital Stock** and **Retained Earnings.** The balance of the **Capital Stock** account is from the Balance Sheet section of the work sheet. The balance of the **Retained Earnings** account is from the statement of retained earnings. Again, the account names are listed at the left edge and the individual balances are listed in the first amount column. "Total Stockholders' Equity" is entered on the line below the last account name, indented about half an inch. The stockholders' equity total is entered in the second amount column.

> ### Key Points
>
> **The Balance Sheet**
> The balance sheet represents the basic accounting equation:
> Assets = Liabilities + Stockholders' (Owners') Equity

On the line following total stockholders' equity, "Total Liabilities and Stockholders' Equity" is entered at the left edge. The total of the Liabilities section and the total of the Stockholders' Equity section are added. The total is entered in the second amount column. This total must agree with the total assets amount. If it does, the balance sheet is double ruled. If it does not, check the addition on the balance sheet. Also check that the accounts and amounts are transferred from the work sheet accurately.

Analyzing Amounts on the Balance Sheet

When analyzing financial statements, you learned that while the dollar amounts provided on the statements are useful, the analysis can be expanded and made more meaningful by expressing the dollar amounts as percentages. In addition to using percentage amounts in vertical analysis as described earlier, they can also be used in horizontal analysis. **Horizontal analysis** is the comparison of the same items on financial statements for two or more accounting periods or dates and the determination of changes from one period or date to the next. With horizontal analysis, each amount on the current statement is compared with its corresponding amount on the previous statement. A **base year** is a year or period that is used for comparison.

Look at the example of a comparative balance sheet in **Figure 19–7**. By comparing the amounts for the two years, you can see that **Cash in Bank** increased by 25.3 percent and **Accounts Payable** decreased by 38.26 percent. The accountant might use this information to assess why cash has increased or why accounts payable have decreased. Perhaps the business is receiving more sales in cash instead of on account. The business may also be purchasing less inventory on account. These are trends that would be of interest to management.

Working Capital

The amount by which current assets exceed current liabilities is known as **working capital** . Because current liabilities are usually paid for out of current assets, working capital represents the excess assets available to continue operations. The working capital for On Your Mark is calculated as follows:

Current Assets — Current Liabilities = Working Capital
$110,182.00 — $17,592.09 = $92,589.91

In this example, current assets include **Cash in Bank, Accounts Receivable, Merchandise Inventory, Supplies**, and **Prepaid Insurance**. Current liabilities are all those listed in the liability section of the balance sheet in **Figure 19–7**.

On Your Mark Athletic Wear
Comparative Balance Sheet
December 31, Current Year and Previous Year

	Current Year	Previous Year	Increase (Decrease) Current over Previous	
			Dollars	Percent
Assets				
Cash in Bank	$ 15,179.00	$ 12,114.57	$ 3,064.43	25.30 %
Accounts Receivable	10,404.00	8,220.00	2,184.00	26.57
Merchandise Inventory	81,385.00	84,921.00	(3,536.00)	(4.16)
Supplies	1,839.00	1,587.00	252.00	15.88
Prepaid Insurance	1,375.00	0.00	1,375.00	—
Delivery Equipment	19,831.00	12,462.00	7,369.00	59.13
Office Equipment	9,825.00	5,854.00	3,971.00	67.83
Store Equipment	5,200.00	3,500.00	1,700.00	48.57
Total Assets	$ 145,038.00	$ 128,658.57	$ 16,379.43	12.73 %
Liabilities				
Accounts Payable	$ 13,850.00	$ 22,433.00	$ (8,583.00)	(38.26)%
Fed. Corp. Inc. Tax Payable	155.00	140.00	15.00	10.71
Employees' Fed. Inc. Tax Pay.	640.00	608.00	32.00	5.26
Employees' State Inc. Tax Pay.	80.00	72.00	8.00	11.11
Social Security Tax Payable	248.00	241.00	7.00	2.90
Medicare Tax Payable	58.00	56.35	1.65	2.93
Federal Unemployment Tax Pay.	18.36	16.50	1.86	11.27
State Unemployment Tax Pay.	114.73	103.17	11.56	11.20
Sales Tax Payable	2,428.00	3,158.00	(730.00)	(23.12)
Total Liabilities	$ 17,592.09	$ 26,828.02	$ (9,235.93)	(34.43)%
Stockholders' Equity				
Capital Stock	$ 75,000.00	$ 75,000.00	$ 0.00	0.00 %
Retained Earnings	52,445.91	26,830.55	25,615.36	95.47
Total Stockholders' Equity	$ 127,445.91	$ 101,830.55	$ 25,615.36	25.15 %
Total Liab. and Stockhldrs' Equity	$ 145,038.00	$ 128,658.57	$ 16,379.43	12.73 %

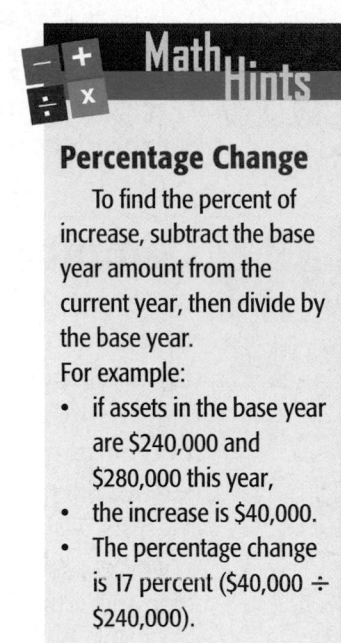

Math Hints

Percentage Change
To find the percent of increase, subtract the base year amount from the current year, then divide by the base year.
For example:
- if assets in the base year are $240,000 and $280,000 this year,
- the increase is $40,000.
- The percentage change is 17 percent ($40,000 ÷ $240,000).

Figure 19–7 Comparative Balance Sheet Showing Horizontal Analysis

---

ANALYZING FINANCIAL REPORTS

Evaluating Stockholders' Equity

Although the balance sheet provides information about stockholders' equity, corporations also prepare a report called the statement of stockholders' equity. This report might also be called a statement of retained earnings.

Look at the consolidated statements of stockholders' equity for Office Depot on pages A-47–A-48. This statement provides details about changes in capital through stock issuance and in retained earnings over a period of years. This information helps investors and analysts get a better picture of the company's capital. Successful companies earn money for future operations (reported as retained earnings) through sales, and rely less on raising new capital through the issuance of stock.

▶ **Analyze the Report:**
Use the consolidated statements of stockholders' equity on pages A-47–A-48 to answer these questions.
1. Explain how retained earnings changed from a balance of $1,516,691,000 in 2000 to a balance of $1,717,734,000 at the end of 2001.
2. How much did additional paid-in capital increase during this same time?

Now that you have studied this section, complete the following questions and problems.

Thinking Critically

1. What is reported on a statement of retained earnings?
2. Explain the use of a horizontal analysis.

Computing in the Business World

Larry Campbell is the owner of Craftsman Furniture, a successful family-owned furniture store. As the accountant for Craftsman Furniture, it is your responsibility to run a vertical analysis on the income statement. Mr. Campbell asks you to prepare an Executive Summary of a three-year vertical analysis. Using the information provided, in your working papers calculate the percentages for each year and complete the columns of the draft report. Mr. Campbell will review the draft with you so he clearly understands the trends in sales for Craftsman Furniture.

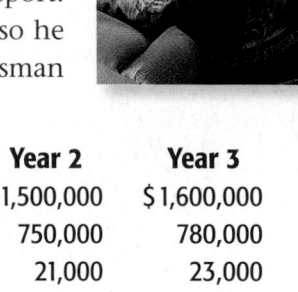

	Year 1	Year 2	Year 3
Net Sales	$1,000,000	$1,500,000	$1,600,000
Gross Profit on Sales	600,000	750,000	780,000
Total Operating Expenses	25,000	21,000	23,000
Net Income	$ 575,000	$ 729,000	$ 757,000

Problem 19–4 Analyzing a Balance Sheet

Use the comparative balance sheet for On Your Mark in **Figure 19–7** to answer the following questions.

1. Which asset account has the greatest percentage increase between the two years? Greatest decrease?
2. Which liability account has the greatest increase between the two years?
3. Did the overall value of the corporation increase or decrease between the two years? What is the dollar amount? What is the percentage?
4. What is the percentage increase in retained earnings between the two years?
5. What conclusions might you draw based on the change in Accounts Receivable? Accounts Payable?
6. Can you provide a possible explanation for the difference in the balance of the **Prepaid Insurance** account?

KEY CONCEPTS

1. Accounting for sole proprietorships and for corporations is very similar except for reporting owner's equity on the balance sheet. Corporations have two stockholders' equity accounts: **Capital Stock** and **Retained Earnings. Capital Stock** represents the stockholders' investments in the corporation. **Retained Earnings** summarizes the profits accumulated less distributions to stockholders.

2. Three financial statements prepared by merchandising corporations are the income statement, the statement of retained earnings, and the balance sheet.

3. Accounting information must be understandable and comparable. Comparability allows information to be compared from one fiscal period to another.

4. Accounting information must also be relevant, reliable, fully-disclosed, and material.

5. The income statement for a merchandising business contains the following elements:
   (a) Net sales, which is total sales less deductions for sales discounts, returns, and allowances
   (b) Net purchases, which is the total cost of merchandise bought plus transportation charges less deductions for purchases discounts, returns, and allowances
   (c) The cost of merchandise sold
   (d) Gross profit on sales, which is net sales minus the cost of merchandise sold.
   (e) Operating expenses
   (f) Operating income
   (g) The federal income tax paid by a corporation, listed separately on the income statement
   (h) Net income or net loss

6. The statement of retained earnings reports the changes in the **Retained Earnings** account due to net income or loss and distributions to stockholders.

7. The cost of merchandise sold is calculated as follows:

   $$
   \begin{array}{l}
   \ \text{Beginning Merchandise Inventory} \\
   +\ \underline{\text{Net Purchases During the Period}} \\
   \ \text{Cost of Merchandise Available for Sale} \\
   -\ \underline{\text{Ending Merchandise Inventory}} \\
   \ \text{Cost of Merchandise Sold}
   \end{array}
   $$

8. The balance sheet reports the financial position of the business on a specific date. The balance sheet includes all the permanent general ledger accounts: assets, liabilities, and stockholders' equity accounts.

9. Vertical analysis helps the accountant determine the relationships among items on a financial statement and the changes in these relationships from one period to the next.

10. Horizontal analysis compares items on a financial statement for two or more accounting periods. Each amount on a current statement is compared with its corresponding amount on the previous statement.

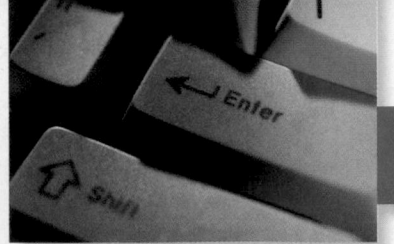

USING **KEY** TERMS

Your company, The Neighborhood Bookworm, was purchased several months ago by an international bookstore chain—The Best Seller. Your new boss, Gabriella Sitta, asks you to create the end-of-year financial statements. Gabriella is not native to the U.S. and does not understand all the English-language business terms. On a separate sheet of paper, write for each term its definition and its relationship to the preparation of financial statements.

administrative expenses	operating income
base year	relevance
Capital Stock	reliability
comparability	retained earnings
full disclosure	selling expenses
gross profit on sales	statement of retained
horizontal analysis	earnings
materiality	stockholders' equity
net purchases	vertical analysis
net sales	working capital
operating expenses	

Understanding Accounting
Concepts and Procedures

Instructions

On a separate sheet of paper, answer the following questions:

1. How does stockholders' equity differ from owner's equity?

2. What three financial statements are prepared by a merchandising corporation?

3. How does an income statement for a merchandising business differ from that for a service business?

4. How is net sales calculated? Net purchases?

5. What is the difference between the cost of merchandise available for sale and the cost of merchandise sold?

6. How is the cost of merchandise sold calculated?

7. Why are the income taxes paid by a corporation listed separately on the income statement?

8. What is the difference between operating income and net income?

9. Why is the net income for the period added to **Retained Earnings** rather than to **Capital Stock?**

10. Why is the income statement prepared before the statement of retained earnings? Why is the statement of retained earnings prepared before the balance sheet?

Case Study...

Merchandising Business: Gourmet Food Gifts

The Gourmet Express sells cookies, candies, food baskets, and other gourmet items. Valentine's Day and Mother's Day are the busiest days. The store sells directly to customers and also ships items through catalog orders. Recently, prices have increased for some food ingredients, such as sugar and chocolate. As a result, net income has decreased. The manager does not want to use lower-priced ingredients because they might change the quality of the finished products.

In preparation for the Valentine's Day rush, you've been asked to suggest some ideas for increasing net income.

Thinking Critically:

1. What items affect net income?
2. Think about the gourmet food gift business, both the retail and the catalog operations. What are some areas for possibly cutting costs?
3. Recommend at least three ideas for cutting costs.

*inter*NET CONNECTION

Corporate Financial Statements

Many corporations publish financial statements online. By accessing a company's financial information, potential investors can locate annual earnings, stock prices, and growth trends for the company.

Do This:

1. Find a well-known company's corporate site on the Web. Try companies like Toys "R" Us, Coca-Cola, Intel, or AT&T. Which company did you choose? What is the Web site address?
2. Locate the company's annual report or earnings release for the current year or the most recent quarter. Did the company have a profit or loss for the period?
3. What is the value of the company's total assets?

Conducting an Audit with Alex

The following account balances are from the Income Statement section of the work sheet.

Account Name	Debit	Credit
Purchases	121,520	
Transportation In	1,306	
Purchases Discounts		4,840
Purchases Returns and Allowances		1,641

The beginning merchandise inventory is $36,813, and the ending merchandise inventory is $54,709.

Instructions

(1) Determine the amount of net purchases for the period.
(2) Determine the cost of merchandise sold.

Workplace Skills

Sociability

Most jobs require you to be adaptable to any situation. Your social skills on the job are equally important. How well you can relate to others, demonstrate an understanding, and respond appropriately to any situation is an indicator of your interpersonal skills development.

On the Job:

Friday night you are attending the annual stockholders' meeting and reception for Big League Sports—a professional-sports merchandising company. Your boss, Lily Chang, asks you to make a presentation about trends in professional sports. She recommends that you keep it colorful, simple, humorous, and appropriate for the event.

Thinking Critically:

Together with several of your colleagues (classmates), develop an outline for your presentation. Decide on visuals to use and topics to cover. Prepare a question and answer segment.

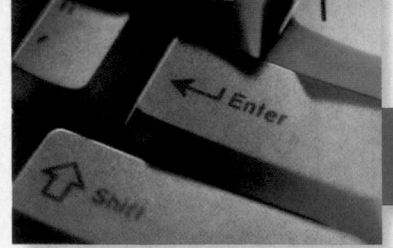

Preparing Financial Statements

Making the Transition from a Manual to a Computerized System

Task	Perform Accounting Procedures Using Manual Methods	Perform Accounting Procedures Using Automated Methods
Preparing financial statements	1. After all business transactions have been journalized and posted, prepare the trial balance. 2. Calculate, journalize, and post the adjusting entries. 3. Prepare the income statement, statement of retained earnings, and balance sheet.	1. After all business transactions have been journalized and posted, print a working trial balance. 2. Journalize the adjusting entries. 3. Print the income statement, statement of retained earnings, and balance sheet.

Preparing Financial Statements

Peachtree Question	Description
Why should I display a financial statement on the screen before printing it?	1. Displaying reports on the screen allows you to review the report before printing. 2. Viewing the report on the screen avoids printing a report that may contain no data or including data that you do not want included. 3. If a transaction in a report is outlined by a blue box, the "drill-down" feature allows you to double-click on the entry and go directly to the Tasks edit screen to make corrections. 4. Changes are reflected in the displayed report before it is printed.
How do I print the Income Statement, Statement of Retained Earnings, and Balance Sheet?	1. Select **Financial Statements** from the ***Reports*** menu. 2. Select Income Statement, Retained Earnings Statement, or Balance Sheet from the Reports list. 3. Click the Screen icon to display the Options window. 4. Select a time frame for the information to be included in the report. Current period is the default. 5. Review the statement on screen. 6. Click *Print*.
What does the software do "behind the scenes"?	• Financial statements are generated from information stored in the general ledger. Selections made at the Options window and the defaults established when the company was set up determine the appearance of the report and the amount of information included.

For detailed instructions: See the Peachtree User Guide in your Glencoe Working Papers.

APPLICATION OPTIONS

 **Problem 19–5 Preparing an Income Statement**

The work sheet for Sunset Surfwear for the year ended December 31 is shown in your working papers.

Instructions Prepare an income statement for Sunset Surfwear in your working papers. Refer to **Figure 19–3** for guidance in setting up the income statement.

Analyze: Which is larger for this period, purchases discounts or purchases returns and allowances?

Problem 19–6 Preparing a Statement of Retained Earnings and a Balance Sheet

Instructions Use the work sheet and the income statement from **Problem 19–5** to prepare a statement of retained earnings and a balance sheet for Sunset Surfwear. Use the accounting stationery provided in your working papers.

Analyze: Calculate working capital for Sunset Surfwear.

Problem 19–7 Preparing Financial Statements

Instructions The partially completed work sheet for Shutterbug Cameras is included in your working papers.
(1) Complete the work sheet.
(2) Prepare an income statement.
(3) Prepare a statement of retained earnings.
(4) Prepare a balance sheet.

Analyze: Was the ending merchandise inventory greater or less than the beginning inventory?

Complete chapter problems one of four ways:

1 **Manual** Glencoe Working Papers

or

2 **Peachtree Complete Accounting** Software

or

3 **QuickBooks** Templates (Problems 19–5, 19–8)

or

4 **Spreadsheet** Templates (Problem 19–5)

SPREADSHEET SMART GUIDE

Step–by–Step Instructions: Problem 19–5

1. Select the spreadsheet template for Problem 19–5.
2. Enter your name and the date in the spaces provided on the template.
3. Complete the spreadsheet using the instructions in your working papers.
4. Print the spreadsheet and proof your work.
5. Save your work and exit the spreadsheet program.

Peachtree®

SMART GUIDE

Step–by–Step Instructions:
Problem 19–6

1. Select the problem set for Sunset Surfwear (Prob. 19–6).
2. Rename the company and set the system date.
3. Print a Statement of Retained Earnings and a Balance Sheet.
4. Answer the Analyze question.
5. End the session.

Peachtree®

SMART GUIDE

Step–by–Step Instructions:
Problem 19–7

1. Select the problem set for Shutterbug Cameras (Prob. 19–7).
2. Rename the company and set the system date.
3. Print the following reports: Adjusted Trial Balance, Balance Sheet, Income Statement, and Statement of Retained Earnings.
4. Answer the Analyze question.
5. End the session.

Problem 19–8
Completing a Work Sheet and Financial Statements

The trial balance for Cycle Tech Bicycles, prepared on a ten-column work sheet, is included in your working papers.

Instructions

(1) Complete the work sheet for the year ended December 31. Use the following information to make the adjustments.

	Cycle Tech Bicycles			
	Work Sheet			
	For the Year Ended December 31, 20--			
ACCT. NO.	ACCOUNT NAME	TRIAL BALANCE		
		DEBIT	CREDIT	
1 101	Cash in Bank	21 931 00		
2 115	Accounts Receivable	1 782 00		
3 125	Merchandise Inventory	24 028 00		
4 130	Supplies	4 159 00		
5 135	Prepaid Insurance	1 800 00		
6 140	Store Equipment	24 895 00		
7 145	Office Equipment	16 113 00		
8 201	Accounts Payable		11 224 00	
9 210	Fed. Corp. Income Tax Payable			
10 211	Emplys' Fed. Inc. Tax Payable		522 00	
11 212	Emplys' State Inc. Tax Payable		144 00	
12 213	Social Security Tax Payable		413 00	
13 214	Medicare Tax Payable		134 00	
14 215	Sales Tax Payable		1 915 00	
15 216	Fed. Unemployment Tax Payable		54 00	
16 217	State Unemployment Tax Payable		271 00	
17 301	Capital Stock		40 000 00	
18 305	Retained Earnings		11 091 00	
19 310	Income Summary			
20 401	Sales		127 151 00	
21 405	Sales Discounts	246 00		
22 410	Sales Returns and Allowances	1 328 00		
23 501	Purchases	66 107 00		
24 505	Transportation In	983 00		
25 510	Purchases Discounts		822 00	
26 515	Purchases Ret. and Allowances		376 00	
27 601	Advertising Expense	2 380 00		
28 605	Bankcard Fees Expense	181 00		
29 625	Fed. Corp. Income Tax Expense	3 340 00		
30 630	Insurance Expense			
31 645	Maintenance Expense	1 950 00		
32 650	Miscellaneous Expense	1 831 00		
33 655	Payroll Tax Expense	834 00		
34 657	Rent Expense	10 800 00		
35 660	Salaries Expense	4 734 00		
36 665	Supplies Expense			
37 675	Utilities Expense	4 695 00		
38				
39		194 117 00	194 117 00	
40	Net Income			
41				
42				

Ending merchandise inventory	$25,191
Ending supplies inventory	1,221
Expired insurance	825
Total federal corporate income taxes for the year	3,472

(2) Prepare an income statement.

(3) Prepare a statement of retained earnings.

(4) Prepare a balance sheet.

Analyze: If the ending value of **Merchandise Inventory** was actually $28,000, would net income be higher or lower?

CHALLENGE PROBLEM
Problem 19–9 Evaluating the Effect of an Error on the Income Statement

Peachtree®

SMART GUIDE

The accounting clerk for River's Edge Canoe & Kayak prepared the income statement for the year ended December 31. The accounting supervisor at River's Edge noticed that the balance of the **Transportation In** account was erroneously omitted from this statement. **Transportation In** has a balance of $562.

Step–by–Step Instructions: Problem 19–8

1. Select the problem set for Cycle Tech Bicycles (Prob. 19–8).
2. Rename the company and set the system date.
3. Print a Working Trial Balance to help you prepare the adjustments.
4. Record the adjustments using the **General Journal Entry** option.
5. Print a General Journal report and proof your work.
6. Print the following reports: Adjusted Trial Balance, Income Statement, Statement of Retained Earnings, and Balance Sheet.
7. Answer the Analyze question.
8. End the session.

Instructions Use the income statement shown in your working papers to answer the following questions.

1. In which section of the income statement is the account **Transportation In** entered?
2. How is net purchases affected by this omission (understated or overstated)? By what amount?
3. How does the omission of the **Transportation In** balance affect gross profit on sales? By what amount?
4. What is the correct amount for the cost of merchandise sold for the period?
5. What is the correct amount for net income?

Analyze: An overstatement of expenses has what effect on net income?

Recording Business Transactions in Special Journals

In-Touch Electronics

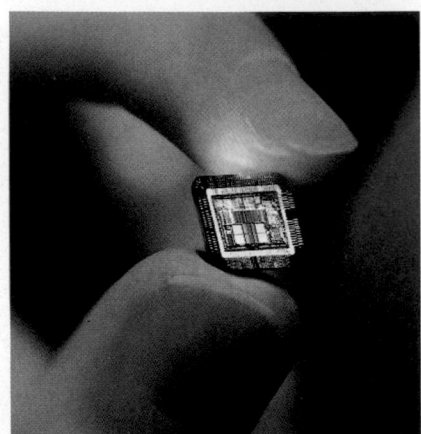

Company Background: Pedro and Tina Cordova own a merchandising business organized as a corporation called In-Touch Electronics. The retail business is a small, electronics store providing a unique service to the local community. This husband and wife team has been operating successfully for ten years.

Keeping the Accounting Records for In-Touch Electronics: Since In-Touch Electronics has a large volume of business transactions, the business uses special journals and a general journal. The previous accounting clerk, Manny Canseco, has journalized and posted the business transactions for May 1 through May 15. Those transactions are included in the accounting stationery in the working papers accompanying this textbook. The transactions that follow took place between May 16 and May 31.

Your Job Responsibilities: The forms for completing this activity are included in the working papers accompanying this textbook.

(1) Record the remaining May transactions in the sales journal (page 18), cash receipts journal (page 15), purchases journal (page 12), cash payments journal (page 14), and general journal (page 7).

(2) Post the individual amounts from the five journals to the accounts receivable and accounts payable subsidiary ledgers on a daily basis.

(3) Post the individual amounts from the General columns of the cash receipts, purchases, cash payments, and general journals on a daily basis.

(4) Foot, prove, total, and rule the special journals.

(5) Post the column totals of the special journals to the general ledger accounts. Use the following order for posting: sales journal, cash receipts journal, purchases journal, and cash payments journal.

(6) Prove cash. The balance shown on check stub 899 is $6109.45.

(7) Prepare a schedule of accounts receivable and a schedule of accounts payable.

(8) Prepare a trial balance.

What You'll Learn

- How to analyze business transactions.
- How to journalize business transactions in the four special journals and in the general journal.
- How to post journal entries to the general ledger and to the accounts receivable and accounts payable subsidiary ledgers.
- How to post the totals of the special journals to the general ledger.
- How to prove cash.
- How to prepare a schedule of accounts receivable and a schedule of accounts payable.
- How to prepare a trial balance.

Why It's Important

In Chapters 16 and 17 you learned how to record the business transactions of a merchandising business in special journals. Now you will have the opportunity to review and apply what you have learned.

APPLICATION OPTIONS

CHART OF ACCOUNTS
In-Touch Electronics

ASSETS

101 Cash in Bank
105 Accounts Receivable
110 Merchandise Inventory
115 Supplies
120 Prepaid Insurance
150 Store Equipment
155 Office Equipment

LIABILITIES

201 Accounts Payable
205 Sales Tax Payable
210 Employees' Federal Income Tax Payable
211 Employees' State Income Tax Payable
212 Social Security Tax Payable
213 Medicare Tax Payable
214 Federal Unemployment Tax Payable
215 State Unemployment Tax Payable

STOCKHOLDERS' EQUITY

301 Capital Stock
302 Retained Earnings
303 Income Summary

REVENUE

401 Sales
405 Sales Discounts
410 Sales Returns and Allowances

COST OF MERCHANDISE

501 Purchases
505 Transportation In
510 Purchases Discounts
515 Purchases Returns and Allowances

EXPENSES

605 Advertising Expense
610 Bankcard Fees Expense
615 Miscellaneous Expense
620 Payroll Tax Expense
625 Rent Expense
630 Salaries Expense
635 Utilities Expense

Complete activities one of three ways:

1 **Manual** Glencoe Working Papers

or

2 **Peachtree Complete Accounting** Software

or

3 **QuickBooks** Templates

Accounts Receivable Subsidiary Ledger

LOR Sam Lorenzo
MAR Marianne Martino
MCC Mark McCormick
SCO Sue Ellen Scott
TRO Tom Trout

Accounts Payable Subsidiary Ledger

COM Computer Systems Inc.
DES Desktop Wholesalers
HIT Hi-Tech Electronics Outlet
LAS Laser & Ink-Jet Products
OFF Office Suppliers Inc.

Peachtree®

SMART GUIDE

Step–by–Step Instructions:

1. Select the problem set for In-Touch Electronics (MP–4).
2. Rename the company and set the system date.
3. Enter all of the sales on account using the **Sales/Invoicing** option.
4. Record and apply any sales returns.
5. Process all of the cash receipts using the **Receipts** option.
6. Enter the purchases on account using the **Purchases/Receive Inventory** option.
7. Record and apply any purchases returns.
8. Process all of the cash payments with the **Payments** option.
9. Use the **General Journal Entry** option to record the error discovered on May 26.
10. Record the employer's payroll taxes using the **General Journal Entry** option.
11. Print the following reports: General Journal, Purchases Journal, Cash Disbursements Journal, Sales Journal, and Cash Receipts Journal.
12. Proof your work.
13. Print the following reports: General Ledger, Vendor Ledgers, and Customer Ledgers.
14. Print a General Ledger Trial Balance.
15. Answer the Analyze questions.
16. End the session.

Business Transactions: In-Touch Electronics had the following transactions in the month of May.

Date	Transactions
May 16	Sold $120.00 in merchandise plus 5% sales tax to Sam Lorenzo on account, Sales Slip 607.
17	Received $126.00 from Tom Trout to apply on his account, Receipt 356.
17	Issued Check 892 for $800.00 to Desktop Wholesalers in payment of our account balance.
18	Issued Debit Memo 38 to Laser & Ink Jet Products for our return of $75.00 in merchandise.
19	Wrote Check 893 for $1,200.00 to Computer Systems Inc. to apply on our account.
19	Paid Hi-Tech Electronics Outlet $1,750.00 in full payment of our account balance by issuing Check 894.
19	Issued Check 895 to Office Suppliers, Inc. for $770.00 in full payment of our account balance.
20	Sold $90.00 in office equipment for cash to an employee, Bob Bell, Receipt 357.
20	Purchased $1,200.00 in store equipment on account from Desktop Wholesalers, DW87, n/30.
20	Received $210.00 from Mark McCormick to apply on his account, Receipt 358.
20	Sue Ellen Scott sent us a check for $308.70 in payment of her $315.00 account less a 2% discount, Receipt 359.
21	Purchased $1,500.00 in merchandise on account from Hi-Tech Electronics Outlet, Invoice HT99, terms 2/10, n/30.
21	Marianne Martino sent us a $94.50 check to apply on her account, Receipt 360.
21	Sold $400.00 in merchandise plus 5% sales tax to Mark McCormick on account, Sales Slip 608, terms 2/10, n/30.
22	Issued Check 896 for $1,200.00 to Desktop Wholesalers, in payment of our account.
23	Sold $500.00 in merchandise to Sue Ellen Scott on account plus 5% sales tax, Sales Slip 609, terms 2/10, n/30.
24	Mark McCormick returned merchandise purchased on account, $100.00, plus 5% sales tax, Credit Memo 55.
25	Paid the annual insurance premium of $1,600.00 by issuing Check 897 to Surfside Insurance Co.
26	Discovered that **Transportation In** account should have been debited last month for $50.00 instead of the **Purchases** account. Recorded the correcting entry, Memorandum 26.
27	Bought $1,400.00 in merchandise on account from Computer Systems, Inc., CS75, terms 2/10, n/30.

Continued ✒

Date	Transactions (cont.)
28	Sold $200.00 in merchandise on account plus 5% sales tax to Marianne Martino, Sales Slip 610, terms 2/10, n/30.
29	Purchased $150.00 in supplies on account from Office Suppliers Inc., Invoice 9489.
30	Issued Check 898 for $1,500.00 in payment for the monthly rent.
31	Recorded cash sales of $1,200.00 plus 5% sales tax, Tape 22.
31	Recorded bankcard sales of $900.00 plus 5% sales tax, Tape 22.
31	Recorded bank service charge of $25.00 and bankcard fees of $100.00, May bank statement (record compound entry).
31	Wrote Check 899 to pay the payroll of $2,500.00 (gross earnings) for the pay period ended May 31. The following amounts were withheld: employees' federal income taxes, $400.00; employees' state income taxes, $50.00; FICA taxes, $155.00 for social security and $36.25 for Medicare.
31	Recorded the employer's payroll taxes for the May 31 payroll: FICA tax rate, 6.2% for social security and 1.45% for Medicare; federal unemployment tax rate, 0.8%; and state unemployment tax rate, 5.4%.

Peachtree®

SMART GUIDE

TIP: To save time entering transactions, group them by type and then enter the transactions in batches.

TIP: Remember that you need to change the G/L Account in the Receipts window to enter a cash receipt for the sale of an asset (e.g., supplies, office equipment.

TIP: Always verify the *G/L Account* field when you enter a purchases on account transaction.

Analyze:
1. How much has **Cash in Bank** increased by throughout the month?
2. What is the amount of the trial balance debit and credit columns on May 31?
3. What is the amount debited to the **Payroll Tax Expense** account on May 31?

CHAPTER 20

Completing the Accounting Cycle for a Merchandising Corporation

Learning Objectives

When you have completed this chapter, you will be able to:

▶ Journalize closing entries for a merchandising corporation.

▶ Post closing entries to the general ledger accounts.

▶ Prepare a post-closing trial balance.

▶ Describe the steps in the accounting cycle.

Bose Corporation

Exploring the Real World of Business

CLOSING THE BOOKS

If you've ever purchased a set of speakers for your stereo system, you've probably heard of **Bose Corporation.** Noted for high-performance audio equipment, **Bose** products are sold in retail stores and found in many luxury automobiles. You'll find **Bose** products in homes as well as in stadiums, arenas, computers, restaurants, public spaces, and even on the space shuttle.

Bose Corporation was started in 1964 by Dr. Amar Bose, a professor at the Massachusetts Institute of Technology. Dr. Bose believes in using research and technology to create the best possible products. Research is expensive, and the company tracks costs through its accounting system.

Making closing entries at the end of each fiscal period helps the company match the specific expenses of developing new loudspeakers or other equipment to a fiscal period and to the products developed.

What do you think?

If you worked for **Bose Corporation,** what accounts would you use to track the costs for a new line of home audio loudspeakers?

Workplace Connections

Applying Your Accounting Knowledge

You've nearly completed another accounting cycle—this time for a merchandising company. After the financial statements are prepared, closing entries are made to get the accounting records ready for the next fiscal period. You might think of closing entries as "wiping the slate clean" to make it ready for more entries. Closing entries for a merchandising business are similar to those you learned about for a service business. There are just more of them.

Investigate:

1. In your job, are there duties that you perform at the end of a night or week that "wipe the slate clean" or "close out" the day's activities?

2. If you were preparing the closing entries for your workplace, what accounts do you imagine would be involved?

Glencoe Accounting *Online*

Visit the *Glencoe Accounting* Web site at **glencoeaccounting.glencoe.com** for additional activities and information.

Journalizing Closing Entries

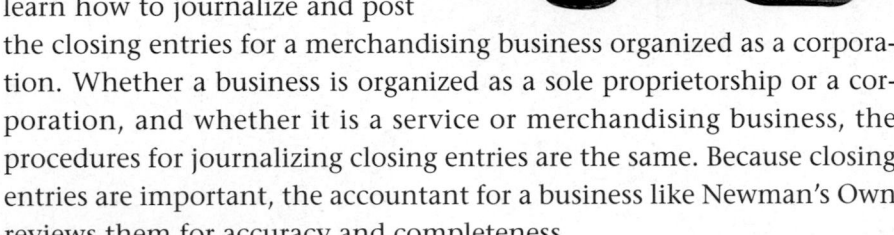

In Chapter 10 you learned how to journalize and post the closing entries for a service business operated as a sole proprietorship. In this chapter you will learn how to journalize and post the closing entries for a merchandising business organized as a corporation. Whether a business is organized as a sole proprietorship or a corporation, and whether it is a service or merchandising business, the procedures for journalizing closing entries are the same. Because closing entries are important, the accountant for a business like Newman's Own reviews them for accuracy and completeness.

Closing entries transfer the balances of all the temporary accounts to a permanent account. After the closing entries are posted, all of the temporary accounts have zero balances. The general ledger is then ready for the next accounting period. Information needed to prepare the

	ACCT. NO.	ACCOUNT NAME	TRIAL BALANCE		ADJUSTMENTS	
			DEBIT	CREDIT	DEBIT	CREDIT
20	310	Income Summary			(a) 3 536 00	
21	401	Sales		320 450 00		
22	405	Sales Discounts	730 00			
23	410	Sales Returns and Allowances	2 000 00			
24	501	Purchases	206 700 00			
25	505	Transportation In	4 036 18			
26	510	Purchases Discounts		1 340 00		
27	515	Purchases Returns and Allow.		1 800 00		
28	601	Advertising Expense	2 450 00			
29	605	Bankcard Fees Expense	4 199 27			
30	630	Fed. Corporate Income Tax Exp.	9 840 00		(d) 155 00	
31	635	Insurance Expense			(c) 125 00	
32	650	Maintenance Expense	3 519 25			
33	655	Miscellaneous Expense	348 28			
34	657	Payroll Tax Expense	3 826 83			
35	660	Rent Expense	14 000 00			
36	665	Salaries Expense	29 374 60			
37	670	Supplies Expense			(b) 3 710 00	
38	680	Utilities Expense	2 364 87			
39			435 798 28	435 798 28	7 526 00	7 526 00
40		Net Income				
41						
42						

On Your Mark
Work
For the Year Ended

Figure 20–1
Closing Entries Needed for a Corporation

closing entries is found in the Income Statement section of the work sheet, which contains the balances of all the temporary accounts.

Steps for Closing the Ledger

In Chapter 10 you made four entries to close the temporary general ledger accounts of a sole proprietorship:

1. close the temporary accounts with credit balances to **Income Summary**
2. close the temporary accounts with debit balances to **Income Summary**
3. close the balance of **Income Summary** to capital
4. close the withdrawals account to capital

Only the first three closing entries are made to close the temporary accounts for a merchandising business organized as a corporation. Since a corporation does not have a withdrawals account, the fourth closing entry is not needed.

The portion of On Your Mark's work sheet in **Figure 20–1** shows the account balances that are closed. Let's look closely at each closing entry.

Sales			Income Summary	
Debit	Credit		Debit	Credit
–	+			
Clos. 320,450.00	Bal. 320,450.00		Adj. 3,536.00	Clos. 323,590.00

1. Close the accounts with balances in the Credit column of the Income Statement section of the work sheet (revenue and contra cost of merchandise accounts) to **Income Summary**.

Purchases Discounts			Purchases Returns and Allowances	
Debit	Credit		Debit	Credit
–	+		–	+
Clos. 1,340.00	Bal. 1,340.00		Clos. 1,800.00	Bal. 1,800.00

Athletic Wear
Sheet
December 31, 20--

ADJUSTED TRIAL BALANCE		INCOME STATEMENT		BALANCE SHEET		
DEBIT	CREDIT	DEBIT	CREDIT	DEBIT	CREDIT	
3 536 00		3 536 00				20
	320 450 00		320 450 00			21
730 00		730 00				22
2 000 00		2 000 00				23
206 700 00		206 700 00				24
4 036 18		4 036 18				25
	1 340 00		1 340 00			26
	1 800 00		1 800 00			27
2 450 00		2 450 00				28
4 199 27		4 199 27				29
9 995 00		9 995 00				30
125 00		125 00				31
3 519 25		3 519 25				32
348 28		348 28				33
3 826 83		3 826 83				34
14 000 00		14 000 00				35
29 374 60		29 374 60				36
3 710 00		3 710 00				37
2 364 87		2 364 87				38
435 953 28	435 953 28	290 915 28	323 59000	145 038 00	112 363 28	39
		32 674 72			32 674 72	40
		323 590 00	323 590 00	145 038 00	145 038 00	41
						42

1 Close temporary accounts with balances in the Income Statement Credit column to Income Summary.

2 Close temporary accounts with balances in the Income Statement Debit column to Income Summary.

3 Close Income Summary to Retained Earnings by the amount of the net income or loss.

Figure 20–1
Closing Entries Needed for a Corporation

The sum of the balances in the Credit column of the Income Statement section of the work sheet, which includes revenue and contra cost of merchandise accounts, is the amount *credited* to **Income Summary.**

GENERAL JOURNAL PAGE ___23___

	DATE	DESCRIPTION	POST. REF.	DEBIT	CREDIT	
1	20--	*Closing Entries*				1
2	Dec. 31	Sales		320 450 00		2
3		Purchases Discounts		1 340 00		3
4		Purchases Returns and Allow.		1 800 00		4
5		Income Summary			323 590 00	5
6						6

After this closing entry is journalized and posted, the **Sales, Purchases Discounts,** and **Purchases Returns and Allowances** accounts have zero balances.

2. Close the accounts with balances in the Debit column of the Income Statement section of the work sheet (contra revenue, cost of merchandise, and expense accounts) to **Income Summary.**

Income Summary	
Debit	Credit
Adj. 3,536.00	Clos. 323,590.00
Clos. 287,379.28	

Insurance Expense	
Debit +	Credit −
Bal. 125.00	Clos. 125.00

Sales Discounts	
Debit +	Credit −
Bal. 730.00	Clos. 730.00

Maintenance Expense	
Debit +	Credit −
Bal. 3,519.25	Clos. 3,519.25

Sales Returns and Allowances	
Debit +	Credit −
Bal. 2,000.00	Clos. 2,000.00

Miscellaneous Expense	
Debit +	Credit −
Bal. 348.28	Clos. 348.28

Purchases	
Debit +	Credit −
Bal. 206,700.00	Clos. 206,700.00

Payroll Tax Expense	
Debit +	Credit −
Bal. 3,826.83	Clos. 3,826.83

Transportation In	
Debit +	Credit −
Bal. 4,036.18	Clos. 4,036.18

Rent Expense	
Debit +	Credit −
Bal. 14,000.00	Clos. 14,000.00

Advertising Expense	
Debit +	Credit −
Bal. 2,450.00	Clos. 2,450.00

Salaries Expense	
Debit +	Credit −
Bal. 29,374.60	Clos. 29,374.60

Bankcard Fees Expense

Debit +	Credit −
Bal. 4,199.27	Clos. 4,199.27

Supplies Expense

Debit +	Credit −
Bal. 3,710.00	Clos. 3,710.00

Federal Corporate Income Tax Expense

Debit +	Credit −
Bal. 9,995.00	Clos. 9,995.00

Utilities Expense

Debit +	Credit −
Bal. 2,364.87	Clos. 2,364.87

GENERAL JOURNAL PAGE __23__

	DATE		DESCRIPTION	POST. REF.	DEBIT	CREDIT	
6	Dec.	31	Income Summary		287 379 28		6
7			Sales Discounts			7 30 00	7
8			Sales Returns and Allow.			2 000 00	8
9			Purchases			206 700 00	9
10			Transportation In			4 036 18	10
11			Advertising Expense			2 450 00	11
12			Bankcard Fees Expense			4 199 27	12
13			Fed. Corp. Inc. Tax Expense			9 995 00	13
14			Insurance Expense			1 25 00	14
15			Maintenance Expense			3 519 25	15
16			Miscellaneous Expense			3 18 38	16
17			Payroll Tax Expense			3 826 83	17
18			Rent Expense			14 000 00	18
19			Salaries Expense			29 374 60	19
20			Supplies Expense			3 710 00	20
21			Utilities Expense			2 364 87	21
22							22

After this closing entry is journalized and posted, contra revenue, cost of merchandise, and expense accounts have zero balances.

After the two preceding closing entries are journalized and posted, **Income Summary** has a credit balance of $32,674.72.

$ 323,590.00   closing credit
−   3,536.00   adjustment debit
−287,379.28   closing debit
$ 32,674.72   credit balance

3. Close **Income Summary** to **Retained Earnings**.

Income Summary

Debit	Credit
Adj. 3,536.00	Clos. 323,590.00
Clos. 287,379.28	
Clos. 32,674.72	

Retained Earnings

Debit −	Credit +
	Bal. 19,771.19
	Clos. 32,674.72

After the entry to close **Income Summary** to **Retained Earnings** is journalized and posted, **Income Summary** has a zero balance. The balance of **Retained Earnings** is increased to $52,445.91.

DATE		DESCRIPTION	POST. REF.	DEBIT	CREDIT	
22	Dec. 31	Income Summary		32 6 7 4 72		22
23		Retained Earnings			32 6 7 4 72	23
24						24

Closing Entry to Transfer a Net Loss

Sometimes businesses incur net losses. For example, suppose the **Income Summary** account of a business after posting the first two entries closing the temporary accounts is as follows:

Income Summary

Debit	Credit
Adj. 3,612.00	Clos. 63,790.00
Clos. 65,178.00	

Before it is closed, **Income Summary** has a debit balance of $5,000.00:

$$\begin{array}{rl} \$\;3,612.00 & \text{adjustment debit} \\ +\;\;65,178.00 & \text{closing debit} \\ -\;\;63,790.00 & \text{closing credit} \\ \hline \$\;5,000.00 & \text{debit balance} \end{array}$$

To close **Income Summary**, it is credited for $5,000. **Retained Earnings** is debited for $5,000. The earnings retained by the business are *decreased* by the amount of the net loss. This closing entry is recorded in the general journal as follows:

DATE		DESCRIPTION	POST. REF.	DEBIT	CREDIT	
1		Closing Entries				1
22	Dec. 31	Retained Earnings		5 0 0 0 00		22
23		Income Summary			5 0 0 0 00	23
24						24

ACCOUNTING TIPS

Entrepreneurs

Entrepreneurs often try more than once to become successful. The owner of Laugh-O-Gram Corporation in Kansas City did so poorly that he filed for bankruptcy after two years. Not discouraged, the owner decided to try again. Walt Disney left Kansas City in 1923 for Hollywood with all his belongings—one set of clothes and some drawings.

A MATTER OF ETHICS

Handling Sales Returns

Most retail stores give employees specific instructions on how to process a sales return. For example, a cash refund can only be given if cash was paid. Imagine that you work for a large sporting goods store like The Sports Authority. Your friend, Martin, comes in to return a sweatshirt he purchased recently. You know he purchased the sweatshirt on sale, but he wants you to give him a full refund.

Ethical Decision Making:

☞ What are the ethical issues?

☞ What are the alternatives?

☞ Who are the affected parties?

☞ How do the alternatives affect the parties?

☞ What would you do?

Now that you have studied this section, complete the following questions and problems.

Thinking Critically

1. During the closing process, which account balances are credited to the **Income Summary** account? Which account balances are debited to the **Income Summary** account?
2. When a business has a net loss, the **Retained Earnings** account is debited for the loss during the closing process. Explain why.

Communicating Accounting

As you are completing the closing entries for the fourth quarter, you realize that your company, Dynamic Sound, has a net loss. You know that your boss is not aware that the fourth quarter financial statements are so bleak. Practice an explanation to your boss of how the **Income Summary** and **Retained Earnings** accounts are affected by the loss. Select a partner from your class and ask him or her to critique your style of delivery and the accuracy of your explanation.

Problem 20–1 Identifying Accounts Affected by Closing Entries

The following account names appear in the chart of accounts of Larkin's Department Store.

General Ledger

Accounts Receivable	Purchases
Bankcard Fees Expense	Purchases Discounts
Capital Stock	Purchases Returns and Allowances
Cash in Bank	Retained Earnings
Equipment	Sales
Fed. Corp. Income Tax Expense	Sales Discounts
Fed. Corp. Income Tax Payable	Sales Returns and Allowances
Income Summary	Sales Tax Payable
Insurance Expense	Supplies
Merchandise Inventory	Supplies Expense
Miscellaneous Expense	Transportation In
Prepaid Insurance	Utilities Expense

Instructions Use the form in your working papers to answer the following questions about each account. Assume that all accounts have normal balances.
(1) Is the account affected by a closing entry?
(2) During closing, is the account debited or credited?
(3) During closing, is **Income Summary** debited or credited?

Posting Closing Entries

- How to post closing entries.
- How to prepare a post-closing trial balance.
- The accounting cycle for a merchandising business.

Why It's Important

To prepare the general ledger for the next period, you need to transfer the temporary account balances to the permanent **Retained Earnings** account.

Key Points

Posting to the General Ledger

Use a systematic procedure when posting. Begin with the date of the transaction. Continue posting by moving from the left of the account to the right. Remember to enter the account number in the Posting Reference column of the journal after you post a transaction to the ledger.

After closing entries are recorded in the general journal, they are posted to the general ledger.

Closing the General Ledger

Figure 20–2 shows the portion of On Your Mark's general ledger affected by the closing process after the closing entries have been posted. For each posting the term "Closing Entry" is written in the Description column of the general ledger account.

ACCOUNT *Retained Earnings*   ACCOUNT NO. *305*

DATE		DESCRIPTION	POST. REF.	DEBIT	CREDIT	BALANCE DEBIT	BALANCE CREDIT
20--							
Dec.	1	Balance	✓				19 7 7 1 19
	31	Clos. Ent.	G23		32 6 7 4 72		52 4 4 5 91

ACCOUNT *Income Summary*   ACCOUNT NO. *310*

DATE		DESCRIPTION	POST. REF.	DEBIT	CREDIT	BALANCE DEBIT	BALANCE CREDIT
20--							
Dec.	31	Adj. Ent	G22	3 5 3 6 00		3 5 3 6 00	
	31	Clos. Ent.	G23		323 5 9 0 00		320 0 5 4 00
	31	Clos. Ent.	G23	287 3 7 9 28			32 6 7 4 72
	31	Clos. Ent.	G23	32 6 7 4 72			

ACCOUNT *Sales*   ACCOUNT NO. *401*

DATE		DESCRIPTION	POST. REF.	DEBIT	CREDIT	BALANCE DEBIT	BALANCE CREDIT
20--							
Dec.	1	Balance	✓				300 0 0 0 00
	31		S12		10 7 5 0 00		310 7 5 0 00
	31		CR13		9 7 0 0 00		320 4 5 0 00
	31	Clos. Ent.	G23	320 4 5 0 00			

Figure 20–2 Partial General Ledger at the End of the Fiscal Period

ACCOUNT *Sales Discounts*   **ACCOUNT NO.** 405

DATE	DESCRIPTION	POST. REF.	DEBIT	CREDIT	BALANCE DEBIT	BALANCE CREDIT
20--						
Dec. 1	Balance	✓			700 00	
31		CR13	30 00		730 00	
31	Clos. Ent.	G23		730 00		

ACCOUNT *Sales Returns and Allowances*   **ACCOUNT NO.** 410

DATE	DESCRIPTION	POST. REF.	DEBIT	CREDIT	BALANCE DEBIT	BALANCE CREDIT
20--						
Dec. 1	Balance	✓			1 850 00	
4		G20	150 00		2 000 00	
31	Clos. Ent.	G23		2 000 00		

ACCOUNT *Purchases*   **ACCOUNT NO.** 501

DATE	DESCRIPTION	POST. REF.	DEBIT	CREDIT	BALANCE DEBIT	BALANCE CREDIT
20--						
Dec. 1	Balance	✓			190 000 00	
19		CP14	1 300 00		191 300 00	
31		P12	15 400 00		206 700 00	
31	Clos. Ent.	G23		206 700 00		

ACCOUNT *Transportation In*   **ACCOUNT NO.** 505

DATE	DESCRIPTION	POST. REF.	DEBIT	CREDIT	BALANCE DEBIT	BALANCE CREDIT
20--						
Dec. 1	Balance	✓			3 761 18	
24		CP14	275 00		4 036 18	
31	Clos. Ent.	G23		4 036 18		

ACCOUNT *Purchases Discounts*   **ACCOUNT NO.** 510

DATE	DESCRIPTION	POST. REF.	DEBIT	CREDIT	BALANCE DEBIT	BALANCE CREDIT
20						
Dec. 1	Balance	✓				1 200 00
31		CP14		140 00		1 340 00
31	Clos. Ent.	G23	1 340 00			

ACCOUNT *Purchases Returns and Allowances*   **ACCOUNT NO.** 515

DATE	DESCRIPTION	POST. REF.	DEBIT	CREDIT	BALANCE DEBIT	BALANCE CREDIT
20--						
Dec. 1	Balance	✓				1 600 00
16		G21		200 00		1 800 00
31	Clos. Ent.	G23	1 800 00			

Figure 20–2 Partial General Ledger at the End of the Fiscal Period (continued)

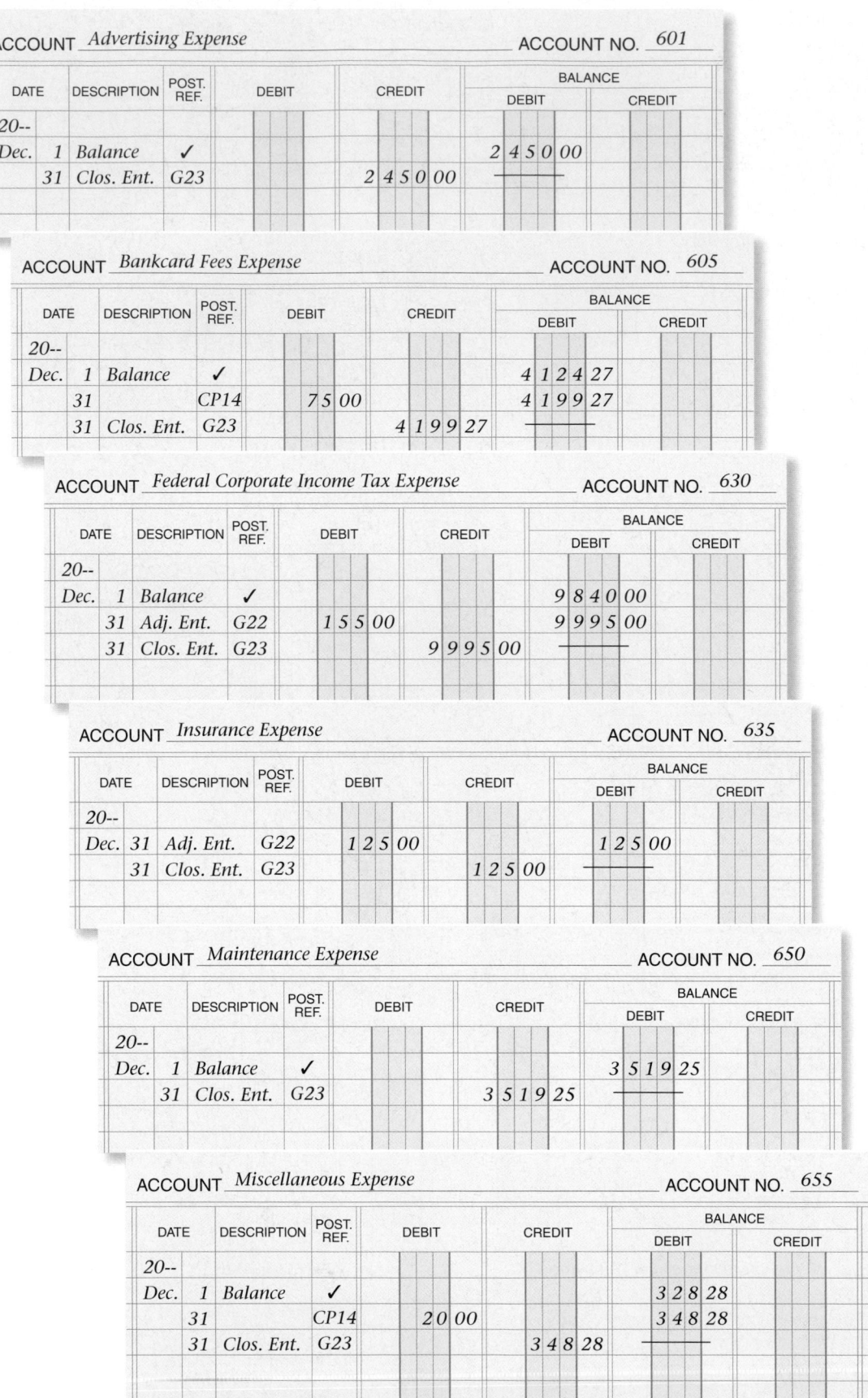

ACCOUNT Advertising Expense   **ACCOUNT NO.** 601

DATE	DESCRIPTION	POST. REF.	DEBIT	CREDIT	BALANCE DEBIT	BALANCE CREDIT
20--						
Dec. 1	Balance	✓			2 4 5 0 00	
31	Clos. Ent.	G23		2 4 5 0 00	—	

ACCOUNT Bankcard Fees Expense   **ACCOUNT NO.** 605

DATE	DESCRIPTION	POST. REF.	DEBIT	CREDIT	BALANCE DEBIT	BALANCE CREDIT
20--						
Dec. 1	Balance	✓			4 1 2 4 27	
31		CP14	7 5 00		4 1 9 9 27	
31	Clos. Ent.	G23		4 1 9 9 27	—	

ACCOUNT Federal Corporate Income Tax Expense   **ACCOUNT NO.** 630

DATE	DESCRIPTION	POST. REF.	DEBIT	CREDIT	BALANCE DEBIT	BALANCE CREDIT
20--						
Dec. 1	Balance	✓			9 8 4 0 00	
31	Adj. Ent.	G22	1 5 5 00		9 9 9 5 00	
31	Clos. Ent.	G23		9 9 9 5 00	—	

ACCOUNT Insurance Expense   **ACCOUNT NO.** 635

DATE	DESCRIPTION	POST. REF.	DEBIT	CREDIT	BALANCE DEBIT	BALANCE CREDIT
20--						
Dec. 31	Adj. Ent.	G22	1 2 5 00		1 2 5 00	
31	Clos. Ent.	G23		1 2 5 00	—	

ACCOUNT Maintenance Expense   **ACCOUNT NO.** 650

DATE	DESCRIPTION	POST. REF.	DEBIT	CREDIT	BALANCE DEBIT	BALANCE CREDIT
20--						
Dec. 1	Balance	✓			3 5 1 9 25	
31	Clos. Ent.	G23		3 5 1 9 25	—	

ACCOUNT Miscellaneous Expense   **ACCOUNT NO.** 655

DATE	DESCRIPTION	POST. REF.	DEBIT	CREDIT	BALANCE DEBIT	BALANCE CREDIT
20--						
Dec. 1	Balance	✓			3 2 8 28	
31		CP14	2 0 00		3 4 8 28	
31	Clos. Ent.	G23		3 4 8 28	—	

Figure 20–2 Partial General Ledger at the End of the Fiscal Period (continued)

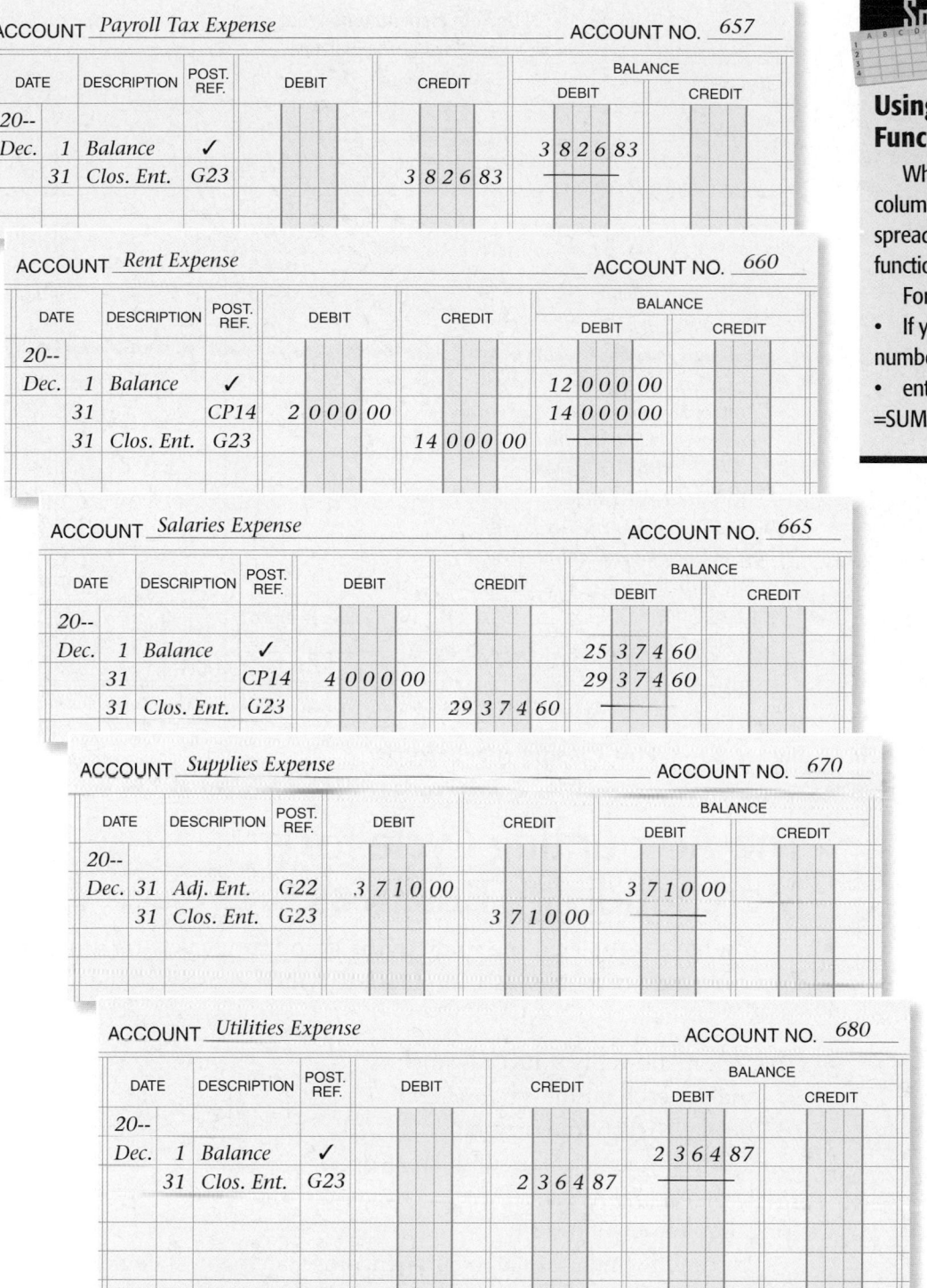

Figure 20–2 Partial General Ledger at the End of the Fiscal Period (continued)

Preparing a Post-Closing Trial Balance

A post-closing trial balance is prepared at the end of the accounting period to prove that the general ledger accounts are in balance after all adjusting and closing entries are posted. **Figure 20–3** shows the post-closing trial balance for On Your Mark.

Key Points

Post-Closing Trial Balance

The same account balances appear on both the post-closing trial balance and the balance sheet.

On Your Mark Athletic Wear
Post-Closing Trial Balance
December 31, 20--

Cash in Bank	15 1 7 9 00	
Accounts Receivable	10 4 0 4 00	
Merchandise Inventory	81 3 8 5 00	
Supplies	1 8 3 9 00	
Prepaid Insurance	1 3 7 5 00	
Delivery Equipment	19 8 3 1 00	
Office Equipment	9 8 2 5 00	
Store Equipment	5 2 0 0 00	
Accounts Payable		13 8 5 0 00
Fed. Corp. Income Tax Payable		1 5 5 00
Employees' Fed. Income Tax Payable		6 4 0 00
Employees' State Income Tax Payable		8 0 00
Social Security Tax Payable		2 4 8 00
Medicare Tax Payable		5 8 00
Fed. Unemployment Tax Payable		1 8 36
State Unemployment Tax Payable		1 1 4 73
Sales Tax Payable		2 4 2 8 00
Capital Stock		75 0 0 0 00
Retained Earnings		52 4 4 5 91
Totals	145 0 3 8 00	145 0 3 8 00

Figure 20–3 Post-Closing Trial Balance

The Accounting Cycle for a Merchandising Business

You have completed the study of the accounting cycle for a merchandising business organized as a corporation, which consists of the following steps:

1. Collect and verify source documents.
2. Analyze each business transaction.
3. Journalize each transaction.
4. Post to the general and subsidiary ledgers.
5. Prepare a trial balance.
6. Complete a work sheet.
7. Prepare the financial statements—income statement, statement of retained earnings, and balance sheet.
8. Journalize and post the adjusting entries.
9. Journalize and post the closing entries.
10. Prepare a post-closing trial balance.

The accounting cycle for other types of businesses, such as a service business, would follow the same steps. Also, regardless of how a business is organized—sole proprietorship, partnership, or corporation—the basic steps of the accounting cycle are the same. **Figure 20–4** illustrates the accounting cycle.

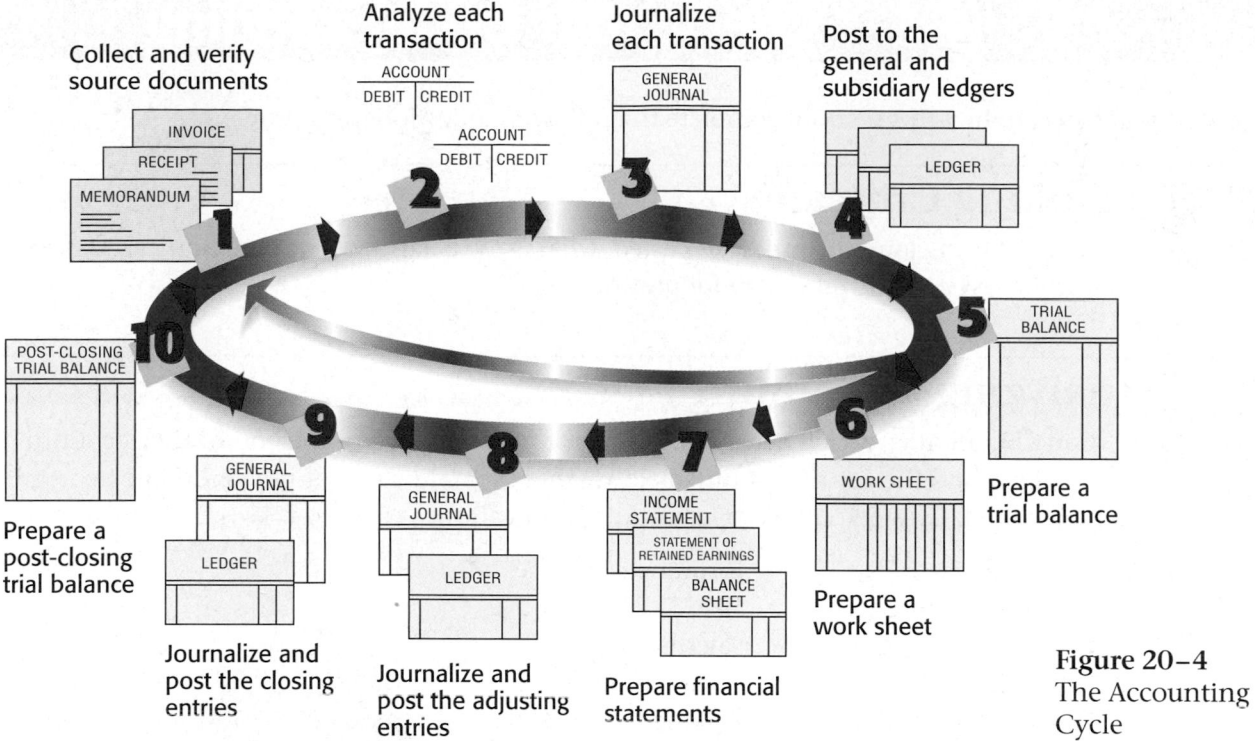

Collect and verify source documents

INVOICE
RECEIPT
MEMORANDUM

Analyze each transaction

ACCOUNT
DEBIT | CREDIT

ACCOUNT
DEBIT | CREDIT

Journalize each transaction

GENERAL JOURNAL

Post to the general and subsidiary ledgers

LEDGER

TRIAL BALANCE

Prepare a trial balance

WORK SHEET

Prepare a work sheet

INCOME STATEMENT
STATEMENT OF RETAINED EARNINGS
BALANCE SHEET

Prepare financial statements

GENERAL JOURNAL
LEDGER

Journalize and post the adjusting entries

GENERAL JOURNAL
LEDGER

Journalize and post the closing entries

POST-CLOSING TRIAL BALANCE

Prepare a post-closing trial balance

Figure 20–4
The Accounting Cycle

The accounting system used, whether manual or computerized, does not affect the steps in the accounting cycle. In a computerized accounting system, however, many of the routine procedures, such as posting, are performed by the computer.

Now that you have studied this section, complete the following questions and problems.

Thinking Critically

1. After all closing journal entries are posted, what is the balance of the temporary accounts?
2. Describe a systematic procedure for posting.

Analyzing Accounting

Can you identify which general ledger accounts are closed at the end of the accounting period? Examine the list of accounts below. On a separate sheet of paper, list the accounts that are closed. Group your lists by account classification.

Rent Expense	Insurance Expense
Delivery Equipment	Sales
Cash in Bank	Sales Discounts
Purchases	Notes Payable
Transportation In	Retained Earnings
Salaries Expense	

Problem 20–2 Analyzing a Source Document

Instructions Review the source document and prepare the journal entry to record this transaction in your working papers. Your Backpack Inc. uses a cash payments journal to record disbursements.

Your Backpack Inc.
29000 White Road
Cold Springs, TX 77282-4513

MEMORANDUM
No. 42

TO: Robert Chan, Chief Accountant
FROM: James Perkins, President
DATE: July 12, 20--
SUBJECT: New Storage Facility Rent

Would you please make a check out to Warehouse Inc. for $750. The check is for the new storage facility we are renting. Please mail the check to:

Mr. James Skiller, Controller
Warehouse Inc.
7576 County Line Highway
Crossplains, TX 77361-8411

Problem 20–3 Organizing the Steps in the Accounting Cycle

Instructions List the following steps of the accounting cycle in their proper order. Use the form provided in your working papers or a separate sheet of paper.

Analyzing business transactions	Journalizing and posting closing entries
Collecting and verifying source documents	Posting journal entries to ledgers
Completing the work sheet	Preparing financial statements
Journalizing business transactions	Preparing a post-closing trial balance
Journalizing and posting adjusting entries	Preparing a trial balance

KEY CONCEPTS

1. Closing entries are made to transfer the balances of the temporary accounts to the permanent **Retained Earnings** account.

2. The information for journalizing closing entries is taken from the Income Statement section of the work sheet.

3. Four entries are made to close the temporary general ledger accounts of a sole proprietorship:
   - close the temporary accounts with credit balances to **Income Summary**
   - close the temporary accounts with debit balances to **Income Summary**
   - close the balance of **Income Summary** to capital
   - close the withdrawals account to capital

4. The first closing entry:

   Debit: All temporary accounts with credit balances

   Credit: **Income Summary**

5. The second closing entry:

   Debit: **Income Summary**

   Credit: All temporary accounts with debit balances

6. The third closing entry:

   Close the balance of **Income Summary** to the **Retained Earnings** account.

Net Income	Net Loss
Debit: **Income Summary**	Debit: **Retained Earnings**
Credit: **Retained Earnings**	Credit: **Income Summary**

7. After posting the closing entries, prepare a post-closing trial balance. The post-closing trial balance contains only Balance Sheet (permanent) accounts.

8. The temporary accounts are ready for the next accounting period after the closing entries are posted.

9. The Accounting Cycle

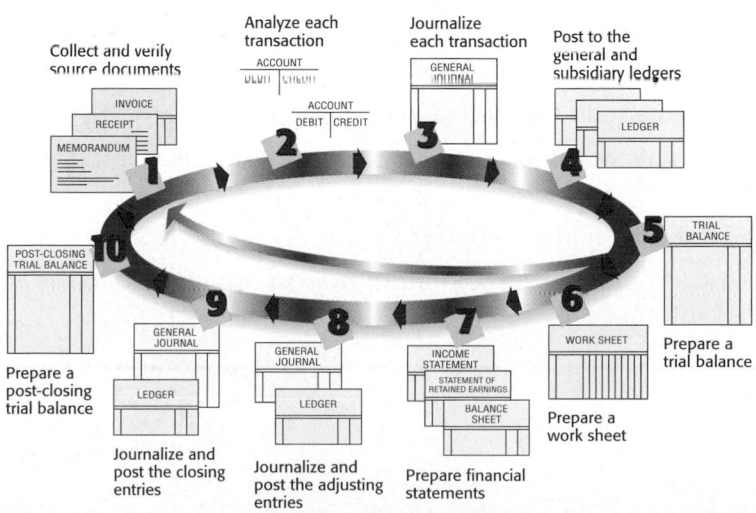

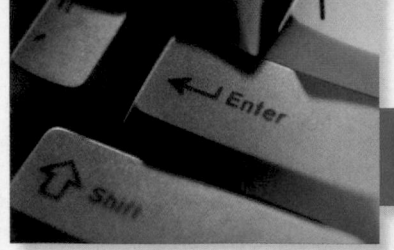

USING KEY TERMS

The following key terms were introduced in Chapter 10. Let's review the terms as they relate to a merchandising corporation such as Bose Corporation. What differences exist between the closing entries for a sole proprietorship and the closing entries for a merchandising corporation? Use the following terms in your explanation.

closing entries	temporary accounts
permanent accounts	

Understanding Accounting Concepts and Procedures

Instructions

On a separate sheet of paper, answer the following questions:

1. What is the purpose of closing entries?

2. Where can you find the information needed to prepare the closing entries?

3. Explain the closing entries for a business organized as a corporation.

4. Why is **Retained Earnings** credited when the business earns a profit?

5. Why is **Retained Earnings** debited when the business has a net loss?

6. Which type of general ledger accounts appear on the post-closing trial balance? On which financial statement do these accounts appear?

7. Does the **Income Summary** account appear on the post-closing trial balance? Why or why not?

8. Name the ten steps in the accounting cycle.

9. When using a computerized accounting system, which tasks in the accounting cycle are performed automatically?

Case Study...

Merchandising Business: Department Store

Pearl's is a department store chain located throughout the southeastern United States. It is known for trendy women's wear and elegant home furnishings.

You work in the accounting department in the Fort Lauderdale location. Your manager asks you to review the work completed by an accounting intern. The intern prepared financial statements and completed the closing process. When looking at the post-closing trial balance, the manager noticed that some of the temporary accounts still have balances.

Thinking Critically:

1. How would you determine which accounts should have zero balances after closing?
2. How would you determine which accounts are closed and which are not?
3. What would you say to the intern to explain why temporary accounts have zero balances after closing?
4. What human-relations skills might you use in your explanation to the intern?

Conducting an Audit with Alex

Mr. Raheev Singh's accountant made the following closing entry.

GENERAL JOURNAL   PAGE ___45___

	DATE	DESCRIPTION	POST. REF.	DEBIT	CREDIT	
1	20--					1
2	Dec. 31	Income Summary		17 000 00		2
3		Purchases Discounts			8 000 00	3
4		Purchases Ret. and Allow.			3 200 00	4
5		Sales Discounts			2 300 00	5
6		Sales Returns and Allow.			3 500 00	6
7						7

Instructions Review the closing entry. On a separate sheet of paper, prepare the closing entries that the accountant should have made.

interNET CONNECTION

Financial Accounting Standards Board

The Financial Accounting Standards Board (FASB) serves an important role in determining how financial information is reported to owners and managers and to stockholders.

Do This:

1. Locate the FASB Web site to learn more about the FASB's work.
2. What is the mission of the FASB?
3. When was the FASB established?
4. List at least three ways the FASB works to achieve its mission.
5. Can an accountant serve on the FASB and continue to work as a practicing accountant?

Workplace Skills

Maintaining and Troubleshooting Technologies

Maintaining and troubleshooting technological equipment is the job of a computer technician. It is also the responsibility of every person who owns or operates computer equipment. To be competent with technology, you should be able to detect problems, generate solutions, and know when to get assistance.

On the Job:

In the accounting department of KidsWear Inc., you are responsible for processing the closing entries. This morning you are having problems with the printer—you are not getting printouts of the ledgers or journals.

Thinking Critically:

What steps do you need to take to troubleshoot this problem? Write down each step and prioritize your list. In one column indicate whom you should call if you can't resolve the problem after each step is completed.

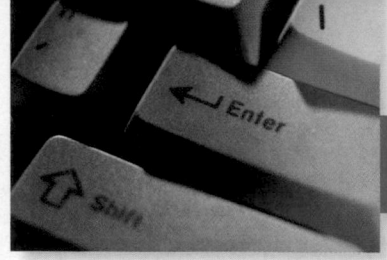

Closing the Fiscal Year

Making the Transition from a Manual to a Computerized System

Task	Perform Accounting Procedures Using Manual Methods	Perform Accounting Procedures Using Automated Methods
Closing a fiscal year	1. Journalize the entry to close the revenue, expense, Income Summary, and Withdrawals accounts. 2. Post the closing entries.	1. Closing the fiscal year is only performed if you want to clear income and expense accounts at the end of the fiscal year. 2. If you have selected the closing option, closing entries are journalized for you.
Post-closing trial balance	1. After the closing entries have been posted to the ledger, prepare a trial balance to verify the equality of debits and credits. 2. All expense and revenue accounts should have zero balances.	1. A post-closing trial balance can be printed to verify that all revenue and expense accounts have been closed.

Closing the Accounting Period

Peachtree Question	Description
What is the difference between changing an accounting period and closing a fiscal year?	1. Typically you will *change* an accounting period when moving from one month to another. 2. You will *close* a fiscal year at the end of a calendar or fiscal year.
What tasks should I perform before closing a fiscal year?	1. Post and print all journal entries before you close the fiscal year. 2. Back up all files before closing. Closing the fiscal year cannot be reversed.
How do I close the fiscal year?	1. From the *Tasks* menu, select **System**. 2. Choose Year-End Wizard. 3. You will be prompted if any procedures need to be completed before the system continues the closing process.
What does the software do "behind the scenes"?	1. Peachtree detects any unposted entries and reminds you to print reports. 2. Peachtree reminds you to back up your files before closing. 3. When you close the fiscal period, the software will create closing entries and post them. All income and expense account balances will be transferred to the **Retained Earnings** account.

For detailed instructions: See the **Peachtree User Guide** in your Glencoe Working Papers.

APPLICATION OPTIONS

Problem 20–4 Journalizing Closing Entries

The following amounts appeared in the Income Statement section of Sunset Surfwear's work sheet.

Instructions In your working papers, record the closing entries for the year ended December 31. Start with general journal page 13.

Complete chapter problems one of four ways:

1 **Manual** Glencoe Working Papers

or

2 **Peachtree Complete Accounting** Software

or

3 **QuickBooks** Templates (Problems 20–5, 20–8)

or

4 **Spreadsheet** Templates (Problem 20–7)

Peachtree®

SMART GUIDE

Step–by–Step Instructions: Problem 20–4

1. Select the problem set for Sunset Surfwear (Prob. 20–4).
2. Rename the company and set the system date.
3. Choose **System** from the **Tasks** menu and then select **Year-End Wizard** to close the fiscal year.
4. Print a Post-Closing Trial Balance.
5. Answer the Analyze question.
6. End the session.

	ACCT. NO.	ACCOUNT NAME	INCOME STATEMENT	
			DEBIT	CREDIT
13	310	Income Summary		7 000 00
14	401	Sales		90 000 00
15	405	Sales Discounts	1 000 00	
16	410	Sales Returns and Allowances	2 400 00	
17	501	Purchases	25 000 00	
18	505	Transportation In	3 000 00	
19	510	Purchases Discounts		500 00
20	515	Purchases Returns and Allowances		1 500 00
21	625	Federal Corporate Income Tax Exp.	5 532 00	
22	635	Insurance Expense	300 00	
23	650	Miscellaneous Expense	600 00	
24	655	Rent Expense	12 000 00	
25	665	Supplies Expense	450 00	
26	675	Utilities Expense	14 000 00	
27			69 682 00	99 000 00
28		Net Income	29 318 00	
29			99 000 00	99 000 00
30				

Analyze: What is the effect of the closing entries on the **Retained Earnings** account?

Peachtree®

Problem 20–5 Journalizing and Posting Closing Entries

The following account balances appeared in the Income Statement section of the work sheet of Shutterbug Cameras.

Instructions

(1) Journalize the closing entries for the year ended December 31. Start with page 14 of a general journal (in your working papers).

(2) Post the closing entries to the general ledger accounts, which are included in your working papers.

	ACCT. NO.	ACCOUNT NAME	INCOME STATEMENT DEBIT	INCOME STATEMENT CREDIT
20	310	Income Summary	4 000 00	
21	401	Sales		150 000 00
22	410	Sales Returns and Allowances	5 000 00	
23	501	Purchases	90 000 00	
24	505	Transportation In	5 000 00	
25	510	Purchases Discounts		1 000 00
26	515	Purchases Returns and Allowances		1 500 00
27	620	Federal Corporate Income Tax Exp.	4 700 00	
28	645	Miscellaneous Expense	300 00	
29	650	Rent Expense	6 000 00	
30	660	Supplies Expense	1 630 00	
31	670	Utilities Expense	3 000 00	
32			119 630 00	152 500 00
33		Net Income	32 870 00	
34			152 500 00	152 500 00
35				

Analyze: What would happen if the accountant for Shutterbug Cameras made a mistake and did not close the **Transportation In** account?

Problem 20–6 Identifying Accounts for Closing Entries

The following is a partial list of the accounts used by Cycle Tech Bicycles. All of the accounts have nonzero balances.

General Ledger

    101 Cash in Bank
    650 Miscellaneous Expense
    125 Merchandise Inventory
    665 Supplies Expense
    215 Sales Tax Payable
    505 Transportation In
    305 Retained Earnings
    401 Sales
    405 Sales Discounts
    310 Income Summary
    501 Purchases
    515 Purchases Returns and Allowances
    601 Advertising Expense
    625 Federal Corporate Income Tax Expense
    657 Rent Expense
    135 Prepaid Insurance

Peachtree®

SMART GUIDE

Step–by–Step Instructions: Problem 20–6

1. Select the problem set for Cycle Tech Bicycles (Prob. 20–6).
2. Rename the company and set the system date.
3. Print a Chart of Accounts report.
4. List the accounts that will be debited and those that will be credited when closed.
5. Answer the Analyze question.
6. End the session.

Instructions In your working papers, list all the account numbers and names for accounts that will be debited when closed. Next, list all the account numbers and names for accounts that will be credited when closed.

Analyze: Did you list all of the accounts? If not, why?

 **Problem 20–7 Completing End-of-Period Activities**

The general ledger accounts for River's Edge Canoe & Kayak as of December 31, the end of the period, appear in the working papers.

SPREADSHEET SMART GUIDE

Step–by–Step Instructions: Problem 20–7

1. Select the spreadsheet template for Problem 20–7.
2. Enter your name and the date in the spaces provided on the template.
3. Complete the spreadsheet using the instructions in your working papers.
4. Print the spreadsheet and proof your work.
5. Save your work and exit the spreadsheet program.

Instructions In your working papers:
(1) Prepare a trial balance on a ten-column work sheet.
(2) Complete the work sheet. Use the following adjustment information.

Merchandise inventory, December 31	$20,000
Supplies inventory, December 31	900
Unexpired insurance, December 31	1,800
Total federal corporate income taxes for the year	2,965

(3) Prepare an income statement from the work sheet information.
(4) Prepare a statement of retained earnings.
(5) Prepare a balance sheet.
(6) Journalize and post the adjusting entries. Begin on general journal page 14.
(7) Journalize and post the closing entries.
(8) Prepare a post-closing trial balance.

Analyze: Did the company make a profit for the year?

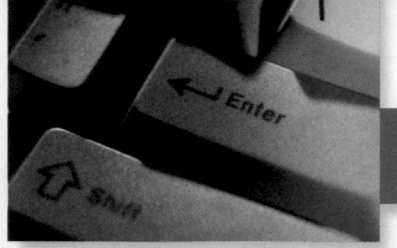

Peachtree®

SMART GUIDE

**Step–by–Step Instructions:
Problem 20–8**

1. Select the problem set for Buzz Newsstand (Prob. 20–8).
2. Rename the company and set the system date.
3. Print a Working Trial Balance to help you prepare the adjustments.
4. Record the adjustments using the **General Journal Entry** option.
5. Print a General Journal report and proof your work.
6. Answer the Analyze question.
7. Close the fiscal year.
8. Print a Post-Closing Trial Balance.
9. End the session.

TIP: Peachtree automatically updates the general ledger accounts when you close the fiscal year.

CHALLENGE PROBLEM

Problem 20–8 Preparing Adjusting and Closing Entries

In the middle of the end-of-period activities, the accountant for Buzz Newsstand was called away because of an illness in the family. Before leaving, the accountant prepared the work sheet and the financial statements. However, the business manager can only locate a trial balance (before adjustments) and the income statement.

Instructions In your working papers:

(1) Journalize the adjusting and closing entries on page 16 of the general journal.
(2) Using the information provided, prepare a post-closing trial balance.

	Buzz Newsstand		
	Trial Balance, Before Adjustments		
	December 31, 20--		
101	Cash in Bank	12 035 00	
115	Accounts Receivable	6 106 00	
130	Merchandise Inventory	64 800 00	
135	Supplies	3 916 00	
140	Prepaid Insurance	5 400 00	
145	Delivery Truck	46 106 00	
201	Accounts Payable		4 690 00
204	Fed. Corp. Income Tax Pay.		
215	Sales Tax Payable		416 00
301	Capital Stock		40 000 00
305	Retained Earnings		24 603 00
310	Income Summary		
401	Sales		299 156 00
410	Sales Returns and Allowances	9 500 00	
501	Purchases	168 624 00	
505	Transportation In	8 236 00	
510	Purchases Discounts		2 950 00
515	Purchases Returns and Allowances		2 108 00
601	Advertising Expense	4 000 00	
625	Fed. Corp. Income Tax Expense	12 500 00	
635	Insurance Expense		
650	Miscellaneous Expense	1 600 00	
660	Salaries Expense	26 900 00	
665	Supplies Expense		
675	Utilities Expense	4 200 00	
	Totals	373 923 00	373 923 00

Buzz Newsstand

Income Statement

For the Year Ended December 31, 20--

Revenue:					
Sales			299 1 5 6 00		
Less: Sales Ret. and Allow.			9 5 0 0 00		
Net Sales				289 6 5 6 00	
Cost of Merch. Sold:					
Merch. Inv., Jan 1, 20--			64 8 0 0 00		
Purchases	168 6 2 4 00				
Plus: Transportation In	8 2 3 6 00				
Cost of Del. Merch.		176 8 6 0 00			
Less: Purch. Discounts	2 9 5 0 00				
Purch. Ret. and Allow.	2 1 0 8 00	5 0 5 8 00			
Net Purchases			171 8 0 2 00		
Cost of Merch. Avail.			236 6 0 2 00		
Merch. Inv., Dec. 31, 20--			60 4 0 0 00		
Cost of Merch. Sold				176 2 0 2 00	
Gross Profit on Sales				113 4 5 4 00	
Operating Expenses:					
Advertising Expense			4 0 0 0 00		
Insurance Expense			1 8 0 0 00		
Miscellaneous Expense			1 6 0 0 00		
Salaries Expense			26 9 0 0 00		
Supplies Expense			2 7 4 4 00		
Utilities Expense			4 2 0 0 00		
Total Oper. Expenses				41 2 4 4 00	
Operating Income				72 2 1 0 00	
Less: Fed. Inc. Tax Exp.				14 9 1 3 00	
Net Income				57 2 9 7 00	

Analyze: What was the impact of adjusting entries on net income?

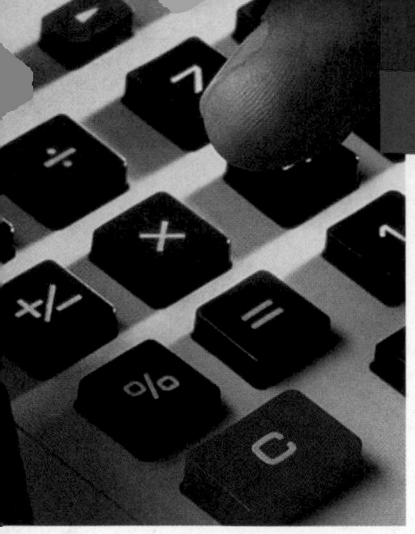

CHAPTER 21

Accounting for Publicly Held Corporations

Learning Objectives

When you have completed this chapter, you will be able to:

▶ Describe the characteristics of the corporate form of business organization.

▶ Prepare journal entries to record the issue of stock to investors.

▶ Prepare journal entries to record the distribution of earnings to owners.

▶ Prepare financial statements for publicly held corporations.

▶ Define the accounting terms introduced in this chapter.

Microsoft

Exploring the Real World of Business

EVALUATING CORPORATE STOCK

Computer technologies affect almost everything we do today—from banking to pumping gas at your local Shell station. Small business owners advertise on the Internet. Database technologies bring stock quotes, weather reports, and airline reservations to our fingertips. One of the biggest companies involved in this technology revolution is **Microsoft.**

Microsoft was started in 1975 by Bill Gates and Paul Allen, based on a belief that every business and home would one day have a personal computer. Rather than building the computer itself, they decided to focus on the software that would run the computer. **Microsoft's** Windows operating systems and computer applications are used in millions of personal computers today. **Microsoft** products are available in 40 languages and are sold in more than 60 countries.

As a public corporation, **Microsoft's** stock is traded on the National Association of Securities Dealers Automated Quotations (NASDAQ). Investors who are interested in buying stock can review the company's financial statements to analyze earnings and dividends paid to preferred stockholders over a period of years.

What do you think?

If you were considering buying stock in **Microsoft,** what financial information would you want to know about the company?

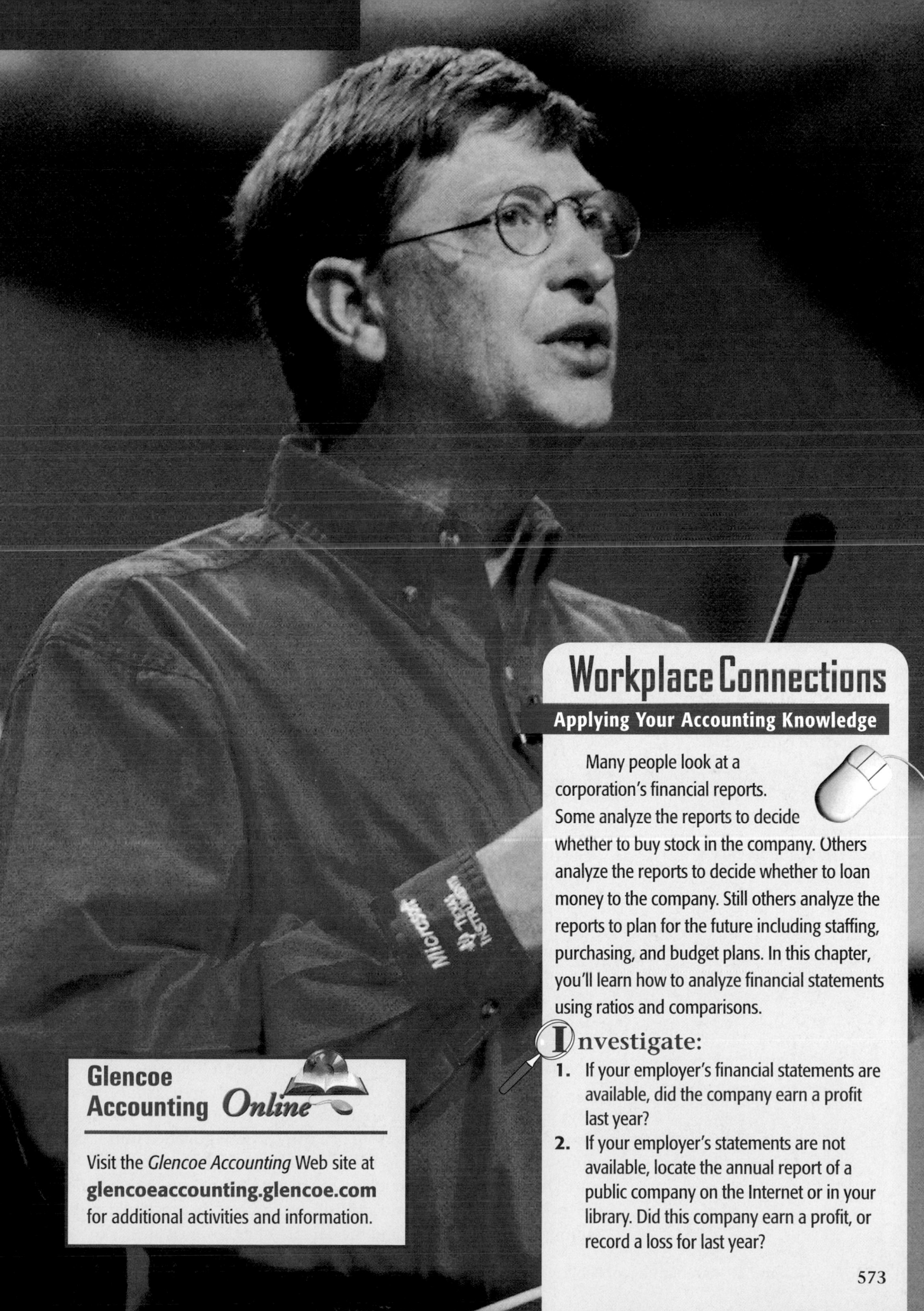

Workplace Connections

Applying Your Accounting Knowledge

Many people look at a corporation's financial reports. Some analyze the reports to decide whether to buy stock in the company. Others analyze the reports to decide whether to loan money to the company. Still others analyze the reports to plan for the future including staffing, purchasing, and budget plans. In this chapter, you'll learn how to analyze financial statements using ratios and comparisons.

Investigate:

1. If your employer's financial statements are available, did the company earn a profit last year?

2. If your employer's statements are not available, locate the annual report of a public company on the Internet or in your library. Did this company earn a profit, or record a loss for last year?

573

Publicly Held Corporations

In the United States, there are more sole proprietorships and partnerships than there are corporations. Corporations, however, account for more business activity than the other two forms of business combined. Many high profile companies like The Coca-Cola Company and General Motors are organized as corporations.

Publicly Held Corporations

In Chapters 14 to 20 you learned how to record the business transactions for a closely held corporation. **Closely held corporations** are corporations owned by a few persons or by a family. The stock of a closely held corporation is not sold to the general public.

In this chapter you will learn about another type of corporation—the publicly held corporation. A **publicly held corporation** is one whose stock is widely held, has a large market, and is usually traded on the New York Stock Exchange or the American Stock Exchange.

Characteristics of a Corporation

The corporation has several unique features:

- **Legal Permission to Operate**—To operate a business as a corporation, the incorporators (organizers) file an application with state officials for permission to operate. Once the application is approved, it becomes the corporation's charter. The charter indicates the purpose of the business and spells out the rules under which the business is to operate. The charter also states the type and amount of stock a corporation is authorized to issue.
- **Separate Legal Entity**—A corporation is a separate legal entity that is created and exists only by law. A corporation may enter into contracts, borrow money, and conduct business in the same manner as a person. It may acquire, own, and sell property in its name. It can also sue and be sued in the courts.
- **Stockholders**—The ownership of a corporation is divided into units called shares of stock. The owners of a corporation are called stockholders. Each stockholder receives a *stock certificate* as proof of ownership. The stock certificate lists the name of the stockholder, the number of shares issued, and the date the shares were issued.

- **Professional Management**—Stockholders own the corporation, but they do not manage it. The stockholders elect a **board of directors**, who govern and are responsible for the affairs of the corporation.

Stockholders' Equity

Stockholders' equity is the value of the stockholders' claims to the assets of the corporation. As you learned in Chapter 19, corporations report stockholders' equity in two parts:

- the equity that is paid into the corporation by stockholders
- the equity earned by the corporation and retained in the business

Let's look at how transactions affecting stockholders' equity are handled.

Capital Stock

The maximum number of shares a corporation may issue is called its **authorized capital stock**. The authorized number of shares is usually much greater than the number of shares the corporation plans to sell right away. This allows the corporation to sell additional shares at a later time.

State laws may require that an amount or value be assigned to each share of stock before it is sold to the public. The amount assigned to each share is referred to as **par value**, the per-share dollar amount printed on the stock certificates. The par value is used to determine the amount credited to the capital stock account. Par values of $1, $5, and $25 are common.

The corporate charter specifies the types of capital stock that a corporation may issue. The two main types of stock are common and preferred.

Common Stock

If the corporation issues only one class of capital stock, it is called **common stock**. The owners of common stock participate in the corporation as follows:

- Elect the board of directors and, through them, exercise control over the operations of the corporation. Stockholders are entitled to one vote for each share of stock they own. The election occurs at the stockholders' meeting, which is usually held once a year. If a stockholder cannot attend the meeting, he or she may send in a **proxy**, which gives the stockholder's voting rights to someone else.
- Share in the earnings of the corporation by receiving dividends declared by the board of directors.
- Entitled to share in the assets of the corporation if it goes out of business.

Preferred Stock

To appeal to as many investors as possible, a corporation may also issue preferred stock. **Preferred stock** has certain privileges (or preferences) over common stock. Preferred stockholders participate as follows:

- Entitled to receive dividends before common stockholders. The preferred stock dividend is stated in specific dollars, such as $6, or as a percentage of the stock's par value, such as 6 percent. The stock itself is then referred to as "preferred $6 stock" or "preferred 6% stock."
- Given preference over common stockholders to the assets of the corporation should it go out of business.

In return for these special privileges, the preferred stockholders give up the right to vote and to participate in the control of the corporation. Usually, investors buy preferred stock to receive the stated dividend.

Issuing Common Stock

When common stock is issued, the **Common Stock** account is credited for the par value of the stock. Let's look at some examples.

Issuing Common Stock at Par Value. When On Your Mark was incorporated, it had the following transaction.

Business Transaction

On January 3 On Your Mark Athletic Wear issued 10,000 shares of $10 par common stock at $10 per share. On Your Mark received $100,000 for the shares, Memorandum 3.

JOURNAL ENTRY

	DATE		DESCRIPTION	POST. REF.	DEBIT	CREDIT	
1	20--						1
2	Jan.	3	Cash in Bank		100 000 00		2
3			Common Stock			100 000 00	3
4			Memorandum 3				4
5							5

GENERAL JOURNAL   PAGE 46

Issuing Common Stock in Excess of Par Value. Investors are often willing to pay more than par value for the stock of a corporation. When a corporation sells its stock at a price that is above par, the excess over par is credited to a separate stockholders' equity account called **Paid-in Capital in Excess of Par**. Paid-in Capital in Excess of Par appears in the chart of accounts immediately following the **Common Stock** account. The amounts recorded in this account are not profits to the corporation. Rather, they represent part of the stockholders' investment in the corporation. This account follows the same rules of debit and credit as other stockholders' equity accounts.

Paid-in Capital in Excess of Par	
Debit	Credit
–	+
Decrease Side	Increase Side
	Normal Balance

One year after On Your Mark was incorporated, it had the following transaction.

On January 5 On Your Mark issued 5,000 shares of $10 par common stock at $11.50 per share, Memorandum 147. On Your Mark received $57,500 for the shares.

Before recording the transaction, determine how much of the $57,500 is credited to **Common Stock** and how much is credited to **Paid-in Capital in Excess of Par.**

Credit to **Common Stock:**
5,000 shares at $10 par value $50,000
Credit to **Paid-in Capital in Excess of Par:**
5,000 shares at $1.50
($11.50 issue price − $10.00 par value) per share   + 7,500
Total cash received $57,500

Remember, the amount credited to the **Common Stock** account is the par value of the shares issued.

JOURNAL ENTRY

		GENERAL JOURNAL			PAGE 99	
	DATE	DESCRIPTION	POST. REF.	DEBIT	CREDIT	
1	20--					1
2	Jan. 5	Cash in Bank		57 500 00		2
3		Common Stock			50 000 00	3
4		Paid-in Cap. in Ex. of Par			7 500 00	4
5		Memorandum 147				5
6						6

Issuing Preferred Stock

When preferred stock is issued, the **Preferred Stock** account is credited for the par value of the stock. Preferred stock is almost always issued at its par value.

On Your Mark was incorporated on January 3, and was authorized to issue 1,000 shares of preferred stock with a par value of $100 and a stated dividend of $6. The next day the company had the following transaction.

On January 4 On Your Mark issued 250 shares of preferred $6 stock, $100 par, at $100 per share. On Your Mark received $25,000 for the shares, Memorandum 5.

JOURNAL ENTRY

		GENERAL JOURNAL			PAGE 47	
	DATE	DESCRIPTION	POST. REF.	DEBIT	CREDIT	
1	20--					1
2	Jan. 4	Cash in Bank		25 000 00		2
3		Preferred Stock			25 000 00	3
4		Memorandum 5				4
5						5

SECTION 1 Check Your Understanding

Now that you have studied this section, complete the following questions and problems.

Thinking Critically

1. What is the difference between a closely held corporation and a publicly held corporation?
2. Describe the difference between common and preferred stock.

Communicating Accounting

You work for a locally owned partnership that was just purchased by a corporation. You decide to share information about corporations with your coworkers. Write a one-page information sheet identifying the characteristics of a corporation. Provide an explanation paragraph for each characteristic.

Problem 21–1 Examining Capital Stock Transactions

The Dublin Corporation was organized and authorized to issue 10,000 shares of $100 par, preferred 8% stock and 500,000 shares of $10 par common stock. The three transactions recorded in the following T accounts took place during the first month of operations.

Instructions In your working papers, describe each of the three transactions.

Cash in Bank

Debit +	Credit −
(1) 300,000	
(2) 200,000	
(3) 700,000	

Preferred Stock

Debit −	Credit +
	(2) 200,000

Common Stock

Debit −	Credit +
	(1) 300,000
	(3) 500,000

Paid-in Capital in Excess of Par

Debit −	Credit +
	(3) 200,000

Distributing the Earnings of a Corporation

In Section 1 you learned to record stock issue transactions for a corporation. In this section you will learn how corporations distribute earnings to the stockholders. Corporations like General Motors have a long history of distributing a portion of earnings to their stockholders every year, making their stock an attractive investment.

Dividends

When an owner of a sole proprietorship or a partnership wishes to take money out of the business, a check is written on the checking account of the business. The amount of the check is recorded as a debit in the owner's withdrawals account, which reduces the owner's equity.

The owners (stockholders) of a publicly held corporation cannot withdraw cash whenever they want. Instead, a **dividend** is a distribution of cash to stockholders. Dividends reduce retained earnings.

The corporation's board of directors declares, or authorizes, dividends. Before a dividend is declared, the corporation should have a sufficient amount of cash available to pay the dividend. In addition, since dividends decrease retained earnings, there must be an adequate balance in the **Retained Earnings** account. **Figure 21–1** illustrates the important dates in the dividend process.

A separate account named **Dividends** is used to record dividends declared. The **Dividends** account is a contra-stockholders' equity account. At the end of the year, the **Dividends** account is closed to the **Retained Earnings** account. The rules of debit and credit for **Dividends** are shown in the T account. Notice that they are the opposite of the rules for the stockholders' equity accounts.

Dividend amounts could be debited directly to the **Retained Earnings** account. Most corporations, however, prefer to use a separate account so that the dividend amounts can be easily determined.

A liability account, **Dividends Payable**, is used to record the amount of dividends that will be paid on the payment date. Like all liability accounts, **Dividends Payable** is increased by credits and decreased by debits. The normal balance of the **Dividends Payable** account is a credit balance.

Dividends	
Debit	Credit
+	−
Increase Side	Decrease Side
Normal Balance	

What You'll Learn

- Why and how corporations distribute their earnings.
- How to record dividends on preferred stock.
- How to record dividends on common stock.

Why It's Important

When the board of directors of a corporation decides to distribute profits in the form of dividends, a general journal entry is recorded.

KEY TERMS

dividend

CONNECT TO . . .
ENGLISH

In 1776, Adam Smith published *The Wealth of Nations.* In his book, the Scots professor argued that individual welfare was more important than national power, and that allowing people to struggle for their own wealth benefits everyone. This was the first written explanation of capitalism and laissez-faire economics.

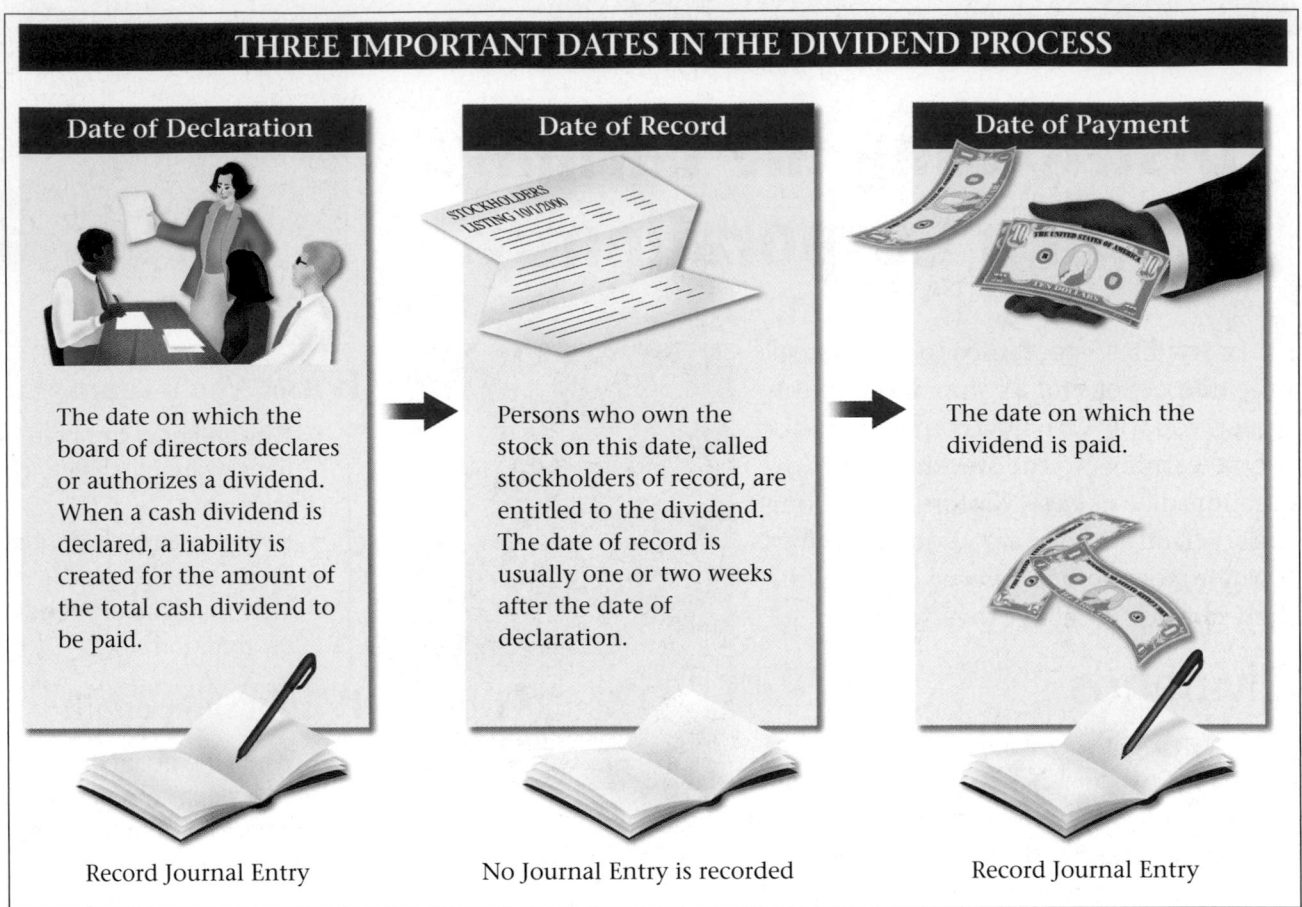

THREE IMPORTANT DATES IN THE DIVIDEND PROCESS

Date of Declaration

The date on which the board of directors declares or authorizes a dividend. When a cash dividend is declared, a liability is created for the amount of the total cash dividend to be paid.

Record Journal Entry

Date of Record

Persons who own the stock on this date, called stockholders of record, are entitled to the dividend. The date of record is usually one or two weeks after the date of declaration.

No Journal Entry is recorded

Date of Payment

The date on which the dividend is paid.

Record Journal Entry

Figure 21–1 Important Dates in the Dividend Process

If a corporation is authorized to issue two types of stock, separate dividend and dividend payable accounts are used for each type of stock. On Your Mark uses the following accounts:

Dividends—Preferred	**Dividends Payable—Preferred**
Dividends—Common	**Dividends Payable—Common**

Let's look at the transactions involved when dividends are declared by the board of directors of On Your Mark during its second year of incorporation.

Dividends on Preferred Stock

As mentioned earlier, preferred stockholders have certain preferences over common stockholders; one preference is the right to receive dividends before common stockholders. The amount of the dividend for preferred stock is predetermined or stated. The stated dividend indicates the amount that will be paid to preferred stockholders per year. On Your Mark issued 250 shares of preferred $6 stock. A $6 dividend will be paid for each share of preferred stock per year. The dividend amount can be paid annually, or in semiannual or quarterly installments.

	Dividend Payment	
Annually	$6.00	
Semiannually	$3.00	($6.00 ÷ 2)
Quarterly	$1.50	($6.00 ÷ 4)

Date of Declaration

A journal entry is made to record the dividend on preferred stock on the date of declaration.

Business Transaction

On November 15 the board of directors for On Your Mark declared an annual cash dividend on the 250 shares of preferred $6 stock issued. The dividend is payable to preferred stockholders of record on November 29. The dividend will be paid on December 15. The total amount of the preferred dividends is $1,500 (250 shares × $6), Memorandum 215.

JOURNAL ENTRY

	DATE		DESCRIPTION	POST. REF.	DEBIT	CREDIT	
1	20--						1
2	Nov.	15	Dividends—Preferred		1 500 00		2
3			Dividends Payable—Preferred			1 500 00	3
4			Memorandum 215				4
5							5

GENERAL JOURNAL — PAGE 72

Date of Record

On November 29 the corporation checks its records and prepares a list of preferred stockholders entitled to receive the dividend. No journal entry is required on this date.

Date of Payment

On December 15 a check for $1,500, the total amount of the dividend payable on preferred stock, is written and then deposited in a special dividends checking account. Separate checks are written on the dividends checking account and are made payable to each preferred stockholder entitled to receive the dividend.

Business Transaction

On December 15 On Your Mark issued Check 1373 for $1,500 in payment of the dividend on preferred stock declared November 15.

JOURNAL ENTRY

	DATE		DESCRIPTION	POST. REF.	DEBIT	CREDIT	
1	20--						1
2	Dec.	15	Dividends Payable—Preferred		1 500 00		2
3			Cash in Bank			1 500 00	3
4			Check 1373				4
5							5

GENERAL JOURNAL — PAGE 81

Dividends on Common Stock

Dividends on common stock may be declared in one of two ways.

(1) The board of directors may declare a dividend amount per common share. For example, the board of directors of On Your Mark declared a 50¢ per common share dividend. Thus, a 50¢ dividend will be paid for each share of common stock.

(2) The board of directors may decide to declare the total cash dividend for both preferred and common stock. In this case the preferred dividends are paid first and the remaining amount is divided equally among the common stockholders. For example, suppose the board of directors of On Your Mark declared a total cash dividend of $3,000. Preferred stockholders will receive $1,500 (250 shares × $6). The remaining amount, $1,500 ($3,000 − $1,500) will be split among the common stockholders. Each share of common stock will receive a 10¢ dividend ($1,500 ÷ 15,000 shares).

Like preferred stock, dividends on common stock can be paid annually, semiannually, or quarterly. Most publicly held corporations pay dividends on a quarterly basis.

ANALYZING FINANCIAL REPORTS

Calculating Return on Stockholders' Equity

Stockholders' equity is used to evaluate a company's profitability. One measure of profitability is the return on common stockholders' equity. You calculated this ratio for a sole proprietorship business in Chapter 10. The calculation for a corporation is similar.

$$\frac{\text{Net Earnings}}{\text{Average Common Stockholders' Equity}} \quad \frac{\$20,990}{\$200,832} = 0.1045 \text{ or } 10.45\%$$

To find the average common stockholders' equity, add the stockholders' equity at the beginning of the year to that at the end of the year and divide by 2. For example:

Beginning stockholders' equity	$186,178
Ending stockholders' equity	215,486
Total	$401,664 ÷ 2 = $200,832

The return on common stockholders' equity shows how much the business earned for each dollar invested by the common stockholders.

▶ **Analyze the Report:**

1. Calculate the return on stockholders' equity for 2001 using Office Depot's balance sheet and income statement on pages A-45–A-46.
2. Why do you think the return on common stockholders' equity would be important to potential buyers of a company's common stock?

Now that you have studied this section, complete the following questions and problems.

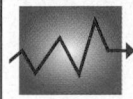

Thinking Critically

1. What two conditions should exist before a cash dividend is declared?
2. Explain how dividends are recorded when a corporation has issued two types of stock.

Computing in the Business World

On January 28 the board of directors for Jelly Bean Works declared an annual cash dividend on 200 shares of preferred $10 stock. What is the total amount of the dividend? How is this dividend accounted for in the company's books?

Problem 21–2   Distributing Corporate Earnings

During its first year of operation, Longhorn Corporation issued 17,500 shares of $10 par common stock. At the end of the year, the corporation had a net income of $350,000. The board of directors declared a cash dividend of $5 per share.

Instructions Answer the following questions in your working papers:
1. How much of the net income was distributed to the stockholders?
2. How much of the net income was retained by the corporation?

Problem 21–3   Analyzing a Source Document

Information related to the first quarter dividend on the common stock of Rob Williams Thrift Market Inc. is provided on the following memorandum.

Instructions Prepare the journal entries required to record the following in your working papers. Use page 18 in a general journal.

* declaration of the first quarter dividend
* payment of the first quarter dividend, Check 221

> **Rob Williams Thrift Market Inc.**
> 2347 Eastern Parkway
> Orange, IA 50322-6922
>
> **MEMORANDUM 37**
>
> TO: Chief Financial Officer
> FROM: Albert MacFish, Chairman of the Board
> DATE: April 8, 20--
> SUBJECT: 1st quarter dividend
>
> On April 1, 20--, the board of directors declared a $1 per share dividend on the 5,679 shares of common stock issued. The date of record is April 15, 20--. The date of payment is April 30, 20--.

JOHNSIE CRAWFORD
Accounting Teacher
Brandon High School

Q: What do you like about your job?
A: Writing the school's accounting curriculum and teaching it are the most exciting things I've done in the 35 years I've been teaching. I feel like I've been on the cutting edge of a revolution in education. I'm helping students step into the real world before they leave high school.

Once students see they can succeed in the accounting class, and get college credit, they realize they do have the skills to succeed in college. They have the motivation and self-esteem to move forward.

Q: Do your students go into the accounting field?
A: Some do. But I emphasize how many careers and fields require at least a year of accounting—doctors, construction workers, farmers, lawyers, mechanics, and so on. Accounting is a valuable course for all students.

Q: Do you need computer skills?
A: Yes. Students learn manual entry first, but then they have to apply those skills to the computer. In addition to training them for business, the computer makes the course come alive.

In 1993, I got 25 new classroom computers. I spent hours learning how to use them. But I learned where the bugs were. Wherever I got stuck, I knew my students might get stuck there too.

Tips from . . .

RHI Robert Half International Inc.

Technology is part of the accounting profession. Spend some time on the Internet and see what's available about accounting. Discover the latest business trends, and learn to research new information about the industry.

CAREER FACTS

Nature of the Work: Create lesson plans and exams, advise students, teach classes, and motivate students and help them achieve mastery.

Training or Education Needed: A bachelor's degree in business education.

Aptitudes, Abilities, and Skills: Accounting, time-management skills, communication skills, and interpersonal skills.

Salary Range: $25,000 to $60,000 depending on your experience.

Career Path: Major in business education, intern in high school, and seek a business education teaching position.

Thinking Critically: What would be the most difficult part of teaching accounting?

Financial Reporting for a Publicly Held Corporation

Many corporations prepare a statement of stockholders' equity instead of a statement of retained earnings. In this section we'll examine the information that is reported on the statement of stockholders' equity and see how this state-

ment is prepared. We'll also see how stockholders' equity is reported on a corporation's balance sheet.

The Income Statement

The income statement of a publicly held corporation is similar to that prepared by a closely held corporation. Remember, the federal corporate income taxes paid by a corporation are reported separately on the income statement.

Statement of Stockholders' Equity

In Chapter 19 you learned how to prepare a statement of retained earnings for a closely held corporation. That statement reports the changes in the **Retained Earnings** account during the period. It showed:

Retained Earnings, beginning balance
+ Net Income
Retained Earnings, ending balance

An increasing number of corporations prepare a statement of stockholders' equity rather than a statement of retained earnings. The **statement of stockholders' equity** reports the changes in all of the stockholders' equity accounts during the period. It also provides information about the transactions affecting stockholders' equity during the period. The information reported on a statement of stockholders' equity includes the number of shares of each type of stock issued and the total amount received for those shares, the net income for the period, and dividends declared during the period.

Figure 21–2 shows the statement of stockholders' equity for On Your Mark at the end of its second year of incorporation. The information needed for the statement comes from the work sheet and from the general ledger accounts. The statement is prepared as follows:

• The names of the four stockholders' equity accounts appear at the top of the amount columns. There is also a Totals column at the far right.

On Your Mark Athletic Wear					
Statement of Stockholders' Equity					
For the Year Ended December 31, 20--					

	$100 Par Preferred $6 Stock	$10 Par Common Stock	Paid-in Capital in Excess of Par	Retained Earnings	Totals
1 Balance, January 1, 20--	25 000 00	100 000 00		27 600 00	152 600 00
2 Issuance of 5,000 shares of common stock		50 000 00	7 500 00		57 500 00
3 Net Income				13 525 00	13 525 00
4 Cash Dividends:					
5 Preferred Stock				(1 500 00)	(1 500 00)
6 Common Stock				(7 500 00)	(7 500 00)
7 Balance, December 31, 20--	25 000 00	150 000 00	7 500 00	32 125 00	214 625 00

Figure 21–2 Statement of Stockholders' Equity

- The first line shows the balance of each account at the beginning of the period.
- The next lines describe various transactions affecting the stockholders' equity accounts, such as issuance of stock, net income, and dividends declared. The transactions are described in the left column. The increase or decrease amounts are recorded in the individual account columns and in the Totals column. For example, the second line on the statement indicates that the company issued 5,000 shares of common stock during the period. The issuance of the 5,000 shares increased the balance of the **Common Stock** account by $50,000. Since the shares were issued at a price above par value, the **Paid-in Capital in Excess of Par** account increased by $7,500.
- The final line shows the balance of each account at the end of the period.

As you review **Figure 21–2**, notice that amounts which decrease account balances, like dividends declared, are enclosed in parentheses. The cash dividends declared on preferred and common stock are each listed separately. Also notice that the Retained Earnings column of the statement of stockholders' equity contains the same information that is reported on a statement of retained earnings. Remember that net income increases retained earnings, and dividends declared decrease retained earnings. The statement of stockholders' equity is used to prepare the corporation's balance sheet.

Balance Sheet

The assets and liabilities sections of a balance sheet for a publicly held corporation are similar to those of a balance sheet for a closely held corporation. Notice in **Figure 21–3** that the **Dividends Payable** accounts are reported in the liabilities section. Since On Your Mark paid the dividends before the end of the year, zero balances are reported in these liability accounts.

The stockholders' equity section of a publicly held corporation's balance sheet is more detailed than that of a closely held corporation. As you can see in **Figure 21–4**, each type of stock issued by On Your Mark is listed separately under the heading "Paid-in Capital." Preferred stock is listed before common stock. Each listing describes:

- the par value,
- the number of shares authorized, and
- the number of shares issued.

The **Dividends** accounts are not listed in the stockholders' equity section because they are closed to **Retained Earnings** at the end of the year. Thus, the retained earnings amount shown on the balance sheet has been reduced by the dividends declared during the period.

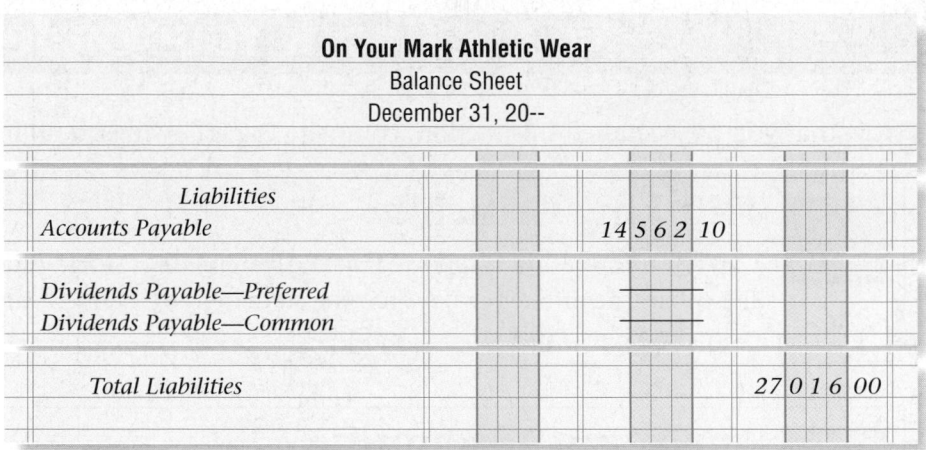

On Your Mark Athletic Wear
Balance Sheet
December 31, 20--

Liabilities		
Accounts Payable	14 5 6 2 10	
Dividends Payable—Preferred	—	
Dividends Payable—Common	—	
Total Liabilities		27 0 1 6 00

Figure 21–3 Reporting the Balances of the Dividends Payable Accounts on the Balance Sheet

On Your Mark Athletic Wear
Balance Sheet
December 31, 20--

Stockholders' Equity			
Paid-in Capital:			
$6 Preferred Stock, $100 par, 1,000 shares authorized,			
250 shares issued	25 0 0 0 00		
Common stock, $10 par, 20,000 shares authorized,			
15,000 shares issued	150 0 0 0 00		
Paid-in Capital in Excess of Par	7 5 0 0 00		
Total Paid-in Capital		182 5 0 0 00	
Retained Earnings		32 1 2 5 00	
Total Stockholders' Equity			214 6 2 5 00
Total Liabilities and Stockholders' Equity			241 6 4 1 00

Figure 21–4 The Stockholders' Equity Section of the Balance Sheet

A MATTER OF ETHICS

Using Insider Information

Imagine that you are an accountant for a large shipping company, like United Parcel Service (UPS). During the course of your work, you learn that the company is planning to buy a company that makes shipping containers. It's a smaller company whose stock is traded on a local stock exchange. You think about purchasing several thousand shares of the smaller company's stock, expecting to make a profit when the purchase goes through.

Ethical Decision Making:

- What are the ethical issues?
- What are the alternatives?
- Who are the affected parties?
- How do the alternatives affect the parties?
- What would you do?

Now that you have studied this section, complete the following questions and problems.

Thinking Critically

1. What information is reported on the statement of stockholders' equity?
2. Explain the difference between the statement of retained earnings and the statement of stockholders' equity.

Analyzing Accounting

As the accounting manager for Sunny Days, a Hawaiian-based sun care products manufacturer and retailer, you are asked to review the stock price and dividends declared over the past three years. The president, Ron Kanai, is looking for a buyer for Sunny Days and thinks an analysis of stock prices and dividends may appeal to potential corporate buyers. Review the following graph and write a one-paragraph report of what may attract potential buyers.

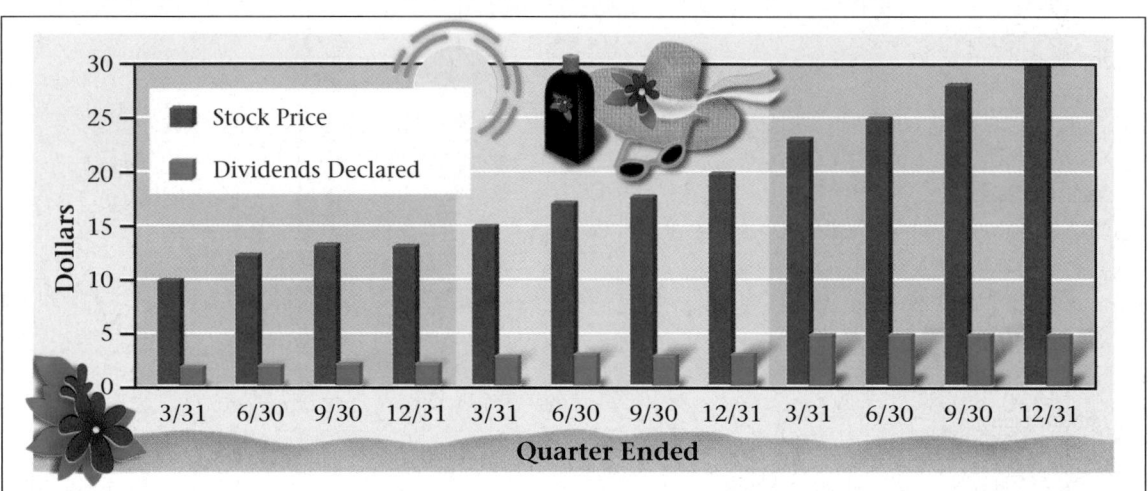

Problem 21–4   Examining the Statement of Stockholders' Equity

The following transactions of Victor Jewelry Corporation took place during the period.

Instructions Use the form in your working papers to indicate which of the transactions is reported on the statement of stockholders' equity.

Transactions:
1. Paid accounts payable of $50,000.
2. Issued 2,000 shares of $10 par common stock, receiving $15 per share.
3. The board of directors declared a cash dividend of $12,000 for all common stockholders.
4. Bought equipment on account at a total cost of $125,000.
5. Paid the cash dividend declared in Transaction 3.
6. Issued 500 shares of $100 par, $7 preferred stock.
7. Paid the federal income tax installment of $5,000.
8. Earned a net income of $150,000 for the period.

KEY CONCEPTS

1. A closely held corporation is one that is owned by a few persons or by a family. A publicly held corporation is one whose stock is widely held, has a large market, and is usually traded on a stock exchange.

2. A corporation must have permission from the state to operate. It is considered to be a separate legal entity, is owned by its stockholders, and is usually run by professional managers.

3. Two types of stock a corporation may issue are common and preferred.

4. The par value of stock is the dollar amount printed on the stock certificate. Par value is used to determine the amount credited to the capital stock account when stock is issued.

5. Common stockholders have the right to vote and elect the board of directors of the corporation, to share in the earnings of the corporation, and to share in the assets of the corporation should it go out of business.

6. Preferred stockholders do not have the right to vote but are entitled to receive dividends before the common stockholders.

7. If stock is issued at a price higher than its par value, the amount received over par is credited to an account called **Paid-in Capital in Excess of Par.**

8. Corporations distribute part of their earnings to stockholders in the form of dividends.

9. Corporations may prepare a statement of stockholders' equity, which reports the changes that occurred in all of the stockholders' equity accounts during the period.

10. T account analysis of typical stock transactions:

    (a) Issuing preferred stock at par value

Cash in Bank		Preferred Stock	
Debit	Credit	Debit	Credit
+	−	−	+
XXX			XXX

    (b) Issuing common stock at par value

Cash in Bank		Common Stock	
Debit	Credit	Debit	Credit
+			+
XXX			XXX

    (c) Declaration of cash dividend

Dividends—Preferred (or Common)		Dividends Payable—Preferred (or Common)	
Debit	Credit	Debit	Credit
+	−	−	+
XXX			XXX

USING KEY TERMS

For each key term, give or find an example of the term in a newspaper, periodical, annual report, or on an Internet site. Then use the example in a sentence.

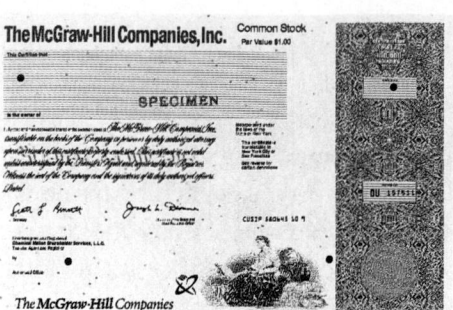

authorized capital stock	par value
board of directors	preferred stock
closely held corporation	proxy
common stock	publicly held corporation
dividend	statement of stockholders'
Paid-in Capital in Excess of Par	equity

Understanding Accounting Concepts and Procedures

Instructions

On a separate sheet of paper, answer the following questions:

1. Explain the difference between a closely held corporation and a publicly held corporation.
2. Name three characteristics of a corporation.
3. What are some of the rights of common stockholders?
4. List the differences between common and preferred stock.
5. When stock is sold at a price above its par value, what amount is credited to the capital stock account?
6. What is the classification of the **Paid-in Capital in Excess of Par** account? What is its normal balance?
7. Name and explain the three dates important to the dividend process.
8. What type of account is **Dividends**?
9. When a dividend is declared, which accounts are debited and which accounts are credited?
10. At what date does a dividend become a liability to the corporation? Explain.
11. What type of information is reported on the statement of stockholders' equity?

Case Study...

Merchandising Business: Coffee Shop

Cyber Café is a retail store that sells a variety of coffees, along with gourmet pastries and other snacks. Besides food and beverages, the store offers computer stations where customers can surf the Web.

The owners of Cyber Café started the business three years ago. Early success helped them decide to incorporate and franchise the business. They now have franchises in 15 cities. The owners want to raise additional money to open cafés in Japan.

Thinking Critically:

1. Name at least three ways the business could raise money for the new franchises.
2. If you were considering investing in Cyber Café, what ratios and analyses would you calculate from their financial statements?
3. How would these calculations help you make an investment decision?

Conducting an Audit with Alex

The balance sheet of Automart Inc. includes the following amounts:

Preferred 6% Stock,	
$100 par value	$ 90,000
Common Stock,	
$10 par value	150,000
Paid-in Capital in	
Excess of Par—Common	40,000
Retained Earnings	55,000

Instructions Audit the balance sheet and report the number of shares of preferred and common stock issued as well as the selling price per share. Prepare a brief memorandum that contains your findings.

interNET CONNECTION

Stocks Online

The Web offers many sites that help investors track their stock holdings. Investors may trade (buy and sell) stocks, check the current prices, or watch trends.

Do This:

1. Locate a Web site that offers online trading capabilities. Use the search terms "stock quote" or "stock reports."
2. What is the current price for Microsoft and Coca Cola stocks? (If you don't know the stock symbol, use the search engine provided on the site.)

Workplace Skills

Working in Teams

Teamwork is essential in any job. Whether you work for a small company or a large corporation, you will seldom make decisions by yourself. If you can work cooperatively with others, contribute to a group, listen and respond accordingly, and take responsibility for accomplishing goals, then your ability to be a team player is definitely an employment strength.

On the Job:

Aussie Diners, owned by Annabelle Brandly, are located in Australia and North America. The corporation is about to go public and offer common stock on the New York Stock Exchange. Ms. Brandly calls you from the corporate office in Perth, Australia. She wants you to invite the North American executive management team to meet before she makes the final decision about going public.

Thinking Critically:

1. What would you do to get all the members of the executive management team together quickly?
2. Group with five students in your class and role play an executive management meeting. Ask each student to assume the role of one of these managers: Marketing, Accounting, Personnel, Facilities, and Purchasing. As a team, make a list of concerns from each department.

Customizing Financial Statements
Making the Transition from a Manual to a Computerized System

Task	Perform Accounting Procedures Using Manual Methods	Perform Accounting Procedures Using Automated Methods
Customizing financial statements	1. Using accounting stationery, you may wish to reorganize information or add details to financial statements.	1. Using the Report Designer option, you may select and sort data that appears on each financial statement. 2. You may also alter information on a report by using the Filter option.

Customizing Financial Reports

Peachtree Question	Description
How do I change the appearance or content of financial reports in Peachtree?	1. Select **Reports** from the *Tasks* menu. 2. Select the report you wish to customize from the Reports list. 3. Display it on the screen. 4. Select the Design icon above the report. 5. The following features can be adjusted: the size of the columns, the types of information displaying in the report, the font style and size of the print, and the location of information on the report. 6. If you wish to save the report in the new format, rename the file, leaving the original files in their original form.
How do I filter information on preformatted reports?	1. After you have selected a report from the Reports list, click the Preview icon to display it on your screen. 2. At the Filter option, you may accept the current settings, or make changes to the displayed fields. 3. The information that can be filtered varies according to the report.
What does the software do "behind the scenes"?	1. Peachtree retrieves general ledger account balances and names and includes them on various financial reports as defined by the parameters of the predefined reports. 2. Changes made to reports are immediately reflected on the screen, ensuring that the printed report will be in a desired format.

For detailed instructions: See the **Peachtree User Guide** in your Glencoe Working Papers.

APPLICATION OPTIONS

Problem 21–5 Distributing Corporate Earnings

During the first year of operations, Sunset Surfwear issued 18,500 shares of $10 par common stock. At the end of the year, the corporation had net income of $380,000. The board of directors declared a $5 cash dividend per share of common stock.

Instructions Answer the following questions in your working papers:
(1) How much of the net income earned for the year was paid to the common stockholders?
(2) How much of the net income was retained by the corporation?

Analyze: The journal entries for this cash dividend are required on which of the following dates: date of declaration, date of record, date of payment? Why are journal entries required on those dates?

Problem 21–6 Journalizing the Issue of Stock

On June 1 InBeat CD Shop was incorporated and authorized to issue 1,000 shares of $100 par, preferred 9% stock, and 10,000 shares of $25 par common stock.

Instructions In your working papers, record the following transactions on general journal page 1.

Date	Transactions
June 1	Issued 200 shares of preferred 9% stock at $100 per share, Memorandum 3.
2	Issued 3,000 shares of common stock at $25 per share, Memorandum 7.
6	Received $31 per share for 2,000 shares of common stock issued, Memorandum 10.
7	Issued 50 shares of preferred 9% stock at par, Memorandum 11.

Analyze: Was any of the stock issued at a price above par? If yes, what amount was credited to the **Paid-in Capital in Excess of Par** account?

Complete chapter problems one of four ways:

1 **Manual** Glencoe Working Papers

or

2 **Peachtree Complete Accounting** Software

or

3 **QuickBooks** Templates (Problems 21–6, 21–9)

or

4 **Spreadsheet** Templates (Problem 21–8)

Peachtree®

SMART GUIDE

Step–by–Step Instructions: Problem 21–6

1. Select the problem set for InBeat CD Shop (Prob. 21–6).
2. Rename the company and set the system date.
3. Record all of the transactions using the **General Journal Entry** option.
4. Print a General Journal report and proof your work.
5. Answer the Analyze question.
6. End the session.

Peachtree®

SMART GUIDE

Step–by–Step Instructions: Problem 21–7

1. Select the problem set for Shutterbug Cameras (Prob. 21–7).
2. Rename the company and set the system date.
3. Record all of the transactions using the **General Journal Entry** option. Remember to enter each transaction in the proper accounting period (month).
4. Print a General Journal report for the entire quarter and proof your work.
5. Print a General Ledger report.
6. Answer the Analyze question.
7. End the session.

TIP: Set the date filter options to print a General Journal report that includes all of the entries for the quarter.

Problem 21–7 Journalizing Common and Preferred Stock Dividend Transactions

Shutterbug Cameras issued 8,000 shares of $80 par, preferred 7% stock and 35,000 shares of $25 par common stock.

Instructions In your working papers:

(1) Record the following transactions on general journal page 14.
(2) Post the transactions to the general ledger accounts provided in your working papers. Net income was $296,490.

Date	Transactions
Oct. 15	The board of directors declared an annual cash dividend on the preferred 7% stock, payable on December 1, Memorandum 407.
Nov. 5	Declared an annual cash dividend of $1.25 on 35,000 shares of common stock, payable on December 17, Memorandum 415.
Dec. 1	Paid the dividend declared on October 15, Check 1163.
17	Paid the dividend declared on November 5, Check 1201.

Analyze: What are the amounts of dividends payable on common stock and dividends payable on preferred stock at the end of December?

Problem 21–8 Preparing Corporate Financial Statements

River's Edge Canoe & Kayak is authorized to issue 10,000 shares of $100 par, preferred 9% stock and 500,000 shares of $5 par common stock. The following balances appeared in the Balance Sheet section of the company's work sheet for the year ended December 31.

Instructions

(1) Prepare the statement of stockholders' equity.
    (a) During the period the corporation issued 500 shares of 9% preferred stock at par and 25,000 shares of common stock at $9.
    (b) The net income for the year was $425,000.
(2) Prepare the balance sheet.

101	Cash in Bank	$506,010
115	Accounts Receivable	850,680
120	Notes Receivable	400,000
130	Merchandise Inventory	388,815
135	Prepaid Ins.	3,600
140	Supplies	10,500
145	Delivery Truck	139,298
150	Store Equipment	363,009
201	Accounts Payable	62,412
202	Dividends Payable—Preferred	22,500

SPREADSHEET SMART GUIDE

Step–by–Step Instructions: Problem 21–8

1. Select the spreadsheet template for Problem 21–8.
2. Enter your name and the date in the spaces provided on the template.
3. Complete the spreadsheet using the instructions in your working papers.
4. Print the spreadsheet and proof your work.
5. Save your work and exit the spreadsheet program.

203	Dividends Payable—Common	$150,000
210	Fed. Corp. Income Tax Payable	20,000
215	Sales Tax Payable	4,500
301	Preferred Stock	500,000
303	Common Stock	750,000
304	Paid-in Capital in Excess of Par	300,000
305	Retained Earnings	735,000
307	Dividends—Common	262,500
308	Dividends—Preferred	45,000

Analyze: What is the total stockholders' equity on December 31?

SOURCE DOCUMENT PROBLEM

Problem 21–9

Use the source documents in your working papers to record the transactions for this problem.

CHALLENGE PROBLEM **Problem 21–9 Recording Stockholders' Equity Transactions** SOURCE DOCUMENT PROBLEM

Buzz Newsstand is authorized to issue 100,000 shares of $5 par common stock and 5,000 shares of $100 par, preferred 8% stock. On January 1, the beginning of the period, the stockholders' equity accounts had the following balances:

301	Preferred Stock	$150,000
302	Paid-in Capital in Excess of Par—Preferred	11,250
303	Common Stock	225,000
304	Paid-in Capital in Excess of Par—Common	112,500
305	Retained Earnings	366,800
307	Dividends—Preferred	0
308	Dividends—Common	0

Instructions In your working papers.

(1) Record the following transactions on general journal page 42. Close the Dividends and Retained Earnings accounts.

(2) Prepare the stockholders' equity section of the balance sheet.

Peachtree®

SMART GUIDE

Step–by–Step Instructions: Problem 21–9

1. Select the problem set for Buzz Newsstand (Prob. 21–9).
2. Rename the company and set the system date.
3. Record all of the transactions. Enter each transaction in the proper accounting period (month).
4. Print a General Journal report and proof your work.
5. Print a Balance Sheet.
6. Answer the Analyze questions.
7. End the session.

Date	Transactions
Mar. 15	The board of directors approved a semiannual cash dividend of $62,250 for both preferred and common stockholders. The dividend is payable to stockholders of record as of April 15 with payment on May 1, Memorandum 635.
Apr. 19	Issued 500 shares of preferred stock at $108, Memorandum 651.
May 1	Paid the dividends declared on March 15, Check 1256.
Sept. 1	The board of directors approved a semiannual cash dividend of $79,250 for both preferred and common stockholders. The dividend is payable to stockholders of record as of October 1 with payment on November 1, Memorandum 828.
Nov. 1	Paid the dividend declared on September 1, Check 2451.

Analyze: What is the December 31 balance of **Retained Earnings**? Why did the balance change from the beginning of the year?

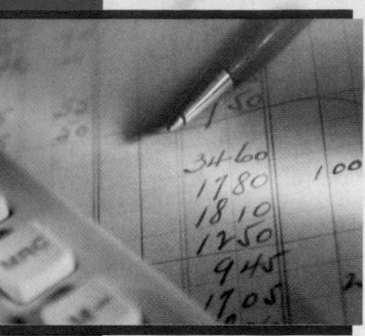

UNIT 5

Accounting for Special Procedures

In this unit. . .

Now that you have learned about the tasks in the accounting cycle for both a service and merchandising business, you will learn how to perform specialized accounting procedures. You will continue to follow the operations of **On Your Mark Athletic Wear,** exploring transactions that include accounting for cash funds, recording the depreciation of assets, accounting for accounts receivable that cannot be collected, and accounting for the cost of inventories. Transactions that include money that is borrowed or loaned to a business will also be analyzed and recorded.

In the middle of difficulty lies opportunity.

—Albert Einstein
Physicist

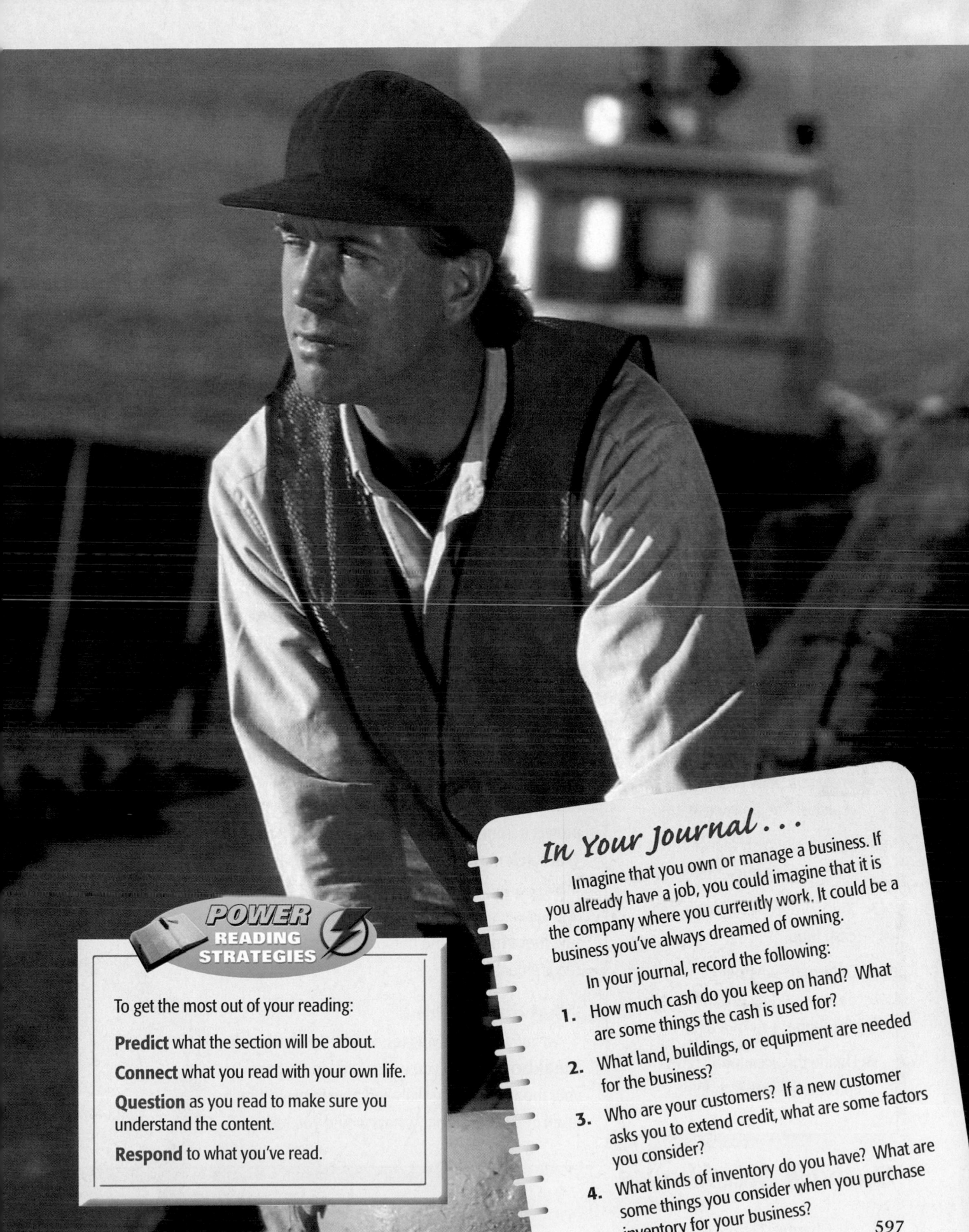

In Your Journal . . .

Imagine that you own or manage a business. If you already have a job, you could imagine that it is the company where you currently work. It could be a business you've always dreamed of owning.

In your journal, record the following:

1. How much cash do you keep on hand? What are some things the cash is used for?

2. What land, buildings, or equipment are needed for the business?

3. Who are your customers? If a new customer asks you to extend credit, what are some factors you consider?

4. What kinds of inventory do you have? What are some things you consider when you purchase inventory for your business?

597

CHAPTER 22

Cash Funds

Learning Objectives

When you have completed this chapter, you will be able to:

▶ Record the entry to establish a change fund.

▶ Prove the cash in the cash register drawers at the end of each business day.

▶ Open and replenish a petty cash fund.

▶ Journalize opening a petty cash fund.

▶ Prepare a petty cash requisition to replenish the petty cash fund.

▶ Use a petty cash register to record petty cash disbursements.

▶ Journalize replenishing a petty cash fund.

▶ Determine whether cash is short or over, and record the amount of the shortage or overage.

▶ Define the accounting terms introduced in this chapter.

Exploring the Real World of Business

PROTECTING CASH

"G'day, mate. Welcome to **Outback Steakhouse.**"

No, you're not really in Australia, but the **Outback Steakhouse** chain of restaurants uses Australia as the theme for decorations and menu items. One of the fastest-growing restaurant chains in the country, **Outback** has opened 750 restaurants around the country since 1988. On average, about 4,000 people eat at an **Outback Steakhouse** every week.

With so many customers and meals served, each restaurant takes in a lot of cash. In any cash business, employees must know how to handle money quickly and accurately, and also how to protect it from theft or loss. Job applicants who want to work for **Outback** must take an aptitude test on basic skills, including making correct change. Ethical questions regarding money handling and business transactions are covered as well. The company also says that a friendly and outgoing personality is an absolute requirement.

What do you think?

If you were applying for a job at an **Outback Steakhouse,** and you were asked to describe your money handling skills and how to protect cash taken in by the company, how would you respond?

Outback Steakhouse

Workplace Connections

Applying Your Accounting Knowledge

Waiters and waitresses are important employees in the restaurant industry. A portion of their earnings is likely to be cash tips from their customers. Businesses that take in a lot of cash need to protect their money from theft or loss. You'll learn about the records used to account for cash funds in this chapter.

Investigate:

1. What measures are taken in your workplace to protect cash?

2. If you were a store manager, how would you prevent employee theft?

The Change Fund

What You'll Learn

- Why a business needs to have a small amount of cash on hand.
- How to record the entry to establish a change fund.
- How to prove the cash in the cash register drawer at the end of each business day.

Why It's Important

Retail businesses that use a cash register need to maintain controls over the change fund and to account for cash shortages and overages.

KEY TERMS

change fund

In earlier chapters you learned that businesses use checking accounts for depositing cash receipts and making cash payments. Merchandising businesses, such as Sears or Blockbuster, keep some cash on hand to make change for customers who pay with cash.

Establishing a Change Fund

A change fund is an amount of money, consisting of varying denominations of bills and coins, that is used to make change in cash transactions. For example, a customer who pays for a $13.80 purchase with a $20 bill will receive $6.20 in change.

When a business first establishes a change fund, the amount needed for the fund is estimated. The size of the fund does not change unless the business finds that it needs more or less change than the original estimate. The change fund is established by writing a check for the amount of the fund. The check is made payable to the person in charge of the change fund. That person cashes the check and places the bills and coins in the cash register drawer. The transaction is recorded in an asset account called **Change Fund.** Let's look at an example.

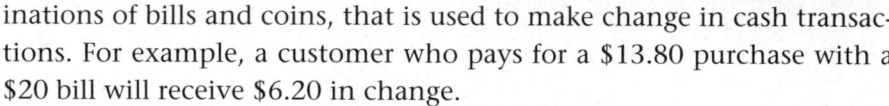

Business Transaction

On May 1 the accountant for On Your Mark wrote Check 2150 for $100 to establish a change fund.

ANALYSIS	*Identify*		
	Classify	1.	The accounts affected are **Change Fund** and **Cash in Bank.**
	+/–	2.	Both **Change Fund** and **Cash in Bank** are asset accounts.
		3.	**Change Fund** is increased by $100. **Cash in Bank** is decreased by $100.

DEBIT-CREDIT RULE	4.	Increases to asset accounts are recorded as debits. Debit **Change Fund** for $100.
	5.	Decreases to asset accounts are recorded as credits. Credit **Cash in Bank** for $100.

T ACCOUNTS	6.	Change Fund		Cash in Bank	

Change Fund		Cash in Bank	
Debit + 100	Credit −	Debit +	Credit − 100

JOURNAL ENTRY

7.

GENERAL JOURNAL PAGE __32__

	DATE		DESCRIPTION	POST. REF.	DEBIT	CREDIT	
1	20--						1
2	May	1	Change Fund		100 00		2
3			Cash in Bank			100 00	3
4			Check 2150				4
5							5

If the business needs to increase the size of the change fund, a check is written for the amount of the cash increase. For example, suppose that On Your Mark needs to increase the change fund from $100 to $125. A check is written for $25. In the journal entry, **Change Fund** is debited for $25 and **Cash in Bank** is credited for $25. This brings the **Change Fund** account balance to $125.

Using the Change Fund

The amount of cash in the change fund is put into the cash register drawer at the beginning of the day. When a cash sale occurs, the salesclerk rings the sale on the cash register. The sale is automatically recorded on the cash register tape. At the end of the day, the cash in the cash register drawer is counted. A cash proof is prepared to verify that the amount of cash in the drawer equals the total cash sales for the day plus the change fund. The amount of cash in the change fund is set aside for use as change for the next day. The balance of the cash from the drawer is deposited in the checking account.

Let's look at an example. Suppose On Your Mark has $470 in the cash register drawer at the end of the day on May 15. The cash register tape shows that cash sales, including sales tax, total $370. **Figure 22–1** shows the cash proof. As you can see, the amount of cash in the drawer at the end of the day minus the amount of cash in the change fund equals the total sales shown on the cash register tape.

Most businesses require that salesclerks sign the cash proof to indicate that they have counted the cash in the drawer and verified its accuracy. The supervisor also checks these amounts and signs the cash proof. The cash proof form is attached to the cash register tape, which is the source document for recording the cash sales for the day.

Figure 22–1 Cash Proof Form

May 15
Tape 71

348.00 CA
22.00 ST
370.00

CASH PROOF

Date ___May 15, 20--___

Cash Register No. ___1___

Total cash sales (from cash register tape)	$	370.00
Cash in drawer	$ 470.00	
Less change fund	100.00	
Net cash received		$ 370.00
Cash short		
Cash over		

Salesclerk   _Tom Blake_

Supervisor   _Greta Keegan_

Recording Cash Short and Over

    Many cash transactions occur during each business day. Occasionally, a salesclerk makes an error and gives the incorrect amount of change to a customer. When this happens, the amount of cash in the cash register drawer, less the beginning change fund, does not agree with the cash sales amount recorded on the cash register tape. If the salesclerk gives a customer too much change, the amount of cash in the drawer at the end of the day is *short*. If the salesclerk gives a customer too little change, the cash amount is *over*.

    The amount of cash either gained or lost because of errors is recorded in the **Cash Short & Over** account. **Cash Short & Over** is a temporary account. Cash shortages are expenses to the business; they are recorded as debits to **Cash Short & Over.** Cash overages are revenue for the business; they are recorded as credits to **Cash Short & Over.** The **Cash Short & Over** account does not have a normal balance.

Cash Short & Over	
Debit	Credit
Cash	Cash
Shortages	Overages

    At the end of the fiscal period, the balance of the **Cash Short & Over** account is closed to Income Summary. Let's look at an example.

On May 2 the cash register tape shows that cash sales are $520 and sales taxes are $26, for a total of $546. The actual cash in the cash register drawer, after subtracting the amount of the change fund, is $545.

T ACCOUNTS

Cash in Bank		Cash Short & Over	
Debit + 545	Credit −	Debit 1	Credit

Sales		Sales Tax Payable	
Debit −	Credit + 520	Debit −	Credit + 26

JOURNAL ENTRY

GENERAL JOURNAL PAGE 33

	DATE		DESCRIPTION	POST. REF.	DEBIT	CREDIT	
1	20--						1
2	May	2	Cash in Bank		545 00		2
3			Cash Short & Over		1 00		3
4			Sales			520 00	4
5			Sales Tax Payable			26 00	5
6			Cash Proof Cash reg. tape				6
7							7

The journal entry to record a cash overage is similar to that for a cash shortage, except that **Cash Short & Over** is *credited* for the amount of the overage. In the previous example, suppose that the amount of cash in the drawer is $547 after the amount of the change fund is subtracted. In the journal entry, **Cash in Bank** would be debited for $547 and **Cash Short & Over** would be credited for $1. The credits to **Sales** and **Sales Tax Payable** would remain the same.

A MATTER OF ETHICS

Petty Cash Funds

You are the petty cashier for a local theater group. The group's petty cash fund is used for taxi fares to and from the airport for actors, directors, and set designers. One day, you forget to bring some cash for your lunch. You consider borrowing five dollars from the petty cash fund and leaving an IOU. After all, you'll pay it back the next day.

Ethical Decision Making:

☞ What are the ethical issues?

☞ What are the alternatives?

☞ Who are the affected parties?

☞ How do the alternatives affect the parties?

☞ What would you do?

Now that you have studied this section, complete the following questions and problems.

Thinking Critically

1. Explain what happens to the cash in a cash register drawer at the end of a business day.
2. Suppose a salesclerk makes an error and gives an incorrect amount of change to a customer. Explain how this error is recorded in the accounting records.

Communicating Accounting

The Children's Consignment Shop operates primarily with cash transactions. The shop is open only on Fridays and Saturdays and does a brisk business. You are hired to maintain the accounting records for the shop. Dorothy Douglas, the owner, wants to increase the change fund from $100 to $200. Write a note to Dorothy explaining the transaction. Remind her to notify the salesclerks that the change fund will be increased by $100.

Problem 22–1 Preparing a Cash Proof

The change fund for Messina's Grocery Store is $200 per cash register. On March 31 total cash sales from cash register six are $964 and sales taxes are $57.84. A count of cash shows $1,216.84 in the cash register drawer.

Instructions

(1) Use the form in your working papers to prepare a cash proof. Sign your name as the salesclerk.
(2) Record the March 31 cash sales on page 2 of a general journal.

```
Mar 31
Tape 49

            964.00  CA
             57.84  ST
```

Problem 22–2 Recording a Cash Overage

The change fund for Visions Hair Salon is $300 per register. On April 14, at the end of the business day, the manager counts the funds in the register. Cash sales total $1,496 and sales taxes amount to $89.77 in register two. The cash drawer contains $1,895.77.

Instructions

(1) Use the form in your working papers to prepare a cash proof. Sign your name as the salesclerk.
(2) Record the April 14 cash sales and overage on page 4 of the general journal.

SECTION 2

The Petty Cash Fund

Businesses often make small cash payments for delivery fees, postage stamps, supplies, and other similar purchases. To handle these payments, businesses establish a special cash fund called petty cash. In this section you will learn how to open and replenish a petty cash fund.

Establishing the Petty Cash Fund

Small, incidental cash payments are made from the **petty cash fund** . The word "petty" indicates that only small amounts of cash are paid out of this fund. When setting up a petty cash fund, each business determines the maximum amount that will be paid out by a petty cash disbursement. A **petty cash disbursement** is any payment made from the petty cash fund. All payments over the maximum amount are paid by check. The person responsible for maintaining the petty cash fund and for making cash disbursements is called the **petty cashier** .

To establish a petty cash fund, a business estimates the amount of cash needed in the fund for a certain period of time, usually a month. This estimate is based on the company's past experiences.

On Your Mark decides to establish a petty cash fund. Crystal Casteel, an office clerk, is appointed petty cashier. The petty cash fund will contain $100. Any payments under $10 will be paid from the petty cash fund. Any payments over $10 will be paid by check. The company accountant, Greta Keegan, prepares a check for $100, payable to "Petty Cashier Crystal Casteel," to establish the fund. The transaction is recorded in an asset account called **Petty Cash Fund.** Crystal cashes the check and places the money, consisting of small denominations of bills and coins, in a petty cash box. For better internal control, the petty cash box is kept in an office safe or a locked desk drawer. Crystal is responsible for the $100 in the petty cash fund. When members of the staff need small amounts of cash for items like stamps or office supplies, Crystal will disburse the cash and store the receipts in the petty cash box. Let's learn how to journalize transactions to open a petty cash fund.

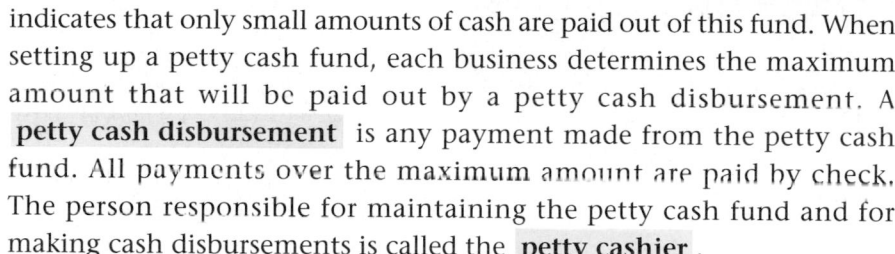

What You'll Learn

- How a business establishes a petty cash fund.
- How to prepare petty cash requisitions to replenish the petty cash fund.
- How to use a petty cash register to record petty cash disbursements.
- How to record the journal entry to replenish the petty cash fund.
- How to determine whether petty cash is short or over and record the amount of the shortage or overage.

Why It's Important

Businesses use petty cash funds because writing checks for small amounts is impractical, costly, and time consuming.

KEY TERMS

petty cash fund
petty cash disbursement
petty cashier
petty cash voucher
petty cash requisition
petty cash register

Business Transaction

On May 1 Check 2151 for $100 was issued to establish the petty cash fund.

ANALYSIS	*Identify*	1.	The accounts affected are **Petty Cash Fund** and **Cash in Bank**.
	Classify	2.	Both **Petty Cash Fund** and **Cash in Bank** are asset accounts.
	+/−	3.	**Petty Cash Fund** is increased by $100. **Cash in Bank** is decreased by $100.

DEBIT-CREDIT RULE	4.	Increases to asset accounts are recorded as debits. Debit **Petty Cash Fund** for $100.
	5.	Decreases to asset accounts are recorded as credits. Credit **Cash in Bank** for $100.

T ACCOUNTS 6.

Petty Cash Fund		Cash in Bank	
Debit + 100	Credit −	Debit +	Credit − 100

JOURNAL ENTRY 7.

		GENERAL JOURNAL				PAGE 32	
	DATE	DESCRIPTION	POST. REF.	DEBIT		CREDIT	
5	May 1	Petty Cash Fund		100 00			5
6		Cash in Bank				100 00	6
7		Check 2151					7
8							8

Sometimes petty cash disbursements occur more often than expected, and the petty cash fund is used up before the end of the specified time period. If this happens often, the company may decide to increase the amount of the fund. To increase the petty cash fund, debit the **Petty Cash Fund** account and credit the **Cash in Bank** account for the amount of the increase.

Making Petty Cash Payments

The petty cashier is responsible for making payments from the petty cash fund. Whenever a cash payment is made, a petty cash voucher is completed. A **petty cash voucher** is a proof of payment from the petty cash fund.

Figure 22–2 shows a petty cash voucher. Petty cash vouchers are usually prenumbered. If they are not, the petty cashier numbers them as they are issued.

The petty cash voucher includes the following information:

1. the date of the payment
2. the person or business to whom the payment is made
3. the amount of the payment
4. the reason for the payment
5. the account to be debited
6. the signature of the person approving the payment (usually the petty cashier)
7. the signature of the person receiving the payment

After the petty cash disbursement is made, the voucher is filed in the petty cash box until the fund is reimbursed.

PETTY CASH VOUCHER

No. 001   Date **May 2, 20--**

Paid to **Premier Office Supply Co.** $ **7.10**

For **Printer paper**

Account **Supplies**

Approved by   Payment received by
6 *Crystal Casteel*   7 *John Marks*

Figure 22–2
Petty Cash Voucher

Replenishing the Petty Cash Fund

To *replenish* a petty cash fund means to restore the fund to its original cash balance. As payments are made from the petty cash fund, the amount of cash in the petty cash box decreases. Some businesses set a minimum amount that must be kept in the petty cash box. When the amount of cash in the petty cash box reaches the minimum amount, the petty cash fund is replenished.

The petty cash fund is replenished once a month, when the balance reaches the minimum amount, or at the end of the fiscal period. When the petty cash fund is replenished, the general ledger accounts affected by petty cash disbursements (such as **Supplies** and **Delivery Fees**) are updated.

To replenish the petty cash fund, you reconcile the cash balance in the fund and then prepare a petty cash requisition form.

Reconciling the Petty Cash Fund

The petty cash fund is reconciled to determine whether or not the fund is in balance. To reconcile the petty cash fund, the petty cashier first adds all the paid petty cash vouchers. This total is then subtracted from the original cash balance of the petty cash fund. The difference is the *reconciled petty cash balance,* or the amount of money that *should be* in the petty cash box. If the count of the cash in the petty cash box agrees with the reconciled balance, the petty cash fund is in balance. If the two amounts do not agree, the petty cash fund is either short or over.

ACCOUNTING Flashbacks

THE BARTER SYSTEM
In Europe, the inconvenience of the barter system for the rising merchant class led to the development of currencies, banking, and the money economy system around 1000 AD.

On May 31 the total of all the petty cash vouchers for the month was $87.75. As you recall, the original petty cash balance was $100. The reconciled petty cash balance is:

Original balance	$100.00
Total of paid petty cash vouchers	− 87.75
Reconciled petty cash balance	$ 12.25

The amount of cash in the petty cash box that Crystal counted was $12.25. The petty cash fund, therefore, is in balance.

Preparing a Petty Cash Requisition Form

After the petty cash fund is reconciled, the petty cashier prepares a petty cash requisition. A **petty cash requisition** is a form requesting money to replenish the petty cash fund. **Figure 22–3** shows a typical petty cash requisition. This form serves as the source of information for the check written to replenish the petty cash fund. The check stub then serves as the source document for the entry recorded in the general journal.

To prepare the petty cash requisition, the petty cashier first sorts the paid petty cash vouchers by account. The vouchers for each account are totaled. The account title and the total amount to be debited to that account are recorded on the petty cash requisition. Look at **Figure 22–3** again. During May, On Your Mark made petty cash disbursements affecting the general ledger accounts **Supplies**, **Advertising Expense**, **Delivery Expense**, and **Miscellaneous Expense**.

The total of all the paid petty cash vouchers is the amount of cash needed to replenish the petty cash fund. When the accountant receives the petty cash requisition from the petty cashier, a check is written for the total of the paid vouchers. The check is made payable to the petty cashier, who cashes the check and places the money in the petty cash box.

PETTY CASH REQUISITION

Accounts for which payments were made:	Amount
Supplies	$24.45
Advertising Expense	14.80
Delivery Expense	19.00
Miscellaneous Expense	29.50
TOTAL CASH NEEDED TO REPLENISH FUND	$87.75

Requested by: *Crystal Casteel* Date *5/31/20--*

Approved by: *Greta Keegan* Date *5/31/20--*

Check No. *2341*

Figure 22–3 Petty Cash Requisition

Using a Petty Cash Register

Some businesses use a **petty cash register** to record all disbursements made from the petty cash fund. The petty cash register is a supplemental record that summarizes the types of petty cash disbursements. It is not an accounting journal because amounts from this register are not posted to general ledger accounts.

Recording Petty Cash Vouchers in a Petty Cash Register

Not all businesses that have a petty cash fund use a petty cash register. Those who do might use a form similar to that shown in **Figure 22–4**. This illustration shows how On Your Mark's petty cash vouchers are recorded. In the example, the establishment of the fund is followed by the month's disbursements.

	DATE	VOU. NO.	DESCRIPTION	PAYMENTS	SUPPLIES	DELIVERY EXPENSE	MISC. EXPENSE	GENERAL ACCOUNT NAME	AMOUNT	
1	20--									1
2	May 1	—	Est. Petty Cash ($100)							2
3	2	1	Printer paper	7 10	7 10					3
4	3	2	Postage on incoming mail	2 50			2 50			4
5	4	3	Newspaper Ad.	9 80				Adv. Expense	9 80	5
6	5	4	Gas & Parking	9 50			9 50			6
7	7	5	Daily newspaper	3 50			3 50			7
8	8	6	Collect telegram	1 25			1 25			8
9	10	7	Pens and pencils	2 50	2 50					9
10	12	8	Dara's Delivery Service	9 50		9 50				10
11	16	9	Daily newspaper	3 50			3 50			11
12	18	10	Memo pads	8 45	8 45					12
13	20	11	Postage stamps	1 00			1 00			13
14	22	12	Ad in H.S. yearbook	5 00				Adv. Expense	5 00	14
15	26	13	File folders	6 40	6 40					15
16	29	14	Dara's Delivery Service	9 50		9 50				16
17	30	15	Gas & tolls	8 25			8 25			17
18	31		Totals	87 75	24 45	19 00	29 50		14 80	18
19										19
20			Reconciled bal. $ 12.25							20
21			Replen. check +87.75							21
22			Total $100.00							22
23										23

Figure 22–4 A Typical Petty Cash Register

Notice that the establishment of the petty cash fund on May 1 is noted on line 2 of the register. On each line that follows, each petty cash payment is identified by date, voucher number, and a brief explanation. The amount of each disbursement is entered in the Payments column *and* in the appropriate Distribution of Payments column. There are three special amount columns: Supplies, Delivery Expense, and Miscellaneous Expense. The General Amount column is used for petty cash payments that do not belong in one of the three special amount columns. The Account Name is written to the left of the amount.

Totaling and Proving the Petty Cash Register

When the petty cash fund is replenished, the petty cash register is totaled and proved. Refer to **Figure 22–4** as you read the following steps on totaling and proving a petty cash register:

1. Enter the date the fund is being replenished in the Date column. Also enter the word "Totals" in the Description column.
2. Single rule the amount columns.
3. Foot each amount column.
4. Verify that the total of the Payments column is equal to the total of the Distribution of Payments columns.

Payments		Distribution of Payments	
		$24.45	Supplies
		14.80	Advertising Expense
		19.00	Delivery Expense
		29.50	Miscellaneous Expense
$87.75	=	$ 87.75	

Once verified, the totals are recorded below the footings.
5. Draw a double rule under the amount columns to show that the totals are proved.
6. You will now enter the petty cash fund replenishment information. Skip one line, then enter the reconciled petty cash balance (the amount of cash that should be in the petty cash box before it is replenished). For On Your Mark, that amount is $12.25.
7. On the next line, write the amount of the check written to replenish the petty cash fund.
8. Add the balance that should be in the petty cash fund and the amount of the check. The sum should equal the original amount of the petty cash fund.

As you can see, the petty cash register helps the petty cashier keep track of the petty cash disbursements by account. When the petty cash fund is replenished, the totals of the special columns and the amounts recorded in the General column are listed on the petty cash requisition form.

Using a Petty Cash Envelope

Small businesses sometimes use petty cash envelopes for recording petty cash disbursements. A form very similar to the petty cash register is printed on the front of the petty cash envelope. Petty cash disbursements are recorded on the form on the envelope.

The paid petty cash vouchers are placed in the petty cash envelope. When the petty cash fund is replenished, the petty cash envelope, containing all the paid vouchers for the period, is sealed and filed. A new envelope is used to record the next period's petty cash disbursements.

Journalizing the Check to Replenish the Petty Cash Fund

When a check is written to replenish the petty cash fund, the check stub and the petty cash requisition are the source documents for recording the journal entry. Let's learn how to journalize transactions to replenish a petty cash fund.

Notice that the **Petty Cash Fund** account is not affected by this transaction. When replenishing petty cash, always credit **Cash in Bank** and debit the accounts for which petty cash payments were made.

Avoiding Errors
To help you find errors:
- use a printing calculator to add column totals or figure account balances,
- then compare the amounts on the calculator tape to those in your accounting records.

Key Points

Petty Cash Fund
The only time the **Petty Cash Fund** account is debited is when the petty cash fund is initially established or when the amount of money in the petty cash fund is increased.

Business Transaction

On May 31 Check 2341 is written to replenish the petty cash fund.

ANALYSIS	*Identify*	1.	The accounts affected are **Supplies, Advertising Expense, Delivery Expense, Miscellaneous Expense**, and **Cash in Bank**.
	Classify	2.	**Supplies** is an asset account. **Advertising Expense, Delivery Expense,** and **Miscellaneous Expense** are expense accounts. **Cash in Bank** is an asset account.
	+/−	3.	**Supplies** is increased by $24.45. **Advertising Expense** is increased by $14.80. **Delivery Expense** is increased by $19. **Miscellaneous Expense** is increased by $29.50. **Cash in Bank** is decreased by $87.75.

DEBIT-CREDIT RULE	4.	Increases in asset accounts are recorded as debits. Debit **Supplies** for $24.45. Increases in expense accounts are recorded as debits. Debit **Advertising Expense** for $14.80. Debit **Delivery Expense** for $19; and **Miscellaneous Expense** for $29.50.
	5.	Decreases in asset accounts are recorded as credits. Credit **Cash in Bank** for $87.75.

T ACCOUNTS 6.

Supplies		Advertising Expense	
Debit	Credit	Debit	Credit
|		|	
24.45		14.80	

Delivery Expense		Cash in Bank	
Debit	Credit	Debit	Credit
+	−	+	−
19.00			87.75

Miscellaneous Expense	
Debit	Credit
+	−
29.50	

JOURNAL ENTRY 7.

GENERAL JOURNAL PAGE __41__

	DATE		DESCRIPTION	POST. REF.	DEBIT	CREDIT	
1	20--						1
2	May	31	Supplies		24 45		2
3			Advertising Expense		14 80		3
4			Delivery Expense		19 00		4
5			Miscellaneous Expense		29 50		5
6			Cash in Bank			87 75	6
7			Check 2341				7
8							8

Handling Cash Short and Over in the Petty Cash Fund

The petty cashier may occasionally make an error when paying out cash from the petty cash fund. When this happens, the amount of cash in the petty cash box will not agree with the reconciled petty cash balance. Any amounts of cash gained or lost through errors made by the petty cashier are recorded in the **Cash Short & Over** account.

Let's look at an example. At the end of June, Crystal Casteel, the petty cashier at On Your Mark, classified and totaled the petty cash vouchers. The accounts affected by the petty cash disbursements are:

Supplies	$15.75
Advertising Expense	25.00
Delivery Expense	20.45
Miscellaneous Expense	21.80

The total petty cash disbursements for June were $83. Crystal then reconciled the petty cash fund.

Original balance	$100
Total of paid petty cash vouchers	− 83
Reconciled petty cash balance	$ 17

When Crystal counted the cash in the petty cash box, she found that there was only $15.50. The petty cash fund was short $1.50. To bring the petty cash fund up to the original $100, $84.50 is needed ($83 + $1.50). The $1.50 cash shortage is an expense and is debited to the **Cash Short & Over** account.

When Crystal prepared the petty cash requisition form, she listed the accounts to be debited for the petty cash disbursements. She also indicated that the **Cash Short & Over** account is to be debited for $1.50. **Figure 22–5** shows the journal entry to record the replenishment.

Figure 22–5 Journal Entry to Replenish the Petty Cash Fund

GENERAL JOURNAL PAGE ___43___

	DATE		DESCRIPTION	POST. REF.	DEBIT	CREDIT	
1	20--						1
2	June	30	Supplies		15 75		2
3			Advertising Expense		25 00		3
4			Delivery Expense		20 45		4
5			Miscellaneous Expense		21 80		5
6			Cash Short & Over		1 50		6
7			Cash in Bank			84 50	7
8							8

A petty cash overage is recorded in a similar manner. If, for example, the cash in the petty cash box is $17.75, there is a cash overage of 75¢. **Cash Short & Over** is credited for that amount in the journal entry. Instead of needing $83 to replenish the fund, only $82.25 is required.

If a business uses a petty cash register, the cash shortage or overage is also reported in that record. **Figure 22–6** shows how the June cash shortage of $1.50 would be recorded in the petty cash register.

	DATE	VOU. NO.	DESCRIPTION	PAYMENTS	DISTRIBUTION OF PAYMENTS					
					SUPPLIES	DELIVERY EXPENSE	MISC. EXPENSE	GENERAL		
								ACCOUNT NAME	AMOUNT	
1	20--									1
2	June 1	16	Postage stamps	5 00			5 00			2
14	30	29	Button	1 25				Adv. Expense	1 25	14
15	30		Totals	83 00	15 75	20 45	21 80		25 00	15
16										16
17			Reconciled bal. $ 17.00							17
18			Cash short (1.50)							18
19			Replen. check 84.50							19
20			Total $100.00							20
21										21

PETTY CASH REGISTER   PAGE ___2___

Figure 22–6 Recording a Cash Shortage in the Petty Cash Register

ANALYZING FINANCIAL REPORTS

Calculating Price-Earnings Ratios

When deciding whether to buy stock, analysts and investors look at stock price information, such as highs and lows over a period of time. They might also calculate the price-earnings (PE) ratio. The PE ratio compares the current market value of a stock with its earnings per share. Usually, the higher the ratio, the less attractive the stock to investors. Here's the formula to calculate the PE ratio:

$$\text{Price-earnings ratio} = \frac{\text{Current market value per share}}{\text{Earnings per share}}$$

You'll find earnings per share reported in the "Financial Highlights" for Office Depot.

▶ **Analyze the Report:**

Use the "Financial Highlights" on page A-42 to answer these questions. Use the "Basic" earnings per share figure and round your answer to the nearest whole number.

1. Calculate the price-earnings ratio for 2001, assuming Office Depot stock is selling at $17.50 per share.
2. Calculate the PE ratio for 2001, assuming Office Depot stock is selling at $20.00 per share.
3. Describe how stock price affects the PE ratio. How would you use this ratio in deciding which stocks to buy?

Now that you have studied this section, complete the following questions and problems.

Thinking Critically

1. How do you determine if a petty cash fund is short or over?
2. When replenishing the petty cash fund, which accounts are debited and which are credited?

Computing in the Business World

It is another busy day at Olde Time Swimming Hole, a private swimming facility for your neighborhood. You have a summer job running the concession stand, and you maintain the petty cash fund. To make your accounting easier, you record the cash sales and the petty cash transactions in one report at the end of the day. You always attach the cash register tape to prove the cash drawer. Using the following figures, determine the revenue and expenses for the day. How much money will remain in the cash drawer?

Opening cash drawer	$225
Petty cash fund	100
Cash sales	600
Pool supplies bought	55
Photocopy paper purchased	8

Problem 22–3   Analyzing a Source Document

The petty cash clerk for Riddle's Card Shop prepared the following petty cash requisition:

Instructions Review the document and prepare Check 973 to replenish the petty cash fund in your working papers.

PETTY CASH REQUISITION

Accounts for which payments were made:	Amount
Office Supplies	$12.40
Postage Expense	12.00
Misc. Expense	16.00
Cash Short and Over	(.89)
TOTAL CASH NEEDED TO REPLENISH FUND	$39.51

Requested by: _Brent Roy_   Date _2/28/20--_

Approved by: _Hugh Morrison_   Date _____

Check No. _941_

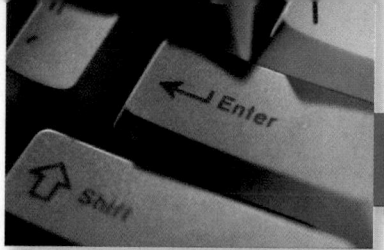

KEY CONCEPTS

1. A change fund is the money used to make change for cash transactions.
2. The asset account **Change Fund** is usually debited only once—when the change fund is established.
3. To record the establishment of a change fund:

    Debit: **Change Fund**   Credit: **Cash in Bank**

4. At the end of each business day, a cash proof is prepared to reconcile the cash in the register to the recorded cash sales.
5. The **Cash Short & Over** account is used to record errors in making change and in petty cash disbursements.
6. To record a cash shortage:

    Debit: **Cash in Bank**   Credit: **Sales**
    Debit: **Cash Short & Over**   Credit: **Sales Tax Payable**

7. To record a cash overage:

    Debit: **Cash in Bank**   Credit: **Sales**
                                          Credit: **Sales Tax Payable**
                                          Credit: **Cash Short & Over**

8. A petty cash fund is the cash a business has on hand for making small, incidental cash payments.
9. The asset account **Petty Cash Fund** is usually debited only once—when the petty cash fund is established.
10. To record the establishment of a petty cash fund:

    Debit: **Petty Cash Fund**   Credit: **Cash in Bank**

11. A petty cash voucher is prepared by the petty cashier when a disbursement is made from the petty cash fund.
12. The petty cashier prepares a petty cash requisition to request that the petty cash fund be replenished.
13. To record the replenishment of the petty cash fund with no shortages or overages:

    Debit: **Various Assets and Expenses**   Credit: **Cash in Bank**

14. To record the replenishment of the petty cash fund with a shortage:

    Debit: **Various Assets and Expenses**   Credit: **Cash in Bank**
    Debit: **Cash Short & Over**

15. To record the replenishment of the petty cash fund with an overage:

    Debit: **Various Assets and Expenses**   Credit: **Cash in Bank**
                                              Credit: **Cash Short & Over**

16. A petty cash register or a petty cash envelope is used to keep a record of all petty cash disbursements on one form.

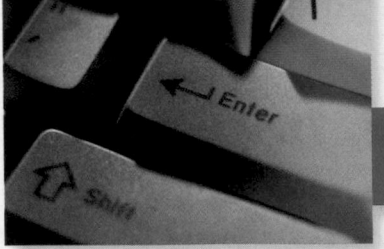

USING KEY TERMS

As the financial manager of The Tennis Center, you believe a petty cash fund should be established. Using the terms below, prepare a one-page memorandum to convince your boss, Megan Long, to open a petty cash fund.

change fund	petty cash requisition
petty cash disbursement	petty cash voucher
petty cash fund	petty cashier
petty cash register	

Understanding Accounting Concepts and Procedures

Instructions

On a separate sheet of paper, answer the following questions:

1. Which accounts are debited and credited when a change fund is established?
2. When does a cash shortage occur?
3. Explain why a cash shortage is treated like an expense.
4. Why would a business set up a petty cash fund?
5. What are the responsibilities of the petty cashier?
6. List three payments that might be made from a petty cash fund.
7. Which accounts are debited and credited to establish a petty cash fund?
8. What information is contained on a petty cash voucher?
9. How often is the **Petty Cash Fund** account debited?
10. Why should the petty cash fund be replenished at the end of the fiscal period?
11. What is meant by reconciling the petty cash fund?
12. Explain the procedure for replenishing the petty cash fund.
13. Why is the petty cash register not considered a journal?
14. How are petty cash envelopes used?

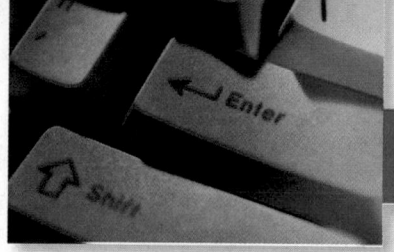

Case Study...

Merchandising Business: Health Foods

The Healthy Alternative is an organic food store that sells vitamins and natural health-care products. The store has two electronic cash registers that track inventory and record sales directly to the computerized accounting system. The owner of the store is concerned because the actual cash on hand is usually short when compared to the sales records.

Thinking Critically:

1. You work for a local CPA firm that is auditing the accounting records for The Healthy Alternative. What advice would you give the owner about cash controls and protection?
2. Explain to the owner why it is important for the cash records to match the accounting records.

*inter*NET CONNECTION

Online Banking

Need to check your bank balance? Apply for a loan? Transfer money from savings to checking? If you have a computer with Internet access, you can do all these things from your home.

Do This:

1. Do the banks in your community have Web sites?
2. List three banks and their Web site addresses.
3. Choose one site listed above. List the services that are provided to online customers.
4. Make a list of the advantages and disadvantages of online banking.

Conducting an Audit with Alex

Alex is auditing the petty cash transactions of Donnell's Decorating. He has asked you to review the journal entry and the list of petty cash vouchers from which the entry was prepared.

Date	Voucher No.	Account	Amount
July 1	1	Misc. Expense	$ 6.25
6	2	Delivery Expense	3.50
8	3	Voided	—
19	4	Samples Expense	8.10
19	5	Misc. Expense	2.10
30	6	Delivery Expense	7.35

GENERAL JOURNAL   PAGE _12_

	DATE	DESCRIPTION	POST. REF.	DEBIT	CREDIT	
1	20--					1
2	July 31	Misc. Expense		16 45		2
3		Delivery Expense		10 85		3
4		Petty Cash Fund			27 30	4
5		Check 327				5
6						6

Instructions Determine if the journal entry is correct. If not, why?

Workplace Skills

Integrity

In the workplace you may face situations where you are asked to make a decision that breaks with commonly held personal or societal values. Your ability to comprehend and choose the ethical course of action is a mark of integrity.

On the Job:

Fun Farm is a hands-on, educational working farm where elementary students learn about planting crops, harvesting, and raising animals. As you review the activity of Fun Farm's petty cash fund, you notice some unusual disbursements and cash shortages.

Thinking Critically:

In the course of your audit, you begin to suspect that someone in the company is taking funds out of petty cash and either not preparing a voucher or falsifying a voucher. Discuss with a partner how you should handle this situation.

Maintaining Cash Funds
Making the Transition from a Manual to a Computerized System

Task	Perform Accounting Procedures Using Manual Methods	Perform Accounting Procedures Using Automated Methods
Maintaining the check register	1. A check stub or deposit slip is the source document for journalizing cash payments. 2. A running balance must be calculated in the check register as deposits are made or checks are written.	1. Checks and deposits are automatically entered in the check register when transactions are journalized and posted. 2. The checking account balance is updated as each transaction is posted.
Reconciling the bank statement	1. Compare the check register with bank statement. 2. Add deposits in transit to the statement balance. 3. Deduct outstanding checks. 4. Deduct bank charges from check register. 5. Journalize and post bank charges.	1. Enter bank statement balance. 2. Verify outstanding checks and deposits not included on statement. 3. Record bank charges as a payment.

Maintaining Cash Funds

Peachtree Question	Description
How do I review the check register in Peachtree?	1. From the *Reports* menu, select **Accounts Payable**. 2. Select Check Register from the Reports list. 3. Select Options. 4. At the Filter window, set the range of checks to be displayed. 5. The register shows the check number, date, payee, cash account, and the amount of the check.
How do I reconcile the bank statement?	1. From the *Tasks* menu, choose **Account Reconciliation**. 2. Enter the Cash in Bank number you wish to reconcile. 3. Enter the ending balance from the bank statement. 4. Mark the *Clear* box for each check listed on the statement. 5. Mark deposits that have cleared. 6. Click *Adjust* to record the journal entry for the service charge. 7. The reconciliation process is complete when the unreconciled difference equals $0.00.
What does the software do "behind the scenes"?	1. During Account Reconciliation, Peachtree will prompt you until the difference between the cash account and the bank statement has been reconciled, thus assuring that the check register is accurate. 2. Each time the Account Reconciliation is accessed, it contains the previously reconciled information.

For detailed instructions: See the **Peachtree User Guide** in your Glencoe Working Papers.

APPLICATION OPTIONS

Problem 22-4 Establishing a Change Fund

On February 1 Sunset Surfwear issued Check 115 to establish a change fund of $150. At the end of the business day on February 2, the shop's cash register tape showed cash sales of $340 plus sales taxes of $17. An actual cash count of the money indicated that $505 was in the cash register drawer.

Instructions

(1) Record the entry to establish the change fund on page 1 of the general journal.

(2) Prepare a cash proof for Feb. 2. Sign your name on the Salesclerk line.

(3) Record the cash sales for Feb. 2 on page 1 of the general journal.

Analyze: Does the shortage or overage represent revenue or expense to the business?

Problem 22-5 Establishing and Replenishing a Petty Cash Fund

InBeat CD Shop established a petty cash fund for $100.

Instructions

(1) In your working papers, record the entry to establish the petty cash fund on page 6 of a general journal.

(2) Record the entry for replenishing the petty cash fund on page 10 of the general journal. There was $5 cash in the petty cash fund box on February 28.

Date	Transactions
Feb. 1	Issued Check 112 for $100 to establish the petty cash fund.
28	Issued Check 146 to replenish the petty cash fund. Paid petty cash vouchers included Supplies, $40; Advertising Expense, $16; Maintenance Expense, $27; and Miscellaneous Expense, $12.

Analyze: Was cash short or over?

Complete chapter problems one of three ways:

1 **Manual** Glencoe Working Papers

or

2 **Peachtree Complete Accounting** Software

or

3 **QuickBooks** Templates (Problems 22-6, 22-7)

Peachtree®

SMART GUIDE

Step-by-Step Instructions: Problem 22-4

1. Select the problem set for Sunset Surfwear (Prob. 22-4).
2. Rename the company and set the system date.
3. Record the entry to establish the change fund using the **General Journal Entry** option.
4. Manually prepare a cash proof.
5. Record the cash sales using the **General Journal Entry** option.
6. Print a General Journal report and proof your work.
7. Answer the Analyze question.
8. End the session.

Peachtree®

SMART GUIDE

Step–by–Step Instructions: Problem 22–5

1. Select the problem set for InBeat CD Shop (Prob. 22–5).
2. Rename the company and set the system date.
3. Record the entry to establish the petty cash fund.
4. Record the entry to replenish the petty cash fund.
5. Print a General Journal report and proof your work.
6. Answer the Analyze question.
7. End the session.

TIP: Use the **General Journal Entry** option to record the cash fund transactions.

Peachtree®

SMART GUIDE

Step–by–Step Instructions: Problem 22–6

1. Select the problem set for Shutterbug Cameras (Prob. 22–6).
2. Rename the company and set the system date.
3. Record the entry to establish the petty cash fund.
4. Make a list of the petty cash vouchers and then manually prepare a petty cash requisition.
5. Record the entry to replenish the petty cash fund.
6. Print a General Journal report and proof your work.
7. Answer the Analyze question.
8. End the session.

TIP: Use the **General Journal Entry** option to record the cash fund transactions.

Problem 22–6 Establishing and Replenishing a Petty Cash Fund

Shutterbug Cameras, a camera store, decided to establish a petty cash fund. On February 1 the accountant, Al Rosen, issued Check 1018 for $70 to establish the fund. The following disbursements were made.

Instructions

(1) In your working papers, record the entry to establish the petty cash fund on page 9 of a general journal.

(2) Make a list of the paid petty cash vouchers.

(3) Classify the petty cash disbursements by account. Calculate the total amount paid out for each account.

(4) Prepare a petty cash requisition, signing your name as the petty cashier. On February 28 there was $1.50 in the petty cash box.

(5) Record the entry in the general journal (page 11) to replenish the petty cash fund on February 28. Use Check 1191.

Date		Transactions
Feb.	1	Purchased memo pads for the office, $2.75, Voucher 101 (**Supplies**).
	3	Prepared Voucher 102 for a newspaper ad, $7.50 (**Advertising Expense**).
	5	Prepared Voucher 103 for the postage on an outgoing package, $1.75 (**Miscellaneous Expense**).
	8	Paid Dandy Delivery Service $5.65, Voucher 104 (**Delivery Expense**).
	10	Prepared Voucher 105 for pens and pencils, $3.75 (**Supplies**).
	12	Paid $2.20 for postage stamps, Voucher 106 (**Miscellaneous Expense**).
	15	Paid Dandy Delivery Service $6.75, Voucher 107 (**Delivery Expense**).
	20	Paid the news carrier $4.25 for delivery of the daily newspaper, Voucher 108 (**Miscellaneous Expense**).
	22	Bought typing paper for $7.50, Voucher 109 (**Supplies**).
	25	Paid $4.50 to Dandy Delivery Service, Voucher 110 (**Delivery Expense**).
	27	Prepared Voucher 111 for an advertisement, $10 (**Advertising Expense**).
	28	Paid $4.40 for postage stamps, Voucher 112 (**Miscellaneous Expense**).
	28	Prepared Voucher 113 for an advertisement, $7.50 (**Advertising Expense**).

Analyze: What were the total petty cash disbursements for **Delivery Expense** during February?

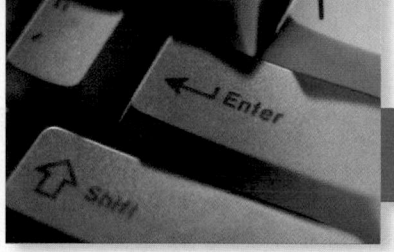

Problem 22–7 Using a Petty Cash Register

Cycle Tech Bicycles decided to establish a petty cash fund. On February 1 the accountant issued Check 3724 for $120 to establish the fund. The following disbursements were made.

Instructions

(1) In your working papers, record the entry to establish the petty cash fund in a general journal, page 5.

(2) Enter the information about the establishment of the petty cash fund on line 1 of a petty cash register, page 1.

(3) Record the petty cash disbursements in the petty cash register.

(4) Foot, total, and prove the petty cash register on February 28.

(5) Record the petty cash fund replenishment information in the explanation column below the totals. On February 28 there was $4.35 in the petty cash box.

(6) Prepare a petty cash requisition form. Use the form provided in your working papers and sign your name as petty cashier.

(7) Record the issuance of Check 3875 to replenish the petty cash fund in the general journal, page 8.

Date	Transactions
Feb. 2	Prepared Voucher 1 for a $9.25 newspaper advertisement (**Advertising Expense**).
5	Prepared Voucher 2 for pens and pencils, $5 (**Supplies**).
9	Paid $12.50 for flowers for an employee's birthday, Voucher 3 (**Miscellaneous Expense**).
12	Bought cash register tape for $3.95, Voucher 4 (**Supplies**).
19	Prepared Voucher 5 for $15 to pay National Express for parts delivered (**Delivery Expense**).
20	Paid $3.90 for postage stamps, Voucher 6 (**Miscellaneous Expense**).
22	Paid $16 to have the show window cleaned, Voucher 7 (**Miscellaneous Expense**).
24	Bought an $11 advertisement in the local newspaper, Voucher 8 (**Advertising Expense**).
25	Bought stationery for $10, Voucher 9 (**Supplies**).
26	Prepared Voucher 10 to National Express for packages delivered, $8.25 (**Delivery Expense**).
27	Prepared Voucher 11 incorrectly and voided it.
27	Purchased memo pads for the office for $3, Voucher 12 (**Supplies**).
28	Paid the news carrier a $4 tip for the daily newspaper delivery, Voucher 13 (**Miscellaneous Expense**).

Continued ✒

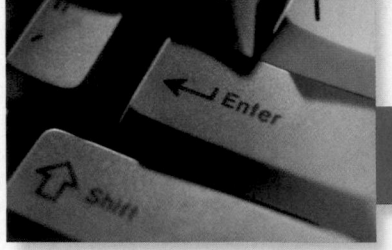

Peachtree®

SMART GUIDE

**Step–by–Step Instructions:
Problem 22–8**

1. Select the problem set for River's Edge Canoe & Kayak (Prob. 22–8).
2. Rename the company and set the system date.
3. Record the entry to establish the petty cash fund.
4. Manually record the petty cash disbursements.
5. Reconcile the petty cash register and prepare a petty cash requisition.
6. Record the entry to replenish the petty cash fund.
7. Record the entry to increase the petty cash fund.
8. Print a General Journal report and proof your work.
9. Answer the Analyze question.
10. End the session.

Date	Problem 22–7 (cont.) Transactions
28	Paid $6.80 for postage stamps, Voucher 14 (**Miscellaneous Expense**).
28	Prepared Voucher 15 for a $10 newspaper advertisement (**Advertising Expense**).

Analyze: How many payments were made from the petty cash fund during the month of February?

Problem 22–8 Handling a Petty Cash Fund

River's Edge Canoe & Kayak petty cash fund was established on February 1 for $100, by writing check 1763. The accounts for which petty cash disbursements are likely to be made include **Supplies, Gas Expense, Advertising Expense, Delivery Expense**, and **Miscellaneous Expense**.

Instructions

(1) In your working papers, record the entry to establish the petty cash fund on page 12 of a general journal.
(2) Record the establishment of the fund on the first line of the petty cash register, page 1.
(3) Record each petty cash disbursement in the petty cash register.
(4) Foot, prove, total, and rule the petty cash register on February 28.
(5) Reconcile the petty cash fund. The amount in the petty cash box is $1.50.
(6) Prepare a petty cash requisition. Sign your name as petty cashier.
(7) Record the entry to replenish the petty cash fund by issuing Check 1798 in the general journal, page 15.
(8) Record the replenishment information in the petty cash register.
(9) The accountant believes the petty cash fund should be increased by $25. Record the issuance of Check 1799 on February 28.

Date		Transactions
Feb.	1	Bought an $8 advertisement in the local newspaper, Voucher 101.
	2	Prepared Voucher 102 for $7.50 to pay Mercury Messenger for packages delivered.
	3	Bought adding machine tape for 75¢, Voucher 103.
	5	Paid $9.50 for flowers for an employee's birthday, Voucher 104.

Continued

Date	Problem 22–8 (cont.) Transactions
7	Prepared Voucher 105 for $5.25 for a typewriter ribbon.
9	Paid $4.40 for postage stamps, Voucher 106.
12	Bought $9 worth of gasoline, Voucher 107.
15	Paid $8.50 to have the shop's windows washed, Voucher 108.
18	Bought memo pads, pencils, and pens for office use, $6.30, Voucher 109.
20	Prepared Voucher 110 for $7.50 to pay Mercury Messenger for packages delivered.
23	Prepared Voucher 111 incorrectly and voided it.
23	Bought stationery for $8, Voucher 112.
27	Paid the news carrier $4.75 for the daily newspaper, Voucher 113.
28	Prepared Voucher 114 for $7.50 to pay Mercury Messenger for packages delivered.
28	Bought gasoline, $5.80, Voucher 115.
28	Prepared Voucher 116 for a newspaper advertisement, $5.

Analyze: List the petty cash disbursements that are charged to the **Miscellaneous Expense** account.

 ## Problem 22–9 Locating Errors in a Petty Cash Register

On February 1 a petty cash fund of $150 was established for Buzz Newsstand, Check 1198. The petty cashier writes a voucher for each petty cash disbursement. The vouchers are entered in a petty cash register, which is included in your working papers. When the petty cash register was totaled on February 28, the accounting clerk discovered that the footings of the Distribution of Payments columns did not equal the total of the Payments column.

Instructions
(1) Compare the following petty cash disbursement information in your working papers with the entries in the petty cash register.
(2) Correct any errors you find in the petty cash register by drawing a line through the incorrect item and writing the correction above it.
(3) Total all columns after the corrections are made.
(4) Record the replenishment information on the register. The amount in the petty cash box on February 28 was $8.10.

Analyze: How did you determine the amount of the check to replenish the petty cash fund on February 28?

CHAPTER 23

Plant Assets and Depreciation

Learning Objectives

When you have completed this chapter, you will be able to:

▶ Identify plant assets.

▶ Explain the need to depreciate plant assets.

▶ Calculate annual depreciation of plant assets.

▶ Calculate partial-year depreciation of plant assets.

▶ Determine the book value of a plant asset.

▶ Record depreciation of plant assets.

▶ Prepare depreciation schedules.

▶ Define the accounting terms introduced in this chapter.

ELECTRONIC ARTS™

Exploring the Real World of Business

DEPRECIATING ASSETS

Have you ever tested your skill as a hot-shot pilot or a professional sports coach? Video games give you the chance to put yourself in many different virtual worlds.

The world's largest interactive entertainment software publisher is **Electronic Arts (EA),** located in Redwood City, California. **EA** or its wholly-owned subsidiaries have created such popular video games as Madden NFL,™ NBA Live,™ Medal of Honor,™ and Ultima Onlines.™ The games run on hardware such as the PlayStation,® Nintendo® GameCube™, and personal computers.

To create their products, **Electronic Arts** uses high-technology equipment, such as professional graphics software and computers. Video editing computers and special sound equipment are also needed. Professional level computer equipment costs thousands of dollars, and the company places each piece of equipment on a depreciation schedule. Because technology changes so quickly, the company frequently needs to upgrade its computers and software so it can remain the premier developer of software video games.

What do you think?

How do you think changes in computer technology affect the useful lives of depreciable assets such as computers?

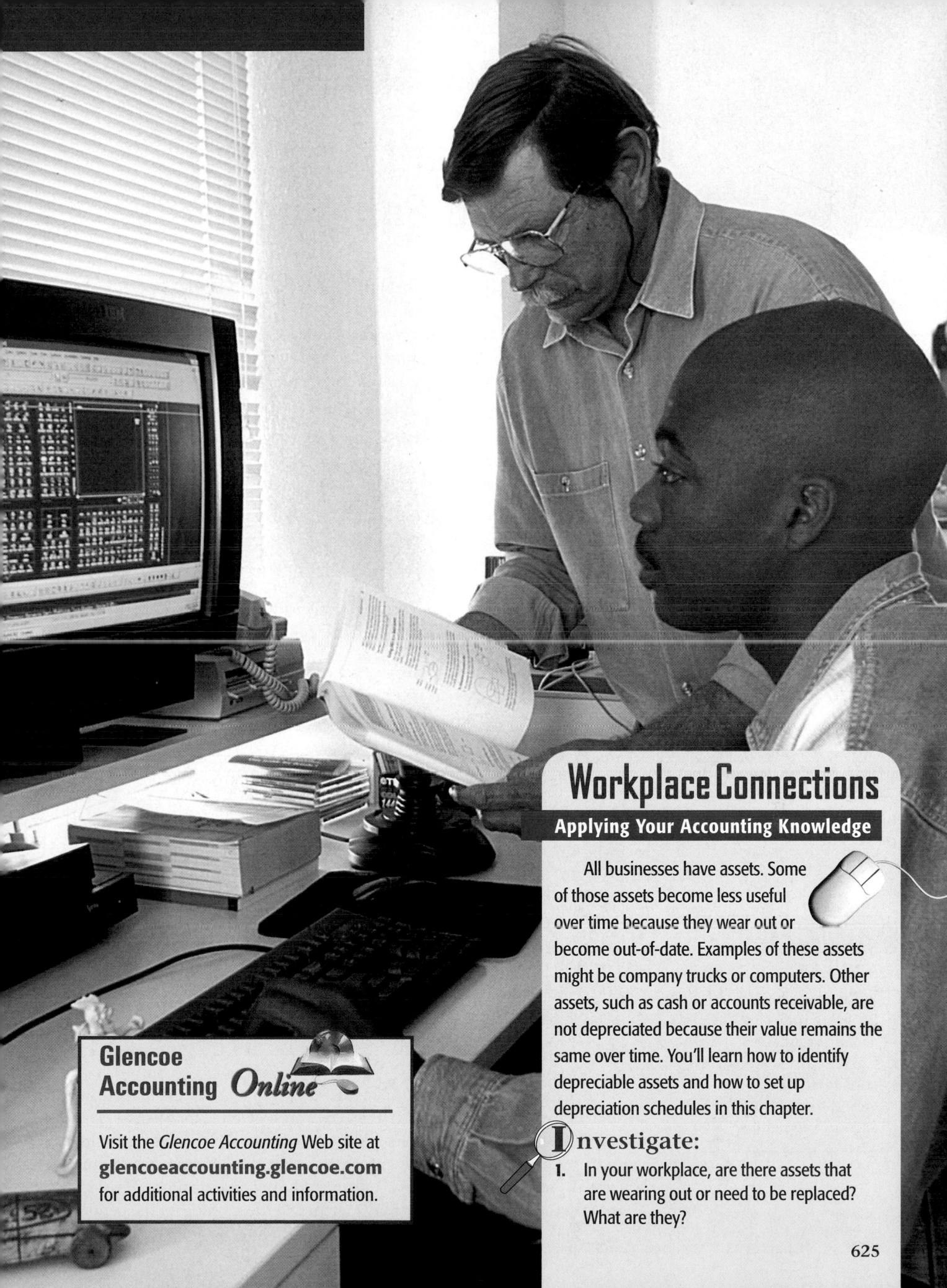

Workplace Connections

Applying Your Accounting Knowledge

All businesses have assets. Some of those assets become less useful over time because they wear out or become out-of-date. Examples of these assets might be company trucks or computers. Other assets, such as cash or accounts receivable, are not depreciated because their value remains the same over time. You'll learn how to identify depreciable assets and how to set up depreciation schedules in this chapter.

Investigate:

1. In your workplace, are there assets that are wearing out or need to be replaced? What are they?

Plant Assets and Equipment

Businesses own many different types of assets. One type of asset requires special treatment in the accounting records. These assets, such as office equipment and buildings, have two things in common:

- They are expected to produce benefits for the business for more than one year.
- They are purchased for use in operating the business, not for resale.

Electronic Arts owns many assets in this category, including computer, office, and delivery equipment. Let's explore how businesses account for these types of assets.

Current and Plant Assets

Throughout this textbook you have learned about various assets that are used in the operation of a business. These assets can be classified as current assets or plant assets.

Current Assets	Plant Assets
Assets that are either consumed or converted to cash during the normal operating cycle of the business, usually one year. Examples are: • cash • accounts receivable (collect cash from charge customers within a short period of time) • merchandise (sold within a short period of time)	Long-lived assets that are used in the production or sale of other assets or services over several accounting periods. Examples are: • land • buildings • delivery equipment • store equipment • office equipment

In Chapter 18 you learned about assets such as supplies and prepaid insurance. As these assets are used, their costs are converted to expenses. This conforms to the matching principle of accounting, which states that during an accounting period expenses must be matched with the revenue earned. Since current assets are consumed during one accounting period, the costs of current assets are easily matched to the revenue for the period.

Plant assets, however, are used over a number of accounting periods. To follow the matching principle, the cost of a plant asset is spread, or allocated, over the periods that the asset will be used to produce revenue.

Allocating the Cost of Plant Assets

Allocating the cost of a plant asset over that asset's useful life is called **depreciation** . For accounting purposes, all plant assets are depreciated, except for land. The cost of land is not depreciated, since land is considered to have an unlimited useful life. In this chapter you will learn how to calculate and record depreciation of plant assets.

For example, suppose that a plant asset costs $40,000 and has a useful life of ten years. The cost of the asset is depreciated over ten years. A portion of the $40,000 is transferred to an expense account each year. At the end of ten years, the cost of the plant asset will have been expensed.

Estimating Depreciation of a Plant Asset

It is important to remember that depreciation is an *estimate*. No one can predict with certainty the useful life or the disposal value of an asset.

Four factors are used to calculate depreciation of plant assets:

- the cost of the plant asset
- the estimated useful life of the asset
- the estimated disposal value of the asset
- the depreciation method used

Plant Asset Cost

The cost of a plant asset is the price paid for the asset plus any sales taxes, delivery charges, and installation charges. The total cost is the amount debited to the plant asset account (for example, **Delivery Equipment**) at the time of purchase.

Estimated Useful Life of a Plant Asset

The *estimated useful life* of a plant asset is the number of years the asset is expected to be used before it wears out, becomes outdated, or is no longer needed by the business. The number of years a plant asset can be used varies from one asset to another. A delivery truck might have a useful life of six years. A building, on the other hand, might have a useful life of thirty years.

In estimating useful life, the accountant considers past experiences with the same type of asset. The Internal Revenue Service (IRS) also publishes guidelines on the estimated useful lives for many types of assets.

Estimated Disposal Value of a Plant Asset

At some point a plant asset will be replaced, sold, or discarded. Usually this occurs while the asset still has some monetary value. For example, if a business buys a new delivery truck, the old delivery truck can often be traded in to reduce the price of the new truck.

The estimated value of a plant asset at its replacement time is called **disposal value** . The disposal value assigned to a plant asset is an estimate that is based on previous experience. The IRS also publishes guidelines on disposal values.

Depreciation Method

There are several depreciation methods. In this course you will learn a simple, widely used depreciation method called the straight-line method. **Straight-line depreciation** equally distributes the depreciation expense over an asset's estimated useful life. Other methods of computing depreciation include units-of-production and accelerated methods.

- Units-of-production method estimates useful life measured in units of *use* rather than units of *time*.
- Accelerated depreciation methods are based on the theory that an asset loses more value in the early years of its useful life than in the later years. Two types of accelerated depreciation are the *sum-of-the-years'-digits* method and the *declining-balance* method.

ANALYZING FINANCIAL REPORTS

The Income Statement: Vertical Analysis

You learned about classified financial statements in earlier chapters. One reason for classifying financial statements is to make it easier to analyze the information they report. One type of analysis used is **vertical analysis.** With vertical analysis, each dollar amount on the statement is stated as a percentage of a base amount. In the case of the income statement, the base amount is net sales. Net sales is 100 percent, and all other amounts for that same year are stated as a percentage of net sales.

Look at Office Depot's Consolidated Statements of Earnings (their income statement). To complete a vertical analysis, each amount is calculated as a percentage of net sales. Here's a sample calculation showing cost of goods sold and gross profit as proportions of net sales.

Sales	$167,155	100.0%
Cost of goods sold	115,212	68.9
Gross profit	$ 51,943	31.1

Calculations:

$115,212 ÷ $167,155 = **68.9%**

$51,943 ÷ $167,155 = **31.1%**

▶ **Analyze the Report:**

Use Office Depot's Consolidated Statements of Earnings on page A-46 to answer these questions:

1. Complete a vertical analysis of net earnings (income) to sales for the past three years as reported on the statement of earnings.
2. Explain how net income has changed in relation to net sales over the three years.

Now that you have studied this section, complete the following questions and problems.

Thinking Critically

1. What is the difference between plant assets and current assets?
2. List three examples of plant assets that are depreciated. Which plant asset should not be depreciated?

Communicating Accounting

As the accounting manager for Small Tykes Playworld, you are trying to convince the owners, Barbara and Bryson Billingsley, to purchase computers for the children to use. You must explain to them that the $20,000 investment can be depreciated and that they will be able to deduct the depreciation on the tax return of the business. Select a classmate with whom you can brainstorm the four factors affecting the estimate of depreciation. Together, prepare your recommendations and practice your presentation for your next meeting with the Billingsleys.

Problem 23–1 Classifying Asset Accounts

Listed below are the assets of New England Sports Equipment Inc.

Accounts Receivable
Building
Cash in Bank
Change Fund
Delivery Equipment
Land
Merchandise Inventory

Office Equipment
Office Furniture
Petty Cash Fund
Prepaid Insurance
Store Equipment
Supplies

Instructions In your working papers, indicate whether each asset listed is a current asset or a plant asset by placing a check mark in the correct column. The first account is completed as an example.

Asset	Current Asset	Plant Asset
Accounts Receivable	✓	

Calculating Depreciation

When an asset is used by a business over a period of several years, depreciation is calculated. Depreciation allocates the cost of the asset over the asset's useful life. This results in the cost of the asset being matched against revenue that the asset generates. In this section you will learn how to calculate depreciation.

Calculating Depreciation

On Your Mark Athletic Wear purchased a delivery truck on January 5 for $16,500 cash. The truck has an estimated disposal value of $1,500 and an estimated useful life of five years. The purchase of the truck is recorded in On Your Mark's general journal as follows:

	DATE		DESCRIPTION	POST. REF.	DEBIT	CREDIT	
	20--						1
	Jan.	5	Delivery Equipment		16 500 00		2
			Cash in Bank			16 500 00	3
			Check 2205				4

GENERAL JOURNAL PAGE ___2___

To calculate depreciation, you need to know the cost of the truck, the estimated useful life, and the estimated disposal value.

First calculate the amount to be depreciated:

Original Cost	−	Estimated Disposal Value	=	Amount to be Depreciated
$16,500	−	$1,500	=	$15,000

The estimated disposal value represents the part of the asset's cost that the business expects to recover. Therefore, the estimated disposal value should not be treated as an expense.

Next calculate the annual depreciation expense using the straight-line method:

Amount to be Depreciated	÷	Estimated Useful Life	=	Annual Depreciation Expense
$15,000	÷	5	=	$3,000

The annual depreciation expense for the delivery truck is $3,000.

Calculating Depreciation Expense for Part of a Year

The $3,000 depreciation expense is for a full year. Suppose that On Your Mark purchased the delivery truck on April 5 instead of January 5. During the first year, the delivery truck will be used for only nine months. Therefore, the depreciation expense is calculated for nine months.

$$\frac{\text{Annual}}{\text{Depreciation Expense}} \times \frac{\text{Fraction}}{\text{of Year}} = \frac{\text{Partial Year}}{\text{Depreciation Expense}}$$

$$\$3,000 \quad \times \quad 9/12 \quad = \quad \$2,250$$

Plant Asset Records

Businesses maintain records for each plant asset and the depreciation taken for that asset. As you can see in **Figure 23–1**, this record provides detailed information about the delivery truck, including:

1. the date of purchase
2. the original cost
3. the estimated useful life
4. annual depreciation
5. accumulated depreciation
6. book value at the end of each year

Use the lower part of the plant asset record to prepare the depreciation schedule. The amount of depreciation expense accumulates from one year to the next. **Accumulated depreciation** is the total amount of depreciation for a plant asset that has been recorded up to a specific point in time. The accumulated depreciation at the end of the third year is $9,000.

The far right column of the depreciation schedule shows the **book value** of the plant asset, the original cost less accumulated depreciation.

At the end of the third year, the book value of the delivery truck is $7,500 ($16,500 − $9,000). Notice that the book value of the delivery truck at the end of five years is $1,500. This is the truck's estimated disposal value. Under the straight-line method, the truck is not depreciated below its estimated disposal value.

> **ACCOUNTING TIPS**
>
> **Book Value**
> Book value = Original cost − Accumulated depreciation

> **Key Points**
>
> **Cost Allocation**
> After a plant asset is purchased, its cost is allocated over its estimated useful life.

PLANT ASSET RECORD

ITEM **Delivery Truck**   GENERAL LEDGER ACCOUNT **Delivery Equipment**

SERIAL NUMBER **2911-50041**   MANUFACTURER **VanPower**

PURCHASED FROM **Winding Creek Auto**   EST. DISPOSAL VALUE **$1,500.00**

ESTIMATED LIFE **5 years 3**   LOCATION **Company Garage**

DEPRECIATION METHOD **Straight-line**   DEPRECIATION PER YEAR **$3,000.00 4**

5

DATE	EXPLANATION	ASSET			ACCUMULATED DEPRECIATION			BOOK VALUE
		DEBIT	CREDIT	BALANCE	DEBIT	CREDIT	BALANCE	
1 1/5/2004	Purchased	16,500 **2**		16,500				**6** 16,500
12/31/2004						3,000	3,000	13,500
12/31/2005						3,000	6,000	10,500
12/31/2006						3,000	9,000	7,500
12/31/2007						3,000	12,000	4,500
12/31/2008						3,000	15,000	1,500

Figure 23–1
Plant Asset Record

Now that you have studied this section, complete the following questions and problems.

Thinking Critically

1. When using the straight-line method, how is the annual depreciation expense calculated?
2. What type of information does the plant asset record contain?

Computing in the Business World

Office furniture for Teen Counseling Center is estimated at a total value of $45,000 with a 10 percent disposal value. The estimated useful life is four years. Calculate the annual depreciation expense for the office furniture.

Problem 23–2 Calculating Depreciation Expense

Instructions

For each of the following plant assets:
(1) calculate the amount to be depreciated,
(2) calculate the annual depreciation expense,
(3) calculate the depreciation expense for the first year.

Use the form provided in your working papers.

Plant Asset	Months Owned First Year	Original Cost	Estimated Disposal Value	Estimated Useful Life
1. Cash register	8	$ 450	$ 30	7 years
2. Computer	2	6,500	1,500	5 years
3. Conference table	6	1,900	100	25 years
4. Delivery truck	3	36,400	6,400	5 years
5. Desk	11	3,180	300	20 years

Problem 23–3 Completing a Plant Asset Record

Use the following information to complete the blank asset record found in your working papers. The company uses the straight-line method for depreciating all plant assets. Item Purchased: Xerox Copier - Serial No. X42599757, $12,500, from K&C Office Equipment.
Purchased: 10/1/2001
Estimated Life: 5 years
Location: Executive Offices
Estimated Disposal Value: $1,700

Accounting for Depreciation Expense at the End of a Year

After depreciation on plant assets is calculated, adjustments are made to record depreciation for the period. These adjustments bring the general ledger in agreement with the plant asset records.

Adjusting for Depreciation Expense

When a plant asset is purchased, the accountant sets up a depreciation schedule for the asset, like the one shown in **Figure 23–1.** The amount of depreciation expense for each plant asset is recorded in the accounting records at the end of the year. The information to record the adjustments for depreciation comes from the plant asset records.

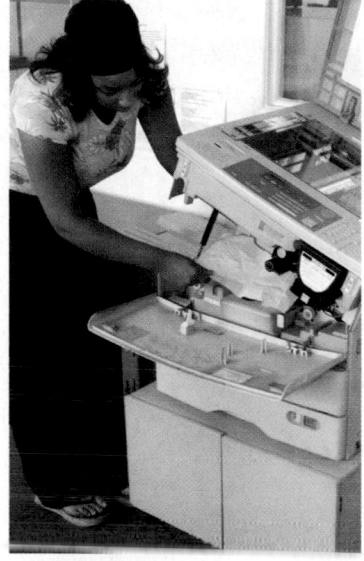

Many businesses prepare a summary of depreciation for each type of plant asset. For example, a business may have ten delivery trucks. Each truck has its own plant asset record. At the end of the year, the depreciation expense for all ten trucks is totaled. This total is entered on a summary form under the name of the asset account, in this case, **Delivery Equipment. Figure 23–2** shows On Your Mark's depreciation summary form for its plant assets.

As you can see, On Your Mark's total depreciation expense for the year is $33,000. This amount includes the depreciation expense for all of the plant assets. The accumulated depreciation for all of On Your Mark's plant assets is $100,250.

What You'll Learn

- How to record adjusting entries in the general journal for depreciation.
- How to record depreciation adjustments on a work sheet.
- How to report **Depreciation Expense** and **Accumulated Depreciation** on financial statements.

Why It's Important

Adjustments are made to record depreciation. This allows businesses to present up-to-date financial information about plant assets.

Figure 23–2 Depreciation Summary Form

2004 SUMMARY OF DEPRECIATION EXPENSE December 31, 2004			
Asset	Cost	Depreciation Expense	Depreciation to Date
Building	50,000	2,500	8,125
Delivery Equipment	16,500	3,000	9,000
Office Equipment	50,000	2,500	8,125
Store Equipment	250,000	25,000	75,000
Totals	366,500	33,000	100,250

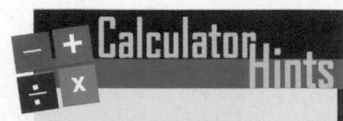
The adjustment for depreciation affects two accounts: **Depreciation Expense** and **Accumulated Depreciation**.

Depreciation Expense

Depreciation Expense is an expense account. During the year the account has a zero balance because the adjustment for depreciation is recorded at the end of the period. **Depreciation Expense** is reported on the income statement. At the end of the year, **Depreciation Expense** is closed to **Income Summary**.

There is a depreciation expense account for each type of plant asset. Some examples are:

• **Depreciation Expense—Delivery Equipment** (trucks, vans, automobiles)
• **Depreciation Expense—Office Furniture** (desks, chairs, filing cabinets)

Accumulated Depreciation

The balance of **Accumulated Depreciation** represents the total amount of depreciation expensed since the asset was purchased. There is an accumulated depreciation account for each type of plant asset. Typical account names are:

• **Accumulated Depreciation—Delivery Equipment**
• **Accumulated Depreciation—Building**

Accumulated Depreciation is classified as a contra asset account. The balance of a contra account reduces the balance of its related account. In the case of an accumulated depreciation account, the related account is a plant asset account. For example, if the asset account is **Delivery Equipment**, the contra asset account is **Accumulated Depreciation—Delivery Equipment**.

Accumulated Depreciation	
Debit	Credit
−	+
Decrease Side	Increase Side Normal Balance Side

The rules of debit and credit for an accumulated depreciation account are opposite those for an asset account. The balance of an accumulated depreciation account is reported on the balance sheet as a decrease to its related plant asset account.

Account Name

Asset	Expense	Contra Asset
Del. Equip.	Depr. Exp.—Del. Equip.	Accum. Depr.—Del. Equip.
Office Equip.	Depr. Exp.—Office Equip.	Accum. Depr.—Office Equip.
Store Equip.	Depr. Exp.—Store Equip.	Accum. Depr.—Store Equip.

Preparing the Adjustment for Depreciation Expense

Let's learn how to record depreciation of plant assets. Look at On Your Mark's depreciation schedule in **Figure 23–1** on page 631. The annual depreciation expense for the delivery truck is $3,000.

Adjustment

On December 31 the accounting clerk for On Your Mark records the depreciation for the delivery truck.

ANALYSIS *Identify*	**1.**	The accounts affected are **Depreciation Expense—Delivery Equipment** and **Accumulated Depreciation—Delivery Equipment**.
Classify	**2.**	**Depreciation Expense—Delivery Equipment** is an expense account. **Accumulated Depreciation—Delivery Equipment** is a contra asset account.
+/–	**3.**	Both **Depreciation Expense—Delivery Equipment** and **Accumulated Depreciation—Delivery Equipment** are increased by $3,000.

⬇

DEBIT-CREDIT RULE	**4.**	Increases to expense accounts are recorded as debits. Debit **Depreciation Expense—Delivery Equipment** for $3,000.
	5.	Increases to contra asset accounts are recorded as credits. Credit **Accumulated Depreciation—Delivery Equipment** for $3,000.

⬇

T ACCOUNTS **6.**

Depreciation Expense— Delivery Equipment		Accumulated Depreciation— Delivery Equipment	
Debit + 3,000	Credit –	Debit –	Credit + 3,000

Similar adjustments are made to record depreciation for other plant assets, such as buildings and office equipment.

Analyzing the Accumulated Depreciation Account

Suppose this is the end of the third year of the estimated useful life of On Your Mark's delivery truck. For each year the same adjustment was made to record the depreciation of the delivery truck:

- a debit to **Depreciation Expense—Delivery Equipment**
- a credit to **Accumulated Depreciation—Delivery Equipment**.

	ACCT. NO.	ACCOUNT NAME	TRIAL BALANCE		ADJUSTMENTS	
			DEBIT	CREDIT	DEBIT	CREDIT
8	140	Delivery Equipment	16 500 00			
9	142	Accum. Depr.—Delivery Equip.		6 000 00		(e) 3 000 00
10	145	Office Equipment	50 000 00			
11	147	Accum. Depr.—Office Equipment		5 625 00		(f) 2 500 00
23	615	Depr. Expense—Delivery Equip.	———		(e) 3 000 00	
24	620	Depr. Expense—Office Equip.	———		(f) 2 500 00	
25						

Figure 23–3 Work Sheet with Depreciation Adjustments

After the books are closed each year, the **Depreciation Expense— Delivery Equipment** account has a zero balance. (Remember that expense accounts are closed at the end of each year.) In contrast, the **Accumulated Depreciation—Delivery Equipment** account shows the total amount of depreciation expensed since the asset was purchased. At the end of the third year, the total is $9,000.

Accumulated Depreciation—
Delivery Equipment

Debit	Credit
–	+
	3,000 (first year depreciation)
	3,000 (second year depreciation)
	3,000 (third year depreciation)
	Bal. 9,000

Recording Depreciation Adjustments on a Work Sheet

After the adjustment for depreciation is prepared, it is entered in the Adjustments section of the work sheet.

Refer to **Figure 23–3**. Locate the accumulated depreciation accounts in the Trial Balance Credit column ($6,000 and $5,625). Notice that the depreciation expense accounts do not have balances in the Trial Balance section. Adjustments (e) and (f) are entered in the Adjustments section to show the depreciation adjustments for the year. Note that the depreciation expense accounts are debited and the accumulated depreciation accounts are credited. Also note that no adjustments are made to the asset accounts.

Each amount is extended to the other work sheet columns.

	Column Extended to	
Account	**Adjusted Trial Balance**	**Financial Statement**
Del. Equip.	Debit (unchanged)	Balance Sheet
Accum. Depr.—Del. Equip.	Credit (increased)	Balance Sheet
Office Equip.	Debit (unchanged)	Balance Sheet
Accum. Depr.—Office Equip.	Credit (increased)	Balance Sheet
Depr. Exp.—Del. Equip.	Debit (increased)	Income Statement
Depr. Exp.—Office Equip.	Debit (increased)	Income Statement

Athletic Wear
Sheet
December 31, 20--

ADJUSTED TRIAL BALANCE		INCOME STATEMENT		BALANCE SHEET		
DEBIT	CREDIT	DEBIT	CREDIT	DEBIT	CREDIT	
16 500 00				16 500 00		8
	9 000 00				9 000 00	9
50 000 00				50 000 00		10
	8 125 00				8 125 00	11
3 000 00		3 000 00				23
2 500 00		2 500 00				24
						25

Figure 23–3 Work Sheet with Depreciation Adjustments (cont.)

Reporting Depreciation Expense and Accumulated Depreciation on Financial Statements

Figure 23–4 shows placement of the depreciation expense accounts on the partial income statement of On Your Mark.

On Your Mark Athletic Wear
Income Statement
For the Year Ended December 31, 20--

Operating Expenses							
Depreciation Expense—Delivery Equip.				3 000 00			
Depreciation Expense—Office Equip.				2 500 00			
Total Operating Expenses						94 351 00	
Operating Income						51 342 00	

Figure 23–4 Income Statement

Figure 23–5 shows placement of the plant asset and related accumulated depreciation accounts. Both types of accounts appear in the Assets section of the balance sheet. Notice that the accumulated depreciation account is listed immediately below the related plant asset account.

For **Delivery Equipment:**

- The original cost is entered in the first amount column ($16,500).
- The accumulated depreciation is entered in the first amount column ($9,000).
- The difference between cost and accumulated depreciation is entered in the second amount column ($7,500).

Figure 23–5
Balance Sheet

On Your Mark Athletic Wear

Balance Sheet

December 31, 20--

Assets				
Delivery Equipment		16 5 0 0 00		
Less: Accum. Depr.—Delivery Equip.		9 0 0 0 00	7 5 0 0 00	
Office Equipment		50 0 0 0 00		
Less: Accum. Depr.—Office Equip.		8 1 2 5 00	41 8 7 5 00	

The $7,500 is the book value of the delivery equipment. The book value of each plant asset reported on the balance sheet should be the same as that shown on the plant asset record.

Journalizing Adjusting Entries for Depreciation Expense

After the work sheet is completed and the financial statements are prepared, adjustments for depreciation expense are recorded in the general journal. The information for the journal entries is taken directly from the Adjustments section of the work sheet.

Adjustment

Record the December 31 adjusting journal entries for depreciation.

ANALYSIS	*Identify*	1.	The accounts affected are **Depreciation Expense—Delivery Equipment, Depreciation Expense—Office Equipment, Accumulated Depreciation—Delivery Equipment**, and **Accumulated Depreciation—Office Equipment**.
	Classify	2.	**Depreciation Expense—Delivery Equipment** and **Depreciation Expense—Office Equipment** are expense accounts. **Accumulated Depreciation—Delivery Equipment** and **Accumulated Depreciation—Office Equipment** are contra asset accounts.
	+/–	3.	**Depreciation Expense—Delivery Equipment** is increased by $3,000. **Depreciation Expense—Office Equipment** is increased by $2,500. **Accumulated Depreciation—Delivery Equipment** is increased by $3,000. **Accumulated Depreciation—Office Equipment** is increased by $2,500.

DEBIT-CREDIT RULE	4.	Increases in expense accounts are recorded as debits. Debit **Depreciation Expense—Delivery Equipment** for $3,000 and **Depreciation Expense—Office Equipment** for $2,500.
	5.	Increases in contra asset accounts are recorded as credits. Credit **Accumulated Depreciation—Delivery Equipment** for $3,000 and **Accumulated Depreciation—Office Equipment** for $2,500.

6.

Depreciation Expense—Delivery Equipment	
Debit + 3,000	Credit –

Accumulated Depreciation—Delivery Equipment	
Debit –	Credit + 3,000

Depreciation Expense—Office Equipment	
Debit + 2,500	Credit –

Accumulated Depreciation—Office Equipment	
Debit –	Credit + 2,500

JOURNAL ENTRY

7.

GENERAL JOURNAL　　　　PAGE _21_

	DATE		DESCRIPTION	POST. REF.	DEBIT	CREDIT	
1	20--						1
2	Dec.	31	Depr. Exp.—Del. Equip.		3 000 00		2
3			Accum. Depr.—Del. Equip.			3 000 00	3
4		31	Depr. Exp.—Office Equip.		2 500 00		4
5			Accum. Depr.—Office Equip.			2 500 00	5
6							6

Journalizing Closing Entries for Depreciation Expense

After adjusting entries are journalized and posted, the next step in the accounting cycle is to close the ledger. In the second closing entry, you'll remember, accounts with debit balances in the Income Statement Debit column of the work sheet are closed to **Income Summary.** This closing entry includes the depreciation expense accounts.

When this closing entry is posted to the general ledger, the balances of the depreciation expense accounts are reduced to zero.

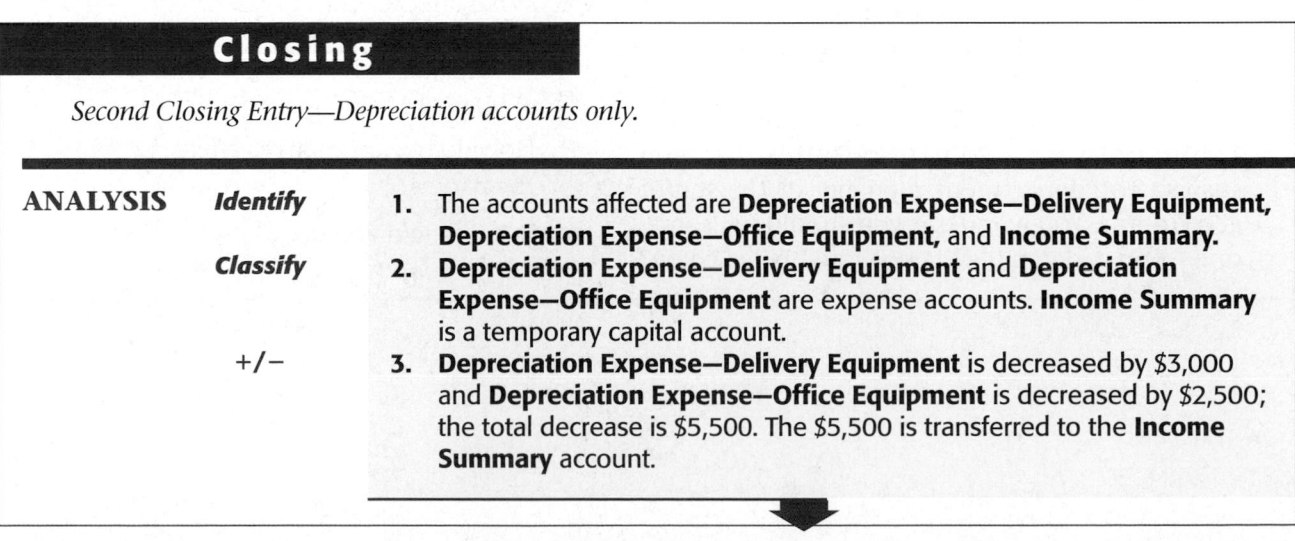

Closing

Second Closing Entry—Depreciation accounts only.

ANALYSIS **Identify**
1. The accounts affected are **Depreciation Expense—Delivery Equipment, Depreciation Expense—Office Equipment,** and **Income Summary.**

Classify
2. **Depreciation Expense—Delivery Equipment** and **Depreciation Expense—Office Equipment** are expense accounts. **Income Summary** is a temporary capital account.

+/–
3. **Depreciation Expense—Delivery Equipment** is decreased by $3,000 and **Depreciation Expense—Office Equipment** is decreased by $2,500; the total decrease is $5,500. The $5,500 is transferred to the **Income Summary** account.

| DEBIT-CREDIT RULE | 4. To transfer the expenses to the **Income Summary** account, debit **Income Summary** for $5,500. |
| | 5. Decreases in expense accounts are recorded as credits. Credit **Depreciation Expense—Delivery Equipment** for $3,000 and **Depreciation Expense—Office Equipment** for $2,500. |

T ACCOUNTS

6.

Income Summary	
Debit	Credit
5,500	

Depreciation Expense—Delivery Equipment	
Debit +	Credit –
3,000	Clos. 3,000

Depreciation Expense—Office Equipment	
Debit +	Credit –
2,500	Clos. 2,500

JOURNAL ENTRY

7.

GENERAL JOURNAL PAGE 22

	DATE	DESCRIPTION	POST. REF.	DEBIT	CREDIT	
1	20--					1
2	Dec. 31	Income Summary		5 500 00		2
3		Depr. Exp.—Del. Equip.			3 000 00	3
4		Depr. Exp.—Office Equip.			2 500 00	4
5						5

A MATTER OF ETHICS

Who Will They Believe?

Imagine that you are the newest employee—an accounting clerk—for a small book publishing company. After nearly a year, you believe you have discovered evidence of embezzlement. You're not sure who is responsible, but you suspect the department manager or the senior accountant. You wonder if you should tell someone. Who can you tell? Who would believe you?

Ethical Decision Making:

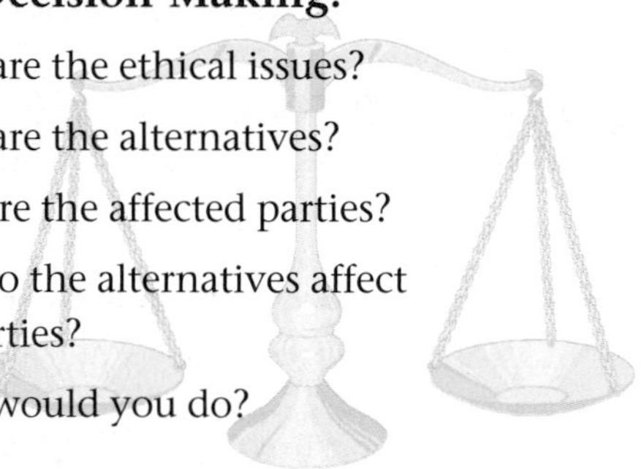

☞ What are the ethical issues?

☞ What are the alternatives?

☞ Who are the affected parties?

☞ How do the alternatives affect the parties?

☞ What would you do?

Now that you have studied this section, complete the following questions and problems.

Thinking Critically

1. Why are depreciation adjusting entries recorded at the end of the period?
2. What does the balance of an accumulated depreciation account represent?

Communicating Accounting

You and your best friend, Paulina, are discussing whether or not to prepare plant asset records and a depreciation summary form for the equipment you purchased to start your screen printing business, Supreme T-Shirt Outfitters. Paulina says it's too much work. What would you say to convince her of the need to prepare and maintain the depreciation records?

Problem 23–4
Analyzing a Source Document

Instructions In your working papers:

(1) Record the purchase in the general journal page 4.
(2) Record the partial depreciation expense for the first year in the general journal, page 7.
  (a) Disposal value—$200
  (b) Estimated useful life—5 years
  (c) The company's fiscal year ends on December 31.
(3) Record the annual depreciation, one year later, in the general journal, page 13.

All Purpose Office Equipment
996 Lake Drive, Sacramento, CA 94203

INVOICE NO. 14492

TO Universal Auto Supply
1422 Central Blvd.
Sacramento, CA 94203

DATE: June 4, 20--
ORDER NO.:   22688
SHIPPED BY: UPS
TERMS: Cash

QTY.	ITEM	UNIT PRICE	TOTAL
1	Xerox Copy Machine Serial Number 24X612987	$ 3,200.00	$ 3,200.00
	Sales Tax		256.00
	Total		$ 3,456.00

Problem 23–5 Preparing a Depreciation Schedule and Journalizing the Depreciation Adjusting Entry

Quade Corporation bought a copy machine on January 7 of the current year for $2,360. It has an estimated useful life of five years and an estimated disposal value of $100.

Instructions In your working papers:

(1) Prepare a depreciation schedule for the copy machine using the straight-line method of depreciation. (Use the form provided in your working papers.)
(2) Journalize the adjustment for depreciation on the copy machine at the end of the first year.
(3) Journalize the closing entry for the expense account affected by the adjusting entry.
(4) What is the book value of the asset after five years? Is this the same as the disposal value?

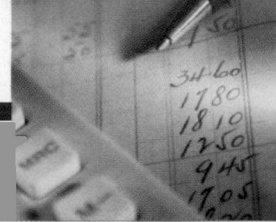

CHRISTINE SPAGNOLA
Controller
SFX Broadcasting of PA, Inc.

Q: How does one get the experience to be a controller?

A: Work for a small company where you perform many functions. I worked for a small company where I didn't make a lot of money, but I did receivables, payables, closings, bad debt, annual reports, auditing, and payroll.

Q: What's difficult about being controller for a broadcasting company?

A: There are frequent buy-outs. Each time the company is sold, I have to do a new chart of accounts, a new budget, and a new projection. So there is a lot of redundant work. It is also hard to motivate a staff under these conditions. They may be determined to prove themselves to the new owners at first, but eventually they get tired of the changes and leave.

Q: How does a person keep his or her job through the changes?

A: Make yourself valuable to the organization. Show them you're an asset. Find the issues that need to be brought to their attention. Don't wait for them to ask you. Call them and tell them what you think.

Q: What skills are most important to a controller?

A: Problem solving. You have to be able to see things other people can't see. If you are given a new problem, you have to be able to complete the task. You have to make things happen.

Tips from . . .

RHI Robert Half International Inc.

Higher positions do not mean shorter hours. Executives surveyed averaged 54 hours a week, with one-third working longer hours now than five years ago. Employees wanting to advance as a company grows will often work additional hours.

CAREER FACTS

Nature of the Work: Oversee staff, make reports, budget, and keep financial reporting on track during transitions.

Training or Education Needed: A bachelor's degree in accounting.

Aptitudes, Abilities, and Skills: Accounting, time-management skills, problem-solving skills, communication skills, and interpersonal skills.

Salary Range: $60,000 and up depending on location and company revenues.

Career Path: Start by working for small company to learn a variety of skills, then move up through other companies to become a controller.

Thinking Critically: In what ways could you demonstrate to a company that you are a valuable employee?

KEY CONCEPTS

1. Plant assets are long-lived assets used in the production or sale of other assets or services over several accounting periods.
2. A plant asset is depreciated so that its cost is spread over its useful life.
3. To calculate the annual depreciation expense of an asset, you must know its cost, estimated useful life, estimated disposal value, and depreciation method.
4. To calculate annual depreciation:

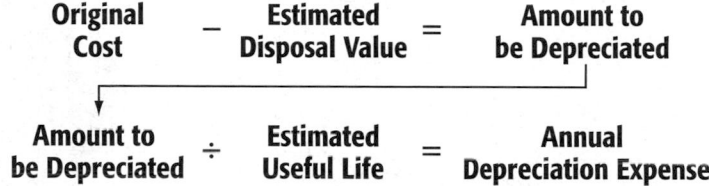

$$\text{Original Cost} - \text{Estimated Disposal Value} = \text{Amount to be Depreciated}$$

$$\text{Amount to be Depreciated} \div \text{Estimated Useful Life} = \text{Annual Depreciation Expense}$$

5. When depreciation is recorded, two accounts are affected:
   Accumulated Depreciation and **Depreciation Expense**.

6. To calculate depreciation for part of a year:

$$\text{Annual Depreciation Expense} \times \text{Fraction of Year} = \text{Partial Year Depreciation Expense}$$

7. To calculate book value:

$$\text{Original Cost} - \text{Accumulated Depreciation} = \text{Book Value}$$

8. To record depreciation:

Depreciation Expense— Description of Asset		Accumulated Depreciation— Description of Asset	
Debit + xx	Credit −	Debit −	Credit + xx

9. On the balance sheet, the accumulated depreciation accounts are listed immediately below their related plant asset accounts.
10. To close depreciation expense accounts:

Income Summary		Depreciation Expense	
Debit xx	Credit	Debit +	Credit − xx

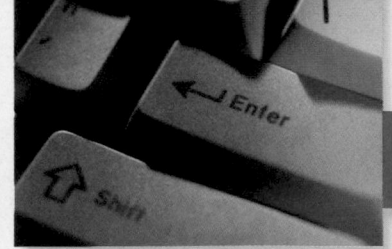

USING KEY TERMS

You have just been hired as the plant accountant for Fast Runner, a large manufacturer of inline skates and skateboards. To do your job well, you must be able to understand and apply accounting procedures for plant assets and depreciation. Your immediate boss is the CEO for Fast Runner, Rob Myers. Rob wants you to define the following terms and give him some examples related to Fast Runner. Pair up with a colleague to discuss each term and find an example. Then write your ideas on a note pad for quick reference during your meeting with Rob. Good luck!

accumulated depreciation	disposal value
book value	plant assets
current assets	straight-line depreciation
depreciation	

Understanding Accounting Concepts and Procedures

Instructions

On a separate sheet of paper, answer the following questions:

1. What distinguishes a plant asset from a current asset?
2. Why is the useful life of a plant asset limited?
3. What is meant by "allocating the cost" of a plant asset?
4. Why is the cost of land not depreciated?
5. What four factors affect the depreciation calculation?
6. How is the annual depreciation expense for a plant asset calculated under the straight-line method?
7. What is the purpose of a plant asset record?
8. When is the depreciation on a plant asset recorded?
9. Which two accounts are affected by an adjusting entry for depreciation?
10. What is the classification of the **Accumulated Depreciation** account?
11. To which account are the depreciation expense accounts closed at the end of the period?

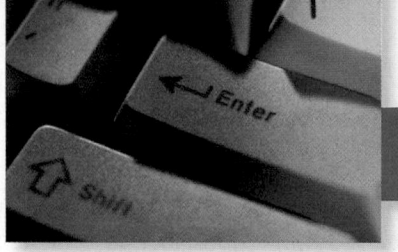

Case Study...

Merchandising Business: Photography Studio

Karina Ludmiko has been photographing weddings and parties as a hobby for several years and has decided to open a business called The Photo Studio. The studio consists of a consultation room, a developing lab, and a portrait studio. Karina has come to you seeking help in setting up the accounting records for the business.

Thinking Critically:

1. Which accounts might be in the chart of accounts for The Photo Studio?
2. Assume that the photography equipment used by The Photo Studio cost $25,000, has a useful life of ten years, and has no salvage value. Set up a depreciation schedule.
3. Explain to Karina how depreciation of the photography equipment appears on the balance sheet and income statement.

*inter*NET CONNECTION

Depreciating Assets

As you learned in this chapter, business furniture and equipment are depreciated over their useful life. For tax purposes the IRS determines the period of time over which to depreciate qualifying property. Do you know what kinds of items can be depreciated? Let's check with the IRS to find out.

Do This:

1. Locate the IRS Web site.
2. Using the site's search feature, locate the IRS publication that provides information about depreciating business equipment and furniture.
3. List five items that can be depreciated according to the IRS.
4. Over what time period should each item be depreciated?

Conducting an Audit with Alex

Brookside Sports Equipment Inc. purchased a new cash register for $3,900 on August 3 from Best Office Equipment. The cash register has an estimated useful life of ten years and an estimated disposal value of $300. Review the journal entry below and answer the following questions.

1. What is wrong with the adjustment for depreciation made on December 31?
2. Because of the error, is the book value of the cash register too high or too low?

	GENERAL JOURNAL			PAGE 61	
DATE	DESCRIPTION	POST. REF.	DEBIT	CREDIT	
1	20--				1
2	Dec. 31	Depr. Exp.—Store Eqp.		3 6 0 00		2
3		Accum. Depr.—Store Eqp.			3 6 0 00	3
4						4

Workplace Skills

Working with Diverse Cultures

An increasing number of businesses are opening international offices. Your ability to work with a variety of ethnic, social, educational, and gender groups indicates your acceptance of cultural diversity.

On the Job:

As the owner of Cool Runnings, a manufacturer of skis, ice skates, and snowboards, you are committed to hiring employees from diverse cultures. You decide to offer workshops on cultural diversity, which will teach your employees techniques for cultural acceptance.

Thinking Critically:

Develop a list of ten items to discuss in your workshops. These should be issues that deal with cultural awareness and gender issues in the workplace.

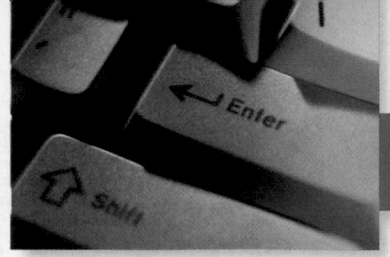

Recording Depreciation
Making the Transition from a Manual to a Computerized System

Task	Perform Accounting Procedures Using Manual Methods	Perform Accounting Procedures Using Automated Methods
Recording depreciation	1. Estimated annual depreciation is calculated when a fixed asset is purchased. 2. Each accounting period, an adjusting entry is journalized and posted for each plant asset account in the general ledger. 3. The Depreciation Expense account is closed at the end of the fiscal year.	1. Estimated annual depreciation is calculated when a fixed asset is purchased. 2. A depreciation journal entry is recorded for the month's amount. The journal entry can be automatically posted each month as a recurring entry. 3. Amounts are posted to the Depreciation Expense and Accumulated Depreciation accounts. Their balances are automatically updated.

Recording Depreciation

Peachtree Question	Description
How do I set up accounts required for depreciation entries in Peachtree?	1. Select **Chart of Accounts** from the ***Maintain*** menu. 2. Enter the account number for the new asset to be depreciated. 3. Enter the account name. For example, Delivery Equipment. 4. Select Fixed Asset as the account type. 5. Set up account numbers and names for the Accumulated Depreciation account and the Depreciation Expense account for this asset in the same manner. Select the appropriate account type for each new account.
How do I record depreciation for fixed assets in Peachtree?	1. Select **General Journal Entry** from the ***Tasks*** menu. 2. Enter the transaction to record the depreciation expense for the current period. 3. Select the Recur icon. 4. Select the number of times and how often you want this transaction to recur. (Each month? Each quarter? Each year?) 5. Click *OK* to save.
What does the software do "behind the scenes"?	1. When you select the account type for accounts such as Fixed Assets, Accumulated Depreciation, or Depreciation Expense, the software then positions these accounts in the appropriate places on the financial statements. 2. Using the Recur option for journal entries tells the system to post the entry at specified intervals to the accounts you have indicated.

For detailed instructions: See the **Peachtree User Guide** in your Glencoe Working Papers.

APPLICATION OPTIONS

Problem 23-6 Opening a Plant Asset Record

On July 10 Sunset Surfwear purchased a scanner from Taunton Equipment for $1,500. Taunton Equipment charged Sunset Surfwear $200 to install the scanner. The scanner has an estimated useful life of four years and an estimated disposal value of $260.

Instructions Prepare a plant asset record, including the depreciation schedule for the new scanner. Use the form provided in your working papers.

> Serial number: TMC46312
> General ledger account: **Office Equipment**
> Location: Main Street store
> Depreciation method: Straight-line
> Manufacturer: Brothers Company

Analyze: How did you determine the book value at the end of each period?

Problem 23-7 Recording Adjusting Entries for Depreciation

The following adjustments for depreciation were entered on the work sheet for InBeat CD Shop for the year ended December 31.

	Adjustments	
	Debit	Credit
Store Equipment		
Accumulated Depreciation—Store Equipment		(e) 3,800
Office Equipment		
Accumulated Depreciation—Office Equipment		(f) 1,400
Depreciation Expense—Store Equipment	(e) 3,800	
Depreciation Expense—Office Equipment	(f) 1,400	

Instructions Record the adjusting entries on general journal page 11.

Analyze: How does the adjustment affect the book value of the store equipment?

Complete chapter problems one of three ways:

1 **Manual** Glencoe Working Papers

or

2 **Peachtree Complete Accounting** Software

or

3 **QuickBooks** Templates (Problems 23–8, 23–10)

Peachtree®

SMART GUIDE

Step–by–Step Instructions: Problem 23–7

1. Select the problem set for InBeat CD Shop (Prob. 23–7).
2. Rename the company and set the system date.
3. Record the depreciation adjusting entries.
4. Print a General Journal report and proof your work.
5. Answer the Analyze question.
6. End the session.

TIP: Use the **General Journal Entry** option to record adjusting entries.

Problem 23–8 Reporting Depreciation Expense on the Work Sheet and Financial Statements

The trial balance of Shutterbug Cameras appears on the work sheet included in your working papers. All adjustments, except those for depreciation, are already recorded on the work sheet.

Instructions

(1) Record the following adjustments for depreciation expense on the work sheet.

   (a) Depreciation for office equipment is $2,500.

   (b) Depreciation for store equipment is $1,200.

(2) Complete the work sheet.

(3) Prepare an income statement, statement of retained earnings, and balance sheet for Shutterbug Cameras for the year ended December 31.

Analyze: What are the total current assets?

Problem 23–9 Calculating and Recording Depreciation Expense

Cycle Tech Bicycles purchased manufacturing equipment on August 1 for $410,000. The equipment has an estimated useful life of 25 years and an estimated disposal value of $20,000. The partial depreciation schedule found in your working papers is set up for the equipment.

Instructions

(1) Calculate annual depreciation, accumulated depreciation, and book value for each of the first two years. The fiscal year ends December 31. Use the form provided in your working papers.

(2) Calculate the depreciation adjustment to be entered on the work sheet at the end of the first year. Use T accounts to show the accounts debited and credited.

(3) Journalize the adjustment for depreciation at the end of the first year, general journal page 21.

(4) Post the adjusting entry to the general ledger accounts.

Analyze: What is the balance of the accumulated depreciation account at the end of the first and second years?

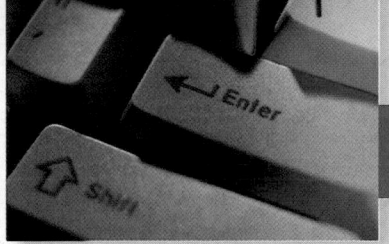

Problem 23–10 Calculating and Recording Adjustments

Peachtree®

SMART GUIDE

Step–by–Step Instructions: Problem 23–10

1. Select the problem set for River's Edge Canoe & Kayak (Prob. 23–10).
2. Rename the company and set the system date.
3. Calculate and record the end-of-period adjustments.
4. Print a General Journal report and proof your work.
5. Print an Income Statement and a Balance Sheet.
6. Close the fiscal year.
7. Print a Post-Closing Trial Balance.
8. Answer the Analyze question.
9. End the session.

The December 31 trial balance of Rivers Edge Canoe & Kayak is included in your working papers.

Instructions

(1) Calculate and record end-of-period adjustments on the work sheet.
  (a) Ending **Merchandise Inventory** is $15,000.
  (b) Supplies on hand total $1,450.
  (c) The amount of the expired insurance premium is $5,000.
  (d) Use the following information to calculate the estimated annual depreciation expense.

Plant Asset	Cost	Estimated Disposal Value	Estimated Useful Life
Store Equipment	$ 13,000	$ 1,000	10 years
Delivery Truck	32,000	2,000	10 years
Building	160,000	10,000	25 years

  (e) The total federal income tax expense for the year is $4,250.
(2) Complete the work sheet.
(3) Journalize and post the adjusting entries on page 16 of the general journal.
(4) Journalize and post the closing entries on page 16 of the general journal.

Analyze: What is the total depreciation expense for the year?

CHALLENGE PROBLEM Problem 23–11 Examining Depreciation Adjustments

On May 2, Buzz Newsstand purchased a new machine from Yong Manufacturing Co. The machine cost $2,700, with an estimated disposal value of $100 and an estimated useful life of eight years.

On December 31 the adjustment for depreciation for the first year was entered: **Accumulated Depreciation—Store Equipment** was credited for $325, and **Depreciation Expense—Store Equipment** was debited for $325.

Instructions

Answer the following questions regarding this adjustment:

(1) What is wrong with the adjustment for depreciation made on December 31? What is the correct entry?
(2) One year from now, another adjustment for this machine will be entered on the work sheet. Assume the error from the previous year is not corrected. What amount should be entered in the Adjustments section for annual depreciation expense?

Analyze: If the original error is not corrected, will the net income for the period be too high or too low?

CHAPTER 24

Uncollectible Accounts Receivable

Learning Objectives

When you have completed this chapter, you will be able to:

▶ Explain the direct write-off method and the allowance method of accounting for uncollectible accounts.

▶ Determine uncollectible accounts receivable.

▶ Record uncollectible accounts receivable using the direct write-off method.

▶ Calculate bad debts expense.

▶ Journalize the adjusting entry for estimated uncollectible accounts.

▶ Record uncollectible accounts receivable using the allowance method.

▶ Journalize the entry to record the collection of an account that was previously written off.

▶ Describe two methods that can be used to estimate uncollectible accounts expense.

Exploring the Real World of Business

ANALYZING CREDIT LOSSES

Personal fitness is a major contributing element to good health and longevity. One company that has made its mark in the personal fitness industry is **Bally Total Fitness,** a national chain of health clubs. **Bally** fitness clubs offer members the use of exercise equipment and free weights, aerobics classes, swimming pools, and racquetball courts. The clubs also sell sports clothing and equipment and nutritional products. The company operates 350 clubs in 29 states and Canada. **Bally** charges its members annual or monthly fees to use the club facilities.

When a company such as **Bally** cannot collect payment for items charged by a club member, they must write off the debt in their accounting records. Too many write-offs will affect earnings and may cause the company to raise membership fees for all members to cover the losses.

What do you think?

If you worked for **Bally Total Fitness,** what would you do to help minimize losses from people who do not pay their debts?

Bally Total Fitness

Workplace Connections

Applying Your Accounting Knowledge

When people cannot pay their debts, businesses have to decide what to do about their losses. Retailers and banks are examples of businesses that are likely to have customers who fail to pay what they owe. When amounts owed to a business cannot be collected, the business records them in the accounting records. In this chapter, you'll learn how to estimate and record uncollectible amounts.

Investigate:

1. In your workplace, does the business have customers who fail to pay what they owe?
2. How does the business handle amounts it cannot collect?

Glencoe Accounting *Online*

Visit the *Glencoe Accounting* Web site at **glencoeaccounting.glencoe.com** for additional activities and information.

651

The Direct Write-Off Method

What You'll Learn

- Why businesses extend credit.
- The direct write-off method of accounting for uncollectible accounts.
- How to record the direct write-off of an uncollectible accounts receivable.
- How to record the collection of an account that was previously written-off under the direct write-off method.

Why It's Important

Sometimes charge customers fail to pay the amounts they owe. Unpaid accounts are eventually removed from the accounting records.

KEY TERMS

uncollectible accounts
direct write-off method

In previous chapters, you learned that many businesses sell goods or services on account. Some charge customers cannot or will not pay the amounts they owe. Businesses such as JCPenney or Mervyn's routinely deal with customers who do not pay their accounts. These uncollectible accounts are eventually removed from the accounting records.

Extending Credit

Selling goods and services on credit is a standard practice for businesses of all sizes and types. Businesses sell on credit because they expect to sell more than if they accepted only cash. The additional sales on account result in higher profits.

Before a business extends credit, it should check each prospective customer's credit rating. This credit check helps the business determine the customer's ability to pay the amounts charged on account. Retail stores often ask customers to complete a credit application. They also rely on reports from credit card companies and local retail credit bureaus. Wholesalers and manufacturers use reports from wholesale credit bureaus and national credit-rating organizations such as Dun & Bradstreet to check their customers' creditworthiness.

An **uncollectible account**, or *bad debt,* is created when a customer fails to pay the amount due on account. An account that is uncollectible becomes an expense to the business. The account receivable is removed from the accounting records, and an expense is recorded.

There are two ways to handle uncollectible accounts: the direct write-off method and the allowance method. In this section, we will look at the direct write-off method.

The Direct Write-Off Method

The direct write-off method is used primarily by small businesses and those with few charge customers. Under the **direct write-off method**, when the business determines that the amount owed is not going to be paid, the uncollectible account is removed from the accounting records. **Uncollectible Accounts Expense** is debited and **Accounts Receivable** (both controlling and subsidiary) is credited.

Let's look at an example of how this method is used to record uncollectible accounts receivable.

Writing Off an Uncollectible Account

On June 4 On Your Mark Athletic Wear sold football equipment on account to Robert Galvin for $250 plus $15 sales tax. The original transaction was recorded as a debit to **Accounts Receivable** (controlling) for $265 and credits to **Sales** for $250 and **Sales Tax Payable** for $15. Also, the subsidiary account **Accounts Receivable—Robert Galvin** was debited for $265.

For over a year, On Your Mark tried to collect this account. The length of time is one consideration used to determine uncollectible accounts receivable. It is now apparent that Robert Galvin is not going to pay the $265.

What this means to On Your Mark is that the business must decrease its **Accounts Receivable** account and increase its expense related to uncollectible accounts. In effect, the business must decrease total assets and increase total expenses when a customer fails to pay a debt.

ACCOUNTING TIPS

Direct Write-Off Method
The direct write-off method is the only method a business can use for income tax purposes.

Business Transaction

On August 25 On Your Mark wrote off as uncollectible Robert Galvin's account for $265, Memorandum 170.

ANALYSIS	*Identify*	1. The accounts affected are **Uncollectible Accounts Expense, Accounts Receivable** (controlling), and **Accounts Receivable—Robert Galvin** (subsidiary).
	Classify	2. **Uncollectible Accounts Expense** is an expense account. **Accounts Receivable** (controlling) and **Accounts Receivable—Robert Galvin** (subsidiary) are asset accounts.
	+/−	3. **Uncollectible Accounts Expense** is increased by $265. **Accounts Receivable** (controlling) and **Accounts Receivable—Robert Galvin** (subsidiary) are decreased by $265.

DEBIT-CREDIT RULE	4. Increases to expense accounts are recorded as debits. Debit **Uncollectible Accounts Expense** for $265.
	5. Decreases to asset accounts are recorded as credits. Credit **Accounts Receivable** (controlling) and **Accounts Receivable—Robert Galvin** (subsidiary) for $265.

T ACCOUNTS

6.

Uncollectible Accounts Expense		Accounts Receivable	
Debit + 265	Credit −	Debit +	Credit − 265

Accounts Receivable Subsidiary Ledger
Robert Galvin

Debit +	Credit − 265

JOURNAL ENTRY

7.

GENERAL JOURNAL PAGE 13

	DATE	DESCRIPTION	POST. REF.	DEBIT	CREDIT	
1	20--					1
2	Aug. 25	Uncollectible Accounts Expense		265 00		2
3		Accts. Rec./Robert Galvin			265 00	3
4		Memorandum 170				4
5						5

Figure 24–1 shows how this transaction is posted to the general ledger and the accounts receivable subsidiary ledger.

ACCOUNT Accounts Receivable ACCOUNT NO. 115

	DATE	DESCRIPTION	POST. REF.	DEBIT	CREDIT	BALANCE DEBIT	BALANCE CREDIT
	2002						
	Aug. 1	Balance	✓			7 821 42	
	25	Write-off	G13		265 00	7 556 42	

ACCOUNT Uncollectible Accounts Expense ACCOUNT NO. 675

	DATE	DESCRIPTION	POST. REF.	DEBIT	CREDIT	BALANCE DEBIT	BALANCE CREDIT
	2002						
	Aug. 25		G13	265 00		265 00	

NAME Robert Galvin
ADDRESS 10223 Riggs Circle, Mesquite, TX 75181

DATE	DESCRIPTION	POST. REF.	DEBIT	CREDIT	BALANCE
2001					
June 4		S14	265 00		265 00
2002					
Aug. 25	Written off as uncollectible	G13		265 00	—

Figure 24–1 Ledger Accounts after an Uncollectible Write-off

Notice the explanation entered in Robert Galvin's account. When an account is written off as uncollectible, it is important to note on the subsidiary ledger that the account was written off, not paid off.

Collecting a Written-Off Account

Occasionally, a charge customer whose account was written off as uncollectible will later pay the amount owed. When this happens:

- First, the customer's account is reinstated, or reentered in the accounting records.
- Second, the cash receipt is recorded.

Business Transaction

On September 5 On Your Mark received $265 from Robert Galvin, whose account was written off as uncollectible on August 25, Memorandum 176 and Receipt 1109. First reinstate the account receivable.

ANALYSIS **Identify** 1. The accounts affected are **Accounts Receivable** (controlling), **Accounts Receivable—Robert Galvin** (subsidiary), and **Uncollectible Accounts Expense.**

Classify 2. **Accounts Receivable** (controlling) and **Accounts Receivable—Robert Galvin** (subsidiary) are asset accounts. **Uncollectible Accounts Expense** is an expense account.

+/− 3. **Accounts Receivable** (controlling) and **Accounts Receivable—Robert Galvin** (subsidiary) are increased by $265. **Uncollectible Accounts Expense** is decreased by $265.

DEBIT-CREDIT RULE 4. Increases to asset accounts are recorded as debits. Debit **Accounts Receivable** (controlling) and **Accounts Receivable—Robert Galvin** (subsidiary) for $265.

5. Decreases to expense accounts are recorded as credits. Credit **Uncollectible Accounts Expense** for $265.

T ACCOUNTS 6.

Accounts Receivable	
Debit	Credit
+	−
265	

Uncollectible Accounts Expense	
Debit	Credit
+	−
	265

Accounts Receivable Subsidiary Ledger
Robert Galvin

Debit	Credit
+	−
265	

GENERAL JOURNAL   PAGE   14

	DATE	DESCRIPTION	POST. REF.	DEBIT	CREDIT	
1	20--					1
2	Sept. 5	Accts. Rec./Robert Galvin		265 00		2
3		Uncollectible Accts. Expense			265 00	3
4		Memorandum 176				4
5						5

After this transaction is posted, the cash receipt is recorded as a debit to **Cash in Bank** for $265 and a credit to **Accounts Receivable** (controlling) for $265. Also, the subsidiary account **Accounts Receivable—Robert Galvin** is credited for $265. Receipt 1109 is the source document for this entry.

Figure 24–2 shows Robert Galvin's subsidiary ledger account, which contains data about: the sale, the write-off, the reinstatement, and the cash receipt.

NAME   *Robert Galvin*

ADDRESS   *10223 Riggs Circle, Mesquite, TX 75181*

DATE		DESCRIPTION	POST. REF.	DEBIT	CREDIT	BALANCE
2001						
June	4		S14	265 00		265 00
2002						
Aug.	25	Written off as uncollectible	G13		265 00	—
Sept.	5	Reinstated	G14	265 00		265 00
	5		G14		265 00	—

Figure 24–2 Robert Galvin Account

A MATTER OF ETHICS

Uncollectible Accounts

Suppose you're an accounts receivable clerk for an advertising agency. Your friend, Hector, owns a deli and has hired your advertising agency to create an ad for a local magazine. Hector's business is having financial difficulties and he wants you to write off his account with your agency, although the account should not be considered uncollectible yet.

Ethical Decision Making:

☞ What are the ethical issues?

☞ What are the alternatives?

☞ Who are the affected parties?

☞ How do the alternatives affect the parties?

☞ What would you do?

Now that you have studied this section, complete the following questions and problems.

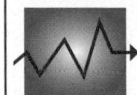

Thinking Critically

1. Before a business extends credit, it needs to approve potential credit customers. What are some items a business needs to evaluate? Why is it important for a business to verify these before extending credit?
2. Explain the use of the direct write-off method of accounting for uncollectible accounts.

Communicating Accounting

As an accounting clerk for The Music Connection, you are responsible for accounts receivable and uncollectible accounts. Six months ago a new dance club in town purchased a high-priced, state-of-the-art music system from your company. This account is still unpaid. Write a letter to the management of the dance club and request payment. In your letter indicate that if payment is not received within 30 days, the account will be turned over to a bill collection agency.

Problem 24–1 Using the Direct Write-Off Method

The Parker Supply Company uses the direct write-off method of accounting for uncollectible accounts.

Instructions In your working papers:
(1) Record the following transactions on page 21 of the general journal.
(2) Post the transactions to the appropriate accounts.

Parker Supply Company   MEMORANDUM 78

TO: Accounting Clerk
FROM: Jon Herbert, Collection Manager
DATE: November 30, 20--
SUBJECT: Account write-off

It has been determined by the collection department that Account No. 4698214, Sonya Dickson, in the amount of $630, is uncollectible. This memo is your authorization to write this amount off as uncollectible.
  Thank you.

Date	Transactions
Apr. 10	Sold merchandise on account to Sonya Dickson, $600 plus $30 sales tax, Sales Slip 928.
Nov. 30	Wrote off Sonya Dickson's account as uncollectible, $630, Memorandum 78.
Dec. 30	Received $630 from Sonya Dickson in full payment of her account. This account was written off on November 30, Memorandum 89 and Receipt 277.

The Allowance Method

What You'll Learn

- The concept of matching uncollectible accounts with revenue.
- The allowance method of accounting for uncollectible accounts.
- How to record the adjustment for uncollectible accounts on the work sheet.
- How to record estimated uncollectible amounts on the financial statements.
- How to journalize the adjusting entry for uncollectible accounts.
- How to write off an uncollectible account receivable using the allowance method.
- How to record the collection of an account written off by the allowance method.

Why It's Important

The allowance method of accounting for uncollectible accounts conforms to the matching principle.

KEY TERMS

allowance method
book value of accounts receivable

In Section 1 you learned that the direct write-off method is used by:

- small businesses
- businesses with few credit customers
- all businesses for tax purposes

Businesses that have many credit customers use the allowance method of accounting for uncollectible accounts. This method allows businesses to match revenue with the expenses incurred to earn that revenue. In this section you will learn about the allowance method and continue to journalize transactions involving uncollectible accounts.

Matching Uncollectible Accounts Expense with Revenue

When the direct write-off method of accounting for uncollectible accounts is used, an unpaid account is written off when the business determines that it will not be paid. Under the direct write-off method, it often happens that the sale is recorded in one period, and the uncollectible accounts expense is recorded in the following period. This violates the matching principle.

One of the fundamental principles of accounting is that *revenue should be matched with the expenses incurred in generating that revenue.* This means that expenses incurred to earn revenue should be deducted in the same period that the revenue is recorded. The uncollectible accounts expense should be reported in the year in which the sale takes place. However, the uncollectible account expense is usually not determined with certainty until some future period. That is, a credit sale in the year 2005 may not be determined to be uncollectible until some time in 2006. In order to conform to the matching principle, the credit sales are recorded in the year 2005 and an *estimate* of the uncollectible accounts expense is also recorded in 2005.

The estimate of uncollectible accounts expense is recorded as an end-of-period adjustment. The adjusting entry meets two objectives:

(1) **Accounts Receivable** is reduced to the amount the business can reasonably expect to receive.

(2) The estimated uncollectible accounts expense is charged to the current period.

Let's look at this method of accounting for uncollectible accounts.

The Allowance Method

The **allowance method** of accounting for uncollectible accounts matches the estimated uncollectible accounts expense with sales made during the same period. At the end of the period, the accountant must calculate bad debts expense that will result from the sales made during the period. The estimated uncollectible accounts expense is recorded as an adjustment on the work sheet. The two accounts affected by this adjustment are **Uncollectible Accounts Expense** and **Allowance for Uncollectible Accounts.**

When the adjustment is made, the business does not know exactly which charge customers will not pay the amounts they owe. Therefore, the estimated uncollectible amount cannot be credited to **Accounts Receivable** (neither controlling nor subsidiary). Since **Accounts Receivable** cannot be used to record the estimated uncollectible amount, another account is opened. This account is **Allowance for Uncollectible Accounts.**

Allowance for Uncollectible Accounts is used to summarize the *estimated* uncollectible accounts receivable of the business. It is classified as a contra asset account.

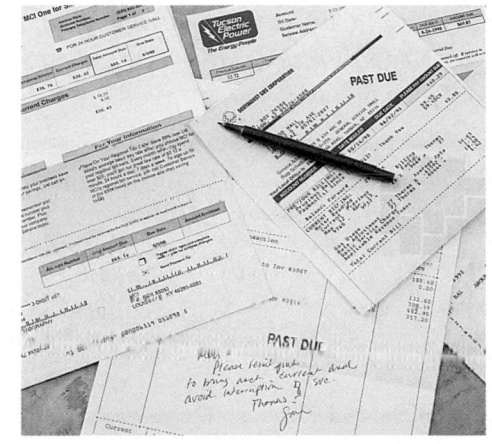

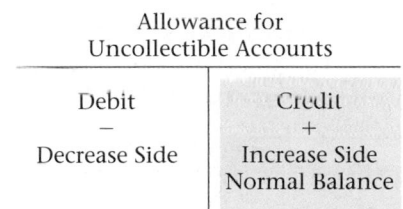

Allowance for Uncollectible Accounts	
Debit	Credit
−	+
Decrease Side	Increase Side
	Normal Balance

Allowance for Uncollectible Accounts appears on the balance sheet as a deduction from **Accounts Receivable.** By using **Allowance for Uncollectible Accounts:**

- The balance of **Accounts Receivable** still equals the total of the customer accounts in the subsidiary ledger.
- The balance of **Allowance for Uncollectible Accounts** represents the amount the business *estimates* to be uncollectible.
- The difference between **Accounts Receivable** and **Allowance for Uncollectible Accounts** represents the book value of accounts receivable.

The **book value of accounts receivable** is the amount the business can reasonably expect to collect from the accounts receivable. **Figure 24–3** illustrates how this adjustment is recorded and extended on the work sheet.

Notice that **Allowance for Uncollectible Accounts** has a $125 balance in the Trial Balance Credit column. This balance is carried over from

Figure 24–3 Recording
the Adjustment for
Uncollectible Accounts
on the Work Sheet

	ACCT. NO.	ACCOUNT NAME	TRIAL BALANCE		ADJUSTMENTS	
			DEBIT	CREDIT	DEBIT	CREDIT
1	101	Cash in Bank	12 650 00			
2	115	Accounts Receivable	44 893 00			
3	117	Allowance for Uncollectible Accts.		125 00		(b)1 350 00
23	670	Supplies Expense	600 00			
24	675	Uncollectible Accounts Expense			(b)1 350 00	
25						

Business Transaction

On December 31 On Your Mark estimates its uncollectible accounts expense for the year ended December 31 to be $1,350. (Various methods are used to estimate uncollectible accounts expense. You will learn about two of these methods later in this chapter.)

ANALYSIS **Identify** 1. The accounts affected are **Uncollectible Accounts Expense** and **Allowance for Uncollectible Accounts.**

Classify 2. **Uncollectible Accounts Expense** is an expense account. **Allowance for Uncollectible Accounts** is a contra asset account.

+/− 3. **Uncollectible Accounts Expense** is increased by $1,350. **Allowance for Uncollectible Accounts** is increased by $1,350.

DEBIT-CREDIT RULE 4. Increases to expense accounts are recorded as debits. Debit **Uncollectible Accounts Expense** for $1,350.

5. Increases to contra asset accounts are recorded as credits. Credit **Allowance for Uncollectible Accounts** for $1,350.

T ACCOUNTS 6.

Uncollectible Accounts Expense		Allowance for Uncollectible Accounts	
Debit + 1,350	Credit −	Debit −	Credit + 1,350

JOURNAL ENTRY 7.

GENERAL JOURNAL PAGE __15__

	DATE		DESCRIPTION	POST. REF.	DEBIT	CREDIT	
1	20--		Adjusting Entries				1
2	Dec.	31	Uncollectible Accts. Expense		1 350 00		2
3			Allow. for Uncollectible Accts.			1 350 00	3
4							4
5							5

Athletic Wear

Sheet

December 31, 20--

	ADJUSTED TRIAL BALANCE		INCOME STATEMENT		BALANCE SHEET		
	DEBIT	CREDIT	DEBIT	CREDIT	DEBIT	CREDIT	
	12 650 00				12 650 00		1
	44 893 00				44 893 00		2
		1 475 00				1 475 00	3
	600 00		600 00				23
	1 350 00		1 350 00				24
							25

previous years. If the previous years' uncollectible accounts exactly equaled the estimate, **Allowance for Uncollectible Accounts** would have a zero balance. This seldom happens.

Also notice that the new balance is extended first to the Adjusted Trial Balance Credit column and then to the Balance Sheet Credit column.

Reporting Estimated Uncollectible Amounts on the Financial Statements

The **Uncollectible Accounts Expense** account appears on On Your Mark's income statement as an expense. The placement of the **Uncollectible Accounts Expense** account is shown in the partial income statement in **Figure 24–4.**

Math Hints

Calculating Percentages

An easier way to calculate percentages or ratios is:
- to round dollar amounts to the nearest whole,
- then use the rounded amounts in your calculations.

Figure 24–4 Reporting Uncollectible Accounts on the Income Statement

On Your Mark Athletic Wear

Income Statement

For the Year Ended December 31, 20--

Operating Expenses				
Supplies Expense			600 00	
Uncollectible Accounts Expense			1 350 00	
Total Operating Expenses				38 345 00
Operating Income				24 698 00

On the balance sheet, **Allowance for Uncollectible Accounts** is listed immediately below **Accounts Receivable** in the Assets section. The partial balance sheet of On Your Mark is shown in **Figure 24–5.**

Figure 24–5 Reporting Allowance for Uncollectible Accounts on the Balance Sheet

On Your Mark Athletic Wear

Balance Sheet

December 31, 20--

Assets				
Cash in Bank			12 650 00	
Accounts Receivable		44 893 00		
Less: Allowance for		1 475 00	43 418 00	
Uncollectible Accounts				

Key Points

Allowance for Uncollectible Accounts

The balance of Allowance for Uncollectible Accounts reduces the balance of **Accounts Receivable**.

Notice that the balances of **Accounts Receivable** and **Allowance for Uncollectible Accounts** are entered in the first amount column. The difference between the two balances—the book value of accounts receivable—is entered in the second amount column.

Journalizing the Adjusting Entry for Uncollectible Accounts

After the work sheet is completed and the financial statements are prepared, the adjusting entries are journalized. The information for the adjusting entries is found in the Adjustments section of the work sheet as shown in **Figure 24–3**.

Figure 24–6 shows how the adjusting entry for the estimated uncollectible accounts expense is recorded in the general journal and posted to the appropriate general ledger accounts.

GENERAL JOURNAL PAGE __14__

	DATE		DESCRIPTION	POST. REF.	DEBIT	CREDIT	
1	20--		*Adjusting Entries*				1
2	Dec.	31	*Uncollectible Accounts Expense*	675	1 3 5 0 00		2
3			*Allowance for Uncollectible Accts.*	117		1 3 5 0 00	3
4							4

ACCOUNT _Allowance for Uncollectible Accounts_   ACCOUNT NO. __117__

DATE		DESCRIPTION	POST. REF.	DEBIT	CREDIT	BALANCE DEBIT	BALANCE CREDIT
20--							
Dec.	1	*Balance*	✓				1 2 5 00
	31	*Adjusting Entry*	G14		1 3 5 0 00		1 4 7 5 00

ACCOUNT _Uncollectible Accounts Expense_   ACCOUNT NO. __675__

DATE		DESCRIPTION	POST. REF.	DEBIT	CREDIT	BALANCE DEBIT	BALANCE CREDIT
20--							
Dec.	31	*Adjusting Entry*	G14	1 3 5 0 00		1 3 5 0 00	

Figure 24–6 Journalizing and Posting the Adjusting Entry for Uncollectible Accounts

At the end of the period, the balance of the **Uncollectible Accounts Expense** account is closed, along with the balances of the other expense accounts, to **Income Summary. Uncollectible Accounts Expense** has a zero balance at the beginning of the next period. The balance of **Allowance for Uncollectible Account**s is not affected by the closing entries. Its balance at the beginning of the next period is $1,475.

Writing Off Uncollectible Accounts Receivable

When it becomes clear that a charge customer is not going to pay the amount owed, the uncollectible account is removed from the accounting records.

Allowance for Uncollectible Accounts acts as a reservoir—at the end of the period, it is "filled up" by the adjusting entry. The account balance is saved until it is needed some time in the future. When a charge customer's account finally proves uncollectible, the business dips into that reservoir to write off the account. In other words, **Allowance for Uncollectible Accounts** is reduced when a specific account is written off. Let's look at an example.

Business Transaction

On April 18, after many attempts to collect the amount owed, On Your Mark decides to write off the account of Megan Sullivan for $150, Memorandum 236.

ANALYSIS	*Identify*	1.	The accounts affected are **Allowance for Uncollectible Accounts, Accounts Receivable** (controlling), and **Accounts Receivable—Megan Sullivan** (subsidiary).
	Classify	2.	**Allowance for Uncollectible Accounts** is a contra asset account. **Accounts Receivable** (controlling) and **Accounts Receivable—Megan Sullivan** (subsidiary) are asset accounts.
	+/−	3.	**Allowance for Uncollectible Accounts** is decreased by $150. **Accounts Receivable** (controlling) and **Accounts Receivable—Megan Sullivan** (subsidiary) are decreased by $150.

DEBIT-CREDIT RULE	4.	Decreases to contra asset accounts are recorded as debits. Debit **Allowance for Uncollectible Accounts** for $150.
	5.	Decreases to asset accounts are recorded as credits. Credit **Accounts Receivable** (controlling) and **Accounts Receivable—Megan Sullivan** (subsidiary) for $150.

T ACCOUNTS 6.

Allowance for Uncollectible Accounts			Accounts Receivable	
Debit	Credit		Debit	Credit
−	+		+	−
150				150

Accounts Receivable Subsidiary Ledger
Megan Sullivan

Debit	Credit
+	−
	150

JOURNAL ENTRY 7.

			GENERAL JOURNAL			PAGE __16__	
	DATE		DESCRIPTION	POST. REF.	DEBIT	CREDIT	
1	20--						1
2	Apr.	18	Allow. for Uncollectible Accts.		150 00		2
3			Accts. Rec./Megan Sullivan			150 00	3
4			Memorandum 236				4
5							5

With the allowance method, an expense account is not affected by the write-off of a specific account. The expense is recorded as an adjusting entry.

Collecting an Account Written Off by the Allowance Method

A charge customer whose account was written off as uncollectible might later pay the amount owed. When this happens:

- First, reinstate the customer's account.
- Second, record the cash receipt.

Business Transaction

On November 19 On Your Mark received a check for $150 from Megan Sullivan, whose account was written off April 18, Memorandum 294 and Receipt 2243.

ANALYSIS *Identify*
1. The accounts affected are **Accounts Receivable** (controlling), **Accounts Receivable—Megan Sullivan** (subsidiary), and **Allowance for Uncollectible Accounts.**

Classify
2. **Accounts Receivable** (controlling) and **Accounts Receivable—Megan Sullivan** (subsidiary) are asset accounts. **Allowance for Uncollectible Accounts** is a contra asset account.

+/−
3. **Accounts Receivable** (controlling) and **Accounts Receivable—Megan Sullivan** (subsidiary) are increased by $150. **Allowance for Uncollectible Accounts** is increased by $150.

DEBIT-CREDIT RULE
4. Increases to asset accounts are recorded as debits. Debit **Accounts Receivable** (controlling) and **Accounts Receivable—Megan Sullivan** (subsidiary) for $150.
5. Increases to contra asset accounts are recorded as credits. Credit **Allowance for Uncollectible Accounts** for $150.

T ACCOUNTS
6.

Accounts Receivable		Allowance for Uncollectible Accounts	
Debit + 150	Credit −	Debit −	Credit + 150

Accounts Receivable Subsidiary Ledger Megan Sullivan	
Debit + 150	Credit −

JOURNAL ENTRY   **7.**

	GENERAL JOURNAL			PAGE 18		
DATE	DESCRIPTION	POST. REF.	DEBIT	CREDIT		
1	20--					1
2	Nov. 19	Accts. Rec./Megan Sullivan		1 5 0 00		2
3		Allow. for Uncollectible Accts.			1 5 0 00	3
4		Memorandum 294				4
5						5

After this transaction is posted, the cash receipt transaction is journalized and posted. **Figure 24–7** shows Megan Sullivan's account after the cash receipt transaction is posted. The account shows that:

(1) The account was declared uncollectible and was written off.
(2) The account was reinstated.
(3) The account was collected in full.

NAME Megan Sullivan

ADDRESS 883 Bisbee Drive, Dallas, TX 75211

DATE		DESCRIPTION	POST. REF.	DEBIT	CREDIT	BALANCE
20--						
Jan.	1	Balance	✓			1 5 0 00
Apr.	18	Written off as uncollectible	G16		1 5 0 00	—
Nov.	19	Reinstated	G18	1 5 0 00		1 5 0 00
	19		G18		1 5 0 00	—

Figure 24–7 Megan Sullivan Account

ANALYZING FINANCIAL REPORTS

The Balance Sheet

In the last chapter, you learned about vertical analysis of the income statement. Another type of analysis is **horizontal analysis.** Horizontal analysis is the comparison of the same items on a financial statement for two or more accounting periods. For example, you might compare changes in depreciation or uncollectible amounts from one year to the next.

Look at the Office Depot balance sheet on page A-45. You'll see financial data for two years. The earlier year is the base year. Amounts in the current year are compared to the base year. To complete a horizontal analysis, the amounts for the base year (2000) are subtracted from the current year (2001). The result is the amount of the increase or decrease over the base year. These amounts are then calculated as percentages of the base year amounts.

▶ **Analyze the Report:**
Use the Office Depot balance sheet to complete the following:
1. By what amount and percentage did total assets and total stockholders' equity change from 2000 to 2001?
2. How does horizontal analysis provide useful information to a reader of an annual report?

Now that you have studied this section, complete the following questions and problems.

 **Thinking Critically**

1. What two objectives are met by the uncollectible accounts adjustment at the end of the period?
2. Explain the use of the allowance method of accounting for uncollectible accounts.

Analyzing Accounting

A review of the books for Mary Sawyer's business, The Secret Garden, revealed a disturbing trend. Her uncollectible accounts continue to increase. You suspect that Mary is far too nice about extending "in store" credit. You strongly recommend that she change her credit policies and collect on the outstanding accounts for this year. However, Mary just doesn't seem to understand the big picture, and she requested an illustration. Using a line graph, map out the uncollectibles for the past five years using the figures given below.

Year 1 $1,500   Year 4 $2,422
Year 2 $1,875   Year 5 $2,800
Year 3 $2,300

 **Problem 24–2 Writing Off Accounts Under the Allowance Method**

Taylor Furniture Company Inc. uses the allowance method of accounting for uncollectible accounts.

Instructions In your working papers:
(1) Record the following transactions in the general journal on page 24.
(2) Post the transactions to the appropriate accounts.
(3) Prepare the Assets section of the balance sheet for Taylor Furniture Company Inc. using the partial general ledger in your working papers. The balance of other asset accounts are **Merchandise Inventory,** $42,000; **Supplies,** $1,500; and **Prepaid Insurance,** $1,200.

Date	Transactions
May 4	Using the allowance method, wrote off the account of Jack Bowers for $1,050 as uncollectible, Memorandum 241.
Nov. 18	Received $1,050 from Jack Bowers in full payment of his account, which was written off May 4, Memorandum 321 and Receipt 1078.
Dec. 31	The adjusting entry for the estimated uncollectible accounts expense for the year ended December 31 was $1,850.

Estimating Uncollectible Accounts Receivable

Under the allowance method of accounting for uncollectible accounts, businesses estimate the uncollectible accounts expense at the end of the period. In this section you will learn about two methods used to estimate uncollectible accounts expense.

Estimating Uncollectible Accounts Expense

The percentage of net sales and the aging of accounts receivable are two ways a business may calculate an estimate of uncollectible accounts expenses. These estimates are based on judgment and past experience.

Percentage of Net Sales Method

When using the **percentage of net sales method** for estimating uncollectible accounts expense, the business assumes that a certain percentage of each year's net sales will be uncollectible. To find the adjustment for uncollectible accounts expense:

(1) Determine the percentage.
(2) Calculate net sales.
(3) Multiply net sales by the percentage.
(4) Enter the amount calculated above on the work sheet.

Let's see how this method works. First, the percentage is determined. As you can see, in recent years On Your Mark's actual uncollectible accounts have been approximately 2 percent of net sales. On this basis, On Your Mark's accountant believes that the 2 percent figure should be used to estimate uncollectible accounts expense.

Year	Net Sales	Uncollectible Accounts	Percentage
2005	$ 59,000	$1,062	(1.8%)
2006	65,000	1,430	(2.2%)
2007	67,000	1,273	(1.9%)
Totals	$191,000	$3,765	(2.0%)

Second, the amount of net sales is calculated. Remember that net sales equals sales minus sales discounts and sales returns and allowances.

What You'll Learn

- How to use the percentage of net sales method to determine the estimated uncollectible accounts expense.
- How to use the aging of accounts receivable method to determine estimated uncollectible accounts expense.

Why It's Important

In order to use the allowance method, uncollectible accounts expense is estimated at the end of the period.

KEY TERMS

percentage of net sales method
aging of accounts receivable method

As shown, net sales for On Your Mark is $67,500.

Sales		$74,500
Less: Sales Discounts	$3,000	
Sales Returns and Allowances	4,000	− 7,000
Net Sales		$67,500

Third, the uncollectible accounts expense for the current year is determined by multiplying net sales by the percentage. On Your Mark's uncollectible accounts expense for the period is estimated to be $1,350 ($67,500 × .02).

Under this method, the amount calculated is recorded as the adjustment on the work sheet and later entered into the accounting records by journalizing the adjusting entry. At the beginning of the next period, **Allowance for Uncollectible Accounts** will have a credit balance of $1,475 ($1,350 adjustment plus $125 existing balance in the account).

The Aging of Accounts Receivable Method

When using the **aging of accounts receivable method**, the uncollectible accounts expense is based on the date each customer account is due. This method assumes that the longer an account is overdue, the less likely it is to be collected. To find the adjustment for uncollectible accounts expense:

(1) "Age," or classify and group, each account according to due date.
(2) Determine a percentage for each group.
(3) Multiply the amount per group by the percentage per group and add the results.
(4) Enter on the work sheet the total estimated uncollectible amount (calculated above) adjusted by any balance in **Allowance for Uncollectible Accounts.**

Let's look at an example. First, each customer account is "aged," or classified and grouped according to its due date.

The computer printout in **Figure 24–8** is an analysis of On Your Mark's "aged" accounts receivable. As you can see, each customer account is placed in a group according to due date.

On Your Mark Athletic Wear
ANALYSIS OF ACCOUNTS RECEIVABLE
December 31, 20--

Account ID	Customer's Name	Total Amount Owed	Not Yet Due	Days Past Due 1–30	31–60	61–90	Over 90
DIM	Joe Dimaio	$ 300.00	$ 300.00				
GAL	Robert Galvin	50.00		$ 50.00			
KLE	Casey Klein	800.00					$ 800.00
MON	Anita Montero	200.00	200.00				
RAH	Shashi Rahim	175.00			$ 175.00		
RAM	Gabriel Ramos	1,000.00	1,000.00				
SUL	Megan Sullivan	40.00				$ 40.00	
TAM	Tammy's Fitness	225.00	225.00				
WON	Kim Wong	306.50		306.50			
YOU	Lara Young	750.00	750.00				
	TOTALS	$ 3,846.50	$ 2,475.00	$ 356.50	$ 175.00	$ 40.00	$ 800.00

Figure 24–8 Computer-Generated Analysis of Accounts Receivable

Next, the accountant for On Your Mark estimates what percentage of each group will be uncollectible. The percentages range from 2 to 80 percent.

Third, the total amount for each group is multiplied by the percentage for that group. The resulting amounts are the estimated uncollectible amounts for each group. The total of all the estimated uncollectible amounts represents the end-of-period balance of **Allowance for Uncollectible Accounts.** The computer printout in **Figure 24–9** illustrates how the estimated uncollectible amount is determined from the accounts receivable analysis in **Figure 24–8.** As you can see, On Your Mark estimates that a total of $729.26 of its accounts will be uncollectible.

On Your Mark Athletic Wear
AGING OF ACCOUNTS RECEIVABLE
Estimated Uncollectible Amount
December 31, 20--

Age Group	Amount	Estimated Percentage Uncollectible	Estimated Uncollectible Amount
Not yet due	$ 2,475.00	2%	$ 49.50
1–30 days past due	356.50	4%	14.26
31–60 days past due	175.00	10%	17.50
61–90 days past due	40.00	20%	8.00
Over 90 days past due	800.00	80%	640.00
Total	$ 3,846.50		$ 729.26

Figure 24–9 Accounts Receivable Aging Schedule

Finally, an adjustment is entered on the work sheet. This adjustment will bring the balance of **Allowance for Uncollectible Accounts** to the estimate of $729.26.

Suppose the balance of **Allowance for Uncollectible Accounts** reported in the Trial Balance Credit column is $49.80. To determine the adjustment, subtract the balance of **Allowance for Uncollectible Accounts** from the total estimated uncollectible amount. The adjustment amount is $679.46 ($729.26 $49.80).

After the adjusting entry is journalized and posted, the balance of **Allowance for Uncollectible Accounts** is $729.26 (the balance as determined by the aging schedule).

Uncollectible Accounts Expense		Allowance for Uncollectible Accounts	
Debit +	Credit −	Debit −	Credit +
Adj. 679.46			Bal. 49.80
			Adj. 679.46
			Bal. 729.26

Now that you have studied this section, complete the following questions and problem.

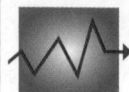

Thinking Critically

1. Explain the aging of accounts receivable method of estimating uncollectible accounts expense.
2. How do you determine the adjustment of uncollectible accounts expense when using the net sales method and the aging of accounts receivable method?

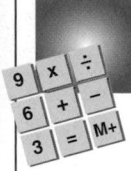

Computing in the Business World

Hernando's Card Shop is planning to expand. Before they expand, the owner wants to review the uncollectible accounts. Hernando asks you to calculate the percentage of uncollectible accounts per year.

	Net Sales	Uncollectible Accounts
Year 1	$23,000	$ 800
Year 2	28,750	1,200
Year 3	46,000	1,345
Year 4	52,000	1,150

Problem 24–3 Estimating Uncollectible Accounts Expense Using the Percentage of Net Sales Method

Listed below are the end-of-period account balances for several stationery and office supply companies. Each company uses the percentage of net sales method to estimate its uncollectible accounts expense. The percentage used by each company is also listed.

Instructions Using the form provided in your working papers:
(1) Calculate the amount of the adjustment for uncollectible accounts expense using the percentage of net sales method.
(2) Record the adjusting entry for the estimated uncollectible accounts expense for Davis Inc.

	Sales	Sales Discounts	Sales Returns and Allowances	Percentage of Net Sales Uncollectible
Andrews Co.	$142,360	$1,423	$ 936	2
The Book Nook	209,100	3,180	1,139	1
Cable Inc.	173,270	1,730	1,540	1½
Davis Inc.	65,460	650	690	2
Ever-Sharp Co.	95,085	900	1,035	1¼

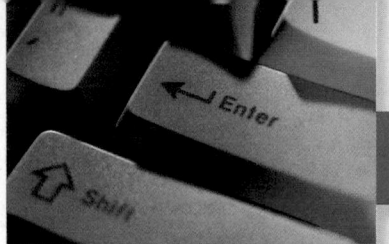

KEY CONCEPTS

1. Customer accounts that are uncollectible are an expense to the business. When it is apparent that a customer account is uncollectible, it is written off using either the direct write-off method or the allowance method.

2. Recording the direct write-off of an accounts receivable:
   Debit: **Uncollectible Accounts Expense** Credit: **Accounts Receivable** (controlling/subsidiary)

3. When a charge customer whose account was previously written off pays the amount owed, the account is first reinstated before the cash receipt is recorded.

4. Recording reinstatement of an account written off using the direct write-off method:
   Debit: **Accounts Receivable** (controlling/subsidiary) Credit: **Uncollectible Accounts Expense**

5. The allowance method of accounting for uncollectible accounts enables the business to match sales and uncollectible accounts expense in the same period.

6. **Allowance for Uncollectible Accounts** is a contra asset account and is shown on the balance sheet as a deduction from **Accounts Receivable.**

7. The book value of accounts receivable is the **Accounts Receivable** balance minus the **Allowance for Uncollectible Accounts** balance. It is the amount the business can reasonably expect to receive from all accounts receivable.

8. Recording the adjusting entry using the allowance method:
   Debit: **Uncollectible Accounts Expense** Credit: **Allowance for Uncollectible Accounts**

9. Recording the write-off of a specific uncollectible account under the allowance method:
   Debit: **Allowance for Uncollectible Accounts** Credit: **Accounts Receivable** (controlling/subsidiary)

10. Recording the reinstatement of an account written off using the allowance method:
    Debit: **Accounts Receivable** (controlling/subsidiary) Credit: **Allowance for Uncollectible Accounts**

11. Two common methods used to estimate uncollectible accounts expense are the percentage of net sales method and the aging of accounts receivable method.

12. Calculating uncollectible accounts expense using the percentage of net sales method:

    Net Sales × Percentage of Net Sales Estimated Uncollectible = Uncollectible Accounts Expense

13. Calculating uncollectible accounts expense using the aging of accounts receivable method:

Age Group	Amount	×	Estimated Percentage Uncollectible	=	Estimated Uncollectible Amount
Not yet due	xxxxx		xx		xxxx
1–30 days past due	xxxxx		xx		xxxx
31–60 days past due	xxxxx		xx		xxxx
61–90 days past due	xxxxx		xx		xxxx
91–180 days past due	xxxxx		xx		xxxx
Over 180 days past due	xxxxx		xx		xxxx
Total					xxxx

Allowance for Uncollectible Accounts, end of period ⟶ xxxx

USING KEY TERMS

You applied for your CPA license and are in the process of studying for the big exam. You need a quick review on uncollectible accounts. You decide to write a description of each key term and show its relationship to **Accounts Receivable.** Your college professor recommends that you teach this unit to his Accounting students as another way to fully comprehend the material. Use the terms below to create your "help sheet."

aging of accounts receivable
   method
allowance method
book value of accounts
   receivable

direct write-off method
percentage of net sales
   method
uncollectible accounts

Understanding Accounting
Concepts and Procedures

Instructions

Answer the following questions on a separate sheet of paper:

1. Name two methods of accounting for uncollectible accounts. Which method is likely to be used by a large business with many charge customers? Which method is likely to be used by a business that sells mainly on a cash basis?

2. Why is an entry made in the Description column of the subsidiary ledger when a customer's account is written off?

3. Describe the two journal entries needed to record the collection of an account that was previously written off.

4. Explain which accounting principle is violated when the direct write-off method of accounting for uncollectible accounts is used.

5. Under the allowance method, which two general ledger accounts are affected by the adjusting entry to record the estimated uncollectible account expense for the period?

6. What is the classification of the account **Allowance for Uncollectible Accounts?**

7. How is the book value of accounts receivable determined?

8. Explain the difference between the write-off of a customer's account using the direct write-off method and the allowance method.

9. Name two methods that can be used to estimate the uncollectible accounts expense.

10. If a company had net sales of $630,000 and estimates that its uncollectible accounts will be 2 percent of net sales, what is the amount of the adjustment?

11. Which method of estimating uncollectible accounts analyzes each customer account?

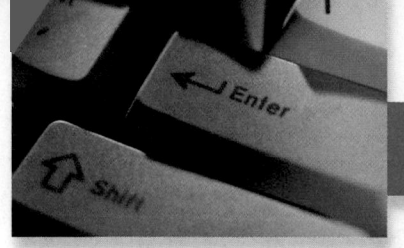

Case Study...

Merchandising Business: Formal Wear

The Black Tie sells and rents tuxedos and formal dresses. They require a down payment to reserve an outfit. The balance is recorded as an account receivable and is due ten days after the outfit is returned.

The Black Tie accepts cash, credit cards, and personal checks. Recently the store has encountered problems collecting accounts receivable. Two customers failed to return their outfits altogether.

Thinking Critically:

1. Suggest a store policy that would help avoid losses from uncollectible accounts and outfits that are not returned.
2. What customer issues might arise if you restrict payment to cash or credit cards only? How can you overcome these issues?

*inter*NET CONNECTION

Outsourcing Accounts Receivable

Outsourcing of accounts receivable is growing at a rapid rate. Since sales on account directly affect cash flow, timely collection of accounts receivable is a measure of a business's success. Businesses seek ways to reduce the expense associated with processing, monitoring, and collecting accounts receivable.

Do This:

1. Conduct research on the Web to find out what it means to outsource accounts receivable. Use search terms like "outsourcing" or "accounts receivable."
2. List three advantages of outsourcing accounts receivable.
3. What is the difference between outsourcing and using a collection agency?

Conducting an Audit with Alex

Peggy Matero, owner of Matero Department Store, uses the allowance method to account for uncollectible accounts. The March 30, 20-- trial balance shows a debit balance of $300 in the Uncollectible Accounts Expense account. You discovered that Jan Anderson's account for $300 was written off on March 1 using the direct write-off method instead of the allowance method.

Instructions

What entry was recorded in the general journal on March 1? Which entry should have been recorded in the general journal on March 1?

Workplace Skills

Interpreting and Communicating Information

Presenting information in the most effective method is a powerful workplace skill.

On the Job:

The Clothes Horse, a well-known retailer of men's apparel, is closing its doors. The store wants to collect all accounts receivable before closing.

Thinking Critically:

1. Design a letter to send to all customers with outstanding balances.
2. Design a second collection letter to send to customers with outstanding balances after four weeks have passed.

Writing Off Uncollectible Accounts Receivable

Making the Transition from a Manual to a Computerized System

Task	Perform Accounting Procedures Using Manual Methods	Perform Accounting Procedures Using Automated Methods
Preparing an Aged Accounts Receivable Report	1. Examine each customer account and organize based on due date. 2. Using accounting stationery, list each customer's account in the appropriate past date columns.	1. A preformatted report feature allows the accountant to generate an aging schedule. The software pulls data from information stored in the accounts receivable ledgers.
Writing off an uncollectible account	1. Determine the method to be used to write-off uncollectible accounts. 2. Record a general journal entry to record the write-off. 3. Post the entry to the general ledger and subsidiary ledger. 4. Calculate new balances for the accounts.	1. Determine the method to be used to write-off uncollectible accounts. 2. Outstanding invoices due are stored in the computerized system and tied to the customer's ID. 3. Using the Customer ID, the invoice due is assigned to the account, Allowance for Uncollectible Accounts.

Accounts Receivable

Peachtree Question	Description
How do I set up defaults for the aging of Accounts Receivable ledgers in Peachtree?	1. From the *Maintain* menu, select **Default** Information. 2. Select Customers to set or to change default information. (In Peachtree, Accounts Receivable ledgers are referred to as customer accounts.) 3. Click on the *Account Aging* tab. 4. Set default for how accounts are to be aged.
How do I write off an uncollectible account in Peachtree?	1. Select **Receipts** from the *Tasks* menu. 2. Enter the Customer ID. 3. In the Cash Account field, select Allowance for Uncollectible Accounts. 4. Click the *Apply to Invoices* tab. 5. Select the *Pay* box next to the invoices you wish to write off. 6. Click *Save*.
What does the software do "behind the scenes"?	The customer's account, the list of unpaid invoices, the Accounts Receivable account, and the Allowance for Uncollectible Accounts are updated.

For detailed instructions: See the Peachtree User Guide in your Glencoe Working Papers.

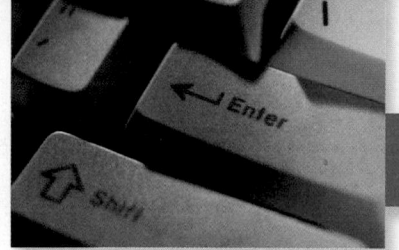

APPLICATION OPTIONS

Problem 24–4 Using the Direct Write-Off Method

Sunset Surfwear uses the direct write-off method of accounting for uncollectible accounts.

Instructions

(1) In your working papers, record the following transactions on page 14 in the general journal.

(2) Post the transactions to the appropriate accounts.

Date	Transactions
June 1	Wrote off the $288.75 account of Alex Hamilton as uncollectible, Memorandum 223.
4	Wrote off the $243.60 account of Helen Jun as uncollectible, Memorandum 249.
14	Wrote off the $57.75 account of Nate Moulder as uncollectible, Memorandum 255.
22	Received $288.75 from Alex Hamilton in full payment of his account, Memorandum 298 and Receipt 944.
29	Wrote off the $100.80 account of Martha Adams as uncollectible, Memorandum 329.

Analyze: When an account is written off, what is the impact on **Accounts Receivable** and **Uncollectible Accounts Expense?**

Problem 24–5 Calculating and Recording Estimated Uncollectible Accounts Expense

InBeat CD Shop uses the percentage of net sales method of accounting for uncollectible accounts. At the end of the period, the following account balances appeared on InBeat's trial balance:

Accts. Rec.	$110,000	Allow. for Uncoll. Accts.	$ 4,000
Sales	900,000	Sales Ret. and Allow.	50,000
Sales Disc.	10,000	Uncoll. Accts. Expense	—

Instructions

(1) In your working papers, determine the amount of the adjustment for uncollectible accounts for the period ended June 30. Management estimates that uncollectible accounts will be 1 percent of net sales.

(2) Journalize the adjusting entry on page 8 in the general journal.

(3) Post the adjusting entry to the general ledger accounts.

Analyze: Determine the book value of accounts receivable.

Complete chapter problems one of three ways:

1 **Manual** Glencoe Working Papers

or

2 **Peachtree Complete Accounting** Software

or

3 **QuickBooks** Templates (Problems 24–4, 24–6)

Peachtree®

SMART GUIDE

Step–by–Step Instructions: Problem 24–4

1. Select the problem set for Sunset Surfwear (Prob. 24–4).
2. Rename the company and set the system date.
3. Record the transactions to write off bad debts using the **Receipts** option.
4. Record the transaction (June 22) to reinstate Alex Hamilton's account **(Sales/Invoicing)** and enter the receipt **(Receipts)**.
5. Print the following reports: Cash Receipts Journal, Sales Journal, Customer Ledgers, and General Ledger.
6. Answer the Analyze question.
7. End the session.

TIP: Remember to set the *Cash Account* field to **Uncollectible Accounts Expense** when you write off a bad debt.

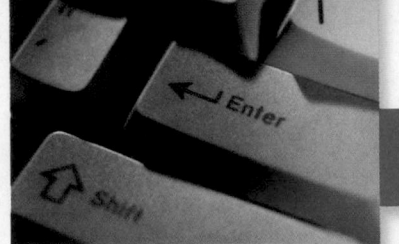

Peachtree®

SMART GUIDE

**Step–by–Step Instructions:
Problem 24–5**

1. Select the problem set for InBeat CD Shop.
2. Rename the company and set the system date.
3. Record the uncollectible accounts adjustment using the **General Journal Entry** option.
4. Print the General Journal and General Ledger reports.
5. Answer the Analyze question.
6. End the session.

Peachtree®

SMART GUIDE

**Step–by–Step Instructions:
Problem 24–6**

1. Select the problem set for Shutterbug Cameras.
2. Record the uncollectible accounts transactions.
3. Record the adjustment for estimated uncollectible accounts.
4. Record the closing entry for **Uncollectible Accounts Expense** using the **General Journal Entry** option.
5. Print reports: Cash Receipts Journal, Sales Journal, Customer Ledgers, General Journal, General Ledger, and Balance Sheet.
6. Answer the Analyze question.
7. End the session.

SOURCE DOCUMENT PROBLEM

Problem 24–6

Use the source documents in your working papers to record the transactions for this problem.

SOURCE DOCUMENT PROBLEM

Problem 24–6 Writing Off Accounts Under the Allowance Method

Shutterbug Cameras uses the allowance method of accounting for uncollectible accounts.

Instructions

(1) In your working papers, record the following transactions on page 9 in the general journal.
(2) Post the transactions to the appropriate accounts.
(3) Prepare the Assets section of the balance sheet for Shutterbug Cameras using the partial general ledger in the working papers. The balances of other asset accounts are **Merchandise Inventory**, $33,000; **Supplies**, $2,000; and **Prepaid Insurance**, $1,200.

Date	Transactions
June 2	Wrote off the $593.25 account of Kalla Booth as uncollectible, Memorandum 329.
9	Wrote off the $840 account of Click Studios as uncollectible, Memorandum 343.
10	Received $131.25 from Jimmy Thompson in full payment of his account, which was written off on November 10, Memorandum 349 and Receipt 210.
12	Wrote off the $945 account of FastForward Productions as uncollectible, Memorandum 474.
30	Recorded the adjusting entry for estimated uncollectible accounts for the period. The uncollectible accounts expense estimate is based on 2 percent of the net sales of $150,000.
30	Recorded the closing entry for **Uncollectible Accounts Expense**.

Analyze: What is the book value of the accounts receivable after the closing entries are posted?

Problem 24–7 Estimating Uncollectible Accounts Expense

Cycle Tech Bicycles uses the allowance method of accounting for uncollectible accounts. The company estimates the uncollectible amount by aging its accounts receivable accounts.

Instructions

(1) Complete the analysis of accounts receivable that is included in your working papers.
(2) Calculate the estimated uncollectible amount. Use the form provided in your working papers.

(3) Journalize the June 30 adjusting entry for uncollectible accounts expense on page 11 of the general journal. Before the adjusting entry, **Allowance for Uncollectible Accounts** had a credit balance of $142.

(4) Post the adjusting entry to the general ledger accounts.

Analyze: Calculate the book value of accounts receivable.

Problem 24–8 Reporting Uncollectible Amounts on the Financial Statements

The work sheet for River's Edge Canoe & Kayak is included in your working papers. The trial balance is complete, and all of the adjustments are entered except the one required for uncollectible accounts.

Instructions

(1) Record the adjustment for uncollectible accounts expense in the Adjustments section of the work sheet. Uncollectible accounts are estimated to be 1.5 percent of net sales. Label the adjustment (a).

(2) Complete the work sheet.

(3) Prepare an income statement, a statement of retained earnings, and a balance sheet.

(4) Record the adjusting entries on page 18 of the general journal.

(5) Post the adjusting entries. Record and post the closing entries.

Analyze: What is the balance of **Allowance for Uncollectible Accounts** before and after the adjusting entry?

 ## Problem 24–9 Using the Allowance Method for Write-Offs

Buzz Newsstand uses the allowance method for uncollectible accounts.

Instructions

In your working papers, journalize the following transactions on page 13 in the general journal. Post the transactions to the account of Lee Adkins.

Date	Transactions
Jan. 14	Wrote off the $194.50 account of Lee Adkins as uncollectible, Memorandum 498.
June 25	Received a check for $30 from Lee Adkins on account, Memorandum 767 and Receipt 98.
Dec. 10	Received notice that Lee Adkins declared bankruptcy. Received 40 percent of the balance not paid, Receipt 288 and Memorandum 941.

Analyze: If the direct write-off method was used instead of the allowance method, which account would you debit when writing off an account?

CHAPTER 25

Inventories

Exploring the Real World of Business

TRACKING INVENTORIES

Have you ever wondered where the **Gap** got its name? The original store, selling jeans and records, was named for a cultural phenomenon known as "the generation gap." Since its beginning in 1969, the **Gap** has expanded to a full line of clothing, kids clothes, and accessories.

With inventories of clothes for its Banana Republic stores, Old Navy locations, GapKids stores, and the **Gap** outlets, you can imagine how important the tracking of merchandise inventory must be. Each store tracks its own inventory and prepares regular reports on items sold and items left in stock. Studying inventory reports helps the store managers decide which items sell best in their particular markets.

What do you think?

If you worked for the **Gap,** what information would you want on an inventory report to help you decide which clothing lines to stock?

Gap

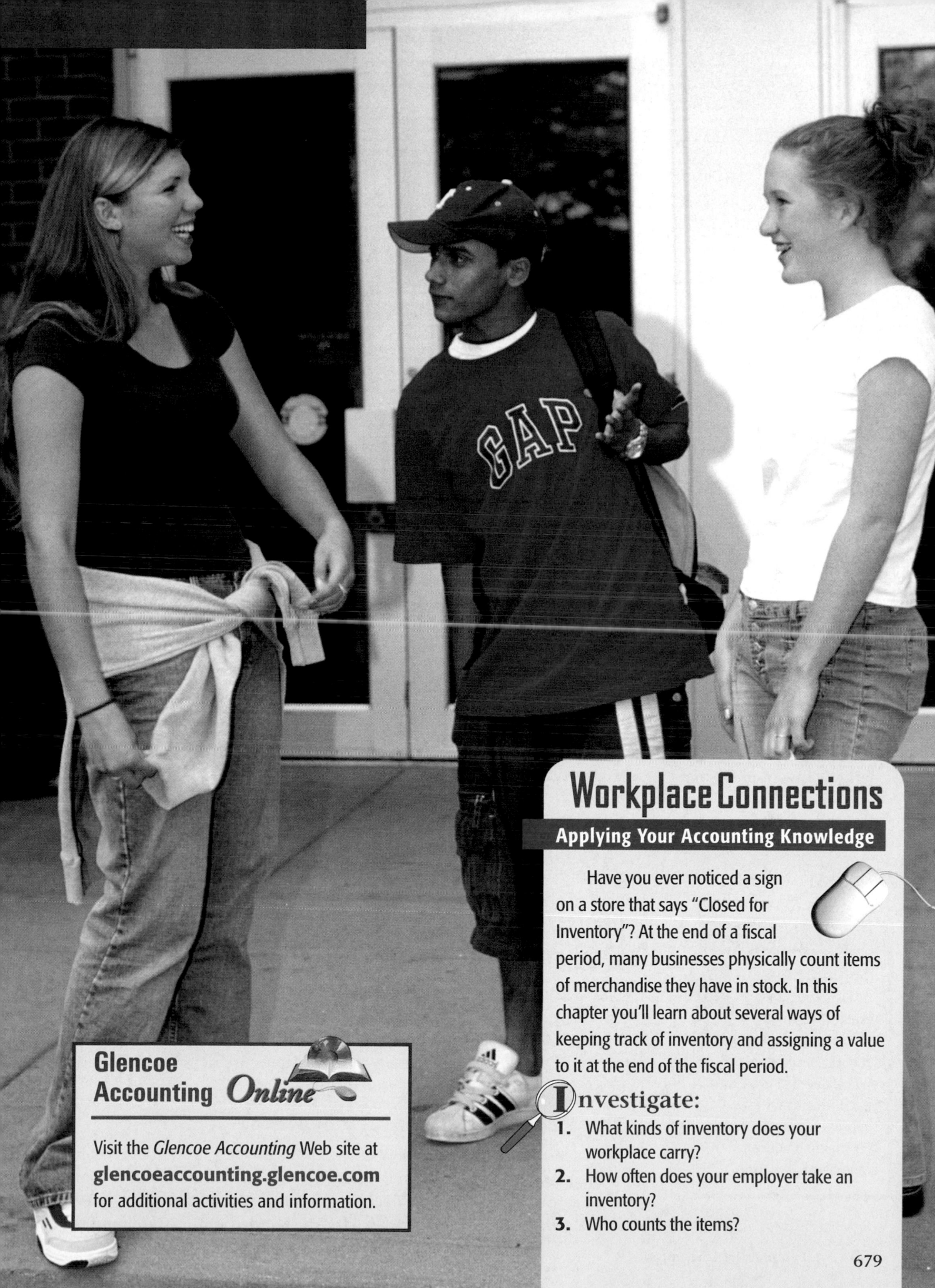

Workplace Connections

Applying Your Accounting Knowledge

Have you ever noticed a sign on a store that says "Closed for Inventory"? At the end of a fiscal period, many businesses physically count items of merchandise they have in stock. In this chapter you'll learn about several ways of keeping track of inventory and assigning a value to it at the end of the fiscal period.

Investigate:

1. What kinds of inventory does your workplace carry?
2. How often does your employer take an inventory?
3. Who counts the items?

Glencoe Accounting *Online*

Visit the *Glencoe Accounting* Web site at **glencoeaccounting.glencoe.com** for additional activities and information.

Determining the Quantity of Inventories

What You'll Learn

- The purpose of the **Merchandise Inventory** account.
- The difference between a periodic and a perpetual inventory system.

Why It's Important

For marketing and financial reporting purposes, a merchandising business needs to know the quantity of merchandise on hand.

KEY TERMS

perpetual inventory system
point-of-sale terminal
online
periodic inventory system

In a merchandising business, it is essential to maintain control over the merchandise that is purchased, stored, and sold. To keep control of its merchandise, a business establishes a system of inventory procedures. Can you imagine the problems that a store like Wal-Mart or a manufacturer like Toyota would encounter if they didn't have an inventory system?

Merchandise Inventory

Earlier you learned that goods purchased by a business for resale to customers are called merchandise. The **Merchandise Inventory** account shows the cost of goods purchased for resale. **Merchandise Inventory** is the only account reported on both the balance sheet (as a current asset) and on the income statement (to calculate the cost of merchandise sold).

Merchandise Inventory typically is one of the largest asset accounts. By tracking merchandise, a business knows:

- how much merchandise is sold,
- which items are selling well, and
- which items, when sold, should not be replaced.

To function efficiently, an inventory control system tracks the quantity and cost of merchandise purchased, on hand, and sold.

Determining the Quantity of Inventories

Two methods are used to track merchandise: the perpetual inventory system and the periodic inventory system. Perpetual inventory systems are used by most large businesses as well as smaller ones with automated accounting systems. Periodic inventory systems are used by small businesses that maintain manual accounting records.

The Perpetual Inventory System

A **perpetual inventory system** keeps a constant, up-to-date record of merchandise on hand. This system reports what merchandise is on hand at any point in time. Under the perpetual inventory system, every time a purchase or sale occurs, an entry is recorded in the **Merchandise**

Did You Know?

Manufacturing

Gap Inc. does not manufacture any of the hundreds of retail products that earn its revenue of around $13 billion a year. The company uses suppliers in several different countries to produce its brand-name products.

Inventory account. Also, after every sale the cost of merchandise sold is recorded in the accounting records.

When a business uses a perpetual inventory system, management can obtain the quantity on hand and cost of any item at any point in time. The business can reorder items when the quantity on hand is low. This avoids loss of sales due to inadequate inventory. **Figure 25–1** shows an example of a computer printout for a perpetual inventory system.

Wilton Outdoor Center
DAILY INVENTORY REPORT
Department 47
October 13, 20--

Stock No.	Item	Unit	Quantity	Unit Cost	Total Value
7651	Kilmer Rods	Each	8	$ 31.80	$ 254.40
7560	Tyon Rods	Each	12	36.40	436.80
7762	Peterson Rods	Each	11	29.75	327.25
7785	K & R Rods	Each	6	26.30	157.80
7208	Weber Reels	Each	5	35.20	176.00
7338	Pro Reels	Each	8	41.40	331.20
7193	Artcraft Reels	Each	4	47.10	188.40
7525	#7 Fishing Hook	Box	26	4.86	126.36
7937	#9 Fishing Hook	Box	31	5.24	162.44
	Total				$ 2,160.65

Figure 25–1 Computer Printout from a Perpetual Inventory System

Computers help to maintain a perpetual inventory system. Many businesses use electronic cash registers, known as **point-of-sale terminals**. These terminals are **online** to a central computer system. Online means that the terminal or cash register is linked to the computer. These machines read bar codes that identify the item being sold. The computer records the sale and automatically updates the inventory information. Also, the cost and quantity of merchandise that is purchased is entered into the computer, and the inventory records are updated.

Businesses that have not yet automated their operations may also use a perpetual inventory system. Instead of point-of-sale terminals and computers, they use stock record sheets or cards. **Figure 25–2** shows a stock card used in a perpetual inventory system. For every purchase and sale, the amount of increase or decrease is recorded on the stock card. For example, when merchandise is purchased, the quantity received is recorded in the In column of the stock card. When items are sold, the quantity is recorded in the Out column.

Figure 25–2 Stock Card Used in a Perpetual Inventory System

The Periodic Inventory System

Another commonly used system of determining the quantity of merchandise on hand is a periodic inventory system. Under the **periodic inventory system**, inventory records are updated only after a physical count of merchandise on hand is made. Under this system, inventory records are not adjusted for every purchase and sale.

STOCK CARD

STOCK NO.	ITEM
C 1297	Altmore Disc Player

SUPPLIER	SUPPLIER'S CATALOGUE NO.
Star Electric	91246

UNIT	MINIMUM	MAXIMUM
Each	15	60

DATE	EXPLANATION	IN	OUT	BALANCE
7/1/20--	Balance on Hand			48
7/8/20--	Shipping Order 21928		6	42
7/12/20--	Shipping Order 22201		10	32
7/20/20--	Shipping Order 22456		8	24
7/24/20--	Shipping Order 22719		12	12
7/24/20--	Purchase Req. 19426			
7/31/20--	Receiving Report 21563	48		60

The Physical Inventory Count

Businesses take a physical count of their merchandise at least once a year. This is called *taking inventory*. Businesses using the periodic inventory system take a physical count to update their accounting records.

For businesses with many items in inventory, the process of identifying and counting all items of merchandise is very time-consuming. For this reason, inventory is usually counted when it is at its lowest level. Seasonal businesses take physical counts and record inventories at the end of the peak selling period after most of the merchandise has been sold. A ski shop, for instance, would probably take inventory in May or June.

The total number of a particular item on hand is recorded on an inventory card or an inventory sheet. **Figure 25–3** shows a typical inventory sheet. The inventory sheet lists the stock number of the item, a description of the item, the quantity on hand, the unit cost, and the total cost of the inventory item on hand.

INVENTORY SHEET

DATE Jan. 5, 20--   CLERK Arlene Stone   PAGE 8

STOCK NO.	ITEM	UNIT	QUANTITY	UNIT COST		TOTAL VALUE	
1901	Needles	Pkg	24	1	14	27	36
2132	Thread	Spool	12		65	7	80
2136	Thread	Spool	18		55	9	90
3245	Zipper	Each	18	1	50	27	00
1917	Pins	Box	24		79	18	96
4971	Buttons	Pkg	12		89	10	68
4993	Tape Measure	Each	15	1	49	22	35
				TOTAL FOR THIS SHEET		789	14

Figure 25–3 Inventory Sheet

A MATTER OF ETHICS

Keeping Promotional Items

Imagine that you just got a job in the cosmetics department of a large department store like Macy's. You have access to free samples—such as shampoo, moisturizer, lipstick, and nail polish—offered by manufacturers to get customers to try their products. This is great! You'll never have to buy these products again. You figure by using them, you're helping to promote them.

Ethical Decision Making:

☛ What are the ethical issues?

☛ What are the alternatives?

☛ Who are the affected parties?

☛ How do the alternatives affect the parties?

☛ What would you do?

Now that you have studied this section, complete the following questions and problems.

Thinking Critically

1. Why do seasonal businesses take inventory at the end of the peak selling period?
2. What is the difference between a periodic and a perpetual inventory system?

Communicating Accounting

Natural Wonder offers products organically grown or made from organic materials. Its products include clothing, jewelry, gardening materials, and hair and body care products. The store is interested in a system that will keep an accurate count of inventory. Discuss the different inventory systems and explain how frequently each system is updated.

Problem 25–1 **Preparing Inventory Reports**

In your working papers, complete the manual inventory sheet for Carole's Gift Shop. Use today's date and your name as the clerk.

Stock No.	Item	Unit	Quantity	Unit Cost
1790	Greeting Cards	Doz.	32	6.00
2217	Plush Toys	Each	20	2.50
1900	Balloons	Doz.	12	.50
1201	Wrapping Paper	Each	30	1.12
1205	Ribbon	Spool	25	.75
3495	Novelty Buttons	Doz.	12	2.50
2722	Music Boxes	Doz.	6	60.00
4200	Party Supplies	Doz.	10	6.50
1907	Gift Boxes	Doz.	5	2.75
1742	Vases	Doz.	2	12.50

Determining the Cost of Inventories

What You'll Learn

- How to determine the cost of the merchandise on hand.
- How to use the four inventory costing methods.

Why It's Important

Much time and effort is spent determining the cost of merchandise inventory because it appears on both the balance sheet and the income statement.

KEY TERMS

specific identification
method
first-in, first-out method
last-in, first-out method
weighted average cost
method

Once the quantity of merchandise on hand is determined, the cost of that merchandise is calculated. There are four inventory costing methods used to assign costs to merchandise.

Methods of Determining Inventory Costs

When merchandise is purchased, it is recorded in the accounting records at cost. However, assigning a cost to each item in inventory can be complicated. A business may purchase the same item many times within a single inventory period, and the cost may change from one purchase to the next. The challenge is to decide which cost applies to each item. To simplify matters businesses use one of four inventory costing methods:

- specific identification
- first-in, first-out
- last-in, first-out
- weighted average cost

The Specific Identification Costing Method

Under the **specific identification method**, the exact cost of each item is determined and assigned to that item. The actual cost of each item is obtained from the invoice.

The specific identification method is most often used by businesses that sell a small number of items with high unit prices. Appliance stores, automobile dealerships, and furniture stores often use this method. Let's look at an example.

The Disk Jockey Electronics Store uses the periodic inventory system. It started the year with a beginning inventory of 15 laser disc players. During the period the store purchased an additional 50 players. When a physical inventory count was taken on May 31, there were 12 players still on hand. The cost of the players was calculated as follows:

Date	Description	Units	Cost		Total
June 1	Beginning inventory	15	$250	=	$ 3,750
Aug. 4	Purchase	20	250	=	5,000
Dec. 8	Purchase	10	253	=	2,530
Feb. 27	Purchase	10	258	=	2,580
May 1	Purchase	10	260	=	2,600
	Total	65			$16,460

Using the specific identification method, the accountant checks the invoices to find the actual cost of each of the 12 players still on hand at the end of May. The accountant found the following:

```
 4  purchased @ $253 each  =  $ 1,012
 5  purchased @ $258 each  =    1,290
 3  purchased @ $260 each  =      780
12  players (ending inventory)   $3,082
```

The cost of ending inventory is $3,082. Once the cost of ending inventory is calculated, the cost of merchandise sold can be computed:

Purchases available for sale
− Cost of ending inventory
Cost of merchandise sold

In this example the cost of the laser disc players sold using the specific identification method is $13,378:

	Units	Cost
Cost of players available for sale	65	$16,460
Less ending inventory	12	3,082
Cost of merchandise sold	53	$13,378

The First-In, First-Out Costing Method

The **first-in, first-out method (FIFO)** of assigning cost assumes that the first items purchased (first in) are the first items sold (first out). The **FIFO** method assumes that the items purchased most recently are the ones on hand at the end of the period. The physical flow of most merchandise is first-in, first out. For example, think about milk that is stocked by a supermarket. Since milk is perishable, the supermarket stocks the shelves with the milk it purchased first. As that milk is sold, later purchases of milk are added at the back of the shelves.

Let's apply the FIFO costing method to our laser disc player example.

Date	Description	Units	Cost	Total
June 1	Beginning inventory	15	$250 =	$ 3,750
Aug. 4	Purchase	20	250 =	5,000
Dec. 8	Purchase	10	253 =	2,530
Feb. 27	Purchase	10	258 =	2,580
May 1	Purchase	10	260 =	2,600
	Total	65		$16,460

Under the FIFO method, the items purchased first are assumed to be the items sold first. In other words, the 53 players sold are assumed to be as follows:

	Units
Beginning inventory	15
Aug. 4	20
Dec. 8	10
Feb. 27	8
Total sold	53

The items remaining in inventory are:

		Units
Feb. 27	(10 − 8 sold)	2
May 1		10
Total		12

The cost of the ending inventory using the FIFO method is:

10 units @ $260 each	=		$2,600
2 units @ $258 each	=		516
12 units			$3,116

The cost of merchandise sold using the FIFO method is $13,344:

	Units	
Cost of players available for sale	65	$16,460
Less ending inventory	12	3,116
Cost of merchandise sold	53	$13,344

The Last-In, First-Out Costing Method

The **last-in, first-out method (LIFO)** of assigning inventory cost assumes that the last items purchased (last in) are the first items sold (first out). The LIFO method assumes that the items purchased first are still on hand at the end of the period. The earliest costs, therefore, are the ones used to assign a cost to the inventory. The physical flow of a stone and gravel company is last-in, first-out. When new gravel is purchased and delivered, it is deposited on top of the existing gravel. As gravel is taken from the top of the pile, the first gravel used is the last gravel delivered.

Let's return to the laser disc player example and apply the LIFO costing method.

Date	Description	Units	Cost		Total
June 1	Beginning inventory	15	$250	=	$ 3,750
Aug. 4	Purchase	20	250	=	5,000
Dec. 8	Purchase	10	253	=	2,530
Feb. 27	Purchase	10	258	=	2,580
May 1	Purchase	10	260	=	2,600
	Total	65			$16,460

Using the LIFO method, the 12 players remaining in stock are from the beginning inventory of 15 units. The cost of the ending inventory is $3,000 (12 units @ $250 each).

The cost of merchandise sold using the LIFO method is $13,460:

	Units	
Cost of players available for sale	65	$16,460
Less ending inventory	12	3,000
Cost of merchandise sold	53	$13,460

The Weighted Average Cost Method

A fourth method of assigning inventory costs is the weighted average cost method. The **weighted average cost method** assigns the average cost to each unit in inventory. The average cost is calculated by:

- adding the number of units on hand at the beginning of the period and the number of units purchased
- adding the cost of the units on hand at the beginning of the period and the cost of the units purchased
- dividing the total cost by the total number of units

The average cost per unit is used to determine the cost of the ending inventory. Again, we will use the Disk Jockey example to apply the weighted average cost method.

Date	Description	Units	Cost		Total
June 1	Beginning inventory	15	$250	=	$ 3,750
Aug. 4	Purchase	20	250	=	5,000
Dec. 8	Purchase	10	253	=	2,530
Feb. 27	Purchase	10	258	=	2,580
May 1	Purchase	10	260	=	2,600
	Total	65			$16,460

The average cost per player is $253.23 ($16,460 ÷ 65 units).

The cost of the ending merchandise inventory using the weighted average cost method is $3,038.76 (12 units × $253.23).

The cost of merchandise sold using the weighted average cost method is $13,421.24:

	Units	
Cost of players available for sale	65	$16,460.00
Less ending inventory	12	3,038.76
Cost of merchandise sold	53	$13,421.24

The following table illustrates the different inventory costing methods for Disk Jockey. Once an inventory costing method is selected, it is applied consistently.

Method	Cost of Players Sold	Ending Inventory
Specific identification	$13,378.00	$3,082.00
FIFO	13,344.00	3,116.00
LIFO	13,460.00	3,000.00
Weighted average	13,421.24	3,038.76

ANALYZING FINANCIAL REPORTS

Inventories

In this chapter, you learned how to count and assign a value to inventory on hand at the end of a fiscal period. Knowing how much inventory is on hand helps managers make decisions about how much product to make. For example, too much inventory means the business has not sold what it has produced, and its money is tied up in the inventory. Managers would want to find out why the product is not selling as well as they expected when they set production numbers.

▶ **Analyze the Report:**

Use the Office Depot balance sheet and "To Our Shareholders" message on pages A-40–A-45 to answer these questions.
1. How did merchandise inventories for Office Depot change from 2000 to 2001?
2. What might be some reasons for this change?

Now that you have studied this section, complete the following questions and problems.

Thinking Critically

1. What type of business would use the specific identification costing method?
2. Contrast the LIFO and FIFO inventory costing methods.

Computing in the Business World

Foxfire Golf Club Pro Shop uses the specific identification method for inventory control. At the beginning of the year, Foxfire had 30 golf club sets on hand. The golf club sets were purchased for $800 each. An additional 12 golf club sets were purchased during the year at $875 each. When inventory was taken at the end of the season, 5 golf sets were still on hand. The remaining 5 sets were valued at $875 each. Using the FIFO method of inventory valuation, what was the total cost of merchandise sold?

Problem 25–2 Determining Inventory Costs

The following items were purchased by Kudos Leather Goods during the month of April:

April 2	34 wallets @ $12.95 each
April 8	24 wallets @ $13.10 each
April 18	15 wallets @ $13.25 each
April 26	20 wallets @ $13.27 each

On April 1 the business had in inventory 19 wallets valued at $12.90 each. On April 30 the business had 36 wallets in inventory; of these wallets, 8 were purchased on April 2, 15 were purchased on April 8, 3 were purchased on April 18, and 10 were purchased on April 26.

Instructions In your working papers, calculate the cost of the ending inventory using:
    (a) the specific identification method
    (b) the FIFO method
    (c) the LIFO method
    (d) the weighted average method

ERIC MONGO
Accounts Payable Accounting Assistant
KICU-TV, Channel 36

Q: How did you get interested in accounting?
A: I developed the interest while working in a family business. I worked as a temp for about three months, then realized that my boss was really smart. I knew I could learn much from her and get more experience than I could get in a class.

Q: What do you do on a typical day?
A: It depends on the week. My functions have recently been expanded to include payroll. If it is a payroll week, from Monday through Wednesday I process payroll in the morning. In the afternoons, I do journal entries. On regular weeks, I pick up the mail and classify the invoices we've received by how each of them is to be paid. I also talk to vendors about payment and to company employees about their checks.

Q: Is a degree necessary for a position as an accounting assistant?
A: Companies often require a bachelor's degree of some kind. They also require some experience, especially if you don't have an accounting or finance degree. You need basic accounting skills. Companies are reluctant to hire someone who has to be taught everything from the beginning.

Q: What is the future like for an accounting assistant?
A: There are quite a lot of openings to go into from here, such as international business or auditing. Accounting is good experience if you want to run your own business.

Tips from . . .

Robert Half International Inc.
Many executives believe a good team player is one who can meet deadlines. Everyone must help keep a project on track. If you don't, everyone else has to work harder to compensate.

CAREER FACTS

Nature of the Work: Organize and process invoices and checks; journal entries; data entry.
Training or Education Needed: A bachelor's degree, and some accounting experience.
Aptitudes, Abilities, and Skills: Accounting, time-management skills, problem-solving skills, accuracy, and communication skills.
Salary Range: $25,000 to $35,000 depending on company size and industry.
Career Path: Start as an entry-level bookkeeper, then take on more difficult tasks and eventually move up as you develop more skills.

Thinking Critically: How might you get the basic accounting experience you need for an entry-level accounting position?

Analyzing the Inventory Costing Methods

A business may use any one of the four inventory costing methods. Careful consideration is given to this choice because it affects the gross profit reported by the business.

Choosing an Inventory Costing Method

When a business applies the same accounting methods from one period to the next, the business is applying the **consistency principle** . Once a business chooses an inventory costing method, the business must use it consistently. This helps owners and creditors compare financial reports from one period to another.

Businesses are permitted to change costing methods but must declare the reasons for changing and how the change will affect the financial statements. In addition, the business must get permission for the change from the Internal Revenue Service.

When making a decision about which inventory costing method to use, the owner or manager compares the four methods and selects the one that is likely to be the most beneficial to the company. The owner or manager will consider the present economic conditions and the future economic outlook. He or she will also consider whether prices and demand for the product will remain stable, will increase, or will decrease.

Comparing the Four Methods of Determining Inventory Cost

The cost of ending inventory affects the cost of merchandise sold, which in turn affects the income or loss reported on the income statement. Remember:

Sales
— Cost of merchandise sold
Gross profit on sales
— Operating expenses
Net income (loss)

The following table compares Disk Jockey's gross profit on sales using the four inventory costing methods. All of the laser disc players were sold for $320 each. Total sales are $16,960 (53 units × $320).

	Specific Identification	First-In, First-Out	Last-In, First-Out	Weighted Average
Sales	$16,960.00	$16,960.00	$16,960.00	$16,960.00
Less: Cost of merchandise sold	13,378.00	13,344.00	13,460.00	13,421.24
Gross profit on sales	$ 3,582.00	$ 3,616.00	$ 3,500.00	$ 3,538.76

Over the year the cost of the laser disc players increased from $250 to $260. As shown in the table, in a period of rising prices, the LIFO method results in the lowest gross profit on sales. The FIFO method results in the highest gross profit on sales.

Businesses pay income taxes on income earned. As shown above, the inventory costing method used by a business can increase or decrease its taxes.

Reporting Inventory Cost Using the Lower-of-Cost-or-Market Rule

The cost of the inventory is reported on the income statement and the balance sheet. The cost of the ending inventory that appears on the financial statements is the lower of cost (calculated using one of the four inventory methods) or market value.

Market value is the current price that is charged for similar items of merchandise in the market. Market value is the cost at which the inventory items could be replaced at the date of the financial statements.

Let's look at an example. Assume that Disk Jockey determines that the current market value of the laser disc players is $248 each. At market the players are worth $2,976 ($248 × 12 units). Assume also that Disk Jockey uses the FIFO inventory costing method. Under this method the cost of the ending inventory was $3,116.

Following the lower-of-cost-or-market rule, Disk Jockey will report inventory at $2,976.

Lower of cost (FIFO)	$3,116
or	
Market	2,976

Cost is the most common basis for reporting inventory. Occasionally inventory may be worth less than its cost. For example, some merchandise items may deteriorate or become obsolete. If the market value of such items is less than the cost, the difference is a loss to the business. In such a case, it is more conservative to report inventory at market value.

The **conservatism principle** is another principle of accounting. To be conservative is to take the safe route. In reporting the financial position of a business, the conservatism principle states that it is best to present amounts that are least likely to result in an overstatement of income or assets. The lower-of-cost-or-market rule is conservative for two reasons:

(1) Decreases in inventory value (losses) are recognized when they occur, but increases in inventory value are not recorded.
(2) Inventory as reported on the balance sheet is never greater, but may be less, than the actual cost of the inventory.

Now that you have studied this section, complete the following questions and problems.

Thinking Critically

1. If a business wants to change its inventory costing method, why must it get permission from the Internal Revenue Service?
2. Explain why the lower-of-cost-or-market rule for inventory valuation is a conservative approach.

Analyzing Accounting

The management of Baby Steps Children's Store wants to report the largest gross profit on sales. Using the graph, compare the gross profit on sales for the four inventory costing methods. Which method results in the largest gross profit on sales?

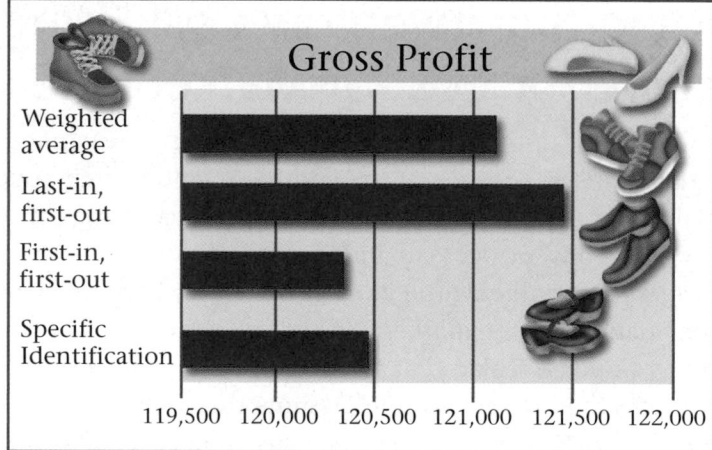

Problem 25–3 Analyzing a Source Document

Read the following memorandum and complete the assigned task.

MEMORANDUM

TO: Accounting Clerk
FROM: Accounting Manager
DATE: June 30, 20--
SUBJECT: Change in Inventory Method

We have received approval to change from the LIFO to the FIFO method of determining our inventory costs. Please calculate the cost of the Walk-A-Long Dolls using the FIFO method. There are 36 dolls in inventory.

Walk-A-Long Dolls	Beginning inventory	8 @ $15.45
	Purchases 6/11	12 @ $15.95
	6/17	10 @ $16.25
	6/22	6 @ $16.40

Instructions

1. What is the new value of the ending inventory?
2. Assume that all 36 dolls were sold for $21.95. What is the gross profit for this item?

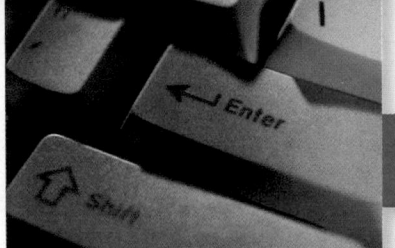

KEY CONCEPTS

1. It is important for a business to keep accurate inventory records so that the financial statements are correct.
2. Most businesses take a physical inventory count at least once a year.
3. Inventory Systems

Perpetual	Periodic
Provides current inventory records at any point in time.	A physical count of all merchandise on hand is required to update inventory records.

4. Perpetual inventory systems are used by most large businesses. Periodic inventory systems are often used by small businesses that maintain manual accounting records.
5. Inventory Costing Methods

Specific identification method	The exact cost of each item is tracked.
First-in, first-out method (FIFO)	Assumes that the first items purchased are the first items sold.
Last-in, first-out method (LIFO)	Assumes that the last items purchased are the first items sold.
Weighted average cost method	Uses an average cost for each inventory item.

6. A company's gross profit on sales and net income are affected by the inventory costing method used.
7. A business must be consistent with the inventory costing method it uses. A change in inventory valuation method must be approved by the Internal Revenue Service.
8. The cost of ending inventory affects the cost of merchandise sold, which in turn affects the income or loss reported on the income statement.
9. The lower-of-cost-or-market rule is a conservative approach to costing inventory. On the financial statements, ending inventory is reported at the lower of cost (using one of the costing methods) or market value.

USING KEY TERMS

Grandma's Toy Attic is in the process of changing from a manual to an automated system of inventory control. You, as the owner, plan to hire an inventory supervisor who understands accounting principles, inventory control, and business economics as well as computer applications. You decide to run an advertisement in your local newspaper to find the most qualified individual. Use the terms listed below and write an advertisement to attract applicants for the inventory supervisor position. You are encouraged to give your newspaper some layout ideas for the advertisement. Also, use these terms to create a job description.

conservatism principle	periodic inventory system
consistency principle	perpetual inventory system
first-in, first-out method	point-of-sale terminal
last-in, first-out method	specific identification method
market value	weighted average cost method
online	

Understanding Accounting Concepts and Procedures

Instructions

On a separate sheet of paper, answer the following questions:

1. Why should a company have a control system for its merchandise inventory?
2. What is the difference between a periodic and a perpetual inventory system?
3. Why is a physical inventory count taken at least once a year?
4. Why is it difficult for some businesses to use a perpetual inventory system?
5. What advantage is there in using a perpetual inventory system?
6. What is meant by the phrase "with the FIFO method, the inventory is based on the most recent costs"?
7. How does the inventory costing method affect gross profit on sales and net income?
8. What is the lower-of-cost-or-market rule, and why is it used?

Case Study...

Merchandising Business: Home Building and Supply

Remodeling a kitchen? Adding a deck to your home? Home Helper is a building supply store that sells everything from lightbulbs to lumber, cabinet fixtures to appliances. Because it stocks many sizes and varieties of building products, the store has a huge inventory.

You work for a local CPA firm that has been hired to evaluate the store's inventory procedures. The store manager wants to make sure the store is using the most appropriate inventory costing method.

Thinking Critically:

Think about the types of products stocked by a home building supply store. Of the four inventory costing methods you have studied in this chapter, recommend the best method for Home Helper. Assume that costs are expected to remain stable over the next few years. Explain the reasons for your recommendation.

inter NET CONNECTION

Inventory Management

Inventory management can be a nightmare without the proper organization and technology. A variety of perpetual inventory management systems exist that help the business owner keep track of inventory quantities as well as sales and product orders. Bar codes and advanced database systems are just two tools available to businesses.

Do This:

Locate Web sites that deal with inventory management products. Try key words like "point-of-sale," "bar codes," and "inventory."

1. List three companies that offer inventory management products.
2. Name one inventory management product.
3. What are the benefits of using inventory technology?

Conducting an Audit with Alex

Instructions Verify the accuracy of the inventory sheet below. Correct any errors on a separate sheet of paper.

INVENTORY SHEET

DATE 11/30/20-- CLERK Janet Milhouse PAGE 17

STOCK NO.	ITEM	UNIT	QUANTITY	UNIT COST		TOTAL VALUE	
2184	Socks	Pair	27	2	19	59	13
2724	Hat	Each	31	7	95	246	54
4163	Gloves	Pair	14	12	40	137	60
2261	Gloves	Pair	9	14	80	133	20
3290	Mittens	Pair	17	14	70	299	90
				TOTAL FOR THIS SHEET		875	47

Workplace Skills

Selecting Equipment and Tools

Many business tasks that are done manually can be performed in a fraction of the time if automated. Selecting equipment and software to achieve desired outcomes demonstrates your evaluation skills.

On the Job:

Your manager, Richard Smythe, has decided to switch from a manual inventory system to an automated perpetual system.

Thinking Critically:

Write a proposal to Mr. Smythe that emphasizes the benefits of using a perpetual inventory system. Specifically address time savings and revenue possibilities.

Inventory Costing

Making the Transition from a Manual to a Computerized System

Task	Perform Accounting Procedures Using Manual Methods	Perform Accounting Procedures Using Automated Methods
Determining the cost of inventories in a perpetual inventory system	1. Enter purchases of merchandise onto stock cards. 2. Enter sales of items onto stock cards. 3. At period end, calculate number and value of remaining inventory items.	1. When the accounting system is set up, the costing method must be determined. Many computerized systems link the cash register to the accounting system. 2. Purchases of merchandise update not only the general ledger but also update the inventory records. 3. As sales are made, the system updates the inventory records. 4. Inventory quantities and values are available when needed.

Maintaining and Costing Inventories

Peachtree Question	Description
How are inventory records set up in Peachtree?	1. Select **Default Inventory** from the **Maintain** menu. 2. Select Inventory Items. 3. Click the *G/L Accts/Costing* tab and enter the G/L account numbers for sales and purchases. 4. Click the *Taxes/Shipping* tab and enter a (✓) if sales taxes are to be collected on items sold. Click *OK*. 5. From the **Maintain** menu, select **Inventory Items.** 6. Enter Item ID codes, descriptions, price, and costing method (FIFO, LIFO, or Average) for all inventory items. 7. The costing method cannot be changed once transactions have been posted against the item.
How do I track inventory?	1. When recording sales or purchases of inventory items, use the established item codes. With each transaction, the system will update the inventory records.
How do I generate inventory reports?	1. From the **Reports** menu, choose **Inventory.** 2. Select Inventory Valuation Report from the Reports list. Quantities on hand and values for each item are displayed based on the costing method default.
What does the software do "behind the scenes"?	1. Peachtree tracks the inventory items and automatically updates the quantities after each transaction. 2. The Cost of Merchandise Sold G/L account will contain all transactions.

For detailed instructions: See the **Peachtree User Guide** in your Glencoe Working Papers.

APPLICATION OPTIONS

Problem 25–4 Calculating the Cost of Ending Inventory

Sunset Surfwear sells wet suits. On January 2 there were 21 wet suits, at a total cost of $4,809 in inventory.

Date	Description	Wet Suits	Cost	Total
Jan. 2	Beginning inventory	21	$229	$ 4,809
Jan. 3	Purchase	10	235	2,350
Mar. 17	Purchase	6	238	1,428
July 27	Purchase	12	240	2,880
Sept. 27	Purchase	10	241	2,410
Nov. 29	Purchase	6	244	1,464
	Total	65		$ 15,341

At the end of the year, there were 17 wet suits in ending inventory. Of these, 1 was purchased on July 27, 10 were purchased on September 27, and 6 were purchased on November 29.

Instructions Assign a cost to the ending inventory using the following:
- (a) the specific identification method
- (b) the FIFO method
- (c) the LIFO method
- (d) the weighted average cost method

Analyze: Which inventory method resulted in the lowest cost of the ending inventory?

Problem 25–5 Completing an Inventory Sheet

InBeat CD Shop assigns a cost to its inventory using the lower of cost-or-market rule. In your working papers, there is a partial inventory record. As an example, the first line of the inventory record has been completed.

INVENTORY RECORD

Item No.	Item	Ending Inventory	Cost per Unit	Current Market Value	Price to be Used	Total Cost
0247	Blank CDs	24	2.67	2.88	2.67	64.08

Complete chapter problems one of four ways:

1 **Manual** Glencoe Working Papers

or

2 **Peachtree Complete Accounting** Software

or

3 **QuickBooks** Templates (Problems 25–4, 25–8)

or

4 **Spreadsheet** Templates (Problem 25–6)

Peachtree®

SMART GUIDE

Step–by–Step Instructions: Problem 25–4

1. Select the problem set for Sunset Surfwear (Prob. 25–4).
2. Rename the company and set the system date.
3. Print the following reports: Inventory Valuation Report, Cost of Goods Sold Journal, and Item Costing Report.
4. End the session.

TIP: Set the date range for the Cost of Goods Sold Journal to include data for the entire year.

Continued

SPREADSHEET SMART GUIDE

Step–by–Step Instructions: Problem 25–6

1. Select the spreadsheet template for Problem 25–6.
2. Enter your name and the date in the spaces provided on the template.
3. Complete the spreadsheet using the instructions in your working papers.
4. Print the spreadsheet and proof your work.
5. Save your work and exit the spreadsheet program.

Instructions Complete the inventory record. Do the following:

(1) Select the lower-of-cost-or-market value. Enter that amount in the Price to be Used column.

(2) Calculate the total cost of each item by multiplying the units in ending inventory by the Price to be Used column.

(3) Add the amounts in the Total Cost column to determine the total cost of the ending inventory.

Analyze: How many of the items used market value rather than actual cost?

 **Problem 25–6 Calculating Gross Profit on Sales**

Using the four inventory costing methods, Shutterbug Cameras summarized the cost of its ending inventory as follows:

Specific Identification	First-In, First-Out	Last-In, First-Out	Weighted Average Cost
$21,476.00	$21,581.40	$21,410.93	$21,447.36

Shutterbug Cameras also reported the following amounts:

Net sales $53,874.92
Purchases available for sale   57,621.31

Instructions Using the above information, determine the cost of merchandise sold and the gross profit on sales for each of the inventory costing methods.

Analyze: Which method resulted in the largest gross profit on sales?

Peachtree®

SMART GUIDE

Step–by–Step Instructions: Problem 25–7

1. Select the problem set for Cycle Tech Bicycles (Prob. 25–7).
2. Rename the company and set the system date.
3. Print the following reports: Inventory Valuation Report, Cost of Goods Sold Journal, and Item Costing Report.
4. Print an Income Statement and a Balance Sheet.
5. End the session.

TIP: Remember to set the date range for the Cost of Goods Sold Journal to include data for the entire year.

Problem 25–7 Reporting Ending Inventory on the Income Statement

Cycle Tech Bicycles operates on a fiscal year beginning January 1. At the beginning of the year, the shop had in stock six Model #8274, ten-speed bicycles, valued at $2,364 (6 bicycles @ $394 each). During the year the business made the following purchases:

Date	Bicycles	Cost		Total
Jan. 20	4	$399	=	$ 1,596
Mar. 5	5	415	=	2,075
Apr. 23	7	419	=	2,933
Aug. 14	4	423	=	1,692
Oct. 3	6	430	=	2,580
Nov. 17	3	435	=	1,305
Total Purchases	29			$12,181

There were seven bicycles in inventory at the end of the period. During the year the bicycles sold for $675 each.

Instructions

(1) Calculate the cost of the ending inventory using the FIFO, LIFO, and weighted average cost methods.

(2) Using the costs calculated in (1), determine the cost of merchandise sold for each inventory costing method.

(3) Prepare a partial income statement for each inventory costing method showing sales and the calculation of gross profit on sales. Assume that the sales and purchases are net amounts.

Analyze: Which method resulted in the lowest cost of merchandise sold?

SOURCE DOCUMENT PROBLEM

Problem 25–8 Calculating Cost of Merchandise Sold and Gross Profit on Sales

CHALLENGE PROBLEM

Buzz Newsstand started the month of May with the following inventory of disposable cameras:

Stock No.	Brand	Units on Hand	Unit Cost	Selling Price
3845	Lenox	4	$9.60	$ 17.95
4931	Lancaster	6	8.40	17.29
9265	Paterson	3	8.10	16.88
4850	McMahon	5	7.60	15.95

Buzz Newsstand uses the FIFO method to calculate the cost of its merchandise inventory. The May 31 physical inventory count indicated:

Lenox	4 cameras	Paterson	7 cameras
Lancaster	5 cameras	McMahon	5 cameras

Instructions

(1) How many units of each of the four cameras were sold during May?

(2) Using the chart provided in your working papers, calculate the gross profit on sales for each type of camera.

Date	Transactions
May 2	Purchased 10 Lancaster cameras at $8.45 each.
4	Purchased 5 McMahon cameras at $7.80 each.
9	Purchased 6 Lenox cameras at $9.95 each plus a $4 transportation charge.
14	Purchased 5 Paterson cameras at $8.25 each.
17	Purchased 8 Lancaster cameras at $8.60 each.
19	Purchased 4 Lenox cameras at $10.10 each plus a $5 transportation charge.
27	Purchased 8 Paterson cameras at $8.30 each.
29	Purchased 4 Lancaster cameras at $8.85 each.

Analyze: Which camera sold the most number of units in May?

Peachtree®

SMART GUIDE

Step–by–Step Instructions: Problem 25–8

1. Select the problem set for Buzz Newsstand (Prob. 25–8).
2. Rename the company and set the system date.
3. Record all of the purchases transactions using the **Purchases/Receive Inventory** option.
4. Record the transportation charges using the **Payments** option.
5. Record the camera sales using the **Receipts** option.
6. Print a Purchases Journal, Cash Disbursements Journal and a Cash Receipts Journal to proof your work.
7. Print the following reports: Inventory Valuation Report, Cost of Goods Sold Journal, and Item Costing Report.
8. Answer the Analyze question.
9. End the session.

TIP: Determine the quantity sold for each camera and enter the sales as a multi-part cash receipt. Record the total sales for each camera on the last day of the month.

SOURCE DOCUMENT PROBLEM

Problem 25–8

Use the source documents in your working papers to record the transactions for this problem.

Notes Payable and Receivable

Learning Objectives

When you have completed this chapter, you will be able to:

▶ Explain how promissory notes are used by businesses.

▶ Calculate and record notes payable and notes receivable.

▶ Explain the difference between interest-bearing and noninterest-bearing notes.

▶ Journalize transactions involving notes payable.

▶ Journalize transactions involving notes receivable.

▶ Define the accounting terms introduced in this chapter.

Exploring the Real World of Business

EVALUATING NOTES

Can you imagine your next vacation aboard a cruise ship? Then check out the cruises offered by **Carnival Cruise Lines. Carnival** is known for its "Fun Ships," which offer on-board entertainment that appeals to all ages. Cruise lines offer fitness facilities, gaming, movies, guest entertainers and shows, musical revues, and of course plenty of food, fresh air, and sunshine. One of **Carnival's** ships, the Conquest, is the largest "Fun Ship" ever constructed, measuring 110,000 tons. This ship has ten decks of passenger rooms and public spaces!

When **Carnival** buys a new cruise ship, the amount of the purchase order is staggering. The **Carnival** Conquest costs $500 million. Like other companies that make very large purchases, the company may choose to borrow money for the purchase by issuing a note payable.

What do you think?

In addition to a note payable, can you think of at least two other ways a company might pay for a large purchase?

Carnival Corporation

Workplace Connections

Applying Your Accounting Knowledge

Have you or your parents ever bought a new or used car? Chances are you made a down payment and then signed a note payable for the rest of the purchase price. When businesses buy costly items, such as manufacturing equipment or even an office building, they also sign a note payable. In this chapter, you'll learn how to calculate the interest on a business note and record the total amount payable.

Investigate:

Have you noticed any items that were purchased by your employer that may have required signing a note payable? This might include purchases like equipment, buildings, vehicles, or land.

Glencoe Accounting *Online*

Visit the *Glencoe Accounting* Web site at **glencoeaccounting.glencoe.com** for additional activities and information.

701

Promissory Notes

If you or a member of your family have ever purchased a car, then you may have signed a note to pay for the vehicle over a certain period of time. You may have signed a note with a company like Ford Motor Credit or with a bank. For large purchases, and sometimes even small ones, customers will promise to pay the debt over a period of time instead of paying for the item at the time of the purchase. In this chapter you'll learn how to calculate and record notes payable and notes receivable.

A Promise to Pay

A **promissory note** is a written promise to pay a certain amount of money at a specific time. "Promissory note" is often shortened to "note." Promissory notes are formal documents that are evidence of credit granted or received.

A **note payable** is a promissory note issued to a creditor. A **note receivable** is a promissory note that a business accepts from a customer.

To be upheld in a court of law, a promissory note must contain certain information, which is shown in **Figure 26–1**.

Determining the Maturity Date of a Note

When a note is signed, the maker agrees to repay the note within a certain period of time, usually expressed in days or months. This period of time is the **term** of the note. Both the term and the **issue date** (date on which the note is signed) are needed to determine the **maturity date** (due date) of a note.

Let's use the promissory note in **Figure 26–1** as our example. In signing this note, Michael Brown, manager of On Your Mark Athletic Wear, agreed to pay Athletic Equipment Inc. the principal plus interest 90 days from September 14. To determine the maturity date:

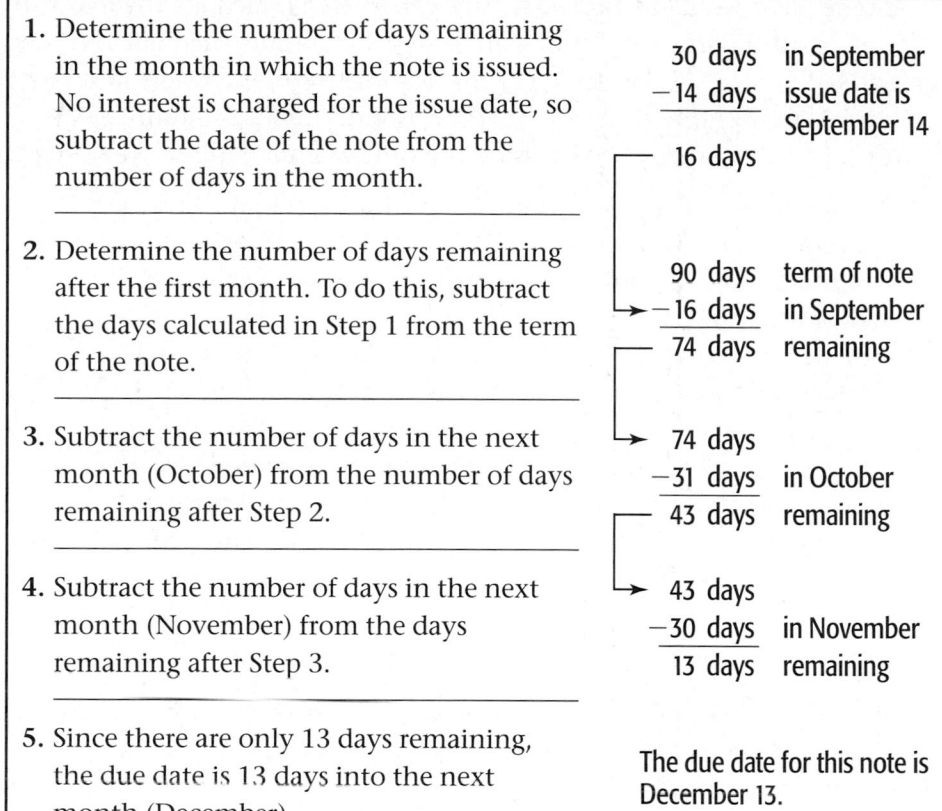

1. Determine the number of days remaining in the month in which the note is issued. No interest is charged for the issue date, so subtract the date of the note from the number of days in the month.

2. Determine the number of days remaining after the first month. To do this, subtract the days calculated in Step 1 from the term of the note.

3. Subtract the number of days in the next month (October) from the number of days remaining after Step 2.

4. Subtract the number of days in the next month (November) from the days remaining after Step 3.

5. Since there are only 13 days remaining, the due date is 13 days into the next month (December).

```
 30 days  in September
−14 days  issue date is
          September 14
 16 days
```

```
 90 days  term of note
−16 days  in September
 74 days  remaining
```

```
 74 days
−31 days  in October
 43 days  remaining
```

```
 43 days
−30 days  in November
 13 days  remaining
```

The due date for this note is December 13.

Key Points

Number of Days in Months

January, March, May, July, August, October, and December have 31 days.

April, June, September, and November have 30 days.

February has 28 days (29 days in a leap year).

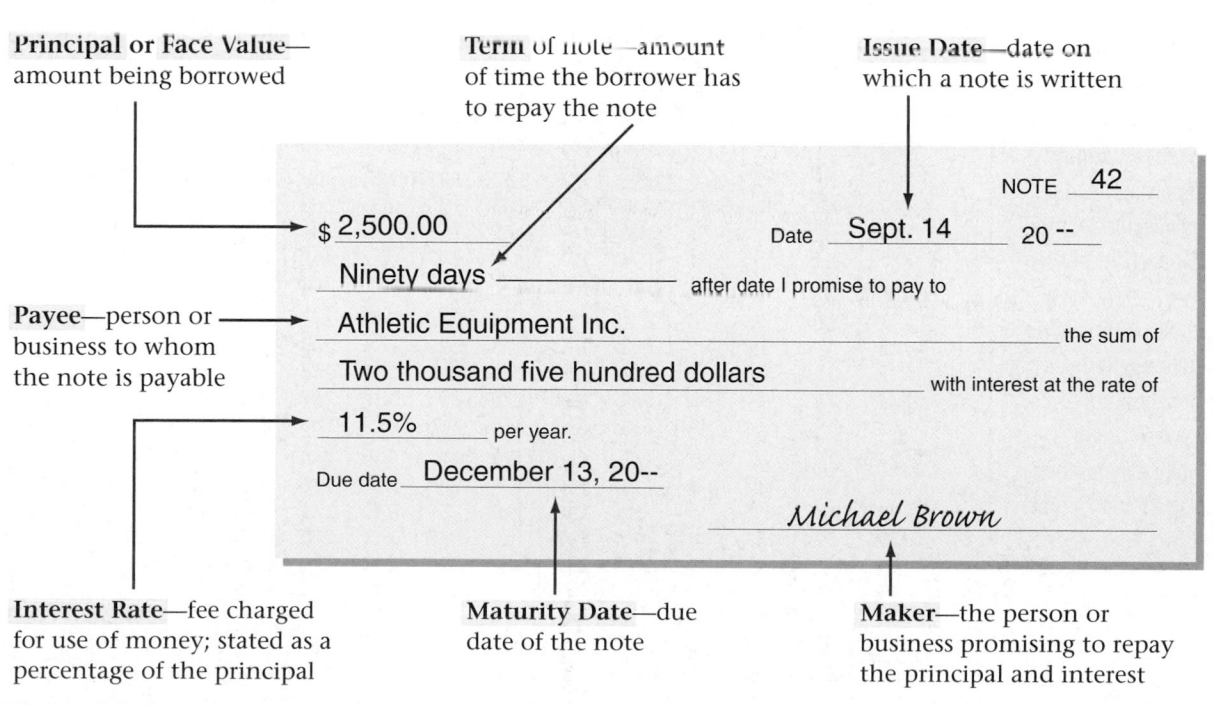

Principal or Face Value—amount being borrowed

Term of note—amount of time the borrower has to repay the note

Issue Date—date on which a note is written

NOTE ___42___

$ 2,500.00   Date ___Sept. 14___ 20 --___

___Ninety days___ after date I promise to pay to

___Athletic Equipment Inc.___ the sum of

___Two thousand five hundred dollars___ with interest at the rate of

___11.5%___ per year.

Due date ___December 13, 20--___

___Michael Brown___

Payee—person or business to whom the note is payable

Interest Rate—fee charged for use of money; stated as a percentage of the principal

Maturity Date—due date of the note

Maker—the person or business promising to repay the principal and interest

Figure 26–1 Promissory Note

Some businesses and banks use time calendars to calculate the maturity date of a note. **Figure 26–2** shows an example of a time calendar. The time calendar has two sets of days: (1) the day of the month (left and right columns), and (2) the day of the year, by month (middle column).

To calculate a maturity date using the time calendar, follow these steps:

1. Locate the issue date of the note (for example, 14) in the Day of month column. Move across the month columns to the issue month (September). In our example September 14 is the 257th day of the year.
2. Add the number of days in the term of the note (90) to the day of the year. The sum of the two numbers is 347 (257 + 90).
3. Find the number 347 in the month columns. The 347th day of the year is in December. The maturity month is December. Move across to the Day of month column. The 347th day of the year corresponds to the 13th day of the month. The due date of the note is December 13.

Day of month	Jan.	Feb.	Mar.	Apr.	May	June	July	Aug.	Sept.	Oct.	Nov.	Dec.	Day of month
1	1	32	60	91	121	152	182	213	244	274	305	335	1
2	2	33	61	92	122	153	183	214	245	275	306	336	2
3	3	34	62	93	123	154	184	215	246	276	307	337	3
4	4	35	63	94	124	155	185	216	247	277	308	338	4
5	5	36	64	95	125	156	186	217	248	278	309	339	5
6	6	37	65	96	126	157	187	218	249	279	310	340	6
7	7	38	66	97	127	158	188	219	250	280	311	341	7
8	8	39	67	98	128	159	189	220	251	281	312	342	8
9	9	40	68	99	129	160	190	221	252	282	313	343	9
10	10	41	69	100	130	161	191	222	253	283	314	344	10
11	11	42	70	101	131	162	192	223	254	284	315	345	11
12	12	43	71	102	132	163	193	224	255	285	316	346	12
13	13	44	72	103	133	164	194	225	256	286	317	347	13
14	14	45	73	104	134	165	195	226	257	287	318	348	14
15	15	46	74	105	135	166	196	227	258	288	319	349	15
16	16	47	75	106	136	167	197	228	259	289	320	350	16
17	17	48	76	107	137	168	198	229	260	290	321	351	17
18	18	49	77	108	138	169	199	230	261	291	322	352	18
19	19	50	78	109	139	170	200	231	262	292	323	353	19
20	20	51	79	110	140	171	201	232	263	293	324	354	20
21	21	52	80	111	141	172	202	233	264	294	325	355	21
22	22	53	81	112	142	173	203	234	265	295	326	356	22
23	23	54	82	113	143	174	204	235	266	296	327	357	23
24	24	55	83	114	144	175	205	236	267	297	328	358	24
25	25	56	84	115	145	176	206	237	268	298	329	359	25
26	26	57	85	116	146	177	207	238	269	299	330	360	26
27	27	58	86	117	147	178	208	239	270	300	331	361	27
28	28	59	87	118	148	179	209	240	271	301	332	362	28
29	29	...	88	119	149	180	210	241	272	302	333	363	29
30	30	...	89	120	150	181	211	242	273	303	334	364	30
31	31	...	90	...	151	...	212	243	...	304	...	365	31

NOTE: For leap years, after February 28, the number of the day is one greater than that given in the table.

Figure 26–2 Time Calendar

Calculating Interest on a Note

Interest is the fee charged for the use of money. The **interest rate** is the interest stated as a percentage of the principal. The interest on a promissory note is based on three factors:

- principal
- interest rate
- term of the note

The formula used to calculate interest is:

Interest = Principal × Interest Rate × Time

Interest rates are usually stated on an annual basis; that is, they are usually based on a borrowing period of one year. To find the interest on a promissory note for one year, multiply the principal by the interest rate. For example, the interest on an 11.5%, $2,500 promissory note for one year is $287.50 ($2,500 × .115 = $287.50).

If the term of a promissory note is less than one year, the time in the calculation is expressed as a fraction of one year. The fraction may be stated in days or months. For example, on September 14 On Your Mark signed a note for $2,500 at 11.5% interest for 90 days. Since the term of the note is expressed in days, 365 days is used as the denominator of the time fraction. The interest is calculated as follows:

Principal	×	Interest Rate	×	Time	=	Interest
$2,500	×	.115	×	90/365	=	$70.89

The interest on the note shown in **Figure 26–1** is $70.89.

On the maturity date, On Your Mark will repay the maturity value of the note. **Maturity value** is the principal plus the interest. In our example the maturity value is $2,570.89 ($2,500.00 + $70.89).

If the term of this note had been three months instead of 90 days, the denominator of the time fraction would be 12. The interest would be calculated as follows:

Principal	×	Interest Rate	×	Time	=	Interest
$2,500	×	.115	×	3/12	=	$71.88

The maturity value would be $2,571.88 ($2,500.00 + $71.88)

Calculating Interest Using an Interest Table

To calculate interest, businesses and banks often use an interest table similar to the one shown in **Figure 26–3**.

SIMPLE INTEREST ON $100 (365 DAY BASIS)

DAY	11.50 % INTEREST	DAY	11.75 % INTEREST	DAY	12.00 % INTEREST	DAY	12.25 % INTEREST	DAY	12.50 % INTEREST	DAY	12.75 % INTEREST
30	0.945205	30	0.965753	30	0.986301	30	1.006849	30	1.027397	30	1.047945
60	1.890411	60	1.931507	60	1.972603	60	2.013699	60	2.054795	60	2.095890
90	2.835616	90	2.897260	90	2.958904	90	3.020548	90	3.082192	90	3.143836
120	3.780822	120	3.863014	120	3.945205	120	4.027397	120	4.109589	120	4.191781
150	4.726027	150	4.828767	150	4.931507	150	5.034247	150	5.136986	150	5.239726
180	5.671233	180	5.794521	180	5.917808	180	6.041096	180	6.164384	180	6.287671
210	6.616438	210	6.760274	210	6.904110	210	7.047945	210	7.191781	210	7.335616
240	7.561644	240	7.726027	240	7.890411	240	8.054795	240	8.219178	240	8.383562
270	8.506849	270	8.691781	270	8.876712	270	9.061644	270	9.246575	270	9.431507
300	9.452055	300	9.657534	300	9.863014	300	10.068493	300	10.273973	300	10.479452
330	10.397260	330	10.623288	330	10.849315	330	11.075342	330	11.301370	330	11.527397
360	11.342466	360	11.589041	360	11.835616	360	12.082192	360	12.328767	360	12.575342
365	11.500000	365	11.750000	365	12.000000	365	12.250000	365	12.500000	365	12.750000
366	11.531507	366	11.782192	366	12.032877	366	12.283562	366	12.534247	366	12.784932

Figure 26–3 Interest Table

Let's use On Your Mark's note as an example. To calculate interest using an interest table:

- Find the term of the note in the Day column, 90.
- Follow the row across until you reach the column for the interest rate, 11.5%. Where the Day row and the Interest column meet is a factor, 2.835616. The factor is based on a principal amount of $100.
- Divide the principal of the note by 100. The result is 25 ($2,500 ÷ 100).
- Multiply the result by the factor to find the interest. The interest is $70.89 (25 × 2.835616).

In this example the interest calculated using the equation and the interest table are the same. Sometimes there are small differences caused by rounding.

A MATTER OF ETHICS

Is the Boss Always Right?

Imagine that you work for a large property management company. Your boss, Joan, is the senior accountant; and her boss, Frank, is vice president. For the past several months, Joan has been coming to work late, taking long lunches, and leaving early. When Frank calls, she has asked you to tell him that she is "away from her desk." You think Frank is getting suspicious, and you're starting to feel guilty for lying.

Ethical Decision Making:

- What are the ethical issues?
- What are the alternatives?
- Who are the affected parties?
- How do the alternatives affect the parties?
- What would you do?

Now that you have studied this section, complete the following questions and problems.

Thinking Critically

1. If the interest rate for a promissory note is stated on an annual basis, and if the promissory note has a term that is less than one year, how is the interest for the note calculated?
2. Explain how to use an interest table to calculate interest on a loan.

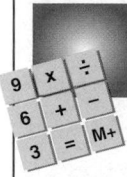

Computing in the Business World

Marty Herick is the owner of CyberAction, a new computer-game store. Marty has just signed a promissory note with Excelsior Bank. He plans to use the loan to purchase and update his interactive computer-game inventory. Using the formula, what is the interest on the $20,000, 90-day note with a 10.5% interest rate? What is the maturity value?

Problem 26–1 Calculating Interest and Finding Maturity Values

Instructions Using the formula, compute the interest and maturity values for each of the following notes. Record your answers in your working papers. Use the interest table to check your computations.

	Principal	Interest Rate	Term
1.	$ 4,000	11.5%	60 days
2.	10,000	11.75%	90 days
3.	6,500	12.75%	60 days
4.	900	12.25%	120 days
5.	2,400	12%	180 days

Problem 26–2 Calculating Interest

Instructions Calculate the interest for each of the following notes. Record your answers in your working papers.

	Principal	Interest Rate	Term
1.	$600	15%	90 days
2.	3,500	12%	60 days
3.	9,600	9%	4 months
4.	2,500	10%	180 days
5.	1,500	11.5%	6 months

Notes Payable

What You'll Learn

- The differences between interest-bearing and noninterest-bearing notes.
- How to record notes payable transactions.
- How to calculate and record bank discounts.

Why It's Important

Many businesses issue and make payment on notes payable.

KEY TERMS

long-term liabilities
interest-bearing note
    payable
noninterest-bearing note
    payable
bank discount
proceeds
other expense

In this section you will journalize transactions involving notes payable. Recall that a note payable is a promissory note issued to a creditor. For example, a note payable may be issued by a business to borrow money from a bank. Notes issued by a business are recorded in the **Notes Payable** account. **Notes Payable** is a liability account; its normal balance is a credit. When the due date of a note extends beyond one year, the note is classified as a long-term liability. **Long-term liabilities** are debts that mature after one year.

There are two types of notes that are frequently issued by businesses: interest-bearing notes and noninterest-bearing notes.

Interest-Bearing Notes Payable

A note that requires the face value plus interest to be paid on the maturity date is called an **interest-bearing note payable** . On an interest-bearing note, the face value and principal are the same amount. The note issued by On Your Mark (in Section 1) is an interest-bearing note. Its maturity value is $2,570.89 ($2,500.00 face value + $70.89 interest).

Let's record an interest-bearing note payable.

Recording the Issuance of an Interest-Bearing Note Payable

Business Transaction

On April 3 On Your Mark borrowed $7,000 from State Street Bank and issued a 90-day, 12% note payable to the bank, Note 6.

ANALYSIS *Identify* 1. The accounts affected are **Cash in Bank** and **Notes Payable.**
            Classify 2. **Cash in Bank** is an asset account. **Notes Payable** is a liability account.
            +/−   3. **Cash in Bank** is increased by $7,000. **Notes Payable** is increased by $7,000.

| DEBIT-CREDIT RULE | **4.** Increases to asset accounts are recorded as debits. Debit **Cash in Bank** for $7,000. |
| | **5.** Increases to liability accounts are recorded as credits. Credit **Notes Payable** for $7,000. |

T ACCOUNTS 6.

Cash in Bank		Notes Payable	
Debit + 7,000	Credit –	Debit –	Credit + 7,000

JOURNAL ENTRY 7.

		GENERAL JOURNAL			PAGE 12	
	DATE	DESCRIPTION	POST. REF.	DEBIT	CREDIT	
1	*20--*					1
2	*Apr.* 3	*Cash in Bank*		7 000 00		2
3		*Notes Payable*			7 000 00	3
4		*Note 6*				4
5						5

Recording the Payment of an Interest-Bearing Note Payable

The maturity date of the note payable is July 2. You can verify this by using the time calendar in **Figure 26–2.** The interest is $207.12:

Principal × Interest Rate × Time = Interest
$7,000 × .12 × 90/365 = $207.12

The maturity value of the note is $7,207.12 ($7,000.00 principal + $207.12 interest).

Business Transaction

On July 2 On Your Mark issued Check 3892 for $7,207.12 payable to State Street Bank in payment of the note payable issued April 3.

ANALYSIS	*Identify*	**1.** The accounts affected are **Notes Payable**, **Interest Expense**, and **Cash in Bank.**
	Classify	**2.** **Notes Payable** is a liability account. **Interest Expense** is an expense account. **Cash in Bank** is an asset account.
	+/–	**3.** **Notes Payable** is decreased by $7,000. **Interest Expense** is increased by $207.12. **Cash in Bank** is decreased by $7,207.12.

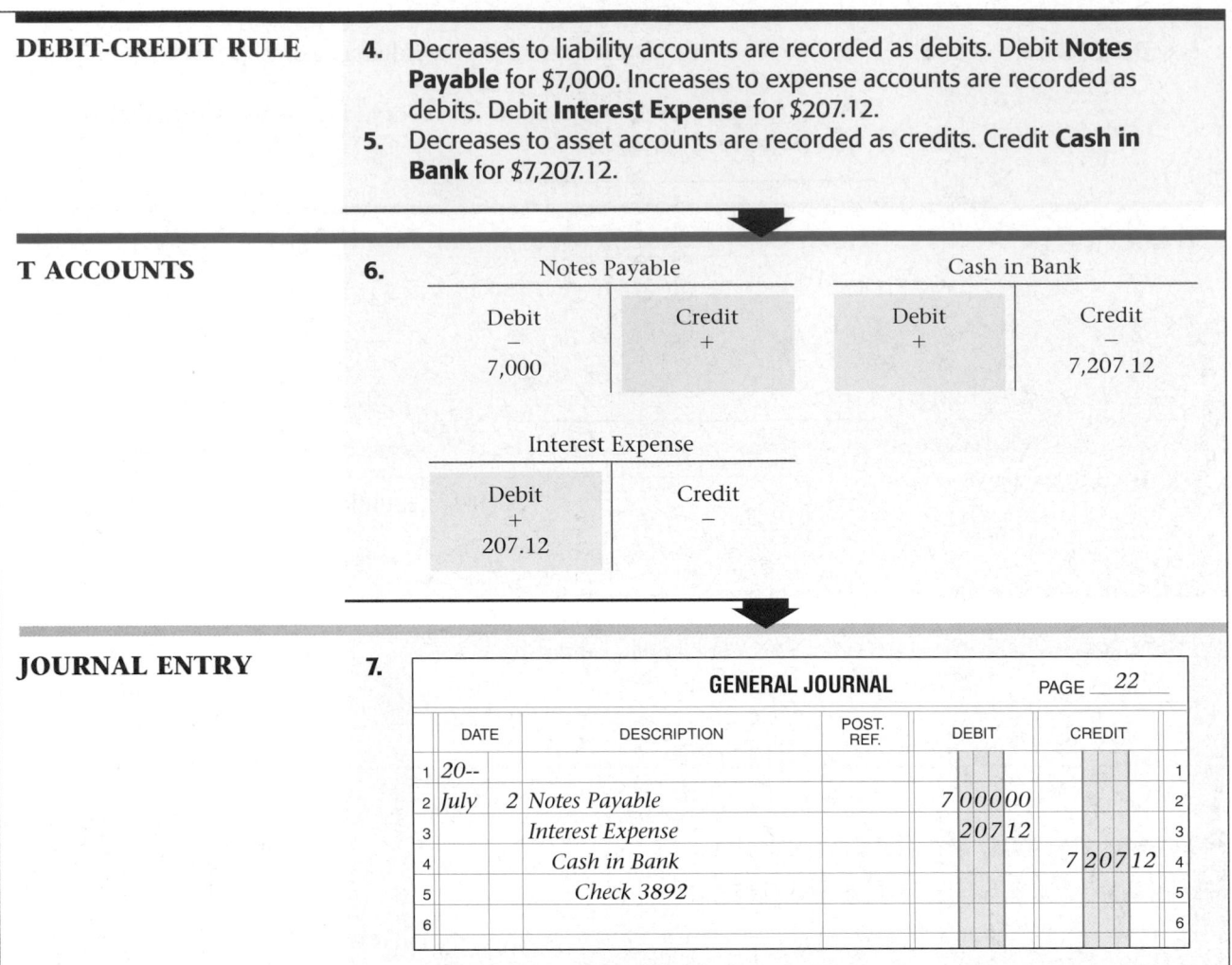

| | DEBIT-CREDIT RULE | | 4. Decreases to liability accounts are recorded as debits. Debit **Notes Payable** for $7,000. Increases to expense accounts are recorded as debits. Debit **Interest Expense** for $207.12. |
| | | | 5. Decreases to asset accounts are recorded as credits. Credit **Cash in Bank** for $7,207.12. |

T ACCOUNTS 6.

Notes Payable			Cash in Bank	
Debit	Credit		Debit	Credit
−	+		+	−
7,000				7,207.12

Interest Expense	
Debit	Credit
+	−
207.12	

JOURNAL ENTRY 7.

GENERAL JOURNAL   PAGE 22

	DATE		DESCRIPTION	POST. REF.	DEBIT	CREDIT	
1	20--						1
2	July	2	Notes Payable		7 000 00		2
3			Interest Expense		207 12		3
4			Cash in Bank			7 207 12	4
5			Check 3892				5
6							6

Noninterest-Bearing Notes Payable

Sometimes a bank requires a borrower to pay the interest on a note in advance. On the issue date, the bank deducts the interest from the face value of the note. This reduces the amount of money received by the borrower. When interest is deducted in advance from the face value of the note, the note is called a **noninterest-bearing note payable**. The note is "noninterest-bearing" because there is no interest rate stated on the note. The interest deducted in advance is called the **bank discount**. The interest rate used to calculate the bank discount is called the discount rate. The cash received by the borrower is called the **proceeds**. The proceeds equal the face value of the note minus the bank discount.

For a noninterest-bearing note payable, the maturity value is the same as the face value. This is because the interest is deducted from the face value on the issue date. **Figure 26–4** shows an example of a noninterest-bearing note payable.

Calculating Noninterest-Bearing Notes Payable

Let's calculate the proceeds of the noninterest-bearing note payable shown in **Figure 26–4**. The note was discounted at a rate of 12% by First Federal Bank, Note 13.

NOTE 13	

$ 1,500.00

Date June 12 20 --

Ninety days ———————— after date I promise to pay to

First Federal Bank ———————————— the sum of

One thousand five hundred ———————— dollars.

Due date September 10, 20--

Michael Brown

Figure 26–4 Noninterest-Bearing Note Payable

The first step is to calculate the bank discount, which is the interest on the note. (Note that the formula is similar to the one used to compute interest on an interest-bearing note.)

Face Value × Discount Rate × Time = Bank Discount
  $1,500 × .12 × 90/365 = $44.38

The bank discount is subtracted from the face value of the note to determine the proceeds. The proceeds are $1,455.62 ($1,500.00 − $44.38).

Recording the Issuance of a Noninterest-Bearing Note Payable

The bank discount is recorded in a contra liability account called **Discount on Notes Payable**. The normal balance of the **Discount on Notes Payable** account is a debit. The bank discount is the future interest expense on the note. However, the bank discount is not recorded in an expense account because the interest expense is not yet incurred.

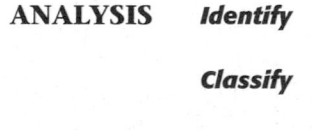

Business Transaction

On June 12 On Your Mark signed a $1,500, 90-day noninterest-bearing note payable that First Federal Bank discounted at a rate of 12%, Note 13.

ANALYSIS	*Identify*	1. The accounts affected are **Cash in Bank**, **Discount on Notes Payable**, and **Notes Payable**.
	Classify	2. **Cash in Bank** is an asset account. **Discount on Notes Payable** is a contra liability account. **Notes Payable** is a liability account.
	+/−	3. **Cash in Bank** is increased by $1,455.62. **Discount on Notes Payable** is increased by $44.38. **Notes Payable** is increased by $1,500.00.

| DEBIT-CREDIT RULE | 4. Increases to asset accounts are recorded as debits. Debit **Cash in Bank** for $1,455.62. Increases to contra liability accounts are recorded as debits. Debit **Discount on Notes Payable** for $44.38. |
| | 5. Increases to liability accounts are recorded as credits. Credit **Notes Payable** for $1,500.00. |

T ACCOUNTS

6.

Cash in Bank		Notes Payable	
Debit + 1,455.62	Credit −	Debit −	Credit + 1,500.00

Discount on Notes Payable	
Debit + 44.38	Credit −

JOURNAL ENTRY

7.

GENERAL JOURNAL   PAGE __20__

	DATE	DESCRIPTION	POST. REF.	DEBIT	CREDIT	
1	20--					1
2	June 12	Cash in Bank		1 455 62		2
3		Discount on Notes Payable		44 38		3
4		Notes Payable			1 500 00	4
5		Note 13				5
6						6

The **Discount on Notes Payable** account is reported on the balance sheet as a deduction from **Notes Payable**. The difference between the **Notes Payable** account and the **Discount on Notes Payable** account is the book value of notes payable. **Figure 26–5** shows the Liabilities section of the balance sheet for On Your Mark on June 30. The book value of notes payable is $1,455.62, ($1,500 − $44.38).

On Your Mark Athletic Wear
Balance Sheet
June 30, 20--

Liabilities					
Notes Payable		1 500 00			
Less: Discount on Notes Payable		44 38		1 455 62	

Figure 26–5 Reporting Noninterest-Bearing Notes Payable on the Balance Sheet

Recording the Payment of a Noninterest-Bearing Note Payable

When the noninterest-bearing note payable is due, On Your Mark will pay First Federal Bank the face value of the note.

Business Transaction

On September 10 On Your Mark issued Check 4241 for $1,500 to First Federal Bank in payment of the June 12 noninterest-bearing note payable.

ANALYSIS	**Identify**	1.	The accounts affected are **Notes Payable** and **Cash in Bank**.
	Classify	2.	**Notes Payable** is a liability account. **Cash in Bank** is an asset account.
	+/−	3.	**Notes Payable** is decreased by $1,500. **Cash in Bank** is decreased by $1,500.

| DEBIT-CREDIT RULE | 4. | Decreases to liability accounts are recorded as debits. Debit **Notes Payable** for $1,500. |
| | 5. | Decreases to asset accounts are recorded as credits. Credit **Cash in Bank** for $1,500. |

T ACCOUNTS 6.

Notes Payable			Cash in Bank	
Debit	Credit		Debit	Credit
−	+		+	−
1,500				1,500

JOURNAL ENTRY 7.

		GENERAL JOURNAL				PAGE 42	
	DATE	DESCRIPTION	POST. REF.	DEBIT		CREDIT	
1	20--						1
2	Sept. 10	Notes Payable		1 500 00			2
3		Cash in Bank				1 500 00	3
4		Check 4241					4
5							5

When a noninterest-bearing note payable matures, the amount of the bank discount is recognized as an expense. The bank discount is transferred from the **Discount on Notes Payable** account to the **Interest Expense** account. As you can see from the T accounts, **Interest Expense** is debited for $44.38 and **Discount on Notes Payable** is credited for $44.38. When this transaction is recorded, the balance of the **Discount on Notes Payable** account is reduced to zero.

	Interest Expense		Discount on Notes Payable	
	Debit +	Credit −	Debit +	Credit −
	9/10 44.38		6/12 44.38	9/10 44.38

You could record two separate journal entries:

(1) the payment of the noninterest-bearing note payable (in the cash payments journal)
(2) the interest expense (in the general journal)

It is simpler, however, to prepare one compound entry:

GENERAL JOURNAL PAGE ___43___

	DATE		DESCRIPTION	POST. REF.	DEBIT	CREDIT	
1	20--						1
2	Sept.	10	Notes Payable		1 500 00		2
3			Interest Expense		44 38		3
4			Cash in Bank			1 500 00	4
5			Discount on Notes Payable			44 38	5
6			Check 4241				6
7							7

The **Interest Expense** account is classified as an other expense account. An **other expense** is a nonoperating expense. This means that the expense does not result from the normal operations of the business. Other expenses appear in a separate section on the income statement, as deductions from operating income.

ANALYZING FINANCIAL REPORTS

Evaluating Debt

Most businesses have debt—both short-term and long-term. Short-term debt refers to liabilities which are expected to be paid off within one year. Examples include accounts payable, short-term notes, and taxes. Long-term debt refers to liabilities which are expected to be paid off in more than one year. Businesses often incur long-term debt when borrowing money to expand business operations.

▶ **Analyze the Report:**

Use the balance sheet for Office Depot on page A-45 to answer these questions:
1. How much has accounts payable increased or decreased from 2000 to 2001?
2. What is the percentage change of the increase or decrease? (Round to the nearest one-tenth of a percent.)
3. How much has long-term debt—net of current maturities—increased or decreased from 2000 to 2001?
4. What is the percentage change of the increase or decrease? (Round to the nearest one-tenth of a percent.)
5. What do you think is meant by the phrase "net of current maturities"?

Now that you have studied this section, complete the following questions and problems.

Thinking Critically

1. How is the interest charge calculated for an interest-bearing note and a noninterest-bearing note?
2. What two journal entries (or one compound entry) are prepared when a noninterest-bearing note payable matures and is paid?

Communicating Accounting

You design brochures to highlight New South Bank's many financial products. Today you were asked to prepare a brochure explaining the value of noninterest-bearing notes. You may design your brochure by hand or on a computer.

Problem 26–3 Recording the Issuance of an Interest-Bearing Note Payable

On June 12 Frank's Lobster Pound issued a $9,000, 120-day, 12% note payable to American Bank of Commerce.

1. Which account is debited? What is the debit amount?
2. Which account is credited? What is the credit amount?
3. What is the classification of each account?
4. What is the maturity value of the note?

Problem 26–4 Recording the Issuance of a Noninterest-Bearing Note Payable

On October 14 Canton Car Care Center issued a $10,000, 60-day, 12% noninterest-bearing note payable to Canton National Bank.

1. Which accounts are debited and which are credited? What are the debit and credit amounts?
2. Compute the bank discount. What are the proceeds?

Notes Receivable

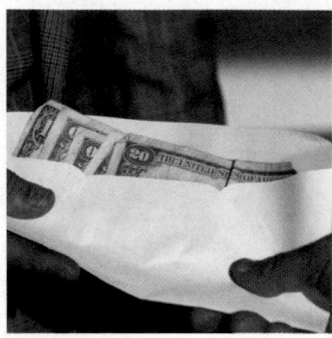

What You'll Learn

- How to record the issuance of a note receivable.
- How to record payments on a note receivable.

Why It's Important

Many businesses accept notes receivable and receive payments on those notes.

KEY TERMS

other revenue

In this section you will journalize transactions involving notes receivable. Have you ever loaned someone money and asked that they repay the loan by a specific date? If so, you understand the basic concept of a note receivable. Sometimes a loan like this may include payment of a specified amount of interest; other times no interest is expected.

Accounting for Notes Receivable

Sometimes a customer needs additional time to pay his or her account receivable. The customer may be asked to sign a promissory note. The customer replaces the account receivable with the note. Promissory notes that a business accepts from customers are called notes receivable.

Notes Receivable is an asset account, and its normal balance is a debit. A note receivable is due on a specific date and carries an interest charge for the term of the note.

The interest earned on a note receivable is recorded in the **Interest Income** account. **Interest Income** is an other revenue account. **Other revenue** accounts track nonoperating revenue that a business receives from activities outside the normal operations of the business. Other revenue appears in a separate section on the income statement, as an increase to operating income.

Recording the Receipt of a Note Receivable

Business Transaction

On March 1 On Your Mark sold $1,750 of merchandise on account to Joe Dimaio. That transaction was recorded in On Your Mark's sales journal. Joe cannot pay his account by the due date. On April 8 On Your Mark received a 60-day, 12.5% note dated April 6 for $1,750 from Joe Dimaio to settle the account receivable, Note 4.

ANALYSIS	Identify	1.	The accounts affected are **Notes Receivable**, **Accounts Receivable** (controlling), and **Accounts Receivable—Joe Dimaio** (subsidiary).
	Classify	2.	**Notes Receivable, Accounts Receivable** (controlling), and **Accounts Receivable—Joe Dimaio** (subsidiary) are asset accounts.
	+/−	3.	**Notes Receivable** is increased by $1,750. **Accounts Receivable** (controlling) and **Accounts Receivable—Joe Dimaio** (subsidiary) are decreased by $1,750.

DEBIT-CREDIT RULE	**4.**	Increases to asset accounts are recorded as debits. Debit **Notes Receivable** for $1,750.	
	5.	Decreases to asset accounts are recorded as credits. Credit **Accounts Receivable** (controlling) for $1,750. Also credit **Accounts Receivable— Joe Dimaio** (subsidiary) for $1,750.	

T ACCOUNTS **6.**

Notes Receivable		Accounts Receivable	
Debit + 1,750	Credit –	Debit +	Credit – 1,750

Accounts Receivable
Subsidiary Ledger
Accounts Receivable—Joe Dimaio

Debit +	Credit – 1,750

JOURNAL ENTRY **7.**

GENERAL JOURNAL PAGE _13_

	DATE	DESCRIPTION	POST. REF.	DEBIT	CREDIT	
1	20--					1
2	Apr. 8	Notes Receivable		1 750 00		2
3		Accts. Rec./Joe Dimaio			1 750 00	3
4		Note 4				4

Recording the Receipt of Cash for a Note

The note from Joe Dimaio is due on June 5. The maturity value of the note is $1,785.96 ($1,750.00 principal + $35.96 interest).

Principal	×	Interest Rate	×	Time	=	Interest
$1,750	×	.125	×	60/365	=	$35.96

Business Transaction

On June 7 On Your Mark received a check dated June 5 for $1,785.96 from Joe Dimaio in payment of the $1,750 note of April 6 plus interest of $35.96, Receipt 996.

JOURNAL ENTRY

GENERAL JOURNAL PAGE _18_

	DATE	DESCRIPTION	POST. REF.	DEBIT	CREDIT	
1	20--					1
2	June 7	Cash in Bank		1 785 96		2
3		Notes Receivable			1 750 00	3
4		Interest Income			35 96	4
5		Receipt 996				5

Now that you have studied this section, complete the following questions and problems.

Thinking Critically

1. Explain the similarities between a note payable and a note receivable.
2. How is interest income recorded in the accounting records?

Analyzing Accounting

Your accounting manager has just finished a graph illustrating the possible interest-bearing notes available from the region's banks. Review the graph and give your boss your recommendation of which bank will provide the best loan value.

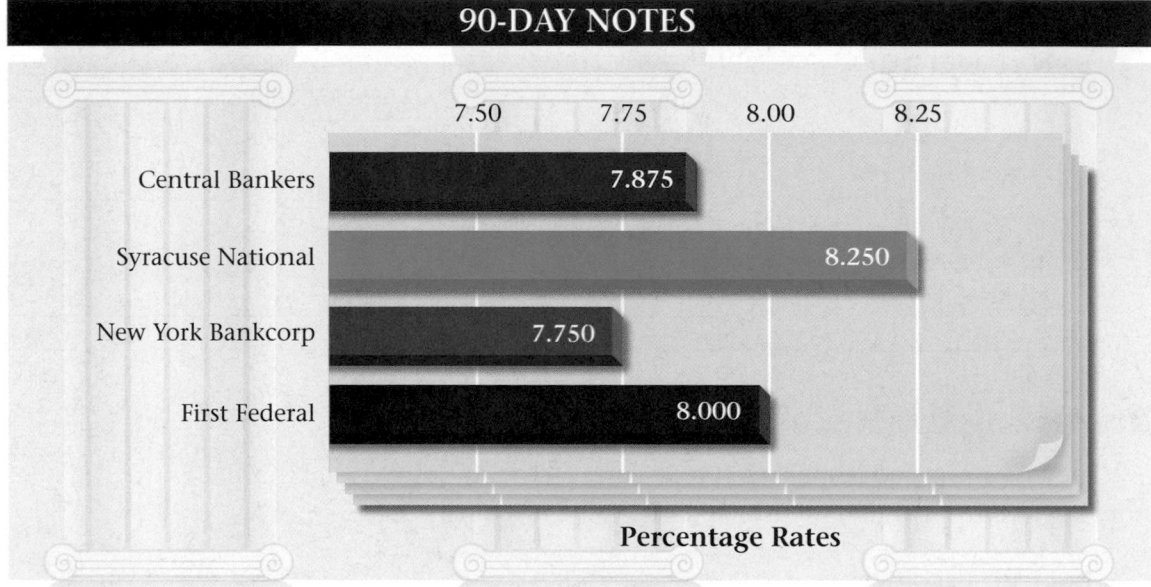

90-DAY NOTES

	7.50	7.75	8.00	8.25

Central Bankers — 7.875
Syracuse National — 8.250
New York Bankcorp — 7.750
First Federal — 8.000

Percentage Rates

Problem 26–5 Analyzing a Source Document

Instructions Examine the note illustrated here. In your working papers, make the appropriate journal entry on page 14 of the general journal for Eli's Catering Company. The note was discounted at a rate of 12% by First Federal Bank.

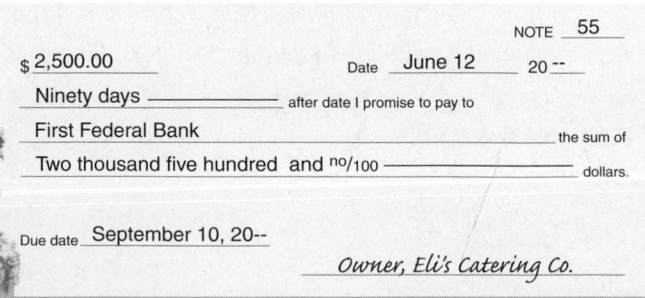

NOTE 55

$ 2,500.00 _____ Date June 12 20 --

Ninety days _____ after date I promise to pay to

First Federal Bank _____ the sum of

Two thousand five hundred and no/100 _____ dollars.

Due date September 10, 20--

Owner, Eli's Catering Co.

KEY CONCEPTS

1. A promissory note is a written promise to pay an amount of money by a specific future date.
2. Promissory notes issued by businesses to creditors or banks to obtain a loan are called notes payable. **Notes Payable** is a liability account.
3. Interest is the fee charged to the issuer of a promissory note for the use of money. Interest is calculated as a percentage of the face value of the note, based on a borrowing period of one year. Borrowing periods of less than one year are expressed as fractions of a year.
4. Calculating interest on a note:
   Interest = Principal × Interest Rate × Time
5. For interest-bearing notes, interest is paid on the maturity date of the note. The maturity value of an interest-bearing note equals the principal (face value) plus the interest.
6. A noninterest-bearing note payable is a note from which the interest is deducted in advance. The interest deducted in advance is called the bank discount. The cash received by the borrower is called the proceeds. For a noninterest-bearing note payable, the maturity value is the same as the face value.
7. Calculating a bank discount:
   Face Value × Discount Rate × Time = Bank Discount
8. When a noninterest-bearing note payable is paid, the bank discount is transferred from **Discount on Notes Payable** to **Interest Expense.**
9. The **Discount on Notes Payable** account is reported on the balance sheet as a deduction from **Notes Payable.** The difference between the two account amounts is the book value of notes payable.
10. Promissory notes accepted by businesses from charge customers are called notes receivable. **Notes Receivable** is an asset account.

USING KEY TERMS

Imagine you are employed by the Carnival Corporation as a staff accountant. You have been asked to discuss the notes payable and receivable of the company with the accounting clerks. Prepare note cards containing the terms below. Arrange these terms in meaningful groups. Explain why you have grouped terms together. Are they related? Are they part of the same thing? Is one the result of another? Are they opposites?

bank discount	noninterest-bearing note
face value	payable
interest	note payable
interest-bearing note	note receivable
payable	other expense
interest rate	other revenue
issue date	payee
long-term liabilities	principal
maker	proceeds
maturity date	promissory note
maturity value	term

Understanding Accounting Concepts and Procedures

Instructions

On a separate sheet of paper, answer the following questions:

1. Name the two parties to a promissory note. Which party issues the note? Which party receives the note?

2. Describe a situation in which a business might (a) receive a promissory note and (b) issue a promissory note.

3. What is the formula to calculate interest?

4. How is the interest on a note calculated if the term is less than one year?

5. Name two types of notes a business may issue. What is the major difference between the two?

6. How is the maturity value of an interest-bearing note determined?

7. What is the difference between interest and a bank discount?

8. When a noninterest-bearing note payable is issued, how are the proceeds calculated?

9. How is the **Discount on Notes Payable** account classified? What is its normal balance?

10. Why are interest income and interest expense reported separately on the income statement?

Case Study...

Merchandising Business: Restaurant/Retail Shop

Moreno's Italian Oven is a local restaurant with a deli that offers takeout pastas and sauces. It is open seven days a week for lunch and dinner. The restaurant seats 60 patrons in a day and averages 90 percent capacity.

The space adjacent to the restaurant is available, and Moreno's is considering expanding. The cost of remodeling the space and buying additional kitchen and restaurant equipment is estimated at $200,000. The rent on the additional space is $1,200 a month.

Thinking Critically:

1. If Moreno's could double the number of customers it serves in a week, how many customers would the restaurant serve?
2. If each customer spends an average of $12 for a meal, how much additional revenue would the restaurant earn in a day if it expands and maintains 90 percent capacity?

inter NET CONNECTION

Notes Payable: Car Loans

Thinking about buying a car? Most of us need a loan to finance the purchase. Wondering how much your monthly payment will be? Let's find out!

Do This:

Assume you are purchasing a used Ford Mustang from a friend and your bank is offering an interest rate of 10.5%. You've agreed to pay $12,500 for the car. You would like to pay the loan over three years.

1. Locate a mortgage or loan calculator on the Internet. You will be asked for the following information:
   - loan term or months to repay the loan: 36 months
   - loan amount: $12,500
   - interest rate: 10.5%
2. What is your monthly payment?

Conducting an Audit with Alex

On May 1 Artist's Loft borrowed $8,000 from American National Bank. The art supply company issued an interest-bearing 90-day, 12% note payable to the bank, Note 5. The following journal entry was made to record the transaction.

		GENERAL JOURNAL		PAGE 18	
	DATE	DESCRIPTION	POST. REF.	DEBIT	CREDIT
1	20--				
2	May 1	Cash in Bank		7 230 40	
3		Notes Payable			7 230 40
4		Note 5			
5					

Instructions Determine whether the entry above is correct. If not, why?

Workplace Skills

Allocating Time, Money, Materials, Space, and Staff

Being resourceful on the job includes allocating time, money, materials, space, and staff efficiently. Budgeting, acquiring materials, assessing employee talents, and allocating time to activities are a few examples of acting competently.

On the Job:

You have been offered a full-time job with Good Times Amusement Park. Before you accept the job, you must purchase a car to get you to and from work.

Thinking Critically:

Make a list of the potential costs involved in owning a car. Make a list of potential costs involved in other modes of transportation. How would owning a car impact the use of your time? How might it affect your budget?

CHAPTER 26 COMPUTERIZED ACCOUNTING

Notes Receivable and Payable

Making the Transition from a Manual to a Computerized System

Task	Perform Accounting Procedures Using Manual Methods	Perform Accounting Procedures Using Automated Methods
Recording notes receivable and payable transactions	1. Using the general journal, record the receipt or issuance of the note. 2. Post the entry to the appropriate accounts in the general ledger and subsidiary ledgers. 3. Journalize and post the entry to record the receipt or payment of cash and interest. 4. Calculate new balances for all accounts affected.	1. Using the general journal, record the receipt or issuance of the note. The entry is automatically posted to the appropriate accounts. 2. Use the Receipts menu item or the Payments menu item to record receipts or payment of notes.

Recording Notes Receivable and Payable

Peachtree Question	Description
How do I record the issuance of a note payable?	1. From the *Tasks* menu, select **Receipts**. 2. Accept the Cash in Bank account number as the G/L account. 3. Enter a Reference number, usually the note number. 4. Click on the *Apply to Revenues* tab. 5. Enter the Notes Payable account number and the note amount.
How do I record the receipt of a note receivable?	1. From the *Tasks* menu, select **Receipts**. 2. Accept the Cash in Bank account number as the G/L account. 3. Enter a Reference number, usually the note number. 4. Enter the Notes Receivable account number and the amount of the note. 5. Enter the Interest Income account number and the amount of interest received.
How do I record the receipt of a note as an extension of an existing account receivable?	1. From the *Tasks* menu, select **Receipts**. 2. Enter the customer ID. 3. Enter a Reference number, usually the note number. 4. Enter the Notes Receivable account number. 5. Click the *Apply to Invoices* tab. 6. Select the *Pay* boxes next to the invoices that the note will pay.
What does the software do "behind the scenes"?	Journal entries are posted to the appropriate G/L accounts and subsidiary accounts for all payments and receipts.

For detailed instructions: See the **Peachtree User Guide** in your Glencoe Working Papers.

APPLICATION OPTIONS

Problem 26–6 Recording Transactions for Interest-Bearing Notes Payable

Instructions In your working papers, record the following transactions in a cash receipts journal (page 22) and a cash payments journal (page 26).

Date	Transactions
Jan. 14	Sunset Surfwear borrowed $1,500 from First One Bank by issuing a 90-day, 12% interest-bearing note payable, Note 78.
Apr. 14	Issued Check 168 for $1,544.38 to First One Bank in payment of the $1,500 note issued on January 14, plus interest of $44.38.
May 31	Borrowed $12,400 from Merchant's Bank and Trust by issuing a 90-day, 12.5% interest-bearing note, Note 79.
Aug. 29	Paid Merchant's Bank and Trust the maturity value of the note issued on May 31, $12,782.19, Check 284.

Analyze: On January 14 the balance in the **Notes Payable** account was zero. What is the balance of the **Notes Payable** account on August 30?

Problem 26–7 Recording Transactions for Noninterest-Bearing Notes Payable

Instructions In your working papers, record the following transactions in a cash receipts journal (page 14) and a cash payments journal (page 16).

Date	Transactions
June 10	InBeat CD Shop borrowed $6,000 from BankOne by issuing a 60-day, noninterest-bearing note payable (proceeds, $5,901.37) that the bank discounted at 10%, Note 67.
Aug. 9	Issued Check 205 for $6,000 in payment of the note issued June 10 and recorded the interest expense.
30	Borrowed $16,000 from Citizens Bank by issuing a 120-day, noninterest-bearing note payable less the 10.5% bank discount of $552.33, Note 68.
Dec. 28	Issued Check 398 in payment of the note issued on August 30 and recorded the interest expense.

Analyze: What is the interest expense associated with these notes?

Complete chapter problems one of three ways:

1 **Manual** Glencoe Working Papers

or

2 **Peachtree Complete Accounting** Software

or

3 **QuickBooks** Templates (Problems 26–6, 26–10)

Peachtree®

SMART GUIDE

Step–by–Step Instructions: Problem 26–6

1. Select the problem set for Sunset Surfwear (Prob. 26–6).
2. Rename the company and set the system date.
3. Record the transactions using the **Receipts** and **Payments** options. Enter each transaction in the proper accounting period (month).
4. Print a Cash Receipts Journal and a Cash Disbursements Journal to proof your work.
5. Answer the Analyze question.
6. End the session.

TIP: Set the date range on the journal reports to print the transactions for all of the periods.

Peachtree®

SMART GUIDE

Step–by–Step Instructions:
Problem 26–7

1. Select the problem set for InBeat CD Shop (Prob. 26–7).
2. Rename the company and set the system date.
3. Record the transactions using the **Receipts** and **Payments** options. Enter each transaction in the proper accounting period (month).
4. Print a Cash Receipts Journal and a Cash Disbursements Journal to proof your work.
5. Answer the Analyze question.
6. End the session.

Peachtree®

SMART GUIDE

Step–by–Step Instructions:
Problem 26–8

1. Select the problem set for Cycle Tech Bicycles (Prob. 26–8).
2. Rename the company and set the system date.
3. Record the transactions using the **Receipts** and **Payments** options.
4. Print a Cash Receipts Journal and a Cash Disbursements Journal to proof your work.
5. Answer the Analyze question.
6. End the session.

TIP: Use the **Receipts** option to record a transaction where a customer replaces an accounts receivable obligation with a promissory note.

Problem 26–8 Recording Notes Payable and Notes Receivable

Instructions In your working papers, record the following transactions in a cash receipts journal (page 47), cash payments journal (page 56), and general journal (page 19) for Cycle Tech Bicycles.

Date	Transactions
Mar. 19	Borrowed $9,000 from Desert Palms Savings and Loan by issuing a 90-day, 12% interest-bearing note payable, Note 87.
June 4	Received a 120-day, 13% note receivable for $1,900 from Greg Kellogg as a time extension on his account receivable, Note 6.
17	Paid Desert Palms Savings and Loan the maturity value of the note issued on March 19, Check 2784.
Sept. 29	Received a check from Greg Kellogg for the maturity value of the note dated June 1, Receipt 628.
Oct. 6	Borrowed $2,700 from Jonesboro Bank and Trust by issuing a 60-day, noninterest-bearing note payable discounted at 11.5%, Note 88.
Dec. 5	Prepared a check for the note issued on October 6 and recorded the interest expense, Check 3954.

Analyze: How much did Cycle Tech pay in interest for the notes payable?

Problem 26–9 Recording Notes Payable and Notes Receivable

The following is a partial list of accounts used by River's Edge Canoe & Kayak.

101	Cash in Bank	205	Notes Payable
115	Accounts Receivable	207	Discount on Notes Payable
120	Notes Receivable	415	Interest Income
201	Accounts Payable	640	Interest Expense

Instructions In your working papers, record the following transactions in a cash receipts journal (page 67), cash payments journal (page 73), and general journal (page 27).

Date	Transactions
May 7	Borrowed $4,000 from Union Bank by issuing a 60-day, 9.5% noninterest-bearing note, Note 284.
15	Issued a $3,000, 90-day, 9% interest-bearing note to Trailhead Canoes in place of the amount owed on account, Note 285.
21	Received a 120-day, 10% note for $1,200 from Cathy Wilcox for an extension of time on her account, Note 94.
July 6	Issued Check 4711 in payment of the noninterest-bearing note given to Union Bank on May 7.
Aug. 13	Issued Check 5044 for the maturity value of the note issued to Trailhead Canoes on May 15.
Sept. 17	Received a check from Cathy Wilcox for the maturity value of the note dated May 21, Receipt 5921.

Analyze: How much interest did Cathy Wilcox pay River's Edge Canoe & Kayak?

Problem 26–10 Renewing a Note Receivable

SOURCE DOCUMENT PROBLEM

Occasionally, on the maturity date, a note may be renewed instead of being paid. When this occurs, (1) the interest on the first note is paid, (2) the first note is canceled, and (3) a new note for the same principal amount is issued, usually at a higher interest rate. Buzz Newsstand had the following transactions.

Instructions In your working papers, record the following transactions on general journal page 24.

Date	Transactions
Mar. 14	Sold merchandise on account to Saba Nadal for $1,800, plus sales tax of $108.00, terms 30 days, Sales Slip 388.
Apr. 13	Accepted a 60-day, 9% note for $1,908.00 from Saba Nadal in place of the account receivable, Note 416.
June 12	Received the interest due from Saba Nadal for the note dated April 13 and agreed to renew the note at 10% for 90 days, Receipt 1387 and Note 417.
Sept. 10	Received a check from Saba Nadal for the maturity value of the note issued June 12, Receipt 1555.

Analyze: On September 10, before the payment was recorded, what was the balance of the Notes Receivable account for Saba Nadal?

Peachtree®

SMART GUIDE

Step–by–Step Instructions: Problem 26–9

1. Select the problem set for River's Edge Canoe & Kayak (Prob. 26–9).
2. Rename the company and set the system date.
3. Record the transactions using the **Receipts** and **Payments** options.
4. Print a Cash Receipts Journal and a Cash Disbursements Journal to proof your work.
5. Answer the Analyze question.
6. End the session.

TIP: Use the **Payments** option to record a transaction where a company issues a promissory note to a vendor to replace an outstanding accounts payable balance.

Peachtree®

SMART GUIDE

Step–by–Step Instructions: Problem 26–10

1. Select the problem set for Buzz Newsstand (Prob. 26–10).
2. Rename the company and set the system date.
3. Record the transactions in the correct period.
4. Print a Sales Journal, Cash Receipts Journal, and a General Journal.
5. Answer the Analyze question.
6. End the session.

SOURCE DOCUMENT PROBLEM

Problem 26–10

Use the source documents in your working papers to record the transactions for this problem.

Completing the Accounting Cycle for a Merchandising Corporation

Kite Loft Inc.

What You'll Learn

- How to analyze, journalize, and post transactions using special journals and the general journal.
- How to prove cash.
- How to prepare a schedule of accounts receivable and a schedule of accounts payable.
- How to prepare a trial balance and a work sheet.
- How to prepare financial statements.
- How to journalize and post adjusting and closing entries.
- How to prepare a post-closing trial balance.
- How to complete the accounting cycle within an assigned time frame.

Why It's Important

In Unit 4, you studied the complete accounting cycle for a merchandising corporation that uses special journals. Now you will apply what you have learned as you work through the accounting cycle for Kite Loft Inc.

Company Background: The Ramspart family owns and operates a wholesale-retail merchandising business organized as a corporation. The business, called Kite Loft Inc., sells a variety of kites and paper airplanes to regional and local toy store businesses.

Your teacher will assign a due date for this project. Working with Kite Loft Inc. will give you an opportunity to complete the accounting cycle within an assigned time frame.

Keeping the Accounting Records for Kite Loft Inc.: Kite Loft Inc. uses special journals and a general journal to record its business activity.

Max Martin, Kite Loft's previous accounting clerk, has already journalized and posted the transactions for December 1 through December 15. The transactions recorded thus far are included in the accounting stationery in your working papers. The transactions for December 16 through December 31 are shown on the following pages.

Your Job Responsibilities: The forms for completing this activity are included in the working papers. As the accountant for Kite Loft:

(1) Record the remaining December transactions in the sales, cash receipts, purchases, cash payments, and general journals.

(2) Post the individual amounts from the five journals to the accounts receivable and accounts payable subsidiary ledgers daily.

(3) Post the individual amounts from the General columns of the cash receipts, purchases, cash payments, and general journal daily.

(4) Foot, prove, total, and rule the special journals at the end of the month.

(5) Post the column totals of the special journals to the general ledger. Use this order for posting: sales, cash receipts, purchases, and cash payments.

(6) Prove cash. The balance shown on check stub 619 is $22,752.83.

(7) Prepare a schedule of accounts receivable and a schedule of accounts payable.

(8) Prepare a trial balance on a ten-column work sheet for the year ended December 31.

Kite Loft Inc.

(9) Complete the work sheet. Use the following December 31 adjustment information.

Merchandise Inventory	$24,850.43
Supplies inventory	120.00
Unexpired insurance	660.00
Total federal income taxes	4,500.00

(10) Prepare the income statement from the work sheet information.

(11) Prepare a statement of retained earnings.

(12) Prepare a balance sheet.

(13) Journalize and post the adjusting entries.

(14) Journalize and post the closing entries.

(15) Prepare a post-closing trial balance.

APPLICATION OPTIONS

CHART OF ACCOUNTS
Kite Loft Inc.

ASSETS

101 Cash in Bank
105 Accounts Receivable
110 Merchandise Inventory
115 Supplies
120 Prepaid Insurance
125 Office Equipment
130 Store Equipment

LIABILITIES

201 Accounts Payable
205 Federal Corp. Income Tax Payable
210 Sales Tax Payable

STOCKHOLDERS' EQUITY

301 Capital Stock
305 Retained Earnings
310 Income Summary

REVENUE

401 Sales
405 Sales Discounts
410 Sales Returns and Allowances

COST OF MERCHANDISE

501 Purchases
505 Transportation In
510 Purchases Discounts
515 Purchases Returns and Allowances

EXPENSES

605 Advertising Expense
610 Bankcard Fees Expense
615 Insurance Expense
620 Miscellaneous Expense
625 Rent Expense
630 Salaries Expense
635 Supplies Expense
640 Utilities Expense
650 Federal Corp. Income Tax Expense

Accounts Receivable Subsidiary Ledger

BES Best Toys
LAR Lars' Specialties
SER Serendipity Shop
SMA Small Town Toys
TOY The Toy Store

Accounts Payable Subsidiary Ledger

BRA Brad's Kites Ltd.
CRE Creative Kites Inc.
EAS Easy Glide Co.
RED Reddi-Bright Manufacturing
STA Stars Kites Outlet
TAY Taylor Office Suppliers

Complete activities one of three ways:

1 **Manual** Glencoe Working Papers

or

2 **Peachtree Complete Accounting** Software

or

3 **QuickBooks** Templates

Peachtree®

Step–by–Step Instructions:

1. Select the problem set for Kite Loft Inc. (MP–5).
2. Rename the company and set the system date.
3. Enter all of the sales on account using the **Sales/Invoicing** option.
4. Record and apply any sales returns.
5. Process all of the cash receipts using the **Receipts** option.
6. Enter the purchases on account using the **Purchases/Receive Inventory** option.
7. Record and apply any purchases returns.
8. Process all of the cash payments with the **Payments** option.
9. Record the adjusting entries.
10. Print the following reports: General Journal, Purchases Journal, Cash Disbursements Journal, Sales Journal, and Cash Receipts Journal.
11. Proof your work.
12. Print the following reports: General Ledger, Vendor Ledgers, and Customer Ledgers.
13. Print a General Ledger Trial Balance.
14. Print an Income Statement.
15. Print a Statement of Retained Earnings.
16. Print a Balance Sheet.
17. Close the fiscal year.
18. Print a Post-Closing Trial Balance.
19. Answer the Analyze questions.
20. End the session.

Business Transactions: Kite Loft Inc. had the following transactions for the month of December.

Date	Transactions
Dec. 16	Received Invoice 410 from Reddi-Bright Manufacturing for merchandise purchased on account, $1,475.00.
16	Paid the quarterly federal income tax installment of $1,050.00, Check 610.
16	Issued Check 611 for $2,548.00 to Brad's Kites Ltd. in payment of Invoice 112 for $2,600.00 less discount of $52.00.
17	Paid the monthly salaries by issuing Check 612 for $4,750.00.
17	Purchased $80.00 of supplies from Taylor Office Suppliers on account, Invoice 830.
17	Received a check for $1,965.60 from Best Toys in payment of Sales Slip 479 for $2,003.40 less a cash discount of $37.80, Receipt 358.
19	Sold merchandise on account to Best Toys, $2,600.00 plus $156.00 sales tax, Sales Slip 484.
19	Prepared Receipt 359 for a $1,716.00 check received from Lars' Specialties in payment of Sales Slip 480 for $1,749.00 less a $33.00 cash discount.
20	Purchased merchandise on account from Brad's Kites Ltd., Invoice 215, $1,560.00.
20	Wrote Check 613 to Creative Kites Inc. to apply on account, $375.00.
21	Prepared Credit Memorandum 44 for $106.00 for the return of $100.00 in merchandise by Best Toys, plus sales tax of $6.00.
23	Sold merchandise to Lars' Specialties on account, $1,580.00 plus sales tax of $94.80, Sales Slip 485.
23	Received a check from Serendipity Shop to apply on account, Receipt 360 for $300.00.
23	Paid Easy Glide Co. for Invoice 326 for $1,890.00 less a $37.80 discount, Check 614 for $1,852.20.
26	Received from The Toy Store a check for $1,102.40 in payment of Sales Slip 483 for $1,123.60 less a cash discount of $21.20, Receipt 361.
26	Returned defective merchandise purchased on account from Brad's Kites Ltd., $150.00, Debit Memorandum 28.
26	Received Invoice 335 from Easy Glide Co. for merchandise purchased on account totaling $1,630.00.
28	Wrote Check 615 for $120.00 to the *Daily Examiner* for a monthly advertisement.
28	Small Town Toys sent a check for $450.00 to apply on account, Receipt 362.
29	Paid Stars Kites Outlet $1,625.00 on account, Check 616.
	Continued

Date	Transactions (cont.)
29	Sold to The Toy Store $1,990.00 of merchandise on account, plus $119.40 sales tax, Sales Slip 486.
30	Issued Check 617 to Reddi-Bright Manufacturing for $700.00 to apply on account.
30	Sold merchandise totaling $560.00 plus $33.60 sales tax to the Serendipity Shop on account, Sales Slip 487.
31	Recorded the bank service charge of $10.00 and the bankcard fee of $150.00, from December bank statement.
31	Paid transportation charges of $51.60 for merchandise shipped from Easy Glide Co., Check 618.
31	Recorded cash sales of $3,995.10 plus $239.71 in sales tax, Tape 41.
31	Recorded bankcard sales of $1,736.27 plus sales tax of $104.18, Tape 41.

Analyze:

1. Which customer owes Kite Loft Inc. the most money at the end of December? How much do they owe?
2. On the cash receipts journal, what is the total amount of the **Cash in Bank** debit that will be posted to the general ledger?
3. On the work sheet, what is the Adjusted Trial Balance debit and credit column total?

Accounting for Partnerships

In this unit...

You will learn how to keep accounting records for a business organized as a partnership. Although accounting for a partnership has many similarities to accounting for a sole proprietorship and a corporation, there are a few different procedures that must be applied as you record transactions for the partnership. You'll learn the procedures involved in accounting for partners' equity and in dividing net income or loss among the partners. You will explore the transactions of **Surfside Bike and Skate Rentals**, a service company owned by Molly Gill and Don Putman. Also in this unit, you will learn about ethics in the accounting profession.

Alone we can do so little; together we can do so much.

—Helen Keller
American Lecturer with Hearing and Visual Impairments

To get the most out of your reading:

Predict what the section will be about.

Connect what you read with your own life.

Question as you read to make sure you understand the content.

Respond to what you've read.

In Your Journal . . .

A business partnership has many unique features and characteristics. It's an association of two or more persons to operate a business as co-owners. Imagine yourself in a couple of years. You and a friend are planning to open a business together.

1. What kind of business will it be?

2. What are the major characteristics of the partnership?

3. What are its advantages? Disadvantages?

4. When you are finished, discuss your responses with a partner in class.

CHAPTER 27

Introduction to Partnerships

Learning Objectives

When you have completed this chapter, you will be able to:

▶ Identify the characteristics of a partnership.

▶ Identify the various accounting functions involved with a partnership.

▶ Account for investments in a partnership.

▶ Account for partners' withdrawals.

▶ Allocate profits and losses to the partners by different methods.

▶ Define the accounting terms introduced in this chapter.

Intersal

Exploring the Real World of Business

LOOKING AT PARTNERSHIPS

Does the name Edward Teach ring a bell? Better known as Blackbeard the Pirate, he was notorious for raiding the East Coast of America in the early 1700s. The wreck of Blackbeard's flagship, *Queen Anne's Revenge,* was recently discovered off the coast of North Carolina. The ship had been lying in the North Carolina waters since it sank in 1718. Among the items found in the shipwreck are a bronze bell dating from 1709, the brass barrel of a blunderbuss, a cannonball, and several cannons.

The search and recovery of Blackbeard's ship is a partnership venture between the state of North Carolina and a private research firm, **Intersal,** that specializes in excavating historic shipwrecks. **Intersal** became interested in *Queen Anne's Revenge* after an eyewitness account of the ship's sinking was found in historical archives in London. This partnership between **Intersal** and North Carolina will last for the length of time it takes **Intersal** to excavate the wreck and recover the ship's artifacts.

What do you think?

What other types of partnerships can you name?

Workplace Connections

Applying Your Accounting Knowledge

Going into business with someone else can be smart when two or more people have complementary business skills and resources that can help a business succeed. Business partners should agree about each person's responsibility in the business and how profits and losses will be shared. In this chapter, you'll learn how a defined partnership agreement helps avoid conflict and benefits the smooth operation of the business.

Investigate:

1. As an employee, you agree to follow the employer's rules. What are some rules in your workplace?
2. How do they help you and your co-workers avoid conflict?
3. If conflicts occur, how are they resolved?

Glencoe Accounting *Online*

Visit the *Glencoe Accounting* Web site at
glencoeaccounting.glencoe.com
for additional activities and information.

733

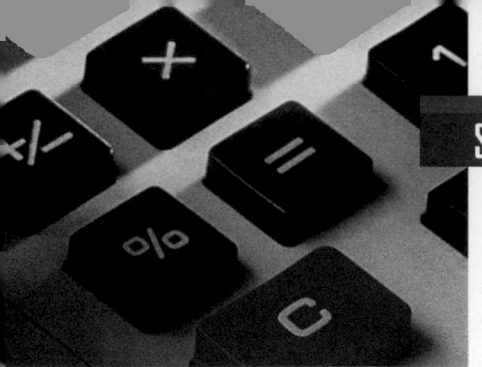

Partnership Equity

As you learned in Chapter 2, a partnership is an association of two or more persons to operate, as co-owners, a business for profit. Any type of business may be organized as a partnership. For example, Intersal is a company that salvages historic shipwrecks. Intersal entered into a partnership with the state of North Carolina to salvage the *Queen Anne's Revenge*, Blackbeard's ship. Partnerships, however, are more common in businesses that provide professional services. For example, accounting and legal firms are often organized as partnerships. Each partner can have his or her own clients, yet share with the other partners the expenses of operating an office.

Characteristics of a Partnership

The partnership form of business organization has certain unique features. Let's look at some of them.

Ease of Formation

Like a sole proprietorship, there are no special legal requirements that must be met to form a partnership. A partnership is automatically formed when two or more persons agree to operate as partners. A partnership is a voluntary arrangement. No one can be forced into a partnership or required to continue as a partner.

Unlimited Liability

Each partner is *personally* liable for the debts of the partnership. This means that if the partnership's creditors cannot be paid out of the assets of the partnership, a partner's personal assets may be used to pay the partnership's debts.

Limited Life

A partnership may end for a number of reasons, including death, withdrawal, bankruptcy, or incapacity of any partner. A partnership may also end when the project for which the partnership was formed is completed, or when the time period set by the partners has expired. For example, two architects may agree to combine their talents to design and oversee the construction of a building. When the building is completed, the partnership is dissolved.

Mutual Agency

Each partner is an agent of the partnership. In other words, any partner can, in the name of the firm, enter into agreements that are binding on all other partners. This relationship is known as **mutual agency**.

Co-ownership of Partnership Property

When a partner invests assets in the partnership, he or she gives up all personal rights of ownership. All of the partnership assets are co-owned by the partners.

Advantages and Disadvantages of a Partnership

One of the most important advantages of a partnership is that it provides the opportunity to bring together the abilities, experiences, and resources of two or more individuals. A partnership is easy to form; the only requirement is the agreement of the partners. Members of a partnership are usually able to make decisions without holding a formal meeting of the partners. Although a partnership must have a legal purpose, there are few other restrictions. Finally, federal and state income taxes are not levied against the partnership. Each partner pays personal income taxes on his or her share of the net income of the business.

There are, of course, disadvantages to the partnership form. As discussed earlier, a partnership has a limited life, each partner is personally liable for the debts of the partnership, and all partners may be held responsible for the decisions of one partner. In addition, a partner cannot transfer his or her interest in the partnership without the consent of the other partners. The ability to work together without major disagreements, however, may be the greatest test of the partnership form of organization.

The Partnership Agreement

A partnership may be formed when two or more individuals orally agree to operate a business as co-owners. However, it is advisable to have a written partnership agreement. A **partnership agreement** is a document that sets out the terms under which the partnership will operate. There is no standard form for a partnership agreement. It should, however, include the following types of information:

1. the name and address of each partner
2. the name, location, and nature of the partnership
3. the date of the agreement and the length of time the partnership is to exist
4. the investment of each partner
5. the duties, rights, and responsibilities of each partner
6. the amount of withdrawals allowed each partner
7. the procedure for sharing profits and losses
8. the procedure for distributing assets when the partnership is dissolved

Each partner should sign the agreement.

Accounting for Partners' Equity

After completing this chapter and Chapter 28, you will be able to identify the various accounting functions involved with a partnership.

Accounting for owners' equity for a partnership is basically the same as for a sole proprietorship. While a sole proprietorship has only one capital account, a partnership has two or more capital accounts. A separate capital account is set up for each partner to record that partner's investment in the business. Each partner also has a separate withdrawals account.

Recording the Investments of the Partners

When a partnership is formed, the value of cash and other assets invested by each partner is listed in the partnership agreement. Separate entries are then made to record each partner's investment in the business. Let's look at an example.

On January 1 Molly Gill and Don Putman agree to form a partnership to operate a business. The name of the partnership is Surfside Bike & Skate Rentals. Each partner agrees to invest the following assets in the new business.

	Gill	Putman
Cash		$12,000
Office supplies		1,000
Office equipment (market value)		12,000
Building (market value)	$30,000	
Land	15,000	
Total assets invested	$45,000	$25,000

When assets other than cash are invested in a partnership, the asset accounts are debited for the market value of the assets.

ACCOUNTING TIPS

Withdrawals

A partnership rewards partners in the form of partnership profits. Partners are not paid as employees of the business. Instead, active partners withdraw money on a weekly or monthly basis in anticipation of their share of annual profits.

Business Transaction

On January 1 Molly Gill and Don Putman contributed cash and other assets to form a partnership, Memorandum 1.

JOURNAL ENTRY

	DATE		DESCRIPTION	POST. REF.	DEBIT	CREDIT	
1	20--						1
2	Jan.	1	Building		30 000 00		2
3			Land		15 000 00		3
4			Molly Gill, Capital			45 000 00	4
5			Memorandum 1				5
6		1	Cash in Bank		12 000 00		6
7			Office Supplies		1 000 00		7
8			Office Equipment		12 000 00		8
9			Don Putman, Capital			25 000 00	9
10			Memorandum 1				10
11							11

GENERAL JOURNAL   PAGE 1

Recording Additional Investments

Any additional investments by the partners are recorded in a similar manner. For example, in April each partner agreed to invest $5,000 cash in the business. **Cash in Bank** is debited for $10,000 and the two partners' capital accounts are credited for $5,000 each.

Recording Withdrawals by the Partners

During the year partners may withdraw cash or other assets for personal use, according to the terms of the partnership agreement. The amount of the withdrawal is debited to the partner's withdrawals account and credited to the appropriate asset account. The amounts withdrawn by the partners do not have to be equal.

Key Points

Partnership Investments

When a partner invests noncash assets in the business, they are recorded in the partnership accounts at the market value of the assets.

Business Transaction

On May 12 Molly Gill withdrew $1,800 cash for personal use, Check 123, and Don Putman withdrew $1,200 cash for personal use, Check 124.

JOURNAL ENTRY

		GENERAL JOURNAL			PAGE 36	
	DATE	DESCRIPTION	POST. REF.	DEBIT	CREDIT	
1	20--					1
2	May 12	Molly Gill, Withdrawals		1 800 00		2
3		Cash in Bank			1 800 00	3
4		Check 123				4
5		Don Putman, Withdrawals		1 200 00		5
6		Cash in Bank			1 200 00	6
7		Check 124				7
8						8

A MATTER OF ETHICS

Partner Loyalty

Imagine that you have started a jewelry business with your best friend Harold. He manages the business while you make the jewelry. Your designs are very successful, but because of Harold's mismanagement, the business isn't making any money. He suggests "doctoring" the financial statements and using them to raise capital by bringing in other investors. You're afraid that the business won't grow as long as Harold is running the business, but he's a good friend and has some good ideas.

Ethical Decision Making:

☞ What are the ethical issues?

☞ What are the alternatives?

☞ Who are the affected parties?

☞ How do the alternatives affect the parties?

☞ What would you do?

Now that you have studied this section, complete the following questions and problem.

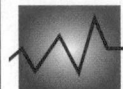

Thinking Critically

1. How is the owners' equity account set up for a partnership?
2. When a partner invests noncash assets in a business, describe how the investment is recorded in the accounting records.

Communicating Accounting

Choose a classmate and discuss a partnership for a business the two of you would like to own and operate. Use your creativity and spell out the details. Prepare a partnership agreement. Include details about what each partner will contribute to the business. Be sure the partners sign the agreement to make it a legal and binding document.

Problem 27–1 Recording Partners' Investments

On June 1 Matthew Deck and Jennifer Rusk agree to combine their sole proprietorships into a new business, Dreamscapes Catering, organized as a partnership. The partnership will take over all the assets of the two proprietorships. The assets invested by Deck and Rusk are listed below.

Instructions Prepare the journal entries required to record the investment by each partner. Use page 1 of the general journal in your working papers. The source document is Memorandum 1.

Investments	Deck	Rusk
Cash	$ 1,200	$ 2,300
Accounts receivable	2,000	7,000
Merchandise	8,000	5,000
Equipment	5,000	12,000
Van	12,000	– –
Office Furniture	1,000	500

Division of Income and Loss

At the end of each accounting period, the net income or net loss from partnership operations is divided among the partners. Partners may divide the income or loss among themselves in any way they choose. The specific method should be defined in the partnership agreement. If it is not, the law provides that net income or net loss be divided equally among the partners.

Dividing Profits and Losses

There are many ways for partners to divide profits and losses. The division is generally based on the services and capital contributed by the partners to the partnership. For example, if the partners share equally in the work of the business, but one partner has invested more capital, it seems only fair that the one who has invested more should profit more.

When the profits of the accounting period are divided, each partner's capital account is increased. If the business incurs a net loss for the accounting period, the capital account of each partner is decreased.

Let's look at three methods that can be used to distribute partnership profits or losses. We'll use two examples for each method: a net income of $24,000 and a net loss of $12,000.

Dividing Profits and Losses Equally

The easiest way to divide a partnership's net income or net loss is equally. This method is often used when all partners invest equal amounts of capital and share equally in the work of the business.

The partnership agreement for Surfside Bike & Skate Rentals states that the profits or losses are to be divided between the two partners equally. During the first year of operation, the partnership earned a net income of $24,000. Each partner's share is $12,000 ($24,000 ÷ 2).

Remember that the balance of the **Income Summary** account is the net income or net loss for the period. In the third closing entry, **Income Summary** is closed to capital. On December 31 the balance of **Income Summary**, a $24,000 credit, is divided equally between the two partners.

What You'll Learn
- How to divide profits and losses equally.
- How to divide profits and losses based on a fractional share.
- How to divide profits and losses based on partners' investments.

Why It's Important
Partnership profits and losses are divided among the partners according to the partnership agreement.

International ACCOUNTING

Business Attire

Learning what is appropriate to wear or not wear when conducting business in another country is important. No matter where you go, it is generally safest to dress in conservative business attire.

	DATE	DESCRIPTION	POST. REF.	DEBIT	CREDIT	
1	20--	Closing Entries				1
2	Dec. 31	Income Summary		24 000 00		2
3		Molly Gill, Capital			12 000 00	3
4		Don Putman, Capital			12 000 00	4
5						5

GENERAL JOURNAL PAGE ___66___

After the journal entry is posted, the balance of Molly Gill's capital account is $62,000 and the balance of Don Putman's capital account is $42,000.

Molly Gill, Capital			Don Putman, Capital	
Debit	Credit		Debit	Credit
−	+		−	+
	Bal. 50,000			Bal. 30,000
	Clos. 12,000			Clos. 12,000
	Bal. 62,000			Bal. 42,000

If the partnership incurs a net loss of $12,000 for the period, each partner's share of the net loss is $6,000 ($12,000 ÷ 2).

On December 31 the balance of **Income Summary**, a $12,000 debit, is divided equally between the two partners.

GENERAL JOURNAL PAGE 66

	DATE	DESCRIPTION	POST. REF.	DEBIT	CREDIT	
1	20--	*Closing Entries*				1
2	*Dec. 31*	*Molly Gill, Capital*		6 000 00		2
3		*Don Putman, Capital*		6 000 00		3
4		*Income Summary*			12 000 00	4
5						5

After the journal entry is posted, the balance of Molly Gill's capital account is $44,000 and the balance of Don Putman's capital account is $24,000.

Molly Gill, Capital			Don Putman, Capital	
Debit	Credit		Debit	Credit
−	+		−	+
Clos. 6,000	Bal. 50,000		Clos. 6,000	Bal. 30,000
	Bal. 44,000			Bal. 24,000

Dividing Profits and Losses on a Fractional Share Basis

Another way to divide net income or loss is to assign each partner a stated fraction of the total. The size of the fraction usually depends on (1) the amount of each partner's investment and (2) the value of each partner's services to the business.

Suppose that the Surfside Bike & Skate Rentals partnership agreement states that the profits or losses are to be divided between the two partners on the following basis: Gill, two-thirds and Putman, one-third.

Key Points

Distribution of Net Income or Net Loss
If the partnership agreement does not explain how net income or net loss is to be distributed, the net income or net loss is shared equally among the partners.

When partners share net income or loss on a fractional share basis, the basis is often stated as a ratio. For example, Gill's two-thirds and Putman's one-third could be expressed as a 2:1 ratio (2 to 1). To turn a ratio into a fraction, add the figures and use the total as the denominator of the fraction.

2:1 = (2 + 1 = 3) = ⅔ and ⅓

The division of the $24,000 net income based on a 2:1 ratio is calculated as follows:

Gill's share:	$24,000 × ⅔ =	$16,000
Putman's share:	$24,000 × ⅓ =	$8,000

The December 31 closing entry is shown below:

GENERAL JOURNAL   PAGE ___66___

	DATE	DESCRIPTION	POST. REF.	DEBIT	CREDIT	
1	20--	*Closing Entries*				1
2	Dec. 31	Income Summary		24 000 00		2
3		Molly Gill, Capital			16 000 00	3
4		Don Putman, Capital			8 000 00	4
5						5

After the journal entry is posted, the balance of Molly Gill's capital account is $66,000 and the balance of Don Putman's capital account is $38,000.

Molly Gill, Capital		Don Putman, Capital	
Debit	Credit	Debit	Credit
−	+	−	+
	Bal. 50,000		Bal. 30,000
	Clos. 16,000		Clos. 8,000
	Bal. 66,000		Bal. 38,000

If the partnership incurs a net loss of $12,000 for the period, the December 31 distribution based on a 2:1 ratio is calculated as follows:

Gill's share:	($12,000) × ⅔ =	($8,000)
Putman's share:	($12,000) × ⅓ =	($4,000)

On December 31 the closing entry is as follows:

GENERAL JOURNAL   PAGE ___66___

	DATE	DESCRIPTION	POST. REF.	DEBIT	CREDIT	
1	20--	*Closing Entries*				1
2	Dec. 31	Molly Gill, Capital		8 000 00		2
3		Don Putman, Capital		4 000 00		3
4		Income Summary			12 000 00	4
5						5

Calculator Hints

Floating Decimal Point

Most calculators have a floating decimal point, which means that the calculator places the decimal in the correct position.
For example:
- if you multiply 0.055 × 1,860
- then the answer will show the decimal in the correct place at 102.3.

After the journal entry is posted, the balance of Molly Gill's capital account is $42,000 and the balance of Don Putman's capital account is $26,000.

Molly Gill, Capital		
Debit	Credit	
–	+	
Clos. 8,000	Bal. 50,000	
	Bal. 42,000	

Don Putman, Capital		
Debit	Credit	
–	+	
Clos. 4,000	Bal. 30,000	
	Bal. 26,000	

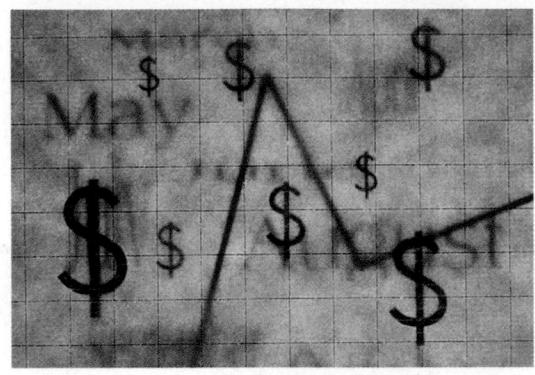

Dividing Profits and Losses Based on Capital Investments

Profits and losses can also be divided on the basis of the capital contributed by the individual partners. To do this, compute the percentage of each partner's capital investment.

$$\frac{\text{Individual Partner's Investment}}{\text{Total Partnership Investment}} = \text{Partner's Percentage}$$

Then multiply the net income or net loss by each partner's percentage.

Molly Gill and Don Putman made the following capital investments:

Molly Gill	$50,000
Don Putman	$30,000
Total investment	$80,000

Gill's Percentage	Putman's Percentage
$\frac{50,000}{80,000} = 62.5\%$	$\frac{30,000}{80,000} = 37.5\%$

Each partner's share of the $24,000 net income is calculated as follows:

Gill's share $24,000 × .625 = $15,000
Putman's share $24,000 × .375 = $9,000

The December 31 closing entry is as follows:

		GENERAL JOURNAL			PAGE 66	
	DATE	DESCRIPTION	POST. REF.	DEBIT	CREDIT	
1	20--	*Closing Entries*				1
2	Dec. 31	*Income Summary*		24 000 00		2
3		*Molly Gill, Capital*			15 000 00	3
4		*Don Putman, Capital*			9 000 00	4
5						5

After the journal entry is posted, the balance of Molly Gill's capital account is $65,000 and the balance of Don Putman's capital account is $39,000.

	Molly Gill, Capital			Don Putman, Capital	
Debit −	Credit +		Debit −	Credit +	
	Bal. 50,000			Bal. 30,000	
	Clos. 15,000			Clos. 9,000	
	Bal. 65,000			Bal. 39,000	

If the partnership incurs a net loss of $12,000 for the period, the December 31 distribution is calculated as follows:

Gill's share   ($12,000) × .625 = ($7,500)
Putman's share   ($12,000) × .375 = ($4,500)

On December 31 the closing entry is as follows:

GENERAL JOURNAL   PAGE _66_

	DATE	DESCRIPTION	POST. REF.	DEBIT	CREDIT	
1	20--	*Closing Entries*				1
2	Dec. 31	*Molly Gill, Capital*		7 500 00		2
3		*Don Putman, Capital*		4 500 00		3
4		*Income Summary*			12 000 00	4
5						5

After the journal entry is posted, the balance of Molly Gill's capital account is $42,500 and the balance of Don Putman's capital account is $25,500.

Molly Gill, Capital			Don Putman, Capital		
Debit −	Credit +		Debit −	Credit +	
Clos. 7,500	Bal. 50,000		Clos. 4,500	Bal. 30,000	
	Bal. 42,500			Bal. 25,500	

ANALYZING FINANCIAL REPORTS

Analyzing Partners' Equity

Financially speaking, the major difference between partnerships and other forms of business ownership is in the equity of the business. In partnerships, two or more people invest equity in the business. When the business earns revenue from its operations, the partners split the revenue in some agreed-upon proportion. The revenue represents a return on their investment of partnership equity.

You learned how to calculate return on equity in Chapters 10 and 21. To review, return on equity is the profit of the business stated as a percentage of equity.

$$\text{Return on Equity} = \frac{\text{Net Income}}{\text{Equity}}$$

In the case of a partnership, each partner may have invested a different amount of equity, so the return might be different for each.

▶ **Analyze the Report:**

Use the balances in the T accounts for partners Putman and Gill on page 741 to answer these questions.
1. Using a total net income of $24,000, calculate the return on total partnership equity.
2. Using an equal split of net income, calculate the return on each partner's equity.
3. Which partner earned the better return? Explain your answer. Why is this percentage different than the return on total equity?

Now that you have studied this section, complete the following questions and problems.

Thinking Critically

1. If the partnership agreement doesn't specify a method, which method is used to divide income and losses among the partners?
2. Describe how to divide net income or net loss to each partner based on a fractional share basis.

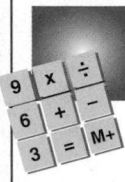

Computing in the Business World

You and your best friend, Mary Jo Perry, operate an ice cream kiosk at the local outdoor shopping mall. You agree to divide profits and losses based on the capital investments made by each partner. Calculate the share of profit and loss due to each partner.

Your investment	$15,000
Mary Jo Perry's investment	25,000
Net income	32,000

1. What is the percentage of investment by each partner?
2. What is your share of the profit?
3. If there is a loss, which partner will have the largest share of the loss?

Problem 27–2 **Determining Partners' Fractional Shares**

Below are the ratios used by several partnerships to divide net income or net loss.

Instructions Determine the fractions that are used to calculate each partner's share of net income or net loss. Use the form provided in your working papers.

1. 3:1   4. 2:1:1
2. 5:3:1   5. 2:1
3. 3:2:2:1

Problem 27–3 **Analyzing a Source Document**

The deposit slips for Mr. Walter's and Ms. Yount's investments in the partnership of Walter and Yount Tax Service are presented here.

Instructions Prepare a journal entry to record the investments by the partners. Use the journal provided in your working papers.

Nations National Bank of U.S.A.
Auburn, Alabama 36831

Date November 13   20 --

Checks and other items are received for deposit subject to the terms and conditions of this bank's collection agreement.

Walter & Yount Tax Service
200 Market Square
Rockford, Alabama 35136

⑈0110065345⑈ 45098 7⑈

	DOLLARS	CENTS
CASH		
CHECKS (List Singly)		
1 234/67	8,000	00
2 Walter		
3		
4		
5		
6		
7		
8		
TOTAL	8,000	00

BE SURE EACH ITEM IS ENDORSED

Nations National Bank of U.S.A.
Auburn, Alabama 36831

Date November 13   20 --

Checks and other items are received for deposit subject to the terms and conditions of this bank's collection agreement.

Walter & Yount Tax Service
200 Market Square
Rockford, Alabama 35136

⑈0110065345⑈ 45098 7⑈

	DOLLARS	CENTS
CASH		
CHECKS (List Singly)		
1 234/89	12,000	00
2 Yount		
3		
4		
5		
6		
7		
8		
TOTAL	12,000	00

BE SURE EACH ITEM IS ENDORSED

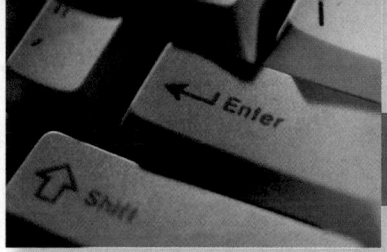

KEY CONCEPTS

1. A partnership is an association of two or more persons to operate, as co-owners, a business for profit.
2. The actions of one partner acting on behalf of the partnership are binding on all partners. This is known as mutual agency.
3. In a partnership a capital account and a withdrawals account are set up for each partner.
4. Recording the investment of partners in a partnership:

Cash in Bank (or other asset)		Individual Partner's Capital	
Debit	Credit	Debit	Credit
+	−	−	+
XX			XX

5. Recording cash withdrawals by partners:

Individual Partner's Withdrawals		Cash in Bank	
Debit	Credit	Debit	Credit
+	−	+	−
XX			XX

6. The net income or net loss of a partnership is divided among the partners according to the terms set forth in the partnership agreement and is usually based on the contribution of services and capital by the partners.
7. Dividing profits among partners:

Individual Partner's Capital		Income Summary	
Debit	Credit	Debit	Credit
−	+		
	XX	XX	

8. Dividing losses among partners:

Individual Partner's Capital		Income Summary	
Debit	Credit	Debit	Credit
−	+		
XX			XX

USING KEY TERMS

You and your friend Marianne Shelton have discussed forming a partnership to provide desktop publishing and layout services to local businesses. You have chosen a business name: The Perfect Paper. You are ready to launch your business idea, but need Marianne to agree so that you can obtain a business loan. Using the terms listed below, write a letter to Marianne and formally invite her to join you in this venture.

mutual agency
partnership agreement

Understanding Accounting Concepts and Procedures

Instructions

On a separate sheet of paper, answer the following questions:

1. List five characteristics of a partnership.

2. List three advantages and three disadvantages of the partnership form of business organization.

3. Why is a written partnership agreement important?

4. What information is usually included in a partnership agreement?

5. When assets other than cash are invested in a partnership, at what amount are the assets recorded?

6. What factors do partners usually consider when deciding on how the profits and losses of the partnership will be divided?

7. Name three methods partners might use to divide profits and losses.

8. How are profits divided when there is no written agreement?

9. What does it mean to share profits at a ratio of 3:4?

10. How do the closing entries of a partnership differ from those of a sole proprietorship?

Case Study...

Partnership: Dentists

Arturo Garcia and Marcela Melendez are partners in Family Dental Center. They share equally the revenue and the costs of office rent, utilities, insurance, and salaries for the four people who work for them.

You just graduated from dental school. Arturo and Marcela offer you a partnership in their practice. Since you lack their years of experience, they offer you a 20 percent interest in return for a $40,000 investment.

Thinking Critically:

1. Assume that the revenue for the dental practice averages $10,000 a week. If you become a partner, you could generate additional revenue of $3,500 a week. Compute your 20 percent share of the revenue.
2. Assume that total expenses for the dental practice are $6,000 a week. Compute your share of the expenses.
3. Do you think that the 20% interest return in the partnership is a good deal? Would you negotiate a different arrangement? Explain.

Conducting an Audit with Alex

The partnership agreement states that partners Mary, Yoto, and Sally are to share profits in the ratio of 3:2:1. Allan, the chief accountant, divided the net income of $86,000 as follows:

Mary's share   = $43,000
Yoto's share   = $28,000
Sally's share   = $15,000

Instructions   Are profits calculated properly? If not, recalculate the partners' shares on a separate sheet of paper.

*inter*NET CONNECTION

Limited Liability Partnership

A Limited Liability Partnership is a hybrid entity—a cross between a partnership and a corporation.

Do This:
1. Search the Web to learn about this form of business ownership. The Limited Liability Partnership (LLP) is referred to as a pass-through entity. What does this mean?
2. Contrast the liability of owners of a Limited Liability Partnership with that of a regular partnership.

Workplace Skills

Negotiating

Can you work toward an agreement between those who disagree? If you can listen to opposing opinions, present facts and arguments, and help bring others to a compromise, then you are able to facilitate negotiations.

On the Job:

Several years ago two of your friends decided to create a business partnership so they could open a sports restaurant—The Gold Medal. You discover that the restaurant now is in jeopardy of closing because the partners are arguing about expansion plans. Because you can negotiate and mediate differences, you were asked to help your friends resolve their conflict.

Thinking Critically:

1. Meet with the partners (two of your classmates) and role-play the conflict. Have the partners talk about the problems connected with the restaurant expansion. Act as the mediator and write down all the issues mentioned.
2. Write down possible solutions for each of the identified problems.
3. Present your recommendations to the partners. Help them decide whether or not it is appropriate to expand the restaurant.

Starting a New Company

Making the Transition from a Manual to a Computerized System

Task	Perform Accounting Procedures Using Manual Methods	Perform Accounting Procedures Using Automated Methods
Starting a new company	1. Determine the form of business ownership. 2. Create a chart of accounts. 3. Open a general ledger account for each account. 4. Record the journal entry for the initial investment by the owner(s). 5. Post the opening entry to the appropriate ledger accounts.	1. Use the New Company Setup routine offered with most computerized accounting systems. 2. You will follow a checklist that will prompt you to enter general information about the business, as well as specific information about the accounting records.

Setting Up a New Company

Peachtree Question	Description
What information will I enter in the New Company Setup routine?	1. Setting up a new company in Peachtree is completed in two parts. 2. Part 1 requires: • company name and address • tax ID • business form (type) • chart of accounts • posting method • accounting period • fiscal year 3. Part 2 requires: • customer defaults • statement and invoice options • vendor defaults • inventory defaults • payroll defaults
What does the software do "behind the scenes"?	1. The company information that you define in Part 1 will appear on all reports, statements, invoices, checks, etc. 2. The business form will determine the type of chart of accounts and relationships of G/L accounts. 3. The defaults that you define for customer and vendor accounts will apply to all transactions that you enter. 4. The accounting period, fiscal year, and posting options that you define set the parameters for the accounting records.

For detailed instructions: See the **Peachtree User Guide** in your Glencoe Working Papers.

APPLICATION OPTIONS

Problem 27–4 Dividing Partnership Earnings

Listed below are the net income and the method of dividing net income or net loss for several partnerships.

Instructions Use the form provided in your working papers to determine each partner's share of the net income.

Net Income	Method of Dividing Partnership Earnings
1. $45,000	Equally: 2 partners
2. $89,700	Fractional share: 2/3, 1/3
3. $22,000	Fractional share: 3:1
4. $32,000	Fractional share: 2/5, 2/5, 1/5
5. $92,700	Equally: 3 partners

Analyze: What accounts are affected when net income is distributed to the partners?

Complete chapter problems one of four ways:

1 **Manual** Glencoe Working Papers

or

2 **Peachtree Complete Accounting** Software

or

3 **QuickBooks** Templates (Problems 27–7, 27–8)

or

4 **Spreadsheet** Templates (Problem 27–5)

Problem 27–5 Calculating the Percentage of Each Partner's Capital Investment

Listed below are the individual partner's investments for several partnerships.

Instructions Using the form provided in your working papers, calculate each partner's percentage ownership in the partnership.

Individual Partner's Investment	Total Partnership Investment
1. $60,000	$180,000
2. 25,000	125,000
3. 11,250	28,125
4. 30,000	40,000

Analyze: Why is it important to know each partner's percentage of the total partnership investment?

SPREADSHEET SMART GUIDE

Step–by–Step Instructions: Problem 27–5

1. Select the spreadsheet template for Problem 27–5.
2. Enter your name and the date in the spaces provided on the template.
3. Complete the spreadsheet using the instructions in your working papers.
4. Print the spreadsheet and proof your work.
5. Save your work and exit the spreadsheet program.

Problem 27–6 Recording Investments of Partners

On May 1, Jason Pua and Roy Nelson formed the partnership called JR Landscaping. Jason contributed $8,100 cash and all of his landscaping equipment. The equipment was purchased by Jason for $2,500 last year. The market value of this equipment is now $1,800. Roy contributed $1,000 cash and his truck that has a market value of $5,600 presently.

Continued

Peachtree®

SMART GUIDE

**Step–by–Step Instructions:
Problem 27–6**

1. Select the problem set for JR Landscaping (Prob. 27–6).
2. Rename the company, change the accounting period to May 1–May 31, 2008, and set the system date.
3. Enter the transactions to record the investment by each partner using the **General Journal Entry** option.
4. Print a General Journal report and proof your work.
5. Answer the Analyze question.
6. End the session.

Instructions Prepare the journal entries required to record the investment by each partner. Use page 1 of the general journal in your working papers. The source document is Memorandum 1.

Analyze: What are the balances in the partners' capital accounts after the formation of the partnership?

Problem 27–7 Sharing Losses Based on Capital Balances

Mariela DeJesus and Natasha Faircloth started the partnership In Shape Fitness with capital balances of $35,000 for Mariela and $45,000 for Natasha. They agreed to share profits and losses on the basis of their capital balances. The net loss for their first year of operation was $28,500.

Instructions Prepare the journal entry required to divide the loss between the partners. Use the journal in your working papers to record your entry.

Analyze: If Mariela took a $1,500 withdrawal, what was her capital account balance on December 31 after the closing entries were posted?

Peachtree®

SMART GUIDE

**Step–by–Step Instructions:
Problem 27–7**

1. Select the problem set for In Shape Fitness (Prob. 27–7).
2. Rename the company and set the system date.
3. Record the entry to divide the loss between the two partners using the **General Journal Entry** option.
4. Print a General Journal report and proof your work.
5. Answer the Analyze question.
6. End the session.

Problem 27–8 Partners' Withdrawals

Graff, Nu, and Pane are partners in Travel Essentials. They agreed that partnership withdrawals would be 10 percent each based upon the profits recorded for the year. In the first year of operation, the partnership reported $25,000 in profits.

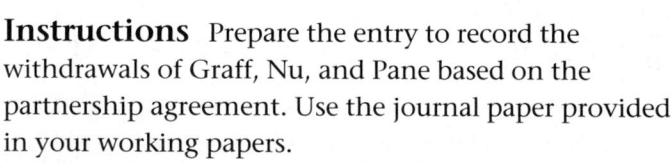

Instructions Prepare the entry to record the withdrawals of Graff, Nu, and Pane based on the partnership agreement. Use the journal paper provided in your working papers.

Analyze: If the partnership had a loss, what account(s) would be debited for the partners' withdrawals?

Problem 27–9 Preparing Closing Entries for a Partnership

Barbara Scott and Martin Towers are partners in the firm of Ten Column Accounting Services. Their partnership agreement states that Scott and Towers share net income or net loss in a 3:2 ratio.

At the end of the period, December 31, the business had a net loss of $9,700. During the period Scott withdrew $6,600 and Towers withdrew $5,400.

Instructions In your working papers, do the following:
(1) Journalize the closing entries to divide the net loss between the partners and to close the withdrawals accounts. Use general journal page 14.
(2) Post the closing entries to the general ledger accounts.

Analyze: What were the ending balances for the Scott and Towers capital accounts?

CHALLENGE PROBLEM ## Problem 27–10 Evaluating Methods of Dividing Partnership Earnings

Jo Garrity, Maureen O'Riley, and David White decided to form a partnership called OnTime Copy Shop. The partners will invest the following assets in the business:

	Garrity	O'Riley	White
Cash	0	$22,000	$40,000
Supplies	0	5,000	2,000
Equipment	0	7,500	4,000
Building	$50,000	0	0
Land	15,000	0	0

They are considering the following plans for the division of net income or net loss:

1. Equally
2. Garrity, 20%; O'Riley, 40%; White, 40%
3. In the same ratio as the beginning balances of their capital accounts

Instructions Assume that the business had a net income of $17,500. Calculate the division of net income under each of the three plans.

Analyze: Which method would O'Riley prefer and why?

CHAPTER 28

Financial Statements and Liquidation of a Partnership

Learning Objectives

When you have completed this chapter, you will be able to:

▶ Prepare an income statement for a partnership.

▶ Prepare a statement of partners' equity.

▶ Prepare the Partners' Equity section of a balance sheet.

▶ Account for partnership liquidation losses.

▶ Account for partnership liquidation gains.

▶ Prepare the final entry to liquidate a partnership.

▶ Define the accounting terms introduced in this chapter.

Exploring the Real World of Business

EVALUATING PARTNERSHIP FINANCIAL STATEMENTS

Look around you and think about the number of products that are made from trees—paper, furniture, homes, and boats. One company that provides raw materials for such products is **Plum Creek Timber Company.** The company owns 7.8 million acres of timberland in the United States (increasing from just two million acres in the last decade) and follows strict environmental principles, including reforestation and soil conservation.

Plum Creek originally started as a partnership in 1989. Its success in timberland ownership and manufacturing is enhanced by its leadership in environmental stewardship. Through the use of habitat conservation plans, the Sustainable Forestry Initiative® Program, and various conservation agreements with local, state, and federal agencies, **Plum Creek** protects wildlife, native fish, and their ecosystems wherever they conduct business.

In 1999 **Plum Creek** became a real estate investment trust, which combines investors' capital for the purpose of purchasing and owning real estate.

Plum Creek

What do you think?

Can you think of at least two other types of partnerships?

Workplace Connections

Applying Your Accounting Knowledge

In previous chapters, you've learned how to prepare financial statements for a sole proprietorship and for a corporation. Preparing financial statements for a partnership is a similar process. A partnership agreement defines how income and loss is to be divided among partners. You'll learn how to calculate and report partners' income or losses in this chapter.

Investigate:

1. Have you ever wondered who receives the profits from the place you work? Who must take the losses?
2. What problems might occur between partners of a business without a signed partnership agreement?

Financial Statements for a Partnership

What You'll Learn

- How to show the division of net income among partners on the income statement.
- How to prepare a statement of changes in partners' equity.
- How to prepare the Partners' Equity section of a balance sheet.

Why It's Important

Partnership financial statements differ from those of a sole proprietorship and a corporation.

KEY TERMS

statement of changes in partners' equity

At the end of the year, Deloitte & Touche LLP, one of the "Big Four" accounting firms, prepares financial statements including an income statement, a statement of changes in partners' equity, and a balance sheet.

The Income Statement

The income statement for a partnership is prepared in the same way as for any service business. Expenses are subtracted from revenue to determine the net income or loss. Although it is not required, the division of net income or net loss among the partners may be shown on the income statement.

The partnership agreement of Surfside Bike & Skate Rentals states that net income or net loss will be divided equally between the partners. At the end of the year, the firm had a net income of $24,000. Each partner's share is $12,000. **Figure 28–1** illustrates how to report the division of net income on the income statement.

Surfside Bike & Skate Rentals			
Income Statement			
For the Year Ended December 31, 20--			
Net Income			24 000 00
Division of Net Income:			
Molly Gill	12 000 00		
Don Putman	12 000 00		
Net Income			24 000 00

Figure 28–1 Reporting the Division of Net Income on the Income Statement

The Statement of Changes in Partners' Equity

The **statement of changes in partners' equity** reports the change in each partner's capital account resulting from business operations. It is similar to the statement of changes in owner's equity for a sole proprietorship, except that there is a separate column for each partner. **Figure 28–2** shows the statement of changes in partners' equity for Surfside Bike & Skate Rentals. Notice that the net income is divided between the partners.

Surfside Bike & Skate Rentals
Statement of Changes in Partners' Equity
For the Year Ended December 31, 20--

	Gill	Putman	Totals
Beginning Capital, Jan. 1, 20--			
Add: Investments	50 000 00	30 000 00	80 000 00
Net Income	12 000 00	12 000 00	24 000 00
Subtotal	62 000 00	42 000 00	104 000 00
Less: Withdrawals	5 000 00	3 000 00	8 000 00
Ending Capital, Dec. 31, 20--	57 000 00	39 000 00	96 000 00

Figure 28–2 Statement of Changes in Partners' Equity

The Balance Sheet

For a partnership the Owners' Equity section of the balance sheet is referred to as the Partners' Equity section. Each partner's capital account is listed separately in the Partners' Equity section. (See **Figure 28–3**.) The capital account amounts reported on the balance sheet are from the statement of changes in partners' equity.

Figure 28–3 The Partners' Equity Section of the Balance Sheet

Surfside Bike & Skate Rentals
Balance Sheet
December 31, 20--

Partners' Equity		
Molly Gill, Capital	57 000 00	
Don Putman, Capital	39 000 00	
Total Partners' Equity		96 000 00
Total Liabilities and Partners' Equity		126 000 00

Now that you have studied this section, complete the following questions and problems.

Thinking Critically

1. What financial statements are prepared for a partnership?
2. What is the difference between a statement of changes in owner's equity and a statement of changes in partners' equity?

Communicating Accounting

Maurice Lance and Terry Klaus are partners in a business called M&T Computer Solutions. Maurice wants to contribute more money to the partnership. Terry, on the other hand, is satisfied with his initial investment. Choose a classmate and role play the partners. Discuss the pros and cons of additional investments.

Problem 28–1 Preparing the Income Statement and Balance Sheet for a Partnership

Information related to the operations of the Goldman and Jones partnership follows.

Instructions In your working papers, prepare the division of income section of the income statement and the Partners' Equity section of the balance sheet.
1. Goldman and Jones share profits in the ratio of 2:3.
2. Net income for the year ended December 31, 20-- was $35,000.
3. The January 1 capital balance for Goldman was $23,000.
4. The January 1 capital balance for Jones was $47,000.

Problem 28–2 Analyzing a Source Document

Instructions In your working papers or on a separate sheet of paper, determine each partner's share of the gain.

N *Buie Norman & Company*
CERTIFIED PUBLIC ACCOUNTANTS

Minutes of the Partners' Meeting
January 12, 20--

The partnership sold equipment for a gain of $26,400. The partners agreed to share the gain as follows:

Larry Bass, CPA	6/22
John Buie, CPA	6/22
Teri Anderson, CPA	3/22
Robert Norman, CPA	3/22
Paula Dunham, CPA	2/22
John Ruppe, CPA	2/22

Liquidation of a Partnership

A partnership does not have an unlimited life. Partnerships end because of death or incapacity of a partner, upon completion of a project, or at the end of a specified time period. In this section you will learn about the procedures followed to dissolve a partnership.

Ending the Partnership

Settling the affairs of the partnership business when it ends is referred to as **partnership liquidation** . In the liquidation process, all partnership assets are converted to cash and all partnership debts are paid. Any remaining cash is then paid to the individual partners. The process involves the following four steps:

1. All noncash assets are sold for cash.
2. All gains or losses from the sale of noncash assets are added to or deducted from the capital accounts of the partners based on the partnership agreement.
3. All partnership creditors are paid.
4. Any cash remaining after the creditors are paid is distributed to the partners based on the final balance in the partners' accounts.

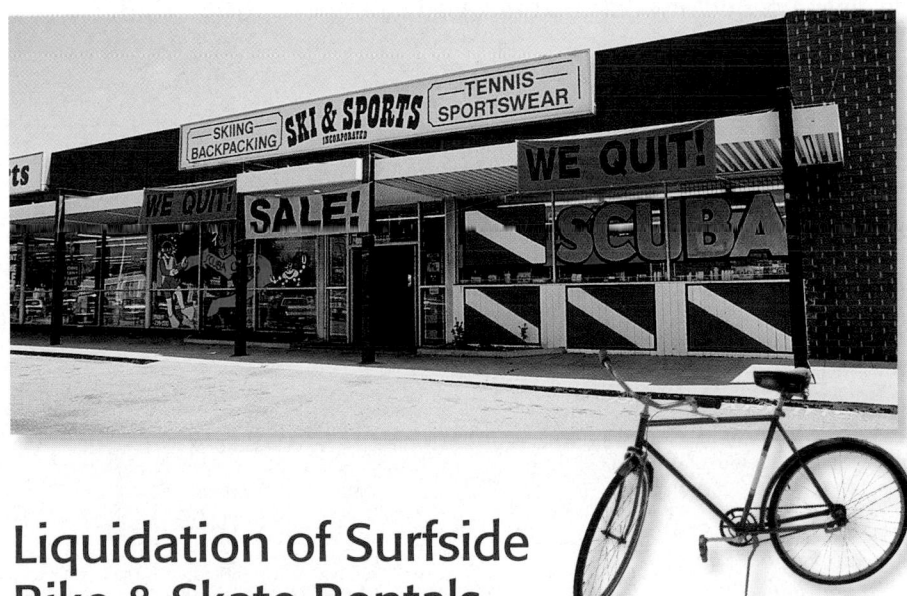

Liquidation of Surfside Bike & Skate Rentals

Let's explore the liquidation of the Surfside Bike & Skate Rentals partnership. **Figure 28–4** shows the balance sheet on the date the partners decided to end Surfside Bike & Skate Rentals.

What You'll Learn

- How to record losses in a partnership liquidation.
- How to record gains in a partnership liquidation.
- How to record the cash distribution required to liquidate a partnership.

Why It's Important

When a partnership is liquidated, the gains or losses from the sale of noncash assets are recognized, the debts of the partnership are paid, and the balance of cash is distributed to the partners.

KEY TERMS

partnership liquidation

ACCOUNTING TIPS

The Seasoned Accountant

What do seasoned accountants know that new recruits do not? Experienced accountants know more about the nature of particular business fields, what can go wrong and why, and what is and is not important. This experience is sometimes called "good judgment."

Figure 28–4 Surfside Bike & Skate Rentals Balance Sheet

Surfside Bike & Skate Rentals					
Balance Sheet					
April 15, 20--					
Assets					
Cash in Bank			18 000 00		
Accounts Receivable			33 000 00		
Merchandise Inventory			35 000 00		
Equipment	48 000 00				
Less: Accumulated Depreciation	(8 000 00)				
			40 000 00		
Total Assets				126 000 00	
Liabilities					
Note Payable			10 000 00		
Accounts Payable			20 000 00		
Total Liabilities				30 000 00	
Partners' Equity					
Molly Gill, Capital			57 000 00		
Don Putman, Capital			39 000 00		
Total Partners' Equity				96 000 00	
Total Liabilities and Partners' Equity				126 000 00	

The Liquidation Process

Gill and Putman share profits and losses equally and agree to end the partnership based on the April 15 balance sheet. The liquidation process requires that all partnership assets be converted to cash, debts be paid, and the remaining cash be distributed to the partners. There were five transactions over a period of weeks that involved ending the partnership.

Sale of Partnership Accounts Receivable at a Loss

On April 20 the $33,000 in accounts receivable are sold to a finance broker for $29,000. The sale of the receivables results in a $4,000 ($29,000 – $33,000) loss to the partnership. The loss is divided equally between Gill and Putman. The entry to record the sale of the receivables and distribute the loss is as follows:

	DATE		DESCRIPTION	POST. REF.	DEBIT	CREDIT	
			GENERAL JOURNAL			PAGE 109	
1	20--						1
2	Apr.	20	Cash in Bank		29 000 00		2
3			Molly Gill, Capital		2 000 00		3
4			Don Putman, Capital		2 000 00		4
5			Accounts Receivable			33 000 00	5
6			Receipt 341				6
7							7

The individual balances in the accounts receivable subsidiary ledger are credited for a total of $33,000.

Sale of Partnership Merchandise at a Loss

On April 29 the merchandise inventory, which cost $35,000, is sold for $32,000 to a discount warehouse. The sale results in a $3,000 ($32,000 − $35,000) loss to the partnership. The loss is divided equally between the partners. The entry to record the sale of the inventory and distribute the loss is as follows:

GENERAL JOURNAL   PAGE _110_

	DATE		DESCRIPTION	POST. REF.	DEBIT	CREDIT	
1	20--						1
2	Apr.	29	Cash in Bank		32 000 00		2
3			Molly Gill, Capital		1 500 00		3
4			Don Putman, Capital		1 500 00		4
5			Merchandise Inventory			35 000 00	5
6			Receipt 363				6
7							7

CONNECT TO . . .
MATHEMATICS

The abacus is an ancient Chinese calculating device with two columns of beads strung on reeds that is still used by many Asians to perform arithmetic. In a 1946 contest between a Japanese abacist and an early computer, the traditional device won easily after two days of competition.

Sale of Partnership Equipment at a Gain

The partnership owns equipment that cost $48,000 and has accumulated depreciation of $8,000. The book value of the equipment is $40,000 ($48,000 − $8,000).

On May 5 the equipment is sold to a dealer for $42,000 resulting in a gain of $2,000 ($42,000 − $40,000). The gain is divided equally between the partners. The entry to record the sale of the equipment and distribute the gain is as follows:

GENERAL JOURNAL   PAGE _111_

	DATE		DESCRIPTION	POST. REF.	DEBIT	CREDIT	
1	20--						1
2	May	5	Accum. Depr.—Equipment		8 000 00		2
3			Cash in Bank		42 000 00		3
4			Molly Gill, Capital			1 000 00	4
5			Don Putman, Capital			1 000 00	5
6			Equipment			48 000 00	6
7			Receipt 371				7
8							8

The Payment of Partnership Liabilities

On May 11 the partnership mails Check 234 to pay the bank note and Checks 235 through 238 to pay the accounts payable balances. The entry to record the transactions is as follows:

	DATE		DESCRIPTION	POST. REF.	DEBIT	CREDIT	
1	20--						1
2	May	11	Notes Payable		10 000 00		2
3			Accounts Payable		20 000 00		3
4			Cash in Bank			30 000 00	4
5			Checks 234–238				5
6							6

GENERAL JOURNAL   PAGE _112_

The individual balances in the accounts payable subsidiary ledger are debited for a total of $20,000. This entry brings the **Accounts Payable** account to zero.

Only three accounts remain in the ledger after all the noncash assets are sold and the debts of the partnership are paid: **Cash in Bank; Molly Gill, Capital;** and **Don Putman, Capital.**

Cash in Bank		
Debit		**Credit**
Bal. 18,000		30,000
29,000		
32,000		
42,000		
Bal. 91,000		

Molly Gill, Capital		
Debit		**Credit**
2,000		Bal. 57,000
1,500		1,000
		Bal. 54,500

Don Putman, Capital		
Debit		**Credit**
2,000		Bal. 39,000
1,500		1,000
		Bal. 36,500

Now cash can be distributed to the partners based on the final balances in their capital accounts: Gill, $54,500 and Putman, $36,500.

Final Distribution of Cash

On May 15 the partnership is ended by distributing the balance of **Cash in Bank** to Gill and Putman. The final transaction to end the partnership is recorded as follows:

GENERAL JOURNAL				PAGE _113_		
DATE	DESCRIPTION	POST. REF.	DEBIT	CREDIT		
1	20--						1
2	May 15	Molly Gill, Capital		54 500 00		2
3		Don Putman, Capital		36 500 00		3
4		Cash in Bank			91 000 00	4
5		Checks 239 and 240				5
6		To dissolve the partnership				6
7						7

Legal Requirements for Dissolving a Partnership

Terms of dissolution may have been stated in the partnership agreement. Any terms laid out in that agreement must be followed when the partnership ends. If the partnership did not have a stated agreement, the laws of the state apply. Most states require that the partnership file a document stating that the entity has been dissolved. If the business has employees, the partnership must also notify the appropriate state and federal tax agencies.

ANALYZING FINANCIAL REPORTS

Evaluating Partnership Operating Results

You learned in earlier chapters how to calculate ratios to help you evaluate the financial health of corporations that publish their operating results in annual reports. Owners and managers of businesses that do not make their financial information public are also interested in these measures of financial health.

$$\text{Return on Sales} = \frac{\text{Net Income}}{\text{Sales}}$$

$$\text{Current Ratio} = \frac{\text{Current Assets}}{\text{Current Liabilities}}$$

$$\text{Quick Ratio} = \frac{\text{Cash \& Receivables}}{\text{Current Liabilities}}$$

Return on sales is a measure of how much profit the business is earning for each dollar of total revenue. Other key measures are the current and quick ratios, which show a company's ability to repay its debts.

▶ **Analyze the Report:**

Use the balance sheet on page 758 to answer these questions:

1. Assume that Surfside Bike & Skate Rentals earned sales revenue of $192,000 and net income of $24,000 for the fiscal period just ended. Calculate the return on sales.
2. Analyze the company's liquidity based on the current ratio and the quick ratio.
3. Write one to two paragraphs describing the financial health of Surfside Bike & Skate Rentals based on your analysis of their financial information.

Now that you have studied this section, complete the following questions and problems.

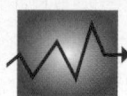

Thinking Critically

1. What steps are involved in liquidating a partnership?
2. Explain how to distribute the cash that remains after a partnership sells all of its noncash assets and pays all of its debts.

Computing in the Business World

Max & Tex novelty store, a partnership, is ending. You are to help liquidate the partnership. Listed below are the remaining assets and liabilities of the business. Max & Tex share profits and losses equally.

Assets		Liabilities	
Cash in Bank	$20,000	Accounts Payable	$15,500
Accounts Receivable	$12,000	**Partners' Equity**	
Merchandise Inventory	$42,000	Marilyn Max, Capital	$59,250
Equipment	$60,000	Tom Tex, Capital	$59,250

Liquidation Transactions:

1. Customers will pay their accounts in full before the liquidation date.
2. Merchandise inventory was sold for $40,000 resulting in a $2,000 loss to the partnership.
3. Equipment was sold to a local retailer for $70,000 resulting in a gain of $10,000.
4. Accounts payable will be paid in full.

Instructions How much cash will each partner receive at final liquidation?

Problem 28–3 Recording a Loss and Gain on the Sale of Noncash Assets by a Partnership

Partners Gunther and Pertee share profits equally. In the process of ending the business, they sell all the partnership's noncash assets. The transactions for the sales follow.

Instructions Record the transactions in general journal form in your working papers. Use general journal page 275.

Date	Transactions
Sept. 4	The merchandise inventory, which cost $45,000, was sold for $38,000.
15	The office equipment, with a book value of $27,000, was sold for $29,000.

KEY CONCEPTS

1. The income statement of a partnership may have a special section showing the division of profits or losses among partners.
2. The balance sheet of a partnership contains a capital section titled Partners' Equity.
3. Partnerships prepare a statement of changes in partners' equity. This statement reflects beginning balances, investments, and withdrawals of each partner.
4. The process of ending a partnership is called partnership liquidation.
5. When partners agree to end the partnership:
   - All noncash assets are sold for cash.
   - All gains or losses from the sale of noncash assets are added to or deducted from the capital accounts of the partners based on the partnership agreement.
   - All partnership creditors are paid.
   - Any cash remaining after creditors are paid is distributed to the partners based on the final balance in the partners' accounts.
6. Each partner's share of gains and losses from the sale of noncash assets is added to or deducted from the partner's capital account.
7. In liquidation, creditors are paid before any partnership assets are distributed to the partners.
8. Terms of dissolution may be stated in a partnership agreement. In lieu of an agreement, laws of the state apply.
9. Upon dissolution, the partnership should notify any applicable taxing authority.

USING KEY TERMS

Imagine that you have been asked to explain the following terms and how they might relate to a timber company organized as a partnership. Review the information about Plum Creek Timber Company on page 752 and prepare a short description of the terms below.

partnership liquidation
statement of changes in
    partners' equity

Understanding Accounting Concepts and Procedures

Instructions

On a separate sheet of paper, answer the following questions:

1. What three financial statements are prepared for a partnership at the end of a period?
2. How does the balance sheet for a partnership differ from that for a sole proprietorship and corporation?
3. What is the meaning of partnership liquidation?
4. List several reasons why partners liquidate a partnership.
5. What are the four steps required to liquidate a partnership?
6. When selling partnership accounts receivable at a loss, what accounts are affected?
7. How are the gains and losses from the sale of noncash assets distributed when a partnership ends?
8. What happens to the partners' capital accounts when noncash assets are sold at a loss? At a gain?
9. When dissolving a partnership, what is the final transaction?

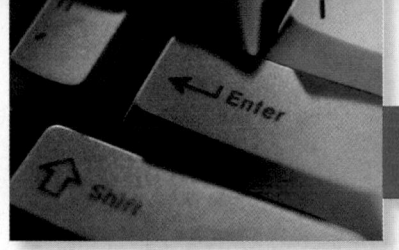

Case Study...

Partnership: Building and Design

Barnes Construction is a homebuilder that wants to expand into commercial real estate. The company has a client who owns 10 acres of land on which she wants to build an apartment complex. Barnes is looking for a partner to help design and build the apartments.

Slater Architectural Design is a firm of architects and builders that has been looking for new projects. Barnes and Slater agree to form a partnership to design and build the apartments. The contract to build the apartments is for $10,400,000. Based on estimated costs, the project should provide net profits of 18 percent.

Thinking Critically:

1. If Barnes and Slater agree to share revenue and expenses equally, how much profit will each partner earn?
2. To limit each partner's liability to this project only, what information should be in the partnership agreement?

interNET CONNECTION

Financial Statements for Partnerships

While the partnerships you studied in this chapter resulted from two or more individuals combining resources and skills to market products or services, partnerships are also possible between corporations.

Competitors AT&T and Sprint have found it profitable to form partnerships and joint ventures with telecommunication companies in other countries to enhance their competitive advantage in the global marketplace.

Do This:

1. Visit the Web sites for AT&T and Sprint.
2. List a partnership or joint venture that each company has formed with another telecommunications company.

Conducting an Audit with Alex

Ann Martha, the accountant for the R&P partnership, made an entry in the partnership books after some of the noncash assets were sold at a loss of $13,000. The remainder of the assets were sold at a gain of $4,000.

The capital balances before the distribution of gains and losses were Roberts, $40,000 and Patrick, $30,000. Roberts and Patrick shared profits and losses based on: Roberts, ⅔; Patrick, ⅓. Martha made the following entry to distribute the balance of cash after all the debts were paid.

Roberts, Capital	$ 34,000
Patrick, Capital	$ 27,000
Total	$ 61,000

Instructions Review Martha's calculations. If incorrect, re-compute the distribution of cash.

Workplace Skills

Self-Esteem

If you are an optimistic thinker and exhibit knowledge of your own skills and abilities, you display the elements of strong self-esteem.

On the Job:

Ten years ago you and your high school teammate opened a small sports and nutrition center. A large national sports center complex has opened in a nearby shopping mall, and your business has dropped significantly. You and your partner have decided to close the center and liquidate the assets.

Thinking Critically:

1. Make a list of all the pros and cons of liquidating a business.
2. Make a list of the tasks necessary to complete the liquidation. Prioritize the items on the list.

Setting Up the General Ledger

Making the Transition from a Manual to a Computerized System

Task	Perform Accounting Procedures Using Manual Methods	Perform Accounting Procedures Using Automated Methods
Setting up general ledger accounts with balances	1. Using accounting stationery, open a general ledger account for accounts based on the expected transactions of the business. 2. Record the balance of each account. Ideally, end-of-period balances should be used, therefore ensuring the accounting records were in balance when transferred.	1. Create a chart of accounts, selecting from predefined charts offered, or by entering select accounts based on the expected transactions for the business. 2. Enter the beginning balance for each account.

Setting up the General Ledger

Peachtree Question	Description
How do I convert a manual accounting general ledger system into Peachtree?	1. Create a general ledger account in Peachtree for each account in the manual system. From the *Maintain* menu, select **Chart of Accounts**. 2. Enter the account number, name, and account type for all accounts. 3. Click the arrow for Beginning Balances. 4. Select the period from which the balance was taken. 5. Enter the beginning balance for each account. 6. Click *Save* when all balances have been entered and the Trial Balance Difference at the bottom of the screen is 0.00.
What does the software do "behind the scenes"?	1. Peachtree will not post the beginning balances to the general ledger accounts until the trial balance is in balance. 2. Once the trial balance is in balance, Peachtree posts the amounts to the general ledger. 3. Transactions for the current period can then be entered.

For detailed instructions: See the **Peachtree User Guide** in your Glencoe Working Papers.

APPLICATION OPTIONS

Problem 28–4 Preparing an Income Statement and Balance Sheet for a Partnership

Joy Webster and Diana Ruiz have been in business since the beginning of the year. Now at the end of the year, they would like to know how the partnership has done in its first year of operation. Joy and Diana stated in the partnership agreement that they will share profits equally. The net income for the year was $5,780. The January 1 capital balances for both partners were $0. Joy invested $6,000 cash in the partnership throughout the year, and withdrew $1,800. Diana invested $5,500 cash in the partnership, and withdrew $1,200.

Instructions In your working papers, prepare the Division of Income section of the income statement and the Partners' Equity section of the balance sheet for the partnership.

Analyze: What are the ending balances in the partners' capital accounts?

Complete chapter problems one of four ways:

1 **Manual** Glencoe Working Papers

or

2 **Peachtree Complete Accounting** Software

or

3 **QuickBooks** Templates (Problems 28–6, 28–8)

or

4 **Spreadsheet** Templates (Problems 28–4, 28–9)

Problem 28–5 Liquidating the Partnership with Losses on the Sale of Noncash Assets

Guice and Ward decide to end their partnership on September 21. They share profits and losses equally. The account balances of the partnership as of that date are listed below.

Cash	$6,500
Inventory	8,800
Equipment (book value)	2,700
Accounts Payable	4,000
Guice, Capital	6,800
Ward, Capital	7,200

The inventory was sold for $5,000. The equipment was sold for $2,000. All of the accounts payable will be paid in full with the cash.

Instructions In your working papers, prepare the journal entries to record the liquidation of this partnership. Use general journal page 85.

Analyze: Before the final distribution to the partners, did the partners' capital account balances increase or decrease as a result of the liquidation of the partnership? Why?

SPREADSHEET SMART GUIDE

Step–by–Step Instructions: Problem 28–4

1. Select the spreadsheet template for Problem 28–4.
2. Enter your name and the date in the spaces provided on the template.
3. Complete the spreadsheet using the instructions in your working papers.
4. Print the spreadsheet and proof your work.
5. Save your work and exit the spreadsheet program.

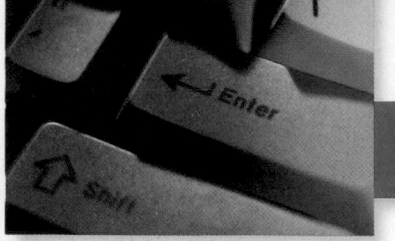
Problem 28–6 Recording a Gain or Loss on the Sale of Noncash Assets by a Partnership

Hudson and Franklin are in the process of liquidating their partnership. They share profits and losses in a 3:1 ratio. They have sold all of the partnership's noncash assets. The transactions for the sales follow.

Date	Transactions
May 29	The equipment, with a book value of $14,500, was sold for $12,775.
June 2	The $7,800 in accounts receivable was sold to a finance broker for $6,900.
4	The merchandise inventory, which cost $2,800 was sold for $1,900.

Instructions In your working papers, record the journal entries for the sale of noncash assets. Use general journal page 120.

Analyze: Why must these losses be distributed to the partners' capital accounts before any cash is paid out to the partners?

Problem 28–7 Preparing a Statement of Changes in Partners' Equity

On January 1 Carol Farmer and Jim Romans formed a partnership called Research Consultants. Each partner invested $50,000 in cash on that date. The partnership agreement stated that the net income or loss would be shared equally.

During the year Farmer invested an additional $2,000 and withdrew $7,500 for personal use. Romans invested an additional $1,500 and withdrew $8,500. Net income for the first year was $33,176.

Instructions In your working papers, prepare a statement of changes in partners' equity for the year ended December 31.

Analyze: What was the balance in Farmer's capital account after earnings were distributed?

Problem 28–8 Liquidating the Partnership

On October 15 Martinez and Royka decide to end their partnership. Their assets consist of $10,000 in cash and inventory that cost $105,000 and was sold for $95,000. Their only liability is a note payable for $10,000 that will be paid in full. Their capital balances are Martinez, $60,000 and Royka, $45,000. They share profits and losses equally.

Instructions In your working papers, prepare the journal entries to record the liquidation of the partnership.

Analyze: If the inventory was sold for $80,000, how much cash would each partner receive at the final dissolution of the partnership?

Peachtree®

SMART GUIDE

Step–by–Step Instructions:
Problem 28–8

1. Select the problem set Problem 28–8.
2. Rename the company and set the system date.
3. Record the transactions to liquidate the partnership using the **General Journal Entry** option.
4. Print a General Journal report and proof your work.
5. Answer the Analyze question.
6. End the session.

Problem 28–9 Completing End-of-Period Activities for a Partnership

CHALLENGE PROBLEM

Richard Smooth and Carrie Overhill are partners in the firm of R&C Roofing. They agreed to divide net income or loss on the following basis: Smooth, ¾; Overhill, ¼.

The completed work sheet for R&C Roofing for the year ended December 31 appears in your working papers.

SPREADSHEET SMART GUIDE

Step–by–Step Instructions:
Problem 28–9

1. Select the spreadsheet template for Problem 28–9.
2. Enter your name and the date in the spaces provided on the template.
3. Complete the spreadsheet using the instructions in your working papers.
4. Print the spreadsheet and proof your work.
5. Save your work and exit the spreadsheet program.

Instructions In your working papers:

(1) Prepare an income statement for the partnership.
(2) Prepare a statement of changes in partners' equity.
(3) Prepare a balance sheet.
(4) Journalize the adjusting and closing entries, beginning on page 27 of the general journal.

Analyze: If Smooth or Overhill had not taken the withdrawals, what would the total equity balance have been at year end?

Completing the Accounting Cycle for a Partnership

Fine Finishes

Fine Finishes

Company Background: Fine Finishes is an interior and exterior painting company organized as a partnership. The partners are Laura Andersen, Sean Woo, and David Ingram. The business earns revenue from consultation and painting fees. The partnership divides income and losses as follows: Laura and Sean each receive 33 percent, and David receives 34 percent.

Your Job Responsibilities: As the accountant for Fine Finishes, use the accounting stationery in your working papers to complete the following activities.

(1) Open a general ledger account for each account in the chart of accounts.
(2) Analyze each business transaction.
(3) Enter each business transaction in the general journal. Begin on journal page 1.
(4) Post each journal entry to the appropriate accounts in the general ledger.
(5) Prepare a trial balance and then complete the work sheet.
(6) Prepare an income statement.
(7) Prepare a statement of partners' equity.
(8) Prepare a balance sheet.
(9) Journalize and post the closing entries.
(10) Prepare a post-closing trial balance.

What You'll Learn

- How to analyze business transactions.
- How to journalize business transactions in the general journal.
- How to post journal entries to the general ledger accounts.
- How to prepare a trial balance and a work sheet.
- How to prepare financial statements.
- How to journalize and post the closing entries.
- How to prepare a post-closing trial balance.

Why It's Important

In Chapters 27 and 28, you learned how to account for partnership equity, divide income and loss among partners, and how to prepare financial statements for a partnership. Now you will have the opportunity to review and apply what you have learned by working through the accounting cycle for Fine Finishes.

Fine Finishes

APPLICATION OPTIONS

CHART OF ACCOUNTS
Fine Finishes

ASSETS

101 Cash in Bank
105 Accts. Rec.—Mountain View City
     School District
120 Computer Equipment
130 Office Supplies
135 Office Equipment
140 Painting Supplies
145 Painting Equipment

LIABILITIES

205 Accts. Pay.—Custom Color
210 Accts. Pay.—J & J Hardware and
     Lumber
215 Accts. Pay.—Paint Palace

PARTNERS' EQUITY

301 Laura Andersen, Capital
302 Laura Andersen, Withdrawals
303 David Ingram, Capital
304 David Ingram, Withdrawals
305 Sean Woo, Capital
306 Sean Woo, Withdrawals
310 Income Summary

REVENUE

401 Painting Fees
405 Consultation Fees

EXPENSES

505 Advertising Expense
510 Miscellaneous Expense
515 Rent Expense
520 Utilities Expense

Complete activities one of three ways:

1 **Manual** Glencoe Working Papers

or

2 **Peachtree Complete Accounting** Software

or

3 **QuickBooks** Templates

Business Transactions: Fine Finishes began business operations on February 1 of this year. During the month of February, the business completed the transactions that follow.

Date	Transactions
Feb. 1	Laura Andersen, David Ingram, and Sean Woo agreed to form a partnership and invest the following assets, Memorandum 1:

Contributed Assets	Andersen	Ingram	Woo
Cash	$1,500	$1,000	$1,200
Computer Equipment	——	2,800	——
Office Equipment	100	——	——
Painting Supplies	150	——	225
Painting Equipment	1,375	——	1,675
Total assets invested	$3,125	$3,800	$3,100

Date	Transactions
1	Signed a one-year rental agreement for a garage at $750 per month. A deposit of one month's rent plus the first month's rent was paid, Check 1101.
1	Put an ad in the Call an Expert section of the newspaper for $25, Check 1102.

Continued ☞

Peachtree®

SMART GUIDE

Step–by–Step Instructions:

1. Select the problem set for Fine Finishes (MP–6).
2. Rename the company and set the system date.
3. Record all of the business transactions using the **General Journal Entry** option.
4. Print a General Journal report and proof your work.
5. Print a General Ledger report.
6. Print a General Ledger Trial Balance.
7. Print an Income statement and a Balance Sheet.
8. Click the save Pre-Closing Balances button in the Glencoe Smart Guide Window.
9. Record the closing entries using the **General Journal Entry** option.
10. Print a general journal report and proof your work.
11. Print a Post-Closing Trial Balance.
12. Answer the Analyze questions.
13. End the session.

TIP: Peachtree can only close a fiscal year. To close a monthly fiscal period, enter the closing entries using the **General Journal Entry** option.

Date	Transactions (cont.)
1	Paid deposit of $100 to utility company to start electric service, Check 1104.
1	Paid telephone company $175 to begin phone service and run dedicated line for computer, Check 1105.
2	Awarded a contract to paint a kitchen and family room for the McGuires. Collected $250 deposit, Receipt 1.
2	Bought paint and border stencils from Custom Color for $200 on account, Invoice 742.
2	Issued check 1103 for $55 for a business license to operate in the city of Mountain View, Colorado (Miscellaneous Expense).
4	Purchased $115 in office supplies, Check 1106.
5	Finished painting the kitchen and family room for the McGuires. Collected final payment of $450, Receipt 2.
6	Joined Mountain View Chamber of Commerce by purchasing membership of $45 (Miscellaneous Expense), Check 1107.
8	Bought painting equipment on account for $375 from Paint Palace, Invoice 1162.
10	Received $60 for color and painting consultation, Receipt 3.
12	Finished painting the cafeteria at the elementary school. Issued Invoice 101 to Mountain View City School District for $835.
14	Sent Check 1108 for $200 to Custom Color on account.
15	Andersen, Ingram, and Woo each made a withdrawal of $650 for personal use, Checks 1109, 1110, and 1111 respectively.
15	Awarded a contract to paint exterior of the Wicker and Hartel law office building. Received deposit of $1,000, Receipt 4.
16	Spent $135 for new paint brushes (Painting Supplies), Check 1112.
16	Bought paint from Custom Color for $395 on account, Invoice 750.
17	Received and paid Invoice 303 from Mountain View Realtors for ad in real estate brochure for $77, Check 1113.
18	Received $125 for painting consultation, Receipt 5.
19	Wrote Check 1114 for $85 to repair computer printer (Miscellaneous Expense).
21	Paid Paint Palace $375 on account, Check 1115.
22	Finished painting the Wicker and Hartel law office building. Collected final payment of $2,000, Receipt 6.
24	Bought $90 of lumber (Painting Supplies) on account from J & J Hardware and Lumber, Invoice 207.
	Continued

Date	Transactions (cont.)
25	Received $575 for painting and making minor repairs to a garage, Receipt 7.
28	Andersen, Ingram, and Woo each made a withdrawal of $650 for personal use, Checks 1116, 1117, and 1118 respectively.

Analyze:

1. What is the balance in the **Laura Andersen, Capital** account after the closing entries have been posted?
2. What is the balance in the **David Ingram, Capital** account after the closing entries have been posted?
3. What is the balance in the **Sean Woo, Capital** account after the closing entries have been posted?
4. What is the net income for the partnership for the month ended February 28, 20--?

CHAPTER 29

Ethics in Accounting

Learning Objectives

When you have completed this chapter, you will be able to:

▶ Explain the meaning of business ethics.

▶ Describe the components of an effective business ethics program.

▶ Identify the role of the accountant in business ethics.

▶ Discuss how ethical behavior benefits individuals, business, and society.

▶ Explain the concepts of integrity, objectivity, independence, competence, and confidentiality as related to the accounting profession.

▶ Identify the professional organizations that establish codes of ethics for accountants.

▶ Define the accounting terms introduced in this chapter.

Exploring the Real World of Business

ASSURING RESPONSIBLE GOVERNANCE

In your school, you probably have a student government organization that influences student body policies and makes decisions on student issues. The term "governance" refers to the exercise of authority, administration, and decision making for a population or an organization.

The success or failure of business depends on ethical corporate governance and accounting practices. The **Institute of Internal Auditors,** an international professional organization, believes that now, more than ever, the internal auditor must play a strong and visible role in governance and internal control processes.

Internal auditors work within a business to review the company's financial, manufacturing, marketing, and human resources data. They make sure that the company operates according to its agreements with suppliers, government, and customers. In addition, the internal auditor establishes plans to safeguard assets and to use resources of the business economically.

What do you think?

Internal auditors evaluate procedures used to safeguard the resources of a business. What are some of these resources?

Institute of Internal Auditors

Workplace Connections

Applying Your Accounting Knowledge

Do you, or anyone you know, work for a fast food restaurant? Whether selling burgers, tacos, or salads, these restaurants must ensure that the food they sell is safe for consumption. They must also provide a safe and sanitary place for their customers to eat.

Investigate:

1. What risks do you think a fast food restaurant faces in regard to customer health?
2. What kinds of internal controls would you suggest to guard against these risks?

Glencoe Accounting *Online*

Visit the *Glencoe Accounting* Web site at **glencoeaccounting.glencoe.com** for additional activities and information.

The Nature of Ethics

What You'll Learn

- The meaning of personal and business ethics.
- The components of an effective business ethics program.
- How the behavior of the accountant contributes to public trust.
- How ethical behavior affects individuals, business, and society.

Why It's Important

Ethical behavior in business and personal life provides the foundation for society.

KEY TERMS

ethics
business ethics
code of ethics
ethics officer

Have you ever been faced with a difficult decision about a particular course of action or behavior? Did you consider how you would feel about the action or how others would view your choice? Did you consider how your behavior would affect others? If so, you've probably encountered an ethical dilemma.

What Are Ethics?

Ethics is the study of our notions of right and wrong. In its broadest sense, ethics deals with human conduct in relation to what is morally good and bad. The term "ethics" often refers to a set of basic principles. Life is complex and individuals are faced with a variety of situations. A person's ethics, or basic principles, can provide guidelines for action when faced with ethical dilemmas.

The basic values found in a system of personal ethics exist in systems of business ethics as well. Business ethics are not very different from ethics in general.

What Are Business Ethics?

Business ethics are the policies and practices that reflect a company's core values such as honesty, trust, respect, and fairness. The ethics of a business can be seen by the way employees and customers are treated and how the company attends to shareholder value, community service, supplier relationships, and regulatory law. Review the following components to understand how a business ethics program can be established.

The Law As a Guide

When discussing ethical performance, the relationship between law and ethics should be considered. While law and ethics both define proper and improper behavior, law attempts to formally define the general public's ideas about what makes something right or wrong. The law describes a minimum acceptable level of correct behavior. Ethical concepts have more subtle implications and are more complex than written rules of law. For example, although a business may be well within the law to advertise certain products to teenagers, it may not be the "right" or "ethical" thing to do. A business may use law as a guide, but must consider ethical principles and standards as well.

Statements of Company Values

If you have heard the phrase, "actions speak louder than words," then you are familiar with one of the best methods of maintaining a strong business ethics program. People learn their standards and values by observing what others do, not necessarily by what they say.

In addition to setting good examples of ethical behavior, a well-defined framework of ethical concerns and core values must be stated. A **code of ethics** is a formal policy of rules and standards that describes the ethical behaviors that a company expects from its management and employees. The following topics are often addressed within a code of ethics:

- Conflicts of interest
- Product quality and testing
- Customer relations
- Employee relations
- Suppliers and consultants
- Expense reports
- Security
- Political contributions
- Environmental actions
- International business
- Workplace safety
- Technology
- Whistle-blowing

International ACCOUNTING

Business Ethics

Knowing about the culture in which a company operates is critical to understanding the subtle points of what is considered unethical. For example, in the U.S. it would not be proper to bring an expensive gift to an initial meeting with a prospective client—it could be viewed as a bribe. In Japan, however, it is considered impolite not to bring a gift.

Key Points

Modeling Behavior

Employees learn ethical standards of an organization by watching the behaviors of their employers and managers.

Training and Outreach

After a code of ethics is created, it is important to communicate that policy properly. Distribution of the written code, along with formal training, helps employees understand the importance of these policies and gives them realistic and concrete examples of what to do when faced with an ethical dilemma.

Ethics Committees

Ethics committees and ethics officers play an important role in developing and enforcing ethical processes. An **ethics officer** is the employee directly responsible for creating business conduct programs, evaluating performance, and enforcing standards of conduct. As ethical dilemmas surface, these officials help settle disputed issues and resolve problems. Once a hearing has been held and all issues have been resolved, an enforcement phase may follow.

Enforcement

Effective enforcement is necessary to achieve an ethical work environment. A company's code of ethics might contain penalties for violations that include performance appraisal notes, probation, suspension, demotion, or termination.

What Is the Accountant's Role?

Accountants play a major role in the operation, management, and development of business. In such roles, they can face many ethical dilemmas. For example, if an accountant's manager gives instructions to record the physical inventory at its original costs when it is obvious that the inventory's value has decreased, what should the accountant do? If an auditor finds questionable accounting practices within a client's financial reporting, yet knows the client is a major source of revenue for his or her firm, what action should be taken?

As you can see, the actions and behaviors of accountants play a critical role in the maintenance of public trust in the business community. The accountant's opinions, practices, and behaviors directly impact how the company is viewed, and how the profession, in turn, is assessed.

In general, the ethically trained accountant should focus on the following goals:

- Avoid harm to stockholders.
- Optimize the interests of the public.
- Adhere to universal standards of what is right.
- Respect the human rights of all.

Specific responsibilities of the accounting profession are expressed in the various codes of ethics created by major organizations. These codes of ethics are addressed in Section 2 of this chapter.

Who Benefits from Ethical Behavior?

While it may seem obvious that ethical behavior naturally benefits individuals, business, and society, the following discussion addresses specific benefits to each group.

Individuals

Acting ethically produces benefits that can affect the course of your life and the lives of others. These benefits include increased self-esteem,

---

Key Points

Public Trust

The practices of the accountant directly reflect the credibility of a business and the integrity of the accounting profession.

Key Points

Positive Returns

Good ethics are good for business. These positive returns include employee loyalty, improved sales and company reputation, strengthened financial performance, and a decrease in consumer complaints.

contentment, and self-respect. Ethical behavior also paves the way for achieving life goals. Your honesty, trustworthiness, and integrity will allow you to find a satisfying career with the type of organization that shares your core values.

As you act ethically, you will also enjoy the benefit of acceptance in a society where appropriate behavior is rewarded and honored. As you focus more on the common good, rather than selfish interests, you will earn trust and respect from friends, co-workers, employers, and society in general. Finally, ethical behavior will dramatically improve the quality of your decisions.

Business

A 1999 DePaul University study indicated that companies that made commitments to an ethics code provided more than twice the value to shareholders than those that did not. A study by Walker Information, a shareholder research firm, supports this finding, reporting that "good corporate behavior" leads to positive business outcomes.

Society

Society can be viewed as the sum of all social relationships between humans. Therefore, it is easy to understand why our individual actions contribute to the overall nature of our society. We cannot expect our society to become more ethical unless individuals and businesses commit to ethical behaviors.

As businesses act in ethical ways, new wealth for society is created. In the realm of ethical financial reporting, the public can be confident in the data provided and make informed investment decisions. In turn, greater capital funding is available for growth and productivity, yielding strong and healthy economies.

Key Points

The Sum of the Parts
The behavior of individuals and business contributes to the overall ethical performance of society.

A MATTER OF ETHICS

Working Conditions

Imagine that you are a stockholder in a corporation that manufactures sports apparel. The company recently moved its operations to a developing country where labor is cheaper. Employees work more than 16 hours per day and the factory conditions are far below those in the U.S. While not comparable to U.S. standards, the conditions are better than those found in other local factories and the rate of pay is nearly double what local workers earned in the past. The company has offered to pay for any work-related injuries. As a stockholder, do you agree with this manufacturing strategy?

Ethical Decision Making:

☞ What are the ethical issues?

☞ What are the alternatives?

☞ Who are the affected parties?

☞ How do the alternatives affect the parties?

☞ What would you do?

Now that you have studied this section, complete the following questions and problems.

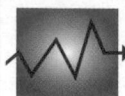

Thinking Critically

1. Supporters of ethical business practices say that good ethics are good for business. Do you agree? What conflicts might arise between the motives for maximum profits and good corporate citizenship?
2. Discuss the components needed to create a strong business ethics program. Which element do you think is most lacking in U.S. business today? Explain your answer.
3. Describe how an ethically trained accountant can contribute to ethical conduct in a business. What challenges might exist in this relationship?

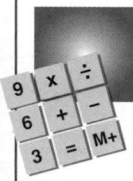

Computing in the Business World

Assume that you are the chief financial officer for a major manufacturer of infant car seats. The lead product designer informs management that installation of a new latch system would improve product safety by 25 percent. The new latch system will add $4 to production costs per car seat. Current production costs are $52.50 per seat and the product sells for $69.50. Management wants to compare the effect on net income if they raise the product price by (a) $1, (b) $2, or (c)$5.

1. If the company sells 8,000 car seats in a year, what is the effect on net income for each proposed price increase scenario? Assume fixed operating costs are $115,000 annually.
2. As an officer of the company, what factors (other than pricing) do you think should be considered when making product design changes?

Problem 29–1 **Reporting Ethics Violations**

Instructions Results from Walker Information's 2001 study on business integrity state that 65 percent of employees who know about an ethical violation choose not to report it. What weaknesses in a company's ethical environment might be responsible for such a finding? Discuss the components of a strong business ethics plan that could be applied to resolve this situation.

Problem 29–2 **Exploring the Difference Between Ethics and Law**

Instructions Adhering to legal regulations is the first step in behaving ethically. Explain why ethical behavior extends beyond the law. Describe one situation in which a company might act within the boundaries of the law, yet still engage in an unethical act.

Ethics in the Accounting Profession

Professional organizations are often separated from other organizations by a code of conduct or a code of ethics. To build public trust, most accountants voluntarily join a professional organization and accept the standards of conduct expected by the organization.

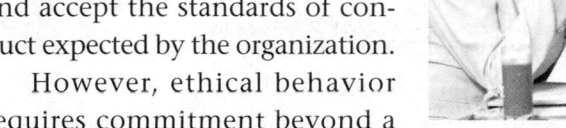

However, ethical behavior requires commitment beyond a few rules of conduct. No ethics code or written rules can apply to all situations that might arise on the job. Day to day job experiences often test an individual's personal judgment and personal ethics.

Written codes of ethics are generally designed to encourage ideal behavior. However, the codes must be both realistic and enforceable. Professional organizations are charged with enforcing the rules of conduct outlined in their codes.

What Are the Key Principles?

Certain principles provide the framework for rules of conduct that an accountant is expected to follow. These principles include integrity, objectivity, independence, competence, and confidentiality.

Integrity

The principle of **integrity** requires that accountants choose what is right and just over what is wrong. Guidance for behaving with integrity suggests the accountant ask the following questions: Is this what a person of integrity would do? Have I made a right and just decision? Have I maintained the spirit of ethical conduct?

How do you explain the concept of integrity as related to the accounting profession? Making false or misleading entries in a client's books violates the accounting principle of integrity. Failing to correct false and misleading financial statements also violates integrity. Integrity helps accountants establish the trust necessary for others to rely on their professional judgment.

Objectivity

Every year publicly traded corporations must submit financial statements to the Securities and Exchange Commission. The financial statements are audited by certified public accountants (CPAs).

CPAs who perform audits are known as "independent auditors." They do not work for the companies they audit. For example, suppose that Paul Corporation needs to give audited financial statements to the SEC. Paul Corporation hires Findlay & Partners, a public accounting firm. Five CPAs who work for Findlay & Partners go to the offices of Paul Corporation and perform the audit. Paul Corporation is the *client* and Findlay & Partners is the *independent auditor*. The work of the independent auditor is critical. Many different users of financial information depend on audited financial statements when making decisions.

The principle of **objectivity** requires that accountants be impartial, honest, and free of conflicts of interest. When forming professional judgments, accountants should not be influenced by personal interests or relationships with others.

Independence

CPAs who audit public companies must maintain a position of independence. **Independence** in this sense means that the CPA does not have a financial interest in the company being audited. An investment in the company or a loan from the company would interfere with the independence required of an auditor. Serving as a director, officer, or employee of the company would also demonstrate a lack of independence.

An accountant must act in such a way that maintains the general public's confidence in the services provided by a professional. Even if the accountant's financial interest is minor and unimportant, the relationship could be suspect, and the accountant would be considered to lack independence. Even non-CPA employees in a public accounting firm may not accept more than token gifts from clients.

Competence

Accountants must engage only in services in which they are competent. **Competence** refers to the knowledge, skills, and experience needed to complete a task. Accountants are expected to maintain an appropriate level of competence through continuing education and to continually improve the quality of professional services. Services should be rendered promptly, carefully, thoroughly, and in accordance with appropriate technical and ethical standards. A commitment to learning and professional improvement must continue throughout the accountant's professional life.

Confidentiality

Accountants learn about everything from individual salaries to business strategies. How do you explain the concept of confidentiality as related to the accounting profession? **Confidentiality** is the requirement that information

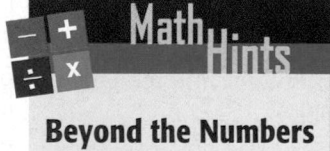

Beyond the Numbers
When weighing alternative actions for an ethical dilemma, remember that not all factors can be measured in numbers or dollars. The effect on morale and potential harm to others must be considered in nonnumeric ways.

acquired in the course of work be protected and not be disclosed without the appropriate legal or professional responsibility to do so. Information should not be used for personal gain.

Who Writes the Codes of Ethics?

Several accounting organizations provide guidelines to assist in ethical decision making.

American Institute of Certified Public Accountants

The AICPA is the national organization of certified public accountants. Members of the AICPA voluntarily accept standards of professional behavior that are much more strict than those required by the law. The following preamble in the AICPA's Code of Professional Conduct emphasizes the importance of ethical standards for CPAs.

AICPA Code of Professional Conduct Preamble

Membership in the American Institute of Certified Public Accountants is voluntary. By accepting membership, a certified public accountant assumes an obligation of self-discipline above and beyond the requirements of laws and regulations.

These Principles of the Code of Professional Conduct of the American Institute of Certified Public Accountants express the profession's recognition of its responsibilities to the public, to clients, and to colleagues. They guide members in the performance of their professional responsibilities and express the basic tenets of ethical and professional conduct. The Principles call for an unswerving commitment to honorable behavior, even at the sacrifice of personal advantage.[1]

Institute of Management Accountants

The IMA is the leading professional organization devoted exclusively to management accountants and financial managers. Unlike accountants in public practice who audit other companies, management accountants usually have a job in a single company.

The IMA helps accountants develop both personally and professionally through education, certification, and association with other professionals. Members of the IMA have a responsibility to maintain professional competence, uphold professional standards of confidentiality, avoid conflicts of interest, and communicate information fairly and objectively.

Institute of Internal Auditors

The IIA was introduced at the beginning of the chapter. Like other professional organizations, the IIA expects its members to demonstrate competence and to follow the principles of integrity, objectivity, and confidentiality. The IIA's code of ethics is necessary and appropriate because of the public trust placed in internal auditors.

[1] Preamble, *Online posting*, AICPA Code of Professional Conduct Section 51, 3 October 2002, <http://www.aicpa.org/about/code/archive/preamble.htm>

Key Points

Guidelines
A code of ethics can't cover the details of every situation that might occur. The code provides principles that can be applied to a variety of unexpected situations.

Now that you have studied this section, complete the following questions and problems.

Thinking Critically

1. Explain the concept of independence as it relates to the profession of accounting.
2. Describe a situation in which the principle of independence might be threatened for an accountant.
3. Describe the role of the internal auditor and how the Institute of Internal Auditors' code of ethics helps establish public trust.

Communicating Accounting

Your friend Samantha recently graduated with a degree in accounting. As a member of the American Institute of Certified Public Accountants, you encourage her to become a CPA and join the organization. Draft an e-mail message to your friend that includes reasons why you think she should join the AICPA and how she will benefit from the membership.

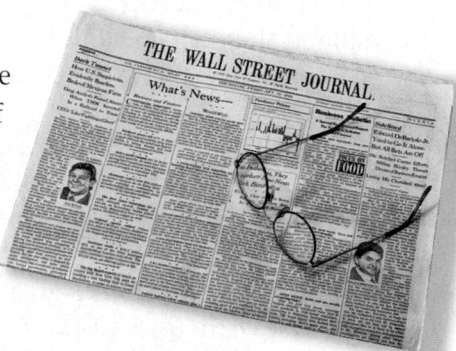

Problem 29–3   Promoting Principles of Conduct

Instructions Read the following scenario. Identify and discuss behaviors that you feel might violate the key principles of conduct for accountants.

In your new position as accounting manager with Triple B Markets, you supervise three staff accountants: Jennifer, Marcus, and Ing. You become aware of the following situations:

- Jennifer, a new employee, has never worked as an accountant, but scored high marks in her college math classes.
- Marcus often records payments of utilities as assets instead of expenses because he wants to show a higher net income for the business.
- You overheard Ing talking with a friend on the phone about the payroll details of the company.

KEY CONCEPTS

1. Ethics is the study of our notions of right and wrong. The term "ethics" also refers to a set of basic principles.

2. Business ethics are the policies and practices that reflect a company's core values such as honesty, trust, respect, and fairness.

3. Components of a business ethics program include adherence to written law, a written and well-communicated code of ethics, training, and enforcement.

4. The behaviors and practices of the accountant are critical to public trust in the business as well as the integrity of the accounting profession.

5. An ethically trained accountant should focus on the following goals: avoiding harm to stockholders, optimizing the interests of the public, adhering to the universal standards of what is right, and respecting the human rights of all.

6. Ethical behavior benefits the individual, business, and society at large.

7. Integrity is the principle that requires accountants to choose what is right and just over what is wrong.

8. Objectivity is the principle that requires accountants to be impartial, honest, and free of conflicts of interest.

9. Independence is the principle that requires CPAs to have no financial interest in the company being audited.

10. Competence is the principle that requires accountants to have the knowledge, skills, and experience needed to complete a task.

11. Confidentiality is the principle that requires accountants to protect and not disclose information acquired in the course of work unless they have a legal or professional responsibility to do so.

12. Professional organizations are often separated from other organizations by a code of professional conduct.

13. Professional accountants are distinguished by their willingness to accept a high degree of responsibility to the public.

14. The American Institute of Certified Public Accountants is the national professional organization of certified public accountants.

15. The Institute of Management Accountants serves management accountants and financial managers.

16. The Institute of Internal Auditors is a worldwide professional group that specializes in internal auditing.

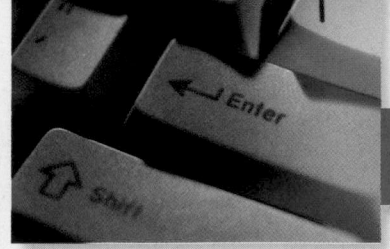

USING KEY TERMS

As the new training director for a public accounting firm, you have been instructed to design and present a program to employees on the importance of ethical behavior. A list of terms, which you are to use in your program, is shown below. Write a complete definition for each term. For each term, write one or two sentences describing its importance to the success of the firm.

business ethics	ethics officer
code of ethics	independence
competence	integrity
confidentiality	objectivity
ethics	

Understanding Accounting Concepts and Procedures

Instructions

On a separate sheet of paper, answer the following questions:

1. Explain what the phrase "actions speak louder than words" means.

2. How can a company communicate a code of ethics to its employees?

3. What kinds of penalties are sometimes imposed on employees who violate a company's code of ethics?

4. What role does the accountant play in maintaining public trust in the business community?

5. List four goals of an ethically trained accountant.

6. How does acting ethically benefit an individual?

7. How does a business benefit from acting ethically?

8. What is the purpose of an ethics code for a professional organization?

9. Explain the concept of integrity as related to the accounting profession.

10. Explain the concepts of objectivity, independence, and competence as related to the accounting profession.

11. Explain the concept of confidentiality as related to the accounting profession.

Case Study...

CPA Firm: Audits

Chris Snyder is an audit supervisor for an accounting firm. She and her staff will be auditing the financial records of Gemma Industries in the near future. The CEO of Gemma has invited Chris and staff to arrive one day earlier than the audit date to play a round of golf at an exclusive country club of which the CEO is a member. They have also been invited for dinner at an expensive restaurant that same evening.

Thinking Critically:

1. Should Chris and her staff accept the invitation?
2. If not, how should Chris turn down the invitation without offending the CEO and possibly losing a client?
3. What ethical issue could arise if Chris accepts the invitation?

*inter*NET CONNECTION

Code of Professional Conduct

Certain principles provide the framework for rules of conduct that an accountant is expected to follow.

Do This:

1. Look at the American Institute of Certified Public Accountants Web site.
2. What guidance is provided to help AICPA members follow the Code of Professional Conduct?
3. List three suggestions given by the AICPA.
4. Explain how the guidelines might help you in your personal behavior.

Conducting an Audit with Alex

One of Alex's clients is a company that owns a hospital. As you review the hospital's various sources of income, you discover the hospital received a large donation from a pharmaceutical company. The hospital's code of ethics states that contributions from suppliers, in this case a pharmaceutical company, are not permitted.

Instructions:

1. Write a memo to Alex that gives your recommendation for action in this situation.
2. In your memo, discuss the reasons you think the hospital's code of ethics does not allow contributions from pharmaceutical companies.

Workplace Skills

Acquiring and Analyzing Information

In order to ensure adequate internal controls for a business, you must be able to acquire and analyze relevant information.

On the Job:

You supervise three accounts payable clerks in your job at Blake's Auto Supply Company. Two clerks routinely process invoices on Friday and mail checks on Monday. The other clerk prepares checks on Monday and mails them on Tuesday. She uses Friday to verify subsidiary ledgers and double-check the calculations on invoices due. All checks must be processed through the data entry department, which has experienced a high turnover lately. Data entry clerks are often absent on Fridays and the entire accounting department must share one printer. You would like all three clerks to follow the same procedures and wonder why there are differences in how they handle their jobs.

Thinking Critically:

1. Prepare a list of questions to ask your employees that will help you assess the situation.
2. What resource factors might influence the way your clerks perform their duties?

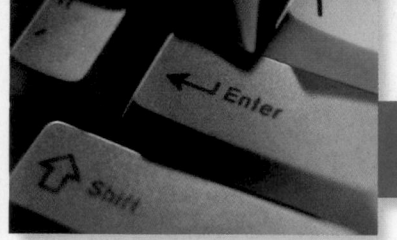

Problem 29–4 Researching Ethics in the News

Instructions Using the library, newspaper, or the Internet, find three recent examples of businesses accused of engaging in unethical practices. For each example, describe the practices of the company, any legal charges involved, and why you think the business chose this course of action.

Problem 29–5 Creating a Business Ethics Program

Instructions Imagine that you are the ethics officer for a national chain of coffeehouses. Prepare a one- or two-page outline for a business ethics plan that covers the main issues you think are relevant to the operations of this company. Include outline headings for a code of ethics, enforcement measures, and how you will communicate the ethics plan to the employees and managers of the company.

Problem 29–6 Making Ethical Decisions

Instructions Sean McGee works as a graphics designer for a large design firm. In his job, he utilizes dozens of expensive software programs that the company purchased for its employees. Because Sean often takes work home to finish for his deadlines, he copied all the software programs and installed them on his personal computer. In addition to the work he does for his employer, he also takes freelance jobs for extra cash. What are the ethical issues? Who are the affected parties? Do you think Sean has made an ethical decision? Why or why not? What actions would you have taken?

Problem 29–7 Making Ethical Decisions

Instructions Randy Simpson and Kyung Won worked as recruiters for a national job placement company. The company provided them with a database filled with potential companies that might use a placement service, as well as qualified applicants who are seeking jobs. After working together for several years, Randy and Kyung decided to open a recruiting agency themselves. They had previously signed agreements not to take any property of the company with them if they left.

When Randy and Kyung were setting up their new offices, Kyung noticed Randy downloading files from floppy disks to his computer. When questioned, Randy said he had copied his list of clients in addition to names of potential new clients and qualified applicants. Kyung was worried that this act

was a violation of the agreement they had signed. Randy maintained that he had built solid relationships with his clients, and that he was entitled to take their contact information. As for the names of applicants, he argued, "These people need jobs. If I can help make that happen, I should." What are the ethical issues? What would you do if you were Kyung?

Problem 29–8 Examining the Impact of Unethical Decisions

Instructions Assume that the accountant for a drug manufacturing company made the decision to record the company's ending drug inventory at an amount higher than its actual worth. How does this decision affect gross profit and net income for that accounting period? In what ways might this decision affect shareholder value? How might this affect confidence in the company's financial statements in the future?

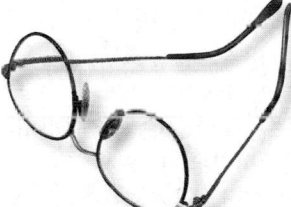

Problem 29–9 Finding Out What Ethical Principles Mean to Your Classmates

Instructions Make a list of the five ethical principles found in the chapter. Take the list with you and ask your friends how they think the principles might influence their everyday life. Report your results in class.

Problem 29–10 Finding Out What Ethical Principles Mean to Adults

Instructions Ask adults how they think the five principles of ethics found in this chapter influence professional behavior. Share your results in class.

Problem 29–11 Applying a Code of Ethics to Personal Behavior

Instructions Write a code of ethics that you feel would help guide the behavior of students in school organizations. Interview students outside your class for help with ideas.

Problem 29–12 Analyzing the AICPA Code of Professional Conduct Preamble

Instructions Look up the AICPA Preamble in the text. List two key points covered in each of the two paragraphs. Are the points important to your everyday behavior? Why or why not?

Adjustments for a Service Business Using a Ten-Column Work Sheet

What You'll Learn

- How to identify general ledger accounts that require adjustments.
- How to calculate end-of-period adjustments for a service business.
- How to record end-of-period adjustments for a service business.
- How to update accounts through adjusting entries for a service business.
- How to enter adjustments on a ten-column work sheet.
- How to complete the Adjusted Trial Balance section of a work sheet.

Why It's Important

Certain general ledger accounts require adjustments before the net income or net loss for the period can be determined and the work sheet completed.

KEY TERMS

adjustment
premium

The ten-column work sheet is prepared in the same manner as the six-column work sheet in Chapter 8. The additional columns are for the Adjustments and Adjusted Trial Balance sections. The ten-column work sheet has five amount sections instead of three.

The Trial Balance Section

The information for the Account Name and Trial Balance sections comes from the general ledger accounts. The end-of-period balance for each account is entered in the appropriate amount column of the Trial Balance section. In Chapter 8 you entered the final account balances in the correct column and completed the Trial Balance section by totaling and ruling the columns.

The Need for Adjustments

Up to this point the general ledger account balances have been changed by journal entries made to record transactions that are supported by source documents. However, not all changes in account balances are the result of daily business transactions. There are no source documents for the changes in account balances caused by the internal operations of a business or the passage of time. Such changes are recorded through adjustments made to the account balances at the end of the accounting period. An **adjustment** is an amount that is added to or subtracted from an account balance to bring that balance up-to-date.

In this appendix you will learn how to calculate end-of-period adjustments for a service business, Maximum Delivery Service. Every adjustment affects at least one permanent account and one temporary account. Two examples of general ledger accounts that need adjusting at the end of the accounting period are **Supplies** and **Prepaid Insurance**.

Adjusting the Supplies Account

All businesses purchase some sort of supplies for the operation of the business. Paper, pens and pencils, ink cartridges, and staples are common business supplies. When supplies are purchased, the asset account **Supplies** is debited (increased). Supplies may be purchased by paying cash or on account.

Purchasing Supplies

When supplies are purchased for cash, the asset account **Supplies** is increased, so it is debited for the amount of the purchase. **Cash in Bank** is also an asset account, and it is decreased (credited). On February 14 Maximum Delivery Service purchased supplies for $300, Check 229.

GENERAL JOURNAL   PAGE __11__

	DATE		DESCRIPTION	POST. REF.	DEBIT	CREDIT	
1	20--						1
2	Feb.	14	Supplies		3 0 0 00		2
3			Cash in Bank			3 0 0 00	3
4			Check 229				4
5							5

When supplies are purchased on account, the **Supplies** account is again debited. Since additional money is owed to a creditor, the liability account, **Accounts Payable**, is credited. On August 21 Maximum Delivery Service purchased $400 worth of supplies on account from Shade Supply Company, Invoice 28714.

GENERAL JOURNAL   PAGE __14__

	DATE		DESCRIPTION	POST. REF.	DEBIT	CREDIT	
1	20--						1
2	Aug.	21	Supplies		4 0 0 00		2
3			Accts. Pay.—Shade Supply Co.			4 0 0 00	3
4			Invoice 28714				4
5							5

Calculating the Adjustment for Supplies

Each time supplies are purchased, the **Supplies** account is debited for the amount of the purchase. For example, Maximum Delivery Service had $100 in supplies on hand at the beginning of the period. During the period the company made two purchases of supplies for $300 and $400. The final balance in the **Supplies** account in the general ledger on December 31 is $800 ($100 + $300 + $400). However, some of these supplies have been used or consumed during the period. Supplies are used every day. It is inefficient to keep daily records of all supplies used on a daily basis.

At the end of the period, Maximum Delivery Service does not have all $800 in supplies. Most of the supplies have been used. By examining the remaining supplies, Maximum determines that only $200 worth of the supplies are still on hand. This means $600 of supplies have been used or consumed during the period ($800 – $200 = $600). The account balance for **Supplies** must be adjusted to report a final balance of $200. The account balance must be reduced by $600.

As supplies are used, they become expenses of the business. At the end of the period, adjustments are made to transfer the costs of the assets consumed from the asset accounts (permanent accounts) to the appropriate expense accounts (temporary accounts).

Entering the Supplies Adjustment on the Work Sheet

The Adjustments section of the work sheet is used to enter the necessary adjustments for the period. Since $600 worth of supplies were used during the period, the **Supplies** account is decreased, or credited, for this amount. The account **Supplies Expense** is increased, or debited, for $600.

Adjustment		
ANALYSIS *Identify* *Classify* +/–	1. The accounts affected are **Supplies** and **Supplies Expense**. 2. **Supplies** is an asset account (permanent). **Supplies Expense** is an expense account (temporary). 3. **Supplies** is decreased by $600. **Supplies Expense** is increased by $600.	
DEBIT-CREDIT RULE	4. Increases to expense accounts are recorded as debits. Debit **Supplies Expense** for $600. 5. Decreases to asset accounts are recorded as credits. Credit **Supplies** for $600.	

T ACCOUNTS   6.

Supplies Expense		Supplies	
Debit + 600	Credit –	Debit +	Credit – 600

The adjustment for **Supplies** in the Adjustments section of the work sheet is shown in **Figure A–1**. To enter the adjustment on the work sheet, follow these steps:

1. In the Adjustments Debit column, enter the debit amount of the adjustment ($600) on the Supplies Expense line.
2. In the Adjustments Credit column, enter the credit amount of the adjustment ($600) on the Supplies line.

On the work sheet, the debit and credit parts of each adjustment are given a unique label. The label consists of a small letter in parentheses and is placed just above and to the left of the adjustment amounts. The supplies adjustment is labeled (a).

	ACCT. NO.	ACCOUNT NAME	TRIAL BALANCE		ADJUSTMENTS		ADJUSTED TRIAL BALANCE	
			DEBIT	CREDIT	DEBIT	CREDIT	DEBIT	CREDIT
1	101	Cash in Bank	7 264 00				7 264 00	
2	105	Accts. Rec.—Wein Corp.	336 00				336 00	
3	110	Accts. Rec.—Mike Cassidy	917 00				917 00	
4	115	Supplies	800 00			(a) 600 00	200 00	
5	120	Prepaid Insurance	750 00			(b) 250 00	500 00	
6	125	Office Equipment	11 364 00				11 364 00	
7	130	Delivery Equipment	14 600 00				14 600 00	
8	201	Accts. Pay.—Gillespie Co.		1 774 00				1 774 00
9	205	Accts. Pay.—Shade Supply Co.		200 00				200 00
10	210	Accts. Pay.—Trip Travel		2 632 00				2 632 00
11	301	Kevin Chan, Capital		16 734 00				16 734 00
12	302	Kevin Chan, Withdrawals	2 500 00				2 500 00	
13	303	Income Summary						
14	401	Delivery Revenue		28 724 00				28 724 00
15	501	Advertising Expense	3 083 00				3 083 00	
16	505	Insurance Expense			(b) 250 00		250 00	
17	510	Maintenance Expense	710 00				710 00	
18	515	Rent Expense	6 500 00				6 500 00	
19	520	Supplies Expense			(a) 600 00		600 00	
20	525	Utilities Expense	1 240 00				1 240 00	
21		Totals	50 064 00	50 064 00	850 00	850 00	50 064 00	50 064 00
22								

Figure A–1 Ten-Column Work Sheet (Partial) Showing the Adjusted Trial Balance

Adjusting the Prepaid Insurance Account

Businesses buy insurance to protect against losses from hazards such as theft, fire, and flood. Insurance policies cover varying time periods, such as six months or one year. The cost of insurance protection is called the **premium**. A premium is paid in advance at the beginning of the covered period. Insurance paid in advance is an asset because, until the insurance protection expires, it represents a benefit to the business. The insurance premium is recorded in the asset account, **Prepaid Insurance**.

On November 1 Maximum Delivery Service paid a six-month insurance premium of $750, Check 314.

	DATE		DESCRIPTION	POST. REF.	DEBIT	CREDIT	
1	20--						1
2	Nov.	1	Prepaid Insurance		7 50 00		2
3			Cash in Bank			7 50 00	3
4			Check 314				4
5							5

GENERAL JOURNAL   PAGE 19

At the end of December, the balance in the **Prepaid Insurance** account is still $750. However, two months of the six months of coverage have expired.

Nov. 1–Dec. 31		Jan. 1–Apr. 30		
Expired		Not Expired		
$250	+	$500	=	$750

The monthly cost of the insurance is $125 ($750 ÷ 6 = $125). Since the coverage for November and December has expired, $250 ($125 x 2) of the $750 in the premium has been used. The asset account **Prepaid Insurance** must be decreased (credited) for $250. The amount of insurance expired is charged to the expense account **Insurance Expense**. In this adjustment **Insurance Expense** is debited for $250.

Adjustment

ANALYSIS	*Identify*	1. The accounts affected are **Prepaid Insurance** and **Insurance Expense**.
	Classify	2. **Prepaid Insurance** is an asset account (permanent). **Insurance Expense** is an expense account (temporary).
	+/–	3. **Prepaid Insurance** is decreased by $250. **Insurance Expense** is increased by $250.

DEBIT-CREDIT RULE	4. Increases to expense accounts are recorded as debits. Debit **Insurance Expense** for $250.
	5. Decreases to asset accounts are recorded as credits. Credit **Prepaid Insurance** for $250.

T ACCOUNTS 6.

Insurance Expense		Prepaid Insurance	
Debit	Credit	Debit	Credit
+	–	+	–
250			250

To enter the adjustment on the work sheet, follow these steps:

1. In the Adjustments Debit column, enter the debit amount of the adjustment ($250) on the Insurance Expense line. Since this is the second adjustment, label it (b).
2. In the Adjustments Credit column, enter the credit amount of the adjustment ($250) on the Prepaid Insurance line. Label it (b) also.

Completing the Work Sheet

After the adjustments are entered on the work sheet, the Adjusted Trial Balance section can be completed. This section of the work sheet shows the updated balances of all the general ledger accounts.

Completing the
Adjusted Trial Balance Section

To complete this section, the balance of each account in the Trial Balance section is combined with the adjustment, if any, in the Adjustments section. The new balance is then entered in the appropriate Adjusted Trial Balance column.

Refer to **Figure A–2** on pages A–7 and A–8 and look at how new balances are computed. If there is no adjustment, the account balance shown on the Trial Balance section is simply extended to the same column (Debit or Credit) in the Adjusted Trial Balance section. After all account balances are extended to the Adjusted Trial Balance section, both columns are totaled. If total debits equal total credits, this section is proved. A double rule is drawn under the totals and across both columns.

Extending Amounts to the Balance Sheet and Income Statement Sections

Beginning with line 1, each account balance in the Adjusted Trial Balance section is extended to the appropriate column of either the Balance Sheet section or the Income Statement section. Remember, the Balance Sheet section includes the asset, liability, and owner's equity accounts. The Income Statement section includes the revenue and expense accounts.

Showing Net Income on the Work Sheet

The Income Statement and Balance Sheet sections of the work sheet are totaled. The net income (or net loss) is entered on the work sheet as shown in **Figure A–2**.

Journalizing and Posting the
Adjusting Entries

The journal entries that update the general ledger accounts at the end of a period are called adjusting entries. The source of information for journalizing the adjusting entries is the Adjustments section of the work sheet. The accounts debited and credited in the Adjustments section are entered in the general journal.

Before recording the first adjusting entry, the words "Adjusting Entries" are written in the Description column of the general journal. This heading eliminates the need to write an explanation after each adjusting entry.

The first adjustment, labeled (a) on the work sheet, is recorded in the general journal as a debit to **Supplies Expense** for $600 and a credit to **Supplies** for $600. The second adjustment is a debit to **Insurance Expense** for $250 and a credit to **Prepaid Insurance** for $250.

After the adjusting entries are recorded in the general journal, they are posted to the general ledger accounts. Once the adjusting entries are posted, the general ledger accounts are up-to-date. Refer to **Figure A–3** on page A–9 to see how to record end-of-period adjustments and update accounts through adjusting entries.

The Steps in the Accounting Cycle

There are additional general ledger accounts that need to be adjusted at the end of the period. You will learn the reasons and procedures for adjusting other accounts throughout this textbook.

Figure A–2 Work Sheet Showing Ending Adjusted Balances and Net Income

Maximum

Work

For Year Ended

	ACCT. NO.	ACCOUNT NAME	TRIAL BALANCE		ADJUSTMENTS	
			DEBIT	CREDIT	DEBIT	CREDIT
1	101	Cash in Bank	7 264 00			
2	105	Accts. Rec.—Wein Corp.	336 00			
3	110	Accts. Rec.—Mike Cassidy	917 00			
4	115	Supplies	800 00			(a) 600 00
5	120	Prepaid Insurance	750 00			(b) 250 00
6	125	Office Equipment	11 364 00			
7	130	Delivery Equipment	14 600 00			
8	201	Accts. Pay.—Gillespie Co.		1 774 00		
9	205	Accts. Pay.—Shade Supply Co.		200 00		
10	210	Accts. Pay.—Trip Travel		2 632 00		
11	301	Kevin Chan, Capital		16 734 00		
12	302	Kevin Chan, Withdrawals	2 500 00			
13	303	Income Summary				
14	401	Delivery Revenue		28 724 00		
15	501	Advertising Expense	3 083 00			
16	505	Insurance Expense			(b) 250 00	
17	510	Maintenance Expense	710 00			
18	515	Rent Expense	6 500 00			
19	520	Supplies Expense			(a) 600 00	
20	525	Utilities Expense	1 240 00			
21			50 064 00	50 064 00	850 00	850 00
22		Net Income				
23						
24						
25						
26						
27						
28						
29						
30						
31						
32						
33						
34						
35						
36						
37						
38						
39						
40						
41						

When adjustments are made at the end of the period, this procedure becomes an additional step in the accounting cycle. After Step 7—*Prepare financial statements*, Step 8 is *Journalize and post the adjusting entries*. The final two steps in the cycle remain the same. We now have a ten-step cycle instead of a nine-step cycle.

Figure A–2 Work Sheet Showing Ending Adjusted Balances and Net Income (continued)

Delivery Service
Sheet
December 31, 20--

	ADJUSTED TRIAL BALANCE		INCOME STATEMENT		BALANCE SHEET		
	DEBIT	CREDIT	DEBIT	CREDIT	DEBIT	CREDIT	
	7 264 00				7 264 00		1
	336 00				336 00		2
	917 00				917 00		3
	200 00				200 00		4
	500 00				500 00		5
	11 364 00				11 364 00		6
	14 600 00				14 600 00		7
		1 774 00				1 774 00	8
		200 00				200 00	9
		2 632 00				2 632 00	10
		16 734 00				16 734 00	11
	2 500 00				2 500 00		12
							13
		28 724 00		28 724 00			14
	3 083 00		3 083 00				15
	250 00		250 00				16
	710 00		710 00				17
	6 500 00		6 500 00				18
	600 00		600 00				19
	1 240 00		1 240 00				20
	50 064 00	50 064 00	12 383 00	28 724 00	37 681 00	21 340 00	21
			16 341 00			16 341 00	22
			28 724 00	28 724 00	37 681 00	37 681 00	23
							24
							25
							26
							27
							28
							29
							30
							31
							32
							33
							34
							35
							36
							37
							38
							39
							40
							41

GENERAL JOURNAL   PAGE ___22___

	DATE		DESCRIPTION	POST. REF.	DEBIT	CREDIT	
1	20--		*Adjusting Entires*				1
2	Dec.	31	Supplies Expense	520	6 0 0 00		2
3			Supplies	115		6 0 0 00	3
4		31	Insurance Expense	505	2 5 0 00		4
5			Prepaid Insurance	120		2 5 0 00	5
6							6

ACCOUNT _Supplies_   ACCOUNT NO. ___115___

DATE		DESCRIPTION	POST. REF.	DEBIT	CREDIT	BALANCE DEBIT	BALANCE CREDIT
20--							
Jan.	1	Balance				1 0 0 00	
Feb.	14		G11	3 0 0 00		4 0 0 00	
Aug.	21		G14	4 0 0 00		8 0 0 00	
Dec.	31	Adjusting Entry	G22		6 0 0 00	2 0 0 00	

ACCOUNT _Prepaid Insurance_   ACCOUNT NO. ___120___

DATE		DESCRIPTION	POST. REF.	DEBIT	CREDIT	BALANCE DEBIT	BALANCE CREDIT
20--							
Nov.	1		G19	7 5 0 00		7 5 0 00	
Dec.	31	Adjusting Entry	G22		2 5 0 00	5 0 0 00	

ACCOUNT _Insurance Expense_   ACCOUNT NO. ___505___

DATE		DESCRIPTION	POST. REF.	DEBIT	CREDIT	BALANCE DEBIT	BALANCE CREDIT
20--							
Dec.	31	Adjusting Entry	G22	2 5 0 00		2 5 0 00	

ACCOUNT _Supplies Expense_   ACCOUNT NO. ___520___

DATE		DESCRIPTION	POST. REF.	DEBIT	CREDIT	BALANCE DEBIT	BALANCE CREDIT
20--							
Dec.	31	Adjusting Entry	G22	6 0 0 00		6 0 0 00	

Figure A–3 Adjusting Entries Posted to the General Ledger

Problem A–1 Analyzing Adjustments

Information related to accounts requiring adjustments on the work sheet for the year ended December 31 for Magner's Advertising Center follows.

Instructions In your working papers, indicate the amount of each adjustment, which account is debited, and which account is credited.

(1) The Trial Balance section shows a balance of $4,239.80 for **Supplies**. The amount of supplies actually on hand at the end of the period is $912.15.

(2) Magner's paid an annual insurance premium of $4,920.00 on October 1.

Problem A–2 Analyzing Adjustments

Ace Advertising Agency has the following information regarding supplies. The beginning balance in the general ledger account **Supplies** on August 1 was $214.00. On August 13, the agency purchased $302.00 worth of supplies. On August 26, they purchased additional supplies for $176.00. At the end of August, Ace counted the supplies and determined that supplies worth $273.00 were still on hand.

Instructions Answer the following questions regarding the **Supplies** account.

(1) What amount should be entered in the Trial Balance section of the work sheet for **Supplies**? Which column should be used?

(2) What amount should be entered in the Adjustments section of the work sheet for **Supplies**? Which column should be used?

(3) Should any other amount be entered in the Adjustments section? If yes, answer these questions:
   a. Which account?
   b. Which column?
   c. What amount?

(4) What amounts should be entered in the Adjusted Trial Balance section? For each amount, list the name of the account and specify which column should be used (Debit or Credit).

Problem A–3 Entering Adjustments and Preparing an Adjusted Trial Balance

The general ledger for Schellhorn's Water Slide shows the following account balances on December 31, the end of the fiscal period.

Instructions In your working papers:
(1) Prepare the Trial Balance section of the work sheet. The account names are entered on the work sheet.
(2) Enter the adjustments for **Office Supplies** and **Prepaid Insurance** in the Adjustments section. The data for the adjustments is as follows:
   (a) The cost of supplies on hand on December 31 is $492.
   (b) The insurance premium expired is $860.
(3) Extend the amounts and complete the Adjusted Trial Balance section.

101	Cash in Bank	$10,230
105	Accts. Rec.—Chiara Adin	519
110	Accts. Rec.—Miguel Hendrickson	207
115	Office Supplies	1,820
120	Prepaid Insurance	1,290
125	Office Equipment	3,117
130	Water Slide Equipment	14,204
201	Accts. Pay.—Northern Slide Co.	6,281
205	Accts. Pay.—Advertising World	1,559
210	Accts. Pay.—Merit Cleaning	332
301	Phil Schellhorn, Capital	12,641
302	Phil Schellhorn, Withdrawals	1,400
303	Income Summary	---
401	Slide Revenue	29,209
501	Advertising Expense	1,350
505	Insurance Expense	---
510	Maintenance Expense	719
515	Rent Expense	12,800
520	Office Supplies Expense	---
525	Utilities Expense	2,366

Problem A–4 Preparing a Ten-Column Work Sheet

The general ledger for Ryan's Canoe Rentals shows the following account balances on December 31, the end of the fiscal period.

Instructions In your working papers:
(1) Prepare the Trial Balance section of the work sheet. The account names are entered on the work sheet.
(2) Enter the adjustments for **Office Supplies** and **Prepaid Insurance** in the Adjustments section. The data for the adjustments is as follows:
    (a) Ryan's determines that 20 percent of the supplies purchased are still on hand on December 31.
    (b) The insurance premium expired is $1,337.
(3) Extend the amounts and complete the Adjusted Trial Balance section.
(4) Extend the appropriate amounts to the Balance Sheet and Income Statement sections and determine the net income or net loss for the period.

101	Cash in Bank	$13,826
105	Accts. Rec.—Nancy Burrows	803
110	Accts. Rec.—Patrick Chang	519
115	Supplies	2,880
120	Prepaid Insurance	2,292
125	Office Equipment	3,117
130	Rental Equipment	14,204
135	Canoes	20,182
201	Accts. Pay.—South Canoe Co.	6,991
205	Accts. Pay.—H & T Advertising	2,046
210	Accts. Pay.—Cassidy's Equipment	855
301	Ryan Gillespie, Capital	38,619
305	Ryan Gillespie, Withdrawals	3,700
310	Income Summary	---
401	Rental Revenue	31,624
402	Lesson Revenue	3,475
501	Advertising Expense	2,730
505	Insurance Expense	---
510	Maintenance Expense	1,664
515	Rent Expense	14,900
520	Supplies Expense	---
525	Utilities Expense	2,793

Using the Numeric Keypad

What You'll Learn

- How to use the numeric keypad by touch.

Why It's Important

Most accounting jobs require the use of a numeric keypad, either for data entry or calculation.

KEY TERMS

home keys

Ten-key numeric keypads are found on electronic calculators and computer keyboards. When you are keying quantities of numerical data, your ability to use the numeric keypad by touch will make your task easier and faster.

Key Locations

The ten-key numeric keypad is usually arranged into four rows of three keys. The locations of the 1 to 9 keys are the same on all equipment. The locations of the 0 (zero), decimal, and Enter keys—as well as other function keys—vary depending on the equipment. Some typical arrangements are illustrated as follows:

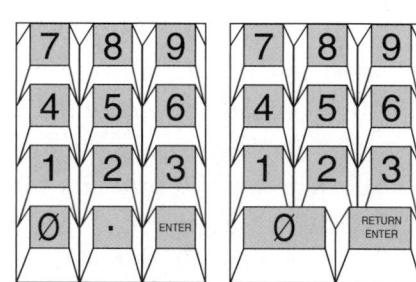

Home Position

On the ten-key numeric keypad, the 4-5-6 keys are called the **home keys.** These keys are the "starting point"

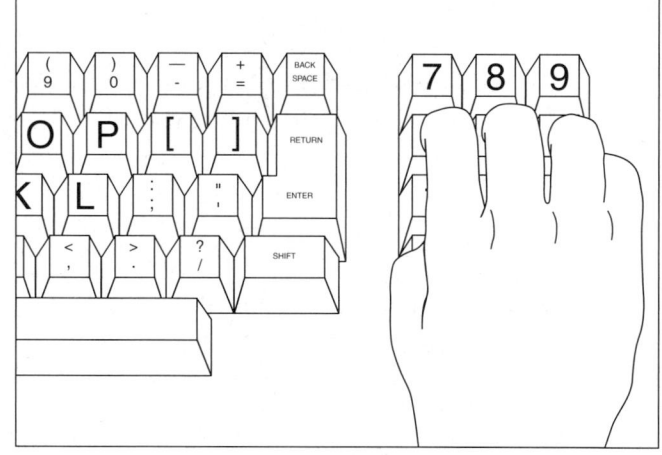

from which you will operate the other number keys. The index finger of your right hand should rest on the 4 key, your middle finger on the 5 key, and your ring finger on the 6 key. Most keypads have a special "help" on the home keys so you can easily locate them: there may be a raised dot on the 5 key or the surfaces of the 4-5-6 keys may be concave (indented).

From the home keys, you reach up or down to tap other keys. The index finger is also used for the 7 and 1 keys. The middle finger is used for the 8 and 2 keys. The ring finger is used for the 9 and 3 keys.

The fingers used for the 0 (zero), decimal, and Enter keys depend on the arrangement of the keypad. On some keypads, the thumb is used to tap the 0 (zero) key and the ring finger for the decimal key. The Enter key on a computer may be operated by the little finger or the thumb, depending on its location.

On an electronic calculator, numbers are entered by using function keys: plus (+), minus (–), multiply (×), divide (÷), and so on. A computer keypad has different function keys for multiply (*) and divide (/). On an electronic calculator, the asterisk (*) is used for the total.

The fingers used to operate these keys depend on the keys' location on the keyboard. Locate these keys on your keypad and determine the correct fingers to use to operate them.

Entering Numbers by Touch

Throughout the remaining pages of this appendix, you will demonstrate use of the numeric keypad by touch. That is, you will enter numbers on the keypad without looking at your fingers.

Your practice consists of adding columns of numbers. If you are using an electronic calculator, tap the plus (+) key after you have entered a number in a column. After entering all the numbers in a column, tap the total (*) key. If you are using a computer spreadsheet program, tap the Enter key after you have entered a number in a column. This will force a line break; each time you strike the Enter key, the cursor will move to the next line. After entering all the numbers in a column, use the software function or formula to add the numbers.

Using the 4-5-6 Keys

1. Demonstrate use of the numeric keypad by touch. Locate the 4-5-6 keys (the home keys) on your keypad. Also locate the Enter key if you're using a computer or the plus key if you're using a calculator.
2. Place your index finger on the 4 key, your middle finger on the 5 key, and your ring finger on the 6 key.
3. To enter a number, tap the number keys, one at a time, in the same order as you read the digits from left to right. Always keep your fingers on the home keys.
4. When you have entered the last digit, tap the Enter key (computer) or the plus key (calculator).
5. Using the following problems, practice entering columns of numbers. Practice at a comfortable pace until you feel confident about each key's location.
6. After entering all of the numbers in a column, add the numbers using the software (computer) or tap the total key once (calculator).

1.	2.	3.	4.	5.	6.
444	555	666	456	554	664
555	666	454	654	445	445
666	444	545	465	564	566
456	654	446	556	664	645
564	546	646	656	565	465
646	465	546	465	655	654

Using the 1, 7 and 0 Keys

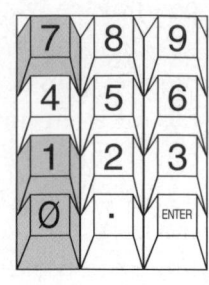

1. Demonstrate use of the numeric keypad by touch. Locate the 1, 7 and 0 (zero) keys on your keypad.
2. Place your fingers on the home keys.
3. Practice the reach from the home keys to each new key. Reach down to the 1 key and up to the 7 key with your index finger. Be sure to return your finger to the home keys after tapping the 1 and 7 keys. Strike the 0 (zero) key with your thumb.
4. Using the following problems, practice adding columns of numbers containing the new keys. Practice at a comfortable pace until you feel confident about each key's location. Be sure to keep your fingers in home-key position.

1.	2.	3.	4.	5.	6.
444	014	140	107	011	141
471	107	701	074	170	117
174	740	701	104	710	417
741	101	704	007	004	047
710	114	471	411	471	104
407	441	117	047	174	114

Using the 3 and 9 Keys

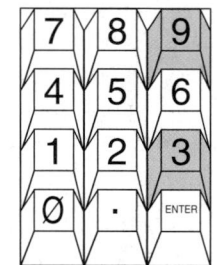

1. Locate the 3 and 9 keys on your keypad.
2. Place your fingers on the home keys.
3. Practice the reach from the home keys to each new key. Reach down to the 3 key and up to the 9 key with your ring finger. Be sure to return your finger to the home keys after tapping the 3 and 9 keys.
4. Using the following problems, practice adding columns of numbers containing the new keys. Practice at a comfortable pace until you feel confident about each key's location. Be sure to keep your fingers in home-key position.

1.	2.	3.	4.	5.	6.
666	669	339	966	939	699
999	663	363	393	363	936
333	936	336	966	393	939
963	396	936	633	639	336
639	936	636	393	369	696
399	363	996	993	369	939

Using the 2 and 8 Keys

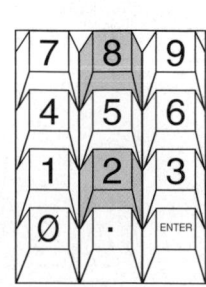

1. Locate the 2 and 8 keys on your keypad.
2. Place your fingers on the home keys.
3. Practice the reach from the home keys to each new key. Reach down to the 2 key and up to the 8 key with your middle finger. Be sure to return your finger to the home keys after tapping the 2 and 8 keys.

4. Using the following problems, practice adding columns of numbers containing the new keys. Practice at a comfortable pace until you feel confident about each key's location. Be sure to keep your fingers in home-key position.

1.	2.	3.	4.	5.	6.
555	228	885	285	582	828
888	852	285	258	558	825
222	522	825	525	582	852
582	252	588	858	825	258
822	528	258	582	525	885
522	855	852	825	582	282

Using the Decimal Key

1. Locate the decimal key on your keypad.
2. Place your fingers on the home keys.
3. Depending on the arrangement of keys on your numeric keypad, you may use your thumb, your middle finger, or your ring finger to tap the decimal key. Practice the reach from the home keys to the decimal key. Be sure to return your finger to the home keys after tapping the decimal key.

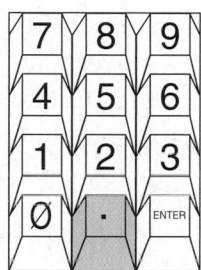

4. Using the following problems, practice adding columns of numbers containing the decimal key. Practice at a comfortable pace until you feel confident about the key's location. Be sure to keep your fingers in home-key position.

1.	2.	3.	4.	5.	6.
.777	.978	.998	8.78	7.88	8.79
.888	.987	.879	8.89	7.87	7.98
.999	.878	.787	8.87	8.97	9.89
.789	.987	.878	7.88	9.77	9.87
.897	.789	.797	9.87	7.97	7.89
.978	.797	.899	7.98	8.79	9.78

7.	8.	9.	10.	11.	12.
468.	48.2	.8	284.0	41.87	154.88
.489	2,537.	5,827.	100.	4,057.4	888.
214.2	852.	.024	8.45	89.45	.0082
7.12	3.978	18.73	56.0	2.25	200.08
6,394.4	257.0	85.00	23.00	20.0	632.48
.58	.2684	1.045	.89	36.248	64.1

13.	14.	15.	16.	17.	18.
267.50	425.21	1.25	467.54	65.27	9.78
4.19	414.50	0.18	95.14	102.38	5.94
87.64	1,684.84	585.56	6,926.95	8,216.58	652.25
654.84	49.95	7.50	35.00	1,852.84	3,782.70
1,750.67	720.65	11.60	7.13	4.60	39.25
141.82	77.61	23.55	154.95	79.15	36.87

Recording Transactions in the Combination Journal

What You'll Learn

The purpose of the combination journal.

- How to record business transactions in a multicolumn journal.
- How to post from the combination journal.
- How to total, prove, and rule the combination journal.

Why It's Important

The combination journal is used primarily by small businesses and professional businesses (doctors, dentists, lawyers, etc.) which usually have one accounting clerk who records repetitious transactions. The accounting concepts, procedures, and applications associated with a combination journal can easily be adapted to a computerized accounting system.

KEY TERMS

combination journal

In earlier chapters you learned that businesses that have a large volume of financial transactions use special journals to record those transactions. Special journals, you'll remember, are designed for recording a "special" kind of business transaction.

Although special journals are ideally used in large businesses, they are not very practical for small service and retail businesses with few employees. Such businesses usually have only one accounting clerk. It is impractical for one clerk to record transactions in five different journals. At the same time, using only a general journal is very time consuming. For many small businesses, one journal is used—a combination journal.

The Combination Journal

As its name implies, a **combination journal** is a multicolumn journal that combines the features of the general journal and the special journals into one book of original entry. Like the special journals, the combination journal has special amount columns that are used to record transactions that occur frequently. In addition, the combination journal has General Debit and Credit columns in which to record transactions for which there are no special amount columns. Therefore, all the transactions of a business can be recorded in a single, multicolumn journal.

A business designs its combination journal to fit its own special needs. The number of columns, the selection of the special columns, and the arrangement of the columns will depend upon the type of business and the transactions that take place. Most businesses, however, use combination journals with between 10 and 13 columns.

The arrangement of the columns varies from one business to another. The columns should be arranged to make recording and posting easy and accurate. For example, look at On Your Mark Athletic Wear's combination journal in **Figure 1**. The Date, Account Name, Document Number, and posting Reference columns are located at the far left. These columns are followed by the General Debit and Credit columns.

COMBINATION

DATE	ACCOUNT NAME	DOC. NO.	POST. REF.	GENERAL		ACCOUNTS RECEIVABLE	
				DEBIT	CREDIT	DEBIT	CREDIT
1							
2							
3							

Figure 1 The Combination Journal

The General columns are followed by the special amount columns for **Accounts Receivable**, **Sales**, **Sales Tax Payable**, **Accounts Payable**, **Purchases**, and **Cash in Bank**.

Notice that the line numbers appear to the left and right sides of each page of the journal. These line numbers help the accounting clerk avoid writing amounts on the wrong lines.

Using the Combination Journal

A properly designed combination journal can be used efficiently for recording every possible business transaction.

- Receipts of cash are recorded in the Cash in Bank Debit column.
- Cash payments are entered in the Cash in Bank Credit column.
- The purchase of merchandise, for cash or on account, is recorded in the Purchases Debit column.
- Transactions affecting creditor accounts are written in the Accounts Payable Debit and Credit columns.
- The sale of merchandise is recorded in the Sales Credit and Sales Tax Payable Credit columns.
- Transactions affecting charge customer accounts are entered in the Accounts Receivable Debit and Credit columns.
- General ledger accounts for which there are no special columns are recorded in the General Debit and Credit columns. Adjusting and closing entries, for example, would be recorded in the General Debit and Credit columns.

On Your Mark Athletic Wear's business transactions for the month of June are recorded in the combination journal shown in Figure 2.

Proving and Posting the Journal

Like special journals, an important feature of the combination journal is that it saves time in both recording and posting transactions. The amounts entered in the General columns are posted on a daily basis to the appropriate general ledger accounts. Amounts entered in the Accounts Receivable and Accounts Payable columns are also posted on a daily basis to the appropriate charge customer or creditor accounts in the accounts receivable and accounts payable subsidiary ledgers. At the end of the month, the combination journal is footed, proved, totaled, and ruled. Totals of the special amount columns of the combination journal are then posted to the general ledger accounts named in the column headings. **Figure 2** shows how the combination journal will look at the end of the month after all postings have been made.

> **Key Points**
>
> **Recording Transactions**
> When recording transactions, use the line numbers as a guide to avoid writing amounts on the wrong line.

> **Key Points**
>
> **Recording Transactions**
> The General columns are used to record any amount for which no special columns are provided.

JOURNAL   PAGE _____

SALES CREDIT	SALES TAX PAYABLE CREDIT	ACCOUNTS PAYABLE		PURCHASES DEBIT	CASH IN BANK		
		DEBIT	CREDIT		DEBIT	CREDIT	
							1
							2
							3

	DATE		ACCOUNT NAME	DOC. NO.	POST. REF.	GENERAL DEBIT	GENERAL CREDIT	ACCOUNTS RECEIVABLE DEBIT	ACCOUNTS RECEIVABLE CREDIT
1	20--								
2	June	6	Cash Sales	T61	—				
3		8	Sales Discounts	R62	405	8 00			
4			Casey Klein		✓				424 00
5		10	Tammy's Fitness Club	S75	✓			530 00	
6		13	Office Equipment	I011	145	650 00			
7			Geary Office Supply		✓				
8		14	Sales Returns and Allowances	CM5	410	90 00			
9			Sales Tax Payable		220	5 40			
10			Lara Young		✓				95 40
11		15	Gabriel Ramos	M12	✓			80 00	
12			Shashi Rahim		✓				80 00
13		16	Computer Solutions	I003	✓				
14		18	Supplies	I214	130	100 00			
15			Geary Office Supplies		✓				
16		21	FastLane Athletics	CK350	✓				
17			Purchases Discounts		510		6 00		
18		23	Utilities Expense	CK351	680	175 00			
19		24	Purchases	CK352	—				
20		26	Salaries Expense	CK353	665	3200 00			
21			Social Security Tax Payable		212		198 40		
22			Medicare Tax Payable		213		46 40		
23			Employees' Federal Income Tax Payable		205		480 00		
24			Employees' State Income Tax Payable		206		70 40		
25		26	Payroll Tax Expense	P.Reg.	657	456 00			
26			Social Security Tax Payable		212		198 40		
27			Medicare Tax Payable		213		46 40		
28			Federal Unemployment Tax Payable		214		25 60		
29			State Unemployment Tax Payable		215		185 60		
30		27	Supplies	CK354	130	500 00			
31		28	Champion Store Supply	DM10	✓				
32			Purchases Returns and Allowances		515		90 00		
33		29	Supplies	M13	130	125 00			
34		30	Purchases		501		125 00		
35			Totals			5309 40	1472 20	610 00	599 40
36						(✓)	(✓)	(115)	(115)
37									

Figure 2 Recording Transactions in a Combination Journal

Daily
Post each amount in the General, Accounts Payable, and Accounts Receivable columns to the general ledger. The account number recorded in the Post Ref. column indicates that posting has been completed.

SALES CREDIT	SALES TAX PAYABLE CREDIT	ACCOUNTS PAYABLE DEBIT	ACCOUNTS PAYABLE CREDIT	PURCHASES DEBIT	CASH IN BANK DEBIT	CASH IN BANK CREDIT	
							1
1 250 00	75 00				1 325 00		2
					416 00		3
							4
500 00	30 00						5
							6
			650 00				7
							8
							9
							10
							11
							12
			4 200 00	4 200 00			13
							14
			100 00				15
		200 00					16
						194 00	17
						175 00	18
				300 00		300 00	19
							20
							21
							22
							23
					2 404 80		24
							25
							26
							27
							28
							29
						500 00	30
		90 00					31
							32
							33
							34
1 750 00	105 00	290 00	4 950 00	4 500 00	1 741 00	3 573 80	35
(401)	(220)	(201)	(201)	(501)	(101)	(101)	36
							37

End of Month
Post the column totals for Sales, Sales Tax Payable, Purchases, and Cash in Bank to the general ledger. Account numbers in parentheses indicate that posting has been completed.

Figure 2 Recording Transactions in a Combination Journal (Cont.)

Problem C–1   Analyzing Transactions for Combination Journal Entries

John Dunn owns The Country Store, a small retail store. He uses a combination journal with the following columns.

General Debit   Accounts Payable Debit
General Credit   Accounts Payable Credit
Accounts Receivable Debit   Purchases Debit
Accounts Receivable Credit   Cash in Bank Debit
Sales Credit   Cash in Bank Credit
Sales Tax Payable Credit

Instructions   Use the form provided in your working papers. For each of the following selected transactions, indicate in which column(s) of the combination journal the debit and credit parts of the entry would be recorded. The first transaction has been completed as an example.

Date	Trans.	General Dr.	General Cr.	Accounts Receivable Dr.	Accounts Receivable Cr.	Sales Cr.	Sales Tax Payable Cr.	Accounts Payable Dr.	Accounts Payable Cr.	Purchases Dr.	Cash in Bank Dr.	Cash in Bank Cr.
Dec. 1	Debit	✓										
	Credit								✓			

Date	Transactions
Dec. 1	Purchased a computer on account from King's Computer Outlet.
2	John Dunn withdrew cash for personal use.
5	Sold merchandise on account to Bernard Peterson, plus sales tax.
10	Issued Credit memo 14 to Tom Tray, a charge customer, for the return of merchandise sold on account plus sales tax.
13	Issued Debit Memo 20 to Cory distributors for the return of merchandise purchased from them on account.
15	Received a check from Bernard Peterson in full payment of his account.
18	Issued a check to Cory Distributors in payment of our account less the purchases return and less a purchases discount.
22	John Dunn invested a calculator in the business.
25	Issued a check for the monthly payroll less deductions for FICA.
25	Recorded the employer's payroll tax liabilities for FICA taxes, federal unemployment tax, and state unemployment tax.
30	Recorded cash sales plus sales tax.
31	Recorded the adjusting entry for the office supplies consumed during the period.

Problem C–2 Recording Transactions/Totaling, Proving, and Ruling the Combination Journal

Craig Glasser is a physician who operates a family medical practice, Glasser Family Medical Center. He uses the combination journal found in your working papers.

Instructions

(1) Record the following transactions on page 17 of the combination journal.

(2) Total, prove, and rule the combination journal.

Date		Transactions
Oct.	1	Received $2,100 in medical fees from patients, Receipt 90.
	2	Issued Check 414 for the cash purchase of $120 of office supplies.
	4	Purchased medical supplies on account from Wharton laboratories, Invoice 14006 for $1,950, terms n/60.
	6	Craig Glasser invested medical equipment valued at $750 in the medical practice, Memorandum 30.
	8	Billed a patient, Daniel O'Connell, $150 for his annual physical, Statement 40.
	9	Completed lab services for Carl Fisher and billed him $160, Statement 41.
	11	Purchased a new examination table (medical equipment) on account from Medical Suppliers, Invoice L163 for $1,452.50, terms n/45.
	13	Billed Patricia Vallano $300 for medical services, Statement 42.
	15	Issued Check 415 for $2,004.81 for the monthly salaries expense of $2,500.00 less deductions: social security tax, $155.00; Medicare tax, $36.25; employees' federal income taxes, $209.00; employees' state income taxes, $94.94.
	15	Recorded the employer's payroll tax liabilities: social security tax, $155; Medicare tax, $36.25; federal unemployment taxes, $20; state unemployment taxes, $145; payroll register.
	18	Issued Debit memo 16 to Wharton Laboratories for $200 for the return of medical supplies purchased on account.
	20	Paid the telephone bill, Check 416 for $110.
	22	A check for $110 was received from John Marshall to apply on his account, Receipt 91.

Continued 🖊

Date	Transactions
25	Craig Glasser withdrew $1,250 cash from the business, Check 417.
28	Received $75 from Daniel O'Connell to apply on his account, Receipt 92.
31	Sent Statement 43 for $95 to Donna Gordon for lab services completed on account.
31	Issued Check 418 for the November rent of $900.

Problem C–3 Recording Transactions, Totaling, Proving, and Ruling the Combination Journal

Sunset Surfwear is a small merchandise business specializing in a variety of surfwear items. Sunset Surfwear uses a combination journal with these amount columns.

General Debit   Accounts Payable Debit
General Credit   Accounts Payable Credit
Accounts Receivable Debit   Purchases Debit
Accounts Receivable Credit   Cash in Bank Debit
Sales Credit   Cash in Bank Credit
Sales Tax Payable Credit

Instructions In your working papers:
(1) Record the following transactions on page 12 of the combination journal.
(2) Total, prove, and rule the combination journal.

Date	Transactions
Dec. 1	Issued Check 151 for $700 to Pine Valley Realty for the monthly rent.
2	Received a check for $204.82 from Martha Adams in payment of her account of $209 less a discount of $4.18, Receipt 303.
3	Purchased $400 of merchandise on account from Kelley Apparel, Invoice 479 dated December 2, terms 2/10, n/30.
4	Issued Check 152 for $75 to The Knight Crier for advertisements.
5	Issued Check 153 for $230.30 to Neilson Store Equipment in payment of their invoice for $235.
6	Sent Credit memo 35 to Alex Hamilton for damaged merchandise returned, $50 plus $2.25 sales tax.
8	Sold merchandise on account to Nate Moulder, $100 plus sales tax of $4.50, Sales Slip 205.

Continued

Date	Transactions (Cont.)
10	Discovered that $95 received on account from Helen Jan on November 16 had been journalized and posted to Harriett Junell's account, Memorandum 16.
11	Recorded the monthly salaries of $2,100 less deductions: social security tax, $130.20; Medicare tax, $30.45; employees' federal income taxes, $326; and employees' state income taxes, $48.09; Check 154 for $1,565.26.
11	Recorded the employer's payroll tax liabilities: social security tax, $130.20; Medicare tax, $30.45; federal unemployment tax, $16.80; state unemployment tax, $121.80; payroll register.
12	Sent Check 155 for $392 to Kelley Apparel in payment of Invoice 479 less a discount of $8.
15	Received $150 from Martha Adams to apply on her account, Receipt 304.
18	Issued Debit Memorandum 20 to Waverunner Designs for $25 for the return of merchandise purchased on account.
24	Sold $200 in merchandise on account to Westwood High School Athletics plus sales tax of $9, Sales Slip 206.
26	Purchased $300 of merchandise on account from Capital Accessories, Invoice 601.
28	Purchased store equipment on account from Neilson Store Equipment, $200, Invoice 609.
29	Paid a $150 electric bill for the month by issuing Check 156 to Dukane Power Company.
31	Recorded cash sales of $3,000, plus $135 sales taxes, Tape 52.

Problem C–4 Recording Adjusting and Closing Entries in a Combination Journal

A partial work sheet for December 31 for In Beat CD Shop is shown in your working papers.

Instructions
(1) Record the adjusting entries in the combination journal. Then total, prove, and rule the General columns of the journal.
(2) Record the closing entries in the combination journal. Then total, prove, and rule the General columns of the journal.

APPENDIX D

The Accrual Basis of Accounting

What You'll Learn

- The difference between a cash and accrual basis of accounting.
- In what instances accruals are needed.
- In what instances deferrals are needed.
- How to record adjusting entries.
- How to record accrual entries.
- How to calculate interest receivable.
- How to calculate interest due and payable.

Why It's Important

Most businesses use the accrual basis of accounting, recognizing revenue when earned and expenses when incurred.

KEY TERMS

cash basis of accounting
accrual basis of
   accounting
accruals
deferrals
accrued revenue
accrued expense
unearned revenue
prepaid expense

Some small businesses keep their financial records on a cash basis. The **cash basis of accounting** recognizes and records revenues when cash is received and expenses only when cash is paid out. Often, however, cash is received and payments are made in an accounting period other than the period in which the original transaction took place. For example, a landscaping service performs work for a client in December, but the customer may not be required to pay until January of the next year. However, if the revenue is not recorded for the service performed in December, the financial statements may not present fairly the business earnings for the year just ended. To overcome this, the accounting profession requires that most businesses use what is called the **accrual basis of accounting**. In accrual accounting, revenues are recognized and recorded when earned, and expenses are recognized and recorded when they are actually incurred. The system for accrual accounting focuses on when earned and incurred rather than on when collected and paid.

Accruals and Deferrals

The accrual basis of accounting requires that accountants recognize revenue when the business makes a sale or performs a service, regardless of when the company receives the cash. Expenses are recognized as incurred, whether or not the business has paid out the cash. To accrue revenue means to record an amount in anticipation of future receipts and to accrue an expense means to record an amount in anticipation of a future payment. Accrual accounting involves two types of revenues and expenses: accruals and deferrals.

Accruals

Accruals relate to *transactions which have not yet been recorded* in the accounts. The word "accrue" means to accumulate or amass. Accruals for unrecorded revenues and expenses are required when:

1. *A revenue has been earned but not yet received.* For example, interest earned on a note receivable in one accounting period but not collected until the next accounting period.
2. *An expense has been incurred but not yet paid.* For example, you may earn wages from April 27 to April 30, but your employer may not pay your check to you until May 5.

Accruals are revenues or expenses that are gradually earned or incurred over time. In order to report a company's financial position fairly, accruals should be recognized in the accounting period in which they belong.

Deferrals

Deferrals are for *transactions that have been recorded* in the accounts. The word "defer" means to wait or delay. Deferrals are for receipts that are not earned and for payments that are not expenses.

1. *Cash may have been received but not yet earned.* For example, rent received in advance when some of the rental time is in one accounting period and the balance is in the next accounting period.
2. *Cash may have been paid but the expenses not incurred.* For example, when premiums on insurance are paid covering part of one accounting period and the balance covers the next accounting period.

Adjusting entries are required to: **(1)** recognize unrecorded accrued revenues and expenses or **(2)** allocate recorded deferred revenues and expenses to the appropriate accounting period.

Accrued Revenue

Accrued revenue is revenue that has been earned but not received or recorded. Examples of unrecorded accrued revenues include unpaid fees for services completed and rent earned but not yet received. The accrued revenue example that follows is for unpaid interest earned on a note receivable.

> ### Key Points
>
> **Accrual Basis of Accounting**
>
> With the accrual basis of accounting, revenue is recorded when it is earned, and expenses are recorded when they are incurred.

Business Transaction

On December 5, Rapid Growth Co. accepted a $5,000, 90-day, 9% note receivable from a charge customer, Janie Pippa. Pippa issued the note as an extension on her charge account. Rapid Growth Co. recorded the transaction as a debit of $5,000 to **Notes Receivable** and a credit of $5,000 to **Accounts Receivable** and Janie Pippa's account in the subsidiary ledger. On December 31, 26 days of interest had been earned (accrued) on the note receivable: $5,000 × .09 × 26/365 = $32.05. An adjusting entry is required on December 31 to record the amount of interest income earned from December 5 to the year ending December 31.

ANALYSIS	*Identify*	1. For the adjusting entry, the accounts **Interest Receivable** and **Interest Income** are affected.
	Classify	2. **Interest Income** is a revenue account. **Interest Receivable** is an asset account.
	+/−	3. **Interest Income** is increased and **Interest Receivable** is increased.

| **DEBIT-CREDIT RULE** | 4. Increases to assets are recorded as debits. Debit **Interest Receivable** for $32.05. |
| | 5. Increases to revenues are recorded as credits. Credit **Interest Income** for $32.05. |

T ACCOUNTS   6.

Interest Receivable		Interest Income	
Debit + Adj. 32.05	Credit −	Debit −	Credit + Adj. 32.05

JOURNAL ENTRY   **7.**

	GENERAL JOURNAL				PAGE 18	
	DATE	DESCRIPTION	POST. REF.	DEBIT	CREDIT	
1	20--	*Adjusting Entries*				1
2	Dec. 31	Interest Receivable		32 05		2
3		Interest Income			32 05	3
4						4

On March 5, Rapid received a check from Janie Pippa for $5,110.96, the maturity value of the note ($5,000.00 principle + $110.96 interest). Of the total interest, $32.05 had been earned and recorded in the previous accounting period. The remaining $78.91 should be recorded as income earned in the *current* fiscal year.

In the entry for the receipt of Janie's payment, **Cash in Bank** is debited for $5,110.96, the total amount of cash received. **Notes Receivable** is credited for $5,000.00. **Interest Receivable** is credited for $32.05 since the amount owed has now been received. **Interest Income** is credited for $78.91, the amount of the interest earned that applies to the current accounting period. The entry for this transaction is shown below.

	GENERAL JOURNAL				PAGE 24	
	DATE	DESCRIPTION	POST. REF.	DEBIT	CREDIT	
1	20--					1
2	Mar. 5	Cash in Bank		5 110 96		2
3		Notes Receivable			5 000 00	3
4		Interest Receivable			32 05	4
5		Interest Income			78 91	5
6		Receipt 416				6
7						7

Accrued Expenses

Most expenses are recorded when they are paid, or a liability is incurred. There are, however, some business expenses that have not been paid—but accrue daily—and are not recorded until an adjusting entry is made at the end of the fiscal period. Some examples of these **accrued expenses** are salaries or wages earned by working employees but not yet paid to them, property taxes owed but not yet paid, and interest accrued on unpaid notes payable. The example that follows shows how to calculate interest due and payable.

Business Transaction

On November 1, Rapid Growth Co. signed a $2,000, 90-day, 12% note payable for the purchase of equipment from Taylor Equipment. Rapid Growth Co. recorded the transaction as a debit of $2,000 to **Equipment** and a credit of $2,000 to **Notes Payable**. On December 31, 60 days of interest was owed (accrued) on the note payable: $2,000 × .12 × 60/365 = $39.45. An adjusting entry is required on December 31 to record the amount of interest expense incurred from November 1 to the year ending December 31.

ANALYSIS	Identify	1. For the adjusting entry, the accounts **Interest Expense** and **Interest Payable** are affected.
	Classify	2. **Interest Expense** is an expense account. **Interest Payable** is a liability account.
	+/−	3. **Interest Expense** is increased and **Interest Payable** is increased.

| DEBIT-CREDIT RULE | | 4. Increases to expenses are recorded as debits. Debit **Interest Expense** for $39.45. |
| | | 5. Increases to liabilities are recorded as credits. Credit **Interest Payable** for $39.45. |

T ACCOUNTS 6.

Interest Expense			Interest Payable	
Debit + Adj. 39.45	Credit −		Debit −	Credit + Adj. 39.45

JOURNAL ENTRY 7.

GENERAL JOURNAL PAGE 18

	DATE	DESCRIPTION	POST REF.	DEBIT	CREDIT	
4	Dec. 31	Interest Expense		39 45		4
5		Interest Payable			39 45	5
6						6

On March 5, Rapid sent a check to Taylor Equipment for $2,059.18, the maturity value of the note ($2,000.00 principle + $59.18 interest). Of the total interest expense, $39.45 had already been owed as of December 31. That amount was recorded as an adjusting entry in the previous accounting period. The remaining $19.73 should be recorded as expense for the *current* fiscal year.

In the entry for the payment of the note, **Notes Payable** is debited for $2,000.00. **Interest Expense** is debited for $19.73, the amount of interest expense incurred that applies to the current accounting period. **Interest Payable** is debited for $39.45 since the amount that was accrued has now been paid. **Cash in Bank** is credited for $2,059.18, the total amount of cash paid. The entry for this transaction is shown below.

GENERAL JOURNAL PAGE 24

	DATE	DESCRIPTION	POST. REF.	DEBIT	CREDIT	
7	Mar. 5	Notes Payable		2 000 00		7
8		Interest Expense		19 73		8
9		Interest Payable		39 45		9
10		Cash in Bank			2 059 18	10
11		Check # 1597				11

To acquire cash with which to provide services, communities impose a tax on real property. Property taxes are usually paid twice a year, with each payment covering a six-month period or one-half the annual tax.

Underwood Merchandisers operates in the building on the land they own. The value of the real property is $300,000. The total annual property taxes are $7,800. Underwood is located in a state where property taxes must be paid in May and November. The May payment covers the first six months of the calendar year, and the November payment covers the last six months of the calendar year.

Underwood's fiscal period ends on April 30. As a result, at the end of its fiscal period, Underwood owes property taxes of $2,600 ($7,800 × 4/12 or $3,900 × 4/6) for the months of January, February, March and April. These taxes, however, are not due to be paid until May.

On April 30, Underwood makes the following adjustment to the accounting records to reflect the correct amount of property tax for the period.

GENERAL JOURNAL PAGE __26__

	DATE		DESCRIPTION	POST. REF.	DEBIT	CREDIT	
1	20--		*Adjusting Entries*				1
2	Apr.	30	Property Tax Expense		2 6 0 0 00		2
3			Property Tax Payable			2 6 0 0 00	3
4							4

On May 15, Underwood wrote a check for the semiannual property tax payment of $3,900. Of this amount, $2,600 is an expense charged to the prior fiscal period and $1,300 is an expense charged to the current accounting period. The entry in May to record this payment is shown in the general journal below.

GENERAL JOURNAL PAGE __33__

	DATE		DESCRIPTION	POST. REF.	DEBIT	CREDIT	
1	20--						1
2	May	15	Property Tax Expense		1 3 0 0 00		2
3			Property Tax Payable		2 6 0 0 00		3
4			Cash in Bank			3 9 0 0 00	4
5			Check 401				5

Deferrals

Sometimes a business receives cash or a receivable for revenue that has not yet been earned. Cash is also paid out for expenses before those expenses are actually incurred. So that a business can more fairly show its financial condition, unearned revenue and prepaid expenses must be deferred (postponed) and allocated to the proper fiscal periods.

Unearned Revenue

Unearned revenue is revenue received before it is actually earned. Examples include cash received in advance for rental properties, for season tickets to various events, for insurance premiums, and for work to be performed in the future. Because the business has an obligation to deliver the merchandise or perform the service for which it has already received payment, unearned revenue represents a current liability for the business.

Boyce Real Estate rents space in its building to a tax accountant. On November 1, the accountant paid Boyce $1,200 in advance for rent covering the months of November through April. The entry to record this transaction is shown below.

GENERAL JOURNAL   PAGE 55

	DATE		DESCRIPTION	POST. REF.	DEBIT	CREDIT	
1	20--						1
2	Nov.	1	Cash in Bank		1 2 0 0 00		2
3			Unearned Rental Income			1 2 0 0 00	3
4			Receipt 181				4

As the business delivers the merchandise or performs the service, it earns a part of the advance payment. The earned portion must be transferred from the liability account to a revenue account through an adjusting entry made at the end of the period.

When Boyce's fiscal period ends on December 31, the company will have earned rental income of $400 for two of the six months paid in advance ($1,200 × 1/3). The adjusting entry to record the rental income is shown below.

GENERAL JOURNAL   PAGE 65

	DATE		DESCRIPTION	POST. REF.	DEBIT	CREDIT	
1	20--		Adjusting Entries				1
2	Dec.	31	Unearned Rental Income		4 0 0 00		2
3			Rental Income			4 0 0 00	3
4							4

Prepaid Expenses

A prepaid expense is an expense paid in advance. Examples include the purchase of office supplies, premiums paid on insurance policies, rent paid in advance on the use of property or equipment, and bank discounts on non-interest-bearing notes payable. Examples of adjustments for prepaid expenses appear in Chapter 18 of this textbook.

APPENDIX D   PROBLEMS

Problem D–1 Identifying Accruals and Deferrals

Instructions Use the form in your working papers that is similar to the one below. For each item listed below, indicate by placing a check mark in the correct column whether the item is a prepaid expense, unearned revenue, an accrued expense, or accrued revenue. The first item has been completed as an example.

1. Rent received in advance for a two-year rental of a computer.
2. A two-year premium paid on a fire insurance policy.
3. Tuition collected in advance by a university.
4. Interest on an interest-bearing note payable due next year.
5. Cash received for a three-year subscription to a magazine.
6. Fees due for the completed designs for three of five buildings.
7. Property taxes incurred for the last three months of the fiscal period.
8. Salaries owed but not yet paid.
9. Interest on an interest-bearing note receivable that matures in the next accounting period.
10. Office supplies purchased.
11. Cash received for season tickets for home football games.

Item	Prepaid Expense	Unearned Revenue	Accrued Expense	Accrued Revenue
1.		✓		

Problem D–2 Recording Adjusting Entries

The Gore Paper Company uses the accrual basis of accounting. Its fiscal period ends on June 30. The following account balances appear in the company's general ledger as of year-end.

Cash in Bank	$34,616	Office Supplies Expense	$0
Interest Receivable	0	Salaries Expense	75,000
Office Supplies	8,335	Rental Income	0
Salaries Payable	0	Interest Income	0
Unearned Rental Income	1,000		

Instructions Record the adjusting entries on general journal page 14 in your working papers.

(1) The office supplies on hand as of June 30 are valued at $935.
(2) Gore's 5-day weekly payroll totals $1,500. Salaries have been earned but not yet paid or recorded for June 28–30.
(3) On June 30, 30 days of interest had accrued on an $8,000, 90-day, 9% note receivable from a charge customer.
(4) Of the $1,000 recorded in the **Unearned Rental Revenue** account, $250 had been earned as of June 30.

Problem D–3 Recording Transactions for Notes Payable

The Villareal Corporation uses the accrual basis of accounting. Its fiscal period ends on December 31. On November 15, the Villareal Corporation borrowed $9,500 from the Second National Bank by issuing a 120-day, 9.5% interest-bearing note payable.

Instructions Record the following transactions on general journal page 41.
(1) The issuance of the note payable (Note 7).
(2) The adjusting entry to record the amount of accrued interest payable at year-end.
(3) The payment of the note on the maturity date (Check 411).

Problem D–4 Recording Accrued Expenses

The Cassenada's Dance Company uses the accrual basis of accounting. Located in Seattle, Washington, the company's fiscal year-end is July 31. Property taxes are paid in June and December. Total annual property taxes on the studio and parking lot are $12,000.

Instructions
(1) Record the payment made on June 30 for the first six months' property tax in the general journal, page 22.
(2) Record the adjusting entry necessary at the fiscal year-end, July 31.

Federal Personal Income Tax

In order to become an informed and contributing member of society, every individual should have a basic knowledge of our federal income tax system. For the system to work fairly and efficiently, everyone must pay their fair share in an accurate and timely manner.

Creating the Federal Income Tax System

When this country was founded in 1776, a federal personal income tax system did not exist. At that time, it was the responsibility of the individual state to tax its residents and raise revenue for needed expenditures. The first personal income tax was created in 1862 in an effort to finance the cost of the Civil War. A commission levied taxes on a small percentage of people in order to generate needed revenue. However, this tax was abolished in 1872, soon after the war ended. A federal personal income tax was again proposed in 1895 but was declared unconstitutional.

It was not until 1913 that Congress ratified the 16th Amendment to the Constitution that enabled the federal government to levy a tax on individuals based on personal income. The income tax system was established under the principle of **voluntary compliance** . This means that all individual taxpayers are responsible for filing their tax return. All taxpayers must report their taxable income, accurately calculate the income tax owed, and file the necessary forms on time.

The Internal Revenue Service (IRS) also has responsibilities under our present tax system. The IRS must administer the tax laws fairly and process tax returns in an efficient manner.

Tax Forms and Procedures

For the federal tax system to run efficiently, certain tax forms must be prepared and filed by all income earning individuals. For personal income tax, the earning period is from January 1 through December 31. Every individual has from January 1 until April 15 of the next year to file a tax return and pay the government all taxes owed for the previous year.

For most taxpayers, the most common and largest form of income is the gross earnings paid to them by employers. Other common forms of taxable income include interest earned on savings accounts and investments, stock dividends, rental income, and profits from business operations run as sole proprietorships or partnerships.

Federal Withholding Tax

A certain amount is withheld from each paycheck by the employer. This system of "pay as you earn" was enacted during the early 1940s.

Since the exact amount earned for the year will not be determined until the end of December, the amount of taxes withheld from each employee's paycheck is an *estimate* of the amount the employee will owe at the end of the year. As you learned in Chapter 12, each employee fills out a **Form W-4** when they begin work. This indicates to the employer how much to withhold for federal income tax from each paycheck. For more information on completing Form W-4, refer back to Chapter 12, pages 293–294.

Reporting Earned Income

Individual taxpayers receive two common federal forms to report income for the year. The first is Form W-2. This form is prepared by employers and reports to employees and the federal government the total gross wages for the year and the amount withheld from employees' wages to pay the federal income tax. This form is given to the employees in the month of January so the information is available for employees to complete their individual tax returns. To review the Form W-2, refer to Chapter 13, page 334.

Reporting Interest Income

The other common form used to report income is **Form 1099** . This form reports interest earned in savings accounts and is prepared by banks or other institutions. Interest from all 1099 forms is added together and the total interest earned for the year is reported on your federal tax return.

Preparing and Filing a Federal Income Tax Return

The most common tax return prepared by students is Form 1040EZ.

Preparing Form 1040EZ

To file **Form 1040EZ** , the following requirements must be met:

1. Taxable income from wages and tips must be less than $50,000.
2. Interest income must be less than $400.

A completed Form 1040EZ is presented in **Figure 2** on page A-36. To complete this form, use the following steps:

1. Enter your name, address, and social security number.
2. Check the box on the next line if you want $3 to go to the Presidential Election Campaign Fund.
3. Add the amount(s) in box 1 of your Form(s) W-2 and put that amount on line 1 of the form. This should be the total gross earnings from **all** of your jobs this year.
4. Add the total interest received, as reported on Form(s) 1099, and enter the total amount of interest on line 2.
5. Add lines 1 and 2 and put the total on line 4. This is your adjusted gross income. Your **adjusted gross income** is your total income for the year.
6. Since you are a student, you are probably claimed as a dependent by your parents or guardians. On line 5, check YES.
7. Go to the worksheet for dependents on the back of the form and complete A through G. Enter the amount from G on line 5 on the front of the form.

| Key Points |

Completing Your Tax Form

You must receive all of your W-2 and 1099 forms before you complete your tax return.

8. Subtract line 5 from line 4 and enter the amount on line 6. This is your **taxable income**.
9. Add the amounts in box 2 of your Form(s) W-2 and enter the amount on line 8. This is the amount *already* deducted from your wages to pay your federal tax liability.
10. Enter the amount from line 8 on line 10.
11. Take the amount entered on line 6, and look up the amount of your actual tax liability on the tax table.
12. Complete the Tax Computation Worksheet for Certain Dependents and enter the amount on line 11 of Form 1040EZ.
13. If line 10 is greater than line 11, then you have paid in more than you owe and are entitled to a **refund.** Enter the amount of the overpayment on line 12a.
14. If line 11 is greater than line 10, then you still owe the federal government more money. Enter the amount you still owe on line 13.

If additional money is owed, you must include a check for the entire amount when you file the tax return. Sign the return and enter the date and your occupation on the designated lines.

Before your file your tax return, Form 1040EZ, make sure you do the following:

1. Check all calculations.
2. Attach Copy B (one copy) of each of your W-2's, which are supplied to you by your employer(s).
3. File the return by April 15.

Using the IRS *e-file* System

You can file electronically by using the **e-file system** . Forms and information are available on the Internet or by fax. By first completing the tax forms, you can use your personal computer to file the return.

Using the IRS *TeleFile* system, you can file your tax return using a Touch-Tone phone. You first complete the ***TeleFile*** *Tax Record,* which is similar to Form 1040EZ, call a toll free number, and follow the instructions on the computerized message. Most taxpayers who use Form 1040EZ can file by phone.

Figure 1 Completed Tax Computation Worksheet

| **Tax Computation Worksheet for Certain Dependents—Line 11** |

1. Figure the tax on the amount on Form 1040EZ, line 6.
   Use the Tax Table. . . . . 1. _**84.00**_

2. Is the amount on line 1 more than the amount shown below for your filing status?
   • Single — $900
   • Married filing jointly — $1,800
   ☐ **Yes.** If **single,** enter $300; if **married**, enter $600 } . . . . 2. _**28.00**_
   ☒ **No.** Divide the amount on line 1 by 3.0.

3. Subtract line 2 from line 1. Enter the result here and
   on Form 1040EZ, line 11. . . . . 3. _**56.00**_

Form 1040EZ

Department of the Treasury–Internal Revenue Service

Income Tax Return for Single and Joint Filers With No Dependents (P) **20--**

OMB No. 1545-0675

Label
(See Page 12.)

Use the IRS label.
Otherwise please print or type

L A B E L

H E R E

Your first name and initial: Joan J.

Last name: Bustelos

If a joint return, spouse's first name and initial

Last name

Home address (number and street). If you have a P.O. box, see page 7. — 84 Elm Street — Apt. no.

City, town or post office, state, and ZIP code. If you have a foreign address, see page 7. — Norwalk, VA 23514

Your social security number
0 3 1 X X X X X X

Spouse's social security number

▲ **Important!** ▲
you **must** enter your SSN(s) above.

Presidential Election Campaign
(See page 12.)

Note: Checking "Yes" will not change your tax or reduce your refund.
Do you, or spouse if a joint return, want $3 to go to this fund? ▶

	You	Spouse
	☑ Yes ☐ No	☐ Yes ☐ No

Income

Attach Form(s) W-2 here.
Enclose, but do not attach, any payment.

1 Total wages, salaries, and tips. This should be shown in box 1 of your W-2 form(s). Attach your W-2 form(s). — 1 — 4,954 | 00

2 Taxable interest. If the total is over $400, you cannot use Form 1040EZ — 2 — 167 | 00

3 Unemployment compensation, qualified state tuition program earnings and Alaska Permanent Fund dividends (see page 14). — 3

4 Add lines 1, 2, and 3. This is your **adjusted gross income.** — 4 — 5,121 | 00

Note. You **must** check Yes or No

5 Can your parents (or someone else) claim you on their return?
Yes. Enter amount from ☑ worksheet on back.
No. If **single,** enter 7,450.00.
If **married,** enter 13,400.00
See back for explanation — 5 — 4,550 | 00

6 Subtract line 5 from line 4. If line 5 is larger than line 4, enter 0. This is your **taxable income.** ▶ 6 — 571 | 00

Credits, payments, and tax

7 Rate reduction credit. See worksheet on page 14. — 7

8 Enter your Federal income tax withheld from box 2 of your W-2 form(s). — 8 — 218 | 00

9a **Earned income credit (EIC).** See page 15. — 9a

b Nontaxable earned income. — 9b

10 Add lines 7, 8, and 9a. These are your **total credits and payments.** ▶ 10 — 218 | 00

11 **Tax.** If you checked "Yes" on line 5, see page 20. Otherwise, use the amount on **line 6 above** to find your tax in the tax table on pages 24–28 of the booklet. Then, enter the tax from the table on this line. — 11 — 56 | 00

Refund
Have it directly deposited! See Page 20 and fill in 12b, 12c, and 12d

12a If line 10 is larger than line 10, subtract line 10 from line 11. This is your **refund.** ▶ 12a — 162 | 00

▶ b Routing number | ▶ c Type: ☐ Checking ☐ Savings

▶ d Account number

Amount you owe

13 If line 11 is larger than line 10, subtract line 10 from line 11. This is the **amount you owe.** See page 21 for details on how to pay. ▶ 13

Third party designee

Do you want to allow another person to discuss this return with the IRS (see page 22)? ☐ **Yes.** Complete the following. ☐ **No**
Designee's name ▶
Phone no. ▶ ( )
Personal identification number(PIN) ▶

Sign here
Joint return?
See page 11.
Keep a copy for your records

Under penalties of perjury, I declare that I have examined this return, and to the best of my knowledge and belief, it is true, correct, and accurately lists all amounts and sources of income I received during the tax year. Declaration of preparer (other than the taxpayer) is based on all information of which the preparer has any knowledge.

Your signature ▶ Joan J. Bustelos — Date 3/19/20-- — Your occupation clerk — Daytime phone number (123) 555-2000

Spouse's signature if a joint return, **both** must sign. — Date — Spouse's occupation

Paid Preparer's use only

Preparer's signature ▶ — Date — Check if self-employed ☐ — Preparer's SSN or PTIN

Firm's name (or yours if self-employed), address, and ZIP code ▶ — EIN — Phone no. ( )

For Disclosure, Privacy Act, and Paperwork Reduction Act Notice, see page 23 — Cat. No. 12616G — Form **1040EZ** 20--

Figure 2 Completed Form 1040EZ

Use this form if

- Your filing status is single or married filing jointly.
- You do not claim any dependents.
- You (and your spouse if married) were under 65 January 1, 20– –, and not blind at the end of 20– –.
- Your taxable income (line 6) is less than $50,000.
- You do not claim a student loan interest deduction (see page 8) or an education credit.
- You had **only** wages, salaries, tips, taxable scholarship or fellowship grants, unemployment compensation, qualified state tuition program earnings, or Alaska Permanent Fund dividends, and your taxable interest was not over $400. **But** if you earned tips, including allocated tips, that are not included in box 5 and box 7 of your W-2, you may not be able to use Form 1040EZ. See page 13. If you are planning to use Form 1040EZ for a child who received Alaska Permanent Fund dividends, see page 14.
- You did not receive any advance earned income credit payments.

If you are not sure about your filing status, see page 11. If you have questions about dependents, use TeleTax topic 354 (see page 6). If you **cannot use this form,** use TeleTax topic 352 (see page 6).

Filling in your return

For tips on how to avoid common mistakes, see page 30

If you received a scholarship or fellowship grant or tax–exempt interest income, such as on municipal bonds, see the booklet before filling in the form. Also, see the booklet if you received a Form 1099–INT showing Federal income tax withheld or if Federal income tax was withheld from your unemployment compensation or Alaska Permanent Fund dividends.

Remember, you must report all wages, salaries, and tips even if you do not get a W–2 form from your employer. You must also report all your taxable interest, including interest from banks, savings and loans, credit unions, etc., even if you do not get a Form 1099–INT.

Worksheet for dependents who checked "Yes" on line 5

(keep a copy for your records)

Use this worksheet to figure the amount to enter on line 5 if someone can claim you (or your spouse if married) as a dependent, even if that person chooses not to do so. To find out if someone can claim you as a dependent, use TeleTax topic 354 (see page 6).

A. Amount, if any, from line 1 on front . . . .   *4,954.00*   + 250.00 Enter total ▶ **A.** *5,204.00*

B. Minimum standard deduction. . . . . **B.** 750.00

C. Enter the **larger** of line A or line B here. . . . . **C.** *5,204.00*

D. Maximum standard deduction. If **single,** enter 4,550.00; if **married,** enter 7,600.00. . . . . **D.** *4,550.00*

E. Enter the **smaller** of line C or line D here. This is your standard deduction. . . . . **E.** *4,550.00*

F. Exemption amount.
- If single, enter 0
- If married and—
  —both you and your spouse can be claimed as dependents, enter 0.
  —only one of you can be claimed as a dependent, enter 2,900.00
} **F.** *0*

G. Add lines E and F. Enter the total here and on line 5 on the front. . . . . **G.** *4,550.00*

If you checked "No" on line 5 because no one can claim you (or your spouse if married) as a dependent, enter on line 5 the amount shown below that applies to you.

- Single, enter 7,450.00. This is the total of your standard deduction (4,550.00) and your exemption (2,900.00).
- Married, enter 13,400.00. This is the total of your standard deduction (7,600.00), your exemption (2,900.00), and your spouse's exemption (2,900.00).

Mailing return

Mail your return by **April 15, 20– –.** Use the envelope that came with your booklet. If you do not have that envelope, see the back cover for the address to use.

Form **1040EZ** (20– –)

Figure 2 Completed Form 1040EZ (continued)

Problem E–1   **Preparing Form 1040EZ**

Michael Feld is a junior at Lewiston High School. He lives with his parents at 274 West Polomia Drive in Hanksville, Ohio, 03856. Mike's social security number is 036-23-8825. If Mike must pay any tax, he wants the $3 to go to the Presidential Election Campaign Fund.

Mike worked full-time last summer at Harriet's Sub Shop as a counter clerk. He received a Form W-2 which stated that he had total gross wages of $4,806.00 and $192.00 was deducted for federal income tax.

Mike also had a savings account. The Kingsman National Bank sent him Form 1099 which stated he had earned interest of $113.00 on his account.

Mike lives at home with his parents and is claimed as a dependent on their tax return.

Instructions Using the information above, prepare Form 1040EZ for Mike Feld. A blank Form 1040EZ is provided in your working papers. Use the tax chart in your working papers to calculate the federal income tax.

Problem E–2   **Preparing Form 1040EZ**

Alicia DeSantis is a senior at Georgetown High School. She lives at 825 Patterson Street in Montville, Texas, 09436. Her social security number is 043-73-8217. She worked part-time during the school year at the Hilltop Deli and full-time during the summer as a lifeguard and swimming instructor at the Montville town pool.

If Alicia must pay some income tax on her earnings this year, she wants the $3 to go to the Presidential Election Campaign Fund. Alicia lives with her mother and is claimed as a dependent on her mother's tax return.

Her Form W-2 from the deli reported that she earned $1,736.00 during the year and $112.00 was deducted for federal income tax. The town of Montville sent her a W-2 that reported she earned $3,927.00 during the summer and $184.00 was deducted for federal income tax.

Alicia opened a savings account at the local bank that sent her a Form 1099 that stated she earned $118.50 in interest last year. She also had another savings account set up for college that paid her $201.70 in interest.

Instructions Prepare Form 1040EZ for Alicia. A blank Form 1040EZ is provided in your working papers. Use the tax charts in your working papers to calculate the tax owed.

Office DEPOT

What you need. What you need to know.℠

Excerpts from the
Office Depot 2001 Annual Report

Intended for Use in Chapters 14–26

In this appendix, we present excerpts from the 2001 Annual Report of Office Depot, a publicly held corporation. These reports were selected to illustrate many of the concepts discussed in this textbook. Since only portions of the Annual Report are presented here, please refer to the Office Depot Web site at www.officedepot.com for the entire 2001 Annual Report. Not all of the terminology and policies appearing in this report are consistent with our text discussions. This illustrates some of the diversity that exists in financial reporting.

Company Profile

O ffice Depot, Inc. is the world's largest supplier of office products and services. The Company sells office supplies, business machines, computers, computer software and office furniture, as well as copy, print, reproduction, mailing and shipping services to small office/home office (SoHo), medium and large businesses in the United States and 17 other countries around the globe. Office Depot operates under brand names Office Depot®, Viking Office Products®, Viking Direct®, 4Sure.com®, Computers4Sure.com®, Solutions4Sure.com®, The Office Place®, and Sands & McDougall™. The Company markets its products through multiple distribution channels, including office supply retail stores, direct mail, global Internet sites, business-to-business e-commerce, and various sales forces. Office Depot has approximately 45,000 employees, and its common stock is traded on the New York Stock Exchange under symbol ODP.

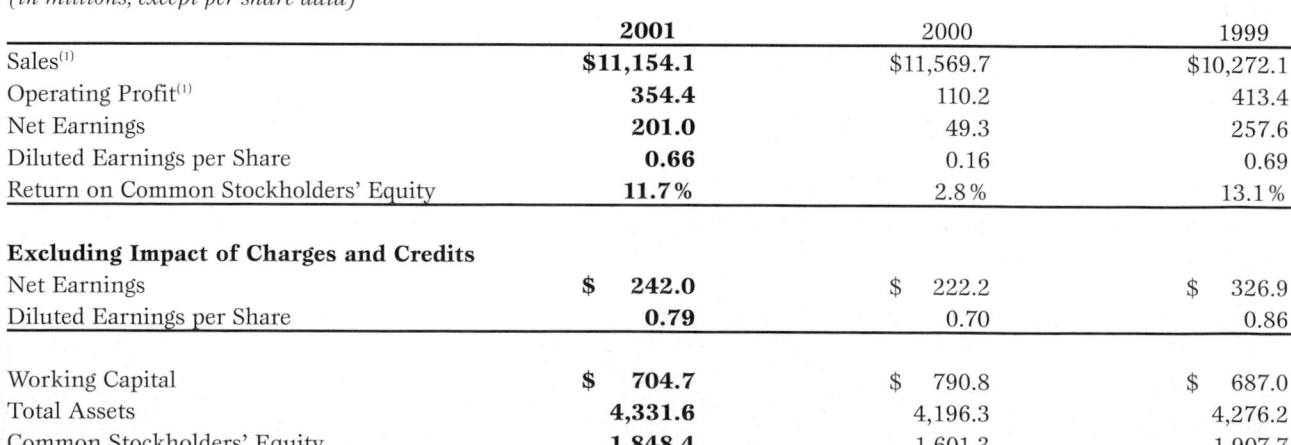

Financial Highlights

(in millions, except per share data)

	2001	2000	1999
Sales[1]	$11,154.1	$11,569.7	$10,272.1
Operating Profit[1]	354.4	110.2	413.4
Net Earnings	201.0	49.3	257.6
Diluted Earnings per Share	0.66	0.16	0.69
Return on Common Stockholders' Equity	11.7%	2.8%	13.1%
Excluding Impact of Charges and Credits			
Net Earnings	$ 242.0	$ 222.2	$ 326.9
Diluted Earnings per Share	0.79	0.70	0.86
Working Capital	$ 704.7	$ 790.8	$ 687.0
Total Assets	4,331.6	4,196.3	4,276.2
Common Stockholders' Equity	1,848.4	1,601.3	1,907.7

[1] *Certain amounts in prior year financial statements have been reclassified to conform to current year presentation.*

To Our Shareholders:

W hen I accepted leadership of Office Depot 20 months ago, our Company faced significant challenges. Growth in the U.S. office supply superstore industry was beginning to mature and we had not responded effectively to the changing competitive environment. We had lost sight of some of our core competencies and competitive advantages, and we had allowed parts of our business to become too complex and inefficient. We had been slow to address issues in underperforming businesses and assets. Worst of all, our Company and our management team had lost the loyalty of our shareholders and the confidence of our employees, who viewed our direction as unclear and our future as uncertain. • These challenges became even more daunting in 2001, as we faced a weak U.S. economy; softness in the computer hardware, software and furniture sectors; unfavorable foreign currency translation; and declining consumer confidence. As our delicate economy teetered on the brink of recession, the tragic events of September 11th gave the final push that sent it over the edge, creating a difficult, stormy and uncertain economic environment.

We are encouraged by Office Depot's progress in 2001, and we firmly believe it demonstrates the strength of our Company's true earnings potential.

Turning the Tide

Our efforts to strengthen Office Depot started in early fall of 2000, when our new leadership team conducted a critical assessment of Office Depot that redefined our destination and plotted a strategic course to get there. Throughout 2001, we continued this process, driving operating improvements that we expect to yield tangible results in the years ahead. • Our initiatives were careful and thorough. We sharpened our focus on our core competencies. We improved efficiencies and instituted disciplined capital spending. We introduced dramatic improvements in the management of our supply chain, our inventory, and our warehouse operations. We closed stores, cut costs in underperforming regions in North America and redeployed capital to our highly profitable and fast-growing international markets. We elevated the delivery of "fanatical" customer service to our first priority, and we established quality indices and ambitious new performance benchmarks. We fostered a management culture that gives our leaders and managers greater responsibility and makes them accountable for results. And we established new corporate values that form the basis for the way we do business and serve as a foundation for our future. • We also devoted significant energy and resources to making Office Depot a more compelling place to work and shop. We improved opportunities across the Company for our employees, and we tied recognition and reward directly to performance. We renewed our commitment to diversity, which appropriately reflects our diverse customers, suppliers and communities in which we live and work. We undertook new measures in our North American Retail stores to make shopping at Office Depot a more informative and customer-friendly experience by remerchandising, upgrading and resigning all 859 of our retail superstores. • These collective management and operating initiatives enabled Office Depot to perform well in light of the difficult economic environment. Total sales declined four percent to $11.2 billion, compared with $11.6 billion in 2000. Comparable worldwide sales in the 849 stores and 39 delivery centers that have been open for more than one year declined two percent, compared with an increase of seven percent in 2000. At the same time, however, our highly profitable International business delivered to record sales and profits, despite negative foreign currency translation. International now accounts for 27 percent of our Company's total segment operating income. Driven by a dramatic improvement in gross margins across our business segments, earnings per share (excluding charges and credits discussed in management's discussion and analysis), rose to $0.79, an increase of 13 percent, compared with $0.70 in 2000. Free cash flow rose to $540 million, a substantial improvement from $49 million in 2000. Stronger cash flow and an emphasis on better cash management enabled us to repay short-term debt, fund working capital needs and build our financial flexibility. • We also achieved marked progress in other vitally important areas of the Company. Employee turnover, a key measure of employee satisfaction, declined 29 percent from a year ago. Our quality and customer satisfaction measurements rose and our retail and warehouse Customer Service Indices hit all-time highs. Our in-stock positions, order-fill rates, line-fill rates and on-time deliveries also improved. In addition, inventory turns rose, accounts receivables declined and

North American warehouse operating costs, as a percentage of sales, decreased to the lowest level in five years. • We are highly encouraged by Office Depot's progress in 2001, and we firmly believe it demonstrates the strength of our Company's true earnings potential once the U.S. and world economies regain stability and return to growth. But Office Depot's story in 2001 is about far more than financial results and operating improvements. It is about a company that has a crystal-clear vision of where it is going and how it is going to get there. It is about a new management team with the experience, skills and financial acumen to help the Company to achieve its goals. It is about our customers who reward us through their loyalty and our shareholders who once again have confidence that we can drive shareholder value. Moreover, it is about our approximately 45,000 worldwide employees, who have regained their trust in Office Depot and reaffirmed their conviction that we can become one of the world's great companies.

Forging Ahead

As we enter 2002, we are sharply focused on leveraging the momentum we have created to expand Office Depot's business. We are seeking new ways to drive sales, manage costs and increase shareholder value. We are undertaking new branding and advertising initiatives that will define the differences between Office Depot and our competitors. We are pursuing fanatical customer service, while leveraging our immense knowledge of our customer base to target our customers more effectively. In addition, we are integrating all of our business channels to make an even more seamless shopping experience for our customers. We expect these actions and others to accelerate growth across all three of our business segments. • At the same time, we are certain that we will continue to face short-term economic challenges that will call for us to make tough decisions and complicated choices. The economy, rapid shifts in technology and fundamental changes in the way Corporate America does business are likely to present new trials at every turn. But we are equally certain that there has never been a better time to invest in our future, as both our Company's foundation and the opportunities to grow our global industry leadership position are stronger than ever before. • As I consider the journey on which Office Depot embarked in 2001, my greatest single surprise is not the fact that our employees responded to the marked change in leadership and direction; rather it is *how* they responded to this change—quickly, willingly, and with enormous teamwork and cooperation. I am extremely grateful to the skilled and talented people at Office Depot for their commitment, loyalty, support, trust and confidence. I look to our Company's future with great enthusiasm, not merely because I know that we can achieve our goals, but also because I know that we will achieve those goals by working harmoniously and synergistically, *together*.

We believe that there has never been a better time to invest in our future, as the opportunities to grow our leadership position are stronger than ever.

Bruce Nelson
Chairman and Chief Executive Officer
March 2002

Office Depot, Inc.

Financial Highlights

(In thousands, except per share amounts and statistical data)

	2001	2000[4]	1999	1998	1997
Statements of Earnings Data:					
Sales[1]	$11,154,081	$11,569,696	$10,272,060	$8,997,738	$8,108,714
Cost of goods sold and occupancy costs	7,983,973	8,479,437	7,450,575	6,484,699	5,963,521
Gross profit	3,170,108	3,090,259	2,821,485	2,513,039	2,145,193
Store and warehouse operating and selling expenses[1]	2,343,394	2,409,478	2,023,055	1,683,973	1,482,179
General and administrative expenses[1]	451,722	453,784	328,108	288,028	241,430
Facility closure costs	8,436	110,038	40,425	—	—
Other operating expenses	12,125	6,733	16,524	136,279	22,703
Operating profit	354,431	110,226	413,373	404,759	398,881
Interest income	13,058	11,502	30,176	25,309	7,570
Interest expense	(44,302)	(33,901)	(26,148)	(22,356)	(21,680)
Miscellaneous income (expense), net	(9,057)	4,632	(3,514)	(18,985)	(13,180)
Earnings before income taxes	314,130	92,459	413,887	388,727	371,591
Income taxes	113,087	43,127	156,249	155,531	136,730
Net earnings	$ 201,043	$ 49,332	$ 257,638	$ 233,196	$ 234,861
Earnings per share[2]:					
Basic	$ 0.67	$ 0.16	$ 0.71	$ 0.64	$ 0.65
Diluted	0.66	0.16	0.69	0.61	0.62
Statistical Data:					
Facilities open at end of period:					
United States and Canada:					
Office supply stores	859	888	825	702	602
Customer service centers	24	25	30	30	33
Call centers	13	7	7	8	8
International[3]:					
Office supply stores	143	132	118	87	39
Customer service centers	23	19	19	18	17
Call centers	15	14	14	13	12
Balance Sheet Data:					
Working capital	$ 704,676	$ 790,752	$ 687,007	$1,293,370	$1,093,463
Total assets	4,331,643	4,196,334	4,276,183	4,025,283	3,498,891
Long-term debt, excluding current maturities	317,552	598,499	321,099	470,711	447,020
Common stockholders' equity	1,848,438	1,601,251	1,907,720	2,028,879	1,717,638

[1] *Certain amounts in prior year financial statements have been reclassified to conform to current year presentation.*

[2] *Earnings per share amounts previously reported for 1997 and 1998 have been restated to reflect the three-for-two stock split declared on February 24, 1999.*

[3] *Includes facilities in our International Division that we wholly own or lease, as well as those that we operate through licensing and joint venture agreements.*

[4] *Includes 53 weeks in accordance with our 52–53 week reporting convention.*

Management's Discussion and Analysis of Financial Condition and Results of Operations

Results of Operations

Fiscal 2001 was a year of improved operational performance across the Company and increased overall earnings compared to 2000, even in the face of difficult economic conditions and a decline in our consolidated sales. Diluted earnings per share improved to $0.66 from $0.16 in 2000, and down from $0.69 in 1999. Fiscal year 2000 was adversely affected by charges associated with a comprehensive business review that resulted in the closing of 70 retail stores, the write-down of certain assets and the elimination of some employee positions. Additional store closure and impairment costs, the write-down of certain Internet investments, settlement of certain employee claims and gain on the sale of our London warehouse were recognized in 2001. Without these charges and credits, EPS was $0.79 in 2001 and $0.70 in 2000. See Charges and Credits section below for additional discussions on these items.

[Note to the student: The Charges and Credits section has been omitted from this selection of excerpts. For the complete 2001 Annual Report, please use the Office Depot Web site (www.officedepot.com).]

Overall

(Dollars in Millions)	2001		2000		1999	
Sales	$11,154.1	100.0%	$11,569.7	100.0%	$10,272.1	100.0%
Cost of goods sold and occupancy costs	7,984.0	71.6%	8,479.4	73.3%	7,450.6	72.5%
Gross profit	3,170.1	28.4%	3,090.3	26.7%	2,821.5	27.5%
Store and warehouse operating and selling expenses	2,343.4	21.0%	2,409.5	20.8%	2,023.1	19.7%
Store and warehouse operating profit	$ 826.7	7.4%	$ 680.8	5.9%	$ 798.4	7.8%

Our overall sales decreased 4% in 2001 and increased 13% in 2000, while comparable sales decreased 2% in 2001 and grew 7% in 2000. Fiscal year 2000 included 53 weeks in accordance with our 52–53 week accounting convention. Adjusting 2000 to a 52-week basis, sales decreased 2% in 2001. The overall sales decrease in 2001 reflects a 10% decrease in our North American Retail Division, a 4% increase in our Business Services Group and a 6% increase in our International Division. Sales across the United States were adversely affected in 2001 by the slowing domestic economy. Additionally, the decline in sales of our North American Retail Division reflects our decision to close 73 stores during 2001, following our comprehensive business review performed in the latter part of 2000. The largest percentage sales increases in 2000 were realized in our BSG segment, driven most significantly by the growth in our contract and Internet businesses. E-commerce sales have improved in all periods, increasing almost 60% in 2001 to $1.6 billion. Also contributing significantly to our sales growth in 2000 was the continued expansion of our store base.

Our worldwide sales by product group were as follows:

	2001	2000	1999
General office supplies	44.2%	41.7%	41.0%
Technology products	46.3%	47.5%	47.5%
Office furniture	9.5%	10.8%	11.5%
	100.0%	100.0%	100.0%

In both 2001 and 2000, our sales mix shifted toward our core office supply items. Sales of technology products decreased significantly in 2001, reflecting to a large extent, a general slowing of technology-related product sales in the overall economy. Moreover, many more general and specialty retailers outside the office products retail segment (including discount retailers, drug store chains and warehouse club retailers) have broadened their assortments of technology products. Technology products generally have lower profit margins compared to many of the core office supplies. Also, within the technology products category, the mix shifted from technology hardware and software towards machine supplies. Sales of office furniture declined, reflecting lower volume and unit prices in 2001 and lower average selling prices during 2000, as many business customers deferred large purchases because of concerns about the economy.

Our overall gross profit percentages fluctuate as a result of numerous factors, including competitive pricing pressures; changes in product, catalog and customer mix; emergence of new technology; suppliers' pricing changes; as well as our ability to improve our net product costs through growth in total merchandise purchases. Additionally, our occupancy costs may vary as we add stores and CSCs in new markets with different rental and other occupancy costs, and as we relocate and/or close existing stores in current markets.

In mid-2000, we reduced prices for paper and machine supplies across all of our domestic sales channels in response to competitive pressures from discount clubs and other non-traditional sellers of those supply items. These price reductions, along with increased product costs, primarily for paper and machine supplies, had the most significant effect on our decreased gross profit percentage in 2000 compared to 1999. These two product groups accounted for approximately 34% of our total sales mix in 2000.

Store and warehouse operating and selling expenses consist of personnel costs; maintenance and other facility costs; advertising expenses; delivery and transportation costs; credit card and bank charges and certain other operating and selling costs. These costs, expressed as a percentage of sales, increased in both 2001 and 2000. The increase in 2001 reflects the impact of declining sales on the ratio, while the increase in 2000 is primarily the result of higher personnel and warehouse costs. In 2001, we scaled back our personnel-related costs in response to weaker sales. Other expenses, such as credit card fees and delivery fees, have also declined along with sales. In 2000, however, we experienced higher delivery- and personnel-related costs in our warehouse operations as third-party carriers increased their rates, and our facility integration efforts took longer to complete than originally planned. We also had a significant increase during 2000 in personnel expenses in our domestic stores, largely related to wage pressures stemming from a tight labor market. Also included in this category are certain charges and credits that affect the comparisons of on-going operations and are more fully discussed below.

[Note to the student: Charges and credits mentioned above have been omitted from this selection of excerpts. For the complete 2001 Annual Report, please use the Office Depot Web site (www.officedepot.com).]

Office Depot, Inc.

Consolidated Balance Sheets

(In thousands, except share and per share amounts)

	December 29, 2001	December 30, 2000
Assets		
Current assets:		
Cash and cash equivalents	$ 563,410	$ 151,482
Receivables, net of allowances of $32,682 in 2001 and $34,461 in 2000	781,476	896,333
Merchandise inventories, net	1,259,522	1,420,825
Deferred income taxes	148,490	157,779
Prepaid expenses	53,292	72,670
Total current assets	2,806,190	2,699,089
Property and equipment, net	1,110,011	1,119,306
Goodwill, net	249,560	219,971
Other assets	165,882	157,968
Total assets	$4,331,643	$4,196,334
Liabilities and Stockholders' Equity		
Current liabilities:		
Accounts payable	$1,060,968	$1,136,994
Accrued expenses and other liabilities	612,999	580,966
Income taxes payable	109,026	37,118
Current maturities of long-term debt	318,521	153,259
Total current liabilities	2,101,514	1,908,337
Deferred income taxes and other credits	64,139	88,247
Long-term debt, net of current maturities	315,331	374,061
Zero coupon, convertible subordinated notes	2,221	224,438
Commitments and contingencies		
Stockholders' equity:		
Common stock—authorized 800,000,000 shares of $.01 par value; issued 385,538,340 in 2001 and 378,688,359 in 2000	3,855	3,787
Additional paid-in capital	1,007,088	939,214
Unamortized value of long-term incentive stock grant	(2,578)	(2,793)
Accumulated other comprehensive loss	(71,273)	(53,490)
Retained earnings	1,717,734	1,516,691
Treasury stock, at cost—82,443,170 shares in 2001 and 82,190,548 shares in 2000	(806,388)	(802,158)
Total stockholders' equity	1,848,438	1,601,251
Total liabilities and stockholders' equity	$4,331,643	$4,196,334

The accompanying notes are an integral part of these statements.

[Note to the student: For complete accompanying notes, refer to the 2001 Annual Report on the Office Depot Web site.]

Assets:
Things the company owns.
- Cash.
- Receivables. Money owed to the company.
- Merchandise Inventories. Products waiting to be sold.
- Property and Equipment. Buildings, machinery, trucks, etc.
- Deferred income taxes, Prepaid expenses, Goodwill, Other assets. These are other assets the company has that have value.

Liabilities:
What the company owes.
- Current liabilities. Bills, payroll due, taxes and other obligations that have to be paid within a year.
- Long-term debt, net of current maturities. This is the amount owed with due dates that are more than one year in the future.
- Deferred income taxes and other credits; Zero coupon, convertible subordinated notes. These are other obligations that are due more than one year in the future.

Office Depot, Inc.

Consolidated Statements of Earnings

(In thousands, except per share amounts)

	2001	2000	1999
Sales	$11,154,081	$11,569,696	$10,272,060
Cost of goods sold and occupancy costs	7,983,973	8,479,437	7,450,575
Gross profit	3,170,108	3,090,259	2,821,485
Store and warehouse operating and selling expenses	2,343,394	2,409,478	2,023,055
General and administrative expenses	451,722	453,784	328,108
Facility closure costs	8,436	110,038	40,425
Other operating expenses	12,125	6,733	16,524
Operating profit	354,431	110,226	413,373
Other income (expense):			
Interest income	13,058	11,502	30,176
Interest expense	(44,302)	(33,901)	(26,148)
Miscellaneous income (expense), net	(9,057)	4,632	(3,514)
Earnings before income taxes	314,130	92,459	413,887
Income taxes	113,087	43,127	156,249
Net earnings	$ 201,043	$ 49,332	$ 257,638
Earnings per share:			
Basic	$ .67	$ .16	$ .71
Diluted	.66	.16	.69

The accompanying notes are an integral part of these statements.

[Note to the student: For complete accompanying notes, refer to the 2001 Annual Report on the Office Depot Web site.]

Statement of Earnings
- Sales. Total sales of the company minus the value of product discounted or returned.
- Cost of goods sold and occupancy costs. Cost of goods sold is the actual cost to the business of the merchandise sold to customers. Occupancy costs include rent, common area maintenance, taxes, and utilities. Cost of goods sold and occupancy costs are reported on the same line based on the industry's general practices.
- Gross profit. Net sales minus cost of goods sold and occupancy costs.
- Store and warehouse operating and selling expenses.
- General and administrative expenses.
- Facility closure costs.
- Other operating expenses.
- Operating profit. Income earned from normal business activities.
- Other income and expense.
- Earnings before income taxes. Income taxes are federal and state taxes paid or due based on the company's taxable income.
- Net earnings. The "bottom line," or final earnings after taxes have been deducted.

Office Depot, Inc.

Consolidated Statements of Stockholders' Equity

(In thousands, except share amounts)

	Common stock shares	Common stock amount	Additional paid-in capital	Unamortized value of long-term incentive stock grant	Accumulated other comprehensive income (loss)	Comprehensive income (loss)	Retained earnings	Treasury stock
Balance at December 26, 1998	373,817,704	$3,738	$ 838,122	$(2,874)	$(18,078)		$1,209,721	$ (1,750)
Comprehensive income:								
Net earnings						$ 257,638	257,638	
Foreign currency translation adjustment					(28,319)	(28,319)		
Unrealized gain on investment securities, net of tax					62,127	62,127		
Comprehensive income						$ 291,446		
Acquisition of treasury stock	(3,245,170)							(501,361)
Retirement of treasury stock	130,000	(32)	(1,718)					1,750
Grant of long-term incentive stock		1	2,127	(2,127)				
Exercise of stock options (including income tax benefits)	4,457,024	45	72,865					
Issuance of stock under employee stock purchase plans	712,431	7	9,240					
Matching contributions under 401(k) and deferred compensation plans	320,906	3	5,423					
Conversion of LYONs® to common stock	23,710		329					
Payment for fractional shares in connection with 3-for-2 stock split	(4,166)		(93)					
Amortization of long-term incentive stock grant				936				
Balance at December 25, 1999	376,212,439	3,762	926,295	(4,065)	15,730		1,467,359	(501,361)
Comprehensive income:								
Net earnings						$ 49,332	49,332	
Foreign currency translation adjustment					(7,093)	(7,093)		
Realized gain on investment securities, net of tax					(62,127)	(62,127)		
Comprehensive income (loss)						$(19,888)		
Acquisition of treasury stock								(300,797)
Grant of long-term incentive stock	25,000		199	(199)				
Cancellation of long-term incentive stock	(50,000)		(819)	600				
Exercise of stock options (including income tax benefits)	424,809	4	(1,984)					
Issuance of stock under employee stock purchase plans	1,372,566	14	9,713					
Matching contributions under 401(k) and deferred compensation plans	703,545	7	5,810					
Amortization of long-term incentive stock grant				871				

Consolidated Statements of Stockholders' Equity *(continued)*

(In thousands, except share amounts)

	Common stock shares	Common stock amount	Additional paid-in capital	Unamortized value of long-term incentive stock grant	Accumulated other comprehensive income (loss)	Comprehensive income (loss)	Retained earnings	Treasury stock
Balance at December 30, 2000	378,688,359	$3,787	$ 939,214	$(2,793)	$(53,490)		$1,516,691	$(802,158)
Comprehensive income:								
Net earnings						$201,043	201,043	
Foreign currency translation adjustment					(17,783)	(17,783)		
Comprehensive income (loss)						$183,260		
Acquisition of treasury stock								(4,254)
Grant of long-term incentive stock	80,000	1	764					
Exercise of stock options (including income tax benefits)	5,604,810	55	56,430					
Issuance of stock under employee stock purchase plans	751,400	8	6,712					
Matching contributions under 401(k) and deferred compensation plans	413,771	4	3,957					
Direct Stock Purchase Plans			11					24
Amortization of long-term incentive stock grant				215				
Balance at December 29, 2001	**385,538,340**	**$3,855**	**$1,007,088**	**$(2,578)**	**$(71,273)**		**$1,717,734**	**$(806,388)**

The accompanying notes are an integral part of these statements.

[Note to the student: For complete accompanying notes, refer to the 2001 Annual Report on the Office Depot Web site.]

Stockholders' Equity

This is called the "book value" of the owners' stake in the company. It includes proceeds the company received from the initial and subsequent sales of stock to the public, plus accumulated profits, called retained earnings.

This book value is not the same as the market value of stock or the public stock market, called "market value." The stock market determines in its own ways whether the company is worth more than the book value of what it owns minus what it owes. For example, a company's stock price changes regularly without regard to the value of the assets and liabilities it uses to run the company.

Additional Reinforcement Problems

APPLICATION OPTIONS

Complete appendix problems one of two ways:

1 **Manual** Glencoe Working Papers

or

2 **Spreadsheet** Templates (Problems 3A, 23A, and 26A)

SPREADSHEET SMART GUIDE

Step–by–Step Instructions: Problem 3A

1. Select the spreadsheet template for Problem 3A.
2. Enter your name and the date in the spaces provided on the template.
3. Complete the spreadsheet using the instructions in your working papers.
4. Print the spreadsheet and proof your work.
5. Save your work and exit the spreadsheet program.

Chapter 3, Problem 3A Determining the Effects of Business Transactions on the Accounting Equation

Pamela Wong started her own business called Thunder Graphics Desktop Publishing.

Instructions Use the form provided in your working papers. For each of the following transactions:

(1) Identify the accounts affected.
(2) Write the amount of the increase (+) or decrease (−) in the space provided on the form.
(3) Determine the new balance for each account.

Trans. No.	Transactions
1	Pamela Wong, the owner, opened a checking account for the business by depositing $48,000 of her personal funds.
2	Paid the monthly rent of $1,500.
3	Bought office furniture on account for $1,000.
4	Pamela Wong invested $3,000 of office equipment in the business.
5	Paid cash for a new computer for the business, $5,000.
6	Paid for an advertisement in the local newspaper, $200.
7	Completed graphic desktop publishing services for a client and sent a bill for $800.
8	Paid $700 on account for the office furniture bought earlier.
9	Received $500 on account from a client.
10	Pamela Wong withdrew $1,000 for personal use.
11	Received $400 cash for desktop publishing services completed for a client.

Analyze: After analyzing all of the transactions, answer the following questions.
(a) What was the total amount of equipment assets?
(b) What is the total amount of assets?
(c) What are the total liabilities and owner's equity?
(d) Is the accounting equation in balance?

Chapter 4, Problem 4A Analyzing Transactions Affecting Assets, Liabilities, and Owner's Equity

Thunder Graphics Desktop Publishing had the following transactions. A partial list of the accounts used to record and report business transactions appear below.

101 Cash in Bank	201 Accounts Payable—
110 Accounts Receivable—	Computer Warehouse, Inc.
Roger McFall	205 Accounts Payable—
125 Office Equipment	Pro Computer Company
130 Office Furniture	301 Pamela Wong, Capital
135 Computer Equipment	

Instructions On the forms provided in your working papers:
(1) Prepare a T account for each account listed above.
(2) Analyze and record each of the following business transactions in the appropriate T accounts. Identify each transaction by number.
(3) After recording all transactions, compute and record the account balance and identify the normal side of each T account.
(4) Add the balances of those accounts with normal debit balances.
(5) Add the balances of those accounts with normal credit balances.

Trans. No.	Transactions
1	Pamela Wong invested $30,000 into the business.
2	Invested office equipment, valued at $650, into the business.
3	Bought a computer on account from Computer Warehouse, Inc. for $9,360.
4	Bought new office equipment for $1,550, Check 100.
5	Bought new office furniture on account from Computer Warehouse, Inc. for $1,250.
6	Sold the older office equipment on account to Roger McFall for $650.
7	Paid $3,000 on account to Computer Warehouse Inc., Check 101.
8	Received $400 on account from Roger McFall.
9	Paid $3,500 on account to Computer Warehouse Inc., Check 102.
10	Bought computer hardware from Pro Computer Company for $775.

Analyze: Is the accounting equation in balance?

Chapter 5, Problem 5A Analyzing Transactions Affecting Revenue, Expenses, and Withdrawals

Pamela Wong owns and operates Thunder Graphics Desktop Publishing. A partial list of the chart of accounts appears in your working papers.

Instructions On the forms provided in your working papers:
(1) Prepare a T account for each account listed above.
(2) Analyze and record each of the following business transactions in the appropriate T accounts. Identify each transaction by number.
(3) After recording all transactions, compute a balance for each account.
(4) Test for the equality of debits and credits.

Continued

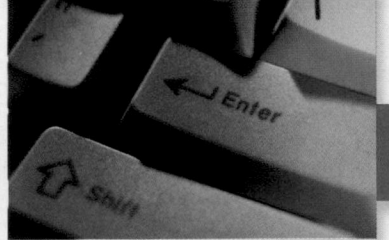

Trans. No.	Transactions
1	Pamela Wong invested $25,000 in the business.
2	Bought a new computer on account from Computer Warehouse, Inc. for $1,400.
3	Ms. Wong invested office equipment, valued at $650, in the business.
4	Paid the rent for the month, $750, Check 207.
5	Wrote Check 208 for $145 for minor repairs to the equipment.
6	Completed graphics design work on account for Adams, Bell, and Cox, Inc., $850.
7	Paid the $175 utility bill, Check 209.
8	Deposited the daily design receipts in the bank, $1,200.
9	Sent Check 210 for $700 to Computer Warehouse, Inc. as payment on account.
10	Received $425 from Adams, Bell, and Cox, Inc.
11	Ms. Wong withdrew $150 for personal needs.
12	Paid the $85 telephone bill, Check 211.

Analyze: How much design income did the business record in the above transactions?

Chapter 6, Problem 6A Recording General Journal Transactions

Instructions On the form provided in your working papers, record the following transactions for the month of January on page 7 of the general journal for Thunder Graphics Desktop Publishing.

Date	Transactions
Jan. 1	Received $900 for completion of design work for Designers Boutique, Receipt 545.
3	Purchased a desk, chairs, and table valued at $2,400 from Computer Warehouse, Inc. Made a down payment of $400 and agreed to pay the balance within 60 days, Check 801/Invoice CW402.
7	Ran a $300 special feature ad in Solutions Software's monthly magazine on account, Invoice SS60.
10	Completed a $3,500 print production job for Adams, Bell, and Cox, Inc. Received a down payment of $500 and agreed to receive the balance within 30 days, Receipt 546/ Invoice TG90.
15	Pamela Wong withdrew $1,500 from the business for personal use, Check 802.
17	Paid a carpenter $175 to install a new office door, Check 803.
20	Purchased a $4,000 computer system from Pro Computer Company on account, Invoice 783.
27	Paid Computer Warehouse, Inc. $1,000 to apply on our account, Check 804.
29	Wrote Check 805 for $300 to Solutions Software in payment of an ad purchased on July 7.
31	Pamela Wong invested a $200 file cabinet in the business, Memo 40.

Analyze: How much cash did the business receive during January?

Chapter 7, Problem 7A Journalizing and Posting Transactions

The balances in the general ledger accounts of Thunder Graphics are shown below.

101	Cash in Bank	$ 10,000
110	Accounts Receivable—Roger McFall	---
125	Office Equipment	2,500
135	Computer Equipment	3,000
201	Accts. Pay.—Computer Warehouse Inc.	---
301	Pamela Wong, Capital	8,000
302	Pamela Wong, Withdrawals	4,000
401	Design Revenue	9,000
405	Print Production Revenue	4,000
505	Maintenance Expense	1,200
510	Miscellaneous Expense	300

Instructions On the forms provided in your working papers:

(1) Open the accounts in the general ledger with their beginning balances as of March 1 of the current year.
(2) Record March transactions on page 15 of the general journal.
(3) Post each journal entry to the appropriate accounts in the ledger.
(4) Prove the ledger by preparing a trial balance.

Date	Transactions
Mar. 1	Pamela Wong invested additional assets in the business: cash, $3,000, and office equipment, $500, Memorandum 75.
5	Paid $600 to Premier Painters for painting the office, Check 912.
7	Discovered that $1,500 in design revenue was incorrectly journalized and posted to the **Print Production Revenue** account last month, Memorandum 76.
9	Purchased $3,600 computer system from Computer Warehouse, Inc. on account, Invoice CW204.
12	Deposited $4,000 into the checking account. $3,000 was earned from design revenue and $1,000 from print production revenue, Receipts 300–310.
15	Completed print production for Roger McFall. Sent him a bill for $600, Invoice TG601.
20	Discovered that $50 in miscellaneous expense was incorrectly journalized and posted to the **Maintenance Expense** account, Memorandum 77.
25	Pamela Wong withdrew $2,000 from the business, Check 913.
28	Received $300 from Roger McFall to apply to his account, Receipt 311.
31	Issued Check 914 for $1,800 to Computer Warehouse, Inc. to apply on our account.

Analyze: What is the balance in the cash account on March 31?

Chapter 8, Problem 8A Preparing a Six-Column Work Sheet

The final balances in the general ledger of Thunder Graphics Desktop Publishing at the end of May are listed below.

101	Cash in Bank	$16,095
105	Accts. Rec.—Adams, Bell, and Cox Inc.	1,729
110	Accts. Rec.—Roger McFall	281
113	Accts. Rec.—Designers Boutique	---
115	Accts. Rec.—Pat Cooper	714
120	Office Supplies	228
125	Office Equipment	5,027
130	Office Furniture	2,940
135	Computer Equipment	8,200
201	Accts. Pay.—Computer Warehouse Inc.	4,027
205	Accts. Pay.—Pro Computer Company	2,441
207	Accts. Pay.—Solutions Software	---
301	Pamela Wong, Capital	24,927
305	Pamela Wong, Withdrawals	2,400
310	Income Summary	---
401	Design Revenue	8,116
405	Print Production Revenue	4,050
501	Advertising Expense	735
505	Maintenance Expense	1,335
510	Miscellaneous Expense	285
520	Rent Expense	3,100
530	Utilities Expense	492

Instructions Use the form in your working papers to prepare a work sheet for the month ended May 30.

Analyze: How much net income or net loss did Thunder Graphics have for the month of May?

Chapter 9, Problem 9A Interpreting Financial Information

You are applying for a job with Thunder Graphics Desktop Publishing. The job includes preparing financial statements. In order to determine your ability to do the job, the owner, Pamela Wong, has given you the following information. At the beginning of the last fiscal period, the **Pamela Wong, Capital** account had a balance of $46,295. At the end of the period, the account showed a balance of $49,152. During the period, Ms. Wong made an additional investment of $2,000 and had withdrawals of $600. The revenue for the period was $12,948.

Analyze: Use the form provided in your working papers to determine the total expenses for the period.

Chapter 10, Problem 10A Preparing Closing Entries

The work sheet of Thunder Graphics Desktop Publishing for the year ended December 31 is presented in your working papers.

Instructions Using the information in the work sheet, prepare the four journal entries to close the temporary capital accounts. Use general journal page 21 provided in your working papers.

Analyze: What is the balance in the **Pamela Wong, Capital** account after the closing entries?

Chapter 11, Problem 11A Recording Deposits in the Checkbook

On October 20, Pamela Wong, owner of Thunder Graphics Desktop Publishing, deposited the following in the checking account of the business.

Cash: $800
Checks: Boyden Company; drawn on National Bank of Commerce; Monroe; ABA No 45-1204; $50.29.
          Gail's Supplies; drawn on Regent Bank; Rayville; ABA No 49-3401; $255.48.
          Clinton Co.; drawn on Sun Federal Savings and Loan; Bastrop; ABA No 52-6429; $788.40.

On October 21, Pamela Wong received the electricity bill from Central Utilities for $314.69 for September 17 to October 18 service.

The October bank statement for Thunder Graphics listed a bank service charge of $21.80, dated October 23.

Instructions On the forms provided in your working papers:
(1) Complete a deposit slip using the October 20 information.
(2) Record the deposit on check stub 1068 using $2,468.14 as the balance brought forward.
(3) Complete check stub 1068 and prepare Check 1068 to Central Utilities. Use October 22 as the date and sign your name as drawer.
(4) Record this service charge in the checkbook on check stub 1069.
(5) Journalize the entry for the bank service charge in the general journal. Use October 25 as the date.
(6) Answer the following questions.
  (a) What was the amount carried forward from check stub 1067?
  (b) What was the checkbook balance before writing Check 1068?
  (c) What was the total amount deposited on October 20?
  (d) Identify the payee of Check 1068.
  (e) What was the balance brought forward on check stub 1069?

Analyze: What is the checkbook balance after all of the above transactions have been recorded?

Chapter 12, Chapter 12A Preparing a Payroll Register

Thunder Graphics Desktop Publishing has four employees. They are paid on a weekly basis with overtime paid for all hours worked over 40. The overtime rate is 1½ times the regular hourly rate of pay. The names of the employees and other information needed to prepare the payroll are as follows.

Employee No.	Employee	Status	Exemptions	Rate/Hour	Union
173	Don Hoffman	M	1	$6.95	No
168	Manual Gongas	S	0	7.10	Yes
167	Riley Sullivan	M	2	7.40	Yes
175	Marcy Jackson	S	1	6.95	Yes

During the week ended Oct. 15, Gongas worked 41 hours, Sullivan worked 39¼ hours, Jackson worked 42½ hours, and Hoffman worked 38¾ hours.

Instructions On the form provided in your working papers:
(1) Prepare a payroll register. The date of payment is October 15. List employees in alphabetical order by last name.
   (a) Compute FICA taxes at 6.2% for social security and 1.45% for Medicare.
   (b) Use the tax table in Chapter 12 to determine federal income taxes. The state income tax is 1.5% of gross earnings.
   (c) All employees have a deduction for hospital insurance that is $4.75 for single employees and $7.85 for married employees.
   (d) Union members pay weekly dues of $3.25.
(2) After the payroll information is entered in the payroll register, total the columns and check the accuracy of the totals.

Analyze: What are the total earnings for the week for all of Thunder Graphics' employees?

Chapter 13, Problem 13A Recording Payroll Transactions

Thunder Graphics Desktop Publishing pays its employees each week. The payroll register for the week ended December 17 is shown in your working papers.

Instructions On the forms provided in your working papers:
(1) Record the payment of the payroll on page 34 of the general journal. Check 831 was written on December 17 to pay the payroll.
(2) Compute the employer's payroll taxes (FICA tax rates, 6.2% social security, 1.45% Medicare; state unemployment tax rate, 5.4%; federal unemployment tax rate, 0.8%).
(3) Record the journal entry for the employer's payroll taxes.
(4) Record the payment of all FICA and employees' federal income taxes, Check 832. The previous account balances were: **Employees' Federal Income Tax Payable**, $189, **Social Security Tax Payable**, $191.48, and **Medicare Tax Payable**, $44.92.
(5) Record the income tax payment to the state, Check 833. The balance in the **Employees' State Income Tax Payable** account before the December 17 payroll was $178.40.

Analyze: What was the amount of Check 832?

Chapter 14, Problem 14A Recording and Posting Sales and Cash Receipt Transactions

On January 1, T-Shirt Trends, a merchandising business, had the following balances in its general ledger and accounts receivable subsidiary ledger.

General Ledger

101	Cash In Bank	$ 7,500
115	Accounts Receivable	10,920
215	Sales Tax Payable	1,500
401	Sales	18,620
405	Sales Discounts	1,400
410	Sales Returns and Allowances	300

Accounts Receivable Subsidiary Ledger

MOR	Morales, Gabriela	$ 420
ROU	Roundabout Fashions	3,150
SAM	Samstead Fashions	5,250
SAN	Sandpiper Sports Club	2,100

Instructions On the forms provided in your working papers:
(1) Open the general ledger accounts and record the January 1 balances.
(2) Open the customer accounts in the accounts receivable subsidiary ledger and record the January 1 balances.
(3) Record the January transactions. Use page 12 in the general journal.
(4) Post the transactions to the general ledger and accounts receivable subsidiary ledger accounts.

Date	Transactions
Jan. 1	Received a check for $3,087 from Roundabout Fashions payment of their $3,150 account less a 2% cash discount of $63, Receipt 82.
4	Gabriela Morales notified us that $40 in T-shirts were defective. Issued Credit Memorandum 20 for $42, which includes a 5% sales tax of $2.
9	Sold $1,000 in merchandise plus a sales tax of $50 to Roundabout Fashions on account, Sales Slip 90.
15	Sandpiper Sports Club sent us a check in payment of their $2,100 account less a 2% cash discount, Receipt 83.
17	Granted Samstead Fashions $252 credit for the return of $240 in merchandise plus a $12 sales tax, Credit Memorandum 21.
20	Received a check from Roundabout Fashions in payment of their $1050 account balance less a cash discount of $21, Receipt 84.
25	Samstead Fashions sent us a check for $2,000 to apply on their account, Receipt 85.
31	Cash sales for the month were $5,000 plus $250 in sales tax, Tape 44.
31	Bankcard transactions for the month were $6,000 plus $300 in sales tax, Tape 44.

Analyze: What is the balance in the **Accounts Receivable** account at the end of January?

Chapter 15, Problem 15A Recording Purchases and Cash Payment Transactions

Business transactions for the month of March for T-Shirt Trends are presented below. A partial general ledger appears in your working papers.

Instructions On the form provided in your working papers, record March transactions on page 11 of the general journal.

Date	Transactions
Mar. 2	Issued Check 5500 for $6,790 to Dancing Wind Clothing Manufacturers in payment of their $7,000 invoice less a 3% cash discount.
4	Purchased $2,800 in merchandise on account from Wilmington Shirt Factory, Invoice WSF123, terms 2/10, n/30.
6	Wrote Check 5501 for $180 to Mario's Trucking for delivery of merchandise shipped from Wilmington Shirt Factory, FOB shipping point.
8	Received a credit allowance of $300 from Wilmington Shirt Factory for damaged merchandise, issued Debit Memo 44.
10	Received a premium notice from Keystone Insurance Company for $3,400, issued Check 5502.
12	Bought $175 in supplies from Carter Office Supply on account, Invoice 97, terms n/30.
14	Paid Wilmington Shirt Factory the $2,500 balance owed less a 2% cash discount, Check 5503.
19	Returned $50 in supplies to Carter Office Supply, issued Debit Memorandum 45.
25	Paid employees gross earnings of $4,000. Rates for taxes withheld are: Employees' Federal Income Tax, 15%; State Income Tax, 6%; Social Security Tax, 6.2%; and Medicare Tax, 1.45%. Issued Check 5504 for the net amount.
30	Wrote Check 5505 to Carter Office Supply for the amount due on our account.

Analyze: How much was the net paid to employees on March 25?

Chapter 16, Problem 16A Recording and Posting Sales, Cash Receipts, and General Journal Transactions

T-Shirt Trends, a retail merchandising store, uses special journals for recording its business transactions. On May 1, the store had the following balances in its general ledger and accounts receivable subsidiary ledger accounts.

Continued

General Ledger

101	Cash in Bank	$ 4,700
115	Accounts Receivable	7,250
135	Supplies	300
215	Sales Tax Payable	600
401	Sales	40,000
405	Sales Discounts	1,500
410	Sales Returns and Allowances	500

Accounts Receivable Subsidiary Ledger

HAL	Hal's Fitness Studios	$ 1,500
HIO	Dave Hioki	200
MOR	Gabriela Morales	100
ROU	Roundabout Fashions	2,000
SAM	Samstead Fashions	2,500
SAN	Sandpiper Sports Club	900
WIL	Virginia Williams	50

Instructions On the forms provided in your working papers:

(1) Open the accounts and enter beginning balances in T-Shirt Trends' general ledger.
(2) Open the customer accounts in the accounts receivable subsidiary ledger and record the beginning balances.
(3) Record the following transactions in the sales journal (page 9), the cash receipts journal (page 10), and the general journal (page 2).
(4) Post to the customer accounts daily from the journals.
(5) Post the entries in the General Credit column of the cash receipts journal daily.
(6) Post general journal entries daily.
(7) Foot, prove, total, and rule the sales and cash receipts journals.
(8) Post the column totals from the special journals.
(9) Prepare a schedule of accounts receivable.

Date	Transactions
May 1	Received a check for $50 from Virginia Williams in payment of her account, Receipt 202.
3	Sandpiper Sports Club sent a check for $882 in payment of their $900 account less 2% cash discount, Receipt 203.
5	Sold Virginia Williams $300 in merchandise plus 5% sales tax of $15, Sales Slip 404.
7	Received a check for $1,470 from Hal's Fitness Studios in payment of their $1,500 account balance less 2% cash discount, Receipt 204.
9	Virginia Williams returned $100 in merchandise plus sales tax of $5, issued Credit Memo 50.
11	Sold $700 in merchandise on account to Sandpiper Sports Club plus sales tax of $35, terms, 2/10, n/30, Sales Slip 405.
13	Dave Hioki sent a check for $100 to apply on his account, Receipt 205.
14	Received $25 from the sale of supplies to Hanson's Market, Receipt 206.
15	Cash sales amounted to $2,000 plus sales tax of $100, Tape 27.
15	Bankcard sales were $1,500 plus sales tax of $75, Tape 27.
18	Issued Credit Memo 51 to Roundabout Fashions for $210, which included $200 in defective merchandise and a sales tax of $10.

Continued

Date	Transactions
22	Sold $3,000 in merchandise on account to Hal's Fitness Studios plus 5% sales tax of $150, Sales Slip 406.
23	Samstead Fashions sent us a check for $1,250 to apply to their account, Receipt 207.
24	Received a check for $100 from Gabriela Morales in payment of her account, Receipt 208.
27	Sold Gabriela Morales $200 in merchandise plus 5% sales tax of $10, Sales Slip 407.
28	Roundabout Fashions sent us a check for $900 to apply on their account, Receipt 209.

Analyze: What is the ending balance in the **Accounts Receivable** account? Does this agree with the total of subsidiary ledgers?

Chapter 17, Problem 17A Recording Special Journal and General Journal Transactions

T-Shirt Trends, a retail merchandising business, uses special journals to record its business transactions.

Instructions On the forms provided in your working papers:
(1) Record the July transactions in the sales journal (page 15), cash receipts journal (page 16), purchases journal (page 15), cash payments journal (page 16), and general journal (page 3).
(2) Foot, prove, total, and rule the special journals.
(3) Prove cash. The beginning cash in bank balance is $7,500. The check stub balance at the end of the month is $13,394.

Date	Transactions
July 2	Sold $500 in merchandise on account to Dave Hioki plus 5% sales tax, Sales Slip 333.
2	Purchased $1,400 in merchandise on account from Cherokee Productions, Inc., Invoice 7001, terms 2/10, n/30.
3	Issued Check 535 for $1,960 in payment of Dancing Wind Clothing Manufacturers $2,000 invoice less a 2% discount.
4	Received $1,764 from Hal's Fitness Studios in payment of our $1,800 invoice less a 2% discount, Receipt 200.
5	Issued Credit Memo 27 to Gabriela Morales for the return of $100 in merchandise plus $5 sales tax.
6	Purchased $2,000 in store equipment on account from Carter Office Supply, Invoice CO123, terms n/30.
6	Received $2,450 from Sandpiper Sports Club in payment of our $2,500 invoice less a 2% discount, Receipt 201.
7	Sold $1,000 in merchandise on account plus 5% sales tax to Virginia Williams, Sales Slip 334.
	Continued

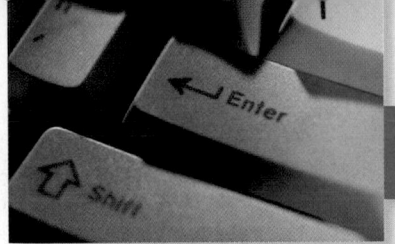
Date	Transactions
7	Issued Debit Memo 14 for $300 to Wilmington Shirt Factory for credit taken on damaged merchandise.
8	Wrote Check 536 to Chapel Hills Realtors in payment of monthly rent of $900.
8	Sold old office equipment for $75 cash to Ann Martin, an employee, Receipt 202.
9	Purchased $3,000 in merchandise on account from CompuRite Solutions, Invoice CR79, terms 2/10, n/30.
10	Sold $3,500 in merchandise plus 5% sales tax on account to Roundabout Fashions, Sales Slip 335.
12	Bought $150 in supplies from Palace Party Supplies, on account, Invoice 876.
13	Issued Check 537 for $1,600 to Academy Insurance Company for annual business insurance premium.
14	Wrote Check 538 to CompuRite Solutions for $2,940 in payment of Invoice CR79 for $3,000 less 2% discount.
15	Cash sales amounted to $3,000 plus 5% sales tax, Tape 29.
15	Bankcard sales were $5,000 plus 5% sales tax, Tape 29.
18	Purchased $1,100 in merchandise on account from Sullivan Screen Printers, Invoice 423, terms 2/10, n/30.
20	Purchased $750 in merchandise for cash from Cherokee Productions, Inc., Check 539.
22	Paid the monthly utility bill, $150, Check 540.
23	Purchased $4,500 in merchandise on account from Dancing Wind Clothing Manufacturers, Invoice 777, terms, 2/10, n/30.
24	Received $525 from Dave Hioki to apply on his account, Receipt 203.
24	Wrote Check 541 to Sullivan Screen Printers for $1,078 in payment of Invoice 423 for $1,100 less a 2% discount.
26	Issued Debit Memo 15 for $200 to Dancing Wind Clothing Manufacturers for the return of merchandise.
31	Cash sales amounted to $2,200 plus $110 sales tax, Tape 30.
31	Bank card sales amounted to $1,500 plus $75.00 sales tax, Tape 30.
31	Wrote Check 542 to pay the payroll of $2,000 (Gross Earnings) for the pay period ended July 31. The following amounts were withheld: employees' federal income taxes, $300; FICA taxes, $124 for social security and $29 for Medicare; employees' state income taxes, $60.
31	Recorded the employer's payroll taxes (FICA tax rate, 6.2% for social security, and 1.45% for Medicare; federal unemployment tax rate, 0.8%; and state unemployment rate, 5.4%).

Analyze: In the purchases journal, what is the total of the Purchases Debit column?

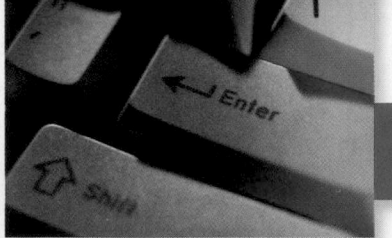

Chapter 18, Problem 18A Calculating Adjustments and Preparing the Ten-Column Work Sheet

A partially completed work sheet for T-Shirt Trends is shown in your working papers. Adjustments need to be made to the following items at year-end.

Data for Adjustments

Merchandise Inventory, December 31	$47,394
Supplies on hand, December 31	678
Insurance premium expired during the period	1,260
Additional federal corporate income tax owed	168

Instructions On the form provided in your working papers, complete the December 31 work sheet for T-Shirt Trends. Make the necessary adjustments on the work sheet.

Analyze: What is the total of the Adjustments columns on the work sheet?

Chapter 19, Problem 19A Preparing Financial Statements

The completed work sheet for T-Shirt Trends for the year ended December 31 appears in your working papers.

Instructions On the forms provided in your working papers, prepare the following financial statements:
(1) The income statement for the fiscal year ended December 31.
(2) A statement of retained earnings.
(3) A balance sheet.

Analyze: What is the balance in the **Retained Earnings** account at December 31?

Chapter 20, Problem 20A Journalizing Closing Entries

The account balances for T-Shirt Trends appear in your working papers as of December 31.

Instructions On the form provided in your working papers, journalize all the closing entries on page 17 in the general journal.

Analyze: What was the balance in the **Income Summary** account before it was closed to **Retained Earnings**?

Chapter 21, Problem 21A Recording Stockholders' Equity Transactions

T-Shirt Trends was organized as a publicly held corporation on September 1 and authorized to issue 10,000 shares of $100 par, $8 preferred stock, and 25,000 shares of $50 par common stock.

Continued

Instructions On the form provided in your working papers, record the following transactions on page 1 of the general journal.

Date	Transactions
2007	
Sept. 1	Issued 4,000 shares of $8 preferred stock at $100 per share, Receipt 101.
12	Issued 12,000 shares of common stock at $50 per share, Receipt 102.
Nov. 15	Received $52.50 per share for 2,500 shares of common stock issued, Receipt 215.
Dec. 16	Received $5,000 for 50 shares of $8 preferred stock issued, Receipt 298.
2008	
Mar. 24	Issued 1,000 shares of common stock at $55 per share, Receipt 389.
Aug.15	Declared a dividend of $32,400 on 4,050 shares of $8 preferred stock outstanding, payable on September 15 to stockholders of record on September 1, Memorandum 316.
15	Declared cash dividend of 25¢ per share on 15,500 shares of common stock outstanding, payable on September 30 to stockholders of record on September 1, Memorandum 317.
Sept.15	Paid preferred stock dividend declared August 15, Check 1763.
30	Paid common stock dividend declared August 15, Check 1802.
Dec. 31	Prepared the closing entries in the general journal to close **Income Summary** for the net income of $102,600 and to close the two **Dividends** accounts.

Analyze: How much was the total dividend declared on preferred stock on August 15? How much was declared on the common stock on August 15?

Chapter 22, Problem 22A Maintaining a Petty Cash Register

Maureen Miller operates T-Shirt Trends, a T-shirt specialty business. She established a petty cash fund on February 1 by writing Check 336 for $100. She also records all petty cash disbursements in a petty cash register. Petty cash disbursements are usually made for expenses such as office supplies, delivery expense, miscellaneous expenses, and advertising expense.

Instructions On the forms provided in your working papers:
(1) Record the establishment of the petty cash fund on the first line of the petty cash register, page 1.
(2) Record each of the following petty cash disbursements in the petty cash register.
(3) Foot, prove, total, and rule the petty cash register at the end of the month.
(4) Reconcile the petty cash fund. An actual cash count of the fund shows a balance of $5.68.
(5) Check 362 was issued to replenish the petty cash fund. Record the replenishment information in the petty cash register.

Continued ✒

Date	Transactions
Feb. 1	Paid $1.20 for postage due on a letter, Voucher 101.
3	Purchased a $9 ad in the *Towne Sentinel* paper, Voucher 102.
5	Bought a ream of typing paper for $4.75, issued Voucher 103.
6	Paid $6 for a mailgram, Voucher 104.
8	Issued Voucher 105 for $9.90 to Express Couriers in payment for the delivery of packages.
10	Paid the newscarrier $4.10 for daily newspapers and issued Voucher 106.
13	Bought pens, pencils, and memo pads for $6.60, Voucher 107.
15	Purchased a $9.50 advertisement in a local trade journal, Voucher 108.
19	Issued Voucher 109 for $8.70 for office supplies.
22	Express Couriers delivered financial data from a client, $9.90, Voucher 110.
26	Issued Voucher 111 for $2.12 for additional postage due on mail.
27	Bought an ad in the *Towne Sentinel* for $8.70 and issued Voucher 112.
28	Purchased a typewriter ribbon for $5.50, issuing Voucher 113.
28	Voided Voucher 114 due to an error.
28	Issued Voucher 115 for $4.10 to the newscarrier.

Analyze: At the end of February, was cash short or over? By what amount? Should this be recorded as a revenue or an expense?

Chapter 23, Problem 23A Calculating and Recording Depreciation Expense

The T-Shirt Trends Company purchased a delivery truck on October 12, 2004, at a cost of $78,900. The delivery truck has an estimated useful life of three years and an estimated disposal value of $900.

Instructions On the forms provided in your working papers:
(1) Prepare a depreciation schedule for the delivery truck using the straight-line method.
(2) Record the following transactions on general journal page 41. Post the transactions to the ledger accounts provided.
(3) Answer the following questions.
   (a) How did you determine the depreciation from October 12 to December 31?
   (b) What was the book value of the truck on December 31, 2004?
   (c) What was the book value of the truck on December 31, 2005?
   (d) How did you determine the annual depreciation on December 31, 2005?

Date	Transactions
2004	
Dec. 31	Recorded the adjusting entry for the year's depreciation expense on the delivery truck.
2005	
Dec. 31	Recorded the adjusting entry for the year's depreciation expense on the delivery truck.

Analyze: How much depreciation expense will be recorded over the useful life of the asset? Which account will show the depreciation recorded over the asset's useful life?

Chapter 24, Problem 24A Calculating and Recording Uncollectible Accounts Expense

T-Shirt Trends uses the allowance method of accounting for uncollectible accounts. At the end of the fiscal period, the following accounts appeared on T-Shirt's trial balance.

Accounts Receivable	$ 18,647.25
Allowance for Uncollectible Accounts	1,060.50
Sales	452,612.00
Sales Discounts	5,431.35
Sales Returns and Allowances	13,578.36
Uncollectible Accounts Expense	0.00

Instructions On the forms provided in your working papers:
(1) Determine the amount of the adjustment for uncollectible accounts for the fiscal period ended December 31. Management estimates that uncollectible accounts will be 1.25% of net sales.
(2) Journalize the adjusting entry in the general journal, page 10.
(3) Post the adjusting entry to the general ledger accounts.
(4) Determine the book value of accounts receivable.

Analyze: When an account is written off in the next fiscal period, what account will be debited?

Chapter 25, Problem 25A Accounting for Inventories

The Shoooot-It Camera Shop uses a one-year fiscal period beginning January 1. At the beginning of the fiscal period, the shop had a beginning inventory of film valued at $867.90 (526 rolls at $1.65 per roll). During the year, the shop made the following purchases:

January 13	400 rolls of film @ $1.67	=	$ 668
March 2	600 rolls of film @ $1.73	=	1,038
April 14	300 rolls of film @ $1.76	=	528
July 8	700 rolls of film @ $1.79	=	1,253
September 3	200 rolls of film @ $1.81	=	362
November 19	300 rolls of film @ $1.83	=	549
Totals	2,500 rolls		$4,398

There were 621 rolls of film in inventory at the end of the fiscal year.

Instructions On the form provided in your working papers, calculate the cost of the ending inventory using the specific identification, FIFO, LIFO, and weighted average cost methods. For the specific identification method, 165 of the rolls were purchased on September 3 and 456 were purchased on July 8.

Analyze: Which inventory valuation method gives the highest value to Shoooot-It's ending inventory?

SPREADSHEET SMART GUIDE

Step–by–Step Instructions: Problem 26A

1. Select the spreadsheet template for Problem 26A.
2. Enter your name and the date in the spaces provided on the template.
3. Complete the spreadsheet using the instructions in your working papers.
4. Print the spreadsheet and proof your work.
5. Save your work and exit the spreadsheet program.

 **Chapter 26, Problem 26A Calculating Current and Future Interest**

Frequently, notes that are issued or received in one fiscal period do not mature until the next fiscal period. As a result, the interest expense paid or the interest income received applies to two different fiscal periods. Listed below is the information for 10 different notes.

Instructions On the form provided in your working papers, determine the following for each note.
(1) Determine the maturity date. Assume February has 28 days.
(2) Determine what portion of the interest applies to the current year and what portion of the interest applies to the following year. December 31 is the end of the fiscal period.

	Amount	Issue Date	Interest Rate	Term
1.	$ 1,100	December 10	9%	30 days
2.	700	November 21	12%	60 days
3.	17,100	October 10	10%	90 days
4.	4,000	December 5	15%	60 days
5.	15,000	November 10	6.5%	120 days
6.	3,000	September 8	7%	180 days
7.	6,600	November 17	10%	70 days
8.	840	October 1	9.5%	6 months
9.	1,200	December 1	10%	3 months
10.	2,700	August 1	8%	9 months

Analyze: Which of the notes will have more interest expense next year than this year?

Chapter 26, Problem 26B Recording Noninterest Bearing Notes Payable

Your company, National Paper Supplies, frequently borrows money for short periods from First Bank by issuing promissory notes.

Instructions In your working papers, record the following transactions on page 6 of the general journal.

Date	Transactions
Jan. 15	Borrowed $12,000 from First Bank by issuing a 90-day, noninterest-bearing note payable that the bank discounted at 12%, Note 45.
Apr. 15	Issued Check 2561 for $12,000 in payment of the note issued Jan.15 and recorded the interest expense.
Oct. 31	Borrowed $18,000 from First Bank by issuing a 120-day, noninterest-bearing note payable that the bank discounted at 13%, Note 46.
Dec. 31	Made an adjusting entry to record the accrued interest expense for Note 46 at year-end.

Analyze: What was the total interest expense incurred in the current year for Notes 45 and 46?

Chapter 27, Problem 27A Recording Partners' Investments

On June 15, Walter Cohen and Janice Connor agreed to combine their individual sole proprietorships into one firm organized as a partnership called Cohen & Connor Legal Services. The partners were to invest all the assets of their two former businesses. Those assets are listed below.

	Cohen	Connor
Cash	$247,000	$517,500
Accounts Receivable	78,000	
Merchandise Inventory	123,000	
Equipment	154,500	

Instructions Prepare the general journal entries (page 1) required to record the partners' investments. The source document is Memorandum 1.

Analyze: What is the total of all the assets contributed to the new partnership?

Chapter 28, Problem 28A Liquidation of a Partnership

The partnership of Joyce, Jane, and Jill is dissolving. The partnership account balances as of November 30, 2004 are:

Cash	$ 8,000	Accounts Payable	$ 8,000
Accounts Receivable	16,000	Joyce, Capital	10,800
Inventory	8,000	Jane, Capital	13,200
Equipment	3,000	Jill, Capital	3,000

Profits and losses are shared 4:5:1 to Joyce, Jane, and Jill respectively.

Date	Transactions
Dec. 1	The accounts receivable are sold for $15,000.
Dec. 8	The inventory is sold for $7,000.
Dec. 15	The equipment is sold for $5,000.
Dec. 23	The accounts payable are paid in full.
Dec. 24	The balance of cash is distributed to the partners.

Instructions Prepare the entries required to liquidate the partnership. Start with general journal page 213.

Analyze: What was the gain or loss on any of the assets that were sold?

Answers to *Check Your Understanding* Problems

Chapter 1

Problem 1-1
Perform an honest analysis of likes and dislikes. Use the chart on page 8 to help identify skills and traits you possess.

Problem 1-2
Use the personal career profile form (Figure 1-1) as a reference for the types of information. List personal information (values, interests, skills, etc.) and then select three possible careers.

Problem 1-3
The possibility for individuals with accounting degrees vary but include careers as: tax accountants, auditors, management accountants, controllers, or chief financial officers.

Problem 1-4
For the accountants mentioned in the section:

> Drew Taylor – Interested in working with numbers and music.
> Maya Cruz – Involved in environmental causes, studied accounting.
> Shelley Hale – Interested in fashion, good with math and logic.

Problem 1-5

PricewaterhouseCoopers	www.pwcglobal.com
Deloitte & Touche	www.deloitte.com/us
Ernst & Young	www.ey.com
KPMG	www.kpmg.com

Problem 1-6
Use local Yellow Pages to find information.

Chapter 2

Problem 2-1
Perform an honest analysis of personal traits. Try to relate the answers to personal activities and experiences that correspond with entrepreneurship.

Problem 2-2
The situations such as these have opposing viewpoints. The drop in sales could be a sign that some improvements are in order. On the other hand, some owners will be reluctant to invest more money in a business where sales are down. More information will be needed in order to make a final decision.

Problem 2-3
Greenwood Sky Divers is the name of the business entity. It has been in business for six years, and is a "going concern." The accounting period for Greenwood Sky Divers is one year.

Chapter 3

Problem 3-1
1. $10,000
2. $26,000
3. $3,000
4. $26,000
5. $6,000
6. $13,000
7. $16,000
8. $8,000
9. $21,000
10. $20,000
11. $35,000
12. $4,500

Problem 3-2
1. Cash in Bank increased $30,000. Jan Swift, Capital increased $30,000.
2. Office Equipment increased $700. Jan Swift, Capital increased $700.
3. Cash in Bank decreased $4,000. Computer Equipment increased $4,000.
4. Office Equipment increased $5,000. Accounts Payable increased $5,000.
5. Accounts Receivable increased by $700. Office Equipment decreased $700.
6. Cash in Bank decreased $2,000. Accounts Payable decreased $2,000.

Problem 3-3
1. Cash in Bank decreased by $50. Jan Swift, Capital decreased by $50.

2. Cash in Bank increased by $1,000. Jan Swift, Capital increased by $1,000.
3. Cash in Bank decreased by $600. Jan Swift, Capital decreased by $600.
4. Cash in Bank decreased by $800. Jan Swift, Capital decreased by $800.
5. Cash in Bank increased by $200. Accounts Receivable decreased by $200.

Chapter 4

Problem 4-1

Office Equipment – asset, debit, credit, debit
Accounts Payable – liability, credit, debit, credit
Accounts Receivable – asset, debit, credit, debit
R. Lewis, Capital – owner's equity, credit, debit, credit

Problem 4-2

1a. The asset Office Equipment is increased. Increases in assets are recorded as debits.
b. The liability Accounts Payable is increased. Increases in liabilities are recorded as credits.
2a. The asset Office Furniture is increased. Increases in assets are recorded as debits.
b. The owner's capital account Alice Roberts, Capital is increased. Increases in the owner's capital account are recorded as credits.
3a. The liability Accounts Payable is decreased. Decreases in liabilities are recorded as debits.
b. The asset Cash in Bank is decreased. Decreases in assets are recorded as credits.

Chapter 5

Problem 5-1

Cash in Bank—asset, debit, credit, debit
Accounts Receivable—asset, debit, credit, debit
Airplanes—asset, debit, credit, debit
Accounts Payable—liability, credit, debit, credit
Caroline Palmer, Capital—owner's equity, credit, debit, credit
Caroline Palmer, Withdrawals—owner's equity, debit, credit, debit
Flying Fees—revenue, credit, debit, credit
Advertising Expense—expense, debit, credit, debit
Food Expense—expense, debit, credit, debit
Fuel and Oil Expense—expense, debit, credit, debit
Repairs Expense—expense, debit, credit, debit

Problem 5-2

1. Dr. Utilities Expense; Cr. Cash in Bank
2. Dr. Accounts Receivable; Cr. Service Fees
3. Dr. John Albers, Withdrawals; Cr. Cash in Bank
4. Dr. Advertising Expense; Cr. Cash in Bank

Chapter 6

Problem 6-1

1. JayMax Office Suppliers
2. Dario's Accounting Firm
3. April 9, 20--
4. $479
5. Fax Machine
6. $299
7. Payable in 30 days

Problem 6-2

Step 1 D
Step 2 F
Step 3 E
Step 4 B
Step 5 A
Step 6 C

Problem 6-3

1. Passenger Van, asset, increase, debit; Cash in Bank, asset, decrease, credit
2. Utilities Expense, expense, increase, debit; Cash in Bank, asset, decrease, credit
3. Cash in Bank, asset, increase, debit; Day Care Fees, revenue, increase, credit

Chapter 7

Problem 7-1

Cash in Bank $10,000 Dr.
Accounts Receivable – Mark Cohen $2,000 Dr.
Accounts Payable – Jenco Industries $1,000 Cr.
Tom Torrie, Capital $35,000 Cr.
Admissions Revenue $0

Problem 7-2

Account Balances:
Cash in Bank $10,000 (Dr.)
David Serlo, Capital $10,000 (Cr.)

Problem 7-3

May 20: Dr. Office Equip. $1,500;
Cr. Computer Equip. $1,500; Memorandum 47

Problem 7-4

July 7: Dr. Advertising Expense $300;
Cr. Rent Expense $300; Memoradum 13

Chapter 8

Problem 8-1

Store Equipment, asset, debit
Rent Expense, expense, debit
Service Fees Revenue, revenue, credit
Accounts Payable–Rubino Supply, liability, credit
Scott Lee, Capital, owner's equity, credit

Advertising Expense, expense, debit
Accounts Receivable–John Langer, asset, debit
Scott Lee, Withdrawals, owner's equity, debit
Maintenance Expense, expense, debit
Office Supplies, asset, debit

Problem 8-2
1. Hailey Office Supply
2. Garmot Electrical Co.
3. June 15
4. $6.23
5. Two
6. The invoice number is 220

Problem 8-3
Store Equipment, Balance Sheet, debit
Rent Expense, Income Statement, debit
Service Fees Revenue, Income Statement, credit
Accounts Payable–Rubino Supply, Balance Sheet, credit
Scott Lee, Capital, Balance Sheet, credit
Advertising Expense, Income Statement, debit
Accounts Receivable–John Langer, Balance Sheet, debit
Scott Lee, Withdrawals, Balance Sheet, debit
Maintenance Expense, Income Statement, debit
Office Supplies, Balance Sheet, debit

Chapter 9

Problem 9-1
1. Stratford Learning Ctr.
2. $832
3. Sandra Miller
4. Payment on account
5. August 21
6. Rose Hughes
7. Roxbury

Problem 9-2
1. $62,500
2. $29,915
3. $29,470
4. $10,630
5. $7,060
6. $25,010

Problem 9-3
Return on Sales = 20.53%

Chapter 10

Problem 10-1
1. Dr. Ticket Revenue $6,000; Cr. Income Summary $6,000
2. Dr. Income Summary $3,100; Cr. Gas and Oil Expense $700, Miscellaneous Expense $600, Utilities Expense $1,800

Problem 10-2
1.,2. Dr. Utilities Expense $129; Cr. Cash in Bank $129
3.,4. Dr. Income Summary $129; Cr. Utilities Exp. $129

Problem 10-3
Accts. Rec.–Linda Brown, Balance Sheet, No, Yes
Advertising Expense, Income Statement, Yes, No

Cash in Bank, Balance Sheet, No, Yes
Exercise Class Revenue, Income Statement, Yes, No
Exercise Equipment, Balance Sheet, No, Yes
Income Summary, N/A, Yes, No
Laundry Equipment, Balance Sheet, No, Yes
Maintenance Expense, Income Statement, Yes, No
Membership fees, Income Statement, Yes, No
Miscellaneous Expense, Income Statement, Yes, No
Office Furniture, Balance Sheet, No, Yes
Rent Expense, Income Statement, Yes, No
Repair Tools, Balance Sheet, No, Yes
Ted Chapman, Capital, Balance Sheet, Yes, Yes
Ted Chapman, Withdrawals, Balance Sheet, Yes, No
Utilities Expense, Income Statement, Yes, No

Chapter 11

Problem 11-1
1.,2. Total Deposit $967.08
3. Balance $2,394.24
4. Balance $2,394.24
5. Balance $2,119.24

Problem 11-2
1. $100
2. $25
3. Miscellaneous Expense

Chapter 12

Problem 12-1
Longas, Jane: 43, $7.25, $290, $32.63, $322.63
Lang, Richard: 38, $7.80, $296.40, $0, $296.40
Quinn, Betty: 44 1/4, $8.30, $332.00, $52.91, $384.91
Sullivan, John: 39 1/2, $8.30, $327.85, $0, $327.85
Talbert, Kelly: 40, $7.50, $300.00, $0, $300.00
Trimbell, Gene: 42 1/2, $9.75, $390.00, $36.56, $426.56
Varney, Heidi: 34 1/4, $8.75, $299.69, $0, $299.69
Wallace, Kevin: 46, $9.25, $370.00, $83.25, $453.25

Problem 12-2
Cleary, Kevin: S, 0, $155.60, $9.65, $2.26, $16, $3.11, $31.02, $124.58
Halley, James: S, 1, $184.10, $11.41, $2.67, $12, $3.68, $29.76, $154.34
Hong, Kim: S, 0, $204.65, $12.69, $2.97, $23, $4.09, $42.75, $161.90
Jackson, Marvin: M, 1, $216.40, $13.42, $3.14, $6, $4.33, $26.89, $189.51
Sell, Richard: M, 2, $196.81, $12.20, $2.85, $0, $3.94, $18.99, $177.82
Totals: $957.56, $59.37, $13.89, $57, $19.15, $149.41, $808.15

Problem 12-3
Medicare $4.57
Social Security $19.53
Federal Income Tax $32
Problem 12-4
Check number 79, net pay $263.94

Chapter 13

Problem 13-1
1. $2,193.40
2. $31.80
3. $503.25
4. $33.75
5. $1,690.15

Problem 13-2
Social Security Tax Payable $299.87
Medicare Tax Payable $70.13
Federal Unemployment Tax Payable $38.69
State Unemployment Tax Payable $261.18

Problem 13-3
Employee's federal income tax, payroll entry
Employer's social security tax, payroll tax entry
U.S. savings bonds, payroll entry
Employers' Medicare tax, payroll tax entry
Federal unemployment tax, payroll tax entry
Employees' state income tax, payroll entry
Union dues, payroll entry
Employees' social security tax, payroll entry
State unemployment tax, payroll tax entry
Employee's Medicare tax, payroll entry

Problem 13-4
April 30: Dr. Social Security Tax Payable $318.55,
Medicare Tax Payable $113.28, Employee's Federal
Income Tax Payable $286; Cr. Cash in Bank $717.83
April 30: Dr. State Income Tax Payable $205.60;
Cr. Cash in Bank $205.60

Problem 13-5
Dr. Payroll Tax Exp. $1,328.07, Cr. Soc. Sec. Tax Pay.
$82.34, Cr. Medicare Tax Payable $19.26, Cr. Fed. Inc.
Tax Pay. $184.00, Cr. State Inc. Tax. Pay. $26.56, Cr.
Hosp. Ins. Prem. Pay. $20.00, Cr. Cash in Bank $995.91

Chapter 14

Problem 14-1
Ending account balances:
Cash in Bank $554
Accounts Receivable $3,000
Sales $3,554

Problem 14-2
Sept. 1: Dr. Accts. Rec.—James Palmer $318; Cr. Sales
$300, Sales Tax Pay. $18; Sales Invoice 101
Sept. 4: Dr. Accts. Rec.—Anna Rodriguez $636; Cr.
Sales $600, Sales Tax Pay. $36; Sales Invoice 102

Sept. 7: Dr. Sales Ret. + Allow. $300, Sales Tax Pay. $18;
Cr. Accts. Rec.—James Palmer $318; Credit Memo. 15
Sept. 19: Dr. Sales Ret. + Allow. $40, Sales Tax Pay.
$2.40; Cr. Accts. Rec.—Anna Rodriguez $42.40;
Credit Memo. 16

Problem 14-3
May 15: Dr. Cash in Bank $1908; Cr. Sales $1800,
Sales Tax Payable $108; Tape 40

Problem 14-4
Mar. 1: Dr. Cash in Bank $140.40; Cr. Sales $130,
Sales Tax Payable $10.40; Sales Slip 49
Mar. 5: Dr. Accts. Rec./Kelly Wilson $324; Cr. Sales
$300, Sales Tax Payable $24; Sales Slip 55
Mar. 17: Dr. Cash in Bank $810; Cr. Sales $750,
Sales Tax Payable $60; Tape 65

Chapter 15

Problem 15-1
1. Case Construction Company
2. Westmoreland Paint and Supply Company
3. 7894
4. November 15, 20--
5. December 1, 20--
6. 25 gallons
7. 5
8. White, gray, brown, beige and peach.
9. $20.00
10. $500.00

Problem 15-2
Sept. 2: Dr. Purchases $900; Cr. Accts. Pay./Sunrise
Novelty Supply $900; Invoice SN110
Sept 7: Dr. Accts. Pay./Sunrise Novelty Supply $50;
Cr. Purchases Returns and Allowances $50; Debit
Memorandum 18

Problem 15-3
Nov. 12: Dr. Accts. Pay./Kaleidoscope Comics $16.00;
Cr. Purchases Ret. and Allow. $16.00; Debit Memo 559

Problem 15-4
May 1: Dr. Purchases $10,500; Cr. Cash in Bank
$10,500; Check 1150
May 5: Dr. Transportation In $325; Cr. Cash in Bank
$325; Check 1151
May 7: Dr. Prepaid Insurance $2,500; Cr. Cash in Bank
$2,500; Check 1152

Chapter 16

Problem 16-1
Post $12,000 to Sales credit column.
Post $720.00 to Sales Tay Pay. credit column.
Post $12,720 to Accts. Rec. debit column.

Problem 16-2
1. Sales credit $820, Sales Tax Payable credit $41, Accounts Receivable debit $861
2. Ending Balance $1,161

Problem 16-3
Totals:
General credit $105
Sales credit $6,200
Sales Tax Payable credit $372
Accounts Receivable credit $5,580
Sales Discounts debit $110
Cash in Bank debit $12,147
Total debits/credits $12,257

Chapter 17

Problem 17-1
Column totals:
Accounts Payable $4,550
Purchases $3,600
General $950

Problem 17-2
Ending Cash in Bank balance $5,610.59

Problem 17-3
Nov. 2: Dr. Accts. Pay./Colonial Products Inc. $900; Cr. Purchases Discounts $27, Cash in Bank $873; Check 104

Chapter 18

Problem 18-1
1. Greater
2. $1,533
3. Merchandise Inventory
4. Income Summary

Problem 18-2
1. Amount $2,454.70
   Account debited, Supplies Expense
   Account credited, Supplies
2. Amount $740
   Account debited, Insurance Expense
   Account credited, Prepaid Insurance
3. Amount $105
   Account debited, Federal Corporate Income Tax Expense
   Account credited, Federal Corporate Income Tax Payable

Problem 18-3
1. $9,995
2. Balance Sheet
3. $3,710
4. $155

Problem 18-4
1. Rotary Supply Corporation
2. 6
3. $177.09
4. Accounts Payable—K & L Electrical
5. Purchases Returns and Allowances

Chapter 19

Problem 19-1
1. Kevin Cleary, Capital
2. Capital Stock
3. Capital Stock and Retained Earnings

Problem 19-2
Subtotal $70.25, sales tax $2.81
Total $73.06

Problem 19-3
1. $96,506
2. $16,703
3. $27,783
4. $17,148

Problem 19-4
1. Office Equipment, Merchandise Inventory.
2. Federal Unemployment Tax Payable.
3. It increased by $16,379.43, or 12.73%.
4. 95.47%
5. The increase in Accounts Receivable indicates that either the company is selling more product or is less efficient at collecting payments. The decrease in Accounts Payable indicates that the company is paying bills earlier. In order to see the whole picture one would need to be able to analyze the data in relation to the other financial statements.
6. The company prepaid for a new insurance contract.

Chapter 20

Problem 20-1
Accounts Receivable, no
Bankcard Fees Expense, yes, credited, debited
Capital Stock, no
Cash in Bank, no
Equipment, no
Fed. Corp. Income Tax Expense, yes, credited, debited
Fed Corp. Income Tax Payable, no
Income Summary, yes, depends (loss = credit), depends (loss = credit)
Insurance Expense, yes, credited, debited
Merchandise Inventory, no
Miscellaneous Expense, yes, credited, debited
Prepaid Insurance, no
Purchases, yes, credited, debited

Purchases Discounts, yes, debited, credited

Purchases Returns and Allowances, yes, debited, credited

Retained Earnings, yes, depends (loss = credit), depends (loss = credit)

Sales, yes, debited, credited

Sales Discounts, yes, credited, debited

Sales Returns and Allowances, yes, credited, debited

Sales Tax Payable, no

Supplies, no

Supplies Expense, yes, credited, debited

Transportation In, yes, credited, debited

Utilities Expense, yes, credited, debited

Problem 20-2

July 12: Dr. Rent Exp. $750; Cr. Cash in Bank $750

Problem 20-3

Collecting and verifying source documents

Analyzing business transactions

Journalizing business transactions

Posting journal entries to ledgers

Preparing a trial balance

Completing the work sheet

Preparing financial statements

Journalizing and posting adjusting entries

Journalizing and posting closing entries

Preparing a post-closing trial balance

Chapter 21

Problem 21-1

1. 30,000 shares of common stock were issued at par, $10 per share in cash.
2. 2,000 shares of preferred stock were issued at par, $100 per share in cash.
3. 50,000 shares of common stock, par $10, were issued at $14 per share.

Problem 21-2

1. $87,500
2. $262,500

Problem 21-3

Apr. 1: Dr. Dividends—Common $5,679; Cr. Dividends Payable—Common $5,679; Memorandum 37

Apr. 30: Dr. Dividends Payable—Common $5,679; Cr. Cash in Bank $5,679; Check 221

Problem 21-4

The transactions that are reported on the statement of stockholders' equity are 2,3,6, and 8.

Chapter 22

Problem 22-1

1. Net cash $1,016.84
   Cash short $5

2. Mar 31: Dr. Cash in Bank $1,016.84, Cash Short and Over $5; Cr. Sales $964, Sales Tax Payable $57.84

Problem 22-2

1. Net cash $1,595.77
   Cash over $10
2. Apr. 14: Dr. Cash in Bank $1,595.77; Cr. Sales $1,496, Sales Tax Pay. $89.77, Cash Short and Over $10

Problem 22-3

Check $39.51

Chapter 23

Problem 23-1

Accounts Receivable, current

Building, plant

Cash in Bank, current

Change Fund, current

Delivery Equipment, plant

Land, plant

Merchandise Inventory, current

Office Equipment, plant

Office Furniture, plant

Petty Cash Fund, current

Prepaid Insurance, current

Store Equipment, plant

Supplies, current

Problem 23-2

Cash register $420, $60, $40

Computer $5,000, $1,000, $166.66

Conference table $1,800, $72, $36

Delivery truck $30,000, $6,000, $1,500

Desk $2,880, $144, $132

Problem 23-3

Book Value:

10/01/2001, $12,500

12/31/2001, $11,960

12/31/2002, $9,800

12/31/2003, $7,640

12/31/2004, $5,480

12/31/2005, $3,320

09/31/2006, $1,700

Problem 23-4

1. June 4: Dr. Office Equipment $3,456; Cr. Cash in Bank $3,456; Invoice 14492
2. Dec. 31: Dr. Depreciation Expense $379.87; Cr. Accumulated Depreciation $379.87
3. Dec. 31: Dr. Depreciation Expense $651.20; Cr. Accumulated Depreciation $651.20

Problem 23-5

1. Book Value:
   Jan. 7, $2,360
   First year, $1,908

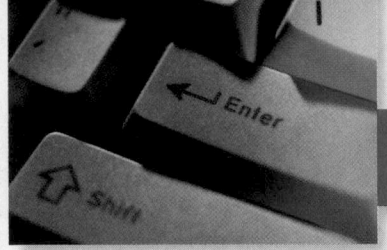

Second year, $1,456
Third year, $1,004
Fourth year, $552
Fifth year, $100

2. Dec. 31: Dr. Depr. Exp.—Office Equip. $452; Cr. Accum. Depr.—Office Equip. $452
3. Dec. 31: Dr. Income Summary $452; Cr. Depr. Exp.—Office Equip. $452
4. $100, Yes

Chapter 24

Problem 24-1
Journal Entries
Apr. 10: Dr. Accts. Rec./Sonya Dickson $630; Cr. Sales $600, Sales Tax Pay. $30; Sales Slip 928
Nov. 30: Dr. Uncollectible Accounts Expense $630; Cr. Accts. Rec./Sonya Dickson $630; Memorandum 78
Dec. 30: Dr. Accts. Rec./Sonya Dickson $630; Cr. Uncollectible Accounts Expense $630; Memorandum 89
Dec. 30: Dr. Cash in Bank $630; Cr. Accts. Rec./Sonya Dickson $630; Receipt 277

Ledger Balances
Ending debit balances:
Cash in Bank $10,058
Accounts Receivable $7,290
Uncollectible Accounts Expense $928
Accts. Rec./Sonya Dickson $0
Ending credit balances:
Sales Tax Pay. $278
Sales $24,760

Problem 24-2
Journal Entries
May 4: Dr. Allowance for Doubtful Accounts $1,050; Cr. Accts. Rec./Jack Bowers $1,050; Memorandum 241
Nov. 18: Dr. Accts. Rec./Jack Bowers $1,050; Cr. Allowance for Doubtful Accounts $1,050; Memorandum 321
Nov. 18: Dr. Cash in Bank $1,050; Cr. Accts. Rec./Jack Bowers $1,050; Receipt 1078
Dec. 31: Dr. Uncollectible Account Expense $1,850; Cr. Allowance for Uncollectible Accounts $1,850

Ledger Balances
Ending debit balances:
Cash in Bank $10,470
Accounts Receivable $19,350
Uncollectible Account Expense $1,850
Accts. Rec./Jack Bowers $0

Ending credit balances:
Allowance for Doubtful Accounts $3,050

Problem 24-3
(1) Uncollectible Accounts Expense:
Andrews Co. $2,800.02
The Book Nook $2,047.81
Cable Inc. $2,550.00
Davis Inc. $1,282.40
Ever-Sharp Co. $1,164.38
(2) Dec. 31: Dr. Uncollectible Account Expense $1,282.40; Cr. Allowance for Uncollectible Accounts $1,282.40

Chapter 25

Problem 25-1
Preparing Inventory Reports
Total value of inventory $794.10

Problem 25-2
Determining Inventory Costs
  a. $472.55
  b. $477.25
  c. $465.25
  d. $470.52

Problem 25-3
  1. Ending inventory $575.90
  2. Gross profit $214.30

Chapter 26

Problem 26-1
  1. Interest $75.62, Maturity value $4,075.62
  2. Interest $289.73, Maturity value $10,289.73
  3. Interest $136.23, Maturity value $6,636.23
  4. Interest $36.25, Maturity value $936.25
  5. Interest $142.03, Maturity value $2,542.03

Problem 26-2
  1. Interest $22.19
  2. Interest $69.04
  3. Interest $288.00
  4. Interest $123.29
  5. Interest $86.25

Problem 26-3
  1. Cash in Bank $9,000
  2. Notes Payable $9,000
  3. Cash in Bank , asset; Notes Payable, liability
  4. $9,355.07

Problem 26-4
  1. Cash in Bank is debited for $9,802.74; Discount on Notes Payable is debited for $197.26; Notes Payable is credited for $10,000.
  2. Discount $197.26, Proceeds $9,802.74

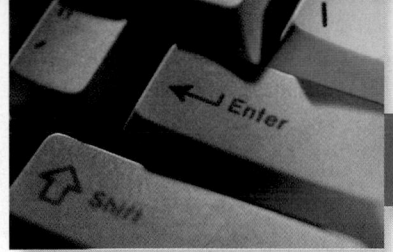

Problem 26-5

June 12: Dr. Cash in Bank $2,426.03, Discount on Notes Payable $73.97; Cr. Notes Payable $2,500; Note 55

Chapter 27

Problem 27-1

June 1: Dr. Cash in Bank $1,200, Accts. Rec. $2,000, Merchandise Inventory $8,000, Equipment $5,000, Van $12,000, Office Furniture $1,000; Cr. Matthew Deck, Capital $29,200; Memorandum 1

June 1: Dr. Cash in Bank $2,300, Accts. Rec. $7,000, Merchandise Inventory $5,000, Equipment $12,000, Office Furniture $500; Cr. Jennifer Rusk, Capital $26,800; Memorandum 1

Problem 27-2

1. 3/4, 1/4
2. 5/9, 3/9, 1/9
3. 3/8, 2/8, 2/8, 1/8
4. 2/4, 1/4, 1/4
5. 2/3, 1/3

Problem 27-3

Nov. 13: Dr. Cash in Bank $20,000; Cr. Walter, Capital $8,000, Yount, Capital $12,000

Chapter 28

Problem 28-1

Division of Net Income:
Goldman $14,000
Jones $21,000
Partners' Equity:
Goldman $37,000
Jones $68,000

Problem 28-2

Shares of gain:
Bass $7,200
Buie $7,200
Anderson $3,600
Norman $3,600
Dunham $2,400
Ruppe $2,400

Problem 28-3

Sept. 4: Dr. Cash in Bank $38,000, Gunther, Capital $3,500, Pertee, Capital $3,500; Cr. Merchandise Inventory $45,000

Sept. 15: Dr. Cash in Bank $29,000; Cr. Gunther, Capital $1,000, Pertee, Capital $1,000, Office Equipment $27,000

Chapter 29

Problem 29-1

Weaknesses might include ethics programs that do not provide clear guidelines for action when faced with various situations. Some employees might not report violations out of fear of retribution. A business ethics plan that includes well-communicated methods for reporting violations (like a Web site, an ethics office, or ethics seminars) could help remedy this problem.

Problem 29-2

The law covers most major ideas about the public's definition of proper and improper behavior, but it does not offer guidance on every dilemma. Ethical concepts cover more subtle instances, where the proper course of action might not be so clear-cut. Use the following resources to find an example in which the actions of a business were legal but might be considered unethical: *Business Week* Online, *The Wall Street Journal*, local newspapers, and business magazines.

Problem 29-3

The following behaviors are possible violations of principles of professional conduct. Marcus appears to be recording transactions in a misleading manner in order to increase the amount of profit reported for the business. This violates the accounting principle of integrity. Jennifer has not been appropriately trained and educated for accounting work. This violates the principle of competence. Ing's behavior violates confidentiality when he shares confidential financial information with anyone not approved to receive it.

Glossary

A

401(k) plan An employee contributes a portion of gross earnings to an account in the 401(k) plan and does not pay income tax on the contributed earnings.

account Subdivision under the three sections of the accounting equation used to summarize increases and decreases in assets, liabilities, and owner's equity.

accountant A person who handles a broad range of jobs related to the making of choices and decisions about the design of a business's accounting system and the preparation and explanation of financial reports.

accounting clerk Entry-level job that can vary with the size of the company from specialization in one part of the system to a wide range of recordkeeping tasks.

accounting cycle The accounting period of a business is separated into activities that help the business keep its accounting records in an orderly fashion.

accounting equation The basis for keeping all accounting records in balance. Assets = liabilities + owner's equity

accounting period A period of time covered by an accounting report.

accounting system A systematic process of recording and reporting the financial information resulting from business transactions.

accounts payable The amount of money owed, or payable, to the creditors of a business.

accounts payable subsidiary ledger A separate ledger that contains accounts for all creditors; it is summarized in the **Accounts Payable** controlling account in the general ledger.

accounts receivable The total amount of money owed to a business.

accounts receivable subsidiary ledger A separate ledger that contains accounts for all charge customers; it is summarized in the **Accounts Receivable** controlling account in the general ledger.

accumulated depreciation The total amount of depreciation for a plant asset that has been recorded up to a specific point in time.

accumulated earnings The employee's year-to-date gross earnings, or the employee's gross earnings from the beginning of the year through the end of each pay period.

adjustment An amount that is added to or subtracted from an account balance to bring that balance up-to-date.

administrative expenses Costs related to the management of a business (for example, office expenses).

aging of accounts receivable method A method of estimating bad debts expense in which each customer's account is examined and classified by age; the age classifications are multiplied by certain percentages; and the total estimated uncollectible amounts are added to determine the end-of-period balance of **Allowance for Uncollectible Accounts.**

allowance Reduces the amount of income tax to be withheld.

allowance method A method of accounting for uncollectible accounts in which an estimate is made of the amount of sales on account for which payment will not be received.

assets Property or items of value owned by a business.

authorized capital stock The maximum number of shares of stock a corporation may issue.

B

balance sheet A report of the balances in all asset, liability, and owner's equity accounts at the end of the period.

bank discount The interest charge deducted in advance on a non-interest-bearing note payable.

bank service charge A fee the bank charges for maintaining bank records and processing bank statement items for the depositor.

bank statement An itemized record of all the transactions in a depositor's account over a given period, usually a month.

bankcard A card issued by a bank that can be used to withdraw cash and to make payments for goods and services at many businesses in place of writing checks.

bankcard fee A fee charged for handling bankcard sales slips; it is usually based on the total dollar volume of the bankcard sales processed.

base year A year or period that is used for comparison in financial statements analysis.

beginning inventory　The merchandise a business has on hand at the beginning of a fiscal period.

board of directors　A group of people, elected by the common stockholders, who are responsible for the affairs of a corporation.

book value　The value of an asset at a specific point in time. For a plant asset, it equals the initial cost of the plant asset minus the accumulated depreciation.

book value of accounts receivable　The amount the business can reasonably expect to receive from all its charge customers.

business entity　Exists independently of its owner's personal holdings. The accounting records and reports are maintained separately and contain financial information related only to the business.

business ethics　The policies and practices that reflect a company's core values such as honesty, trust, respect, and fairness.

business transaction　A business event, such as the buying, selling, or exchange of goods, that causes a change in the assets, liabilities, or owner's equity of a business.

C

calendar year　Period for which a business begins on January 1 and ends on December 31.

canceled checks　Checks paid by the bank and deducted from the depositor's account.

capital　Money supplied by investors, banks, or owners of a business. Refers to the dollar value of assets contributed to the business.

Capital Stock　The account that represents the total amount of investment in the corporation by its stockholders (owners).

cash discount　The amount a customer can deduct from the amount owed for purchased merchandise if payment is made within a certain time.

cash payments journal　A special journal used to record all transactions in which cash is paid out or decreased.

cash receipt　The cash received by a business.

cash receipts journal　A special journal used to record all transactions in which cash is received.

cash sale　A transaction in which the business receives full payment for the merchandise sold at the time of the sale.

certified public accountant　A public accountant who has passed the licensing exam on accounting theory, practice, auditing, and business law. (CPA)

change fund　An amount of money, consisting of varying denominations of bills and coins, that is used to make change in cash transactions.

charge customer　A customer to whom a sale on account is made.

chart of accounts　A list of all the accounts and their assigned account numbers, used in journalizing transactions.

charter　A legal written permission that gives a corporation certain rights and privileges and spells out the rules under which the corporation is to operate.

check　A written order from a depositor telling the bank to pay a stated amount of cash to the person or business named on the check.

check stub　A source document that lists the same information that appears on a check and shows the balance in the checking account before and after each check is written.

checking account　Allows a person or business to deposit cash in a bank and to write checks against the account balance.

closely held corporation　A corporation, often owned by a few people or by a family, that does not offer its stock for sale to the general public.

closing entries　Journal entries made to close, or reduce to zero, the balances in the temporary capital accounts and to transfer the net income or net loss for the period to the capital account.

code of ethics　A formal policy of rules and standards that describe the ethical behaviors that a company expects from its management and employees.

commission　An amount paid to an employee based on a percentage of the employee's sales.

common stock　The stock issued by a corporation when it is authorized to issue only one class of stock.

comparability　The accounting principle that allows the financial information from one period to be compared to that of another period; also, the comparison of financial information of two or more businesses.

competence　The principle that requires accountants to have the knowledge, skills, and experience needed to complete a task.

Glossary

compound entry   A journal entry with two or more debits or two or more credits.

computerized accounting system   A system in which financial information is recorded by entering it into a computer.

confidentiality   The principle that requires accountants to protect and not disclose information acquired in the course of work unless they have a legal or professional responsibility to do so.

conservatism principle   Accounting guideline requiring that accountants choose the safer, or more conservative, method when there is a choice of procedures.

consistency principle   The consistent use of an inventory costing method helps owners and creditors compare financial reports from one period to another.

contra account   An account whose balance is a decrease to another account.

controlling account   An account that acts as a control on the accuracy of the accounts in a related subsidiary ledger; its balance must equal the total of all the account balances in the subsidiary ledger.

corporation   Business organization that is recognized by law to have a life of its own.

correcting entry   An entry made to correct an error in a journal entry discovered after posting.

cost of merchandise   The actual cost to the business of the merchandise sold to customers.

credit   An agreement to pay for a purchase at a later time; an entry to the right side of a T account.

credit cards   Cards containing a customer's name and account number presented when buying merchandise on account.

credit memorandum   A form that lists the details of a sales return or sales allowance.

credit terms   Terms that set out the time allowed for payment for a sale on account.

creditor   A person or business that has a claim to the assets of a business; a person or business to which money is owed.

current assets   Assets that are either used up or converted to cash during the normal operating cycle of the business, usually one year.

current liabilities   Debts of the business that must be paid within the next accounting period.

current ratio   The relationship between current assets and current liabilities; calculated by dividing the dollar amount of current assets by the dollar amount of current liabilities.

D

debit   An amount entered on the *left* side of the T account.

debit memorandum   The form a business uses to notify its supplier (creditor) of a return or allowance.

deduction   An amount that is subtracted from an employee's gross earnings.

deposit slip   A bank form listing the cash and checks to be deposited.

depositor   A person or business that has cash on deposit in a bank.

depreciation   Allocating the cost of a plant asset over an asset's useful life.

direct deposit   The depositing of an employee's net pay directly into her or his personal bank account; usually made through electronic funds transfer.

direct write-off method   A procedure in which an uncollectible account is removed from the accounts receivable subsidiary ledger and the controlling account in the general ledger when a business determines that the amount owed is not going to be paid.

discount period   The period of time within which an invoice must be paid if a discount is to be taken.

disposal value   The estimated value of a plant asset at its replacement time; often called trade-in value or salvage value.

dividend   A return on the investments by the stockholders of a corporation; charged against the corporation's retained earnings.

double-entry accounting   A financial recordkeeping system in which each transaction affects at least two accounts; for each debit there must be an equal credit.

drawee   The bank on which a check is written.

drawer   The person who signs a check.

due dates   The date by which an invoice must be paid.

E

electronic badge readers   Employee is issued an identification badge with a magnetic strip that contains employee information. When the employee inserts the identification badge into the badge reader, the magnetic strip is scanned and information is transferred directly to the computer.

Electronic Federal Tax Payment System (EFTPS) Larger businesses deposit income tax payments by electronic funds transfer.

Electronic Funds Transfer System (EFTS)   Allows banks to transfer funds among accounts quickly and accurately without the exchange of checks.

employee's earnings record   An individual payroll record prepared for each employee; includes data on earnings, deductions, net pay, and accumulated earnings.

ending inventory   The merchandise a business has on hand at the end of a fiscal period.

endorsement   An authorized signature written or stamped on the back of a check representing receipt and deposit or payment of check.

entrepreneur   A person who transforms ideas for products or services into real-world businesses.

equity   The total financial claims to the assets, or property, of a business.

ethics   The study of our notions of right and wrong; a set of basic principles.

ethics officer   The employee directly responsible for creating business conduct programs, evaluating performance, and enforcing standards of conduct.

expense   The cost of the goods or services that are used to operate a business; expenses decrease owner's equity.

external controls   The measures and procedures provided outside the business to protect cash and other assets.

F

face value   The amount written on the face of a promissory note; usually the same as the principal.

Federal Tax Deposit Coupon   A form sent with payment for FICA and federal income taxes or federal unemployment taxes to indicate the total amount of taxes being paid.

Federal Unemployment Tax Act (FUTA)   Requires employers to pay unemployment taxes.

financial accounting   Reporting information to external users (individuals not directly involved in the day-to-day operations of the business).

financial claims   Legal rights to an item.

financial reports   Summarized information about the financial status of a business.

financial statements   Prepared to summarize the changes resulting from business transactions that occur during an accounting period.

first-in, first-out method   An inventory costing method that assumes that the first items purchased (first in) were the first items sold (first out).

fiscal year   An accounting period of twelve months.

FOB destination   Shipping terms specifying that the supplier pays the shipping cost to the buyer's destination.

FOB shipping point   Shipping terms specifying that the buyer pays the shipping charge from the supplier's shipping point.

footing   A column total written in small pencil figures.

Form 940   The employer's unemployment tax return; it includes both federal and state unemployment taxes paid during the year.

Form 941   The employer's quarterly federal tax return; it reports the accumulated amounts of FICA and federal income tax withheld from employees' earnings for the quarter, as well as FICA tax owed by the employer.

Form W-2   A form that provides the employee with a summary of earnings and amounts withheld for federal, state, and local taxes; also called a wage and tax statement.

Form W-3   The Transmittal of Wage and Tax Statements, filed with the federal government to summarize the information contained on the employees' Forms W-2.

for-profit business   Business that operates to earn money for its owners.

free enterprise system   A system in which people are free to produce the goods and services they choose.

full disclosure   Accounting guideline requiring that a financial report include enough information so that it is complete.

Glossary

G

general journal An all-purpose journal in which all the transactions of a business may be recorded.

general ledger The group of accounts used by a business.

generally accepted accounting principles (GAAP) A set of rules used by accountants to prepare financial reports.

going concern The assumption that a business entity will continue to operate for an indefinite time.

gross earnings The total amount of money an employee earns in a pay period.

gross profit on sales The amount of profit made during the fiscal period before expenses are deducted; it is found by subtracting the cost of merchandise sold from net sales.

H

home keys The 4-5-6 keys on a numeric keypad.

horizontal analysis The comparison of the same items on financial statements for two or more accounting periods and the analysis of changes from one period to the next.

I

income statement A report of the net income or net loss for a fiscal period; sometimes called a "profit and loss" statement.

Income Summary account The account in the general ledger used to summarize the revenue and expenses for the fiscal period.

independence The principle that requires CPAs to have no financial interest in the company being audited.

integrity The principle that requires accountants to choose what is right and just over what is wrong.

interest The fee charged for the use of money.

interest rate The fee charged for the use of the principal when a loan is made.

interest-bearing note payable A note that requires the face value plus interest to be paid at maturity.

internal controls Steps a business takes to protect cash (for example, limiting the number of persons handling cash).

inventory The items of merchandise a business has in stock.

investments Those assets owned by a business but not used in the operation of the business.

invoice A bill; a form that lists the quantity, description, unit price, and total cost of the items sold and shipped to a buyer.

issue date The date on which a promissory note is written.

J

journal A chronological record of all of the transactions of a business.

journalizing The process of recording business transactions in a journal.

L

last-in, first-out method An inventory costing method that assumes that the last items purchased are the first items sold.

ledger A book or file containing a separate page for each business account; serves as a permanent record of financial transactions.

ledger account form The accounting stationery used to record financial information about specific accounts.

liabilities Amounts owed to creditors; the claims of creditors to the assets of the business.

lifestyle The way you use your time, energy, and resources.

liquidity ratio The measure of a business's ability to pay its current debts as they become due and to provide for unexpected needs of cash.

long-term liabilities Debts that are not required to be paid within the next accounting period.

loss The result of a company's spending more than it receives in revenue.

M

maker   The person or business promising to repay the principal and interest when a loan is made.

management accounting   Reporting information to management, often referred to as accounting for *internal* users of accounting information.

manual accounting system   A system in which accounting information is recorded and processed by hand.

manufacturing business   A business that transforms raw materials into finished products through the use of labor and machinery.

market value   The current price that is being charged for similar items of merchandise in the market.

matching principle   Principle stating that expenses are compared to revenues for the same period.

materiality   An accounting guideline stating that relatively important data should be included in financial reports.

maturity date   The due date of a promissory note; the date on which the principal and interest must be paid.

maturity value   The principal plus interest on a note that must be paid on the maturity date.

memorandum   A brief written message that describes a transaction that takes place within a business.

merchandise   Goods bought for resale to customers.

merchandising business   A business that buys goods (for example, books or clothing) and then sells those goods for a profit.

mutual agency   The characteristic of partnerships under which any partner can enter into agreements for the business that are binding on all other partners.

N

net income   The amount of revenue that remains after expenses for the period are subtracted.

net loss   The amount by which total expenses exceed total revenue.

net pay   The amount left after total deductions are subtracted from gross earnings.

net purchases   The total cost of all merchandise purchased during a fiscal period, less any purchases discounts, returns, or allowances.

net sales   The amount of sales for the period less any sales discounts, returns, or allowances.

networking   Making contacts with people to share information and advice.

noninterest-bearing note payable   A note from which the interest is deducted at the time the note is made; a promissory note that has no stated rate of interest on its face.

normal balance   The increase side of an account: assets, debit side; liabilities and capital, credit side. The word *normal* used here means usual.

note payable   A promissory note issued to a creditor.

note receivable   A promissory note that a business accepts from a customer or other person who owes the business money.

not-for-profit organization   An organization that does not operate for the purpose of making a profit.

NSF check   A check returned to the depositor by the bank because there are not sufficient funds in the drawer's checking account to cover the check.

O

objectivity   The principle that requires accountants to be impartial, honest, and free of conflicts of interest.

on account   When a business or individual buys an item on credit.

online   The direct link-up of a terminal or cash register to a centralized computer system.

operating expenses   The cash spent or assets consumed to earn revenue for a business; operating expenses do not include federal income tax expense.

operating income   The taxable income of a corporation.

other expense   A non-operating expense; an expense that does not result from the normal operations of the business.

other revenue   Non-operating revenue that a business receives from activities outside its normal operations.

outstanding checks   Checks that have been written but have not yet been presented to the bank for payment.

Glossary

outstanding deposits Deposits that have been made and recorded in the checkbook but do not appear on the bank statement.

overtime rate Employers are required to pay overtime when employees covered by these laws work more than 40 hours per week.

owner's equity Owner's claims to the assets of the business.

P

packing slip A form that lists the items included in the shipment.

Paid-in Capital in Excess of Par The account that represents the amount of cash received by a corporation over the stock's par value.

par value The dollar amount assigned to each share of stock when the corporation's charter is approved; used to determine the amount credited to the capital stock account.

partnership Business owned by two or more persons, called partners, who agree to operate the business as co-owners.

partnership agreement A written document that sets out the terms under which the partnership will operate.

partnership liquidation Ending a partnership involves winding up the affairs of the partnership business.

pay period The amount of time over which an employee is paid.

payee The person or business to whom a check is written or a note is payable.

payroll A list of the employees and the payments due to each employee for a specific pay period.

payroll clerk Responsible for preparing the payroll.

payroll register A form that summarizes information about employees' earnings for each pay period.

Payroll Tax Expense Account where the employer's payroll taxes are recorded.

percentage of net sales method A method of estimating uncollectible debts expense in which a business assumes that a certain percentage of each year's net sales will be uncollectible.

periodic inventory system An inventory system in which the number of items on hand is determined by a physical count.

permanent accounts Accounts that are continuous from one accounting period to the next; balances are carried forward to the next period (for example, assets, liabilities, and owner's capital accounts).

perpetual inventory system An inventory system in which a constant, up-to-date record of the amount of merchandise on hand is maintained.

personal interest tests Tests that uncover personal preferences you can use to research potential careers and determine which ones match your particular interests.

personality A set of unique qualities that makes us different from all other people.

petty cash disbursement A payment made from the petty cash fund.

petty cash fund Cash kept on hand for making small, incidental cash payments.

petty cash register A record of all disbursements made from the petty cash fund.

petty cash requisition A form requesting money to replenish the petty cash fund.

petty cash voucher A form that provides proof of payment from the petty cash fund.

petty cashier The person responsible for maintaining the petty cash fund and for making petty cash disbursements.

physical inventory An actual count of all the merchandise on hand and available for sale.

plant assets Long-lived assets that are used in the production or sale of other assets or services over several accounting periods.

point-of-sale terminal Electronic cash register.

post-closing trial balance Prepared to verify that total debits equal total credits after the closing entries are posted.

posting The process of transferring information from the general journal to individual general ledger accounts, the fourth step in the accounting cycle.

preferred stock Stock whose owners have certain privileges over common stockholders.

premium The amount paid for insurance.

principal　The amount of money being borrowed on a promissory note.

proceeds　The amount of cash actually received by a borrower on a non-interest-bearing note payable.

processing stamp　A stamp placed on a creditor's invoice that outlines the steps to be followed in processing the invoice for payment.

profit　The amount of revenue earned above the expenses incurred to operate the business.

profitability ratio　Ratios used to evaluate the earnings performance of a business during the accounting period (for example, return on common stockholders' equity).

promissory note　A written promise to pay a certain amount of money at a specific future time.

property　Items of value that are owned or controlled by a business; economic resources of a business.

property rights　Creditors' and owners' financial claims to the assets of a business.

proving cash　The process of determining whether the amounts of cash recorded in the accounting records of a business and in its checkbook agree.

proving the ledger　Adding all debit balances and all credit balances of ledger accounts and then comparing the two totals to see whether they are equal.

proxy　A document that transfers a stockholder's voting rights to someone else.

public accounting　Accounting services that range from tax preparation to merger and acquisition consultation; a variety of accounting services offered to businesses.

publicly held corporation　A corporation whose stock is widely held, has a large market, and is usually traded on a stock exchange.

purchase order　A written offer to a supplier to buy certain items.

purchase requisition　A written request that a certain item or items be ordered.

Purchases account　The account used to record the cost of merchandise purchased during a fiscal period.

purchases allowances　A price reduction given when a business keeps unsatisfactory merchandise it has bought.

purchases discount　Term used by the buyer to refer to a cash discount offered for early payment.

purchases journal　A special journal used to record all transactions in which items are bought on account.

purchases returns　The return to the supplier for full credit of merchandise bought on account.

Q

quick ratio　A measure of the relationship between short-term assets and current liabilities.

R

ratio analysis　Involves the comparison of two amounts on a financial statement and the evaluation of the relationship between these amounts.

receipt　A form that serves as a record of cash received.

reconciling the bank statement　The process of determining any differences between a bank statement balance and a checkbook balance.

relevance　A characteristic of accounting requiring that information "make a difference" in reaching a business decision.

reliability　A characteristic requiring that accounting information be reasonably free of bias and error.

report form　A format for preparing the balance sheet in which the classifications of accounts are listed one under another.

restrictive endorsement　A check endorsement that restricts or limits how a check may be handled (for example, "For Deposit Only").

retailer　A business that sells to the final user, the consumer.

retained earnings　Earnings held by a corporation and not paid to stockholders as a return on their investment.

return on sales　The portion of each sales dollar that represents profit. To calculate this ratio, divide net income by sales.

revenue　Income earned from the sale of goods and services.

revenue recognition　Accounting principle that states that revenue is recognized and recorded on the date it is earned even if cash has not been received.

ruling　A single line drawn under a column of figures to signify that the entries above the rule are to be added or subtracted; a double rule under an amount signifies a total.

Glossary

S

Salaries Expense The expense account used to record employees' earnings.

salary A fixed amount of money paid to an employee for each pay period.

sale on account The sale of merchandise that will be paid for at a later date.

Sales A revenue account to record the amount of the merchandise sold.

sales allowance A price reduction granted for damaged goods kept by the customer.

sales discount A cash discount.

sales journal A special journal used to record only the sale of merchandise on account.

sales return Any merchandise returned for credit or a cash refund.

sales slip A form that lists the details of a sale.

sales tax A tax levied by a city or state on the retail sale of merchandise.

schedule of accounts payable A list of all creditors in the accounts payable ledger, the balance in each account, and the total amount owed to all creditors.

schedule of accounts receivable A list of each charge customer, the balance in the customer's account, and the total amount due from all customers.

selling expenses Expenses incurred in selling or marketing the merchandise or services sold by a business.

service business Provides a needed service for a fee.

signature card A card containing the signature(s) of the person(s) authorized to write checks on a checking account.

skills Activities that you perform well.

slide error Accidental misplacement of a decimal point in an amount.

sole proprietorship A business owned by one person.

source document A paper prepared as evidence that a transaction occurred.

special journals Multicolumn journals that have columns reserved for the recording of specific types of transactions.

specific identification method An inventory costing method in which the exact cost of each item in inventory is determined and assigned; used most often by businesses that have a low unit volume of merchandise with high unit prices.

State Unemployment Tax Act (SUTA) Requires employers to pay unemployment taxes.

statement of changes in owner's equity A financial statement prepared to summarize the effects of business transactions on the capital account.

statement of changes in partners' equity A financial statement that reports the changes in each partner's capital account as a result of business operations.

statement of retained earnings A statement that reports the changes that have taken place in the **Retained Earnings** account during the fiscal period; prepared as a supporting document for the balance sheet.

statement of stockholders' equity A statement that reports the changes that have taken place in all of the stockholders' equity accounts during the period.

stockholders' equity The value of the stockholders' claims to the assets of the corporation.

stop payment order A demand by the drawer that the bank not honor a certain check.

straight-line depreciation A method of equally distributing the cost of a plant asset over the asset's estimated useful life.

subsidiary ledger A ledger that is summarized in a controlling account in the general ledger.

T

T account   An account shaped like a "T" that is used for analyzing transactions.

temporary capital accounts   Accounts used to record information during the fiscal period that will be transferred to a permanent capital account at the end of the period.

term   The length of time the borrower has to repay a promissory note.

tickler file   A file that contains a folder for each day of the month; invoices are placed in the folders according to their due dates.

time card   A record of the time an employee arrives at work, the time the employee leaves, and the total number of hours worked each day.

transposition error   Occurs when two digits within an amount are accidentally reversed, or transposed.

trial balance   A proof of the equality of total debits and credits, the fifth step in the accounting cycle.

U

uncollectible accounts   An account receivable that cannot be collected, sometimes called a bad debt.

unemployment taxes   Taxes collected to provide funds for workers who are temporarily out of work; usually paid only by the employer.

V

values   Concepts or ideas held important or worthwhile.

vertical analysis   A method of analysis that requires the restating of each dollar amount reported on a financial statement as a percentage of a base amount reported on the same statement.

voiding a check   Canceling a check by writing the word "Void" across the front in ink.

W

wage   An amount of money paid to an employee at a specified rate per hour worked.

weighted average cost method   An inventory costing method in which all purchases of an item are added to the beginning inventory of that item; the total cost is then divided by the total units to obtain the average cost per unit.

wholesaler   A business that sells to retailers.

withdrawal   The removal of cash or another asset from the business by the owner for personal use.

work sheet   A working paper used to collect information from ledger accounts for use in completing end-of-fiscal-period work.

working capital   The amount by which current assets exceed current liabilities.

Index A

A

Index

B

C

Index A

D

E

F

Index A

financial claim, 46, 47, 48
financial position, 484
financial statements, 72, 204. *See also specific
    financial statements*
    analyzing, 221, 245, 272, 297, 336, 375, 399,
        439, 470, 503, 535, 561, 582, 613, 628, 665,
        687, 714, 743, 761
    balance sheet, 216–218, 665
    customizing, 592
    end-of-period, 519–520
    income statement, 205–208
    preparing computerized, 226, 540
    preparing manual, 205, 522
    recording depreciation on, 637–638
    statement of changes in owner's equity,
        210–213
    statement of changes in partner's equity,
        754–755
    statement of retained earnings, 531–532
finding errors. *See also* errors
    in trial balance, 108, 167–168
first-in, first-out method (FIFO), 685–686
fiscal year (period), 124
    closing the, 566
FOB, 405–406
footing, 423
for-profit business, 15
Form 940, 334
Form 941, 334, 335
Form 8109, 327
Form W-2, 334
Form W-3, 336
Form W-4, 293–294
four-column ledger account form, 153
fractional share basis, 740–742
free enterprise system, 26
full disclosure, 519
FUTA (Federal Unemployment Tax Act), 323, 330

G

GAAP (generally accepted accounting principles),
    32, 34
    conservatism, 691
    consistency, 690
    revenue recognition, 106
general journal, 126
    adjusting entries in, 126
    closing entries in, 232
    correcting errors in, 139
    recording entries in, 126–130
general ledger, 153
    closing, 551–554, 556–559
    posting closing entries to the, 243–244

posting payroll to the, 319–320
    setting up the, 153–155, 174, 766
generally accepted accounting principles. *See* GAAP
going concern, 34
gross earnings, 289
gross pay. *See* gross earnings
gross profit on sales, 526

H

heading
    on financial statements, 205, 210, 216
    work sheet, 183
home keys, A-13
horizontal analysis, 534
hourly wage, 290

I

income statement, 204, 205, 503, 522
    analysis of, 527–528, 628
    cost of merchandise sold, 523, 524, 525
    expenses section, 207–208
    gross profit on sales, 526
    net income section, 208, 526–527
    operating expenses, 526
    for partnership, 75
    revenue section, 206–207, 523
    section of a work sheet, 187, 189
Income Summary, 235–236
    closing to capital, 238–240
    closing entries to, 236–238
independence, 782
Institute of Internal Auditors (IIA), 774, 783
Institute of Management Accountants (IMA), 783
insurance
    prepaid, 402
    recording payment of, 402, 403
integrity, 781
interest,
    calculating due and payable, A-25, A-27
    calculating note, 705–706
    payable, A-25, A-26–A-27
    receivable, A-25, A-27–A-28
interest rate, 705
interest table, 706
interest-bearing notes payable, 708–710
interests, personal, 7
internal controls, 258, 259
inventory
    beginning, 487
    determining quantity of, 680–682
    ending, 487
    merchandise, 487–489

physical, 682
    recording, 682
    sheet, 682
inventory costing, 696
    choosing, 690–691
    FIFO, 685–686
    LIFO, 686
    specific identification, 684–685
    weighted average cost, 686–687
investments, 47, 52
invoice, 123
    processing supplier's, 390
issue date, 702

J

journalizing, 124
    cash payments, 458, 466–467
    cash receipts, 429, 435
    closing entries, 232–235, 550–554
    correcting entries, 168
    employer's payroll taxes, 323–324
    payroll, 316–318
    purchases, 450–451, 454, 455
    sales, 420, 421, 423, 424
    work sheet adjustments, 500
journals, 124
    closing entries in, 232–235, 236
    special, 420
    usefulness of, 155
    See also specific journals

K

keeping the books, 72

L

last in, first out (LIFO) method, 686
ledger, 72. *See also specific ledgers*
ledger account form, 153
ledger accounts
    opening, 154–155
ledger, general. *See* general ledger
ledgers
    usefulness of, 155
liabilities, 48
    current, 220
    long term, 708
    payroll, 316–317
    rules of debit and credit, 74–75
liabilities section
    on balance sheet, 218
liability accounts, 75–76
lifestyle, 9
LIFO (last-in, first-out), 686

liquidation. *See* partnership
liquidity ratios, 220–221
local taxes, 296
loss, 26
lower-of-cost-or-market method, inventory
    valuation, 691

M

management
    and payroll accounting, 303
    use of income statements, 528
    use of journals and ledgers, 155
    use of work sheet, 189
management accounting, 33
manual accounting system, 32, 72, 394
    accounts receivable subsidiary ledger in a, 360
    general ledger in a, 153
manufacturing business, 28
market value, 691
matching principle, 189
materiality, 520
maturity date, 702–704
maturity value, 705
memorandum, 123
    credit, 362, 363
    debit, 397
merchandise
    cost of, 391
    purchase of, 388–398, 403, 404
    sale of, 354–365, 372
merchandise inventory, 356, 487–489, 680
merchandising business, 28, 354
    contrasting with a service business, 354
    operating cycle, 354, 356
    Sales, 356
MICR number, on check, 260
mutual agency, 735

N

net income, 190
    closing entry for, 551
    division of, for partnership, 739–743
    on an income statement, 205
    on a work sheet, 189
net loss, 192
    at closing, 239–240, 554
    on an income statement, 208
    on a work sheet, 192–193
net pay, 300
net purchases, 524
net sales, 523
networking, 10
noninterest-bearing notes payable, 710–714
non-profit. *See* not-for-profit organization

Index A

Index A

sales allowances, 362–363
sales and cash receipts, 444
sales credit column
    posting to Sales, 424
sales discounts, 369
sales journal, 420, 421, 423, 424
    posting to ledger, 422–423
    posting totals of, 424–426
    recording sales of merchandise on account, 421–422
sales of merchandise on account
    recording, 421–422
sales returns, 362–363
Sales Returns and Allowances account, 363
sales slips, 358
    bankcard, 368
sales tax, 359
schedule of accounts payable, 468
schedule of accounts receivable, 438
selling expenses, 526
service business, 28
    contrasting with a merchandising business, 354
service change, bank, 267
shareholders, 30
shipping charge, 406
showing net income, 189
showing net loss, 192
signature card, 259
six-column work sheet
    account name section, 184
    completing the, 191–192
    heading for, 183
    preparing the, 183–185, 193
    showing net income, 189–191
    showing net loss, 192
    See also ten-column work sheet; work sheet
skills, 7, 8, 12
slide error, 167
social security tax, 296. *See also* FICA
sole proprietorship, 29, 30
    accounting functions involved with a, 97–102
source documents, 123
    applying information from, 124
    bank statements as, 269, 270
    for cash payments journal, 458
    cash register tapes as, 367, 601
    credit memos as, 363
    debit memos as, 397
    examination of, 124
    sales slips as, 358
special journals, 420. *See also specific journals*
specific identification costing method, 684–685
spreadsheets, electronic, 64
state taxes, 296, 329
State Unemployment Tax Act (SUTA), 323, 331

statement of changes in owner's equity, 204, 210–213
statement of changes in partners' equity, 754–755
statement of retained earnings, 531–532
statement of stockholders' equity, 585–586
stock
    capital, 516, 517, 575
    common, 575, 576, 577
    dividends, 579–582
    preferred, 575, 577
stockholders, 30, 574
stockholders' equity, 575, 582
    reporting, 517–518
    statement of, 585–586
stop payment order, 270
stopping payment on a check, 270
straight-line depreciation, 628, 631
subsidiary ledgers, 359
    errors in the, 438, 439
    preparing schedules for, 438, 468
summary of depreciation, 633
SUTA (State Unemployment Tax Act), 323, 331

T

T accounts, 73–74, 78
tax reports,
    payroll, 334–336
tax tables, 294–295
taxes
    EFTPS, 328
    employer's payroll, 322–325
    federal income, 293–296
    FICA, 296, 322–323
    sales, 359
    social security, 296
    state and local, 296
    unemployment, 323
temporary accounts, 245
temporary capital accounts, 96–97, 98–102
    closing entries for, 236–241
ten-column work sheet, 484, A-1
    adjustments in, 486–489, 491–494, A-3–A-5
    extending amounts, 498–499, A-6
    journalizing adjustments of, 500, A-9
    trial balance section, 485, 496–497, A-1
    See also six-column work sheet; work sheet
term, of promissory note, 702
tickler file, 395
time calendar, 704
time card, 290
traits
    of entrepreneurs, 27, 28, 29
    personal, 7, 8
Transmittal of Wage and Tax statements (Form W-3), 336

Index B

Real-World Applications and Connections

Real-World Applications and Connections

Index B

Index B

Real-World Applications and Connections

Index B

Real-World Applications and Connections

Photo Credits

Cover photography by: Masterfile/Imtek Imagineering(b); Jordon Miller(t)

Selected spot photography provided by: Corbis Digital Stock; EyeWire Image Library; & Photo Disc, Inc.

AFP/Corbis xv, 573; Thomas J. Abercrombie/National Geographic Society 734(b); Adam Smith/FPG International LLC 142(b); Lori Adamski Peek/Tony Stone Images 360; American Airlines 96(c); Amwell/Tony Stone Images 556(b); Eric Antoniou/Corbis 32; Bill Aron/Photo Edit 101, 327(b), 393(b), 629, 776(t), 631; Robert Aschenbrenner/Tony Stone Images 621(b); Joe Atlas/Artville 482(bl); Bruce Ayres/Tony Stone Images 67(b), 79; Bill Bachman/Leo de Wys 166(b); Bill Bachmann/Photo Edit 614(t), 701; Davis Barber/Photo Edit 89(b); Barros & Barros/The Image Bank 9(b), 632(t); Harry Bartlett/Stone xix; 775; Paul Barton/The Stock Market 715(t); Ben & Jerry's Homemade, Inc. 122(b), 796, 799; Brain Bielmann/Index Stock 619(b); Ken Biggs Tony Stone Images 215(b); Nathan Bilow/Tony Stone Images 438; Warren Bolster/Tony Stone Images 381(c); D. Boone/Corbis-Westlight 75; Mathew Borkoski/Index Stock 782; Daniel Bosler/Tony Stone Images 164, 358(b), 601(t), 744; Deborah Boyd/World Wildlife Fund 5; Robert Brenner/Photo Edit 323, 367(b); Gary Brettracher/Image State xiii(b), 483; Michelle D. Bridwell/PhotoEdit 679; P. Broze/Leo de Wys 605(b); Peter Cade/Tony Stone Images 769, Melanie Carr/Image State 781; Melanie Carr/Index Stock 616(c); Tom Carroll/International Stock 299(b); Aaron Chang/The Stock Market 172(b); Ron Chapple/FPG International LLC 340(c); Steve Chenn/Corbis-Westlight 694(b), 768(c); Ken Chernnus/FPG International LLC 663; Cleo/Photo Edit 595(b); Dennis Cody/FPG International LLC 366; Stewart Cohen/Tony Stone Images 216(b), 521, 681; Connie Coleman/Tony Stone Images 30; Comstock, Inc. xii(m), 350(t), 401(t), 472, 530(t), 584(t); Corbis 777(t); Gary Conner/Corbis 597; Gary A. Conner/Photo Edit 157(b), 235; Tom Craig/FPG International LLC 322(t); David K. Crow/Photo Edit 98; Jim Cummins/FPG International LLC 16(b); Robert E. Daemmrich/Tony Stone Images 92(b), 170, 276(b); Michael Kevin Dal/The Stock Market 415(b); Michael Daly/The Stock Market 207(t), 428; Dennis Degnan/Westlight 582; Uli Degwert/International Stock 73; Danita DeJane viii(b), 120(bl), 628(b), 687(b); David de Lossy/The Image Bank 136(b); Thomas Del Brase/Tony Stone Images(m), 284(t), 338(t); Dewys & Japack/Leo de Wys 495(b); Dewys/D & J Heaton/Leo de Wys 517; George Diebold/The Stock Market 338(b); Digital Vision 50(b), 287; Joseph Drivas/The Image Bank 532; Robert Essel/Corbis 776(b); Eyewire/Stone 95 638; Jon Feingersh/The Stock Market 403, 495(t); Myrleen Ferguson/Photo Edit 8(t), 555; Bob Firth/

International Stock 192; Kim Fowler/Leo de Wys 46(c); David Fraizer Photolibrary 316(b), 689(b), 754(b), 759; David R. Frazier/Tony Stone Images, 136(t); Tony Freeman/Photo Edit 57(b), 60, 83, 104(b), 224(b), 757(c); Robert Frerck/Tony Stone Images 14(b); Tim Fuller Photography xv(b), 6(b), 12 (all except br) 52 , 56, 59, 106(b), 117(c), 128, 129, 133, 139, 153, 194, 201(b), 210(b), 212, 225(br), 260, 264, 270, 309(b), 322(b), 357, 378(c), 387, 410(b), 421, 492, 564(b), 570(b), 579(b), 614(b), 659, 685, 738(t), 746(c); Robert Ginn/Photo Edit 199(b); GK & Vikki Hart/Petco Inc. 474(b); Spencer Grant/Photo Edit 258(b), 292, 449; Ernst Grasser/Stone 126(b); Vincent Graziani/ International Stock 265(b); Jeff Greenberg/Photo Edit 22(t), 103; Brain Haimer/Photo Edit 627(b), 755; David Hanilton/The Image Bank 90(c); Chris Harvey/Stone ix(b), 231; John Henley/The Stock Market 672(b); Ed Honowitz/Tony Stone Images 18, 49; Ted Horowitz/The Stock Market 15, 596(b); Richard Hutchings/Photo Edit 391; Miwako Ikeda/International Stock 306(b); Index Stock 9(t), 50(b), 65(b), 148(b), 196(b), 271, 291, 372, 451, 463, 518, 622(b), 750(b); David Joel/Tony Stone Images 707; Johnny Stockshooter/International Stock 484(b); Mark A. Johnson/The Stock Market 688(t); Chris Jones/The Stock Market/538(b); R.W. Jones/Corbis-Westlight 408, 543(b), 750(c); Mark Joseph/Tony Stone Images 490; Kalunzy & Thatcher/FPG International LLC 487(t); Bonnie Kamin/Photo Edit 326; Ronnie Kaufman/Corbis 121; Chuck Keeler/Tony Stone Images 99; Michael A. Keller/The Stock Market 369; John P. Kelley/The Image Bank 350(b); Michael Krasowitz/FPG International LLC 20, 33, 186, 269; Bob Krist/Leo de Wys 13; Gary D. Landsman/The Stock Market/Corbis xii(b), 419, 691; Brian Leng/Corbis-Westlight xix(tl), 4(t), 6(t), 14(t), 24(t), 26(t), 32(t), 44(t), 46(t), 50(t), 57(t), 70(t), 72(t), 78(t), 96(t), 120(t), 122(t), 126(t), 150(t), 152(t), 157(t), 166(t), 180(t), 182(t), 202(t), 204(t), 210(t), 256(t), 258(t), 265(t), 286(t), 288(t), 293(t), 299(t), 314, 316(t), 322(t), 327(t), 352(t), 354(t), 358(t), 367(t), 386(t), 388(t), 393(t), 402(t), 418(t), 420(t), 429(t), 448(t), 450(t), 458(t), 482(t), 484(t), 491(t), 493, 514(t), 516(t), 522, 531(t), 548(t), 550(t), 556(t), 572(t), 574(t), 579(t), 585(t), 600(t), 605(t), 624(t), 626(t), 630, 633(t), 650(t), 652(t), 658(t), 667(t), 678(t), 680(t), 684, 690(t), 700(t), 702(t), 708(t), 730(t), 732(t), 734(t), 739, 752(t), 754(t), 757(t), 774, 782, 790, 806, 824; Larry Levine/Washington Metropolitan Area Transit Authority viii(b), 181; RobLewine/Corbis 549; Romilly Lockyer/The Image Bank 214; Dick Luria/FPG International LLC 458(b), 612; Renee Lynn/Tony Stone Images 343(b); David Madison/Tony Stone Images 273; Nadine Markova/The Stock Market 187(b); Chuck Mason/International Stock xi(b), 246, 287, 513(b); Don Mason/The Stock Market xi(t), 257, 356; Masterfile xvi(c), 642(t), 689(t); Dennis MacDonald/Photo Edit 138, 653(t);

Glencoe's
Business Transaction Analysis Model

Business Transaction

On October 1 Maria Sanchez took $25,000 from personal savings and deposited that amount to open a business checking account in the name of Roadrunner Delivery Service, Memorandum 1.

Roadrunner Delivery Service
155 Gateway Blvd.
Sacramento, CA 94230

MEMORANDUM 1

TO: Accounting Clerk
FROM: Maria Sanchez
DATE: October 1, 20--
SUBJECT: Contributed personal funds to the business

I have contributed $25,000 from my personal savings for a deposit to the business, Roadrunner Delivery Service.

ANALYSIS	Identify	1.	The accounts **Cash in Bank** and **Maria Sanchez, Capital** are affected.
	Classify	2.	**Cash in Bank** is an asset account. **Maria Sanchez, Capital** is an owner's capital account.
	+/−	3.	**Cash in Bank** is increased by $25,000. **Maria Sanchez, Capital** is increased by $25,000.

| DEBIT-CREDIT RULE | 4. | Increases in asset accounts are recorded as debits. Debit **Cash in Bank** for $25,000. |
| | 5. | Increases in the owner's capital account are recorded as credits. Credit **Maria Sanchez, Capital** for $25,000. |

T ACCOUNTS 6.

Cash in Bank		Maria Sanchez, Capital	
Debit + 25,000	Credit −	Debit −	Credit + 25,000

JOURNAL ENTRY 7.

		GENERAL JOURNAL		PAGE _1_		
	DATE	DESCRIPTION	POST. REF.	DEBIT	CREDIT	
1	20--					1
2	Oct. 1	Cash in Bank		25 000 00		2
3		Maria Sanchez, Capital			25 000 00	3
4		Memorandum 1				4
5						5